BOOKS BY CLAY BLAIR

NONFICTION

The Atomic Submarine and Admiral Rickover
The Hydrogen Bomb, with James R. Shepley
Beyond Courage
Valley of the Shadow, for Ward M. Millar
Nautilus 90 North, with William R. Anderson
Diving for Pleasure and Treasure
Always Another Dawn, with A. Scott Crossfield
The Voyage of Nina II, for Robert Marx
The Strange Case of James Earl Ray
Survive!
Silent Victory: The U.S. Submarine War Against Japan
The Search for JFK, with Joan Blair
MacArthur
Combat Patrol
Return From the River Kwai, with Joan Blair
A General's Life, with Omar N. Bradley
Ridgway's Paratroopers
The Forgotten War: America in Korea 1950–1953
Hitler's U-boat War: The Hunters, 1939–1942

FICTION

The Board Room
The Archbishop
Pentagon Country
Scuba!, with Joan Blair
Mission Tokyo Bay, with Joan Blair
Swordray's First Three Patrols, with Joan Blair

HITLER'S U-BOAT WAR

HITLER'S U-BOAT WAR

THE HUNTED

1942–1945

★ ★

CLAY BLAIR

RANDOM HOUSE
NEW YORK

Published in the United States by Random House, Inc., New York, and simultaneously in Canada by Random House of Canada Limited, Toronto.

Grateful acknowledgment is made to the following for permission to reprint previously published material:

Henry Holt and Company Inc.: Excerpts from *Iron Coffins* by Herbert A. Werner. Copyright © 1969 by Herbert A. Werner. Reprinted by permission of Henry Holt and Company, Inc.

U.S. Naval Institute: Excerpts from *My Life* by Eric Raeder, translated by Henry W. Drexel. Copyright © 1960, 1988 by U.S. Naval Institute. Reprinted by permission of U.S. Naval Institute.

Library of Congress Cataloging-in-Publication Data

Blair, Clay.
Hitler's U-boat war / Clay Blair.
p. cm.
Includes index.
Contents: v. 2. The hunted, 1942–1945.
ISBN 0-679-45742-9
1. World War, 1939–1945—Naval operations—Submarine. 2. World War, 1939–1945—Naval operations, German. I. Title.
D781.B53 1996
940.54'51—dc20 96-2275

Random House website address: www.randomhouse.com
Printed in the United States of America on acid-free paper

2 4 6 8 9 7 5 3

First Edition

Book design by Caroline Cunningham

Once again, to Joan—my wife,
best friend, and loyal and
patient collaborator

FOREWORD

In Volume I of this history, *The Hunters,* I described, analyzed, and assessed in great detail the first three years of the German U-boat war: August 1939 to August 1942. This volume, *The Hunted,* is a continuation of the U-boat story from September 1942 to the surrender of Germany in May 1945.

Like the U-boat war itself, Volume I was subdivided into two sequential books: the U-boat war against the British Empire (1939–1941) and the U-boat war against the Americas (December 1941–August 1942). This second volume contains but one book: the U-boat war against the naval forces of the British Commonwealth, including notably Canada, and those of the United States.

Adolf Hitler's Third Reich was absurdly unprepared for a naval war with the Allies. Therefore, for the second time in the twentieth century, German navalists were compelled to resort to cheap, mass-produced submarines, manned mostly by civilian volunteers, to conduct the war at sea, often and somewhat misleadingly called the "Battle of the Atlantic." They conceived and waged a *guerre de course,* or war against British-controlled merchant shipping, designed to blockade the British Isles so tightly that the starved-out British government would be forced to lay down arms and withdraw from the war.

The commander in chief of the U-boat force, Karl Dönitz, characterized this German naval strategy as a "tonnage war." The objective was the destruction of British-controlled merchant ships wherever they could be found with the least risk to the U-boats. It did not matter whether the ships were large, medium, or small, laden or empty, close to or distant from the battlefronts. The goal was to sink merchant ships (tonnage) at a rate much faster than the British could replace them with new ships, thereby whittling down the existing tonnage to a decisively unworkable level.

As described in Volume I, this "tonnage war" against the British-controlled merchant fleet failed in the period from 1939 to 1941 for various reasons. There were not enough U-boats to bring it off and those deployed to the battlefronts had so many shortcomings that they were not suitable for the task. They sank 1,125 ships for about 5.3 million tons, but the British Commonwealth more than made good these losses by new construction and by acquisition of shipping from the United States, German-occupied nations such as Norway, France, Belgium, the Netherlands, and Greece, and by captures of Axis-controlled vessels. At the end of 1941, the British-controlled merchant fleet, including tankers, was larger by about three million tons than it was in 1939.

After the United States formally entered the war against the Axis powers in December 1941, Dönitz viewed the British and American merchant-marine fleets as a single entity and continued the "tonnage war" as before. Sensing an opportunity to strike a heavy blow at low risk, he threw the main weight of the U-boat force at the Americas for about eight months, from December 1941 to August 1942. That campaign destroyed about six hundred Allied ships for about three million tons, but by that time American shipyards, employing tens of thousands of women, were mass-producing "Liberty ships," tankers, and other types at a prodigious rate, not only making good all Allied merchant-ship losses but also swelling the size of the combined Allied fleet to undreamed of tonnage levels.

As in World War I, strategists at the British Admiralty and senior fleet commanders of the Royal Navy were slow to recognize and to properly come to grips with the U-boat threat. They believed that by convoying and by arming merchant ships with 4" or larger guns, and employing secret asdic (sonar) technology, which was developed between the wars, any U-boat force the Germans deployed could be neutralized and quickly defeated. This smugness did not last for long. It turned out that the besieged Royal Navy, committed to an overabundance of tasks, had nowhere near enough blue-water escorts to properly protect convoys and, furthermore, the smallish *Hunt*-class destroyer escort, specifically designed for that purpose and rushed into production, failed to live up to its promise and could not be employed on the vital North Atlantic run between the Americas and the British Isles.

Hard-pressed on land and sea and in the air, the British chose brains over brawn. To counter the *Luftwaffe,* British scientists perfected a radar-warning net, then miniaturized radar to fit into aircraft, sharing this ingenious, war-decisive technology with Canada and the United States. At the same time, other British intellectuals, capitalizing on technical help from the defeated Poles, broke into the German Enigma military encoding-machine system. Still other British scientists and engineers developed an astonishingly accurate land-based high-frequency direction-finding network (Huff Duff), then miniaturized the devices to fit on ships. Radar, codebreaking, and to a limited extent Huff

Duff,* and other scientific breakthroughs, enabled the Royal Navy and Royal Air Force to thwart "wolf pack" attacks by the Atlantic-based U-boats on convoys in 1941, in large part, by simply routing convoys around known U-boat positions.

That same year, 1941, the United States gradually—and illegally—entered the "Battle of the Atlantic." Having already loaned the British sixty warships for convoy escort (fifty old destroyers and ten Coast Guard cutters), the United States occupied the Avalon Peninsula of Newfoundland and built a naval base at Argentia. It then occupied Greenland and Iceland and built substantial naval and air bases on Iceland. It commenced building a naval base in Londonderry, Northern Ireland, and slated about fifty more destroyers to escort fast convoys on the North Atlantic run between Canada and Iceland and the reverse. The passage of the Lend-Lease Act enabled America to build warships ("jeep" carriers, destroyer escorts, and frigates, among other types) and Liberty-type merchant ships for Britain and Canada and to repair warships of those nations in American naval shipyards. A relaxation of the Neutrality Act authorized American merchant ships to enter the war zones in Europe to deliver Lend-Lease war matériel and oil.

When the United States formally entered the war in December 1941, President Roosevelt and his military chiefs, adhering to prior secret agreements, revalidated a war policy of defeating Germany and Italy first, then Japan. Notwithstanding the losses incurred in the Japanese attack on Pearl Harbor and other places in the Pacific and Far East, the United States retained substantial naval forces in the Atlantic Ocean area to combat the U-boats, to insure that the vital North Atlantic cargo run to the British Isles and the Arctic cargo route to northern Russia continued to operate effectively, and to transport tens of thousands of troops to Iceland, Northern Ireland, and the British Isles. Owing to its prior gift of sixty warships to the Canadian and British navies, the United States did not have enough escorts to initiate convoying in the waters of the East Coast, Gulf of Mexico, and the Caribbean Sea in the first four months of 1942, during which time the Allies incurred grievous merchant-ship and crew losses to U-boats.

By the end of August 1942, when Volume I of this history, *The Hunters,* concludes, the U-boats in three years of naval warfare had sunk in all waters about two thousand Allied ships of all sizes, shapes, and types, for about 9.3 million gross tons. While these figures are quite impressive—indisputably a notable chapter in the history of naval warfare—they were not anywhere near enough. New merchant-ship production in American yards alone had reached a level of about six million gross tons a year and was rising dramatically; the Commonwealth turned out another million-plus gross tons of new shipping and repaired a great number of ships that had been laid up with damage.

Moreover, by August 1942, the Allies, in a reverse tonnage war, had in hand sufficient naval and air assets not only to defend convoys but also to kill U-boats faster than the Germans could replace them or produce meaningful numbers of radically improved models. Those assets included growing numbers of antisubmarine warfare (ASW) aircraft and experienced convoy surface-ship escorts (destroy-

* For more on Huff Duff, see Appendix 8.

ers, destroyer escorts, corvettes, catapult merchant ships, and with merchant aircraft carriers and "jeep" carriers in the offing), centimetric-wavelength (microwave) radar, land-based and shipboard Huff Duff, forward-firing Hedgehog antisubmarine bombs, improved conventional shipboard and air-dropped depth charges with Torpex warheads, and a large number of experts on both sides of the Atlantic working to break back into German naval Enigma.

Nevertheless, in the remaining years of the war, from August 1942 to May 1945, the U-boat force sank about one thousand more Allied ships for about 5.7 million gross tons. Most of those sinkings (seven hundred ships for about four million gross tons) were achieved in the nine months from September 1942 to June 1943, a result comparable to the eight-month onslaught in the Americas from January to August 1942. These new sinkings brought the final toll of the German tonnage war to about three thousand ships of all types for about fourteen million gross tons.*

What lies ahead in these pages are further accounts of intense and exhausting battles between convoys and "wolf packs"—few days in the North Atlantic were ever easy—and the story of how the Allied navies learned that electronic intelligence combined with aircraft was the most effective anti–U-boat weapon system, how those navies finally acquired the correct aircraft to do the job, and how the Germans sought desperately to produce radically new submarines to counteract these Allied technical advances—and failed.

As the term implies, a "tonnage war" is by its very nature a naval war entailing an analysis of many statistics. Only a very few historians and readers welcome the intrusion of statistics, and partly as a result, this aspect of the U-boat war has been egregiously neglected. This neglect, in turn, has led to serious distortions in the perception of the results of the U-boat war. Although I have sought to include as few statistics as possible, this account is the first attempt by anyone to prove by statistical analysis that, contrary to the accepted wisdom—and mythology—at no time did the German U-boat force ever come close to winning the "Battle of the Atlantic," bringing on the collapse of Great Britain and, in such case, a different shape and outcome of the war in Europe.

I did not set out beforehand to prove this revolutionary conclusion. It became obvious along the way. I was at first startled and skeptical, even disbelieving. I invested years of study, analysis, and writing before I became fully convinced of these findings and was willing to present them to the community of naval historians and to the public.

CLAY BLAIR
Washington, D.C., London, Hamburg,
and Washington Island, Wisconsin,
1987–98

* See Volume II, Appendix 15, and Volume I, Appendix 18, based on Tarrant (1989).

CONTENTS

BOOK THREE

THE U-BOAT CAMPAIGN AGAINST THE BRITISH COMMONWEALTH AND THE UNITED STATES

SEPTEMBER 1942–MAY 1945

ONE

TWO

THREE

FOUR

FIVE

SIX

SEVEN

LIST OF MAPS

Faeroes
Norwegian
Sea
Shetlands
ATLANTIC
OCEAN
Orkneys
Scapa Flow
Hebrides
The Minches
Loch Ewe
Cromarty Firth
Moray Firth
Firth of Forth
Glasgow
North Channel
Firth of Clyde
North Sea
Londonderry
NORTHERN
IRELAND
Hartlepool
Barrow-
in-Furness
Irish Sea
Galway
Bay
Liverpool
IRELAND
St. George's Channel
GREAT
BRITAIN
Lowestoft
Milford
Haven
Harwich
Bristol Channel
London
Folkestone
Dover
B
Calais
Portsmouth
Lands End
Plymouth
Portland
Scillies
English Channel
Dieppe
FRANCE

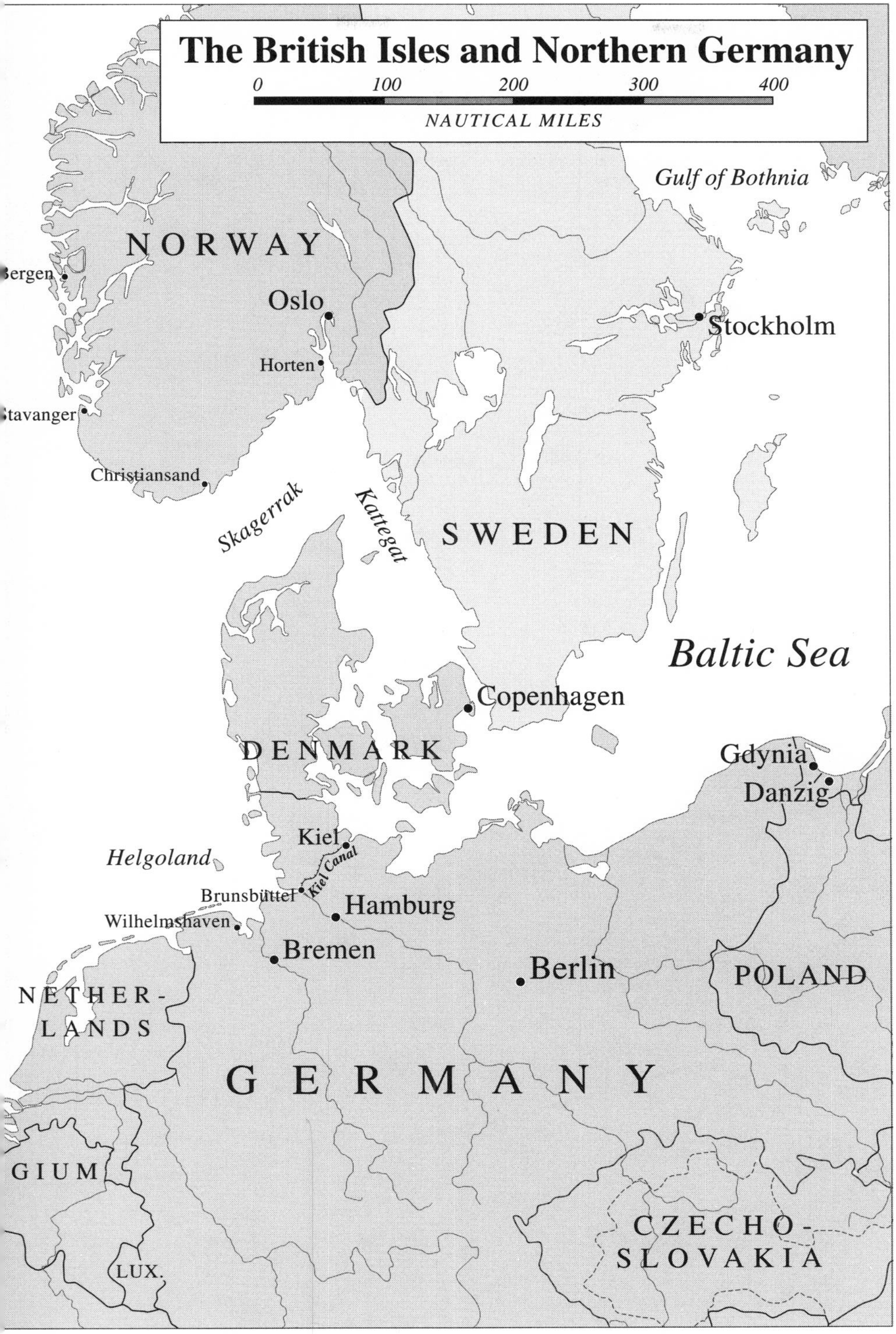
The British Isles and Northern Germany
0 100 200 300 400
NAUTICAL MILES
Gulf of Bothnia
NORWAY
ergen
Oslo
Horten
Stockholm
tavanger
Christiansand
Skagerrak
Kattegat
SWEDEN
Baltic Sea
Copenhagen
DENMARK
Gdynia
Danzig
Kiel
Helgoland
Kiel Canal
Brunsbüttel
Hamburg
Wilhelmshaven
Bremen
Berlin
POLAND
NETHER-
LANDS
GERMANY
GIUM
CZECHO-
SLOVAKIA
LUX.

North Atlantic Convoy Routes
0 100 200 300 400
NAUTICAL MILES
(at 50° North Latitude)
Greenland
Cape Farewell
CANADA
Belle Isle Strait
Newfoundland
Argentia
St. John's
Gulf of St. Lawrence
Quebec
St. Lawrence R.
Montreal
Nova Scotia
Sydney
Halifax
Cape Race
Cape Sable
Cape Cod
ATLANTIC
New York
UNITED STATES
Norfolk
Middle Atlantic Convoy Route
after November 8, 1942
Bermuda
UG—GU

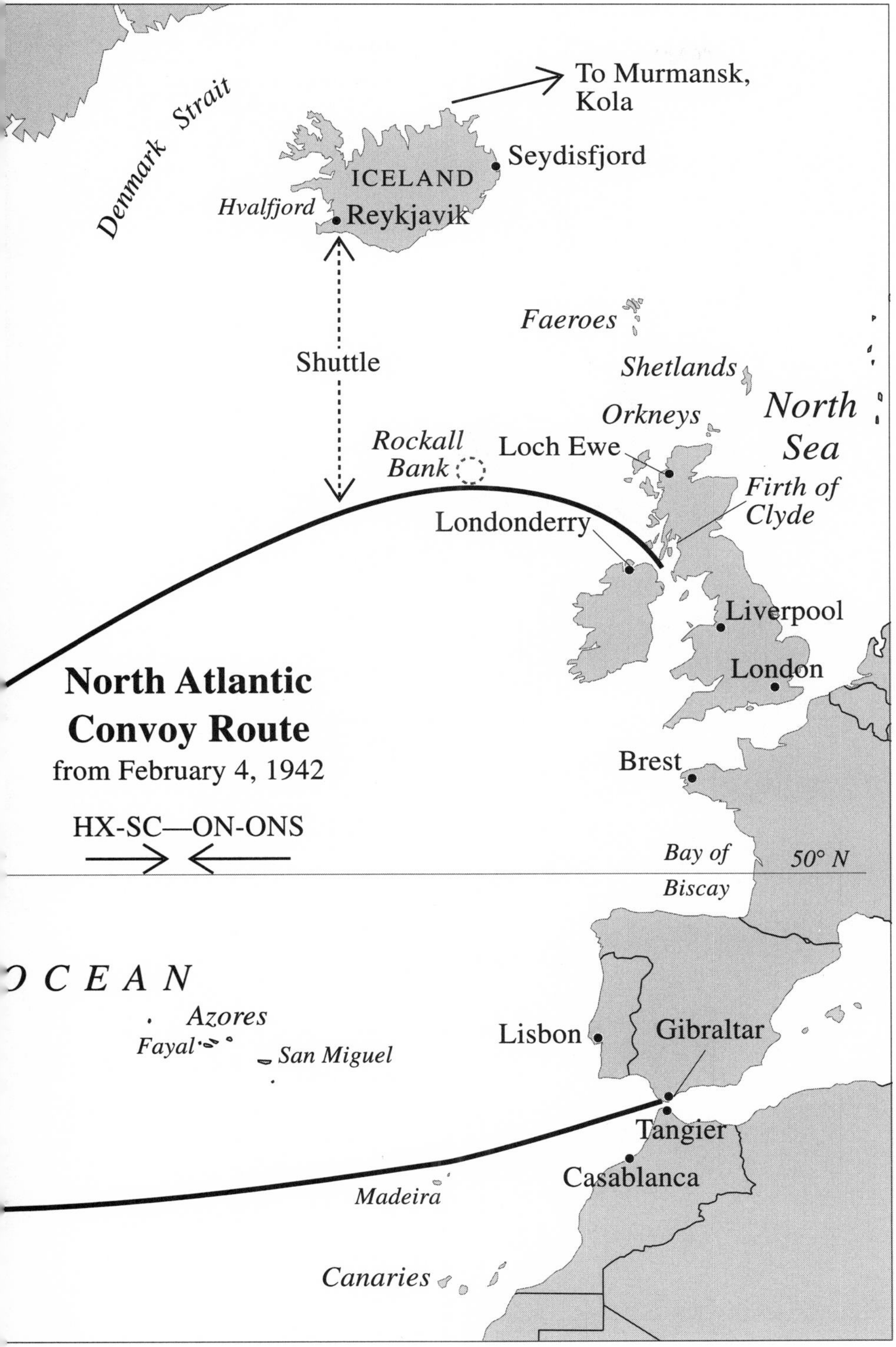
Denmark Strait
To Murmansk,
Kola
ICELAND
Seydisfjord
Hvalfjord
Reykjavik
Shuttle
Faeroes
Shetlands
Orkneys
North
Sea
Rockall
Bank
Loch Ewe
Firth of
Clyde
Londonderry
Liverpool
London
North Atlantic
Convoy Route
from February 4, 1942
HX-SC—ON-ONS
Brest
Bay of
Biscay
50° N
OCEAN
Azores
Fayal
San Miguel
Lisbon
Gibraltar
Tangier
Casablanca
Madeira
Canaries

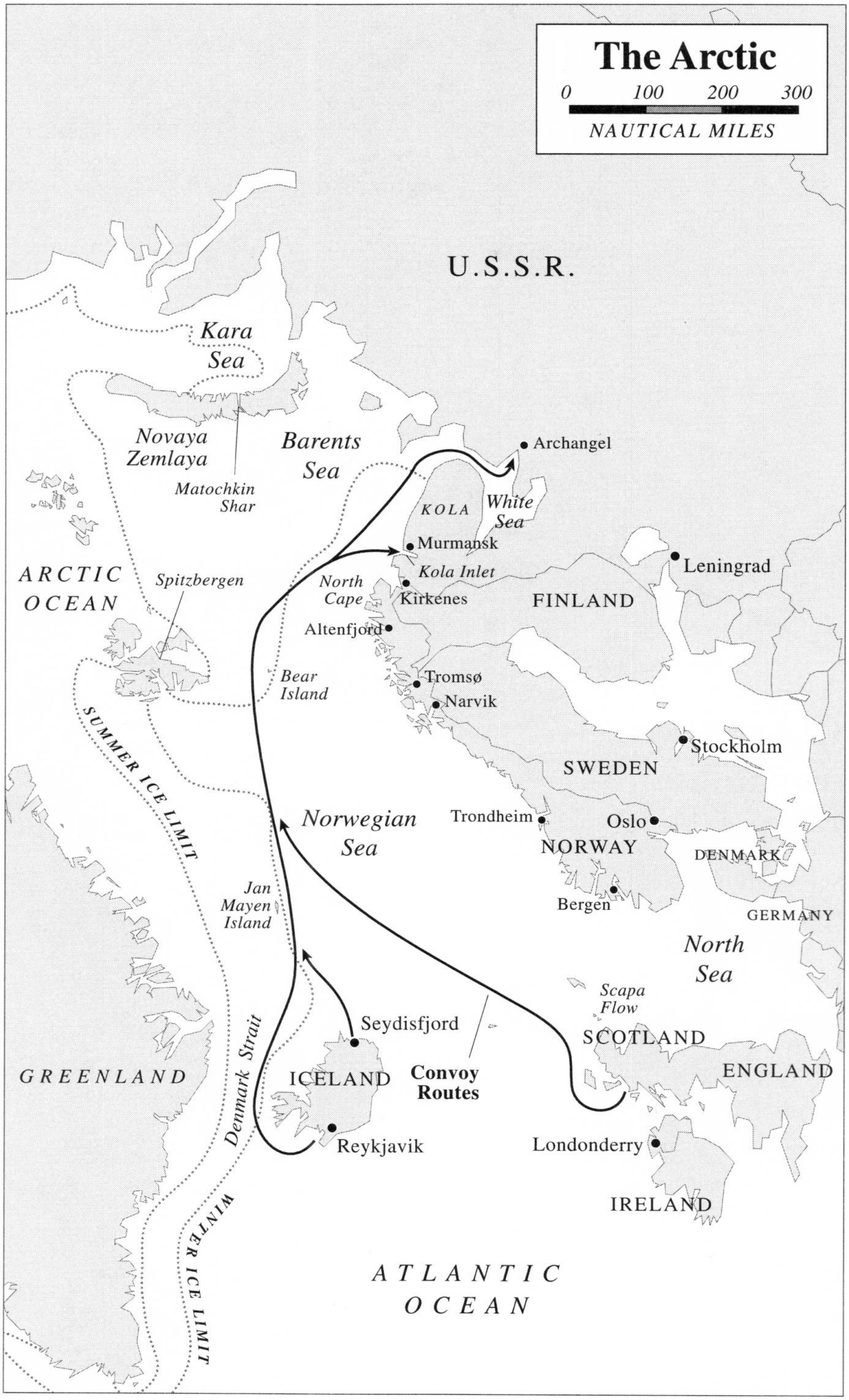
The Arctic
0 100 200 300
NAUTICAL MILES
U.S.S.R.
Kara Sea
Novaya Zemlaya
Matochkin Shar
Barents Sea
Archangel
KOLA
White Sea
Murmansk
Kola Inlet
Leningrad
ARCTIC OCEAN
Spitzbergen
North Cape
Kirkenes
FINLAND
Altenfjord
Bear Island
Tromsø
Narvik
Stockholm
SUMMER ICE LIMIT
SWEDEN
Norwegian Sea
Trondheim
Oslo
NORWAY
DENMARK
Jan Mayen Island
Bergen
GERMANY
North Sea
Scapa Flow
Seydisfjord
SCOTLAND
ENGLAND
GREENLAND
Denmark Strait
ICELAND
Convoy Routes
Reykjavik
Londonderry
IRELAND
WINTER ICE LIMIT
ATLANTIC OCEAN

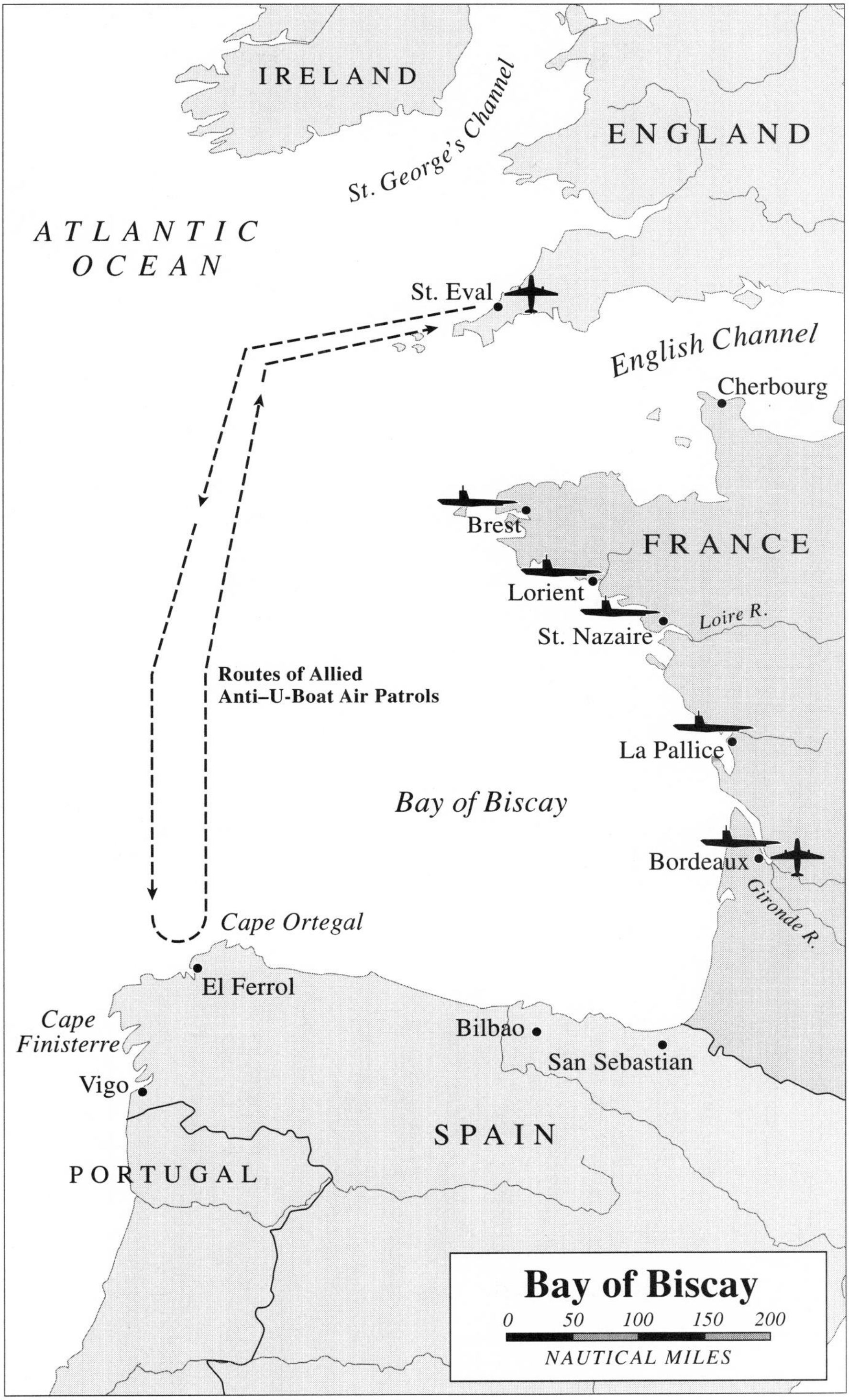
IRELAND
ENGLAND
St. George's Channel
ATLANTIC OCEAN
St. Eval
English Channel
Cherbourg
Brest
FRANCE
Lorient
St. Nazaire
Loire R.
Routes of Allied Anti–U-Boat Air Patrols
La Pallice
Bay of Biscay
Bordeaux
Gironde R.
Cape Ortegal
El Ferrol
Cape Finisterre
Bilbao
San Sebastian
Vigo
SPAIN
PORTUGAL
Bay of Biscay
0 50 100 150 200
NAUTICAL MILES

IRELAND
GREAT BRITAIN
DENMARK
GERMA
FRANCE
SPAIN
PORTUGAL
Marseilles
Toulon
La Spezia
Pola
Corsica
Rome
Sardinia
I T
Sicil
Gibraltar
Tangier
SP. MOROCCO
Oran
Algiers
Tunis
MOROCCO
TUNISIA
Tripo
ALGERIA
The Mediterranean
0 100 200 300 400
NAUTICAL MILES

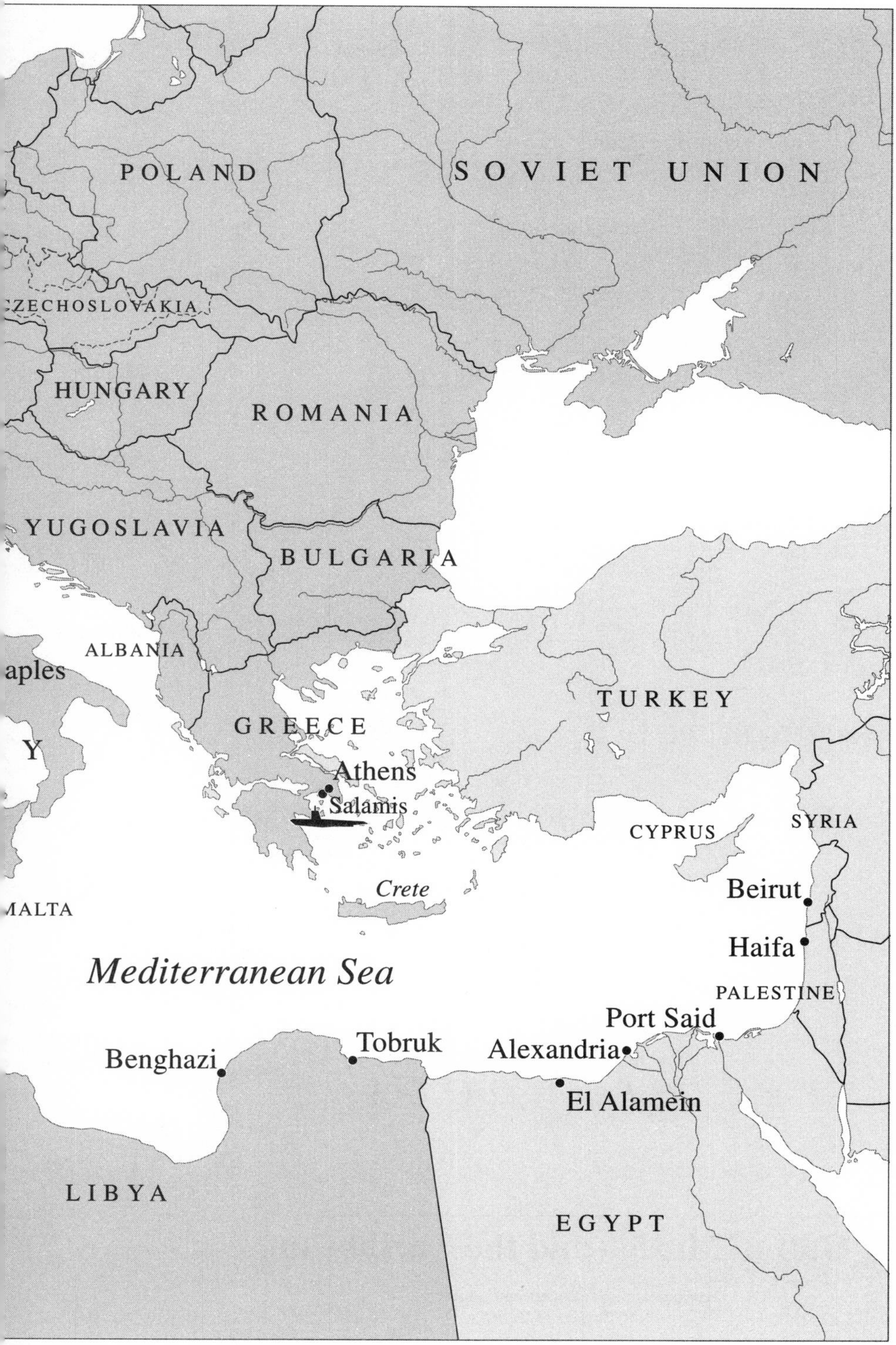
POLAND
SOVIET UNION
CZECHOSLOVAKIA
HUNGARY
ROMANIA
YUGOSLAVIA
BULGARIA
ALBANIA
aples
Y
GREECE
Athens
Salamis
TURKEY
CYPRUS
SYRIA
Crete
MALTA
Beirut
Haifa
Mediterranean Sea
PALESTINE
Port Said
Benghazi
Tobruk
Alexandria
El Alamein
LIBYA
EGYPT

Gulf of Mexico and the Caribbean

0 100 200 300 400

NAUTICAL MILES

ATLANTIC OCEAN
The Bahamas
hama Channel
Guantánamo
Windward Passage
DOMINICAN REPUBLIC
HAITI
AMAICA
Mona Passage
PUERTO RICO
Anegada Passage
Martinique
St. Lucia
Barbados
Caribbean Sea
Aruba
Curaçao
Trinidad
Gulf of Venezuela
Lake Maracaibo
VENEZUELA
COLOMBIA
BRAZIL

United States East Coast
0 100 200 300
NAUTICAL MILES
CANADA
CANADA
UNITED STATES
Halifax
Portland
Casco Bay
Boston
Cape Cod
Long Island
New York
Philadelphia
Washington, D.C.
Delaware Bay
Chesapeake Bay
Norfolk
Bermuda
Cape Hatteras
Cape Lookout
Cape Fear
100 FATHOM CURVE
Charleston
Savannah
Jacksonville
ATLANTIC OCEAN
Miami
The Bahamas

LIST OF PLATES

Cutaway illustrations of Type VIIC and Type IXC U-boats appear on pages xxx and xxxi.

Medium Type VII C

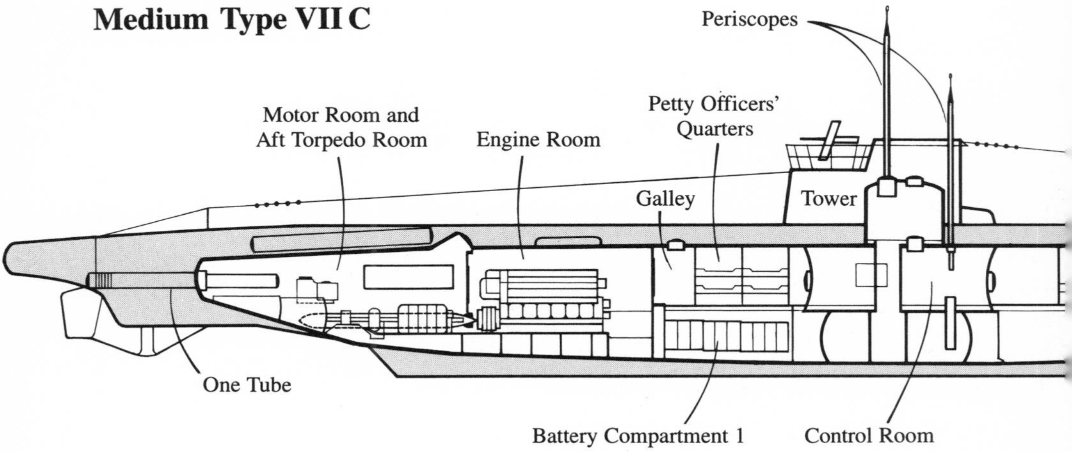

(Note: Tower, bridge, and antiaircraft gun configurations were often altered during the war.)

Large Type IX C

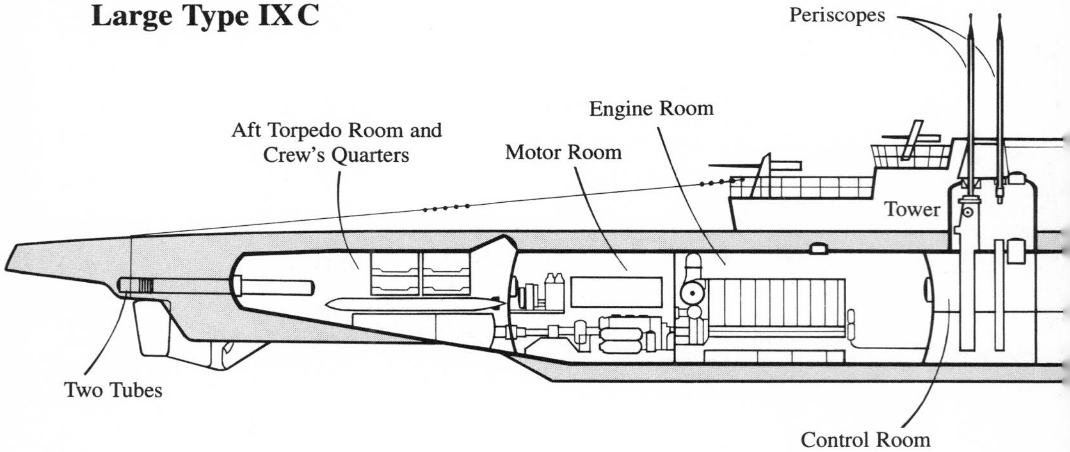

Principal German Attack Submarines of World War II

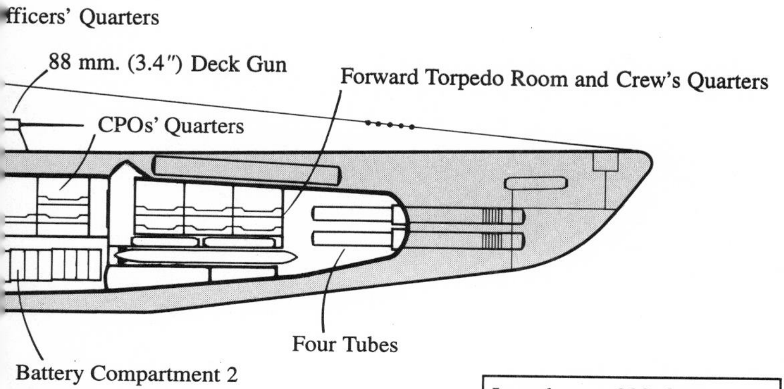

Length	220	feet
Fuel	113	tons
Speed	17	knots
Range at 12 knots	6,500	naut. miles
Torpedoes	12	

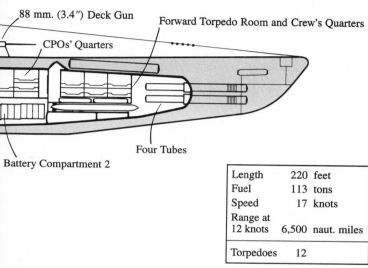

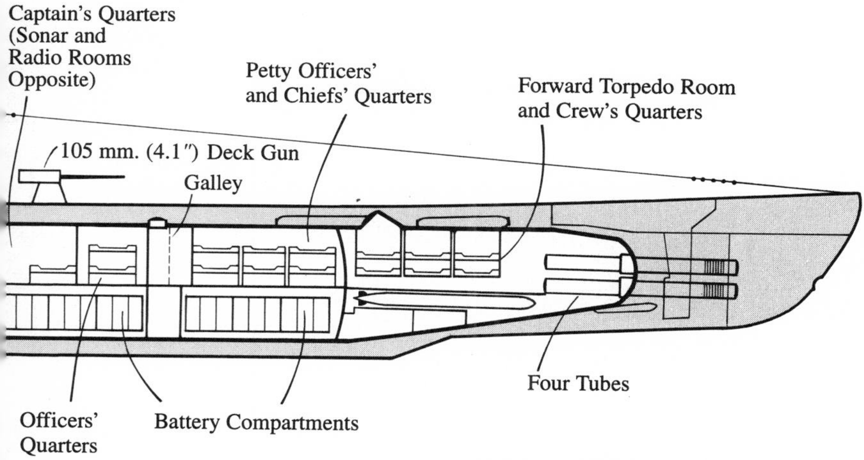

Length	252	feet
Fuel	208	tons
Speed	18.3	knots
Range at 12 knots	11,000	naut. miles
Torpedoes	14	

HITLER'S U-BOAT WAR

BOOK THREE

THE U-BOAT CAMPAIGN AGAINST THE BRITISH COMMONWEALTH AND THE UNITED STATES

SEPTEMBER 1942–MAY 1945

ONE

Overviews

At the beginning of the fourth year of World War II, September 3, 1942, Allied and Axis leaders were preoccupied with the following major military operations:

- **Stalingrad and the Caucasus.** Still dominating all else, the massive German armies and air forces in the southern regions of the Soviet Union had advanced steadily over the summer. Owing to the great symbolic importance of Stalingrad, Hitler insisted on its capture. Toward that end he diverted forces from the Caucasus Mountain area, thus slowing the German drive toward the Soviet oil fields to a crawl.

When Hitler's intentions became clear, Stalin and his generals rushed reinforcements to Stalingrad, setting the stage for one of the greatest battles of the war. As German forces closed on the city in early September, Stalin's chief military commander, Georgi Zhukov, saw an opportunity developing for a counterattack and obtained permission from Stalin to strike in early November.

- **Allied Aid to the Soviet Union.** Still doubtful that the Soviet armies could hold out alone, President Roosevelt insisted that Washington and London do everything possible to provide Moscow with assistance. Chief among the measures agreed to were a renewal of PQ convoys to Murmansk in September, a diversion of American fighters and bombers to the southern regions of the Soviet Union, and upgrades of port facilities in the Persian Gulf area and the railroad running through Iran to the Soviet Union.

• **North Africa.** At the end of August, Erwin Rommel attempted to break deeper into Egypt through British lines at Alam Halfa, but he failed. Dispirited and ill, he requested relief. On September 22, Georg Stumme, a tank specialist from the German campaign in the Soviet Union, replaced Rommel, who hospitalized himself in Germany. Meanwhile, the new British commanders, Harold Alexander and Bernard Montgomery, prepared the growing British Eighth Army (powerfully supplied with American tanks and aircraft) for an attack out of Egypt to the west designed to destroy the Axis forces, in particular Germany's shrinking and exhausted *Afrika Korps.*

• **Torch.** Preparations for Torch, the Allied invasion of French Northwest Africa, which had supplanted Sledgehammer, the first planned invasion of France, as a "second front" in 1942, proceeded apace. Commanded by Dwight D. Eisenhower, Torch forces were to land at three places: the Atlantic coast of Morocco and inside the Mediterranean at Algiers and Oran.

Torch was a risky undertaking. Some of the chief dangers:

1. Should the secret leak, the Germans might pre-position as many as fifty to one hundred U-boats west of Gibraltar to repel the Allied invasion forces.
2. The Germans might occupy Vichy France and Spain, capture Gibraltar, seize the neutralized French fleet at Toulon, and trap Allied forces inside the western Mediterranean.
3. The shy Italian surface fleet, supported by the Italian Air Force, the *Luftwaffe,* and Italian submarines, might finally mount an aggressive attack against Allied naval forces in the Mediterranean.
4. Rather than extending a friendly welcome, as hoped, French military forces in Morocco and Algeria might oppose the Allied landings vigorously, as they had opposed the recent British landing in Madagascar.
5. The notoriously rough seas on the open Atlantic coast of Morocco might well foil the attempts to mount an amphibious assault and occupy that country.

Influenced in part by the shortage of merchant shipping and warships for escort, the Torch D day fluctuated. It was first set for October 7, then postponed to November 8. In a message on September 4, Roosevelt informed Churchill that the U.S. Navy would provide Torch the bulk of the fighting power of the Atlantic Fleet. *Viz.*

3	battleships (1 modern)
1	fleet carrier *(Ranger)*
2	"jeep" carriers (later, increased to 4)
5	cruisers (2 heavy)
40	destroyers
6	minesweepers

The American forces landing in Morocco were to be supported by six new, prepositioned fleet submarines. They were to provide weather reports and homing beacons and later to blockade the unfinished but armed French battleship *Richelieu* at Dakar, Senegal. These six fleet boats were the first American-manned submarines assigned to combat in European waters.*

• **Guadalcanal.** The efforts by the Japanese to drive American forces from Guadalcanal intensified in the fall of 1942. In addition to the devastating losses the American Navy incurred in August and September, as related in Volume I, the Americans suffered further heavy warship losses during several naval battles in the Solomon Islands chain in October and November. These included the carrier *Hornet* and three more modern destroyers, *Duncan, Meredith,* and *Porter* sunk, the carrier *Enterprise,* the new battleship *South Dakota,* the light cruiser *Boise,* the modern destroyers *Farenholt* and *Smith* severely damaged. The battleship *South Dakota* and the modern destroyer *Mahan* collided, resulting in heavy damage to *Mahan.*

• **Atlantic Convoys.** Owing to several factors, including the commitment of warships for Murmansk convoy PQ 18 and for Torch, the Allies made major changes in the North Atlantic convoy networks. The most important was to designate New York rather than Canadian seaports as the primary assembly and sailing point for Halifax and Sydney (or Slow) convoys. This change, which took effect on September 17, enabled the Allies to eliminate most of the Boston-Halifax (BX) and Halifax-Boston (XB) convoys, to shrink the Canadian local escort force, and to reduce drastically the heavy ship traffic in the Cape Cod Canal, where the possibility of another lengthy shutdown due to an accident was still a matter of serious concern.

At this same time, the Allies approved final plans for a second major transatlantic convoy route. Designed initially to directly support Torch and other Mediterranean operations, this route was located in the more southerly latitudes of the Middle Atlantic. Fast and slow convoys outbound from America to support Torch were designated United States–Gibraltar (UGF and UGS). The reverse fast and slow convoys for returning ships were designated Gibraltar–United States (GUF and GUS). In addition to surface-ship escorts, these convoys were to be provided with long-range air escort from bases on the East Coast of the United States, Bermuda, Morocco, and Gibraltar.

In very short order, this all-American Middle Atlantic convoy route would become a major line of communications from the Arsenal of Democracy to the Mediterranean theater of war. Scarcely mentioned in accounts of the U-boat war, from its inception in the late fall of 1942 to the surrender of Germany in May 1945, about 12,300 Allied ships in about three hundred different convoys crossed the Atlantic east or west by that route.

These convoys were at first escorted by American destroyers, later by American destroyers and destroyer escorts, supported by American "jeep" carrier hunter-killer forces. The close escorts—usually about eight per convoy—refueled from tankers at sea. Because of the great distances entailed, the shortage of Type VII attack U-boats and U-tankers, and the decision to concentrate maximum force on the

---

* Designated Submarine Squadron 50, the first boats were *Barb, Blackfish, Gunnel, Gurnard, Herring,* and *Shad.* After Torch operations, the boats and the tender *Beaver* were to base in Roseneath, Scotland, and conduct anti–U-boat patrols.

North Atlantic run, the Germans could not simultaneously wage a U-boat war against the Middle Atlantic route. The best they could do was to mount glancing attacks on the eastern end of the route between the Azores and Gibraltar, but that area was soon saturated with radar-equipped Allied air and surface escorts based at Gibraltar and Morocco (and later, the Azores), making U-boat operations no less perilous than operations in the Iceland–British Isles area. As a result, in twenty-eight months of combat operations, the Middle Atlantic convoys lost only about twenty-five merchant ships (.002 percent), another remarkable and unheralded victory by the U.S. Navy.*

The final and absolute cancellation of Sledgehammer for 1942 and the decreasing likelihood of Roundup, the next planned invasion of France, in 1943, because of the demands of Torch, led Washington to make major changes in shipbuilding programs. Chief among these was the lowering of priorities for landing craft and the raising of priorities for the much-delayed destroyer escort and "jeep" carrier programs. On October 24, President Roosevelt notified Churchill that these and other adjustments would enable American shipyards to produce in 1943 seventy more destroyer escorts than planned (to a total of 336) and an additional two million deadweight tons of merchant ships (from about eighteen million deadweight tons to about twenty million).

This message was crossed in passing by a letter from Churchill to Roosevelt, which was hand-delivered on November 4 by the British war production czar, Oliver Lyttelton. Among other "major points," Churchill stressed the British requirement for additional merchant shipping from American production in 1943 (one million deadweight tons of tankers and 2.5 million deadweight tons of cargo ships) to provide a rock-bottom twenty-seven million tons of imports.

No less important, Churchill implored Roosevelt to provide long-range convoy escorts on the North Atlantic run. "It is *escorts* that we need," Churchill emphasized in italics, "even more than merchant ships. We want both, but I am all with those who say 'A ship not sunk in 1943 is worth two built for 1944.' " He urged the "maximum construction of escort vessels which engine [manufacturing] capacity will allow" and a distribution of 1 escort to the British for every 1.37 escorts to the Americans.

In pressing his case, Churchill continued to greatly inflate the "U-boat menace." It was, he was sure, "our worst danger." He went on in the bleakest possible language:

> It is horrible to me that we should be budgeting jointly for a balance of shipping on the basis of 700,000 tons a month loss. True, it is not yet as bad as that. But the spectacle of all these splendid ships being built, sent to sea crammed with priceless food and munitions, and being sunk—three or four every day—torments me day and night. Not only does this attack cripple our war energies and threaten our life,

* See Plate 12.

> but it arbitrarily limits the might of the United States coming into the struggle. The Oceans, which were your shields, threaten to become your cage.
>
> Next year there will be many more U-boats and they will range far more widely. No ocean passage will be safe. All focal points will be beset and will require long range air protection.

The Views from Berlin

Coinciding with the beginning of the fourth year of the war, the commander in chief of the *Kriegsmarine,* Grand Admiral Erich Raeder, met with Hitler on August 26 and September 28, 1942, to review the German naval picture. The U-boat commander in chief, Admiral Karl Dönitz, attended the second meeting to give Hitler a special presentation on the U-boat war.

Hitler opened the second meeting by heaping praise on the U-boat arm for its great achievements. A stenographer noted that Hitler dismissed the recently released American shipbuilding figures* as propaganda, adding:

> He is convinced that the monthly rate of sinkings will continue to be so high that the enemy will not be able to replace his losses by new construction. He considers it impossible that the increase in production of the enemy shipyards comes anywhere near what propaganda would have us believe. Even if the enemy should succeed in launching ships relatively fast, he would still not have the necessary engines, auxiliary engines, other equipment and, most of all, crews for the ships.

Dönitz began his presentation to Hitler by explaining that U-boats "fighting off the American coast [were] no longer sufficiently profitable." American ASW measures—air patrols in particular—and the extension of the convoy network were the main reasons. Except for a couple of "hot spots" (e.g., the Gulf of St. Lawrence, the Atlantic Ocean east and southeast of Trinidad), henceforth the U-boats were to move back to the North Atlantic and to the west coast of Africa near Freetown and south to Cape Town.

Dönitz stressed the extreme difficulties his boats faced attacking convoys on the North Atlantic run. Growing numbers of radar-equipped, long- and very-long-range Allied aircraft (B-24 Liberators, B-17 Flying Fortresses, PBY Catalinas, Sunderlands) based in the British Isles, Iceland, and Newfoundland were able to provide convoys with air cover nearly all the way across the North Atlantic.† The presence of these aircraft made it very difficult for the U-boats to stay on the surface and shadow a convoy so that other boats could gather, or to haul around to a better or second shooting position ahead of the convoy. Distant and close radar-

---

* A public forecast by the Deputy Director of the U.S. Maritime Commission, Howard L. Vickery, that in 1942 and 1943 American yards alone would produce over 2,500 ships for 27.4 million deadweight tons. It was an accurate prediction. In 1942 and 1943, American yards produced 2,709 ships for 27.21 million deadweight tons, or 18.435 million gross registered tons.

† See Appendix 10.

equipped surface escorts made it difficult for the U-boats to get close enough to the convoy formation to shoot.*

As a result of intensified and improved Allied ASW measures, the inexperience of the U-boat crews, foul weather, and other factors, the tonnage sunk per boat in North Atlantic convoy battles was certain to decline. In order to reverse the decline—indeed, to return to the previous high levels of sinkings per U-boat—Dönitz said the U-boat arm urgently required:

- A very-long-range, high-performance bomber, such as the prototype Heinkel 177 (HE-177), to scout out convoys and to warn of an approaching Allied air threat and to deal with that threat when it arrived.
- An entirely new attack submarine with very high submerged speed to enable it to catch up to a convoy submerged, outmaneuver and outrun escorts during the attack and withdrawal phases, and shadow a convoy submerged long enough to bring up other members of the pack.

In response to these sweeping proposals, Hitler had two very different reactions. On the one hand, he ducked any "definite promises" for a new aircraft, such as the HE-177, to support the submarines. To be sure, he recognized the need for the "best possible aircraft" for that purpose, but the German aircraft industry was already swamped by demands and could not take on mass production of a large bomber. On the other hand, Hitler strongly endorsed the construction of new U-boats with high underwater sprint speed. Such a submarine, Hitler enthused, "would have a revolutionary effect. It would immediately render ineffective the whole apparatus of enemy escort vessels and the construction programs of the relatively slow corvettes."

The idea for a German submarine with high submerged sprint speed was not new. In the early 1930s, a brilliant German engineer, Helmuth Walter, had proposed to the Berlin naval command a small, experimental design that in theory could run submerged at thirty knots for brief periods. It was to have diesel engines for surface cruising and a turbine propelled by decomposed hydrogen peroxide (H_2O_2) and water for submerged cruising. To reduce underwater drag, the hull was to be smooth, streamlined, and fish-shaped.

Although the Germans had settled on conventional diesel-electric propulsion plants for the new generation of VIIs and IXs, the OKM† did not slam the door on Walter. In 1939 Berlin awarded him a contract for an eighty-ton, seventy-two-foot test vehicle, designated *V-80.* Built in the greatest secrecy in a screened-off area of the Krupp Germania-Werft yards in Kiel, the boat very much resembled a huge fish. Viewed bow on in cross section, she formed a figure eight. The living, working, and fighting areas were in the upper half of the eight; the lower half was used to store volatile hydrogen-peroxide fuel. In trials at Hela in 1940, the sleek *V-80* achieved a sensational submerged sprint speed of 28.1 knots.

---

* Dönitz was still unaware that usually one or more ships in every convoy had Huff Duff or of the increasingly important role shipboard and land-based Huff Duff played in convoy defense. See Appendix 8.

† *Oberkommando der Kriegsmarine,* i.e., naval headquarters, Berlin.

Owing to the great success of the Types VII and IX in 1940 and 1941, and to lingering technical doubts about "Walter boats," the OKM was not keen to increase support for the program. However, in January 1942, when Walter presented improved designs for large and small hydrogen-peroxide-powered submarines, Dönitz endorsed them enthusiastically and urged the OKM to back Walter to the fullest. In the wake of the intensified RAF Coastal Command ASW operations in the Bay of Biscay, Dönitz repeated that request on June 24, 1942. In lukewarm response, the OKM awarded Walter contracts for five experimental hydrogen-peroxide prototypes: one 170-foot, 600-ton "Atlantic" boat *(U-791)* and four small coastal boats *(U-792* to *U-795).* On paper, all were capable of bursts of speed to twenty-five knots or slightly more while submerged.

Although Walter had been designing hydrogen-peroxide submarines for ten years and one test bed *(V-80)* had been built and tried out with considerable success, by September 1942 none of the five boats under contract had progressed much beyond the design stage. Formidable technical problems remained to be solved, not the least of which was the construction of several plants capable of producing vast quantities of the hydrogen-peroxide fuel. Nonetheless, with Hitler's enthusiastic approval, Raeder and Dönitz decided in the September 28 meeting to place orders for twenty-four of the small boats (*U-1405* to *U-1416* and *U-1081* to *U-1092*) and "hoped to be able to make a decision within two months regarding mass production of the larger type." In any case, Raeder stated, "mass production of these submarines is to be started as soon as possible, with corresponding adjustment of the present submarine construction program."

These little-noted decisions in the early fall of 1942 were among the most important of the U-boat war. They contain the profound implication that Raeder and Dönitz had concluded that Allied detection technology and air and sea supremacy had rendered the Type VIIs and IXs inadequate and obsolescent weapon systems. To successfully prosecute the U-boat war, an entirely new generation of U-boats, embodying quantum leaps in technology, was required. The most promising possibility was the Walter boat. Hence the huge gamble on the professor's visionary ideas at this time.

Obviously the fleets of Walter boats could not be produced overnight. It would take at least a year to complete, test, and debug the four small prototypes. The knowledge and experience gained from these four boats, as well as the twenty-four additional small boats on order were to be applied promptly to two big Walter "Atlantic" prototypes *(U-796* and *U-797),* which were to be built in parallel with the smaller boats. That way, it was believed, many of the expected R&D delays could be avoided and the big "Atlantic" boats could be rushed into mass production.

Pending the completion of large and small Walter boats in meaningful numbers, German yards were to continue production of Type VIIs and IXs. With patched-on improvements, these boats were to carry on the U-boat war to the best of their ability until Allied ASW measures completely checked or defeated them. Although it was expected that the sinkings by these boats would gradually diminish and that losses would climb, the continuing presence of Type VIIs and IXs in many separate areas of the world was to serve several important war aims apart from sinkings: to insure a continuation of wasteful Allied convoying, to tie down substantial numbers of Allied military assets in an ASW role, and to train and battle-harden a new generation of German submariners who were to man the Walter boats.

The Codebreakers

In September 1942, the Germans still enjoyed the advantage in the seesaw battle of naval codebreaking. In February 1942, they had introduced a fourth rotor to the naval Enigma machine in use on the Atlantic U-boat radio networks, again blinding Allied codebreakers. The Germans called this new cipher *Triton;* the British called it Shark. Absent "four-rotor bombes"* and "physical captures" (of short-signal weather and battle codebooks or Enigma key settings), the codebreakers at Bletchley Park in England had made little or no progress in breaking into four-rotor Enigma. On the other side of the hill, since February 1942 the swelling staff of the German codebreaking organization, *B-dienst,* was reading the Allied Cypher Number 3, employed jointly by the Americans, the Canadians, and the British for North Atlantic convoy operations. By September 1942, *B-dienst* daily produced an unprecedented picture of Allied convoy sailings and the routes they followed sufficiently current for Dönitz to use the information tactically.

The U.S. Navy was by this time thoroughly fed up with those Britons who still held tightly to the secrets of the bombe technology and had not yet provided the Americans with a long-promised bombe to copy for purposes of breaking *Kriegsmarine* (or naval) Enigma. The reasons for the delay were usually attributed to genuine British fears that the Americans would not keep secret the breaking of Enigma, as a consequence of which the Germans would turn to an entirely new and more difficult to break encoding system, blinding the British to the *Luftwaffe* Red and other Enigma ciphers they were reading. Doubtless the time-honored British custom of total secrecy regarding dissemination of codebreaking technology also played a role in the delay.

British fears of losing all Enigma product were perfectly understandable and, furthermore, they were fueled by a startling new challenge in the ether. British radio-interception stations picked up increasingly heavy German traffic on a new, sophisticated non-Morse (Baudot) encoded automatic-teletype system. The German name for this high-level cryptographic system was *Geheimschreiber;* the British called it Fish. Some feared it would in part replace the Enigma system. The British had built a machine to help break into Fish that was so complicated in appearance that it was christened "Robinson," after Heath Robinson, the British version of the American cartoonist Rube Goldberg, who devised fantastic machines to perform ludicrous tasks. Beyond that, and far more importantly, they had com-

---

* A "bombe" was an ingenious Allied electromechanical machine, first developed by the Poles in prewar years, that was used to help break German Enigma codes. (See photo insert.)

menced work on an experimental, mammoth new Fish bombe aptly named Colossus, which had 2,400 vacuum tubes!*

During the summer of 1942, the British authorized the semipermanent attachment of two U.S. Navy officers to Hut 8, the naval cryptography section at Bletchley Park—reservist Joseph J. Eachus and Robert Bellville Ely, III. In a history of the U.S. Navy bombe project, its chief designer, Howard T. Engstrom,† wrote that Ely and Eachus were sent to England in July of 1942

> for the primary purpose of studying [general] British cryptanalytical research methods but with additional instructions to find out all details possible concerning the British "E" [Enigma] problem. Under the impetus of the presence of these two officers, considerable detailed information was forthcoming concerning the British bombe and wiring diagrams.‡

That is, the British were much more forthcoming than they had been when U.S. Navy officers Prescott H. Currier and Robert H. Weeks visited Bletchley Park in February of 1941.§

Engstrom continued:

> As the months passed, it became more and more evident from reports received from our representatives in England [Eachus and Gaschk] that the British would be unable to supply us a machine [bombe] by the promised date.# It became evident, furthermore, that the British were having considerable difficulty in building any workable high-speed machine. Accordingly, early in September after continuous conferences, we reached the conclusion that American methods and design showed sufficient probability of success to inaugurate the bombe program.

After clearing it with superiors up the line, in "early September" Joseph Wenger, head of the U.S. Navy's codebreaking outfit, OP20G, met with Edward G. G. Hastings, the Bletchley Park representative on the British Joint Staff Mission in Wash-

---

* The story of Fish and Colossus is beyond the scope of this book. See articles in the bibliography under "Colossus."

† For biographical and professional information on Engstrom, see Volume I, pp. 243–44 and 557.

‡ See unpublished documents in NARA, RG 457, NSA History Collection, Box 705, especially NR 1736, dated April 24, 1944, "Memorandum for the Director of Naval Communications, History of the Bombe Project," by Joseph N. Wenger, Engstrom, and Ralph I. Meader (hereafter Engstrom Memo), and chapter 11 of George E. Howe's *United States Cryptographic History, NSA* (1980). In a 1998 taped interview with the author, Eachus clarified: He and Ely flew to England, remained at Bletchley Park about three weeks, then flew back to the States with blueprints for an Enigma machine. At the specific request of Gordon Welchman, almost immediately the U.S. Navy sent Eachus back by air to Bletchley Park where he and a U.S. Navy coworker, Milton Gaschk, remained on semipermanent duty for about one year, submitting reports on various British projects at the GC&CS.

§ See Volume I, pp. 240–44.

On May 13, 1942, Bletchley Park's deputy director, Edward Travis, had promised in writing to deliver to the Americans "by August or September" a bombe and "a mechanic to instruct in the maintenance and operation."

ington. Wenger told Hastings that since the British "had shown no evidence of being able to live up to their promises," the U.S. Navy would proceed alone with development and production of a high-speed four-rotor bombe to attack four-rotor naval Enigma. Hastings countered that the British had indeed lived up to their promises, but his protests fell on deaf ears. On September 3, 1942, Wenger formally proposed to the Director of Naval Communications, Joseph R. Redman,* that the U.S. Navy proceed with a bombe project. Redman readily approved, as did the Assistant Chief of Naval Operations, Frederick J. Horne, who signed off officially on September 4.

From a technical standpoint, the addition of a fourth rotor to naval Enigma "introduced a factor of twenty-six in the time required for a solution," Engstrom wrote. To find the daily key settings "necessitated either twenty-six times as many [three-rotor] bombes or a bombe which would go twenty-six times as fast." Based on his theoretical work in 1941 and 1942, Engstrom had concluded that the American effort should be directed "to high-speed approaches to the problem," as he wrote Wenger.

The OP20G proposal did not specify how many bombes should be built. The Americans thought at first that the figure should be 336. In his memo to Wenger, Engstrom explained why:

> In the original concept of the problem it appeared that 336 units were desirable since there are 336 possible wheel settings. In forming preliminary notions of the size and power requirements for the equipment, the British 3-wheel bombe was in mind. The British 3-wheel bombes have three levels in each physical piece of equipment. Thus the concept of 336 bombes led to the notion of 112 separate pieces of equipment.
>
> The early decision to build 336 units was predicated upon the belief that we should have to provide for running all 336 wheel orders. As study of the problem progressed, it became evident that there were analytical ways of ruling out many of the wheel orders, thus reducing the bombe requirements. The possibilities of making this reduction were given very serious study for the reason that materials at the time were exceedingly critical. . . . Meanwhile, certain changes in German communications which affected cross-cribbing and indications of procedure changes involving the use of the fourth wheel arose. These changes made it impossible to arrive at a definite decision on the number of machines required before it became necessary to proceed with designs for housing the equipment.†

The Americans chose the National Cash Register (NCR) Company in Dayton, Ohio, to manufacture the bombes. A Dartmouth College graduate (1919), inventor, and Navy reservist, Ralph I. Meader, then serving in the Bureau of Ships, went to NCR in Dayton to represent the Navy. On November 11, 1942, the Navy began construction at NCR of the U.S. Naval Computing Machine Laboratory, "for the purpose of assisting the contractor in the production of these bombes and in the

---

* Redman had replaced Leigh Noyes as Director of Naval Communications in March 1942.

† The official British intelligence historian F. H. Hinsley presents a quite inaccurate account of the American decisions with respect to the number of American bombes contemplated and why. See his *British Intelligence in the Second World War,* vol. 2, p. 57.

training of maintenance and operational personnel." Meader became officer in charge of this facility, which soon grew to include hundreds of enlisted men and Waves who actually built the bombes.

The National Cash Register Company, which invented and produced the first such "cash register" to bear its name, was the most prominent of numerous Dayton manufacturing facilities, almost all engaged in war production. In addition to the cash register, Daytonians had invented or exploited a variety of mechanical and electromechanical devices: the airplane (Wright Brothers), the automobile starter, bicycles, refrigerators, and radios.

Another reason the Navy chose NCR was because of the presence there of a remarkably inventive thirty-five-year-old electrical engineer named Joseph R. Desch. A graduate of the University of Dayton (1928), Desch came from one of the city's many large German families. In the darkest of the Depression years, from 1930 to 1938, Desch had worked as a practical inventor/designer for three prominent Dayton firms: General Motors Radio, Telecom Laboratories, and Frigidaire. In 1938, when NCR's visionary president, Colonel Edward Deeds, established an electrical research laboratory, Desch came aboard to experiment with all kinds of exotic new electronic devices. His brilliant contributions in this field gained him many honors and association with other leading American inventors and scientists, such as Vannevar Bush at MIT, who rose to direct the nation's military science projects in World War II.

Dayton was the ideal place to make bombes but it was not a good place to operate them. It was too far from Washington and the "users" of the output of the bombes. Foreseeing this problem, Wenger and Engstrom were already carrying out plans to transfer all the bombes to Washington. To house them, Wenger had acquired a former girls' school, Mount Vernon Seminary, at 3801 Nebraska Avenue, in the heart of residential northwest Washington at Ward Circle. Work was under way on a strongly built two-story building for the bombes and also quarters for the hundreds of Waves who were to operate and repair the machines, much as British "Wrens"* operated and repaired the British bombes at Bletchley Park. The new Navy installation was merely fifteen minutes by automobile from the Navy Department offices, located downtown on Constitution Avenue.

By coincidence perhaps, at this time the British made some sweeping changes in the Naval Intelligence Division and at Bletchley Park.

- Winston Churchill directed First Sea Lord Dudley Pound to sack the Director of the Admiralty's Naval Intelligence Division, John H. Godfrey.† Promoted to vice admiral, Godfrey departed England by flying boat on September 24 to carry out a preplanned visit to Washington and Ottawa. He was replaced by Edmund G. N. Rushbrooke.

---

* Nickname for members of the Women's Royal Naval Service (WRNS), formally incorporated into the Royal Navy in 1949.

† See Beesly, *Very Special Admiral* (1980).

- At Bletchley Park, deputy director Edward Travis replaced deputy director Alastair Denniston as operating head of that swelling establishment. The era of quaint eccentricity had passed, the codebreaking historian David Kahn wrote. A "table thumper" who had risen through the "codebreaking side," Travis was "a manager who could bring it into the modern era of cryptanalytic mass production." Denniston remained as a deputy director of the civil side, a much smaller outfit.
- The brilliant, eccentric British mathematician and coinventor, with Gordon Welchman, of the first British bombe, Alan Turing, proved—not surprisingly—to be a poor administrator. In September, he was eased out of his job as chief of the naval Enigma codebreakers in Hut 8 at Bletchley Park, in due course replaced by a mathematician (and chess champion), Hugh Alexander. After working briefly on Fish and the teletype-decoding machines Robinson and Colossus, Turing left for the United States on the giant troopship *Queen Elizabeth,* arriving in New York on November 13, 1942. He remained in the States for the next four and a half months.

In Washington on October 2, the Royal Navy's Captain Carl Holden and the U.S. Navy's Captain Joseph Wenger entered into a written agreement outlining a complete and open exchange of information and technology regarding four-rotor U-boat Enigma and Italian and Japanese naval codes. A brief summary of this agreement in Howe's NSA history was deleted by censors. However, it was presumably a document that finally opened the way for a truly complete exchange of intelligence on U-boats.

The importance of this Anglo-American naval agreement cannot be too strongly stressed. The historian Bradley F. Smith wrote*:

> It broke with the age-old tradition of caution and suspicion which admonished even closely allied states not to open their most secret cupboards because today's comrades in arms could well be tomorrow's dangerous opponents.

Even though the U.S. Army was shortly to face German armies in Torch (the Anglo-American invasion of French Northwest Africa set for November 8), the British refused to enter into a similar exchange with the Americans of German Army and *Luftwaffe* Enigma out of fear that the Americans would leak the secrets. Accordingly, Howe wrote, the U.S. Army entered into a contract with Bell Telephone Laboratories on September 30 to produce 144 bombes for a unilateral attack on German Army and Air Force (three-rotor) Enigma. These bombes were known as "Rapid Analytical Machines" (or RAMs) and rather than "rotors" they employed "relay switching" (stepping switches) similar to the Army's clones of the Japanese "Purple" machines. In a little over one month, Bell Labs demonstrated a successful sample model, Howe wrote, and expected to fulfill half of the order (seventy-two machines) by April 1943.

The Army Chief of Staff, George C. Marshall, agreed with the British that at least for the time being there was no pressing reason why the British should share the fruits of German Army and *Luftwaffe* codes with the U.S. Army headquarters

---

* *The Ultra-Magic Deals* (1992).

in Washington. Rather than run the risk of leaks in transmission or in Washington itself, Marshall arranged with the British to send a meticulously selected and screened cadre of U.S. Army officers to England. These officers were to be put in the Ultra picture at Bletchley Park, then head up small Special Liaison Units (SLUs) that were to be attached to U.S. Army headquarters in the Mediterranean and Europe, serving as conduits for British-produced German Army and Air Force Ultra information.

These arrangements between the British and the U.S. Navy in October 1942 would at last lead to a close working relationship between the two nations in naval intelligence matters. The U.S. Navy's OP20G would work hand in glove with Bletchley Park to break into the *Kriegsmarine*'s *Triton* traffic. The U.S. Army codebreakers in Washington would concentrate on breaking Japanese military codes. The British were to provide to the American forces in Europe Ultra material from German Army, *Luftwaffe,* and other Enigma networks, appropriate to the prosecution of land and air warfare.

Alan Turing's biographer, Andrew Hodges, wrote that the purpose of his trip to the United States in the fall of 1942 was to help American scientists and engineers at Bell Laboratories (in New York City) develop an absolutely secure high-level telephone link between London and Washington, the technology for which later became known to laymen as a "scrambler." This very well may have been the case, but much more about this trip needs to be brought to light. Turing spent most of the first two months of his visit in Washington with Howard Engstrom and other U.S. Navy codebreakers, who were in the process of refining the design of the bombes to attack naval Enigma then under construction at NCR in Dayton. He did not report for work at Bell Labs, Hodges wrote, until January 1943. At first he was denied access to classified work, but after a dust-up on the highest levels he was cleared. Thereafter, he was allowed complete access to everything Bell Labs had undertaken, including, of course, its most important project, the RAM (or bombe), of which the U.S. Army had ordered 144.

Turing would no longer play a freewheeling and dominant role at Bletchley Park, which had grown to thousands of rigidly isolated workers in closely administered Ultra production lines. On this trip to America, the U.S. Army and Navy, both recently embarked upon producing an aggregate of about 250 different bombes, milked Turing's brain profitably.

In his history of the U.S. Navy bombe project, Engstrom wrote that Alan Turing visited OP20G and the naval bombe facility at NCR, in Dayton, in December 1942. Afterward, Turing wrote a report in which he criticized several aspects of the American technical approach to the problem, although he conceded that *"starting from scratch* on the design of a bombe, this method is about as good as our own." In his bombe history, Engstrom quoted criticisms from the Turing memo and remarked: "These quotations and other comments in the report indicate the considerable extent to which our design was at variance with British ideas and experience."

Gordon Welchman, the coinventor of the original British bombe, wrote in his memoir* that the new Bletchley Park chief, Edward Travis, also removed him from his old haunts. Concluding his work in Hut 6, Welchman became Assistant Director for Mechanization at Government Code & Cipher School (GC&CS). Emulating Alan Turing, he sailed to the States on February 17, 1943, aboard the troopship-liner *Queen Mary* for an extended visit. He wrote that he established himself in the New York office of the senior British spymaster in the States, William Stephenson (the subject of *A Man Called Intrepid*). He spent Mondays to Fridays in Washington and weekends in New York, "where cipher machines were being built." In Washington, he worked with U.S. military cryptographic experts, such as the Army's Frank B. Rowlett and the Navy's Howard Engstrom. Like Turing, he probably contributed ideas to the Army's RAM program and the Navy's bombe project.†

The Arctic: Convoys PQ 18 and QP 14

Unaware of the Allied decision to halt convoys to northern Russia in the months of July and August 1942, the Germans wasted many U-boat patrols and aircraft sorties in a futile search for convoy PQ 18 to Murmansk and its reverse, convoy QP 14 from Murmansk. Finally, on September 5, the Germans learned of the postponement and new scheduled sailing, from documents recovered in a British Hampden aircraft that crashed near Vardø, Norway, and from decrypts of some Russian Air Force radio transmissions.

The long delayed PQ 18, consisting of forty heavily laden cargo ships, some towing tethered blimps for protection from low-flying aircraft, and others streaming Admiralty Net Defense,‡ sailed from Scotland on September 2. The close escort and support force was massive: fifty-two British vessels, consisting of:

1	"jeep" carrier, *Avenger*
2	antiaircraft light cruisers
1	light cruiser, *Scylla*
21	destroyers
4	corvettes
7	minesweepers
9	submarines
4	ASW trawlers
2	tankers
1	rescue ship

* *The Hut Six Story* (1982).

† After the war, Welchman immigrated to the United States and became an American citizen. He joined a private firm, Engineering Research Associates (ERA), which was founded by Howard Engstrom, Ralph Meader, and others to build codebreaking machines for the Navy and early commercial mainframe computers for private industry. Because in his book Welchman described technically some ways wartime Enigma was penetrated, London and Washington were furious. Washington rescinded his security clearance, thereby denying him the ability to ply his trade, and threatened to prosecute him by U.S. laws for leaking British secrets. The British writer "Nigel West" (*The Sigint Secrets,* 1988) wrote that the stress brought on by this governmental "harassment" aggravated a heart condition and led to his premature death in October 1985.

‡ Strong steel-mesh nets to stop or deflect submarine torpedoes.

Another twenty-five British warships and support vessels provided distant cover or carried out special missions in conjunction with the voyage of PQ 18. These included three battleships and six cruisers with appropriate destroyer screens and two tankers. By Churchill's reckoning, PQ 18 required altogether "seventy-seven escorts" (as he told Roosevelt), a heavy strain on the Royal Navy, which also had to carry out a large assignment in Torch on November 8.

The "jeep" carrier *Avenger* was included not to defend the convoy from torpedo planes and dive-bombers, as many supposed, but rather to destroy or drive off *Luftwaffe* shadowers and U-boats. For that purpose she embarked a dozen old Sea Hurricanes (and another half dozen in storage) and three old radar-equipped Swordfish biplanes. Neither type of aircraft was suitable for the task. The Sea Hurricanes were too lightly armed. Owing to the slow speed of *Avenger* in convoy, the Swordfish could not take off with a load of depth charges. They could only reconnoiter, drop flares, and hope to guide destroyers to the U-boats.

The opposite-sailing convoy, QP 14, assembled at the northern Russian port of Archangel, which was more distant than Murmansk from the Norway-based *Luftwaffe* aircraft and is ice-free from July to September. Composed of fifteen cargo ships, the convoy was ordered to sail on September 13. It was guarded by twelve other British warships: two destroyers, four corvettes, three minesweepers, and three ASW trawlers.

The new German admiral commanding the Arctic area, Otto Klüber, planned to bring all available German sea power to bear against PQ 18 and QP 14. This time, the U-boats were to attack both convoys. The "pocket" battleship *Admiral Scheer,* the heavy cruiser *Hipper,* the light cruiser *Köln,* and five destroyers were to attack QP 14.* While *Admiral Scheer* was shifting from Narvik to Altenfiord to prepare for this mission, the British submarine *Tigris* spotted and attacked her but the four torpedoes missed. However, *Scheer* developed serious engine problems and was forced to abort. Later, when Hitler again cautioned Admiral Raeder not to unduly risk the big ships, the OKM canceled the entire surface-ship mission. The attacks on PQ 18 and QP 14 were thus to be restricted to U-boats and aircraft.

German reconnaissance aircraft found and shadowed PQ 18 on September 6 and 8. In response, Klüber brought to bear fifteen Norway-based U-boats. Initially, eleven boats that were ready (or soon to be ready) were to operate against PQ 18, and four boats in (or soon to be in) the eastern area were to operate against QP 14. On the OKM's order, Dönitz temporarily diverted seven new Type VIIs sailing from Kiel to the Atlantic to positions near Iceland to intercept QP 14 and its heavy escorts at the end of the voyage. One of these, *U-606,* aborted to Bergen with an ailing skipper.†

---

* Owing to a defective main bearing, the battleship *Tirpitz* could not participate.

† The *U-606* skipper, Hans Klatt, was temporarily replaced by Dietrich von der Esch of *U-586,* which was in refit. He brought ten of his crew to *U-606,* displacing a like number of that ship's green crew. At the end of this brief patrol, Hans Döhler was appointed commander of *U-606* and sailed it onward to join the Atlantic force.

Counting the *U-606,* Klüber had twenty-two U-boats ready or near ready for battle. Seven rushed at maximum speed to intercept PQ 18. Since Klüber had declared the primary target to be the "jeep" carrier *Avenger,* the boats were dubbed group *Traegertod* (Carrier Killer). Rolf-Heinrich Hopmann in *U-405* was the first to make contact with the carrier on September 13. His beacon signals brought in Reinhard von Hymmen in *U-408* and Hans-Joachim Horrer in *U-589.* All three skippers claimed they hit and sank 7,000-ton freighters, and Horrer claimed two hits on *Avenger* as well. Postwar analysis credited von Hymmen with sinking the 7,209-ton American freighter *Oliver Ellsworth* and Horrer with sinking the 3,600-ton Russian freighter *Stalingrad,* but no boat hit *Avenger.*

The Sea Hurricanes on *Avenger* focused on shooting down the German shadow aircraft, but they failed. Vectored in by the shadowers, that afternoon the *Luftwaffe* hit PQ 18 in a mass torpedo-plane and dive-bomber attack, "like a huge flight of nightmare locusts," as one participant put it. Notwithstanding the heavy flak from the convoy and escorts, the tethered blimps, and some interference by the Sea Hurricanes, the German planes sank eight confirmed ships for 43,256 tons.

The next day, September 14, Karl Brandenburg in *U-457* got around the escorts. He claimed he sank a tanker and a freighter for 10,000 tons and got two hits on a "destroyer," but postwar analysis credited him with damage only to one ship, the 9,000-ton British tanker *Atheltemplar.* She was so badly wrecked that she had to be sunk by the escorts. The next day, Brandenburg reported that he missed another "destroyer" with a three-torpedo salvo.

The massive escort for PQ 18 delivered numerous attacks on the U-boats. Hunting cooperatively, British Swordfish from Squadron 825 on *Avenger* and destroyers, or destroyers alone, sank three.

- On September 12, a Swordfish spotted a U-boat six miles south of the convoy. This was *U-88,* commanded by Heino Bohmann. The destroyer *Onslow* peeled off to investigate. At a distance she saw exhaust "smoke," then a conning tower. The boat dived, but *Onslow* got a good sonar contact and threw over thirty-six depth charges. Nothing more was ever heard from *U-88.* As proof of her kill, *Onslow* recovered wood deck gratings, green vegetables, boxes, and a sock.
- On September 14, another Swordfish from *Avenger* reported that a U-boat had dived four miles ahead of the convoy. This was *U-589,* commanded by Hans-Joachim Horrer. Sent to investigate, the destroyer *Faulkner* got a good sonar contact and dropped a salvo of five depth charges. *Faulkner*'s sonar operator heard a "loud noise," then the contact diminished to "faint" and disappeared. No conclusive proof was found but the kill was deduced from Enigma intercepts. Four German airmen whom Horrer had rescued died in the sinking.*
- On September 16, the destroyer *Impulsive* of the close escort got a good sonar contact at eight hundred yards. This was *U-457,* commanded by Karl Brandenburg. *Impulsive* attacked immediately, throwing over five depth charges. Later

* The official British naval historian writes at odds with the Admiralty assessment committee, and perhaps in error, that *Faulkner* killed *U-88* and *Onslow* killed *U-589.* Other British naval historians have copied Roskill, but without noting the discrepancies or attempting to resolve them.

she found an oil slick and "various pieces of wreckage," which included numerous pieces of wood, some scraps of paper, and one black leather glove. The kill was also deduced from Enigma. There were no survivors.

The opposite-sailing convoys PQ 18 and QP 14 passed in the Barents Sea on September 15 and 16. There were twelve U-boats in the vicinity, tracking one or the other of the convoys. Klüber directed five to stay with PQ 18 and seven to attack QP 14. Reinhard Reche in *U-255* reported two failed attacks against *Avenger.* Otto Köhler in *U-377* reported a possible hit on a freighter. Rolf-Heinrich Hopmann in *U-405* reported a possible hit on a fleet destroyer. Heinz-Ehlert Clausen in *U-403* reported heavy depth-charge damage from a British escort, two failed attacks on his boat by confused German airmen, and a botched attack by a Soviet submarine. Reinhard von Hymmen in *U-408* reported a failed attack by a British submarine.

Beginning on September 17, four Soviet destroyers joined PQ 18 to help escort the convoy into Archangel, which was still ice-free and less vulnerable to German aircraft. In a final attack, *Luftwaffe* aircraft hit and sank another ship, the 5,400-ton *Kentucky,* and wrecked the 6,500-ton freighter *Troubador,* which was beached to save her cargo. Allied losses in PQ 18: thirteen ships for 76,000 tons, of which three for 21,000 tons were sunk by U-boats only, the other ten by the *Luftwaffe.**

The seven U-boats stalking QP 14 also achieved some successes. In two separate attacks, the leading shooter of the Norway-based boats, Siegfried Strelow in *U-435,* sank one of the escorts, the 835-ton British minesweeper *Leda,* and three freighters for 15,800 tons (two British and one American). For this exceptional achievement in the teeth of numerous escorts, and for past claims, Strelow was awarded a *Ritterkreuz,*† the first such honor for a Norway-based skipper. Heinz Bielfeld in *U-703* hit the *Tribal*-class destroyer *Somali.* Taken in tow by her sister ship *Ashanti, Somali* foundered in heavy weather with the loss of forty-five men of her salvage crew. Reinhardt Reche in *U-255* sank the 5,000-ton American freighter *Silver Sword.* Dietrich von der Esch in the newly arrived *U-606* hit a British Catalina with his flak guns and forced it to land. Reinhard von Hymmen in *U-408* reported hits on a fleet destroyer and a freighter, but they could not be confirmed. Alfred Hoschatt in *U-378* reported firing four torpedoes at *Avenger* and four at a destroyer, but all missed.‡ Sinkings in QP 14 by U-boats: two escorts, *Leda* and *Somali,* and four merchant ships for 20,800 tons.

The sixteen Arctic U-boats that operated against PQ 18 and QP 14 sank nine ships for 43,216 tons, including the escorts *Leda* and *Somali.*§ In return, three

---

* The *Luftwaffe* mounted about three hundred torpedo and bombing sorties against PQ 18. The Germans lost forty-one aircraft, mostly to flak.

† The *"Ritterkreuz"* was the Knight's Cross of the Iron Cross, a much-prized decoration in the German military. At the time of the award, Strelow's confirmed score was seven ships for 34,914 tons.

‡ When Hoschatt returned to port, Hans-Jürgen Zetzsche, who had run his *U-591* on some rocks, was given temporary command of *U-378.* Erich Mäder soon replaced Zetzsche as permanent skipper. Zetzsche's *U-591* required two months in the Bergen shipyard to repair the damage. A *Kriegsmarine* Board of Inquiry sentenced Zetzsche and his quartermaster to four days confinement in quarters.

§ The *Luftwaffe* sank ten merchant ships, all from PQ 18. See Plate 13.

U-boats were lost with all hands (plus the rescued German airmen on board) in the attack on PQ 18. Arctic commander Otto Klüber aptly commented to the OKM that three U-boats lost to sink three freighters in PQ 18 was "too high a price" to pay. In addition, four boats incurred heavy battle damage: Heinrich Timm's *U-251,* Reinhardt Reche's *U-255,* Heinz-Ehlert Clausen's *U-403,* and Rolf-Heinrich Hopmann's *U-405.*

The diversion of British warships to prepare for and carry out Torch again shut down the Murmansk convoys, this time until mid-December. At the suggestion of President Roosevelt, some fast freighters attempted the voyage singly. Thirteen sailed, but only five arrived. Three aborted, two were sunk by U-boats unassisted, two by the *Luftwaffe* and U-boats combined, and one, hit by aircraft, wrecked on Spitzbergen. Upon the arrival of near twenty-four-hour Arctic darkness in November, QP 15, composed of twenty-eight empty ships of PQ 18 and earlier convoys, sailed from northern Russia to Iceland. Two U-boats, *U-601* and the newly arrived *U-625,* commanded by Peter-Ottmar Grau and Hans Benker, respectively, each sank one freighter from QP 15, for an aggregate of 9,800 tons.

During the hunt for Murmansk-bound convoys, *U-408,* commanded by Reinhard von Hymmen, patrolled close off the north coast of Iceland. On November 5, a Catalina of the U.S. Navy's Patrol Squadron VP 84, piloted by Robert C. Millard, caught *U-408* on the surface and sank her. The Catalina crew reported seven Germans in the water, together with "quantities of wood splinters, oil, and other objects," but none of the Germans survived.

The loss in a period of about eighty days of forty-three* valuable ships in convoys PQ 17 (twenty-four) and PQ 18/QP 14 (nineteen), came as physical and psychological shocks to the Allies, and deservedly so. The news and newsreel reports and Allied and Axis propaganda that summer and fall, and talk among Allied merchant mariners and, later, war feature films, led to the impression that the "Murmansk Run" was the most dangerous convoy route of all. However, as Dönitz repeatedly informed Berlin, the Arctic was the *least* remunerative hunting ground for U-boats. Only a very few sank any more ships in that area. After the summer of 1942, the *Luftwaffe* was also ineffective against Allied shipping in the Arctic.

Eyes on the North Atlantic Run

Karl Dönitz knew well that U-boat warfare by the obsolescent Type VIIs in the North Atlantic would be extremely difficult and that German losses were sure to mount to very high levels, but he remained convinced that that inhospitable arena was the decisive one in the naval war. If his Atlantic U-boat force could shut down the vital Allied North Atlantic convoy run, it was still possible that the British Isles could be isolated and starved out, denying the Allies a launching pad for an amphibious invasion of Occupied France. Therefore, despite the failures in the past to

* Eighteen by aircraft alone, sixteen by U-boats alone, and nine by aircraft and U-boats combined.

do so, Dönitz directed that every possible effort must be made to destroy that sea link.

For the first time in the war, the Atlantic U-boat force had what appeared to the Germans to be sufficient numbers of U-boats to carry out this difficult task. The clearing out of the logjam of U-boats in the Baltic in the summer of 1942 led to the first significant jump in the size of the Atlantic U-boat force. On September 3—the beginning of the fourth year of continuous U-boat warfare—Dönitz had 126 attack boats* at his Atlantic front: seventy-seven Type VIIs, forty-seven Type IXs, the IXD2 U-cruiser *U-179,* and *U-A.*

Dönitz counted on additional large increases of Atlantic U-boats in September and October 1942, but it was not to be. Again the flow of new boats was whittled down by accidents and other delays in the Baltic,† and by further diversions. To replace losses in the Arctic force and to assist in the hunt for PQ/QP convoys, in September and October the OKM sent eight new VIIs to northern Norway for permanent and temporary duty,‡ and routed three to the Atlantic via slow transits of the Denmark Strait, where one, the new *U-253,* commanded by Adolf Friedrichs, age twenty-eight, hit a mine northwest of Iceland and sank with the loss of all hands. Furthermore, in order to rebuild the gutted Mediterranean force, the OKM ordered that six more Type VIIs were to be sent there in October. These diversions were to remove seventeen VIIs from the Atlantic force, ten permanently and seven temporarily. Owing to these diversions and to battle losses, the Atlantic force was to increase by only twenty-eight attack boats during September and October to a total of 152 on November 1: one hundred VIIs and fifty-two IXs.

Even though the growth of the Atlantic force was disappointingly slow, Dönitz was able to mount an unprecedented 109 war patrols by attack boats in September and October 1942. The great preponderance of these boats (seventy-three) went to the North Atlantic to hunt convoys sailing to and from the British Isles. The other attack-boat patrols (thirty-six) were divided equally between American waters and those off West and South Africa.§

In some histories of the "Battle of the Atlantic," the authors segue from one convoy battle to the next, omitting all the failed interceptions and/or attacks. This selectiv-

---

* Including about a dozen boats undergoing battle-damage repairs. For Order of Battle, see Appendix 1.

† The VII *U-626,* commanded by Hans-Botho Bade, rammed and sank the VII *U-222,* commanded by Rolf von Jessen. Only Jessen and two others survived. Jessen went to another new VII. The VII *U-446,* commanded by Hellmut-Bert Richard, hit a mine near Danzig and sank with the loss of twenty-three men. A freighter rammed the VII *U-450,* commanded by Kurt Böhme. The IXC *U-523,* commanded by Werner Pietzsch, rammed *Scharnhorst.* Repairs to *U-626, U-450,* and *U-523* delayed their departures to the front for several months. The *U-446* was salvaged but held in the Baltic as a school boat.

‡ The *U-212, U-354, U-606, U-622,* and *U-663* were sent for permanent duty and the *U-262, U-611,* and *U-625* for temporary duty, but the *U-625* remained in the Arctic. Two days after leaving Bergen on September 24, two Hudsons of British Squadron 48, piloted by E. Tammes and R. Horney, dropped eight depth charges near *U-262,* commanded by Heinz Franke, age twenty-six. The damage forced Franke to abort to Bergen. He resailed on October 3.

§ See appendices 2, 4, and 5.

PLATE I

DEPLOYMENT OF U-BOATS BY BATTLEFRONT[1]

SEPTEMBER 1 TO DECEMBER 31, 1942

		ATLANTIC	MEDITERRANEAN	ARCTIC	TOTAL
9/1	VII	77	15	23	115
	IX	47			47
		124	15	23	162
10/1	VII	98	15	24	137
	IX	47			47
		145	15	24	184
11/1	VII	101	18	23	142
	IX	49			49
		150	18	23	191
12/1	VII	100	20	21	141
	IX	48			48
		148	20	21	189
12/31	VII	106	23	19	148
	IX	51			51
		157	23	19	199
Net gain or Loss	VII	+29	+8	(-)4	+33
	IX	+ 4			+ 4
		+33	+8	(-)4	+37

1. Includes new attack boats assigned, transfers between the Atlantic, Arctic, and Mediterranean U-boat forces, and boats under repair, less battle losses, retirements, and internments. The IXs do not include U-cruisers. Source: Author's calculations.

ity gives the quite wrong impression that the U-boats in the North Atlantic in September and October 1942 inflicted an absolute massacre on Allied shipping. In spite of the good information on Allied convoys derived from the German break into British Naval Cypher Number 3, which *B-dienst* provided Dönitz, for various reasons the U-boats were able to mount notable attacks on only six of thirty-five convoys that sailed to and from the British Isles in those two months, and to sink only fifty-seven of about 1,700 merchant ships (3 percent) in those convoys, of which thirty-nine (2 percent) were eastbound.* This was another tough blow for the Allies but hardly a massacre. From the German point of view, the renewed campaign on the North Atlantic run to cut this vital sea link had to be judged a failure.

Cargo convoys on the North Atlantic run in this period were heavily protected by Allied warships and aircraft.

The warships were divided into three commands: the Canadian Western Local

* For details of North Atlantic convoys, September 1942–May 1943, see Appendix 3.

Escort Force (WLEF), the Allied Mid-Ocean Escort Force (MOEF), and the British Eastern Local Escort Force (ELEF). The Canadian WLEF protected convoys in Canadian waters to and from the Western Ocean Meeting Point (WESTOMP). Warships of the Allied MOEF sailing east from St. John's, Newfoundland, took over at the WOMP and protected eastbound convoys to the East Ocean Meeting Point (EASTOMP), where the British ELEF took over. In the reverse process, warships of the British ELEF, sailing west, escorted westbound convoys to the EOMP, where warships of the MOEF, sailing west from Londonderry, Northern Ireland, took over the task.

The heaviest ocean-escort responsibilities fell on the warships of the Allied MOEF. These were subdivided into eleven close escort groups, six British (B-1 to B-6),* four Canadian (C-1 to C-4), and one American (A-3). Under optimal circumstances, the British and Canadian groups were comprised of about seven ships: two or three destroyers and four or five corvettes. The American group usually included one or two big, *Treasury*-class Coast Guard cutters (*Bibb, Campbell, Duane, Ingham,* or *Spencer*), a mixture of British and Canadian corvettes, and, from time to time, a British or Canadian destroyer.

The MOEF groups sailed on a thirty-three-day cycle, commonly known as "Newfie to 'Derry." Eastbound from St. John's, Newfoundland, they crossed the Atlantic to Londonderry in nine and one-half days. They laid over in Londonderry for eight days for refit or upgrading and crew R&R. Westbound from Londonderry, they crossed the Atlantic in nine and one-half days to St. John's, where they laid over for six days before restarting the cycle.

Most of the British and American escorts were fitted with improved sonar and with rotating centimetric-wavelength radar (Type 271), with Planned Position Indicator (PPI) scopes, which displayed surface ships and U-boats in relation to the escort. The Canadian warships had the older sonar and meter-wavelength radar (Type 286). At least one and usually two ships in the convoy were fitted with high-frequency direction-finding gear (Huff Duff), which enabled the escorts to detect and home on the radio reports from a shadowing U-boat and to attack. All escorts carried depth charges with the more powerful Torpex warheads, which could be set to explode down to six hundred feet. Many of the British escorts were fitted with the Hedgehog, a foward-firing contact mortar. Land-based submarine attack simulators and sophisticated radar and sonar shipboard attack plotters were in "mass" production.

The Western Local Escort Force (WLEF), manned and commanded exclusively by the Royal Canadian Navy, was comprised of forty-six warships—eighteen Canadian and British destroyers, and twenty-eight corvettes. These were assigned to eight Canadian escort groups, usually with four ships per group, the rest being in training, refit, or overhaul. A number of the destroyers were old (World War I) Royal Navy *"V"* and *"W"* class, which were unsuitable for operations in the cold, harsh northwest Atlantic waters in winter, because they lacked sufficient reserve stability to allow for the inevitable buildup of ice topside. The hope therefore was

* The British and Canadian groups B-5 and C-5 were serving temporarily in the Caribbean.

to replace the *V*s and *W*s with the winterized ex-American four-stack (or *Town*-class) destroyers acquired by the Commonwealth in the 1940 "Destroyer Deal."

At a Canadian-American "Convoy Conference" in Ottawa in the summer of 1942, senior naval officials had hashed over the escort situation in great detail. They agreed that with the onset of winter weather, on or about November 1, the harsh conditions would force the North Atlantic convoys to slow down, extending the escort's time at sea. In order to compensate for this slowdown and for the need to repair storm and ice damage to the escorts, the conferees estimated that at least one more escort group would be required for the MOEF and that the groups in the WLEF should be increased from four ships to six. Hence, the Allied convoy experts calculated that come winter they faced a shortage of forty-seven warships, nine destroyers, and thirty-eight corvettes, of which twenty-six vessels (six destroyers and twenty corvettes) were to be allotted to the WLEF, the rest to the MOEF.

In the meantime, the plan to sail all transatlantic convoys from New York commencing in mid-September was revalidated. As one step of this process, the Canadians closed Sydney, Nova Scotia, after the departure of Slow Convoy 94. From August 4 on, succeeding Slow Convoys (95 through 101) consisting of an aggregate of 318 vessels, departed from Halifax, reducing the need for the cumbersome, time-wasting Halifax-Sydney convoy run. On September 19, Slow Convoy 102 became the first of this category to sail from New York. On September 17, the fast Halifax 208 was the first of that category.*

The protection of North Atlantic convoys by Allied aircraft had grown dramatically—far more so than the Germans realized. In September–October 1942, there were about seven hundred planes assigned to frontline ASW units around the perimeter of the North Atlantic (North America, Greenland, Iceland, and the British Isles†). Counting squadron reserves (not shown here), these included almost three hundred aircraft capable of long-range or very-long-range missions:

138	Catalinas or Cansos (a Canadian version of the Catalina)
48	Sunderlands
42	B-24 Liberators
36	B-17 Flying Fortresses
12	Halifaxes

These ASW aircraft and others were being equipped as rapidly as possible with the latest weaponry and electronic gear. The standard armament, the Mark XIII aerial depth charge with Torpex warhead, had been reshaped, strengthened, and fitted

* The official Canadian Navy historian wrote that convoys HX 1 to HX 207 from Halifax had sailed with 8,501 ships, and SC 1 to SC 94 had sailed with 3,652 ships. Convoys SC 95 to SC 101 (from Halifax) sailed with 318 ships. All told: 12,471 vessels sailed in these eastbound convoys in three full years of operations. See Volume I, Plate 10, and Plate 13.

† For a detailed list of Allied airborne ASW units in the North Atlantic area, see Appendix 10.

with shallow-set pistols (fuses), that exploded at a depth of twenty-five feet, giving the aircraft the improved ability to attack a crash-diving U-boat. Some planes had been fitted with the more powerful and effective Mark III ASV centimeter-wavelength radar, replacing the Mark II ASV meter-plus wavelength model. The American-made Fido homing torpedo, disguised as the "Mark XXIV mine," was in high-priority production, as were the hydrophone sonobuoys, which could be dropped into the water to detect U-boat noises and positions.*

After leaving the heavily patrolled waters of the United States East Coast, the eastbound convoys fell under protection of the Royal Canadian Air Force (RCAF). This organization, like the Royal Canadian Navy, was a relatively inexperienced and impoverished stepchild. There were nine frontline RCAF ASW squadrons based in Nova Scotia and Newfoundland. These were comprised of over one hundred combat-ready aircraft: forty-eight Catalinas-Cansos, twelve Digbys (a Canadian version of the USAAF B-18), and forty-eight Hudsons. The RCAF was backed up by twenty-four U.S.–manned aircraft: twelve B-18s of USAAF Squadron 20 at Gander, and twelve Catalinas of the U.S. Navy's VP 84 at Argentia.†

The sixty Cansos and Catalinas in Nova Scotia and Newfoundland could effectively escort Allied convoys out to about five or six hundred miles, depending on a number of factors, including weather. In a stretch, the B-18s and the Digbys could reach to about four hundred miles, the Hudsons about three hundred miles. Although there were glaring gaps and inefficiencies, the Allied convoy air escort in the northwest Atlantic was a steadily growing force with which to reckon.

In September 1942, the so-called Battle of the St. Lawrence was still in progress. Several U-boats had penetrated the relatively confined waters of the Gulf of St. Lawrence and had sunk a number of ships.‡ These enemy excursions into the "home" waters of the Maritime Provinces had caused local panic and a political uproar in Ottawa. As a consequence, the Canadian Prime Minister, W. L. Mackenzie King, closed the gulf to oceangoing ship traffic indefinitely and redeployed a substantial number of frontline aircraft to offensive ASW patrols over the gulf, thus reducing air forces available for ocean-convoy air escort. During this "crisis," United States Army Air Forces B-25s from a base in Westover, Massachusetts, assisted the RCAF, flying from Yarmouth, Nova Scotia.

From Canadian waters, most eastbound convoys crossed the extensive and shallow waters of the Grand Banks. This area, where the warm Gulf Stream meets the cold Labrador Current, is almost perpetually fogbound and often cluttered with icebergs, and therefore it was a hazardous place for merchant ships and warships and especially so for RCAF escort aircraft. Aircraft operating in this foggy area faced an additional hazard: prevailing westerly winds on the return legs, which increased fuel consumption and thus curtailed the efficiency of the missions.

---

* See Volume I, pp. 475–481.

† The U.S. Navy's PBY-5A Catalinas and the Canadian Canso "A" flying boats operating in Newfoundland and Nova Scotia were fitted with retractable wheels and could therefore fly from land bases in icy winter months.

‡ See Volume I, p. 687.

For the next one thousand miles (or four or five days) of the voyage, eastbound convoys in the fall of 1942 had no air escort. This area was the so-called Air Gap or Greenland Gap or Black Hole. Fortunately for the Allies, this was a difficult area for U-boat "wolf pack" operations. Ignoring this fact, historians and popular writers have greatly inflated U-boat successes in the "Gap" just as they have done on the Murmansk run.

Eastward of the "Air Gap," the convoys fell under the protection of Allied aircraft based at Iceland. This, too, was a formidable force, consisting of about fifty radar-equipped frontline aircraft with experienced aircrews: twenty-four Catalinas in U.S. Navy Squadron VP 73* and British Squadron 330, twenty Hudsons in British Squadron 269, and six B-24 Liberators in British Squadron 120. The Catalinas could provide convoy protection out to about six hundred miles, the Hudsons to about four hundred miles, the B-24s to eight hundred to one thousand miles. Where formerly the Iceland-based aircraft attempted to provide all transatlantic convoys with protection, in the fall of 1942 they protected only the relatively few convoys known to be—or about to be—under U-boat attack.

From Iceland easterly toward the British Isles, the Iceland air escort was reinforced and ultimately replaced by RAF Coastal Command aircraft in about ten squadrons based in the Hebrides, Faeroes, northwest Scotland, and Northern Ireland. These units were equipped with over one hundred frontline aircraft: twenty-four B-17s (Squadrons 206 and 220), twenty-four Sunderlands (Squadrons 201 and 228), twelve Catalinas (Squadron 210), twenty-eight Whitleys (Squadrons 58 and 612), twenty Hudsons (Squadron 48), six Wellingtons (Squadron 179), and three B-24s (Squadron 120).

There were a further ten ASW RAF Coastal Command squadrons based in south and southwest England. These comprised 150 frontline aircraft: twelve B-24 Liberators (Squadron 224), twelve Halifaxes (Squadron 502), twenty-four Sunderlands (Australian Squadrons 10 and 461), forty-two Wellingtons (Squadrons 172, 304, and 311), twenty Hudsons (Squadron 500), and forty Whitleys (Squadrons 51 and 77). RAF Bomber Command Operational Training Unit 10 in southwest England provided another eight Whitleys for ASW.

In the literature of the "Battle of the Atlantic," an abundance of pages is devoted to describing the miserable and perilous duty on surface escorts in the north, especially life on board the corvettes. But a picture of life on board the long- and very-long-range aircraft is difficult to find. The missions of the B-24s, B-17s, Catalinas, and Sunderlands were usually prolonged, often twelve to sixteen hours or more. In order to maximize the effectiveness of ASV radar, the planes usually flew at low altitudes (two thousand to four thousand feet), where rough air was commonplace. Radio or radar altimeters were not yet standard; most of the pilots

---

* On October 29, VP 73 deployed to Morocco for Torch via Ballykelly, Northern Ireland. U.S. Navy Squadron VP 84 (Catalinas) in Argentia replaced VP 73 in Iceland and VP 82, reequipped with PV-3 Venturas, replaced VP 84 in Argentia. The Ventura was envisioned as an upgraded Hudson (top speed 318 m.p.h. versus 250 m.p.h.; payload six depth charges versus four), but the plane was crippled with defects and deficiencies in 1942 and was therefore unsuitable for its ASW mission.

had to rely on old-technology altimeters that were not always accurate, especially at the very low attack altitudes. Visibility was often poor to terrible. Occasionally these aircraft unintentionally flew right into the sea.

The ASW air patrols were relatively safe from enemy attack at this time, and therefore not unattractive to some airmen. However, the overwhelming majority of Coastal Command and aircrews found the missions to be monumentally boring and physically and mentally exhausting. Most crews flew thousands of hours over gray seas searching for or suppressing U-boats without ever seeing any sign of one.

An actual attack on a U-boat was a rare event, and usually it failed. In three years of antisubmarine warfare on the North Atlantic run—through September 3, 1942—Coastal Command aircraft had captured one U-boat (the Type VIIC *U-570)* with surface-ship assistance* but had positively accounted for only one kill unassisted by surface craft. That one (the "Milk Cow" Type XIV supply boat *U-464*) had been forced to scuttle by a U.S. Navy Catalina crew of VP 73, based on Iceland.† U.S. Navy Catalinas of VP 74 and Hudsons of VP 82 had sunk three others in North Atlantic waters: *U-158, U-656,* and *U-503.*

In view of the enormous air-escort effort expended on the North Atlantic convoy run, the confirmed kill or capture of five U-boats in those waters (four by U.S. Navy forces) in three years of warfare was not impressive, to say the least. However, the Allied strategic policy of the time stressed the "safe and timely" arrival of convoys rather than U-boat kills. Wherever and whenever possible, convoys evaded known U-boat positions, reducing the odds of ASW aircraft finding U-boats. Nonetheless, Allied aircraft had suppressed untold scores of U-boats that were shadowing or attacking North Atlantic convoys and had damaged more than a few. These were notable protective (or defensive) achievements of the air escorts that seldom made the front pages or earned decorations.

The glory days for the Allied airmen in the Atlantic area engaged in ASW had obviously not yet arrived. But they lay just ahead. When they did finally arrive, the results were astounding.

German Successes and Failures

The seventy-three attack U-boats deployed against the North Atlantic run in September and October were assigned to groups or "wolf packs." There were usually several groups operating simultaneously, raking east or west along the Great Circle convoy routes. Dönitz or his staff rigidly controlled their operations by freely using radios. As in 1941, the composition of the groups changed almost daily as boats fell out with battle damage or ran low on fuel and/or torpedoes and left for a

---

* See Volume I, p. 341.

† Coastal Command aircraft had also sunk three U-boats in the Bay of Biscay unassisted by surface craft *(U-502, U-578, U-751),* and Royal Navy aircraft had sunk two *(U-64, U-451).* U.S. Army and Navy aircraft had sunk six others in American waters, three in cooperation with surface ships: *U-94, U-153, U-166, U-576, U-654,* and *U-701.*

U-tanker or France, and new boats arrived from France or Germany to replace them. Entirely new groups sprang into being from week to week and old groups faded away or were renamed. Hence the Germans made no attempt to propagandize groups by name and the U-boats developed no lasting identification with or loyalty to any group.

The North Atlantic boats were supported in September and October by five U-tankers. These included two Type XIV "Milk Cows," Wolf Stiebler's *U-461* and Leo Wolfbauer's *U-463,* and three big Type XB minelayers on temporary tanker duty: the *U-116,* commanded by a new skipper, Wilhelm Grimme, age thirty-five, which sailed on September 22 and disappeared without a trace, probably the victim of an as yet unidentified Allied aircraft; the new *U-117,* commanded by Hans-Werner Neumann, age thirty-six, who first laid a nonproductive minefield off the northwestern coast of Iceland; and the new *U-118,* commanded by Werner Czygan, age thirty-seven.

All the U-boats sailing in September and October were equipped with the meter-wavelength FuMB radar detector made by Metox. The primitive but remarkably successful Metox ("Biscay Cross") reduced U-boat losses, damage, and delays in crossing the Bay of Biscay to such a marked degree that on October 1 the British canceled the intense ASW aircraft offensive in the bay. But Metox gear was not able to detect centimetric-wavelength radar, which was fitted in the British surface escorts and the long- and very-long-range aircraft in the North Atlantic area. Although few in number, those radar-equipped aircraft were able to catch U-boats by surprise, disrupt numerous group attacks, and sink or damage an ever-increasing number of U-boats.

In the first days of September 1942, there were already three groups operating against the North Atlantic convoys: *Loss, Vorwärts,* and *Pfeil.* Acting on *B-dienst* information, on September 9, one of a dozen boats in the *Vorwärts* group, *U-584,* commanded by Joachim Deecke, sighted convoy Outbound North 127, about five hundred miles west of Ireland. Composed of thirty-two ships, the convoy was escorted by Canadian Escort Group C-4: two destroyers (the modern *Ottawa* and the ex-American four-stack *St. Croix),* three Canadian corvettes, and one British corvette. The Canadian vessels were equipped with the obsolescent Type 286 meter-wavelength radar, but all sets were out of commission. Only the British corvette *Celandine* had Type 271 centimetric-wavelength radar. None of the ships had Huff Duff.

Based on Deecke's information, several boats got ahead of the convoy on September 10, submerged, and lay in wait in fine weather to make daylight submerged attacks. Seven boats fired torpedoes in the first attacks that day and on the surface at night. Shooting first, the experienced Hans-Jürgen Hellriegel in the famous but aging *U-96* severely damaged two tankers in ballast and a freighter. Next, Hans Stock, age twenty-seven, in the new *U-659* damaged the 8,000-ton British tanker *Empire Oil,* which was sunk later by Deecke in *U-584,* who also sank a freighter. Then came the experienced Otto von Bülow in *U-404,* who damaged another tanker in ballast. Richard Becker, age thirty-one, in the new Type VIID (minelayer) *U-218* damaged yet another tanker in ballast. Rolf Struckmeier in the new *U-608* and Adolf Oelrich, age twenty-six, in the new *U-92* shot at targets but missed.

Five of the six escorts counterattacked, throwing out depth charges. One escort hit Hans Stock in *U-659.* He reported "a loud knocking" in the tankage or propeller shafts, which forced him to abort to France. One corvette, *Sherbrooke,* was designated to fall back and sink by gun two ships damaged by Hellriegel in *U-96:* the 4,200-ton Belgian freighter *Elisabeth van Belgie* and the 6,300-ton British tanker *Sveve.* The British at Western Approaches sarcastically criticized the Canadians for, as they put it, "helping to reduce our tonnage by weakening the escort and completing the enemy's work." The other three damaged tankers limped to port and were saved.

In the second wave of attacks during the next forty-eight hours, five boats fired torpedoes. Von Bülow in *U-404* claimed sinking three freighters for 17,000 tons with a full bow salvo, but only damage to a 9,300-ton tanker in ballast was confirmed in postwar records. Karl Hause in the new *U-211* fired four torpedoes at four ships and damaged two, a 14,000-ton British whale factory ship and a 6,800-ton British freighter, both of which were subsequently sunk by Struckmeier in *U-608.* Josef Röther in the new *U-380* fired four torpedoes at three targets and heard three detonations, but the hits could not be confirmed. Friedrich Mumm in *U-594* also missed with four torpedoes. Oelrich in *U-92* fired four torpedoes at a "destroyer" and claimed sinking it, but this success was never confirmed either.

Again the escorts counterattacked vigorously. One found and depth-charged Becker's big, clumsy VIID (minelayer) *U-218,* inflicting such heavy damage that he was forced to haul out, then abort to France. In the melee, Röther in *U-380* lost a diesel engine, which he could not repair and he was also forced to haul away. An escort fired at Heinz Walkerling, age twenty-seven, in the new *U-91,* causing "slight" damage, but Walkerling pressed on. Another escort thwarted a third attack by Struckmeier in *U-608.* Hellriegel in *U-96* lost a diesel engine chasing down a 400-ton Portuguese sailing trawler and, as a result, declared himself temporarily unfit for convoy attacks.

In a noteworthy achievement, two Canadian Cansos from Botwood, Newfoundland, made contact with Outbound North 127 six hundred miles out on September 13. They drove the U-boats under and off, but two boats continued the battle under cover of darkness. Oelrich in *U-92* fired three torpedoes and claimed hits on three freighters, but these hits could not be confirmed. Firing two torpedoes, Walkerling in *U-91* hit and sank the Canadian destroyer *Ottawa,* with the loss of 114 men. Shortly thereafter, two other destroyers from Halifax, the ex-American four-stack *Annapolis* and the old British *Witch,* joined the escort and, helped by the fog on the Newfoundland Bank, thwarted any further attacks.

Based on the flash reports from the boats of group *Vorwärts,* Dönitz had good reason to be pleased. He believed that twelve of the thirteen boats of the group—eight of them on maiden patrols—had attacked Outbound North 127 successfully, sinking nineteen ships for about 118,000 tons, including two destroyers and a corvette, and damaging six or more other ships. No U-boats had been lost. It was believed that only one boat, *U-659,* had been forced to abort with battle damage. The captains deserved "special recognition" for efficiency and tenacity, Dönitz logged. The one regrettable aspect of the battle was that torpedoes fitted with impact pistols had "such small effect." Would the technicians ever release the newly designed magnetic pistol for combat service?

The confirmed score from convoy Outbound North 127 was substantially less than the claims: the destroyer *Ottawa* and seven merchant ships for about 51,500 tons sunk and four tankers for about 27,000 tons damaged. Not one but two boats, *U-659* and *U-218,* aborted with battle damage, and *U-608* also limped home prematurely.

One of the boats of group *Pfeil,* the new Type VIID (minelayer) *U-216,* commanded by Karl-Otto Schultz, age twenty-seven, found a fast eastbound convoy on September 13. This was Halifax 206, comprised of forty-six heavily laden merchant ships protected by the well-equipped, experienced British Escort Group B-1: two destroyers (*Hurricane* and *Watchman*) and four corvettes. Schultz attempted to shadow, but the escorts used direction-finding gear to locate his signals and drove him under. Nonetheless, Dönitz directed the rest of group *Pfeil* to close on the convoy. Another *Pfeil* boat, the new *U-440,* commanded by Hans Geissler, age twenty-five, not yet two weeks out from Kiel, attempted to attack, but an escort also drove this boat off and down, inflicting such heavy damage that Geissler was forced to abort to France. Inasmuch as the convoy reached air cover from Iceland before group *Pfeil* could properly assemble, Dönitz canceled the attack. The British praised the good performance of Huff Duff in this engagement.

Another *Pfeil* boat, the new *U-221,* commanded by Hans Trojer, age twenty-six, found a convoy sailing in the opposite direction on September 15. It was Outbound North 129, protected by Canadian Escort Group C-2: two British destroyers, four Canadian corvettes, and a British corvette. Dönitz ordered the other *Pfeil* boats to converge on Trojer, but foul weather blew up, preventing a mass attack, and all but one ship of the convoy got away. She was the 3,000-ton Norwegian freighter *Olaf Fostenes,* sunk by thirty-four-year-old Josef Röther in the new *U-380.* Rushing to join *Pfeil* for this attack on September 15, the new *U-261,* commanded by Hans Lange, age twenty-seven, merely one week out from Kiel, was caught and sunk near Rosemary Bank by a Whitley of RAF Squadron 58, piloted by B. F. Snell. There were no survivors of *U-261.*

Acting on *B-dienst* information, a boat of group *Loss, U-599,* commanded by Wolfgang Breithaupt, age twenty-nine, intercepted another eastbound convoy on September 18. This was Slow Convoy 100, a group of twenty-four heavily laden merchant ships, escorted by Paul R. Heineman's American Escort Group A-3: the big *Treasury*-class Coast Guard cutters *Campbell* and *Spencer* and five corvettes, plus two Canadian corvettes en route to the British Isles for duty in Torch.*

---

* The Canadians provided seventeen corvettes for Torch.

At this time the Admiralty deployed to the North Atlantic an experimental hunter-killer group, designated the 20th Support Group. It originally included a "jeep" carrier, but that had been diverted to augment Torch forces. Now composed of ten warships (four destroyers, four *River*-class frigates, and two sloops), the group sailed from the British Isles in late September in conjunction with convoy Outbound North (Slow) 132, which included a tanker, *Laurelwood,* to refuel the group at sea. Unattached to any convoy, the purpose of the experimental 20th Support Group was to patrol the convoy routes and to rush in on call and attack any U-boats that might find Outbound North (Slow) 132 and/or the inbound Slow Convoys 100 and 102.

Breithaupt in *U-599* shadowed and sent beacon signals to bring up the other boats of group *Loss* to eastbound Slow Convoy 100. Next to arrive was the new *U-755,* commanded by Walter Göing, age twenty-eight, fresh from sinking an American warship.* Next came Klaus Köpke, age twenty-seven, in the new *U-259* and Hans Peter Hinsch in the veteran *U-569.* While attempting to attack submerged, Köpke collided with a merchant ship and had to break off the attack and surface. Later a "destroyer" came out of the fog, forced Köpke and Hinsch to dive, then pasted both boats with numerous depth charges. Low on fuel, Hinsch in *U-569* headed for France; Köpke in *U-259* remained with the pack.

Eager for another big convoy victory, Dönitz ordered the boats of group *Pfeil* to join group *Loss* for a combined attack of about twenty-one U-boats. Meanwhile, the *Loss* boats still in contact with the convoy were authorized to shoot. Paul-Karl Loeser, age twenty-seven, in the new *U-373,* and Günter Jahn, age thirty-two, in the new *U-596* fired almost simultaneously. Loeser thought he hit a corvette (the Canadian *Rosthern*), but he missed. Jahn hit and sank a 5,700-ton British freighter.

A massive storm, described by the U-boat skippers as a "hurricane," blew into the battle scene, spoiling the merger of *Loss* and *Pfeil.* Hanging on doggedly, Breithaupt in *U-599,* Jahn in *U-596,* Göing in *U-755,* and Ralph Kapitzky, age twenty-six, in the new *U-615* sought to outmaneuver or outguess the escorts and shoot. Kapitzky had to forgo an opportunity to shoot at "two destroyers," he reported, because "the seas were too big." In truth, the seas were so wild that the convoy had to heave to and ride out the storm. Unaware that several boats were still in contact, Dönitz prematurely canceled operations because of the hurricane.

On the third day of the storm, one of the *Pfeil* boats, *U-617,* commanded by Albrecht Brandi, age twenty-eight, making his maiden patrol, relocated Slow Convoy 100. He shot at and sank three ships: the 8,900-ton British tanker *Athelsultan,* the 2,300-ton British freighter *Tennessee,* and a straggler, the 3,600-ton Belgian freighter *Roumanie.* Brandi reported his successes and the position of the convoy, but U-boat headquarters did not receive the message. As a result, no boats came up to assist him.

A *Loss* boat and a *Pfeil* boat made contact with the convoy in clearing weather the next day, September 24. The *Loss* boat was the veteran *U-432,* commanded by

* The 1,800-ton Coast Guard cutter *Muskeget,* reporting weather from a station south of Greenland. All 121 men on board perished.

the *Ritterkreuz* holder Heinz-Otto Schultze. The *Pfeil* boat was the new *U-258,* commanded by Wilhelm von Mässenhausen, age twenty-seven. Schultze sank a 5,900-ton American freighter. Mässenhausen fired a full bow salvo at overlapping ships and claimed damage to two freighters, but the hits could not be confirmed.

On the next day, Coastal Command aircraft gave Slow Convoy 100 saturation coverage, which drove the U-boats under and held others at bay. Upon learning of this, Dönitz canceled a plan to resume operations, blaming the storm, poor radio reception, and aggressive escorts for the failure of the joint *Loss-Pfeil* attack. The confirmed losses in Slow Convoy 100: five ships for 26,300 tons. Three of the five were sunk by one of the twenty-one U-boats assigned to the battle, Brandi in *U-617.*

Caught up in the same hurricane, the British 20th Support Group was unable to carry out its hunter-killer mission. After the weather cleared, the group remained briefly in support of Convoy 100 and Slow Convoy 102 (the first of this type to sail from New York), but for naught since the U-boats did not find and attack that convoy. In early October the hunter-killer group returned to the British Isles to prepare for Torch missions. Although it had not made contact with the enemy, the group gained valuable operating experience, which was passed on for the benefit of hunter-killer groups to be formed in the future.

Farther to the west, meanwhile, the seven remaining boats of group *Vorwärts* refueled from Wolf Stiebler's tanker, *U-461,* on September 20 and established a patrol line to intercept an eastbound convoy predicted by *B-dienst.* After the storm had swept through, one of these boats, the new *U-380,* commanded by Josef Röther (who had sunk a lone 3,000-ton Norwegian freighter from Outbound North 129 but lost that convoy in foul weather), found what he reported to be an eastbound convoy of big "troop transports." Owing to the "great value" of these supposed troopships, all remaining boats of groups *Pfeil, Vorwärts,* and the boats of a newly formed group, *Blitz,* were ordered to converge on Röther's convoy.

Röther had found not a convoy of big "troop transports," but rather a formation of moderate-size vessels similar in silhouette to big two-funnel ocean liners. In actuality, they were American Great Lakes steamers sold to the British en route from the St. Lawrence River to England in a special fast convoy, River to Britain, or RB 1. A dozen or more U-boats responded to Röther's contact, all hungrily seeking a formation of ocean liners of 15,000 to 20,000 tons filled with troops.

Ten U-boats were in contact with convoy RB 1 by September 23. Two boats, Hellriegel's *U-96* and Röther's *U-380,* incurred diesel-engine failures that spoiled any chance of hauling ahead for an attack. Six other boats attempted to shoot, but only two managed to do so: Karl Hause, age twenty-six, in the new *U-211* and the *Ritterkreuz* holder Ernst Mengersen in *U-607.* Neither skipper claimed a hit. Mengersen reported that while maneuvering for a submerged daylight attack, he was rammed by a destroyer but sustained only slight damage. By happenstance, Hause in *U-211* encountered the 11,200-ton American tanker *Esso Williamsburg,* which was sailing alone, and sank her.

A dozen boats held contact with the RB convoy. On September 25 and 26 half of them attacked. Karl-Otto Schultz in the new VIID (minelayer) *U-216* claimed sinking a 19,000-ton liner. His victim was later identified as the 5,000-ton laker *Boston.* Hellriegel in *U-96* claimed that his torpedoes "exploded" a 17,700-ton liner. His victim was later identified as the 5,000-ton laker *New York.* Kurt Makowski, age twenty-seven, in the new *U-618,* claimed sinking a 11,660-ton vessel, which proved to be the 1,500-ton laker *Yorktown.* Heinz Walkerling in *U-91* claimed a hit on a steamer, but it could not be confirmed. Kurt Sturm, age thirty-six, in the new *U-410* reported four misses. Georg Wallas, age thirty-seven, in the new *U-356* reported three misses. Otto von Bülow in *U-404* reported that his attack failed. A half dozen boats lying in wait ahead of the convoy in daylight were outfoxed when the convoy suddenly zigged away.

Von Bülow in *U-404* hung on tenaciously. The next day he regained contact and attacked, firing three torpedoes at a destroyer, the old 1,100-ton British *Veteran.* Two torpedoes hit *Veteran;* the third hit a freighter. The destroyer blew apart and sank with heavy loss of life. The hit on the freighter could not be confirmed.*

Shortly afterward von Bülow returned to France. He claimed sinking three freighters and a tanker for 23,000 tons, the destroyer *Veteran,* and probable hits on two other freighters during this patrol. Postwar records confirmed the sinking of *Veteran* but not the other ships, plus hits on two tankers in ballast for 16,700 tons. Counting past claims and overclaims, von Bülow was awarded a *Ritterkreuz.*† He was the only skipper in the North Atlantic to win that high decoration in the fall of 1942.

Dönitz was convinced that this attack on RB 1 was successful: three big "ocean liners" for about 50,000 tons and *Veteran* sunk. When aircraft from Iceland appeared at the site, he wrongly assumed that they must be assisting in the rescue of the hundreds of soldiers embarked in the liners and canceled further operations. The OKM diarist—and Berlin radio—gloated that the loss of the "three big ocean liners" was "a severe blow to the enemy." In reality, the U-boats had sunk three ancient lakers and *Veteran,* comprising 12,600 tons in all.

A boat of group *Pfeil,* the *U-617,* commanded by Albrecht Brandi, came upon another convoy in foul weather on September 26. It was Outbound North 131, escorted by Canadian Escort Group C-3, the destroyers *Saguenay* and *Skeena* and five corvettes. Brandi's contact report drew in seventeen other boats of groups *Vorwärts* and *Blitz,* which hurriedly reorganized into a single new group, *Tiger.*

While the boats gathered, Brandi was authorized to shoot. He claimed that three torpedoes sank two freighters and damaged another, but none of these sinkings or hits have been confirmed in postwar records. One of the radar-equipped escorts drove Brandi off and prevented a second attack. Thereafter another massive

---

* Three destroyers of the hunter-killer 20th Support Group raced to the assistance of RB 1 but had no success.

† At the time of the award, his confirmed score was twelve ships, including *Veteran,* sunk for 61,700 tons and damage to the two tankers.

storm swept the area, fouling the operations of group *Tiger.* The old hand Werner Schulte in *U-582* sank a 3,000-ton Norwegian freighter that strayed from this convoy. Kurt Makowski in the new *U-619* found and sank another, a 7,200-ton American freighter. Georg Wallas in *U-356* hit and stopped yet another straggler from the convoy, but he missed and the ship steamed off into foul weather and escaped. Another boat of this group, *U-595,* commanded by Jürgen Quaet-Faslem, was disabled by a fire in a battery cable and forced to abort to France. Due to the storm, operations versus Outbound North 131 were canceled.

Altogether, the Allies sailed nineteen convoys across the North Atlantic run east or west in September, comprised of about 580 merchant ships.* The great congregation of U-boats mounted decisive attacks on only three convoys in the month of September: the eastbound Slow Convoy 100 and RB 1, and the westbound Outbound North 127. From these convoys, the boats sank nineteen merchant ships (3 percent) and two destroyers (the Canadian *Ottawa* and the British *Veteran*) for about 89,000 tons. Nine of the merchant ships sunk (1.5 percent) were eastbound to the British Isles.

German casualties in the North Atlantic in the month of September were not light. Five new boats were lost: the IX *U-165,* and the VIIs *U-253, U-261, U-705,* and *U-756.* Four VIIs aborted with battle damage: *U-218, U-440, U-595,* and *U-659.* In addition, one of the two highest scorers, the aging *U-96* (four ships for 16,000 tons), had to go into yard overhaul.

Heavy U-boat Losses

By October 1942, the *Queen Mary, Queen Elizabeth,* and *Acquitania* were operating fulltime on the North Atlantic run transporting American personnel to the British Isles. Sailing with as many as fifteen thousand troops, these fast liner troopships were escorted away from the American coast by American destroyers, then zigzagging at high speed, crossed the Atlantic unescorted. Upon nearing the British Isles, an escort of British warships met the liners and shepherded them through North Channel to the Firth of Clyde.

On the night of October 1, the *Queen Mary,* captained by C. G. Illingworth, with about fifteen thousand American troops embarked, picked up her British escort about sixty miles northwest of Bloody Foreland. The warships included the light antiaircraft cruiser *Curaçao,* commanded by John Boutwood. As it happened, that night the new Type VII *U-407,* commanded by twenty-five-year-old Ernst-Ulrich Brüller, which had sailed to the North Atlantic from Kiel on August 15 and was inbound to Brest, came upon the 81,235-ton *Queen Mary,* with a fair chance to shoot.

Apparently, lookouts or the radar watch on *Curaçao* or *Queen Mary* saw *U-407*

---

* Halifax 205 to 208; Slow Convoy 98 to 102; RB 1; Outbound North and Outbound North (Slow) 126 to 134. HX 208 was the first of this type to sail from New York, on September 17. See Appendix 3.

and gave the alarm. Turning to run down *U-407*'s bearing, *Curaçao* crossed into the zigzagging path of *Queen Mary.* The sharp bow of the big liner struck *Curaçao* amidships at about twenty-six knots and cut her clean in half. The two sections of *Curaçao* drifted apart and sank within five minutes. Captain Illingworth could not risk the *Queen Mary* to rescue *Curaçao*'s survivors, and 338 men perished. Brüller deserved credit for indirectly causing the loss of *Curaçao,* but the British kept the mishap secret until after the war.

In compliance with Hitler's orders, six Type VIIs of the Atlantic force were directed to penetrate the Strait of Gibraltar during the period of the October new moon and permanently join the Mediterranean U-boat force, commanded by Leo Karl Kreisch. For administrative purposes, Dönitz organized the boats into group *Tümmler.* After passing through the strait, they were to patrol the western Mediterranean before proceeding to bases at La Spezia, Pola, or Salamis.

Group *Tümmler* sailed from French bases from October 1 to October 4. En route, two boats reported "radio failures" and did not attempt the strait: Dietrich Lohmann in *U-89* and Rudolf Franzius in *U-438.* Both skippers subsequently repaired their radios and joined groups operating on the North Atlantic run. Four boats successfully penetrated the strait on the nights of October 10 and 11: Kurt Diggins in *U-458,* Gerd Kelbling in *U-593,* Herbert-Viktor Schütze in *U-605,* and Götz Baur in *U-660.* Schütze in *U-605* reported that upon entering the Mediterranean, a British submarine shot at him but missed. The addition of these four boats increased the German U-boat force in the Mediterranean to nineteen.

The "loss" of these four boats from the Atlantic force to the Mediterranean was partially offset by the return of two boats that had been loaned recently to the Norway/Arctic commands to attack PQ/QP convoys and repel possible invaders of Norway. These were the *U-606,* with a third skipper in as many months, Hans Döhler, age twenty-four, and the *U-436,* commanded by Günther Seibicke. Both boats proceeded directly from Norway to groups operating on the North Atlantic run.

A boat of group *Luchs,* the new *U-610,* commanded by Walter von Freyberg-Eisenberg-Allmendingen, age twenty-six, found an eastbound convoy on October 2. This was the fast Halifax 209, protected by British Escort Group B-4. Acting on *U-610*'s signals, other boats of group *Luchs* converged, but the weather again turned foul and a solar storm drastically impeded radio transmissions. Nonetheless, a dozen boats got close to the Allied ships and a few were able to shoot. Odo Loewe, from the wrecked *U-256,* substituting in *U-254* for the regular captain, Hans Gilardone, who was ill, reported that he sank the burned-out hulk of the 11,700-ton abandoned American tanker *Robert H. Colley,* but no other boats had any success.

One reason, U-boat skippers reported, was that "seaplanes" were swarming over Halifax 209, preventing attacks. These were probably Catalinas based in Iceland, working at extreme range. The air escorts sank two U-boats with the loss of all hands: Werner Schulte in *U-582* and Kurt Makowski in the new *U-619.** A Catalina of U.S. Navy Squadron VP 73 sank *U-582.*† A Hudson of British Squadron 269, piloted by J. Markham, sank *U-619.* Another British aircraft depth-charged Heinz Rahe in the new *U-257* so badly that he was forced to abort to France, where battle-damage repairs required weeks.

In the days following, Dönitz jockeyed groups *Leopard, Wotan,* and *Panter* to intercept westbound convoys, based on a good flow of information from *B-dienst.* Several boats made contact with one or more of these convoys, but owing to heavy storms, poor communications, misidentifications, erroneous position reports, and other factors, the outcome was less than satisfactory.

A new boat of group *Leopard, U-620,* commanded by Heinz Stein, age twenty-nine, reported a westbound convoy in very rough seas on October 12. This was Outbound North (Slow) 136, which had come apart in the storm. In response to Stein's signals, the new *U-382,* commanded by Herbert Juli, age twenty-six, and the *U-597,* commanded by Eberhard Bopst, came up and made contact with scattered sections of the convoy, which was escorted by British group B-3. Juli in *U-382* fired a salvo of three torpedoes at a "flush-deck destroyer." He claimed she sank, but no hits on a destroyer could be confirmed. Bopst in *U-597* fired four torpedoes at a 7,000-ton freighter and claimed hits, but these were never confirmed either.

Four different U-boats each picked off a straggling freighter of Outbound North (Slow) 136: Ralph Kapitzky in the new *U-615* got a 4,200-ton Panamanian and captured the captain and chief engineer; Horst Schünemann, age twenty-eight, in the new *U-621* got a 6,100-ton Britisher; Horst Kessler in the *U-704,* making his second patrol, got a 4,200-ton Britisher; and Alexander Zitzewitz, age twenty-six, in the new *U-706,* also got a 4,200-ton Britisher.

The convoy escorts and long-range Coastal Command aircraft from Iceland counterattacked the boats of group *Leopard.* Coastal Command aircraft continued to have successes:

- At about noon on October 12, a B-24, piloted by the commander of British Squadron 120, Terence M. Bulloch, spotted Bopst in *U-597* on the surface. In a straight-in, diving attack, Bulloch dropped six shallow-set depth charges on *U-597* in a close pattern. Bulloch reported that the U-boat literally blew up, hurling a "large oval chunk" of steel skyward that almost hit his rear gun turret. There were no German survivors.
- Another (unidentified) aircraft caught and depth-charged Herbert Juli in *U-382,* disabling three of his four bow torpedo tubes. Upon reporting this damage,

* At the time, the Admiralty credited a Hudson of British Squadron 269 with sinking *U-582* and the British destroyer *Viscount* with sinking *U-619.* However, according to Franks (1995), in the postwar reappraisal, credit for sinking both boats went to aircraft, as described herein.

† The identity of the Catalina and pilot is difficult to establish. Remarkably, four different Catalinas (Nos. 8, 9, 10, 12) of VP 73 carried out attacks on U-boats in that area on October 5 and 6. The pilots were C. F. Swanson, M. Luke, W. Mercer, and W. B. Huey, Jr. Niestlé credits Swanson.

Juli was ordered to leave the combat zone and to find and provide escort for the inbound blockade-runner *Tannenfels.* When he finally reached France at the end of October, the boat went into repair for over three months.

Surface escorts of convoy Outbound North (Slow) 136 pounced on Heinz Stein in *U-620* and Klaus Rudloff in *U-609.* They depth-charged Stein for six hours, but he survived to fight on. Battle damage forced Rudloff in *U-609,* who had only just arrived from France, to abort.

On that same day, October 12, the new *U-258* of group *Wotan,* commanded by Wilhelm von Mässenhausen, found an anticipated eastbound convoy. This was Slow Convoy 104, composed of forty-eight ships, which had sailed from New York on October 3. It was protected by British Escort Group B-6, the battle-wise British destroyers *Fame* and *Viscount* and four corvettes manned by Norwegian crews. The British destroyers were equipped with Type 271 centimetric-wavelength radar; at least two ships had Huff Duff.

Von Mässenhausen shadowed Slow Convoy 104 and brought up group *Wotan.* Next to arrive were the new *U-221* and *U-356,* commanded by Hans Trojer and Georg Wallas, respectively. The destroyers and corvettes drove von Mässenhausen and Wallas off, but Trojer in *U-221* found an opening and shot a full salvo of five torpedoes. He claimed sinking four freighters for 20,000 tons and leaving another in flames, but only three sinkings for 11,354 tons could be confirmed in this first attack.

Five *Wotan* boats got into position to launch a second attack on Slow Convoy 104 on October 14. Leading the pack was Trojer in *U-221,* who claimed sinking four more ships for 27,547 tons, including the British whale factory ship *Southern Empress.* Only two of these sinkings were confirmed, a 5,900-ton American freighter and the 12,398-ton *Southern Empress.** The *Ritterkreuz* holder Ernst Mengersen in *U-607* hit and sank a 4,800-ton Greek freighter, but an escort counterattacked him, causing so much damage that he was forced to abort to France. Erich von Lilienfeldt, age twenty-six, in the new *U-661,* sank a 3,700-ton Greek freighter. Yet another new skipper, Kurt Baberg, age twenty-five, in *U-618,* claimed two sinkings for 11,000 tons plus damage to a third ship, but only one sinking, a 5,800-ton British freighter, could be confirmed. Finally, another new skipper, Kurt Sturm in *U-410,* claimed to have sunk a 3,000-ton freighter that had been damaged by another boat.

In retaliation, each of the two British destroyers of the escort sank a Type VIIC U-boat.

- *Viscount,* commanded by John Waterman, got a radar contact at six thousand yards on the new *U-661* in the early hours of October 15. Waterman immediately rang up twenty-six knots and set a course to ram. He missed on the first try,

---

* Trojer's claims in two attacks on Slow Convoy 104 were eight ships sunk for 43,547 tons. His confirmed score was five ships sunk for 29,681 tons, the highest confirmed score of any U-boat on the North Atlantic run in the fall of 1942.

but, as he put it, "for reasons which will never be discovered," the U-boat turned and cut right across *Viscount*'s bow. This time the destroyer hit *U-661* a hard blow abaft the conning tower and rode up on her superstructure. When the two ships disengaged, Waterman wrote, the U-boat had "a broken back" and "*Viscount* opened fire and obtained numerous hits with the close-range weapons." Fourteen minutes after the original contact, Waterman dropped a "heavy charge" on *U-661*. Destroyed by these depth charges, the boat upended and sank stern first with no survivors. Heavily damaged by the collision, *Viscount* reduced speed to seven knots and eased inside the convoy formation.

• In the afternoon of the next day, October 16, the destroyer *Fame*, commanded by R. Heathcote, which was sweeping ahead of the convoy, got a firm sonar contact at two thousand yards. This was the new boat *U-353*, commanded by twenty-six-year-old Wolfgang Römer, twenty-five days out from Kiel. Römer was hovering at sixty-five feet—not deep enough to pass under the convoy and too deep to use his periscope. Before he could collect his wits and evade, *Fame* was on top of *U-353*, throwing off ten depth charges set for fifty to 140 feet. These explosions wrecked *U-353*. Römer ordered her to the surface to scuttle.

As *Fame* was coming about for a Hedgehog attack, *U-353* suddenly popped up. When Römer and his crew rushed topside, Heathcote and his men opened fire with every weapon that would bear and rang up eighteen knots to ram. *Fame* hit *U-353* a glancing blow and scraped down her starboard side, tearing a "long rent" in her own plating. When *U-353* drew astern, *Fame* plastered her with five more depth charges set for fifty feet. Meanwhile, the entire convoy overtook the combatants and every ship in it that could bring a weapon to bear opened fire on the U-boat.

Amid this tumult, Römer and his crew jumped overboard. Heathcote sent a boarding party to ransack *U-353* for intelligence documents, but the party, commanded by P. M. Jones, had only five minutes inside the sinking boat and it found nothing of value. *Fame* and the Norwegian-manned corvette *Acanthus* picked up Römer and thirty-seven other survivors. Six Germans died in the sinking. Too badly damaged by the collision to provide further escort, *Fame* limped alone to the British Isles.

British interrogators discovered that Römer had previously commanded the school duck *U-56*. After Werner Pfeifer of *U-581* and Otto Harms of *U-464*, Römer was the third skipper of *U-56* to be captured, a record of sorts. The interrogators wrote that Römer complained bitterly about the shortage of qualified personnel to man the U-boats. His engineer was the only officer with prior experience in submarines, and that experience had been gained in a school boat. About 80 percent of the enlisted men of *U-353* were raw recruits with scant training, the British reported.

The damage to *Viscount* and the departure of *Fame* left only the four Norwegian-manned corvettes to protect Slow Convoy 104. Command responsibility fell on the senior Norwegian, C. A. Monsen in *Potentilla*. Late in the evening of October 16, he got a radar contact at 2,800 yards and unhesitatingly turned to ram. The U-boat reversed course and came directly at *Potentilla* at full speed. Fearing that his corvette might be fatally damaged in a head-to-head collision with a U-boat at a combined speed of about thirty knots, Monsen veered off. As the U-boat passed close down his port side, he threw over five depth charges set for fifty to 140 feet. When the boat dived, Monsen ran at the swirl and dropped thirteen more depth charges.

No positive identification of this boat can be made. Very likely it was the *U-254,* which Odo Loewe commanded temporarily in place of the ill Hans Gilardone. After making contact with Slow Convoy 104, Loewe reported that escorts had forced him under three times and that he had incurred heavy depth-charge damage and was forced to abort for the second time in as many patrols.

Homebound, Loewe linked up with another battle-damaged boat, Klaus Rudloff in *U-609,* who provided Loewe with Metox radar-detector protection while crossing the Bay of Biscay. Upon reaching France, Loewe turned *U-254* back over to Gilardone. In the meantime, his own battle-damaged boat, *U-256,* had been declared nonserviceable, and as a result, Loewe returned to Germany to commission a new Type VII. This was *U-954,* to which Dönitz's youngest son, twenty-year-old Peter, had been assigned as a junior watch officer.

Eight Catalinas and B-24 Liberators based in Iceland flew out to provide Slow Convoy 104 with air escort on October 16 and 17. Upon learning of this saturation coverage, Dönitz canceled operations and put the boats back on the trail of Outbound North convoys.

Upon analysis of the attacks and the sinking reports on Slow Convoy 104, Dönitz had ambivalent feelings. He praised Trojer in *U-221* for good tracking in foul weather and for sinking (as was believed) eight ships for 45,000 tons, making the supposed sinkings eleven out of what was erroneously believed to be a convoy of only nineteen ships. At the same time, Dönitz again went out of his way to comment bitterly that convoy battles had become "much more difficult." It was therefore "intensely important"—even "decisive"—that new German weapons, such as search radar and improved radar detectors, heavier flak guns, and reliable torpedo pistols be developed as soon as possible. Unaware of the loss of *U-353* in this action or of the heavy damage to *U-254,* he logged German casualties as *U-661* sunk and *U-607* damaged. The confirmed Allied losses from Slow Convoy 104 were eight of forty-eight ships for about 44,000 tons. The confirmed German losses were *U-353* and *U-661* sunk, and *U-254* and *U-607* damaged.

In the days following, several of the U-boats again made contact with westbound convoys. For various reasons, including foul weather, Dönitz was not able to mobilize an effective group attack on any of them. However, a half dozen boats from several different groups picked off seven ships for nearly 60,000 tons. Old hand Günther Heydemann in *U-575* achieved the most notable success by sinking the 11,300-ton British troopship *Abosso,* which was loaded with Allied military personnel, including a number of Dutch submariners. Walter von Freyberg-Eisenberg-Allmendingen in the new *U-610* and Kurt Baberg in the new *U-618* each sank an American freighter, stragglers from Outbound North 137.

The U-boats also found Outbound North (Slow) 138. It was composed of forty-eight merchant ships, protected by the crack British Escort Group B-2, commanded by Donald Macintyre. The escort group consisted of three British destroyers (*Hesperus, Whitehall,* and *Vanessa*) and three British corvettes. Every warship had Type 271 centimetric-wavelength radar; *Hesperus* and the rescue vessel, *Accrington,* had Huff Duff.

The convoy had sailed from Liverpool on October 11 and was almost immediately scattered in a raging storm. A week later Macintyre finally got the ships into proper formation. Three days later, on October 21—Trafalgar Day—the weather cleared beautifully and the escorts refueled from a tanker in the convoy, a technique the British had only just begun to master. On the night of October 23, British land-based Huff Duff picked up the now familiar urgent beginning of a U-boat convoy-contact report ("Beta Beta," colloquially dubbed "B-bar"), and Macintyre girded for a pack attack.

The destroyers *Hesperus* and *Vanessa* ran out a Huff Duff bearing but found nothing. For the next several days, Macintyre wrote,* all three destroyers responded to local Huff Duff contacts by running down bearings, and by this means and by radical changes of course by the convoy, prevented a full-scale U-boat assembly. The underway refueling and a shift to a "more southerly" convoy course (for New York) also helped. The result was that no U-boat attacked any ship in Outbound North (Slow) 138.

At about this time, a boat of the *Puma* group, the new *U-443,* commanded by Konstantin von Puttkamer, age twenty-five, found convoy Outbound North 139. This was an odd-numbered "fast" formation, the reverse of the fast Halifax convoys; therefore it was more difficult to bring up U-boats for a mass attack.

In view of that fact, Dönitz had recently made an important change in convoy-attack doctrine: If the convoy speed of advance was eleven knots or more, the U-boat first making contact was authorized to shoot after sending a contact report. Von Puttkamer reported and shot, sinking two big British ships: a 9,800-ton freighter and the 8,000-ton tanker *Donax.* Escorts promptly counterattacked with depth charges and held *U-443* down until the convoy escaped. Over the next several days six other *Puma* boats made contact, but none had any success.

During this same period, land-based aircraft assigned to Coastal Command inflicted further heavy losses on the Atlantic U-boat force: four boats sunk, two severely damaged. Two were accounted for by Coastal Command Squadron 224, based in southern England and newly equipped with twelve B-24 Liberators.†

- On October 20, a B-24 Liberator of Squadron 224, piloted by D. M. Sleep, sank the new Type VIID (minelayer) *U-216,* commanded by Karl-Otto Schultz, directly west of the Bay of Biscay.‡ There were no survivors. The debris from the exploding U-boat severely damaged the aircraft, which crashed while attempting an emergency landing at a base.

---

* *U-boat Killer* (1956).

† Bringing the number of RAF B-24s assigned to operational Coastal Command ASW squadrons to twenty-one.

‡ After *U-213* and *U-215,* she was the third of the six clumsy Type VIID minelayers to be sunk within four months.

• On October 22, a Leigh Light–equipped Wellington of Squadron 179, piloted by A.D.S. Martin, sank the new Type VII *U-412,* commanded by Walter Jahrmärker, age twenty-five, as she entered the Atlantic northeast of the Faeroes, six days out from Kiel. There were no survivors.

• On October 24, another B-24 of Squadron 224, piloted by B. P. Liddington, sank the new Type VII *U-599,* commanded by Wolfgang Breithaupt, directly west of the Bay of Biscay. There were no survivors.

• On October 24, an unidentified land-based aircraft hit and severely damaged the new *U-620,* commanded by Heinz Stein, who was pursuing Outbound North 139. The boat aborted and, on orders from Dönitz, withdrew from the North Atlantic to the quiet Gulf of Cadiz.

• On October 27, one of the newly assigned B-17 Flying Fortress of Squadron 206, piloted by R. L. Cowey, sank the new *U-627,* commanded by Robert Kindelbacher, age twenty-seven, south of Iceland, shortly after she entered the Atlantic. There were no survivors.

• On November 1, a Catalina of U.S. Navy Squadron VP 84, newly arrived in Iceland and piloted by R. C. Child, hit the new *U-664,* commanded by Adolf Graef, age twenty-six, with depth charges, four of which exploded nearby and caused severe damage. Only thirteen days out of Kiel, Graef was forced to jettison his two stern torpedoes and abort to France.

A recent transfer from the Arctic assigned to group *Puma* in the North Atlantic, the *U-436,* commanded by Günther Seibicke, came upon a fast eastbound convoy on October 26. This was Halifax 212, protected by Paul Heineman's American Escort Group A-3, consisting of the big Coast Guard cutter *Campbell,* the four-stack destroyer *Badger,* and six corvettes—five Canadian and one British. Three of the Canadian corvettes were en route to the British Isles for assignment to Torch forces. One of the latter, *Summerside,* had Type 271 centimetric-wavelength radar, but most of the other escorts lacked modern electronic-detection gear.

Seibicke in *U-436* shadowed and brought up other *Puma* boats. During the night of October 27–28, three boats attacked. Shooting first, Seibicke fired a full salvo of five torpedoes. He claimed sinking a 5,000-ton freighter and a 10,000-ton tanker and damage to three freighters for 18,000 tons. In reality, he sank the 10,000-ton British tanker *Sourabaya* and damaged two other tankers, the 7,400-ton Norwegian *Frontenac,* which reached port, and the 8,200-ton American *Gurney E. Newlin.* Horst Schnemann, age twenty-eight, in the new *U-621,* shot two torpedoes at two freighters and claimed two hits, but the hits could not be verified. Hans Döhler, new skipper of *U-606,* which had been diverted to the Arctic for one patrol, sank the damaged *Gurney E. Newlin* and damaged the big 17,000-ton Norwegian whale factory ship, *Kosmos II.*

In a second attack on the following night, three skippers had successes. In spite of five misses, Ulrich von Soden-Fraunhafen, age twenty-nine, in the new *U-624,* sank the damaged *Kosmos II,* as well as the 7,700-ton American tanker *Pan New York.* Günther Seibicke in *U-436* sank a 5,000-ton British freighter that had fallen back to assist *Kosmos II.* Hans Karl Kosbadt, age twenty-four, in the new boat *U-224,* sank a 4,000-ton Canadian freighter.

By the morning of October 29, Halifax 212 was close enough to Iceland to get B-24 support. Upon learning this, Dönitz canceled operations. He logged that ten of the twelve boats of *Puma* made contact and sank nine ships for 68,500 tons and damaged three other ships. The confirmed score was six ships (including four tankers) for 52,000 tons sunk and one tanker damaged.*

Three new Type IXCs sailed directly from the Baltic to patrol the Gulf of St. Lawrence before the cold weather shut down shipping operations. One skipper, Klaus Bargsten in *U-521,* had previously commanded the Type VII *U-563,* which was badly wrecked in December 1941 when Bargsten attempted to slip into the Mediterranean through the Strait of Gibraltar. He sailed from Kiel on October 3. The other two skippers, Volkmar Schwartzkopff, age twenty-eight, in *U-520* and Herbert Schneider, age twenty-seven, in *U-522,* were new to command of ocean-going boats. They sailed from Kiel on October 3 and 8, respectively.

Near Cape Race, Newfoundland, on October 29, Schneider in *U-522* spotted smoke on the horizon. This was Slow Convoy 107, comprised of forty-two ships, twenty from New York and twenty-two from Sydney and Halifax. The convoy was protected by an ad hoc Canadian escort group, C-4: one modern Canadian destroyer, *Restigouche,* commanded by Desmond W. Piers, and five corvettes—four Canadian and one British.† One Canadian corvette, *Regina,* aborted with engine problems. Another, *Moosejaw,* sailed to take her place. *Restigouche* had the older Type 286 meter-wavelength radar; the British corvette *Celandine* had the newer Type 271 centimetric-wavelength radar, but it broke down. *Restigouche* and the rescue ship *Stockport* had Huff Duff.

Upon receiving the contact report from Schneider in *U-522,* Dönitz directed the fourteen U-boats of group *Veilchen* to home on his signals. Allied land-based direction-finding stations and Huff Duff sets in the convoy picked up the heavy German radio traffic. As a result, Canadian authorities intensified ASW sea and air patrols. The four-stack Canadian destroyer *Columbia* (of the local escort group) found *U-522* tailing the convoy and attempted to attack, but Schneider dived and drove her away with two torpedoes, which missed. The British destroyer *Walker* (also of the local escort) briefly extended her stay with the convoy.

Canadian Air Force aircraft supporting Slow Convoy 107 achieved two remarkable victories that went largely unheralded at the time:

• On October 30, while sweeping ahead of the convoy, E. L. Robinson, the pilot of one of two Hudsons of Squadron 145 supporting the convoy, saw a U-boat on the surface two miles off. This was the Type VII *Veilchen* boat *U-658,* com-

---

* This was the heaviest damage inflicted on a Halifax convoy by U-boats since the attack on Halifax 133 sixteen months earlier, from June 24 to June 29, 1941.

† Two regular warships of Escort Group C-4, the ex-American four-stack destroyer *St. Croix* and corvette *Sherbrooke,* were in the dock for refits.

manded by Hans Senkel, making his second patrol. Robinson ran in and dropped four 250-pound Mark VIII depth charges, set at twenty-five feet. These straddled *U-658* and blasted her to bits. There were no survivors.

• Eight hours later, a Digby of Squadron 10, homebound after providing escort to convoy Outbound North (Slow) 140, also saw a U-boat on the surface. This was one of the three new Type IXCs, *U-520,* commanded by Volkmar Schwartzkopff, racing up to join the *Veilchen* group. Attacking from 3,200 feet, the pilot, D. F. Raymes, dropped four 450-pound Mark VII depth charges on *U-520.* Nothing further was ever heard from that boat.

• On the day following, October 31, one of four Hudsons of Squadron 145 supporting Slow Convoy 107 found and attacked Klaus Bargsten in *U-521,* but he got away with minor damage.

One of the *Veilchen* boats, the new *U-381,* commanded by Wilhelm-Heinrich von Pückler und Limpurg, age twenty-nine, made contact with Slow Convoy 107 on November 1 in deteriorating weather and shadowed. During the afternoon and evening, the *Veilchen* boats, as well as the two surviving IXCs, *U-521* and *U-522,* closed on the convoy. That night and the next morning, November 1–2, the two IXCs and four VIIs of the *Veilchen* group attacked. The shadower, *U-381,* fired a spread at *Restigouche,* but missed.

The experienced Siegfried von Forstner in *U-402,* who had incurred heavy battle damage off Cape Hatteras on his prior patrol, closed to shoot. In three separate night-surface attacks over six hours, von Forstner claimed sinking six freighters for 40,000 tons and damage to one of 7,000 tons. His impressive confirmed score was four freighters sunk for about 20,000 tons and half credit for the 7,500-ton British freighter *Empire Sunrise,* which was sunk three hours later by the veteran Horst Uphoff in *U-84.*

The five corvettes raced hither and yon, firing guns at various U-boats and dropping depth charges. Star shells and flaming ships lit the seascape. The two Type IXs attacked next. Schneider in *U-522* sank two freighters, a 5,800-ton Britisher and a 5,700-ton Greek, and damaged another 5,500-ton Britisher. Klaus Bargsten in *U-521* claimed a possible hit on a corvette and the sinking of a stopped freighter. In actuality he missed the corvette *Moosejaw* and hit the 5,500-ton British freighter *Hartington,* which was sunk later by Herbert Schneider in *U-522* and Rudolf Franzius in *U-438,* to share credit three ways.

Both sides ordered reinforcements into the battle during November 2. The Allies directed four warships to join Slow Convoy 107: the British destroyer *Vanessa,* which was escorting Halifax 213 astern of Slow Convoy 107; the American four-stack destroyers *Leary* and *Schenck;* and the *Treasury*-class Coast Guard cutter *Ingham,* from Iceland. Dönitz in turn directed a newly formed group, *Natter,* composed of a dozen boats, to join *Veilchen.*

On the second and third nights of the battle, November 2–3 and 3–4, seven U-boats attacked Slow Convoy 107. The experienced Dietrich Lohmann in *U-89* sank two British freighters, the 5,300-ton *Jeypore,* serving as the convoy commodore's flagship, and the 4,600-ton *Daleby.* Another experienced hand, Ernst Vogelsang in *U-132,* sank two ships, the 5,500-ton Dutch tanker *Hobbema* and a

6,400-ton British freighter, and damaged the 6,700-ton British freighter *Hatimura.* Soon after, Hans-Joachim Hesse, age thirty-six, in the new boat *U-442,* also hit the *Hatimura,* which blew up in a thunderous explosion. Later, it was postulated that the explosion of *Hatimura* most likely destroyed Vogelsang's *U-132.** Herbert Schneider in the Type IXC *U-522* claimed sinking two more freighters for 6,200 tons, bringing his claimed bag on this patrol to nine ships sunk for 51,665 tons, but only a 3,200-ton Greek could be confirmed. Klaus Bargsten in the Type IXC *U-521* claimed sinking a tanker and a freighter for 11,115 tons, but only the 6,900-ton American tanker *Hahira* could be confirmed.

The rescue ship *Stockport* fished out 350 survivors from the ships that went down. When she reported she had no more space, the American Navy seagoing tugs *Uncas* and *Pessacus* were pressed into service and collected 240 more survivors. Late on the evening of November 4, the two Navy tugs and the American Navy oiler *Gauger,* escorted by two corvettes, left the convoy to land about six hundred survivors in Iceland. Still later, eight of the surviving merchant ships, escorted by the destroyers *Leary* and *Schenck* and the Coast Guard cutter *Ingham,* also put into Iceland.

By the morning of November 5, B-24s and Catalinas from Iceland arrived to provide an air umbrella for Slow Convoy 107. Upon learning this, Dönitz canceled operations for the seven boats of group *Veilchen* and redirected the thirteen boats of group *Natter* to yet another Outbound North convoy. He was very well pleased with the destruction in Slow Convoy 107. Based on flash reports, he logged that the U-boats had sunk twenty-three merchant ships for 136,115 tons and damaged a destroyer, a corvette, and four other freighters. The confirmed score—the fourth most successful North Atlantic convoy attack of the war—was fifteen ships sunk for about 83,000 tons. Three boats were lost: the Type VIIs *U-132* and *U-658,* and the Type IXC *U-520.* Severely depth-charged by Terence Bulloch in a B-24, Lohmann in *U-89* was disabled and forced to abort to France.

It had become standard operating procedure at Western Approaches to denigrate the performance of Canadian escort groups, not to say Canadians in general. The after-action report of Slow Convoy 107 drew the usual negative endorsements. Furthermore, an inspector from Coastal Command, then in Newfoundland, concluded his visit with a damning indictment of Canadian Air Force ASW operations.

Neither of those reports adequately took into consideration the growing pains of the Canadian military forces or the shortcomings of their weaponry. The Canadian surface escorts were still making do with too few unimproved corvettes, green crews, and antiquated radar and sonar. The Atlantic forces had been pared to the bone to provide the seventeen most experienced and best-equipped Canadian corvettes for Torch. As for the air escorts, only two Canadian squadrons (5 and 116) had Cansos/Catalinas, and one of those units (116) had only just arrived in

---

* Credit for her kill went initially to Squadron Leader Terence Bulloch in a British B-24 of Squadron 120 based in Iceland, but a postwar Admiralty analysis identified the explosion of *Hatimura* as the likely cause.

Newfoundland for duty. The other squadrons made do with limited-range Digbys and Hudsons.*

Assessments

In the month of October, the Allies sailed sixteen convoys across the Atlantic, east and west,† comprised of about 725 merchant ships. The great congregation of U-boats on the North Atlantic convoy run mounted truly noteworthy attacks on only three convoys, all eastbound to the British Isles: Slow Convoy 104, Slow Convoy 107, and Halifax 212. From these three convoys the U-boats sank twenty-nine merchant ships for about 179,000 tons, all loaded with food and war matériel. Of the 725 merchant ships in all sixteen convoys, U-boats sank thirty-eight ships (5 percent).

German U-boat casualties in October were unusually heavy, indeed, by far the worst of the war to then. Twelve boats were lost on the North Atlantic run alone: the XB minelayer *U-116,* serving as a temporary tanker; the Type IXC *U-520;* and ten Type VIICs.‡ Remarkably, nine and maybe ten of the boats were sunk by Allied aircraft, unassisted by surface ships. Moreover, ten Type VIIs aborted in the month of October.§

In their rush to describe the "massacre" of merchant ships on the North Atlantic run, historians seldom, if ever, tabulate and stress the twenty U-boat casualties (sinkings and aborts) in the month of October. Doubtless these casualties provoked alarm and deeply troubling questions at U-boat headquarters. Over five hundred U-boat crewmen on the twelve lost boats had been killed or captured, not to mention other U-boat losses elsewhere in October.

When the months of September and October 1942 are combined, we see that the numerous groups of U-boats operating on the North Atlantic run mounted noteworthy attacks on six of the thirty-five convoys# that crossed the Atlantic in those months. From these convoys, comprising about 1,700 merchant ships, the U-boats sank fifty-seven cargo vessels (3 percent) plus the destroyers *Ottawa* and *Veteran* for 343,535 tons. In return, sixteen U-boats and about 720 German submariners were lost (or captured) in those two months, including *U-116,* the valuable XB minelayer serving as a provisional tanker. This was an intolerable exchange rate of

* Squadron 145 was preparing to reequip from Hudsons to Cansos, but this would take quite some time. The new Squadron 162 was scheduled for Cansos.

† Halifax 209 to 212; Slow Convoy 103 to 107; Outbound North and Outbound North (Slow) 135 to 141. See Appendix 3.

‡ *U-216, U-353, U-412, U-582, U-597, U-599, U-619, U-627, U-658, U-661.* The VIIC *U-132,* sunk on November 5 in action against Slow Convoy 107, would raise the loss of VIICs to eleven.

§ *U-89, U-254, U-257, U-382, U-440, U-595, U-607, U-609, U-620, U-664.* The *U-620,* shifted to the Gulf of Cadiz, was at sea on this patrol for sixty days.

\# Including special convoy RB 1.

about 3.5 merchant ships sunk for each U-boat lost. In addition, in the same two months, twelve U-boats on the North Atlantic run were forced to abort, bringing U-boat casualties (sinkings and aborts) to twenty-eight.

In this same period, American shipyards alone increased production of new merchant vessels to an astonishing rate, turning out nearly four times the gross tonnage of the ships lost in those six convoys:

Month	*New Ships*	*Gross Tons*
September	94	691,000
October	84	599,000
Totals	178	1,290,000*

A further close analysis of anticonvoy operations in all areas of the North Atlantic by the seventy-three attack boats sailing in September and October is also revealing. Forty-three of these patrols (59 percent) were carried out by new boats or new skippers. The fifty-seven merchant ships sunk by all the boats came to an average of .78 ships per boat per patrol. This was a marked decrease from the average .92 ships per boat per patrol achieved by the boats sailing to the North Atlantic in July and August.† Forty attack boats, or well over half of the seventy-three putting out (55 percent), sank no ships, an increase in the nonproductive trend, so ominous for the Germans:‡

	Patrols	*New C.O.*	*Ships Sunk*	*Per Boat*	*Boats Lost*	*No Sinkings*
September	33	22 (67%)	21½	.65	5	20 (60%)
October	40	21 (53%)§	36½	.91	13#	20 (50%)
Totals	73	43 (59%)	58	.78	18	40 (55%)

These figures show that even without reading the four-rotor naval Enigma, *Triton,* by the fall of 1942 the Allies were fast gaining the upper hand over the U-boat threat on the North Atlantic run. Lacking search radar, a reliable magnetic pistol for torpedoes, and adequate numbers of U-tankers, unaware of shipboard Huff Duff and harassed by radar-equipped Allied aircraft, skippers of the Type VII and Type IX U-boats fought convoy battles under increasingly severe handicaps. In truth, notwithstanding the slowly growing strength of the Atlantic U-boat force, there was no longer any possibility that the obsolescent Type VIIs and IXs could pose a meaningful, let alone decisive, threat to Allied shipping on the North Atlantic run. The much-vaunted "wolf pack" tactic was a failure on many levels.

Nonetheless, Dönitz insisted upon continuing the convoy battles in the North

---

* Stated in the more commonly cited deadweight tons: 1,886,000.

† See chart in Volume I, p. 666.

‡ See Appendix 2. Twenty of thirty-three U-boats that sailed in September and twenty of forty that sailed in October.

§ Includes four experienced attack boats commanded by new skippers.

\# Not including provisional U-tanker *U-116.*

Atlantic. Apart from the Allied shiping losses achieved and the propaganda opportunities these offered, the presence of U-boats perpetuated the reign of terror at sea and compelled the Allies to continue using convoys, which cut imports and delayed some military operations. However, Dönitz's plan had to be canceled. On November 8, when Berlin became aware of the Torch landings in Northwest Africa, Hitler directed that every available U-boat of the Atlantic force be employed to repel the Allied invaders.

Thus the U-boat campaign on the North Atlantic run was again abruptly halted, this time after merely four months into the renewed assault. In canceling this campaign, Hitler provided the Allies another "breathing space" in the North Atlantic, largely free of U-boats. During that breather, hundreds upon hundreds of loaded ships in Halifax and Slow convoys delivered huge quantities of oil, food, and supplies to the British Isles.

Patrols to the Americas

To exploit Allied shipping traffic in the Gulf of St. Lawrence and in the area of Trinidad—and to freeze ASW forces in those places and force the Allies to continue convoying—Dönitz deployed eighteen U-boats to American waters in September and October: thirteen Type IXs and five Type VIIs.

Four Type IXs sailed in September to Canadian waters for torpedo patrols within a period of one week, from September 19 to 26. One, *U-518,* was assigned the additional task of landing an agent of the *Abwehr,* the German intelligence agency, on the coast of New Brunswick.

Leaving from France, Hans-Joachim Schwantke in the aging IX *U-43* and Hermann Rasch in the XB *U-106* arrived in Canadian waters first. Both reported intense air patrols. Rasch likened them to the air threat in the Bay of Biscay. Newly installed Metox gear gave warning of aircraft using meter-wavelength ASV radar, but Rasch, who dived and surfaced *U-106* so often that he felt like a "dolphin," suggested that if at all possible, Metox should be upgraded to provide the range to the detected aircraft.

Both Schwantke and Rasch cruised boldly up the St. Lawrence River—Schwantke farther upstream that any U-boat skipper ever had—but attentive air patrols and noticeably improved cooperation between air and surface ASW forces thwarted attacks on convoys and single ships. Moreover, it was at about this time that Canadian authorities closed the St. Lawrence River to ocean shipping. In these arduous, nerve-racking operations, Schwantke sank no ships and Rasch sank but one: the 2,100-ton ore boat *Waterton,* escorted by the armed yacht *Vison* and an RCAF Canso. After the attack, *Vison* got *U-106* on sonar and dropped twelve well-placed depth charges, forcing Rasch to lie doggo on the bottom at 607 feet for eight hours. Upon withdrawing from the Gulf of St. Lawrence, Schwantke advised Dönitz that Canadian ASW measures were now so effective that he should not send any more boats to the area. Rasch concurred, but Dönitz did not.

Harassed by aircraft, neither Schwantke nor Rasch had any further success.

Homebound, the boats were to meet the tanker *U-460,* commanded by Ebe Schnoor, for replenishment. A raging storm delayed the refueling for six days, during which time they—and some other U-boats—literally ran out of fuel and drifted. Finally the refueling was carried out on November 29 and most of the boats returned to France, but Rasch in *U-106* was temporarily diverted to help repel the Torch invasion convoys. For past successes and for his tenacity and aggressiveness in the St. Lawrence River, Dönitz awarded Rasch a *Ritterkreuz.**

Homebound on November 17, Schwantke in *U-43* found the eastbound Slow Convoy 109, whose Canadian escort had been weakened by the abort of the modern destroyer *Saguenay,* severely damaged in a collision with a merchant ship. An RCAF Canso drove *U-43* off, but Schwantke regained contact the following day and got in one full salvo. He claimed he sank two freighters for 10,000 tons and damaged the 9,100-ton American tanker *Brilliant,* in ballast. The sinkings could not be confirmed, but *Brilliant* was indeed hit and damaged and later sank under tow.

Outbound from Germany to Canada, the new IXC/40 *U-183* and IXC *U-518,* commanded by Heinrich Schäfer, age thirty-five, and Friedrich-Wilhelm Wissmann, age twenty-six, respectively, were diverted temporarily to a group on the North Atlantic run. While awaiting action, Schäfer was twice bombed by aircraft, but the damage was slight. After they were released from the group, both boats proceeded to the north outlet of Belle Isle Strait, to again check out Dönitz's firm but wrong conviction that the Slow and Halifax convoys were exiting the Gulf of St. Lawrence through the strait, when, in actuality, they were leaving from New York. During ten days of lying in wait off the north exit, neither skipper found a convoy, of course, but Wissmann shot four torpedoes at a lone "destroyer." However, all missed.

After the two boats had patrolled that area for ten fruitless days, Dönitz released them to penetrate the Gulf of St. Lawrence, via Cabot Strait. Proceeding slowly south along the east coast of Newfoundland toward St. John's, Wissmann boldly entered Conception Bay, where he sank the 5,600-ton Canadian freighter *Rose Castle* and a 5,600-ton British ore carrier in the Wabana Roadstead. Schäfer fired two torpedoes at a tanker and a destroyer. He heard two detonations and claimed the tanker sank, but it could not be confirmed in postwar records.

Wissmann entered the gulf via Cabot Strait on November 2, en route to New Brunswick to land the *Abwehr* agent. A radar-equipped Canadian ASW aircraft caught *U-518* in the strait and dropped four shallow-set depth charges, but Wissmann crash-dived and went deep. That maneuver and the sudden onset of fog thwarted a second air attack.

Running submerged most of the time to avoid ASW aircraft, Wissmann slowly proceeded westerly to Baie des Chaleurs. In the early hours of November 9, he carefully beached the bow of *U-518* on a sandbar and landed the agent, Werner Alfred Waldmar von Janowski, on a deserted shore via an inflatable dinghy. When the dinghy returned, Wissmann backed off the sandbar and ran for the open waters of

* At the time of the award (December 29, 1942), his confirmed score, all on *U-106,* was eleven ships for 73,413 tons, plus damage to the tanker *Salinas* and an American freighter for 12,885 tons.

the gulf that same night. He reported to Dönitz that his special mission had been carried out without notable incident.* Finding no targets inside the gulf, Wissmann departed the area on November 17.

That same day, Schäfer in *U-183* found the westbound convoy Outbound North (Slow) 142 on the Grand Banks. As he was preparing to attack, an RCAF aircraft escorting the convoy saw *U-183* and dropped six close depth charges. Schäfer survived, but he had no further opportunity to get at the convoy. Furthermore, he reported mechanical defects that precluded any immediate convoy attacks.

Four days later, on November 21, Wissmann in *U-518* found and attacked another incoming convoy, Outbound North 145, which, owing to a foul-up in communications between Canadian and American ASW forces, had no air cover. Wissmann sank the 6,100-ton British freighter *Empire Sailor* and damaged two tankers sailing in ballast, but his boat, too, was badly damaged.

Homebound, both skippers sank ships: Schäfer in *U-183* got the 6,000-ton British freighter *Empire Dabchink* from convoy Outbound North (Slow) 146; Wissmann in *U-518* got a lone 10,200-ton American tanker, *Caddo,* from which he captured the captain and first mate. Schäfer in *U-183,* like Rasch in *U-106,* was temporarily diverted to help repel Torch invasion convoys.

This four-boat foray into Canadian waters thus had to be deemed a failure. Only one boat, *U-106,* sank a ship inside the Gulf of St. Lawrence and that ship, *Waterton,* was merely 2,100 tons. Two boats, *U-43* and *U-183,* sank one ship each outside the gulf. Apart from landing the agent, Wissmann in *U-518* sank four ships for 29,748 tons—and damaged two tankers—all outside the gulf.

Before learning of the poor returns from these September IXs, Dönitz ordered three new IXCs sailing in October *(U-520, U-521, U- 522)* to patrol the Gulf of St. Lawrence. As related, while en route to Canada, all three boats became entangled in North Atlantic convoy battles; none reached Canada, and *U-520* was lost. In the event, with icing, the closure of the St. Lawrence River to oceangoing traffic, and the onset of another bitterly cold winter, U-boat incursions became impractical.

Seven U-boats sailed to the area near Trinidad in September: four Type VIIs and three Type IXs. These four VIIs were the last of that type to conduct strictly torpedo patrols in American waters in 1942.

Rolf Mützelburg in *U-203,* who wore Oak Leaves on his *Ritterkreuz,* was the first of the VIIs to sail. After he crossed the Bay of Biscay, U-boat Control assigned him to chase a couple of convoys, but owing to foul weather, the chases came to naught, and upon release he proceeded to a rendezvous with Ebe Schnoor's tanker, *U-460.*

---

* After changing into civilian clothes, Janowski made his way to New Carlisle with two heavy suitcases, and checked into a hotel to bathe and rest for a few hours. He then checked out, paying in obsolete Canadian bills, and boarded a local train, the first stage in a journey to Montreal. A suspicious hotel clerk notified police, who arrested Janowski at the first train stop, nine miles away. Some sources say the Canadians "turned" Janowski and used him and his radio gear and codes to transmit disinformation to Berlin.

Fourteen days out from France on September 11, Mützelburg hove to and announced a swim call. When he dived overboard, he slipped and hit his head on a saddle tank, incurring fatal injuries. Assuming temporary command of the boat, the first watch officer, Hans Seidel, age twenty-four, elected to head at maximum speed for Schnoor's tanker, *U-460,* which had a doctor. However, after only a few hours, Mützelburg died and Dönitz directed Seidel in *U-203* to return to France. When this melancholy boat reentered Lorient on September 18, Seidel left to commission and command a new Type VII in Germany. His predecessor as first watch officer, Hermann Kottmann, who had returned to Germany to command a new boat, was recalled to command *U-203.*

The other three VIIs followed *U-203* from France by a week. While outbound in the Bay of Biscay, one, *U-202,* was bombed by a Coastal Command aircraft. Although two torpedoes were damaged, the boat continued its voyage. On September 17, all three boats refueled in mid-Atlantic from Schnoor's *U-460.*

These three VIIs patrolled east and southeast of Trinidad. The experienced Johannes Liebe in *U-332* was first to sink a ship: the 6,000-ton British freighter *Registan.* That same day, September 29, Günther Poser, age twenty-six, the new skipper of *U-202,* shot at but missed a big tanker and was in turn bombed by an aircraft on ASW patrol. The shock of the depth-charge explosions knocked out an air compressor, limiting *U-202*'s diving ability and forcing Poser to remain well to the east of Trinidad. On October 1, Günther Rosenberg, age twenty-five, the new skipper of *U-201,* and Poser in *U-202* sank two small freighters sailing in company: the 2,100-ton American *Alcoa Transport,* and the 1,800-ton Dutch *Achilles.* Attempting to mount a second attack, Rosenberg was heavily depth-charged and driven off. Still working together on October 7 and 8, Rosenberg and Poser each got two hits to sink the 7,200-ton American Liberty ship *John Carter Rose.* On the following day, October 9, Rosenberg missed a big freighter, the 6,400-ton Dutch *Flensburg,* but after a hard chase, sank it by torpedo and gun. Reporting a double miss on a lone freighter, Poser informed U-boat Control that all his torpedoes were expended and that he was homebound. Rosenberg followed by a day or so.

These departures left one Type VII in American waters, Liebe's *U-332.* An ASW aircraft knocked out his attack periscope, but Liebe pressed on, sinking a second freighter, the 5,000-ton British *Rothley* on October 19. Assured of a second refueling on the homebound leg, Liebe remained in waters off Trinidad until November 1, but he sank no more ships. Total bag for the three Type VIIs on this foray to Trinidad waters: six ships for 28,500 tons.

Liebe crossed the Atlantic to the Freetown area, where he refueled from the tanker *U-462,* which was supporting U-boats in the South Atlantic. Owing to the diversion of U-boats to the Torch invasion in November, and to his abundance of fuel and torpedoes, Liebe's patrol was extended a full month, a very great hardship on the crew.

Three veteran Type IXs sailed from France to areas near Trinidad in mid- to late September. En route, Hans Witt in *U-129,* who had sunk eleven ships on his one prior patrol to the Americas, got the 5,500-ton Norwegian freighter *Trafalgar.*

Arriving in the area first, *Ritterkreuz* holder Georg Lassen in *U-160* promptly picked up a small convoy outbound from Trinidad via the Tobago Passage. After flashing an alert, which was heard by another of the arriving skippers, Günther Müller-Stöckheim in *U-67,* Lassen lay in wait submerged and attacked. He managed to sink only one 730-ton British freighter and to damage a 6,200-ton American freighter before the escorts picked him up on sonar and pounded him with depth charges in shallow water. Müller-Stöckheim arrived too late to help.

All three IXs patrolled the Atlantic east and southeast of Trinidad during the last days of October. Witt in *U-129* sank two American freighters for 12,400 tons. Müller-Stöckheim in *U-67* hit the 4,400-ton Norwegian vessel *Primero* with two torpedoes. Seeing that it did not sink, he dived and approached his victim to inspect her at periscope depth. Then, as he was preparing to surface for a gun action, *Primero* veered into *U-67*'s path and smashed into the conning tower, crippling both periscopes. Rising to the surface, Müller-Stöckheim sank *Primero* with two more torpedoes, then hauled away to repair damage and to download the topside torpedoes. During the latter operation, a crewman was killed when excessive air pressure in a topside-storage canister blew the door into his chest.

Witt in *U-129* and Lassen in *U-160* entered the Caribbean, Witt via Mona Passage, Lassen via Tobago Passage. Encouraged to shell the refineries and tank farms on Aruba and Curaçao, Witt planned to cruise far to the west, but that plan was shelved when Lassen in *U-160* reported a westbound convoy, TAG 18, en route from Trinidad to Guantánamo Bay via Aruba.

Lassen estimated that the convoy consisted of about twenty freighters and tankers. On November 3, he attacked with great skill and coolness. He claimed sinking five ships for 31,500 tons; four for 25,600 tons were confirmed. Witt in *U-129* raced up and attacked the convoy on November 5. He thought he sank five ships (three tankers, two freighters) for 31,000 tons within the space of ten minutes, but only two tankers for 14,600 tons were confirmed. Accepting the overclaims, Dönitz awarded Witt a *Ritterkreuz.**

Hauling back to Atlantic waters east of Trinidad, Lassen in *U-160* operated in loose cooperation with Müller-Stöckheim in *U-67* from time to time in the ensuing days. Lassen sank three more freighters for 18,200 tons, bringing his confirmed bag to an impressive eight ships for 44,900 tons. Müller-Stöckheim sank three ships for 16,000 tons and damaged two others for 11,700 tons. These successes raised Müller-Stöckheim's confirmed sinkings for the patrol to four vessels for 20,500 tons, which, combined with past claims and overclaims, was sufficient to earn a *Ritterkreuz.*†

Six of the seven boats sailing in October reached American waters. Four IXs patrolled the Trinidad area. Two IXs set off for Brazil. One of them, *U-511,* was recalled and diverted to attack Torch forces; the other, *U-174,* continued as planned.

---

* At the time of the award, his confirmed score was sixteen ships for 74,184 tons.

† At the time of the award, his confirmed score was thirteen ships for 71,704 tons, plus damage to five for about 30,000 tons.

A single Type VII, *U-608,* was ordered to plant a minefield in the approaches to New York harbor.

The first of the four IXs sailing to the Trinidad area was the IXC *U-505,* commanded by a young new skipper, Peter Zschech, who had been first watch officer of the famous *U-124.* Born October 1, 1918, Zschech was only twenty-three years old when he assumed command of *U-505* on September 15 and celebrated his twenty-fourth birthday three days before he sailed. On November 7 he sank a 7,200-ton British freighter sixty miles due east of Trinidad. That sinking drew saturation air coverage to the site. Nonetheless, on November 9, Zschech attacked another freighter, firing four torpedoes. All missed.

While *U-505* was cruising on the surface on the afternoon of November 10, a twin-engine aircraft came out of the sun and attacked before the boat could dive. The plane dropped a string of shallow-set depth charges, which savaged the boat, blew up the plane, and severely wounded two Germans, including the second watch officer and a crewman. Another crewman, Hans Joachim Decker, wrote:

> It looked as if a bulldozer had run over the deck—twisted steel, crumpled sheet metal, broken and twisted pipelines. Sections of the false hull [superstructure] had disappeared. The 37mm antiaircraft cannon had been blown overboard. And from behind the ship streamed an ever widening ribbon of thick, black substance. The bombs had split open our fuel tanks. A nice track that was. . . . Below, we discovered that the after bulkhead of the engine room had buckled; the water had come from our fresh water cooling pipes, smashed in by a huge dent in the pressure hull over the port diesel.

No U-boat had ever sustained such massive damage and survived, Decker wrote. Running east on one engine to elude other Trinidad-based aircraft, the crew worked feverishly to repair the worst of the damage so that the boat could dive. Thirteen long days later, on November 22, *U-505* rendezvoused with the tanker *U-462.* Zschech left the wounded second watch officer in the care of the doctor on *U-462,* which was returning to France, took on fuel and a Metox set, and limped onward to France, arriving on December 12. The *U-505* was in battle-damage repair and modification for the next seven months.

The other three IXs sailing for the Trinidad area in October were badly in need of successes. In a prior eighty-one-day patrol to the Caribbean under the command of Walther Kölle, *U-154* had sunk only one 65-ton trawler. Her new skipper, Heinrich Schuch, came from the *U-105,* which had been badly damaged in the Bay of Biscay by a Coastal Command Sunderland in June. In a prior patrol to the Caribbean, Kurt-Edward Engelmann, in *U-163,* had been forced to abort and sank nothing, and Georg Staats in *U-508* had sunk only two Cuban coasters for 2,700 tons.

The three boats arrived in the Trinidad area in early November. East of the Windward Islands chain, Engelmann in *U-163* sank the first ship, a 5,200-ton British freighter. Nearby, on November 8 and 9, Heinrich Schuch in *U-154* sank two British freighters for 12,700 tons.

Two of the boats slipped into the Caribbean via the Mona Passage: Staats in *U-508* and Engelmann in *U-163.* West of Trinidad, on November 7, Staats sank two freighters for 12,400 tons, one American and one British. On November 12, Engelmann found and attacked a Trinidad–Aruba–Guantánamo Bay convoy, TAG 20. He claimed sinking a 5,000-ton freighter and a fleet destroyer and damage to a 6,000-ton freighter, but, in fact, he only hit and severely damaged one of the escorts. She was the big (328-foot, 2,000-ton) U.S. Navy gunboat *Erie* (prototype of the *Treasury*-class Coast Guard cutters), awesomely armed with four 6" guns. Fires ignited *Erie*'s ammo locker, killing seven men and wounding eleven, and forcing the rest of the crew to abandon ship. Several days later, fire-fighting specialists boarded *Erie,* and a tug towed her into the harbor at Curaçao, where she capsized and sank on December 5.

These attacks froze traffic inside the Caribbean temporarily and drew heavy air patrols. Accordingly, Engelmann, whose Metox was out, and Staats withdrew to the fruitful hunting grounds in the Atlantic east and southeast of Trinidad. There Engelmann sank two freighters for 9,800 tons, bringing his confirmed bag for the patrol to four ships for 17,000 tons, plus damage to a 7,100-ton American tanker. Remaining in the area east of the Windward Islands chain, Schuch sank one other British freighter for 5,200 tons, raising his confirmed bag to three ships for about 18,000 tons. In an impressive display of seamanship and fighting skill, Staats sank by torpedo alone seven more freighters for 37,800 tons in the Atlantic between Trinidad and British Guiana from November 17 to December 8. These successes raised Staats's confirmed bag for this patrol to an impressive nine ships for 50,300 tons, the fourth-best U-boat patrol to American waters.*

Ulrich Thilo in *U-174,* who had made one luckless patrol in the North Atlantic, carried the U-boat war to Brazilian waters. In three days, from October 31 to November 2, he sank three freighters for 20,300 tons, but a long, arduous month passed before he sank another ship, a 5,000-ton Norwegian freighter. After refueling from the tanker *U-461* in mid-Atlantic, Thilo returned to Brazilian waters and on December 15 sank the 5,500-ton American freighter *Alcoa Rambler.* That success raised his sinkings for the patrol to five ships for 30,800 tons.

The sinking of the *Alcoa Rambler* drew an Allied counterattack. Possibly, two Catalinas of U.S. Navy Squadron VP 83 based at Natal found *U-174.* Pilot Wall first spotted the U-boat on the surface. He attacked with depth charges, forcing the boat to crash dive. Near this site later in the day, another Catalina of VP 83 piloted by Bertram J. Prueher attacked a surfaced U-boat, perhaps *U-174.* Prueher reported "evidence of considerable damage" but claimed no definite kill. Thilo in *U-174* reported to U-boat Control that "a number of depth charges" fell after the sinking and that owing to a shortage of fuel, he was headed home. About two weeks after this incident, Prueher was named commander of Squadron VP 83. As will be described, later in the year he was killed in a daring attack on another U-boat.

To carry out the oft-delayed—and hazardous—mission of mining New York harbor, Dönitz chose Rolf Struckmeier in the Type VII *U-608,* who had made one

---

* See Plate 2.

promising patrol in the North Atlantic versus convoy Outbound North 127. Struckmeier took aboard ten TMA mines,* plus as many torpedoes as he could carry, and sailed on October 20. He planted the field near the Ambrose lightship in the approaches to New York on November 10, but it was discovered and swept and did not produce any sinkings. While loitering off New York on November 16, Struckmeier sank a 5,600-ton British freighter that was sailing alone.

Struckmeier's return voyage was a nightmare. Promised a refueling from Ebe Schnoor's *U-460,* he, too, was caught in the raging storm that delayed the tanker's refueling operations for six days. As a consequence, on November 27 Struckmeier ran dry of fuel and could only drift. In response to his call for help, Klaus Bargsten in the Type IXC *U-521* found *U-608* and gave her fuel enough to reach the tanker, *U-460.* After replenishment, Struckmeier took *U-608* home to France without further incident.

Although the patrol of the Type VII *U-608* yielded little, the patrols by Type IXs to Trinidad and Latin America were remunerative. Altogether, the five Type IXs that sailed to those areas in October sank twenty-two ships for 123,200 tons, an average of 4.4 ships for 24,600 tons per boat per patrol.

PLATE 2

MOST PRODUCTIVE U-BOAT PATROLS TO AMERICAN WATERS

(BY CONFIRMED GROSS TONNAGE SUNK OVER 40,000 IN 1942)[1]

BOAT	TYPE	SKIPPER	SHIPS SUNK	TONS
U-158	IXC	Erwin Rostin	13	65,108
U-68	IXC	Karl-Friedrich Merten	7	50,898
U-159	IXC	Helmut Witte	10	50,354
U-508	IXC	Georg Staats	9	50,265
U-66	IXC	Friedrich Markworth	9	48,896
U-162	IXC	Jürgen Wattenberg	9	47,181
U-123	IXB	Reinhard Hardegen	7	46,744
U-507	IXC	Harro Schacht	9	44,055
U-66	IXC	Richard Zapp	6	43,946
U-155	IXC	Adolf-Cornelius Piening	10	43,892
U-103	IXB	Werner Winter	9	42,169
U-515	IXC	Werner Henke	8	42,114
U-124	IXB	Johann Hendrick Mohr	7	42,048
U-129	IXC	Hans Ludwig Witt	11	41,571
U-172	IXC	Carl Emmermann	10	40,745
		Totals:	134	699,986

1. Source: Rohwer, *Axis Submarine Successes.*

* The TMA was an anchored or moored mine that could be launched from a torpedo tube in depths to 885 feet. Owing to the weight and bulk of the anchor and chain, its warhead was only 474 pounds.

The combined results of the eighteen patrols mounted to the Americas in September and October (including aborts) came to fifty-three confirmed ships sunk for 302,400 tons. This was only four ships shy of the fifty-seven ships sunk by the seventy-three attack boats (including aborts) that sailed to the North Atlantic run in the same two months. Inasmuch as neither side reported sinkings by geographic area, sinkings in the Caribbean and southwest Atlantic—especially those in November—helped foster the wrong impression that the U-boats on the North Atlantic run were carrying out a "massacre."

After analyzing the returns from American waters, which resulted in no U-boat losses, naturally Dönitz planned to continue the campaign in the same areas—but only by long-range Type IXs and Type VIID minelayers. As will be seen, notwithstanding Torch, eleven U-boats sailed to American waters in November. However, three Type IXs were lost and only one boat produced a worthwhile return, and after November 1942, the U-boat campaign to American waters was curtailed drastically.

The *Laconia* Affair

The very good returns of the twenty-eight boats that sailed to the South Atlantic during the early summer of 1942 and the increased availability of U-tankers prompted Dönitz to continue U-boat patrols in that area during the late summer and fall. Most of the boats bound for southern waters were attached to three groups:

- ***Iltis.*** Comprised of the Type IXB *U-107* and five Type VIIs formerly of group *Blücher,* group *Iltis* (Pole Cat) was ordered to rake southward for Sierra Leone convoys from an area near the Azores to Freetown. Two of the ex-*Blücher* Type VIIs, Horst Dieterichs in *U-406* and Günther Reeder in the Type VIID (minelayer) *U-214,* soon turned back for France. The other four boats continued to Freetown, but found no convoys.
- ***Eisbär.*** Comprised of four veteran Type IXCs, supported by the tanker *U-459,* group *Eisbär* (Polar Bear) was to carry out a surprise attack at Cape Town, South Africa, and if feasible and advisable, go farther eastward into the Indian Ocean. While southbound near the Azores on August 27, one of the *Eisbär* boats, Werner Hartenstein's *U-156,* joined group Blücher's attack on convoy Sierra Leone 119 and sank the 6,000-ton British freighter *Clan Macwirter,* a straggler. South of the equator, Karl-Friedrich Merten in *U-68* torpedoed the 5,300-ton British vessel *Trevilley,* captured her captain and chief engineer, and put her under with one hundred rounds from his deck gun.
- **The U-Cruiser Force.** Not really a formal group—hence it sailed unnamed—the force was comprised of four big, new Type IXD2s, commanded by two senior ex-flotilla commanders, Hans Ibbeken in *U-178* and Ernst Sobe in *U-179,* and by two younger *Ritterkreuz* holders, Robert Gysae in *U-177** and

* Injured during an Allied air raid on Bremen, Gysae returned to *U-177* from the hospital on crutches. Hence the crew adopted a crutch for its conning-tower emblem.

Wolfgang Lüth in *U-181*. The force was to round the Cape of Good Hope more or less at the same time and operate against unconvoyed Allied shipping in the Indian Ocean. En route to the Atlantic, Gysae in *U-177* lost a man overboard in heavy seas and was attacked by a Coastal Command aircraft, but its bombs fell wide. Nearing the Atlantic, Lüth in *U-181* was also attacked by a Coastal Command aircraft. It dropped one "close" bomb and summoned several surface warships, which dropped thirty depth charges at *U-181* during a ten-hour search.

In addition to the foregoing, Dönitz directed that five other veteran boats (four Type IXCs and one Type VII), sailing singly, patrol to Freetown or farther south along the African coast to the Gulf of Guinea. These brought the number of attack boats sailing southward in late August and September to Freetown or beyond to seventeen.* The boats were to be supported by three U-tankers and by two ex-Dutch submarines converted to torpedo-supply boats. Three Italian submarines, *Barbarigo, Archimede,* and *Cappellini,* also independently patrolled southern Atlantic waters at this time.

On the morning of September 12, Werner Hartenstein in *U-156,* a Type IXC of group *Eisbär* en route to Cape Town, spotted the second enemy ship of his patrol. She was a big one: the 19,700-ton British Cunard White Star passenger liner *Laconia,* serving as a troopship. Northbound from Cape Town to the British Isles, *Laconia* was sailing alone about nine hundred miles south of Freetown. There were about 2,700 people on board, including 1,800 Italian POWs, 268 British military personnel, 103 Free Poles who were guarding the Italians, and about 80 women and children.

Remaining hull-down beyond the horizon, Hartenstein tracked *Laconia* until dark, then ran in by the light of a full moon to make a surface attack. He fired two bow torpedoes. One hit forward, the other amidships. *Laconia* stopped dead in the water. The crew lowered lifeboats and threw over rafts. The radio operator sent out a submarine warning *(SSS),* giving the name of the ship and her position, adding that *Laconia* had been torpedoed. No Allied radio monitors picked up this warning or the distress message, or a second one *Laconia* broadcast four minutes later. But Hartenstein heard them and doubtless his pulse quickened. Counting confirmed claims on his two prior patrols to the Caribbean and the *Clan Macwirter* sunk in Sierra Leone 119, *Laconia*'s 20,000 tons brought his sinkings to 100,000 tons and made him eligible for a *Ritterkreuz.*

Laconia had enough lifeboats and rafts to support all 2,700 persons aboard her, including the POWs. But owing to the sharp list of the ship, many boats and rafts could not be launched. Others were improperly launched and capsized or swamped. Chaos reigned on the boat decks. Many lifeboats entered the water and

* Four Type VIIs, nine Type IXs, and four Type IXD2 U-cruisers. Five of the seventeen boats were commanded by *Ritterkreuz* holders. These were, in addition to Gysae and Lüth in the U-cruisers, Karl Friedrich Merten and Ernst Bauer in the Type IXCs *U-68* and *U-126,* respectively, and Peter Cremer in the Type VII *U-333.*

pulled away half full or less. *Laconia*'s captain, Rudolph Sharp, brave and defiant to the end, chose to go down with his ship, which sank about an hour and a half after the torpedoes hit. The noise of her exploding boilers attracted scores of sharks to the scene. They attacked the hundreds of survivors who had jumped into the sea wearing life preservers.

Circling the sinking ship in the darkness at a safe distance, Hartenstein watched her lowering away lifeboats. Then he heard men shouting in Italian, *"Aiuto! Aiuto!"* ("Help! Help!"). He fished out several of the Italians and from them learned to his shock and dismay that they were survivors of a shipment of hundreds of Italian POWs from North Africa. They told Hartenstein that both torpedoes exploded in POW pens deep in the ship's hold, killing hundreds. The Poles who were assigned to guard the POWs refused to unbolt the doors on the pens and consequently hundreds of Italians who survived the torpedoes went down with the ship. Several hundred or more broke out of one pen and scrambled topside, but they were refused places in lifeboats at gun and bayonet point.

According to the rules of war being observed by Axis and Allies alike, Hartenstein was in no way guilty of any infraction. *Laconia* was armed (two 4.7" naval guns, six 3" antiaircraft guns, and so on), zigzagging, and blacked out, hence a legitimate submarine target. Inasmuch as the U-boat rules discouraged—or even prohibited—rescue or capture of survivors of sunken ships (except captains and chief engineers), Hartenstein was free to resume his journey to Cape Town, leaving all the survivors, including the Italians, to fend for themselves. But he did not. Perhaps concerned that the accidental killing and stranding of so many Italian soldiers could cause a serious political rupture in the Axis high command, and/or deeply moved by humanitarian considerations, Hartenstein launched a rescue operation. In two hours, he fished out ninety Italians, many suffering from bayonet wounds or shark bites.

There were "hundreds" more Italians floating in the water, many without life jackets, clinging to wreckage. Hartenstein soon realized he could not take them all on board. Nor could he leave them behind. What they urgently needed were more U-boats. He therefore notified Dönitz of the situation—that *Laconia* "unfortunately" carried "1,500 Italian POWs"—and requested instructions. Approving Hartenstein's rescue operation, Dönitz immediately directed seven other U-boats to proceed at high speed to the disaster scene: the other four U-boats of group *Eisbär,* including the tanker *U-459,* plus Erich Würdemann's *U-506,* in the Gulf of Guinea, and Harro Schacht's *U-507,* homebound from a foray to Brazil, and the Italian submarine *Cappellini,* commanded by Marco Revedin. Dönitz then notified Berlin of the situation, the action he had taken, and of a hastily concocted plan to have the eight rescue submarines land the survivors in the port of Bingerville, on the Vichy French Ivory Coast, about six hundred miles to the northeast.

Berlin had other ideas. Professing to be humiliated and outraged by the loss of Italian comrades, Hitler declared that Hartenstein should have said nothing, quietly submerged, and left the scene. He insisted that nothing was to interfere with *Eisbär*'s surprise attack on Cape Town, which was designed to deliver a crippling blow to military supplies destined for the British in Egypt and the Soviets, via the

Persian Gulf. In response to this tirade, Admiral Raeder directed Dönitz to disengage all *Eisbär* boats from the *Laconia* rescue, including Hartenstein's *U-156,* and send them onward to Cape Town, per the original plan. Würdemann's *U-506,* Schacht's *U-507,* and Revedin's *Cappellini* were to take on Hartenstein's Italian survivors and to pick up other Italians if they could be rescued without endangering the boats. No British or other Allied survivors were to be rescued, only Italians. In place of landing the survivors in Bingerville, Raeder was to request that the Vichy French send warships from Dakar and/or the Ivory Coast to meet the U-boats at sea and take off the survivors.

In the meantime, Hartenstein fished out about four hundred survivors. He took 193, including 172 Italians and twenty-one British men and women, on board *U-156* and put the others in lifeboats. In response to queries from Dönitz, he described the sinking and the scene in detail and suggested "a diplomatic neutralization" (i.e., a temporary cease-fire) in the area in order to effect a safe rescue of both Allied and Axis survivors. Dönitz relayed this unusual proposal to Berlin, but Admiral Raeder and the OKM rejected it, in part because Hitler in his rage had directed that no word of the *Laconia* sinking or the proposed Axis rescue be transmitted to the Allies, and in part because Raeder did not think it wise to enter into a "deal" with the untrustworthy Allies.

No one told Hartenstein that his "neutralization" proposal had been rejected. In any case, he did not wait for approval. On his own initiative on the morning of September 13, he broadcast this extraordinary message in plain English three times:

> If any ship will assist the shipwrecked *Laconia* crew I will not attack her, providing I am not attacked by ship or air force. I picked up 193 men. 4°-52" south. 11°-26" west. German Submarine.

The British in Freetown intercepted this message, but believing it might be a *ruse de guerre,* refused to credit it or to act. While waiting for a response, Hartenstein cruised about, rescuing and redistributing the survivors. To relieve the crowding on *U-156,* he transferred thirty-one English and Italians to lifeboats but kept four British women. To prevent lifeboats from swamping, he redistributed about one hundred survivors from overloaded lifeboats to those with more space. Later in the day, Dönitz canceled orders to the four oncoming *Eisbär* boats to assist in the rescue and specifically directed Hartenstein to turn over all survivors to the first U-boat to arrive at the scene—probably Würdemann's *U-506*—and then head south to rejoin group *Eisbär* for the attack on Cape Town. In response to Berlin's request, the 7,500-ton Vichy French cruiser *Gloire* sailed from Dakar, and two sloops, the fast 650-ton *Annamite* and the slower 2,000-ton *Dumont d'Urville,* sailed from Conakry, French Guinea, and Cotonou, Dahomey, respectively.

During September 14 Hartenstein continued to play the role of shepherd. He logged that in addition to the 162 survivors on board *U-159,* he was surrounded by "roughly twenty-two large fully filled boats and a large number of small rafts." He retrieved and righted swamped boats, doled out water and food to British and Italians alike, and shifted survivors around to equalize the loads in the boats. He intercepted messages from Dönitz to the four *Eisbär* boats ordering them to cancel rescue operations, turn about, and go on to Cape Town, to Helmut Witte in *U-159,* alerting him to prepare to relieve Hartenstein for operations with group *Eisbär,* and detailed instructions to Hartenstein and to Würdemann in *U-506* and Schacht in *U-507* for conducting rescues and meeting the Vichy French ships. Dönitz warned the three German rescue submarines: "All boats, including Hartenstein, only take as many men into the boat as will allow it to be fully ready for action when submerged."

On the following day, September 15, Würdemann and Schacht arrived at the scene. By then Dönitz had formally substituted Helmut Witte in *U-159* for Hartenstein in group *Eisbär* and had directed Hartenstein to continue the rescue operations until the Vichy French ships arrived. In compliance with Dönitz's order not to overcrowd the U-boats, Hartenstein transferred 132 Italians to Würdemann's *U-506,* retaining 131, including five women. In addition, Würdemann took in tow four lifeboats, containing, he logged, "about 250 people." Schacht took on board from the lifeboats or rafts 149 Italians, two English officers, and two women. In addition, he also took in tow four lifeboats containing, he logged, "eighty-six Englishmen and nine Poles."

After these rescues had been carried out, Würdemann and Schacht gave Dönitz brief descriptions of their situations. In reporting that he had four lifeboats containing 250 people in tow, Würdemann did not say the boats contained British and Poles. Dönitz assumed they were some of the hundreds of Italian survivors. In reporting that he also had four lifeboats in tow, Schacht stated that they contained ninety-five British and Poles. Upon receipt of this message, Dönitz directed Schacht but not Würdemann to cut the lifeboats loose.

Unknown to Berlin and to all but a few Allied personnel, the Americans had only recently established an airfield on the British island of Ascension, 250 miles southwest of the *Laconia* sinking. Its primary purpose was to serve as a refueling stop for combat and transport aircraft en route to Africa via the Brazil–South Atlantic route. Its secondary purpose was to provide limited air escort and rescue for Allied shipping in this remote area of the South Atlantic. For the secondary task—and for self-defense against Axis air or sea attack—a squadron of twenty-three Air Force planes (eighteen P-39 fighters and five B-25 medium bombers) had recently arrived for permanent duty. Although the squadron had been supplied with the latest ASW depth charges and bombs, none of the airmen had been trained in ASW.

On the morning of September 15, five transient aircraft en route from Ascension to Accra, British Ghana, spotted two U-boats on the surface. When one of the aircraft descended for a closer look, one of the U-boats shot at it with flak guns, or so said the Americans. The plane evaded and resumed its flight to Accra. Another of the planes at a higher altitude radioed Ascension to report the U-boat sighting and the brief encounter. Within ten minutes of this notice, Ascension had two B-25s in the air on a search-and-destroy mission, but they could not find the U-boats. The records do not reveal which U-boats they were.

That same day—September 15—British authorities in Freetown for the first time notified Ascension of the *Laconia* sinking and of a plan to divert a British merchant ship, *Empire Haven,* to the scene to rescue the survivors. The garbled or poorly composed message gave the impression that *Laconia* had only just been sunk that day. It did not mention Hartenstein's ongoing rescue efforts or his proposal for a diplomatic "neutralization" (or cease-fire) in the rescue area or that Vichy French ships were en route to the scene. The heart of the message was a request for Ascension to provide air cover during *Empire Haven*'s rescue efforts. Ascension replied that the sinking site (as given in the message) was too far away for its twin-engine B-25 medium bombers to effectively assist, but that a transient B-24 Liberator would be pressed into service on the following day.

The next morning, September 16, Hartenstein reported to Dönitz that he had turned over 132 survivors to Würdemann and that he was attempting to corral the lifeboats, which were drifting over a wide area. Per orders from Dönitz, he intended to remain at the site until the arrival of the Vichy French ships. Beyond Hartenstein's ken, Würdemann fished out another twelve Italian survivors, bringing his total on board to 142. He also had nine women and children on board and the four lifeboats in tow. Schacht had transferred twenty-three Italians and one British officer from *U-507* to the lifeboats, to make room to take on board thirteen more women and sixteen children, bringing the number of survivors on *U-507* to an excessive 161 (129 Italians, sixteen children, fifteen women, one British officer). Near *U-507* were seven lifeboats containing about 330 people, including about 35 Italians.

That morning—September 16—the transient B-24 Liberator, commanded by James D. Harden, took off from Ascension laden with depth charges and bombs. Two and a half hours later, at 9:30 A.M., Harden sighted *U-156.* At that time Hartenstein had 115 survivors on board (fifty-five Italians, fifty-five British males, and five British females), and was towing four crowded lifeboats and preparing to tie on another. Upon seeing the plane, Hartenstein displayed a homemade six-foot-by-six-foot Red Cross flag over his bridge and attempted to talk to Harden by signal lamp, but in vain. Harden flew off to a safe distance, described the situation to Ascension, and asked for instructions. Unaware of Hartenstein's proposal for a temporary cease-fire during the rescue, or anything about the ongoing rescues by *U-506, U-507,* and *Cappellini,* the squadron commander, Robert C. Richardson III,* replied: "Sink sub."

Harden returned to *U-156* and circled to attack. He later reported officially that the "lifeboats had moved away from sub," and that on the first pass he dropped three depth charges. Two fell wide but one "hit ten feet astern." In his official report, Hartenstein stated that when the B-24 reappeared, the four lifeboats were still in tow. When he saw the plane's bomb-bay doors open, he ordered the towline cut so

* West Point–educated son of the general commanding all Army forces in the central Pacific under Admiral Nimitz.

that he could crash dive. One of the three bombs fell amid the lifeboats, Hartenstein wrote, capsizing one of them and flinging the survivors into the sea. Harden reported that he made four more runs at *U-156.* On the first three, the depth charges or bombs failed to release. On the fourth and last, Harden dropped two bombs that fell very close. "The sub rolled over and was last seen bottom up," Harden said, claiming a kill. "Crew had abandoned sub and taken to surrounding lifeboats."

During Harden's three abortive runs, Hartenstein concluded that the plane's "bomb racks were empty." Hence, he remained on the surface. On the last run, Hartenstein reported, one of the two bombs exploded "immediately below the control room." When the Germans below reported heavy flooding and chlorine gas, Hartenstein ordered all survivors (British and Italians alike) overboard and directed his crew to don life jackets and to prepare to abandon ship. He broadcast a U-boat "distress signal" three times on four different frequencies.

Fortunately for the Germans, the initial damage reports were exaggerated. The flooding was easily checked; no dangerous chlorine gas developed. Both periscopes were damaged but not seriously; seven battery cells were broken. Hartenstein pulled away and dived, furious at the American airmen for failing to honor the Red Cross flag and for bombing the lifeboats. Later he reported the attack to Dönitz, concluding, "Am discontinuing help. All men [survivors] overboard. Am moving away to the west. Am repairing damage."*

When Dönitz learned of the attack on *U-156* he, too, was furious. Some of his equally enraged staffers urged him to break off the rescue. In his memoirs, Dönitz wrote that having set his hand to the task, he could not abandon it and put an end to all such discussion with these words: "I cannot put those people into the water. I shall carry on." He ordered Hartenstein to "take no further part in salvage operations." He directed Würdemann and Schacht not to rely on Red Cross flags, to transfer to the lifeboats all survivors except Italians, to keep their U-boats in "instant readiness" to dive and conduct submerged combat.

Not fully informed of what was going on, Revedin in *Cappellini* arrived at the scene that same day. He saw hundreds of "dots" in the water, which proved to be shark-bitten corpses. Later he found two lifeboats under sail. One contained fifty British males, the other, forty-one British males and forty-three British females and children. Revedin offered to take aboard all survivors in both boats, but all refused. In lieu of rescue, Revedin gave them food, water, cigarettes, and so on and directions to the African coast, six hundred miles away.

In the late afternoon, Revedin found other half-sunk lifeboats. These contained many Italians as well as British and others. He picked up forty-nine of the weakest Italians and put them belowdecks. He then brought aboard "a lot" of British and Poles, who remained topside on the deck while Revedin sought to find one of the Vichy French rescue ships. The Italian POWs told Revedin that the British had

---

* These and other details of the event, as recorded at the time by Hartenstein, are taken from an English translation of the war diary of *U-156,* which was presented at Dönitz's trial in Nuremberg and included as an appendix in the published record of the war crimes trial of Heinz Eck et al. (See bibliography listing for Cameron.)

treated them barbarically and that probably 1,400 of their number had gone down with the ship, still locked in the holding pens.*

On the following day, September 17, Ascension reverberated with bellicose activity. The five B-25s of the permanent squadron and Harden's transient B-24 Liberator flew ASW missions from dawn to dusk. Squadron commander Richardson in a B-25 found a group of *Laconia* lifeboats and informed the British rescue ship *Empire Haven* of their position. Harden in the B-24 caught sight of Würdemann in *U-506,* who still had 142 Italians and nine women and children on board, and attacked. Würdemann belatedly crash-dived, but his conning tower was still exposed when Harden made his pass. Luckily for the Germans (and the 151 *Laconia* survivors), Harden's depth charges or bombs again fouled and refused to fall. On a second pass, Harden dropped two 500-pound bombs and two 350-pound depth charges, but by then Würdemann was deep and the shallow-set missiles caused no serious damage.† Upon receiving another garbled or unclear message from the British at Freetown, advising that three Vichy French ships were en route from Dakar, Ascension wrongly assumed that these French intended to invade and seize Ascension Island. Therefore the entire garrison girded to repel invaders.

That same day—September 17—the three Vichy French ships arrived at the *Laconia* sinking site and began picking up the survivors, who had been in the lifeboats or water or U-boats for five days. *Gloire* rescued fifty-two British from a lifeboat and directed Würdemann and Schacht to put their three hundred–plus survivors on board the sloop *Annamite* while she, *Gloire,* hunted for others. During that afternoon and the night of September 17–18, *Gloire* found 684 more survivors in lifeboats or on rafts or clinging to boards. On September 18, *Gloire* again met *Annamite* to take off her three hundred–plus survivors, bringing the number of survivors on *Gloire* to 1,041, of which 597 were British (including 48 women and children), 373 were Italian, 70 were Poles, and one was a Greek. *Gloire* then set sail for Casablanca via Dakar, leaving the two sloops to conduct further rescues.

Revedin in *Cappellini* made contact with the sloop *Dumont d'Urville* on September 19. He transferred forty-two Italians to the sloop, but as instructed, he retained two British officers (as POWs) and six Italian survivors to guard the British and went directly to Bordeaux. Later that day, *Dumont* transferred the forty-two Italian POWs to *Annamite,* who took them to Dakar. *Dumont* continued searching the area until September 21, in vain, then returned to Cotonou, Dahomey. Two *Laconia* lifeboats containing twenty survivors later reached the African coast. Thus, it

---

* The exact fate of the Italian POWs and the approximate number who drowned locked in holding pens, if any, has not been established. The assertion here of callous inhumanity is taken from an excellent but incomplete account of the disaster, *The Laconia Affair* (1963), by a French author, Léonce Peillard. In several other places in his account, Peillard states (or quotes others as stating) that the Polish guards refused to unlock the pens. Elsewhere, he writes that hundreds of fear-crazed Italian POWs escaped by rushing the bars en masse and smashing them down. He depicts one *Laconia* officer leading a group of Italian POWs from the hold to the boat deck. Citing Italians, both Hartenstein and Schacht logged—and informed Dönitz by radio—that the British had badly mistreated the Italian POWs.

† Harden and crew were awarded Air Medals for the "destruction" of one submarine *(U-156)* and "probable destruction" of another *(U-506).*

was reckoned roughly, about 1,600 out of about 2,700 persons were lost in the disaster, including about 1,000 of the 1,800 Italian POWs.*

After transferring their survivors to *Annamite, U-506* and *U-507* reported same to Dönitz. In addition, Schacht sent off several long-winded messages, passing on the Italian allegations of British mistreatment of the POWs and other information of no tactical urgency. In one message, Schacht described the help he had given the British and Polish survivors. That message drew a stern rebuke from Dönitz:

> Action was wrong. Boat was dispatched to rescue Italian Allies not for rescue and care of Englishmen and Poles.

At the conclusion of these rescue operations on September 17, Dönitz was exasperated. He thought Hartenstein had shown poor judgment in assuming that a "tacit truce" existed. The Allies could not be trusted. All three German skippers involved in the rescue had unduly risked their U-boats by taking on too many survivors and by towing strings of lifeboats that interfered with crash dives. As a consequence, *U-156* and *U-506* were nearly lost to air attack. All three skippers likewise erred by showing excessive compassion and humanity to the British and Poles. Schacht erred by sending unnecessarily garrulous reports, which could be DFed.

Dönitz had long since admonished his captains (in Standing Orders 154 and 173) not to put their boats at risk by attempting rescues of survivors. They were to suppress their natural humanitarian instincts and be as hard-hearted as the enemy. Feeling the need to again emphasize these points, that night—September 17—Dönitz issued a more toughly worded repetition of the earlier admonitions:

> 1. No attempt of any kind must be made at rescuing members of ships sunk; and this includes picking up persons in the water and putting them in lifeboats, righting capsized lifeboats and handing over food and water. Rescue runs counter to the rudimentary demands of warfare for the destruction of enemy ships and crews.
> 2. Orders for bringing in captains and chief engineers still apply.
> 3. Rescue the shipwrecked only if their statements will be of importance to your boat.
> 4. Be harsh, having in mind that the enemy takes no regard of women and children in his bombing attacks on German cities.

This admonition was to achieve fleeting notoriety as the "Laconia Order." The British prosecutor at Dönitz's trial in Nuremberg introduced it as the centerpiece in the catalog of "evidence" to prove the charge that Dönitz encouraged inhumane naval warfare in violation of the Submarine Protocol. The prosecutor charged that the admonition was a thinly veiled order for U-boat skippers "deliberately to anni-

* All survivors rescued by *Gloire* were interned at Casablanca. Torch forces released the British and Polish survivors, but the fate of the Italians is not known. If not already repatriated, they were recaptured by Torch forces. In gratitude for the French role in the rescue of the Italians, the Axis offered to release an equal number of imprisoned Frenchmen named by the crews of the French ships. On June 10, 1944, the Germans turned over 385 Frenchmen listed by *Gloire* crewmen, but failed to act on lists submitted by *Annamite* and *Dumont.*

hilate" merchant-ship survivors, as Hitler had proposed earlier in the year. But this "evidence" backfired.

The introduction of the admonition at Nuremberg gave the Dönitz defense team an opportunity to depict at length German submariners behaving with unprecedented humanity at great personal risk, while in the same event Allied forces behaved callously, or worse. Speaking with cool restraint, Dönitz showed how the need for the "Laconia Order" arose in light of the *Laconia* experience and convincingly refuted the charge that it was designed to encourage his skippers to kill survivors.

Hartenstein repaired the damage to *U-156* and continued his patrol in the Freetown area. To his delight, word came that he had been awarded a *Ritterkreuz.** On September 19, he sank by torpedo and gun his third ship of the patrol, the 4,700-ton British freighter *Quebec City,* sailing alone, but in the month of October he had no successes. When he returned to France, Dönitz criticized his role in the *Laconia* affair—for assuming he could arrange a "tacit truce"—but otherwise praised him for conducting a "well-executed" patrol.

Würdemann in *U-506,* who had sunk four ships off Freetown and in the Gulf of Guinea before engaging in the *Laconia* rescue, obtained some fuel from Hartenstein and returned to patrol near Freetown. Like Hartenstein, he sank only one other ship before returning to France, but that one brought his bag for the patrol to five ships for 28,000 tons. Schacht in *U-507* returned directly from the *Laconia* rescue to France without sinking any more ships. The confirmed aggregate returns of *U-156, U-506,* and *U-507* came to thirteen ships sunk for 76,500 tons.

Other Patrols to the South Atlantic

The four boats of the disbanded group *Iltis,* which raked south from the Azores to Freetown in search of Sierra Leone convoys, arrived in southern waters in early October. None had found any targets. *Ritterkreuz* holder Peter Cremer in *U-333* wrote in his memoir that he suffered a dangerous exhaust-valve failure that was later attributed to "sabotage" by French workers.

Based on sighting, sinking, and Huff Duff reports, and other slim intelligence, early in the fall Rodger Winn in the Admiralty's Submarine Tracking Room had warned of the growing buildup of U-boats in the South Atlantic. On October 5, he estimated with uncanny accuracy that there were about fourteen German and four Italian submarines off Freetown, Ascension Island, and farther south. German records show there were fourteen attack U-boats,† three or four Italian boats, plus

* At the time of the award, Hartenstein's confirmed score was seventeen ships for 88,198 tons, including *Laconia.*

† The four Type IXs of group *Eisbär,* preparing to attack Cape Town, two of the four Type IXD2s bound for the Indian Ocean, five Type IXs, and three Type VIIs patrolling independently.

the U-tanker *U-459* and the torpedo-supply boat *U-D5* in the Freetown area or farther south.

The Admiralty passed along Winn's estimate to Freetown, Cape Town, and to other Allied bases on the west and east coasts of Africa, along with his "hunch" that a group of U-boats might attack shipping in Cape Town and the heavily traveled six-hundred-mile-wide Mozambique Channel, separating the island of Madagascar from the African mainland. Freetown and Cape Town increased ASW air patrols, but owing to the requirements for Torch, they were short of surface ships of all categories. In fact, there were scarcely enough warships to provide an adequate escort for Sierra Leone 125, the last convoy to sail north to the British Isles until French Northwest Africa was in Allied hands.

The senior escort for Sierra Leone 125 was to be the hard-working corvette *Petunia,* commanded by J. M. Rayner. On the night of October 5, when *Petunia* was inbound to Freetown to assume this responsibility, the Italian submarine *Barbarigo,* commanded by Enzo Grossi, who had claimed sinking an American battleship off Brazil the previous May, spotted the corvette. Wittingly or unwittingly identifying *Petunia* as another American "battleship," Grossi fired at least five torpedoes at her. Steaming along with both her Type 271 centimetric-wavelength radar and her sonar temporarily out of commission, *Petunia* was oblivious to the danger until the bridge watch saw the torpedo wakes. *Petunia* turned to parallel the torpedoes, avoiding a hit, and threw over a depth charge to discourage another attack. Hearing that explosion, Grossi claimed sinking his second American battleship. Rome happily accepted this claim and announced that Grossi had been awarded a German *Ritterkreuz* as well as appropriate Italian honors.*

That same night, October 5, another corvette based in Freetown was ordered out to help sink or drive away "probably seven" U-boats believed to be patrolling off the coast. She was the British *Crocus,* commanded by a former New Zealand merchant-marine officer, J. F. Holm. Early on the following morning, *Crocus* got a weak contact on her Type 271 centimetric-wavelength radar at 2,800 yards. Believing it to be a U-boat, without hesitation Holm rang up full speed and turned to ram.

The U-boat was *U-333,* commanded by *Ritterkreuz* holder Peter Cremer, who had come in close to Freetown to reconnoiter the harbor. Cremer's unalert bridge watch saw *Crocus* too late to dive. The only chance of escape was to outmaneuver or outrun the corvette in darkness, or shoot it out on the surface. Guns blazing, *Crocus* closed at maximum speed, while Cremer attempted to turn inside, close aboard. The gunfire, Cremer wrote, killed, wounded, or incapacitated every man on *U-333*'s bridge. The *Crocus* smashed into *U-333* abaft the conning tower, wrecking the superstructure. The U-boat hung up on the bow momentarily, then broke loose and banged and scraped down the port side of *Crocus,* ripping a large hole in her at the waterline.

---

* Credit to Grossi for sinking two battleships was withdrawn after the war. His confirmed bag in the war was two ships sunk for 10,309 tons and one ship damaged for 5,000 tons. One of the ships sunk was the Spanish neutral *Navemar,* which had delivered a load of 1,120 Jewish refugees from France to New York and was returning empty to Spain.

The nearly continuous gunfire from *Crocus* riddled *U-333*'s conning tower. It killed the first watch officer and two seamen, knocked a bosun's mate overboard, and badly wounded Cremer. Bleeding and in pain, Cremer remained on the bridge alone, twisting and turning the boat at maximum speed to avoid the gunfire and a second ramming. He failed. *Crocus* again smashed into *U-333* at maximum speed. This time the U-boat banged and scraped down the starboard side. When she broke loose, Holm let fly depth charges.

Barely in possession of his senses, Cremer elected to dive. Smashed and riddled and leaking fore and aft, the boat hit bottom at sixty-six feet. Thereupon Holm unleashed a heavy barrage of depth charges. Many fell close, savaging the boat so badly that Cremer ordered the crew to prepare to abandon ship. He surfaced *U-333* to scuttle, but *Crocus* lost him momentarily and Cremer limped off into the darkness and got away.

Bruised and battered, Cremer had incurred eight shell-splinter wounds. The worst and most painful was a fingerlong splinter in his chest, which impaired his breathing. The splinter had to come out. After Cremer anesthetized himself with two cups of rum, his chief engineer removed the splinter with "a great pair of pincers from a tool box."

The nearest German doctor was on board the tanker *U-459,* which was about nine hundred miles south providing support for the Cape Town foray. After confining Cremer to his bunk, the senior surviving line officer, the second watch officer, Wilhelm Pohl, who had been shot in the throat, took command of *U-333* and ran at high speed to *U-459.* En route, Pohl buried the first watch officer and two seamen. When Cremer reached *U-459,* the doctor found that his blood pressure was dangerously low, that his pulse was irregular and barely perceptible, and that he had lost much blood. However, he was able to save Cremer's life and that of the wounded second watch officer, Pohl, as well.

The commander of *U-459,* Georg von Wilamowitz-Möllendorf, gave *U-333* one of his officers, a qualified U-boat skipper, Lorenz Kasch, age twenty-eight, who assumed command of *U-333* and immediately headed for France. One day out, in the Bay of Biscay, on October 21, a British submarine fired four torpedoes at *U-333,* but the watch was able to evade and avoided a disaster. Long after the war, Cremer ascertained (at least to his satisfaction) that the British submarine that shot at him was the captured *U-570,* renamed HMS *Graph,* commanded by Peter B. Marriot, on her first combat patrol for the Royal Navy.

Upon arrival in France, Cremer and Pohl were hospitalized, Cremer for many weeks. After two months of repairs, the *U-333* sailed under a new skipper. Upon his discharge from the hospital, Cremer was assigned as second staff officer to Dönitz. Kasch returned to Germany to take command of a new Type IX.

The other boats patrolling off Freetown in October found the hunting poor. In the month of October, they sank only five ships, all sailing alone between Freetown and/or Cape Town and Trinidad. Harald Gelhaus in *U-107* got the impressive 15,000-ton British freighter *Andalucia Star.* Guido Saccardo in *Archimede* got the

20,000-ton British liner/troopship *Oronsay,* homebound from Suez. Fortunately for the Allies, the loss of life was small. Ulrich Folkers in *U-125* sank the 4,400-ton British freighter *Glendene.* Her crew was rescued by the 7,400-ton British freighter *Agapenor,* which Joachim Berger in *U-87* sank the next day. The busy corvette *Petunia* rescued the combined crews and took them into Freetown. Bruno Mahn in the ex-Dutch torpedo-supply boat *U-D5,* which Mahn pronounced unfit for combat operations, got the 7,600-ton British freighter *Primrose Hill* on the way home. Heinrich Müller-Edzards in the *U-590* sank no ships. These boats returned to France in November.

Unobserved by the numerous U-boats in the area, convoy Sierra Leone 125 sailed from Freetown. It was composed of forty-two ships, many of them transporting military personnel home to the British Isles. Its escort was scandalously inadequate: one sloop, four corvettes, and one ASW trawler. En route, the sloop and trawler peeled off for other assignments, leaving only the four corvettes, commanded by Rayner in the doughty *Petunia.*

B-dienst intercepted and decoded valuable tactical information on Sierra Leone 125. In response, on October 23 Dönitz deployed a new group, *Streitaxt* (Battle Axe), composed of ten boats (three IXs, seven VIIs) newly sailed from France, to the west of the Canary Islands to intercept the convoy.

Four of the seven Type VIIs were veterans. One, the *U-203,* was newly commanded by her onetime first watch officer, Hermann Kottmann, age twenty-six, who had returned to Germany to commission and command a new boat, but who was called back to *U-203* upon the accidental death of her skipper, Rolf Mützelburg. The son of a *Wehrmacht* officer, Kottmann was serving on the *Admiral Graf Spee* in 1940 when she was scuttled in Uruguay, but escaped internment and returned to Germany via Vladivostok and the trans-Siberian railway. Another Type VII, *U-572,* was commanded by Heinz Hirsacker, one of the most experienced skippers in the U-boat force. However, having sunk only three ships for 14,800 tons in a full year of combat, Hirsacker was in the Dönitz doghouse.

Kottmann was first to find Sierra Leone 125. After reporting its location on October 25, he attacked a tanker, but two of the four corvettes drove him off. Their depth-charge attack damaged *U-203*'s diesel engines, forcing Kottmann to haul away for repairs. Acting on a report from another of the veteran skippers, Rudolf Schendel in *U-134,* Werner Witte, age twenty-seven, new skipper of the Type IXC *U-509,* attacked and damaged the 7,700-ton British tanker *Anglo Maersk.* Hans Stock in the Type VII *U-659* attempted to attack the convoy, but two corvettes drove him off and depth-charged him.

By the evening of October 27, nine of the ten boats had converged on Sierra Leone 125, but none had yet sunk a ship. That night in bright moonlight, however, the battle shifted in favor of the U-boats. Horst Höltring in the Type VII *U-604* sank the damaged tanker *Anglo Maersk* and Witte sank two big British freighters, the 8,000-ton *Pacific Star* and the 6,100-ton *Stentor.* The corvette *Woodruff* rescued 202 of *Stentor*'s 246 crew and passengers, while *Petunia* and the other two corvettes, using to advantage the moonlight, the Type 271 centimetric-wavelength radar, and Huff Duff, prevented any more sinkings.

Several boats attempted daylight submerged attacks on October 28, but none succeeded. After dark, Kottmann and Witte got by the corvettes and attacked again. Witte claimed sinking four more ships (in all, six for 42,500 tons), but the records confirm only one sinking in this attack, the 5,300-ton British freighter *Nagpore,* and probable damage to the 5,200-ton British freighter *Hopecastle.* Kottmann reported sinking *Nagpore,* but it is more likely that he hit and sank the damaged *Hopecastle.*

Foul weather crimped operations on the night of October 29–30, but four U-boats overwhelmed the four corvettes and mounted attacks. Witte claimed he sank two more ships for 18,000 tons (bringing his claims in this convoy to eight for 60,500 tons), but the records confirm only one sinking that night, the 4,800-ton British freighter *Brittany,* plus damage to the 7,100-ton British freighter *Corinaldo.* Hans-Ferdinand Massmann in *U-409* claimed sinking an 8,000-ton freighter, but his victim was actually the 7,500-ton British tanker *Bullmouth,* which he only damaged. Hans Stock in *U-659* came up and put two finishing shots in *Corinaldo* and two in *Bullmouth,* but only the latter sank. Kottmann finally put *Corinaldo* under with his deck gun.

The weather improved dramatically on October 30, and that night five boats attacked the convoy. Höltring in *U-604* claimed three ships sunk for 20,000 tons, but only two could be confirmed, the 11,900-ton *President Doumer* and the 3,600-ton *Baron Vernon.* Massmann in *U-409* and Karl Neitzel in *U-510* both claimed sinking 6,000-ton freighters. Massmann's claim was confirmed as the 6,400-ton *Silverwillow,* but Neitzel's victim, the 5,700-ton Norwegian freighter *Alaska,* was only damaged and reached port. Stock claimed one ship sunk and one ship damaged, but only damage to the 6,400-ton British freighter *Tasmania* was confirmed. Gustav-Adolf Janssen in *U-103* put *Tasmania* under and claimed another sinking for 9,000 tons, but the latter could not be confirmed.

RAF Coastal Command saturated the air over Sierra Leone 125 with long-range land-based aircraft on the morning of November 1. Mindful of the heavy damage long-range ASW aircraft had inflicted on the U-boats that attacked Sierra Leone 119 in late August,* Dönitz promptly canceled operations, but not without satisfaction. He calculated that seven of the ten U-boats in group *Streitaxt* had attacked, sinking eighteen ships for 133,131 tons. No boats had been lost. Only one, Stock's *U-659,* had incurred battle damage grave enough to force an abort. The confirmed score was twelve ships sunk for 85,686 tons and one ship of 5,681 tons damaged. British naval historian Stephen Roskill wrote that the loss of life in this convoy was "severe," but did not amplify.

The long, hard chase had carried group *Streitaxt* to an area west of Gibraltar. From there, three other Type VIIs *(U-203, U-409, U-604)* that were low on fuel returned to France along with Stock in the battle-damaged *U-659.* Hirsacker in *U-572* was ordered to patrol off Lisbon, joined by the *U-620,* which had been damaged in a convoy battle on the North Atlantic run. The *U-134* and *U-510* were ordered to about-face and patrol to Freetown, refueling from the tanker *U-462* on the way. The *U-103* and the newly sailed *U-440* were to refuel from Werner Witte's

---

* See Volume I, pp. 673–74.

Type IXC *U-509,* which was homebound and almost out of torpedoes, and then proceed to Freetown.

By November 1, some of the Torch naval task forces and convoys from the British Isles were converging on Gibraltar. German aircraft and U-boats spotted some of these forces but Berlin was slow to grasp their significance. When the Germans belatedly realized what was in the wind, they altered the orders to most of the *Streitaxt* boats. As a result, only one boat sailing in October, the aforementioned veteran VII *U-134,* went on to the Freetown area. Commanded by Rudolf Schendel, *U-134* joined four other veteran boats (three IXs, one VII) that had sailed to the Freetown area in September for extended patrols.

These boats, soon reinforced by Liebe's Type VII *U-332* coming from the waters near Trinidad, also found poor hunting. Cruising mostly off harbors in the Gulf of Guinea, Achilles in *U-161* sank two freighters for 11,300 tons, damaged the 5,500-ton British light cruiser *Phoebe,* and damaged a 5,500-ton British freighter. In that same area, *Ritterkreuz* holder Ernst Bauer in *U-126* sank three freighters for 14,500 tons. Far to the west of Freetown, Ulrich Heyse in *U-128* sank three freighters for 15,600 tons and captured three senior ships' officers, whom he turned over to U-tankers. Klaus Popp, age twenty-five, who had replaced Erich Topp as commander of *U-552,* sank the 500-ton British ASW trawler *Alouette* and a 3,200-ton British freighter. Schendel in *U-134* sank one 4,800-ton freighter; Liebe in *U-332* sank none. Total: eleven ships for about 50,000 tons, plus damage.*

Liebe and Popp soon left for France. Liebe arrived on December 6, completing a patrol of ninety-three days, a new endurance record for a Type VII. But that record stood only nine days. Popp in the Type VII *U-552* arrived on December 15, completing a patrol of ninety-seven days. Liebe went to other duty; Popp remained in command of *U-552,* but as the inside joke went, "Popp was no Topp."

In early December, Dönitz logged, *B-dienst* broke a British code and discovered "new routes" for Allied shipping in the South Atlantic. In preparation for an assault on these routes, Dönitz arranged for all boats in the immediate area to resupply west of Freetown in the mid-Atlantic from Wolf Stiebler's tanker, *U-461,* and from the other ex-Dutch torpedo-supply boat, *U-D3,* commanded by Hermann Rigele, age fifty-one. Remarkably, on December 9, ten U-boats† met at the designated grid square, ER50. Seven attack boats, including the last four of the "Freetown boats," proceeded to Brazilian waters to exploit the *B-dienst* intelligence. Achilles in *U-161* sank the 5,000-ton British freighter *Ripley,* but the other "Freetown boats" had no luck.‡ Upon return to France, Heyse and Achilles were

* The Italian skipper Gianfranco Gazzana-Priaroggia in *Da Vinci* sank four freighters for 26,000 tons.

† In addition to the two supply boats, these were Bauer in *U-126;* Heyse in *U-128;* Schendel in *U-134;* Achilles in *U-161;* two boats patrolling Brazilian waters, Thilo's *U-174* and Dierksen's *U-176;* and two returning *Eisbär* boats, Helmut Witte's *U-159* and Emmermann's *U-172.*

‡ Three other attack boats that proceeded from the replenishment to Brazilian waters sank five other ships.

awarded the *Ritterkreuz*.* Heyse left *U-128* for duty in Training Command. Bauer in *U-126* and Schendel in *U-134,* who tied Popp's Type VII endurance record of ninety-seven days, also went on to other duties.

The Attack on Cape Town, South Africa

Nine big attack U-boats were en route to or approaching Cape Town, South Africa, by October 1. These were the four IXCs of group *Eisbär,* which had refueled from the tanker *U-459* after the canceled diversion to *Laconia,* the four very-long-range Type IXD2 U-cruisers, and the new, 1,700-ton Italian U-cruiser *Ammiraglio Cagni,* on her maiden voyage in the Atlantic. One *Eisbär* boat, Karl-Friedrich Merten's *U-68,* had encountered and sunk by torpedo and gun two big freighters for 12,200 tons on the way. All others had full loads of armament, about 225 torpedoes,† plus gun ammo. Discounting 10 percent for torpedo misses and malfunctions, and allowing two torpedoes per victim, it was believed the nine boats had enough torpedoes to sink one hundred Allied ships totaling half a million tons.

South Africa was no more prepared to repel a U-boat attack than the United States had been in early 1942. The British naval authorities at Cape Town controlled four destroyers and several corvettes—some on loan from the British Eastern Fleet based in Mombasa—but these were insufficient to establish convoys between the Cape and Freetown and/or the Cape and Suez, and points in between. Likewise, there were only a few aircraft available for ASW patrols.

Owing to heavy commitments to Torch, the British were hard-pressed to reinforce the South African ASW forces. In due course, London and Washington sent thirty British ASW trawlers, twelve from Western Approaches and the eighteen still left in American waters. In addition, London directed the Eastern Fleet to send ten warships (six destroyers, four corvettes) and the RAF to send Catalinas of Coastal Command Squadron 209 to Cape Town and Durban. But all these forces were slow to arrive: the eighteen ASW trawlers from the United States did not report for duty until the end of the year.

Rodger Winn in the Admiralty's Submarine Tracking Room monitored the eight oncoming U-boats—and *Cagni*—with "prescient accuracy," as the official British naval historian put it. Reacting to his forecasts, the Admiralty directed that shipping at Cape Town be drastically reduced by making the East African city of Durban—rather than Cape Town—the final port of call for vessels homebound from the Suez Canal, Persian Gulf, and India. During Torch operations, upon leaving Durban, ships were to pass well to the south of Cape Town, cross the Atlantic

---

* At the time of the award, Heyse's confirmed score was twelve ships sunk for 83,639 tons. Achilles's confirmed score was eleven ships sunk for 58,518 tons, plus damage to seven ships for 44,427 tons, including the light cruiser *Phoebe,* which was repaired in an American shipyard and thus out of action for months.

† The four IXCs each set out with twenty-two torpedoes, the four IXD2s each with twenty-four. The *Cagni,* which had eight bow tubes and six stern tubes, carried an astonishing total of forty-two Italian-made, 17.7" torpedoes on this patrol.

northwestward to Brazil, thence go to Trinidad and United States waters and from those places, in convoy, to the British Isles.

The final attack plan as drawn by the OKM, Dönitz, and the skippers, was as follows. Commencing on or about October 5, Karl-Friedrich Merten in *U-68* and Carl Emmermann in *U-172* were to reconnoiter the Cape Town anchorage, Table Bay, mindful of the offensive mines planted earlier in the year by the German raider *Doggerbank* and defensive minefields planted by the British, known to the Germans through Emmermann's capture of papers from the freighter *Santa Rita* on his prior patrol to the Caribbean. At thirty minutes past midnight on October 8—a period of new moon—they were to enter Table Bay and simultaneously commence attacking what was thought likely to be "fifty ships" anchored in the roadstead. While this surprise attack was in progress, Helmut Witte in *U-159,* Fritz Poske in *U-504,* and Ernst Sobe in the U-cruiser *U-179,* which was well ahead of the other U-cruisers, were to lie outside the harbor and pick off ships fleeing the massacre.

Per plan, Merten and Emmermann closed Table Bay on the night of October 5, traveling on the surface to avoid undisclosed defensive mines. To minimize loss of life should *U-172* hit a mine, Emmermann ordered as many crew as possible topside in life jackets. What the two skippers found was deeply disappointing. The Table Bay anchorage was "empty," Emmermann reported. Not only that, Merten elaborated, but the anchorage was bathed by a "searchlight barrage" and land-based radar, which made it impossible for the boats to attack on the surface. Under these circumstances he doubted that the surprise attack would work.

Both skippers requested release from the plan and freedom of action. In reply, Dönitz asked the two skippers to try again, in case the "empty" anchorage was a fluke of shipping schedules. If on the second try they found the anchorage still empty, then they would be released from the plan and have freedom of action from midnight, October 8.

Claiming later that he received a garbled version of those orders, Emmermann wrote that he proceeded on the basis that he had freedom of action from 4 A.M., October 7, onward. Hence, he jumped the gun by nineteen hours and sank the outbound 6,200-ton American freighter *Chickasaw City* with two torpedoes. Three hours later he sank an inbound freighter, the 4,700-ton *Firethorn* with two torpedoes. Perhaps with crossed fingers or tongue in cheek, Dönitz later reprimanded Emmermann for this premature attack: "The fact that the captain struck prematurely could easily have wrecked the whole operation and for Command reasons it must be condemned."

The other four boats waited impatiently for the midnight deadline. Helmut Witte in *U-159* also jumped the gun, by five minutes, to sink the 5,800-ton British freighter *Boringia* with a single torpedo. Neither she nor the two ships sunk prematurely by Emmermann in *U-172* got off distress signals. Thus when H-hour arrived at midnight, October 8, Cape Town was lit up "as in peace time" and still unaware that a U-boat attack was in progress.

The U-boats continued the attack into the early hours of October 8. Emmermann sank his third ship, the 3,800-ton Greek *Pantelis* with a single torpedo. Close by, Merten in *U-68* sank two ships in quick succession, expending seven torpedoes: the 3,600-ton Greek *Koumoundouros* and the 8,600-ton Dutch *Gaasterkerk.* Both of these vessels had time to get off distress signals, alerting Cape Town, but authorities there still had no idea the U-boats had sunk six ships.

At first light on October 8, Cape Town deployed its weak ASW forces. The British destroyers *Active, Arrow,* and *Foxhound,* the Australian destroyer *Nizam,* and the British corvette *Rockrose* sailed out to do battle, but spent most of the day rescuing survivors of the six ships. Every available military aircraft, including those of a basic training school, took to the air to assist in the rescues.

The U-boats sank one more ship during that day. Witte found the 7,600-ton British freighter *Clan Mactavish* imprudently stopped dead in the water, picking up survivors of the *Boringia,* which he had sunk earlier. Witte put the *Clan Mactavish* under with two torpedoes. Aircraft on ASW patrols guided another freighter, *Matheran,* to the scene, and she rescued the crews of both ships.

After dark that day, Ernst Sobe in the U-cruiser *U-179,* which was close by *U-68* and *U-172,* torpedoed the 6,600-ton British freighter *City of Athens.* Still later that evening, the British destroyer *Active* reached the site and rescued ninety-nine persons. While she was doing so, her radar operator reported a contact at 2,500 yards. This was Sobe in *U-179,* who had loitered at the scene apparently in hopes of sinking another freighter on a rescue mission. When *Active*'s sonar operator also reported a contact, her skipper, M. W. Tomkinson, rang up full speed and ran down the bearing.

Soon *Active*'s lookouts discerned a "large" U-boat on the surface, which appeared to be stopped. Closing to eight hundred yards, Tomkinson turned on his searchlight and opened fire with his main battery. It is likely that *U-179*'s lookouts had seen *Active* before she opened fire and that Sobe had dived immediately. However, his big, clumsy, slow-diving U-cruiser was no match for a radar-equipped fleet destroyer. As the seas closed over *U-179*'s conning tower, *Active* raced over her swirl at twenty-five knots and fired "by eye" ten depth charges set for fifty to one hundred feet. These blew *U-179* back to the surface, Tomkinson logged. She hung momentarily, then plunged under, never to be seen again, an expensive loss in weaponry and manpower for the Germans.*

Close by, Merten in *U-68* and Emmermann in *U-172* heard *Active*'s attack on *U-179.* Emmermann logged that he picked up the sinking noises of *U-179* "quite clearly." At about this same time, the corvette *Rockrose* detected and doggedly chased Emmermann, dropping twelve depth charges, which Emmermann described as "too close for comfort." The explosions slightly damaged one bow torpedo tube but were otherwise "ineffective," Emmermann continued.

While that was going on, Merten sank two ships. The first was the fully loaded, 8,200-ton American tanker *Swiftsure.* One torpedo turned her into an inferno, sending "pitch dark clouds of smoke . . . hundreds of meters skyward." Even so, she did not sink immediately and the British tried to tow her into port, but in vain. The sec-

* Not having heard from Sobe since September 18, and unaware that he had reached the Cape, Dönitz logged that there was "no clue" as to the *U-179*'s loss. Some staffers wrongly presumed that *U-179* had been sunk by Allied aircraft near Ascension Island.

ond ship was the 5,300-ton British freighter *Sarthe,* which Merten put under with two torpedoes.

Merten's massacre continued past midnight into the wee hours of October 9, when he attacked two more ships: the 5,000-ton American freighter *Examelia,* sunk with one torpedo, and the 5,400-ton freighter *Belgian Fighter,* sunk with two torpedoes. In the second attack, Merten lost control of *U-68* in a routine dive and plunged at a terrifying angle to 656 feet before his emergency measures restored control. This near-fatal accident dampened somewhat the celebrations over the boat's remarkable successes at the Cape: six confirmed ships for 36,000 tons sunk within twenty-four hours, bringing his total for this patrol to eight ships for 48,200 tons.

That afternoon, October 9, in that same area, Helmut Witte in *U-159* sank yet another ship with a single torpedo. She was the 6,600-ton American freighter *Coloradan.* That victory brought the sinkings off the Cape by Merten, Emmermann, Witte, and Sobe in about forty-eight hours to eleven vessels for 77,300 tons, far exceeding U-boat successes off the American coast over a comparable time period. Berlin propagandists praised the skippers for this extraordinary achievement in such far distant waters, releasing their combined score as a conservative twelve ships sunk for 74,000 tons.

By the next day, October 10, the Cape Town authorities had diverted or frozen most shipping in South African waters, but the Germans scored two more impressive victories. Operating that morning near the Cape in foul, rainy weather and heavy seas, Emmermann in *U-172* spotted the 23,456-ton liner *Orcades,* sailing alone to the British Isles with 1,300 Allied troops and Axis POWs. After a brief chase, Emmermann hit her with three bow torpedoes. The crew abandoned ship, but with the help of fifty-two volunteers who reboarded, the captain attempted to limp into Table Bay. Emmermann chased, reloaded his bow tubes, and put *Orcades* under with three more hits from close range. That same morning the southbound U-cruiser *U-178,* commanded by Hans Ibbeken, sank another crowded homebound British liner, the 20,119-ton *Duchess of Atholl,* sailing alone a little north of Ascension Island. Fortunately for the Allies, the loss of life in the sinking of these two troopships was light: forty on *Orcades.**

The fifteenth—and last—ship to fall victim to the *Eisbär* boats and the U-cruiser *U-179* off Cape Town was the 7,200-ton British freighter *Empire Nomad.* Helmut Witte in *U-159* sank her with four torpedoes. When added to the victories achieved on his outstanding first patrol to the Caribbean, Witte's sinkings off Cape Town qualified him for a *Ritterkreuz.*† One day after the award of his *Ritterkreuz* by radio, on October 23, Witte requested a rendezvous with Ibbeken's oncoming U-cruiser, *U-178,* to transfer a sick crewman to the latter, which had a doctor on board.

---

* Within a period of about one month, Axis submarines in the South Atlantic sank four big British liners in service as troopships for about 84,000 tons: *Laconia, Oronsay, Orcades,* and *Duchess of Atholl.* The 11,330-ton British *Abosso,* sunk on October 30 by *U-575* in the North Atlantic, raised British troopship losses to five by November 1, 1942. Seldom mentioned, these troopship losses stand in stark contrast to the nearly perfect safety record of troopships escorted by American warships.

† At the time of the award, his confirmed score was fourteen ships for 77,530 tons.

Believing the South African traffic had been diverted far to the south of the Cape, one by one the *Eisbär* boats proceeded to that area. This took them to the notorious "Roaring Forties" (i.e., 40 degrees south latitude) where for over a week they were slammed around by hurricane-force storms and mountainous seas. Nonetheless, Witte sank with five torpedoes two British freighters on October 29 in those inhospitable waters: the 5,000-ton *Ross* and the 7,300-ton *Laplace.*

Fritz Poske in *U-504* got off to a wobbly start at the Cape, but his luck began to change when he reached the Roaring Forties. There, on October 17, he sank the 6,000-ton British freighter *Empire Chaucer.* Since he had freedom of action, he elected to go north to Durban on the southeast coast of Africa, where, as he knew, the U-cruisers were headed. En route, he attacked two ships off East London on October 23 and 26. His torpedoes sank the 5,700-ton British freighter *City of Johannesburg* and broke in half the 7,200-ton American Liberty ship *Anne Hutchinson.* Her stern eventually sank, but a minesweeper and a tugboat towed the bow into Port Elizabeth, a complete loss.

Remaining about 250 miles east of the coastline to minimize attacks from ASW aircraft, Poske beat the U-cruisers into Durban waters. On October 31 he sank two British freighters: the 7,000-ton *Empire Guidon* and the 5,100-ton *Reynolds.* With only two torpedoes remaining, he about-faced and headed home. While rounding the Cape on November 3, he expended his last torpedoes to sink the 5,200-ton Brazilian freighter *Porto Alegre.* These successes raised Poske's bag in eighteen days to the level of Merten in *U-68:* six ships sunk for 36,000 tons. When these sinkings were added to his claims on two prior patrols, Poske qualified for and received a *Ritterkreuz** by radio on November 6.

The four *Eisbär* boats departed the Cape Town area in high spirits. Merten and Poske went directly up the center of the Atlantic to France. Witte and Emmermann went to a rendezvous with the tanker *U-461* and the torpedo-supply boat *U-D3.*

Homebound in the middle of the South Atlantic on November 6, Merten found and sank the 8,000-ton British freighter *City of Cairo,* which carried 125 passengers, including women and children. This sinking raised his score for the patrol to nine ships for 56,200 tons and qualified him for Oak Leaves to his *Ritterkreuz,* which came from Hitler via radio.† Upon reaching France, both Merten and Poske left their boats and did not return to combat. Merten was assigned to command the 24th Flotilla in the Training Command.

Witte in *U-159* and Emmermann in *U-172,* who had become arch rivals in the tonnage competition, proceeded northwestward to the U-tanker rendezvous, raking likely Allied shipping routes between Cape Town and Trinidad. On the way Witte found and sank two lone American ships. The first was the 5,500-ton *La Salle,* loaded with ammo. The torpedo exploded her cargo with an awesome blast that was heard three hundred miles away at Cape Town and that "atomized" the ship and rained debris on *U-159,* slightly injuring Witte and three crewmen. The second

* At the time of the award, his confirmed score was sixteen ships for 82,135 tons.

† At the time of the award, his confirmed score was twenty-seven ships for 170,175 tons. He stood eighth in tonnage sunk among all U-boat skippers.

was the posh but aged (1887) six-masted, 2,300-ton sailing vessel *Star of Scotland* (ex-*Kenilworth*), which was en route to Brazil with a load of guns. Witte stripped her of food, cigarettes, and other useful commodities, then sank her by gun. Cutting across the South Atlantic into Brazilian waters, Emmermann sank four freighters, the British *Aldington Court, Llandilo,* and *Benlomond,** of 4,900, 5,000, and 6,600 tons, respectively, and the 5,400-ton American *Alaskan.* These sinkings raised Emmermann's bag to eight ships for 60,000 tons and qualified him for a *Ritterkreuz.*†

As related earlier, Witte and Emmermann rendezvoused with the tanker *U-461* and the torpedo-supply boat *U-D3* and eight other U-boats on December 9. In addition to fuel, Witte took on eight air torpedoes and joined six other Type IXs for a concerted attack on Allied shipping in Brazilian waters. In a period of three days, from December 13 to 16, he sank three freighters for 18,600 tons, two British and—awkwardly—one neutral 5,000-ton Argentine, the *Star of Suez.* These sinkings raised Witte's score for this patrol to an impressive eleven ships for 63,700 tons.

Homebound with but two torpedoes on December 11, Emmermann in *U-172* found a Cape Town to Trinidad convoy at a grid position exactly predicted by *B-dienst.* Emmermann attacked, firing one torpedo at each of two ships. He claimed both torpedoes hit and that, based on the noise he heard, both ships probably sank. He was credited with one sinking for about 8,000 tons, raising his bag to nine ships for 68,000 tons, thereby besting his rival, Helmut Witte in *U-159,* but the last sinking could not be confirmed in postwar records and Witte came out the winner after all.

The attack by group *Eisbär* on South Africa was one of the most successful U-boat operations of the war. The four Type IXs sank twenty-three ships for 155,335 tons off Cape Town and Durban. In addition, three of the four sank eleven ships for 60,829 tons en route to and from the Cape, raising the number of sinkings to thirty-four ships for 216,164 tons. This was an average of 8.5 ships for 54,041 tons per boat per patrol,‡ a substantially greater return than the best month in the U-boat attack on the United States.

The other three IXD2 U-cruisers arrived off the Cape in late October. *Cagni* tarried in the Gulf of Guinea, where she sank a ship on November 3, and came later. The

---

* The *Benlomond* was en route from Cape Town to Dutch Guinea (Surinam). Hit by two torpedoes, she sank instantly about 750 miles east of the mouth of the Amazon River. There was one survivor, Poon Lim, a Chinese mess steward. After a record 133 days on a raft, he was rescued by a Brazilian fishing trawler near Belem, Brazil.

† At the time of the award, his confirmed score was eighteen ships for 100,793 tons. It was noted that with this award, four of the five skippers of the attack boats originally assigned to group *Eisbär,* including Hartenstein in *U-156,* won a *Ritterkreuz,* and the fifth skipper, Merten, won Oak Leaves to his *Ritterkreuz.*

‡ The patrols averaged 122 days or about four months. Witte in *U-159* and Emmermann in *U-172* were at sea 135 and 131 days, respectively. All boats refueled twice, once outbound and once inbound.

U-cruisers confronted intensified ASW measures, but these did not significantly impede the Germans.

Leading the pack, Hans Ibbeken in *U-178,* who had sunk the 20,119-ton troopship *Duchess of Atholl* en route, skirted the Cape and went north to Durban. In his first two days in those waters, he vainly chased a tanker, missed a freighter with two torpedoes, and narrowly escaped an aircraft attack. However, on November 1, he attacked "a big passenger ship," which he identified "quite definitely" as the 18,700-ton *Laurentic,* a "nice present after so long a time." His first two torpedoes missed. The next two hit and sank what proved to be a troopship half the size of *Laurentic,* the British *Mendoza,* 8,200 tons. About 150 of the four hundred persons on board were killed or never found.*

Earlier in the war, Ibbeken recalled, Dönitz had promised that he would be the first German U-boat skipper to circumnavigate the island of Madagascar. He did so, sinking two freighters along the way: the 2,600-ton Norwegian *Hai Hing* and the 5,200-ton British *Trekieve.* Bedeviled by engine trouble, the voyage around Madagascar itself was unproductive.

The second and third IXD2 U-cruisers reached the Cape Town area nearly simultaneously. *Ritterkreuz* holder Robert Gysae in *U-177* was first to find a target. On November 2, he chased and fired four torpedoes at the 4,500-ton Greek freighter *Aegeus,* which had a load of ammo. Two torpedoes missed but two hit, and the ship literally disappeared in an immense explosion that showered debris on *U-177,* injuring a lookout. The next day, *Ritterkreuz* holder Wolfgang Lüth in *U-181* found and attacked the 8,200-ton American ore carrier *East Indian.* As with Gysae, two torpedoes missed but two hit and the ship went down. Thirty-four of her fifty-man crew were never found.

The two boats hunted off the Cape for about ten days. Gysae attacked only one other ship, the 2,600-ton British tanker *Cerion,* sailing in ballast. In a frustrating daylong chase, he shot five torpedoes at her, all of which missed. He then surfaced to sink the ship with his deck gun, but *Cerion* shot back and finally Gysae was forced to let her go. Lüth in *U-181* sank three more freighters (two American, one Norwegian) for 14,000 tons, enough, Dönitz ruled, to qualify him for Oak Leaves to his *Ritterkreuz.* The award came in a personal message from Hitler on November 13.†

Gysae and Lüth cruised north toward Durban, where Ibbeken in *U-178* concluded his disappointing journey around Madagascar. In the period from November 13 to 15, Ibbeken attacked two British freighters off Durban: the 3,800-ton *Louise Moller* and the 6,300-ton *Adviser.* He sank the former, but the latter was salvaged and towed into Durban. In reaction, ASW aircraft twice attacked *U-178,* driving Ibbeken down and thwarting an attack on another ship. "Three aerial bombs," Ibbeken logged, "very close [but] no damage." Still bedeviled by engine and other mechanical troubles, Ibbeken hauled well offshore to make extended re-

---

* This raised the loss of British troopships in this foray to five.

† At the time of the award, Lüth's confirmed score on the ducks *U-9* and *U-138,* the IX *U-43,* and *U-181* was twenty-nine ships for 147,256 tons, including the French submarine *Doris.*

pairs, then headed for home. While rounding the Cape, he missed one ship but sank another, the 7,200-ton American Liberty ship *Jeremiah Wadsworth,* raising his confirmed sinkings to six ships for 47,000 tons. Upon arrival in France on January 9, completing a voyage of 124 days, Ibbeken left *U-178* for other duty.

On the day Ibbeken departed the Durban area, November 15, the British destroyer *Inconstant,* responding to alarms from ASW aircraft, caught Lüth in *U-181.* Lüth dived deep (573 feet) to evade, but the skipper of *Inconstant,* W. S. Clouston, mounted a dogged nine-hour chase, dropping thirty depth charges. Late in the afternoon, two corvettes, *Jasmine* and *Nigella,* arrived to relieve *Inconstant. Jasmine* got a sonar contact and dropped five more depth charges but she lost *U-181* in the noise and, finally, Lüth escaped in darkness and repaired the considerable damage. It was a close call. Had the two corvettes pursued *U-181* as persistently as had *Inconstant* and had aircraft assisted them the following day, they might well have forced *U-181* to the surface for a kill.

After completing repairs, Lüth cruised north about 250 miles to the magnificent neutral port of Lourenço Marques, situated on Delagoa Bay, Portuguese East Africa. Patrolling near this port over the next two weeks, from November 19 to December 2, Lüth sank by gun and torpedo eight ships for 23,800 tons, four principally by deck gun, expending his entire stock of 355 rounds of 4.1" ammo. A recent biographer of Lüth* characterized the prodigal expenditure of shells as "callous," "malicious," and "unprofessional," in that the gunfire killed many seamen needlessly and that Lüth recklessly exposed *U-181* in these attacks.

Saving two torpedoes for self-defense, Lüth returned to France on January 18, completing a voyage of 129 days in which he traveled 21,369 miles without refueling. His confirmed bag for this patrol was twelve ships for 58,381 tons. This was twice the number of ships that were sunk by Ibbeken in *U-178,* but 5,350 fewer tons than were sunk by Witte in *U-159* and 1,700 fewer tons than were sunk by Merten in *U-68* and Emmermann in *U-172.* Thus a big, expensive U-cruiser in the hands of a veteran skipper wearing Oak Leaves did not sink significantly more tonnage in the same area than any one of the three Type IXCs.

Commencing on November 19, Gysae in *U-177* also patrolled the area near Lourenço Marques, but usually at a considerable distance from Lüth. Over a period of twenty-six days he expended all of his torpedoes to sink seven ships (including one tanker) for 44,800 tons. One of these was another unescorted British troopship: the homeward-bound, armed, 6,800-ton *Nova Scotia,* the sixth British troopship to be lost to unassisted Axis submarines within two months.† In addition to her crew, *Nova Scotia* carried 899 passengers: 765 Italian civilian internees and 134 South African soldiers. Upon learning that he, like Hartenstein in *U-156,* had sunk a ship carrying hundreds of Italian allies, Gysae radioed Dönitz for instructions: "Sank

---

* The American Jordan Vause, in *U-boat Ace* (1990).

† Not counting troopships assigned to Torch forces or those sunk in the Mediterranean, or the *Abosso* sunk in the North Atlantic, but including *Oronsay,* sunk by *Archimede* near Freetown. These lamentable troopship losses are not described in full by the official British naval historians or by other British authors. For details, see Plate 4.

auxiliary cruiser *Nova Scotia* with over 1,000 Italian civil internees ex [from] Massaua [Ethiopia]. Two survivors taken on board. Still about 400 on boats or rafts. Moved away because of air [craft]." In his reply, Dönitz, in effect, evoked the "Laconia Order": "Continue operating. Waging war comes first. No rescue attempts."

Dönitz notified the Portuguese, who dispatched vessels from Lourenço Marques. A Portuguese sloop rescued 192 survivors (including forty-three South Africans) in boats or rafts, surrounded by ravenous sharks. Including the crewmen, about 750 persons perished. One hundred and twenty corpses washed up on Durban beaches. Sharks consumed many of the other 630 dead. At Gysae's request, the crew of *U-177* signed a pledge never to discuss the catastrophe.

Gysae returned *U-177* to France on January 22, completing a patrol of 128 days. His confirmed score was eight ships for 49,371 tons. Like Lüth, he remained with his boat to prepare for another patrol to the Indian Ocean. Dönitz awarded his engineer, Gerhard Bieleg, a *Ritterkreuz,* noting that he had served 454 days on patrol on three U-boats and had "saved his boats three times."

The big Italian U-cruiser *Cagni* contributed almost nothing to this attack on South Africa. On November 29 she sank one ship off Cape Town, the 2,000-ton Greek *Argo.* Encountering intensified ASW measures near the Cape, she soon reversed course and headed home. Near the equator on January 10, she refueled from the tanker *U-459,* then proceeded to Bordeaux.

Four German U-cruisers had operated off Cape Town and Durban. In all they sank twenty-seven confirmed ships for 161,407 tons, an average of 6.75 ships for 40,350 tons per boat per patrol. Considering that one boat, Sobe's *U-179,* had been lost after sinking only one ship, this was an exceptionally good average return. The single success of the Italian U-cruiser *Cagni* raised the total for all Axis U-cruisers to twenty-eight ships for 163,400 tons.

When the successes of the four Type IXs of group *Eisbär* were added to those of the four Type IXD2 U-cruisers, the number was impressive indeed: sixty-two ships for 379,566 tons, including the six British troopships. This was an average of 7.8 ships for 47,446 tons sunk per boat per patrol, exceeding the best performance of the Type IXs in American waters.

Altogether, in the second half of 1942 about fifty U-boats patrolled to the Azores, the Canaries, Freetown, to African waters farther south, and to Cape Town and Durban. These sank about 150 ships for about 900,000 tons, for the loss of merely three boats* with all hands. This was an "exchange rate" of about fifty ships sunk for each U-boat, an extraordinary German achievement but also a rarely mentioned and embarrassing failure of Commonwealth ASW forces in those waters.

Like the sinkings in American waters, these German successes in South African waters during October and November 1942 also added substantially to the aggregate Allied ship losses to U-boats in those months. Since, as related, Allied losses were not identified by geographical area, the figures also tended to reinforce the wrong impression that U-boats were conducting a "massacre" on the North Atlantic run.

* The VIIC *U-136,* the VIID minelayer *U-213,* and the IXD2 U-cruiser *U-179.*

PLATE 3

U-BOAT SUCCESSES IN SOUTH AFRICAN WATERS[1]

OCTOBER–NOVEMBER 1942

BOAT	TYPE	SKIPPER	SHIPS SUNK	GRT
U-68	IXC	Karl-Friedrich Merten	9	56,230
U-156	IXC	Werner Hartenstein	3	30,381[2]
U-159	IXC	Helmut Witte	11	63,730
U-172	IXC	Carl Emmermann	8	60,048[3]
U-177	IXD2	Robert Gysae	8	49,371[4]
U-178	IXD2	Hans Ibbeken	6	47,097[5]
U-179	IXD2	Ernst Sobe	1	6,558[6]
U-181	IXD2	Wolfgang Lüth	12	58,381[7]
U-504	IXC	Friedrich Poske	6	36,156
Cagni	Italian	Carlo Liannazza	1	1,995[8]
Totals:	9 Patrols (less *U-156*)		65	409,947

1. Source: Turner et al., *War in the Southern Oceans;* Rohwer, *Axis Submarine Successes,* and Rohwer and Hümmelchen, *Chronology.* Figures include sinkings en route to and from South Africa.

2. Including the 19,700-ton British troopship *Laconia* on September 12, after which *U-156* aborted her voyage to South Africa.

3. Including the 23,500-ton British troopship *Orcades* on October 10.

4. Including the 6,800-ton British troopship *Nova Scotia* on November 28.

5. Including the 20,100-ton British troopship *Duchess of Atholl* on October 10, and the 8,233-ton British troopship *Mendoza* on November 1.

6. U-boat was sunk off Cape Town by ASW forces on October 8, 1942.

7. All but one ship of 4,328 tons sunk in November.

8. Another Italian boat, *Archimede,* sank the 20,000-ton British troopship *Oronsay* on October 9, off Freetown.

THE MEDITERRANEAN: PRICELESS CAPTURES

At ten o'clock on the evening of October 23, the British Eighth Army, commanded by Bernard Law Montgomery, launched a massive attack on the Axis forces at El Alamein. On the following day, when Hitler was informed, he telephoned Erwin Rommel, who was still in a hospital, and asked if he was well enough to return to North Africa to resume command of his *Afrika Korps.* Rommel arrived on the second day, October 25, to find Axis forces cracking under the weight of Montgomery's attack, which profited greatly from the reading of *Luftwaffe* Enigma and some timely breaks in German Army Enigma. Rommel proposed a strategic withdrawal westward toward Benghazi, but Hitler demurred and foolishly directed Rommel to "stand fast!" whatever the cost.

At that time, the Mediterranean U-boat force, commanded by Leo Karl

Kreisch, numbered nineteen Type VIICs. This number included four new arrivals from the Atlantic *(U-458, U-593, U-605, U-660),* which had slipped through the Strait of Gibraltar on the nights of October 10 and 11. One of these, *U-605,* commanded by Herbert-Viktor Schütze, age twenty-five, had had a harrowing transit. An unidentified submerged Allied submarine had shot torpedoes at *U-605* but missed. Schütze had dived and the two submarines had played cat and mouse for three hours. Schütze had shot a full bow salvo—four torpedoes—at the enemy submarine, but he, too, had missed. These four boats had arrived at the Italian naval base at La Spezia, Italy, on October 14 and 15, where Kreisch indoctrinated the men in fighting in the hazardous waters of the Mediterranean.

The Mediterranean U-boat force was in its worst slump yet. Apart from several small sailing vessels, in all of September and October the U-boats had sunk only one ship, a 600-ton Palestinian freighter.

When Montgomery attacked on October 23–24, there were seven U-boats at sea. Four patrolled in western sectors off Algeria and Tunisia and three in the eastern sectors off Egypt and Palestine. The plan was to maintain that deployment scheme in case the Allies staged an amphibious assault in North Africa behind (or west) of Rommel or in the more extreme west at Algeria or Oran or on the island of Sardinia. Three U-boats *(U-458, U-565, U-660)* were due to sail from La Spezia to the eastern sector to relieve the three boats in that area *(U-77, U-205, U-559).*

On October 25, Hitler personally intervened and changed the deployment of the Mediterranean U-boats. Based on German intelligence reports indicating that the British carrier *Furious* and other warships were gathering at Gibraltar, perhaps to invade Sardinia or fly off fighters to Malta, the Führer directed that "all available" U-boats be sent to the western Mediterranean immediately. Leo Kreisch, therefore, redirected the three newly sailed U-boats intended for the eastern Mediterranean to go to the western Mediterranean. Furthermore, Kreisch ordered two of the three U-boats in the east *(U-77, U-205)* to make for Messina, Sicily, to replenish and prepare to join the other U-boats in the west.

What the British had afoot was yet another fighter-aircraft reinforcement of Malta. At Gibraltar on October 27, the carrier *Furious* took on the aircraft. The next day the task force, which included the cruisers *Charybdis* and *Penelope* and six destroyers, set sail. By then the Axis naval commands had deployed fourteen submarines in the narrow neck of the western Mediterranean: seven German U-boats* and a separate force of seven Italian submarines blocking the channel between Cape Antonio, Spain, and the island of Ibiza, in case the British elected to go north of the Balearic Islands, then eastward.

In the late evening of October 28, two U-boats sighted and reported the task force: *Ritterkreuz* holder Friedrich (Fritz) Guggenberger in *U-81,* who had sunk the British carrier *Ark Royal* the year before, and the new arrival Schütze in *U-605.*

---

* The veterans *U-73, U-81, U-431, U-565,* and three of the four new arrivals, *U-458, U-605,* and *U-660.*

Nearby, at about the same time, another Mediterranean veteran, Wilhelm Franken in *U-565,* shot four torpedoes at *Furious* but, he reported, all were duds. Inasmuch as Guggenberger had reported the task force speed as twenty-one knots, Leo Kreisch logged: "It is hopeless for the U-boats to pursue."

The new German plan was to sink *Furious* on her return voyage to Gibraltar. Kreisch redeployed the seven U-boats to likely waiting spots, while Axis aircraft reconnoitered and found the task force. Several U-boats spotted the formation. One, *U-431,* commanded by another Mediterranean veteran, Wilhelm Dommes, shot four torpedoes at *Furious* but all missed. Still making about twenty knots, the task force returned to Gibraltar without incurring any losses.

Leo Kreisch logged:

> The operation is thus concluded. It has been quite unsuccessful. . . . Of the seven boats available, five different boats have had altogether six encounters with the enemy. Two boats each fired a fan of four, no hits were obtained. To attack a heavily defended aircraft carrier, proceeding at high speed, is not simply a question of opportunity but also luck. . . .

As a result of Hitler's personal intervention, only one U-boat was left in the eastern Mediterranean. She was *U-559,* commanded by twenty-eight-year-old Hans-Otto Heidtmann. He had commanded three school ducks* in the last half of 1940, after which he commissioned *U-559* on February 27, 1941. Reporting to the Atlantic force in June 1941, Heidtmann had sunk one 1,600-ton British freighter during the attack on convoy Outbound Gibraltar 71 in August.† A month later, *U-559* was one of the six U-boats that pioneered the way into the Mediterranean. In a full year of combat operations in those dangerous waters, Heidtmann had sunk four confirmed ships: the 1,100-ton Australian sloop *Parramatta,* two freighters, and the 4,700-ton Norwegian tanker *Athene.*

Heidtmann was quite familiar with the waters of the eastern Mediterranean. He had conducted a barren thirty-eight-day patrol there from August 15 to September 21, returning to Messina. After merely eight days in that port for replenishing and crew R&R, he had resailed for the eastern Mediterranean on September 29.

The senior German naval commander in the Mediterranean Basin, Eberhard Weichold, wrote:

> Leaving *U-559* behind in the Eastern Mediterranean after the other boats operating there had been recalled, was done deliberately. The boat had been operating against the enemy since August with only one break of a few days [in Messina] and

---

* "Ducks" were very small (141-foot, 300-ton) German submarines designed for North Sea operations and the Training Command. Six Type IIB ducks *(U-9, U-18, U-19, U-20, U-23, U-24)* were dismantled and floated on river barges to Galatic, Romania, reassembled, and organized into Combat Flotilla 30, which operated from Constanta. According to Rohwer *(Successes),* the little flotilla sank six confirmed Soviet freighters for 28,303 tons and maybe two minesweepers and a submarine. No ducks returned from the Black Sea.

† See Volume I, pp. 337–38.

> as it is in need of repairs it was out of the question to put it into operation in the Western Mediterranean. But the boat can be of use in the Eastern Mediterranean a few days longer until it has exhausted all its resources.

Heidtmann's orders were to attack shipping "anywhere" in the eastern Mediterranean (the Levant). Like other boats before him, he focused his efforts on the short Allied convoy route running between Port Said, the Mediterranean terminus of the Suez Canal, and the British naval base at Haifa, Palestine. In the early hours of October 30, when *U-559* was about seventy miles north by northeast of Port Said, a radar-equipped Sunderland on ASW patrol found *U-559* and reported a contact, "possibly a submarine." The British destroyer *Hero,* which was about twenty miles from the reported position, proceeded there and commenced a sonar search, but she found nothing. Other British aircraft arrived to assist *Hero* in the hunt, but they could not find anything either.

Upon receiving the initial report from the Sunderland, the commander of Destroyer Squadron 12, Eric B. K. Stevens in *Pakenham,* sailed from Port Said with three other destroyers: *Petard, Dulverton,* and *Hurworth.* Seven hours later, at about thirty minutes after noon, the four destroyers arrived near the reported site. Just as they did so, a British Wellesley aircraft seven miles distant sighted a periscope and the "clearly visible" outline of a submerged submarine. The pilot attacked from low altitude, dropping three depth charges and firing Very flares to alert the destroyers. Absorbing *Hero* into his formation, Stevens raced the five destroyers to the circling aircraft at thirty-one knots. Upon slowing to sonar-search speed, *Dulverton* almost immediately reported a submarine contact.

The U-boat hunt that ensued resembled the tenacious thirteen-hour hunt (and kill) of *U-372* by four destroyers and aircraft in early August in nearly the same spot.* The five destroyers and aircraft hunting *U-559* doggedly clung to the contact for almost ten hours. Alternating passes, *Dulverton* attacked six times, with fifty-six depth charges; *Pakenham* and *Petard* each attacked four times, dropping thirty-two and thirty charges, respectively; *Hero* attacked three times, with seventeen charges; and *Hurworth* attacked twice, dropping fifteen charges. Totals: nineteen separate attacks in which 150 depth charges were dropped at depths ranging between 150 and 600 feet.†

Earlier on his second Atlantic patrol, Heidtmann had been detected and hunted for hours by a tenacious team of British destroyers. He escaped by taking *U-559* to 590 feet and lying doggo. He repeated this tactic, but he could not shake these five destroyers. After nearly ten hours of pursuit, the air in the boat was foul. Moreover, the last five of the 150 depth charges—dropped by *Petard*—had caused severe damage and flooding. Therefore, at about 10:40 P.M., Heidtmann surfaced, hoping to slip away in darkness.

The instant *U-559* reached the surface, *Hurworth* picked her up on radar and caught her in a big searchlight. Too close to depress the main 4" guns, *Hurworth*

---

* See Volume I, pp. 652–53.

† *Petard*'s crew reached six hundred feet with some missiles of a ten-charge pattern by plugging the holes in the hydrostatic pistols with soap.

and *Petard* opened fire with 20 and 40mm cannons. *Petard*'s fire, officially described as "a murderous barrage," raked the *U-559*'s bridge, probably killing several Germans, possibly including Heidtmann (the record is not clear), and wounding others. With no possibility of escape, the Germans scuttled *U-559* and began jumping into the sea. In the rush to abandon ship, they failed to jettison all Enigma material in accordance with regulations.

Petard's captain, Mark Thornton, sensed an opportunity to ransack and possibly even capture *U-559*. He brought his ship to starboard of *U-559*, pointed in the opposite direction, his bow to her stern. As *Petard* eased close alongside the U-boat, some of her crew, including Lieutenant Spens-Black, Able Seamen K. Lacroix and G. W. MacFarlane, and Canteen Assistant Thomas Brown, jumped down onto the deck of *U-559* to shackle on a towline. The first line parted, as did the second, but finally they attached a big manila line to the *U-559*'s stern that held.

In the meantime, Thornton called away his boarding party and put over two whaleboats. Due to a misunderstanding of his orders, one whaler diverted to pick up German survivors, collecting fourteen. The leader of the boarding party, *Petard*'s second-in-command, Francis Anthony Blair Fasson, turned the other whaler over to another officer, G. Gordon Connell, then stripped naked, dived overboard, and swam to *U-559*. Able Seaman Colin Grazier also shed his clothes and dived in to assist Fasson.

Fasson, Grazier, and Canteen Assistant Brown went down inside *U-559* to the control room. It was dark, Brown remembered, but Fasson had a flashlight and a machine gun. Fasson went directly forward to Heidtmann's quarters and the radio room and smashed open cabinets with the butt of the machine gun. He found a set of keys hanging on the back of the door, Brown said, and these opened a locked drawer. Fasson took some "confidential books" from the drawer and gave them to Brown, who took them topside and rigged a line to lift others. He returned to help Fasson, who gave him another load of documents, which Brown stacked at the bottom of the conning-tower ladder. He then returned to Heidtmann's quarters and the radio room, where Fasson had found yet more confidential books. Brown took these to the conning-tower hatch as well and then climbed topside and gave the documents to Spens-Black, Lacroix, and MacFarlane. They, in turn, passed the documents to the men in the whaler.

When Brown returned to the control room, he found Fasson attempting to break an unidentified "apparatus" from a bulkhead. Fasson pried it off, but he could not cut the wires leading into the apparatus, "so we gave up," Brown remembered. Fasson then handed Brown yet another load of confidential books. On this third trip topside, Brown gave these directly to the men in the whaler. Meanwhile, Spens-Black, Lacroix, and MacFarlane were hauling up a "box" which Fasson had secured to the lifting line that Brown had rigged. Fasson twice shouted up to them to be very careful as the "instrument" was "very delicate" and "important." It could have been an Enigma machine.

The *U-559* suddenly began to sink rapidly by the stern. Thornton ordered *Petard*'s engines ahead, to put a strain on the towline and hold up the U-boat's stern, but when he saw he might hit and capsize the whaler and lose the documents, he canceled the order and chopped the towline. Spens-Black, Brown, and others on the U-boat deck and in the whaler all shouted "Abandon ship! Abandon ship!" Brown remembered seeing Fasson and Grazier at the foot of the conning-tower ladder and twice shouted: "You'd better come up." They "had just started up," Brown said, when "the submarine started to sink very quickly." Vainly fighting against the flood of water pouring down the conning-tower hatch, neither man made it. The "instrument" was lost as well. "I had to leave it," MacFarlane remembered, "as the water was rising above the conning tower." As *U-559* upended and sank stern first, he and Brown and others of the topside group swam to the whaler.*

The British destroyers rescued forty-one of the forty-eight Germans on *U-559*. Heidtmann was not among the survivors. One other survivor died of wounds, leaving forty. *Petard* took some of these Germans, as well as all the documents recovered from *U-559*, directly to the eastern Mediterranean naval intelligence center, which had withdrawn from Alexandria and relocated in Haifa.

Among the intelligence documents recovered from *U-559* were two that were priceless to British codebreakers:

- A current edition of the short-signal codebook for weather reports.
- A current edition of the short-signal codebook for reporting enemy ships, battle results, and other tactical information.

For the skippers of *Petard* and *U-559* there were ironic aftermaths. Six weeks later, on December 15, *Petard*, in company with the Greek destroyer *Queen Olga*, discovered and attacked the Italian submarine *Uarsciek*. In keeping with Admiralty policy, during this action *Petard* drove the submarine to the surface and inflicted merciless casualties on the Italians in an attempt to keep them belowdecks and prevent scuttling. Moreover, for the second time, *Petard* got a boarding party on an enemy warship and again captured an impressive haul of "confidential books" of all kinds and almost succeeded in towing the captured vessel into port.

Notwithstanding this second outstanding achievement, according to a published history of *Petard*, the doctor on board the ship, William Finbar Prendergast, concluded that *Petard*'s captain, Mark Thornton, had gone over the edge and that he should have a "medical checkup and rest." In effect sacked, Thornton abruptly left his command without the usual farewell ceremonies.† In contrast, for reasons never made clear, *U-559*'s skipper Heidtmann, who had committed gross negligence in failing to insure destruction of his Enigma papers, was awarded a *Ritterkreuz* on April 14, 1943.‡

---

* For their bravery, Fasson and Grazier were posthumously awarded the George Cross, and Canteen Assistant Tommy Brown was awarded the George Medal. When it was learned that Brown was only sixteen years old and had falsified his age by a year in order to join the Royal Navy, he was discharged immediately. In 1944, Brown was killed attempting to rescue his younger sister, who was trapped in a burning building.

† See *Fighting Destroyer* (1976), by one of *Petard*'s officers, G. Gordon Connell. In a candid afterword, Rear Admiral G. C. Leslie, R.N., wrote that only a "few" destroyer captains in the Royal Navy went through the war "without a breakdown" and that during Thornton's command of *Petard*, "the strain became too great to bear." Later, however, Thornton was given command of another destroyer.

‡ At the time of the award, his confirmed score was five ships sunk for 14,542 tons, including the Australian sloop *Parramatta*.

When the short-signal weather codebook reached Bletchley Park, it offered British codebreakers who could decode weather reports the possibility of cribs to break weather reports reenciphered into four-rotor Enigma. However, it defied them until December 13. That day, the codebreakers discovered to their astonishment that the Germans had made a terrible lapse in code security. In weather reporting, U-boats put the fourth rotor in "neutral," using their four-rotor Enigma like three-rotor Enigma. Obtaining three of the four Enigma keys of the day from this source, it was not difficult to cycle the bombes through twenty-six more possibilities to obtain the fourth wheel setting.

This break into four-rotor Enigma enabled Bletchley Park to read immediately eight days of November traffic and all the early days of December with little delay. Still fearful of a leak by the Americans, First Sea Lord Pound notified Admiral Ernest J. King in patronizing language:

> As the result of months of the most strenuous endeavour, a few days' U-boat traffic will be readable in the immediate future and this may lead to better results in the near future.
>
> You will, I am sure, appreciate the care necessary in making use of this information to prevent suspicion being aroused as to its source. We have found this especially difficult when action by [ship] routing authorities outside the Admiralty is required. It would be a tragedy if we had to start all over again on what would undoubtedly be a still more difficult problem.

The captures from *U-559* thus equaled in importance those from *U-110* in May 1941 as a source for cribs. The short-signal codebook for weather reports was to remain operational until March 1943. By the time it expired, the British had perfected a method of obtaining cribs from the other (tactical) short-signal codebook, which remained in use until the end of the war. Even so, it was to take six months or more for the British codebreakers to completely master *Triton.* Until then, it was often a nail-biting, hit-or-miss enterprise.

Bletchley Park immediately telexed the Admiralty's Operational Intelligence Center its first decoded intercepts. The chief of the Submarine Tracking Room, Rodger Winn, was not present to join in the celebration. Never robust, he had recently suffered a temporary collapse caused by the pressures and strains of his job. His assistant, Patrick Beesly, plotted in the first confirmed U-boat positions, which, amazingly, did not differ markedly from Winn's guesstimates, Beesly wrote.

TWO

Torch

The vast Allied armada for Torch closed on Gibraltar and Morocco in the last days of October and the beginning of November. The Axis had only vague intimations as to what was afoot.

German forces stumbled upon two British units by happenstance. On October 31, Focke-Wulf FW-200 Condors reported a southbound Allied task force, composed of "two carriers and two cruisers," 280 miles west of Portugal. On November 2, Hans-Jürgen Auffermann in *U-514,* returning from Trinidad to France, reported "seven large troop transports" in approximately the same area.

Upon receiving the Condor report, Dönitz directed five boats from the disbanded group *Streitaxt,* which had been attacking convoy Sierra Leone 125, to attempt to intercept the "carrier group." The Condors failed to follow up the contact and, as a result, none of the boats could find the "carrier group." As related, Massmann in *U-409,* low on fuel, returned to France and the other four boats of *Streitaxt* were ordered onward to Freetown.

In response to the November 2 report of seven southbound transports by Auffermann in *U-514,* Dönitz directed five boats in the area to intercept. All attempted to comply, but Auffermann lost contact. *Ritterkreuz* holder Ernst Kals in *U-130,* Hans Geissler in *U-440,* and Heinz Stein in *U-620* reported temporary mechanical difficulties or battle damage, and Heinz Hirsacker in *U-572* failed again to react aggressively. Geissler in *U-440* came upon an eastbound convoy that may—or may not—have been the one reported by Auffermann. In the event, he was unable to attack or shadow, he reported, owing to diesel-engine difficulties.

These two sightings, and reports by German and Italian spies of a mounting assemblage of warships and merchantmen of all kinds at Gibraltar, convinced Berlin belatedly that the Allies were staging for a large amphibious operation inside the Mediterranean. Inasmuch as Hitler believed the Allies would not antagonize the Vichy French and drive them into a closer relationship with the Axis, Berlin ruled out Allied landings in French Northwest Africa (Morocco, Algeria, and Tunisia). At first, Berlin believed the likeliest Allied objectives were positions close behind Rommel, perhaps at Tripoli or Benghazi in Libya, together with yet another reinforcement of Malta.

On November 4—four days prior to Torch D day—Berlin asked Dönitz to immediately send seven Type VIIs of the Atlantic force to reinforce the Mediterranean U-boats. In compliance, Dönitz hurriedly formed group *Delphin* from six boats already at sea plus Jürgen Quaet-Faslem's *U-595,* which sailed from France that day. Owing to engine problems, two of the seven boats at sea, *U-440* and *U-662,* could not carry out the mission and were replaced by Klaus Köpke in *U-259* and Josef Röther in *U-380,* both of whom sailed from France on November 5. The first five boats of group *Delphin** were to slip through the Strait of Gibraltar on the night of November 8–9, when the moon was new, the *U-259* and *U-380* to sail later, on the night of November 10–11. These additions were to increase the German Mediterranean force to twenty-five U-boats.

At the insistence of Dönitz, some torpedoes of the Mediterranean boats were to be equipped at all possible speed with two exotic new features from the torpedo technicians:

- A new and better magnetic pistol, designated MZ-Pi39H, but generally referred to as the Pi2. The first fifty of these pistols from the production line in Germany went to the U-boat bases at La Spezia and Pola. Until the new pistols were available in quantity, the skippers were directed to fire these torpedoes only at important targets, such as battleships and carriers.
- A new steering device, which could be set to drive the standard air (G7a) or electric (G7e) torpedo on a looping path (left or right, short or long) through a convoy or naval task force. Designated *Federapparat,* the device was generally referred to as FAT. Its looping path increased the possibility of a hit in a large ship formation. The twenty-four FAT air (G7a) torpedoes in Kiel ready for service were sent to La Spezia and Pola.

The use of a FAT torpedo required a minor modification to the torpedo tube from which it was to be fired. Since there were only twenty-four FATs on hand, it was decided to allot these to only four U-boats, all veterans of Mediterranean duty: *U-83, U-375, U-453,* and *U-562.* To speed up the departure of the boats, it was further decided to modify at first only two bow tubes in each of these four boats. They were to sail with six FATs in the bow compartment, plus four G7e electrics with Pi2 magnetic pistols in the stern compartment. Since the air FAT left a highly visible bubble wake like an ordinary air torpedo, it was to be used sparingly in day-

---

* Ernst-Ulrich Brüller's *U-407,* Quaet-Faslem's *U-595,* Günter Jahn's *U-596,* Albrecht Brandi's *U-617,* and Walter Göing's *U-755.*

time, in order to keep the FAT secret from the Allies for as long as possible. On the first patrols, the boats were to load the bow tubes with one FAT and three electrics with Pi2 pistols for daytime operations and two FATs and two electrics with Pi2 pistols for night operations.

Much was expected of the Axis submarines inside the Mediterranean. But Berlin had evidently forgotten the lessons of Norway two and a half years past: U-boats were virtually useless for stopping massively escorted invasion forces fully alert to possible submarine attacks. Inasmuch as the Torch naval forces included thirteen aircraft carriers (five fleet, eight light—"jeep" or semi-"jeep"), and scores of the warships were fitted with the British Type 271 or the American Type SG centimetric-wavelength radar as well as Huff Duff, the task would be that much more difficult, and perhaps impossible.

In the period preceding Torch, the Allies made a secret deal with an anti-Axis French hero, General Henri Giraud. He was to enter Algiers on D day, assume command of the French colonial government and armed forces in North Africa, and direct those French to lay aside arms and welcome their liberation by the Allies. However, in arranging this deal, the Allies made three mistakes: They overestimated Giraud's prestige and appeal to the colonial French and underestimated the loyalty of many to Vichy; they failed to draw the French Navy into the scheme; and in their determination to keep secret the time and places of the landings, they confided in only a few of the senior French military commanders on the scene. The upshot was to be a decidedly mixed reception for the Allies on Torch D day, November 8.

The Royal Navy delivered a mixture of American and British amphibious forces to Algiers and Oran. For that job, it organized three task forces: a Main Covering Force of big ships to repel a possible attack by the Italian or Vichy French navies, or both; an Eastern Task Force to occupy Algiers; and a Center Task Force to occupy Oran. The official Admiralty historian wrote that the British utilized 229 ships for these operations. They included the battleships *Nelson, Rodney,* and *Duke of York;* the battle cruiser *Renown;* the modern carriers *Formidable* and *Victorious,* and the old carriers *Argus* and *Furious;* the new (American-built) "jeep" carriers *Avenger, Biter, Dasher,* and *Archer* (the last serving only as an aircraft ferry); and 217 other vessels of all types.

By happenstance, Admiral Jean François Darlan, the heir apparent to Marshal Pétain in the Vichy government, was in Algiers combining business with a visit with his son, who had been hospitalized with poliomyelitis. When the Allied military and political leaders perceived that General Giraud carried little weight with the French in North Africa, they quickly turned to Darlan. After a series of byzantine political maneuvers, Darlan defected to the Allies, who named him High Commissioner of French Northwest Africa. Many in America and Britain roundly criticized Eisenhower for making a "deal" with the "odious Nazi collaborator" Darlan, but the admiral's exhortations to the French colonials in the days ahead to lay arms aside doubtless saved Allied lives in Algeria and Morocco. Darlan could not, however, deliver Vichy Tunisia or, as Churchill devoutly hoped, those elements of the French fleet neutralized at Toulon and other warships at Dakar.*

Remarkably, the Allied armada destined for Algiers and Oran suffered only one serious casualty en route. At 6:50 A.M. on November 7, the American troopship *Thomas Stone,* with 1,450 American shock troops embarked, was hit in the stern by one torpedo, which disabled her rudder and screws. Contemporary accounts credited a German U-boat with the hit, but it has not been confirmed in postwar German records. Nor could Italian naval historians attribute the hit to an Italian submarine. It may have been delivered by a submarine of another nation (France? Spain?), that was lost at sea before reporting, or concealed the attack for various reasons. Or it may have been a loose mine.

The convoy proceeded, but the British destroyers *Wishart* and *Velox,* the corvette *Spey,* and a tug stood by the damaged vessel. About eight hundred of the soldiers on *Thomas Stone* bravely set off for Algeria in twenty-four landing craft, escorted by *Spey.* One by one all the landing craft broke down or foundered during the 150-mile voyage, but *Spey* took all eight hundred soldiers on board and delivered them to Algiers, a day and a half late. The destroyers and the tug eventually got *Thomas Stone* to Algiers, where she disembarked the rest of her troops but sailed no more.

During the Allied landings to the east and west of Algiers early on November 8, two British destroyers, *Broke* and *Malcolm,* were detailed to crash through the booms in the main harbor and land commando teams, which were to seize the waterfront and prevent ship scuttlings. That operation was a disaster. Both destroyers encountered heavy damage and casualties from French shore-based naval guns and were forced to withdraw to sea, where *Broke* later sank, the single serious naval casualty in the Algiers landings. Thereafter the only two French warships left in the Algiers harbor, the submarines *Caïman* and *Marsouin,* boldly sailed out to repel the invaders. British aircraft and surface ships spotted and pounded the submarines, forcing them off. Both eventually escaped to Toulon, *Caïman* severely damaged.

Inasmuch as a pro-Allied French general was in command of the defenders at Algiers, the main landings east and west of the city were virtually unopposed and the French surrendered by nightfall of the first day. According to the plan, these Allied forces were to race east and capture Tunisia before the Axis could reinforce it, but the Allies botched this important phase of the operation. Reacting with astonishing speed, the Axis rushed heavy armored and infantry units from Italy to Tunisia, wrested control of the nation from the Vichy French, and deployed troops at the western border who solidly blocked the Allies for months, thus creating an escape corridor for the retreating *Afrika Korps.*†

---

* Eisenhower's naval aide, Harry C. Butcher, noted in his diary, *My Three Years with Eisenhower* (1946), that Churchill said: "Kiss Darlan's stern if you have to, but get the French Navy."

† When a British naval task force leapfrogged about one hundred miles east to Bougie on November 11–14, Axis aircraft sank three big troop transports, a cargo vessel, and two warships and badly damaged the new 8,000-ton monitor *Roberts,* which mounted two 15" guns, eight 4" guns, and many smaller weapons.

The Allied landings at Oran were more difficult than those at Algiers. The local Army commander was pro-Vichy, and the harbor was jammed with Vichy French warships that refused to defect to the Allies. As at Algiers, two Allied vessels were assigned to crack the main harbor boom and land commando teams to seize the waterfront and prevent scuttlings. The vessels designated for this task were the ex-American, 250-foot Coast Guard cutters *Pontchartrain* and *Sebago,* rechristened by the Royal Navy as *Hartland* and *Walney.* French shore- and ship-based guns blasted the two vessels to pieces, killing hundreds of Allied commandos and ships' crewmen.

Eight French warships in the harbor at Oran sailed out to repel the invaders: the super-destroyer *Epervier;* the destroyers *Tramontane, Tornade,* and *Typhon;* the sloop *Surprise;* and the submarines *Argonaute, Actéon,* and *Fresnel.* British warships and aircraft met these ships head-on with murderous fire. Four of the five surface ships were driven back or forced to beach. The British destroyer *Brilliant* sank the *Surprise.* The veteran British destroyers *Wescott* and *Achates* sank the submarines *Argonaute* and *Actéon,* respectively. The defiant crewmen of the destroyer *Typhon* blew up their ship in the harbor. The French also scuttled five other drydocked or decommissioned submarines. Only the submarine *Fresnel* escaped to Toulon.

The third leg of Torch was the American invasion of Morocco. For that purpose, the U.S. Navy's commander in chief, Admiral King, created the Western Task Force, commanded by Henry Kent Hewitt, which sailed directly from the United States. The armada consisted of three battleships (the new *Massachusetts,* the aged *New York,* and *Texas*), the carrier *Ranger,* four new, thinly trained light carriers (*Suwanee, Sangamon, Santee,* and *Chenango,* the latter serving only as an aircraft ferry),* and ninety-six other vessels of all kinds, including thirty-eight American destroyers. Hewitt's task was to put ashore about 35,000 Army troops, commanded by General George S. Patton, at three sites: Fedala and Mehdia–Port Lyautey, fourteen and sixty-five miles north of Casablanca, respectively, and Safi, 125 miles south of Casablanca.

The largest and most powerful of the American amphibious forces struck at Fedala to encircle and capture Casablanca. The new battleship *Massachusetts* (on her shakedown cruise), the veteran fleet carrier *Ranger,* the new light carrier *Suwanee,* and numerous cruisers and destroyers provided offensive and defensive support for the twelve big troop transports and three cargo vessels. The very unfriendly French forces in Casablanca harbor included the battleship *Jean Bart,* unfinished but with one operable turret of four 15" guns, the light cruiser *Primauguet,* two super-destroyers, fifteen conventional destroyers and sloops, and eleven submarines.

A tough naval battle ensued off Casablanca on D day. The *Jean Bart* and

* These four U.S. Navy carriers were hurried conversions of big tankers. They were longer than the "jeep" carriers (about 555 feet versus 495 feet) and carried more aircraft (thirty-two versus fifteen to twenty-five). They had two elevators to the hangar deck and two catapults.

coastal batteries opened fire on the *Massachusetts* and other covering ships. Remarkably, in return fire, *Massachusetts* hit *Jean Bart* five times in sixteen minutes, knocking out her single operating big-gun turret. Thereafter, eight French surface ships valorously sailed out to repel the invaders: the cruiser *Primauguet,* the super-destroyers *Milan* and *Albatros,* and five conventional destroyers. American ships and aircraft sank at sea the destroyers *Boulonnais, Brestois,* and *Fougueux,* and forced the *Primauguet, Milan, Albatros,* and *Frondeur* to withdraw to anchorages close inshore or to beach outside Casablanca. Subsequently, American aircraft destroyed these four ships as well. Only one of the eight ships, the destroyer *Alcyon,* returned to Casablanca harbor undamaged.

The eleven submarines at Casablanca were likewise roughly handled. American gunfire in the early actions sank three *(Amphitrite, Psyché, Oréade)* in the harbor. The other eight sailed out to repel the invaders. The *Amazone* shot five or more torpedoes at the cruiser *Brooklyn,* but all were evaded. *Tonnant* shot at the carrier *Ranger,* but missed. *Méduse* and *Antiope* attacked the transports at Fedala, but they also missed. Four of the eight submarines were lost. Three aircraft from the light carrier *Suwanee* sank *Sidi-Ferruch,* thus becoming the first Allied carrier-based planes to destroy a submarine unassisted by surface craft. Two U.S. Navy Catalinas arriving at Casablanca found *Conquérant* on the surface and sank her with three shallow-set, 325-pound Mark XVII depth charges. Under fire from a British aircraft, *Tonnant* scuttled. *Sibylle* disappeared without a trace. *Amazone, Antiope,* and *Méduse* set off to join French naval forces at Dakar; *Orphée* returned to Casablanca without serious damage and eventually joined Allied forces.

To the north, at Mehdia–Port Lyautey, American forces also met a hot reception. The battleship *Texas,* the new light carriers *Sangamon* and *Chenango* (the aircraft ferry), and other vessels provided offensive and defensive support for the six troop transports and two cargo vessels. In a remarkable, bold, and innovative operation, the four-stack destroyer *Dallas* won high honors for pushing deep up a river to land troops at the airport. There were no French naval forces present to challenge the Americans, but French shore batteries and ground forces put up a stiff fight before Admiral Darlan's exhortations to cease firing reached them and could be verified. The capture of Mehdia–Port Lyautey provided the Allies with the only airfield with paved runways in Morocco.

To the south at Safi, the least important of the American objectives, "everything clicked," American naval historian Samuel Eliot Morison wrote. The battleship *New York,* the cruiser *Philadelphia,* and the greenest of the new light carriers, *Santee,* provided offensive and defensive support for five troop transports and one cargo vessel. As at Algiers and Oran, two ships, the four-stack destroyers *Bernadou* and *Cole,* crammed with commandos, crashed the harbor to capture the waterfront and prevent scuttlings. Both slipped in undetected and successfully carried out this difficult mission with no losses. The Vichy submarine *Méduse,* southbound to Dakar, diverted to attack Allied forces, but an aircraft from *Philadelphia* drove her onto the beach. Owing to the inexperience of the pilots, to an unreliable catapult, and to insufficient winds for launching and recovering aircraft, *Santee* lost twenty-one of her thirty-one aircraft to accidents, the greatest Allied setback at Safi.

The six American fleet submarines assigned to Torch contributed little. Two,

Gurnard and *Gunnel,* had newly designed diesel engines that proved to be defective. *Gurnard* was forced to abort with engine problems. *Gunnel,* commanded by John S. McCain, Jr., the son of an admiral, carried out the first part of her mission off Fedala. Later in the day, per plan, she and *Blackfish* and *Herring* set off to the south to establish a patrol line to intercept the battleship *Richelieu* or other Vichy warships that might sail north from Dakar. An Army Air Forces plane mistook *Gunnel* for a Vichy or Axis submarine and bombed her, knocking out all four temperamental diesel engines and causing other damage. By ingeniously rigging a small, reliable, auxiliary diesel engine to charge batteries, McCain was able to coax *Gunnel* at three knots on her electric motors all the way to Falmouth, England. *Herring,* commanded by Raymond W. Johnson, was the only one of the five American submarines to sink a ship, the 5,000-ton Vichy freighter *Ville du Havre.**

On the whole, the five Torch landings on November 8 were ragged but immensely successful. Allied naval losses to French or Axis forces on D day were slight: the British destroyer *Broke;* the ex–Coast Guard cutters *Hartland* and *Walney,* deliberately savaged or sunk at Algiers and Oran; and the American troopship *Leedstown,* badly bombed by Axis aircraft off Algiers after disembarking her troops, then sunk by a U-boat. No Allied ships were lost on D day at Casablanca, Mehdia–Port Lyautey, or Safi. Except for the loss of the commandos in the harbor attacks at Algiers and Oran, Allied army casualties were also light.

The Germans had long before drawn up a plan, *Attila,* for the occupation of the Vichy, or free, zone of southern France in an emergency. Believing the French fleet at Toulon might obey Darlan and defect to the Allies, on November 11 Hitler ordered plan *Attila* to be implemented. German forces quickly overran Vichy France; Italian amphibious forces, long in training to invade Malta, captured the Vichy French island of Corsica.

The Vichy French naval chiefs fell into dispute over what to do. Paul Auphan, who had succeeded Darlan as Minister of Marine, wanted the fleet at Toulon to sail out and defect to the Allies. Jean de Laborde, commander in chief of the Mediterranean Fleet, and a rabid Anglophobe, wanted the fleet to sail out and attack the Allies. To avoid provoking the Vichy French into scuttling the fleet, the Germans approached Toulon with olive branches extended and halted short of the city to negotiate. Nonetheless, on November 27, Laborde ordered the fleet to scuttle.†

During the thirty months that France had been divided, the chief of French codebreakers, Gustave Bertrand, and the refugee Polish codebreakers he had sheltered, had continued attacks on certain Enigma nets in hiding at a château near Avignon. When Hitler ordered *Attila* to commence, all hands fled for Spain or

* Dakar fell to the Allies without a fight on November 23. Subsequently, the unfinished battleship *Richelieu* and a half dozen French cruisers and other vessels sailed to the United States for refits and modernization.

† Down went seventy-seven warships: the old battleship *Provence,* two modern battle cruisers, *Dunkerque* and *Strasbourg,* seven cruisers, thirty-two destroyers, sixteen submarines, including *Caïman* and *Fresnel,* which had just escaped from North Africa, a seaplane tender, and eighteen sloops and smaller craft. Four other submarines sailed from Toulon: *Glorieux, Iris, Marsouin,* and *Casabianca. Iris* reached Spain, where she was interned for the rest of the war. The other three reached Algiers.

Gibraltar, intending to go on to Britain. The Gestapo caught some, including Bertrand; the chief engineer, Antoni Palluth; and one of the Poles, Guido Langer. Although all those captured were subjected to brutal interrogation, not one gave away the secret that Enigma had been broken.

Axis Submarines Versus Torch Inside the Mediterranean

The U-boat force commander in the Mediterranean, Leo Kreisch, first became aware on November 5 that the Allies were about to launch something big inside the Mediterranean. That evening, he logged, an Italian spy reported that a great congregation of ships at Gibraltar began sailing east at 8:00 P.M. Included:

3	Aircraft carriers
1	Battleship
7	Light cruisers
1	Monitor
17	Destroyers
11	Gunboats
1	Liner
40	Freighters
15	Tankers

Later that evening, the same or another Italian spy reported that sixty or more blacked-out ships, including two aircraft carriers and two battleships, had passed abreast of Tarifa, Spain, eastbound through the Strait of Gibraltar.

Kreisch and other senior Germans, of course, did not know precisely what was afoot. It might be another convoy to deliver fighter aircraft to Malta, as did a *Furious* task force on October 28–29. Or it might be a large-scale amphibious landing behind (or west of) Rommel's *Afrika Korps.* The German naval commander in chief, Mediterranean, Eberhard Weichold, and Kreisch leaned strongly to the latter possibility. Inasmuch as they believed the Vichy French would vigorously repel an Allied landing at Oran or Algiers and that the water was unfavorably deep right up to the North African coastline in most areas, they concluded that a landing probably would take place at Bougie Bay, about one hundred miles east of Algiers.

Berlin received the same spy reports. From Adolf Hitler came another exhortation:

> To all [Mediterranean] U-boats: The existence of the *Afrika Korps* depends on the destruction of the Gibraltar force. I expect a ruthless, victorious operation.

By November 7, Leo Kreisch had deployed nine of his remaining force of eighteen boats to waiting positions in the narrow neck of the western Mediterranean. Of the nine, four *(U-81, U-565, U-593, U-605)* formed a "first wave" of defense, three *(U-77, U-205, U-660)* a "second wave," and two *(U-73* and *U-458)* backstopped the waves. Three others *(U-331, U-431, U-561)* were proceeding westward as fast as possible.*

In the afternoon and evening of D day minus one, November 7, five U-boats made contact with fast-moving British amphibious forces. The veteran *U-77*, commanded by Otto Hartmann, was first, but he reported that enemy forces bombed and gunned him under and inflicted personnel casualties. Another veteran, *U-73*, commanded by the new skipper Horst Deckert, attempted to attack several big ocean liner/troopships, but escorts depth-charged the boat and forced her off. Yet another veteran, *U-205*, also with a new skipper, Friedrich Bürgel, was the first to shoot. He fired a full bow salvo at an 18,000-ton liner/troopship, but the torpedoes missed or malfunctioned. A fourth veteran, *U-81*, commanded by the *Ritterkreuz* holder Friedrich (Fritz) Guggenberger, attempted to attack two aircraft carriers, *Furious* and *Argus*, but escorts foiled his setup and drove him off. One of the recent arrivals, *U-458*, commanded by Kurt Diggins, shot a two-fan at a light cruiser. He claimed one hit, but it could not be confirmed. Aircraft bombed the boat twice, and escorts drove her under with gunfire.

In the early hours of D day, November 8, London radio (BBC) announced that Allied troops would be landing in North Africa in a few hours. Fooled by British deceptive moves at sea and still believing that Bougie Bay was the likeliest landing area, Leo Kreisch directed eight U-boats to the bay at maximum speed. These were the veterans *U-73, U-77, U-81*, and *U-205*, one of the recent arrivals, Götz Baur in *U-660*, and three more veterans, newly sailed from La Spezia, *U-331, U-431*, and *U-561*. This movement to the east left only four U-boats in the Algiers area: the veteran *U-565* and three of the most recent arrivals, *U-458, U-593*, and *U-605*.

By noon on D day, the Germans realized they had erred badly. Intelligence reported that there had obviously been a big amphibious landing at Algiers, certainly supported by heavy naval forces, and that there were no enemy forces east of Algiers at Bougie, where Leo Kreisch had sent the bulk of his veteran U-boat force. Inasmuch as Kreisch still believed Bougie Bay certainly had to be one of the main targets, he was reluctant to turn the boats around and send them back to Algiers. However, the senior German naval officer at Rome, Eberhard Weichold, overruled Kreisch and ordered him to do exactly that.

This was easier said than done. To avoid enemy detection and attack, the U-boats heading east to Bougie in daylight were running submerged half the time. Some did not receive the new orders. The first to arrive at Bougie Bay, Hartmann in *U-77*, reported: "No enemy forces." Kreisch, no doubt sheepishly, radioed all boats on the evening of D day:

> Landings of strong enemy forces at many points, principally at Oran and Algiers. . . . Algiers apparently in enemy hands, stronger resistance at Oran. Innumer-

---

* Six veteran boats undergoing refit, overhaul, upgrade, or battle-damage repair could not sail: *U-83* and *U-97* at Salamis; *U-371* and *U-375* at Pola; *U-453* and *U-562* at La Spezia. However, by December 1, 1942, five of these six were at sea in combat operations, except for the badly damaged *U-97*.

able transports in [Algiers area], covered by aircraft carrier and battleships. Go to it! All out! Dare everything.*

Fortuitously, Berlin had ordered seven U-boats (group *Delphin*) into the Mediterranean on November 4. In its early reaction to Torch, Berlin directed Dönitz to send another group of Type VIIs into the Mediterranean, but he demurred. The Allies were virtually certain to detect the passage of the seven *Delphin* boats through the Strait of Gibraltar from November 8 to 11. With the advantage of surprise, the *Delphin* boats might get through safely but the Allies would be on full alert for other U-boats thereafter. Moreover, by November 15 or 16, when the boats of a second wave could reach the strait, moonlight conditions would be unfavorable for a passage. Finally, Dönitz argued, the three Italian-managed U-boat bases (La Spezia, Pola, Salamis) could not efficiently handle the U-boats already in the Mediterranean, let alone another substantial increase. In the face of these objections, the OKM agreed for the time being that no more U-boats were to enter the Mediterranean.

The seven U-boats of group *Delphin* commenced the transit of Gibraltar Strait on D day night, November 8–9. To throw off the British ASW forces, the skippers were under orders to delay a report of a safe transit ("Yes") until they had reached wide open seas east of Algiers. However, Weichold and Kreisch decided to deploy the *Delphin* boats against the Allied amphibious forces at Oran. Hence they were directed to report "Yes" when they reached the meridian of 1 degree west. Jürgen Quaet-Faslem in *U-595* spoke up from there shortly after midnight on November 9, but there was no word from the other six reinforcements from the Atlantic.

Kreisch continued to micromanage the U-boats. Since Axis reconnaissance aircraft had been unable to pinpoint the exact location of Allied landing sites and other naval forces, in the early hours of November 9, he assigned the dozen boats between Algiers and Bougie Bay to search for the enemy task forces. These orders sent some boats east of Algiers and some boats west of Algiers along the coast, futile missions all.

At noon on November 9, Kreisch again reversed himself and issued yet another set of orders. By that time, a second *Delphin* boat, *U-617,* commanded by Albrecht Brandi, had reported in off Oran, but no others. As a result, Kreisch decided to send six of the boats off Algiers to Oran. He therefore formed all the boats into two named groups:

Hai (Shark) at Algiers (6)		*Delphin (Dolphin) at Oran (8)*	
U-77	*U-561*	*U-73*	*U-593*
U-205	*U-660*	*U-81*	*U-595* (new)
U-331		*U-458*	*U-605*
U-431		*U-565*	*U-617* (new)

* Kreisch added that U-boats were not, as was customary, to give highest priority to aircraft carriers and battleships but to amphibious forces and merchant ships.

Toward evening on November 9, two U-boats shot torpedoes at targets. Fresh from La Spezia, *Ritterkreuz* holder Hans-Dietrich von Tiesenhausen in the veteran *U-331,* who had sunk the battleship *Barham* a year past, sank the 9,100-ton American freighter *Leedstown,* which was anchored, already damaged by air attack. The big ship settled to the bottom, but almost all of her cargo and gear was saved. The recently arrived *U-605,* commanded by Herbert-Viktor Schütze, shot at an "escort" and claimed a sinking, but it could not be confirmed.

Schütze's shots caused controversy. A petty officer in Götz Baur's recently arrived *U-660* remembered that while his boat was maneuvering submerged to fire at the carrier *Furious,* Schütze's *U-605* "shot four torpedoes" at one of the destroyers screening *Furious,* and that all four passed directly over *U-660*'s conning tower. After dark, Baur surfaced and berated Schütze by radio: *"Schafskopf!"* ("Fool!"). Leo Kreisch chimed in from Italy to reprimand Baur for breaking radio silence with "stupid remarks." Still later, the petty officer in *U-660* remembered that when Baur reported missing a destroyer with four torpedoes, Kreisch castigated him for attacking such "insignificant" targets when so many battleships and carriers were present.

While searching close along the coast between Algiers and Oran in the early hours of November 10, the veteran *U-81,* commanded by *Ritterkreuz* holder Fritz Guggenberger, came upon a small convoy and attacked. He hit and sank the 2,000-ton British freighter *Garlinge* and thought he got a hit on an escort. The *Garlinge* was the first merchant ship of the Allied invasion force to be sunk at sea by a U-boat and one of the very few. The supposed hit on the escort could not be confirmed.

Two hours later another veteran, *U-431,* commanded by Wilhelm Dommes, newly arrived from La Spezia, came upon a convoy farther out at sea. He shot a full bow salvo at what he believed to be a 7,200-ton British cruiser. The torpedoes hit solidly, and the target—actually the modern (1941) 2,000-ton British destroyer *Martin*—sank swiftly beneath the waves. *Martin* was the only Allied warship to be sunk in the Mediterranean by a U-boat in the early days of the invasion. A mechanical failure compelled Dommes to withdraw to the north.

Still later that day, four other U-boats shot at British warships, but all the torpedoes malfunctioned or missed.

- The recently arrived *U-458,* commanded by Kurt Diggins, fired a three-fan at an unidentified "large destroyer."
- The veteran *U-561,* commanded by Heinz Schomburg, fired a four-fan at the ancient carrier *Argus.*
- The veteran *U-77,* commanded by Otto Hartmann, fired a four-fan at the aircraft carrier *Furious.*
- The veteran *U-73,* commanded by Horst Deckert, fired a four-fan at the fast-moving battleship *Rodney* from a range of five thousand meters (nearly three miles). His nonsuccess report drew a rebuke from Kreisch for shooting at such extreme range.

By D plus three, November 11, Kreisch had seventeen U-boats in the Algiers/Oran area. The new German tactical plan was: (1) blockade Algeria with group *Hai* (five boats); (2) blockade Oran with group *Delphin* (five boats); (3) position a mobile "attack group," *Wal* (seven boats), in the narrow neck of the western Mediterranean between Oran and Cartagena, Spain (near the zero meridian). On second thought, Kreisch canceled group *Hai*'s blockade of Algiers and sent it seaward to operate as an attack group like *Wal.*

That day, November 11, six U-boats attacked Allied shipping. Deckert in *U-73,* Bürgel in *U-205,* and Walter Göing in the newly arrived *Delphin* boat *U-755* all missed or were driven off. However, three newly arrived *Delphin* boats achieved noteworthy successes:

- The *U-407,* commanded by Ernst-Ulrich Brüller, sank the 20,000-ton British liner/troopship *Viceroy of India.* Brüller hit her with a four-fan, but she sank slowly, and he polished her off with a finishing shot. Fortunately for the Allies, the loss of life was slight.
- The *U-380,* commanded by Josef Röther, sank the 11,000-ton Dutch liner/troopship *Nieuw Zeeland.*
- The *U-595,* commanded by Jürgen Quaet-Faslem, sank the 5,300-ton British freighter *Browning.* In return, British escorts depth-charged *U-595* for sixteen hours.

British forces intensified ASW measures, and by November 12, six boats that incurred heavy battle damage or mechanical failures had been compelled to abort.* These were three veterans (Fritz Guggenberger in *U-81,* Heinz Schomburg in *U-561,* and Wilhelm Franken in *U-565*), two boats recently arrived (Kurt Diggins in *U-458* and Gerd Kelbling in *U-593*), and a newly arrived *Delphin* boat (Günter Jahn in *U-596*).

On D plus five, November 13, the U-boat force operating against Torch forces was reduced by another abort. Wilhelm Dommes in the veteran *U-431,* who had sunk the British destroyer *Martin,* but had been forced by mechanical difficulties to withdraw northward off the coast, came upon an enemy convoy and attacked. He thought he sank a big British *Tribal*-class destroyer. In fact, it was the old 1,600-ton Dutch destroyer *Isaac Sweers.* In this same attack, Dommes claimed he hit a tanker and set it afire, but that hit could not be confirmed. A Hudson of British Squadron 500, piloted by New Zealander Mike A. Ensor, attacked *U-458* with four depth charges, one ASW bomb, and machine-gun fire. Dommes reported casualties and very extensive damage as well as mechanical failures and aborted to Messina, then Pola, where he received a *Ritterkreuz.*†

That same day, November 13, Fritz Guggenberger in the aborting veteran *U-81* came upon a convoy. He claimed torpedo hits on two ships for 11,000 tons. One of these, the 6,500-ton British vessel *Maron* sank; the other hit could not be confirmed. This was Guggenberger's second success against Torch merchantmen,

---

* An attempt by the Germans to establish a temporary forward U-boat base at Cagliari, on the southern coast of Sardinia, failed. On November 11, a British submarine sank the U-boat mother ship, *Bengasi,* off Cape Ferrato, northeast Sardinia. Lost were forty G7e electric torpedoes, a year's supply of food for U-boat crews, plus U-boat fuel and lube oil.

† At the time of the award, his confirmed score was only five ships for 13,000 tons. The fact that his was the only U-boat to sink Torch warships—the destroyers *Martin* and *Isaac Sweers*—doubtless figured strongly in the award.

a total bag of about 8,500 tons. For this achievement, Hitler awarded him Oak Leaves to his *Ritterkreuz.* Detached from *U-81* at La Spezia, he returned to Germany to commission a new U-cruiser.*

In the early days of Torch, Allied forces destroyed five U-boats.

- In the wee hours of November 12, Götz Baur in *U-660* carried out a submerged attack on a convoy off Oran, firing a full bow salvo at four different ships. The British destroyers *Wescott, Verity,* and *Wivern* and corvettes *Starwort* and *Lotus* pounced on *U-660.* Baur ejected *Bolde*† noisemakers and went deep—to 656 feet, one crewman said—but *Starwort* and *Lotus* clung to the sonar contact, dropping depth charges, which caused severe damage and flooding. After four hours, Baur conceded defeat and surfaced to scuttle. The British fished out Baur and forty-five others. Two Germans were killed by British gunfire in the sinking. The survivors bitterly criticized U-boat force commander Leo Kreisch for his poor leadership and professional ineptitude.
- On the next afternoon, November 14, a Hudson of British Squadron 233, piloted by New Zealander John W. Barling, sighted a U-boat north of Oran. Barling attacked and sank the recently arrived *U-605,* commanded by Herbert-Viktor Schütze. There were no survivors. The Admiralty credited the kill to the corvettes *Lotus* and *Poppy,* but after a more thorough postwar analysis, gave it to Barling's Hudson.
- That same day, in the same area, a swarm of British Hudsons based in Algeria found and attacked the newly arrived *Delphin* boat *U-595,* commanded by Jürgen Quaet-Faslem. Two Hudsons of Squadron 608, piloted by G. Williams and C. A. Livingstone, attacked *U-595,* dropping eight depth charges that damaged the boat and left her unable to dive. Later in the day, five Hudsons of Squadron 500 found *U-595* on the surface, "a sitting duck," as one pilot later wrote. Led by Wing Commander Denis Spotswood (later RAF Air Marshal), they attacked in the teeth of heavy flak. The Germans hit four of the Hudsons, including Spotswood's, and, amazingly, *U-595* survived all these attacks.

Believing he might escape with help from the Vichy French ashore, Quaet-Faslem dumped his Enigma machine and all secret documents and ran at full speed for the beach at Cape Tenes. His plan was to put most of the crew ashore, then return to deep water and scuttle, but the plan went awry. He unintentionally ran *U-595* hard aground at Cape Khamis—seventy miles northeast of Oran—and could not get her off. The captain and crew attempted to destroy the boat with demolition charges, then all but one enlisted man, who was captured by the British destroyer *Wivern,* swam ashore and made contact with a Vichy French officer. Believing him

* At the time of the award, his confirmed score, all on *U-81,* was five ships for about 40,000 tons, including, of course, the British carrier *Ark Royal,* plus five sailing ships. His new ship was the IXD2 *U-847,* the first of a special series of six U-cruisers (*U-847* to *U-852*) that were to be commanded only by *Ritterkreuz* holders, including Wilhelm Rollmann and Heinz-Otto Schultze. Almost immediately after commissioning *U-847,* however, Guggenberger was transferred to France to take command of an IXC whose skipper had been sacked.

† A submerged noisemaker, designed to confuse enemy sonar operators.

to be an ally, the Germans surrendered their arms. Collecting reinforcements along the way, the Frenchman led the forty-four Germans to the village of Picard, where he made arrangements to feed and house them for the night. Alerted by British air and naval forces, at about midnight, a U.S. Army tank unit arrived and captured Quaet-Faslem and his forty-three men, the only instance to this point in the war in which a U-boat crew fell to Allied ground forces. By the end of the month, the survivors of *U-595* were in the United States, undergoing interrogations.

• On the following day, November 15, Hudson pilot Mike Ensor of Squadron 500, who had severely damaged *U-458,* found on the surface the newly arrived *Delphin* boat *U-259,* commanded by Klaus Köpke. Ensor attacked with four depth charges, one of which fell directly on the topside deck and caused a violent secondary explosion that threw the deck gun and entire conning tower skyward. The boat then sank swiftly, leaving no survivors. The flying debris wrecked the low-flying Hudson, forcing Ensor and his three crewmen to bail out into the sea about twenty miles north of Algiers. Ensor and one other man survived this perilous victory and were rescued by British surface ships. The other two crewmen perished.

• Two days later, November 17, in the same area, Squadron Leader Ian C. Patterson in another Hudson of Squadron 500 found and attacked the veteran *U-331,* commanded by *Ritterkreuz* holder Hans-Dietrich von Tiesenhausen, who had sunk the British battleship *Barham* in 1941. Three depth charges and one ASW bomb wrecked the boat and blew open the torpedo-loading hatch in the bow compartment, flooding that space. Two other Hudsons of Squadron 500, piloted by Andrew W. Barwood and a Sergeant Young joined Patterson and carried out depth-charge and strafing attacks, which killed and wounded some Germans who had come topside. Von Tiesenhausen ran up a white flag.* The Hudson airmen cheered this second surrender (after *U-570*) of a U-boat to British aircraft.

The celebration was short-lived. A Royal Navy Martlet fighter suddenly appeared on the scene and strafed the boat, killing more Germans and wounding von Tiesenhausen, his second watch officer, Irwin A. K. Hartwig, and others. Then, to the further dismay of Patterson in the Hudson, a Royal Navy Albacore torpedo-bomber of Squadron 820 on the carrier *Formidable* came out of nowhere and sank *U-331* with a torpedo, killing many Germans who were still belowdecks. The British destroyer *Wilton,* racing from Algiers to assist in the capture, and a British Walrus flying boat fished out von Tiesenhausen and sixteen other Germans, one of whom was later killed while attempting to escape at Gibraltar. Although the Hudson airmen of Squadron 500 were furious at this botched U-boat "capture" (as they thought), they were rightly pleased when they learned the British had in custody the German "hero" who had sunk the *Barham.*†

When it learned of the first four of the five U-boat losses inside the Mediter-

---

* The white flag was probably raised to deter the killing and wounding of German crewmen and to invite rescue of the survivors. Doubtless the loyal, defiant, and resourceful von Tiesenhausen would have scuttled upon the arrival of a surface ship.

† Allied forces also sank three Italian submarines in the Mediterranean in the first two weeks of November: *Antonio Sciesa* by United States Army Air Forces aircraft, *Granito* by the British submarine *Saracen* (which had earlier sunk *U-335* near the Shetlands), and *Emo* by the British ASW trawler *Lord Nuffield.*

ranean, the OKM directed Dönitz to replace them with Type VIIs from the Atlantic force. Dönitz registered the familiar protests—the high risks for poor returns, the overcrowded bases—but in view of the perilous position of the *Afrika Korps,* he complied as swiftly as possible. The four VIIs sailed for the Mediterranean in the last days of November and early days of December. They were to slip through the Strait of Gibraltar during the new moon, from December 4 to 9. Only three of the four made it: Willy-Roderich Körner in *U-301,* Konstantin von Puttkamer in *U-443,* and Philipp Schüler in *U-602.** These additions were to put the Mediterranean U-boat force at twenty-three boats at the end of 1942, of which at least four (*U-73, U-97, U-458,* and *U-561*) were in the yards for extensive battle-damage repair.

On the whole, the U-boat opposition to Torch inside the Mediterranean was pitiful. It replicated the U-boat defense of Norway in April 1940.† It proved once again that submarines of that era were not suitable weapons systems for use against an alert, fast, heavily defended naval task force engaged in an amphibious assault. In Torch, Weichold and Kreisch compounded the problem by attempting to micromanage the U-boat defense by radio from various headquarters nearly one thousand miles from the scene. They shunted the U-boats back and forth willy-nilly, changing their orders or groups every few hours, or so it seemed. Given this, it is astonishing that Allied forces sank only five of the U-boats.

To recapitulate, the Mediterranean U-boat force in the month of November sank eight ships (including two destroyers) for 57,200 tons. In addition, they damaged two ships, the 1,200-ton British sloop *Stork* and the 7,500-ton British freighter *Lalande.* Apart from the destroyers, the big prize was the British liner/troopship *Viceroy of India.*‡

Harassed by the teeming Allied aircraft and naval task forces, the U-boat skippers usually could get only a brief glimpse of their targets and the results of their torpedo attacks. Doubtless, depth-charge explosions were often reported as torpedo hits. These and other factors led to many overclaims. The chief overclaimer was Albrecht Brandi in the newly arrived *Delphin* boat *U-617.* He reported hits on a battleship, a cruiser, a destroyer, and a 5,500-ton freighter, none of which was confirmed in the postwar accounting.

The Mediterranean U-boats went on to achieve several notable victories in December. The top honors went to two veterans, *U-565,* commanded by Wilhelm Franken, and *U-562,* commanded by Horst Hamm. Franken sank the 1,500-ton

---

* The other, *U-258,* aborted owing to the "illness" of the skipper, Wilhelm von Mässenhausen, who temporarily left the boat on returning to France. She was replaced by *U-257,* commanded by Heinz Rahe, who also aborted owing to the "illness" of the engineering officer and a serious leak.

† And the U.S. submarine defense of the Philippines in 1941 and Midway Island in 1942.

‡ Twenty-two Italian submarines deployed against Torch forces. These sank or polished off four ships at or near Bougie Bay: the 16,600-ton troopship *Narkunda,* the 13,482-ton troopship *Awatea,* the 2,400-ton antiaircraft cruiser *Tynwald,* and the 850-ton minesweeper *Algerine. Awatea* and *Tynwald* had previously been damaged by the *Luftwaffe,* Jürgen Rohwer wrote, and "settled to the bottom."

British destroyer *Partridge* and damaged the 16,300-ton British troopship *Cameronia.* The latter, sailing in convoy KMF 5, was polished off by the *Luftwaffe.* Hamm in *U-562* sank the 23,700-ton troopship *Strathallan,* the newest prewar Pacific and Orient liner, also sailing in convoy KMF 5. There were five thousand troops on board *Strathallan,* but the ship sank slowly and the loss of life, the official Admiralty historian wrote, was "small." Two newly arrived boats also had successes: *U-602,* commanded by thirty-one-year-old Philipp Schüler, sank the 1,500-ton British destroyer *Porcupine; U-443,* commanded by Konstantin von Puttkamer, sank the 1,000-ton British *Hunt*-class destroyer *Blean.**

The usual overclaims continued, notably those of Albrecht Brandi in *U-617.* He reported sinking four ships, including a 1,500-ton destroyer, and damage to two 7,000-ton freighters. His confirmed bag was only one 1,000-ton British fleet tug, *St. Issey,* sunk. Jürgen Könenkamp in *U-375* claimed sinking a 10,000-ton *London*-class cruiser, but only damage to the 2,650-ton cruiser/minelayer *Manxman* was confirmed. Von Puttkamer claimed sinking a 6,000-ton freighter, which proved to be the 1,600-ton British *Edencrag.*

American B-24 ASW Squadrons Deploy for Torch

Chafing under the restrictions imposed upon it, in September 1942, the U.S. Army Air Forces bluntly and officially informed the Navy's commander in chief, Admiral King, that the fragmentation of ASW aircraft by sea frontiers was not the best way to fight U-boats.† Therefore, it intended to reorganize planes of the First Bomber Command engaged in ASW into a single autonomous unit known as the First Antisubmarine Army Air Command. The command was to be controlled from Washington so that it could be promptly dispatched to areas of heavy enemy submarine activity wherever it might occur. In keeping with the earlier Army-Navy agreement, the paper declared disingenuously, the ASW aircraft "naturally will be under the operational control of the sea frontier concerned."

Choosing to ignore the obvious implication that the establishment of this command was the first step in an Army Air Forces bid to regain operational control of all land-based aircraft engaged in ASW, King did not object to the formation of the centralized command. However, he stressed that he still believed the "preferable method" of employing aircraft versus U-boats was the more or less permanent allocation of ASW aircraft to individual sea frontiers. In any case, King wrote, *he*

---

* In all of 1942, U-boats in the Mediterranean sank twelve warships, eleven of them British: the aircraft carrier *Eagle;* two light cruisers, *Naiad* and *Hermione;* five destroyers *(Gurkha, Jaguar, Martin, Partridge, Porcupine),* and three *Hunt*-class destroyers *(Blean, Grove, Heythrop).* The other warship was the Dutch destroyer *Isaac Sweers.*

† "Experience with the First Bomber Command in antisubmarine operations since March indicates that the effective employment of air forces against submarines demands rapid communication, mobility, *and freedom from the restrictions inherent in command systems based upon area responsibility"* (emphasis added).

would continue to exercise operational control over Army Air Forces planes through the various sea frontiers.

Henry H. (Hap) Arnold, the commander of the U.S. Army Air Forces, (USAAF), officially activated the Army Air Forces antisubmarine unit on October 15, 1942. Commanded by Westside T. Larson, it drew its cadres from First Bomber Command. Relieved of any further responsibility for strategic bombing, its singular mission was to attack hostile submarines "wherever they may be operating in opposition to our war effort." Its principal combat aircraft were to be the long-range B-24 Liberator and the medium-range B-25 Mitchell, both equipped with centimetric-wavelength radar and shallow-fused depth charges. It initiated combat in its new status on the United States East Coast and in the Gulf of Mexico with the 25th and 26th Wings, cooperatively merging operation rooms with those of the Navy in New York and Miami, respectively. Apparently unknown to Admiral King, Secretary of War Henry L. Stimson and Army Chief of Staff George C. Marshall approved an important provision in its charter, specifying that its elements could be transferred "to extracontinental areas on a detached service basis." That is, its units could be sent overseas to fight U-boats.

The upshot of this action by the Army Air Forces was the creation of *two* separate and distinct ASW air commands, the one controlled by the Navy through the sea frontiers and the other controlled by the Army Air Forces. The former primarily escorted convoys, the latter primarily patrolled offensively and secondarily escorted convoys. The official Air Force historian wrote that this arrangement was so loose that it

> left undefined the nature and extent of the operational control to be exercised by the Navy; and it left untouched the problem of duplication, the parallel development of two land-based air forces for the same task. Consequently, within this undefined area there remained ample room for continued debate and confusion, especially in view of the fact that differences also remained concerning the most effective way of employing long-range land-based aircraft in the antisubmarine campaign.

At the time of Torch, the Antisubmarine Command consisted of eighteen squadrons operating about two hundred aircraft, all based in the United States, the Caribbean, or Newfoundland. In eleven months of ASW patrolling, these aircraft had positively sunk three U-boats unassisted *(U-512, U-654, U-701)* and had shared credit with the U.S. Navy destroyer *Lansdowne* for another *(U-153),* and had wrecked the *U-505,* forcing her to abort a Caribbean patrol.

For Torch backup, Marshall directed Arnold to prepare to deploy to Morocco two ASW squadrons equipped with long-range B-24 Liberators. These big land-based aircraft were to fly hunter-killer missions and provide air cover for the all-American convoys UGS and GUS in the waters of the Azores-Madeira-Gibraltar triangle.

This little-known ASW deployment has been described recently by the historian Max Schoenfeld.* In its initial stages, it was not a model of perfection.

---

* *Stalking the U-boat* (1994).

Everything was done in a frenetic rush. The aircrews picked up the B-24s as they came off the factory production lines. They then flew them to Wright-Patterson Field in Dayton, Ohio, for installation of centimetric-wavelength ASV radar (SCR-517C) and other gear. They then flew onward to Langley Field, Virginia (near Norfolk), to stage for overseas deployment. In all, there were twenty-one B-24s, nine in the 1st ASW Squadron, commanded by Jack Roberts, and twelve in the 2nd ASW Squadron, commanded by Wilkie A. Rambo.

Westside Larson directed Roberts and Rambo to cross the Atlantic to North Africa via the "northern route": Newfoundland–Iceland–England–Morocco. The nine aircraft of Roberts's 1st ASW Squadron went first, assembling at the airfield in Gander, Newfoundland, from which the first three planes left on November 6. Despite hideous weather and other obstacles, all three arrived safely at a British airfield in the Hebrides, then flew on to another British airfield in southwest England, St. Eval.

Meanwhile, Prime Minister Churchill prevailed upon President Roosevelt to delay the deployment to Morocco of these two American squadrons in order to temporarily reinforce Coastal Command ASW operations with these twenty-one radar-equipped B-24s. In the interim, the five British ASW squadrons at Gibraltar and in North Africa* and U.S. Navy Catalina squadrons arriving in Morocco would provide the American UGS and GUS convoys with air cover.

The airfield at St. Eval was jammed. Coastal Command's Squadron 502, which based there, was in the process of reequipping from Whitleys to four-engine Halifaxes. Bomber Command's Operational Training Unit 10, which also based there, flew Whitleys on ASW missions before graduating the crews to frontline bomber units. In addition, Spitfires of British Photo Squadron 543, as well as other miscellaneous aircraft, were based at St. Eval.

Inasmuch as the diversion of the two American ASW squadrons to St. Eval had been hastily arranged, there was no American infrastructure. The American crews had to be billeted off-base, an inconvenient arrangement. They ate at the British mess, which they found "unbelievably bad," being oversupplied as it was with cabbage, brussels sprouts, and cauliflower. The England-based American Eighth Air Force had to lend the ASW squadrons mechanics and other ground personnel, pending the arrival of their own.

Nonetheless, on November 16—nine days after reaching St. Eval—Army Air Forces pilot Isaac J. Haviland flew the first American B-24 ASW mission over the Bay of Biscay.

Delayed by bad weather, the other six B-24s of ASW Squadron 1 finally got away from Newfoundland on November 23. These six ran into severe turbulence and icing conditions. Only two made it across the Atlantic. Three were forced back, and one disappeared without a trace. The two that reached Europe arrived at St. Eval on November 27, bringing the American ASW B-24 force to five. The

---

* Three squadrons of Hudsons (48, 233, 500), one squadron of Catalinas and Sunderlands (202), and one squadron (179) of Leigh Light–equipped Wellingtons.

other three B-24s of the squadron followed the Catalinas of the Navy's Squadron VP 92, going by way of the longer but friendlier skies of the "southern route": Florida–Trinidad–Brazil–Ascension Island–Accra–Morocco–England. One of the three was delayed in Morocco for want of a spare tire and did not reach St. Eval until January 5, 1943, two months after the first B-24s staged from Langley Field.

Based on the erratic experience of ASW Squadron 1, the dozen B-24s of Rambo's ASW Squadron 2 left Langley by the "southern route": December 10 to 24. After a stop in Trinidad, one plane disappeared, but the other eleven eventually reached St. Eval in January 1943. The ground personnel crossed the Atlantic on the *Queen Elizabeth* from New York to the Firth of Clyde, arriving on January 12. ASW Squadron 2 flew its first ASW mission on January 16, 1943.*

At the suggestion of Jack Roberts, on January 15 the two USAAF ASW squadrons at St. Eval were consolidated under his command. This single unit was designated the 1st Antisubmarine Group (Provisional), a detached unit of the 25th Antisubmarine Wing of the Army Air Forces Antisubmarine Command.† Alfred J. Hanlon, Jr., replaced Roberts as commander of Squadron 1; Isaac Haviland replaced Rambo as commander of Squadron 2. Rambo moved up to serve as Roberts's engineering and supply officer.

The somewhat tattered arrival of these two American squadrons raised the number of B-24s in ASW squadrons controlled by Coastal Command in January 1943 to almost fifty: twenty-four in British Squadrons 120 and 224, and ultimately twenty-four in USAAF Squadrons 1 and 2. In addition, at this time Coastal Command had twenty-four B-17 Flying Fortresses in British Squadrons 206 and 220 and twenty-four Halifaxes in British Squadrons 405 (on loan from Bomber Command) and 502, all told about ninety-six four-engine heavy-bomber types. These long-range and very-long-range land-based bombers significantly increased the offshore offensive and defensive capabilities of Coastal Command.

Further U-boat Diversions to Attack Torch Forces

At the time of the Torch landings, there were ninety-six German U-boats of the Atlantic force at sea, including three U-tankers. Fifty-one boats were operating to the north of the Bay of Biscay, forty-five to the south. Forty in the north were at or going to and from attack areas on the North Atlantic convoy run, four were in Canadian waters, one was planting a minefield off New York harbor, two were bound for the Mediterranean, and four new boats were outbound from Germany. Five in the south were bound for the Mediterranean. The other forty were at or in

* These ASW B-24s were stripped of standard gear required for high-altitude daylight bombing—armor, self-sealing fuel tanks, engine turbochargers, machine-gun turrets, and so on—and were fitted with four forward-firing 20mm cannons. A part of the bomb bay was modified to carry extra fuel, greatly extending the range but cutting the depth-charge payload to about sixteen.

† Confusingly, on March 1, 1943, the consolidated unit was redesignated USAAF 2037th Wing (Provisional) and finally, on June 21, 1943, 480th Group.

transit to or from attack areas off the coasts of Iberia, the Azores, West Africa, Trinidad, and South America.

In addition to the seven boats already on transfer to the Mediterranean in response to the urgent demands of Berlin, Dönitz rushed twenty-five more Atlantic boats to the Atlantic waters immediately *west* of the Strait of Gibraltar and Morocco. This brought the number of Atlantic U-boats reassigned to attack Torch forces to thirty-two, or about one-third of all the boats of that force at sea on November 8.

Of the twenty-five boats that rushed to the Strait of Gibraltar–Morocco area, thirteen were recently sailed boats assigned to the North Atlantic convoy run, nine were recently sailed boats operating in areas south of Biscay, and three were boats that had sailed from French bases on November 7. Six of the twenty-five were on maiden patrols from Germany; three were veteran boats from France with new skippers.

Inasmuch as thirteen of the remaining forty-one boats patrolling the North Atlantic run were low on fuel or torpedoes and were compelled to return to France by about November 20, the withdrawal of the thirteen boats newly assigned to that area to attack Torch forces crippled the U-boat war in the North Atlantic. Not counting the four new boats still outbound from Germany, Dönitz was left with only ten boats (two IXs, eight VIIs) to carry on the North Atlantic convoy war, the campaign he had deemed "decisive." Three of the VIIs *(U-454, U-606, U-624)* had first to refuel from the homebound *U-117,* a Type XB minelayer temporarily serving as a tanker. On November 9, another VII, *U-704,* commanded by Horst Kessler, diverted to chase the giant ocean liner *Queen Elizabeth,* westbound at high speed. Kessler got close enough to fire four torpedoes at the liner,* but soon thereafter he reported that he was forced to abort to France, owing to the severe illness of a crewman. The departure of *U-704* on November 11 left merely nine U-boats to carry on the U-boat war on the North Atlantic run, three of them temporarily out of action to refuel. Of this drastically depleted campaign, more later.

The first nine boats of the Atlantic force to reach the Strait of Gibraltar–Morocco area were designated group *Schlagetot* (Death Blow). Seven of the nine were Type IXs, ill suited for attacking the fast, heavily guarded Allied invasion convoys or for operating in those waters, which are very shallow out to twenty or thirty miles. Three of the IXs had only just been released from group *Streitaxt,* which had attacked convoy Sierra Leone 125 near the Azores. The other four IXs, recently sailed from French bases, were diverted from missions to distant waters. The two VIIs, *U-572* and *U-752,* both veteran boats, also had only just been released from group *Streitaxt.*

* Kessler claimed one hit on the *Queen Elizabeth* but failed to specify it was the ocean liner, not the battleship of the same name, thereby causing considerable confusion at U-boat headquarters. The hit could not be confirmed. Among the passengers on the liner was the senior codebreaker and bombe designer Alan Turing, who, as related, was embarked on an official visit to the United States.

The first boat of group *Schlagetot* to reach Moroccan waters was Heinz Hirsacker in *U-572.* He encountered intense surface and air ASW patrols. Even so, he had several opportunities to attack Allied shipping, but, according to his officers and crewmen, he cravenly shied off. Counting his balk at the Strait of Gibraltar in January 1942, this was the second time Hirsacker had failed the *Afrika Korps.* As a consequence, when the boat returned to France on November 22, Dönitz directed that Hirsacker be arrested and tried for cowardice. Found guilty, he was condemned to death. Reinhard Hardegen, the celebrated shipper of *U-123,* famous for his Drumbeat patrols, remembered that, in order to avoid the disgrace of a Nazi execution, close friends slipped a pistol into Hirsacker's jail cell and he committed suicide on April 24, 1943.

The other Type VII was the *U-752,* commanded by Karl-Ernst Schroeter, who had patrolled successfully in the Arctic, in American waters, and in the Freetown area. Hounded and harassed by Allied ASW forces before he could mount an attack, Schroeter incurred heavy depth-charge damage. Granted authority to withdraw to safer waters to make repairs, Schroeter headed west. After patching up the boat, he found—and chased—a high-speed convoy, but before he could vector in other boats or attack, it got away. Still leaking oil, Schroeter was again granted authority to withdraw to a "remote" area for repairs. Unable to stop the leak, he aborted and returned to France on December 3, having inflicted no damage on Torch forces.

The failure of the two Type VIIs of group *Schlagetot* left the anti-Torch job to the seven less suitable Type IXs. The three that came from the attack by group *Streitaxt* on convoy Sierra Leone 125 were *U-103, U-509,* and *U-510.* Commanded by the new skipper Gustav-Adolf Janssen, the aging IXB *U-103* had sunk one ship and was low on fuel. Commanded by the new skipper Werner Witte, the IXC *U-509* had sunk four ships and damaged three, but she still had plenty of fuel and eight torpedoes. The IXC *U-510,* commanded by Karl Neitzel, had damaged one ship and had plenty of fuel and nearly a full load of torpedoes. These three were joined near the Azores by the newly sailed, aging IXB *U-108,* commanded by a new skipper, Ralf-Reimar Wolfram, age thirty, who had hoped to join group *Streitaxt* for the attack on Sierra Leone 125 but had arrived too late.

Prior to the Torch crisis, Dönitz had planned for *U-509* to give *U-103* and *U-108* much of her surplus fuel and then come home. Then the replenished *U-103* and *U-108,* together with the *U-510,* were to rake southward as far as the Freetown area in search of other Sierra Leone convoys. Per plan, the *U-509* refueled *U-103* and *U-108,* but upon learning of the Torch landings, Dönitz redirected these three IXs as well as the *U-510* to Moroccan waters.

Werner Witte in *U-509* boldly closed on the Mehdia–Port Lyautey area on November 11, cruising in waters less than two hundred feet deep. For the next three days, he reported, he was hunted, depth-charged, and bombed by swarms of surface ships and aircraft. During one encounter with the enemy, Witte—and everyone else on board *U-509*—heard what was believed to be a mine cable scraping down the entire length of the hull; then a terrifying explosion close under the stern. In this or another encounter, depth charges cracked a fuel-oil tank and caused a leak, which forced Witte to pull out to the west, then abort to France, where he arrived—to great praise for his attacks on Sierra Leone 125—on November 26. He also had had no opportunity to attack Torch forces.

By November 13, two squadrons of U.S. Navy amphibious Catalinas, comprising twenty-two aircraft, had arrived in Morocco.* Squadron VP 73 (from Iceland) based at Port Lyautey; VP 92 (from the States) based at Casablanca. On November 14, Navy pilot A. S. Allbritton of VP 73 was the first to attack a U-boat. The results were uncertain.

Karl Neitzel in *U-510* patrolled off Mehdia–Port Lyautey as well. On November 15, he spotted a fast convoy of transports, escorted by "a battleship, a carrier, and ten destroyers." Neitzel bravely but futilely chased the battleship submerged, then in desperation fired three torpedoes at her from "extreme" range, his sole attack on Torch forces in Moroccan waters. All torpedoes missed. Later an aircraft bombed *U-510,* causing "a serious oil leak," forcing Neitzel to withdraw well to the west to attempt repairs. He did not inflict any damage on Torch forces either.

After taking on fuel from Witte in *U-509,* the new skippers Janssen in *U-103* and Wolfram in *U-108* closed on Morocco. Janssen reconnoitered Safi; Wolfram, Casablanca. Other than numerous "destroyers" and aircraft on ASW patrol, neither skipper saw a thing. On November 11, a destroyer detected and aggressively hunted Wolfram in *U-108,* dropping depth charges nearby. The explosions damaged his "diving gear," forcing him to withdraw well to the west for repairs. On November 16, when he reported the damage could be only "partly repaired," he was ordered to abort to France. He arrived there on November 26, having done nothing to repel the Torch landings.

Of the other three recently sailed Type IXs that were hurriedly diverted from missions in distant waters to group *Schlagetot,* yet another failed. This was the IXC *U-511,* commanded by Friedrich Steinhoff, the older, onetime merchant marine officer who had made one disappointing patrol to the Caribbean. By November 8, Steinhoff had refueled from the tanker *U-462* and was west of Freetown en route to Brazil. Directed to about-face and run for Morocco at the highest possible speed, Steinhoff reached Agadir in southern Morocco on November 15. There, he fell "ill" and *U-511* was forced to abort to France without having fired a shot. Steinhoff left the boat to become a staff officer in a combat flotilla, then later returned to Germany to commission a U-cruiser that was under conversion to a cargo-carrier.

The other two IXs recently sailed from France were the only boats of group *Schlagetot* to mount successful attacks on Allied forces in Moroccan waters, but one of these was lost.

The *U-173,* which had made one unsatisfactory patrol to the Caribbean under Heinz-Ehler Beucke, sailed from France on November 1 with a new skipper, Hans-Adolph Schweichel, age twenty-seven. On the night of November 11, Schweichel

* From November 1, 1942, U.S. Navy Patrol Wings, usually composed of a headquarters and three aircraft squadrons, were redesignated Fleet Air Wings or Fairwings. The one in Morocco, Fairwing 15, was commanded by George A. Seitz.

adroitly—and bravely—slipped through the ASW screen protecting the fifteen transports and cargo vessels anchored in Fedala. The transports had put all their troops ashore, but others were still laboriously unloading supplies and equipment. Schweichel shot first at the 9,400-ton U.S. Navy transport *Joseph Hewes.* The torpedo hit in Number 2 hold and the ship sank bow first, taking the lives of her captain, Robert McL. Smith, and several crewmen, plus "over 93 percent" of her cargo.

Schweichel next put his sights on the 10,600-ton U.S. Navy tanker *Winooski* and the new destroyer *Hambleton,* which was anchored nearby, awaiting clearance to refuel. Luckily for the Allies, the torpedo hit *Winooski* in a tank emptied of fuel and ballasted with seawater. Although the hole was twenty-five feet square, the crew was able to patch it temporarily, and by the following morning *Winooski* was back in business. The torpedo aimed at *Hambleton* hit in the forward engine room, killing or fatally injuring about twenty men. Remarkably, *Hambleton* remained afloat, and the redoubtable oceangoing tug *Cherokee* was able to tow her into Casablanca. There, Navy SeaBees ingeniously cut away forty feet of the damaged hull and patched the two halves together. Months later, *Hambleton,* escorted by another tug, sailed to Boston, where she was properly rebuilt in time to participate in Overlord.

Of the numerous radar-equipped American destroyers in or off Fedala that night, only one, the new *Bristol,* detected *U-173.* However, *Bristol*'s skipper, concerned that the contact might be a friendly landing craft, hesitated and turned on his searchlight to make a positive identification. That delay gave Schweichel time to dive *U-173* and avoid *Bristol*'s belated gunfire. Even though the water was very shallow and *Bristol* delivered two salvos of depth charges, Schweichel was able to slip away undamaged.

That same night, November 11, the *Ritterkreuz* holder Ernst Kals in *U-130,* who had sailed from France on October 29, approached Fedala. Rather than attempting to slip through the radar-equipped destroyer screen from seaward, Kals elected to hug the coastline submerged in sixty feet of water, barely enough to conceal his top hamper. Grazing bottom, Kals reached the anchorage undetected and while submerged in daylight on November 12, he boldly fired five torpedoes, four from the bow tubes and one from a stern tube. His torpedoes hit and sank three large American transports: the 9,400-ton *Edward Rutledge,* the 12,600-ton *Tasker H. Bliss,* and the 12,500-ton *Hugh L. Scott.* All three ships (for 34,400 tons) sank. About 115 men of the 1,607 crew and others on the three ships were lost. *Rutledge* also lost "97 percent" of her Army supplies and equipment; *Bliss* and *Scott,* "about 65 percent" each. Undetected, Kals slipped away submerged, still hugging the coastline.

In view of the loss of four valuable transports at Fedala, the Allies shifted most of the unloading to Casablanca. On November 13, five big ships from Fedala entered Casablanca. Two days later the other six big ships from Fedala and about five from Mehdia–Port Lyautey got under way for Casablanca. Early that morning off Casablanca, Schweichel in *U-173* intercepted and torpedoed one of the American ships, the 8,100-ton *Electra.* Although badly holed, the ship managed to beach near Casablanca and was later salvaged and returned to service.

The next day, November 16, three American destroyers, *Quick, Swanson,* and *Woolsey,* patrolled off Casablanca. At about noon, *Woolsey* reported a good sonar contact close aboard and immediately fired two depth charges by eye. Her target was *U-173.* In two more carefully executed follow-up attacks, *Woolsey* dropped eight more depth charges, bringing up oil and air bubbles. She then had to break off to refuel in Casablanca, leaving her quarry to *Swanson* and *Quick,* both of which were highly skeptical about this "contact." Nonetheless, *Swanson* fired two depth-charge salvos at the rising bubbles and *Quick* let go a special single charge, set to explode on the bottom. If *U-173* was not already fatally holed, these attacks destroyed her. There were no survivors.

The second wave of sixteen U-boats of the Atlantic force congregated in the dangerously confined and shallow waters immediately west of the Strait of Gibraltar. The aim was to create a "wall" to block completely all Allied ship traffic going in and out of the strait. It was an impossible mission. In anticipation of a strong U-boat assault, the Allies had saturated that area with radar-equipped aircraft and surface ships. One U-boat skipper reported that Allied ASW measures were so intense that he was forced to remain submerged twenty hours a day and could not properly air the boat and charge batteries.

These sixteen boats included three that had sailed directly from France on November 7: two Type IXs and one Type VII. All three tangled with Allied forces.

The first to contact the enemy was Werner Henke in the Type IXC *U-515,* who had made an outstanding maiden patrol to the Caribbean. On the night of November 12, while about 180 miles due west of the Strait of Gibraltar, Henke spotted what he believed to be two big British cruisers, escorted by three fleet destroyers. In actuality, it was one British cruiser, *Vindictive,* and the big British destroyer tender *Hecla,* escorted by two destroyers. One of the destroyers, *Venomous,* which had Type 271 centimetric-wavelength radar, got a contact on *U-515* at four thousand yards but inexplicably failed to inform the other vessels.

After an arduous five-hour chase at full speed, Henke gained a good shooting position. He fired a full bow salvo at the "*Birmingham*-class cruiser," but two of the four torpedoes went astray. The cruiser *Vindictive* saw the wakes of these or the other two torpedoes and zigged to avoid. She had time to warn the destroyer tender *Hecla,* but, inexplicably, she failed to do so. As a result, two torpedoes slammed into *Hecla* but did not sink her. *Vindictive* fled the area; the destroyers *Venomous* and *Marne* commenced a U-boat hunt, but *Marne* soon broke off to stand by *Hecla.* Closing in, Henke fired two more torpedoes at *Hecla.* One hit her with a violent explosion; the other hit *Marne* and blew off her stern. *Hecla* sank, but *Marne* remained afloat. Of the 847 men on *Hecla,* 279 perished.

The destroyer *Venomous* gave up her U-boat hunt and took *Marne* in tow, stern first. Mistaking *Marne* for the "cruiser" he had been attempting to sink, Henke closed for yet another attack. When *Venomous* reported a radar contact, both destroyers opened up on *U-515* with main batteries. *Venomous* then cut the towline and chased *U-515* under, dropping five depth charges. The Admiralty later concluded that *Venomous*'s attack doubtless saved *Marne.* Inasmuch as the depth charges knocked out her sonar, *Venomous* again broke off the U-boat hunt and commenced rescuing the survivors of *Hecla.* Henke, meanwhile, mounted yet another attack, firing two torpedoes at *Venomous,* which evaded and speeded up to ram *U-515.* Henke dived to avoid *Venomous,* which dropped ten depth charges. He then slipped away in deep water. Since *Venomous* was low on fuel, a corvette in the area, *Jonquil,* took over the escort of *Marne. Venomous* went on to Casablanca with *Hecla*'s 568 survivors; *Marne* was eventually towed to Gibraltar.

The next boat of the second wave to make contact with the enemy was the new Type VII *U-413,* commanded by Gustav Poel, who was still on his maiden patrol from Kiel. While southbound on November 14, he ran into a northbound convoy, MK 1, consisting of British troopships returning from the Mediterranean to the British Isles with the new "jeep" carriers *Biter* and *Dasher* in company. In his first attack as captain, Poel hit and sank the valuable 20,000-ton troopship *Warwick Castle.*

In the early hours of November 14, several boats of the second wave found another homebound British convoy, Mediterranean–United Kingdom Fast Number 1 (MKF 1), about eighty miles due west of Gibraltar Strait. It was composed of eight big, fast transports and cargo vessels, escorted by five British destroyers, including the old (1918) but modernized *Wrestler.* The new "jeep" carrier *Avenger* and the small, old carrier *Argus,* both returning to England, sailed in company.

The British destroyer *Wrestler* picked up a surfaced U-boat on radar, five miles ahead. *Wrestler* raced in to ram, but at seven hundred yards, she aborted the attempt and the U-boat crash-dived, merely one hundred yards ahead. *Wrestler* fired fourteen depth charges "by eye" at the swirls and, while the convoy made an emergency turn, she lagged behind to hunt the U-boat. The official Admiralty assessment was "U-boat probably sunk," and, in fact, *Wrestler* had destroyed *U-98,* commanded by a new skipper, Kurt Eichmann, age twenty-five, who had sailed from France on October 22. There were no survivors.*

When the convoy made its belated emergency turn to starboard, the maneuver greatly helped another U-boat. This was the Type IXC *U-155,* commanded by the *Ritterkreuz* holder Adolf-Cornelius Piening, who had sailed from France on November 7. Upon making contact, Piening fired a full bow salvo into the dense convoy formation. His torpedoes blew up and sank the 13,800-ton "jeep" carrier *Avenger* and the 11,300-ton British troop transport *Ettrick,* and damaged the 6,700-ton U.S. Navy cargo ship *Almaak.* The loss of life on the "jeep" carrier *Avenger* was horrific. Only twelve of the crew were rescued. The British withheld news of her loss.†

---

* The Admiralty initially credited the kill of *U-98* to a Hudson. This wrong assessment led to confusion and to further wrong assessments and misplaced kill credits at this time. To avoid further confusion the Admiralty errors are not detailed here.

† The seven other "jeep" and light carriers survived Torch but were not immediately available for Atlantic convoy escort as originally intended. The Admiralty was not satisfied with the aircraft fuel-handling systems on the American-built "jeep" carriers, to say nothing of the ill-performing main-propulsion plants. Hence, upon arrival in the British Isles, *Archer, Biter,* and *Dasher* went into shipyards for extensive modification, or "anglicization." Ironically, *Dasher*'s modified fuel-handling system blew

Nearby was the VIIC *U-411,* which had left France on November 7, commanded by a new skipper, Johann Spindlegger, age twenty-seven. A Hudson of Squadron 500, based at Gibraltar and piloted by another Ensor of the unit, John B., spotted *U-411* on the surface about five miles distant. From an altitude of fifty feet, John Ensor dropped four depth charges on the boat, which crash-dived. She was never heard from again. Since the results of this attack were not known at the time, the Admiralty wrongly credited others for sinking *U-411,* but in recent years, it gave the kill to Ensor and his crew.

Only two other boats of the second wave—both new Type VIIs—had any success. On November 16, Adolf Oelrich in *U-92,* who had made one luckless North Atlantic patrol, sank the 7,700-ton British freighter *Clan Mactaggart.* On November 20, Kurt Nölke, age twenty-eight, in *U-263,* still on his maiden voyage from Kiel, sank two heavily laden freighters from Gibraltar-bound convoy KR-S 3: the 7,200-ton Norwegian *Prins Harald* and the 5,100-ton British *Grangepark.*

Throughout the deployment of these U-boats directly west of Gibraltar, Allied ASW measures—particularly air patrols—remained intense. In addition to the loss of the Type VIIs *U-98* and *U-411,* five boats incurred such severe damage that they were forced to abort.

- On November 15, Allied aircraft and surface ships teamed up on the Type VIID (minelayer) *U-218,* commanded by Richard Becker, who was attempting to sink a British destroyer. The damage inflicted was so great that Becker was forced to abort to France, concluding a fruitless patrol of twenty-seven days.
- On November 17, the veteran Type VII *U-566,* commanded by Gerhard Remus, which had been severely damaged in August, again incurred heavy damage. This time her nemesis was a Hudson of British Squadron 233, piloted by a sergeant, Eric Harold Smith. As a result of the air attack, *U-566* developed an irreparable oil leak that forced Remus to abort to France. Repairs kept the boat out of action for over two months.
- On November 18, a Hudson of British Squadron 608, piloted by J.B.R. Petrie, hit the new Type VII *U-613,* commanded by Helmut Köppe, age thirty-three, still on her maiden patrol from Kiel. The explosion severely damaged the boat. Dönitz directed four nearby U-boats to assist *U-613,* including the aborting IXC *U-509.* Unable to repair the damage, Köppe too was forced to abort to France, escorted by the *U-509.* Repairs kept the boat out of action for forty-four days.
- On November 19, a Hudson of British Squadron 608, piloted by A. F. Wilcox, found the new Type VII *U-413,* commanded by Gustav Poel, who was chasing another convoy. Poel crash-dived, but Wilcox dropped four depth charges on the swirl. These destroyed Poel's periscopes, forcing him to abort to France, where he received high praise for his earlier sinking of the British troopship *Warwick Castle.*

---

up and sank the carrier in the Firth of Clyde on March 27, 1943. The two survivors, *Archer* and *Biter,* finally began convoy escort in April 1943. Three of the four American semi-"jeeps," *Sangamon, Suwannee,* and *Chenango* (heavily damaged in a storm on the homeward voyage), went from Torch to the States to the Pacific. The fourth, *Santee,* remained in the Atlantic Fleet for ASW missions, but she, too, had first to undergo refit, modernization, and aircrew training, which required about six months.

• The next day, November 20, the new Type VII *U-263,* commanded by Kurt Nölke, reported that while attempting to attack two freighters, escorts pounced on the boat, dropping 119 depth charges during a prolonged hunt. The damage was so severe that Nölke was forced to abort to France.

Four days later, November 24, a Hudson of British Squadron 233, piloted by the sergeant Eric Smith, who had damaged *U-566* a week earlier, attacked the aborting *U-263* with four depth charges. These explosions caused so much additional damage that Nölke could not dive. As a result, Dönitz proposed that the boat put into El Ferrol, Spain, for internment. However, after receiving assistance from the aborting IXC *U-511* and air cover from JU-88s, Nölke bypassed El Ferrol and limped into La Pallice, arriving on November 29. This wrecked boat was in repair and modification for thirteen months.

Five other boats incurred damage but remained on patrol.

• On November 19, another aircraft hit the *U-91,* commanded by Heinz Walkerling, who had sunk the Canadian destroyer *Ottawa* on his prior patrol. He reported the attack, adding that only one of his torpedoes was in firing condition. Nonetheless, Dönitz told him to withdraw to the west, repair damage, and continue the patrol as a lookout.

• On November 21, the new Type IXC *U-519,* commanded by Günter Eppen, age thirty, still on her maiden patrol from Germany, was damaged by ASW forces during a convoy battle. Eppen pulled out to the west and repaired the damage.

• That same day, the Type VII *U-564,* made famous by Reinhard Suhren but commanded by a new skipper, Hans Fiedler, age twenty-eight, also incurred damage during a convoy battle. Fiedler also ran west to repair damage.

• In the period from November 22 to 25, the Type VII *U-92,* commanded by Adolf Oelrich, who had sunk the *Clan Mactaggart,* was hit once by surface ships and twice by Catalinas. He too repaired damage.

• On November 24, the new Type IXC40 *U-185,* commanded by August Maus, still on her maiden patrol from Kiel, incurred "heavy damage" from an unidentified aircraft. Maus withdrew to the southwest to a rendezvous with the Type XB minelayer *U-118,* temporarily pressed into service as a U-tanker for the boats operating off the Strait of Gibraltar and Morocco. With assistance from *U-118,* commanded by Werner Czygan, Maus made repairs.

The twenty-five U-boats of the Atlantic force that rushed to the areas just west of the Strait of Gibraltar and Morocco during the first two weeks of Torch failed to impede that operation to any significant degree. They sank eleven ships for 119,000 tons and damaged five ships for 29,000 tons. The *Ritterkreuz* holder Ernst Kals in the Type IXB *U-130,* who slipped into the Fedala anchorage to sink three big American transports for 34,407 tons, achieved the greatest tonnage successes. Upon his return to France, he was promoted to command Combat Flotilla 2. The *Ritterkreuz* holder Adolf-Cornelius Piening in the Type IXC *U-155,* who sank the British "jeep" carrier *Avenger* and a big British transport for 25,000 tons, ran second in tonnage, but the sinking of *Avenger* was concealed from the Germans.

In return for eleven Allied ships sunk and five damaged, Dönitz had lost three U-boats of the Atlantic force *(U-98, U-173, U-411)* with all hands. This was a ruinous "exchange rate" of 3.6 ships sunk for each U-boat lost. Ten other boats of the Atlantic force were forced to abort, eight with battle damage,* and two with serious skipper problems *(U-511, U-572).* Five other boats sustained battle damage but were able to make repairs and continue patrols.†

For Dönitz and the U-boat staff, the losses of and damage to the U-boat force as a result of Torch were devastating and eerily reminiscent of the heavy losses and damage during the same period the year before in the same areas.‡ When the five boats lost *inside* the Mediterranean were added to those lost *outside,* the grim total was eight.

Even before a full reckoning had been made, on November 18 Dönitz registered his dismay and displeasure in his daily war diary, which circulated in the highest levels in Berlin. The entry was similar in tone and substance to his earlier repeated objections to operating Type VII and Type IX U-boats so close to the Strait of Gibraltar where Allied airpower was so formidable—and, with Northwest Africa now available for bases, it was bound to grow even greater in strength. The boats had achieved little in the anti-Torch operations, and the prospects for the future were dim.

Moreover, to maintain twenty U-boats in the Atlantic west of Gibraltar, as Berlin continued to insist, Dönitz would have to earmark thirty boats of the Atlantic force for that purpose, to allow for travel time to and from the area. And besides that, if the U-boat force inside the Mediterranean was to be kept at a level of twenty-four Type VIIs, as Berlin also insisted, Dönitz would have to transfer yet another six or eight boats there, further diluting the Atlantic force, which, of course, he believed, could achieve much greater success on the "decisive" North Atlantic run.

There was no doubt about it: Just as it had fully resumed, the U-boat campaign on the North Atlantic run had been gutted by the wholesale transfer of U-boats to the anti-Torch operations in November. However, the larger truth was that the existing Type VIIs and IXs were too obsolescent and lacking in electronics to properly wage submarine warfare in any area where the Allies had established even the most modest defenses. The resumption of full-scale U-boat warfare by groups (or "wolf packs") on the North Atlantic run might well send more Allied tonnage to the bottom with less risk to the German submariners, but not enough tonnage to appreciably affect the course of the war. The Germans had already lost the contest at sea, but it was not in Dönitz's nature to concede defeat or grant that there was no hope, no victory just over the horizon.

Berlin was not yet ready to concede the approaches to Gibraltar. Hence, a dozen boats remained on patrol in that area through the month of December. To minimize

* *U-108, U-218, U-263, U-413, U-509, U-566, U-613, U-752.*

† *U-91, U-92, U-185, U-519, U-564.*

‡ See Volume I, pp. 395–404.

losses and battle damage, Dönitz was granted authority to move the boats westward, beyond range of the Hudsons and Wellingtons. Dönitz designated the remaining boats group *Westwall.* They achieved little.

Werner Henke in *U-515* took the prize. On the night of December 7–8, he came upon the 18,700-ton British troopship *Ceramic,* an ocean liner launched in 1913. Bound for Cape Town and beyond, she had left Liverpool with convoy Outbound North 149 on November 23, peeled off in mid-Atlantic with six other ships, and headed south. There were 656 persons on board *Ceramic,* including ninety-two women and children. After an eight-hour chase, Henke caught up and fired five torpedoes, sending *Ceramic* to the bottom. The survivors launched lifeboats and rafts, but a violent and prolonged storm soon arose. Henke took one prisoner, a British soldier, Eric Munday, but the other 655 persons perished.* Added to past claims and overclaims, Henke earned a *Ritterkreuz,* the only such honor awarded to Atlantic force skippers contesting Torch.†

Three other *Westwall* Type IX boats came upon the other southbound ships that had peeled off from Outbound North 149.

- *Ritterkreuz* holder Adolf-Cornelius Piening in the IXC *U-155* sank the 8,500-ton Dutch vessel *Serooskerk.* This raised Piening's bag to an impressive three ships sunk for 33,500 tons, but he and Dönitz were unaware that he had sunk the 13,800-ton "jeep" carrier *Avenger.*
- The new skipper of the IXB *U-103,* Gustav-Adolph Janssen, who had had no luck in Moroccan waters, sank the 5,000-ton British freighter *Henry Stanley* and damaged another, the 14,000-ton *Hororata.*‡ Janssen captured the captain of *Henry Stanley,* Richard Jones, but the other seventy-one persons on the ship perished.
- August Maus in the new IXC40 *U-185* sank the 5,500-ton British freighter *Peter Maersk.*

These additional successes raised the bag of the original twenty-five Atlantic boats deployed to oppose Torch forces to fifteen ships sunk for 156,700 tons plus six damaged for about 43,000 tons.

In a postscript to these operations, Dönitz sent a task force of two Type VIIs into Moroccan waters to attack a special Allied convoy, reported to be composed of thirty to forty ships. The boats were the veteran *U-432,* commanded by *Ritterkreuz* holder Heinz-Otto Schultze, and the *U-618,* commanded by Kurt Baberg, a rising star who had sunk two freighters on his maiden Atlantic patrol. Arriving in December, both boats encountered intense ASW measures. As a result, Baberg sank nothing; Schultze sank one 300-ton French trawler. Upon his return to France, Schultze left the *U-432* and went to Germany to commission a new IXD2 U-cruiser.

Counting all forces operating inside and outside the Mediterranean, the Ger-

---

* Counting the 279 persons lost on the destroyer tender *Hecla* and those on the damaged destroyer *Marne,* Henke had caused the deaths of about one thousand persons on this single anti-Torch patrol.

† At the time of the award, his confirmed score was ten ships for 71,677 tons.

‡ Believing *Hororata* had run into the island of Flores in the Azores for repairs, Dönitz directed Walter Schug in the Type VIIB *U-86* to secretly cut her mooring chains and when she drifted into international waters, sink her. However, Schug could not find *Hororata,* and the scheme was abandoned.

mans deployed about fifty U-boats against Torch forces. The Italians contributed another twenty-two boats, for a total of seventy-two Axis submarines. To about December 15, all the German U-boats had sunk twenty-four ships for 218,000 tons and damaged eight for 51,600 tons. Four different Italian submarines and Axis aircraft in the Mediterranean sank four ships for 33,300 tons and damaged the 5,500-ton British light cruiser *Argonaut.**

In order to maintain group *Westwall* at twelve boats, Dönitz had to further deplete the North Atlantic force. He attached the recently sailed Type VIIs *U-563, U-615,* and *U-706,* and temporarily attached two Type IXs returning from long patrols to Canada, Hermann Rasch in *U-106* and Heinrich Schäfer in *U-183.* Since five of the original boats, including *U-91,* as well as the newly attached *U-183,* were low on fuel, he had to divert another tanker, *U-463,* to the area, replacing the provisional XB (minelayer) *U-118.* During these operations the Type VII *U-91* was again hit by Allied aircraft and so "badly damaged" she "could not dive." Piening in *U-155* came to her rescue, giving her spare parts and sufficient fuel to reach France. Finally—on December 23—the OKM conceded that group *Westwall* was not sufficiently rewarding and allowed Dönitz to disband it.

Dönitz logged with obvious relief that the OKM concession would free the Atlantic U-boat force of "a rather thankless task." He sent two of the recently sailed VIIs, *U-563* and *U-706,* to groups on the North Atlantic run. All others returned to France without further loss or mishap.

The senior American strategists were never quite pleased with Torch. The failure of the British-led forces in Algiers to promptly move east and seize Tunisia resulted in a prolonged and miserable struggle for that strategic territory and to a commensurate delay in the destruction of the *Afrika Korps.* At the insistence of Prime Minister Churchill, the Allies were to prolong operations in the Mediterranean even further by invasions of Sicily and southern Italy, all of which the impatient Americans viewed as peripheral and diversionary to the main task of defeating Germany, and to the secondary task of defeating Japan.

In the view of Dönitz, the permanent diversion of the ten U-boats to the Mediterranean in the fall of 1942, when the Allies were not yet overwhelmingly strong in ASW forces, robbed the U-boat arm of an opportunity to deliver a decisive blow to the vital North Atlantic convoys at the least risk. In all, by the end of 1942, Berlin had sent sixty Type VII U-boats to the Mediterranean. Forty-two of these got through the Strait of Gibraltar, none ever to return.†

The Return of U-boats to the North Atlantic Run

The redeployment of U-boats of the Atlantic force to Morocco and west of the Strait of Gibraltar left only nine boats (two IXs, seven VIIs) in the North Atlantic

---

* In addition, on the night of December 11–12, Italian frogmen swimming from the submarine *Ambra* with attachable, timed explosives, sank one 1,500-ton freighter and damaged three others for 18,800 tons in Algiers harbor.

† See Volume I, Appendix 6 and Volume II, Appendix 7.

on November 10. Three of the VIIs refueled from the departing XB (minelayer) *U-117,* temporarily serving as a tanker. Since this was not really sufficient force with which to attack a convoy, the boats were given freedom to search for and sink single ships, but none found any.

The paucity of boats was gradually overcome by several means. First, the tanker *U-460,* commanded by Ebe Schnoor, sailed from France at top speed to replenish those boats already in the area that still had a good supply of torpedoes. Second, four new boats outbound from Kiel (one IX, three VIIs) were integrated with the others. Third, three VIIs *(U-262, U-611, U-663)* that had been briefly halted for the defense of Norway, were released from that task to the North Atlantic. By November 15, the North Atlantic force, including those boats refueling or waiting to refuel, had increased to sixteen boats (three IXs, thirteen VIIs), enough to form one group, *Kreuzotter* (Viper).

On that day, Klaus Bargsten in the Type IXC *U-521,* still on his maiden patrol from Kiel, found a convoy. It was the relatively small Outbound North (Slow) 144, composed of thirty-three ships, guarded by British Escort Group B-6 less its two destroyers, *Fame* and *Viscount,* both damaged when they had rammed U-boats on the earlier eastbound voyage with Slow Convoy 104. Absent these, the escort was quite weak: five corvettes—one British, *Vervain,* and four Norwegian. Nominally British, the group was commanded by the Norwegian C. A. Monsen in *Potentilla.* All ships had Type 271 centimetric-wavelength radar, and the convoy-rescue ship *Perth* had Huff Duff.

Bargsten in *U-521* reported and shadowed the convoy, but his vector signal was defective and the other boats could not home on him. Granted permission to attack, Bargsten fired a full salvo of six torpedoes, but all missed.

Bargsten hung on for the next twenty-four hours, repaired his vector signal, and brought up some other boats. After dark on November 17, three of these—all on maiden patrols—attacked. The first was *U-262,* one of the Type VIIs released from Norway, commanded by Heinz Franke, age twenty-six. He shot three torpedoes, but all missed. Second was Hartwig Looks, age twenty-five, in *U-264,* a new Type VII from Kiel, who sank a 6,700-ton Greek freighter. Third was Günther Dangschat, age twenty-seven, in the new Type IXC40 from Kiel, *U-184,* who claimed sinking two ships and probably a third, but who actually sank only one 3,200-ton freighter.

For the next six hours a furious battle ensued. Using Type 271 radar to advantage, the five corvettes, notably the Norwegians in *Potentilla, Rose,* and *Montbretia,* held the gathering U-boats at bay or drove them under and delivered depth-charge attacks. It is possible that one of these attacks caught and destroyed the green Type IXC40 *U-184,* with the loss of all hands, ten days into her first patrol.* Several other U-boats also reported persistent and heavy depth-charge attacks.

---

* The Norwegian corvette *Potentilla* was credited with the kill on November 20, but in a postwar analysis, the Admiralty concluded that that assessment was "doubtful." During the chaotic action on the night of November 17–18, any of the several corvettes could have done the deed. The Norwegians saw—and reported—oil and debris that night, but no corvette had time to recover the debris to substantiate a kill.

In the early hours of November 18, ten boats shot at the convoy. Ulrich von Soden-Fraunhofen, age twenty-nine, in the new Type VII *U-624,* sank the 5,300-ton British tanker *President Sergent* and the 4,700-ton American freighter *Parismina,* and damaged the 5,400-ton American freighter *Yaka.* Herbert Schneider, age twenty-seven, in the new Type IXC *U-522,* put *Yaka* under with a finishing shot. Heinz Franke in the *U-262* hit and sank the Norwegian corvette *Montbretia,* which plowed under at full speed. Twenty-nine of the crew were rescued, but her captain and forty-six others could not be found. Klaus Bargsten in *U-521;* Hans-Karl Kosbadt, age twenty-four, in the new VII *U-224;* Hartwig Looks in the new VII *U-264;* Horst Kremser, age twenty-five, in the new VII *U-383;* Burkhard Hackländer in the veteran VII *U-454;* and Alfred Manhardt von Mannstein in another veteran VII, *U-753,* all shot torpedoes but missed.

The four remaining corvettes—one British, three Norwegian—closed in tight on the convoy and attacked the U-boats with astonishing courage, persistence, and skill, taking advantage of radar and a bright moon. On November 19, Allied authorities ordered two destroyers, the British *Firedrake* and the American four-stack *Badger,* to reinforce the escort, but by that time the U-boats had fallen away. On November 20, a local coastal Canadian group took over Outbound North (Slow) 144 and escorted the convoy onward to New York.

Based on flash reports from the boats, Dönitz was well satisfied with the attack on Outbound North (Slow) 144. They claimed to have sunk eighteen ships for 82,800 tons (including two destroyers and a corvette) and to have damaged six other ships. The confirmed score was about one-third of the claims: five ships (including one tanker) for 25,400 tons sunk plus the corvette *Montbretia.* Allied authorities again "warmly congratulated" Norwegian escort commander Monsen in *Potentilla* for "magnificent" aggressiveness, which prevented what could have been a major convoy disaster.

Following this action, the nine boats that had constituted the entire North Atlantic force on November 10 and one of the recently joined, *U-264,* began the return to France. About six of the nine, as well as several boats returning from patrols to the Americas, were to refuel from Schnoor's *U-460* in a grid about five hundred miles northwest of the Azores. As related, a massive, prolonged storm swept into this area, preventing the refueling, Dönitz logged, for six days. Some of the boats ran completely out of fuel and drifted helplessly, unable even to charge batteries for lighting and cooking. What was even more frustrating, Dönitz added, was that there were indications from *B-dienst* that a section of a large westbound convoy dispersed nearby. Had the boats been able to refuel earlier as scheduled, they would have been ready to attack these unescorted targets.

Unaware that the *U-184* had been lost, Dönitz formed a new, small group, *Drachen* (Dragon), comprised of (as he thought) the three boats recently transferred from Norway, plus two new ones from Kiel. He positioned these on a line running southeast from Greenland and alerted them to expect an eastbound Slow Convoy. But *Drachen* did not find this, or any other convoy. One of the recently arrived boats from Norway, Heinz Franke's *U-262,* which had sunk the corvette *Montbre-*

tia in convoy Outbound North (Slow) 144, sank a lone 7,200-ton British Liberty ship, *Ocean Crusade,* with its last torpedoes and went home, leaving *Drachen* with merely four boats. Another boat recently transferred from Norway, *U-663,* commanded by Heinrich Schmid, sank the 5,200-ton British freighter *Barberrys.* When Dönitz became aware that *Drachen* had been reduced to four boats, he dissolved it and assigned the boats to new groups forming in the North Atlantic.

Drastically reduced by anti-Torch redeployments, after November 5 the U-boat groups operating on the North Atlantic run mounted telling attacks on only one of the fifteen convoys* comprising about seven hundred merchant ships that sailed east and west across the Atlantic during that month: Outbound North (Slow) 144. The U-boats sank six ships for 26,300 tons from that convoy (including the corvette *Montbretia*). In addition, U-boats sank one ship from each of three other convoys that sailed in November (Slow 109, Outbound North 143 and 145) and five loners, a total of eight other ships for 57,500 tons.† That brought the bag for November on this vital lifeline to twenty-nine ships for about 166,660 tons.‡ Sixteen of these losses were loaded, eastbound ships in convoy. Two U-boats were lost with all hands on the North Atlantic run in November: the Type VII *U-132* and the Type IX *U-184.*

Both sides declared November 1942 to be the high-water mark for Axis submarines. During the war, Dönitz claimed that all Axis submarines in all waters sank about 900,000 tons of Allied shipping. The Admiralty's postwar analysis put the merchant-ship losses to Axis submarines at 119 for 729,160 tons.§ As shown, twenty-nine were sunk on the North Atlantic run; ninety were sunk in waters elsewhere.

Some accounts of the Battle of the Atlantic imply that because of the heavy shipping losses incurred in November, Churchill and Pound sacked Percy Noble, the commander of Western Approaches. He was replaced on November 17 by Max Kennedy Horton, who had commanded the British submarine force for almost three years. Noble, in turn, was appointed chief of the Admiralty delegation in Washington, a position of the utmost importance and sensitivity.

In his history of the British Royal Navy in World War II,# Correlli Barnett wrote that Admiral

> Noble, an elegant, courteous, charming man, lacked aggressive drive either in regard to his own command or London's naval and political hierarchies. Horton could hardly have stood in greater contrast. Himself a veteran submariner . . . he could match Dönitz in first-hand understanding of U-boat operations—and the psy-

---

* Halifax 213 to 216; Slow 108 to 110; Outbound North (Fast and Slow) 142 to 149.

† The ship in Slow Convoy 109, the 9,100-ton American tanker *Brilliant,* was only damaged. However, she sank under tow on December 25, 1943, so she is shown as a loss in November.

‡ Including, as related, fifteen ships for 82,800 tons from Slow Convoy 107, which sailed in late October; they were sunk in November.

§ In his analysis, Jürgen Rohwer put the loss from Axis submarines at 131 Allied ships for 817,385 tons, of which 120 for 737,675 tons were accounted for by German U-boats. The tables in Tarrant (1989), which are utilized in this account, put the figure for Axis submarines at 126 ships for 802,160 tons.

\# *Engage the Enemy More Closely* (1991).

LOSSES OF TROOPSHIPS AND OTHER LARGE NON-TANKER BRITISH-CONTROLLED VESSELS

SEPTEMBER–DECEMBER 1942[1]

In November 1942, Axis submarines sunk more Allied tonnage than in any other month in the war: 802,160. This figure was achieved, in part, by the sinking of an unusual number of large British ships, most of them troopships sailing independently or in convoys supporting Torch, the Allied invasion of northwest Africa. The list below shows British ships of about 10,000 gross tons or more lost in the fall of 1942, plus two troopships, *Mendoza* and *Nova Scotia,* sunk in the Indian Ocean. Unassisted Axis submarines accounted for twenty-one of the ships; unassisted Axis aircraft in the Mediterranean got four (*Cathay, Karanja, Narkunda, Scythia*). Axis submarines and aircraft in the Mediterranean jointly destroyed two (*Awatea, Cameronia*). Note that in November alone the Axis accounted for over 208,000 gross tons of large vessels but none on the North Atlantic run. ("T" signifies troopship.)

DATE	SHIP	TONNAGE	AREA	AIRCRAFT (AC) OR U-BOAT
SEPTEMBER:				
9	*Tuscan Star*	11,449	South Atlantic	*U-109*
12	*Laconia* (T)	19,695	South Atlantic	*U-156*
Total:	2	31,144		
OCTOBER:				
6	*Andalucia Star*	14,943	Freetown	*U-107*
9	*Oronsay* (T)	20,043	Freetown	*Archimede*
10	*Duchess of Atholl* (T)	20,119	South Atlantic	*U-178*
10	*Orcades* (T)	23,456	Cape Town	*U-172*
23	*Empire Star*	12,656	North Atlantic	*U-615*
29	*Abosso* (T)	11,330	North Atlantic	*U-575*
Total:	6	102,547		
NOVEMBER:				
1	*Mendoza* (T)	8,233	Indian Ocean	*U-178*
2	*Zaandam*	10,909	Brazil	*U-174*
11	*Viceroy of India* (T)	19,627	Mediterranean	*U-407*
11	*Nieuw Zeeland* (T)	11,069	Mediterranean	*U-380*
11	*Awatea* (T)	13,482	Mediterranean	*Argo*/AC
11	*Cathay* (T)	15,225	Mediterranean	AC
12	*Hecla*	10,850	West of Gibralter	*U-515*
12	*Karanja* (T)	9,890	Mediterranean	AC
14	*Narkunda* (T)	16,632	Mediterranean	AC
14	*Warwick Castle* (T)	20,107	West of Gibralter	*U-413*
15	*Ettrick* (T)	11,279	West of Gibralter	*U-155*
15	*Avenger* (T)	13,785	West of Gibralter	*U-155*
23	*Tilawa*	10,006	Indian Ocean	*I-29* (IJN)
23	*Scythia* (T)[2]	19,761	Mediterranean	AC
28	*Nova Scotia* (T)	6,796	Indian Ocean	*U-177*
30	*Landaff Castle*	10,799	Indian Ocean	*U-177*
Total:	16	208,450		
DECEMBER:				
6	*Ceramic* (T)	18,713	North Atlantic	*U-515*
21	*Strathallan* (T)	23,722	Mediterranean	*U-562*
23	*Cameronia* (T)[3]	16,297	Mediterranean	*U-565*/AC
Total:	3	58,732		

1. Source: Rower, *Axis Submarine Successes;* Admirality, *British Vessels Lost at Sea, 1939–45;* Roskill, *The War at Sea, 1939–1945.* Note: This table does not include tankers. For worldwide Allied tanker losses in this period (thirty-four vessels), see Volume I, Appendix 17.

2. Officially listed as seriously damaged.

3. Officially listed as seriously damaged.

> chology of U-boat crews. He no less matched Dönitz in ruthless will to win, though perhaps not in power of mind. Horton drove his command hard, his displeasure expressed in ways which reduced his less robust subordinates to nervous wrecks; and only the bravest dared approach him on days when he had lost at his regular game of golf. Every ship's company in Western Approaches Command could feel the grip and impulse of such harsh leadership. . . .

It hardly seems fair to slur Percy Noble and the achievements of his staff of about one thousand at Derby House, Liverpool, in order to deify Max Horton. As we have seen, by the time Horton arrived, Noble and staff had made quite substantial progress in checking the U-boats on the vital North Atlantic convoy run, Noble's primary area of responsibility. Derby House had achieved this near victory notwithstanding the acute shortage of suitable air and surface escorts and proper training time for them, the diversion of naval assets to Torch, the loss of naval Enigma, the shift of American destroyers in the Atlantic from cargo convoys to troop convoys, the inexperience of the Canadians, and dozens of other handicaps. Noble had developed the key ideas of independent hunter-killer groups (support groups) to aid threatened convoys and to kill more U-boats, and the use of very-long-range four-engine heavy bombers (B-17s, B-24s, Halifaxes) in an ASW role. He had established the escort-group training center (HMS *Western Isles*) at Tobermory on the island of Mull, under G. O. Stephenson and the convoy tactical trainer ("Anti–U-boat School") on the top floor of Derby House under Gilbert H. Roberts. He had formed the closest possible working relationship in a unified plot with the commanders of Coastal Command Groups 15 and 19, the former under J. M. Robb, succeeded by Leonard H. Slatter, the latter under Geoffrey Bromet.

At about this same time, on November 4, Churchill convened a new, high-level body, the Anti–U-boat Committee. A subdivision of the War Cabinet, it replaced the moribund Battle of the Atlantic committee. Its primary purpose was to focus the top minds and political powers in the British and Canadian governments on the task of providing very-long-range air escort for North Atlantic convoys while in the Greenland "Air Gap." Max Horton was invited to serve on this committee, giving him a voice at the highest levels.* In pursuit of its mandate, the committee delved into all challenges presented by the U-boat forces in all waters.

Thus it was that the dynamic and flamboyant Max Horton entered the ASW business at a time when most of its weaknesses had been defined and the solutions to them were clear and nearly at hand.

Dönitz commenced rebuilding U-boat forces on the North Atlantic run as fast as possible. In the three weeks from November 10 to December 1, twenty-eight fresh attack boats (two IXs, twenty-six VIIs) arrived in the hunting grounds from Germany, Norway, and France. One *(U-184)* had been lost and two *(U-262, U-264)* had

---

* Churchill also invited President Roosevelt's two most senior American advisers in London, Averell Harriman and Admiral Stark, to attend the committee meetings.

run out of torpedoes and gone home. The remaining twenty-five were assigned to two new groups, *Draufgänger* (Daredevil) and *Panzer* (Armor), and to cadre a third.

All operations were hampered by wildly unfavorable weather—the worst Atlantic winter in memory, according to a Coast Guard officer, John M. Waters, Jr. He wrote in his 1987 war memoir:

> In that terrible winter, the weather would break records of fifty-years standing, and 116 days out of 140 would see storms of gale force or greater on the northern ocean. Many years and dozens of storms later, veteran seamen would still hark back to the storms of that winter to define the superlatives of weather at sea.

Notwithstanding the hostile weather, the buildup of U-boats on the North Atlantic run—and elsewhere—continued at a remarkable pace. In all, fifty fresh attack boats sailed to the North Atlantic areas in December: thirty-six from France (five IXs, thirty-one VIIs), thirteen new boats from Germany (three IXs, ten VIIs), and one VII *(U-591)* from Norway.* Formed into a special group, *Delphin* (Dolphin), six of the VIIs sailed in December from France to mount a surprise attack in Brazilian waters, but that mission was canceled and the boats remained in the North Atlantic. Much against the wishes of Dönitz, the OKM insisted that four boats (two IXs, two VIIs) escort the blockade runner *Germania,* which was departing for the Far East, through the Bay of Biscay to safe seas. One provisional tanker, the Type XB (minelayer) *U-117,* and the Type XIV "Milk Cow," *U-463,* commanded by Leo Wolfbauer, sailed in support of all North Atlantic operations.

In view of the return of sunless days in the Arctic zone—and the continued low rate of sinkings in that area—Dönitz renewed his long-standing campaign to reduce the number of U-boats assigned there. On December 9, the OKM finally—and still reluctantly—agreed to release provisionally eleven of the twenty-three Arctic/Norway boats to Dönitz, provided he deployed them only in North Atlantic waters so that in event of an emergency need in Norway, they could quickly return to that area. Six of the twelve boats remaining in the Arctic/Norway area were to be ready for action—against Murmansk convoys or an Allied invasion—at all times.†

One of the new VIIs, *U-603,* which sailed from Germany to the North Atlantic in late November, reported a serious problem: The skipper, Hans-Joachim Bertelsmann, age twenty-six, fell ill and could not continue the patrol. While inbound to France on December 4, the boat came upon a southbound convoy en route to

---

* Two new VIIs, *U-302,* commanded by Herbert Sickel, and *U-629,* commanded by Hans-Helmut Bugs, were assigned directly to the Norway Arctic command to conform to Hitler's minimum force requirements. Another, *U-272,* commanded by Horst Hepp, collided in the Baltic with *U-634,* commanded by Hans-Günther Brosin. Both boats sank, but *U-634* was later salvaged. Seventy-nine of 108 crewmen were rescued including Hepp and Brosin. Twenty-nine died.

† The eleven boats provisionally released to Dönitz had first to be overhauled and modified for Atlantic duty. As a result, the transfers were slow: four in January 1943, one in March, two in April, etc.

Gibraltar. Bertelsmann shadowed and reported, but escorts drove him off and down and depth-charged the boat for two hours.

The beacon signals from *U-603* drew in four other boats. Philipp Schüler in *U-602,* outbound to the Mediterranean, made contact, but the escorts drove him off and down and delivered what Schüler described as a "prolonged" depth-charge attack. Nonetheless, he surfaced, chased, regained contact, and brought up the other two boats. One of these, the outbound IXC *U-175,* commanded by Heinrich Bruns, was forced to haul off with "leaky exhaust pipes." When the fourth boat reported heavy air and surface escorts, Dönitz canceled operations on December 6 and directed the ailing Bertelsmann in *U-603* to continue to France at high speed.

The next day, December 7, a new Type IXC in group *Panzer, U-524,* commanded by Walter von Steinaecker, age twenty-five, made contact with an eastbound convoy about three hundred miles due south of Greenland. The Germans believed this to be a Slow Convoy, but, in fact, it was the fast convoy Halifax 217, which had departed New York on November 27. Originally consisting of thirty-three heavily laden ships, the convoy was guarded by the British Escort Group 6, consisting of the destroyer *Fame,* the Polish destroyer *Burza,* four corvettes (three Norwegian, one British), and the rescue ship *Perth,* equipped with Huff Duff. On December 3 and 4, the convoy had run into a howling storm and had become intermingled with scattered ships of Slow Convoy 111. By December 7, eight of its thirty-three merchant ships had run into St. John's, Newfoundland, to escape the storm, leaving twenty-five in the convoy.

Von Steinaecker in *U-524* homed in six other *Panzer* boats that night. The weather was miserable: high winds, heavy rain, and snow. After the others had made contact, von Steinaecker carried out several attacks, firing nine torpedoes at various ships, including the destroyer *Fame.* Most of his torpedoes missed, but some hit the 8,200-ton British tanker *Empire Spencer,* which burst into flames and sank. The rescue ship *Perth* picked up all but one of her fifty-eight crewmen. Hans Gilardone in *U-254* fired a single torpedo, but it missed.

During that night, the six escorts, all equipped with Type 271 centimetric-wavelength radar, conducted a brilliant defense of convoy Halifax 217. The three Norwegian corvettes, *Rose, Potentilla,* and *Eglantine,* looking to revenge the loss of their sister ship *Montbretia* on the westbound voyage to New York with Convoy Outbound North (Slow) 144, were again outstandingly aggressive. While *Rose* was chasing one U-boat with her main gun, another U-boat surfaced merely 150 yards away. Without missing a beat, *Rose* shifted targets, forcing both boats under. All seven U-boats, however, survived the night.

From the contact reports, Dönitz concluded correctly that the convoy was a fast one, not a slow one. Nonetheless, on the night of December 7, he directed group *Draufgänger,* which had failed to find an expected Outbound North convoy, and four other boats newly arrived in the area to join group *Panzer.* Dönitz later logged that he had put twenty-two U-boats on the trail of Halifax 217. However, atmospheric conditions were not favorable for radio communications, and the boats reported so many conflicting positions that he was unable to organize an effective mass attack.

On the following day, December 8, three long-range B-24 Liberators from British Squadron 120 on Iceland, eight hundred miles distant, arrived over the convoy. By exercising rigid fuel economies, one of the aircraft was able to remain in the vicinity of the convoy for seven hours. With the help of centimetric-wavelength ASV radar, the B-24s found and repeatedly attacked the massing U-boats. In the face of this harassment, the shadowing U-boats were unable to get ahead of the convoy for better shooting positions and those boats coming up on the flanks to make contact were thwarted.

After dark that evening, there occurred another German "first" in the Atlantic U-boat war. The *U-221* of group *Draufgänger,* commanded by Hans Trojer, rammed *U-254* of group *Panzer,* commanded by Hans Gilardone. Hit hard and holed, the *U-254* sank immediately, taking down Gilardone and most of his crew. Trojer managed to rescue four survivors, but the damage he sustained rendered *U-221* incapable of diving and he was forced to abort to France and did not sail again until the end of February. Coming upon "wreckage and human remains" at the site, C. A. Monsen in the Norwegian corvette *Potentilla* speculated that a B-24 must have sunk a U-boat earlier in the day. Unaware of the collision, the Admiralty credited Squadron 120 with a kill but corrected the error in a postwar analysis. Commenting on this mishap, Dönitz exonerated Trojer of any blame: "Generally speaking, it's not practical to have more than thirteen to fifteen U-boats on a single convoy."

Owing to the skilled and courageous work of the six escorts during the night of December 8–9, only two U-boats could get into position to shoot at Halifax 217. The first was the new Type VII *U-758,* commanded by Helmut Manseck, age twenty-five. He fired a full salvo of five torpedoes at two different ships, but all missed. The next was one of the few *Ritterkreuz* holders still in active combat, Karl Thurmann in *U-553,* who carried the first FATs—the pattern-running or looping torpedoes—issued to the Atlantic force. He hit and blew up the 5,300-ton British ammunition ship *Charles L.D.,* from which only twelve crew were rescued. Whether Thurmann hit her with a FAT or an ordinary torpedo is not clear. In the event, Thurmann was forced to abort, he logged, because an experimental spray deflector that had been installed on the forward end of his conning tower was a complete failure. While the boat was cruising on the surface, the deflected spray was highly visible at a distance, giving away the boat's location to the enemy. When the boat cruised submerged, it was destabilized by the deflector.*

Bad weather on December 9 forced Coastal Command to cancel all air escorts for North Atlantic convoys. The stand-down gave the twenty-odd boats operating against Halifax 217 not only a breather but also an opportunity to maneuver on the surface to better shooting positions. It was all for naught. Acting on radar and Huff Duff contacts, the convoy's six escorts beat off the U-boats. Remarkably, not one boat was able to shoot on the night of December 9–10.

---

* The deflector was by then a standard modification on production-line boats. Upon receiving Thurmann's report, Dönitz canceled the modification and ordered that all deflectors of this type be removed.

The next day, December 10, the weather cleared and Coastal Command saturated the skies with aircraft basing temporarily or permanently in Iceland. The planes included B-24s from Squadron 120, B-17s from Squadrons 206 and 220; Sunderlands from Squadrons 201 and 423; Catalinas from the American Navy's Squadron VP 84, recently arrived from Argentia; and six Hudsons from Squadron 269. One of the B-24s, piloted by Terence M. Bulloch, hit with depth charges one of the new Type VIIs recently transferred from the Arctic, *U-611,* commanded by Nikolaus von Jacobs, age twenty-nine. The U-boat sank with the loss of all hands.

In view of the saturation air coverage, Dönitz canceled operations versus Halifax 217. It was a disappointing battle, he logged. He believed that the twenty-two U-boats involved had sunk only six ships for 36,600 tons, plus damage to a destroyer and three other merchant ships. The confirmed score probably would have dismayed him: two ships sunk for 13,500 tons. Western Approaches was ecstatic: The defense mounted by the Norwegian-manned escorts was one of the best of the war.

The four boats (two IXs, two VIIs) reluctantly assigned, at the OKM's insistence, to escort the outbound blockade-runner *Germania* to safe waters sailed from France on December 8 and 9. On December 12, Dönitz again groused in his diary that the diversion of U-boats to escort duties of this kind significantly diminished the Allied shipping tonnage that could be sunk. The OKM responded huffily that the eight thousand tons of rubber that *Germania* could bring back from the Far East was far more valuable to the war effort than the amount of tonnage the four U-boat escorts might sink.

After *Germania* sailed and her U-boat escorts got into positions close by on December 15, she unintentionally ran into a British convoy en route to or from Gibraltar. Two of the convoy escorts, including the sloop *Egret,* challenged *Germania,* which promptly scuttled. Her U-boat escorts—and other U-boats nearby—searched for *Germania* survivors for several days, but found none. Thereafter, the two VIIs of the escort, *U-563,* commanded by Götz von Hartmann, and *U-706,* commanded by Alexander von Zitzewitz, went on to join groups on the North Atlantic run. Von Hartmann in *U-563* promptly ran into military convoy MKS 3-Y, en route from Gibraltar to the British Isles. He sank the 4,900-ton British freighter *Bretwalda,* but several of the new Pi2 magnetic pistols failed (Dönitz speculated) and "destroyers" thwarted a second attack. The two IXs of the escort, the veteran *U-125,* commanded by the Drumbeater Ulrich Folkers, and *U-514,* commanded by Hans-Jürgen Auffermann, headed for American waters but were soon recalled to carry out operations on the Middle Atlantic convoy run.

More Hideous Weather in the North

In the second week of December, Dönitz reorganized the U-boats assigned to the North Atlantic run into two groups, *Ungestüm* (Impetuous) and *Raufbold*

(Brawler), and provided a cadre of three boats for a third, *Büffel* (Sideboard). These groups occupied positions astride the probable convoy routes south of Greenland and Iceland. All were provided plentiful *B-dienst* information on specific eastbound and westbound convoys.

In foul weather on December 13, the three-boat cadre of group *Büffel* found an eastbound convoy. It was believed to be the fast Halifax 218, but it may have been Slow Convoy 112. All three VIIs established contact: Paul-Karl Loeser in the veteran *U-373,* Heinz-Konrad Fenn, age twenty-four, in the new *U-445,* and Heinrich Schmid in *U-663.* Aggressive escorts drove all three boats off and down and blasted them with depth charges. Schmid in *U-663* incurred "considerable damage" and was forced to abort to France. The boat did not sail again until March.

Although the three boats lost contact with the convoy, Dönitz ordered group *Ungestüm,* less three boats that were low on fuel, to home on the remaining two boats of group *Büffel:* Loeser's *U-373* and Fenn's *U-445.* The three *Ungestüm* boats low on fuel, *U-610, U-611* (actually lost), and *U-623,* were transferred to group *Raufbold,* which was farther east and closer to the proposed positions of the U-tankers. These realignments gave group *Ungestüm* eleven boats and group *Raufbold* thirteen boats. Dönitz directed another new VII, *U-626,* commanded by a thirty-three-year-old former merchant-marine captain, Hans-Botho Bade, to join group *Ungestüm* in the hunt for the reported eastbound convoy.

During this time, three American warships had set out from Iceland in foul weather, escorting twelve merchant ships that were to join the westbound convoy Outbound North (Slow) 152. The warships were the four-stack destroyers *Babbitt* and *Leary* and the *Treasury*-class Coast Guard cutter *Ingham,* the latter commanded by George E. McCabe. Owing to the dirty weather and to poor navigation and communications, the two formations were unable to find each other, so on December 15, Allied authorities in Iceland sent out a radar-equipped Catalina to help bring them together.

Leading the formation from Iceland at about noon that day, the cutter *Ingham* got a solid sonar contact about 3,500 yards ahead. This was Hans-Botho Bade in *U-626,* one week out of Bergen, on orders to join group *Ungestüm*'s hunt for the eastbound convoy. McCabe on *Ingham* did not put much store in this sonar contact, but he dutifully ran in and rolled a single, shallow-set, 720-pound Mark VII depth charge off the stern. The close explosion was so violent that it lifted the china on the wardroom table. Preoccupied with establishing contact with the Catalina and Outbound North (Slow) 152, McCabe cruised on, unaware that this perfunctorily launched single depth charge—surely the luckiest Allied shot of the war—had destroyed Bade's *U-626* with the loss of all hands.

With the help of the Catalina, McCabe found Outbound North (Slow) 152, escorted by Canadian Escort Group C-3, and merged the twelve merchant ships from Iceland. Since this convoy was not under U-boat attack, *Ingham, Babbitt,* and *Leary* were shifted to the eastbound Slow Convoy 112, escorted by Canadian group C-4, which had reported U-boat shadowers. In his memoir, *Bloody Winter,* the Coast Guard officer John Waters writes that on December 17—not December 15—*Ingham* found and sank *U-626* with massive salvos of big and small depth charges. The Admiralty's assessment committee doubted this kill—rating it only as "possible"—but in the postwar accounting, it credited *Ingham* with the kill of *U-626* by single depth charge on December 15.*

Despite the hideous weather, the eleven boats of group *Ungestüm* intercepted and pursued the eastbound convoy (Halifax 218 or Slow Convoy 112), which had been discovered by the cadre of group *Büffel.* Horst Höltring in the VII *U-604* of *Ungestüm,* who had sunk a lone 7,100-ton American vessel, *Coamo,* which was returning to the British Isles, clung to the formation in wild seas, but the escorts drove him off before he could bring up the other boats. Groping for the ships in gales on December 16, Loeser in *U-373* of the group *Büffel* cadre reported that he had found the convoy again. He brought up three other boats: Fenn in *U-445,* also formerly of the *Büffel* cadre, and two *Ungestüm* boats, Ralph Kapitzky in the VII *U-615* and Walter von Steinaecker in the new Type IXC *U-524.*

Upon analysis of the reports from the boats, Dönitz concluded that Loeser had found not the eastbound convoy (Halifax 218 or Slow Convoy 112) but an Outbound North convoy, sailing in the opposite direction. However, the weather was so ghastly that he ordered group *Ungestüm* to temporarily give up the chase, heave to, and ride out the storm. After the storm dissipated on December 21, Hans-Jürgen Zetzsche in the VII *U-591,* another recent transfer from the Arctic, found and sank the 3,100-ton British freighter *Montreal City,* a straggler from convoy Outbound North 152. That proved to be the sole success of the dozen boats of the stillborn group *Büffel* and of group *Ungestüm* in these operations.

The other group, *Raufbold,* underwent a minor change in composition. Slightly damaged by enemy bombs or depth charges, the new boat *U-465,* commanded by Heinz Wolf, age twenty-eight, was forced to abort to France, reducing the group to ten boats. However, the transfer of the VIIs *U-610* and *U-623* from *Ungestüm* increased the group to twelve boats. Still unaware of the loss of *U-611,* Dönitz believed the group had thirteen boats.

In the terrible weather of December 15, one of the *Raufbold* VIIs, *U-621,* commanded by a new skipper, Max Kruschka, age twenty-three, found another convoy. It was Outbound North 153, composed of thirty-eight merchant ships, guarded by British Escort Group B-7, comprised of seven warships: the destroyers *Firedrake* and the ex-American four-stack *Chesterfield,* and five British corvettes. Kruschka in *U-621* brought up five other boats. Despite the gales and mountainous seas, five boats were able to attack.

- Karl Hause in *U-211* hit one of the escorts, the 1,350-ton British destroyer *Firedrake,* which broke in half.

---

* Waters apparently adhered to the Coast Guard view that the December 15 kill was improbable. In contrast, official Coast Guard historians have accepted the Admiralty's assessment. The *U-626* was the last of eighteen U-boats sunk by American forces in their first year of the war, 1942—one of them, *U-94,* shared by U.S. Navy aircraft and the Canadian corvette *Oakville.* Unassisted Navy aircraft accounted for seven; unassisted destroyers accounted for one; unassisted Army Air Forces aircraft accounted for three; Army aircraft and a Navy destroyer shared one; Navy aircraft and a merchant ship shared one; Coast Guard forces (three cutters, one aircraft) sank the other four.

• Walter von Freyberg-Eisenberg-Allmendingen in *U-610* sank the 6,100-ton Norwegian tanker *Bello* and damaged the 9,600-ton British tanker *Regent Lion.*

• Adolph Graef in *U-664* sank the 5,900-ton Belgian freighter *Emile Francqui.*

• Günther Ruppelt, age twenty-three, new skipper of *U-356,* claimed sinking a tanker with three hits, but it could not be confirmed.

Verified results against convoy Outbound North 153: three ships (including one tanker) sunk for 13,334 tons, including the destroyer *Firedrake;* one tanker for 9,600 tons damaged.

The bow section of *Firedrake* sank within a half hour, taking down the escort commander and scores of men, but the stern remained afloat for about three and a half hours. Thirty-five men on the stern section jettisoned depth charges and torpedoes to lighten ship and prepared rafts to abandon ship. Responding to a distress flare, the corvette *Sunflower* closed the stern section by radar, but her captain decided to wait until daylight to mount the rescue. However, the stern section soon began to sink and in towering seas and pitch darkness, *Sunflower* rescued twenty-five of thirty-five survivors.

Although this epic storm, with waves of "40 to 50 feet," as the corvette *Pink* reported, raged unabated through December 16, Klaus Rudloff in *U-609* hung on to the convoy, sending beacon signals. These helped five other boats maintain contact, but all reported "heavy" Catalina and B-24 Liberator air cover. Rudloff fired six torpedoes at several ships, but he wrote that all missed "despite perfect firing data." No other boats had an opportunity to shoot. Although there was no chance that he could reorganize group *Raufbold* for a concerted attack, Dönitz continued the chase in case the weather had scattered the convoy and the boats might yet find and sink singles. Kruschka in *U-621* found and sank the 6,200-ton British tanker *Otina* from this convoy, Outbound North 153, as well as another ship, a 4,500-ton Greek sailing alone. Massively reinforced by warships putting out from Canadian ports (American four-stack destroyers *Cole* and *Dallas,* four-stack ex-American Canadian *Annapolis,* three Canadian corvettes, and a minesweeper), convoy Outbound North 153 reorganized and proceeded westward to New York without further losses.

After this brutal, frustrating, and largely futile chase, three skippers of *Raufbold* VIIs were detached for a special OKM mission although Dönitz had done his utmost to prevent it. Hans-Ferdinand Massmann in the newly joined *U-409,* from France; Kurt Sturm in *U-410;* and Max Kruschka in *U-621* were to escort the blockade-runner *Rhakotis* into France on the last leg of her journey from the Far East. Sturm and Kruschka complied, albeit grudgingly, but inexplicably Massmann in *U-409* diverted to a futile chase of a reported convoy. As a consequence, Dönitz was compelled to assign yet another VII to the task, *U-659,* commanded by Hans Stock, recently sailed from France. Massmann, Dönitz logged angrily, "will have to answer for this arbitrary behavior on his return."

By this time, British codebreakers and Rodger Winn in the Submarine Tracking Room had developed sufficient information on blockade-runners returning from the Far East to predict their courses and positions with a fair degree of accuracy. After deploying the British cruiser *Scylla* along the predicted path of *Rhakotis,* on January 1 Coastal Command sent a Sunderland of Australian Squadron 10 out to find her. Guided by the Sunderland, *Scylla* intercepted *Rhakotis,* per plan. The German crew scuttled and took to the lifeboats. The escorts, *U-410, U-621,* and *U-659,* cruising just over the horizon, never saw a thing. When the Germans learned that the British had "sunk" the *Rhakotis,* the red-faced U-boat escorts, as well as several other U-boats that Dönitz diverted to the scene, searched for survivors for several days. Kurt Sturm in *U-410* found two lifeboats containing eighty men, took them aboard, and returned to France. Two other lifeboats reached Spain, where the Germans were "interned," but soon repatriated.

Several days before Christmas there were three groups deployed against convoys on the North Atlantic run: the aging *Ungestüm* (nine boats), the new *Spitz* (eight boats), and a cadre for *Falke* (Falcon), initially to be composed of three new boats from Germany and three veterans from France. Groups *Ungestüm* and *Spitz* were positioned to intercept convoy Outbound North (Slow) 154. When fully formed, group *Falke* was to intercept the fast Outbound North 155.

The three new boats from Germany assigned to cadre group *Falke* were two VIIs, *U-357* and *U-384,* and the IXC40 *U-525,* all of which sailed from Kiel at about the same time. Approaching the designated assembly area near Rockall Bank on the day after Christmas, the twenty-eight-year-old skipper of *U-357,* Adolf Kellner, unexpectedly spotted—and reported—an *eastbound* convoy, which he erroneously described as "poorly defended." This was Halifax 219, guarded by the crack British Escort Group 2, commanded by Donald Macintyre, which had earlier captured Otto Kretschmer in *U-99* and killed Joachim Schepke in *U-100.* Well within range of Coastal Command Hudsons, the ships of the convoy were preparing to disperse to their various final destinations.

Macintyre in the destroyer *Hesperus* picked up Kellner's Beta Beta or "B-bar" contact report on his Huff Duff. He calculated the U-boat was about fifteen miles astern of the convoy. Informing the convoy commodore of this threat, Macintyre left the merchant ships in the care of six corvettes of the group and directed another destroyer, *Vanessa,* commanded by C. E. Sheen, to form on *Hesperus.* Thereupon both warships raced down the Huff Duff bearing at maximum speed with Type 271 centimetric-wavelength radars on line.

Upon receiving the report of this inbound convoy from *U-357,* Dönitz was not overjoyed. The convoy was too close to the British Isles to mount a group attack; there was not enough time or sea room. The only U-boats within reach were the other two that had sailed from Germany with Kellner to cadre group *Falke, U-384* and *U-525.* Although he saw little possibility of success and the risks were great, Dönitz nonetheless directed these three green boats to attack the convoy. Despite several serious mechanical defects, Kellner in *U-357* did not hesitate to comply, but neither *U-384* nor *U-525* ever found the convoy.

Running down the Huff Duff bearing, *Hesperus* and *Vanessa* found *U-357* on the surface and drove her under. Kellner boldly fired a single torpedo at *Vanessa,* but it missed. Spotting *U-357*'s periscope, Macintyre charged it and threw over a pattern of depth charges to distract and frighten Kellner and ruin his aim. Thereafter *Hesperus* and *Vanessa* conducted a well-organized and prolonged hunt, which finally brought *U-357* to the surface after dark. When she came into view on radar, Macintyre in *Hesperus* rammed *U-357,* cutting the U-boat in half and badly damaging the bottom of his own ship. The British could find only eight German survivors; Kellner and about thirty-five others perished. After makeshift repairs, Macintyre got *Hesperus* into Liverpool on her own steam to a cheering reception, but the ship was in repair and refit for the next three months. British intelligence officers who interrogated the survivors of *U-357* reported that only four of the crew had made prior war patrols; all others were fresh from U-boat school.

On the day Macintyre sank *U-357,* December 26, Adolph Graef in the VII *U-664* of group *Spitz* found convoy Outbound North (Slow) 154 about six hundred miles due west of Brest. It was "three days late," Dönitz logged, probably because of the stormy weather. The convoy consisted of forty-four merchant ships, the rescue ship *Toward,* and a small, French-manned catapult merchant ship, *Fidelity* (the former *Le Rhin*), equipped with two floatplanes. The escort was the Canadian group C-1, commanded by the new skipper of the destroyer *St. Laurent,* Guy S. Windeyer. Normally the ex-American four-stack British destroyer *Burwell* sailed with C-1, but she was forced to abort at the eleventh hour with mechanical defects and no replacement destroyer was provided. *St. Laurent* and the five Canadian corvettes of the group were newly fitted with Type 271 centimetric-wavelength radar, but the operators were green. *St. Laurent, Toward,* and *Fidelity* had Huff Duff, but not all the sets were properly calibrated.

Dönitz ordered groups *Spitz* and *Ungestüm,* comprising about twenty boats, to attack the convoy. Graef in *U-664* hung on tenaciously and brought up three VIIs: *U-356, U-441,* and *U-662.* In the early hours of December 27, Günther Ruppelt in *U-356* launched the attack. Shooting with skill—and the advantage of surprise—he sank three British freighters for 13,600 tons and damaged a 7,100-ton Dutch freighter, which Klaus Hartmann in *U-441* sank later in the day. Windeyer in *St. Laurent* and some of the corvettes counterattacked and one of them unknowingly sank Günther Ruppelt in *U-356* with the loss of all hands. After the war, when the kill was discovered in German records, the Admiralty credited it to the Canadians: the destroyer *St. Laurent* and three of the corvettes, *Battleford, Chilliwack,* and *Napanee.**

The Admiralty had routed the convoy southwesterly toward the Azores to avoid the North Atlantic storms. The route was too long for the corvettes to travel without refueling, so the convoy included a British oiler, the 7,100-ton *Scottish Heather.* On December 27, while the corvette *Chilliwack* was alongside, refueling—a first for the Canadian Navy—Wolfgang Leimkühler in the new VII *U-225* torpedoed *Scottish Heather.* The oiler was not seriously damaged, but she was forced to return to the British Isles. Resorting to a contingency plan, Windeyer

---

* In the year 1942, Canadian forces sank nine U-boats, including *U-94,* shared with the U.S. Navy. Including *U-94,* Canadian surface ships accounted for six; unassisted aircraft, for three.

made arrangements for some of the corvettes to temporarily fall out and refuel in the Azores.

The U-boats lost track of convoy Outbound North (Slow) 154 for about twenty-four hours, but on the morning of December 28, Hubertus Purkhold in *U-260* found it again and cannily hung on through a densely foggy day. His beacon signals brought up nine other boats, six from group *Spitz* and three from group *Ungestüm.* Later that evening, three other boats of group *Ungestüm* also made contact, bringing the number of U-boats stalking the convoy to thirteen. In an emergency measure to reinforce the weak and dwindling escort, the Admiralty shifted the British destroyers *Milne* and *Meteor* from a Torch convoy to Outbound North (Slow) 154, but these ships were not to arrive until December 29.

During the night of December 28–29, the U-boats attacked from all quarters, completely overwhelming the escorts. A slaughter ensued:

- In two separate attacks, Leimkühler in *U-225* sank the 5,300-ton British freighter *Melmore Head* and damaged and stopped three other ships: the 5,100-ton British freighter *Ville de Rouen,* the 5,000-ton Belgian tanker *President Francqui,* and the 7,100-ton British freighter *Empire Shackleton.*
- Wolfgang Hermann in *U-662* sank the damaged *Ville de Rouen.*
- Hans Hunger in *U-336* sank the damaged *President Francqui.*
- Horst von Schroeter, age twenty-three, new skipper of the famous Type IXB *U-123,** further damaged the *Empire Shackleton,* which was finally sunk by the *Ritterkreuz* holder Siegfried Strelow in the veteran *U-435,* another recent transfer from the Arctic.
- Horst Dieterichs in the veteran *U-406,* who carried some pattern-running FAT torpedoes, damaged and stopped three British freighters: the 3,400-ton *Baron Cochrane,* the 4,500-ton *Zarian,* and the 5,000-ton *Lynton Grange.*
- Von Schroeter in *U-123* sank the damaged *Baron Cochrane.*
- Hans-Jürgen Zetzsche in *U-591* sank the damaged *Zarian* and damaged the 5,700-ton Norwegian freighter *Norse King.*
- Heinz Hasenschar, age twenty-six, in the new *U-628,* sank the damaged *Lynton Grange.*
- The tenacious shadower, Hubertus Purkhold in *U-260,* sank the 4,900-ton British freighter *Empire Wagtail.*
- Strelow in *U-435* sank the damaged *Norse King.*
- Hermann Kottmann, age twenty-seven, new skipper of the veteran *U-203,* shot at a 9,000-ton "ocean liner" but missed.
- Strelow and Hasenschar missed the destroyer *St. Laurent* and a corvette, which had stopped to rescue survivors.
- Ralph Kapitzky in *U-615* fired five torpedoes at the catapult merchant ship *Fidelity,* which he identified as a "Q" ship, but all missed or hung up in *Fidelity*'s net defense.

---

* Reinhard Hardegen had commanded her on his two celebrated Drumbeat patrols to the United States. She sailed from Germany on December 5, after six months of battle-damage repairs. Her new commander, Horst von Schroeter, had been Hardegen's first watch officer.

• Hans-Martin Scheibe, age twenty-four, new skipper of *U-455,* fired a full bow salvo at overlapping ships, all of which missed.

Losses in this mass attack: nine ships for 46,200 tons. In addition, one of two floatplanes from the catapult ship *Fidelity* crashed during its launching. The destroyer *St. Laurent* rescued its two aircrew.

After daylight on December 29, the U-boats veered off to avoid the escorts and to submit shooting reports to Dönitz. During the forenoon, the modern British destroyers *Milne* and *Meteor* arrived, increasing the escort to three destroyers and five corvettes. *Milne* and *Meteor* drove off the shadowing U-boats and helped to thwart a third attack on the night of December 29–30. But both destroyers were low on fuel and on the afternoon of December 30, they and the corvettes *Battleford* and *Shediac* had to divert to the Azores, leaving only the destroyer *St. Laurent* and three corvettes to cope with the U-boats. Later that day, Strelow in *U-435* sank the 2,500-ton catapult merchant ship *Fidelity,* with the loss of her Free French crew, in all 334 men. Anticipating another savage attack that night, Windeyer gave permission to the ships *Calgary* and *Adrastus*—both carrying large numbers of passengers—to proceed independently, but they remained in formation.

During this long, hard chase, the U-boats had also consumed much fuel. One by one they were forced to fall out and return to France. By the night of December 30–31, only five boats had sufficient fuel to continue the hunt and none had the convoy in sight. Unaware that there were only four escorts left to guard the convoy—all critically low on fuel—Dönitz canceled further operations. That same day the veteran destroyer *Fame,* flagship of British Escort Group B-6, was shifted from convoy Outbound North 155 to reinforce the escort. Her experienced commander, R. Heathcote, assumed command of the escort from Canadian Guy Windeyer in *St. Laurent,* who collapsed from stress and exhaustion and on arrival in Canada was sent to other duty.

In all, convoy Outbound North (Slow) 154 lost fourteen ships of about 69,378 tons (plus two 10-ton LCV landing craft) and 486 men killed. Those numbers ranked it as one of the half dozen worst North Atlantic convoy disasters of the war. Even though the Admiralty had sailed the convoy shy a veteran British destroyer, had routed it beyond reach of air escort in the areas of highest risk, and had not made adequate provisions for refueling the escorts at sea, the British put all the blame for the disaster on the Canadians for failing to aggressively and efficiently repel the U-boats. Doubtless, too, the loss of the 334 men of the small Free French catapult merchant ship *Fidelity* tainted the Canadians. Had it been known that the Canadians had sunk *U-356,* the criticism might have been muted somewhat.

The investigation into the disaster led the Admiralty to a drastic decision: Three of the four Canadian ocean-escort groups were to be withdrawn and intensively trained at the British "escort school" at Tobermory. Until the Admiralty deemed them qualified for combat, they were to be replaced by British escort groups, which were to be backstopped by about five British hunter-killer groups (support groups), comprised of warships released from Torch duties, including, in due course, the several "jeep" carriers. The Canadians welcomed the opportunity for intense group training, but they also renewed long-standing demands for modern radar-equipped long-range aircraft and more modern destroyers, the latter to be fitted with the latest and best radar, sonar, and Huff Duff. They also demanded a larger voice in the command and routing of transatlantic convoys and the assignment of escort groups.

With the exception of the success against convoy Outbound North (Slow) 154, the month of December 1942 was another difficult and disappointing time for U-boats on the North Atlantic run. Sixteen Allied convoys comprised of about 650 merchant ships sailed across the Atlantic east and west.* The U-boats were able to mount noteworthy attacks on only three convoys: Halifax 217, Outbound North 153, and Outbound North (Slow) 154. These three battles resulted in the sinking of twenty ships for about 102,400 tons, fourteen for about 70,000 tons from one convoy, Outbound North (Slow) 154. In addition, the boats on the North Atlantic run in December sank seven ships of about 48,400 tons from other convoys and/or singles.† Grand total: twenty-seven ships for about 150,800 tons.

Assessments

Because of the lack of precision in most histories of the battles on the North Atlantic convoy run in the fall of 1942, a statistical review of the months of November and December is appropriate.

Owing to the diversions to Torch and the initiation of fast and slow Torch convoys (UGS and GUS), and to the temporary shutdown of Murmansk convoys, Allied convoy traffic on the North Atlantic run in November and December 1942 fell off slightly. A total of 1,218 ships in thirty-one east- and westbound convoys sailed across the Atlantic. Three hundred and twenty ships sailed from New York in eight fast Halifax convoys (213 to 220), and 307 ships sailed from New York in seven Slow convoys (108 to 114). U-boats sank only three—repeat three—of the 627 loaded ships that sailed in eastbound convoys in those two months, a little-noted but absolutely disastrous German naval failure. In the same two months, 591 ships sailed from the British Isles to North America in sixteen fast and slow Outbound North convoys (142 to 157). U-boats sank thirty-one of these empty westbound ships, running up impressive "tonnage war" figures for propaganda purposes, but these westbound losses did not impede imports to the British Isles. Total losses in both eastbound and westbound convoys: thirty-four ships.‡

In this welter of eye-glazing statistics, which Winston Churchill so deplored, it is easy to lose sight of the human factor. Literally hundreds of merchant seamen, sailors, naval gunners, and passengers died ghastly deaths in these sinkings or in lifeboats or on floats or in the icy waters. Particularly noteworthy in December

---

* Halifax 217 to 220; Slow Convoy 111 to 114; Outbound North and Outbound North (Slow) 150 to 157.

† Including, notably, the 18,700-ton British liner/troopship *Ceramic*.

‡ See Appendix 3. In the same two-month period, U.S. shipyards alone turned out well over five times these losses: 214 ships of 1.3 million gross tons.

were the 655 deaths incurred when Werner Henke in *U-515* sank the liner/troopship *Ceramic,* after she detached from convoy Outbound North 149. Many of the dead as well as the survivors performed countless acts of heroism that also should not be overlooked.

On the other side of the hill, confirmed U-boat kills by Allied ASW forces on the North Atlantic run in November and December 1942 were among the lowest for any two-month period in the war: five Type VIIs. U.S. Navy air and surface forces accounted for two (*U-408, U-626*), British air and surface forces, two (*U-357, U-611*), and Canadian Navy surface forces for one (*U-356*). Three other U-boats also failed to return: the VII *U-132* (likely the victim of an explosion), the VII *U-254* (accidentally rammed and sunk by *U-221*), and the IXC40 *U-184* (perhaps sunk by a Norwegian-manned corvette).* Only eight of the four hundred Germans on these eight boats survived to be captured, all from *U-357.*

As in prior months, a look at the results achieved by all U-boats sailing in all areas of the North Atlantic in November and December is instructive. The number of new boats and/or new skippers dropped sharply from an average of about 63 percent to about 43 percent, but the average sinkings per boat per patrol declined further to .69 ships. Forty-three boats of the eighty-four putting out (51 percent) sank no ships, continuing a nonproductive trend ominous for the Germans. *Viz.*

	Patrols†	*New C.O.*	*Ships Sunk*	*Per Boat*	*Boats Lost*	*No Sinkings*
November	34	16 (47%)‡	21 1/3	.63	5	18 (53%)
December	50	20 (40%)§	37 2/3	.75	8#	25 (50%)
Totals	84	36 (43%)	59	.69	13 (15%)	43 (51%)

These figures further reinforce the case that even without reading four-rotor naval Enigma, the Allies held an increasingly dominant hand over the U-boat threat in the North Atlantic area. Note especially the forty-three "No Sinkings." To laboriously prepare eighty-four boats and crews for patrols and have about half of them fail to sink any ships whatsoever was an increasingly futile and wasteful enterprise. Although the terrible winter weather greatly impeded Allied flight operations in this period in that area, sharply reducing the number of U-boats found and killed by aircraft, it equally impeded U-boat operations.

Patrols to the Americas

The anti-Torch and North Atlantic convoy battles absorbed the great majority of U-boats of the Atlantic force. Nonetheless, Dönitz remained convinced that patrols

---

* British forces sank three other boats in the Bay of Biscay or the approaches to the Strait of Gibraltar: the VIIs *U-98, U-411,* and the IXC *U-517.*

† See Appendix 2.

‡ Includes four experienced boats with new skippers.

§ Includes six experienced boats with new skippers.

\# Includes *U-96,* which was retired to the Training Command.

to the waters of Trinidad and Brazil could significantly interrupt the flow of oil and other war matériel to the Mediterranean Basin via Gibraltar and the Indian Ocean. He therefore sailed eleven boats to these waters in November: six IXCs, three aging IXBs, and two VIID (minelayers), which had extended range. Three of the eleven did not get far:

• On the second day out from France, a mechanical failure in the IXC *U-66,* commanded by Friedrich Markworth, caused serious flooding when the boat dived. Some salt water leaked into a battery compartment, causing chlorine gas to form. Forced to abort, Markworth reversed course, running at maximum speed to France on the surface at night. A Coastal Command radar-equipped Wellington with a Leigh Light, piloted by D. E. Dixon, detected the boat and dropped four depth charges. Unable to dive, Markworth zigzagged wildly to confuse the bombardier, a tactic that worked and enabled the boat to reach port without incurring further damage. Consigned to overhaul—and modification—*U-66* did not sail again for two months.

• While crossing the Bay of Biscay, Paul Hartwig in the IXC *U-517,* who had made a notable first patrol in the Gulf of St. Lawrence, reported diesel-engine failures. During repairs the mechanics found dirt in the fuel system, believed to be the work of saboteurs. Hartwig was tempted to abort, but he pressed on.

On the fifth day of the voyage, November 21, Hartwig concluded he was beyond the dangers posed by Coastal Command's Biscay patrols and elected to remain on the surface with his Metox rigged. That device picked up aircraft radar signals and Hartwig crash-dived, but it was too late. While on routine defensive ASW patrol, an Albacore torpedo bomber of Squadron 817, based on the carrier *Victorious,* which was returning to the British Isles, had found *U-517.* Attacking from the stern, the Albacore dropped three shallow-set depth charges, which blew away the bridge and part of the conning tower and knocked the diesels off their mounts. With no hope of saving the boat, Hartwig surfaced, informed Dönitz of the disaster, and scuttled. Dönitz ordered the outbound *U-211* and other boats nearby to render assistance, but they could do nothing. Covered by *Victorious* aircraft, two destroyers of the British task force fished Hartwig and forty-nine of his crew from the water and took them to England.

• Outbound to Trinidad, the IXC *U-513,* commanded by Rolf Rüggeberg, who had limped home from his first patrol to the St. Lawrence with a damaged conning tower, also developed trouble in the fuel-oil system. The filters and injectors clogged, he reported. Arrangements were made for Rüggeberg to rendezvous with Karl-Friedrich Merten in *U-68,* who was returning from Cape Town, to obtain spare parts, including three fuel-injector pumps. Thereupon, Rüggeberg was to overhaul and thoroughly clean both diesels, then run continuously at high speed for twenty-four hours.

Rüggeberg got the pumps from Merten and cleaned the diesels, but nothing worked and he was compelled to abort. The return trip was a nightmare. By using some spare parts carried on board and some parts from the number two engine, the mechanics were able to run on the other engine for a while. When number one failed, Rüggeberg submerged and ran on the electric motors while the mechanics used parts from the number one engine to rebuild and restart the other engine. By this method, the boat finally reached Lorient on December 18, after twenty-eight anxious—and fruitless—days at sea. Upon investigation, it was discovered that when the boat was in refit, the interior of her fuel tanks had been painted with an aluminum paint that was either of inferior quality or not allowed to dry adequately. The paint had flaked off and clogged the oil lines, filters, and pumps. The boat did not sail again until late February.

Yet another skipper bound for the Americas developed serious fuel problems. This was the youthful *Ritterkreuz* holder, Johann Mohr, in the IXB *U-124,* returning to combat after five months of overhaul and battle-damage repairs. In a history of *U-124,** Elizabeth B. Gasaway asserted that the boat's fuel supply had been "sabotaged" in Lorient with a chemical that caused the fuel pumps to corrode, jamming the fuel-injector valves. Perhaps so, but it may well have been that the aluminum paint inside *U-124*'s fuel tanks had flaked like that in *U-513.*

As with *U-513,* Dönitz directed Mohr to thoroughly clean his engines, then run at full speed for twenty-four hours. Upon completion of the run, Mohr reported that the port diesel was clear but he had to replace a fuel pump and two valves on the starboard engine. Reluctant to abort, he requested a rendezvous with the big XB (minelayer) *U-118,* temporarily serving as a tanker for the *Westwall* boats, to pick up a new fuel pump and valves and some fresh, clean fuel oil. After this had been done, Mohr ran on the "sabotaged" oil, saving the "clean" oil obtained from *U-118* for battle. Despite these measures, Gasaway wrote, "one diesel or the other was being repaired nearly every day," an unspeakable ordeal for the mechanics, working in the heat and humidity of the tropics.

There was also trouble of a different kind in this group of boats. Heinrich Bleichrodt in the cranky old Type IXB *U-109,* who wore Oak Leaves on his *Ritterkreuz,* was cracking from the strain of eighteen months of sustained war patrolling. Westbound out of Biscay, he found and boldly attacked a British naval task force, but he was driven off by "destroyers," who heavily depth-charged the boat. Approaching Trinidad on December 26, Bleichrodt attacked a lone freighter, firing six torpedoes, all of which missed. The freighter in turn dropped "one to three" depth charges, leading Bleichrodt to conclude his quarry was probably a "Q" ship, to be avoided.

That same report contained a shocking postscript. Bleichrodt requested authority to abort the patrol, as Dönitz logged it, "because of his own nervous state." To help Bleichrodt avoid disgrace and professional ruin—and possibly a Nazi firing squad—Dönitz denied the request, advising *U-109* to "carry out operations no matter what happens." However, four days later, on December 30, *U-109* reported that Bleichrodt was no longer capable of complying with those orders. Dönitz responded that *U-109 must* remain on patrol, "even if it was necessary to hand over command to the first watch officer." Apparently, the first watch officer did take temporary command and notwithstanding the orders, aborted the patrol. To assist with administration and watch-keeping en route home, *U-109* rendezvoused with

* *Grey Wolf, Grey Sea* (1970).

Ritterkreuz holder Günther Krech in *U-558* and took aboard a warrant quartermaster. Upon arrival in France, Bleichrodt was hospitalized and rehabilitated. Later he was transferred to the Training Command, where he was appointed commander of Flotilla 22.*

As a result of these mishaps, only seven, not eleven, patrols were conducted in American waters by the boats sailing in November, including that of Mohr's *U-124* with defective diesels. Moreover, two of the seven boats were lost soon after reaching their patrol areas, leaving only five.

En route to Brazil, the Type IXC *U-164,* commanded by Otto Fechner, who had made one disappointing patrol to the Caribbean in late summer, developed two small holes in her pressure hull between a battery compartment and a ballast tank. In an attempt to repair the leak, Fechner moored in the lee of remote—and deserted—St. Paul's Rocks, in the South Atlantic. Although no satisfactory means could be found to stop the leak, Fechner continued to Brazilian waters. After he reached the area on December 27, he requested permission to abort. The request was denied, but he was authorized to withdraw from the coastal shipping lanes and to patrol "remote areas." In the course of complying with these instructions, Fechner found, stopped—and sank—the 2,600-ton Swedish neutral *Brageland,* en route to New York with a load of coffee and wool.

By this time, the U.S. Navy had substantially increased ASW air patrols in the Caribbean and Latin America. Long based at San Juan, Puerto Rico, Fleet Air Wing (Fairwing) 11 provided convoy coverage in the Caribbean and also in the waters of Trinidad and as far south as Brazil.† On February 16, 1943, the Navy established Fairwing 16 at Norfolk. Deployed to Natal, Brazil, in April 1943, it took over responsibility from Fairwing 11 for Latin American waters.‡ The British assisted in this area by transferring RAF Squadron 53 of Coastal Command (equipped with Hudsons) to Trinidad.

On January 6, a Catalina of Navy Patrol Squadron VP 83, forward based in Natal, Brazil, found *U-164* cruising on the surface, sixty-five miles off the Brazilian coast. The pilot, William R. Ford, attacked immediately, diving to wave-top altitude. The unalert bridge watch on *U-164* crash-dived too late. Ford dropped four shallow-set Mark XVII depth charges. Three hit close, apparently blowing *U-164* into two halves, which sank immediately. Two seamen who were topside bathing when the attack occurred survived, clinging to torpedo canisters that had been blown overboard. Ford dropped them an inflatable dinghy and seven days later they washed ashore at a fishing village. There, Brazilian authorities took them into custody and turned them over to the U.S. Navy detachment at Natal.

Harro Schacht in the Type IXC *U-507,* who had pioneered patrols in the Gulf

---

* Bleichrodt did not return to combat. In total ships and tonnage sunk (28 for 162,491 tons) he stood tenth among all U-boats skippers in the war.

† In early 1943, Patrol Squadrons VP 32, VP 34, VP 53, VP 74, VP 81, VP 83, VP 94, and six of the VP 200–VP 212 series served in Fairwing 11.

‡ Fairwing 16 absorbed four patrol squadrons from Fairwing 11: VP 74, VP 83, VP 94, and VP 203. Both wings were equipped with Catalinas, Mariners, and Venturas, the latter two aircraft types plagued with serious defects.

of Mexico and Brazilian waters and participated in the rescue of the *Laconia* survivors, patrolled the same area off Brazil as did Fechner. In the two weeks from December 27 to January 8, Schacht sank three lone British freighters for 14,200 tons, and captured the captains of two. These sinkings and past claims and overclaims qualified Schacht for a *Ritterkreuz,* awarded by radio on January 9.* On January 13, in nearly the same place that *U-164* was sunk a week earlier, Schacht reported that he had sighted a southbound convoy. It was the first to operate on a newly organized run from Trinidad to Bahia (Salvador), Brazil. Apart from its surface escort of Canadian corvettes and American patrol craft (PCs), the convoy had protection from Catalinas of Patrol Squadron VP 83. One of the Catalinas, piloted by L. Ludwig, spotted *U-507* while she was diving, dropped four bombs, and sank her with the loss of all hands as well as the two British POWs. It went down about twenty miles due north of *U-164.* Schacht had enjoyed the prestige of his *Ritterkreuz* for merely four days.

Of the five remaining boats, one, the Type IXC *U-176,* went to Brazilian waters, and the other four patrolled near Trinidad to interdict traffic leaving there for the Mediterranean or Brazil.

While outbound in the South Atlantic to Brazil on November 25, Reiner Dierksen in *U-176,* who had made one impressive patrol in the North Atlantic, came upon the 6,000-ton Dutch freighter *Polydorus.* She had sailed on November 8 from the British Isles with convoy Outbound North 145, but a week later, she and fifteen other ships had left the convoy to sail independently to Freetown and elsewhere.

Dierksen had sunk five and a half ships on his maiden patrol and knew what he was about. But *Polydorus* proved to be one of the most stubborn victims of the U-boat war. In his first attack from a submerged position, on the afternoon of November 25, Dierksen fired four torpedoes. One prematured, and the other three missed. After dark, Dierksen surfaced and attacked *Polydorus* with his 4.1" deck gun and other topside weapons. The captain of *Polydorus,* H. Brouwer, evaded and returned fire with his slightly smaller 4" gun, laid a smoke screen, then escaped into a rain squall.

Dierksen continued the chase through the night. At dawn he mounted a second submerged attack, firing two torpedoes, but the alert Dutch crew saw the torpedoes and evaded. Shortly afterward, *U-176* surfaced in broad daylight and again opened fire with her deck gun. *Polydorus* returned fire with her gun, forcing Dierksen to fall back beyond range. He kept the top hamper of *Polydorus* in sight and tracked through the day, then, after dark, he pulled ahead slowly. In the early hours of November 27—after nearly forty-eight hours of pursuit—Dierksen got into good position, and undetected, fired two more torpedoes (the seventh and eighth) at this ship. Both hit and *Polydorus* sank slowly, giving eighty survivors of the eighty-one-man crew time to organize and provision three lifeboats. After merely one day

* At the time of the award, his confirmed score was nineteen ships for 77,144 tons.

in the boats, a Spanish ship came along, rescued the men, and landed them in the Canary Islands.

Dierksen proceeded westward to Brazilian waters. On December 13 and 16 he sank two other ships. The first, which he boarded and scuttled, was the insignificant 1,600-ton Swedish neutral *Scania,* which he deemed to be carrying contraband. The second was the 5,900-ton British freighter *Observer,* which Dierksen sank near Natal. In the second attack, he reported, a "B-24" (if true, a USAAF aircraft) caught and bombed *U-176,* causing serious damage. Forced to haul far out to sea to make repairs, it was not until January 9 that Dierksen reported that *U-176* was again "fully operational." Thereafter he commenced a long voyage home, slowly crossing the South Atlantic to Freetown, thence northward to a site west of the Canary Islands, where *U-176* met the XB (minelayer) *U-118* to take on fuel and Metox apparatus to further hand over to two other inbound boats. The *U-176* arrived in France on February 18, completing a voyage of 102 days, during which she sank three ships for 12,400 tons, or an average of one ship every thirty-four days.

The aging IXB *U-105,* severely damaged in June by British aircraft, sailed in late November, commanded by a new skipper, Jürgen Nissen, age twenty-six. Approaching the West Indies, Nissen sank the 6,600-ton British freighter *Orfor.* When Bleichrodt in *U-109* aborted, Nissen replaced him in an area north of Trinidad. Harassed by heavy air patrols day and night, Nissen sank nothing in this area except the 67-ton British sailing ship *C. S. Flight,* which he boarded and scuttled near the island of St. Lucia.*

Three other boats patrolled near Trinidad at this time. These were Mohr in *U-124,* crippled by malfunctioning diesel engines, and two Type VIID minelayers, *U-214* and *U-217.* Kurt Reichenbach-Klinke in *U-217,* who boarded and scuttled the 2,600-ton Swedish neutral *Etna,* was under orders to enter the Caribbean and patrol off Aruba and Curaçao. However, following his claim of sinking a 6,000-ton freighter and several hits on another big freighter near Trinidad, Reichenbach-Klinke reported his Metox was out and requested cancellation of his Caribbean assignment. As a result, the other VIID, *U-214,* commanded by Günther Reeder, who had sunk a 4,400-ton Polish freighter, was assigned to the area near Aruba and Curaçao and *U-217* patrolled a less hazardous area off British Guiana.

Reeder in *U-214* entered the Caribbean, but almost immediately he incurred a gyro-compass failure. He arranged a rendezvous with Nissen in *U-105,* who had compass spare parts. After that, Reeder returned to Aruba and Curaçao, the first

---

* As one step in an apparent attempt to terrorize British ship crews, on March 11, 1943, a German radio propagandist bragged about Nissen's attack on the *C. S. Flight.* He said that Nissen poured "streams of tracer bullets" and lobbed hand grenades into the sails and rigging, forcing the "Negro crew" to leap into the sea. At Dönitz's trial at Nuremberg, British prosecutors introduced a précis of the broadcast as one more example of alleged atrocities committed by U-boats. Probably because no witnesses could be found to corroborate the hearsay radio broadcast, the British prosecutors did not pursue this incident further.

U-boat to patrol those waters in many months. Off Curaçao on January 8, he attempted a daylight submerged attack on a convoy of eight tankers, but one of the ships saw a "torpedo splash" (as Reeder reported), spoiling the attack. Altogether Reeder patrolled for nineteen arduous days inside the Caribbean, but he had abysmal luck. Having sunk only the Polish ship of 4,400 tons, he headed for home.

Reichenbach-Klinke in *U-217* patrolled off the coast of British Guiana for the entire month of January without seeing any shipping. He reported that there were "systematic" Catalina patrols extending up to two hundred miles off the coast.* On his return trip to France, Reichenbach-Klinke found and sank by torpedo and gun a 8,000-ton British freighter and captured one officer. Owing to an unscheduled early return of the "Milk Cow" tanker *U-462,* the recently sailed Type IXC *U-504* was directed to replenish *U-217,* an operation twice delayed by inclement weather. Reichenbach-Klinke arrived in France after ninety-two days at sea—a near record for a Type VIID—having sunk two ships for 10,600 tons.

Nissen in *U-105* patrolled off Trinidad for a full month, from December 15 to January 15, without sinking anything other than the sailing ship. On the return voyage to France, he found and sank the abandoned hulk of the 8,100-ton tanker *British Vigilance,* damaged earlier by *U-514.* Three days later, on January 27, he sank the lone 5,100-ton American freighter *Cape Decision,* heavily laden with war matériel. Like *U-217,* Nissen refueled from the IXC *U-504.* In this eighty-four-day patrol, Nissen sank three confirmed ships for about 11,900 tons, plus the 8,100-ton hulk of the *British Vigilance.*

Approaching Trinidad on December 16, Johann Mohr in *U-124,* beset by intermittent engine failure, found a northbound convoy. He counted six big tankers escorted by five "destroyers." With scarcely a pause, Mohr attacked, shooting a salvo at one of the escorts and at two tankers. He reported that two torpedoes missed the escort, but two hit an 8,000-ton tanker and one hit a 6,000-ton tanker. One tanker sank in five minutes, the other in fifteen minutes, Mohr reported, but neither of these sinkings could be confirmed in Allied records. After reloading his torpedo tubes, Mohr attempted a second attack, but it was thwarted by ASW aircraft.

During the next dozen days, Mohr patrolled off Trinidad and Tobago. He spent much of the time nursing his failing diesels. On one occasion, a small amount of salt water from the distiller contaminated some battery cells, causing the formation of chlorine gas. It took twelve hours to fix this problem and ventilate the boat. Engine failure, Mohr reported, thwarted effective attacks on two other small convoys. A Catalina air patrol drove him off another convoy. During these trying days he destroyed only one confirmed ship, a 4,700-ton British freighter, sunk by a single torpedo fired from a submerged position on a bright moonlit night.

Mohr's luck changed dramatically on January 9. That night he found a south-

* Patrol Squadron VP 83 of Fairwing 11, based at Natal, had been reinforced early in January 1943 by two other U.S. Navy patrol squadrons from Fairwing 11, Squadrons 74 and 94. U.S. Army Air Forces aircraft also patrolled this area.

bound convoy, Trinidad-Bahia 1 (TB 1). Tracking close with faltering engines, he counted nine ships and four escorts, and dived to conduct a daylight submerged attack. In two separate, bold, well-executed approaches, he sank four American ships for 23,567 tons, the 7,700-ton tanker *Broad Arrow* and three cargo ships. These and past sinkings and overclaims qualified Mohr for Oak Leaves to his *Ritterkreuz,* later awarded by Hitler at his headquarters in the Ukraine.*

The rest of the patrol brought more frustration. On January 10, Mohr chased a lone freighter on one engine. When he finally got close enough to shoot, he missed. A Catalina appeared to spoil a second attack. A week later, on January 16, he shot a single torpedo at a tanker. Fortunately it missed: The ship turned out to be a neutral. After that chase, Mohr's engineer warned him that if he did not head for home immediately, the diesels might fail beyond repair. While homebound, Mohr refueled from the IXC *U-504,* in the wake of *U-105* and *U-217.* In this arduous, eighty-one-day patrol, Mohr claimed sinking eight ships (three tankers, five freighters) for 46,000 tons. His confirmed score—by far the best of the eight boats to reach American waters—was five ships for 28,259 tons. Although Mohr could have chosen a safe job ashore, he elected to remain in command of *U-124.*

Apart from Mohr's patrol, the eleven boats assigned to American waters in November turned in disappointing results. Three boats never got beyond the Bay of Biscay, and Bleichrodt in *U-109* aborted with no sinkings. The seven other boats that reached American waters, including Mohr's crippled *U-124,* sank nineteen ships for about 92,400 tons, including the 8,100-ton abandoned hulk *British Vigilance.* In all, the eleven boats sank an average of only 1.7 ships for 8,400 tons per boat per patrol. Three of the Type IXs did not return: *U-164, U-507,* and *U-517.*

From the reports of these and other boats it was clear that the hunting grounds east and southeast of Trinidad and in the waters off British, Dutch, and French Guiana no longer offered easy prey. The Allies had extended the convoy network to those areas with Catalinas and other aircraft escorting most of the way. Yet it was vital for the Germans to interdict that traffic. Most of the loaded tankers and freighters forming into convoys at Trinidad were headed for the Mediterranean, either directly east across the Atlantic or south-southeast via Cape Town. Every one of those Allied ships that was sunk directly helped the retreating *Afrika Korps* in North Africa.

Action in the Middle Atlantic

During the year 1942, British oil stocks (reserves or stockpiles) fell from seven million tons to 5.2 million tons. The reasons were several:

- Petroleum products for all British forces involved in Torch were drawn directly from reserves in the British Isles. The failure of the Allies to promptly seize Tunisia, prolonging the campaign, produced a further, unanticipated drain on the reserves.

---

* At the time of the award, his confirmed score was twenty-seven ships for 125,520 tons.

• The establishment of the extensive convoy network in American waters at midyear, in which most Allied tankers were required to sail, significantly slowed the flow of oil to the British Isles via Halifax convoys sailing from New York.

• The loss to Axis submarines of 185 Allied tankers from January 1 to September 1, 1942,* while not a crippling blow, nonetheless contributed to the decline in British stocks.†

• The hideous weather in the fall and winter in the North Atlantic caused heavy damage to many merchant ships, especially to tankers. At the end of 1942, the official British oil historian wrote, nearly one quarter of the British-controlled tanker fleet (1.7 million of 7.6 million deadweight tons) was in repair, awaiting repair, or otherwise immobilized (a few ships, of course, by torpedo damage).

The drawdown of British oil reserves in 1942 caused great alarm in London. Battle plans for 1943 were contingent upon healthy oil reserves. On December 17, Churchill proposed to Roosevelt a number of drastic measures to arrest the decline and rebuild the stocks:

• Special oil convoys to sail directly from the Caribbean to the British Isles (or United Kingdom) every three weeks (CU and the reverse, UC). The eighteen inbound convoys per year were to deliver about 1.2 million tons of petroleum products in 1943, enough to arrest the decline. To provide escorts for these special convoys, the British Royal Navy would assume all escort duties on the North Atlantic run with eight close escort groups, releasing three Canadian groups and the American group, A-3, for other convoy duty.

• Special oil convoys to sail directly from the Caribbean to various Allied-controlled ports in the Mediterranean in support of Torch. These convoys (Oil-Torch, or OT, and the reverse, TO) would enable the British to substantially reduce the flow of oil from British stocks and, in effect, contribute to their rebuilding. Composed only of fast tankers ("Greyhounds" of 14 1/2 knots plus), these convoys were to be escorted by a special detachment of modern American destroyers from the Atlantic Fleet.

• Further rebuilding of stocks by the sailing of Greyhounds from the Caribbean to the British Isles, unescorted.

These proposals raised serious questions in Washington. Uppermost was this one: Why should British oil reserves be maintained at seven million tons? Even at the December 1942 figure, 5.2 million tons, the British had more than a six-month supply of one hundred octane aviation gasoline and a comparable supply of fuel oil. No American or Pacific war zone had more than ten weeks of aviation gasoline, and the northeastern United States had a fuel oil reserve of only four weeks. In order to meet Churchill's proposal for aviation fuel, the training of military pilots in the United States would have to be curtailed appreciably, resulting in a senseless production of aircraft for which no aircrews were to be available.

Roosevelt responded tactfully that he would continue to help the British in

---

* See Volume I, Appendix 17.

† From September 1 to December 31, 1942, the Allies lost thirty-three tankers to Axis submarines, nineteen in North Atlantic convoys.

every way he possibly could, but . . . He opposed opening out the North Atlantic convoys from eight to ten days, the shifting around of the escort groups already in service in that area, the sailing of fast tankers unescorted, and the sailing of tankers into Mediterranean ports, often bombed by the *Luftwaffe.* New measures already in train, such as special oil convoys directly from the Caribbean to the "New York oil pool," which were to increase the number of escorted tanker round-trips in fast Halifax convoys, would provide the British with 1.25 million tons of petroleum products a month from the Americas or fifteen million tons per year. This, said Roosevelt's oil king, Harold Ickes, was enough not only to stop the erosion of British stocks but also, possibly, to rebuild them.

The discussions about the decline of British imports, including oil, continued with mounting intensity into 1943. In the meantime, the British War Cabinet, more deeply concerned than ever about the so-called oil shortage, directed the Admiralty to sail at least three tanker convoys, protected by British escorts, directly from Trinidad or the Caribbean to the Mediterranean. These were TM 1, a slow convoy with corvettes in the escort, which sailed from Trinidad on December 28, 1942, and TM (Fast) 1 and TM (Fast) 2, both of which had sailed by mid-January 1943, escorted by British destroyers.

Owing to the prolongation of Torch operations, Washington did, in fact, finally organize and sail OT (Oil-Torch) convoys directly from the Caribbean to Northwest Africa. The first, OT 1, composed of Greyhounds and escorted by American destroyers, sailed from Aruba on February 2 for Dakar. The second, OT 2, sailed from Aruba on February 20 for Gibraltar and Casablanca, but not to Allied ports deep inside the Mediterranean. Delayed by the need to refit or overhaul the American destroyers engaged in the escort, the OT convoys sailed about every two months, delivering an average of about 200,000 tons of petroleum products in each convoy.

The Americans also finally yielded and commenced sailing oil convoys direct from the Caribbean to the United Kingdom. The first, CU 1, comprised of nine Greyhound tankers escorted by American destroyers, sailed from Curaçao on March 20 and arrived in the British Isles thirteen days later. The second, CU 2, similarly composed, sailed sixty-three days after the first, on May 22. These two convoys delivered 130,000 tons of oil to further replenish British stockpiles.*

The Type IXs and VIID (minelayers) that patrolled American waters possessed the endurance for the task, but they were not really suitable for attacking convoys or capable of quick dives to elude aircraft. Therefore, Dönitz decided to send, in addition to two IXs, a special task force of a half dozen VIIs to the waters near Natal, Brazil, to attack along the newly organized convoy routes. Adopting the much used codename group *Delphin* (Dolphin), the boats sailed during the week from December 17 to 22. The task force was to be supported by the "Milk Cow" tanker *U-463,* commnded by Leo Wolfbauer, which had sailed earlier.

---

* See Plate 5.

The two IXs assigned to American waters in December were *U-125* and *U-514*, which, as related, had first to escort the outbound blockade-runner *Germania* through the Bay of Biscay to safer waters. After the British sank *Germania* on December 15, and the search for survivors was called off, the two boats were diverted to attack a southbound convoy discovered west of Biscay on December 18 by the outbound VII *U-441*. When all efforts to assemble a U-boat group strong enough to attack this convoy failed, on December 21 *U-125* and *U-514* were directed to resume their voyages to the Trinidad area. However, when Ulrich Folkers in *U-125* reported serious diesel-engine problems and a lack of the necessary spare parts, he was diverted to a rendezvous first with the "Milk Cow" tanker *U-461*, then with Helmut Witte in the IXC *U-159*, returning from his notable patrol to Cape Town. As a result of these delays to pick up spare parts, *U-125* lagged about 250 miles behind *U-514*.

In the meantime, *B-dienst* alerted Dönitz to a UGS convoy en route from the Americas to Gibraltar, which was to sail an unusual route to the *south* of the Azores. Acting on this information, Dönitz halted the Brazil-bound group *Delphin* and redeployed its six VIIs on a patrol line southwest of the Azores. After one full week of futile searching, on January 2 Dönitz canceled this diversion and directed the *Delphin* boats to refuel from the group's tanker, *U-463*, then resume the voyage to Brazil.

On the following day, January 3, the Trinidad-bound *U-514*, commanded by Hans-Jürgen Auffermann, encountered by chance a convoy of nine fully laden, big, fast tankers en route from Trinidad to the Mediterranean. This was TM 1, the first special British oil convoy, too thinly escorted by British Escort Group 5, commanded by Richard C. Boyle: the destroyer *Havelock* and three British corvettes, *Pimpernel, Godetia,* and *Saxifrage*. The tankers were fast ones, but the need to stretch the fuel of the corvettes reduced the speed of the convoy to about eight knots, leaving it much more vulnerable to U-boat attack.

Upon receiving Auffermann's report, Dönitz told him to shadow "without fail" but also authorized him to attack. Folkers in *U-125* (250 miles east) and group *Delphin* (nine hundred miles east) were to close on the convoy at high speed. Dönitz believed Folkers could help Auffermann, but, as he logged, he felt there was "little hope" that group *Delphin* could. Nonetheless, owing to the "pressing need" to shut down Torch oil traffic, every possible effort had to be made.

Auffermann attacked and hit the 8,100-ton tanker *British Vigilance*. It exploded in a fireball but did not sink.* Auffermann mistakenly reported his victim to be the 17,000-ton whale factory ship *Kosmos II*, serving as a tanker. Owing to the weakness of the escort group and to failures in the radar and/or Huff Duff sets, the four British warships were unable to take effective action against the lone shadower, *U-514*. Unfortunately for the Germans, Auffermann's radio and his diesels partly failed. Thus most of his contact reports were unreadable and he could only make 13 knots. Nonetheless, he hung on. As a result of Auffermann's radio failures,

---

* As related, Nissen in *U-105*, homebound from Trinidad, later found and sank the hulk.

Folkers in *U-125,* still beset with diesel-engine problems, could not find Auffermann or the convoy and played no further role in the battle.

At this time a number of U-boats, both inbound and outbound, were in the vicinity. Among the outbound boats were several of another group, *Seehund* (Seal), en route to Cape Town and the Indian Ocean.* At the same time that Auffermann reported convoy TM 1, the new U-cruiser *U-182,* commanded by *Ritterkreuz* holder Nikolaus Clausen, which was loosely attached to group *Seehund,* found and reported a westbound convoy. Since Clausen's convoy was merely 360 miles from the center boat of the group *Delphin* patrol line, Dönitz canceled the orders for them to attack *U-514*'s convoy (TM 1) and directed the group to attack *U-182*'s convoy.

The convoy that Clausen came upon was GUF (Gibraltar–United States Fast) 3, which sailed from Casablanca on December 29. It was composed of twenty-four ships, powerfully escorted by American men-of-war: the battleship *New York,* the light cruiser *Philadelphia,* and nine destroyers. The new destroyer *Earle,* commanded by Hamilton W. Howe, who, as skipper of *Roper* had sunk *U-85* off Cape Hatteras, got *U-182* on radar, ran down the bearing, and opened fire by searchlight. Joined by another new destroyer, *Parker, Earle* hunted *U-182* for ten hours, Howe logged.

As a result of this long and persistent chase, Clausen lost contact with the GUF convoy. Nonetheless, based on his reports and good guesses, the next night four of the *Delphin* boats found it and reported. But before they could attack, the destroyers *Earle* and *Parker* and others drove the U-boats off and under. After receiving reports from these boats, including one from Günther Heydemann in *U-575,* who reported a "very heavy" depth-charge attack, Dönitz decided to cancel *Delphin* operations against this heavily escorted convoy and shift the group back to *U-514*'s weakly escorted convoy (TM 1), even though the latter was at least four days distant and might never be found.

It was a risky decision but it paid off. Stubbornly dismissing a recommendation from London to divert to the north of the Azores, escort commander Boyle held to his original game plan. As a consequence, on the afternoon of January 8, convoy TM 1 sailed right into the center of the *Delphin* patrol line. Wilhelm-Heinrich von Pückler und Limpurg in *U-381* found, reported, and tracked the convoy. Upon receipt of his report, the five other *Delphin* boats closed. In addition, Dönitz ordered four other boats in the area to join the hunt: two Type IXCs of the outbound *Seehund* group (*U-511* and *U-522*) and two boats inbound from prolonged patrols in the South Atlantic (*U-128* and *U-134*). Later, Dönitz also directed Wolfgang Lüth in the IXD2 U-cruiser *U-181,* inbound from the Indian Ocean, to join. These orders put thirteen attack boats (five IXs, seven VIIs, one U-cruiser) on the trail of the eight remaining tankers of TM 1. However, three of the IXs (*U-125, U-128,* and *U-514*) had no hope of catching up with the convoy and of getting into the battle.

That night, January 8–9, and in the day and night following, the U-boats made

---

* Initially *Seehund* was composed of five experienced IXC40s and the new IXD2 U-cruiser *U-182.* The IXC40s were to be supported by the tanker *U-459.*

contact and attacked. From Paris Dönitz exhorted: "Be hard in the attack! Help your comrades in Tunis . . . operate tenaciously . . . go after the slightest opportunity with all your energy!"

All ten boats shot at targets.

- Günther Seibicke in the VII *U-436,* a veteran of the Arctic, sank by torpedo and gun two British tankers: the 8,300-ton *Albert L. Ellsworth* and the 6,400-ton *Oltenia II.*
- Herbert Schneider in the IXC *U-522* also sank two tankers: the 10,000-ton Panamanian *Norvik* and the 6,800-ton Norwegian *Minister Wedel.* Schneider damaged another tanker, the 7,000-ton *British Dominion.*
- Heinz Stein in the VII *U-620* sank the tanker *British Dominion.*
- Hans-Joachim Hesse in the VII *U-442* sank the 9,800-ton British tanker *Empire Lytton.*
- Fritz Schneewind, new skipper of the IXC *U-511,* sank the 5,000-ton British freighter *William Wilberforce,* but it turned out she was not part of the convoy, merely an unlucky loner that happened by.

The other five boats in contact with the convoy shot but missed Günther Heydemann with a bow salvo of four FATs. Only two of the nine tankers that formed the original convoy, the Norwegians *Vanja* and *Cliona,* reached Gibraltar.

The U-boats suffered no loses and except for Rudolf Schendel in *U-134,* only slight battle damage or mechanical failures. Reporting "heavy" damage from a depth-charge attack, Schendel resumed his homeward voyage. Wolfgang Lüth in *U-181,* Günther Seibicke in *U-436,* Helmut Möhlmann in *U-571,* and Heinz Stein in *U-620* reported depth-charge attacks but only minor damage. Lüth also resumed his homeward voyage. Von Pückler und Limpurg in *U-381,* Hesse in *U-442,* and Heydemann in *U-575* reported repairable diesel-engine failures. The six VIIs of group *Delphin* replenished from the tanker *U-463* on January 14. Heydemann in *U-575,* who had fired all twelve of his internal torpedoes in the battle, met Bleichrodt's aborting *U-109* and got five torpedoes from her, downloading two more torpedoes from his deck canisters.

It was difficult for Dönitz and the OKM to assess the damage to convoy TM 1. In aggregate, the U-boats claimed hits on twenty-five ships and that fifteen of these ships had sunk. Although it was obvious that different U-boats claimed hitting and sinking the same ships, Dönitz and the OKM let the inflated claims stand.* In a personal message, Admiral Raeder congratulated Dönitz and the skippers of group *Delphin* and others for a "brilliant joint success." German propagandists boasted that the U-boats sank fifteen ships for 142,000 tons. The confirmed score was seven of nine tankers for 56,453 tons sunk from the convoy. Adding in the hapless freighter that happened by made eight ships for 61,457 tons.†

---

* Heydemann in *U-575* claimed his original twelve internal torpedoes had sunk six ships for 41,000 tons, none of which could be confirmed.

† On January 16, Herbert Schneider in *U-522,* who had sunk two tankers in TM 1 for 16,867 tons and damaged another, was awarded a *Ritterkreuz.* At the time of the award his confirmed score was six ships for about 37,000 tons, plus damage to two others.

The battle with TM 1 significantly altered the deployment plan for many of the December U-boats. None of those headed for the Americas got there. The foray of group *Delphin* to Brazil was canceled, as were the patrols of *U-125* and *U-514* to the West Indies. Having shot off many torpedoes and used up a lot of fuel, the *U-511* and *U-522* had to be deleted from group *Seehund,* bound for Cape Town and the Indian Ocean.* Group *Delphin,* enlarged to include the IXs that were drawn into the battle (*U-125, U-511, U-514,* and *U-522*) and by five VIIs that sailed in January, remained in the area near the Azores to intercept inbound or outbound Torch convoys, in effect replacing the disbanded group *Westwall.*

In the early days of January 1943, Allied codebreakers had not yet mastered the four-rotor Enigma, *Triton.* Hence the Submarine Tracking Rooms were unable to provide Torch convoy commanders with much assistance. But from January 9 onward the codebreakers began to read *Triton,* sometimes with little delay. As a result, the Allies were able to route most UG and GU Torch convoys around group *Delphin.*

Such was the case of convoy UGS 4, inbound to Gibraltar from the United States. Fully alive to the presence of group *Delphin* south of the Azores, Allied authorities diverted this convoy to the north of the Azores. However, three American stragglers of the convoy failed to get the word, or elected to ignore it and went south of the Azores, directly into the *Delphin* patrol line. As a result, Hesse in *U-442* and Auffermann in *U-514* sank 7,200-ton Liberty ships, *Julia Ward Howe* and *Charles C. Pinckney,* respectively, and Heydemann in *U-575* sank the 5,000-ton freighter *City of Flint.* These successes increased the score of the expanded *Delphin* group to ten ships for 80,900 tons.†

The horrific losses in British oil convoy TM 1 was a humiliating setback for London and, of course, did nothing to slow the drawdown of British oil reserves or contribute to rebuilding them. However, the two fast, heavily escorted oil convoys immediately following, TMF 1 and TMF 2, which reached Gibraltar by the end of January with no losses, did significantly help the situation. Thereafter London contributed only a slight trickle of petrol to Torch from reserves in the British Isles, most of it in cans, which were in great demand in the desert.

Allied Strategic Bombing

In three years of warfare, Prime Minister Churchill and a majority of the British War Cabinet had become resolutely convinced that the Allies could decisively erode Germany's ability and will to fight by a massive and relentless bomber offensive against German war plants and the civilian population. The chief of the RAF,

* The IXC *U-160,* which sailed in early January, replaced *U-522* in group *Seehund,* but *U-511* was not replaced. Hence, *Seehund* was reduced to five boats: *U-160,* the IXCs *U-506, U-509,* and *U-516,* and Clausen's IXD2 U-cruiser *U-182,* all supported by the tanker *U-459.*

† If Auffermann in *U-514* rather than Nissen in *U-105* is credited the 8,100-ton tanker *British Vigilance* of TM 1, the expanded *Delphin* group sank eleven ships for 89,000 tons.

Charles Portal, and the chief of Bomber Command, Arthur Harris, pressed this strategic concept with undiminished vigor. They stressed that it was a relatively cheap option that would also grind down the existing *Luftwaffe* fighter force at home, draw *Luftwaffe* elements from the Russian front, possibly obviate a direct, bloody confrontation between Allied ground forces and the German army on the continent, as in World War I, and, of course, exact revenge for *Luftwaffe* attacks on British cities. American airmen and others held similar views.

While the senior British and American airmen agreed on the strategic need for a combined bomber offensive, they differed markedly over tactics. Lacking a long-range fighter to protect its heavy bombers and a high-altitude precision aiming device, Bomber Command had elected to conduct "area" raids on German cities at night. Unable to pinpoint the location of military installations or war plants in the dark, the main targets became by default the civilian populations. In contrast, the Americans, employing heavily armed, rugged, heavy bombers (B-17 Flying Fortresses; B-24 Liberators) equipped with the wondrous (top secret) Norden bombsights, elected to raid German cities by day, bombing visible war plants and military installations from high altitudes, sparing, to the extent possible, the civilian population.

During the early years of the war (1939–1941) Bomber Command incurred heavy losses and, other than exacting revenge, it achieved little. By 1942, however, it had grown to the point that it could stage awesome "Thousand Plane Raids."* Mesmerized by the propaganda and other advantages such raids promised, in the summer of 1942 Prime Minister Churchill authorized a hefty increase in the size of Bomber Command (from thirty-two to fifty squadrons) by January 1, 1943. The new heavy-bomber groups were to have greatly improved British aircraft (Lancasters and Halifaxes) and American-built Lend-Lease B-17s and B-24s.† Pathfinder aircraft, guided to the target by an electronic "beam" navigational system (Gee) and equipped with a ground-mapping centimetric-wavelength radar (H2S), were to insure greater accuracy—and devastation—by the oncoming heavy-bomber formations.

To carry out their share of the bomber offensive, in June 1942, the Americans established the Eighth Air Force in the British Isles. Its chief was Carl Spaatz, who reported directly to Dwight Eisenhower, the newly appointed commander of all

---

* The first RAF "Thousand Plane Raid" hit Cologne on the night of May 30–31, 1942. The bombers killed 474 people, destroyed 3,300 homes, and left 45,000 homeless. Two further "Thousand Plane Raids" followed: at Essen on June 1 (956 aircraft) and at Bremen on June 25 (904 aircraft). On analysis, the second two raids were deemed to be failures and, partly as a consequence, Bomber Command mounted no other "Thousand Plane Raids" in 1942.

† Heavy-bomber production in Britain and the United States was still relatively modest. In the month of July 1942, for example, British factories turned out 179 such aircraft, fifty less than planned. In 1942 the United States produced 2,576 heavy bombers, an average of 214 per month, which was about 6 percent of the total 42,000 aircraft deliveries. In compliance with the American Army-Navy Agreement of March 1942, the Army Air Forces grudgingly began delivery of B-24s to the American Navy in August. By the end of 1942, the Navy had received fifty-two B-24s, but Admiral King had sent all of them to the Pacific. In 1943 the Americans produced 9,393 heavy bombers, an average of 783 per month, which was about 14 percent of the 67,000 aircraft deliveries.

American Army and Army Air Forces units in the European Theater. Eisenhower did not share the view of the air zealots that the bomber offensive alone could defeat Germany, but in the belief that it could be a decisive factor in achieving an Allied victory, he gave it strong support.

The Eighth Air Force commenced combat operations on Independence Day, July 4, 1942. Six American crews, flying light American-designed RAF Boston attack bombers, joined a Bomber Command raid on four German airfields in the Netherlands. (Two of the American-manned planes were lost.) On August 17, Eighth Air Force carried out its first independent operation: a B-17 raid on the railroad yards in Rouen, France. By September, Spaatz was mounting ever larger attacks on German targets in France, Belgium, and the Netherlands (but not Germany), employing as many as thirty to fifty B-17s per raid. Eisenhower commended these early operations and concurred with Spaatz that the American tactic of high-level daylight bombing using the Norden bombsight was not only valid but superior to Bomber Command's nighttime "area" raids on German cities. British airmen continued to hold the opposite view and to urge the Americans to bomb at night.

The combined Anglo-American bomber offensive had only just begun when Torch shut it down. First, the British and the Americans transferred a substantial number of heavy bombers from the British Isles to the Mediterranean—the Americans to flesh out the newly formed Twelfth Air Force. Second, Dwight Eisenhower, concerned for the safety of the many Torch convoys, directed Eighth Air Force commander Carl Spaatz to throw most of the remaining weight of his outfit against the U-boat pens in western France.

"I want you to know," Eisenhower wrote Spaatz in explanation, "that I consider the defeat of the submarine to be one of the basic requirements of the winning of the war." Eisenhower appreciated the need to bomb Germany—and to draw *Luftwaffe* fighter elements from the Russian front and grind them down—but none of these air missions, he insisted, "should rank above the effort to defeat the German submarine."

The American airmen were not overjoyed at Eisenhower's directive, yet they, as well as the British airmen, conceded the necessity of protecting Torch convoys and of curtailing shipping losses by U-boats in all waters to the fullest possible extent. Meeting on October 14, Portal, Spaatz, Harris, and other senior Allied airmen agreed that Axis "submarines should be first priority targets at this time." Bomber Command was to concentrate its night bombing raids on German cities known to have U-boat building yards.* In compliance with Eisenhower's orders, the Eighth Air Force was to focus on the submarine pens at Lorient, St. Nazaire, La Pallice, and Brest.

Owing to the transfers of heavy bombers to the Twelfth Air Force in support of Torch, Spaatz was hard-pressed to mount "mass" attacks on the U-boat pens.

---

* Bomber Command had already raided Rostock, Lübeck, Emden, Bremen, Hamburg, and Wilhelmshaven. As was learned after the war, none of the hundreds of planes involved in these raids had hit a U-boat building yard or any U-boat.

Nonetheless, on October 21, a force of ninety heavy bombers (of which seventeen carried out diversionary sorties) left bases in the British Isles with about 231 tons of bombs. Meeting unexpectedly strong, skilled, radar-directed *Luftwaffe* fighters and heavy flak, only fifteen of the ninety bombers actually attacked Lorient. The aircrews claimed to have dropped thirty tons of bombs on the target. Based on photo reconnaissance, air intelligence concluded that only about half of the bombs dropped (fifteen tons) hit the target. No bomb penetrated the thick (twelve-to fourteen-foot) reinforced concrete roofs of the U-boat pens, but, as related, the IXB *U-124,* commanded by the *Ritterkreuz* holder Johann Mohr, caught in the open while shifting berths, was damaged and thus delayed in departing on patrol. Three American bombers were lost.

The Eighth Air Force conducted only that one raid in October, but during the initial Torch operations, from November 7 to 23, it attacked the U-boat pens seven more times. The November campaign comprised 411 sorties, of which fifty-five were diversionary. Two hundred and thirty-four sorties actually attacked the targets (Lorient, St. Nazaire, La Pallice, Brest) dropping 575 tons of bombs. Air intelligence estimated that about sixty tons of bombs hit the targets, but no bomb did any appreciable damage to any pen or U-boat. The Americans lost twelve heavy bombers in the seven raids in November.

In early December, Eisenhower summoned Spaatz to Algeria to temporarily direct Torch air operations. Spaatz's deputy, Ira C. Eaker (soon promoted to command the Eighth Air Force), assumed responsibility for continuing the raids on the U-boat pens. However, the shortage of available aircraft, terrible flying weather, and other factors restricted Eaker to merely one raid during the month of December. Seventy-seven aircraft, carrying about 146 tons of bombs, flew at the target (Lorient, for the fourth time). Forty of the seventy-seven aircraft actually attacked Lorient, dropping about eighty tons of bombs, but air intelligence calculated that only nine tons hit the target. The city of Lorient was flattened, but none of the bombs did any appreciable damage to the pens or the U-boats. Three bombers were lost.*

First Sea Lord Dudley Pound dutifully and graciously thanked Eaker and his aircrews for the November offensive against the pens, but all concerned suspected (correctly) that the raids were a failure, that at most they had only slightly inconvenienced the U-boat force. The Admiralty concluded that the raids could be truly effective only if Eighth Air Force mounted them in irregular order twice daily, employing not less than fifty heavy bombers in each attack. However, in view of the atrocious winter weather, which aborted takeoffs and obscured or hid the targets, it was not practical to attempt daylight raids on anything like that scale with any hope of success. Nonetheless, Allied authorities ruled that the raids on the U-boat pens were to continue indefinitely, with the greatest possible intensity, and

* Bomber Command managed only three raids on German cities with U-boat building yards in October, and no raids in November or December, in part because of terrible weather. Allied intelligence authorities characterized these three raids as "small and inconsequential." In a memo of January 4, 1943, Churchill groused that "the Americans have not yet succeeded in dropping a single bomb on Germany."

that commencing in January 1943, RAF Bomber Command was to assist Eighth Air Force with those targets.

The extent to which Allied strategic bombing contributed to the defeat of the Third Reich was, and still is, moot, and will probably remain unresolved forever. What is indisputable, however, is that had the War Cabinet assigned more of Bomber Command's four-engine, long-range, radar-equipped, land-based aircraft to Coastal Command from the summer of 1942 on, the "U-boat peril" could have been reduced dramatically that year. Given the loss of Allied shipping to U-boats in 1942, the failure to take that step (as Admiral King repeatedly urged) was yet another painful lapse by Prime Minister Churchill and others in London who were bedazzled and blinded by the enticing doctrines of the airmen, who promised a cheap, easy victory over Germany through airpower alone.

Hitler Sacks Raeder and Promotes Dönitz

With the winding down of Torch naval operations and the onset of twenty-four-hour darkness in the Arctic, which worked to the disadvantage of German aircraft and submarines, the Allies resumed convoys to Murmansk in December 1942. Inasmuch as naval aviators had not yet fully mastered night landings on carriers and the Germans had transferred most of their aircraft from Norway to the Russian or Mediterranean theaters, the Royal Navy's "jeep" carriers were not included in the escort.

At this time the roster of big German ships in Norwegian waters had altered somewhat. The battleship *Tirpitz,* the heavy cruiser *Hipper,* and the light cruisers *Köln* and *Nuremberg* were present but the "pocket" battleship *Admiral Scheer* had returned to the Baltic for repairs, replaced by her sister ship *Lützow* (ex-*Deutschland*). The latter was to remain in Norwegian waters until early January when, it was planned, she was to join the battle cruiser *Scharnhorst* and the heavy cruiser *Prinz Eugen* (both still in the Baltic) for a foray into the Atlantic, provided Hitler approved. *Hipper* and *Köln* were based in Altenfiord for possible attacks on Murmansk convoys.

British codebreakers, reading *Luftwaffe* Red and the three-rotor naval Enigma still in use on naval nets in Norway, provided good information on most of the big-ship movements as well as the German decision to provisionally transfer U-boats from the Arctic force to the Atlantic force. The codebreakers reported that *Hipper* and *Köln* were in Altenfiord and that *Lützow* arrived in Narvik on December 12.

The Admiralty, which was responsible for Murmansk convoys, decided to sail the December convoy (PQ 19) in two sections of about fifteen ships each. The first section, designated by new coding procedures as JW 51-A and composed of fifteen ships plus an oiler for the escorts, sailed from Loch Ewe, Scotland, on December 15.* It was closely escorted by seven fleet destroyers and four smaller vessels plus

---

* Loch Ewe was a more convenient and comfortable departure port for Murmansk convoys than Iceland, especially in the icy winter months. Ships from the United States bound for Murmansk crossed the Atlantic in fast Halifax convoys, which sailed from New York.

the cruisers *Sheffield* and *Jamaica* and two more destroyers to screen the cruisers. A force from the Home Fleet, comprised of the battleship *King George V,* the heavy cruiser *Berwick,* and three more destroyers, provided distant cover. Four British submarines laid off Altenfiord to watch for movements by *Hipper* and *Köln.*

The German admiral commanding Arctic operations, Otto Klüber, who had only three U-boats and no aircraft on patrol, failed to detect JW 51-A. Under cover of Arctic darkness, the convoy reached Kola Inlet, the waterway to Murmansk, on Christmas Day with no enemy encounters. Five cargo ships went on to Molotovsk, near icebound Archangel. Two days later, the opposite-sailing convoy, redesignated RA 51, with its close escort plus the cruisers *Sheffield* and *Jamaica* and their two-destroyer screen sailed from Kola Inlet. Since there were seven destroyers with JW 51-A and seven with RA 51, the two destroyers in RA 51 serving as screens for the cruisers were detached and proceeded independently to Iceland.

The second section of the convoy to Murmansk, JW 51-B, sailed from Loch Ewe on December 22. Comprised of fourteen merchant ships, it was escorted by six fleet destroyers and five other smaller vessels—two corvettes, a minesweeper *(Bramble),* and two ASW trawlers. The battleship *Anson,* the heavy cruiser *Cumberland,* and destroyer screens of the Home Fleet provided distant cover. On the fifth day out, December 27, this convoy ran into a heavy storm. In the dark, heavy seas and howling Arctic wind, five merchant ships and two escorts separated from the main body. Later three ships rejoined and one ship, escorted by the destroyer *Oribi,* proceeded independently to Kola Inlet. The other ship, escorted by an ASW trawler, sought to rejoin the convoy.

One of four German U-boats on Arctic patrol, the newly arrived *U-354,* commanded by Karl-Heinz Herbschleb, detected convoy JW 51-B. Upon receiving Herbschleb's report, Admiral Raeder directed Otto Klüber to attack JW 51-B with the "pocket" battleship *Lützow,* which had shifted from Narvik to Altenfiord on December 19, the heavy cruiser *Hipper,* and six destroyers. Maintaining radio silence, this force sailed from Altenfiord on December 30, undetected by British codebreakers or by the four British submarines that were scouting off the fjord. The force was commanded by Oskar Kummetz, the officer whom Dönitz had praised for correcting many of the defects in German torpedoes in 1940. Like the big-ship commanders preceding him in Arctic waters, Kummetz was under orders from the OKM to avoid contact with an enemy of equal or superior strength because Hitler did not wish to risk a blow to German prestige by the loss of another big ship.

Unaware of the close presence of *Sheffield* and *Jamaica,* Kummetz had conceived an unusual—and controversial—plan of action, which divided his forces. *Hipper* and three destroyers were to attack the convoy from the port quarter during the two and a half hours of feeble twilight before noon. Kummetz believed that *Hipper* and her three destroyers would draw off the fleet destroyers of the close escort and that the convoy itself would turn away, or south, right into the waiting arms of *Lützow* and her three destroyers.

These German and British forces met in a wild melee in the morning twilight of December 31. Per plan, *Hipper* and her three destroyers drew off the convoy escorts. *Hipper* hit three destroyers (*Onslow, Obedient,* and the aged *Achates*) and the minesweeper *Bramble. Achates* sank. The German destroyer *Eckholdt* of

Hipper's group sank the damaged *Bramble*. Hearing the gunfire, the cruisers *Sheffield* and *Jamaica*, with the westbound convoy RA 51, valorously came up at full speed to counterattack the larger-gunned *Hipper* (6" versus 8") and her three destroyers. The British cruisers sank the destroyer *Eckholdt* and severely damaged *Hipper*. Mindful of Hitler's orders not to risk a big-ship loss and fearful of an enemy torpedo attack in the darkness, which might cause damage and dash her planned Atlantic sortie with *Scharnhorst* and *Prinz Eugen*, *Lützow* (six 11" guns, eight 5.9" guns, and six 4.1" guns) and her three destroyers timidly lobbed a few rounds at the convoy, slightly damaging the destroyer *Obdurate* and the merchant ship *Calobre*. *Lützow* then forswore a golden opportunity not only to destroy the entire convoy but also to sink *Sheffield* and *Jamaica* and perhaps the remaining five British destroyers and smaller escorts, and shamefully fled with *Hipper* and the five surviving German destroyers to Altenfiord. Herbschleb in *U-354* twice attacked the convoy, but both times he failed. No other U-boat attempted an attack.

The merchant ships of both convoys, JW 51-B and RA 51, reached their respective destinations essentially unharmed. In the battle of December 31, the British lost one old destroyer *(Achates)* and a minesweeper *(Bramble)*. *Hipper* severely damaged the destroyer *Onslow*. The Germans lost one destroyer *(Eckholdt)* and incurred severe damage to *Hipper*. As a result, *Hipper* was forced to return (with *Köln*) to Germany for repairs and she did not again leave the Baltic.

Berlin gained the impression from a grossly misleading message from Herbschleb in *U-354* that the Germans had achieved a great victory. While preparing a boastful New Year's Day propaganda message, Hitler heard a radio broadcast from London, announcing that Allied convoy escorts had repulsed a determined attack by big German surface vessels and that the convoy had reached Murmansk without the loss of a single merchant ship.

Hitler was stunned. Absent any word from Kummetz, who was still maintaining radio silence and reporting via a landline to Berlin that proved to be defective, Hitler "flew into an uncontrollable rage," Admiral Raeder wrote in his memoir, "unjustly claiming that information had been deliberately withheld from him." Raeder continued:

> He announced his intentions of immediately having all the heavy ships laid up, and recorded in the War Diary his view that the heavy ships were utterly useless—an entry made so that his opinion on the matter should be on record in black and white. He would not listen to any explanations by Vice Admiral [Theodor] Krancke, my personal representative at his headquarters, but ordered me by telephone to report to him immediately. I requested time to obtain the necessary, accurate details but . . . [some days elapsed] before I had the full picture of what had happened.

Raeder met with Hitler and the Führer's trusted military adviser Wilhelm Keitel in the evening of January 6 at *Wolfschanze*. Raeder briefly described the extraordinary scene:

> For one whole hour Hitler, in the presence of Field Marshal Keitel, gave me a thorough dressing down.* He reiterated his complaint about getting insufficient information. He went on to attack the Navy in a vicious and impertinent way. He disparaged its founding, belittled its every role since 1804 and stated that except for the submarines the entire history of the German Navy had been one of futility. Göring's hand and influence were evident in everything Hitler said. Heretofore the heavy ships had been Hitler's pride and interest. Now he dammed them as being utterly worthless, needing the Air Force and the smaller ships to protect them every time they went to sea. He added, further, that in case of any Allied attack on Norway, the Air Force could be put to better use attacking the British Fleet than flying air cover for our ships.
>
> Next, he stated that the large ships no longer had any operational value and that they should be laid up so that their guns could be put to use elsewhere—ashore, where guns were so urgently needed. Lastly he even criticized the scuttling of the German Fleet at Scapa Flow [in 1919] and attacked the spirit and morale of the Navy, which up to then he had always praised.
>
> It was glaringly obvious that this whole diatribe against the Navy which I commanded was intended but for one thing—to insult me personally. Hitler concluded by inviting me to hand in a memorandum in which I would be permitted to explain any views to the contrary that I might have as to the role of the heavy ships. Throughout his remarks I had exerted my utmost self-control to keep silent. I felt it beneath the dignity of the senior officer of the Navy to attempt to contradict in detail such utterly prejudiced statements. When he finished speaking, I quietly asked to be allowed to speak to him by myself. Field Marshal Keitel and the two stenographers left the room.

In his meeting alone with Hitler, Raeder wrote, the time had come "for a parting of the ways." Since Hitler in his remarks "had indicated that he was dissatisfied [and] no longer had confidence in me," Raeder wrote that he "very quietly" asked to be relieved from the position of commander in chief of the Navy. Hitler "began to calm down" and "begged" Raeder to stay on the job, but Raeder refused, he wrote. It was finally decided that Raeder was to step down on January 30, 1943, the tenth anniversary of his service under Hitler. Asked to propose two men who were best qualified to succeed him, Raeder named fifty-seven-year-old Rolf Carls, then commanding Naval Group North, and fifty-one-year-old Karl Dönitz. Hitler chose Dönitz.

In response to Hitler's demand that the big ships be decommissioned and scrapped, the OKM drew up a tentative schedule for 1943:

Hipper and *Köln,* March 1
Schleswig-Holstein, April 1
Schlesien, May 1
Scharnhorst, July 1
Tirpitz, Autumn

---

* The official stenographer wrote that it was "an hour and a half."

Admiral Raeder revealed his reassignment and the appointment of Dönitz to succeed him in three radio broadcasts on January 30, 31, and February 1. To avoid the impression that he had been summarily sacked (like so many *Wehrmacht* generals on the Russian front), he said that he had asked for reassignment owing to ill health, but that he would continue to serve in the less demanding post of Inspector General of the *Kriegsmarine.* Briefly reviewing his role in the growth of the *Kriegsmarine* under "our beloved Führer," Raeder concluded:

> As I have dedicated my whole life to the Navy in the past, so will I continue to serve it in the future and to take part with all my heart in its heavy battle. I know that the Navy will carry on this battle under its new Commander-in-Chief with the same obdurate determination, with the same unshakable will to conquer, and with the same loyalty as heretofore. I know that each man will give all that he has in him, to the end that believing in good and trusting in our Führer, he may win the victory for our people and *Reich.* Long live the Führer!

Raeder's public broadcast was followed by a message from Dönitz:

> At the order of the Führer I today take over the high command of the Navy. To the U-boat arm, which I have been hitherto privileged to command, I extend my thanks for its courageous readiness to fight to the death and for its loyalty. I shall continue personally to command the U-boat war.
>
> I intend to command the Navy in the same firm martial spirit. From every individual I expect unqualified obedience, extreme courage, and devotion to the last breath. It is in these things that we uphold our honor. Gathered about our Führer, we will not lay down our arms until victory and peace shall have been won. Hail our Führer!*

Dönitz assumed his new responsibilities without missing a beat. He moved from Paris to Berlin, occupying an imposing residence in a suburb, Dahlem, about fifteen miles west of his birthplace, Grünau. He established U-boat headquarters in a building in Charlottenburg,† four miles north of his home, and named Admiral Hans-Georg von Friedeburg to be commander in chief (FdU) of U-boats. The chief staffers were housed nearby in the Hotel am Steinplatz. These remained forty-two-year-old Eberhard Godt, promoted to rear admiral, and Dönitz's son-in-law, Günther Hessler, first staff officer, or right-hand man to Godt. They were closely assisted in operations by Adalbert Schnee and Peter Cremer, the communications specialist Hans Meckel, and the engineer Gerhard Suhren, older brother of Reinhard Suhren. The thirty-seven-year-old Hans-Rudolf Rösing was promoted to the exalted post of administrative chief of the eight combat flotillas based in France.

Peter Cremer wrote in his memoir:

---

* This message was widely repeated, not only on various naval Engima nets, but also in lower codes, such as the "dockyard" net, *Werft,* thus providing Allied codebreakers with cribs.

† Dönitz wrote that he spent most of his time as C in C, *Kriegsmarine,* at a "somewhat isolated" headquarters in Koralle, about twenty miles north of Berlin center, between Bernau and Eberswalde.

> Every morning the new C in C Navy left his desk and turned up shortly after at our HQ in the Steinplatz . . . the [U-boat] battles were fought at the legendary green baize table . . . [on which U-boat] positions were symbolized by little flags and plotted on the big situation charts, the oceans on paper. . . . There were no fixed hours of duty. We relieved one another, but individual operations [versus convoys] often lasted for days. At night our work was interrupted more and more often [by Allied heavy bomber attacks that] forced us into the air-raid shelter. The place, according to eyewitnesses, was "swarming with Knight's Crosses."

The Allies assumed from the Raeder-Dönitz change of command and the bellicose tone of the Dönitz broadcast that the Germans were going to wage all-out U-boat warfare to the exclusion of major big-ship operations. At first the assumption was correct. Dönitz hastened to agree with Hitler's order to scrap all the big ships and, in turn, received the Führer's enthusiastic approval for another substantial increase in U-boat production and *Luftwaffe* support in the Atlantic. On second thought, however, Dönitz concluded that if the commanders were given greater freedom to take risks, a task force consisting of *Tirpitz, Scharnhorst,* and *Lützow,* basing in Norway, might carry out effective raids against convoys in the Arctic—and possibly in the North Atlantic—thereby tying down a comparable or greater force of Allied big ships that might be used elsewhere. In one of his first sessions with Hitler—reportedly a tempestuous one—Dönitz convinced the Führer of his revised views. Accordingly, as originally planned, *Scharnhorst* shifted from the Baltic to Norway. Thus she, *Tirpitz,* and *Lützow* escaped Hitler's axe, but none of the other big ships ever left the Baltic again. Some were scrapped (as was the unfinished carrier *Graf Zeppelin*), but some were retained as training ships.

Dönitz had promised in his broadcast to the *Kriegsmarine* that he was to continue "personally to command the U-boat war." But he was hard-pressed to keep that promise. In replacing Raeder, he had assumed immense, new, and time-consuming responsibilities. Not the least of these was to establish closer personal ties to Hitler and the arms-production chief, Albert Speer, and other Nazi leaders and to neutralize or diminish the influence of the *Luftwaffe* chief, Hermann Göring, in order to gain for the *Kriegsmarine* a greater share of Germany's shrinking resources for war fighting.

THREE

The Casablanca Conference

The Axis suffered four defeats in January 1943 that collectively marked an unrecognized but decisive turning point in the war. From that time onward, there was not the slightest possibility that the Axis could prevail. *Viz.*

- **Stalingrad.** The prolonged Soviet counterattack in numbing cold weather finally trapped the German forces holding the pile of rubble that was once a great city and forced them to surrender. In this first clear-cut Soviet victory of the war, the German casualties (dead, captured, missing) in the Stalingrad battle exceeded 250,000. Moreover, this devastating and humiliating defeat compelled the German forces in the Caucasus, which had reached the prized Baku oil fields on the Caspian Sea, to withdraw, relinquishing one of the main objectives of that arduous campaign.
- **North Africa.** Axis forces under Erwin Rommel, in full retreat to the west before Bernard Montgomery's British Eighth Army, abandoned the strategic seaport of Tripoli, Libya, and finally stopped at the prewar fortifications known as the Mareth Line on the Libya-Tunisia border. The loss of Italian Libya, yet another humiliating setback for the Pact of Steel, precluded any possibility of another Axis counterstrike across Libya to threaten Egypt, the Suez Canal, or oil resources in the Persian Gulf area. The newly arrived German forces in Tunisia held Eisenhower's lackluster Torch forces at bay and reinforced the Mareth Line, but the Allied vise was closing inexorably. It appeared to be merely a matter of weeks before all Axis forces in North Africa were evacuated or annihilated.

• **Southwest Pacific.** Allied forces on Guadalcanal and in Papua New Guinea decisively defeated Japanese forces, eliminating entirely the Axis threat to Australia and to the Allied line of communication to that continent. The unforeseen but epic six-month struggle for Guadalcanal resulted in an Allied victory in the Pacific, ranking in strategic importance with the Battle of Midway. The struggle cost the Japanese about thirty thousand killed, the Allies about seven thousand killed, including casualties at sea and in the air.*

• **Signals Intelligence.** With the help of captured materials, a great increase in the number of bombes and other mechanical devices, and inspired mathematical and intellectual solutions, Allied codebreakers at Bletchley Park and in Washington and elsewhere slowly but steadily broke deeper into Axis military, diplomatic, and merchant-marine codes. Setbacks continued to occur but they came less frequently and were overcome more quickly. The quantity of precise information that the Allies amassed on the enemy forces and intentions in 1943 and later was without precedent in history, and it became an increasingly larger factor in Allied military decisions.

No less important, decrypts of *Triton* led to a growing suspicion among Allied codebreakers that *B-dienst* was reading Allied Atlantic convoy codes, as was the case. The clues recovered led those responsible for Allied communications security to launch an investigation that was to confirm those suspicions and cause a sweeping modification of Allied naval codes, leaving the German codebreakers at *B-dienst* virtually blind and deaf for the rest of the war.

As the New Year arrived, President Roosevelt and Prime Minister Churchill both felt the need for another face-to-face strategy conference—their fourth. Code-named Symbol, it was held in Casablanca, Morocco, from January 14 to 24. Because of the critical battle at Stalingrad, Joseph Stalin declined to attend. The Free French were represented by General Henri Giraud, replacing Admiral Darlan, who had been assassinated in Algiers on Christmas Eve. President Roosevelt flew via the "southern" route, Brazil to Dakar to Morocco. Churchill flew far into the Atlantic west of France to avoid German aircraft, then doubled back to Africa.

The British arrived with clear objectives and well-prepared position papers. They urged these courses of action:

• A substantial reinforcement of Allied forces in North Africa to assure an early, decisive defeat of the Axis in Tunisia.

---

* In the numerous naval battles associated with the fighting on Guadalcanal, the Americans incurred very heavy warship losses: two fleet carriers (*Wasp, Hornet*); five heavy cruisers (*Astoria, Chicago, Quincy, Northampton, Vincennes*); two light cruisers (*Atlanta, Juneau*); fifteen destroyers; three destroyer/transports; and one troopship. The Australians lost the heavy cruiser *Canberra.* Many other Allied warships were damaged, some heavily. The Japanese lost one fleet carrier (*Ryujo*), two battleships (*Hiei, Kirishima*), three heavy cruisers (*Kako, Furutaka, Kingugasa*), one light cruiser (*Yura*), eleven destroyers, six submarines, and twelve troop transports. Comparative warship losses: Allies 29, Japanese 36.

• Intensified military operations in the Mediterranean Basin, designed to knock Italy out of the war and to regain safe convoy routes from Gibraltar to the Suez Canal. These operations were to include invasions of Sicily and Italy in 1943.

• An all-out effort to defeat the U-boats in the Atlantic, which was to include a single Allied commander of all ASW forces.

• A massive, combined bomber offensive against Germany. The Americans were to bomb by day, the British by night.

• A postponement of Overlord, the invasion of Occupied France, to May of 1944.

• Utmost matériel support for the military forces of the Soviet Union, to be shipped via Murmansk, the Persian Gulf, and Vladivostok, unless shipping losses became prohibitive.

The Americans arrived with murky or conflicting objectives and ill-prepared position papers. They urged these courses of action:

• A drastic diminution of Mediterranean operations after the defeat of the Axis in Tunisia. No invasions of Sicily or Italy.

• An all-out Allied effort to defeat the U-boats in the Atlantic, but no single, unified commander of ASW forces.

• A massive, combined bomber offensive against Germany.

• Overlord to be staged as early as possible in 1943.

• An intensification of operations in the Pacific against the Japanese, backed by a 100 percent increase in men and matériel (i.e., from about 15 percent of the Allied war effort to about 30 percent).

Prolonged and sometimes heated debates ensued. Against the advice of his military chiefs, Roosevelt sided with Churchill and approved further Allied operations in the Mediterranean Basin. The conferees finally agreed that:

• After the defeat of the Axis in Tunisia, the Allies were to promptly invade Sicily (Operation Husky), probably in early July during the new moon, which favored paratroopers. Proposals for the invasion of Italy were tabled.

• Owing to the delays in the capture of Tunisia and the decision to invade Sicily—and possibly Italy—Overlord was to be postponed to about May 1944. George Marshall, Dwight Eisenhower, and other American Army strategists regarded this postponement in favor of the Mediterranean operations a major mistake.

• The Allies were to mount an all-out offensive against the German U-boat force. At the insistence of Admiral King, who was still loath to place American ships under "foreign" (i.e., Commonwealth) command, there was to be no single Allied ASW commander, on the Atlantic, presiding over a unified force.

• Concurrent with the campaign against the U-boats, Bomber Command and the U.S. Eighth Air Force were to begin the combined bomber offensive (Sickle) against Germany.

• Military forces of the Soviet Union were to be supplied matériel, but not at "prohibitive cost" to other operations. However, during the period of complete daylight in the Arctic and the invasion of Sicily, shipments via the Arctic route were to be curtailed.

• Operations against Japan were to be intensified in five ways: in the Southwest Pacific, a two-pronged assault on the stronghold of Rabaul, staged from New

Guinea and the Solomon Islands; an island-hopping campaign across the central Pacific, beginning at Tarawa in the Gilberts; the recapture of Burma by Allied forces staging from India; matériel support to the Chinese Nationalists, who were fighting Japanese armies on the Asian mainland; and maximum support of the American submarine force in the Pacific.

- The Allies were to accept nothing less than the "unconditional surrender" of the Axis.

Throughout the Casablanca conference, the acute shortage of Allied shipping remained the "controlling factor" in most decisions. The loss of Allied merchant shipping to all causes in 1942 had been a hard blow: 1,664 vessels for 7.8 million gross tons. Of this number, it was calculated, Axis submarines sank about 1,160 ships for about 6.25 million gross tons, well over half of that in North American waters. All Allied shipyards had worked frenetically to overcome the losses. American yards turned out an astounding 760 ships for about 5.4 million gross tons in 1942. British Commonwealth yards had produced about 1.1 million gross tons, raising the total to 6.5 million gross tons by all Allied yards, almost exactly offsetting losses to Axis submarines. The net loss in Allied shipping in 1942 was therefore about 1.3 million gross tons.*

Convoying and the shipping losses to U-boats in 1942 plus diversions of shipping for offensive operations (Torch, Guadalcanal, Papua New Guinea) had sharply reduced imports to sustain the people and war-production facilities in the British Isles. From a comfortable prewar level of fifty million tons, British imports had fallen to forty-two million tons in 1940, to thirty-one million in 1941, and to an absolutely intolerable twenty-three million tons in 1942. In response to a strongly worded request from Churchill that additional shipping be allotted for British imports, Roosevelt had replied on November 30, 1942, that he had ordered an increase in American shipbuilding goals for 1943 from about sixteen million (deadweight) tons to about 18.8 million (deadweight) tons, and if the steel could be spared he might possibly order twenty million (deadweight) tons.† He had assured Churchill that the United States would Lend-Lease the British sufficient extra shipping from the increased American production to guarantee that imports to the British Isles would not fall below twenty-seven million tons in 1943.

Owing to a breakdown in communications—and to loose language and terms—the American military chiefs came to Casablanca with a large misunder-

---

* Allied and neutral merchant-ship losses are Admiralty figures, which require refinement. In boasting about American ship production, officials such as War Shipping Administrator Admiral Emory S. (Jerry) Land invariably used the larger "deadweight" tonnage figures rather than the smaller "gross" tonnage figures. Hence, on January 5, 1943, Land announced that the United States had built 746 ships (later corrected to 760 ships) for 8 million tons in 1942. The failure of some Allied officials and some historians of the Battle of the Atlantic to draw a distinction between deadweight and gross tonnage figures led to considerable confusion during the war and later. (The *gross tonnage* of a ship is arrived at by measuring the cubic capacity of the enclosed spaces of the ship and allowing one gross ton for every 100 cubic feet. The *deadweight tonnage* of a ship is the weight [in tons of 2,240 lbs.] of the cargo she can carry, including fuel, stores, and water.)

† American yards were to produce 1,949 ships of 19.2 million deadweight or 13 million gross tons in 1943.

standing of Roosevelt's guarantee of extra American shipping to raise British imports to twenty-seven million tons in 1943. The Americans not only thought the increase in Lend-Lease shipping for that purpose was to be far, far less, but also that the British were to provide extra shipping for military operations. Because there were no shipping experts at Casablanca, the conferees did not discuss maritime allocations in any significant detail and therefore the misunderstanding remained unrevealed for several weeks. When it finally came to light, it was to cause temporary difficulties in Anglo-American relations and force revisions in some plans agreed upon at Casablanca.

Of the many decisions reached at Casablanca, none ranked more urgently in the minds of the conferees than the protection of shipping and the destruction of the German U-boat force. That mission was explicitly and officially granted "first charge" (or priority) on Allied military assets. Among the numerous measures to be taken:

- American and British heavy-bomber forces were to greatly intensify the attacks on the U-boat bases on the French Atlantic coast.
- American and British heavy-bomber forces were to bomb German cities known to have U-boat building yards or factories producing important U-boat components, such as diesel engines and batteries.
- Coastal Command was to remount hunter-killer operations in the Bay of Biscay in order to interdict U-boats going to and from the French bases. The two Army Air Forces squadrons (numbers 1 and 2) of the Antisubmarine Command, based at St. Eval in southwest England and equipped with B-24 Liberators fitted with centimetric-wavelength radar, were to operate in cooperation with Coastal Command in the extension of the Biscay hunter-killer missions.
- Because of the shortage of surface escorts, beginning in January 1943, eastbound cargo convoys on the North Atlantic run were to sail from New York on a ten-day cycle rather than eight days, guarded mostly by British and Canadian warships but still including one American escort group, A-3. The British and Canadians were to increase convoy defenses by providing a minimum of five offensive or hunter-killer groups (support groups). Comprised of about six to eight ships each (destroyers, sloops, ex-American Coast Guard cutters, frigates, and, when available, "jeep" carriers) the hunter-killer groups were to patrol the convoy routes and rush to the support of those convoys threatened by U-boats, killing as many as possible, rather than merely suppressing them as in prior years.
- North Atlantic convoys known to be under direct threat of U-boat attack were to be provided with air escort to the maximum extent possible. The early model B-24s of Coastal Command's Squadron 120 were to be upgraded to very-long-range aircraft by the addition of extra fuel tanks in the bomb bays, and other measures. Meanwhile, the B-17 Flying Fortresses and Halifax bombers and the less lethal, more vulnerable, shorter range Catalina and Sunderland flying boats were to provide the main weight of long-range coverage, operating as far as possible toward the Greenland "Air Gap."
- The newly established Middle Atlantic convoys from the United States to Gibraltar and the return (UG and GU Fast and Slow), in support of Torch opera-

tions, were to be escorted exclusively by American warships. These were mainly cruisers, *Treasury*-class Coast Guard cutters, and a host of destroyers, but since many troopships sailed in the UGF convoys, the escort also included the old battleships *Arkansas, New York,* and *Texas,* the carrier *Ranger,* and later, offensive "jeep" carrier hunter-killer support groups.*

- The Allies also established two other convoy routes in the Middle Atlantic area, protected by American destroyers. These were exclusively "oil" convoys, comprised of seven big, fast tankers, which cruised at 14.5 knots. The first, OT ("Oil for Torch"), sailed directly from the Caribbean to Gibraltar and the Mediterranean, returning in ballast to the Caribbean as convoy TO. The second, CU ("Oil from Curaçao for the United Kingdom"), sailed directly from the Caribbean to the British Isles, returning in ballast to the Caribbean as UC convoys. Scarcely ever mentioned in popular accounts of the Battle of the Atlantic, the Middle Atlantic convoy system grew to be an enormous enterprise and was to require large numbers of American warships and aircraft for escort.†
- By decision of the highest British officials, Coastal Command was to be allotted forty H2S centimetric-wavelength aircraft-radar sets, theretofore designated for Bomber Command.‡ Fearing that the Germans would recover an H2S from a crashed British bomber and quickly devise a centimetric-wavelength radar-detection device (FuMB) for U-boats before Coastal Command could exploit the new radar, John Slessor, the new chief of Coastal Command,§ requested that Bomber Command not fly H2S sets over Germany or German-occupied territory for at least several months. The request was denied. The Germans recovered an H2S from a Stirling that was shot down near Rotterdam on the night of February 1–2, only the second time the H2S was employed in combat.
- Priority for construction of destroyer escorts (DEs) in American yards, which had been downgraded in 1942 in favor of landing craft and merchant ships, was to be upgraded. However, as a result of the low building priority in 1942, only fifty-five DEs were to be commissioned in the first half of 1943. Twenty-one were to be sent directly to the Pacific to release fleet destroyers from convoy duties. Of the remaining thirty-four, seven were to go to the Royal Navy and five to U.S. Navy schools, leaving only twenty-two for Atlantic convoy escort.#

---

* UGF 1 (thirty-eight ships, fifty-six escorts) was the Torch assualt convoy, Task Force 34. UGF 2 (twenty-four ships, ten escorts) sailed from the United States on November 13, 1942, and arrived at Casablanca on November 18, designated Task Force 38. There was no UGS 1. UGS 2 (eighty-three ships including escorts) sailed on November 25, designated Task Forces 37 and 39. Thereafter UGF and UGS convoys sailed about every twenty-five days.

† See Appendix 15 and Plate 5.

‡ At the time of the Casablanca conference, January 1943, only twenty-four aircraft of Bomber Command were equipped with H2S radar sets: twelve Stirlings of Squadron 7, and twelve Halifaxes of Squadron 38. The H2S radar was first used in combat over Germany on the night of January 30–31 by six pathfinder aircraft (four Stirlings, two Halifaxes), which found Hamburg in foul weather and marked it with incendiaries for the main bomber formations.

§ He officially replaced Philip de la Ferté Joubert on February 5, 1943.

See Appendix 14.

• • •

In the first quarter of 1943, Allied heavy-bomber forces carried out twenty separate raids on the U-boat bases in France, thirteen by Bomber Command and seven by the Eighth Air Force.* The combined air forces flew 3,124 sorties. Some of the Bomber Command raids were massive: 302 aircraft to Lorient on the night of February 7–8, 437 to St. Nazaire on the night of February 13–14, 363 to Lorient on the night of February 16–17, and 413 to St. Nazaire on the night of February 28–March 1. These and the other raids destroyed the thinly built exterior base facilities and utterly leveled the cities of St. Nazaire and Lorient, but no bombs penetrated the U-boat pens or damaged any U-boats outside the pens. Similarly, the smaller raids on Brest failed to dent those pens.

The airmen dreaded and hated these missions. Invariably aircraft and aircrew losses were heavy. The failure to inflict any damage on the pens—even with 2,000-pound bombs—was humiliating and demoralizing. Berlin propagandists ridiculed the campaign, boasting of the invulnerability of the structures and steadfastness of the submariners. But, in fact, the Allied airmen made an important contribution to the anti–U-boat campaign, unrecognized at the time or later, even by the Air Force historians. The air raids significantly delayed or halted construction of *other* U-boat pens that were urgently needed to adequately accommodate the swelling Atlantic U-boat force.

Bomber Command continued to carry the weight of the Allied air attack on the U-boat pens and the building yards in Germany in the first quarter of 1943. In nine separate raids comprising 1,443 sorties, RAF bombers hit Wilhelmshaven four times, Hamburg three times, and Bremen and Emden one time each. These raids also failed: No bombs hit any U-boat building facilities or U-boats.

Owing to the slow arrival of aircraft and to the diversion of bombers to the Twelfth Air Force supporting Torch, the Eighth Air Force grew only slowly. It flew its first mission against German soil (Wilhelmshaven) on January 27, a token raid of fifty-three aircraft. In February and March, it mounted four other raids on Germany, two more against Wilhelmshaven and one each against Bremen and Emden. Not until March 18 was it capable of mounting a raid of up to one hundred bombers and its fighter support remained inadequate. The raids in Germany, which also failed to damage any U-boat building yards or U-boats, were "largely experimental," the official American Air Force historians wrote. Thus the combined bomber offensive (Sickle) against German targets other than the U-boat building yards proceeded haltingly.

1943: Myths Versus Facts

For many years after World War II, naval historians and popular authors alike depicted the Battle of the Atlantic in the months January through April 1943 in a melodramatic fashion. The story line was that the Germans, having finally accu-

---

* See Appendix 13.

mulated "four hundred" or "over four hundred" U-boats "in service," came within a whisker of closing down the vital North Atlantic convoy run in March, thereby "winning" that long-fought naval struggle, and that as a consequence, all Allied operations in that sector of the globe were thrown into peril. Then in May 1943, the U-boat war suddenly and almost inexplicably collapsed.

That view of this period in the Battle of the Atlantic apparently was first committed to paper in the British Admiralty's authoritative and secret "Monthly Anti-Submarine Report" for December 1943. Reviewing the year 1943, the author wrote:

> Up to the 20th March 1943, there seemed real danger that the enemy would achieve his aim of severing the routes which united Great Britain with the North American continent. After that date his strength seemed to ebb. . . .

Two paragraphs later, the author painted an even more apocalyptic picture:

> The significance of the period up to the 20th March was that it appeared possible that we should not be able to continue convoy as an effective system of defence against the enemy's pack attacks. . . .

In Volume I of Samuel Eliot Morison's semiofficial fifteen-volume history of U.S. naval operations in World War II, published in 1947, Morison cited this Admiralty source and wrote:

> The enemy never came so near to disrupting communications between the New World and the Old as in the first twenty days of March 1943.

In Volume II of Stephen W. Roskill's four-volume history of Royal Navy operations in World War II, published ten years later in 1957, he quoted directly and extensively from the same Admiralty source, and wrote that this period was the "crisis of crises" and that

> [f]or what it is worth this writer's view is that in the early spring of 1943 we had a very narrow escape from defeat in the Atlantic. . . . [One cannot] look back on that month [of March] without feeling something approaching horror over the losses we suffered. . . . Where could the Admiralty turn if the convoy system had lost its effectiveness? They did not know; but they must have felt, though no one admitted it, that defeat stared them in the face. . . .

Although later scholarship showed that lugubrious story line to be quite wrong, vestiges of it still appear from time to time, even in the most serious works. For example, American naval historian David Syrett wrote* of this period:

> The Allies' strategic situation in the North Atlantic was bleak with no end in sight to the sinkings and U-boat attacks on transatlantic convoys. . . . March 1943

---

* In *The Defeat of the German U-boats* (1994).

> marked the point at which the German U-boats came closest to disrupting seaborne communications between North America and Great Britain. . . . [The shipping shortage was such that] the Allies found it almost impossible to provide the required vessels to maintain essential civilian programs such as imports of food and raw materials into Great Britain while at the same time provide the ships required to support military operations.

In order to put this matter in truer perspective, it is appropriate to set forth a number of relevant facts fully and clearly.

First, the strength of the U-boat force.

While it is true that by January 1, 1943, there were "400 U-boats in service," according to the most reliable German sources, that figure demands close analysis. Less about twelve specialty boats (XIV "Milk Cow" U-tankers, XB minelayers, IXD2 U-cruisers), only about half of the "four hundred" were considered to be in "operational" status; all the rest were in workup or refit or icebound in the Baltic or assigned to the schools. Moreover, if we accept the repeated contention of Dönitz that the operational boats assigned to the Arctic and Mediterranean were wrongly placed and virtually useless except as a "threat in being," then the only U-boats that posed a meaningful peril to the Allies were those of the Atlantic force, based at the five French Atlantic ports.

That force was still quite modest in size in January 1943. Counting gains and losses, the number of attack boats had grown by only thirty-three since late summer of 1942. This growth had developed as follows:

	*9/1/42**	*10/1*	*11/1*	*12/1*	*1/1/43*
Type VII:	77	98	101	100	106
Type IX:	47	47	49	48	51
Totals	124	145	150	148	157

Nor was there to be a dramatic growth in the number of attack boats of the Atlantic U-boat force in the first four months of 1943.

	1/1/43	*2/1*	*3/1*	*4/1*	*5/1*
Type VII	106	114	125	123	134
Type IX	51	53	54	54	52
Totals	157	167	179	177	186†

* See Plate 1.

† Mishaps and setbacks continued in the Baltic, delaying the flow of new U-boats to the Atlantic. The worst setback was the delay of the XIV tanker *U-490,* commanded by Wilhelm Gerlach, age thirty-eight. She sank off Gotenhafen during workup and was in salvage and repair for eight months, a blow to the thin, hard-pressed Atlantic refueler fleet. The VII *U-231,* commanded by Wolfgang Wenzel, age thirty-five, failed her tactical exercise and had to repeat the test. During another tactical exercise, her sister ship, *U-232,* commanded by Ernst Ziehm, age twenty-eight, collided with *U-649,* commanded by Raimund Tiesler, age twenty- three. The *U-649* sank with the loss of thirty-five of forty-six crew. Rescued, Tiesler commissioned another VII. The new VII *U-416,* commanded by Christian Reich, age twenty-seven, hit a mine laid by British aircraft and sank. She was salvaged but relegated to a school boat. Reich commissioned another VII. The new VII *U-421,* commanded by Hans Kolbus, age twenty-

In the four months under analysis, January through April 1943, the Germans deployed the overwhelming majority of the Type VII and IX attack boats and XB minelayers in the Atlantic force to the North Atlantic convoy run:

	January	*February*	*March*	*April*
North Atlantic	42	55*	40	72†
Middle Atlantic	14‡	12	7§	12
South Atlantic	1	1	3	—
Americas	4	3	4	6#
Totals	61	71	54	90

Second, Allied losses.

In the same four months, the Allies sailed fifty-nine cargo convoys composed of about 2,400 merchant ships east and west across the North Atlantic run.** Over half, about 1,320 ships, left from New York eastbound in Halifax and Slow Convoys. The others, 1,081 ships, left from the British Isles to the Americas in Outbound North and Outbound North (Slow) convoys.

U-boats sank 111 of these 2,401 ships: seventy-three en route to the British Isles; thirty-eight on the return voyages to North America. This was about 5 percent of all ships that crossed the Atlantic in convoys in that area. Therefore, in these four months, 95 percent of the ships sailing in those fifty-nine convoys arrived at their destinations.

In the first twenty days of March, the U-boats operating against the North Atlantic run achieved unusual success against four eastbound convoys: Halifax 228 and 229 and Slow Convoys 121 and 122, sinking thirty-nine of the approximately two hundred merchant ships (20 percent) in these convoys and the British destroyer *Harvester.* It was this harsh blow that so rattled the Admiralty. The fact that eleven other convoys got through unscathed in the month of March in that area and only one other convoy lost one ship to U-boats is seldom if ever mentioned in the apocalyptic scenarios.

The loss of thirty-nine merchant ships in these four eastbound convoys in March cannot be dismissed lightly. No complete reckoning of the loss of life and

---

three, also hit a British mine and was severely damaged. The *U-643,* commanded by Hans-Harald Speidel, age twenty-five, incurred a horrendous series of mechanical difficulties, including a battery explosion, which delayed her readiness for over six months. Rammed the previous fall in a tactical exercise by the IXC40 *U-168,* commanded by Helmut Pich, *U-643* finally sailed after months of repairs.

* Including the XB *U-119,* which laid an unsuccessful minefield off Iceland.

† Including the VIIDs *U-217* and *U-218,* which laid unsuccessful minefields off the coast of England, and *U-303, U-410, U-414,* and *U-616,* which entered the Mediterranean.

‡ Including the XB *U-118,* which laid a successful minefield off Gibraltar Strait, and *U-224,* which entered the Mediterranean.

§ Including the VII *U-455* and the XB *U-117,* which laid minefields off Casablanca on April 10 and April 11. These fields resulted in the sinking of one 3,800-ton French freighter and damage to two other Liberty-type vessels.

\# Including XB *U-119,* which laid a minefield off Halifax that sank one 3,000-ton freighter and damaged another of 7,100 tons.

** See Appendix 3.

food, weaponry, and raw material has come to light, but it was obviously serious. Yet not serious enough to cause, in Roskill's words, the "crisis of crises." In contrast to his assertions and those of other historians, the official historian of British merchant shipping during World War II, C.B.A. Behrens,* wrote that although stockpiles shrank throughout the first quarter of the year, "they began to rise" and "the United Kingdom import program suffered no disasters in the first half of 1943."

Although Allied shipping losses on the North Atlantic run in the first four months of 1943 were of overriding importance, they were not the whole story. U-boats operating in other areas (Middle Atlantic, Arctic, Mediterranean, West Africa, Indian Ocean, Americas) achieved some successes as well. The Admiralty has calculated that all merchant ship losses to Axis submarines in the period under analysis were as follows:†

1943	*Ships Lost*	*Gross Tons*
January	37	203,128
February	63	359,328
March	108	627,377
April	56	327,943
Totals	264	1,517,776

In the interest of putting the Allied merchant ship situation of this period into better perspective, it is also pertinent to note the output of new vessels in Allied yards. By the winter of 1942–43, the rate of production of ships in American yards alone was truly phenomenal—over twice the rate of losses to all Axis submarines:

1943	*Ships Built*	*Gross Tons*
January	106	647,000
February	132	792,000
March	149	1,005,000
April	159	1,076,000
Totals	546	3,520,000

From the German perspective, there was certainly no sign that the U-boats in the North Atlantic came close to cutting the line of communications between North America and the British Isles and West Africa in this four-month period. On the contrary, except for the spike in March, achieved by boats sailing mostly in February, successes of the U-boats against North Atlantic convoys in this period steadily declined. The number of nonproductive patrols by attack boats—that trend so ominous for the Germans—continued to rise:

* *Merchant Shipping and the Demands of War* (1955).

† In this instance, the calculations of Allied shipping losses by Jürgen Rohwer closely match those of the Admiralty.

	Patrols	*New C.O.*	*Ships Sunk*	*Per Boat*	*Boats Lost*	*No Sinkings*
January	56	14 (25%)*	41.5	.74	12	32 (57%)
February	67	31 (46%)†	61	.91	8	36 (54%)
March	47	14 (30%)‡	26	.55	15§	27 (57%)
April	86	22 (25%)#	19	.22	31**	66 (76%)
Totals	56	81 (32%)	147.5	.58	66 (26%)	61 (63%)

As in 1941 and 1942, Churchill and the Admiralty expressed the gravest concern over Allied shipping losses and continued to raise the possibility of an import crisis in the British Isles, which would force the British to draw down stockpiles to a dangerous level. As in those two earlier years, President Roosevelt's response to the cries of alarm from London in 1943 was prompt and generous. He directed Admiral Emory S. (Jerry) Land at the War Shipping Administration to transfer to Great Britain under the Lend-Lease Act fifteen new cargo ships per month for ten months, or 150 ships of about one million gross tons, which were to be manned by the estimated ten thousand British merchant mariners who had lost their ships. Furthermore, Roosevelt informed Churchill, he had suggested to Land that the transfers "be increased to twenty" per month for ten months, or two hundred ships of nearly 1.5 million gross tons.††

From this analysis, it is clear that the U-boats of the Atlantic force scored heavily against four eastbound convoys on the North Atlantic run in the first twenty days of March. As stated, the losses in those convoys cannot be dismissed as inconsequential—indeed, they were devastating—but in the overall picture they did not justify the retrospective conclusions at the Admiralty to the effect that the U-boats never came so close to severing the Atlantic lifeline and that possibly convoys were no longer an effective means of defense against U-boats.

The authoritative, contemporaneous British document, the secret "Monthly Anti-Submarine Report" of March 1943, put it this way: "Considering the weight of attacks developed, the convoys came through for the most part remarkably well."

More U-boat Failures on the North Atlantic Run

German U-boat Control‡‡ sailed fifty-six boats against Allied convoy routes in the North and Middle Atlantic in the month of January 1943. These consisted of forty-

* Includes one experienced boat with a new skipper.

† Includes eight experienced boats with new skippers.

‡ Includes four experienced boats with new skippers.

§ Includes *U-71* and *U-704,* retired to Training Command.

Includes two experienced boats with new skippers.

** Includes *U-108,* retired to Training Command.

†† Known as SAM ships, 182 were actually transferred to the British.

‡‡ From February 1943, nominally Admiral Friedeberg, C in C, U-boats, but in reality Rear Admiral Eberhard Godt, head of U-boat operations; his first staff officer, Günther Hessler; Adalbert Schnee; Peter Cremer; and a few others.

six VIIs* and even though they were not suitable for convoy attacks, nine IXs and one XB minelayer, *U-118.* One of the VIIs, *U-439,* commanded by Wolfgang Sporn, was assigned to carry out a special mission, but that task was canceled and she returned to France after five days. Her skipper went on to other duty and, as one consequence, the boat did not resail until late February.

Another myth that arose in later years was that from 1943 to the end of the war the German U-boat skippers were quite young, age twenty-one or twenty-two, and therefore too immature and inexperienced for command. The German authors Michael Salewski and Lothar-Günther Buchheim were the chief purveyors of this myth. Buchheim, echoing a statement by Dönitz, wrote that "the majority of submariners in the later war years were little more than children."

Numerous academic and statistical studies have thoroughly refuted these assertions.† As can be seen from the dates of birth column in Appendix 1 of this volume, the skippers of the approximately two hundred new boats that reported to battlefronts in 1943 averaged about age twenty-eight. The overwhelming majority (148) averaged age twenty-six.‡ One skipper (in the XB minelayer *U-219)* was age fifty-two(!), two were in their forties, forty-two were in their thirties. Only six were age twenty-three and one was twenty-two.

As related, in order to properly wage submarine warfare against convoys in the North Atlantic beyond range of most Allied aircraft, it was necessary to refuel many of the Type VIIs. This requirement presented the Germans with a number of difficulties. There were not enough U-tankers to adequately support the large number of VIIs deployed. Refueling in winter weather was chancy, because of the difficulty of navigating and locating the boat's position when skies were overcast for days on end, and putting oil hoses across in stormy weather and heavy seas.

At that time, January 1943, there were five Type XIV U-tankers, or "Milk Cows," in the Atlantic force, plus the XB minelayer *U-117,* serving as a provisional tanker. The XIV *U-463* and the *U-117* were already at sea supporting VIIs in the North Atlantic, and due to return by the end of the month. The XIV *U-459* had just sailed on a special mission to support the second U-boat foray to Cape Town, group *Seehund.* The XIV *U-461,* which put out in November, was nearly home, due at St. Nazaire on January 3 for refit and crew leave. Two XIVs, *U-460* and *U-462,* were to sail in January, but *U-462* developed mechanical difficulties and had to abort for repairs, and *U-460* could not get away until the last day of the month. Therefore, U-boat Control directed that after she laid her minefield, the XB minelayer *U-118* was to serve as a provisional tanker in the Middle Atlantic area.

---

* Including four transfers from the Arctic: *U-376, U-377, U-403, U-456.*

† See especially Rolf Güth (with documentation by Jochen Brennecke) in the German periodical *Schiff und Zeit,* no. 28 (1988) and Dr. Timothy P. Mulligan, "German U-boat Crews in World War II: Sociology of an Elite," *Journal of Military History* (April 1992), as corrected in reprints. Invaluable to the study of this controversy is a list of all U-boat commanders with their date of birth compiled and published by R. Busch and H. J. Röll in the German periodical *Der Landser Grosshand,* based on data provided by Horst Bredow and staff at the U-boat Archive, Cuxhaven.

‡

Year of Birth:	1914	1915	1916	1917	1918	1919
Number of COs:	17	18	26	33	28	26

All U-boats assigned to the North Atlantic run sailed into appalling winter storms. The discomfort encountered was unspeakable: massive waves, howling winds, near-freezing temperatures inside the steel hulls. Yet morale on all but a few boats remained high. U-boat Control constantly reminded the crews that every ship sunk helped their comrades on the Eastern Front and elsewhere. They had within their grasp the best, indeed the only, chance to win the war for the Führer and the Fatherland.

Many boats sailing in January carried new weapons:

- Pattern-running or looping FAT air (G7a) torpedoes.
- Electric torpedoes (G7e) fitted with the new Pi2 magnetic pistols.
- "Acoustic" torpedoes. Long in development and issued to only a few boats for battle testing, the "acoustic" torpedo T-3, called *Falke* (Falcon) was a modified electric (G7e) designed to go into a short circle pattern upon "hearing" the noise of a merchant ship's propeller at close quarters, improving the chances of a poorly aimed torpedo hitting its target. With a speed of about twenty knots and a range of about 7,200 yards, the T-3 *Falke* was believed to be effective against ships traveling at speeds up to twelve knots.*
- Increased numbers of antiaircraft guns, including twin 20mm cannons on fore and aft bridge mounts and a new rapid fire 37mm gun mounted on the lower deck immediately aft of the conning tower. To offset the increase in topside weight and underwater resistance, most of the 88mm deck guns on the Type VIIs, now used quite infrequently, were being removed. To enhance concealment while surface running, the bridge and conning-tower profiles of all U-boats were being cut down and smoothed, the first known application of antiradar "stealth" technology.
- Improved passive sonar (or hydrophone) gear. Known as "array" sonar, its "ears" consisted of scores of sensors fitted on the port and starboard bow sections of the boats. In good sea conditions, array sonar could detect the propeller noises of ships in convoys as far as ten to twenty miles away. In foggy weather on the Grand Banks and around Greenland and Iceland when visibility was often merely a few yards, array sonar provided the Germans with a means of detecting and shadowing convoys and of evading escorts.

Unknown or unconfirmed as yet in Germany, the Allies also had promising new assets:

- More and more ships and aircraft fitted with centimetric-wavelength radar, which the Metox FuMB gear *could not detect.*
- Ever-increasing numbers of convoy escorts and convoy rescue vessels fitted with Huff Duff, which convoy commanders regarded as equally effective as radar, if not more so, in detecting the presence of shadowing and gathering U-boats.
- More frequent breaks in four-rotor naval Enigma, which yielded sufficient information to enable the Allies to recommence evasive convoy routing.
- An entirely new weapon for aircraft: the solid-propellant rocket. These missiles were 3" in diameter, weighed sixty-six pounds, had a twenty-five-pound, solid

* A more sophisticated version, the T-5, called *Zaunkönig* (Wren), which was designed to "home" straight at the propeller noise of a target and hit the propeller, was under development.

steel, armor-piercing warhead and traveled close to the speed of sound. Mounted in racks on the undersides of the aircraft wings, they could be fired singly or in salvos. For optimum results, the rockets were aimed to hit about sixty feet short of the target, entering the water at an angle of about 13 degrees. The unusual shape of the warhead caused the rocket to run shallow—no more than about eight feet—then curve upward to blow a hole in a surfaced U-boat pressure hull below the water line. Of course, the rockets could also be fired "dry," directly at the exposed superstructure of the U-boat, but that method was considered less effective because it was more difficult to punch through both the superstructure *and* the pressure hull.

As a result of the transfers and diversions and the prolonged battle with convoy Outbound North (Slow) 154 in December, and the ghastly winter weather, there were not enough U-boats patrolling the North Atlantic on January 1, 1943, to form two full attack groups ("wolf packs") of thirteen to fifteen boats each. Pending the arrival of the first January boats, U-boat Control directed five boats to refuel from the XB minelayer *U-117,* then cadre a new group, *Jaguar,* northeast of Newfoundland to intercept eastbound convoys (Halifax or Slow) and directed fourteen boats to form a full group, *Falke* (Falcon), southeast of Greenland to intercept Outbound North and Outbound North (Slow) convoys.

The plan to cadre *Jaguar* and build it up with January boats ran into trouble. The weather was so bad that *U-117* could refuel only one of the five boats, the *U-662,* commanded by Wolfgang Hermann. He, in turn, was forced into an emergency refueling of the *U-664,* commanded by Adolf Graef, so that the latter could get to France. In view of *U-117*'s dwindling supply of fuel oil, U-boat Control ordered *U-440,* commanded by Hans Geissler, to abort his proposed refueling and to come home.

Because of its inability to refuel, the cadre for *Jaguar* fell apart. Of the five boats, only Horst von Schroeter in the IXB *U-123,* which had adequate fuel, and Hermann's refueled *U-662* were able to continue operations with *Jaguar.* In due course, six fresh boats from France and Germany joined the group. These included *U-96,* the boat that inspired Buchheim's novel (and film) *Das Boot,* homebound under command of Hans-Jürgen Hellriegel for retirement to the Training Command. She and the other seven *Jaguar* boats loitered off Newfoundland for days and days without seeing—or hearing—any sign of a convoy.

Group *Falke* formed a line running southeast from Greenland beyond range of most aircraft on Iceland. Its fourteen boats, seeking westbound convoys, included the *Ritterkreuz* holder Otto von Bülow in the veteran VII *U-404.*

One of the converging *Falke* boats suffered a calamity. She was the new IXC40 *U-167,* commanded by Kurt Neubert, age thirty-two. Heavy seas smashed the bridge, washing the quartermaster overboard and so badly injuring Neubert that he was forced to abort. The boat arrived in France on January 16, completing a patrol of twenty-seven days. Control appointed a new skipper to command the boat for its next patrol, which was to be even more calamitous.

Hans Karpf, age twenty-six, in the new VII *U-632,* reported a convoy on January 9. At first U-boat Control believed it to be the Outbound North convoy *Falke* had been positioned to intercept. Consequently, five other *Falke* boats in the vicinity closed on Karpf's signals. As it turned out, there was no Outbound North convoy—it had evaded the patrol line—but in a period of about twenty-four hours, four *Falke* boats, including Karpf in *U-632,* encountered and sank four loners, a tanker and three freighters, for about 25,000 tons. These four ships were the only enemy vessels sunk by all the U-boats on the North Atlantic run in the first half of January.

While escorting convoy Outbound North (Slow) 160 on January 15, a B-17 Flying Fortress of British Squadron 206, piloted by Leslie G. Clark, came upon a surfaced U-boat. This was the new *Falke* boat, *U-632,* commanded by Hans Karpf. Pilot Clark attacked from an altitude of eighty feet, toggling seven shallow-set depth charges. Three hung up, but the other four fell close to *U-632* and damaged her. Clark claimed a U-boat kill—believed to be the first Coastal Command success in the North Atlantic area in nearly three months.*

Days and days passed as *Falke* searched in vain for the evading westbound convoys. Thoroughly frustrated, Godt wrote testily in the Control war diary that U-boats were "totally unsuitable" for *finding* convoys. To do so required a very great number of U-boats engaged in wasteful, fruitless waiting. What was urgently needed to find convoys was long-range search aircraft. "If we had airplanes," Godt wrote, echoing Dönitz, "the war would be very different."

Inasmuch as *Falke* had no luck in locating westbound convoys, U-boat Control extended its length by replacing the several boats that had to leave and by the addition of a new group, *Habicht* (Hawk), which soon grew to nine boats. At its peak strength, *Falke-Habicht* comprised twenty-seven boats patrolling a line nearly five hundred miles long.

Finally, one of the *Habicht* boats found a big, fast convoy on January 17. The boat was a new VII, *U-268,* commanded by Ernst Heydemann, age twenty-six, seventeen days out from Kiel. The convoy was the eastbound Halifax 222, escorted by Canadian group C-1, temporarily comprised of two British destroyers (ex-American four-stack *Chesterfield* and the *Vansittart*), an ex-American Canadian four-stack destroyer (*St. Croix*), and five Canadian corvettes. The big handicap for the Germans was that the convoy was merely 180 miles southwest of Iceland, within easy range of Hudsons or other medium-range aircraft. U-boat Control authorized Heydemann to shoot, but not the other boats of *Falke-Habicht.* Heydemann chose the biggest target in sight, the 14,500-ton whale factory ship *Vestfold,* loaded with oil and all kinds of war matériel, including three 150-ton tank landing craft (LCTs). In the massive explosion that destroyed the whale factory, all three LCTs sank, giving Heydemann a score of "four ships" for about 15,000 tons.

U-boat Control was baffled and unhappy. The twenty-seven boats of *Falke-Habicht* had found no sign of the expected Outbound North (Slow) convoy. By January 19, many of the boats were running low on fuel. Control therefore split the boats (plus about ten new arrivals) into two groups, *Haudegen* (Broadsword) and

---

* The Admiralty credited Clark with sinking the new *U-337,* en route to group *Jaguar.* In a revised edition of his *Search, Find and Kill* (1995), Franks writes that that "kill" was actually the failed attack on *U-632* and that *U-337,* commanded by Kurt Ruwiedel, was lost to unknown causes.

Landsknecht (Mercenary). Boats with adequate fuel joined *Haudegen* on a line running from the southeast tip of Greenland, Cape Farewell. Boats low on fuel joined *Landsknecht* on a similar line farther southeast but still distant from Coastal Command patrol areas. Counting *Jaguar* (twelve boats), still in place northeast of Newfoundland, there were then three groups deployed on the North Atlantic run.

Four boats sailed from France on January 16 to join group *Landsknecht.* One of these was the VII *U-553,* commanded by *Ritterkreuz* holder Karl Thurmann, which had been in port since September 17—four months. On January 20, he met Heinz Wolf in the outbound VII *U-465* and passed him a nautical yearbook. That was the last anyone saw or heard from Thurmann and *U-553.* The place and cause of his loss were never determined or at least not disclosed. Possibly he was a victim of a yet to be determined Coastal Command air patrol.*

Six new boats (one IX and five VIIs) that sailed from Kiel on January 12 were directed to join group *Haudegen* southeast of Greenland. While proceeding there, Rolf Manke, age twenty-seven, in the new VII *U-358,* found a small convoy, UR 59, en route from the British Isles to Iceland (United Kingdom to Reykjavik). Manke tracked in foul weather, then shot. He claimed a 3,500-ton freighter, but in the postwar accounting it was found to be a 1,500-ton Swede. She was only the sixth ship sunk by all the North Atlantic boats in January. No other boat found the convoy. Manke lost it in rainy weather close to the coast and gave up the chase.

The reconstituted group *Jaguar* and the new group *Haudegen* were in place in the area east of Newfoundland and southeast of Greenland by January 22. The weather, visibility, and communications were rotten. A *Jaguar* boat, the aged, Germany-bound VII *U-96,* commanded by Hans-Jürgen Hellriegel, reported numerous mechanical difficulties. In response, U-boat Control released *U-96* for the return trip to Germany and retirement to the Training Command. The other boats searched diligently by eye and sonar for eastbound convoys.

Confusingly, a *Haudegen* boat, Ulrich Gräf in *U-69,* and Hellriegel in the aborting *U-96* both reported convoy contacts on January 22. Although communications remained poor, U-boat Control concluded correctly that these were two different eastbound convoys, sailing on nearly parallel tracks three hundred miles apart. They were Slow Convoy 117, guarded by British Escort Group B-3 on the southernmost track, and Halifax 223, guarded by American Escort Group A-3, on the northernmost track.

Over the next four days, U-boat Control attempted to micromanage groups *Jaguar* and *Haudegen* into positions to attack both convoys. Owing to the poor communications, foul weather, and inexperience of the U-boat crews, the effort was a failure. The two groups sank four ships from the two convoys:

- Gustav Poel in the *Jaguar* VII *U-413,* got a 3,600-ton Greek straggler from Slow Convoy 117.
- Ulrich von Soden-Fraunhofen in the *Haudegen* VII *U-624* sank a 5,100-ton British freighter from the same convoy.
- Rolf Manke in the *Haudegen* boat *U-358* sank an 8,200-ton Norwegian tanker from Halifax 223.

---

* Thurmann was credited with sinking fifteen confirmed ships for 85,500 tons.

• The *Haudegen* VIIs *U-607,* commanded by *Ritterkreuz* holder Ernst Mengersen, and *U-594,* commanded by Friedrich Mumm, teamed up to sink the bow of the 8,300-ton Norwegian tanker *Kollbjörg,* which had broken in half in heavy weather.

The operation against Slow Convoy 117 and Halifax 223 was another frustrating setback for U-boat Control. Upon cancellation of the chase on January 27, the groups on the North Atlantic run were reshuffled or disbanded. The boats of *Jaguar* were withdrawn to refuel or to return to France. A new group, *Pfeil* (Arrow), replaced *Jaguar* east of Newfoundland. Group *Haudegen,* increased to twenty-one boats, remained on a 300-mile patrol line running southeast from Greenland. Group *Landsknecht,* farther east, which had not sunk a single ship, was disbanded. Its boats with a good fuel supply went to *Pfeil.* Those low on fuel returned to France.

Two veteran VIIs of the returning *Landsknecht* group that had adequate fuel were assigned to a high-risk special mission: a sudden, surprise attack on shipping in the shallow water close to Land's End and the Scilly Islands during the dark of the new moon.

Nothing came of this foray. Harassed by Coastal Command Leigh Light–equipped Wellingtons with centimetric-wavelength ASV III radar, von Bülow in *U-404* struck a rock, disabled his bow planes, and returned to France, completing a fallow patrol of forty-nine days. Kurt Nölke in *U-584* received permission to abort owing to a noisy propeller shaft. A plan to have Hardo Rodler von Roithberg in the homebound *U-71* replace *U-404* was shelved.

In the last days of January, *B-dienst* alerted U-boat Control to a special convoy sailing from the British Isles to Gibraltar. Although Admiral Dönitz and U-boat Control were still reluctant to attack the heavily escorted Gibraltar-bound convoys, this one could not be ignored because of the increasingly desperate situation of Axis forces in Tunisia. Accordingly, U-boat Control hastily organized a group, *Hartherz* (Stouthearted), at the extreme western edge of the Bay of Biscay.

Group *Hartherz* was composed of twelve boats (nine VIIs, three IXs), nine of which were newly sailed from France and three of which were inbound to France, including two VIIs, Nölke in the aborting *U-584* and Rodler von Roithberg in *U-71.* One of the outbound VIIs, *U-590,* commanded by Heinrich Müller-Edzards, was diverted to assist another boat disabled by an aircraft, then was compelled to abort owing to corroded fuel pumps. Rodler von Roithberg in *U-71* found and shot at a lone corvette, but he missed. The IXC40 *U-183,* commanded by Heinrich Schäfer, picked up propeller noises on hydrophones. The reports from *U-71* and *U-183* were thought to be indications of the expected convoy but, in fact, the British were alerted to *Hartherz* from decrypts of naval Enigma and they diverted the convoy around the group. In addition, the convoy's surface escorts sank one of the U-boats, the IXC *U-519,* commanded by Günter Eppen, on February 10.*

Group *Hartherz* also failed. When U-boat Control finally realized it had missed

* The Admiralty originally credited a B-24 of the newly arrived American Army Air Forces Antisubmarine Squadron 2, piloted by William L. Sanford, with the kill of *U-519.* In a postwar review, Admiralty historians concluded that British convoy escorts, *Eva* and the heavy cruiser *Cornwall,* sank *U-519.* Later yet they declared *U-519* lost to unknown causes.

the Gibraltar-bound convoy, the group was dissolved, a complete waste of twelve boats for ten days, not to mention the loss of one IXC. Five of the outbound VIIs joined other groups on the North Atlantic run. The IXs *U-107* and *U-183* went southward, the former to join anti-Torch groups west of Gibraltar, the latter to American waters. The three VIIs that were low on fuel resumed their homebound voyages.

Owing to the decision to "open out" the sailing cycle from eight to ten days, only thirteen convoys, comprised of about 520 merchant ships, sailed across the stormy Atlantic east or west on the North Atlantic run in January 1943. Although Allied codebreakers read naval Enigma imperfectly in that month, its output enabled the Allies to divert most convoys around the U-boat groups. The large force of U-boats patrolling that area in hideous weather made fleeting contact with ships of only three of the transatlantic convoys (Halifax 222 and 223, Slow 117) and sank only four ships for 31,865 gross tons, plus the bow of the wrecked *Kollbjörg,* the least remunerative month of the entire war.* Due to the lack of contact with the enemy, U-boat losses on the North Atlantic run in January were slight: Ruwiedel's new *U-337* and Thurmann's veteran *U-553,* both to unknown causes.

U-boat Successes on the North Atlantic Run

U-boat Control sailed a record sixty-seven attack boats against Allied convoy routes in the North and Middle Atlantic in the month of February 1943. These consisted of fifty-four VIIs,† twelve more Type IXs unsuitable for hard convoy battles, and one XB minelayer, *U-119.* As in January, one-half of these boats were new or were commanded by new skippers.

The boats sailing in the first half of February had to contend with Coastal Command's new and intensified Bay of Biscay offensive, Gondola. However, Allied aircraft hit only one of the sixty-seven outbound attack U-boats. She was the *U-211,* commanded by Karl Hause. The attacking aircraft was a B-24 of Army Air Forces Antisubmarine Squadron 1, piloted by Wayne S. Johnson. He dropped six depth charges in a close straddle. The explosion severely damaged *U-211* and forced Hause to abort and return to Brest.

There were not nearly enough U-tankers to support the large number of VIIs at sea. Of the five "Milk Cow" XIV tankers, *U-459* was in the South Atlantic supporting the Cape Town foray, *Seehund,* and the *U-463* had just returned to France. The *U-460* sailed to the North Atlantic the last day of January; the other two, *U-461* and *U-462* (delayed by repairs), sailed on February 13 and 19, respectively. Therefore U-boat Control directed that after she laid her minefield, the XB *U-119* was to serve as a provisional tanker for VIIs in the North Atlantic.

The Allied breaks into naval Enigma continued into February. To process the

* In convoy Outbound North (Slow) 160, huge seas capsized and sank the commodore's flagship, *Ville de Tamatave,* with the loss of all hands.

† Including two from the Arctic: *U-405* and *U-591.*

flow of information on U-boats obtained from Enigma intercepts by British and American codebreakers, Admiral King established a "Secret Room" adjacent to the U.S. Navy's Submarine Tracking Room. A reserve lieutenant, John E. Parsons, was in charge of the room, which was kept locked at all times. Only Parsons, his assistant, John V. Boland, another reservist, two yeomen, and the Navy's principal U-boat tracker, Kenneth Knowles, had keys to the room.

There were large charts of the North and South Atlantic and Indian Oceans and the Caribbean Sea on three walls. A symbol representing the date and last known position of every U-boat was pinned on the charts. Different colored tabs were used to indicate the type of U-boat (VII, IX, XB minelayer, and so on). Each wall also had a "Port Board" showing the location of all U-boat forward bases and symbols representing the U-boats in that port, plus the date of their arrival. The information from these charts and boards enabled Knowles to plot the daily *estimated* positions of U-boats at sea (as opposed to the last *known* position) on similar ocean charts in the Submarine Tracking Room without revealing the source of his information.

The first challenging task for Parsons and Boland was to positively identify newly sailing U-boats by number and by their skippers. This process began when the U-boat sent a short-signal "passage report" indicating it had safely crossed the Bay of Biscay or the Iceland-Faeroes gap and entered the broad reaches of the Atlantic. These signals were signed not by skipper name or the actual number of the U-boat but by a bigram. Later, however, it might happen that U-boat Control would slip up and respond to a U-boat signal signed by a number with a signal addressed to the skipper by name or vice versa; the U-boat might respond to a skipper message with a number. By consulting a card catalog in the Secret Room library, it was usually possible from accumulated information to know that a certain skipper commanded a certain U-boat and what type it was. Hence most boats and skippers could be identified fairly quickly—and always within three weeks.

To avoid direct references to individual U-boats in the London-Washington secret traffic (which might be broken by the Germans), each U-boat was permanently designated in Allied records by a bigram, or two-letter code. The first letter in the bigram designated the type and the second letter the specific boat within that type series. Every second letter of the alphabet was used in the bigrams to designate Type VIIs (A, C, E, G, I, and so on) and the intervening letters to designate Type IXs (B, D, F, H, J, L). The M was reserved for minelayers, the S for U- cruisers, the W for cargo boats, and the Z for U-tankers and torpedo-resupply boats.* As more information accumulated from all sources, the Allies, where possible, assigned a skipper name to the bigram. Hence, hypothetically, bigram "GD" might represent the Type VII *U- 598* commanded by Gottfried Holtorf.

The next important challenge was to determine where each U-boat was bound: North Atlantic "wolf pack"? South Atlantic? Americas? This was not easy because the Germans then disguised their system of oceanic bigram grid squares (AK, AL,

* As examples, AA, AB, AC, AD and CA, CB, CD represented specific Type VIIs; BA, BB, BC, BD and DA, DB, DC represented specific Type IXs. MA might be the XB (minelayer) *U-116,* MB the *U-117,* etc.

etc.) by colors and by additives. Hence U-boat Control might order a certain VII, "EB," to a group forming in oceanic grid square AL 22 in the North Atlantic (south of Iceland) by using "Blue 72," the additive in this example being fifty. By comparing the files of short signals from other identified U-boats, such as convoy contacts, reports of sinkings, damage, weather, and soon with Huff Duff bearings and other information it was possible to puzzle out that "Blue 72" was grid square AL 22. But it was tedious work requiring codebreakers with uncanny intuition and infinite patience.

At the same time Parsons and Knowles were solving these riddles, so were Rodger Winn and his associates in the Admiralty's Submarine Tracking Room. Knowles and Winn exchanged messages almost daily. ("We think GD in Blue 72 is Holtorf in *U-598*" might elicit a response such as "Agree" or "Do not agree. We show Holtorf in GR in Lorient.") About once a week Knowles and Winn exchanged provisional lists of all U-boats at sea, the skippers, type bigrams, status of fuel and torpedoes, location, group assignments, and so on, and then conducted a transatlantic vetting of the lists until reaching complete agreement. All these data were promptly entered on the U-boat file cards, along with all other information.*

The American codebreaking historian George Howe wrote that the Allies read U-boat traffic steadily from February 5 to February 28, 1943, with an average decoding delay of one day. That intelligence was so up to the minute that it could be used tactically, to evade U-boat groups or for Allied aircraft to "discover" a rendezvous between one or several boats and/or U-tankers and to attack.

The U-boats were likewise the beneficiaries of a flow of information on North Atlantic convoys from *B-dienst.* On the first day of February, the veteran VII *U-456,* commanded by Max-Martin Teichert, newly transferred from the Arctic, found a big, fast convoy in mid-Atlantic. This was Halifax 224, consisting of fifty-eight merchant ships guarded by the seven warships of Canadian group C-4: the ex-American British four-stack destroyer *Churchill,* the Canadian destroyer *Restigouche,* and five Canadian and British corvettes.

Teichert shadowed and brought up several nearby boats. He then attacked and sank a 7,200-ton American Liberty ship and the 9,500-ton British tanker *Inverilen.* One other boat, the new *U-632,* commanded by Hans Karpf, who was low on fuel and inbound to France, found and sank a straggler from the convoy, the 8,200-ton British tanker *Cordelia.* It was Karpf's second tanker kill on his first patrol, a total of 16,000 tons.

In all, six boats made contact with convoy Halifax 224. U-boat Control ordered four that had sufficient fuel to continue tracking. One of these was the new VII

* See NARA unpublished documents in Record Group 457. These are the tens of thousands of pages of the files from the "Secret Room," a huge store of information in English, so utterly complete for 1943, 1944, and 1945 that one could almost write a history of the U-boat war from them alone. The files also contain English translations of all messages between U-boat Control and the U-boats at sea and vice versa.

U-265, commanded by Leonhard Auffhammer, age twenty-five, two weeks out from Kiel. On February 3, a B-17 Flying Fortress of British Squadron 220, piloted by K. Ramsden, which had come out to escort Halifax 224, caught and dropped seven depth charges on *U-265.* She went down with the loss of all hands about five hundred miles west of Scotland.

Karpf in *U-632* rescued the chief engineer of the British tanker *Cordelia.* According to German accounts, he revealed that another big convoy was following exactly in the wake of Halifax 224 and Karpf radioed this information to U-boat Control. It confirmed guesses that the Allies might send a Slow Convoy along the same path, in the belief that all the U-boats were trailing Halifax 224 eastwardly and the waters behind it were apt to be clear. Acting on Karpf's report, U-boat Control shifted into the wake of Halifax 224 the newly forming group *Pfeil* (Arrow), consisting of thirteen boats: three already in the area, six from the dissolved group *Landsknecht,* and four recently sailed from France.

While this redeployment was taking place, a boat on the extreme northern end of the reconstituted *Haudegen* group also reported an eastbound convoy. She was the new *U-223,* commanded by Karl-Jürgen Wächter, age twenty-six, three weeks out from Kiel. At first U-boat Control believed this contact to be the expected Slow Convoy and ordered the entire northern half of group *Haudegen* (nine boats) to home on *U-223.* But Wächter's second report correctly surmised that the convoy, which he said was comprised of merely five ships, was probably a local one en route to an Allied base in Greenland. Accepting this assessment, U-boat Control reduced the reinforcements for *U-223* to four boats (three VIIs, one IX), all of them on maiden patrols from Kiel.

Wächter had indeed found a "local" convoy en route from Newfoundland to Greenland. It consisted of one 5,600-ton U.S. Army troopship, *Dorchester,* which carried 904 men (130 crew, 751 military personnel, 23 naval armed guardsmen) plus one thousand tons of cargo, and two smaller Norwegian freighters, *Lutz* and *Biscaya.* These three merchant ships were escorted by three ice-encrusted Coast Guard cutters: the 240-foot *Tampa,* and two 165-footers, *Comanche* and *Escanaba.* In a night surface attack on this formation, Wächter shot all five torpedoes in his five tubes singly. Three torpedoes missed but two hit *Dorchester* which, unaccountably, made no distress signals. The other five ships sailed on in the darkness.

On *Dorchester* there was mass panic and disorder as the 904 men abandoned ship in near-freezing water. Only two of fourteen lifeboats were used to full advantage. When the escort belatedly realized that *Dorchester* was missing, the senior vessel, *Tampa,* commanded by Joseph Greenspun, went on to Greenland with the two Norwegian freighters and sent *Comanche* and *Escanaba* back to hunt for U-boats and rescue the survivors of *Dorchester.* After a futile U-boat hunt, the crews of the two cutters heroically plunged into the water to tow rafts and/or individual survivors to waiting hands. But they were able to rescue only 229 of the 904 persons on *Dorchester.* In this rare American troopship disaster, 675 men died, 404 of them U.S. Army personnel.

On that same day, February 4, U-boat Control redistributed the twenty boats of group *Haudegen.* The five boats on maiden patrols that had been sent after the

Dorchester convoy, redesignated group *Nortstrum,* remained on a likely shipping lane midway between Newfoundland and Greenland. Five experienced boats that had sailed from France from January 7 to 9 were detached to group *Pfeil* for the attack on the expected Slow Convoy. The remaining ten boats (four on maiden patrols) were deployed very close off St. John's, along the Newfoundland coast.

Alerted by Enigma decrypts, Allied aircraft (as yet unidentified) caught and bombed two of these ten boats, Heinz-Ehlert Clausen's *U-403,* newly transferred from the Arctic, and the new *U-414,* commanded by Walter Huth. The latter incurred such heavy damage that Huth was forced to abort to France. The boat was out of action until April.

The expected Slow Convoy trailing Halifax 224 was SC 118. It sailed from New York on January 24 with forty-four ships. Nineteen ships from Newfoundland joined, making sixty-three. She was guarded by the crack British group B-2, usually commanded by Donald Macintyre in *Hesperus,* but his ship, which had rammed and sunk *U-357* on a prior trip, was in repair in Liverpool. The temporary group commander was F. B. Proudfoot, new skipper of the British destroyer *Vanessa.* The group was quite strong: *Vanessa,* and three other British destroyers, *Vimy, Witch,* and the ex-American four-stack *Beverley;* the big American *Treasury*-class Coast Guard cutter *Bibb;* and four corvettes, one British, three French. All nine escorts had radar. *Vanessa, Bibb,* and the indefatigable rescue ship *Toward* also had Huff Duff.

The convoy sailed through the *Pfeil* patrol line undetected in the early hours of February 4. Then, as luck would have it, a seaman on the Norwegian freighter *Annik* accidentally fired a brilliant snowflake flare. One of the *Pfeil* boats, Ralph Münnich's new IXC40 *U-187,* about three weeks out from Kiel, saw the flare. He closed on the convoy from ahead and radioed a contact report for the benefit of the dozen other boats of group *Pfeil. Bibb,* commanded by Roy L. Raney, and *Toward* DFed Münnich's B-bar short-signal contact report.

Proudfoot directed two of the British destroyers to run down the Huff Duff bearing of the U-boat: the four-stack *Beverley* (ex-U.S.S. *Branch*), and the *Vimy,* commanded by Richard Stannard, who had earlier won Great Britain's highest award, the Victoria Cross. The two destroyers raced out. *Beverley* spotted *U-187* at about five thousand yards, but owing to the rough seas, she could not fire her main battery. In the event, when he saw the destroyers gaining, Münnich dived and went deep.

Vimy got *U-187* on sonar and, with *Beverley,* commenced a methodical attack with Hedgehog and depth charges. Münnich released a *Bolde* noisemaker and attempted to creep away on his motors, but the destroyers held fast. *Vimy*'s Hedgehog did no damage but some of her thirty depth charges cracked the boat's pressure hull center and aft, flooding the control room with fuel oil and the aft areas with salt water. Much too heavy aft, the boat nosed up at a terrifying 45 degree angle. Two and a half hours into the hunt, when he saw that *U-187* was doomed, Münnich ordered the crew to surface and scuttle. Most of the crew concluded that escape was impossible and shook hands in lugubrious farewells. But their luck held. With the last gasp of high-pressure air, Münnich achieved sufficient positive buoyancy to reach the surface.

When *U-187* appeared, *Beverley* and *Vimy* opened fire with main batteries and antiaircraft cannons. The fire killed nine Germans, including Münnich and probably his chief engineer. The *U-187* upended and sank stern first, leaving the rest of the crew in the water. *Beverley* and *Vimy* rescued forty-five men, including three officers, after which the two destroyers rejoined the convoy.

Acting on Münnich's contact report, U-boat Control reinforced the thirteen boats of group *Pfeil* with seven more: five from group *Haudegen* and two that had been chasing Halifax 224. In the late afternoon of February 4, four *Pfeil* boats reported contact. Three, including Siegfried von Forstner in *U-402,* were experienced skippers, the other, *U-267,* commanded by Otto Tinschert, age twenty-seven, was a new boat three weeks out from Kiel. All reported that the strong, aggressive escort and foul weather (snow, hail, high winds, heavy seas) made shadowing difficult. No boat was able to mount an effective attack on the convoy during the night of February 4–5.

Over the next twenty-four hours, Klaus Rudloff in *U-609* made contact and shadowed tenaciously. During that time, three boats attacked the convoy. Heinz Franke in the *U-262,* making his second patrol, claimed that he sank a 12,000-ton tanker with three hits, but the sinking was never confirmed. In a second attack, Franke claimed sinking another tanker of 9,000 tons and possible hits on a third tanker. In all likelihood he sank only the 2,900-ton Polish freighter *Zagloba.* Gustav Poel in the *U-413,* also on his second patrol, sank a straggler, the 5,400-ton American freighter *West Portal.* Rolf von Jessen in the new *U-266* sank another straggler, the 4,100-ton Greek *Polyktor* and captured the captain and chief engineer.

By the evening of February 5, Slow Convoy 118 had reached a point about seven hundred miles from Iceland. One escort, the British destroyer *Witch,* had run short of fuel and had left. However, that night three escorts from Iceland joined the convoy: the big *Treasury*-class Coast Guard cutter *Ingham* (with defective sonar) and two American four-stack destroyers, *Babbitt* and *Schenck.* This increased the surface escort to eleven warships: five destroyers, two *Treasury*-class Coast Guard cutters, and the four corvettes. Although Rudloff in *U-609* held on, sending contact reports for which he received high praise, no U-boats got through the screen that night, prompting testy exhortations from U-boat Control: "At 'em! Operate ruthlessly to relieve the Eastern Front!"

Long-range aircraft from Iceland and/or Northern Ireland provided air escort on the morning of February 6. Working closely with the eleven surface escorts, the aircraft scattered the U-boats and drove them under. Five VIIs reported battle damage by destroyers or aircraft or both, and aborted to France: Franke in *U-262* (who was out of torpedoes anyway); Otto Tinschert in the new *U-267;* Rudolf Franzius in *U-438;* Heinz Wolf in *U-465;* and Karl-Ernst Schroeter in *U-752.* Two B-24s of British Squadron 120, piloted by Desmond J. Isted and Donald C. Fleming-Williams, carried out close attacks on U-boats that afternoon, possibly on Wolf's *U-465,* but the U-boat survived.

In response to the exhortations from Berlin, a half dozen boats risked all to attack Slow Convoy 118 on February 7. Two VIIs met with disaster. The Free French corvette *Lobelia,* commanded by Pierre de Morsier, got Rudloff's *U-609* on radar, chased her under with gunfire, then destroyed her with depth charges. A B-17 Flying Fortress of British Squadron 220, piloted by G. Roberson, sank with seven depth charges *U-624,* commanded by Ulrich von Soden-Fraunhofen. There were no survivors from either U-boat.

Two boats evaded the escorts and closed the convoy that night: Siegfried von Forstner in the veteran *U-402* and Wolfgang Sträter in the new *U-614.* In a classic four-hour attack, von Forstner sank five confirmed ships for about 28,000 tons and damaged the 9,300-ton Norwegian tanker *Daghild.* During the same four hours, Sträter in *U-614* sank one 5,700-ton British freighter and later hit *Daghild,* which still refused to sink.* In the chaos von Forstner created, the merchant ship *Samuel Huntington* rammed and disabled the Greek freighter *Adamas,* which had veered out of her assigned column. While attempting to sink *Adamas* with her guns, the Free French corvette *Lobelia* disabled herself, and *Vimy* had to tow her to the British Isles.

Two of the ships von Forstner sank resulted in heavy loss of life. The first was the valiant 1,600-ton rescue ship *Toward.* Of the seventy-four men on board, fifty-eight were killed or died in the icy water. The second was the 6,100-ton American vessel *Henry R. Mallory,* serving as a troopship. Although she went down slowly, the abandon-ship procedure was marked by the usual panic and ineptitude. As a result, 228 of the 495 men on board perished. Valorously ignoring the danger of a U-boat attack, Roy Raney in the Coast Guard cutter *Bibb* launched a rescue of *Mallory*'s 267 survivors.

When the British escort commander, F. B. Proudfoot on *Vanessa,* realized that *Bibb* had lagged behind to rescue survivors, he repeatedly ordered Raney to cease and desist and to rejoin the convoy at once. Raney ignored those orders and launched whaleboats, determined to rescue every American soldier and sailor he could possibly find. Under the direction of a deck officer, Henry C. Keene, Jr., over the next several hours Raney's men picked up 202 of the 267 *Mallory* survivors, plus the cook's dog, "Rickey," found all alone on a raft. Raney then rescued thirty-three survivors of the Greek *Kalliopi* (sunk by von Forstner in *U-402*)—altogether 235 men, of whom three later died.†

Puzzled and angry that so few of the twenty U-boats had reported contact, U-boat Control exhorted the skippers to press the killing and pointedly radioed congratulations to von Forstner in *U-402* and Franke in *U-262* for their aggressive attacks and to the lost Klaus Rudloff in *U-609* for his dogged shadowing. Notwithstanding the heavy air and surface escorts, von Forstner got in again and sank yet another freighter, a 5,000-ton Greek. This sinking raised von Forstner's claims in

---

* One of the corvettes attempted to sink *Daghild* with gunfire, but failed. Rolf Struckmeier in *U-608* finally sank the hulk with a torpedo.

† When this rescue story leaked, it was widely publicized in the wartime media, which featured Raney (who later rose to vice admiral) and Keene—and the dog "Rickey." See Webster article, "Someone Get That Damned Dog!"

Slow Convoy 118 to seven ships for 62,200 tons, which earned him personal congratulations from Dönitz and a *Ritterkreuz,* one of the very few awarded to skippers on the North Atlantic run in the winter of 1942–1943.*

Coastal Command was able to provide Slow Convoy 118 with saturation air cover, and U-boat Control was forced to cancel operations by February 9. The Germans claimed sinking fourteen merchant ships for 109,000 tons. The actual score was eleven ships for about 60,000 tons (over half of that sunk by von Forstner) plus the Greek *Adamas,* lost in collision as a result of the battle. Allied forces sank three U-boats: the IXC *U-187,* and the VIIs *U-609, U-624.*

British aircraft very nearly sank three more U-boats of this group. On February 8, a B-24 of British Squadron 120, piloted by New Zealander Bryan W. Turnbull, hit the *U-135,* commanded by Heinz Schütt. The next day a B-17 Flying Fortress of British Squadron 206, piloted by R. C. Patrick, hit the *U-614,* commanded by Wolfgang Sträter. On February 10, a B-24 of American Squadron 2, piloted by William L. Sanford, hit the aborting *U-752,* commanded by Karl-Ernst Schroeter.† Schütt in *U-135* repaired his damage and continued operations, but Sträter in *U-614,* who reported "severe" damage, aborted to France, and Schroeter in *U-752* continued his homeward voyage.

That the twenty U-boats assigned to Slow Convoy 118 had not achieved greater success led to disappointment, displeasure, and concern in Berlin. Godt explained in the war diary that "only experienced boats could succeed" against such a heavily escorted convoy. Increasingly that observation applied to all heavily escorted Allied convoys. Only rarely could green boats get by the escorts to shoot.

Too late to help Slow Convoy 118 evade the U-boat groups, Allied codebreakers recovered naval Enigma on February 5 and, as related, read it steadily to the last day of the month. The information thus gained enabled the Allies to route the many ships and escorts of eastbound convoys Halifax 225 and 226 and Slow Convoys 119 and 120 around U-boat patrol lines without any losses to the Germans.

Patrolling off fogbound Newfoundland in search of eastbound convoys, group *Haudegen,* reduced to nine boats by February 9, reorganized. The five boats of *Haudegen* that were detached to form group *Nortstrum,* northeast of Newfoundland, were returned to *Haudegen,* except for Ernst Heydemann in the new *U-268,* who was low on fuel and had to return to France. While he was inbound to Brest, a Leigh Light–equipped Wellington of British Squadron 172, piloted by G. D. Lundon, caught the boat and savaged her with four close depth charges. In response to Heydemann's final, desperate request for help, U-boat Control sent

---

* Von Forstner's confirmed bag in Slow Convoy 118 was six ships for 32,446 tons, plus a Landing Craft, Infantry (LCI) from *Daghild.* His confirmed score at the time of the award, all on *U-402,* was thirteen ships sunk for 63,409 tons, plus severe damage to two tankers for 16,731 tons, which were abandoned and sunk by other U-boats.

† According to Franks in *Search, Find and Kill* (1995), originally it was erroneously believed that in this attack Sanford sank *U-519.*

out aircraft and patrol boats, but they could find no sign of *U-268.* The boat and all hands had perished.

The reorganization of *Haudegen* increased the group to thirteen boats. Other than local ASW vessels, in the next seven days only one boat saw a target. She was the VII *U-607,* commanded by the *Ritterkreuz* holder Ernst Mengersen. He came upon a lone American tanker on February 15. She was the fast 11,400-ton *Atlantic Sun* (of Sun Oil Company) en route from Iceland to join convoy Outbound North (Slow) 165, but she had not yet caught up. At about midday, Mengersen attacked submerged and exploded the ship with three torpedoes. As she broke into pieces, the sixty-six men on board (including a nineteen-man naval armed-guard crew) scrambled for the lifeboats and rafts. Mengersen captured a twenty-three-year-old merchant seaman, William Golobich, but the other sixty-five men perished.

Golobich falsely told Mengersen that the tanker was a straggler from a "fast convoy," probably the eastbound Halifax 225 for which group *Haudegen* was lying in wait. The news that the convoy had apparently slipped by, plus the realization that many of the boats were critically low on fuel, led U-boat Control to disband the luckless *Haudegen.* Eight of the thirteen boats set sail for France; five with adequate fuel remained off Newfoundland to cadre a new group, *Taifun* (Typhoon).

While homebound, one of the ex-*Haudegen* boats, the *U-69,* commanded by Ulrich Gräf, discovered convoy Outbound North (Slow) 165 on February 17. Gräf got off a B-bar contact report and set up a beacon for other homebound *Haudegen* boats. The signals brought up *U-201,* commanded by Günther Rosenberg. Warships of British Escort Group B-6, commanded by R. Heathcote, detected the gathering U-boats on Huff Duff and radar. Heathcote's two veteran destroyers, *Fame* and *Viscount,* ran down the bearings, firing and dropping depth charges. *Fame* sank *U-69,* which had gained renown under *Ritterkreuz* holder Jost Metzler for her pioneering voyage in 1941 to Freetown and Takorodi.* *Viscount* sank *U-201,* which had gained renown under Adalbert Schnee, who won the *Ritterkreuz* with Oak Leaves on her. There were no survivors from either U-boat.

Several other boats made contact with Outbound North (Slow) 165 in foul weather. Three of these were homebound and low on fuel: Rolf von Jessen in *U-266;* Heinz-Ehlert Clausen in *U-403;* and *Ritterkreuz* holder Ernst Mengersen in *U-607.* Neither Jessen nor Mengersen had a chance to shoot, but Clausen sank a 6,000-ton Greek. Hans-Joachim Drewitz, age thirty-five, in the new IXC40 *U-525,* assigned to the newly formed group *Taifun,* sank a 3,500-ton British freighter. While *U-525* was homebound in Biscay on March 3, a Leigh Light–equipped Wellington of British Squadron 172, piloted by J. W. Tweddle, bombed and severely damaged her. Drewitz limped into Lorient, escorted by two JU-88s and several small vessels. The boat was out of action until April.

By the middle of February, U-boat Control had deployed three new groups on the North Atlantic run between Greenland and Iceland. These were *Ritter* (Knight), *Knappen* (Shieldbearer), and *Neptun,* comprising in all thirty-two boats.

---

* See Volume I, p. 301.

Allied codebreakers were aware of the positions of these new groups. Perhaps as a consequence, group *Ritter* lost two of eleven boats on the same day, February 15. One was the new IXC 40 *U-529,* commanded by Georg-Werner Fraatz, the skipper who had commanded *U-652* in her historic engagement with the American destroyer *Greer* in the Denmark Strait on September 4, 1941. Subsequently, Fraatz had sunk two British destroyers *(Heythrop, Jaguar)* in the Mediterranean before Allied aircraft savaged his *U-652* so badly that she had to be sunk by *U-81,* who rescued Fraatz and his crew, many of whom remained with him to commission *U-529.* The other boat lost that day was the VII *U-225,* commanded by Wolfgang Leimkühler, out from France on his second patrol with group *Ritter.* There were no survivors from either boat.*

A Focke-Wulf FW-200 Condor reported a westbound convoy well to the east of these three groups on February 18. For the purpose of intercepting this convoy, U-boat Control split off five of the ten boats of group *Knappen* to cadre a new group, *Burggraf* (Fortress Chief). The remaining five boats of group *Knappen* were then attached to group *Ritter,* extending its line southeast. Three boats newly sailed from France joined the *Burggraf* cadre, raising its strength to eight boats.

One of the *Knappen* boats, *U-604,* commanded by Horst Höltring, reported a westbound convoy on the morning of February 20. This was the fast Outbound North 166, composed of about sixty merchant ships. The convoy was guarded by the American Escort Group A-3, commanded by the veteran Paul Heineman. His group consisted of seven warships: two *Treasury*-class Coast Guard cutters, *Campbell* and *Spencer,* both equipped with centimetric-wavelength radar and Huff Duff, four Canadian corvettes, and one British corvette, all with centimetric-wavelength radar. The rescue ship, *Stockport,* was equipped with Huff Duff.

Groups *Knappen* and *Ritter* combined consisted of fourteen boats. U-boat Control ordered all but one, *U-377,* commanded by Otto Köhler, who was too far to the east, to close on the convoy. In addition, Control directed six boats of the Newfoundland group *Taifun,* which were refueling from the XIV "Milk Cow" tanker *U-460,* to come northeast and join the attack. These orders were to put nineteen boats into the battle with Outbound North 166, one of the largest U-boat operations of the war.

During the night of February 20–21, while Höltring in *U-604* shadowed, the boats gathered. In the early hours of February 21, two VIIs of group *Ritter,* Eberhard Hüttemann in *U-332* and Hans Joachim Bertelsmann in *U-603,* and one VII of *Knappen,* Adolf Oelrich in *U-92,* got inside the screen and attacked. Hüttemann and Bertelsmann both claimed sinking 6,000-ton freighters, but as it turned out, they had hit the same ship, the 6,000-ton Norwegian tanker *Stigstad,* which sank. Hüttemann in *U-332* later reported that a corvette hunted him for thirteen hours. In

---

* Credit for these kills remains uncertain. Originally the Admiralty credited a B-24 of Squadron 120, based in Iceland, for the kill of Fraatz's *U-529.* In the postwar analysis, it withdrew the credit and speculated that the loss was probably due to an "accident." According to the war diary of U-boat Control, *U-529* was probably at or close to the place where the aircraft claimed a kill that day. Wartime credit for the kill of *U-225* (nearby *U-529)* was certainly wrongly attributed. In the postwar revision, the Admiralty credited the kill of *U-225* to a B-24 of Squadron 120, piloted by Reginald T. F. Turner, who was escorting Slow Convoy 119.

his attack, Oelrich in *U-92* damaged the 10,000-ton British freighter *Empire Trader.* The escort commander, Paul Heineman, directed the Canadian corvette *Dauphin* to escort this big, valuable ship to the Azores. Subsequently the Admiralty countermanded these orders and directed *Dauphin* to sink *Empire Trader* by gun and rejoin the besieged convoy as soon as possible.

A B-24 Liberator of British Squadron 120, piloted by Desmond J. Isted, found the VII *U-623* on the surface on the afternoon of February 21. Commanded by Hermann Schröder, *U-623* was making her second Atlantic patrol. Isted dived out of a cloud and dropped six shallow-set depth charges in a close straddle. Nothing further was ever heard from *U-623.** Three other VIIs reported aircraft had forced them down: the *Knappen* boats *U-91,* commanded by Heinz Walkerling, and *U-604,* commanded by Horst Höltring; and the *U-454,* an ex-Arctic VII commanded by Burkhard Hackländer in group *Ritter.* Walkerling in *U-91* later reported that a rain of aircraft bombs and depth charges from surface escorts caused such damage to the boat that he had to withdraw temporarily for repairs. He later resumed the chase, but he did not again make contact with this convoy.

In view of the large numbers of U-boats converging on Outbound North 166, and the temporary absence of the corvette *Dauphin,* Western Approaches ordered the ex-French, Polish-manned destroyer *Burza,* commanded by Franciszek Pitulko, of group B-3, escorting the oncoming convoy Outbound North (Slow) 167, to run ahead and reinforce the American escort group. Until she arrived and *Dauphin* rejoined, Heineman, with merely six escorts, had his hands full. Nonetheless, that night, Heineman believed, the escort evened the score. The *Treasury*-class Coast Guard cutter *Spencer,* commanded by the aptly named sailor Harold Sloop Berdine, chased down and, it was thought, sank one U-boat, identified later in official records as the *U-225,* commanded by Wolfgang Leimkühler.†

Three U-boats evaded the screen and attacked the convoy on the night of February 22. The first two were Oelrich in the *Knappen* boat *U-92* and Alfred Manhardt von Mannstein in the *Ritter* boat *U-753.* Oelrich claimed sinking two freighters for 11,000 tons and possible hits on a third ship. In fact, he hit only the big 9,300-ton Norwegian freighter *N.T. Nielsen Alonso* with two FATs. Manhardt von Mannstein in *U-753* also hit the *Alonso,* leaving her a floating wreck. The big Coast Guard cutter *Campbell* removed *Alonso*'s fifty-man crew, then the destroyer *Burza* put the hulk under by gunfire. Meanwhile *Campbell* found *U-753* and depth-charged the boat so savagely that von Mannstein was compelled to withdraw from the battle. Upon learning of his damage (both periscopes and one diesel out), U-boat Control directed von Mannstein to head homeward and, if feasible, join a group preparing to attack the oncoming convoy, Outbound North (Slow) 167.

The third boat to attack that night was the first VII to arrive from group *Taifun,* the *U-606,* commanded by twenty-five-year-old Hans Döhler. He sank the 5,700-

* Initially the Admiralty attributed the loss of *U-623* to "unknown causes," date also unknown. Much later in the postwar analysis, British historians concluded that Isted did the deed.

† As related, in the postwar analysis, the Admiralty withdrew credit for the kill of *U-225* from *Spencer* and gave it to pilot Turner in a B-24 of British Squadron 120.

ton American freighter *Chattanooga City,* and damaged the 5,000-ton American freighter *Expositor* and the 6,600-ton British freighter *Empire Redshank.* The Canadian corvette *Trillium* put the *Redshank* under with her gun, but was unable to do the same with the hulk of *Expositor.* The second *Taifun* VII to arrive, the new *U-303,* commanded by Karl-Franz Heine, age twenty-seven, sank *Expositor* with a finishing shot.

Three escorts counterattacked Döhler in *U-606:* the Canadian corvette *Chilliwack,* the Polish destroyer *Burza,* and the U.S. Coast Guard cutter *Campbell.* Franciszek Pitulko in *Burza* carried the weight of the initial attack, doggedly holding the sonar contact and firing about forty depth charges. These charges drove *U-606* to the scary depth of 787 feet and caused so much external and internal damage that *U-606*'s chief engineer insisted that Döhler surface to escape or to scuttle.

When *U-606* popped up, the cutter *Campbell* got her on radar at 4,600 yards. The skipper, James A. Hirschfield, who was accidentally wounded by his own gunners, ran down the bearing firing every weapon that could bear, then, as he was throwing over two shallow-set depth charges, he unintentionally rammed *U-606.* The U-boat dragged down the side of *Campbell,* cutting a fifteen-foot gash in her plating and flooding the engine room. When the ships separated, *Campbell* fixed *U-606* in her searchlight and again raked her with every possible weapon. Thereupon the flooding caused *Campbell*'s power to fail and, like *U-606,* she lay helpless, drifting with the currents.

There was chaos on *U-606.* The gunfire from *Campbell* wrecked the boat and killed most of the Germans who got topside, including Döhler. Many survivors jumped overboard to escape the gunfire, drifted off, and drowned. *Campbell* sent a whaler to the sinking U-boat to take off survivors, but only five of them got in the boat. Later in the night *Burza* found *U-606,* decks awash but still afloat, with eight Germans on board. These Germans opened the last vents to sink *U-606,* then jumped into the water and swam to *Burza.* One survivor failed to make it, leaving the Germans captured alive from *U-606* at only twelve.*

Nothing could be done to get *Campbell* under way on her own steam. She had to be sunk or towed to Newfoundland. Hirschfield transferred the fifty survivors of the freighter *Nielsen Alonso,* the five German POWs, and 112 of the *Campbell* crew to *Burza.* Although he was low on fuel, Pitulko on *Burza* volunteered to tow *Campbell* to Newfoundland. Reluctant to offer the many U-boats present two sitting ducks in a towing operation, Hirschfield declined the offer. Crowded with survivors, *Burza* then departed the convoy for St. John's, arriving with very little fuel. The corvette *Dauphin* came up to stand by *Campbell* until the tug *Tenacity* arrived to tow *Campbell* to St. John's, protected by yet another corvette. For his cool heroism and for carrying on to sink *U-606* in spite of his wounds, Hirschfield was awarded a Navy Cross.

Convoy Outbound North 166 continued westward. Soon the British corvette *Dianthus,* critically low on fuel, was compelled to break off for St. John's, reduced

---

* The damage that *Campbell* incurred in her unintentional ramming of *U-606* precluded any hope of her putting over a boarding party.

to burning gunnery and mineral oil and paint thinner. Her departure left only the cutter *Spencer* and four corvettes to deal with the sixteen U-boats tenaciously tracking the convoy.

During the night of February 23–24, no less than a dozen boats overwhelmed the thin escort and ran in and shot torpedoes. Horst Höltring in the *Knappen* VII *U-604* sank the 1,700-ton rescue ship *Stockport,* reducing the ability of the escorts to locate the U-boats by Huff Duff. Partly as a result, the U-boats sank six ships that night:

- Heinz Hasenschar in the *Ritter* VII *U-628* hit and damaged two tankers in ballast, the 7,000-ton *Winkler* and the 6,400-ton *Glittore.*
- Karl-Jürgen Wächter in the *Taifun* VII *U-223,* on his maiden patrol, finished off the *Winkler.*
- Hans-Joachim Bertelsmann in the *Ritter* boat *U-603,* finished off the *Glittore.*
- Siegfried Hesemann, age thirty, in the *Taifun* boat *U-186,* an IXC40 on her maiden patrol, sank the 5,400-ton American freighter *Hastings* and the 6,200-ton British freighter *Eulima.*
- Günther Gretschel in the *Taifun* VII *U-707,* also on her maiden patrol, sank the 7,200-ton American Liberty ship *Jonathan Sturges.*

Convoy Outbound North 166 reached the outer limits of Newfoundland-based ASW aircraft by February 24, and four Cansos (Catalinas) of Canadian Squadron 5 came out to provide cover. One of the planes, piloted by F. C. Colborne, hit and severely damaged the *Knappen* VII *U-604,* commanded by Horst Höltring. Another Canso, piloted by D. G. Baldwin, hit the *Ritter* VII *U-621,* commanded by Max Kruschka. Höltring in *U-604* was compelled to abort to France. Kruschka in *U-621* fell out, repaired the damage, and remained on patrol.

Over the next forty-eight hours, as the weather deteriorated, seven more U-boats got through the thin screen and shot. The *Ritter* VII *U-628,* commanded by Heinz Hasenschar, and the *Knappen* VII *U-600,* commanded by Bernard Zurmühlen, both hit the same ship, the 4,400-ton Norwegian freighter *Ingria,* which sank. Later Hasenschar sank the 7,200-ton British Liberty ship *Manchester Merchant.* The veteran Gerhard Feiler in the *Ritter* VII *U-653* hit the 9,400-ton Dutch freighter *Madoera,* which was abandoned, but she survived and was towed to port.* Oelrich in the *Knappen* VII *U-92,* Zurmühlen in the *Knappen* VII *U-600,* and Kruschka in the *Ritter* VII *U-621* all missed in second attacks and *U-92* aborted to France.

When the boats crossed the 100-fathom (600-foot) line off Newfoundland in impenetrable fog, U-boat Control canceled operations against Outbound North 166. Admiral Godt proudly logged the reported results: Nineteen boats had chased

---

* Several days later during a howling gale, Manhardt von Mannstein in *U-753* found a crowded *Madoera* lifeboat. He ordered six white men to *U-753* but left "a number" of black Lascars in the boat. Upon learning of this episode, British propagandists branded Manhardt von Mannstein an "atrocity monger." Hans-Jürgen Zetzsche in *U-591* found and captured *Madoera's* first mate in another lifeboat, leaving the other survivors to their fate, but he was not publicly branded.

the convoy westward for six gruelling days over 1,100 miles. Thirteen of the nineteen boats "fired successfully," sinking twenty-three ships for 132,171 tons and damaging seven others. Only one U-boat, *U-606,* had been lost.

The confirmed figures were less impressive, but the total constituted one of the worst fast-convoy disasters of the war: fourteen (of sixty) merchant ships for 78,700 tons sunk by eleven boats; two tankers *(N. T. Nielson Alonso, Madoera)* hit for damage, and one escort disabled (the Coast Guard cutter *Campbell* was laid up for repairs until May 19). Counting the two *Ritter* boats (*U-225* and *U-529)* sunk on February 15 while awaiting the convoy on the patrol line and *U-606* and *U-623,* not one but four U-boats had been lost, three VIIs and one IX. Only twelve of the approximately two hundred men on those boats survived, all to become POWs.

At the conclusion of this epic battle, eight of the remaining boats headed directly to France with battle damage or fuel shortages or both. Manhardt von Mannstein in *U-753,* who had been ordered to make repairs and to attack Outbound North (Slow) 167, was unable to comply on account of battle damage. He and Höltring in *U-604* were the most severely damaged boats. Both reached France, but Manhardt von Mannstein did not sail again until May; Höltring did not sail again until late June. The other boats, quickly repaired, all resailed in April.

Convoy Outbound North (Slow) 167, which followed closely behind the fast Outbound North 166, was comprised of twenty-five ships. It was thinly guarded by British Escort Group B-3, commanded by A. A. Tait, which consisted of two British destroyers *(Harvester, Escapade),* two Polish destroyers *(Garland, Burza),* and four corvettes, three Free French and one British. As related, the *Burza* was detached to reinforce the preceding convoy, Outbound North 166.

Adolf Graef in the experienced VII *U-664* found Outbound North (Slow) 167 on the morning of February 21. The boat was one of five newly arrived to join group *Burggraf.* Graef shadowed well, bringing up Helmut Manseck in *U-758.* After Manseck reported contact, Graef attacked and sank two ships, the 4,700-ton American freighter *Rosario* and the 8,800-ton Panamanian tanker *H. H. Rogers.*

To capitalize on this contact, U-boat Control dissolved the embryo group *Burggraf* and created a new group, *Sturmbock* (Battering Ram). It was to be comprised of the five newly arrived VIIs of *Burggraf,* plus two damaged boats from the battle with Outbound North 166, and three homebound ex-*Haudegen* boats. The plan was that *Sturmbock* was to shadow and nibble away at the convoy as it waddled west. Then all the boats returning from the chase of Outbound North 166 with sufficient fuel and torpedoes were to be shifted to attack Outbound North (Slow) 167.

Allied codebreakers learned of this plan from Enigma decrypts and the Admiralty initiated an evasion plan. When the escorts forced Graef in *U-664* and Manseck in *U-758* under and held them there, the convoy made a radical turn and then followed a more southerly route than had Outbound North 166. As a result of these maneuvers, group *Sturmbock* lost the convoy and did not regain contact. The boats continued hunting west toward Newfoundland until U-boat Control realized it had been outwitted and canceled the pursuit. The five homebound boats that were diverted to join group *Sturmbock* were released. These included *Ritterkreuz* holder Ernst Mengersen in the ex-*Haudegen* boat *U-607*. Upon arrival in France, Mengersen left the boat to command the 20th Flotilla in the Training Command.*

Group *Neptun,* which assembled between Greenland and Iceland from February 15 to 20, consisted of eleven boats, including three recent transfers from the Arctic. Assailed by hideous winter storms, *Neptun* patrolled for twelve miserable days without finding anything. Finally on February 27, the new VII *U-759,* commanded by Rudolf Friedrich, age twenty-eight, came upon Halifax 227, comprised of sixty-two ships. It was thinly guarded by British Escort Group B-6, commanded by R. Heathcote: two veteran destroyers, *Fame* and *Viscount,* and four corvettes. The convoy had been routed very far to the north to avoid the U-boats pursuing the more southerly westbound convoys Outbound North 166 and Outbound North (Slow) 167.

Owing to the wild storms raging through this area, Friedrich in *U-759* had difficulty getting his contact report to Berlin. When the message finally arrived (relayed by *U-405),* U-boat Control directed group *Neptun,* less the new but tardy VII *U-638,* commanded by Hinrich-Oskar Bernbeck, age twenty-eight, to home on *U-759*'s beacon. By that time, however, Heathcote had detected *U-759* by Huff Duff and driven her under. The shadower thus lost contact with the convoy.

Bucking huge seas and howling winds, group *Neptun* could not organize for a coordinated attack. Only four boats made contact with the convoy or its stragglers. Rolf-Heinrich Hopmann in the Arctic transfer *U-405* found a group of five stragglers and sank one, the 7,200-ton British Liberty ship *Wade Hampton,* plus two patrol boats she was transporting on her deck. Regaining contact with the convoy, Rudolf Friedrich in *U-759* shot at the straggling 7,200-ton American Liberty ship *Meriwether Lewis,* but he missed and could not chase further owing to a diesel-engine failure. Another boat newly arrived from Kiel, *U-634,* was commanded by Eberhard Dahlhaus, age twenty-two, the youngest skipper in the Atlantic force.† Benefiting from Friedrich's reports, Dahlhaus found and sank the *Lewis* with three torpedoes. Two *Neptun* VIIs, Heinz Schütt's *U-135* and another Arctic transfer, Friedrich-Karl Marks's *U-376,* were compelled to abort to France, *U-135* because of a shortage of fuel and *U-376* due to battle damage. The *U-135* was out of action until early June; Schütt went to other duty.

A reconstituted *Neptun* remained in the area immediately south of Greenland. Two of its VIIs, Marks's aborting *U-376* and the *U-608,* commanded by Rolf Struckmeier, found the fast Outbound North 168, fifty-two merchant ships, which had also been rerouted to the north to avoid the U-boats attacking convoys Outbound North 166 and Outbound North (Slow) 167. Two destroyers, *Havelock* and

---

* Mengersen's confirmed score on the duck *U-18,* and the VIIs *U-101* and *U-607* was sixteen ships for 84,961 tons.

† Dahlhaus, crew of 1938, had served as a watch officer for eighteen months on the VII *U-753,* commanded by Manhardt von Mannstein.

Volunteer, of the British Escort Group B-5, commanded by Richard C. Boyle, got the boats on Huff Duff and drove them under. No other boats could find convoy Outbound North 168, but on March 7, the new VII *U-638,* commanded by Hinrich-Oskar Bernbeck, found and shot at a straggler in ballast, the 6,500-ton British tanker *Empire Light.* He reported that his torpedoes missed, but, in fact, he hit the ship and the crew abandoned her.

Twelve convoys comprised of about 550 merchant ships crossed the Atlantic between the Americas and the British Isles on the North Atlantic run in February. The falloff in traffic was the result of several factors: the increase in the eastbound convoy sailing schedule from every eight days to every ten days; the short month (twenty-eight days); hostile weather; the transfer of some surface escorts to the Fast and Slow Torch convoys (UG-GU) and to northern Russia convoys (JW-RA); the further diversion of merchant ships to northern Russia via Iceland; the withdrawal of three Canadian MOEF groups (C-1, C-2, C-4) for training at Tobermory and workup on the Gibraltar run.

The fact that both sides were reading the other's encoded radio transmissions fairly consistently in February led to a gigantic game of naval chess on the North Atlantic run. The convoys changed routes to avoid U-boat patrol lines. The patrol lines shifted to intercept convoys on the new routes, each side continually reacting to information in enemy decrypts.

In this perilous game, the U-boats had located about half the Allied convoys and had mounted truly devastating attacks on two of them or their stragglers: the eastbound Slow Convoy 118 (with British escort B-2) and the fast westbound convoy Outbound North 166 (with American escort A-3). The U-boats sank twenty-four confirmed merchant ships from these two convoys, plus eight other ships from five other North Atlantic convoys and three ships (one tanker) sailing alone. Grand total: thirty-five sinkings (nine tankers). About one-third of the lost ships (twelve) were eastbound, loaded with war matériel and food, the rest westbound vessels in ballast.* About 94 percent of all merchant ships and escorts in these convoys reached their destinations.

German losses on the North Atlantic run in February were very heavy: twelve boats (nine VIIs and three IXs). Aircraft probably accounted for six boats; surface escorts the other six. The "exchange rate" that month in that "decisive" area was thus about one U-boat sunk for three merchant ships sunk, a ruinous trend for the Germans. Of the approximately six hundred Germans serving on the twelve lost U-boats, only twelve men from *U-606* survived, all to become POWs.

When the figures on the North Atlantic run for the months of January and February are combined, there is no convincing evidence that the U-boats were anywhere close to severing this decisive lifeline. Altogether, twenty-five convoys, comprising about 1,100 merchant ships, sailed east and west in those two months.

---

* The three losses in Halifax 224 in February are counted in the January figures. See Appendix 3.

The U-boats sank forty ships from those convoys or convoy stragglers (4 percent), half of them eastbound, and seven other ships sailing alone, a total of forty-seven ships. In return, fourteen U-boats on patrol in that area failed to return, an "exchange rate" of one U-boat lost per 3.3 merchant ships sunk.*

U-boat Failures Against the New Middle Atlantic Convoy Runs

Not including the initial Torch invasion convoys, by January 1, 1943, seven fast and slow convoys had sailed between the United States and Gibraltar (UGS, UGF) and vice versa (GUF). These convoys consisted of 152 merchant ships (including troopships) and sixty-one escorts. As with the initial inbound Torch invasion convoys, no losses were incurred.

In the year 1943, 106 convoys comprised of 3,657 merchant ships and 878 escorts crossed east and west via the Middle Atlantic routes. These included twenty-seven slow and nine fast UG convoys, twenty-eight slow and eight fast GU convoys, twenty-four Torch tanker convoys (TM, OT, and TO), and ten tanker convoys between the Caribbean and the United Kingdom (CU, UC). One hundred and fifty-three tankers sailed east and west in the Torch convoys; another 192 tankers in the CU-UC convoys between the Caribbean and the British Isles.

Allied ship losses to Axis forces in the Middle Atlantic convoys in 1943 were practically infinitesimal. Axis submarines and air attacks in the Atlantic Ocean and Mediterranean Sea sank altogether nineteen merchant vessels, seven of them in the hapless British tanker convoy TM 1 in early January. Thereafter Axis forces sank only a dozen more merchant ships from Middle Atlantic convoys during the rest of the year.†

The overwhelming strength of the Atlantic U-boat force sailed against the North Atlantic run in January and February 1943. However, U-boat Control could not ignore their new Middle Atlantic routes.

In the three months from January through March, Control sent thirty-six fresh U-boats to the Gibraltar-Azores area. These consisted of twenty-one Type IXs‡ that were unsuitable for hard anticonvoy operations, thirteen VIIs, and two XB minelayers, *U-117* and *U-118.* These thirty-six joined two IXCs, *U-511* and *U-522,* which had sailed on the last day of December 1942 for the second Cape Town foray, *Seehund,* had then been diverted to attack the tanker convoy TM 1, and were subsequently held in the Gibraltar-Azores area.

Owing to the shortage of XIV tankers, only one, *U-461,* could be spared to support the boats in the Gibraltar-Azores area. She sailed on February 13. Since

---

* See Appendix 2 and Appendix 3.

† In addition, nine escorts were lost, all of them to U-boats inside the Mediterranean in the last third of 1943.

‡ Three, *U-105, U-123,* and *U-515,* embarked for West Africa but were temporarily diverted to the Gibraltar-Azores area.

this was not sufficient tanker support for the thirty-eight boats operating in that area, U-boat Control diverted the XB minelayers *U-117* and *U-118* to serve as provisional tankers upon completion of their primary tasks. In addition, Control directed that all attack boats homebound from this area with surplus fuel, including VIIs, were to give all they could to those boats remaining in the combat zone.

The first half dozen of these attack boats relieved the boats of the original group *Delphin.* These first boats, together with the IXs *U-511* and *U-522,* and the boats to follow in January and February, were variously organized into a second group *Delphin,* and two other groups, *Rochen* (Ray) and *Robbe* (Seal).

Seven of the newly sailed boats had first to conduct special missions:

- The IXC *U-66,* commanded by Friedrich Markworth, was directed to land a "French saboteur," Jean Marie Lallart, on the coast of Spanish Sahara near Mauritania–Río de Oro on January 20. Two crewmen put Lallart ashore in *U-66*'s dinghy, but the boat overturned in the surf and the crewmen were unable to recover from the mishap and return to the U-boat. Subsequently, French military personnel captured the two *U-66* crewmen in Port Etienne, Morocco, and turned them over to the British. The fate of Lallart has not come to light.
- The XB minelayer *U-118,* commanded by thirty-eight-year-old Werner Czygan, laid a field in an Allied safe lane at Gibraltar on the night of February 1. In a hair-raising few hours, Czygan planted sixty-six SMA mines. The field proved to be one of the most fertile of the war. The mines sank three British freighters for 14,000 tons and the Canadian corvette *Weyburn* and damaged a 10,000-ton Norwegian tanker and (awkwardly) a 2,000-ton neutral Spanish freighter. While attempting to assist the sinking *Weyburn* at close quarters, the British destroyer *Wivern* was damaged either by another mine or (more likely) by several of *Weyburn*'s depth charges, which detonated as she went down stern first. Afterward, *U-118* served as a provisional U-tanker, providing fuel for nine boats.
- The veteran Type VII *U-455,* commanded by a new skipper, Hans-Martin Scheibe, laid a minefield in the Allied safe lanes at Fedala (Casablanca), Morocco, on April 10. The twelve TMB mines sank one 3,800-ton French freighter.
- The XB minelayer *U-117,* commanded by Hans-Werner Neumann, was also directed to lay mines at Fedala. While approaching the harbor, Allied ASW patrols detected and hunted Neumann. Nonetheless, on the night of April 11, *U-117* planted sixty-six SMA mines. These mines damaged two 7,200-ton Liberty ships, one American, one British. Afterward, *U-117* also served as a provisional U-tanker, providing fuel for nine boats.
- The IXC *U-163,* commanded by Kurt-Edward Engelmann, was assigned to meet the inbound blockade-runner *Regensburg* and give her instructions. On March 13, while making his way out of the Bay of Biscay, Engelmann responded to a *Luftwaffe* convoy sighting—Outbound South 44—and attempted to run in and attack. One of the seven escorts, the Canadian corvette *Prescott,* picked up *U-163* on radar and sank her with depth charges.* There were no survivors. When U-boat

---

* Many published works credit the American submarine *Herring* with the kill of *U-163,* but after a meticulous reappraisal, Admiralty historians credit *Prescott.*

Control realized that *U-163* had been lost, it temporarily diverted the Americas-bound *U-161,* commanded by Albrecht Achilles, to carry out the rendezvous.

• Directed to provide submarine escorts for the blockade-runner *Hohenfriedburg,* inbound from the Far East to France, U-boat Control assigned three VIIs: the inbound *U-264,* commanded by Hartwig Looks; the inbound *U-258,* commanded by Leopold Koch, temporarily replacing the regular skipper Wilhelm von Mässenhausen, who was hospitalized; and the outbound veteran *U-437,* commanded by a new skipper, Hermann Lamby, age twenty-seven.

Based on information from Allied codebreakers, the British heavy cruiser *Sussex* lay in wait for the Germans about 720 miles west northwest of Lisbon. Adhering to the procedure for protecting the secrets of codebreaking, on the morning of February 26, an American B-24 "found" *Hohenfriedburg* and its alert ostensibly "brought up" *Sussex,* which forced the Germans to scuttle. Looks in *U-264* boldly attacked *Sussex* with a full bow salvo, but all torpedoes missed. After *Sussex* hauled out, Looks rescued the entire crew of *Hohenfriedburg* and took the men to France.

One of the boats originally assigned to meet *Hohenfriedburg* had a difficult patrol. This was Hermann Lamby, new skipper of the VII *U-437,* who discovered a serious crack in the diesel-exhaust flange, which barred the boat from diving deep, thereby robbing her of the most important means of escaping the enemy. Therefore Control, on April 13, directed Lamby to withdraw southward to "a less dangerous area" near the Azores, where he could serve as a lookout for UG-GU convoys. A week later, the outbound VII *U-409* met Lamby in *U-437* and gave him some spare parts, but Lamby aborted and returned to France on March 5, completing an utterly frustrating and useless voyage of thirty-one days.

The VIID (minelayer) *U-218,* commanded by Richard Becker, found a convoy northeast of the Canaries on February 7. U-boat Control directed five of the new *Delphin* boats and the new group *Rochen* to attack. Including *U-218,* nine U-boats made contact with the convoy, drawing heavy air attacks. Only three could get into position to shoot. Two missed, but the third, Klaus Bargsten in the IXC *U-521,* claimed sinking a 10,000-ton tanker and a corvette, and damage to an 8,000-ton freighter. Postwar records confirmed only the 750-ton British ASW trawler *Bredon.*

The IXB *U-108,* commanded by Ralf-Reimar Wolfram, reported a convoy north of the Canaries on February 10. U-boat Control rushed seven other boats of group *Rochen* to join *U-108.* Responding to the U-boat alarm, a Catalina of the Gibraltar-based British Squadron 202, piloted by William Ogle-Skan, drove *U-108* down and bombed her, Wolfram reported, "at great depth." The bombs disabled *U-108*'s four bow tubes, rendering the boat incapable of torpedo attacks. She loitered in the area for several days, giving other boats her spare fuel, then aborted to France for the second time in as many patrols. Declared unfit for further combat, *U-108* made ready to sail home to Germany for duty in the Training Command. No other boat found this convoy. Owing to the "heavy" Allied air patrols, U-boat Control temporarily suspended anticonvoy operations north and northeast of the Canaries.

Two days later, on February 12, a VII outbound from France to join group *Rochen* reported a southbound convoy near Cape Finisterre. She was *U-569,* a veteran that had come out to the Atlantic in August of 1941, commanded by Peter Hinsch, but had sunk only three ships for 8,800 tons in nearly eighteen months of operations. Deemed to be "too cautious" to be a U-boat skipper, Hinsch had finally been relieved by thirty-two-year-old Hans Johannsen, a prewar merchant-marine officer. The first watch officer, Fritz Otto Paschen, merely twenty-one-years old, had made one prior patrol in that capacity.

Although U-boat Control expected heavy Allied air cover, it directed the six new boats of group *Delphin* plus the Americas-bound IXC40 *U-185* to home on *U-569* and attack the convoy. August Maus in *U-185,* who was not far away, made contact and reported the convoy was composed of "five large troopships," heavily escorted by surface ships and aircraft. Maus boldly closed for a daylight submerged attack, but when he ordered "fire," owing to an error by the first watch officer or a mechanical failure, no torpedoes left the tubes. While maneuvering into position to shoot, Johannsen in *U-569* was detected by the alert escorts and driven off. The IXC *U-511,* under her new commander, Fritz Schneewind, who had been in the area for six weeks, made contact with the convoy, but she too was driven off by escorts who damaged her with depth charges. Owing to the very heavy escort, U-boat Control canceled further operations against this convoy.

Hitler's famous "intuition" led him to believe that the Allies were on the verge of occupying Portugal. To repel this supposed occupation force, Hitler directed Dönitz to rush a group of U-boats to blocking positions directly west of Lisbon. Dönitz doubted that the Allies had designs on Portugal, but he complied with the order by sending the original six Type VIIs of group *Delphin* plus three of the added Type IXs *(U-125, U-511, U-522)* to the area, even though all six VIIs and the *U-125* were very low on fuel.

Allied codebreakers detected this redeployment of group *Delphin* to an area within easy reach of Gibraltar-based British ASW aircraft. Commencing on February 12, Coastal Command saturated the skies with radar-equipped British planes. Two found lively action:

- On February 12, a Hudson of Squadron 48, piloted by Geoffrey Richard Mayhew, came upon the VIIC *U-442,* commanded by Hans-Joachim Hesse. Mayhew attacked, dropping four depth charges and strafing with machine guns. Savaged, *U-442* sank with the loss of all hands.
- In the early evening of February 14, a Catalina of Squadron 202, piloted by Canadian Harry R. Sheardown, escorting the southbound convoy KMS 9, found and attacked a U-boat with five depth charges. This was the VIIC *U-381,* commanded by Wilhelm-Heinrich von Pückler und Limpurg, who had sailed from France on December 19. The damage sustained in this attack and a shortage of fuel forced von Pückler und Limpurg to return to France. He arrived on February 19, completing an arduous patrol of sixty-two days without a success.

Later that evening, pilot Sheardown got another radar contact. He turned on his landing lights and attacked another U-boat with his remaining two depth charges. This was the VIIC *U-620,* commanded by Heinz Stein, who had sailed from France on December 19. The attack destroyed *U-620* with the loss of all hands.

Sheardown returned to Gibraltar having been airborne for twenty-two hours and twenty minutes, doubtless a Catalina endurance record.

Low on fuel, the four surviving VIIs and the IXC *U-125* returned to France.* The IXCs *U-511* and *U-522,* which had been detached from group *Seehund* to reinforce group *Delphin*'s attack on TM 1, remained in the Portugal-Gibraltar-Azores area to reinforce other newly forming groups.

Commanded by Herbert Schneider, the IXC *U-522,* which also had been on patrol in the Azores-Madeira area for six weeks, ran critically low on fuel. Upon learning this, U-boat Control arranged for her to refuel from the newly sailed XIV tanker *U-461.* En route to this rendezvous on February 17, *U-522* made contact with a fast convoy east of the Azores, reported as "five large ships" with three escorts making twelve knots. Schneider shadowed—and reported—but owing to the high speed of the quarry, Control was unable to bring up either group *Rochen* or group *Robbe,* and Schneider finally had to give up the chase because of his acute fuel shortage.

B-dienst reported that a large Torch convoy inbound from the United States was to pass close to the Azores on about February 17. Control made elaborate plans to intercept. It deployed two groups, composed of newly arrived boats and the remnants of group *Delphin,* some of which had refueled from the XB minelayer *U-118: Rochen* (ten boats) and *Robbe* (eight boats). Upon forming patrol lines, the boats were to "lie to" submerged to avoid being spotted by aircraft and attempt to intercept the convoy by picking up its propeller noises on hydrophones.

Aware of these U-boat formations from breaks in naval Enigma, Allied authorities rerouted this big Africa-bound convoy around groups *Rochen* and *Robbe.* By February 19, U-boat Control realized that it had missed the prize and canceled both patrol lines. Declaring with italicized emphasis that Torch convoys *"must be stopped,"* U-boat Control concluded that the groups could not do so efficiently in the vast and wide-open seas in the Azores area and that therefore they had to operate "much closer" to the Strait of Gibraltar.

Group *Robbe* was to lead the way eastward. After refueling from *U-461,* group *Rochen* was to follow. En route to this hazardous new assignment, on February 22, one of the *Robbe* IXBs, *U-107,* commanded by Harald Gelhaus, encountered and sank the 7,800-ton British vessel *Roxborough Castle,* which was sailing alone. Other than the ASW trawler bagged by Bargsten in *U-521,* this was the first ship to be sunk in the month of February by any of the dozen and a half U-boats in those waters.

After refueling from *U-461,* Herbert Schneider in *U-522* received orders to intercept a convoy that was expected to hug the coast of Morocco. En route to that special task on February 22, Schneider happened upon a big British southbound convoy. This was the fast (9.5 knots) oil convoy UC 1, consisting of thirty-two

---

* Before resailing, Günther Seibicke in *U-436,* who sank two tankers in convoy TM 1, was awarded a *Ritterkreuz* on March 27. At that time his confirmed score was five ships for 33,091 tons, plus damage to two other tankers in the North Atlantic. On the same day, Drumbeater Ulrich Folkers in *U-125,* who had sunk no ships on this patrol nor contributed to the chase of TM 1 or other Torch convoys, also received a *Ritterkreuz.* At the time of the award his confirmed score was sixteen ships for 78,136 tons.

ships —seventeen of them tankers in ballast—en route from the British Isles to Curaçao. It was closely guarded by British Escort Group 42, commanded by L. F. Durnford-Slater, comprised of six warships: the new 1,400-ton frigate *Ness,* the sloop *Folkstone,* the former American Coast Guard cutter *Totland,* and three corvettes. The close escort was backed up by an American hunter-killer group (support group) consisting of four new (1940) fleet destroyers. All ten escorts were equipped with centimetric-wavelength radar and some warships had Huff Duff.

Upon receiving the report from Schneider in *U-522,* U-boat Control directed seven boats of group *Rochen* to cancel the refueling operation and home on *U-522* at high speed, without regard for fuel consumption. The VII *U-202* of group *Rochen,* which had already fueled, and three boats of group *Robbe,* which were close enough to catch the convoy, were also told to join the chase. However, one of these *Robbe* boats, Gelhaus in the IXB *U-107,* did not receive the message in time and could not join. Thus eleven attack boats (six VIIs; five IXs) pursued this rich but massively guarded target. The XIV tanker *U-461* closely trailed the U-boats, prepared to refuel any boat that required replenishment. "The enemy must not be left in peace," U-boat Control exhorted. "The hardest fighter carries the day. No slacking off!"

Schneider in *U-522* lost contact with convoy UC 1 but regained it at dawn on the morning of February 23. Inasmuch as another boat had reported contact, Schneider attacked and sank the 8,900-ton British tanker *Athelprincess* sailing in ballast. By noon that day, four other boats were in contact, including the *Ritterkreuz* holder Günther Krech in the VII *U-558.* Meanwhile, Schneider had pulled ahead of the convoy and dived to make a daylight periscope attack. He was detected by the escorts, who pounced with great fury and destroyed the *U-522.* There were no survivors. The Admiralty gave sole credit for the kill to the former American Coast Guard cutter *Totland* (ex-*Cayuga*).

In the afternoon five other U-boats made contact with the convoy, bringing the number of attackers to nine. The other pursuing boat, Richard Becker in the VIID (minelayer) *U-218,* reported delays due to engine and rudder failures, but he pressed on gamely. That night seven of the nine boats in contact attempted to attack.

- Günter Poser in the VII *U-202* sank the 8,000-ton American tanker *Esso Baton Rouge* and damaged the British tankers *Empire Norseman* and *British Fortitude.*
- The *Ritterkreuz* holder Günther Krech in the VII *U-558* sank the damaged 9,800-ton *Empire Norseman* but missed "three destroyers."
- In two separate attacks, in which he fired one FAT, one "acoustic," and two electric torpedoes, Herbert Juli in the VII *U-382* claimed sinking two 8,000-ton tankers, but in reality he only damaged the Dutch tanker *Murena,* which reached port.
- Hans Johannsen in the VII *U-569* fired three torpedoes and claimed hits on as many ships, but none could be confirmed.
- Attacks by Hans-Joachim Schwantke in the old IX *U-43;* Wilhelm Luis, age twenty-seven, new skipper of the IXC *U-504;* and Klaus Bargsten in the IXC *U-521* were thwarted by aggressive escorts.

The boats hung on doggedly for the next two days. Several boldly attempted to penetrate the heavy screen and attack, but only two fired torpedoes: Günter Poser in *U-202,* who reported four misses, and Friedrich Markworth in *U-66,* who claimed a hit on a "destroyer" and possibly hits on two other ships, but no hit was ever confirmed. Becker in the VIID (minelayer) *U-218* finally caught up, but his rudder failed again and he was forced to abort to France. Juli in *U-382* and Johannsen in *U-569* suffered severe depth-charge damage. After pausing at the XIV tanker *U-461* for repairs and fuel, they too aborted to France. These three boats were out of action until mid-April.

Berlin propagandists claimed a smashing victory for the U-boats against UC 1: one "destroyer" and eight tankers sunk. The confirmed score was far less: three tankers (in ballast) for 26,700 tons sunk and two tankers (in ballast) damaged, but both of the latter remained with the convoy and reached port. One U-boat, the IXC *U-522,* was lost with all hands. Appraising the performance of the four American destroyers of the support group, the commander of British Escort Group 42, Durnford-Slater, paid the Americans a rare compliment: "No escort group has ever been better supported."

The British TM 1 and British UC 1 were the only two special tanker convoys to lose ships to U-boats in 1943. The combined loss was ten vessels sunk and two vessels damaged out of 345 sailing east and west on the Middle Atlantic routes. The Americans soon assumed responsibility for escorting all special oil convoys. From mid-year 1943, the CU-UC convoys sailed via the United States East Coast and North Atlantic route. Seven such convoys, comprised of 133 tankers, crossed east and west with no losses to Axis forces.*

The veteran Joachim Berger in *U-87,* assigned to group *Rochen,* developed a lube-oil leak that could not be fixed and crippled his attack on the convoy UC 1. After a brief stop at the tanker *U-461,* he proceeded to France. On March 4, when *U-87* was about two hundred miles west of Portugal, the *Luftwaffe* reported a convoy en route from the United Kingdom to the Mediterranean, designated KMS 10.

Berger found this slow convoy. It was guarded by Canadian Escort Group C-1, which had just completed two weeks of intense training at the Royal Navy's ASW school at Tobermory. Escort Group C-1 was comprised of a British destroyer, the four-stack Canadian destroyer *St. Croix,* and four Canadian corvettes, including *Shediac,* all newly equipped with centimetric-wavelength radar. Berger in *U-87,* who had a full load of torpedoes, boldly attempted to attack the convoy all alone, but the escorts detected him and counterattacked with skill and tenacity, destroying *U-87* with the loss of all hands. The Admiralty credited the Canadian vessels *St. Croix* and *Shediac* with the kill.

Several boats of group *Robbe* took up the hunt for convoy KMS 10. Three found it: Harald Gelhaus in *U-107;* the veteran *U-410,* commanded by a new skipper, Horst-Arno Fenski, age twenty-four; and the *U-445,* commanded by Heinz-Konrad Fenn. Escorts thwarted Gelhaus and Fenn, but Fenski got in and hit two

---

* See Appendix 15.

7,100-ton British freighters. One sank but the other, *Fort Paskoyac,* equipped with a net defense, survived. The Canadian escorts counterattacked Fenski and forced him to haul to westward to repair damage.

Based on intelligence from *B-dienst,* U-boat Control formed a new group, *Tümmler* (Porpoise) on March 1 to intercept a convoy about six hundred miles southwest of the Azores. Comprised of seven boats (five IXs, two VIIs), *Tümmler* waited on a patrol line for three days but saw nothing. Very likely Allied code-breakers decrypted the formation orders to this group and the convoy authorities rerouted the ships to evade the boats.

U-boat Control abandoned the search for this convoy on March 3 and shifted group *Tümmler,* less *Ritterkreuz* holder Hermann Rasch in *U-106,* to the narrow waters between the Canaries and the mainland of Africa. While proceeding to this new area, Hans-Joachim Schwantke in *U-43* came upon a lone ship, which he took to be a British freighter. In actuality it was the 5,200-ton German raider-minelayer *Doggerbank* (ex-British *Speybank*), returning to France after a round-trip voyage of thirteen months to the Orient and Japan. Loaded with seven thousand tons of rubber and other scarce raw materials, *Doggerbank* was inexplicably sailing well ahead of the moving safety grid for her homebound leg. Schwantke hit *Doggerbank* with three torpedoes; she blew up and sank in about three minutes. Later, when U-boat Control learned of this terrible mistake, all mention of the sinking was expunged from the log of *U-43.*

A twenty-four-year-old survivor of *Doggerbank,* Fritz Kürt, climbed into a skiff that had floated free. He then rescued a dog, "Leo," and fourteen survivors, including *Doggerbank*'s captain, Paul Schneidewind. The survivors fashioned a sail and in order to take fullest advantage of the trade winds, set a course westerly to the Caribbean. Eleven days later a gale capsized the skiff and eight of the fifteen men and the dog drowned. Subsequently, four of the seven survivors, crazed by thirst, asked to be shot. Schneidewind reluctantly complied with these requests, Kürt said later, then shot himself, leaving Kürt and one other survivor alive. On March 20 the latter died, leaving only Kürt, who was found unconscious and "near death" on March 29 by the Spanish tanker *Campoamor,* bound for Aruba. Upon arrival at that island, Kürt, by then recovered from his ordeal, was turned over to American naval intelligence officers, who took him to the States for exhaustive interrogation.*

As group *Tümmler* was occupying its new positions, U-boat Control released the remaining boats of group *Robbe,* which had been patrolling off the mouth of the Strait of Gibraltar under heavy air attacks. While they were withdrawing westward to less dangerous waters, the *Luftwaffe* reported a convoy. This was Outbound South 44, consisting of forty-six ships and eight escorts en route from the

---

* Kürt revealed that he was on *Doggerbank* in Yokohama harbor on November 30, 1942, when the German tanker/supply ship *Uckermark* blew up, destroying the German raider *Thor* and the German supply ship *Leuthen,* and damaging several other Axis vessels. He confused the names of the German ships that were lost in the explosion and fire, but his information helped Allied intelligence sort out that disaster and puzzle out which German ships were probably left to raid in the Far East or Indian Ocean or to run the blockade into France.

British Isles to Sierra Leone. Harald Gelhaus in *U-107,* Horst-Arno Fenski in *U-410,* and Heinz-Konrad Fenn in *U-445* raced to the reported position. Gelhaus in *U-107* got there first and attacked, firing all six torpedoes in his tubes at multiple targets.

With this single, well-executed salvo Gelhaus hit and sank four freighters for 17,400 tons. Harassed by surface and air escorts, neither Fenski in *U-410* nor Fenn in *U-445* could get in to shoot. Gelhaus pursued and attempted a second attack the next day, but aircraft drove him off. In return for past victories and claims and for sinking five ships for 25,000 tons on this patrol, Gelhaus earned a *Ritterkreuz.**

THE NEW YORK TASK FORCE

Owing to the lack of success and to the heavy air patrols in the Gibraltar-Morocco area, U-boat Control concluded it might achieve better results against Middle Atlantic convoys by attacking them as they sailed out of New York. Accordingly, a task force of six Type IXs was assigned to this operation, including the former *Tümmler* boat *U-106,* commanded by Hermann Rasch, who was to first refuel near Madeira from the tanker *U-461.*

One of these boats did not get far: the IXC *U-508,* commanded by Georg Staats. Five days out from France, on February 26, a B-24 of British Squadron 224, piloted by Peter J. Cundy, caught Staats on the surface and bombed the boat, causing heavy damage. Unable to dive, Staats went *west* at high speed, to get beyond range of Coastal Command aircraft on Biscay patrols. In response to his calls for help, U-boat Control ordered two boats to assist: the IXC *U-172,* commanded by *Ritterkreuz* holder Carl Emmermann, outbound to join the New York task force, and the Type VII *U-590,* commanded by Heinrich Müller-Edzards, outbound to the North Atlantic run with a doctor on board.†

Emmermann reached the *U-508* first and stood by for several days, providing assistance until Müller-Edzards arrived in *U-590* with the doctor. Forced to abort, Staats gave Emmermann and Müller-Edzards most of his fuel, then limped back across the Bay of Biscay to France. As a result of the battle damage, the *U-508* was out of action for nearly three months. Emmermann in *U-172* proceeded toward New York, pausing to sink two lone freighters in the Middle Atlantic for an aggregate of 11,000 tons.

Another boat assigned to the New York task force was the famous *U-130,* with a new skipper, Siegfried Keller, age twenty-five, former watch officer on Bleichrodt's *U-109.* On his fifth day out from France, March 4, the *Luftwaffe* reported a convoy en route from Gibraltar to the British Isles. Keller found it the next day and with skill and aplomb, he mounted a lone attack on the convoy, XK 2, firing four bow torpedoes. Remarkably, this single salvo sank four British freighters

* At the time of the award, his score was sixteen confirmed ships sunk for 86,500 tons.

† Normally Type VIIs did not carry doctors. Perhaps *U-590* was to transfer the doctor to a U-tanker (*U-460* or *U-462)* on the North Atlantic run.

for 16,400 tons. After he reported that a second attack had been thwarted by escorts, U-boat Control ordered him to break off and to resume his course to join the New York task force.

Increased to seven boats, the New York task force continued westward across the Middle Atlantic. Several days later, *B-dienst* provided precise information on a big Africa-bound Torch convoy, United States–Gibraltar Slow 6 (UGS 6), which had departed New York on March 4. Originally it had been composed of forty-five heavily laden ships, but an accident had reduced it to forty-three. A Norwegian freighter sailing alone had blundered into the convoy in darkness and collided with a freighter. The Norwegian had gone down; her disabled victim had been forced to fall out of the convoy. Another merchantman had also fallen out to stand by the damaged ship.

Like all the American convoys sailing between the United States and Africa and vice versa, UGS 6 was very heavily guarded. Commanded by Charles Wellborn, Jr. (who later rose to vice admiral), the escort consisted of seven modern (1935–1942) fleet destroyers, one of which was fresh from workup. All were equipped with the latest centimetric-wavelength radar. None had Huff Duff, but the improved Allied shore-based Huff Duff network in the Atlantic Ocean area provided the Allies with fairly fast and precise information on the locations of the U-boats that were transmitting radio traffic.

Upon receiving the *B-dienst* report, U-boat Control directed the New York task force, five boats of which were organized into group *Unverzaget* (Intrepid) to alter course and intercept UGS 6. The eager new skipper Siegfried Keller in *U-130*—still flush from his four sinkings from convoy XK 2—found UGS 6 on the evening of March 12. Per doctrine, U-boat Control ordered Keller to shadow and not to attack until other boats had established contact. Shore-based Huff Duff stations alerted Wellborn to the presence of *U-130* and the probability that she would draw in other U-boats.

At about that same time, the skipper of the second newest of the destroyers, Charles L. Melson (later, a four-star admiral and in 1958–1960, superintendent of the U.S. Naval Academy) in *Champlin,* got a radar contact at two miles. Ringing up flank speed, Melson ran down the bearing and opened fire with his 5" guns in the forward turret at a range of one mile. Too late, Keller in *U-130* dived, catching two close depth charges before he could get deep. Temporarily detached from the convoy, Melson in *Champlin* hunted the U-boat for four hours, carrying out four separate, well-executed depth-charge attacks. Nothing further was ever heard from *U-130.**

Forced by another destroyer to drop back, *Ritterkreuz* holder Carl Emmermann in *U-172,* who had already sunk two loners, found a straggler fifty miles astern of the formation, the 5,600-ton American freighter *Keystone.* Emmermann easily sank this sitting duck with torpedoes, then put on speed to haul ahead of the convoy to gain a better shooting position. Meanwhile, five other Type IXs reported contact

---

* Under Kals and Keller, *U-130* sank twenty-five confirmed ships for 167,350 tons to rank twelfth among all U-boats in the war. See Appendix 17.

with the convoy: *Ritterkreuz* holder Hermann Rasch in *U-106;* Kurt Sturm, who had replaced the injured Neubert as skipper of the *U-167;* Rolf Rüggeberg in *U-513* (delayed again by engine problems); *Ritterkreuz* holder Werner Henke in *U-515* (who was bound for Freetown and had earlier sunk a lone 8,300-ton British freighter); and Walter von Steinaecker in *U-524.* Aggressive escorts, sweeping ahead and astern and on the flanks of the convoy as far out as ten miles, "damaged" Henke's *U-515,* he reported, but he was not a skipper easily cowed.

Sensing an opportunity for a big kill that would help the Axis forces in Tunisia, U-boat Control organized a second group, *Wohlgemut* (Optimistic), to backstop group *Unverzaget.* On the charts in Berlin the two groups were neatly organized into five and six boats, respectively, but by sunset on March 14, the boats were all mixed up. Attempting to attack in the dark, they were repeatedly detected and driven off by the destroyers. The *Ritterkreuz* holder Helmut Witte in *U-159* and Walter von Steinaecker in *U-524* managed to haul ahead for submerged attacks; however, both attacks were thwarted when the convoy suddenly zigged away. Shooting with small hope of success, von Steinaecker hit and sank the 8,100-ton French freighter *Wyoming.* While the newest of the destroyers, *Hobby,* drove off the U-boats, skipper Melson in *Champlin* rescued *Wyoming*'s entire crew of 127 men.

To increase the possibilities of a decisive success versus UGS 6, on March 16 U-boat Control ordered those boats of the distant group *Tümmler* that had sufficient fuel to join the chase. This raised the number of U-boats assigned to the operation to seventeen, less the lost *U-130.* That same day Emmermann in *U-172* and von Steinaecker in *U-524,* using Metox to help elude those escorts with meter-wavelength radar, gained positions to attack submerged. Von Steinaecker clearly missed and made no claims. Emmermann fired six torpedoes (four bow, two stern) and claimed two freighters for 18,000 tons sunk and two others for 12,000 tons probably sunk. In reality, Emmermann hit only one vessel, the 7,200-ton American Liberty ship *Benjamin Harrison,* which was abandoned and sunk by one of the destroyers.

By noon on March 17, the convoy had reached a position about seven hundred miles west of the Strait of Gibraltar. Later that day several flights of Sunderlands and Catalinas from Gibraltar and Morocco met the convoy and drove the U-boats under. Nonetheless, after dark Kurt Sturm in the IXC *U-167* and the *Ritterkreuz* holder Günther Krech in the VII *U-558* attacked. Sturm claimed he sank the 7,200-ton American Liberty ship *Molly Pitcher,* but he only damaged her. Klaus Bargsten in *U-521* came up and put the abandoned hulk under with a finishing shot. Krech reported possible hits, but they could not be confirmed. In view of the saturation air coverage and the exhaustion of the U-boat crews, U-boat Control canceled further operations versus UGS 6 in the early hours of March 19.

Proudly stressing its assistance to Axis forces in Tunisia, U-boat Control informed the OKM that the German submariners had sunk eight ships for 56,565 tons and hit or damaged five other ships from UGS 6. The confirmed ships sunk were less than half the claim: four for 28,000 tons. No other ships were damaged. The other thirty-nine ships of the convoy—and all seven American destroyers—reached African ports without further incident.

Eight of the boats involved in the battle with UGS 6 immediately set course for

France. They were joined by the IXB *U-109,* commanded by a new skipper, her former first watch officer, Hans Joachim Schramm, age twenty-six, who had only just arrived in the area but was forced by a mechanical failure to abort. He gave his spare fuel to the homebound boats *U-43, U-202,* and *U-558.* The *Ritterkreuz* holder Hermann Rasch in *U-106,* who had sunk no ships on this patrol, gave all of his spare fuel to Helmut Witte in *U-159* and Werner Henke in *U-515.* When *U-106* reached France, Rasch left the boat and went to other duty. U-boat Control directed three of the homebound boats *(U-103, U-504, U-521)* to intercept a Gibraltar-bound convoy, but none could find it. After reaching France, Klaus Bargsten in the IXC *U-521,* who had conducted a relentlessly aggressive patrol and boldly attacked three separate convoys, was awarded a *Ritterkreuz.** These departures left eight IXs in the Gibraltar-Morocco area, including the newly arrived IXB *U-105,* commanded by Jürgen Nissen.

Upon conclusion of Gondola (the Biscay air offensive, from February 6 to 15), the two American B-24 squadrons (numbers 1 and 2) left St. Eval and proceeded, as originally planned, to Port Lyautey, Morocco. The combined outfit, ultimately known as the 480th Group, had flown 218 hunter-killer missions in the Bay of Biscay, comprising nearly two thousand hours flying time. Of the original nineteen aircraft that had finally reached St. Eval, five had been lost on operations: one shot down by a German JU-88, two failed to return for undetermined reasons, and two crashed. Sixty-five airmen had perished. The group's planes had carried out eight separate attacks on U-boats and had been credited with severe damage to the VII *U-211* and one kill, *U-519*—but, as related, that kill was subsequently withdrawn.

The 480th Group, commanded by Jack Roberts, began operations from Port Lyautey on March 19 with about one thousand personnel and sixteen aircraft, eight shy of authorized strength. In accordance with the latest agreement between the U.S. Army and U.S. Navy, the group was controlled by the commander of the Navy's newly established Moroccan Sea Frontier, who also commanded Fleet Air Wing (Fairwing) 15, consisting of two squadrons of Catalinas, VP 73 and VP 92. The B-24s were to fly "defensive" missions in support of Torch convoys, rather than the preferred "offensive" hunter-killer missions.

Pilot William L. Sanford of Squadron 2, flying the B-24 "Tidewater Tillie" (mistakenly credited with sinking *U-519* earlier), made a low-level attack on a fully surfaced U-boat northwest of the Canary Islands on March 22. This was the IXC *U-524,* commanded by Walter von Steinaecker, en route to a new patrol area. Sanford's crew dropped four 650-pound Mark XXXVII depth charges in a tight straddle. These big missiles destroyed *U-524.* The airmen saw "nine" German survivors "on a raft," but they, as well as the rest of the Germans on *U-524,* perished.

Having shelved the idea of a New York task force, U-boat Control repositioned

---

* At the time of the award, his confirmed score on *U-563* and *U-521* was six ships for 23,613 tons, including the damaged hulk *Molly Pitcher.*

the seven remaining boats in a large reconnaissance arc running from west to southeast of the Canary Islands in hopes of snagging another UGS convoy. The reconnaissance arc proved to be futile; no boat intercepted a UGS convoy.

Acting on *B-dienst* information, U-boat Control shifted all the boats in the arc, plus, temporarily, the Freetown-bound *U-123,* commanded by Horst von Schroeter, to the narrow waters between the Canaries and the African coast. Designated group *Seeräuber* (Pirate), these eight boats found the convoy on March 28. It was RS 3, southbound from Rabat to Sierra Leone, supported by land-based air patrols. As a result of the close protection provided by the aircraft, only three of the nine boats were able to mount successful attacks.

- *Ritterkreuz* holder Helmut Witte in *U-159* sank a 5,500-ton British freighter.
- Kurt Sturm in *U-167* sank a 4,600-ton British freighter.
- *Ritterkreuz* holder Carl Emmermann in *U-172* sank a 5,300-ton British freighter, raising his total for this patrol to an impressive five confirmed ships sunk for about 29,000 tons.

Allied aircraft damaged three U-boats in this brief battle, all commanded by *Ritterkreuz* holders: Günther Müller-Stöckheim in *U-67,* Witte in *U-159,* and Emmermann in *U-172.* Hit hard by aerial depth charges, the *U-67* plunged to 750 feet before the crew could regain control. Upon surfacing later, it was discovered that the six topside torpedo canisters and great chunks of the superstructure had been ripped away. In a similar near-disaster, Witte in *U-159* plunged to 689 feet before regaining control. Emmermann in *U-172* stood by *U-67* until it was reckoned that the latter could make it back to France. Before leaving the area, *U-67* gave spare fuel to Henke in *U-515,* who proceeded south to Dakar in place of Witte's badly damaged *U-159,* which went to a "quiet" area in the Azores.

By then, the U.S. Navy's Fairwing 15 at Craw Field, Port Lyautey, Morocco, had become a formidable and busy force: twenty-four Catalinas of Squadrons VP 73 and 92, and twenty-four B-24s of the Army Air Forces ASW Squadrons 1 and 2. On April 7, a B-24 of Squadron 1, piloted by Walter E. Thorne, got a radar contact on Emmermann's surfaced *U-172* thirty miles away. Thorne attacked but, to his surprise, Emmermann remained on the surface, zigzagging and shooting back with his rapid-fire 37mm cannon and other antiaircraft weaponry. When Thorne called for assistance, another B-24 of Squadron 1, piloted by H. C. Easterling, responded. Low on fuel, both aircraft finally ran in and dropped a total of twelve depth charges, but none fell close enough to harm *U-172.**

Two boats, Kurt Sturm in *U-167* and Rolf Rüggeberg in *U-513,* remained in the narrow waters between the Canaries and the mainland. On April 5, two Hudsons of British Squadron 233, piloted by Donald D. Lipman and William E. Willets, hit *U-167* and so badly damaged the boat that Sturm was forced to run in close to Grand Canary Island and scuttle in seventy-two feet of water.† About

* To extend the Allied convoy coverage farther southward, the U.S. Navy created a base for flying boats at Agadir, in southern Morocco. On April 17, six Catalinas of Squadron VP 73 transferred to Agadir.

† In January 1952, salvors refloated *U-167,* towed her into Las Palmas, and scrapped her.

fifty men of *U-167* got ashore. After extensive diplomatic negotiations with Spanish authorities in the Canary Islands and Madrid, the crew was released for repatriation.

Carrying out the first step of a complicated and oft-delayed plan, on the night of April 13–14 the crew embarked at Las Palmas on a tugboat, which ferried the Germans out to a rendezvous with Hans-Martin Scheibe in the VII *U-455,* who, as related, had laid a minefield off Fedala. Scheibe took the *U-167* crew on board, then later met *Ritterkreuz* holder Helmut Witte in the damaged *U-159* and Friedrich-Wilhelm Wissmann in *U-518,* returning from Brazil. Witte, Wissmann, who refueled from the newly arrived XB minelayer *U-117,* and Scheibe divided the fifty *U-167* survivors among their three boats and returned to France. Upon reaching Germany, Sturm and some of the *U-167* crew were assigned to commission a new Type IX.

Other boats in the Middle Atlantic also began the return voyage to France. On the way, Rolf Rüggeberg in *U-513,* who had sunk no ships, was diverted to help escort the inbound blockade-runner *Irene* (ex-*Silvaplana*), as was Müller-Stöckheim in *U-67,* until Control learned that *U-67* was severely damaged. Two IXCs outbound from France, *U-174* and *U-176,* were also to meet *Irene* to give her instructions for crossing the Bay of Biscay. None of the boats homebound from the south was able to find *Irene.*

Approaching Lorient on April 14, Rüggeberg in *U-513* met the German escorts and also the new IXC40 *U-526,* commanded by Hans Möglich, age twenty-seven, inbound from her maiden patrol from Germany. As the senior skipper, Rüggeberg was entitled to follow immediately behind the minesweeper escort into Lorient, but heedless of protocol, Möglich pushed ahead of Rüggeberg. One mile from home, the minesweeper peeled off and Möglich maneuvered toward the dock, where the commander of Combat Flotilla 10, Günter Kuhnke, together with an honor guard, a band, and other greeters, waited.

Suddenly there was chaos. *U-526* hit a newly planted British mine and blew sky-high. Forty-two of her men were killed, including Möglich; twelve men, including nine injured, were saved. The two halves of *U-526* were salvaged for their engines and other valuables. Spared by a breach of protocol, Rüggeberg and the crew of *U-513* moored safely amid the frantic rescue operations. Having made two and a half unsuccessful patrols, Rüggeberg left *U-513* to command Combat Flotilla 13 in Norway.

Owing to strong Allied surface and air escorts and to information from naval Enigma decrypts, which enabled many convoys to evade U-boat reconnaissance lines, the U-boat patrols to the Gibraltar-Azores area in the first quarter of 1943 were extremely hazardous and not very productive. Including ten attack boats that sailed to or were diverted to that area in December* and thirty-six more in January, February, and March, the forty-six patrols resulted in the sinking of forty ships for 252,000 tons, an average of less than one ship sunk per boat per patrol.

* The six VIIs of Brazil-bound group *Delphin,* two IXs bound for the Americas, and two IXs of group *Seehund* bound for Cape Town.

Twenty of the forty-six attack boats (47 percent) sank no ships. Nine boats (six IXs, three VIIs) were lost. Most of the crew of the *U-167,* scuttled in the Canaries, was saved, but there were no survivors from the approximately four hundred men on the other eight boats. Seven other boats incurred battle damage that forced them to abort.

In all, these boats were able to mount really meaningful attacks on only six of the scores of Torch convoys which plied that area from January through April 1943.* In March, when ten big eastbound and westbound UG and GU convoys passed through, the U-boats had managed to sink ships from only one, UGS 6. Although the Admiralty was rattled, there was never the slightest possibility that U-boats might sever the Middle Atlantic All-American UG-GU, OT-TO, and CU-UC convoy routes.

Three boats that engaged in these futile attacks and had ample fuel stocks continued southward for prolonged patrols off Freetown and the Gulf of Guinea, replacing Heinrich Bruns in the IXC *U-175,* who had sunk merely one ship and had endured a punishing depth-charge attack. The replacements were Jürgen Nissen in the IXB *U-105,* Horst von Schroeter in the IXB *U-123,* and *Ritterkreuz* holder Werner Henke in the IXC *U-515.* They were joined by the newly sailed IXC *U-126,* commanded by a new skipper, Siegfried Kietz, age twenty-six. Nissen and Kietz each sank one ship and Kietz damaged the American tanker *Standella,* previously hit by a U-boat in the Caribbean. Von Schroeter in *U-123* sank five ships for 24,900 tons, including the 680-ton British submarine *P-615.*† Counting the 8,300-ton British freighter he sank en route to join the canceled New York task force and another of 2,400 tons while southbound off Dakar, Werner Henke in *U-515* turned in the best patrol of 1943: ten confirmed ships sunk for 58,456 tons.

In running up his big score, Henke mounted one of the most remarkable convoy attacks of the war. En route from Takoradi, Ghana, to Freetown, Sierra Leone, the convoy (TS 37) consisted of fourteen freighters weakly guarded by four escorts, one corvette and three ASW trawlers. After fending off a Catalina with a single 20mm flak gun, Henke found the convoy on the moonless night of April 30, ninety miles south of Freetown. Attacking from dead astern, Henke aimed a salvo of six electrics with new Pi2 magnetic pistols at six different ships. He claimed all six torpedoes hit, but in actuality, the two stern shots missed. In a second attack toward dawn on May 1, Henke fired three more electrics with Pi2 magnetic pistols at three different ships. These all hit as well, Henke reported. This time he was right.

His claim was nine ships sunk from the convoy for 62,000 tons, but the confirmed number was seven ships sunk for 43,300 tons. Adding another 4,500-ton ship to his bag in the following week earned Henke Oak Leaves for his *Ritterkreuz*

* TM 1, UC 1, XK 2, KMS 10, UGS 6, RS 3.

† Originally christened the *Uluc Ali Reis,* she was one of four submarines built in Great Britain for Turkey in 1940. Two boats went to Turkey (a gesture to entice her into the war on the side of the Allies), but the British retained the other two, rechristened *P-614* and *P-615.*

from Hitler.* Inbound, he refueled from a XIV U-tanker, and returned to France on June 24, completing an arduous but highly productive patrol of 124 days.

Two boats were lost while homebound from these extended Freetown patrols. On June 2, Jürgen Nissen in the IXB *U-105,* passing close to Dakar, was caught and sunk by an aircraft of Free French Squadron 141. There were no survivors. Severely damaged by aircraft off Freetown, Siegfried Kietz in the IXC *U-126* was detected by a plane, bombed, and sunk in the Bay of Biscay on the night of July 2–3. The plane was a Leigh Light–equipped Wellington of British Squadron 172, piloted by the Rhodesian Alex Coumbis, who had earlier sunk *U-566.* There were no survivors of this boat either.

Young Johann Mohr in the IXB *U-124,* who wore Oak Leaves on his *Ritterkreuz,* sailed from France to the Gibraltar-Morocco area on March 27. On the seventh night out, April 2, while west of Cape Finisterre, Mohr encountered a big convoy, Outbound South 45, en route from the British Isles to Sierra Leone. Per doctrine, Mohr reported the convoy and shadowed to bring up other boats. Since there were no other boats in the immediate vicinity, U-boat Control authorized Mohr to attack, but only once and not to shadow because of the heavy Allied air patrols from Gibraltar and Morocco, which extended far to the west of Portugal. Taking advantage of the darkness, Mohr attacked on the surface and sank two British freighters for an aggregate 9,500 tons.

Immediately after these sinkings, one of the escorts, the sloop *Black Swan,* commanded by Rodney Thomson, got *U-124* on her centimetric-wavelength radar. Thomson ran down the bearing with both twin 4" forward turrets primed. At a range of not more than one hundred feet—too close to depress the turret guns—a lookout saw *U-124*'s conning tower go under. Passing over the swirl, Thomson fired a salvo of shallow-set depth charges by eye. He then directed another escort, the corvette *Stonecrop,* commanded by Patrick Smythe, to fall out and hunt down the U-boat. Smythe got *U-124* on sonar and dropped a depth-charge salvo, but lost contact in the noise of the explosions. Nothing further was ever heard from *U-124.* The Admiralty credited *Black Swan* and *Stonecrop* with the kill, a loss keenly felt by Dönitz and others in the U-boat arm.†

As a result of the small returns, the high risks, and of the "shortage of U-boats" for convoy battles on the North Atlantic run (as U-boat Control put it), on April 6, Dönitz ordered that *all* Type IXs, theretofore regarded as less suitable for warfare against heavily escorted convoys in rough waters, were to reinforce the U-boats operating on the North Atlantic run. The U-boat patrols to the Gibraltar-Azores

---

* At the time of the award, his confirmed score was twenty ships for 130,133 tons.

† After *U-48, U-99,* and *U-123,* the *U-124* was the fourth most successful U-boat of the war. Under command of Georg-Wilhelm Schulz and Mohr, she sank forty-eight confirmed ships for 224,000 tons, including two warships: the British cruiser *Dunedin* and the French corvette *Mimose.* Credited with sinking twenty-nine confirmed ships for 135,000 tons, including both of the warships, Mohr stood nineteenth among all skippers in the war.

area, which had produced so few sinkings at such great risk and cost, were again to be temporarily suspended.

Futile U-boat Operations in the Mediterranean

East of Gibraltar, the Mediterranean U-boat force, commanded by Leo Kreisch, focused almost all of its available strength on Torch shipping in the area between Oran and Tripoli. Counting the losses and new arrivals in the last quarter of 1942, on January 1, 1943, Kreisch had a net strength of twenty-three boats,* of which several were undergoing battle-damage repairs. In place of the two boats that had aborted attempts to transit the Strait of Gibraltar in December, Berlin sent one more boat in January 1943. She was the *U-224,* commanded by Hans-Karl Kosbadt, who got into the Mediterranean on January 12, temporarily increasing the force to twenty-four boats.

U-boat patrols in the Mediterranean in 1943 were more hazardous than ever. As the Allies closed the vise on the Axis armies in Tunisia, they established a line of airfields along the north coast of Africa, reaching from Oran to Alexandria. Some of these airfields were used by ASW aircraft to protect the convoys sailing in those waters. Other ASW aircraft, based on the island of Malta, provided additional convoy support. These newly arrived aircraft and the growing numbers of surface-ship convoy escorts and a few newly established destroyer hunter-killer groups based in North African seaports became so formidable that U-boat attacks failed time and time again, and more often than ever, drew devastating reprisals.

The OKM issued new submarine-torpedo policies that applied to the Mediterranean U-boats. Owing to the phosphorescence in the Mediterranean waters, the looping air torpedo (G7a, FAT),† which could only be used at night, was to be withdrawn because its highly visible bubble track gave away the position of the U-boat. The plan was that by April 1943, a new looping electric torpedo (G7e, FAT), which left no bubble wake (day or night), was to be issued to U-boats in the Mediterranean and the Arctic and by June to U-boats in the Atlantic force. The FAT production goals called for one hundred of each type per month, but owing to unforeseen "assembly difficulties," considerable delays were encountered. When sufficient electric FATs became available, the Mediterranean boats were to load four of these forward and two aft, as well as six T-3 *(Falke)* "homing torpedoes" forward.

Owing to the extremely hazardous nature of U-boat operations in the Mediterranean, force commander Leo Kreisch was less demanding of proof of successes and more generous with awards to skippers. A notable case was that of Albrecht Brandi in *U-617,* one of the boats that had arrived in November 1942 in reaction to Torch.

---

* See Appendix 7.

† There were two types of FATs: FAT I, which made a long and a short loop, and FAT II, which made a long loop and then a circle.

On his first Mediterranean patrol in November, Brandi claimed that he sank a 5,500-ton freighter and damaged another of the same tonnage and also that he hit and damaged three important warships: a 33,950-ton battleship, a 6,496-ton light cruiser, and a 1,500-ton destroyer. None of these claims has been officially verified.

On his second patrol, Brandi claimed that he sank eight ships for 25,600 tons (including a fleet destroyer) and damaged two freighters for 14,000 tons. Three of the sinkings for 6,996 tons were confirmed: a 4,324-ton Greek freighter, the British ocean tug *St. Issey,* and a 1,862-ton Norwegian freighter. The hits for damage have not been officially verified. On January 21, Brandi was awarded a *Ritterkreuz.**

On his third patrol, Brandi claimed he sank three ships for 12,450 tons, including a 5,450-ton light cruiser. All three sinkings were confirmed, but the tonnage was almost halved (to 7,264), including the 2,650-ton British minelayer/cruiser *Welshman* and two medium Norwegian freighters, for an aggregate 4,614 tons.

On his fourth patrol in April, Brandi claimed that he sank an 8,000-ton "*Uganda*-class" cruiser and damaged two destroyers, and a 23,500-ton "*Orcades*-class" ocean liner, serving as a troopship. None of these claims has been officially verified. On April 11, Brandi was awarded Oak Leaves to his *Ritterkreuz.*†

Apart from Brandi in *U-617,* three veteran Mediterranean U-boats sank three oceangoing vessels for 13,600 tons during January 1943. These included the 545-ton British ASW trawler *Jura,* by Waldemar Mehl in *U-371,* who also damaged the 7,200-ton British freighter *Ville de Strasbourg;* the 7,200-ton American Liberty ship *Arthur Middleton,* by Horst Deckert in *U-73;* and the 5,859-ton Belgian freighter *Jean Jadot,* by Egon-Reiner von Schlippenbach in *U-453.* In addition, the veteran *U-431,* commanded by a new skipper, Dietrich Schöneboom, age twenty-five, sank four sailing ships for an aggregate 265 tons. The most significant Axis sinking of that month was achieved by Vittorio Patrelli-Camgagnano in *Platino,* who got the British corvette *Samphire.*

In the month of February, three Mediterranean U-boats sank four oceangoing ships for 16,211 tons. Otto Hartmann in *U-77* got two big British freighters for an aggregate 13,742 tons. Waldemar Mehl in *U-371* got a 2,100-ton British freighter and also damaged an American Liberty ship. Günter Jahn in *U-596* got a 380-ton British LCI. Wilhelm Franken in the veteran *U-565* shared credit with the *Luftwaffe* for destroying the 7,200-ton American Liberty ship *Nathanael Greene* and damaged the 10,400-ton British tanker *Seminole.* In addition, the famous *U-81,* commanded by a new skipper, Johann-Otto Krieg, age twenty-three, sank three sailing vessels for an aggregate 352 tons. The Italian Pasquale Beltrami, commanding *Acciaio,* sank the 409-ton British ASW trawler *Tervani.*

---

* At the time of the award, Brandi claimed fifteen ships, including a destroyer, for 58,700 tons sunk, plus six ships damaged for 61,500 tons. The confirmed score was seven freighters (no destroyer) sunk for 22,100 tons.

† At the time of the award, Brandi's claims were nineteen ships sunk for about 80,000 tons, including two cruisers and a fleet destroyer, plus nine ships damaged for about 88,500 tons, including a battleship, a big troopship, a cruiser, and three destroyers. His confirmed score was ten ships sunk for 29,339 tons, including one warship, the 2,650-ton British minelayer/cruiser *Welshman.*

The Mediterranean U-boat force reached its high-water mark in the month of March 1943. Six skippers sank nine oceangoing vessels. Günter Jahn in *U-596* was the highest tonnage scorer with the 9,600-ton Norwegian tanker *Hallanger* and the 7,100-ton British freighter *Fort à la Corhe,* plus damage to two other big British ships, *Fort Norman* and *Empire Standard,* for an aggregate 14,180 tons. Subsequently Jahn was awarded a *Ritterkreuz* and promoted to command the (Mediterranean) 29th Flotilla.* Second best in tonnage was Gerd Kelbling in *U-593,* who got three British freighters for 9,723 tons. Otto Hartmann in *U-77* got the 5,222-ton British freighter *Hadleigh* and damaged another of similar size. Josef Röther in *U-380* (who had earlier sunk the Dutch troopship *Nieuw Zeeland*) got the 7,200-ton British Liberty ship *Ocean Seaman.* Dietrich Schöneboom in *U-431* sank the 6,400-ton British freighter *City of Perth.* Walter Göing in *U-755* got a 1,100-ton French freighter. In addition, Johann-Otto Krieg in *U-81* sank two sailboats and a small vessel for an aggregate 454 tons.†

Thus twelve vessels that were sunk by U-boats in the Mediterranean during March 1943 totaled 46,800 tons. Since the positions of lost merchant ships were not announced, this tonnage loss contributed to the general misimpression that U-boats in March 1943 came close to cutting the vital lifeline between the Americas and the British Isles.

In the months of April and May 1943, when the Allies finally closed the vise on Axis forces in Tunisia, thereby gaining control of all of North Africa, the Mediterranean U-boats achieved very little. The high scorer was Wilhelm Franken in *U-565,* who sank the 5,600-ton American freighter *Michigan* and the 4,400-ton Free French vessel *Sidi-Bel-Abbés,* employed as a troopship for Senegalese infantry. Five hundred and sixty-seven men perished in the troopship sinking. These victories earned Franken a *Ritterkreuz.*‡ Walther Huth in *U-414* hit two British freighters, the 6,000-ton *Empire Eve,* which sank, and the 7,100-ton *Fort Anne,* which limped into port. Mehl in *U-371,* Kelbling in *U-593,* and Göing in *U-755* each got a small freighter.

In summary, during the five months from January to June 1943, the twenty-odd U-boats in the Mediterranean force sank thirty Allied ships and nine sailing craft. The vessels included two British warships (minelayer/cruiser *Welshman, LCI 162*) and one ASW trawler *(Jura).* Italian submarines sank one other British warship (corvette *Samphire*) and the ASW trawler *Tervani.* These thin results were of no real help to the besieged Axis armies in North Africa and, as Dönitz continued to insist, doubtless the boats could have achieved much more on the "decisive" North Atlantic run. Even so, Hitler insisted that the Mediterranean force be maintained at twenty-plus U-boats.

---

* At the time of the award, his confirmed score in the Atlantic and Mediterranean was four ships for 27,326 tons, plus damages.

† On March 19, Mediterranean skipper Baron Egon-Reiner von Schlippenbach in *U-453* was awarded a *Ritterkreuz.* His confirmed score was two ships for 10,061 tons plus damage to the 9,700-ton British hospital ship *Somersetshire,* which the Germans classified as a troopship.

‡ At the time of the award, his confirmed score was four ships for 12,887 tons, including the British destroyer *Partridge,* shared credit with the *Luftwaffe* for an American Liberty ship, plus damage to two other large vessels for 26,686 tons, one a troopship, *Cameronia.*

• • •

As in prior months, losses in the Mediterranean force were heavy in the period from January 1 to June 1, 1943: eleven U-boats and about five hundred crew, many of them the most experienced submariners in the *Kriegsmarine.**

• On the afternoon of January 13, *Ville de Québec,* one of the sixteen Canadian corvettes participating in Torch, got a strong sonar contact about ninety miles east of Oran while escorting the sixteen ships of convoy TE 13 eastbound from Gibraltar to North African ports. Her skipper, A.R.E. Coleman, notified the other four Canadian corvettes of the convoy escort group, then let go a pattern of depth charges.

His target was the *U-224,* commanded by Hans-Karl Kosbadt, who had only just entered the Mediterranean on January 9 and had a tanker in his periscope crosshairs. The explosion blew *U-224* to the surface, bow first. Turning to ram, Coleman opened fire with his cannons and machine guns and smashed into *U-224* forward of the conning tower. Within four minutes, *U-224* had disappeared. Coleman reported that a "tremendous underwater explosion" followed and that "pieces of clothing, insulating material and woodwork" rose to the surface amid a "great pool of oil." It was only ten minutes from first contact to kill. Another Canadian corvette, *Port Arthur,* rescued the sole survivor, the first watch officer Wolf Dietrich Danckworth.

• On January 20, the *U-301,* commanded by Willy-Roderich Körner, sailed from La Spezia on her second Mediterranean patrol. Körner had orders to intercept an Allied convoy eastbound from Gibraltar. In order to do so, he had to drive full speed on the surface. Shortly after dawn the next morning, the British submarine *Sahib,* commanded by J. H. Bromage, who was returning from a war patrol to his tender in Algiers, spotted *U-301* running on the surface toward his periscope. When the range had closed to four thousand yards, Bromage fired a full bow salvo. One or two torpedoes hit, and the *U-301* blew up and sank immediately. *Sahib* rescued one nineteen-year-old German, the midshipman Wilhelm Rahn, a lookout who had been thrown into the water by the force of the explosion.†

• While approaching a small coastal convoy about one hundred miles west of Tobruk on February 17, *U-205,* commanded by Friedrich Bürgel, was detected on sonar by one of the four escorts, the British destroyer *Paladin.* The destroyer ran down the sonar bearing and threw over a salvo of five depth charges set for one hundred feet. Some of these exploded close to *U-205* and the damage they inflicted compelled Bürgel to surface and scuttle.

When the U-boat suddenly came into view, the *Paladin* and another escort, the destroyer *Jervis,* and a South African Air Force plane pounced. This as yet uniden-

---

* During the same period, the Allies sank eight Italian submarines in the Mediterranean (*Narvalo, Santorre Santarosa, Tritone, Avorio, Malachite, Asteria, Mocenigo, Gorgo*). The Canadian corvettes *Port Arthur* and *Regina* each sank one, as did the new American destroyer *Nields* and the Dutch submarine *Dolfyn.* An Army Air Forces raid on Sardinia got one. British surface ships and aircraft got three. A ninth submarine, *Delfino,* was lost in a collision off Sicily.

† On February 6, *Luftwaffe* aircraft torpedoed and sank the Canadian corvette *Louisburg,* one of fifteen such vessels escorting convoy KMS 8, en route from Gibraltar to Boné. The British destroyer *Lookout* rescued forty men; thirty-eight were lost.

tified aircraft delivered a well-executed attack with guns and depth charges, forcing some Germans on the deck to jump into the water. The wild hurricane of gunfire from *Paladin,* which by accident killed four of her own men and seriously wounded four others, drove the rest of the Germans over the side. The abandoned *U-205* remained on the surface, circling at about nine knots on her electric motors. Unable to bring *Paladin* alongside, her skipper launched a whaler with a two-man boarding party, Sidney Constable and Kenneth J. Toy. While the party boarded *U-205, Paladin* and *Jervis* fished out forty-two German survivors, including Bürgel.

Although *U-205* appeared to be slowly flooding, Constable entered her and went below. In his official report, *Paladin*'s skipper wrote:

> On descending [Mr. Constable] found the boat in almost complete darkness and loose gear in considerable confusion. . . . [He] then proceeded forward to try and find the captain's cabin. This he found on the port side, his orders being to search for [confidential] books. These were found in a small cupboard near the deck and was shut but not locked. These were passed up the conning tower together with the commanding officer's binoculars, a superb pair, and a small wireless set. In the Control Room a small cupboard was found of which half was open, the other locked. This was full of books and these in their turn were passed up. In a desk a number of files and notebooks were found. . . . In all, a very large number of books were recovered.*

Meanwhile the British authorities present at the scene decided that there was a slim chance that *U-205* could be "captured." Accordingly, the British corvette *Gloxinia* was detached from another small convoy passing nearby and ordered to serve as the towing vessel. After an arduous struggle, *Gloxinia* finally managed to attach a three-and-a-half-inch steel cable to the still slowly circling *U-205* and headed directly for shore at Ras el Hilab Bay, one hundred miles west of Tobruk. About three hours later *Gloxinia* entered the bay with her tow but by that time *U-205* was heavily flooded, and when *Gloxinia* reduced speed, the U-boat sank stern first in ninety-six feet of water.†

• In the same area two days later, February 19, a Wellington of British Squadron 38, piloted by I. B. Butler, who was providing air escort for a small British convoy, XT 3, spotted another Mediterranean veteran, *U-562,* commanded by Horst Hamm. Butler's attack was not successful, but he dropped two smoke floats and one of the convoy escorts, the destroyer *Isis,* fell out to investigate. *Isis* could not get a sonar contact, but nonetheless she threw over a single depth charge. The senior escort, the destroyer *Derwent,* joined *Isis* but could not get a sonar con-

---

* A full description of these books or of the "small wireless set" has not been published. Enigma historian Ralph Erskine says that bigram tables *Strom* were recovered "but no other captures of consequence." For a description of how these tables were used, see his article, "Naval Enigma: The Missing Link. . . ."

† The Admiralty has not revealed whether or not it attempted to refloat *U-205* or to further search the wreck for other valuables, such as FAT and homing torpedoes or those fitted with the new Pi2 magnetic pistols.

tact either. *Derwent* ordered yet another destroyer of the escort group, *Hursley,* to join *Isis* for a protracted hunt, whereupon *Derwent* returned to the convoy.

After searching for about one hour, the new arrival, *Hursley,* got a sonar contact and attacked with a single salvo of depth charges. Thereupon *Isis* came up and carried out four consecutive attacks. Then *Hursley* ran in and fired the sixth salvo of depth charges but before they exploded, *U-562* suddenly surfaced momentarily, merely one hundred feet away. In this brief glimpse, the British saw that *U-562*'s conning tower was "badly buckled." Doubtless she incurred further damage as she dived again directly into the sixth depth charge salvo. *Hursley* carried out two further attacks and *Isis* one before the sonar contact faded away.

Altogether *Isis* and *Hursley* conducted nine separate depth-charge attacks, firing fifty-nine missiles. They were certain that they had killed the U-boat, but naval authorities ordered them to remain in the area and hunt for positive evidence. The corvette *Hyacinth* and two other Royal Navy vessels joined this hunt, but none of the ships could find a thing. Later, however, the Admiralty credited Butler's Wellington and the *Isis* and *Hursley* with the kill of *U-562* at that time and place. There were no survivors.

• On the morning of February 23, an Allied aircraft reported a U-boat on the surface off the port of Algiers. This was the newly arrived *U-443,* commanded by Konstantin von Puttkamer. The British ordered a hunter-killer group of four destroyers to carry out a chase: *Bicester, Lamerton, Wheatland,* and *Wilton.*

Bicester found *U-443* by sonar and attacked immediately, dropping a salvo of ten depth charges set for one hundred to 225 feet. Thereafter she crept back to the point of attack and saw some "wreckage." Before she could recover it, *Wheatland* also got a sonar contact and attacked with a salvo of ten depth charges set for the same depths. *Lamerton* followed with five depth charges set for one hundred feet. For good measure, *Bicester* fired a second salvo of ten depth charges, bringing the number of missiles fired to thirty-five.

Bicester returned and stopped in the area where she had seen wreckage. Her crew fished out two locker lids, a big (26"-by-46") cupboard door, other pieces of wood, and "possible human remains." Aware from decrypts of naval Enigma that a U-boat had been lost on this date, the Admiralty credited *Bicester* with "major" credit for the kill, with "some share" to *Wheatland* and *Lamerton.*

• While patrolling the seas about eighty miles northeast of Oran on March 4, a Hudson of Squadron 500, piloted by G. Jackimov, spotted a U-boat. This was the veteran *U-83,* commanded by Ulrich Wörishoffer. Jackimov attacked into flak from *U-83* with three 100-pound ASW bombs, but these inflicted no damage. On a second attack run at thirty-five feet above the wave tops, with guns blazing, Jackimov dropped three shallow-set depth charges, which exploded close around *U-83.* The aircrew reported that the U-boat began to sink on an even keel, that about fifteen Germans floated free, and that they saw "at least twenty-five bodies" that rose to the surface in "large bubbles and oil." Jackimov dropped two dinghies to the survivors, but these craft "appeared to sink" on impact. Nothing further was ever heard from *U-83* or its survivors, if any. Based on Enigma decrypts, the Admiralty confirmed this remarkable kill.

• On the morning of March 28, a Hudson of Squadron 48, piloted by J. B. Harrop, found a U-boat off the east coast of Spain. She was the Mediterranean veteran *U-77,* commanded by Otto Hartmann, homebound from a successful patrol off Oran, where she sank one 5,200-ton British freighter and damaged another of similar size. The Hudson attacked out of cloud cover, dropping four shallow-set depth charges on the swirl *U-77* created when she dived. Low on fuel, the Hudson was unable to loiter to assess the attack.

Later in the day, a Hudson of Squadron 233, piloted by Edgar F. Castell, relocated *U-77* on the surface about thirty miles northeast of the first attack. When the plane dived to attack, it met a hot flak reception from *U-77,* which remained on the surface. The Hudson returned fire with machine guns (three thousand rounds), then braved the flak to mount two bombing attacks. On the first it dropped a single 100-pound bomb; on the second, four depth charges. This plane also had to break off because of a fuel shortage.

These attacks so badly savaged *U-77* that Hartmann was compelled to declare a dire emergency. The force commander, Leo Kreisch, told Hartmann that if possible he should head for Alicante, Spain, and exercise his right under international law to repair his ship. Meanwhile Kreisch requested Spanish authorities, via Berlin, to send a vessel to meet *U-77* off that port and, if necessary, tow her the rest of the way. At the same time, Kreisch directed Josef Röther in the *U-380* to rendezvous with *U-77* and take off forty of her crew, leaving the rest to man the boat during the tow into Alicante.

On the next day, March 29, another Hudson of Squadron 48 found *U-77* on the surface in the narrow waters between Calo de San Antonia and the island of Ibiza. Upon sighting the Hudson, *U-77* fired flak, until probably she ran out of ammo, then dived. Before the periscope was fully under, the Hudson dropped four shallow-set depth charges on the swirl. This attack destroyed the heavily damaged *U-77.* Nine German survivors drifted ashore near Denia, Spain, and were eventually repatriated to Germany. The rest of the crew, including Hartmann, died in the sinking.

• On April 23, a Hudson of Squadron 500, piloted by R. Obee, found a U-boat patrolling off Oran. Obee attacked into flak from an altitude of two hundred feet, dropping four shallow-set depth charges that fell close. Some flak exploded in the cockpit, killing Obee. Two other airmen, Alfred S. Kempster and A. F. Blackwell, took over the controls and nursed the badly damaged plane back to its base at Tafaraouri, near Oran, where all hands bailed out and the plane crashed with Obee's body still on board. Initially the Admiralty credited this Hudson with the kill of *U-602,* commanded by Philipp Schüler, but subsequently declared *U-602* lost to unknown causes.

These eight losses gradually whittled the Mediterranean U-boat force down to sixteen boats. In response to urgent requests from senior German and Italian authorities in the Mediterranean Basin, Berlin again directed that the Atlantic U-boat force reinforce the Mediterranean U-boat force, to assist Axis forces trapped in Tunisia by the closing Allied vise. Five boats set out but only four made it: *U-303,* commanded by Karl-Franz Heine, and *U-414,* commanded by Walther Huth, both of which entered the Mediterranean on April 9; *U-410,* commanded by Horst-Arno

Fenski; and *U-616,* commanded by Siegfried Koitschka, which entered the Mediterranean on the night of May 6–7.

While patrolling west of the Strait of Gibraltar on the evening of May 7, two Hudsons of Gibraltar-based Squadron 233 sighted a U-boat on the surface. This was the fifth boat, *U-447,* commanded by Friedrich-Wilhelm Bothe, who was preparing to run the strait that night. The planes, piloted by J. V. Holland and J. W. McQueen, attacked, each dropping four shallow-set depth charges and strafing. Nothing further was ever heard from *U-447.*

Two of the four boats that got into the Mediterranean on April 9 were lost:

- While patrolling off Toulon on May 21, the British submarine *Sickle,* commanded by J. R. Drummond (son of a vice admiral), hit and sank Heine's *U-303,* which had sailed from Toulon for sea trials. Amazingly, Heine, his first watch officer, Erwin Coupette, and nine other Germans on board survived and were rescued by an Axis minesweeper.*
- While escorting the westbound convoy GTX 1 off Oran on May 25, the British corvette *Vetch* got a sonar contact. This was *U-414,* commanded by Walther Huth, age twenty-four, who had served as first watch officer of Horst Hamm's *U-562* for six months in the Mediterranean before getting command of his own boat. Five days earlier, May 18, Huth had sunk a 6,000-ton British freighter and damaged a 7,100-ton British freighter.

Unaware of *Vetch,* which had closed to about one hundred feet, Huth raised his periscope to shoot into the convoy. Scarcely able to believe his eyes, *Vetch*'s skipper, H. J. Beauly, quick fired a salvo of five depth charges set for fifty to 140 feet at point-blank range. When the first one exploded, Huth's periscope was still visible. Very likely the charges closely straddled *U-414,* destroying the boat. For good measure, Beauly fired four more depth charges by eye. Other than huge air and oil bubbles and a deep explosion, *Vetch* had no evidence to substantiate a kill, but as was learned later, she had sunk *U-414,* for which she received sole credit. There were no survivors.

Another of the boats that had entered the Mediterranean in November to attack Torch forces was also sunk in late May. This was the *U-755,* commanded by Walter Göing. On the morning of May 28, a Hudson of British Squadron 608, based near Algiers and piloted by G.A.K. Ogilvie, found *U-755* on the surface in the narrow waters between the Spanish coast and the island of Majorca. This Hudson carried the new air-to-surface rockets.

Göing elected to stay on the surface and fight it out. Ogilvie came in low and fired a two-rocket salvo. One missile failed to release but the other performed perfectly, hitting the underside of the U-boat pressure hull dead center. Circling the damaged boat, Ogilvie came in for a second attack and fired a four-rocket salvo. Astonishingly, three of the four rockets hit the underside of the pressure hull.

When he saw that these hits had fatally holed *U-755,* Göing gave orders to abandon ship. As the crew rushed topside, the Hudson attacked the men and the U-boat,

* Heine returned to France to command a new VII.

firing about seven thousand rounds from the machine guns. Nine minutes after it was first sighted, *U-755* upended and sank stern first. The Spanish destroyer *Churruca* rescued nine Germans—all wounded—who were eventually repatriated to Germany. The rest of the crew of *U-755,* including Göing, perished in the sinking.

These three losses in May reduced the Mediterranean force on June 1 to seventeen U-boats, including several undergoing battle-damage repairs. One other VII entered the Mediterranean on June 5, the *U-409,* commanded by Hans-Ferdinand Massmann, raising the force to eighteen boats. No others entered the Mediterranean during the summer of 1943.

In return for the thirty confirmed ships for about 110,000 tons and nine sailing vessels sunk during the five-month period from January 1 to June 1, 1943, the Mediterranean force lost eleven boats, plus *U-447,* sunk while preparing to run Gibraltar Strait. That was a ruinous "exchange rate" of 2.5 ships sunk for each U-boat lost. About five hundred men manning these boats perished.*

The sinkings amounted to no more than a pinprick in the dense Allied traffic in the Mediterranean. It failed to make any difference whatsoever in the climactic land battle in Tunisia. On May 13, the Allied vise finally clamped shut on the Axis forces, less Erwin Rommel and his staff who earlier had been evacuated by air. Rommel's replacement, Jürgen von Arnim, and his Italian counterpart, Giovanni Messe, surrendered themselves and about 275,000 Axis soldiers. It was an Allied victory comparable to Stalingrad and thus another grave humiliation for Hitler and an unmitigated disaster for his erstwhile ally, Benito Mussolini.

The maritime benefits of this land victory were incalculable. For the first time since 1941, Allied convoys, hugging the coast of North Africa and continuously protected by land-based aircraft, could sail the Mediterranean in relative safety from Gibraltar to the Suez Canal. Merchant ships bound for Egypt or the Levant (Palestine, Lebanon, Syria) or for India no longer had to go the long way via Cape Town, a savings of nine thousand sea miles and about forty-five days steaming per ship, as Churchill was wont to emphasize when enumerating the naval fruits of this victory. Moreover, the ensuing reduction of shipping via Freetown, Cape Town, and Durban made available convoy-escort vessels for use elsewhere.

Most of the remaining eighteen Mediterranean U-boats were based at La Spezia to facilitate patrols to the western Mediterranean against Torch shipping. Neither the OKM nor Leo Kreisch had ever been satisfied with the arrangements in La Spezia. The port was crowded with Italian ships and submarines; the facilities were overburdened; the Italians had not welcomed the Germans with open arms. The only real advantage of the base was its proximity to Germany.

With the fall of Tunisia, Berlin correctly sensed that the Italian king, Victor Emmanuel III, and the Fascist Grand Council might oust or assassinate Mussolini

* Twelve boats times forty-seven crew, less sixty-five men: Forty-five from *U-205, U-224,* and *U-301* were captured and twenty rescued by Axis forces or neutral Spain and returned to Germany.

and defect or surrender Italy to the Allies. Berlin therefore directed Kreisch to move the German 29th Combat Flotilla from La Spezia to the magnificent French naval base at Toulon by August 1. At that time, *Ritterkreuz* holder Günter Jahn, the outstanding commander of the veteran *U-596,* was to relieve *Ritterkreuz* holder Fritz Frauenheim as commander of the flotilla.

Diminishing Returns in American Waters

The decision to divert a large number of Type IXs to convoy battles in the North and Middle Atlantic sharply reduced the number of this type available for patrols to the Americas.

In the first four months of 1943, U-boat Control sailed only thirteen Type IXs to the Americas: four in January, three in February, four in March, and two in early April. They confronted plentiful and well-organized ASW forces and convoying. Returns were thin and four of the thirteen were lost.

The first to sail in January was the *U-518,* commanded by Friedrich-Wilhelm Wissmann, making his second patrol. His maiden outing to Canadian waters had been outstanding: an agent landed safely, four ships for about 30,000 tons sunk, two tankers for about 15,000 tons damaged.

After a temporary diversion to the groups patrolling west of Gibraltar, Wissmann proceeded to Brazil. By that time few merchant ships sailed alone in Brazilian waters. Most were assigned to coastal convoys running between Trinidad and Bahia (Salvador) designated TB, or the reverse BT, with a stop at Recife. Brazilian naval forces provided escorts from Recife to Bahia and the reverse. American naval vessels and aircraft provided escort between Recife and Trinidad and the reverse. The U.S. Navy's Fleet Air Wing 16, comprised of three patrol squadrons, VP 74, VP 83, and VP 94, equipped with Catalinas and the troublesome, lethal (to their aircrews) Mariners, covered the convoy route from Recife to Trinidad and the reverse.

Owing to the convoying, Wissmann found the seas nearly empty of loners. Finally on February 18, he sank the 6,000-ton Brazilian *Brasiloide,* which was sailing alone. Another ten long days passed with no sightings. Then on March 1 he found a submariner's dream: convoy BT 6, northbound from Bahia (Salvador) to Recife en route to Trinidad. It was composed of twenty-nine merchant ships thinly escorted by three Brazilian warships.

Wissmann tracked and planned his attack with utmost care. Choosing several American Liberty ships for his first targets, he closed the convoy at night on the surface. In repeated attacks throughout the night, Wissmann fired fourteen electrics with Pi2 magnetic pistols. The result was a German fiasco. He sank one 7,200-ton American Liberty ship, the *Fitz-John Porter,* but, he reported, at least eight torpedoes ran too deep. Several others simply missed. As a consequence, this golden opportunity to decimate a convoy was lost.

Karl Neitzel in the *U-510,* who had sailed for Brazil five days after Wissmann, picked up the latter's convoy report. He maneuvered his boat into a likely position to intercept convoy BT 6 farther north off the coast of French Guiana. Having sunk only two confirmed ships in two prior patrols, Neitzel was under the gun to produce. On the night of March 9, he found the convoy and, like Wissmann, he gazed in awe at this submariner's dream.

Neitzel reported the convoy to U-boat Control, which authorized him to attack immediately. After a series of wild night-surface shots, Neitzel reported that he sank six ships for 70,000 tons, left another ship of 5,000 tons sinking, and hit yet another of 6,000 tons (81,000 tons sunk or damaged). This electrifying report drew high praise from U-boat Control and, on March 27, a *Ritterkreuz* for Neitzel. But Neitzel's claims were much too rosy. His confirmed score was three ships for 18,300 tons sunk: two 7,200-ton American Liberty ships, *James K. Polk* and *Thomas Ruffin,* and one British freighter of 3,900 tons. In addition, he hit five other American Liberty ships for 36,000 tons, but all of these made port.*

Wissmann and Neitzel continued to patrol Brazilian waters but Neitzel soon headed home with an oil leak. Upon arrival in France, he left the boat to command Flotilla 25 in the Training Command. Wissmann sank two more ships in Brazilian waters, a 7,700-ton Dutchman and a 1,700-ton Swede, then returned to France via the Canary Islands where, as related, he picked up a part of the crew of the scuttled *U-167* and refueled from the XB minelayer *U-117.*

The other two boats that sailed to the Americas in January were the *U-156,* commanded by the *Ritterkreuz* holder Werner Hartenstein (who sank *Laconia* and initiated the famous rescue), and the *U-183,* commanded by Heinrich Schäfer, making his second patrol. Hartenstein was sent to Trinidad; Schäfer was to enter the Caribbean Sea via the Windward Passage.

By the time Hartenstein in *U-156* reached Trinidad it was, like Iceland, an ASW stronghold. Army and Navy aircraft equipped with centimetric-wavelength radar patrolled the area nearly continuously, escorting convoys converging on the island from numerous points and leaving for Guantánamo, Cuba, and other destinations. Harassed by these aircraft, Hartenstein informed U-boat Control that the Allies were employing a "new radar" that Metox could not detect. The proof of that important assertion was that he had been subjected to "precise" night attacks by aircraft *without* searchlights.

U-boat Control notified Hartenstein of the oncoming convoy BT 6, which Wissmann and Neitzel had attacked. Accordingly, Hartenstein proceeded to an area southeast of Trinidad to attempt to intercept. Doubtless Allied Huff Duff stations picked up Hartenstein's transmissions and fixed his position. On March 8, a Catalina of Navy Squadron VP 53, a part of Fleet Air Wing 11, based on Trinidad, found *U-156* on ASV radar about 270 miles east of Barbados. Ghosting silently out of the clouds, the Catalina descended to one hundred feet and caught *U-156* completely unawares. The pilot, J. E. Dryden, dropped four 350-pound Torpex depth charges. Two straddled the conning tower and broke the boat into three pieces that sank quickly, one by one. The airmen counted eleven survivors in the

* At the time of the award, Neitzel's confirmed score was five ships sunk for about 28,400 tons and seven ships damaged for about 42,000 tons.

water clinging to wreckage. They dropped a raft and emergency supplies, but notwithstanding a prolonged search over the ensuing days, not one of the survivors of *U-156* was ever found.

The three IXs that sailed in February joined Schäfer in *U-183* to enter the Caribbean and Gulf of Mexico for a loosely coordinated and timed four-boat "surprise attack." These were the famous *U-68,* commanded by a new skipper, Albert Lauzemis, age twenty-five, the *Ritterkreuz* holder Adolf-Cornelius Piening in the veteran *U-155,* and August Maus in *U-185,* making his second patrol.

The four boats reached their assigned areas in the first week of March. On March 10, Maus in *U-185* opened the campaign by attacking in the Windward Passage a convoy, KG 123, southbound from Key West to Guantánamo. He sank two American ships, the 6,200-ton tanker *Virginia Sinclair* and the 7,200-ton Liberty ship *James Sprunt.* Tenacious escorts diverted from a nearby convoy northbound to Key West thwarted a second attack and heavily depth-charged Maus, forcing him to withdraw. In the Yucatan Channel on March 11, Schäfer in *U-183* sank what he claimed to be a 7,000-ton freighter but what in reality was the 2,500-ton Honduran banana boat *Olancho.* South of the Windward Passage on March 13, Lauzemis in *U-68* found a Guantánamo-Aruba-Trinidad convoy, GAT 49, and sank two ships from it, a 2,700-ton Dutch freighter and the 7,500-ton American tanker *Cities Service Missouri.* Entering the Gulf of Mexico via the Straits of Florida, Piening in *U-155* found no targets to kick off this "surprise attack."

Detected and tracked by Enigma decrypts, Huff Duff, and radar, none of these four boats achieved much more. Lauzemis in *U-68* shot at a fast freighter but missed. He was then forced to withdraw to the Atlantic because, as he said, his "Metox failed." He sank no more ships and returned to France after refueling from the provisional tanker, XB minelayer *U-117.*

Braving strong aircraft and blimp patrols in the Florida Straits on April 1 and 3, *Ritterkreuz* holder Piening in *U-155,* who had found no targets in the Gulf of Mexico, sank a 1,000-ton Norwegian freighter and atomized the 6,900-ton American tanker *Gulfstate,* which was loaded with gasoline. On his return to France he was bombed in the Bay of Biscay by an unidentified Allied aircraft on the night of April 27, but he remained on the surface and repelled the aircraft with his flak guns and reached Lorient.

Although Maus in *U-185* was also harassed—and bombed—by aircraft and blimps, he sank another American Liberty ship, the 7,200-ton *John Sevier,* in the Windward Passage, bringing his bag to three ships for 20, 000 tons. He then returned to France.

Schäfer in *U-183* sank no ships other than the 2,500-ton Honduran.

In all, this four-boat "surprise attack" and subsequent actions netted eight ships for 41,200 tons, a disappointing average of two ships per boat per patrol.

The IXs operating in the Gulf of Mexico, Caribbean, and South American waters in March 1943 sank eleven ships for 60,800 tons. The Italian submarine *Barbarigo,* commanded by Roberto Rigoli, sank two other freighters for 12,131 tons off the Brazilian coast. The total sinkings, thirteen ships for 72,900 tons, also contributed to the general impression that in March 1943, U-boats nearly cut the vital lifeline between the Americas and the British Isles.

Six IXs sailed to American waters in March and early April. One, the *U-129,* commanded by *Ritterkreuz* holder Hans Witt, was to enter the Caribbean and patrol off Panama, but owing to excessively high battery temperatures, he had to cancel that plan. He joined three other boats, *U-161, U-174,* and *U-176,* to attack shipping in Canadian and United States coastal waters, which had not been patrolled for six months. The other two IXs, *U-128* and *U-154,* were to patrol off Brazil.

After the voyage to Panama was canceled, Witt in *U-129* was directed to reconnoiter Bermuda, then Cape Hatteras. En route to Bermuda he found and sank the impressive 12,800-ton British vessel *Melbourne Star.* Off Bermuda he saw no targets and was harassed by intense air and surface ASW patrols. Finding thin traffic off Cape Hatteras, Witt went farther south. On April 24 he sank the 6,500-ton American freighter *Santa Catalina.* On April 26 he missed a large American submarine with three torpedoes, misidentified as a "*Narwhal*-class." Off North Carolina on May 5, he sank the 7,300-ton Panamanian tanker *Panam.* He then returned to France, having bagged three ships for 26,590 tons, the best patrol by tonnage sunk of any boat in American waters in the first half of 1943.

The next two boats to sail were *Ritterkreuz* holder Albrecht Achilles in *U-161* and a new skipper, Wolfgang Grandefeld, age twenty-six, in *U-174.* Both had to first carry out special missions. Substituting for the lost *U-163,* Achilles in *U-161* was directed to meet the inbound blockade-runner *Regensburg,* to give her special instructions. Grandefeld in *U-174* was directed to meet the inbound blockade-runner *Karin* (ex-*Kota Nopan*) for the same task. Unknown to the Germans, on March 10 the American cruiser *Savannah* and destroyer *Eberle* had intercepted *Karin* in the Middle Atlantic and forced her to scuttle.

Not without difficulties, Achilles and Grandefeld attempted to carry out these special tasks. On March 23, Achilles found *Regensburg* and passed to her documents and verbal instructions. Achilles was then directed to meet the inbound Italian blockade-runner *Pietro Orseolo,* and give her instructions. He performed this task on March 27, then went west to patrol the area between Nova Scotia and New York. A submarine torpedo hit the *Pietro Orseolo,* but she limped into Bordeaux on April 1. Unable to find the lost *Karin,* Grandefeld in *U-174* was directed to rendezvous with another inbound blockade-runner, *Irene* (ex-*Silvaplana*). Grandefeld met *Irene* on April 6 and carried out his task.

The British tracked *Regensburg* closely, benefitting from the many Enigma decrypts concerning her routing and U-boat protection and rescue assignments. The *Regensburg* was to transit the Denmark Strait, then proceed to Norway, then to the Baltic. Berlin ordered U-boat Control to deploy three new Atlantic boats along her projected path: the IXC40 *U-191,* commanded by Helmut Fiehn, age twenty-seven, and the VIIs *U-469* and *U-635,* commanded respectively by Emil Claussen, age twenty-five, and Heinz Eckelmann, age twenty-six. On March 25, an Ireland-based B-17 of British Squadron 206, piloted by Willis Roxburg, sank the *U-469* with depth charges. On March 30, a British task force, including the heavy cruiser *Glasgow,* intercepted and sank *Regensburg.* There were no survivors of these German losses.

The British also closely tracked the next blockade-runner, *Irene,* inbound to Bordeaux. Owing to the embarrassing loss of *Regensburg,* when Dönitz learned that *U-174* had met *Irene,* he issued a "personal order" to U-boat Control to sail at once four U-boats (two IXs, two VIIs) specifically to escort *Irene* across the Bay of Biscay. Control selected four boats that had been detailed to make patrols to the Americas. The two IXs, *U-128* and *U-176,* sailed from Lorient on April 6; the two VIIs, *U-262* and *U-376,* sailed from La Pallice the same day. Subsequently Dönitz ordered these U-boats to escort *Irene* into Vigo, Spain, for temporary refuge.

The British, meanwhile, rushed aircraft and a naval task force of light vessels to the scene. On April 10, the minelayer *Adventure,* en route from the Mediterranean to the British Isles, came upon *Irene* and opened fire, forcing the Germans to scuttle and take to the lifeboats. The British captured the *Irene* crew and cast off the empty lifeboats.

When Dönitz got word of this latest *Kriegsmarine* fiasco, he directed that German aircraft and the four U-boats sent to escort *Irene* were to search thoroughly for German survivors. Meanwhile, he recalled one of four outbound blockade-runners, the Italian-manned *Himalaya,* escorted by four German destroyers, which had sailed from Bordeaux on March 29. The other three proceeded to the Far East, but one, *Portland,* was intercepted on April 13 and sunk by the Free French cruiser *Georges Leygues.**

German aircraft found eight lifeboats from *Irene* but no sign of life. The four U-boats searched until April 12, but they too could find nothing of *Irene* or her crew. Control thereafter ordered the two IXs, *U-128* and *U-176,* and the two VIIs, *U-262* and *U-376,* to proceed to the Americas. However, one VII did not respond: the ex-Arctic *U-376,* commanded by Friedrich Marks. The Admiralty initially credited a Leigh Light–equipped Wellington of British Squadron 172, piloted by G. H. Whiteley, with the kill of *U-376,* but subsequently declared her lost to unknown causes.

Achilles in *U-161* had a miserable patrol to the Americas. Hunted relentlessly by strong surface and air ASW forces in Canadian waters, he was forced under time and again. Finally, on April 26, he found a fast convoy southeast of Nova Scotia. He got off a contact report and shadowed but a diesel engine failed and he lost the convoy. On May 19 he found the 255-ton Canadian sailing ship *Angelus.* After the crew had abandoned ship, Achilles sank her by gun and returned to France, ending

---

* In the first quarter of 1943, the Axis sailed ten blockade-runners from the Far East to Europe. Four were recalled to Japan for various reasons but six proceeded. Of these, five were lost: *Hohenfriedburg* (sunk by *Sussex*), *Doggerbank* (by *U-43*), *Karin* (by *Savannah*), *Regensburg* (by *Glasgow*), *Irene* (by *Adventure*). Although damaged, the sixth ship, *Pietro Orseolo,* reached Bordeaux on April 1. In the same quarter, four blockade-runners sailed from Europe to the Far East. *Himalaya* aborted; *Portland* was lost (to *Georges Leygues*), *Osorno* and *Alsterufer* reached Japan on June 4 and June 19, respectively. In summary, of the fourteen sailings, only three vessels reached their destinations.

an unsuccessful patrol, his first. Owing to the intense ASW measures, he declared, U-boat patrols to the Canadian and United States coasts were "hopeless."*

Grandefeld in *U-174* literally followed in the wake of *U-161* by about ten days. Patrolling southeast of Nova Scotia, on April 17 he found what he believed to be a subsection of a Halifax convoy. He shadowed and attempted to attack, he reported, but he was thwarted by foul weather and escorts. Nine days later, on April 26, he probably picked up the convoy report of Achilles in *U-161*. He was in a good position to intercept it southeast of Nova Scotia, but on the next day, April 27, a Ventura of Navy Squadron VP 125, newly based in Newfoundland to provide convoy support, found *U-174* running on the surface. The pilot, Thomas Kinaszczuk, commenced an attack, but Grandefeld remained on the surface, shooting at the Ventura with all topside weapons. Braving the flak smashing into his wings and fuselage, Kinaszczuk came in very low and dropped four shallow-set depth charges. Three exploded in a close straddle, hurtling *U-174* bow up. She sank stern first, straight up, with the loss of all hands. Kinaszczuk earned a Navy Cross.

Reiner Dierksen in *U-176,* who had diverted to escort the doomed blockade-runner *Irene,* was ordered to patrol the Gulf of Mexico. In the Middle Atlantic on April 20, he rendezvoused with Piening, homebound in *U-155,* to learn firsthand about conditions in the gulf.

The first watch officer on *U-155*'s first two patrols, Alfred Eick, who had left to replace Neitzel as commander of *U-510,* worried that Dierksen was too headstrong and incautious, that he would soon come to grief. Eick's premonition proved to be correct. On the night of May 13, Dierksen sank two small tankers in the Old Bahama Channel off the north coast of Cuba, the 2,200-ton American *Nickeliner,* and the 2,000-ton Cuban *Mambu.* The sinkings prompted the Caribbean Sea Frontier to mount a vigorous U-boat hunt. As a result, on the morning of May 15, an American OS2U Kingfisher floatplane of Navy Scouting Squadron VS 62 spotted *U-176* in the Old Bahama Channel about one hundred miles east of Havana. Seeing a small convoy approaching, the scout plane dropped a smoke bomb where *U-176* had crash-dived, then coaxed one of the three convoy escorts to the scene, the Cuban Sub Chaser (*SC*) *13,* one of a dozen ex-American eighty-three-foot Coast Guard cutters given to Cuba.

The *SC 13* reported an excellent sonar contact at four hundred yards and she ran in and dropped three depth charges, set for 100, 150, and 200 feet. After the third explosion, the *SC 13* heard a "loud" secondary explosion. When the noise abated and the roiling water settled, *SC 13* regained sonar contact at five hundred yards and dropped two more depth charges set for 200 and 250 feet. These explosions brought up "brown" or "muddy" water and slight traces of oil. The escort

* See Appendix 11. On April 1, 1943, there were in Newfoundland and Nova Scotia eight frontline ASW squadrons of American and Canadian aircraft, comprising over one hundred B-24 Liberators, Cansos, Catalinas, plus two U.S. Navy squadrons of PV-1 Venturas, and five RCAF squadrons of Hudsons and Digbys.

puttered around some more, then rejoined the convoy after an absence of merely one hour. Incensed by the lack of tenacity shown by the Cuban escort, American naval authorities recommended that the skipper be censured. No credit for a kill was granted, but, remarkably, this eighty-three-foot Cuban cutter had sunk *U-176* with the loss of all hands with merely five depth charges.

Had the *U-176* survived, she might have encountered a special American troop convoy. This was BT 203, which sailed from New York to the Pacific—the first troopship convoy in over a year to leave from an Atlantic port for the Pacific. The convoy, comprised of four big liners escorted by four American destroyers (*Buck, Nicholson, Swanson,* and *Wilkes*), arrived in Panama unmolested by U-boats and proceeded onward to the Pacific.

The two IXs bound for Brazil were veterans, both commanded by new skippers: Hermann Steinert, age twenty-six, in *U-128* and Oskar Heinz Kusch, age twenty-five, in *U-154.*

Steinert in *U-128,* who also had diverted to escort the *Irene,* was first to find a target. On May 8 he encountered a loner and attacked her at night, firing three salvos of two torpedoes each. To Steinert's chagrin, all six torpedoes missed and the ship got away. After this puzzling failure, the crew downloaded four (of eight) air torpedoes from the topside canisters.

A week later, on May 16, while patrolling off Bahia (Salvador) in support of convoy TB 13, southbound from Trinidad to Bahia, a Mariner flying boat of the Navy's Squadron VP 74 found *U-128* and attacked. Steinert crash-dived; the depth charges fell wide, causing no damage. That night a Catalina flew out to re-establish contact—and hold the U-boat down—but the plane had no radar and could not find *U-128.* Charging batteries, Steinert cruised northward on the surface toward Recife during the night. Near dawn he submerged and promptly picked up the convoy on sonar at about ten miles. After he had established its course and speed by sonar, Steinert surfaced in order to run to a better shooting position.

That morning—May 17—two other Mariners of Squadron VP 74, equipped with centimetric-wavelength radar, were assigned to provide air escort for the convoy. Both aircraft detected *U-128* on radar, one at eighteen miles, the other at twenty-eight miles. The closest Mariner, flown by Howland S. Davis, attacked first, dropping six shallow-set depth charges from an altitude of sixty feet. Steinert saw the plane coming and attempted to crash-dive, but the hydraulic system malfunctioned and the ballast-tank vents had to be opened by hand, a slow process. While she was still struggling to get under, the depth charges exploded around *U-128.* The other Mariner, flown by Harold C. Carey, arrived and dropped six more shallow-set depth charges from an altitude of one hundred feet. The twelve depth charges wrecked *U-128.* The aircrews added four thousand rounds of 50-caliber machine-gun fire.

In response to requests from the airmen for assistance, two modern American destroyers, *Moffett* (1936) and *Jouett* (1939), came charging up at flank speed.

Both destroyers opened up with 5" guns, firing an astonishing 247 rounds. This fire and/or scuttling sank the wrecked *U-128*. *Moffett* fished out fifty-one of *U-128*'s fifty-four-man crew, including Steinert. Four of the survivors, including *U-128*'s chief engineer, died on board *Moffett*. The remaining forty-seven POWs were delivered to naval authorities at Recife. Steinert, his first watch officer, Siegfried Sterzing, and eleven others were flown immediately to the United States for interrogation. The POWs wondered why neither *Moffett* nor *Jouett* had made an effort to board *U-128* to gather intelligence documents. The reason was that those destroyers had no parties trained for boarding sinking U-boats.

Left alone in these distant waters, Oskar-Heinz Kusch, new skipper of *U-154*, conducted an aggressive patrol. In late May he intercepted convoy BT 14, northbound from Bahia to Trinidad and attacked it on the surface at night. He claimed sinking three freighters for 21,500 tons, plus possibly a 6,000-ton tanker and damage to an 8,000-ton tanker. His confirmed score was one 8,200-ton American tanker, *John Worthington*, sunk and two American ships (one tanker, one freighter) for 15,800 tons damaged.

When Kusch reported that his Metox was "permanently out," U-boat Control authorized him to slowly withdraw from American waters on a homebound course. In the meantime, Control directed Siegfried Kietz in *U-126*, which was severely damaged by an air attack off Freetown on June 15, to meet Kusch in *U-154* and return to France in company. These two veteran boats with green skippers met near the Azores on June 29, where Kusch missed a fast freighter with two torpedoes.

A Leigh Light–equipped Wellington of British Squadron 172, piloted by the Rhodesian Alex Coumbis, got *U-126* or *U-154* on radar in the Bay of Biscay in the early hours of July 3. Coumbis lined up and attacked a U-boat that proved to be Kietz in *U-126*. Nothing more was ever heard from *U-126*. Kusch in *U-154* witnessed the attack from close quarters. Incorrectly surmising that *U-126* had dived to safety, Kusch reported the attack to be "unsuccessful." The *U-154* then proceeded to Lorient alone, arriving safely three days later.

The commander of Combat Flotilla 2, *Ritterkreuz* holder Ernst Kals, wrote that Kusch, who had served as a watch officer on *U-103* under *Ritterkreuz* holder Werner Winter and Gustav-Adolf Janssen for eighteen months, had made a good first patrol and was well qualified to be a U-boat commander. However, Kusch's first watch officer, the reservist Ulrich Abel, a doctor of laws and fanatical Nazi, was of the opposite opinion and because of that, very big trouble lay ahead for Kusch.

The thirteen Type IXs that sailed to the Americas from January through early April sank twenty-two confirmed ships for 121,200 tons. This was an average of about 1.7 ships for 9,300 tons sunk per boat per patrol, a drastic decline from the same period the year before, when the IXs ranged freely in American waters. Four of the thirteen boats were lost: *Ritterkreuz* holder Werner Hartenstein's *U-156*, Wolfgang Grandefeld's *U-174*, Reiner Dierksen's *U-176*, and Hermann Steinert's *U-128*. Since the drastic decline in returns was obscured by gross overclaims, such as those of Neitzel in *U-510*, U-boat Control planned to continue—and perhaps even increase—patrols to American waters despite the heavy losses.

The Italians sent five large Bordeaux-based submarines to patrol Brazilian waters from February to April 1943. As related, only one of these boats, *Barbarigo,* commanded by Roberto Rigoli, had any success. She sank three confirmed freighters for 15,600 tons: a Spaniard, a Brazilian, and the American *Stag Hound,* 8,600 tons.

One of the Italian boats was lost: *Archimede,* commanded by Guido Saccardo. On April 15, a Catalina of U.S. Navy Squadron VP 83, based in Natal, Brazil, spotted *Archimede* running on the surface. The pilot, T. E. Robertson, attacked with bombs and depth charges in the face of flak from *Archimede,* which dived, then resurfaced, circling uncontrollably. A second Catalina of VP 83, piloted by G. Bradford, Jr., arrived and attacked with four depth charges from fifty feet. Thereafter, both aircraft strafed *Archimede* until she sank, leaving nineteen survivors in the water. Each Catalina dropped a raft, then departed. Twenty-nine days later, one raft containing a lone survivor, coxswain Giuseppe Lococo, washed ashore near the mouth of the Amazon River. Subsequently, Brazilian authorities turned him over to the Americans at Belem. All other Italians perished.

During this period U-boat Control mounted one special mission to Canada. It was supervised by the second staff officer, *Ritterkreuz* holder Peter Cremer, recovering from the severe injuries he incurred on his boat, *U-333.*

Most U-boat POWs captured by British or Commonwealth forces were eventually transferred to camps in Canada. Some of them continued to communicate with Admiral Dönitz or U-boat Control by encoded messages in letters to their families. Fully alive to these "secret" communications, Allied intelligence officers continued to break the simple code *(Irland)* and monitor the messages, taking care not to reveal that they were doing so because the information gained from them was sometimes of military value. Copies of the decrypted letters were exchanged between Washington, London, and Ottawa. Some letters were stopped, but most were allowed to go forward to Germany through Red Cross channels.

For a long period of time, some German U-boat POWs incarcerated at Camp 70, near the city of Fredericton, New Brunswick, Canada, had been planning an intricate escape. The plan was to break out and make their way to the East Coast (110 air miles), thence by stolen small boat across Northumberland Strait (fifteen miles) to thinly populated Prince Edward Island in the Gulf of St. Lawrence, where a U-boat could pick them up.

By means of encoded messages in the return mail of the families, Dönitz encouraged this scheme, code-named *Elster* (Magpie). He promised by encoded mail that a U-boat would appear off North Point, Prince Edward Island, in the first week of May 1943, when, it was presumed, the ice in the Gulf of St. Lawrence had melted. Whether or not Allied authorities became aware of this scheme from decrypting POW mail is unclear. In the event, the escape attempt became known to the Allies by some means and it failed. So far as is known, no POW ever reached Prince Edward Island.

At U-boat Control, Peter Cremer selected two VIIs to carry out *Elster:* a lead boat, *U-376,* and a backup, *U-262.* As related, both had been diverted to escort *Irene* and, as also related, the *U-376* was lost to unknown causes while she was searching for *Irene* survivors. Responsibility for the mission therefore went to the backup, *U-262,* commanded by Heinz Franke. On April 15, he came upon convoy Halifax 233 and shadowed, but escorts drove him off and down with guns and depth charges. When other boats responded to Franke's report, a fierce battle ensued, as will be described later. However, U-boat Control directed Franke to break off and proceed to Prince Edward Island and carry out "special task" *Elster,* per the secret orders he had been provided before he sailed.

Franke reached Cabot Strait on April 25 in fair weather.* He continued north into the Gulf of St. Lawrence, where the ice became progressively worse. At one point the *U-262* was trapped beneath a heavy layer of ice and Franke was forced to crash through it by blowing all ballast tanks simultaneously. The upward thrust of the boat broke the ice and the boat "surfaced," but the effort knocked out three of *U-262*'s bow tubes, her deck gun, and other topside gear. Per plan, on May 2 Franke took up station off North Point, Prince Edward Island, awaiting some kind of signal from the POW escapees. He lingered there for five days, finally departing on May 6, logging that the failure of *Elster* was "a shame," but not through any fault of *U-262.*

After withdrawing from the gulf through Cabot Strait, on May 10 Franke signalled U-boat Control, giving his position and fuel supply and reporting that *Elster* had failed and that three of his bow tubes were unusable because of ice damage. In reply, U-boat Control directed Franke to return to France, refueling on the way from the XIV tanker *U-459.* Allied codebreakers, who had puzzled mightily over Franke's often-mentioned but unidentified "special task," belatedly figured it out during his homeward voyage and logged: "He is thought to have been involved in a proposed escape of German P/Ws from Canada and may have been in Gulf of Maine or even Gulf of St. Lawrence."

Elster failed but the most famous U-boat POW, Otto Kretschmer, incarcerated in Camp 30 at Bowmanville, Ontario (forty miles east of Toronto), had set in motion a similar escape plan, which the Allies learned of in advance. Also encouraged by Admiral Dönitz and U-boat Control, it was to be attempted later in the summer.

The Second Foray to the Indian Ocean

After it was reconstituted at sea in January 1943, group *Seehund* (Seal), the second foray to Cape Town and the Indian Ocean, resumed its long voyage. The XIV tanker *U-459* accompanied the boats to the South Atlantic, where it refueled the four IXs,† then returned to France on March 8. Although designated a group, the five boats of *Seehund* were to patrol independently, like those of its predecessor, *Eisbär.*

The first of the IXs of *Seehund* to sink a ship in the South Atlantic was the last to join the group, *Ritterkreuz* holder Georg Lassen's *U-160.* It was not an easy kill. In the first attack on February 7, Lassen fired two torpedoes; one missed, one hit.

---

* Achilles in *U-161* and Grandefeld in *U-174* were not far from Nova Scotia on April 26, perhaps with collateral duty to provide backup for *U-262.* That backup evaporated on April 26 when, as related, Achilles found a convoy and, perhaps in pursuit of same, *U-174* was sunk on April 27.

† Plus the Italian submarine *Cagni* and the Americas-bound IXC *U-161.*

The Armed Guard gun crew of the vessel, the 7,200-ton American Liberty ship *Roger B. Taney,* shot back, forcing Lassen to dive. In his second attack, Lassen again fired two torpedoes. Again he missed with one and hit with the other. This second hit put *Taney* under. Most of the ship's crew perished in the sinking or thereafter, but a few were rescued from lifeboats about a month later.

Lassen proceeded to an area southeast of Cape Town. On the night of March 2 he found the poorly organized, thinly escorted convoy DN 21, en route from Durban north to the Suez Canal. It was comprised of ten or eleven big, heavily laden merchant ships and four escorts, the British corvette *Nigella* and three ASW trawlers.

Favored with a dark, moonless night and good weather, Lassen launched his attack after midnight on March 3. In all, he shot eight torpedoes, an initial salvo of six, plus two reloads. He claimed he sank six ships for 37,000 tons and possibly sank one of 5,000 tons; altogether seven ships for 42,000 tons put out of action, a telling blow of direct benefit to Axis forces in Tunisia. In reality, he sank four ships (the American *Harvey W. Scott* and the British *Nipura, Empire Mahseer,* and *Marietta*) for 25,900 tons and damaged two ships (the Dutch tanker *Tibia,* the British freighter *Sheaf Crown*) for 15,200 tons—altogether, hits on six ships of about 41,000 tons.

Lassen's flash report electrified U-boat Control. This kind of single-handed convoy devastation was what Dönitz and the U-boat staff prized, but it was all too rare. Dönitz immediately initiated steps leading to the award of Oak Leaves to Lassen's *Ritterkreuz.* The award—and the usual message of congratulations from Hitler—arrived on March 7.*

In the week following, Lassen remained off Durban. In the four-day period from March 8 to 11, he sank the 7,200-ton American Liberty ship *James B. Stephens* and the 5,000-ton British freighter *Aelybryn.* Having sunk seven confirmed ships for 45,200 tons and damaged two others, Lassen advised U-boat Control that he was down to three torpedoes and coming home. En route he found a fast lone freighter near Freetown and shot two of his three torpedoes at her, but they missed. He arrived in France on May 10 after 125 days at sea. U-boat Control credited him with ten ships sunk for 66,800 tons and characterized his patrol as "brilliantly executed." His confirmed bag on this patrol was six ships sunk for about 38,000 tons, plus damage to two others. He left the boat for a job in the Training Command.†

East of Cape Town on March 7, Würdemann in the IXC *U-506* sank the 5,200-ton British freighter *Sabor,* firing five torpedoes. While edging up submerged to the sinking ship to look her over, Würdemann hit an "unidentified object." The collision damaged a periscope and fouled a propeller, forcing him to withdraw far to the south of Cape Town to make repairs. While so engaged on March 9, the 4,800-ton Norwegian freighter *Tabor* happened by and Würdemann sank her with three

---

* At the time of the award, his confirmed score was twenty-four ships sunk for 143,920 tons, plus damage to five others.

† Credited with sinking twenty-six confirmed ships for 156,000 tons, Lassen ranked twelfth among all skippers in the war.

torpedoes and gunfire. When added to the sinkings—and overclaims—on prior patrols to the Gulf of Mexico and to the Caribbean, Würdemann qualified for a *Ritterkreuz,* awarded by radio on March 14.*

After making repairs, Würdemann returned to the area east of Cape Town to interdict coastal convoys. Inasmuch as his presence was known through Enigma decrypts and DFing, the Allies rerouted convoys to avoid him. On March 19, he notified U-boat Control that the area was unpromising and that he was returning. After refueling from the XB (minelayer) *U-117* near the Azores, he reached France on May 8, completing a patrol of 146 days. Crediting Würdemann with two ships sunk for about 10,000 tons, U-boat Control characterized Würdemann as a "proven captain" but the patrol as "somewhat disappointing."

Werner Witte in the IXC *U-509,* embarked on his third patrol, sank his first ship off Cape Town on February 11. She was the 5,000-ton British *Queen Anne,* which Witte hit with a single torpedo from four hundred yards. The British ASW trawler *St. Zeno*† counterattacked *U-509* with gunfire and seven depth charges, but Witte slipped away undamaged. Remaining off the Cape Town area through March 13, he shot at several ships but had no further success. Acting on a suggestion from U-boat Control, Witte doubled back to Saldanha Bay, northwest of Cape Town.

Witte patrolled near Saldanha Bay for two more weeks without sinking a ship. Running short of food, he commenced his return voyage on March 28, holding close to the west coast of Africa. On April 2, he found a small convoy south of Walvis Bay. Approaching the ships submerged, Witte fired four torpedoes by sonar bearings at extreme range. Astonishingly, two of the four hit the 7,200-ton British freighter *City of Baroda,* which limped into Lüderitz Bay, Southwest Africa, and beached, a complete loss. After refueling from the provisional tanker XB (minelayer) *U-117, U-509* reached France on May 11, completing a frustrating 140-day patrol. Witte was credited with two ships for about 12,000 tons.

The other IXC, *U-516,* commanded by Gerhard Wiebe, making his second patrol, sank three ships south and southeast of Cape Town from February 11 to February 27. They were the British and American freighters *Helmsprey* and *Deer Lodge,* respectively, and the valuable 11,000-ton Dutch submarine tender *Colombia.* The latter ship, returning from refit in East London and escorted by the corvette *Genista,* sank in thirteen minutes, taking down several Dutch submarine crews. *Genista*'s cursory counterattack did no damage to *U-516.*

Wiebe reported on March 5 that he had accidentally rammed wreckage and was withdrawing to the south to make repairs and to fix an oil trace. Then, five days later, *U-516* reported that she had withdrawn because Wiebe had "stomach pains" so severe that it was necessary to abort the patrol. Temporarily commanded by the first

* At the time of the award, his score was sixteen confirmed ships sunk for 86,911 tons.

† ASW forces in South African waters had been reinforced to thirty ASW trawlers, eighteen of them released from duty on the U.S. East Coast.

watch officer, *U-516* sailed northward, like *U-509,* close to the west coast of Africa. On March 20, *U-516* sank the 3,700-ton Panamanian freighter *Nortun.* Subsequently, Wiebe's engineering gang discovered "severe corrosion" in the pressure hull, adjacent to a battery compartment. Since the sea pressure of a deep dive might crack the hull and flood the battery compartment with salt water, causing deadly chlorine gas to form, the boat sped home at the highest practical speed. She arrived in France on May 3, completing a 132-day patrol. Although Wiebe had sunk six ships on his first patrol to the Caribbean and four for 25,600 tons on this patrol, the illness and other factors led to his transfer from *U-516* to other duty.

The new IXD2 U-cruiser *U-182,* loosely attached to *Seehund,* was commanded by the old hand Nikolaus Clausen, who had sunk eighteen confirmed ships on the VII *U-37* and the IX *U-129,* and had won a *Ritterkreuz.* He sailed *U-182* from Norway on December 9, intending to patrol to Madagascar to attack shipping directly supporting the British Eighth Army in North Africa. Southbound in the area west of Freetown, Clausen sank the 7,200-ton British Liberty ship *Ocean Courage.* Rounding the Cape of Good Hope on February 17, he sank the 4,800-ton British freighter *Llanashe.*

Clausen cruised Mozambique Channel to Durban, Lourenço Marques, and the west coast of Madagascar. The outcome was a great disappointment. In a full month of operations—all of March—Clausen sank only one ship, the 7,200-ton American Liberty ship *Richard D. Spaight.* On the return voyage Clausen got two more freighters: the 5,000-ton British *Aloe* and the 5,800-ton Greek *Adelfotis* and captured both captains. These sinkings raised Clausen's score on this patrol to five ships for 30,000 tons.

By the night of May 16–17, the 160th day of *U-182*'s voyage, Clausen had reached a point about 250 miles west of the island of Madeira. Apparently by chance he met a subsection of convoy UGS 8, en route from the United States to Gibraltar. Two warships of the escort, the new (1942) American destroyers *Laub* and *MacKenzie,* were guarding fourteen LSTs. *MacKenzie* got *U-182* on radar at 7,200 yards. Reacting promptly and efficiently, *MacKenzie* notified *Laub* and raced down the bearing, but for reasons unrevealed, she did not open fire with her main batteries as required by operational doctrine. At 2,700 yards, the radar contact disappeared, indicating that the target had dived. *MacKenzie* soon got a good sonar contact and carried out several attacks, dropping fifteen depth charges.

Laub, which had not had a radar or sonar contact, joined the hunt skeptically. From that point onward, neither destroyer could get a sonar contact. Then, mysteriously, at forty-five minutes and fifty-four minutes after *MacKenzie*'s depth-charge attack, the ships heard and felt "heavy explosions." The destroyers remained in the area nearly three hours, searching in vain for evidence of a U-boat kill or an explanation for the explosions. Impatiently, the senior vessel, *Laub,* canceled the search at dawn, and the two ships rejoined the convoy and went on to Casablanca.

Allied ASW authorities were irate when they received reports of this encounter. "A sad pair of attacks," one assessor wrote. *MacKenzie* should have opened fire with her main batteries at four thousand yards. *Laub* should have reacted more quickly and joined the attack. Moreover, the destroyers should have remained at the scene for at least twelve hours, hunting the U-boat to exhaustion. This episode, wrote another assessor, "brings up forcibly the need for better [ASW] training." The conclusion of the highest assessor was: "No evidence of damage."

However, in the postwar analysis, Allied naval authorities concluded that *MacKenzie* had in fact sunk *U-182* with the two Allied POWs on board. How *MacKenzie* sank *U-182* is not known. Nor is there a satisfactory explanation of the two "heavy explosions" that occurred nearly an hour after *MacKenzie*'s attack. Possibly the depth charges weakened some of *U-182*'s twelve topside torpedo canisters, causing them to belatedly implode at great depth and flood, sinking the boat. Or perhaps Clausen fired two torpedoes at the *MacKenzie* that malfunctioned and circled back to hit and sink *U-182*. Whatever the case, nothing further was ever heard from *U-182*.*

On the whole, *Seehund*, the second foray to the Indian Ocean, was judged to be only a modest success. The five boats sank twenty confirmed ships for about 123,000 tons, about half the bag of *Seehund*'s predecessor, *Eisbär*. Lassen in *U-160* sank seven; Clausen in the IXD2 U-cruiser *U-182*, five; the ailing Wiebe in *U-516*, four; and Würdemann in *U-506* and Witte in *U-509*, two apiece. That was an average of about four ships per boat per patrol, but the patrols of these IXs averaged 136 days, nearly four and a half months.†

Like the boats patrolling to American waters, those of group *Seehund* were frustrated by intensified ASW measures, by convoying, and by information derived from Enigma decrypts that enabled naval authorities in the Cape Town and Durban areas to hold up shipping or to divert it around known U-boat positions. However, no U-boats had been lost in South Atlantic waters: *U-182* went down in the dangerous Madeira-Azores area in the Middle Atlantic.

Altogether, these IXs had sunk twelve ships for 71,000 tons in the month of March. A Japanese submarine, *I-27*, operating off India in March, sank one 7,100-ton British ship, *Fort Mumford*. That brought the Allied losses in March in this area to thirteen ships for 78,000 tons, contributing to the misimpression that U-boats nearly cut the lifeline between the Americas and the British Isles.

U-boat Control mounted a special mission in the Indian Ocean at this time. The task was to meet a Japanese submarine at sea for the purpose of exchanging personnel and cargo, including weaponry.

---

* Clausen was credited with sinking twenty-three confirmed ships for about 75,000 tons on *U-37*, *U-129*, and *U-182*. Ten of the ships displaced less than 2,000 tons. Had they been as large as claimed, he would have ranked high among all skippers.

† The big Italian submarine *Da Vinci*, with eight 21" torpedo tubes and two 4.1" deck guns, sailed independently to Cape Town on February 20, under command of Gianfranco Gazzana-Priaroggia. She sank six ships for 58,973 tons, including the 21,517-ton British troopship *Empress of Canada*, earning Gazzana-Priaroggia high Italian awards and a *Ritterkreuz*. On May 23, as she was entering the Bay of Biscay, *Da Vinci* was sunk by the British destroyer *Active* and the British frigate *Ness* with the loss of all hands.

The German boat chosen for this mission was a U-cruiser, the new IXD1 *U-180,* commanded by Werner Musenberg, age thirty-eight. The boat was a failed design. Powered by six Mercedes-Benz 1,500 horsepower, water-cooled diesels, adapted from the engines in German PT boats, the 1,600-ton *U-180* had a top speed of 20.8 knots, making her the fastest diesel U-boat built by the Germans in World War II. But the engines were not suitable for submarines. They smoked "like an old coal-burning tramp," as Musenberg put it, and generated nearly unbearable heat throughout the boat, particularly in tropical waters. Like the other U-cruisers, *U-180* had four bow and two stern torpedo tubes, could carry twenty-seven torpedoes (including twelve in topside canisters), and mounted a 4.1" gun on the forward deck. She had a crew of sixty-three men, including a physician.

On the eve of his departure from Kiel, Musenberg embarked a VIP and his aide, who were to be transferred to the Japanese submarine. The VIP was the leftist Indian political activist Subhas Chandra Bose, son of a knighted Indian scientist and president of the Indian National Congress party and, as such, a protégé of Mohandas Gandhi, who was then "interned" in India. Jailed in Britain in 1940 for his pro-Axis (i.e., outspoken anti-British) views, Bose had escaped and fled to Germany. His ambition was to create and lead an "army of liberation," cadred by Indian soldiers captured by the Japanese in Southeast Asia. Although Tokyo doubtless viewed this grandiose scheme with skepticism, some Japanese believed Bose might be useful for fomenting anti-British sentiment in India and had arranged to transfer him and his aide, Abid Hasan, from *U-180* and carry them onward to Singapore or to Japan.

Allied codebreakers who were decrypting Japanese diplomatic codes picked up Japanese messages from Berlin to Tokyo reporting the departure of Bose by U-boat from Kiel on February 9. This and other information from diplomatic traffic was passed to Kenneth Knowles and Rodger Winn in the American and British Submarine Tracking Rooms. They were able to identify the departing boat as "U-Musenberg" and tracked it as it made its way to meet the Japanese submarine in the Indian Ocean.

The Japanese submarine was the *I-29,* commanded by Juichi Izu. Like the *I-30* (code-named "Cherry Blossom"), which had briefly called at Lorient in August 1942,* the *I-29* was a large U-cruiser, 354 feet long, displacing 2,500 tons. It had a floatplane stored in a hangar on the deck immediately forward of the conning

* The huge *I-30,* commanded by Shinobu Endo, left Japan on April 4, 1942, patrolled in the Indian Ocean, replenished from an armed merchant cruiser, then reached Lorient on August 5, where she was greeted with great fanfare by Admiral Raeder and other high naval officers. In compliance with a prior request from Berlin, she delivered 3,300 pounds (1,500 kilograms) of mica and 1,452 pounds (660 kilograms) of shellac. She departed Lorient on August 22 with a valuable load of German naval equipment: a submarine torpedo fire-control system (or data computer), five G7a (air) and three G7e (electric) torpedoes, 240 rounds of the sonar deflector *Bolde,* a search radar, a Metox, a hydrophone array, fifty Enigma machines, and other gear. The *I-30* reached Singapore on the morning of October 13 and after only six and one-half hours, resailed to Japan. Outbound from Singapore, she hit a Japanese defensive mine and sank with the loss of fourteen of her 110 men. Later the Japanese salvaged some German gear from the wreck.

tower as well as a catapult. It was armed with six torpedo tubes with eleven reloads in the bow compartment and a 5.5" gun on the deck aft of the conning tower. A veteran of several Indian Ocean patrols, *I-29* had sunk six Allied ships.

Musenberg in *U-180* entered the Atlantic and sailed southward toward Cape Town. Inasmuch as the six engines consumed large amounts of fuel, it was necessary to replenish *U-180* from a U-tanker. Accordingly, Musenberg met the XIV *U-462* in the Middle Atlantic on March 3. Allied codebreakers saw that on March 20, Musenberg was to meet an Italian U-cruiser (probably *Da Vinci*) near the equator and provide unspecified medical assistance, but Musenberg could not find the Italian and the rendezvous was canceled. After rounding the Cape of Good Hope and sailing onward to the southeast, on April 18 Musenberg found and sank a loner, the 8,200-ton British tanker *Corbis.* Two days later, during a submerged attack on another loner, *U-180* broached and her victim escaped.

As planned, the *U-180* and *I-29* met on April 23 at a point in the Indian Ocean about 450 miles southeast of Madagascar. The weather that day was too rough to carry out the exchanges of men and matériel, Musenberg reported, so the two boats traveled in company for several days until the waters were calm. The transfers finally took place on April 27.

Apart from the two passengers, Bose and Hasan, the Germans passed cargo to *I-29.* It included a torpedo tube containing a gun barrel (of unspecified type) and ammunition; cases of documents and construction drawings for military weapons, aircraft, and submarines; and three cases containing 432 *Bolde* noisemakers.

The *I-29* in turn passed two men to *U-180,* plus an astounding quantity of cargo. The men were submarine commander Tetsusiro Emi and a submarine designer/engineer, Hideo Tomogaga. The cargo consisted of three 21" aerial torpedoes (Model No. 2); several cases of quinine; 1.3 tons of Japanese weaponry and drawings; over half a ton of mail, documents, and drawings from the German embassy in Tokyo; and two tons of gold ingots in 146 large cases. In all, the Japanese cargo transferred to *U-180* weighed eleven tons, and it took up every inch of spare space in the boat. With it, Musenberg logged testily, came cockroaches, beetles, and all kinds of "very small mites."

Authorized to attack loners only, Musenberg closed the coast of South Africa near East London. Two British aircraft approached *U-180.* The first was an unarmed twin-engine Avro Anson on a training flight, attracted by the smoke of *U-180*'s engines. Musenberg drove it off with flak. The second was a twin-engine Handley Page Hampden bomber, loaded for combat. It attacked *U-180,* Musenberg logged, but the Germans shot it down. Handicapped by smoking engines and defective engine-cooling systems, Musenberg soon gave up his antiship patrol and headed home. On the way he found and sank a second loner, the 5,200-ton Greek *Boris* on June 3. After refueling a second time (from the IXC 40 *U-530,* serving as a provisional U-tanker) west of the Canaries on June 19, Musenberg reached Bordeaux on July 3.

The meeting of *U-180* and *I-29* in the Indian Ocean was an Axis submarine "first" and therefore notable. The *I-29* delivered Bose and his aide to Singapore and returned to Japan. Of course, Bose was never able to raise a nationalist army.

He became a nuisance to the Japanese until he was killed in an airplane crash in 1945. Declared unfit for combat after this one patrol, the IXD1 *U-180* was decommissioned on September 30, 1943, for conversion to a cargo submarine powered by two conventional (i.e., 1,400 horsepower) diesels and capable of transporting 252 tons of goods. Musenberg went to other duty. Contrary to postwar rumors that *U-180* had sunk with the two tons of gold on board near Bordeaux, all the gold reached the Japanese Embassy in Berlin safely. It was used to pay for Japanese expenses in Germany and elsewhere in Europe.

FOUR

Shifting Tides

When Grand Admiral Karl Dönitz assumed the post of commander in chief of the *Kriegsmarine* in early 1943, Adolf Hitler was fixated on the titanic struggle to conquer the Soviet Union. That struggle was slowly shifting in favor of the Red Army. After the victory at Stalingrad, Soviet ground and air forces in that area launched a massive winter offensive on a five-hundred-mile front between Orel and Rostov. On February 8 they recaptured Kursk; on February 16, Kharkov and Rostov. The Germans in turn unleashed a massive counterattack on February 20. On March 15 they retook Kharkov and laid plans to inflict a decisive defeat on the Red Army, which was holding what appeared to be a vulnerable salient at Kursk. However, the massing of German matériel and forces for this huge attack (Citadel) required weeks, partly because of an early spring thaw, which again turned the primitive roads into quagmires.

The impending battle for Kursk was a last, great gamble for Hitler. If the Germans won the battle, he believed, it might be possible to destroy the Red Army in a series of follow-up hammer blows. If the Germans lost, the consequences would be disastrous: the despised Red Army again triumphant, the German Army in ruins, Hitler humiliated, perhaps even toppled or assassinated.

In preparing for this battle, Hitler and his generals failed to appreciate the unheralded but very real growth in the fighting power of the Red Army, which numbered about six million men and women. Working at frantic speed on three shifts in defense factories that had been moved eastward into or beyond the Ural Mountains, Soviet civilians were turning out astounding numbers of heavy T-34 tanks, self-propelled and towed artillery pieces, fighters and fighter-bombers, rifles, ammunition, and other armaments. (Soviet tank production was to peak at four thousand units per month.) Fully aware of the importance of holding Kursk and the salient, Stalin deployed prodigious quantities of these armaments into that area for use by hundreds of thousands of Red Army troops massing there.

Overcommitted in North Africa and elsewhere around the globe, the Allied navies were reluctant or unable to sustain the flow of armaments to the Red Army via Murmansk at this time. In January and February 1943, only two convoys sailed to Murmansk.

The shrinking German U-boat force in the Arctic/Norway area had a new commander, Rudolf Peters, who assumed that duty officially on January 18, 1943. Like his predecessor, Hubert Schmundt, he maintained his headquarters on the yacht *Grille,* based in Narvik. On the day he took over, the Arctic/Norway U-boat force consisted of twenty boats, including two in Germany undergoing refits or overhauls (*U-586, U-601*) and one transferring to the Atlantic force (*U-209*). Two others in Norway (*U-376, U-377*) were to transfer directly to the Atlantic force before the end of January, leaving a net Arctic/Norway force of seventeen U-boats on February 1.

The Arctic convoys that sailed, in brief:

• Convoy JW 52, composed of fourteen merchant ships, left Loch Ewe on January 17. One merchant ship aborted but the other thirteen reached Soviet ports safely. The escorts repelled feeble German aircraft and U-boat attacks. The return convoy, RA 52, composed of eleven merchant ships, which left on January 26, was found and attacked by the weakened Arctic U-boat force. Torpedoes from Hans Benker in *U-625* missed or malfunctioned, but Reinhard Reche in *U-255,* who had earlier sunk two small Russian freighters for 4,300 tons, hit and sank the 7,200-ton American Liberty ship *Greylock.* The other ten ships reached Loch Ewe safely.

• Convoy JW 53, composed of twenty-eight merchant ships left Loch Ewe on February 15. The very strong escort included the British "jeep" carrier *Dasher* and the cruiser *Sheffield.* Early in the voyage a powerful Arctic storm struck the convoy. It severely damaged *Dasher, Sheffield,* and six merchant ships, and forced them to abort.* Utilizing its radar, one of the distant cover ships, the battleship *King George V,* reassembled the convoy and the escorts, which repelled desultory German air and U-boat attacks and reached Soviet ports without losses to German forces.

The return convoy, RA 53, comprised of thirty merchant ships that left on March 1, was also found and attacked by German aircraft and U-boats. Reche in *U-255* sank two American ships: the 7,200-ton Liberty ship *Richard Bland* and the 5,000-ton *Executive.*† A fierce Arctic gale dispersed the convoy and broke the

---

* After she was repaired, *Dasher,* anchored in the Firth of Clyde, blew up on March 27 and sank with the loss of 378 men. The Admiralty blamed the accident on a faulty aviation-gasoline system and, to minimize accidents, insisted that other American-built "jeep" carriers for the Royal Navy be modified, triggering another Anglo-American naval controversy.

† For these and past victories and claims, Reche was awarded a *Ritterkreuz,* the second skipper in the Arctic force after Siegfried Strelow to be so honored. At the time of the award, Reche's score was ten confirmed ships sunk for 53,519 tons.

American *J.L.M. Curry* in half. Dietrich von der Esch in *U-586* sank a straggler, the 6,100-ton American freighter *Puerto Rican,* about three hundred miles north of Iceland. One of the sixty-two men on this ship, August Wallenhaupt, survived on a raft and was rescued by the British destroyer *Elistin,* but he lost both legs and most of seven fingers. Counting the disabled American *J. H. Latrobe,* which had to be towed, twenty-six of the thirty merchant ships in RA 53 reached British ports.

Owing to the coming of some daylight hours in the Arctic in March, and the unforeseen demands of Torch and the forthcoming invasion of Sicily (Husky), the British were reluctant to sail any more convoys to Murmansk. When the Admiralty discovered from Enigma intercepts in early March that the battleship *Tirpitz,* the battle cruiser *Scharnhorst,* and the "pocket" battleship *Lützow* had moved forward to Narvik, then to Altenfiord to attack Murmansk convoys (per Dönitz's plan), Churchill informed Stalin that Murmansk convoys had to be canceled. For the time being, Allied military supplies for the Soviet Union had to go the longer route via the Persian Gulf and Iran or via the Sea of Japan to Vladivostok.

Admiral Dönitz met with the Führer four times in February and March 1943. On each occasion, Hitler and Dönitz discussed the U-boat war in detail. In February, Dönitz explained that the campaign on the decisive North Atlantic run was *not* succeeding for numerous reasons. Among the most important were:

• The Allies appeared to know the location of the U-boat groups and routed the convoys around them. At first Dönitz and U-boat Control again suspected that the Allies had broken naval Enigma and had demanded that the chief of *Kriegsmarine* communications security, Erhard Maertens, conduct another investigation. When Maertens had again assured Dönitz that Enigma was not compromised, Dönitz concluded—and U-boat Control concurred—that, as Dönitz told Hitler, the Allies must have some new long-range radar or other electronic-location device in patrol aircraft that pinpointed the U-boat groups.

Dönitz thus remained ignorant of the two most important Allied U-boat location tools in the war: penetration of four-rotor naval Enigma and shore-base and shipboard high-frequency direction finding, Huff Duff.

• In spite of long-standing and repeated requests from Dönitz, the *Luftwaffe* had not yet provided the Atlantic U-boat force with adequate support. That force urgently required very-long-range aircraft to locate the evading convoys and to shoot down the radar-equipped long- and very-long-range Allied aircraft that apparently were pinpointing the U-boat groups. It also urgently required many aircraft, such as JU-88s, to base in western France to repel Coastal Command aircraft carrying out the intensified ASW patrols in the Bay of Biscay.

Hitler expressed doubt that very-long-range aircraft could be produced in time to be of help to the U-boat force, but he promised to find out if three big Blohm & Voss BV-222 flying boats* were available for convoy locating. Also, despite the ur-

---

* Conceived in prewar years as passenger planes, they were then under consideration for bombing the United States by refueling from U-boats.

gent needs on the Eastern Front, he promised to base more JU-88s in western France, and did.

• There were still not enough U-boats. To find and sink Allied convoys, Dönitz asserted that he needed an increase in U-boat production to twenty-seven attack boats (VIIs and IXs) per month for the second half of 1943 and for all of 1944 and 1945. This would amount to an awesome 810 U-boats to be built in thirty months, requiring about forty thousand submariners to arm and man them and an appropriate number of new looping and homing torpedoes.

Hitler readily approved this grandiose plan and again assured Dönitz that sufficient steel and other scarce metals (e.g., copper) would be made available to meet the increased goals. He also promised he would again issue a directive prohibiting the mindless drafting of shipwrights into the army, in order to ensure that the existing labor shortages in the U-boat yards and subsidiary factories (twenty-seven thousand men) could be filled and the new labor needed for the increase in U-boat production (fourteen thousand men) could be met. Albert Speer, who admired Dönitz, promised to do everything possible to meet these new production goals.

• In view of the drastic curtailment of the Allied Murmansk convoys and the Baltic ice and Arctic darkness, Dönitz persuaded Hitler to allow a delay in the replacement of the half dozen Arctic/Norway VIIs that had transferred to the Atlantic force from December 1942 to February 1943.* Hitler agreed that the replacement boats need not report until April, when the Baltic thawed and daylight returned to the Arctic. As a consequence, on March 1, 1943, the Arctic/Norway force at sea on war patrols fell to merely four boats.

During these four meetings, Hitler and Dönitz discussed several matters regarding submarines in the Italian and Japanese navies.

First, Dönitz proposed that, in view of the losses suffered by the German surface-ship blockade-runners, the ten big Italian submarines operating in the Atlantic (to small purpose) be converted to cargo submarines. They could meet Axis surface-ship blockade-runners in the western Indian Ocean and take aboard rubber, tin, wolfram, quinine, and so on, and carry it north in mid-Atlantic to Bordeaux more safely than surface ships.

For reasons not clear, Hitler at first objected to this proposal. But after Dönitz flew to Rome to confer with the dictator Benito Mussolini and with his naval counterpart, Commander in Chief Arturo Riccardi,† and returned to Berlin with Italian approval, Hitler also approved. The Italians agreed to convert nine of the ten Bordeaux-based submarines, sparing the only surviving 1,700-ton Italian

---

* See Appendix 6.

† Riccardi had replaced Domenico Cavagnari on December 11, 1940, and remained in that post until Italy capitulated. His formal jaw-breaking title was *Capo di Stato Maggiore della Marina e Sottosegretario di Stato alla Marina.*

U-cruiser, *Cagni.** In return, Dönitz agreed to give the Italians ten Type VIIs and train the Italian crews in the Baltic.†

The Italian cargo submarines, Dönitz stated, could in time be replaced by a fleet of German cargo submarines, to operate over the complete route between France and the Far East. As a result of an earlier demand by Hitler for a fleet of U-boats to be used in a scheme to capture—and hold—Iceland as a German air base to attack Allied convoys, the design for a German cargo U-boat was already in hand. Designated Type XX, the "U-cargo" was to be a 253-foot vessel, displacing 2,700 tons, and capable of cruising thirteen thousand miles at 12 knots with a cargo of about eight hundred tons. On March 15, Hitler approved the building of thirty such U-boats (*U-1601* to *U-1615* and *U-1701* to *U-1715*), the first to be delivered in August 1944, and three per month thereafter, raising the approved U-boat construction plan to thirty boats per month.‡ In the interim, four Type VIICs (*U-1059* to *U-1062,* designated Type VIIF) that had been converted to torpedo-supply boats by the addition of a thirty-three-foot storage compartment and were to be commissioned within several months could be used on the Far East cargo run.

The nine Italian boats§ designated as cargo carriers fared poorly. As related, two U.S. Navy Catalinas of Squadron VP 83 sank *Archimede* 350 miles east of Natal, Brazil, on April 15. As also related, Allied forces sank *Da Vinci* on May 23, inbound from her maiden patrol to Cape Town. *Cappellini,* commanded by Walter Auconi, which sailed on May 11, was the first to reach the Far East. She carried 150 tons of "precious" German war matériel, documents, and so on, for the Japanese. *Tazzoli, Giuliani, Torelli,* and *Barbarigo* sailed between May 16 and June 15. The Allies sank *Tazzoli* and *Barbarigo,* but *Giuliani* and *Torelli* reached the Far East with German cargoes for the Japanese.

After the Italian submarine situation had been resolved, Hitler revealed that the Imperial Japanese Navy had requested the gift of two U-boats through its naval attaché in Berlin, Admiral Kichisaburo Nomura (the phony "peace negotiator" in Washington when the Japanese bombed Pearl Harbor). Ostensibly the Japanese were to copy and mass-produce these U-boats for use in the Pacific against American naval forces. Dönitz objected to the gift on the grounds that the Japanese were incapable of mass-producing German-designed U-boats in time to influence the war. However, Hitler insisted that Dönitz turn over at least one boat as a gesture of friendship and compensation for the enormous quantities of tin, rubber, and other raw materials the Japanese had generously provided the German blockade-runners.

---

* Four 1,700-ton Italian "U-cruisers" were built and named for Italian admirals: *Cagni, Caracciolo, Millo,* and *Saint Bon.* They were armed with eight torpedo tubes forward and six aft and carried a normal load of thirty-six 18" torpedoes. All but *Cagni* were sunk by Allied forces in the Mediterranean in 1941 and 1942 while on cargo runs between Italy and North Africa.

† The ten VIICs designated for transfer to the Italians were *U-428* to *U-430, U-746* to *U-750,* and *U-1161* and *U-1162,* all to be commissioned in the summer of 1943 and named *S-1* to *S-10.* Owing to the collapse of Italy, none was ever transferred to Italy; all became German school boats.

‡ The Type XX was never built.

§ *Archimede, Da Vinci, Tazzoli, Giuliani, Cappellini, Torelli, Barbarigo, Bagnolini,* and *Finzi.*

The U-boat chosen for transfer to Japan was the IXC *U-511,* commanded by Fritz Schneewind and redesignated "Marco Polo I." Schneewind sailed in *U-511* on May 10 with cargo and six passengers, including Admiral Nomura. After refueling from the XIV tanker *U-460,* the boat reached the island of Penang, Malaysia, on July 17. There Nomura left the boat and flew on to Japan. Schneewind took aboard a Japanese officer to serve as pilot and communicator and reached Japan on September 16.* Subsequently Schneewind and his crew returned by surface ship to Penang, where the Germans were in the process of establishing a U-boat base to accommodate Italian cargo and German attack and cargo submarines.

The Atlantic Convoy Conference: March 1–12, 1943

For a variety of expressed and unexpressed motives, the Allies convened in Washington on March 1 what would prove to be a historic meeting that came to be known as "the Atlantic Convoy Conference." Some of the motives were:

- The British wished to raise anew the issue of a single ASW command structure for the entire Atlantic, to be controlled by Max Horton at Western Approaches in Liverpool. The British also wished to have Washington navalists reaffirm Roosevelt's promise of a minimum of twenty-seven million tons of imports to the British Isles in 1943, the Lend-Lease gift to the British of "15 to 20" new cargo ships per month for ten months (150 to 200 vessels), as well as a buildup of British oil stocks, depleted by Torch. To press the importance and urgency of these issues, Churchill sent the Secretary of State for Foreign Affairs, Anthony Eden, to confer directly with President Roosevelt.
- The Canadians, long treated dismissively by both London and Washington, but who then bore about half of the large burden of cargo convoy escort on the North Atlantic run, wished to close down the U.S. Navy convoy-escort command structures at Argentia, Newfoundland, Task Force 24, and to establish an all-Canadian "Northwest Atlantic" command in its place. They also wanted the return of the three MOEF escort groups (C-l, C-2, C-4) that had been withdrawn to the British Isles for training and the fourteen surviving corvettes assigned to Torch.†
- The Americans, who bore sole responsibility for the escort of the transatlantic fast and slow UG-GU convoys, as well as the CU-UC and OT-TO tanker convoys and the huge "Interlocking Convoy System" in the Western Hemisphere, wanted to withdraw from convoy-escort responsibilities on the North Atlantic run provided they were satisfied that the Canadians and British could do the job.

---

* The Japanese renamed the boat *RO-500.*

† After two weeks of intense training at Tobermory, the three Canadian MOEF escort groups got actual combat operational training by joining the British escort groups (37, 38, 39, 40) guarding Torch convoys between the British Isles and the Mediterranean (KMF, KMS, MKF, MKS). The original sixteen Canadian corvettes assigned to Torch duties were formed into three Canadian escort groups (CEG 25, 26, and 27) and also joined British escorts protecting Torch convoys. Axis forces sank two of the sixteen Canadian corvettes, *Louisburg* and *Weyburn.* Another, *Lunenburg,* remained in the British Isles until August for overhaul and upgrading.

• Unanimous in the belief that an increase in the number of B-24 Liberators in very-long-range (VLR) configurations was necessary to protect Atlantic convoys and kill U-boats, London, Washington, and Ottawa were nonetheless still at sixes and sevens over the allocation of these aircraft between strategic bombing and ASW and between the various branches of the armed forces of the three nations. Since all hands wished to have a larger and larger share of these aircraft, it was necessary to formulate a systematic division of them among nations and air forces and theaters of war.

• After years in development, construction, and workup, American and British "jeep" carrier hunter-killer groups (support groups), as well as the destroyer escorts (or frigates), were finally ready for ASW duty in the Atlantic. Like the B-24 bombers, these ASW assets had to be allocated among the three nations for use in specific operating areas and on convoy routes in the Atlantic.

Throughout the Atlantic Convoy Conference, those in attendance labored under two grim intelligence assumptions that, however, proved to be utterly wrong: that the U-boat force was to increase in size dramatically in 1943, and that Allied codebreakers would again lose four-rotor Enigma for at least several months.

As to the first assumption, on March 1, 1943, senior Allied intelligence officers projected that by the end of the year, December 31, 1943, the Germans would have in commission a force of 613 U-boats. This figure was arrived at by assuming that the Germans would commission 320 new U-boats in 1943 (26.6 per month), and that the Allies would sink 124 U-boats during the year (10.3 per month). When the projected net gain of 196 U-boats (320 new, less 124 sunk) was added to the 417 U-boats assumed to be in commission on January 1, 1943, the result was 613 U-boats.

Owing to an unanticipated great increase in Allied U-boat kills in 1943, these figures were to be well off the mark. According to records at U-boat Control, on December 31, 1943, the U-boat force had not 613 but only 436 boats in commission, a gain of but nineteen boats in 1943. These included eighty-seven school boats, 181 boats in Baltic workup and R&D ("on trials, training and experiments"), but only 168 boats "on active service" at all battlefronts. The latter figure included thirty-two VIIs in the Mediterranean and Arctic, 130 VIIs and IXs in the Atlantic force, and six ducks in the Black Sea.

The Atlantic U-boat force did not grow in the summer of 1943; rather, it shrank. The proximate force levels :

	5/1	*6/1*	*7/1*	*8/1*	*9/1*
Type VII	134	119	112	98	93
Type IX	52	46	45	33	30
Total	186*	165	157	131	123†

* Not counting XB minelayers, XIV U-tankers, and IXD 1 and IXD 2 U-cruisers, but counting all VIIs and IXs in France undergoing battle-damage repairs, modification, or refits, however extensive.

† Note well that, in the crucial year, September 1, 1942, to September 1, 1943, the Atlantic force shrank from 124 U-Boats to 123. Compare Plate 1.

As to the second grim assumption, the loss of four-rotor naval Enigma, it was British codebreakers who made this forecast. They had learned from Enigma decrypts that on March 10 the Germans were to introduce a new short-signal codebook for weather reports, superseding that recovered from *U-559* the previous October. Since the weather codebook was an indispensable part of the crib-finding process for the British bombe programmers, Bletchley Park "feared that the consequences would be fatal," as the official British intelligence historian put it.

During the convoy conference, on March 9, the Admiralty's Assistant Chief of Staff for Trade, John H. Edelsten, memoed First Sea Lord Pound: "The foreseen has come to pass. DNI [Director of Naval Intelligence] reported on March 8 that the Tracking Room will be 'blinded' in regard to U-boat movements, for some considerable period, perhaps extending to months." Pound relayed this bad news to the Vice Chief of Naval Staff, Henry R. Moore, who was in Washington for the Atlantic Convoy Conference, in these words: "U-boat Special Intelligence has received a severe setback. After 10th March it is unlikely that we shall obtain [break] more than 2 to 3 pairs of days per month and these will not be current." Pound added a hopeful postscript: "After 2 to 3 months the situation should improve considerably."

However, the Allies lost four-rotor Enigma for only about ten days. In one of the great intelligence feats of the war, British codebreakers at Bletchley Park, who had sixty three-rotor bombes on line, broke back into four-rotor Enigma on March 19. The official intelligence historian wrote that in the 112 days from March 10 to June 30, the British read four-rotor Enigma for 90 days, or 80 percent of the time.

The senior conferees of the Atlantic Convoy Conference included Admiral King (Chair); his chief of Staff, Richard S. Edwards; British Admiral Percy Noble, fresh from command of Western Approaches, then serving as senior British naval officer in Washington; the aforementioned Vice Chief of the British Naval Staff, Henry R. Moore; and the senior Canadian officer in Washington, Rear Admiral V. G. Brodeur.

King opened the conference with brief remarks, then turned the chair over to Edwards. In his remarks, King said that he still believed that convoying was not only the best way to protect Allied shipping but the *only* way. "A ship saved," he emphasized, "is worth two built." The "safe and timely arrival" of convoys should continue to be the guiding strategic principle; hunter-killer operations, secondary.

King also expressed grave concern over the dangerously increasing congestion in New York harbor. From September 1942, when the North Atlantic convoys shifted to New York for departures and arrivals, to February 1, 1943, there had been 123 collisions of oceangoing vessels (involving 246 ships) in the harbor. Of greatest importance, King stressed, the old battleship *Arkansas* had nearly been rammed twice while at anchor.*

---

* In the month of February 1943, there were another thirty-one collisions (involving sixty-two ships) in New York harbor, including the U.S. Navy fleet destroyers *Cowie* and *Tillman*. In the early dark hours of April 1, convoys Halifax 232 and UGS 7 departed three hours apart in heavy fog and became intermingled. Six collisions occurred; fourteen other ships did not sail or aborted, reducing Halifax 232 by sixteen ships and UGS 7 by ten ships, serious setbacks.

The conferees reached a number of important decisions that were promptly ratified by the three governments. Among the most important:

The North Atlantic Run

The British and Canadians were to assume full—and sole—responsibility for the escort of cargo convoys on the North Atlantic run. The American command, Task Force 24 in Argentia, would withdraw as would the last American escort group, A-3, and the American "shuttle" based in Iceland.* Ships bound to and from Iceland were to sail between the Americas and British Isles in North Atlantic convoys, thence to and from Iceland in the existing convoys, UR-RU (United Kingdom to Reykjavik and reverse), escorted by British-controlled warships.

The Halifax and Slow and Outbound North convoys on the North Atlantic run would continue generally as before but with several modifications. As Admiral King had suggested, to relieve the congestion in New York, Slow Convoys (SC) and Outbound North (Slow) convoys (ONS) would originate and terminate in Halifax, Nova Scotia, commencing on March 31.† As earlier, ships for Halifax would travel to and from that port in the existing convoys HB-BX (Halifax-Boston and reverse) escorted by Canadian warships and by U.S. and Canadian aircraft. Ships would travel to and from Boston in the U.S. interlocking convoy system.

The Mid-Ocean Escort Force (MOEF), to be controlled by the Admiralty, was to consist of fourteen escort groups of six ships each (eighty-four warships), seven groups to be provided by the Canadians and seven groups to be provided by the British. To accommodate Canadian needs, the three Canadian MOEF escort groups that had been withdrawn for training in the British Isles and the fourteen surviving Canadian corvettes assigned to three Torch escort groups were to be returned to Canada.

Upon the withdrawal of the American Task Force 24, the Canadians would assume operational control of the western portion of the North Atlantic run and XB-BX convoys. Designated Canadian Northwest Atlantic Command, the area comprised all waters west of a line at 47 degrees west longitude and south to 42 degrees north latitude (Boston). A Canadian Western Escort Force comprised of eleven groups (increased from the existing eight) would guard the convoys in this area. To man these groups, in addition to the return of Torch and other corvettes, the Canadians would retain the eleven British destroyers on loan in Canadian waters.‡

---

* The Iceland shuttle consisted of eight American warships: four destroyers, three Coast Guard cutters, and one minesweeper. Coast Guard cutters would continue to man the Greenland Patrol and escort supply ships from Canada to American bases in Greenland.

† In the period September 19, 1942, to March 20, 1943, twenty Slow Convoys, comprised of 1,184 merchant ships, sailed from New York.

‡ The old *Witherington* and ten old ex-American *Town*-class. These destroyers were in "relatively poor shape," Task Force 24 reported to Atlantic Fleet commander Royal Ingersoll. Two were in extended overhaul; four in refit but to be available between March 2–22; one scheduled for refit beginning March 10; and only four in operation, one of which (*Leamington*) was unsuitable for open-ocean sailing due to her very limited endurance. In addition, the Canadians still had seven old ex-American *Town*-class destroyers that they had received directly from the U.S. Navy. (See Volume I, appendices 9 and 10.)

The Slow Convoys were to sail from Halifax every eight days, commencing with convoy SC 125 on March 31. The HB-BX convoys were to sail from Halifax to Boston every four days, commencing with XB 38 on or about March 23, after Outbound North (Slow) 171 arrived in Halifax. Thereafter, Outbound North (Slow) convoys to Halifax were to be renumbered from 1, to distinguish them from the (fast) Outbound North (ON) convoys to and from New York.

To meet the urgent British demands for an increase in imports, which President Roosevelt had promised, the sailings of the fast HX convoys from New York and the reverse, ON, from the British Isles were stepped up and the size of the convoys was increased in most instances to about sixty merchant ships plus eastbound Landing Ships, Tank (LSTs). Admiral King stoutly resisted a British proposal to increase the size of convoys on that route to eighty ships. That was too many merchant ships for one escort group (of six ships) to properly guard, he asserted. He warned that the external and internal repercussions over "heavy American ship losses in excessively large and inadequately protected convoys" would be strident and difficult.

The stepped-up pace of convoy sailings on the fast HX-ON route was to take place as follows. Commencing with HX 230 on March 18, the next two convoys were to sail every seven days. Convoy HX 233 was to sail five days after HX 232. Convoys HX 234 to HX 236 were to sail every six days. Convoy HX 237, sailing on April 30, and all succeeding HX convoys were to sail every five days. In addition, in March a "special" (or extra) convoy, HX 229A, was to sail. Commencing with ON 173, fast westbound convoys were to sail on a similar schedule, until reaching a five-day interval after ON 178, which was to sail on April 12.

The British were to continue sole responsibility for the convoy routes between the British Isles and the Mediterranean (KM-MK), Sierra Leone and other West African ports (Outbound South or OS and the reverse, SL), and for the Winston Special (WS) military convoys. To maximize the use of British escorts on these routes, the Admiralty was to combine KMS and OS convoys on a twenty-day cycle, and KMF and WS on a thirty-day cycle. To further economize on local escort deployment at Gibraltar, every effort was to be made to synchronize the sailings of UGF and KMF convoys as well as UGS and KMS convoys. When sufficient escorts became available, the British were to resume the sailing of medium and small shallow-draft vessels in Outbound Gibraltar (OG) and Homebound Gibraltar (HG) convoys.

The British were also to continue sole responsibility for the JW-RA convoy routes to and from northern Russia (Murmansk, Archangel). These were to be comprised mostly of American cargo ships, such as the Liberty ships, but there were to be no American warships in the escort. Consisting of a maximum of thirty cargo ships, these convoys were to sail on a forty-two-day cycle.

The British and Canadians were to provide five hunter-killer groups (support groups) to reinforce threatened convoys on the North Atlantic run. These were to consist of three to five destroyers, sloops, or frigates, and, as they became available, the British "jeep" carriers *Archer, Avenger, Biter,* and *Tracker,* one carrier per group. The first of the American hunter-killer groups scheduled to become combat ready, consisting of the "jeep" carrier *Bogue* and five destroyers, was to be loaned to the British-Canadian North Atlantic run. British merchant aircraft carriers (MAC ships with three or four Swordfish airplanes but no catapult) were to sail in each of the slower convoys (SC, ONS), commencing in May, when the weather was more favorable for aircraft operations.

The Middle Atlantic Runs

The Americans were to assume full—and sole—responsibility for the escort of convoys on the three routes in the Middle Atlantic: UG-GU, OT-TO, and CU-UC. Since these convoys sailed at much greater intervals than those on the North Atlantic run, fewer escort groups were required to guard them. These groups were made up of the five Atlantic-based *Treasury*-class Coast Guard cutters, new and old destroyers, and when they were to be available, destroyer escorts.

The UG-GU convoys between New York and Gibraltar sailed on fast (fifteen-knot) and slow schedules, like the convoys on the North Atlantic run. Fast convoys (UGF, GUF), which were comprised of troopships as well as cargo ships, sailed every twenty-five days. The slow convoys (UGS, GUS) then sailing every twenty-five days, were to sail every fifteen days commencing in May.

The fast (14.5 knots) OT-TO tanker convoys sailed between Aruba in the Caribbean and Gibraltar every twenty-eight days. Upon returning in ballast to the Caribbean, the tankers were to reload with oil and sail without escort to New York, deposit that load of oil in the "New York Oil Pool," then return to the Caribbean to reload for Gibraltar. Slower tankers on the North Atlantic run were to transship the oil in the New York pool to the British Isles. Meanwhile, the transatlantic escort groups (six destroyers per group) were to put into the U.S. Navy base at Guantánamo, Cuba, for refits, upgrades, and crew training.

The fast (14.5 knots) CU-UC convoys, delivering oil directly from the Caribbean to the British Isles, sailed from the Caribbean every fifty-four days. The round-trip cycle consisted of a fifteen-day voyage to the British Isles, a six-day layover there, a fifteen-day return voyage to the Caribbean, and an eighteen-day layover. During the layover in the Americas, the tankers also were to make an unescorted round-trip to New York to deliver a shipload to the New York pool while the transatlantic escort groups refitted at Guantánamo.

The Middle Atlantic convoy routes were to be reinforced by five hunter-killer groups (support groups). Each of these was to consist of four or five destroyers and American "jeep" carriers as they became combat ready. These were the *Block Island, Card, Core, Croatan,* and *Santee.* As more British "jeep" carriers became available, the *Bogue* support group on loan to the British-Canadian North Atlantic run was to be shifted to the American Middle Atlantic runs.

The Atlantic Convoy Conference reached these decisions during early March when ship losses in the North Atlantic convoys were much heavier than usual. Appropriate concern was expressed over these heavy losses, but it is noteworthy that nothing was said remotely comparable to the fear expressed at the Admiralty about how the Allies faced the "crisis of crises" or that, owing to U-boat attacks, convoys might no longer be a viable means of protecting merchant shipping.

PLATE 5

NORTH AND MIDDLE ATLANTIC CONVOY ROUTES REAFFIRMED AT THE ATLANTIC CONVOY CONFERENCE

MARCH 1 TO MARCH 12, 1943

- HX, SC, ON, and ONS convoys from New York and Halifax to the British Isles and return. A maximum of sixty ships per convoy; to be protected by fourteen British and Canadian MOEF escort groups and five support groups, plus one American "jeep" carrier hunter-killer group (*Bogue*) on loan. Canadians to provide local escort from a line at 47 degrees west longitude. To relieve congestion in New York harbor, from June 17 on Slow Convoys departed from Halifax, Nova Scotia.
- HB-BX convoys between Halifax and Boston. Canadian escort.
- UGF, UGS, GUF, and GUS convoys from New York and Norfolk to Gibraltar and return. (From June 1943, the UGF convoys were suspended for one year, to July 1, 1944. To further relieve congestion in New York harbor, from November 1943 UGS convoys sailed from Norfolk.) American escorts to include remaining five big Coast Guard cutters, destroyers (later, also destroyer escorts), and five (later six) "jeep" carriers.
- Interlocking convoy system, U.S. East Coast, Gulf of Mexico, Caribbean Sea, and southwest Atlantic. American and Brazilian escort.
- CU-UC fast (14.5 knots) tanker convoys from the Caribbean to the British Isles and return and to New York pool and return. From November 1943, CU sailed from New York and in 1944, many were combined with 14.5-knot UT troop convoys sailing from New York to the British Isles or France. American escort.
- OT-TO tanker convoys from the Caribbean to Gibraltar and return and to New York pool and return. American escort.
- KMF, KMS, MFK, and MKS convoys between the British Isles and the Mediterranean. KMF to combine with WS military convoys. British escort.
- OS and SL slow convoys to and from the British Isles and Sierra Leone and other West African ports and/or beyond. OS to combine with KMS. British escort.
- UR and RU convoys between the British Isles and Iceland and return. British escort.
- JW-RA convoys between the British Isles or Iceland and northern Russia and return. British escort.

Long- and Very-Long-Range ASW Aircraft

By March 1, 1943, when the Atlantic Convoy Conference convened, the Allies had in place a powerful and growing force of long- and very-long-range ASW aircraft in the North Atlantic. It was far more impressive than is depicted in most accounts of the Battle of the Atlantic.*

In the first half of 1943, there were no U-boats operating in waters of the Eastern Sea Frontier.† Ably commanded by Admiral Adolphus Andrews, that battlefront encompassed the entire United States East Coast from Maine to Florida. All merchant shipping in that area sailed in convoys guarded by escort groups drawn from a fleet of about two hundred warships.

Since there were no U-boats along the East Coast and the convoys sailed close

* See Appendix 11.

† See Appendix 5.

to shore, there was very little need for long-range ASW aircraft. However, Andrews maintained continuous air patrols to protect these unthreatened convoys. On February 25, 1943, he reported, he exercised operational control over 328 aircraft of which 192 were Navy and Coast Guard and 136 were Army Air Forces. The Navy and Coast Guard aircraft included ten Catalinas of Patrol Squadron VP 31 (deployed at Rhode Island, North Carolina, and Florida), six PBM-3C Mariners (at Norfolk), and eighteen blimps. The rest were short-range single-engine floatplanes, such as the Navy's OS2U Kingfisher. The Army Air Forces planes included twenty-five B-18s (of Squadrons 4, 7, 12), twelve B-17 Flying Fortresses (of Squadron 20), thirty-eight B-25 long-range Mitchells (of Squadrons 3, 5, 6, 13, 14), and forty-four B-34 Lexingtons, the Army's version of the Navy's Ventura (of Squadrons 7, 11, 15, 16).

In Canadian waters, north of the Eastern Sea Frontier where U-boats still operated, the Royal Canadian Air Force (RCAF), like the Royal Canadian Navy (RCN), was growing slowly and steadily gaining in effectiveness.

The RCAF deployed nine ASW squadrons at the battlefront. Four (5, 116, 117, 162) were equipped with Catalinas/Cansos, one (10) with Digbys (USAAF B-18s), and four with Hudsons (11, 113, 119, 145). In addition, scores of Ansons in the Training Command flew practice missions over the Gulf of St. Lawrence, adding to the air coverage.

The United States contribution of ASW aircraft in the Maritime Provinces remained substantial. One reason was that duty there was like a postgraduate course in ASW. U.S. Army and Navy aircraft crews could gain actual battle experience without fear of reprisal from Axis aircraft.

The American units continued to rotate. As related, U.S. Navy Catalina Patrol Squadron VP 84 moved east to Iceland in the fall of 1942. Catalina Patrol Squadrons VP 82 and VP 93 returned to the United States to be reequipped with a different aircraft, the Lockheed Ventura, of which more later. These departing squadrons were in part temporarily replaced by six Catalinas of Squadrons VP 31 and VP 52 from the States. As will be described, the Army Air Forces B-17 ASW Squadron 20 at Gander, Newfoundland, returned to the States, replaced by other Army and Navy aviation units.

Clockwise around the North Atlantic, next came the vital Allied ASW aircraft bases in Iceland. By March 1943, the whole of Terence Bulloch's pioneering RAF Squadron 120, comprised of a dozen to fifteen B-24 Liberators, had deployed there. These stripped-down, very-long-range aircraft reinforced threatened convoys in the Greenland "Air Gap." The dozen Catalinas of U.S. Navy Patrol Squadron VP 84 provided escort for threatened convoys east of the "Air Gap," as did the Catalinas of RAF Squadron 330, manned by Norwegian crews.

Continuing farther east across the North Atlantic, RAF Coastal Command deployed ninety-six long- and very-long-range aircraft at bases in Scotland and Northern Ireland. These were all four-engine planes: a dozen very-long-range B-24 Liberators (Squadron 86), two dozen B-17 Flying Fortresses (Squadrons 206 and 220), and sixty Sunderlands (British Squadrons 201, 228, and 246, and Canadian Squadrons 422 and 423). These planes provided escort for convoys to the northwest, west, and southwest of the British Isles.

In southern England, RAF Coastal Command deployed about seventy-two other four-engine aircraft, most of which conducted patrols in the Bay of Biscay or southward toward Portugal. These were a dozen B-24 Liberators (Squadron 224), two dozen Halifaxes (Squadrons 58 and 502), and three dozen Sunderlands (British Squadron 119, Australian Air Force Squadrons 10 and 461). As related, the twenty-four B-24 Liberators of U.S. Army Air Forces ASW Squadrons 1 and 2 redeployed from southwest England to Morocco in March 1943. (Otherwise the total in southern England would have been ninety-six four-engine aircraft.)

Also in southern England were three squadrons of the twin-engine workhorse Wellingtons, comprising thirty-six aircraft. Many of these planes had been fitted with Leigh Lights, the powerful searchlight that was utilized in the final mile of a low-level night attack on a U-boat. One of the squadrons (RAF 304) was manned by Poles, another (RAF 311) by Czechs, the third (RAF 172) by British crews.

Finally, at Gibraltar and Port Lyautey, Morocco, there were seventy-two long-range aircraft. These were the twenty-four B-24s of the U.S. Army Air Forces's 480th Group (ASW Squadrons 1 and 2), thirty-six Catalinas (British Squadron 202 at Gibraltar, USN Squadrons VP 73 and VP 92 at Port Lyautey), and twelve Wellingtons (British Squadron 179 at Gibraltar). These aircraft provided protection for the UG-GU convoys to the westward as well as convoys going to and from West African ports.

This formidable Allied ASW force in the North Atlantic comprised fifty-seven squadrons of 684 aircraft, not counting Hudsons, Whitleys, and other low-performance aircraft in frontline units. Yet many problems remained. Four different agencies controlled these planes: RAF Coastal Command, the Royal Canadian Air Force, the U.S. Navy, and the U.S. Army Air Forces. Coordination and cooperation between these agencies left much to be desired. The U.S. Navy and U.S. Army ASW air forces were still at sixes and sevens over doctrine and command, studiously and determinedly avoiding a Navy-controlled operational merger somewhat similar to that of RAF Coastal Command. The British and Americans continued to deny the Canadians a fair share of modern ASW aircraft and ASV radar and other electronics.

By far the most efficient U-boat killers were the B-24 Liberators. By March 1943, the Allies had deployed five squadrons of these killers, comprising sixty-odd planes:

RAF	120	in Iceland
RAF	86	in Northern Ireland
RAF	224	in southern England
USAAF	1	in Morocco
USAAF	2	in Morocco

Eleven other Allied B-24 squadrons, comprising 132-plus aircraft, were fitting out or working up for ASW duty in the Atlantic. Five were U.S. Navy (Bombing Squadrons VB 103, VB 105, VB 110, VB 111, VB 112), four were U.S. Army Air Forces (4, 6, 19, 22), one was British (59), and one was Canadian (10).

The conferees at the Atlantic Convoy Conference naturally wished to rush into combat these eleven B-24 squadrons that were fitting out or working up. In particular, they believed the most urgent task was to do everything possible to close the Greenland "Air Gap." However, the B-24s were complicated aircraft and all required substantial modification for ASW. Therefore the eleven squadrons designated to receive B-24s for ASW in the North Atlantic in 1943 deployed only slowly:

RAF	59	to Northern Ireland 5/43
USAAF	4	to southern England 7/43
USAAF	19	to southern England 7/43
RCAF	10	at Newfoundland 7/43*
USN	VB 103	to southern England 8/43
USN	VB 105	to southern England 9/43
USN	VB 110	to southern England 9/43
USAAF	6	to southern England 9/43
USAAF	22	to southern England 9/43
USN	VB 111	to Morocco 11/43
USN	VB 112	to Morocco 11/43

When all of these squadrons had been deployed, there were two hundred B-24s on ASW duty in the North Atlantic, 132 of them (66 percent) manned by U.S. Army or Navy crews.

The U.S. Navy had intended to substantially reinforce its North Atlantic ASW squadrons in 1943 with two new aircraft types. However, one type was a technological failure; the other, like the B-24, entered service all too slowly. These were:

- The PBM-3 Mariner twin-engine, gull-wing flying boat, in production by the Glenn L. Martin Company. This plane was conceived as a sort of upgraded Catalina. On paper it had much more powerful engines (2,100 h.p. versus 1,200 h.p.), twice the fuel capacity (3,488 versus 1,705 gallons), twice the combat radius (1,200 versus 600 nautical miles), and over three times the payload (14,600 versus 4,000 pounds).

By January 1943, Martin had delivered only sixty-four PBM-3s to the U.S. Navy. These had been distributed as follows: twelve to Patrol Squadron VP 32 in the Caribbean; six each to the newly commissioned patrol squadrons in the U.S., VP 201 through VP 208; and four to R&D agencies.

However, the PBM-3 was plagued by innumerable faults: severe engine weaknesses, poor aerodynamic characteristics, erratic performance of the bombing system, and inadequate spare parts, to name only the most important. Exasperated, the Atlantic Fleet aviation authorities officially recommended (on April 8, 1943) that the contract with Martin be canceled and that the squadrons that had or expected these aircraft be reequipped with PBY-5A (amphibian) Catalinas. Admiral King rejected this proposal and directed the naval authorities to drastically modify the PBM-3 so that it could carry out its intended ASW mission. Accordingly, the au-

* From its 1943 allotment of B-24s, the RAF gave the RCAF five a month in April, May, and June.

thorities issued orders to "relieve the overload condition" of this aircraft. They were to eliminate armor, waist guns, ammo, oxygen equipment, bombsight and stabilizer, mattresses, and so on. The first modified aircraft, PBM-3S (stripped), was delivered on June 1, 1943, the second aircraft on July 27.

An official Navy aviation historian wrote that "the plane as stripped left much to be desired in an efficient Anti-Submarine Warfare type of aircraft." Therefore naval aviation authorities gave Martin a new contract for yet another new model, the PBM-3D. The first of these was delivered on December 3, 1943. But, the historian continued, "considerable difficulty was experienced with this model as well."

So stripped, these aircraft could not be deployed where there was even a slight chance of meeting enemy aircraft. Therefore, as the newly equipped Mariner squadrons were commissioned, most were deployed to patrol the waters of the Gulf of Mexico, Caribbean, and Latin America.*

- The PV-1 Ventura, a twin-engine, land-based, medium bomber, in production by Lockheed. This plane, a substantially upgraded Lockheed PBO Hudson, the Navy's version of the U.S. Army Air Forces B-34 medium bomber, had a combat radius of about five hundred nautical miles. Conceived initially for service in the Pacific where strong Japanese fighter opposition was expected, it was also employed over waters in North, Central, and South America, and West Africa in an ASW role.

The big disappointment—and headache—for the U.S. Navy was the slow—very slow—delivery schedule of the PV-1 Ventura, its first official allocation of land-based bombers. The Army Air Forces retained first priority for acquiring these planes (as B-34s); the Navy a lesser priority. By January 1943, the Navy had in hand fewer than fifty Venturas. As related, with these it reequipped the Newfoundland-based Catalina Patrol Squadrons VP 82 and VP 93, which were redesignated Bomber Squadrons VB 125 and VB 126. As other Venturas slowly came into service, they were assigned to Bomber Squadrons VB 127, VB 128, and so on.†

The North Atlantic Run: March 1943

In the month of March 1943, U-boat Control sailed forty-seven boats against Allied convoy routes in the North and Middle Atlantic. These consisted of thirty-five VIIs,‡ eleven old and new IXs, unsuitable for hard convoy battles, and one XB minelayer, *U-117*. Thirteen of the attack boats were new or commanded by new skippers. Like the sixty-seven boats that sailed in February, all the March boats reached assigned operating areas in spite of Coastal Command's intensified air of-

---

* Fulfilling wartime contracts, Martin produced 1,312 Mariners.

† Squadrons VB 125 and VB 126 (formerly VP 82 and VP 93) arrived in Canada on March 1, 1943, and rotated back to the United States on June 18, 1943. Squadron VB 127 relieved Catalina Squadron VP 92 in Morocco on September 6, 1943; VB 128 relieved Catalina Squadrin VP 84 in Iceland on September 5, 1943.

‡ Including one from the Arctic, *U-592*.

fensive in Biscay Bay, which culminated in Operation Enclose I, from March 20 to 28. Assigned to reinforce groups then composed largely of February boats, about half of the March boats participated in the unusual German successes achieved against convoys that month.

One outbound VII, the *U-333,* still commanded by Werner Schwaff, very nearly met catastrophe. Two days out from La Pallice on the night of March 5, an unidentified Leigh Light–equipped Wellington of Squadron 172, newly fitted with centimetric-wavelength radar (ASV III), attacked *U-333* seemingly out of nowhere. Schwaff's Metox had given no warning, but his flak guns were manned and the gunners were exceptionally alert. They hit a fuel tank in a wing of the Wellington with incendiary bullets, and it burst into flames. The plane continued its run, dropped four depth charges, then plunged aflame into the sea. Two missiles hit *U-333.* One bounced overboard to no effect. Another crashed through and lodged in the aft superstructure but failed to detonate, a very lucky break for the Germans.

Schwaff's report, combined with similar Metox failure reports about this time from Werner Hartenstein in *U-156* near Trinidad and Günther Reeder in *U-214* in the Caribbean, led U-boat Control on March 5 to suspect (correctly) that the Allies had a new airborne radar that Metox could not detect. This suspicion was more or less confirmed by the recovery of the H2S centimetric-wavelength radar from a crashed British Stirling near Rotterdam on February 2. Moreover, at about this same time a captured British airman cleverly misled the Germans into believing that Metox itself emitted a strong signal on which Allied airmen could "home" and therefore its use was dangerous.

The failure of the Metox FuMB against airborne centimetric-wavelength radar led the Germans to pursue urgent R&D on a new detector and to mount clumsy experimental versions of meter-wavelength search radar on U-boats. However, until these electronic devices were more fully developed and in hand, Dönitz and U-boat Control had no choice other than to beef up the flak arrangements on U-boats and to strongly urge (i.e., order) skippers to remain surfaced and fight off enemy aircraft, especially in the Bay of Biscay where the Leigh Light–equipped Wellingtons patrolled.

The flak arrangement on all U-boats by March 1943 had been improved. The guns were mounted aft of the conning tower on two separate, open, semicircular platforms, an upper one, and a lower one called the "Winter Garden." The flak guns on each platform were either single or twin rapid-fire 20mm cannons. The 20mm weapons were not always reliable and did not have much punch. The goal was to put a pair of improved (C/38) twin 20mm guns on the upper platform and a more powerful rapid-fire 37mm gun on the Winter Garden. Until that goal could be realized, various mixes of flak guns were the rule, but no boat had a gun greater in caliber than a 20mm.

Unless they were unaware and unalert, most U-boats stood a fair chance against the thinly armored, slow, and somewhat ponderous Catalina and Sunderland flying boats and the old and slow Wellingtons and Whitleys. Not so the much faster and more heavily armed B-17s, B-24s, and Halifaxes. The U-boats were highly vulnerable in a fight with these aircraft. They had no armor to protect the relatively thin pressure hulls; the flak guns had no protective splinter shields; the German gunners were completely exposed, and the reloading of ammo was slow at best. Should two aircraft attack the U-boat simultaneously from different angles, the German gunners would be hard-pressed to deal with both. Moreover, owing to the position of the conning tower, it was almost impossible to fire the flak guns from aft to fore, so the skipper had to maneuver the boat in order to obtain a clear field of fire.

More difficulties for the U-boats lay just ahead. British-built aircraft rockets and the American-built Fido air-dropped homing torpedo were then being distributed to a number of Allied ASW aircraft units. Fido was rightly viewed as a highly promising weapon, especially for "jeep" carrier operations. The tactical doctrine worked out by the navalists was that one or more high-speed Grumman F4F Wildcat fighters (Martlets in the Royal Navy) would attack the surfaced U-boat with six wing-mounted .50-caliber machine guns, wiping out the German flak guns and gunners, thereby forcing the U-boat to dive. Thereupon a loitering Grumman TBF Avenger torpedo bomber would drop a Fido on the swirl.

As in prior months, there were not nearly enough Type XIV "Milk Cow" U-tankers to support so great a number of Type VIIs in March. Of the six tankers of this class, two, the *U-459* and *U-460,* which returned to France in the first week of March, were undergoing long refits and did not resail until late April. The *U-461* and *U-462* were at sea refueling February boats and returned to France on March 11 and 22 for refits. The other two XIVs, *U-463* and the new *U-487,** sailed on March 4 and 27, respectively.

What this meant was that only one XIV tanker, *U-463,* sailed afresh in the month of March in time to replenish the numerous VIIs at sea. Therefore it was necessary to order the XB minelayer *U-117* to serve as a provisional tanker after she laid her minefield.

Like the February boats, the boats that sailed in March were the beneficiaries of an exceptionally precise flow of convoy information from *B-dienst.* Oppositely, as related, the Allied codebreakers were unable to break four-rotor naval Enigma consistently during the first ten days of March, and not at all from March 10 to March 19.

The boats sailing in March also faced hideous winter weather. Herbert Werner, author of *Iron Coffins,* who departed from Germany in February as first watch officer of the new VII *U-230,* remembered March this way:

> The sea boiled and foamed and leaped continually under the lash of gales that chased one another across the Atlantic from west to east. *U-230* struggled through gurgling whirlpools, up and down mountainous seas; she was pitched into the air by

---

* The first of a new series of fourteen U-tankers, *U-487* to *U-500,* of which only four, *U-487, U-488, U-489,* and *U-490,* were completed and reached the Atlantic.

> one towering wave and caught by another and buried under tons of water by still another. The cruel winds whipped across the wild surface at speeds up to 150 miles an hour, whistling in the highest treble and snarling in the lowest base.
>
> When we were on watch, the wind punished us with driving snow, sleet, hail, and frozen spray. It beat against our rubber diver's suits, cut our faces like a razor, and threatened to tear away our eye masks; only the steel belts around our waists secured us to boat and life. Below, inside the bobbing steel cockleshell, the boat's violent up-and-down motion drove us to the floorplates and hurled us straight up and threw us around like puppets. And yet we managed to survive the furious wind and water, and to arrive in our designated [grid] square in one piece.

Acting on information from *B-dienst,* U-boat Control deployed twenty-three boats in three groups: *Wildfang* (Madcap), *Burggraf,* and *Neuland* south and southeast of Greenland to intercept an eastbound convoy. This was Slow Convoy 121, which sailed from New York on February 24, with eighty merchant ships, plus LSTs. Twenty-one of these ships put into Halifax to await the sailing of the next Slow Convoy. Finally comprised of fifty-nine merchant ships plus the LSTs, the convoy was too thinly guarded by the sole American escort group, A-3, commanded by Paul Heineman. The warships consisted of the *Treasury*-class Coast Guard cutter *Spencer;* the old four-stack destroyer *Greer;* and three corvettes, two Canadian, one British.

Aware of the U-boat groups from Enigma intercepts, Allied authorities adroitly slipped the convoy between groups *Wildfang* and *Burggraf.* However, a recent Arctic transfer, the *U-405,* commanded by Rolf-Heinrich Hopmann, one of four boats backstopping *Wildfang,* found the convoy on March 6. Upon receipt of Hopmann's report, U-boat Control redeployed the twenty-three boats of the three groups and the four backstoppers into two attack groups: *Westmark* (seventeen boats, including the four backstoppers), and *Ostmark* (ten boats). Elsewhere on the North Atlantic run, fourteen other boats (six from *Wildfang,* six from refueling from the tanker *U-462,* and two from *Burggraf*) formed a new group, *Raubgraf* (Robber Baron). Thirteen others, well to the east, rebuilt group *Neuland,* which had been gutted to form group *Ostmark.*

There was a high percentage of green skippers in groups *Westmark* and *Ostmark,* assigned to attack Slow Convoy 121. Eighteen of the twenty-seven boats (66 percent) were on maiden patrols from Germany, ten assigned to *Westmark* and eight to *Ostmark.* In addition, there were three veteran boats with new skippers, two in *Westmark* and one in *Ostmark.* Therefore, twelve of the seventeen boats in *Westmark* (70 percent) were new or had new skippers and nine of the ten *Ostmark* boats (90 percent) were new or had new skippers. Only six of the twenty-seven skippers (22 percent) had made one or more prior patrols.

U-boat Control directed the seventeen boats of *Westmark* to close on Hopmann's *U-405,* attack Slow Convoy 121 immediately, and hold tightly to the formation. The ten boats of *Ostmark* were to remain east of the opening action and wait for the convoy to come to them. The *Westmark* boats attempted to comply with these instructions but miserable weather (snow, sleet, hail, gale-force winds) and poor communications thwarted a coordinated attack.

During the night, six of the seventeen *Westmark* boats found Slow Convoy 121 or parts of it. The green skipper Paul Siegmann, age twenty-nine, in the new VII *U-230,* shot at what he described as two 5,000-ton freighters and claimed both sank, but in reality, he put down only the 2,900-ton British freighter *Egyptian.* The veteran transfer from the Arctic, Hans-Jürgen Zetzsche in *U-591,* sank the 6,100-ton British freighter *Empire Impala,* which had humanely but unwisely stopped to rescue survivors of the *Egyptian.* Two new VIIs, *U-448,* commanded by Helmut Dauter, age twenty-three, and the experienced *U-659,* commanded by Hans Stock, age twenty-seven, were forced to break off the chase on account of engine failures and head for the newly sailed tanker, Leo Wolfbauer's *U-463.* Neither boat sank a ship on these patrols.

The weather worsened to nearly hurricane force. Even so, about six boats (four new, two veteran) of the fifteen left in *Westmark* managed to hold contact with the core of Slow Convoy 121, which was disorganized by the weather. Over the next forty-eight hours—through March 9—the storm abated. During that period, the *Westmark* boats got six more ships.

- Hans-Ferdinand Massmann in *U-409* sank two, the 3,800-ton American freighter *Malantic* and the 6,000-ton British tanker *Rosewood.*
- Hans-Jürgen Zetzsche in *U-591* sank the 5,900-ton Yugoslavian *Vojvoda Putnik,* which had incurred heavy storm damage and had been abandoned.
- Rolf-Heinrich Hopmann in *U-405,* who had originally found the convoy, sank the convoy commander's flagship, the 4,700-ton Norwegian vessel *Bonneville* (and one LCT landing craft alongside).
- Herbert Uhlig in the new IXC40 *U-527* sank the 5,200-ton British freighter *Fort Lamy* and one LCT landing craft on board.
- Either the new IXC40 *U-526,* commanded by Hans Möglich, or the veteran VII *U-432,* commanded by a new skipper, Hermann Eckhardt, age twenty-six, sank the 4,000-ton British freighter *Guido.*

Total bag from Slow Convoy 121 for the seventeen *Westmark* boats: eight ships for 38,500 tons plus the two 143-ton LCTs. One new VII, *U-709,* commanded by Karl-Otto Weber, age twenty-eight, suffered a radio-transmitter failure and had to abort.

The convoy proceeded easterly in more reasonable weather, straight into the line of the ten *Ostmark* boats. On March 8 and 9, four boats of this group got four more ships for about 19,000 tons and damaged another.

- Max Wintermeyer in the new IXC40 *U-190* sank the 7,000-ton British freighter *Empire Lakeland.*
- Robert Schetelig in the new VII *U-229* sank the 5,000-ton British freighter *Nailsea Court* (and damaged the 3,700-ton British freighter *Coulmore*).
- Kurt Lange in the new IXC40 *U-530* sank the 3,100-ton Swedish freighter *Milos.*
- Herbert Brünning in the *U-642* sank the 2,100-ton British freighter *Leadgate.*

Meanwhile, Allied authorities had ordered air and surface escorts from Iceland to reinforce Slow Convoy 121. Aircraft arrived early on March 9. Later in the day two *Treasury*-class Coast Guard cutters, *Bibb* and *Ingham,* an American four-stack destroyer, *Babbitt,* and two British corvettes, *Campion* and *Mallow,* joined, increasing the escort to ten warships: three American *Treasury*-class cutters, two American four-stack destroyers, and five corvettes, three British and two Canadian. These plus heavy air cover forced U-boat Control to cancel operations.

One U-boat was lost on March 10. Commanded by Bernhard Müller, age twenty-six, she was the new VII *U-633,* which sailed from Kiel on February 20 in company with seven other new boats. She and the others had been assigned to the first Neuland group, then to *Ostmark.* In wartime, the Admiralty credited a B-17 of Squadron 220 with the kill. In a postwar reassessment, however, it credited the British merchant ship *Scorton,* commanded by T. Glover, with her destruction by ramming. The *U-633* went down with all hands, reducing group *Ostmark* to nine boats.

Based on flash reports from the boats, U-boat Control sent along to the OKM a conservative estimate of successes: thirteen ships sunk for 73,000 tons, plus three for 19,500 tons hit and possibly sunk. The confirmed number was twelve of the fifty-nine ships in the convoy sunk for 55,661 tons (plus the two 143-ton LCTs) and one ship of 3,700 tons damaged. Unaware that the new VII *U-633* had been sunk en route to join *Ostmark,* U-boat Control reported no losses. Eleven other boats had been attacked by air and surface escorts with depth charges and bombs, but none had incurred serious damage.

The Americans of Escort Group A-3 met polite but stinging criticism in the British Isles. In two consecutive Atlantic crossings the group had run up a dubious record of sorts: fourteen ships for 80,000 tons lost from Outbound North 166 en route to the States (February 21–25) and on the return voyage (March 7–10), twelve ships for about 56,000 tons from Slow Convoy 121—altogether twenty-six ships for about 144,000 tons. Unaware that they had run a gauntlet of twenty-six U-boats, the Americans blamed the losses in Slow Convoy 121 on the fact that apart from too few escorts they had not had sufficient turnaround time at Argentia and St. John's to repair defective sonar, radar, radios, and Huff Duff sets and to properly rest the crews.

Coming behind Slow Convoy 121 was the fast Halifax 228, which sailed from New York on February 27 with eighty ships, but twenty put into Halifax. Comprised of sixty merchant ships plus LCTs, it was guarded by British Escort Group B-3, commanded by the skilled veteran A. A. Tait in the destroyer *Harvester.* Besides *Harvester,* the close escort included the British destroyer *Escapade;* two Polish-manned destroyers, *Burza* and *Garland;* and five corvettes, two British and three French. All told, nine warships: four destroyers and five corvettes.

The convoy was backed up by the first American "jeep" carrier support group to sail: the 10,000-ton *Bogue,* which carried twenty-one aircraft of Squadron VC 9, nine Wildcat fighters and twelve Avenger torpedo bombers. She was escorted by two four-stack destroyers, *Belknap* and *George E. Badger,* which had been converted to seaplane tenders, based at Argentia, Newfoundland. This group sailed from Argentia on March 5. Owing to the brutal weather on the North Atlantic run, the inability of the short-legged destroyers to refuel at sea, and the difficulty of launching and recovering aircraft as well as to defective depth-charge and bomb releases in the Avengers, on March 10 *Bogue* aborted to Argentia. En route the group rescued twenty-one desperate survivors of the merchant ship *Jonathan Sturges,* sunk from convoy Outbound North 166 on February 24 by Günter Gretschel in *U-707.**

Allied authorities routed Halifax 228 well north of Slow Convoy 121 to avoid the teeming U-boats on the latter's trail. The evasive rerouting sent the convoy directly into the patrol line of the rebuilt group *Neuland,* which on March 10 consisted of thirteen boats, twelve of which had made one or more prior patrols. One of the boats, *U-221,* commanded by Hans Trojer, had sunk the 3,000-ton Norwegian *Jamaica* while en route to join the *Neuland* group.

The first of the *Neuland* boats to contact convoy Halifax 228 was the *U-336,* commanded by Hans Hunger, one week into his second patrol. He found it on March 10, mere hours after the *Bogue* group had departed. Upon receiving Hunger's report on March 10, U-boat Control directed five other boats—the outbound *U-333* and four inbound—to join *Neuland,* raising its strength to eighteen boats, of which only two (Heinz Förster's *U-359* and Helmut Dauter's *U-448*) were new boats on first patrols.

During the first night, March 10–11, Hunger in *U-336* brought up nine boats. Hans Trojer in *U-221* opened the assault in a snow squall. His torpedoes hit and demolished two ships loaded with ammunition, the 5,400-ton British *Tucurinca* and the 6,600-ton American *Andrea F. Luckenbach,* and damaged the 7,200-ton American Liberty ship *Lawton B. Edwards.* Trojer logged that the *Tucurinca* blew apart with awesome force, hurling "hundreds of steel plates . . . through the air like sheets of paper." Some of the debris hit Trojer's attack periscope, bending it so that it would not lower fully. Thereafter, he wrote, escorts counterattacked *U-221,* dropping eight depth charges. These caused a serious leak in the conning-tower hatch, allowing "a mass of water" to enter the boat. Thoroughly shaken by the ammo explosions, the depth charges, and the flooding, Trojer broke off the chase to make repairs.

In the early hours of March 11, four other boats got hits.

- Albert Langfeld in the VII *U-444,* eleven days into his second patrol, damaged the 7,200-ton American Liberty ship *William M. Gorgas.*
- Friedrich Deetz in the VII *U-757* sank that ship with a finishing shot as well as the 5,000-ton Norwegian ammunition freighter *Brant County.* The force of the ammo explosion "seriously damaged" *U-757* and injured some personnel on the bridge. Deetz made contact with Heinrich Müller-Edzards in *U-590* who still had a doctor on board, then aborted to France at high speed. Crossing Biscay, Deetz teamed up with Heinz Förster in the VII *U-359,* who had refueled from the XB

* Astonishingly, over a month later, on April 5, the homebound *U-336,* commanded by Hans Hunger, picked up six other survivors of the *Jonathan Sturges* and took them to France. This act of humanity was apparently overlooked and therefore not introduced in the Dönitz trial.

minelayer *U-119,* and their combined flak power repelled an attack by an unidentified B-24 Liberator on March 16. The *U-757* was out of action for four months.

• Walter Schug in *U-86* and Horst Dieterichs in *U-406* both claimed FAT hits on ships that, if valid, had to include the 5,500-ton British freighter *Jamaica Producer.* Despite the damage, she reached port.

The nine warships of Tait's escort group had a frenetic night chasing radar, Huff Duff, and sonar contacts. Near dawn, Tait, in the destroyer *Harvester,* sighted a U-boat on the surface. This was Albert Langfeld in the VII *U-444.* Ordering his gunners to open fire, Tait rang up full speed and rammed *U-444,* riding up and over her afterdeck. Somehow the blow failed to hole *U-444* sufficiently to sink her immediately and she became entangled in *Harvester*'s propeller shaft. By the time the two vessels broke free, *Harvester*'s propeller shafts and propellers were so badly damaged that she could only crawl on one engine, a perilous predicament with eighteen U-boats converging on the area. Busy saving his own ship, Tait rescued only one of the forty-five Germans of *U-444* and later, fifty American survivors of the *William M. Gorgas.*

One of the four homebound boats diverted to reinforce group *Neuland* was the VII *U-432,* a veteran with a new skipper, Hermann Eckhardt, age twenty-six, who came from command of the 600-ton Italian-built Romanian submarine *Delfinul* in the Black Sea. Longtime crewmen such as the first watch officer, Josef Bröhl, who had helped the former skipper of *U-432,* Heinz-Otto Schultze, win his *Ritterkreuz,* believed Eckhardt was too overconfident and undertrained for combat on the North Atlantic run. Nonetheless, when he found *Harvester* lying-to dead in the water, Eckhardt fired two conventional electrics at her by periscope from a distance of six hundred and seven hundred yards. Both hit and *Harvester* sank with the loss of 149 men, including Tait.

Earlier, Tait had summoned the Free French corvette *Aconit,* commanded by Jean Levasseur, to close and screen *Harvester. Aconit* belatedly arrived to find no *Harvester,* but a sea teeming with her survivors and those of the *William M. Gorgas* and one German clinging to rafts and wreckage. At the same time, *Aconit* spotted the *U-444,* which *Harvester* had rammed, still afloat. Leaving the survivors temporarily, Levasseur raced at *U-444* and rammed her so hard the U-boat split in two and sank immediately. Levasseur fished out three Germans, making four men (all enlisted) picked up from *U-444* by Escort Group B-3.

Returning to the scene where *Harvester* had sunk, *Aconit* unexpectedly got a good sonar contact. This was *Harvester*'s killer, *U-432,* still at periscope depth. After sinking *Harvester,* Eckhardt had opened a bottle of champagne so the officers could celebrate, after which the officers and crew had begun to eat lunch or to sleep. When the first two salvos (ten depth charges) from *Aconit* fell, *U-432* was deaf and blind. The hydrophone operator was washing the champagne glasses; the first watch officer had gone to bed. The close explosions caused extensive damage and drove *U-432* to a record one thousand feet.

The depth to which *U-432* plunged so terrified all hands that Eckhardt decided to surface in broad daylight and attempt to outrun his attacker. When *U-432* popped up, *Aconit* was merely a half mile away. The French spotted the U-boat and instantly opened fire with the 4" gun and other weapons. This heavy gunfire probably killed Eckhardt and many other Germans who were topside. *Aconit* closed *U-432* slowly, intending to put a boarding party on her directly from her bow, but the heavy seas threw her at the U-boat. Unintentionally, *Aconit* rammed *U-432,* which sank instantly, taking down over half of the forty-six men of the crew. *Aconit* rescued twenty Germans, including first watch officer Bröhl. She then returned to the area where the survivors of *Harvester* and *Gorgas* were adrift and took them all aboard. The rescued included twenty-four Germans—four from *U-444,* twenty from *U-432.*

By March 12, Halifax 228 was too close to aircraft bases in Iceland to risk further U-boat operations. U-boat Control reported six ships (including a tanker) sunk for nearly 50,000 tons, plus hits on two other ships, which presumably sank, and probable hits on four other ships. The confirmed result was four merchant ships (no tankers) for about 24,000 tons sunk, plus *Harvester.* The U-boats hit two other merchant ships, but both reached port. The Germans presumed *U-444* to have been lost in the battle but did not learn of the loss of *U-432* until later.

The battle with Halifax 228 was actually a humiliating defeat for the U-boat force. The eighteen U-boats of *Neuland,* operating in fair weather, had sunk only four merchant ships out of sixty, plus *Harvester.* In return, two boats had been lost, a ruinous "exchange rate" of two merchant ships sunk for each U-boat lost. In this case, as in others, radar-equipped Allied aircraft swarming over the convoy had been the decisive factor, even though none of the aircraft sank or even damaged a U-boat.

Several of the *Neuland* boats refueled from the XB minelayer *U-119* before heading homeward. U-boat Control ordered one of these VIIs, the *U-659,* commanded by Hans Stock, to meet and escort Weber in *U-709,* who was still without a radio transmitter. The two boats were to travel at "high speed." Both reached Brest, *U-709* on March 18, *U-659* on March 20.

In the first fifteen days of March 1943, while the Atlantic Convoy Conference met in Washington, the dozens of U-boats on the North Atlantic run managed to mount telling attacks on only two sixty-ship eastbound convoys: Slow Convoy 121 and Halifax 228. Of these 120 ships (plus LSTs), the U-boats sank twelve from Slow Convoy 121 and four plus *Harvester* from Halifax 228. One hundred and four eastbound merchant ships in these convoys (86 percent) reached their destinations.

As related, in March the German codebreakers at *B-dienst* provided an unprecedented flow of data on nearly all of the Atlantic convoys. They may well have benefitted from the heavy Allied radio traffic generated in connection with various aspects of the Atlantic Convoy Conference, including the specific sailing dates and routing of convoys and stragglers. As also related, owing to the issuance of a new German short-signal weather-reporting codebook, the Allied codebreakers lost four-rotor naval Enigma from March 10 to March 19. This temporary loss, plus the unprecedented number of U-boats operating against the North Atlantic run, made it more difficult for the Allies to evade the various attack groups.

The loss of these sixteen loaded eastbound merchant ships on the "decisive" North Atlantic lifeline was a tough blow, but it hardly justified the doom-and-gloom view of convoying at the Admiralty. Moreover, to make good the loss of British imports, a special Halifax convoy (229A) was added in March* and by April, Halifax and Outbound North convoys of sixty merchant ships each were to sail every five days. However, as related, Allied merchant-ship losses in the Middle Atlantic, Pacific Ocean, Mediterranean Sea, and elsewhere during the first half of March were also unusually heavy, adding to the alarm at the Admiralty. Moreover, in the immediate days ahead a true disaster took place on the North Atlantic run.

The Greatest Convoy Battles of the War

Group *Raubgraf* (Robber Baron) was created to intercept the flow of Outbound North and Outbound North (Slow) convoys sailing to the Americas. Composed of thirteen boats detached from groups *Wildfang, Burggraf,* and the original group *Neuland,* it was positioned in the "Air Gap" on a line running south from Greenland.

The anticipated prey for group *Raubgraf* were convoys Outbound North (Slow) 169 (thirty-seven merchant ships) and Outbound North 170 (fifty-two merchant ships). The first, ONS 169, was guarded by the British Escort Group B-4, commanded by E.C.L. Day in the destroyer *Highlander.* The group consisted of seven warships: three destroyers and four corvettes. However, one of the destroyers, *Vimy,* aborted to Iceland for repairs. The second convoy, ON 170, was guarded by the British Escort Group B-2, under a temporary commander, inasmuch as Donald Macintyre's flagship, the destroyer *Hesperus,* was in repair after ramming *U-357.* The group thus consisted of only six warships: two destroyers, a new 1,500-ton sloop, *Whimbrel* (flagship), and three British corvettes.

To avoid group *Neuland*'s battle with Halifax 228, the Admiralty routed Outbound North (Slow) 169 on a northerly track. Off Greenland the convoy ran into a violent storm that scattered its ships all over the ocean and damaged many. In such weather it was impossible for the U-boats to carry out a coordinated hunt. Consequently, group *Raubgraf* could not find that convoy. However, three of the VIIs found and sank three stragglers.

- Klemens Schamong, age twenty-six in the new VII *U-468,* got the abandoned 6,500-ton British tanker *Empire Light* of Outbound North 168, previously damaged by Hinrich-Oskar Bernbeck in the new VII *U-638.*
- Max Kruschka in *U-621,* embarked on his third patrol, sank the 3,400-ton British freighter *Baron Kinnard* from Outbound North (Slow) 169.
- Gerhard Feiler, on his second patrol in *U-653,* sank the 7,200-ton American Liberty ship *Thomas Hooker,* from the same convoy.

Owing to the storm, Outbound North (Slow) 169 arrived off Cape Cod piecemeal. The escort group, including the destroyers *Highlander* and *Beverley* and the

* See Appendix 3.

Canadian corvette *Sherbrooke,* put into St. John's, Newfoundland, on March 11. *Highlander* and *Sherbrooke* had incurred such heavy storm damage that they had to go into dry dock for rushed repairs. They were thus to be delayed in departing St. John's to escort the eastbound convoy, Halifax 229.

The fast Outbound North 170 came right in the wake of 169. Two of its merchant ships aborted and one, *Empire Puma,* straggled, leaving forty-nine ships in the formation. This convoy also followed a northerly track and ran into violent storms that demasted some ships and smashed the top hamper of others. Having DFed sinking and other reports from the *Raubgraf* boats, the temporary escort group commander employed clever evasive courses to get around the group. Even so, five *Raubgraf* boats made contact with Outbound North 170. In response, Allied authorities ordered seven warships (three destroyers, two corvettes, and two minesweepers) to sail at once from St. John's, as well as the American four-stack destroyer *Upshur,* which was already at sea in the area, en route to Iceland. When the skies partially cleared on March 14, long-range aircraft (Cansos, B-17s) from Newfoundland commenced patrols over the convoy.

Although he only had six warships when the U-boats found the convoy, the escort commander in the sloop *Whimbrel* utilized them skillfully. He directed one corvette, *Heather,* to haul well away from the convoy and fire snowflakes (star shells), thereby creating a diversion, then changed the convoy's course to dead south. He directed another corvette, *Gentian,* to attack the green skipper Klemens Schamong in *U-468,* who was shadowing and broadcasting position reports. *Gentian* held *U-468* down for several hours, carrying out three depth-charge attacks. Faulty position reports from Bernhard Zurmühlen in *U-600* and Schamong in *U-468* led U-boat Control to believe the convoy was headed southwest rather than due south, as was the case. Thus *Raubgraf* chased in the wrong direction and Outbound North 170 eventually reached the jurisdiction of the local Canadian escort without loss of a single ship to U-boats.

After this action, two *Raubgraf* VIIs reported "engine damage" and set a course to France. These were Dietrich Lohmann in *U-89* and Gerhard Feiler in *U-653,* both of whom had earlier refueled in the operational area. Lohmann reached home on March 28, completing a barren patrol of sixty-four days. Feiler, who had sunk one straggling American Liberty ship and damaged a tanker, helped locate a convoy that led to the greatest battle in the Atlantic naval war.

The eastbound Slow Convoy 122, composed of fifty merchant ships, sailed from New York with a Canadian local escort on March 5. On the second day out, the convoy ran into a gale. Three ships aborted to New York and six to Halifax, Nova Scotia. Three, including *Clarissa Radcliffe,* were declared stragglers. On March 9, a feeder convoy of fourteen ships from Halifax, including the rescue ship *Zamalek,* joined the convoy. After all the aborts and the comings and goings, the convoy consisted of fifty laden merchant ships, including five bound for Iceland and forty-five for the British Isles (two of the latter were LSTs).

The British Escort Group B-5, commanded by Richard C. Boyle, which had brought Outbound North 168 across, was assigned to guard Slow Convoy 122. The group sailed from St. John's on March 11 and joined the convoy a day later. It was composed of nine warships: two destroyers (the British *Havelock* and the American four-stack *Upshur*), a new 1,500-ton frigate (the British *Swale*), five corvettes (two manned by Belgians), and the ASW trawler *Campobello.* The *Upshur* was to peel off halfway across and escort the five ships of the convoy that were bound for Iceland.

On March 12, Allied intelligence DFed a message from a *Raubgraf* boat, Max Kruschka in *U-621,* reporting the sinking of the *Baron Kinnard,* a straggler from Outbound North (Slow) 169. As a result, Allied authorities redirected Slow Convoy 122 to a more southerly route to evade *Raubgraf.* The maneuver worked. No boat of *Raubgraf* found Slow Convoy 122. However, lying ahead on a newly created north-south line were two big groups: *Stürmer* (Daredevil), eighteen boats; and *Dränger* (Harrier), eleven boats, deployed south from *Stürmer.* Owing to the loss of naval Enigma from March 10 to 19, Allied authorities were not fully aware of the size and locations of groups *Stürmer* and *Dränger* and were thus unable to divert Slow Convoy 122 to a safe course.

Three days after Slow Convoy 122 sailed on March 8, the fast convoy Halifax 229 departed New York. It consisted of forty merchant ships plus a local escort group of five vessels. Two merchant ships aborted, leaving thirty-eight, one of which, the 7,200-ton American Liberty ship *Hugh Williamson,* straggled but eventually reached Northern Ireland on her own.

From St. John's, some warships of close Escort Group B-4, commanded by E.C.L. Day, which had brought Outbound North (Slow) 169 across, began to join convoy Halifax 229 on March 13. The group was short of Day's flagship, the destroyer *Highlander,* and the Canadian corvette *Sherbrooke,* both delayed in dry dock. Pending the arrival of those two warships, B-4, temporarily commanded by Gordon J. Luther in the British destroyer *Volunteer* (borrowed from Escort Group B-5), consisted of the latter, plus two short-legged, temporarily attached British destroyers (*Witherington* and the ex-American four-stack *Mansfield*), the ex-American four-stack British destroyer *Beverley,* and two British corvettes. The escort for this valuable convoy was thus pitifully thin: four destroyers (two on temporary duty) and two corvettes.

The day after Halifax 229 sailed, on March 9, a "second section," Halifax 229A, departed New York. It was comprised of twenty-eight ships, four of them bound for Halifax, plus a local Canadian escort. A feeder convoy of sixteen ships from Halifax joined 229A, including the *Lady Rodney,* which went only as far as St. John's, Newfoundland. The final composition of Halifax 229A was thus thirty-nine merchant ships. It was guarded by a thin escort group, 40, commanded by John S. Dallison, which normally guarded KM-MK Torch convoys, but had sailed to St. John's specifically to escort Halifax 229A to the British Isles. Escort Group 40 consisted of but six warships, all below fleet-destroyer class: two new 1,500-ton *River*-class frigates *(Moyola, Waveney),* two old 260-foot sloops, and two ex-American 250-foot Coast Guard cutters, *Lulworth* and *Landguard.*

The lead convoy of these eastbound three, Slow 122, plodded along at about seven knots. On March 15 it ran into a furious gale. The storm was quite hard on the two smallest ships in the convoy, the 755-ton Icelandic freighter *Selfoss,* which had joined at Halifax, and the 550-ton Canadian-built ASW trawler *Campobello,* of the escort group. *Selfoss* left the convoy and reached Iceland safely via a direct route. *Campobello* developed leaks in a coal bin that could not be stopped. Escort commander Boyle sent the Belgian-manned corvette *Godetia* back to take off the *Campobello* crew and sink her. After all the crew had been transferred, *Godetia* destroyed *Campobello* with a single depth charge.

The codebreakers at *B-dienst* intercepted and decrypted the orders to Slow Convoy 122 and Halifax 229 to follow a more southerly route to avoid *Raubgraf.* Accordingly, U-boat Control ordered *Raubgraf* to break off the frustrating and unrewarding attack on Outbound North 170 and to intercept eastbound convoys Slow 122 and Halifax 229.

Racing south, the *Raubgraf* boat *U-91,* commanded by Heinz Walkerling, who was embarked on his third patrol, found a convoy on March 15. U-boat Control wrongly assumed it to be Slow Convoy 122. In actuality, it was Halifax 229, which was overtaking Slow 122. U-boat Control ordered three experienced *Raubgraf* boats to close on *U-91* and attack the convoy: Horst Uphoff in *U-84,* Adolf Graef in *U-664,* and Helmut Manseck in *U-758.*

While seeking a U-tanker, Gerhard Feiler in the homebound *U-653* came upon the other eastbound convoy, also believed to be Slow Convoy 122. His position report put the convoy slightly east of *U-91*'s position report, which appeared to be perfectly logical. Acting on this report, U-boat Control directed the nine remaining boats of *Raubgraf,* plus two new additions coming from the U-tanker, to close on Feiler in *U-653.* In addition, Control directed eleven boats of group *Stürmer,* six of group *Dränger,* and eleven others to run west at high speed to assist *Raubgraf,* making thirty-eight boats. The weather was ghastly: gale-force winds and huge seas.

The *U-91* and *U-653* had not found Slow Convoy 122, but rather the fast, overtaking Halifax 229, which was about one hundred miles behind, or southwest, of Slow 122, following approximately the same route. On March 16 and 17, eight U-boats (five of *Raubgraf,* two of *Stürmer,* and one, *U-288,* passing by homebound) attacked Halifax 229 in the mistaken belief that it was Slow Convoy 122. Results:

- Hans-Joachim Bertelsmann in *U-603,* who had sunk one and a half ships from Outbound North 166, shot three FATs and one electric and sank the 5,200-ton Norwegian *Elin K.*
- Helmut Manseck in *U-758* sank the 6,800-ton Dutchman *Zaanland* and damaged the 7,200-ton American Liberty ship *James Oglethorpe.*
- Siegfried Strelow, who had won a *Ritterkreuz* in *U-435* on Arctic duty, shot two double FAT salvos and damaged the 7,200-ton American Liberty ship *William Eustis.*
- Bernhard Zurmühlen in *U-600* sank the 12,200-ton British whale factory ship-cum-tanker *Southern Princess* and damaged the 8,700-ton British freighter *Nariva* as well as the 6,100-ton American freighter *Irenée Du Pont.*

- Heinz Walkerling in *U-91* sank the 6,400-ton American freighter *Harry Luckenbach* and then the four damaged and abandoned ships *Oglethorpe, Eustis, Nariva,* and *Du Pont.*
- Hans-Achim von Rosenberg-Gruszczynski in *U-384* sank the 7,200-ton British Liberty ship *Coracero.*
- Jürgen Krüger in *U-631* sank the 5,200-ton Dutch freighter *Terkoelei.*

The claims amounted to twelve ships for 77,500 tons sunk and six other ships damaged. The confirmed figures to this point were ten ships for 72,200 tons sunk by seven different U-boats.

There was no rescue ship with Halifax 229, a terrible lapse, as it turned out. One consequence was that only two of the escorts remained continuously with the convoy; the rest were trying their best to pick up survivors from the ten lost ships, American observers in London reported later. These acts of humanity, of course, further exposed Halifax 229.

In the aftermath of these attacks, all twelve of the U-boats then comprising *Raubgraf* broke off the attack, six for want of fuel, six with battle damage or mechanical problems. As a result of depth-charge attacks, Manseck in *U-758* had a stern tube and an air compressor out of order. Graef in *U-664* said that owing to worn bearings in one or both electric propulsion motors, his port shaft was knocking loudly. Ralph Kapitzky in *U-615* had incurred slight topside damage and one periscope was frozen. Bertelsmann in *U-603* said his topside stern torpedo canister had washed overboard and one diesel engine was out of commission. Zurmühlen in *U-600* requested permission to abort to France because both diesel engines were in need of a major overhaul and because there was chlorine gas in the number 2 battery compartment. *Ritterkreuz* holder Strelow in *U-435* also requested permission to abort to France because of diesel-engine and electric propulsion-motor defects. He "urgently required" a major overhaul of his diesel engines and battery compartments.

Five of these boats reached France from March 25 to March 30, but Kapitzky in *U-615* repaired his damage and continued to patrol. Feiler in *U-653* arrived in France on March 31, completing a patrol of sixty-three days.

The *Stürmer* and *Dränger* boats assigned to the battle went west at high speed. On the night of March 16–17, one of the *Stürmer* VIIs, the new *U-338,* commanded by Manfred Kinzel, just ten days short of his twenty-eighth birthday, unexpectedly came upon the actual Slow Convoy 122 and what remained of its close escort. The alert and opportunistic Kinzel, three weeks out from Kiel on his first patrol, slipped through the thinned-out escort (seven warships) and fired a full salvo into the convoy. Remarkably, his five torpedoes sank two British freighters for about 10,000 tons, *Kingsbury* and *King Gruffydd,* and a 7,900-ton Dutchman, *Alderamin,* and damaged the 7,200-ton British freighter *Fort Cedar Lake.* The Slow Convoy 122 rescue ship *Zamalek,* screened by the British corvette *Saxifrage,* fell out to pick up survivors.

Kinzel's battle report caused confusion at U-boat Control. The position he gave was more than one hundred miles from what Control believed to be (the lone) Slow Convoy 122. In the ensuing hours, reports from other boats correctly suggested that there were actually two eastbound convoys about one hundred to 125 miles apart. Control wrongly surmised that Kinzel had attacked the fast convoy, Halifax 229, and the *Raubgraf* boats had attacked Slow Convoy 122. In reality, it was the other way around.

After Kinzel's attack, the escort commander of Slow Convoy 122, Richard Boyle, reported that he was under attack and requested that surface-ship reinforcements sail at once from Iceland; he also asked for heavy air cover at first light. In response, Allied authorities sent the *Treasury*-class Coast Guard cutter *Ingham* and the American four-stack destroyer *Babbitt* to Slow Convoy 122. When Allied authorities realized Halifax 229 was also under heavy attack, they diverted *Babbitt* as well as the British destroyer *Vimy,* which also sailed from Iceland, to assist that convoy. Meanwhile the B-4 escort commander, E.C.L. Day in the destroyer *Highlander,* with the Canadian corvette *Sherbrooke* (both delayed in dry dock), raced east to join the very thin escort of Halifax 229. The five reinforcing warships ran into hurricane-force winds (70 knots, *Ingham* reported), which slowed them considerably.

Convoy Halifax 229 had sailed with six MOEF escorts—four British destroyers and two British corvettes. Two of the short-legged destroyers (*Witherington* and *Mansfield*) returned to Newfoundland, to be replaced by the British destroyers *Highlander* and *Vimy.* When the American destroyer *Babbitt* arrived from Iceland and two more corvettes arrived from Newfoundland, the escort numbered nine warships: five destroyers and four corvettes, but most escorts were still picking up survivors.

During the early hours of March 17, Coastal Command launched the first of what was to become a powerful air umbrella over both convoys. Very-long-range B-24s from British Squadrons 120 (at Iceland) and 86 (Northern Ireland) covered Slow Convoy 122 in the morning and afternoon. Very-long-range B-24s (from Iceland) covered convoy Halifax 229 in the late evening. These aircraft sighted numerous U-boats and carried out depth-charge attacks on five. They did not score a kill, but they harassed the U-boats, making it difficult for them to shadow or to home on the shadower, upsetting the massing of U-boats for battle.

Despite the addition of surface escorts and heavy air cover from March 17, three more U-boats had successes against the remaining twenty-eight ships of Halifax 229.

• Hans Trojer in *U-221,* who had sunk five ships for about 30,000 tons in Slow Convoy 104 on his first patrol in October and rammed and sank *U-254* on his second, got two big ships: the 7,200-ton American Liberty ship *Walter O. Gresham* and the fast British refrigerator ship *Canadian Star,* which usually sailed alone but was ordered into convoy because her 4" gun was broken. Thirty of her eighty-seven passengers and crew perished in the sinking. For these two successes and prior sinkings and claims on this patrol, Dönitz awarded Trojer a *Ritterkreuz* by radio on March 24.*

* At the time of the award his confirmed score was ten ships for 60,157 tons, all sunk on the North Atlantic run, plus damage to an American Liberty ship. It was a success that almost exactly duplicated that of Siegfried Forstner in *U-402,* who sank ten and one-half ships for 57,000 tons during that difficult winter to win a *Ritterkreuz.*

• Herbert Uhlig, age twenty-seven, in the new IXC40 *U-527* of the *Stürmer* group, got two hits and seriously disabled the American freighter *Mathew Luckenbach* (not to be confused with the lost *Harry Luckenbach,* also in Halifax 229). She was a "romper"* from the convoy, which had fled ahead after the attack of the first wave of U-boats. The Coast Guard cutter *Ingham* and the American destroyer *Upshur,* assigned to protect Slow Convoy 122, came upon the abandoned ship and rescued her entire crew from lifeboats. After dark, Uhlig in *U-527* returned to the scene to give his victim a finishing shot, but another new *Stürmer* IXC, *U-523,* commanded by Werner Pietzsch, age twenty-five, got there first and sank the derelict *Mathew Luckenbach* with one torpedo.

By March 18, the two convoys were about 250 to three hundred miles west of Iceland. Coastal Command sent four very-long-range B-24s of Squadron 120 to meet convoy Halifax 229, but owing to a failure of homing procedures, they could not find the convoy. However, one B-24 spotted a U-boat and attacked, but made no kill. Five B-24s of Squadron 120 provided cover for Slow Convoy 122 for a period of ten hours. These made four attacks but no kills.

The next day, March 19, Coastal Command mounted the largest air umbrella yet to protect a North Atlantic convoy. It consisted of eleven sorties by B-24s of Squadrons 86 and 120 and long-range B-17s of Squadrons 206 and 220, plus five by Sunderlands. These aircraft carried out six attacks on U-boats, but achieved no kills.

The heavy air and sea escorts thwarted further U-boat attacks on Halifax 229. Altogether, ten U-boats were credited with sinking thirteen confirmed ships for 93,502 tons, making this battle (after PQ 17) the second most remunerative in tonnage—repeat tonnage—sunk by German U-boats in the war. Moreover, the victory was achieved with the loss of only one U-boat: von Rosenberg-Gruszczynski in the new VII *U-384,* sunk with the loss of all hands by a B-17 Flying Fortress of British Squadron 206, flown by Leslie G. Clark, who had damaged *U-632* two months earlier.

After Kinzel in the new *U-338* found Slow Convoy 122 on March 16–17 and sank three and damaged one of its merchant ships, U-boat Control directed other boats of groups *Stürmer* and *Dränger* to close on *U-338* at maximum speed, without concern for fuel consumption. For those boats critically low on fuel, Control promised to send a U-tanker northward, closer to the battle scene, or to designate a newly arrived boat to share its fuel.

Two *Stürmer* boats, Hans-Jürgen Haupt, age thirty-two, in the new VII *U-665,* and Rudolf Bahr, age twenty-six, in the new VII *U-305,* arrived at the convoy first. Haupt sank the ship Kinzel in *U-338* had damaged, the 7,200-ton British Liberty ship *Fort Cedar Lake.* Bahr sank two British vessels: the 8,800-ton refrigerator ship *Port Auckland* and the 4,300-ton *Zouave,* loaded with iron filings. Kinzel in *U-338* sank his fourth ship from this convoy, the 4,100-ton Panamanian freighter

* A "romper," as opposed to a "straggler," was a vessel that violated orders and left its assigned convoy and proceeded ahead all alone.

Granville. These attacks raised the losses in Slow Convoy 122 to seven ships for 42,106 tons sunk by three U-boats.

During the night of March 17–18, a storm of "near hurricane" fury struck Slow Convoy 122 and the thirteen pursuing U-boats. After daylight, when the B-24 aircraft appeared over the convoy, they drove the U-boats off and under. Thirsting for a dramatic massacre of this slow formation, U-boat Control directed the boats to ignore the aircraft, maintain contact at all costs, and haul ahead of the convoy to obtain a good position for night attacks. While exhorting the boats, Control did not spare feelings. It singled out the veteran Walter Schug in the *Dränger* boat *U-86* for unbridled criticism, which all boats could read: "Your position 120 miles behind convoy without [any] action can be explained only as absolute faulty operation. Pursue at top speed."

The *Treasury*-class cutter *Ingham,* from Iceland, reinforced the escort of Slow Convoy 122 on March 18 and the corvette *Godetia* rejoined after picking up survivors. These additions raised the close escort back to nine warships: *Ingham,* two destroyers (British *Havelock* and American *Upshur*), one frigate (*Swale*), and five corvettes. The air and surface escorts hounded the *Stürmer* and *Dränger* boats. Kinzel in the new *U-338* and Haupt in the new *U-665* reported major depth-charge damage that forced them to abort. While Haupt in *U-665* was inbound in Biscay on the night of March 22, a Whitley of Bomber Command's Operational Training Unit 10, piloted by J. A. Marsden, found and, with six depth charges, sank her with the loss of all hands.* Helmut von Tippelskirch, age twenty-five, new skipper of the VII *U-439,* reported that he had been hunted and depth-charged for eight hours. Max Wintermeyer in the new IXC40 *U-190* said he had been hunted and depth-charged for nine hours. Hans Möglich in the new IXC40 *U-526* and Herbert Uhlig in the new IXC40 *U-527* reported diesel-engine problems that forced them to break off pursuit. Four other Type VIIs also reported diesel-engine breakdowns.

U-boat Control did not achieve a massacre of Slow Convoy 122. In this second assault, a half dozen boats got into shooting positions, but only three managed hits:

- Herbert Engel in the new VII *U-666* severely damaged the 5,200-ton Greek *Carras.* In return, a B-17 of Squadron 220, piloted by William Knowles, who had sunk *U-633* earlier in March, hit *U-666* with a close straddle of four depth charges, forcing Engel to abort to France.
- Werner Schwaff in the veteran *U-333* came along and sank the abandoned hulk of *Carras.*
- Heinrich Schmid in the VII *U-663,* fresh from France, probably sank the 5,800-ton British freighter *Clarissa Radcliffe,* which had been straggling for days.

Confirmed sinkings in Slow Convoy 122: nine ships for 53,094 tons by six U-boats.

Wittingly or unwittingly the Germans viewed Slow Convoy 122 and Halifax 229 as a single convoy. Berlin propagandists gloated that the thirty-eight to forty

---

* At the time, the kill was credited to a Leigh Light–equipped Wellington, but in a postwar reassessment, the Admiralty credited the Whitley.

U-boats engaged sank thirty-two enemy merchant ships for 186,000 tons. U-boat Control also bestowed effusive private praise:

> Appreciation and recognition for the greatest success yet achieved against a convoy. After the extraordinarily successful surprise blow on the first night, tough and energetic pursuit despite strong air and surface defense brought splendid successes to the submarines in their attacks both by day and night.

If viewed as a single convoy, the battle was indeed by far the "greatest success" ever achieved by the Atlantic U-boat force, as Dönitz claimed in his memoir. But the combined confirmed sinkings were significantly less than the Germans claimed: twenty-two ships for 146,596 tons. If viewed as two separate convoys, attacked for the most part by three separate U-boat groups (*Raubgraf, Stürmer, Dränger*) plus a few nonassigned boats in the area, the results are less spectacular and not records: nine ships for 53,000 tons sunk in Slow Convoy 122; thirteen ships for 93,500 tons sunk in Halifax 229. In any case, assuming forty boats participated, the confirmed sinkings came to an average of about one-half ship per U-boat, no greater success rate than usual.

These two ill-fated convoys sailed during the closing days of the Atlantic Convoy Conference, a time of substantial change in the Atlantic convoy network, an increase in convoy size to sixty ships (plus LSTs) despite the critical shortage of escorts, and the loss of four-rotor naval Enigma. Neither British escort group (B-4 or B-5) was strong enough. Convoy Halifax 229 should have had a rescue ship. Moreover, Western Approaches made a serious mistake in sailing them one after the other on the same track so closely that they appeared to be a single convoy and thus a very rich target worth any risk. Fortunately, the Allies were able to prevent a really hideous massacre by sending surface-ship reinforcements from Iceland and by deploying an umbrella of very-long-range B-24 and long-range B-17 and Sunderland aircraft, which made altogether fifty-four sorties, forcing U-boats off and down and killing one, *U-384.**

While homebound from these battles on March 18, Max Kruschka in the VII *U-621* happened upon a convoy about four hundred miles west of Lorient. This was southbound KMS 111, en route to the Mediterranean. Upon receiving Kruschka's report, U-boat Control directed all boats and FW-200 Condors that could to home on *U-621* and to track and attack these laden ships.

Kruschka doggedly shadowed this rich prey. Three other VIIs, the inbound *U-332* and *U-634* and the outbound *U-632,* attempted to close on *U-621,* but Allied ASW aircraft thwarted them. Hans Karpf in *U-632* said he had been forced down "several times," but he continued his outbound passage. Eberhard Hüttemann in *U-332* reported contact, but he was "very low" on fuel and had "no success." Four homebound IXs and two more homebound VIIs were unable or unwilling to find the convoy and it steamed on, unharmed.

Two nights later, on March 21, a Leigh Light–equipped Wellington of

* The British calculated that in the fifty-four sorties, British aircraft sighted thirty-two U-boats and conducted twenty-one attacks.

Squadron 172, piloted by I. D. Prebble, caught Hüttemann in the homebound *U-332* on the surface in the Bay of Biscay by moonlight. Prebble dropped six depth charges and severely damaged *U-332*. Hüttemann played possum until the Wellington left the area, then appealed to U-boat Control for "urgent" assistance.

At dawn, Control sent four JU-88s to provide escort for *U-332,* which could not dive. British Beaufighters also responded, and they shot down two of the four German planes and chased the other two away.* Hüttemann, meanwhile, had repaired *U-332* sufficiently to dive to shallow depths. She reached France on March 24, a lucky boat, at least for the present.

During this tough battle on the North Atlantic run, the twenty-eight merchant ships of the "second section" of convoy Halifax 229—designated Halifax 229A—steered a route that was much farther to the north of the U-boats. As planned, four ships put into Halifax and one into St. John's and a feeder convoy of sixteen ships from Halifax joined the convoy. Of these, one, *Lady Rodney,* went only as far as St. John's. After passing that place, Halifax 229A consisted of thirty-eight ships. Four of the thirty-eight aborted (two to Halifax, two to St. John's), leaving thirty-four. Two others, the American *Lone Star* and the British *Belgian Airman,* incurred ice damage and were "detached," leaving thirty-two merchant ships.

While in far northern waters, the 14,800-ton British whale factory ship-cum-tanker *Svend Foyn* of Halifax 229A collided with an iceberg on March 19. The sloop *Hastings* of the convoy's thin Escort Group 40 fell out to protect her while the crew attempted repairs. Meanwhile, the *Treasury*-class Coast Guard cutter *Bibb,* which sailed from Iceland, temporarily reinforced the escort.

All efforts to save the valuable whale factory ship *Svend Foyn* continued. Four American Coast Guard vessels from Greenland, led by the 240-foot *Medoc,* arrived to relieve the sloop *Hastings.* The *Svend Foyn*'s captain insisted that he could save the ship, but during the night a gale swept the area and she abruptly sank. Of the 195 men on board *Svend Foyn,* 152 were rescued (128 by *Medoc*); forty-three were lost.

After *Bibb* peeled off for Iceland, Halifax 229A was reduced to thirty merchant ships plus its close escort. All these vessels arrived at destinations in the British Isles. In summary, one ship sank after colliding with an iceberg, six aborted to Nova Scotia or Newfoundland because of mechanical or other difficulties or ice damage, but none fell victim to a U-boat.

B-dienst continued to supply timely information to U-boat Control about the convoys on the North Atlantic run. When the Allies commenced renumbering the slow westbound convoys after Outbound North (Slow) 171—to Outbound North (Slow) 1—*B-dienst* promptly decrypted the change and gave U-boat Control the convoy's

---

* Control logged that Beaufighters were "superior" to the JU-88 Model 6C. The German planes were too slow, underarmed, and had water-cooled engines that were vulnerable to enemy fire.

predicted position and routing. At the same time, it provided routing information on the eastbound convoys Halifax 230 and Slow Convoy 123, each comprised of sixty merchant ships.

As related, Allied codebreakers broke back into *Triton* by March 20. This was a loss of merely ten days of U-boat signal traffic, during which U-boats sank twenty-two ships from Slow Convoy 122 and Halifax 229. The new break provided information on U-boats with about a two-day lag, but since U-boat groups were formed and ordered to specific areas several days in advance, the breaks were sufficiently current to be of extraordinary tactical value.

U-boat Control formed two new large groups, *Seeteufel* (Sea Devil) and *Seewolf,* on March 20. Consisting of sixteen boats (twelve VIIs, four IXC40s), *Seeteufel* was positioned to intercept Outbound North (Slow) 1. It was made up of three boats from group *Stürmer,* one boat from group *Dränger,* one veteran transfer from the Arctic, four new boats from Germany (two IXC40s, two VIIs), and seven boats newly sailed from France, all of which had made one or more patrols. *Seewolf,* consisting of nineteen boats (seventeen VIIs, two IXC40s), was positioned to intercept the eastbound Slow Convoy 123 and/or Halifax 230. It was made up of one boat from group *Westmark* and two boats from group *Raubgraf* that had refueled, eight boats from group *Stürmer,* seven boats from group *Dränger,* and one veteran boat newly sailed from France.

All told, the two groups, *Seeteufel* and *Seewolf,* numbered thirty-five U-boats. About one-third (twelve) were on maiden patrols from Germany. Six of those twelve were clumsy IXC40s, unsuitable for convoy warfare in the North Atlantic, but utilized nonetheless to help alleviate the shortage of VIIs and to augment the U-tankers in refueling operations if necessary.

Convoy Outbound North (Slow) 1 sailed from the British Isles on March 17. It was joined the following day by the British Escort Group B-6, commanded by R. Heathcote in the destroyer *Fame.* His group was also thin: *Fame* and another destroyer, *Viscount,* and four corvettes, one of which was manned by Norwegians.

Two of the *Seeteufel* VIIs made contact with "destroyers" of Outbound North (Slow) 1: the new *U-306,* commanded by Claus von Trotha, age twenty-nine, and the veteran *U-572,* commanded by Heinz Kummetat. Control directed four other *Seeteufel* boats to join *U-306* and two other *Seeteufel* boats to join *U-572.* The other eight boats of *Seeteufel* marked time in place.

Two of the eight *Seeteufel* boats searching for the ships seen by *U-306* and *U-572* reported enemy forces. The veteran VII *U-564,* commanded by Hans Fiedler, saw flares and gunfire. He ran at high speed toward the lights and noise but lost them and could not reestablish contact. The VII *U-592,* a veteran transfer from the Arctic, commanded by Carl Borm, saw what was believed to be a big freighter, guarded by two escorts, but lost sight of the ships in a snow storm. Helmut Pich in the new IXC40 *U-168* found Borm's three "ships," but, he reported, they turned out to be three icebergs with an uncanny resemblance to ships.

Correctly assuming Outbound North (Slow) 1 had slipped by group *Seeteufel,* U-boat Control redeployed the whole of that group as well as the whole of group *Seewolf* to intercept the next two eastbound formations, Slow Convoy 123 and Halifax 230. The redeployments resulted in a line of thirty-five U-boats six hundred miles long(!) running southeast from the southern tip of Greenland.

One of the northernmost of the *Seeteufel* VIIs, Hans Fiedler in *U-564,* reported a convoy about 150 miles southeast of Greenland. U-boat Control believed it might be Outbound North (Slow) 2, but in reality, it was the opposite-sailing Slow Convoy 123, guarded by the British Escort Group B-2, with a temporary commander in the sloop *Whimbrel.* The escort was composed of seven warships: two destroyers, the *Whimbrel,* and four corvettes. In addition, the American Support Group 6, consisting of the "jeep" carrier *Bogue* and her two American four-stack destroyers (*Belknap* and *George E. Badger*), sailed from Argentia on March 20 to reinforce this convoy, catching up the next day.

Two other *Seeteufel* VIIs closed on Fiedler's position: the new *U-415,* commanded by Kurt Neide, age twenty-six, and the veteran *U-663,* commanded by Heinrich Schmid. Fiedler and Schmid saw and reported the carrier *Bogue* sailing in the center of the convoy. U-boat Control responded that the sinking of the carrier was "particularly important for the progress of convoy operations" but the U-boats were not to pursue it to the point that they "let other chances slip."

The *Bogue,* commanded by Giles E. Short, contributed little to nothing on this, her second patrol. One reason was the wretched weather. As on her first patrol, gale-force winds and heaving seas restricted aircraft operations, this time to only four days. By coincidence, on the day U-boats discovered her, March 26, she aborted and returned to Argentia with her two four-stack destroyer screen. Owing to weather damage and a faulty catapult, she went onward to the Boston Navy Yard for several weeks of repairs. Contrary to some accounts, *Bogue* had not yet helped close the Greenland "Air Gap."

On the following day, March 27, Halifax 230 overtook Slow Convoy 123. This fast convoy was guarded by the British Escort Group B-1, commanded by E. C. Bayldon in the destroyer *Hurricane.* The group consisted of eight warships: *Hurricane* and two other destroyers, one frigate, and four corvettes. Bayldon had anticipated assistance from *Bogue* and her screening destroyers, but *Bogue*'s abort precluded any warship augmentation.

The northernmost of the *Seewolf* boats, the new VII *U-305,* commanded by Rudolf Bahr, found Halifax 230. She shadowed the convoy for a few hours but lost it in foul weather. Nonetheless U-boat Control directed that all sixteen boats of group *Seeteufel* and the ten most northerly boats of group *Seewolf*—twenty-six boats—were to seek out and attack the convoy, Halifax 230. One boat of each group could not comply owing to the need to refuel from a U-tanker, but the other twenty-four closed on *U-305.* Four boats (*U-523, U-591, U-610, U-631*) made contact with the convoy, but its escorts, responding to Huff Duff, sonar, or radar contacts, drove them off. Six other boats (three IXC40s and three VIIs) were low on fuel and broke off to find the U-tanker.

The remaining twenty U-boats trailing Halifax 230 ran into atrocious weather, a gale of near hurricane force, on March 28. Moreover, that day long-range and very-long-range aircraft from Iceland appeared, forcing the boats to submerge. On top of that, high winds and pitching seas scattered the convoy. As a result, the reports to

U-boat Control were fragmentary and unhelpful. The *U-591* saw seven freighters and five "destroyers," but aircraft drove her down. The *U-632* saw a tanker with "aircraft escort" but lost it almost immediately. The *U-618* saw a freighter escorted by a "destroyer" but could not attain a shooting position before the ship pulled away.

By March 29 the winds were blowing from the southwest at hurricane force. U-boat Control urged the boats to put the wind at their backs and use its force to help them pull ahead of the convoy for one last attack before it reached Hudson-range from Iceland. This was an impossible order. Hubertus Purkhold in the experienced *U-260* logged:

> Pursuit broken off. While trying to run before the storm at full speed, the boat plunged [under] twice. By blowing tanks, putting my helm hard over and reducing speed I managed to hold her reasonably well on the surface. To remain on the bridge was impossible. In just half an hour the captain and the watch were half drowned. Within a short time five tons of water cascaded into the U-boat through the conning-tower hatch, the voice pipe and the diesel air intake.

The chase turned into a first-class fiasco. Few boats could catch up with the convoy. One *Seeteufel* boat that did, the experienced *U-610,* commanded by Walter von Freyberg-Eisenberg-Allmendingen, sank one ship, the 7,200-ton American Liberty ship *William Pierce Frye.* None of the other thirty-four boats comprising groups *Seeteufel* and *Seewolf* sank a ship. Nor were any U-boats of these groups lost.

As related, on March 25, a B-17 of British Squadron 206 sank the VII *U-469,* which was awaiting escort duty with the blockade-runner *Regensberg,* subsequently lost. Two days later, the same B-17 with a new aircrew, commanded by A.C.I. Samuel, got the IXC40 *U-169,* commanded by Hermann Bauer, age twenty-five, also ten days out from Kiel. In what was doubtless the least memorable battle cry of Coastal Command in the entire war, Samuel reported that the U-boat sank almost vertically, "like a dose of Enos's," the trademark of an English brand of liver salts.

British Coastal Command Squadron 190, a Catalina outfit based at bleak Sullom Voe in the Faroe Islands, was favorably placed to kill U-boats outbound from Germany to join the Atlantic force or boats of the Arctic Norway force in nearby waters. On March 26, one of the Catalinas of Squadron 190, piloted by J. Fish, found a new VII of the Arctic Norway force unalertly traveling from Bergen on the surface. She was the *U-339,* commanded by Georg-Wilhelm Basse, age twenty-five. Fish dropped six depth charges which savaged *U-339,* forcing Basse to abort and limp to Trondheim. From there *U-339* returned to the Baltic, where, owing to the damage, she was retired to the Training Command, a school boat that never left the Baltic again. Basse was assigned to commission and command another new VII destined for the Arctic force.

The last Allied convoy to be found and attacked in the North Atlantic in March 1943 was Sierra Leone 126, the first convoy from that place since the previous October. It was thinly guarded by five warships: three frigates and two sloops. A Focke-Wulf

Condor patrol found it on March 27, west northwest of Cape Finisterre. U-boat Control directed five boats outbound from France to attempt an interception.

Two of the five U-boats locked onto the convoy and chased it for four days. These were *Ritterkreuz* holder Otto von Bülow in the veteran *U-404* and the experienced *U-662,* commanded by a new skipper, Heinz-Eberhard Müller, age twenty-seven. Aided by radar the frigate *Rother* carried out six separate attacks, dropping seventy-five depth charges. Nonetheless, in a remarkable five-torpedo salvo on March 29, Müller in *U-662* sank the 6,200-ton British freighter *Empire Whale,* wrecked another 6,900-ton British freighter, the *Umaria* (sunk by the escorts), and damaged yet another British freighter, the 7,200-ton Liberty ship *Ocean Viceroy.* On that day and the next, von Bülow in *U-404* sank two British freighters: the 8,800-ton *Nagara* and the 7,000-ton *Empire Bowman.* Totals: four ships for about 29,000 tons sunk, one ship of 7,200 tons damaged.

U-boat Control was naturally pleased with the outcome, noting the excellent cooperation between the *Luftwaffe* and the U-boats. Control expressed the hope that this tenacious attack would persuade the Allies to sail Gibraltar and Sierra Leone convoys farther to the west, beyond range of most Allied ASW aircraft and where the U-boats had greater sea room for operations.

Notwithstanding the unfavorable weather on the North Atlantic run, the Atlantic U-boat force ran up a noteworthy record of sinkings in the month of March: eighty-four merchant ships for 505,000 tons, plus the British destroyer *Harvester.* As a result, Axis submarine successes in all areas of the world in the month of March were 110 merchant ships for 635,600 tons, the third-highest monthly total of the war after June and November 1942. Twenty-eight of the victims (25 percent) for 190,000 tons (38 percent) were United States vessels, the rest British or British-controlled.

The breakdown of all sinkings by Axis submarines in March by areas of operation:

	Ships	*G.R.T.*
Arctic	3	18,245
Atlantic	84	504,575
Mediterranean	12	46,823
Indian Ocean	11	65,966
Total	110	635,609*

The numerous reasons for the sharp spike in sinkings in the North Atlantic run in March bear repeating:

* Figures as compiled by Professor Rohwer. Berlin propagandists claimed that Axis forces sank one million gross tons of shipping in March, bringing the claims for the war to thirty million gross tons. The actual figure for the war was about eighteen million gross tons. A Senate investigating committee, chaired by Harry S. Truman, imprudently seemed to confirm the outlandish claims of German propagandists, reporting that Axis forces sank an average one million tons per month in 1942, or twelve million tons that year alone.

• The accurate and timely flow of information on Allied convoys from the codebreakers at *B-dienst* and, oppositely, the temporary loss of naval Enigma by Allied codebreakers.

• The gradual expansion of the Atlantic U-boat force to a peak strength of 171 U-boats by April 1, which enabled Control to deploy enough boats to form several patrol lines up to six hundred miles long simultaneously.

• The concentration of U-boat groups in the Allied "Air Gap" southeastward of Greenland, which in March only the handful of very-long-range B-24s of Coastal Command Squadron 120 in Iceland could reach and patrol effectively.

• The presence of two XIV tankers *(U-461; U-463)* near the North Atlantic run, which permitted some VIIs to remain on station longer and to chase convoys at their highest speed.

• The more effective communications and cooperation between the *Luftwaffe* Condors and the U-boats in eastern Atlantic waters.

• The unflagging zeal of nearly all U-boat crews to achieve successes against the Allies in order to offset the German setbacks in the Soviet Union and North Africa and to avenge the intensified Allied heavy-bomber raids (Sickle) on civilians in the large German cities.

• Possibly a greater number of torpedo hits with the looping FAT torpedoes and a higher percentage of lethal hits with the Pi2 magnetic pistols in the nose of the electrics.

• In too many instances, the thinning out of close convoy escorts and the inability of aircraft from the "jeep" carrier *Bogue* to fly on account of foul weather and/or mechanical defects.

Although obviously a terrible spike indeed, the U-boat successes on the North Atlantic run in March did not come close to cutting this vital lifeline to the British Isles. The sinking figures also bear repeating. Sixteen convoys composed of about nine hundred merchant ships, plus escorts, sailed east and west over this route in March. The scores upon scores of U-boats were able to mount decisive attacks on only four of the eight eastbound convoys: Halifax 228 and 229, and Slow Convoys 121 and 122. These attacks resulted in the sinking of thirty-nine out of about 450 merchant ships in the eight eastbound convoys.* The loss of 8.5 percent of all the laden merchant ships sailing east that month hardly constitutes a "crisis of crises." Ninety-one and a half percent of all merchant ships that sailed east on that route in March got through to destinations. The cargoes in the thirty merchant ships of the "extra" eastbound convoy, Halifax 229A, which was not attacked by U-boats, nearly offset the cargoes lost in the four eastbound convoys that came under attack by U-boats.

Nine German U-boats assigned to the North Atlantic run were lost, seven VIIs and two IXs. Five U-boats were sunk by British aircraft, four of these by American-built B-17s of Squadrons 206 and 220, the other by a Whitley of OTU

---

* One ship of the eastbound Halifax 227 that sailed in February was lost to U-boats. None of the eight westbound convoys, comprised of 450 ships, sailing in March lost a ship to U-boats. One ship from Outbound North (Slow) 168 and two ships from Outbound North 169 that sailed in February were lost to U-boats. See Appendix 3.

10. Four were sunk by British and Canadian surface ships and the Free French corvette *Aconit.* These lost nine were manned by about four hundred men, of which twenty-four (from *U-432* and *U-444*) were captured. The rest of the Germans perished. The U-boats sank one escort, the British destroyer *Harvester,* on March 11, the first loss of an escort on the North Atlantic run since the British destroyer *Firedrake* in convoy Outbound North (Slow) 153 on December 16, 1942.

In all waters, Allied forces sank fourteen U-boats in March, nine VIIs and five IXs, manned by about 650 men, of whom only the aforementioned twenty-four were captured. For the first time in the war, aircraft sank more U-boats in a given month than surface ships: nine versus five, a portent of things to come.

More German Failures in the North Atlantic

The arrival in April of twenty-one new boats from Germany and two transfers from the Arctic force enabled U-boat Control to sail an unprecedented eighty-seven attack boats that month against Allied convoys in the North and Middle Atlantic. This great mass of U-boats consisted of seventy-two VIIs and fifteen Type IXs. Two of the VIIs, *U-217* and *U-218,* both Model D minelayers, were to lay fields in the waters off England. One of the IXs, *U-108,* was homebound to retirement in Germany.

Five of the VIIs were to sail from France to reinforce the Mediterranean force. The *U-303* and *U-414,* commanded by Karl-Franz Heine and Walter Huth, respectively, got through Gibraltar Strait on the night of April 9. Horst-Arno Fenski in *U-410* and Siegfried Koitschka in *U-616* got through on the nights of May 6 and 7, respectively. The fifth and last boat, Friedrich-Wilhelm Bothe's *U-447,* did not make it. On the night of May 7, two Gibraltar-based Hudsons of British Squadron 233, piloted by J. V. Holland and J. W. McQueen, found her in the western approaches to the strait and sank her with depth charges. There were no survivors.

Four Type XIV "Milk Cow" U-tankers backed up the swarm of attack boats in the North Atlantic. These were Bruno Vowe's *U-462,* which sailed on April 1; Helmut Metz's new *U-487,* which sailed from Kiel on March 27 and entered the Atlantic in early April; and two that sailed later in the month, Wolf Stiebler's *U-461* on April 20 and Georg von Wilamowitz's *U-459* on April 21. In addition, the XB minelayer *U-119,* which sailed on April 25 to plant a field off Halifax, was to refuel VIIs in the North Atlantic on her outward leg. After planting a minefield off Casablanca, the XB minelayer *U-117,* which sailed on March 31, was to refuel about ten IXs in the Azores area.

Most of the new VIIs sailing from Kiel were commanded by officers twenty-five or twenty-six years old who had prior experience in the Atlantic. However, the skippers of three new VIIs were younger. Gerhard Lange in *U-418,* age twenty-two, tied Eberhard Dahlhaus in *U-634* for the dubious distinction of youngest skipper in the Atlantic force. (Lange, actually two months older than Dahlhaus, did not survive his first patrol.) Claus-Peter Carlsen in *U-732* was twenty-three years old, and Werner Techand in *U-731* was twenty-four.

Dönitz and U-boat Control expected that this awesome deployment of subma-

PLATE 6

RESULTS OF RAF COASTAL COMMAND'S BAY OF BISCAY OFFENSIVES (DERANGE, MUSKETRY, SEASLUG, AND PERCUSSION) BY 19 GROUP

April 10–September 21, 1943[1]

U-BOATS SUNK			U-BOATS DAMAGED		
April 1943		(Derange 4/13–6/6)			
4/10	*U-376*	VIIC	4/10	*U-465*	VIIC
4/29	*U-332*	VIIC	4/26	*U-566*	VIIC
			4/29	*U-437*	VIIC
May 1943		(Derange to 6/6)			
5/2	*U-465*	VIIC	5/1	*U-415*	VIIC
5/7	*U-663*	VIIC	5/6	*U-214*	VIID (minelayer)
5/11	*U-528*	IXC40	5/9	*U-405*	VIIC
5/15	*U-266*	VIIC	5/15	*U-591*	VIIC
5/16	*U-463*	XIV (tanker)	5/24	*U-523*	IXC
5/31	*U-563*	VIIC	5/24	*U-441*	VII (flak)
5/31	*U-440*	VIIC	5/29	*U-552*	VIIC
			5/31	*U-261*	VIIC
June 1943		(Derange to 6/6; Musketry-Seaslug (6/14–8/21)			
6/1	*U-418*	VIIC	6/14	*U-155*	IXC
6/14	*U-564*	VIIC	6/14	*U-68*	IXC
6/24	*U-119*	IXB (SG-2)[2]	6/17	*U-338*	VIIC
6/24	*U-449*	VIIC (SG-2)	6/21	*U-462*	XIV (tanker)
			6/27	*U-518*	IXC
July 1943		(Musketry-Seaslug to 8/21)			
7/3	*U-126*	IXC	7/2	*U-462*	XIV (tanker)
7/3	*U-628*	VIIC	7/3	*U-267*	VIIC
7/5	*U-535*	IXC40	7/7	*U-386*	VIIC
7/8	*U-514*	ISC	7/12	*U-441*	VII (flak)
7/13	*U-607*	VIIC			
7/20	*U-558*	VIIC			
7/24	*U-459*	XIV (tanker)			
7/28	*U-404*	VIIC			
7/29	*U-614*	VIIC			
7/30	*U-461*	XIV (tanker)			
7/30	*U-462*	XIV (tanker)			
7/30	*U-504*	IXC (SG-2)			
August 1943		(Musketry-Seaslug to 8/21)			
8/1	*U-383*	VIIC	8/2	*U-218*	VIID (minelayer)
8/1	*U-454*	VIIC			
8/2	*U-706*	VIIC			
8/2	*U-106*	IXB			
September 1943		(Percussion 8/21–9/21)			
9/7	*U-669*	VIIC			
Totals:		30 Sunk	19 Damaged		

1. Sources: U-boat Control War Diary (BdU KTB); Franks, *Search, Find and Kill* (1995); Milner, *The U-Boat Hunters* (1994); Niestlé (1998); and others.

2. Johnny Walker's Support Group 2 (five sloops), assigned to the Bay of Biscay offensive, cooperated with aircraft of 19 Group and sank three U-boats, as shown. Walker's group was relieved by John S. Dallison's Support Group 40. Also cooperating was the newly formed "Canadian" Support Group 5. It was composed of five upgraded Canadian corvettes, a British corvette, and two British frigates, *Nene* and *Tweed.* This "Canadian" group was commanded by a Britisher, J. D. Birch, in *Nene.* The British Support Group 1, commanded by G. N. Brewer in the sloop *Egret,* was backed up by two British destroyers, *Athabaskan* and *Grenville* and relieved Dallison's Support Group 40. Off Cape Finisterre (in the Percussion Area) on August 23 and 28, flights of *Luftwaffe* DO-217s, fitted with "smart bombs," supported by JU-88s, attacked the various ships of these last-named support groups. Most of the bombs missed the wildly dodging warships but on August 28, one hit and sank Brewer's flagship, the sloop *Egret,* with the loss of 200 of her 225-man crew. Another hit and damaged the big *Tribal*-class *Athabaskan,* which, after about two months of repairs, was turned over to the Royal Canadian Navy.

rine power to the North Atlantic would decisively interdict and possibly shut down the flow of cargoes to the British Isles and to Torch forces. Nothing of the kind occurred. To the contrary, the U-boats failed dramatically and decisively. For starters, ten of the eighty-seven attack boats did not reach the convoy lanes.

As a result of the intensified Coastal Command air offensive, including that in the Bay of Biscay,* five boats sailing to the North Atlantic in April were sunk by British aircraft soon after leaving port or before reaching their assigned groups.

- The VII *U-465,* commanded by Heinz Wolf, age twenty-eight, sailed from Lorient for its third patrol on April 7 to join a group on the North Atlantic run. On April 10 a Catalina of British Squadron 210, piloted by Frank Squire, depth-charged the boat in Biscay and forced her to abort. After repairs at Lorient, Wolf resailed on April 29. On May 2, at the western edge of Biscay, a Sunderland of Australian Squadron 461, piloted by E. C. Smith, sank the boat with machine-gun fire and eight shallow-set depth charges. Smith's crew saw "about fifteen" Germans in the water, but all perished.
- The new VII *U-710,* commanded by Dietrich von Carlowitz, age twenty-six, sailed from Kiel on April 15. Ten days later, as she was entering the Atlantic in the Iceland-Faeroes gap, a B-17 of British Squadron 206, piloted by Robert L. Cowey (who had sunk *U-627* in October), sighted the boat on the surface. Cowey attacked in the teeth of flak and dropped six shallow-set depth charges. After the boat sank, Cowey reported twenty-five Germans swimming near the debris but none was rescued.
- The new VII *U-227,* commanded by Jürgen Kuntze, age twenty-five, departed Kiel on April 24. As she was entering the Atlantic in the Iceland-Faeroes gap on April 30, a Hampden of Australian Squadron 455, piloted by J. S. Freeth, age twenty-two, caught her on the surface and sank her with eight shallow-set depth charges. The aircrew reported thirty Germans amongst the debris, but there were no survivors. Pilot Freeth was killed three weeks later in a flying accident, the day after his twenty-third birthday.
- The VII *U-332,* commanded by Eberhard Hüttemann, age twenty-three, embarked on his second patrol, sailed from France to the Middle Atlantic on April 26. On the morning of April 29, a long-range B-24 of British Squadron 224, piloted by A. Russell Laughland, attacked *U-332* on the surface in the southwest edge of the Bay of Biscay. In two runs, Laughland dropped twelve shallow-set depth charges that fell close and sank *U-332.* The aircrew saw "wood and canvas" in a huge circle of oil. There were no survivors.†
- The veteran IXB *U-109,* commanded by her former first watch officer Hans Joachim Schramm, age twenty-six, sailed from St. Nazaire for the North Atlantic on April 28. Seven days later on May 4, a very-long-range B-24 of British Squadron 86 found *U-109* on the surface, while still en route to her assigned area. The pilot, J. C. Green, caught Schramm's bridge watch unalert and dropped four shallow-set depth charges from an altitude of eighty feet. The depth charges fell

---

* Enclose II, from April 6 to April 13; and thereafter Derange, see Plate 6.

† The Admiralty originally credited a Sunderland of RAAF Squadron 461 for this kill.

very close and blew up *U-109.* After the water subsided, the aircrew saw much debris, including twenty-four wooden planks about eight feet long (U-boat decking) and several floating "cylinders" (topside torpedo-storage canisters?). There were no survivors. The Admiralty assessment committee praised Green for conducting "a well executed approach and a perfect attack." *

Four other boats that departed on patrols in April returned prematurely to France. Three were damaged by the enemy or incurred mechanical problems. The fourth escorted one of the damaged boats back to base.

• The veteran VII *U-604,* commanded by Horst Höltring, sailed from France on April 22. On the second day out, the diesel engines failed and she returned to France on April 26. Höltring suspected that the engines had been sabotaged, but no saboteurs were ever found. During an inspection of the boat before repairs commenced, workers found several dead rats in the drinking-water storage tank, which reinforced the theory that the boat had been sabotaged. The engine repairs were lengthy, and *U-604* did not resail until late June.

• The often-damaged veteran VII *U-566,* commanded by Hans Hornkohl, embarked on his second patrol, sailed from Brest on April 22. On the western edge of Biscay, five days later, on April 26, a Leigh Light–equipped Wellington of Squadron 172, piloted by the Rhodesian Alex Coumbis, caught and damaged her with six depth charges. Unable to dive, she limped back to Brest, escorted by JU-88s and surface craft. She did not sail again until July.

• The veteran VII *U-437,* commanded by Hermann Lamby, embarked on his second patrol, sailed from St. Nazaire to the Middle Atlantic on April 26. On Lamby's first patrol he had been forced to abort with a cracked diesel-exhaust flange. Five days out from France at the western edge of Biscay, a Leigh Light–equipped Wellington of Squadron 172, piloted by Peter H. Stembridge, caught and straddled *U-437.* Lamby sent out an SOS, stating he "urgently" required help.

U-boat Control directed all boats in the vicinity to respond to the SOS at high speed without regard for fuel consumption. In addition, German airmen provided two flights of JU-88s. The *U-445,* commanded by Heinz-Konrad Fenn, which sailed from France to the Middle Atlantic on April 27, found *U-437* and nursed her back to St. Nazaire on April 30. The heavily damaged *U-437* did not resail until late September. An epidemic of diphtheria on Fenn's *U-445* and other factors delayed her resailing to July.

Three boats sailing in April carried out special missions before joining the other boats on torpedo patrols.

• The XB minelayer *U-119,* commanded by a new skipper, Horst-Tessen von Kameke, age twenty-seven, sailed from France on her second combat mission on April 25. While she was outbound in Biscay on April 29, two unidentified enemy aircraft attacked her, killing one petty officer, but von Kameke pressed on to the Americas. After refueling six VIIs in the North Atlantic, *U-119* planted sixty-six

* However, the Admiralty erroneously credited a Sunderland of Australian Squadron 10 for the kill of *U-109,* later corrected in a postwar analysis.

SMA (moored) mines off Halifax, Nova Scotia. The fields probably produced one sinking, the 3,000-ton Panamanian freighter *Halma* and possibly damaged an American Liberty ship, *John A. Poor.* Subsequently, von Kameke proceeded to the central Atlantic to fuel other VIIs if required and/or to attack Allied ships with his two loaded stern torpedo tubes and nine reloads.

- The VIID minelayer *U-217,* commanded by Kurt Reichenbach-Klinke, sailed from France on April 19 to lay a field of fifteen SMA (moored) mines off Land's End, the southwestern tip of England. On May 6, she withdrew from that location owing to "heavy enemy opposition" and Reichenbach-Klinke laid the fifteen mines in other areas of St. George's Channel. However, these mines produced no sinkings. After obtaining potash cartridges for the individual respirators and binoculars from an inbound boat, *U-217* set off to patrol Canadian waters near Nova Scotia, but U-boat Control diverted her to the Middle Atlantic.
- The VIID minelayer *U-218,* commanded by Richard Becker, sailed from France on April 20 to lay a field of fifteen SMA (moored) mines in the North Channel. Becker planted the field on May 4 but it produced no sinkings. Afterward, *U-218* sailed west to transfer an ill crewman to the XIV U-tanker *U-459* and to join the groups engaged in anticonvoy operations.

U-boat Control directed fifteen boats (four IXs, eleven VIIs) that had sailed in February or March to form a new group, *Löwenherz* (Lionhearted). However, as related, one of these boats, the IXC40 *U-169,* had been sunk in late March by a B-17 of British Squadron 206. Thus, unknown to U-boat Control, group *Löwenherz* had been reduced to fourteen boats. Its purpose was to intercept eastbound Slow or Halifax convoys.

A new IXC40, *U-530,* commanded by Kurt Lange, age thirty-nine, spotted Halifax 231 on April 4. Composed of sixty-one ships (twenty-two loaded tankers), the convoy was thinly guarded by British Escort Group B-7, commanded by Peter W. Gretton. It consisted of the destroyer *Vidette,* the new frigate *Tay,* and four corvettes.

While Lange in *U-530* shadowed and reported the convoy's composition, course, and speed, U-boat Control ordered the other boats of *Löwenherz,* plus (fuel permitting) nine other boats in the area to join in the attack, including the new VII *U-229,* which had been diverted to weather-reporting duty near Greenland, and the newly arriving IXC40 *U-532.* Three of the nine additional boats were unable to make contact. Hence the reinforced *Löwenherz* consisted of seventeen boats.

Upon learning that U-boats had discovered Halifax 231, Allied authorities directed the British Support Group 4, refueling at Iceland, and Coastal Command Squadron 120, based at Iceland and Northern Ireland, to reinforce Gretton's thin escort group. Newly created with four destroyers from the Home Fleet (*Icarus, Inglefield, Eclipse, Fury*), Support Group 4 was slow off the mark, ran into heavy weather, and did not meet the convoy for three days.

Several boats attacked the first night. The new VII *U-630,* commanded by Werner Winkler, age twenty-five, claimed sinking two ships, but only the 9,400-ton

British freighter *Waroonga,* which stayed with the convoy for thirty-six hours before sinking, was confirmed. Another new VII, *U-635,* commanded by Heinz Eckelmann, age twenty-seven (released from *Regensberg* escort duty), also claimed sinking two ships, but only the 5,500-ton British freighter *Shillong* was confirmed. The *U-229,* commanded by Robert Schetelig, sank a straggler from the convoy, the 3,400-ton Swedish *Vaalaren.*

The surface escorts spotted and fought off the mass of U-boats near the convoy. Nonetheless, three more boats were able to shoot. The veteran VII *U-706,* commanded by Alexander von Zitzewitz, sank the 7,100-ton tanker *British Ardour.* Another veteran VII, *U-563,* commanded by Götz von Hartmann, hit the 9,000-ton American tanker *Sunoil,* which was straggling with engine trouble. Kurt Lange in *U-530,* who had discovered the convoy, put *Sunoil* under with three torpedoes. The VII *U-632,* commanded by Hans Karpf, sank the 7,100-ton Dutchman *Blitar,* also straggling.

British aircraft from Iceland and Northern Ireland arrived on the afternoon of April 5 to support convoy Halifax 231. Over the next forty-eight hours the aircraft drove the U-boats down or off and sank two VIIs:

- On April 5, an Iceland-based very-long-range B-24 of British Squadron 120, piloted by Gordon L. Hatherly, got the new *U-635,* commanded by Heinz Eckelmann, three weeks out of Kiel. Hatherly dropped six shallow-set depth charges, which destroyed the boat with the loss of all hands.*
- On April 6, a very-long-range B-24 of British Squadron 86, piloted by Cyril W. Burcher, got the *U-632,* commanded by Hans Karpf, embarked on his second patrol. In two attacks, Burcher dropped eight shallow-set depth charges. There were no survivors.

Gretton's British Escort Group B-7, finally reinforced by the four destroyers of British Support Group 4 from Iceland and Coastal Command aircraft, thwarted further U-boat attacks on convoy Halifax 231, and on the evening of April 7, U-boat Control unhappily canceled this operation. It chided the *Löwenherz* skippers for broadcasting too many nonessential messages and for too much chasing of stragglers rather than the main body. It credited the seventeen U-boats operating on or near the convoy with sinking eight ships for 58,000 tons, plus a "destroyer," and hits on three other ships. The confirmed score was six merchant ships sunk (two tankers) for 41,600 tons and no warships. The other fifty-five ships (twenty tankers) of the convoy reached their destinations.†

The attack on Halifax 231 was costly for the Germans. In addition to the loss of the VIIs *U-632* and *U-635* with all hands, Control noted "a further five U-boats were heavily damaged by aircraft bombs or by depth charges." A "destroyer" attacked and "rammed" one of these five, the *U-572,* formerly commanded by the disgraced Heinz Hirsacker. Presumably the new skipper, Heinz Kummetat, age

---

* The Admiralty wrongly credited the kill of *U-635* to the frigate *Tay* of Gretton's Escort Group B-7, which had attacked a U-boat. Long after the war, the Admiralty shifted the credit to Hatherly's B-24.

† Doubtless by coincidence, on April 7, at the conclusion of this battle, Hitler awarded Dönitz Oak Leaves to his *Ritterkreuz.*

twenty-four, embarked on his second patrol, was seeking to restore the boat's honor. Ironically, he sank no ships on either of these patrols and was forced to abort the second.

Three other VIIs also aborted: the *U-563, U-564,* and *U-594.* The last named, commanded by Hans Fiedler, was hit by a B-24 of British Squadron 120, piloted by John K. Moffatt, but the boat reached France on April 13.

U-boat Control directed ten of the boats that attacked Halifax 231 to form a new group, *Lerche* (Lark). On April 11, one of the ten, the veteran *U-584,* commanded by Joachim Deecke, found the next eastbound convoy, Halifax 232. Composed of forty-seven merchant ships, it was guarded by the British Escort Group B-3, commanded by M. J. Evans, replacing A. A. Tait, who had been killed when his flagship, the destroyer *Harvester,* was sunk on March 11 defending Halifax 228. The group consisted of seven warships: three destroyers (British *Escapade* and *Witherington,* Polish *Garland*) and two British and two Free French corvettes. The British Support Group 4 (four Home Fleet destroyers) provided backup.

Adroitly shadowing, Deecke in *U-584* brought up three other *Lerche* boats. Helmut Pich in the new IXC40 *U-168* attacked first, firing a salvo of six torpedoes. He heard two explosions and believed he had hit two ships, but these were not confirmed. Götz von Hartmann in the aborting VII *U-563,* who had survived a close air attack in the battle with Halifax 231 (and lost two men overboard), attacked next. He claimed sinking three ships for 26,000 tons and damage to a fourth. In reality he sank two freighters for 9,800 tons and damaged the 7,300-ton British freighter *Fresno City,* which Alexander von Zitzewitz in *U-706* put under with a finishing shot. Upon return to France, Götz von Hartmann, who had made three patrols and sunk only two ships (plus damage to *Sunoil*), left *U-706* and was assigned to another boat.

By April 10 the *U-615,* commanded by Ralph Kapitzky, had been at sea for fifty-two days, assigned to three different groups, and had sunk no ships. En route to yet another group, Kapitzky found a straggler from Halifax 232, the 7,200-ton American Liberty ship *Edward B. Dudley.* Kapitzky fired a full bow salvo at the ship, but apparently he got only one hit and that one was a dud. The Liberty ship rang up flank speed; Kapitzky commenced a prolonged stern chase. Finally *U-615* caught up, closed to point-blank range, and again shot torpedoes. These hit and the ship, loaded with ammunition, blew up with an awesome explosion. Some of the debris landed on the bridge of *U-615,* severely injuring Kapitzky. He recovered in a Paris hospital, but the boat was out of action for nearly two months.

One of the *Lerche* boats, the new IXC40 *U-191,* commanded by Helmut Fiehn, age twenty-seven, reported that on April 13 he had repelled several attacks by a Sunderland using "both MG C/38" 20mm flak guns. U-boat Control immediately put this news on the U-boat network "in order to give all boats necessary encouragement for similar action."*

---

* In early April, similar reports of flak-gun successes had come from three other IXs: Emmermann in *U-172* and Helmut Pich in *U-168,* both IXC40s, and Karl Neitzel in the IXC *U-510.*

• • •

Acting on *B-dienst* information, U-boat Control formed another new group, *Adler* (Eagle), to intercept Slow Convoy 125, the first of these convoys to resume departures from Halifax in order to reduce congestion in New York harbor. The group was composed of sixteen boats, all veterans that had sailed from France, including the *Ritterkreuz* holder Otto von Bülow in *U-404*. Reading naval Enigma, Allied authorities rerouted Slow Convoy 125 to the south of group *Adler* and its ships arrived at their destinations without interference from the U-boats.

Based on further information from *B-dienst,* U-boat Control repositioned *Adler* to intercept an eastbound Halifax convoy. This interception also failed, but by happenstance, von Bülow in *U-404* discovered an opposite-sailing convoy, Outbound North 176. It was composed of forty-six merchant ships guarded by British Escort Group B-4, commanded by E.C.L. Day, comprised of three destroyers (*Highlander, Vimy,* and the ex-American four-stack *Beverley*) and five corvettes. U-boat Control directed eight of the northernmost *Adler* boats to join von Bülow for an attack on this convoy. The remaining six boats of *Adler,* plus the new *U-415,* commanded by Kurt Neide, were directed to cadre a new group, *Meise* (Titmouse).

Several *Adler* boats attacked Outbound North 176 but only two had any success.

- Siegfried Lüdden in the new IXC40 *U-188* claimed sinking three freighters for 18,000 tons plus a hit on a fourth ship. In reality, he sank only one vessel, the Norwegian-manned four-stack British destroyer *Beverley,* which had earlier incurred heavy damage to her sonar in a collision with the cargo ship *Cairnvalona. Beverley* could not "hear" and could make only fifteen knots. Four of *Beverley*'s 152-man crew were rescued; the rest perished.
- Von Bülow in *U-404* fired a full bow salvo (two FATs, two electrics) and claimed two ships for 14,000 tons sunk, plus one ship of 10,000 tons damaged. In reality he sank only the 1,900-ton British freighter *Lancastrain Prince* in ballast.
- Helmut Köppe in *U-613* also claimed a sinking from this convoy, but it could not be confirmed.

Racing north at top speed, the veteran Helmut Möhlmann in the *Adler* boat *U-571* came upon a convoy, but it was not the targeted Outbound North 176. Rather, it was Outbound North (Slow) 2, following the same course. Composed of thirty-seven merchant ships, it was guarded by Canadian Escort Group C-1, commanded by A. H. Dobson. Horst Uphoff in the *Adler* VII *U-84* joined Möhlmann to attack. Möhlmann fired four torpedoes and claimed two sinkings for 13,500 tons and damage to another ship. He was credited with sinking the 3,800-ton Norwegian freighter *Ingerfire,* but no other damage was confirmed. Even so, Möhlmann was awarded a *Ritterkreuz.** Uphoff in *U-84* claimed one sinking and damage to another ship, but neither claim could be confirmed.

---

* At the time of the award, Möhlmann had commanded *U-571* at the battlefronts for almost two full years. His confirmed score was six ships (one tanker) for 37,346 tons sunk, two ships (one tanker) for 13,658 tons wrecked beyond repair, eight ships for about 51,000 tons destroyed plus damage to another tanker of 11,400 tons. Upon arrival in France, he left the boat for other duties and later was appointed commander of Training Flotilla 14.

Unaware that the ships under attack by the *Adler* boats were attached to two separate convoys, Outbound North 176 and Outbound North (Slow) 2, U-boat Control informed Berlin that these boats had sunk nine ships for 56,500 tons and damaged four others. In reality the *Adler* boats had sunk merely three ships for about 7,000 tons: one by von Bülow in *U-404,* one by Möhlmann in *U-571,* and the destroyer *Beverley* by Lüdden in *U-188.*

As related, the *U-262,* commanded by Heinz Franke, en route to the Gulf of St. Lawrence on a secret mission to pick up escaped German POWs, by happenstance found a convoy on April 15. She shadowed for a while, bringing up seven other boats outbound from France, then proceeded to her special mission in Canadian waters. This convoy was Halifax 233, composed of fifty-seven merchant ships, guarded by the last American escort group on the North Atlantic run, A-3, commanded by Paul Heineman, on its last mission. The escort consisted of eight warships: two big *Treasury*-class Coast Guard cutters, *Duane* and *Spencer;* the Canadian destroyer *Skeena;* and five corvettes, three British and two Canadian.

On the morning of April 17, one of the seven boats, *U-628,* commanded by Heinz Hasenschar, who was embarked on his third patrol, launched the attack on Halifax 233. He fired torpedoes at two ships and claimed hits on both, sinking one and badly damaging one. In reality he hit only one, the 7,100-ton British *Fort Rampart.* She fell out of the convoy screened by one of the corvettes, which took off the crew. Hasenschar in *U-628* and Rolf Borchers in *U-226,* making his second patrol, both fired finishing shots and hit *Fort Rampart,* and she sank immediately.

At that time the veteran cutter *Spencer,* commanded by Harold Sloop Berdine, was well away from the convoy, pursuing a sonar contact. Upon learning that a ship had been sunk, *Spencer* rejoined the convoy and soon got a sonar contact five thousand yards ahead. Berdine rang up full speed and dropped two salvos of eleven depth charges each.

The charges closely straddled the IXC *U-175,* commanded by the promising skipper Heinrich Bruns, who had sunk ten ships for 40,600 tons in two prior patrols. He was attempting a risky daylight submerged attack. The depth charges wrecked *U-175* internally and cracked the pressure hull. Flooding fore and aft, *U-175* plunged deeper and deeper, out of control. Inasmuch as Bruns appeared to be shocked senseless, at a depth of nine hundred feet the engineer took over and blew all ballast tanks in a last-ditch effort to stop the descent and save the crew.

The *Spencer* and her sister ship, *Duane,* commanded by H. B. Bradbury, held sonar contact on *U-175* and anticipated her rapid rise to the surface. When she popped up, both vessels opened fire with guns at close range, as did a number of merchant ships in the rear positions of the convoy. A shell from one of the merchant ships hit *Spencer,* wounding eight men, one fatally. *Spencer*'s fire at *U-175* wrecked the bridge and conning tower and killed the skipper, Bruns, and a half dozen others. Berdine brought *Spencer* around to a course to ram *U-175,* but the escort commander, Paul Heineman, perhaps recalling the severe damage her sister ship *Campbell* sustained in ramming *U-606,* told *Spencer* to heave to and put over a boarding party. Commanded by Ross P. Bullard, the party got into the conning tower, but *U-175* was rapidly sinking stern first and there was no opportunity to search for documents or souvenirs.

In the meantime the surviving Germans had jumped into the sea and, as Berdine reported, "acted in a very hysterical manner." *Spencer* picked up nineteen Germans, *Duane* twenty-two, altogether forty-one of the fifty-four-man crew. A photographer on *Spencer* took numerous shots of the bewildered and frightened Germans, including a famous one of a survivor in the water, arms raised in a prayerful plea for rescue.*

Other escorts found and attacked other U-boats. Leopold Koch in the *U-382* was hunted and depth-charged for sixteen hours. He incurred such heavy damage that he was forced to abort to France for the second time in as many patrols. Rolf Borchers in *U-226* and Hartwig Looks in *U-264* reported heavy depth-charge damage but both boats were able to make repairs and continue their patrols.

Upon learning that seven or eight newly sailed, experienced U-boats were gathering around Halifax 233, Allied authorities directed the new British Support Group 3, commanded by J. W. McCoy, to assist. McCoy sailed with four destroyers, recently obtained from the Home Fleet: *Offa, Oribi, Penn,* and *Panther.* These powerful vessels raised the escort of Halifax 233 to twelve warships: seven of destroyer class or larger and five corvettes. All had new radar and several had Huff Duff.

With its twelve warships and very-long-range aircraft support commencing on April 18, Halifax 233 was no longer a sensible target. U-boat Control canceled operations and sent the remaining U-boats to a newly forming group, *Specht* (Woodpecker). Halifax 233 completed its voyage in the British Isles, having lost only the one ship of its fifty-seven, the *Fort Rampart.* It was a fitting swan song for Paul Heineman and A-3, the last American close escort group to operate on the long-established North Atlantic run.

The seven U-boats from group *Adler* that cadred the new group *Meise* (Titmouse) were soon reinforced by the other ten boats of *Adler* that had attacked Outbound North 176 and Outbound North (Slow) 2. Control logged that "Italian codebreakers" provided the location and course of Slow Convoy 126, adding that it was "one day behind schedule."† It was composed of thirty-eight merchant ships, escorted by Richard Boyle's British close Escort Group 5 (the destroyers *Havelock, Volunter,* frigate *Swale,* and five corvettes).

Control positioned *Meise* to intercept Slow Convoy 126. However, on April 14, Allied aircraft detected two *Ritterkreuz* holders of group *Meise,* von Bülow in *U-404* and Möhlmann in *U-571.* This forced U-boat Control to shift the group northeastward where it believed the evading convoy was likely to be found. Six other boats joined the group, bringing *Meise* to twenty-three U-boats. It was to be supported by Helmut Metz's new Type XIV tanker *U-487,* which had sailed from Kiel on March 27 to relieve *U-462.*

---

* See photo opposite p. 497, Volume I.

† Control logged further that this unusual Italian report was "confirmed" by *B-dienst* on April 13.

During the shifting about and recomposition of *Meise,* the newly joined VII *U-631,* commanded by Jürgen Krüger, which had sailed from France on her second patrol on March 6, rammed the veteran VII *U-71,* the second-oldest boat in the Atlantic force after the IX *U-43.* No one was seriously injured in the collision, but *U-71* incurred heavy damage. Upon learning of the incident, U-boat Control decided to retire *U-71* to the Training Command, along with the IXB *U-108* and the VII *U-704.** The *U-71* aborted then and there and headed for Germany via Norway for emergency repairs. Upon reaching Germany, her skipper, Hardo Rodler von Roithberg, and some of the crew were assigned to commission a new VIIC. The rammer, *U-631,* made repairs and remained at sea.

It soon became apparent that Slow Convoy 126 had eluded group *Meise* by going south rather than north as the Germans anticipated. However, the shift of *Meise* to the north put the group on the paths of three other convoys: Halifax 234, Outbound North 178, and Outbound North (Slow) 4.

One of the newly joined *Meise* boats, *U-306,* commanded by Claus von Trotha, found Halifax 234 on April 21. It was composed of forty-three merchant ships and was closely guarded by British Escort Group B-4, commanded by E.C.L. Day, consisting of two destroyers (*Highlander, Vimy*) and five corvettes. U-boat Control directed all *Meise* boats that could reasonably do so to close this convoy. Von Trotha brought up six boats, two IXs and four other newly joined VIIs. The IXs were the *U-108,* commanded by Ralf-Reimar Wolfram, preparing to depart for retirement to the Training Command, and the new IXC40 *U-189,* commanded by Helmut Kurrer, age twenty-seven. Five other VIIs took up backstopping positions east of the von Trotha group. These included two veteran VIIs recently transferred from the Arctic: *U-209,* commanded by Heinrich Brodda, and *U-378,* commanded by Erich Mäder. The other three were new boats from Germany. On one, the *U-954,* commanded by Odo Loewe, Dönitz's younger son Peter, age twenty-one, was the second watch officer.

Loewe was an experienced skipper. He had commissioned and commanded the *U-256* for one Atlantic war patrol, at the end of which the boat was wrecked by British aircraft and decommissioned in Lorient. He then commanded *U-254* for one Atlantic patrol, substituting for Hans Gilardone, who was ill. He sank two ships for about 17,700 tons on that patrol, then returned to Germany to commission *U-954.* The reason Peter Dönitz was assigned to this particular boat has not been established.

Allied authorities DFed the U-boats massing to attack Halifax 234 and promptly provided the convoy with very-long-range air cover. As a result, the U-boats achieved little. Von Trotha in *U-306* sank two big freighters, the 10, 200-ton British *Amerika* and the 7,200-ton American Liberty ship *Robert Gray.* Loewe in the new, backstopping *U-954* damaged the 5,300-ton British freighter *Silvermaple.* Walter von Freyberg in the newly joined *U-610* thought he hit a ship with FATs, but it was not confirmed.

---

* In three prior Atlantic patrols, Horst Hessler in *U-704* had sunk only one confirmed ship, a 4,200-ton British freighter. It is not clear why the boat was retired so soon. After reaching the Baltic in early April, Hessler was reassigned to commission a new VII.

Von Trotha in *U-306* continued to deliver what U-boat Control characterized as "perfect shadowing." His reports kept a dozen boats on the convoy over several days, but intense Allied air cover, the veteran warships of Day's Escort Group B-4, and Support Group 4 thwarted all U-boat attacks.

The aircraft hit two boats.

- A very-long-range B-24 of Squadron 120 from Iceland, piloted by John K. Moffatt, who had earlier damaged the VII *U-594,* found and sank the new IXC40 *U-189,* commanded by Helmut Kurrer, age twenty-seven, merely three weeks out from Kiel. Moffatt reported "about fifty" Germans in the water, but there were no survivors.
- On April 22, another aircraft so heavily damaged the newly refueled veteran, *U-134,* commanded by a new skipper, Hans-Günther Brosin, age twenty-six, that she was forced to abort to France. She arrived on May 2, completing an arduous but unsuccessful patrol of fifty-eight days. After repairs, she sailed again, a month later.

Another Great Convoy Battle

The experienced VII *U-706* of group *Meise* (Titmouse), commanded by Alexander von Zitzewitz, who had sunk one ship each from Halifax 231 and Halifax 232 on this patrol, found convoy Outbound North 178 on April 21. Composed of fifty-eight merchant ships, it was guarded by British Escort Group B-1, commanded by E. C. Bayldon in the destroyer *Hurricane.* It consisted of another destroyer, the ex-American four-stack *Rockingham;* a frigate, *Kale;* and five corvettes.

At nearly the same hour, the new VII *U-415,* commanded by Kurt Neide, reported the same convoy. Von Zitzewitz lost it in the foul weather, but Neide hung on and attacked. His torpedoes sank two British freighters, the 4,900-ton *Ashantian* and the 5,500-ton *Wanstead.* Helmut Fiehn, age twenty-seven, in the new IXC40 *U-191* came up and sank the 3,000-ton Norwegian *Scebeli.*

Neide in *U-415,* who had been at sea since March 7, broke off operations and headed for France. He met the new XIV tanker *U-487* for a small drink of fuel on April 26, then proceeded easterly to the Bay of Biscay. In the early hours of May 1, a Leigh Light–equipped Wellington of Squadron 172, piloted by Peter W. Phillips, got *U-415* on centimetric-wavelength radar. Phillips turned on his light and attacked in the teeth of flak, dropping six depth charges, forcing the U-boat under. The flak blew the Wellington's left tire and upon returning to base, the plane crash-landed, but no one was hurt.

Later in the morning of May 1, a Sunderland of Australian Squadron 461, piloted by E. C. Smith, who had earlier sunk *U-465,* found *U-415* on the surface. As Smith commenced his attack, *U-415* dived. Smith toggled a salvo of depth charges at the swirl but these caused no apparent damage.

Still later that day, yet another aircraft found *U-415* on the surface. She was a Whitley of British Squadron 612, piloted by Norman Earnshaw, participating in the renewed British Biscay air offensive, Derange. He nursed this slow, clumsy aircraft into an attack glide, notwithstanding heavy flak from *U-415,* which crash-dived. He then dropped six depth charges at the swirl but these fell somewhat wide. In a second, more calmly conducted run, Earnshaw dropped his last two depth charges and these caused "heavy damage," Neide reported. However, *U-415* could still dive and thus was able to limp into Brest on May 5.

Another *Meise* boat, the veteran VII *U-438,* reported another westbound convoy about eighty miles behind Outbound North 178. The *U-438* was commanded by a new but experienced skipper: Heinrich Heinsohn, former captain of the Mediterranean boat *U-573,* which had been hit by aircraft and had limped into Spain, where Heinsohn and his crew had been briefly "interned," then "repatriated."

At about the same time another *Meise* VII, *U-613,* commanded by Helmut Köppe, reported the same convoy. It was Outbound North (Slow) 4, composed of thirty-two merchant ships, escorted by British Escort Group B-2, commanded by Donald Macintyre in his refurbished destroyer *Hesperus.* It consisted of another destroyer, *Whitehall,* five corvettes, and an ASW trawler. The B-2 close escort was augmented by British Support Group 5, commanded by E.M.C. Abel-Smith, consisting of the "anglicized" "jeep" carrier *Biter* on her maiden voyage, screened by four destroyers. The combined escort thus consisted of thirteen warships: *Biter,* six destroyers, five corvettes, and an ASW trawler. Sailing from Iceland on April 21, *Biter* had nine Swordfish biplanes and two American-built Martlets, the British version of the F4F Wildcat.

To mount a better planned and more concentrated attack on Outbound North (Slow) 4, U-boat Control canceled the attack on Outbound North 178. The new VII *U-732,* commanded by young Claus-Peter Carlsen, age twenty-three, was the next boat to locate this preferred convoy. Carlsen attempted to attack, he reported, but a "biplane" drove him off. The "biplane" was a Swordfish from the carrier *Biter,* one of the eleven aircraft of ASW Squadron 811. Then an escort depth-charged *U-732,* knocking out a periscope and forcing Carlsen to abort to France. Carlsen sank no ships, but his report brought up four other *Meise* boats, three IXs (the Germany-bound *U-108,* the experienced *U-514,* and the newly arrived *U-191*) and one VII, the *U-404,* commanded by *Ritterkreuz* holder Otto von Bülow. Fiehn in *U-191* carried out a daylight submerged attack, firing four torpedoes, but all missed. Wolfram in *U-108* was subjected to a "fairly long" depth-charge attack, but he continued to shadow.

Donald Macintyre in *Hesperus* DFed a radio message from Fiehn in the new IXC40 *U-191* on April 23. Signaling the corvette *Clematis* to join him, Macintyre raced down the bearing. Too late, Fiehn saw *Hesperus* approaching at high speed and dived. In what Macintyre later described as "perfect" sonar conditions, *Hesperus* got a solid contact. Unfortunately the green and undertrained crew on the newly installed Hedgehog launcher had not yet removed the safety pins and when Macintyre ordered the Hedgehog to be fired, "nothing happened." While the safety pins were being removed, *Hesperus* and *Clematis* both carried out depth-charge attacks. On his second depth-charge run, Macintyre also fired from a torpedo tube an awesome, experimental, 2,000-pound depth charge and then—finally—a full salvo of twenty-four mortar missiles from the Hedgehog. The sonar operator reported two definite Hedgehog explosions, indicating they hit *U-191*. Nothing further was ever heard from that boat. The Admiralty credited her loss to *Hesperus*.

By this time, group *Specht* (Woodpecker) had formed up about two hundred miles southeast of Outbound North (Slow) 4 to attack the opposite-sailing Slow Convoy 127. It was comprised of eighteen boats, ten of the southernmost boats of *Meise* (including six that had refueled) and eight of the newly sailed boats that had attacked the American-escorted Halifax 233, including the IXC *U-125,* one of the original Drumbeat boats, still commanded by *Ritterkreuz* holder Ulrich Folkers. U-boat Control directed group *Specht,* less three boats that had to refuel, to race north to join in the attack on Outbound North (Slow) 4. Should it fail to locate that convoy, *Specht,* now composed of seventeen boats, was to remain in the more northerly waters on a patrol line running southeast from Greenland.

Otto von Bülow in *U-404* held firmly to Outbound North (Slow) 4. On April 24 he spotted *Biter* and her screen of four destroyers. His report brought up three other boats (two IXs, one VII). That night when one of these had made contact, von Bülow boldly slipped through the destroyer screen and fired all five torpedo tubes at *Biter* (two FATs, two electrics, and one electric with a Pi2 magnetic pistol). While retreating on the surface, von Bülow heard four hits, he reported, and saw "two tongues of flame" rising from *Biter.* He thought it was the American fleet carrier *Ranger,* and he "presumed" it sank. The response from U-boat Control and Dönitz was immediate. The next day Hitler awarded von Bülow Oak Leaves to his *Ritterkreuz,* which the Führer later presented in person.* After the presentation, von Bülow left *U-404* to command Flotilla 23 in the Training Command.

On Easter Sunday, April 25, *Hesperus* DFed another U-boat nearby. This was the *U-203,* made famous by Rolf Mützelburg, now commanded by Hermann Kottmann, who was preparing to attack *Biter.* When Macintyre notified *Biter,* she diverted a Swordfish to run down the DF bearing. The aircraft spotted the diving U-boat and dropped two shallow-set depth charges on the swirl from an altitude of fifty feet. The plane then remained over the spot until the destroyer *Pathfinder* of *Biter*'s screen arrived. In the hurried dive, one of *U-203*'s diesel-exhaust valves had not properly seated and was leaking. Kottmann was therefore reluctant to go deeper than two hundred feet.

Pathfinder held sonar contact and carried out several depth-charge runs, dropping over forty missiles. The close explosions increased the flooding aft to the point that Kottmann became convinced *U-203* was doomed. He blew all main-ballast tanks and surfaced close to *Pathfinder.* The engineer stayed below to open the vents to scuttle the boat and was never seen again. Nine other Germans died in the sinking from shock, hypothermia, or failure to properly don escape apparatus, the British reported. *Pathfinder* rescued Kottmann and thirty-seven other crew. *Biter*—not *Bogue*—was thus the first "jeep" carrier to participate in a confirmed U-boat kill.

---

* At the time of the award, his confirmed score was fifteen ships for 77,483 tons, including the British destroyer *Veteran.* The hits on *Biter* could not be confirmed.

Evasive routing, skilled escort work, *Biter*'s local air cover, and very-long-range aircraft from Iceland and Newfoundland thwarted any further U-boat attacks on Outbound North (Slow) 4. After threading through a dangerous field of icebergs, the convoy was further reinforced by British Support Group 1, commanded by Godfrey N. Brewer, consisting of five warships: three frigates (*Wear, Jed, Spey*), a sloop (*Pelican*), and an ex-Coast Guard cutter (*Sennen*). Every merchant ship of the convoy reached its destination. Macintyre's escort group, B-2, and the *Biter* support group, 5, put into Canada to prepare for a return trip to the British Isles.

The Germans were disappointed in these three convoy operations, to say the least. The forty-odd U-boats of groups *Meise* and *Specht* sank only three ships for 13,400 tons from Outbound North 178 and only two ships for 17,400 tons from Halifax 234, and none from Outbound North (Slow) 4. Total sinkings by these big groups: five ships for about 31,000 tons. U-boat losses: three (the new IXs *U-189* and *U-191* and the VII *U-203*). This was a catastrophic "exchange rate" of 1.7 merchant ships sunk for each U-boat lost.

By April 25, U-boat Control had dissolved group *Meise*. Three groups remained on the North Atlantic run: two new ones, *Amsel* (Blackbird) and *Star* (Starling), and a reorganized *Specht* (Woodpecker). The *Amsel* patrol line of thirteen boats began at a point northeast of Newfoundland and ran to the southeast. The nineteen boats of *Specht* extended *Amsel*'s line farther southeastward, so that the combined *Amsel-Specht* line of thirty-two U-boats was nearly five hundred miles long. These boats were to trap eastbound Halifax or Slow Convoys. *Star,* composed of sixteen boats, was deployed on a line east of *Amsel-Specht.* These boats were to trap the oppositely sailing Outbound North and Outbound North (Slow) convoys. In keeping with the new policy, the three groups included ten of the unsuitable Type IXs.

At that time, two big and important convoys were en route to the British Isles: Slow Convoy 127 (fifty-seven merchant ships) and Halifax 235 (thirty-six fast merchant ships). The first convoy, Slow 127, was guarded by Canadian Escort Group C-1, composed of six warships: two Canadian destroyers, a British frigate, and three Canadian corvettes. The second convoy, Halifax 235, was guarded by Canadian Escort Group C-4, composed of five warships: two destroyers (one British, one Canadian) and three corvettes. The American Support Group 6—the "jeep" carrier *Bogue* and five destroyers—augmented the close escort of Halifax 235, bringing the warships with it to eleven: *Bogue,* seven destroyers, and three corvettes.

Based on complete and current breaks into naval Enigma, Allied authorities were able to thread Slow Convoy 127 and Halifax 235 through the long *Amsel-Specht* patrol line. Equipped with twenty-one aircraft (including six Wildcats and twelve Avengers), *Bogue,* still commanded by Giles E. Short, occupied a position *inside* the convoy. Taking advantage of improving weather, she launched Wildcats and Avengers daily to scout for U-boats ahead and on the flanks of the convoy. One Avenger found and attacked a U-boat with four depth charges, but no sinking was claimed or credited. Halifax 235 and Slow Convoy 127 crossed the Atlantic without the loss of any ships. *Bogue* and her destroyer screen attended the Royal

Navy's ASW schools in Liverpool and Northern Ireland, and *Bogue* was fitted with Huff Duff.

Outwitted by Allied decrypts of Enigma, on April 29 U-boat Control shifted the *Amsel-Specht* line southwest. *Amsel* was reinforced by the arrival of two experienced VIIs, increasing its strength to seventeen boats. Two of the nineteen boats of *Specht* fell out (the veteran IX *U-108* to retirement in Germany and the experienced VII *U-706* to refuel), reducing its strength to seventeen boats. The thirty-four boats of the *Amsel-Specht* patrol line searched for eastbound convoys but found none.

The new German U-boat group, *Star* (Starling), was to be deployed on a 250-mile north-south line midway between Iceland and Greenland. The group was to be composed of sixteen boats: four new IXs and twelve VIIs, of which six were new, four were experienced boats from France, and two were veteran transfers from the Arctic.

One of the VIIs of *Star,* the new *U-650,* commanded by Ernst von Witzendorff, age twenty-six, reported a westbound convoy about 250 miles southwest of Iceland on April 28. This was Outbound North (Slow) 5, composed of forty-three merchant ships. It was guarded by British Escort Group B-7, commanded by Peter Gretton in the newly upgraded destroyer *Duncan.* The group was comprised of seven warships: *Duncan* and another destroyer, *Vidette;* the frigate *Tay;* and four corvettes. The escort was supported by two tankers, one (*British Lady*) well equipped to refuel escorts, the other (*Argon*) inadequately equipped. Two ASW trawlers, *Northern Spray* and *Northern Gem,* were attached to the convoy to serve as rescue vessels.

The Allies lost four-rotor naval Enigma on April 26. As a result, they were "blind" for about a week and with the passing of each day, the exact deployment of U-boat groups became less and less certain. This intelligence loss profoundly influenced the fate of convoy Outbound North (Slow) 5.

The weather was so atrocious that the escort vessels could not refuel. This handicap led to a decision to follow the shortest route to Canada. The green skipper von Witzendorff in *U-650* hung on to the convoy. On instructions from Control, he broadcast beacon signals to bring up the other fourteen boats of *Star.* The first two VIIs to arrive were the Arctic transfer *U-378,* commanded by Erich Mäder, and the new *U-386,* commanded by Hans-Albrecht Kandler, age twenty-five. On the way from Kiel, Kandler had sunk the 2,000-ton British freighter *Rosenborg,* a straggler from convoy RU 71, en route from Iceland to the British Isles.

The weather remained terrible, limiting Allied air cover and convoy and U-boat operations alike. After some other boats arrived, von Witzendorff in *U-650* attempted to attack the convoy, but Peter Gretton in the destroyer *Duncan* drove him off. In retaliation, von Witzendorff fired three torpedoes at *Duncan,* but all missed. Otto-Heinrich Junker in the new IXC40 *U-532* fired a full salvo of six torpedoes. He claimed hits on two ships, but they were not confirmed. All six torpedoes apparently missed or malfunctioned. Wilhelm von Mässenhausen in the veteran VII *U-258,* who had earlier patrolled with groups *Amsel* and *Meise,* fired a full bow salvo into the convoy. He claimed three hits on two freighters. In actuality, only

National Archives 242HB20583

Notoriously ignorant of naval strategy and tactics, and prone to seasickness, Adolf Hitler pays a rare visit to a warship.

National Archives 208PU-52D-3

Albert Speer, director of German arms production, and Grand Admiral Karl Dönitz, commander in chief of the German Navy.

Angus MacLean Thuermer

Helmut Walter, chief German submarine designer in the prewar and wartime years.

National Archives 306NT1342

Admiral Hans-Georg von Friedeberg, who succeeded Karl Dönitz in February 1943 as chief of U-boats and as commander in chief of the German Navy in April 1945, shown here signing surrender papers in Berlin.

U-boot-Archiv Horst Bredow, Cuxhaven, Germany

Admiral Eberhard Godt, chief of U-boat Control from February 1943, when Dönitz was promoted to commander in chief.

U-boot-Archiv Horst Bredow, Cuxhaven, Germany

Dönitz's son-in-law, Günther Hessler, U-boat ace and principal tactician at U-boat Control.

National Archives 80G164070

Big Three at Teheran: General Joseph Stalin, President Franklin D. Roosevelt, and Prime Minister Winston S. Churchill.

National Archives RG 38MCN-122-1

Admiral Andrew B. Cunningham, First Sea Lord, succeeding Admiral Dudley Pound upon the death of the latter in 1943.

Imperial War Museum A18476

Admiral Max Horton, commander in chief, Western Approaches, who directed the British end of the Atlantic convoy system from Liverpool.

National Archives 306NT202B1

Air Marshal John Slessor, chief of RAF Coastal Command in 1943, when Allied air power decimated the U-boat force.

National Archives 80G473448

Admiral Ernest J. King, commander in chief of the U.S. Navy in World War II.

Admiral Francis S. ("Frog") Low, King's chief deputy for antisubmarine warfare.

Admiral Jonas H. Ingram, commander in chief of the U.S. Atlantic fleet, succeeding Royal E. Ingersoll.

Admiral George C. Jones, chief of the Royal Canadian Navy from January 1944, succeeding Percy W. Nelles.

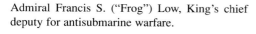

Admiral L. W. Murray, commander of the Royal Canadian Navy's Northwest Atlantic Command.

National Archives 357G Fldr. 336, No. 1640

Admiral Emory S. Land, chairman of the U.S. Maritime Commission, who directed the construction of more than five thousand ships during World War II, shown here with models of various types, including the famous "Liberty."

National Archives 80G179267

From 1943, the principal nemesis of the U-boat was a radar-equipped aircraft on offensive or defensive patrol. Here, an Allied aircraft attacks the big IXD2 cruiser submarine *U-848*. Note the unmanned antiaircraft gun array on the U-boat's bridge.

National Archives 242GAP102M8

Johann Hendrick Mohr, skipper of the Type IXB *U-124*.

National Archives 242GAP101B20

Otto von Bülow, skipper of the Type VIIC *U-404*.

National Archives 242GAP103V35

Richard Zapp, skipper of the Type IXC *U-66*.

National Archives 242GAP102M11

Rolf Mützelburg, skipper of the Type VIIC *U-203*. Destined to become one of the prominent U-boat aces, he died in a swimming accident before realizing that honor.

Carl Emmermann

Carl Emmermann, skipper of the Type IXC *U-172*.

National Archives 242GAP101A4

Young Otto Ites, skipper of the Type VIIC *U-94*. He discovered hidden flaws in the German torpedoes.

T. R. Mulligan

Werner Henke, skipper of the Type IXC *U-515*. Captured, he committed suicide at the secret American POW interrogation center, Fort Hunt, Virginia.

Alfred Eick

Alfred Eick, skipper of the Type IXC *U-510,* who made a successful patrol to the Far East and back.

National Archives 306NY1342

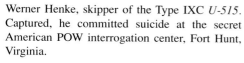

Heinrich Bleichrodt (right), skipper of the VIIC *U-48,* the IXC *U-67,* and the IXB *U-109*. On his last war patrol he requested—then demanded—relief of command.

Imperial War Museum A21988

Frederic J. (Johnny) Walker, commander of the Royal Navy's famed hunter-killer Support Group 2, composed of sloops, which sank about twenty U-boats.

Imperial War Museum A15601

Donald Macintyre, commander of the Royal Navy's Escort Group 5, composed of old destroyers, which also ran up an impressive number of U-boat kills.

Imperial War Museum A12427

Peter Gretton, commander of Escort Group 7, which defended convoy Outbound North 5 in May 1943, in a series of fierce battles on the Newfoundland Grand Banks. Gretton's group and others sank six U-boats.

Imperial War Museum CH4017A

Shown here with his flight crew, Terence M. Bulloch (seated, center), commander of RAF Coastal Command's Squadron 120, pioneered antisubmarine tactics for the B-24 Liberator.

Imperial War Museum CH14506

Wilfred E. Oulton, another outstanding RAF U-boat killer.

National Archives of Canada PA151743

James D. Prentice developed and taught antisubmarine tactics for the Royal Canadian Navy.

National Archives RG 457, NSA Box 1431

Edward W. Travis, who replaced Alastair Denniston as chief of Britain's codebreaking unit, the Government Code and Cipher School (GC&CS) at Bletchley Park in 1942.

National Archives RG 457, NSA Box 1431

Captain Joseph N. Wenger, who replaced Laurence F. Safford as head of the U.S. Navy's codebreaking unit, OP20G, in 1942.

Elliott & Fry, National Portrait Gallery 47918

Alan Turing, brilliant British mathematician, who with another brilliant British mathematician, Gordon Welchman, designed a machine (bombe) to break German naval Enigma.

U.S. Navy via Kristina Engstrom

Captain Howard T. Engstrom, chief of the OP20G research and development section, who played a key role in the design and manufacture of the American four-rotor bombe used for breaking German naval Enigma. He is shown here accepting the award of a Distinguished Service Medal from Secretary of the Navy James V. Forrestal.

National Archives RG 457, NSA Box 584

U.S. Navy WAVES, who operated the bombes, sit for a "working portrait" at desks adjoining the bombes, which were housed at a former girls' school in Washington, D.C. The machines were manned twenty-four hours a day.

Smithsonian 90-3650

A Navy WAVE poses before the workhorse Model 1530 U.S. Navy four-rotor bombe. In strictest secrecy, the engineers and technicians at National Cash Register Company, Dayton, Ohio, manufactured about 120 such bombes during the war. From October 1943, U.S. Navy codebreakers assumed full responsibility for breaking U-boat codes with these machines.

U.S. Navy/Knowles Family

Commander Kenneth A. Knowles, who managed the U.S. Navy's Submarine Tracking Room in Washington, relied to a great extent on signals intelligence.

National Archives RG457, NSA Box 1431

Captain Rodger Winn, who managed the Royal Navy's Submarine Tracking Room in London utilizing signals intelligence.

one torpedo hit and wrecked a ship, the aged, 6,200-ton American kerosene tanker *McKeesport,* sunk later by the frigate *Tay.*

The well-trained and aggressive escorts and the occasional Allied aircraft that got through bad weather attacked and severely damaged three new U-boats, forcing them to abort to France: Kandler in *U-386,* Georg von Rabenau in the IXC40 *U-528,* and Junker in the IXC40 *U-532,* who was hunted and depth-charged for fifteen hours.

Kandler in *U-386* and Junker in *U-532* eventually made it home to France, but von Rabenau in *U-528* did not. Pilot W. A. Shevlin in a U.S. Navy Catalina of Squadron VP 84, based on Iceland, had hit *U-528* with a close straddle of four depth charges and forced her to abort. When the damaged boat reached the western edge of the Bay of Biscay on May 11, pilot James B. Stark, in a Halifax of Squadron 58, who was providing air cover for convoy Outbound South 47, caught *U-528* on the surface. Before von Rabenau could dive deep, Stark attacked, dropping five shallow-set depth charges.

Believing he had sunk the U-boat, Stark dropped a smoke flare at the site and notified the convoy's Escort Group 39, commanded by H. V. King in the sloop *Scarborough.* King immediately sent the other sloop of the group, *Fleetwood,* to the sinking site to look for survivors or debris, to make sure a kill had occurred and that the U-boat posed no danger to the convoy.

When *Fleetwood,* commanded by W. B. Piggot, reached the smoke flare, she got a sonar contact. Piggot carried out eight attacks on the target, dropping about sixty depth charges. These blasts further damaged *U-528,* forcing her to a depth of seven hundred feet. After assessing the damage, von Rabenau concluded *U-528* could not remain submerged, and he ordered the crew to surface and attempt to escape.

Meanwhile, Piggot in *Fleetwood,* who had no more depth charges, was reinforced by another of the convoy escorts, the corvette *Mignonette.* When *U-528* surfaced, both *Fleetwood* and *Mignonette* immediately saw her close by and opened fire with all guns that could bear. This fire forced the Germans topside to jump overboard. Von Rabenau gave orders to abandon ship and scuttle. Forty-five Germans survived. *Fleetwood* fished out von Rabenau and thirty-eight others; *Mignonette* picked up six. The Admiralty gave equal credit for the kill to the Halifax aircraft and to *Fleetwood.*

Reduced to thirteen boats, group *Star* groped westerly for Outbound North (Slow) 5 in the foulest possible weather and waves thirty feet high. On April 30, Wilhelm-Heinrich Pückler und Limpurg in the experienced *U-381* caught sight of the convoy, but lost it one hour later. In fact, the storm had scattered the convoy over a wide area. In spite of the weather and small icebergs ("growlers"), Gretton in the fuel-guzzling *Duncan* and the other destroyer, *Vidette,* were able to refuel from *British Lady.* To assist in reforming and protecting the convoy, Allied authorities ordered British Support Group 3, consisting of five Home Fleet destroyers commanded by J. W. McCoy, to reinforce Gretton. The first of these destroyers, *Oribi,* arrived from Iceland on April 30.

The weather remained foul. The other four destroyers of McCoy's support group (*Offa, Impulsive, Penn, Panther*), which sailed from Newfoundland, found the nucleus of the convoy (about thirty-two ships) and joined. This raised the escort to twelve warships: seven destroyers, one frigate, and four corvettes. It was sufficient strength to enable Gretton in *Duncan,* who, owing to a leak, was again critically low on fuel, to fall out to refuel in Newfoundland. He left R. E. Sherwood in the frigate *Tay* in charge of close Escort Group B-7. Three of the support group destroyers also had to fall out to refuel: *Impulsive* to Iceland, *Penn* and *Panther* to St. John's. These departures reduced the escort to eight warships: three destroyers *(Vidette, Offa, Oribi),* the frigate *Tay,* and the four corvettes.

Max Horton at Western Approaches ordered up yet more reinforcements: Godfrey N. Brewer's British Support Group 1 at St. John's, Newfoundland: the sloop *Pelican,* three frigates, and the ex–Coast Guard cutter *Sennen.* In view of the foul weather and poor visibility and communications, on May 1 U-boat Control canceled group *Star*'s pursuit of Outbound North (Slow) 5.

To this point, *Star*'s chase had produced little. Von Mässenhausen in *U-258* had sunk one old 6,200-ton kerosene tanker in ballast. In return, British warships and aircraft sank one *Star* boat, von Rabenau's *U-528,* and had severely damaged two others: Kandler's *U-386* and Junker's *U-532.*

Acting on information from *B-dienst,* U-boat Control was on the lookout for two big, eastbound convoys, Slow Convoy 128 and Halifax 236, guarded by British escorts. To be certain of intercepting these convoys, Control organized and deployed two very large groups between Newfoundland and Greenland:

- *Fink* (Finch), which comprised twenty-nine boats, of which eleven (38 percent) were on maiden patrols from Germany. *Fink* was made up of sixteen boats from the dissolved group *Specht* (three new VIIs; one new IX; two veteran VIIs with new skippers, *U-438* and *U-662;* two veteran IXs; and eight veteran VIIs). To these were added twelve boats from the dissolved group *Star* (three new IXs, four new VIIs, five veteran VIIs). In addition, one new IXC40, *U-531,* came from the dissolved group *Meise.* In sum, twenty-nine boats: seven IXs (five new) and twenty-two VIIs (seven new). One of the skippers was a *Ritterkreuz* holder, Ulrich Folkers in the veteran Drumbeater IXC *U-125.*
- *Amsel* (Blackbird), which was comprised of twenty-four boats from France (five IXs, nineteen VIIs), all experienced or veterans. As an experiment designed to confuse the Allies, *Amsel* was subdivided into four task forces of six boats each. There were two *Ritterkreuz* holders in *Amsel:* Siegfried von Forstner in the VII *U-402* of *Amsel* 1 and Harald Gelhaus in the IXB *U-107* of *Amsel* 2.

Fink-Amsel was the largest congregation of U-boats to be assembled in the same patrol area during the war. Together *Fink-Amsel* comprised fifty-three U-boats: twelve IXs (five new) and forty-one VIIs (seven new).

Aware from fragmented Enigma decrypts that a very large deployment of U-boats had occurred, threatening Outbound North (Slow) 5, Allied authorities launched Canadian and American aircraft sweeps when the weather permitted. On May 4 the sweeps yielded a kill: a Canso (Catalina) of Canadian Squadron 5 caught the VII *U-209* of group *Fink,* commanded by Werner Winkler, on the surface. The pilot, B. H. Moffit, dived to wave-top altitude and dropped four shallow-set depth charges. One missed, but three straddled the boat closely. On a second attack run, the aircrew saw a large oil patch and pieces of wood with "fresh breaks" and claimed a sinking.

That same day, another Canso of Squadron 5 caught an unalert boat on the surface, believed to be *U-438* of group *Fink,* commanded by Heinrich Heinsohn. The pilot, John W. C. Langmuir, attacked *U-438* three times at wave-top altitude, but Heinsohn remained on the surface and fought back with his flak guns. The Canso nose gunner claimed he killed or wounded three Germans on the bridge, but the depth charges fell too wide to inflict any major damage and *U-438* escaped, at least for the time being.

The valuable, rerouted Slow Convoy 128 and Halifax 236 slipped through or around the fifty-two surviving U-boats of *Fink-Amsel,* a dismaying setback for the Germans. However, on the afternoon of May 4, the westbound convoy Outbound North (Slow) 5, disorganized by storms, unwittingly sailed right into this mass of U-boats. At that time, the convoy's main body consisted of about thirty merchant ships, escorted by seven warships: three destroyers (*Oribi, Offa,* and *Vidette,* all low on fuel), the frigate *Tay,* and three corvettes. The other corvette, *Pink,* was far astern, escorting a miniconvoy of six ships; six other ships were stragglers.

Within two hours, three *Fink* VIIs reported the convoy contact: Rolf Manke in *U-358,* Paul-Friedrich Otto in *U-270,* and Heinz Hasenschar in *U-628.* In response, U-boat Control directed forty U-boats to attack the convoy: all of *Fink* (twenty-eight boats) plus the twelve boats of *Amsel* 1 and *Amsel* 2. Control exhorted: "I am certain that you will fight with everything you've got. Don't overestimate your opponent . . . strike him dead!"

During the next forty-eight hours, May 5–6, a furious naval battle raged amid icebergs and fog. In a notable success, the U-boats sank twelve confirmed ships (two American, ten British or British-controlled) for about 55,800 tons. The high scorer was the *Fink* VII *U-264,* commanded by Hartwig Looks, who sank three ships for 15,228 tons, including one damaged earlier by Heinz Hasenschar in *U-628.* Hasenschar in turn sank one ship for 5,200 tons damaged earlier by the *Fink* VII *U-358,* commanded by Rolf Manke, who also hit and sank a 2,900-tonner. The second-highest scorer was the *Amsel* 2 VII *U-266,* commanded by Ralf von Jessen, who sank three ships for 12,000 tons. Four other boats sank one ship each.

During the battle, Godfrey Brewer's British Support Group 1 (the sloop *Pelican,* frigates *Weir, Spey, Jed,* and the former Coast Guard cutter *Sennen*) sailed from St. John's, and the destroyers *Oribi* and *Offa* of J. W. McCoy's British Support Group 3, both low on fuel, prepared to depart for St. John's. In the period May 5–6, Allied forces sank six more U-boats, three VIIs and three IXs:

- The VII *U-630* of *Fink,* an Arctic transfer on her first Atlantic patrol, commanded by Heinrich Brodda. She was believed to have been sunk by Canadian Canso or American B-17 aircraft based in Newfoundland.* There were no survivors.

---

* In a 1991 reassessment, the Admiralty credited the British destroyer *Vidette* of B-7, commanded by Raymond Hart, with the kill of *U-630.*

• The IXC40 *U-192* of *Fink,* a new boat commanded by Werner Happe, age twenty-seven, merely twenty-three days out from Kiel. She was sunk by *Loostrife,* a corvette of Escort Group B-7, commanded by Harold A. Stonehouse. There were no survivors.

• The VII *U-638* of *Amsel* 1, commanded by Oskar Staudinger, on her second patrol. She sank one 5,500-ton British freighter from the convoy, but was in turn sunk by the corvette *Sunflower* of Escort Group B-7, commanded by Canadian J. Plomer. There were no survivors.

• The veteran IXC *U-125* of *Fink,* commanded by the Drumbeater and *Ritterkreuz* holder Ulrich Folkers, who had probably sunk one 4,700-ton British freighter, the *Lorient.* He was rammed and sunk by the destroyer *Oribi,* commanded by J.C.A. Ingram with help from the corvette *Snowflake,* commanded by H. G. Chesterman.

• The new IXC40 *U-531* of *Fink,* commanded by Herbert Neckel, age twenty-six, also twenty-three days out from Kiel. While en route from Kiel to join *Fink,* Neckel had been attacked by an unidentified aircraft near Iceland that had dropped four bombs or depth charges and had caused "some damage." She was sunk by the destroyer *Vidette,* that ship's second kill in as many days. There were no survivors.

• The VII *U-438* of *Fink,* a veteran boat commanded by the new skipper Heinrich Heinsohn, believed to have been damaged earlier by a Canso of Canadian Squadron 5. The boat was sunk by the sloop *Pelican,* commanded by Godfrey Brewer of British Support Group 1. There were no survivors.

In addition to these six sinkings on May 5–6, the escorts damaged about a dozen other U-boats, forcing many to abort to a U-tanker and four or five to abort to France. One of the latter was the new IXC40 of *Fink, U-533,* commanded by Helmut Hennig, rammed by the British corvette *Sunflower,* commanded by J. Plomer, who was making his first Atlantic crossing in an escort group. Another was the VII *U-270,* commanded by Paul-Friedrich Otto, who refueled and had been out forty-three days, attached to several groups. Otto reached France on May 15.

One other Amsel boat was lost while homebound. She was the VII *U-266,* commanded by Ralf von Jessen, the second-highest scorer against Outbound North (Slow) 5. On May 15, while on an ASW patrol over the Bay of Biscay, a Halifax of British Squadron 58, piloted by Wilfred E. Oulton, came out of the sun and sank the inbound *U-266* with a salvo of depth charges.

U-boat Control never did sort out exactly which convoy the *Fink-Amsel* boats attacked nor did Control realize that it was the same convoy that the dissolved group *Star* had found and chased earlier. The Germans wrongly identified the convoy as Outbound North 180 and claimed that the U-boats had sunk sixteen ships for 90,500 tons from it and also got hits on a corvette and three other freighters. Six U-boats had been lost, Control logged, "a high and grave" number considering the brevity of operations. Control attributed the losses to enemy radar, which enabled the surface escorts to pinpoint surfaced U-boats at night and in the Grand Banks fog and to air escorts that were able to hide in low-lying clouds and pounce with the advantage of complete surprise.

In summary, the correct story was as follows. Group *Star* found Outbound North (Slow) 5 on April 27, during an Enigma blackout. On April 27–28, one *Star* VII, the veteran *U-258,* commanded by Wilhelm von Mässenhausen, sank one confirmed ship from the convoy, the 6,200-ton American kerosene tanker *McKeesport.* In turn, Peter Gretton's Escort Group B-7 and Allied aircraft severely damaged the VII *U-386* and the new IXC40s *U-528* and *U-532.* While limping home to France, the *U-528* was sunk in Biscay by cooperating British aircraft and surface ships.

After *Fink-Amsel* had been formed by fifty-three U-boats to attack eastbound convoys, the Outbound North (Slow) 5 blundered into that massive German formation. On May 5–6, eight of these U-boats sank twelve more confirmed ships for about 56,000 tons, raising the grand total of confirmed sinkings in Outbound North (Slow) 5 to thirteen ships for about 62,000 tons. The shrunken Escort Group B-7, temporarily commanded by R. E. Sherwood in the frigate *Tay,* was reinforced by two British support groups and by Canadian and American aircraft from Newfoundland. These forces sank six more U-boats from May 4 to May 6. Counting *U-710,* assigned to *Star, U-528* of *Star,* and *U-266* of *Amsel,* German losses in all operations versus Outbound North (Slow) 5 came to a ruinous nine boats (four IXs, five VIIs) and about 450 submariners, including *Ritterkreuz* holder Ulrich Folkers, killed or left to die in the icy waters. The Allies made no attempt to rescue Germans of these boats in the western Atlantic.

The sinking of what was believed to be six U-boats plus the heavy damage to four or five others in a single convoy battle was viewed as a classic naval victory in the British Isles, and those who fought it drew praise from Winston Churchill, Max Horton, and other high officials. In the postwar years, British and German historians and authors and navalists (including B-7 commander Peter Gretton) were to write extensively about the battle. It thus gradually acquired a string of adjectives such as "fiercest" and "decisive" and was cited by some authors as "a major turning point" in the Battle of the Atlantic. But of course, there was never a defining "turning point," only a gradually accelerating German defeat from September 1942 onward.

On the German side, when the full extent of the losses became evident, there was alarm and dismay. U-boat Control logged that the "worst enemy" was Allied radar. It not only impeded U-boat attacks but also enabled the convoys to evade U-boat patrol lines. In particular, airborne radar was a menace. It enabled land-based ASW aircraft, which could escort eastbound and westbound convoys nearly all the way across the Atlantic, to find and keep in close contact with the merchant ships, to drive the shadowers off and/or down, and prevent other U-boats from pulling ahead of the convoy to better shooting positions. Worse yet for the Germans, it appeared that the Allies were to assign "jeep" carrier support groups to accompany all the convoys on the North Atlantic run.

To reassure the skippers and crews, Dönitz signaled all U-boats: "I expect you to continue your determined struggle with the enemy and by pitting your ingenuity, ability and toughness against his tricks and technical developments, finally to finish him off." Remember, Dönitz added, that the enemy has "weak spots everywhere" and was not so efficient as he appeared at first sight. "I believe," he concluded, "that I shall shortly be able to give you better weapons for this hard struggle of yours."

The loss of four IXs in this action, plus eleven other IXs in March and April—a total of fifteen—stressed the long-held view that the clumsy, slow-diving IXs were unsuitable for hard anticonvoy operations in the North Atlantic. After obtaining authorization from Dönitz, U-boat Control rescinded the recent order that *all* IXs were to patrol the North Atlantic convoy run. The new IXs outbound from Germany to France were to carry out maiden patrols in the North Atlantic, but those already based in France were to be sent only south or southwest to Freetown, the West Indies, and Brazil.

The study of the IX losses in the North Atlantic in this period led German engineers to tentatively conclude that the more powerful and deeper-sinking Allied depth charges were rupturing and flooding the topside torpedo-storage canisters on both the VIIs and IXs, destabilizing the boats and causing losses. The OKM therefore issued new rules regarding topside canisters. Without exception, VIIs at the battlefronts were to remove *all* topside canisters. New VIIs under construction were to be fitted with much stronger steel canisters. The IXBs and IXCs were also to remove all canisters. With special permission, IXs patrolling south to West Africa or to the Americas could mount six canisters in place of the usual eight. The new XB minelayers were to be issued six canisters as before, but no XB could install the canisters without special permission. The IXD2 U-cruisers going to distant waters (such as the Indian Ocean) were permitted to retain all twelve topside canisters loaded with G7a air torpedoes.

The Allies sailed eighteen convoys east and west on the North Atlantic run in April,* comprising about nine hundred merchant ships. Thanks to the work of *B-dienst,* the U-boat groups were able to intercept a great number of these convoys. Yet the convoy defenses in that area had become so formidable with the addition of destroyer and "jeep" carrier support groups and very-long-range aircraft that the masses of U-boats on the North Atlantic run were able to sink only thirty-one ships (including the British destroyer *Beverley*) from seven of these convoys, most notably six from Halifax 231 and thirteen from Outbound North (Slow) 5. Halifax 232 yielded four victims, the other four convoys merely one to three ships.

In all waters of the world, all Axis submarines sank fifty-six merchant ships for about 328,000 gross tons in April.† This was only about one-half of the merchant ship sinkings achieved in March, a disastrous setback for the Germans, as yet only dimly perceived owing to the overclaims of U-boat skippers. Against the fifty-six Allied ships sunk worldwide, the Germans lost fifteen U-boats in all waters in April (seven IXs, eight VIIs), another ruinous "exchange rate" of 3.7 ships sunk for each U-boat. As in March, the output of American shipyards alone in April was prodigious: 159 ships for about one million gross tons, or nearly three times the number of ships and tonnage lost to U-boats that month.

* Halifax 231 to 235; Slow Convoys 125 to 128; Outbound North 176 to 181; Outbound North (Slow) 3 to 5. See Appendix 3.

† According to Admiralty figures. In a close match, Professor Rohwer has calculated fifty-five merchant ships lost in April for 312,612 tons.

GROUP *DROSSEL*: A FUTILE AND COSTLY GESTURE

In the third week of April, the British First and Eighth armies commenced the final encirclement of the dispirited and defeated Axis ground forces in Tunisia, North Africa—the long-delayed culmination of Torch. The Germans and Italians had not the slightest chance of escape. Neither Berlin nor Rome made any effort to evacuate these tens of thousands of defeated troops.

Perhaps for political or psychological reasons, Dönitz directed U-boat Control to send a special group of a dozen VIIs to attack Allied convoys supporting Allied forces in North Africa. It was not a prudent idea to send another attack group to the risky Gibraltar-Azores waters, but apparently Dönitz felt he had no other choice; the *Kriegsmarine* had to make a final gesture of support for the *Afrika Korps*.

Designated group *Drossel* (Thrush), these dozen VIIs sailed from French bases from April 24 to April 27. Among them was the veteran *U-436,* commanded by Günther Seibecke, who had recently won a *Ritterkreuz*. As related, three *Drossel* VIICs did not get out of the Bay of Biscay. Allied aircraft sank *U-332* with the loss of all hands and severely damaged the *U-437,* which was escorted back to France by the *U-445*.

The nine remaining *Drossel* boats were to work in close cooperation with Condors based at Bordeaux. On May 3, the aircraft reported two southbound convoys: one composed of twenty-four to twenty-seven "freight barges" and three escorts, the other composed of eleven freighters and six escorts.

The *Drossel* veterans, *U-89,* commanded by Dietrich Lohmann, and *U-456,* commanded by Max-Martin Teichert, found the convoy of "freight barges." The ships turned out to be landing craft (LCTs) en route to the Mediterranean for the proposed invasion of Sicily (Husky). Because of their shallow draft, the landing craft were unsuitable torpedo targets. Nonetheless, Lohmann in *U-89* shot three torpedoes into the formation. None hit. Inasmuch as no boat found the more promising convoy of eleven freighters and because heavy Allied air cover from Gibraltar to support it was expected, U-boat Control prohibited further searching for that formation.

During that night, May 3–4, two other *Drossel* boats found the landing-craft convoy: Hans Stock in the veteran *U-659,* who had just received an emergency change in orders to enter the Mediterranean, and Helmut von Tippelskirch in the experienced *U-439*. Momentarily distracted by a sudden burst of gunfire from an escort, von Tippelskirch in *U-439* rammed Stock in *U-659*. The impact flooded the bow compartment of *U-439,* and she began to sink. Von Tippelskirch flashed Stock an SOS by signal lamp, but Stock's *U-659* was also fatally holed and sinking. One of the four convoy escorts, a British PT boat (*MGB 670*), commanded by R.R.W. Ashby, rescued twelve Germans, three from *U-659* and nine from *U-439*. Both U-boat captains were killed. One of the survivors of *U-439* said that the first watch officer was so remorseful over the collision—or so fearful of a Nazi court-martial—that he refused a life preserver, held firmly to a bridge stanchion, and deliberately went down with the boat.

This latest misfortune reduced *Drossel* from nine boats to seven. This was insufficient strength to tackle a major convoy, yet U-boat Control left the boats in place, west of Cape Finisterre, to provide whatever help they could to Axis forces in Tunisia. On the evening of May 5, *Drossel* suffered yet another misfortune. The veteran boats *U-406,* commanded by Horst Dieterichs, and *U-600,* commanded by Bernhard Zurmühlen, also collided. No one was seriously injured, but both boats incurred "major damage" and were forced to abort to France, reducing the snake-bit group *Drossel* to merely five boats.

B-dienst predicted that a big convoy, Sierra Leone 128, was steaming northbound right at group *Drossel*'s position. Condors from Bordeaux confirmed the intelligence, reporting forty-eight ships and three escorts. On May 6, Wolf Jeschonnek, age twenty-three, who had only just inherited command of the veteran VII *U-607* from *Ritterkreuz* holder Ernst Mengersen, found the convoy. His signals brought up the other four boats of *Drossel,* which included the VII *U-436,* commanded by *Ritterkreuz* holder Günther Seibicke. Two boats shot torpedoes. Lohmann in the VII *U-89* hit and sank the 3,800-ton Greek freighter *Laconikos* with a torpedo fitted with a magnetic pistol. Jeschonnek in the VII *U-607* fired a full bow salvo into the formation. He reported one FAT hit, but it was not confirmed.

Three of the five remaining boats of *Drossel* were counterattacked by the convoy escorts and land-based aircraft. Max-Martin Teichert in *U-456* was severely damaged by depth charges or bombs, but after repairs, he reported he could continue his patrol. Paul Siegmann in *U-230* expertly shadowed the convoy all the next day. According to his first watch officer, Herbert Werner,* the sustained air attacks *U-230* endured were almost beyond belief. Owing to the weakness of *Drossel,* U-boat Control canceled operations against Sierra Leone 128 on May 7 and sent the remaining five boats northwestward to join groups on the North Atlantic run. As will be described, only two of these five survived and returned to France. In sum, ten of twelve *Drossel* boats were sunk or forced to abort. Only one VII, Lohmann in *U-89,* sank an Allied ship, the Greek freighter *Laconikos*.

The Third U-cruiser Foray to the Indian Ocean

Dönitz directed U-boat Control to mount a major foray of U-cruisers to the Indian Ocean in March and April.† Seven U-cruisers (three old, four new) were to participate: the ill-engined sister ship of *U-180,* the IXD1 *U-195,* and six IXD2s. All were commanded by older, conservative skippers; five of the six by *Ritterkreuz* holders. Dönitz believed that with the resupply of food, water, and fuel from a victim and/or an Axis raider or tanker, the U-cruisers could remain in the Indian Ocean for a prolonged time, preying on lone or thinly escorted Allied shipping at small risk.

The first of the seven U-cruisers to sail on this extraordinary foray was the new

---

* In his book *Iron Coffins.*

† Hitler's gift to Tojo, the IXC *U-511* ("Marco Polo I"), sailed to Japan on May 10, but separately. Her skipper, Fritz Schneewind, sank the 7,200-ton American Liberty ship *Sebastiano Cermeno.*

IXD2 *U-198*. She was commanded by forty-year-old Werner Hartmann (crew of 1921) who had gained fame and a *Ritterkreuz* on the *U-37* in 1939 and 1940. Since leaving *U-37*, Hartmann had held down several desk jobs in France and Germany, and he was pleased to return to sea as commander of an exalted U-cruiser.

Allied codebreakers in due course provided details on this seven-boat foray and the Admiralty notified appropriate naval commands. On May 4 the war diary of the British South Atlantic command recorded:

> In view of the approaching U-boat threat, complete convoy system round South Africa coast reintroduced. All independent sailings suspended except fast ships. All vessels approaching Cape Town diverted to reach coastal area early.

Hartmann in *U-198* rounded the Cape of Good Hope into the lower Mozambique Channel, and on May 17 he found a southbound convoy en route from Lourenço Marques to Durban (LMD 17). It was comprised of six big freighters, very thinly escorted by two ASW trawlers and one aircraft. Hartmann tracked and sank the 4,400-ton British freighter *Northmoor*, his first sinking in about three years.* The ASW trawlers pounded him with about fifty depth charges, he logged, and the aircraft dropped five. None did any noteworthy damage but the convoy got away.

On the following day, thirty miles east of Durban, Hartmann found and chased two freighters sailing in company. As he reached a favorable firing position, an aircraft spotted him and attacked, botching Hartmann's setup. Thereafter, aircraft and small surface craft hounded Hartmann all day and well into the night. Hartmann held his ground and fought back. He missed a submarine chaser with two torpedoes but repelled a Catalina of RAF Squadron 262 that night with his flak guns and forced it to abort on one engine.

After a frustrating and fallow week, on May 26 Hartmann found yet another convoy near Durban. It was heavily escorted by warships and aircraft. Hartmann attempted to attack, but the escorts drove him off and he lost this prize. The heavy air cover over the waters near Durban persuaded him to leave the area. He cruised about four hundred miles eastward into the Indian Ocean, where on May 29 he found and sank the lone 5,200-ton British freighter *Hopetarn* and captured her second mate. Two days later in the same area, Hartmann found yet another small but heavily escorted convoy. He attempted to attack, but a corvette got *U-198* on sonar and forced her very deep. Later, when Hartmann surfaced, he discovered that the pressure of the depth-charge explosions had crushed one of his topside torpedo canisters.

Returning to the Durban area, Hartmann found better hunting. On June 5 he sank the 2,300-ton British freighter *Dumra* and captured her chief engineer. The next day he sank the 7,200-ton American Liberty ship *William King* and captured her captain. These two sinkings brought Hartmann's bag in the ninety days since he had sailed from Kiel to four ships for about 19,000 tons, a modest return for the investment of time, men, and resources.

---

* Since April 12, 1940, on *U-37*.

On or about June 1, U-boat Control had decided that the U-cruisers, all of which had plenty of torpedoes, should extend their patrols. It was therefore arranged that the boats were to replenish from a German tanker in the Indian Ocean, the *Charlotte Schliemann.* The rendezvous was to take place en masse on June 22 at a remote site about 1,800 miles due east of Durban and about six hundred miles due south of the island of Mauritius.

The second of the new U-cruisers to leave Kiel was the *U-196.* She was commanded by the thirty-six-year-old Eitel-Friedrich Kentrat, who had won a *Ritterkreuz* on *U-74,* operating in the North Atlantic, before taking that boat to the Mediterranean. He had not been to sea for almost exactly one year. Sixteen months had passed since he had sunk his last confirmed ship.*

Kentrat rounded the British Isles and went south down the middle of the Atlantic. He skirted the Cape of Good Hope to the south, then swung northward to an area near Durban. On May 11 he shot two torpedoes and sank the 5,000-ton British freighter *Nailsea Meadow.* Two long and frustrating weeks later, in this same area, Kentrat finally found a convoy and attacked, firing two electric torpedoes with Pi2 magnetic pistols. One torpedo ejected as designed, but the other hung up in the tube, its motor running and turning the propeller. The *U-196* crew expected the magnetic pistol to trigger the torpedo and blow up the boat. To prevent this terrible fate, Kentrat put the bow down steeply, and the torpedo slid out of the tube. A desultory counterattack (four depth charges) by one of the escorts during this crisis was scarcely noticed.

The *U-196* patrolled the waters near Durban for another week, to about June 1. Then Kentrat turned east to carry out the replenishment rendezvous with the *Charlotte Schliemann.* Since leaving Kiel on March 13, *U-196* had sunk only one ship.

The third new U-cruiser to leave Kiel was the IXD1 *U-195,* commanded by thirty-four-year-old Heinz Buchholz. He had carried out a successful mine-laying mission early in the war on the duck *U-15,* but ever since he had been in high-level shore jobs, the last as commander of Combat Flotilla 1 in Brest. Like her sister ship *U-180,* the *U-195* was powered by six high-performance, fuel-guzzling, and temperamental Mercedes-Benz engines, which generated nearly unbearable heat inside the boat in tropical waters.

Buchholz followed approximately the same course in the Atlantic as had Hartmann and Kentrat. West of the Canary Islands on April 12, the *U-195* found and sank the lone 7,200-ton American Liberty ship *James W. Denver.* After crossing the equator on May 7, Buchholz found and sank another 7,200-ton American Liberty ship sailing alone, *Samuel Jordan Kirkwood.* Five days later, off Cape Town, Buchholz encountered yet another lone American vessel, the 6,800-ton *Cape Neddick.* He hit and damaged her, but *Neddick*'s captain, Harry Stark, counterattacked with his guns and tried to ram *U-195.* Rattled by this unusual display of ferocity, Buchholz dived to avoid the shelling and shot another torpedo at *Neddick,* but it missed. Stark turned tail, ran at full speed, escaped, and eventually delivered his cargo of tanks, locomotives, and aviation gasoline to British forces in Egypt.

---

* On November 7, 1941.

Thereafter Buchholz patrolled off Cape Town, but he found no more targets. On May 30, he not surprisingly reported severe engine problems and requested permission to abort the patrol. U-boat Control approved and Buchholz reached Bordeaux on July 23. As related, both of the failed IXD1s, *U-180* and *U-195,* were reengined with two conventional, 1,400-horsepower diesels and converted to cargo carriers. The thirty-nine-year-old Musenberg retained command of *U-180,* but Buchholz left *U-195* to command a IXD2 U-cruiser.

The fourth and last of the new U-cruisers to leave Kiel was the *U-197.* Her skipper was thirty-two-year-old Robert Bartels, who had commanded the new VII *U-561* for sixteen months in the Atlantic and the Mediterranean, laying a successful minefield in a British harbor in the latter area. On the forty-eighth day out from Kiel, Bartels found the 4,800-ton Dutch tanker *Benakat* sailing alone in the middle of the South Atlantic and sank her. By the time he rounded the Cape of Good Hope, it was time to proceed to the refueling rendezvous with *Charlotte Schliemann.* Five days shy of the rendezvous, an aircraft attacked *U-197.* One German was killed, but the boat survived to carry out the replenishment on June 22. In eighty-one days at sea, Bartels, like Kentrat in *U-196,* had sunk but one ship.

Of the three experienced U-cruisers departing Bordeaux, the first to sail was the IXD2 *U-181,* commanded by Wolfgang Lüth, who wore Oak Leaves on his *Ritterkreuz.* On his twentieth day at sea, April 11, Lüth spotted the lone 6,000-ton British refrigerator ship *Empire Whimbrel* about four hundred miles south of Freetown. Lüth fired four torpedoes at this ship and two hit. After the crew abandoned the sinking hulk, Lüth ordered a gun action to polish her off. A shell in the 37mm gun on the deck aft of the conning tower jammed in the barrel and blew up, severely wounding three men, one of whom died later in the day and was buried at sea. Lüth arranged to transfer the other two wounded the next day to the homebound *Seehund* boat, *U-516,* commanded by Gerhard Wiebe. Lüth finally sank *Empire Whimbrel* with twenty rounds from his 4.1" deck gun.

Upon learning of this sinking, Dönitz arranged with Hitler to add Crossed Swords to the Oak Leaves of Lüth's *Ritterkreuz.* Lüth thus became the twenty-ninth man in all the German armed forces and the fourth submariner (after Kretschmer, Topp, and Suhren) to receive this high decoration. When the news reached *U-181* by an encoded radio message, the crew celebrated with beer and cognac.*

Lüth rounded the Cape of Good Hope and went north up the lower Mozambique Channel to patrol off the Portuguese harbor of Lourenço Marques, where he had had success on his first patrol to the Indian Ocean. Close inshore, he fouled his propellers on a steel fishing net. For a few anxious hours Lüth and his men believed they were goners, but one of his men, wearing a clumsy deep-sea diving suit, cut the steel wires away with an electric torch. While the diver was at this work, the crew caught and killed a big shark that posed a threat to the diver.

---

* At the time of the award, his confirmed score was thirty-eight ships sunk for 189,633 tons, second in (confirmed) ships and tonnage after Kretschmer.

Lüth patrolled lower Mozambique Channel from Lourenço Marques to Durban for a full month, from May 11 to June 11. In that time he sank three more lone ships: the 5,200-ton British freighter *Tinhow;* the 1,600-ton Swedish neutral *Sicilia* (which Lüth deemed to be carrying contraband); and the small (200-ton) South African coaster *Harrier,* filled with ammunition. He sank *Tinhow* with two torpedoes and *Harrier* (which vaporized) with one torpedo. He first stopped the Swede with ten rounds from *U-181*'s 4.1" deck gun. After the Swedes abandoned the *Sicilia,* Lüth sank her with one torpedo fired at point-blank range.

During these actions, on May 18, U-boat Control informed Lüth that his wife had given birth to a son with this doggerel:

As far as Capetown
Be it known:
A little Lüth
Has been born.

Now see in this,
As ever taught,
Tough guts gets
Whatever sought.

Per plan, Lüth arrived at the rendezvous with *Charlotte Schliemann* on June 22. In his ninety-two days at sea, he had sunk four ships for 13,000 tons, a tie with Hartmann in *U-198* in numbers of ships, but about 6,000 fewer tons. It was also a poor return on the investment of time, men, and resources.

The next experienced U-cruiser to leave Bordeaux was the IXD2 *U-177,* commanded by thirty-two-year-old *Ritterkreuz* holder Robert Gysae. Like Lüth, this was to be Gysae's second patrol to Cape Town and the Indian Ocean in a U-cruiser.

On this trip, Gysae's *U-177* was equipped with a new day-search device: a primitive, one-man, three-rotor, motorless helicopter, known as the *Bachstelze* (Wagtail). Stowed knocked-down in topside canisters, it could be assembled by three well-trained men in less than ten minutes and disassembled and restowed in five minutes. It was tethered to the U-boat by a one-thousand-foot steel cable wound on an air-powered winch. With the U-boat towing at fifteen knots, its whirling rotors could lift it to about five hundred feet altitude. Equipped with binoculars, a helmet with a two-way telephone, and a parachute, upon attaining maximum altitude the pilot could search a radius of about twenty-five miles. The helicopter was very tricky to launch, operate, and recover and, of course, it could only be utilized in areas where sudden aircraft attacks were unlikely. Otherwise, the pilot and his machine were expendable.

Off the Cape of Good Hope on May 28, Gysae came upon a convoy en route from Cape Town to Durban, designated CD 20. It was composed of sixteen merchant ships, thinly escorted by seven warships of dubious value: a South African gunboat, *Vereeniging,* two Indian minesweepers lacking sonar, three British ASW trawlers, and a British tugboat for rescues. Gysae fired numerous torpedoes at the mass of merchant ships and sank two: the 6,700-ton American freighter *Agwinonte* and the 7,900-ton Norwegian tanker *Storaas.* On June 1, Dönitz radioed Gysae congratulations and the news that Hitler had awarded him Oak Leaves to his *Ritterkreuz.**

At the suggestion of U-boat Control, Gysae doubled back to Saldanha, on the lower west coast of Africa. In the week following, he found a convoy and commenced tracking it in foggy weather. On June 6, the fog suddenly lifted and Gysae found himself completely exposed on the surface in the "middle" of the convoy. All ships that could bring guns to bear without hitting a friendly ship opened fire, and a Catalina arrived to drop three depth charges. Gysae escaped by a very thin margin. Thereafter he met Buchholz's aborting IXD1 *U-195* and transferred to her one of his crewmen who was ill. He then set off for the rendezvous with *Charlotte Schliemann,* arriving a day late on June 23. In his eighty-three days at sea, he had sunk two ships for 14,600 tons, second in tonnage after Hartmann in *U-198,* but also not nearly enough to justify the expenditure of time, men, and resources. Often launched, the helicopter (*Bachstelze*) had not yet produced.

The third and last experienced U-cruiser of this foray to sail from France was the IXD2 *U-178.* It was to be her second cruise to the Indian Ocean but she had a new skipper. He was thirty-six-year-old Wilhelm Dommes, who had commanded the VII *U-431* in the Atlantic and Mediterranean, winning a *Ritterkreuz* in the latter area.

Dommes reached Cape Town waters in early May. Thereupon the boat developed an oil leak so serious that he was forced to pull far away to make repairs. While returning to the coast on May 24, he found a small convoy. He pursued but a Catalina manned by a Dutch crew attacked *U-178* with depth charges. Dommes returned fire but when a second aircraft appeared, he dived and lost the convoy.

In the last days of May, Dommes heard Gysae in *U-177* report the convoy en route from Cape Town to Durban. As he was not far away, Dommes set a course to intercept this formation and found it cruising close to shore about sixty miles south of Durban. Despite the surface escorts and Catalinas, Dommes attacked on June 1 and hit the 6,600-ton Dutch freighter *Salabangka.* The convoy's tug took the damaged ship in tow, but a storm arose and she broke up and sank.

Dommes patrolled the lower Mozambique Channel for several more days, then turned east to rendezvous with the *Charlotte Schliemann.* He arrived on the eighty-seventh day of his patrol, June 22. Like Kentrat in *U-196* and Bartels in *U-197,* in all that time Dommes had sunk only one ship.

To this point in the U-cruiser foray, the returns from the seven boats were thin. They had sunk fifteen ships for 77,400 tons, an overall average of two ships for 11,000 tons per U-boat in about three months at sea. One boat, *U-195,* had aborted, leaving six to carry on the mission.

The skippers of the six U-cruisers replenishing at *Charlotte Schliemann* visited back and forth, exchanging experiences. All topped off fuel, water, and lube-oil

---

* At the time of the award, his confirmed score on the VII *U-98* and *U-177* was twenty ships for about 116,000 tons.

tanks, but all were disappointed at the "Japanese" food provided by the German tanker. Beyond that, Lüth logged, none of the U-boats really got sufficient quantities of food.

U-boat Control issued new orders to the six U-cruisers. They were to remain in the Indian Ocean and mount a simultaneous surprise attack on Allied shipping in a variety of areas. Lüth in *U-181,* who left his three POWs with *Charlotte Schliemann,* was to go to the island of Mauritius. Hartmann in *U-198* was to go to Lourenço Marques. Kentrat in *U-196* was to sweep north to south down the Mozambique Channel while Dommes in *U-178* swept south to north. Gysae in *U-177* was to patrol south of Madagascar. Bartels in *U-197* was to patrol close inshore in the area between Lourenço Marques and Durban.

Sporting shiny new Oak Leaves on his *Ritterkreuz,* Gysae in *U-177* patrolled well south of Madagascar, where it was safer to operate the helicopter. In the period from July 5 to July 10, he carried out attacks on three lone freighters. In the first, he missed with two torpedoes and the ship got away. In the second, he sank the 7,200-ton Canadian *Jasper Park* with three torpedoes. In the third, closer to Madagascar, he sank the 7,200-ton American Liberty ship *Alice F. Palmer* with two torpedoes and ninety-nine rounds from his 4.1" deck gun.

Returning to the areas well south and southeast of Madagascar, Gysae saw nothing for days on end, despite frequent use of the helicopter. Finally, on July 29, he found and sank the 5,000-ton British freighter *Cornish City* and almost got an American Liberty ship as well. A protracted but vain chase of the latter took *U-177* to within sixty miles of the southern tip of Madagascar. There, on August 5, the helicopter pilot spotted his first victim, a 4,200-ton Greek, *Efthalia Mari,* which Gysae sank. The next day the helicopter pilot spotted another lone ship, but a fire broke out in *U-177*'s engine room and while Gysae was busy dealing with the emergency, the ship escaped. Having sunk six ships for 38,000 tons on this cruise, Gysae went on to France.

The return trip took fifty-eight days; the entire patrol, 184 days. On arrival in Bordeaux on October 1, Gysae left *U-177* to command Training Flotilla 25 in the Baltic.* Heinz Buchholz, the skipper of *U-195,* which was undergoing conversion to a cargo vessel, replaced Gysae as skipper of *U-177,* but two and a half months passed before he sailed on January 1, 1944.

Dommes in *U-178* went southabout Madagascar and cruised slowly north in the Mozambique Channel. North of Lourenço Marques on July 4, he sank two freighters: the 2,700-ton Norwegian *Breiviken* and the 4,800-ton Greek *Michael Livanos.* He chased another freighter and fired six torpedoes at her but all missed. Reporting these actions to U-boat Control, he added that he was ill but he would carry on.

Convinced that the area north of Lourenço Marques was a rich hunting ground,

---

* Having sunk twenty-four confirmed ships for about 140,000 tons on the VII *U-98* and *U-177,* Gysae ranked seventeenth among all skippers in the war.

the ailing Dommes remained more or less in place. His instinct was correct. In the week from July 11 to 16, he torpedoed and sank three more big freighters: the 4,800-ton Greek *Mary Livanos,* the 7,200-ton American Liberty ship *Robert Bacon,* and the 6,700-ton British *City of Canton.*

Having expended all of his torpedoes, per new orders, on August 12 Dommes met the eastbound Italian cargo submarine *Torelli* southeast of Madagascar to give her some fuel. In the interim, U-boat Control had asked Dommes if he and his *U-178* were sufficiently fit to go to the island of Penang, Malaysia, for refit and then conduct a full-blown patrol homeward through the Indian Ocean. Dommes had replied in the affirmative. After refueling *Torelli,* both boats proceeded in company to Penang, arriving on August 29, Dommes completing a patrol of 155 days.* He had sunk six ships for 32,800 tons.

As Dommes was nearing Penang, Dönitz and the OKM decided to establish a U-boat base at that island to accommodate the big German U-cruisers and cargo boats and Italian cargo boats and crews. Subsequently that assignment went to Dommes, who left *U-178* in Penang because of illness. The boat's first watch officer, Hans Spahr, who had been the quartermaster on Prien's legendary 1939 foray into Scapa Flow in *U-47,* was named to replace Dommes. Spahr sailed to France on November 27, arriving 178 days later, May 24, 1944. The boat never sailed again.

Werner Hartmann in *U-198* also patrolled north of Lourenço Marques. On July 4, he almost committed the sin of sinking a Portuguese neutral. At the last minute of his approach, a sixth sense caused him to abort the attack. Several days later, on July 6 and 7, he sank two freighters: the 4,500-ton Greek *Hydraios* and the 4,700-ton British *Leana.* He torpedoed the first and attacked the second with his 4.1" deck gun. After 147 rounds, he sank the battered *Leana* with a torpedo and captured her captain. Thereafter aircraft based near Durban harassed *U-198* almost daily and sometimes several times daily. Nonetheless, on August 1, Hartmann sank another ship, the 8,500-ton Dutch *Mangkalibat.*

Hartmann then set a course for France. He arrived on September 25, after a voyage of 201 days. His bag was seven confirmed ships for 36,778 tons, which brought his complete bag for the war on *U-37* and *U-198* to twenty-six ships sunk for 115,778 tons, including one trawler. This was not enough tonnage for Oak Leaves, but Dönitz had another promotion for Hartmann: effective January 1, 1944, he was to command U-boats in the Mediterranean, replacing Leo Kreisch.

After recruiting one merchant seaman from *Charlotte Schliemann* to replace the three men he had lost early in his patrol, Lüth in *U-181* proceeded northward to the island of Mauritius. On July 1, he surveyed the harbor, Port Louis, and saw three freighters, all beyond reach. Over the following two days he sank the 2,800-ton British freighter *Hoihow,* escaped an air attack, wasted two torpedoes on small coasters, and chased a cruiser westward toward Madagascar. This vain pursuit took *U-181* to Tamatave, on the east coast of Madagascar, where on July 15 and 16 Lüth

* Hitler's gift to Japan, the IXC *U-511* ("Marco Polo I"), and the Italian cargo submarines *Cappellini* and *Giuliani* had reached Penang in July with spare torpedoes for the returning German U-cruisers.

sank two more British freighters sailing alone: the 2,900-ton *Empire Lake* and the 7,200-ton *Fort Franklin.*

When U-boat Control learned that Lüth was operating off the east coast of Madagascar, it ordered him to return to Mauritius. In compliance, Lüth headed eastward slowly. Near the island on August 4, 7, and 11, Lüth sank three more British ships sailing alone: the 4,600-ton *Dalfram,* the 4,400-ton *Umvuma,* and the 10,500-ton refrigerator ship *Clan Macarthur.*

Upon learning of these successes, Dönitz recommended to Hitler that Lüth be given Germany's highest award: Diamonds to the Oak Leaves and Crossed Swords of his *Ritterkreuz.* Hitler approved and effective August 9, Lüth became the seventh man in the Third Reich and the first in the *Kriegsmarine* to be so honored.* When Dönitz radioed the news and his congratulations to Lüth, the officers and crew, bursting with pride, celebrated with beer and cognac. Thereafter Control directed Lüth to rendezvous with Bartels in *U-197* at a site several hundred miles southeast of Madagascar to obtain new Enigma keys for his voyage home.

By August 15, a serious morale problem had developed on *U-197.* In the fifty-one days since leaving the *Charlotte Schliemann,* Bartels had sunk only one confirmed ship, the 9,600-ton Swedish tanker *Pegasus.* On July 30, he had found, stalked, and attacked a convoy, damaging the 7,200-ton American Liberty ship *William Ellery,* later towed into Durban. An aircraft thwarted a second attack. When he complained to U-boat Control that he had not only been bombed but also had had two torpedo-pistol failures, Control replied curtly: "Vent your rage" upon the enemy.

Lüth in *U-181* reached the rendezvous site on August 17, but there was no sign of Bartels in *U-197.* Later that night Lüth intercepted a report from Bartels to Control stating that he had sunk another ship (his third on this patrol), the 7,000-ton British *Empire Stanley.* This action had delayed him and since he was some distance from Lüth, he requested a new rendezvous site more convenient to both U-cruisers.

In the early hours of August 19, Lüth and Bartels met at the new rendezvous. Bartels gave Lüth the new Enigma keys and a second set to pass to Kentrat in *U-196.* Lüth told Bartels that he had seen four unescorted freighters in the rendezvous area and had shot his last torpedo at one, to no avail. In reply, Bartels said he would remain in the area and try to sink these and/or other ships. Inasmuch as Lüth was low on fuel, he could not tarry a day longer to help spot traffic. He waved good-bye to Bartels and sailed off to the southwest to meet with Kentrat in *U-196.*

The Allies DFed much of this U-boat chatter and got a rough fix on the site where *U-181* and *U-197* had met and where Bartels in *U-197* had elected to remain. On August 20 several Catalinas of two RAF squadrons flew from a base near Durban to search the site. In the afternoon that day, a Catalina of RAF Squadron 259, piloted by O. Barnett, found *U-197* casually cruising on the surface and at-

* At the time of the award, Lüth's score on the ducks *U-9* and *U-138* and the IXs *U-43* and *U-181* was forty-seven ships sunk for about 229,000 tons, including the French submarine *Doris.* He was the second-ranking U-boat skipper in the war after Otto Kretschmer who, as related, sank forty-five ships for about 270,000 tons and captured one for about 2,000 tons.

tacked. Barnett raked the U-cruiser with machine-gun fire and dropped six shallow-set depth charges from an altitude of fifty feet. Bartels responded with his flak guns, then crash-dived. Barnett dropped a smoke float near the swirl, radioed for reinforcements, then circled the smoke for nearly an hour.

Suddenly *U-197* surfaced, manned flak guns, and sent out several distress signals, stating that she was under aircraft attack and was "unable to submerge." At about that time, a Catalina from RAF Squadron 265, piloted by C. E. Robin, arrived and attacked. Like Barnett, pilot Robin raked the U-boat with machine-gun fire and dropped six shallow-set depth charges from an altitude of seventy-five feet. The *U-197* blew up, flinging debris high into the air. The two Catalinas circled an ever-widening oil patch, then returned to base, claiming a kill. The claim was correct. The *U-197* was lost this day with all hands, the second U-cruiser after Sobe's *U-179* to go down in South African waters.

Meanwhile, that same day, Lüth in *U-181* and Kentrat in *U-196* met per plan and Lüth gave Kentrat a set of the Enigma keys. Although Kentrat had sunk only one ship since leaving *Charlotte Schliemann,* the 7,300-ton British *City of Oran,* he generously offered Lüth five torpedoes and some food to extend his patrol, but Lüth declined, stating he barely had enough fuel to reach France. While they were still side by side, they heard the distress signals from Bartels in *U-197* and hastily drew up a rescue attempt, communicating visually. When it issued formal orders for the rescue attempt, U-boat Control suggested that the three U-boats cruising homeward very close together on the surface with all flak guns manned could repel any and all air attacks.

Assuming Bartels might still be afloat and coming south in the dark toward them, Lüth and Kentrat plotted the best search pattern to intercept him. Finally it was decided that Kentrat should stay put while Lüth went north toward the site of the attack. Perhaps fortunately for Lüth in *U-181* and Kentrat in *U-196,* foul weather on August 21 grounded all aircraft. After a futile search August from 21 to 24, *U-181* and *U-196* turned to a course south by west and headed for France.

Both boats got home. Completing a voyage of 206 days, Lüth in *U-181* arrived in Bordeaux one day before his thirtieth birthday, October 14, having sunk ten confirmed ships for 45,331 tons. Completing a record voyage of 225 days (that had begun earlier from Kiel), Kentrat in *U-196* arrived in Bordeaux on October 23, having sunk only two confirmed ships for 12,285 tons. Lüth went to Hitler's headquarters on October 25 to receive the two awards won on this patrol (Crossed Swords and the Diamonds)* and later to the Baltic to command Training Flotilla 22. Subsequently, he published a book in collaboration with *Ritterkreuz* holder Claus Korth. Despite his lackluster performance, *Ritterkreuz* holder Kentrat was left in command of *U-196.* However, he did not resail until March 1944.

The overall returns of this extraordinary U-cruiser foray to the Indian Ocean were mixed. Seven U-cruisers sailed. One (*U-197*) was sunk and one (*U-195*) aborted. Including the days at sea and ships sunk by those two boats, the foray

---

* The crew of *U-181* received high decorations as well. The chief engineer, Carl-August Landfehrmann, was awarded a *Ritterkreuz,* the seventh presented to U-boat engineers to that time.

bagged thirty-six ships for about 200,000 tons in 1,237 patrol days. Thanks to Lüth, Hartmann, Gysae, and Dommes, the overall average return per boat was five ships for about 28,500 tons per patrol. However, the three U-cruisers (*U-195, U-196, U-197*) sank only seven ships. Not incidentally, the foray caused deep consternation in those waters as well as great disruption in Allied maritime traffic and a diversion of warships to provide added protection.

FIVE

TRIDENT

On the eve of Allied victory in North Africa, Prime Minister Churchill and a large group of senior advisers secretly departed England on the liner/troopship *Queen Mary* to confer with President Roosevelt and his senior advisers on future courses of action. The ship arrived at New York without incident on May 11,* and the British party went on to Washington by special train. At Roosevelt's insistence, Churchill again quartered at the White House.

This Anglo-American conference, code-named Trident, took place over fourteen days from May 12 to 25. In contrast to the conference at Casablanca in January (Symbol), this time the senior American and British military got along well and were in closer agreement as to what to do next in most theaters of the war. The chief decisions were:

- The war against the U-boat force was to continue "with every possible means." As one measure, the British were to intensify diplomatic pressure on Portugal for authorization to operate aircraft and ships from the Azores to hunt down U-boats more efficiently and protect Allied convoys en route to and from the United States and Gibraltar.† As another measure, John Slessor's Coastal Command was to mount an all-out series of intense hunter-killer operations (Musketry,

---

* There were five thousand German POWs on board, including some submariners, en route to camps in North America, confined to the lower deck under guard.

† This elusive objective was finally attained in October 1943, by the far-fetched "recognition" of an ancient Anglo-Portuguese treaty. American reinforcements soon eased into the Azores under British

Seaslug, Percussion) during the summer months in the Bay of Biscay while the American Eighth Air Force increased daylight bombing raids on the U-boat building yards in Germany.

• As scheduled, Husky, the massive Allied invasion of Sicily, was to take place on the night of July 9–10.

• After the conquest of Sicily, the Allies were to continue operations on a limited scale in the Mediterranean to keep their military forces keenly attuned and, if possible, knock Italy out of the war. Churchill made a strong and emotional case for an invasion of Italy, but Roosevelt and the other Americans opposed it and the matter was tabled. One possibility after Sicily was a simultaneous invasion of the islands of (Italian) Sardinia and (Vichy) Corsica. Reluctant to mount any more land battles in the Mediterranean Basin, the Americans preferred—and offered—a scheme to knock Italy out of the war by airpower alone, but it was tabled as well.

• The colossal Allied invasion of Occupied France, Overlord, was to take place in about one year, on or about May 1, 1944. All other military operations were to be secondary to this undertaking. As a prelude, the combined heavy-bomber offensive against the German war industry and the civilian population (Sickle-Pointblank) was to proceed as designed, building to a climax to coincide with the invasion.

• American forces in the southwest and central Pacific and the Alaska area were to step up counterattacks against Japanese forces. The main objective in the southwest Pacific was still to capture the stronghold of Rabaul, which was to be approached by separate campaigns in New Guinea and the Solomon Islands. The first objective in the central Pacific was the capture of the Gilbert Islands (Tarawa, in particular). The objective in the Alaska area was to eject the Japanese from the Aleutian islands of Attu and Kiska.

• The Soviet Union and China were to be supported to the greatest possible extent. The Soviet Union was to bring massive pressure on Germany from the east while the Allies brought pressure from the west. China was to be a launching site for a massive heavy-bomber offensive against the Japanese home islands. However, a proposed amphibious invasion of Burma, which would facilitate that objective, was tabled.

Churchill left Washington via Boeing Clipper on May 25. At President Roosevelt's request, George Marshall accompanied the Prime Minister to North Africa to confer with Eisenhower, Montgomery, and other military leaders. Marshall was still fundamentally opposed to "periphery-pecking" in the Mediterranean Basin and was determined to do all in his power to limit operations in that area, especially an invasion of the Italian peninsula. Churchill was no less determined to mount an invasion of Italy and hoped to change Marshall's mind during this trip.

In the middle of the Trident meetings—on May 18—Admiral King revealed to the conferees that he had taken a significant new step to deal with the U-boat menace.

---

flag. In 1944, the Portuguese allowed the Americans to openly build air and naval bases on the island of Terceira.

He had created within his headquarters a new centralized paper command—designated the Tenth Fleet—which was empowered to coordinate all available information on U-boat operations and to direct American naval countermeasures, such as convoy evasions or hunter-killer operations. For administrative purposes (training, refitting, manning, and so on) American naval forces in the Atlantic, Caribbean, and Gulf of Mexico were to remain under the jurisdiction of Royal Ingersoll's Atlantic Fleet, the various sea frontiers, and/or special naval commands, but the commander of the Tenth Fleet had authority at any time to order any of these forces to take whatever action he thought necessary, simply by notifying the subordinate commanders and the forces concerned.

The British delegates and the American Army and Army Air Forces chiefs were delighted with this news. As the many historians hostile to King were to emphasize, it seemed that at long last this myopic admiral, fixated on the Pacific war, had recognized the lethality of the U-boat threat and had done something about it. The truth of the matter was that the creation of a Tenth Fleet or a similar organization before the spring of 1943 would have been virtually useless in view of the lack of the oft-mentioned "tools" (land-based aircraft, "jeep" carriers and suitable carrier aircraft and weaponry, destroyers, destroyer escorts, and so on) to carry out its mission.

The organization of Tenth Fleet served another purpose. It became the direct recipient of all naval Enigma intelligence, which had to be so very closely guarded against leaks. Its senior personnel in Washington, liaising with London over a secure teletype, digested the daily flow of naval Enigma, recommended convoy diversions, and directed other highly secret ASW operations without the need to divulge the reasons for them to subordinate commanders.

On paper, King himself commanded the Tenth Fleet. In actuality it was run by King's assistant chief of staff, forty-eight-year-old Francis S. ("Frog") Low, a bright, inventive, and tough-minded Naval Academy graduate, class of 1915. Low had served in submarines in World War I and between the wars. When King was named to command Atlantic naval forces to carry out the Neutrality Patrol in 1941, he chose Low to be his operations officer. When King moved up to commander in chief of the Navy, he brought Low to the Navy Department in the same capacity. During this Washington stint, Low conceived and urged the plan for the Doolittle raid on Tokyo, after which he commanded the cruiser *Wichita* during Torch. Upon his return to the Navy Department in 1943 to run Tenth Fleet and match wits with Dönitz and U-boat Control, Low was promoted to rear admiral.

There was one large weakness in the Tenth Fleet. The Army Air Forces ASW command, which had grown to twenty-seven squadrons and was scheduled for substantial expansion by year's end, was not directly and fully under Tenth Fleet control. There still existed an awkward—and hugely wasteful—internal struggle between the Army and Navy over control of land-based ASW aircraft. However, in the continuing and prolonged discussions of this issue in May and June 1943, Secretary of the Navy Frank Knox and King finally persuaded Stimson, Marshall, and Arnold that all ASW, including land-based air, should be exclusively a Navy responsibility.

Admiral King resolved another sensitive issue at Trident. As related, he had sent six fleet boats of American Submarine Squadron 50 to Scotland in December

1942 to augment British submarine ASW patrols. Two of these boats with defective diesels returned to the States, replaced in April 1943 by two others, *Haddo* and *Hake,* which also had defective engines. By May 1943, only one of these eight fleet boats had sunk a confirmed ship after about twenty-four war patrols.* Believing the boats to be unsuited for ASW or other missions in European/Arctic waters, on April 20 King had proposed that they be clandestinely employed in special hunter-killer operations against U-tankers, utilizing Enigma decrypts.

First Sea Lord Pound—and doubtless Churchill as well—had objected to this proposed tactical use of Enigma intelligence, fearing the Germans might realize naval Enigma had been broken. "We should not risk what is so valuable to us," Pound had cabled. If Enigma "failed us at the present time," Pound continued in a follow-up cable, "it would, I am sure, result in our shipping losses going up by anything from 50 to 100 percent."

King persisted. Off went another cable to Pound:

> While I am equally concerned with you as to security of Zebra [Enigma] information it is my belief that we are not deriving from it fullest value. The refueling submarine is the key to high speed, long range U-boat operations. To deprive the enemy of refuelers would at once decrease the effectiveness and radius of entire U-boat deployment. With careful preparations it seems not unlikely that their destruction might be accomplished without trace. While there is risk of compromise it would be a matter of lasting regret to all if Zebra [Enigma] security were jeopardized in some less worthy cause. . . .

When Pound again objected to this scheme, King proposed at Trident that owing to the unsuitability of big American submarines for other missions in European waters, Submarine Squadron 50 should be returned to the States and thereafter its six remaining boats be shifted to the Pacific theater. This proposal was approved. Deprived of a job, the squadron commander, Norman S. Ives, took a staff post in London and later was killed by German mortar fire in Normandy during Overlord.

Historians of the Battle of the Atlantic have slighted or ignored Submarine Squadron 50. And yet, ironically and unintentionally, at the time it made a great contribution to the war, which has only recently come to light in the declassified American Enigma documents.

For several months in 1943, Allied codebreakers suspected that German codebreakers were reading the combined Anglo-American Naval Cypher Number 3. In view of this possibility, British and American task forces combed through old and current Enigma decrypts for clues. They found a half dozen possibilities, but most cases were too ambiguous and were not sufficiently convincing to set in train a change of codes, a large and complex undertaking.

While this search was in progress, on May 25, 27, and 31, U-boat Control committed three horrendous breaches of communications security.† *B-dienst* had inter-

---

* As related, *Herring* sank the 7,000-ton Vichy freighter *Ville du Havre* during the Torch invasion. The *Shad* damaged the inbound blockade-runner *Pietro Orselo* on April 1.

† See U-boat Control (BdU) War Diary (KTB) on those dates and at NARA in RG 457: SRMN 35, p. 45; SRMN 37, pp. 58–137; SRH 208, pp. 70–93.

cepted and decrypted Allied warnings in Naval Cypher Number 3 to all Allied convoys that three of the Submarine Squadron 50 submarines, *Haddo, Hake,* and *Herring,* were to operate at certain positions along the North Atlantic run during their return to the States. Believing that German U-boats in that area should also be warned of these American submarines, Control relayed the Allied information, giving the nearly exact grid squares (latitudes and longitudes) where the three were or were supposed to be, without any exceptional measure to disguise the information with interior codes or by some other means.

These Enigma decrypts were unequivocal confirmation that, as suspected, *B-dienst* was reading Naval Cypher Number 3. The discovery assumed added force and urgency because American crews on the three submarines were believed to be at imminent risk. Hence on June 10, Allied communication authorities directed all naval commands and ships to switch to Allied Naval Code Number 5. This switch came as a devastating setback for *B-dienst.* After months of reading Allied convoy codes with sufficient currency to be of tactical value, in June 1943 German codebreakers suddenly went virtually blind and deaf. In the future they were to regain some Allied convoy codes sporadically, but thanks in large part to the seemingly fruitless patrols of *Haddo, Hake,* and *Herring,* the glory days for German codebreakers were over.

Technological Revolutions and Interim Upgrades

By the end of April 1943, the Germans confronted a naval rout in the Atlantic. Allied centimetric-wavelength radar, land- and ship-based Huff Duff, land-based aircraft, skilled surface escort and support groups, Enigma codebreaking, and superb intelligence evaluation and operational-research teams in London and Washington had finally defeated the U-boat force. No existing production U-boat could enter combat in the North Atlantic with even the slightest degree of confidence. Attacks on Allied convoys had become near-suicidal endeavors and would only become more dangerous.

The defeat of the existing U-boat force was no surprise. Dönitz and U-boat Control had seen it coming for a year or perhaps longer. The increased Allied air power was an important reason, but the "determining factor," Dönitz explained to Hitler, was "a new [Allied] location device, evidently also used by surface vessels, by means of which planes are now in a position to locate submarines." That explanation, of course, was only partly correct and it reflected the lack of technological sophistication in Hitler's Germany, particularly in the *Kriegsmarine.*

Both Hitler and Dönitz were in full agreement that the U-boat war must continue. "There can be no talk of a letup in submarine warfare," Hitler said, according to a stenographer. "The Atlantic is my first line of defense in the West, and even if I have to fight a defensive battle there, that is preferable to waiting to defend myself on the coast of Europe. The enemy forces tied up by our submarine warfare are tremendous, even though the actual losses inflicted by us are no longer great. I cannot afford to release these forces by discontinuing submarine warfare."

What was desperately needed was a quantum leap in U-boat technology. That was why Raeder and Dönitz had encouraged and supported the ideas of the inventive engineer Helmut Walter, who had proposed a high-speed, "true" submarine, powered when submerged by engines that obtained oxygen from hydrogen peroxide (code-named "Ingolin").* As related, Hitler had earlier authorized the construction of two oceangoing Walter prototypes (*U-796* and *U-797*) and twenty-four Walter coastal boats or "ducks" (*U-1405* to *U-1416; U-1081* to *U-1092*).

This radical submarine program, going forward in utmost secrecy, had run into many difficulties. One, ironically, was the overwhelming success of the conventional VIIs and IXs in American waters in the first half of 1942. That heady success, which seemed to portend others, tended to undermine the urgency of the Walter-boat program. Another was the growing number of technical problems. Chief among these was the acute shortage of hydrogen peroxide, which was also used in the V-2 ballistic missile program, likewise under high-priority development. It had become apparent that a big oceangoing Walter U-boat fleet would require several large-scale hydrogen-peroxide production plants for which there were nowhere near sufficient resources. Yet another reason was the intensifying Allied bomber offensive against U-boat building yards. An RAF raid on Kiel on March 12, 1942, had so damaged the first oceangoing Walter test bed, *U-791,* that it was scrapped.

It also became apparent that there was a tactical weakness in the hydrogen-peroxide submarine. Unlike conventional storage batteries, which could be recharged for submerged operations (used again and again), hydrogen peroxide was a nonrecyclable power source. Once burned, it was gone. Since there was not enough room in the Walter boat for both a big rechargeable storage battery *and* hydrogen-peroxide tankage, and that tankage was not, of course, unlimited in size, the submerged endurance of such a boat was restricted. Hence until some means could be devised to replenish this exotic fuel supply at sea (hydrogen-peroxide U-tankers?), the operating radius was quite limited.

For these reasons and others, by May 1943 it was clear that neither the oceangoing nor the coastal Walter boats powered by hydrogen peroxide could be produced in sufficient quantity to influence the outcome of the war. However, Walter came up with another idea that held great promise. The large internal hydrogen-peroxide fuel tanks in the lower half of the figure-eight hull of the large and small Walter boats could be used to add additional storage batteries that could provide about three times the power of those in a VII, IX, or a Type II duck. Wind-tunnel tests and mathematical computations showed that with streamlining and the elimination of deck guns these boats could sprint submerged on batteries at an amazing 18 knots for brief periods. This increase in battery power would give U-boats the ability to overtake and strike convoys at high sprint speed submerged and withdraw at equal sprint speed for several hours, outrunning most surface escorts.

Owing to the many, many years of R&D invested in the design of the high-speed Walter hydrogen-peroxide boats, it was a relatively simple matter to produce quickly a radically new submarine design, substituting batteries for hydrogen-

* Partly an inside joke: Walter's young son was named Ingol.

peroxide tankage. Hence mass production could commence in a matter of mere weeks and the first boats might be ready by the summer of 1944.

After Hitler approved this scheme, Dönitz ordered about seven hundred such submarines: 450 1,600-ton oceangoing types (based on plans for the Walter Type XVIII "Atlantic boats," *U-796* and *U-797*), which were designated XXI, and about 250 250-ton coastal types (based on the Walter Type XVIIA and B "Coastal boats"), which were designated Type XXIII. Owing to their massive battery power, the Germans called these two new submarine types "electro boats" to distinguish them from the conventional "diesel boats" or the hydrogen-peroxide "Walter boats."

Notwithstanding all the problems, work on the Walter hydrogen-peroxide boats continued to the end of the war. Apart from the test beds *V-80* and *V-300* (*U-791*), seven Walter boats were commissioned in the war, all ducks of 300 tons or less that had a load of four torpedoes (two in bow tubes and two reloads) and a submerged range of about 100–150 miles.*

Numerous historians and engineers have extolled this achievement and some have speculated that had they been perfected and built earlier, the hydrogen-peroxide U-boats could have had a decisive impact on the war. This is nonsense. The hydrogen-peroxide boats were impossibly complex and dangerous and, in any case, Germany was in no position to provide the exotic fuel. For these and other reasons, in the postwar years the United States, Great Britain, and other nations declined to pursue this line of submarine technology.

However, if they lived up to expectations, the "electro boats" were well positioned to provide the "new generation" of U-boats required to decisively outfight convoy air and surface escorts. But they were not to be ready in sufficient numbers for a year or more. In the interim, a radical upgrade was required to enhance the survivability of the VIIs and IXs.

Professor Walter provided that upgrade as well: the *Schnorchel,* or in the English spelling, snorkel, known among all submariners colloquially as the "snort." This was a double-barrel tube that could be raised above the water or lowered beneath it like a periscope while the boat was running submerged. One barrel of the tube sucked in air to run the diesel engines submerged; the other barrel expelled the diesel exhaust. Conceived primarily as a defense against enemy radar-equipped aircraft, the snort allowed U-boats to charge batteries submerged with the diesels at a speed of up to 5 or 6 knots, offering only a very small radar target.

The snort was not a new idea. In the previous fifty years, numerous submarine designers had incorporated snorts in their proposals. The Dutch had built several submarines in the 1930s with snorts, some of which were captured by the Germans. However, it was believed that snorts could only be used effectively in relatively calm seas, never in the rough North Atlantic where the snorts would be continuously "dunked" by the big waves. When that occurred, the diesels would suck an enormous quantity of air from inside the boat, perhaps even from the lungs of the crewmen, and/or the carbon-monoxide exhaust would back up inside the hull and kill the crew. Besides those horrifying possibilities, snorting boats running submerged on diesels made a tremendous racket, easily detected by enemy hy-

* The XVIIAs *U-792, U-793, U-794,* and *U-795* and the XVIIBs *U-1405, U-1406,* and *U-1407.*

drophones and other passive sonar devices, while at the same time "deafening" the submarine. A submerged snorting boat thrusting its full girth against resisting seas also would use almost twice the fuel oil of a surfaced U-boat.

Incorporating some features of the Dutch model, Walter's snort was of advanced engineering design, which eliminated many of the weaknesses and drawbacks of earlier versions. Both ends of the tube had sensitive valves and floats to prevent spray inhalation or flooding and exhaust backup. Walter demonstrated that even if the air intake "dunked" and closed for a full minute, the air sucked from inside the boat would not be physically harmful to the crew, merely annoying. Accordingly, in June 1943, Dönitz and the OKM directed that the school ducks *U-57* (Erich Topp's old command, which had been rammed, sunk, and salvaged) and *U-58,* and the VIICs *U-235* and *U-236,* which had been sunk during an Allied air raid on Kiel on May 14 and salvaged, be fitted with snorts for test purposes.

The tests were far from satisfactory. Mounted on the port side just forward of the bridge, the exhaust or wake of the snorts on the two VIIs clouded the raised periscopes, reducing submerged visibility. When the snort dunked, the suction inside the boat was much greater and more rapid than predicted. Hence it became necessary when snorting for one engineer to maintain a continuous close watch on a barometer. When the pressure inside the boat suddenly dropped below a normal 1020 millibars to 850 millibars, he shut down one diesel. If the pressure fell another 100 millibars to 750, he shut down the other diesel and shifted to battery power. Notwithstanding all efforts to prevent it, diesel fumes seeped into the boat, causing crewmen headaches and blurred vision or more serious illnesses.

Hailed by some historians and engineers as another great technical achievement, the snort was not that by a long shot. Rather it was a miserable, temporary device that German U-boat crews hated absolutely. They resisted its installation on their boats and used it *not continuously,* as often depicted, but only very sparingly (ordinarily about four hours a day) to charge batteries, owing to the high fuel-oil consumption experienced when running submerged on diesels. In his memoir, *Iron Coffins,* Herbert Werner described what happened when the ball float in the snort air intake jammed shut, creating a vacuum in the boat:

> The men gasped for air, their eyes bulging. The Chief [engineer] lowered the boat, bringing the *Schnorchel* head below surface in an effort to loosen the float. To no avail. Breathing became ever more difficult; suffocation seemed imminent. The Chief gesticulated wildly, trying to tell his men to lay down the air mast, which might result in unlocking the float. With agonizing effort, the mechanics turned handles, lowered the mast by cable, then erected it again with the primitive winch.* Painful minutes passed, but then the mast drained and the seawater gurgled down into the bilges. The float cleared with a snap and air was sucked into the boat with a long sigh. The sudden change in pressure burst many an eardrum. Some of the men covered their faces in pain and sagged to the deck plates. Others swallowed violently to equalize the pressure.

* Ordinarily the snort was raised and laid down flat into a slot on the upper deck almost effortlessly by hydraulic devices. In this instance the hydraulic system must have malfunctioned.

Owing to crew complaints and technical bottlenecks, the Germans fitted the snort much more slowly than usually described. The OKM ordered the first twenty snorts for operational boats in August 1943, and another 140 in late September. First priority went to boats already at the battlefronts and secondly to new construction. The "electro boats" were also to have snorts.

Pending the arrival of "electro boats" and "snort boats," Dönitz proposed to continue the U-boat war on a reduced scale with upgraded Type VIIs and IXs, employing some changes in tactics. The upgrading and new tactics were as follow:

- A new FuMB, or radar detector, called *Wanze,* built by the German company Hagenuk, to replace Metox. Still doubtful that the Allies had adapted an airborne centimetric-wavelength ASW radar and convinced that the Allies were "homing" on the electronic emanations from Metox, the Germans put the supposedly nonradiating *Wanze,* which searched in the eighty-centimeter range, into production. But, of course, it was useless against the centimeter-wavelength ASV radar that had become standard issue in Coastal Command and the American ASW commands. Until *Wanze* arrived, U-boat Control directed that U-boats were only to operate on the surface with one electric motor at night or in foggy weather so the bridge watch could "hear" enemy aircraft approaching.
- The new T-5 *Zaunkönig* (Wren) antiescort acoustic or homing torpedo, a "wonder weapon" to replace the less than satisfactory T-3 *Falke.* Capable of homing on ships traveling at speeds of up to 15 knots, the faster *Zaunkönig,* it was believed, would at the very least put U-boats on an even footing with most escorts.
- Increased numbers of G7a FAT I (looping) torpedoes made possible by the conversion of G7as formerly carried in topside canisters, which had been abolished. The FAT I was to be fired only at night and was fitted with only an impact pistol (AZ).
- The new FAT II, a G7e electric torpedo that could be fired submerged. It was designed not only to loop but also to circle. It was to be used against escorts until the *Zaunkönig* was debugged and fully operational.*
- An improved version of the Pi2 pistol for G7e (electric) torpedoes that could be set for either impact (AZ) or magnetic (MZ) detonation.
- Increased numbers of flak guns, notably a new quad 20mm (aft of the bridge on a bandstand) to allow U-boats to better counter Allied air attacks. The interim goal was to modify and equip the bridges of all Atlantic force U-boats with a quad 20mm gun, two single or twin barrel 20mm guns, and four dismountable .50-caliber machine guns. The fact that the bulky quad 20mm, which had splinter shields, somewhat destabilized and slowed the boats while diving and running submerged had to be accepted.
- Improved search radar for U-boats, including sets modified from the *Luftwaffe*'s somewhat primitive meter-wavelength airborne *Hohentwiel.*

---

* The FAT II (electric) was to be introduced first in the Mediterranean and Arctic, where the FAT I (air) could not be used owing to phosphorescent water in the former and too much daylight in the latter. If all went well, FAT IIs were to be issued to the Atlantic U-boat force in May. The production rate was modest: one hundred torpedoes per month to start, gradually increasing after August 1943.

- A convoy contact buoy. This device enabled the convoy shadower to mark the path of the convoy for the other boats assembling for the attack, even if submerged. After being launched, the buoy intermittently fired off red, green, or yellow star shells, or combinations thereof that imparted certain prearranged tracking information to the other boats.
- Radar deceivers known as *Aphrodite* and *Thetis.* Fitted with metal reflectors, these devices were designed (like Allied chaff) to confuse enemy radar operators at night and lead them to think the reflector was the U-boat, giving the boat time to escape. *Aphrodite* was mounted on a balloon and wafted along just above the water. *Thetis* was "moored" on the water's surface by means of ballasting gear.

For the future, German electronic engineers were to produce all-frequency radar "jamming gear," small enough to fit in a Type VII. Technicians at I. G. Farben were convinced that a radar-absorbing material and/or some other porous materials (*Schwaemme*) under study would make U-boats invisible to radar, an R&D stealth project dubbed "the black submarine."

The Germans had also conceived a devilish weapons system known as a "flak trap," or "flak U-boat." The veteran VII *U-441* was the first. She was fitted with two shielded, quadruple 20mm cannons (quad 20s) on bandstands fore and aft of the conning tower, a rapid-fire 37mm on a second, lower bandstand aft, plus nests of machine guns on the bridge. Her task was to escort U-boats across the Bay of Biscay and U-tankers in more distant waters and to sucker unsuspecting Allied aircraft into an attack. Seven other VIIs were likewise converted, but only one other, *U-621,* sailed as such that summer.*

As for new tactics, the most important was put into effect on May 1. All U-boats that already had dismountable single or twin 20mm cannons on the bridge were to remain on the surface and "fight it out" when attacked by enemy aircraft. Meanwhile, the *Kriegsmarine* had rushed production of the quad 20s and a new 37mm Skoda rapid-fire antiaircraft gun for U-boats, which Hitler favored.

At this same time, on May 5, due to heavy losses, Dönitz directed U-boat Control to withdraw all Type IXs from groups on anticonvoy operations in the North Atlantic. Older IXs in France were only to patrol distant waters where it was thought that ASW measures were less intense. New IXs outbound from Germany to join the Atlantic force were to exercise extreme caution until clear of the North Atlantic area and to attack enemy ships only if conditions were entirely favorable.

U-boat Losses and Aborts

U-boat Control sailed forty-six attack boats against Allied convoys in the North and Middle Atlantic in May: forty VIIs,† four IXs, one VIID minelayer, *U-214,*

---

* The others: *U-211, U-256, U-263, U-271, U-650,* and *U-953.* Four first sailed in October 1943. The *U-263* and *U-650* did not ever sail as flak boats.

† Including *U-636,* which made her maiden patrol in the Atlantic but was transferred to the Arctic at its conclusion, and two boats that sailed for the Mediterranean, *U-409* and *U-594.* The *U-409* got

and one XB minelayer, *U-118.** These boats joined or attempted to join boats that sailed in April and were still at sea. Eighteen of the forty-six boats sailing in May (40 percent) did not return.

The U-tanker fleet was still inadequate to replenish so many VIIs. Of the seven XIV tankers then in service, one (*U-460*) was supporting a foray to the distant South Atlantic, and two (*U-459, U-461*) were at sea backing up the April boats. One (*U-487*) was inbound to France from the North Atlantic and one (*U-462*) was in port for refit. Therefore only two Type XIVs were available to sail in May: the *U-463,* which left France on May 8, and the new *U-488,* commanded by Erwin Bartke, age thirty-four, which left Kiel May 18. Allied aircraft were to sink *U-463* and as one consequence, Control had to divert three of the four Type IXs that sailed in May (*U-170, U-530, U-535*), as well as the XB minelayer *U-118,* to duty as provisional tankers.

Many historians of the U-boat war were to write that by the summer of 1943, most U-boats were commanded by very young and inexperienced officers. Doubtless this view derived partly from an ill-considered and exaggerated statement by Dönitz, cited by the German naval historian Michael Salewski, to the effect that in the later years of the war German submariners "were little more than children." However, recent age studies have refuted that assertion.† German submariners in 1943 were no younger than they were in the earlier years of the war. There were very few skippers under the age of twenty-five.

The boats sailing to the North Atlantic in May were armed with three types of production torpedoes. The Type VII boats, no longer fitted with topside storage canisters, had twelve torpedoes belowdecks: six electric (G7e) T-3 *Faulkes* ("homing") and four air (G7a) FAT I ("looping") in the bow compartment for night surface attacks, and two electric (G7e) FAT II ("looping and circling") in the stern compartment for daylight submerged attacks. The Type IX boats, also stripped of topside canisters, had fourteen torpedoes belowdecks: six electric T-3 and four air FAT I in the bow compartment and two air FAT I and two electric FAT II in the stern compartment.‡

The onboard maintenance and the firing of this array of torpedoes had become quite complex. The majority of torpedoes carried were battery-powered "electrics."

---

into the Mediterranean, but a Hudson of British Squadron 48, piloted by H. C. Bailey, sank with rockets the *U-594,* commanded by Friedrich Mumm, on June 4.

* Including three transfers from the Arctic, *U-467, U-646,* and *U-657.* The usual setbacks and delays in the Baltic continued. An Eighth Air Force raid (126 bombers) on Kiel on May 14 sank at dockside the VIIs *U-235, U-236,* and *U-237* and damaged the VIIs *U-244* and *U-1051,* two VIIF transport boats, *U-1061* and *U-1062,* and the XB minelayer *U-234.* Another Eighth Air Force raid (ninety-seven bombers) on Vegesack (Bremen), on May 18, severely damaged *U-287* and *U-295.* The VII *U-450,* which had been rammed at a Kiel dock in the fall of 1942, was rammed a second time near Danzig during workup. The IXC40 *U-528* twice collided with other boats in tactical exercises. Found wanting for various reasons, her original skipper and that of the VII *U-671* had to be replaced.

† See second footnote, p. 170.

‡ Type IXs going to calmer Middle Atlantic waters or to more remote areas carried twenty torpedoes, six of them G7as, in topside canisters. The fourteen belowdecks consisted of six T-3s and four conventional G7es in the bow and two FAT II and two conventional G7es in the stern.

These were slow moving and, if the batteries were not kept properly heated, slower still. Owing to the need for extended "patrol lines" to find convoys, fewer and fewer boats actually shot torpedoes, so the jam-packed bow compartment remained an inhospitable living space. When preparing to shoot a FAT I or FAT II, the boats in a group had to radio a "FAT warning" to other boats at or near the convoy fifteen minutes in advance so they could get out of the way or submerge to at least 164 feet. One, two, or more simultaneous or nearly so "FAT warnings" could easily confuse or foul a group attack.

All boats sailing in May confronted the intensified Coastal Command hunter-killer operation in the Bay of Biscay, Derange. Conceived by Air Marshal John Slessor and Geoffrey Bromet, chief of Coastal Command's 19 Group based in southern England, this powerful air offensive took place from April 13 to June 6. Although the British air commanders sorely missed the B-24s of U.S. Army Air Forces ASW Squadrons 1 and 2 (transferred to Morocco), they were not without improved resources:

- A new model Leigh Light–equipped Wellington, fitted with more powerful Hercules engines and featherable propellers, which enabled the plane to fly on one engine in emergencies. Importantly, these aircraft were also fitted with the latest ASV III centimetric radar with a PPI display.

Two Coastal Command squadrons, consisting of about fifteen aircraft each, got these new Wellingtons: British Squadron 172 and Canadian Squadron 407. The primary task of the Leigh Light–equipped Wellingtons was to saturate the Bay of Biscay at night, forcing as many U-boats as possible to dive and run submerged and then to surface in daylight hours to charge batteries. By this tactic Slessor and Bromet were able to increase the effectiveness of the Derange daylight air patrols of the Whitleys, Sunderlands, Catalinas, and other aircraft fitted with less sophisticated radar, whose crews relied heavily on daytime visual spottings. Of course, a nighttime kill by a Leigh Light–equipped Wellington was an added bonus.

- Two Coastal Command squadrons, each consisting of about fifteen four-engine Halifax aircraft, also fitted with ASV III centimetric-wavelength radar with PPI display. These were British Squadron 58 (only recently upgraded from older model Wellingtons) and British Squadron 502 (upgraded earlier from Whitleys).
- One Coastal Command squadron of about fifteen B-24s, also fitted with ASV III centimetric-wavelength radar with PPI display. This was British Squadron 224, based at Beaulieu near St. Eval in southwest England. Theretofore the B-24s had been utilized in defensive roles as convoy escorts far out in the Atlantic. The crews welcomed the switch to a predominantly offensive role.

Altogether then, Slessor and Bromet had five squadrons consisting of seventy to seventy-five modern two- and four-engine aircraft fitted with centimetric radar with PPI display for Derange. In addition, in 19 Group there were available three squadrons of Sunderlands (RAF 228, Australian 10 and 461), one squadron of British Catalinas (210), and two squadrons of British Whitleys (612 and OTU 10). These planes were variously equipped with improved Torpex depth charges, Fidos, ASW bombs, and rockets.

Eleven May boats were sunk or forced to abort shortly after sailing and did not reach operational areas. Five sinkings:

- The VII *U-663,* commanded by Heinrich Schmid, age twenty-seven, who sailed from France on his third patrol on May 5. Two days later, in the Bay of Biscay, Geoffrey G. Rossiter of Australian Squadron 10, piloting a four-engine Sunderland on Derange patrol, spotted *U-663* on the surface and straddled her with six 250-pound depth charges. Nothing further was ever heard from this boat.*
- The XIV tanker *U-463,* commanded by Leo Wolfbauer, age forty-seven, who sailed on his fifth patrol from France on May 8. A week later, on May 15, a Halifax of British Squadron 58, piloted by Anthony J. W. Birch, spotted *U-463* on the western edge of the Bay of Biscay. Birch attacked with six 250-pound depth charges, sinking *U-463* with no survivors. The loss of this valuable U-tanker, on top of the accidental sinking of the new XIV tanker *U-490* during workup in the Baltic and other losses and mishaps, was to lead to acute complications in U-boat refueling operations in May as well as June and July.
- The new VII *U-308,* commanded by Karl Mühlenpfort, age thirty-three, who sailed from Kiel on May 29. Seven days later, as *U-308* was rounding the Faeroes to enter the Atlantic, the big new British submarine *Truculent,* commanded by Robert L. Alexander, probably acting on an Enigma decrypt or other intelligence, found her on the surface. Alexander dived and fired a spread of six torpedoes, some of which hit and blew up *U-308.* When *Truculent* surfaced to recover proof of a kill, the crew found, in the words of the British writer Geoffrey P. Jones† "a large patch of fuel oil" and "a considerable amount of wreckage, shattered woodwork, watch coats, sea boots, paper and loaves of bread." There were no survivors.
- The veteran VII *U-563,* which earlier had spent a year in Germany undergoing battle-damage repairs. Commanded for one Atlantic patrol by Götz von Hartmann, age twenty-nine, she sailed from France on her second patrol under a new skipper, Gustav Borchardt, age twenty-six. Two days later, on May 31, the commander of Squadron 58, Wilfred E. Oulton, piloting a Halifax, spotted *U-563* on the surface and attacked with machine guns and nine depth charges in two runs.

The *U-563* appeared to be fatally wounded, but she refused to sink. Moreover, Borchardt shot back at Oulton with flak guns during several strafing runs. A second Halifax of Squadron 58, piloted by Eric L. Hartley, arrived and carried out two nearly identical attacks, dropping nine depth charges, but they fell wide and *U-563* still refused to sink. She was finally put down by two Sunderlands, one piloted by William M. French of British Squadron 228 and the other by Maxwell S. Mainprize of Australian Squadron 10. The Allied airmen reported "thirty or forty Germans" in the water from *U-563*—perhaps living survivors—but a search on the following day by JU-88s carrying life rafts proved futile.

In response to Borchardt's appeal for help, the inbound, fuel-low *U-621,* commanded by Max Kruschka, age twenty-four, briefly searched for survivors of *U-563* but found none and was herself attacked by a B-24 of British Squadron 224,

---

* The Admiralty originally attributed the kill of *U-663* to a Halifax of British Squadron 58, but Alex Niestlé (1998) credits Rossiter.

† *Submarines Versus U-boats* (1986).

piloted by an American, Robert V. Sweeny, who toggled twelve depth charges in two runs. These severely damaged *U-621* but she reached France on June 3, completing a patrol of forty-three days. Due to the heavy damage, *U-621* was selected for conversion to a "flak" boat.

• The veteran but luckless VII *U-440,* commanded by a new skipper, Werner Schwaff, age twenty-eight, from whom *Ritterkreuz* holder Peter Cremer had reclaimed *U-333.* Schwaff sailed *U-440* from France on May 26. Five days later, on May 31, while on the western edge of the Bay of Biscay, a Sunderland of British Squadron 201, piloted by Douglas M. Gall, saw *U-440* on the surface. Gall attacked in the face of heavy flak from *U-440* and dropped four depth charges in a good straddle near the U-boat's stern. The explosion must have badly holed *U-440* aft for her bow raised vertically and she sank stern first. There were no survivors.

The four U-boat losses recounted above, which were credited to British aircraft, were the direct result of Coastal Command's intense Biscay offensive, Derange. It was believed at the time that a single British Halifax pilot, Wilfred Oulton, commander of British Squadron 58, was responsible for three of the four kills: the XIV tanker *U-463* and the VIIs *U-563* and *U-663.* For this achievement, the Admiralty awarded Oulton the DFC and DSO, but in the postwar reappraisal, Oulton's kills in this outbound group were reduced to one, *U-563.**

Six boats that sailed in May were forced to abort shortly after leaving port, all by British aircraft. These aborts:

• The VIID (minelayer) *U-214,* commanded by Günther Reeder, age twenty-seven. He sailed to lay a field of fifteen SMA (moored) mines off Dakar. While crossing the Bay of Biscay on May 6, a Whitley of Bomber Command's OTU 10 on Derange patrol piloted by S. J. Barnett hit the boat with a straddle of depth charges and heavy machine-gun fire, severely wounding Reeder and forcing *U-214* to abort. Commanded by a new skipper, Rupprecht Stock, also age twenty-seven, she resailed on May 19 and laid the field at Dakar on June 6. The mines damaged one ship, the 6,500-ton American freighter *Santa Maria,* which was repaired and eventually returned to service.

• The VII *U-405,* a former Arctic boat, commanded by Rolf-Heinrich Hopmann, age thirty-seven. Two days out from France, on May 9, an unidentified Allied aircraft hit *U-405.* Hopmann repaired some of the damage, but he could not stop a bad oil leak. On May 12, he aborted the patrol, arriving in France on May 21. The boat did not sail again until October.

• Yet another onetime Arctic boat, the VII *U-591,* commanded by Hans-Jürgen Zetzsche, age twenty-seven. Four days out from France, a Whitley of Bomber Command's OTU 10, piloted by G. W. Brookes, hit *U-591,* wounding Zetzsche and a seaman. Unable to carry on, Zetzsche aborted the patrol, arriving in France on May 16. While hospitalized, Zetzsche lost command of *U-591,* which resailed in June. He did not return to Atlantic combat.

• The Type VII "flak boat" *U-441.* Commanded by a new skipper, twenty-nine-year-old Götz von Hartmann from *U-563,* who (confusingly) relieved Klaus

* The attribution of these kills is derived from Franks, *Search, Find and Kill* (1995), a revision of his edition of 1990. At this time, Oulton also sank an inbound VII, as will be described.

Hartmann, age thirty, she sailed from France into the Bay of Biscay on May 22. She carried sixty-seven men, including a doctor, two engineers to test radar-detection gear, and a team of highly trained gunners to man her two quad 20s and the 37mm flak guns.

Three days out, on May 24, a Sunderland of British Squadron 228, piloted by H. J. Debden, spotted *U-441,* took the bait, and attacked with a salvo of depth charges. Handicapped by the loss of one quad 20, which failed owing to a poor weld in the bandstand, *U-441* nonetheless hit and shot down the Sunderland with the loss of all hands. Badly damaged in the bow area by the depth charges, *U-441* was forced to abort to France, arriving in Brest on May 26, a voyage of but five days. This inauspicious debut of the first "flak trap" appeared not to have discouraged the Germans; the conversion of the other seven flak boats proceeded apace.

• The IXC *U-523,* commanded by Werner Pietzsch, age twenty-six, bound for the Americas. She too sailed from France on May 22 and was not far from *U-441* on May 24 when the latter was hit. A Whitley of Bomber Command's OTU 10, piloted by S. C. Chatton, attacked *U-523,* inflicting such severe damage that Pietzsch was also forced to abort, arriving in Lorient on May 26. The boat did not resail until August.

• The new VII *U-450,* commanded by Kurt Böhme, age twenty-six, who sailed from Kiel on May 25. Two weeks later, on June 6, a B-17 of British Squadron 220, piloted by H. Warren, attacked *U-450* in the Iceland-Faeroes gap. The machine-gun fire and depth charges seriously wounded four men, including Böhme, slightly wounded three others, and wrecked the boat.

In response to *U-450*'s SOS, U-boat Control authorized Böhme to abandon ship, if necessary, and directed four new VIIs from Kiel and the VII *U-592,* which had sailed from France with a doctor, to assist. Three of the four new VIIs from Kiel reached *U-450* on June 9 and helped with the wounded and with repairs. When it appeared that *U-450* could reach port after all, U-boat Control released all boats except the inbound *U-645,* commanded by Otto Ferro, which escorted *U-450* to the rendezvous with the doctor on *U-592* on June 13. The doctor swam across to *U-450* and treated the wounded, after which *U-592* went on her way. From there Otto Ferro in *U-645* escorted *U-450* into Brest, arriving June 22. Böhme retained command of *U-450* but the boat did not resail until mid-October.

These eleven losses or aborts of the outgoing May boats were only one part of the devastation of the Atlantic U-boat force. As has been or will be told, numerous other inbound U-boats were sunk or destroyed in May.

The mounting success of Derange provided John Slessor with the necessary clout to pressure Washington into contributing significantly more aircraft to the Bay of Biscay offensive, specifically for an even more intense campaign planned for the summer months, code-named Musketry followed by Seaslug followed by Percussion. To urge his case, Slessor flew to Washington and met with President Roosevelt, the Secretaries of War and Navy, and the Joint Chiefs of Staff, Generals Marshall and Arnold and Admiral King.

Slessor arrived in Washington at a climactic moment in the prolonged and vastly troubling history of the Army and Navy struggle over control of land-based ASW aircraft. Those services were finally working toward a logical, long overdue—even historic—deal whereby the Army would, in effect, get out of the antisubmarine business worldwide and leave that task exclusively to the Navy. As part of the deal, the Army Air Forces agreed to turn over to the Navy its trained B-24 squadrons, provided King allowed the Army Air Forces to receive an equal number of B-24s from the Navy's paltry 1943 allotment.* When King agreed to this, a schedule for the gradual swap was drawn with a completion date of September 1, 1943.

The Army Air Forces and Navy's ASW B-24 squadrons were to be operationally controlled by Tenth Fleet. Thus in order to accomplish his mission of obtaining more American B-24s for the Musketry-Seaslug-Percussion summer offensive in the Bay of Biscay, Slessor had then to coax them out of the fearsome and supposed Anglophobe, Admiral King.

As Slessor tells it, King was not very helpful. He offered to send Squadron VB 128 (upgraded from Hudsons to Venturas) and Squadron VP 63 (Catalinas with MAD gear)† temporarily to Iceland so that Slessor could shift British aircraft from Iceland to southern England to reinforce the Bay of Biscay offensive. Slessor was not satisfied with his offer since what he really wanted for Musketry-Seaslug-Percussion were very-long-range B-24s with centimetric-wavelength radar. Nonetheless King loaned these two Navy squadrons to Coastal Command, sending the Venturas to Iceland and the Catalinas, which were not wheeled (amphibious), to Wales for the Biscay offensive. The Catalinas arrived the last week of July; the Venturas in August.

Nor was that all. King, who had been pressing the British to mount an intense Biscay air offensive for almost two years, eagerly approved of Musketry-Seaslug-Percussion. To support the offensive he did, in fact, agree to transfer temporarily to Coastal Command five squadrons of very-long-range B-24s fitted with centimetric-wavelength radar with PPI displays. These units, which comprised about seventy-five aircraft, were:

- The Army Air Forces ASW Squadrons 4 and 19, based at Gander in Newfoundland. All twenty-four B-24s of these two squadrons arrived safely at St. Eval, thirteen planes on June 30 and eleven on July 7. These squadrons, not yet integrated into Tenth Fleet and commanded by Howard Moore, were designated 479th Group. The group began flying missions over the bay on July 13. Subsequently it moved to a new RAF field at Dunkeswell in adjacent Devonshire.
- Two more Army Air Forces ASW Squadrons, 6 and 22. These twenty-four very-long-range B-24s arrived at Dunkeswell in August. However, Squadron 6, less its aircraft, was soon reassigned to another command.
- Two U.S. Navy very-long-range B-24 squadrons, VB 103 and VB 105, comprising advance elements of Fleet Air Wing 7. According to Slessor, VB 103

* Deliveries of B-24s to the U.S. Navy commenced in August 1942. That year the Navy received fifty-two new B-24s; in 1943 it received 308 new B-24s and in 1944, 604 new B-24s.

† See Volume I, pp. 478–479. MAD stood for Magnetic Airborne Detector. Employed by low-flying aircraft, the gear could detect magnetic anomalies made by a submerged U-boat.

relieved Army Air Forces Squadron 6 at Dunkeswell, leaving a total of five new American very-long-range ASW B-24 squadrons (about seventy-five aircraft) to reach England between July 7 and September 1, at which time the Army Air Forces Antisubmarine Command was deactivated.*

By September 1, John Slessor at Coastal Command had about 150 American-built VLR B-24s in ten squadrons. Five were British units (53, 59, 86, 120, 224) and five were American (USAAF 4, 19, 22, and USN VB 103 and VB 105). Over the following two months, another U.S. Navy B-24 squadron (VB 110) arrived in southwest England to join Fleet Air Wing 7.† Thereupon the three former Army Air Forces squadrons (4, 19, 22) comprising the 479th Group, transferred to the England-based American Eighth Air Force. At the same time, Tenth Fleet shifted the (MAD-equipped) Catalina Squadron VP 63 from Wales to Morocco to mount experimental MAD ASW patrols over the approaches to the Strait of Gibraltar.

Slessor wrote ungraciously that owing to Admiral King's foot-dragging, most of these American ASW squadrons arrived too late to be of any real help in Operation Derange or Musketry-Seaslug-Percussion. "Actually, as it happened, it did not make much difference because we were able to defeat the U-boat by ourselves," he wrote.‡ In his attack on the Americans—especially Admiral King—Slessor omitted to recall Churchill's famous commitment to Washington—"Give us the tools and we'll finish the job"—or that the two hundred aircraft in Coastal Command's ten B-24 squadrons, two Catalina squadrons, the Ventura squadron, and the remaining three of the original British "jeep" carriers (*Archer, Biter, Tracker*) were indeed tools from the Arsenal of Democracy.

"Adam" and "Eve"

The U.S. Navy's crash program to build one hundred four-rotor bombes for breaking four-rotor naval Enigma proceeded at a frenetic pace at the National Cash Register Company in Dayton, Ohio. The goal was daunting: to produce, virtually on an assembly-line basis, the most complicated and fastest electromechanical devices ever created. Not surprisingly, there was constant friction as to method, design, and manufacturing technique among the four principals running this program: Joe Wenger and Howard Engstrom in Washington and Ralph Meader and Joe

---

* The Army Air Forces transferred 217 ASW aircraft to the U.S. Navy: 77 B-24s, 140 B-17s, B-18s, and B-25s.

† One pilot in VB 110 was Joseph P. Kennedy, Jr., eldest son of former Ambassador Joseph P. Kennedy and brother of the future President of the United States, John Fitzgerald Kennedy.

‡ Contrarily, the official USAAF historians wrote that in the period July 13–August 2, American Squadrons 4 and 19 of 479th Group played "an extremely active part" in the Biscay campaign. The Americans sighted twelve U-boats, attacked eight, sank one, *U-404,* and shared credit with the RAF and RCAF for sinking *U-558* and *U-706*. Five B-24s were lost, one to U-boat flak. Thirty-seven airmen perished.

Desch in Dayton. Furthermore, Engstrom wrote,* OP20G was engaged in a "constant battle" for priority materials, "always hampered by the fact that the purpose of the machines had to be kept secret from the various agencies controlling priorities."

By the end of 1997, the NSA still had not publicly released sufficient documents to recount this epic struggle in detail. However, the American historian Colin B. Burke, who was a scholar in residence at the NSA in 1994–95, was allowed private access to the unreleased material and published his version of the struggle.† Burke's version gives great credit to the genius of electrical engineer Joe Desch of NCR, less so to the genius of mathematician Howard Engstrom, chief of OP20G R&D. This thesis cannot be tested for accuracy and balance without the availability of the actual documents; however, as of this writing, it must do.

Burke asserts that at the beginning of 1943 the American bombe was "tragically behind schedule" and that the Americans had yet to make a "real contribution" to the Enigma problem. There was no bombe prototype and there was growing concern about the "practicability" of some of the components. "Tragically behind" seems to be an overly harsh assessment; after all, the Naval Computing Machine Laboratory (NCML) at NCR, established on November 11, 1942, was less than two months old. Moreover, the four men running the program had yet to absolutely agree on the final bombe design.

What made the American bombe situation somewhat embarrassing was, as previously related, that in December 1942 the British codebreakers at Bletchley Park had finally broken into *Triton* utilizing their three-rotor bombes. As also related, they were able to do this by exploiting the Enigma materials seized from the sinking *U-559* in the Mediterranean. However, the British three-rotor bombes were maddeningly slow and not sufficiently sophisticated to deal with the anticipated German upgrades in the complexity of naval Enigma.

By March 1943, Burke explains, NCR had produced two "wheezy" prototypes, "Adam" and "Eve." However, he states, these machines were full of bugs. "The group at NCR could not even tempt the two Bombe prototypes to run for more than a few inadequate minutes." Even with improvements, Burke says, Adam and Eve "refused to run for more than a few hours without spurting oil or developing incurable cases of faulty electrical contacts." The latter problem was caused when the fundamental elements of the bombe, the very-high-speed commutators (large rotors) overheated and lost their shapes. As June approached, says Burke, the American bombe "seemed to be too much of a challenge, even for the talented Joe Desch."

* In the previously cited NSA document NR 1736, Box 705, RG 457, "Bombe History," signed by Wenger, Engstrom, and Meader.

† The misleadingly titled *Information and Secrecy* (1994). The unreleased documents are cited under the general rubric "NSA RAM File." RAM is an acronym for Rapid Analytical Machines. Of course, Burke also relies on many NSA documents that have been released to NARA (RG 457) as well as an impressive list of other documents and published works.

In his history of the bombe project, Howard Engstrom wrote contrarily that

> The first two experimental models of the American 4-wheel Bombes [Adam and Eve] were put into operation at the U.S. Naval Computing Machine Laboratory in May 1943, and were immediately successful. Secure means of communications were established between Washington and Dayton and the machines were operated there in order to be under observation by the maintenance and design engineers. [Meanwhile] production models started to be put into operation in early June.

The big high-speed commutators did, indeed, cause problems, Engstrom continued. He and Joe Desch fell into dispute over the method to eliminate this serious defect. Desch urged that greatly improved sets of small wheels like those in Adam and Eve were the solution. However, Engstrom calculated that the use of small-wheel sets would double the number of wheels to be employed to forty thousand and "would present extreme difficulties in maintenance and in rewiring" in case the Germans made changes. "To make the machines workable it was imperative that we use a single size wheel for all four positions in the machine," Engstrom wrote. Although the Engstrom solution had yet to be tested, he was confident that it could be made to work and rather than "holding up the entire project," he ordered that production of the bombes proceed forthwith "against the advice of the engineers."

What emerged from these debates was an electromechanical marvel, designated "Bombe, Model 530." These bombes were big: eight feet long, seven feet high, and two feet wide. Each weighed five thousand pounds. Each contained thousands of high-tolerance parts, including 1,500 vacuum tubes arranged in what was "very high advanced circuitry," as Burke put it. Each generated tremendous heat, so much so that powerful air conditioners were required to maintain a reasonably comfortable work environment. Each machine cost $45,000.

Not without justification, Burke rhapsodized that each bombe

> housed sixteen four-wheel sets of Enigma analogs [i.e., clones] and the Welchman diagonal board [i.e., the powerful plug-board system conceived for the original Turing British bombe]. It had all the circuits needed to link them together and test the hundreds of thousands of possible combinations of wheel positions against a text crib for inconsistencies. Its sixty-four double Enigma wheel commutators each contained 104 contact points which had to be perfectly aligned when they touched the copper and silver sensing brushes. Such alignment and synchronization were difficult to achieve, especially for the fast wheel which rotated close to two thousand RPM.

That is only a crude glimpse into the interior of Model 530. Notably, it also contained some "truly distinctive" digital electronics, designed by Joe Desch and his engineering aides. Burke again:

> The sixty-four double commutators on the Bombes could be driven at very high speeds by mechanical means, but motors and shafts and electromechanical counters were unable to track their position. . . . [Desch] created a digital electronic tracking and control system that amazed the Navy's engineers. His 1,500-tube system did

> more than record the position of a hit: It exercised control. It was able to track the wheel positions, signal the motor and the clutches, then reverse the machine's action until it had returned all the wheels to their hit position. At that point the wheel locations were [automatically] printed and the operator could signal the machine to restart its search for consistencies.

During May and June 1943, Navy personnel who were to operate and maintain the bombes reported to Dayton. These included a large contingent of Waves who were to program and run the machines twenty-four hours a day on three shifts. The new men and women were astonished at the power and speed of the bombe. Given a "crib" (known or assumed plain text) a bombe could carry out 20,280 "trys" per second. It required merely fifty seconds to carry out a complete short three-rotor "run" and twenty minutes to do a "long" four-rotor run.

Inasmuch as the buildings to house the bombes on Nebraska Avenue in Washington* were not yet ready and the bombes were undergoing nearly continuous mechanical revision and improvement, the codebreakers first used them operationally at NCR, Dayton. Mathematician Joseph Eachus, the Engstrom protégé who had served a highly productive tour at Bletchley Park, reported there to help establish a temporary message-analysis center. Washington sent Dayton the Enigma intercepts by secure teletype; Dayton replied with decrypts that were delivered immediately to "Frog" Low and Kenneth Knowles of the Tenth Fleet staff.

The British, meanwhile, had completed four-rotor bombes of two different designs. They were slower than the American bombe, requiring thirty minutes for a full run compared to twenty minutes. They were also much less reliable.† The British built sixty-nine four-rotor bombes.

The early erratic yields of the NCR four-rotor bombes at Dayton in May 1943 probably helped confirm the long-held suspicion that the Germans were reading the Allied convoy code. As related, in June 1943, the Allies made emergency alterations to that code that left German codebreakers blind and deaf and later in the summer introduced a new convoy code that the Germans were unable to break.

Action in the North Atlantic in May: I

The Allied convoy traffic on the North Atlantic run in May 1943 was about average: fifteen sailings, eight eastbound and seven westbound. There were about seven hundred ships in these fifteen convoys. Three "jeep" carrier support groups (British *Archer* and *Biter;* American *Bogue*) operated in the North Atlantic during the month. U-boats sank only six of the approximately seven hundred ships in the fifteen convoys.‡

---

* Benignly known as Communications Supplementary Activities Washington (CSAW, pronounced "See-Saw") and later, the Naval Security Station.

† The official British intelligence historian wrote that "the earliest British four-wheel Bombes proved to have low serviceability, owing to the shortage of good quality raw materials." See Hinsley, vol. 2 (1981), p. 752n.

‡ See Appendix 3.

As related, in the opening days of May, two German groups, *Amsel* and *Fink,* consisting of about forty boats, were attacking convoy Outbound North (Slow) 5, in the waters between Greenland and Newfoundland. Owing mainly to heavy fog, which favored the radar-equipped air and surface escorts, on May 7 U-boat Control canceled the operation and dissolved *Amsel* and *Fink.* As a result, some boats headed for France, some to a U-tanker.

U-boat Control organized the remaining twenty-nine boats, including some that were damaged, into two new groups named for German rivers. These were *Elbe* (seventeen boats) and *Rhein* (twelve boats). Based on *B-dienst* information, U-boat Control shifted the groups southeastward to intercept two eastbound convoys, Halifax 237 and Slow Convoy 129. The damaged boats, or those low on fuel, were to serve only as convoy spotters. In order to bring greater force to bear, Control directed the five remaining boats of the ill-fated group *Drossel,* which, as related, had patrolled west of Cape Finisterre, where two pairs of its boats had collided, to go west at highest speed.

B-dienst provided quite specific and current information on the routes and positions of these two convoys. Acting on this information, a *Rhein* VII, *U-359,* commanded by Heinz Förster, age thirty-three, making his second patrol, found Halifax 237 on May 9. It was composed of forty-six ships, guarded by Canadian Escort Group C-2, commanded by E. H. Chavasse, who at first had but five warships: the ex-American four-stack British destroyer *Broadway,* the new British frigate *Lagan,* and three corvettes, two Canadian and one British. In due course, another Canadian corvette joined. When Western Approaches deduced from Förster's contact report that Halifax 237 was in danger, it ordered British Support Group 5, the "jeep" carrier *Biter* and her screen, to reinforce the convoy.

At first U-boat Control directed all three groups, *Rhein, Elbe,* and *Drossel,* to attack Halifax 237, but almost immediately it modified these orders. The twelve boats of group *Rhein* and seven of group *Drossel* (the latter reinforced by the recently sailed VIIs *U-221* and *U-753*) were to attack Halifax 237. Group *Elbe,* reduced to sixteen boats by the departure of *U-266,* but reinforced by eleven other boats to twenty-seven (seven of them IXs), was to hunt for and attack Slow Convoy 129. Commanded by Ralf von Jessen, age twenty-six, making his second patrol, *U-266* refueled from the tanker *U-461* on May 12. While homebound two days later, a Halifax of British Squadron 58, piloted by Wilfred Oulton, sank her with depth charges. There were no survivors.*

Escorts of Halifax 237 drove Heinz Förster in *U-359* off and down and he lost touch. But on the next day, May 10, another *Rhein* boat, the Arctic veteran *U-454,* commanded by Burkhard Hackländer, age twenty-eight, relocated the convoy, which was covered by Swordfish biplanes from *Biter.* One of the Swordfish forced Hackländer under, but his contact report brought up several other boats.

Despite the air cover from *Biter,* four boats attacked Halifax 237. Two other Arctic veterans, Max-Martin Teichert in *U-456* (of *Drossel*), age twenty-eight, and Heinz-Ehlert Clausen, age thirty-three, in *U-403* (of *Rhein*), shared credit for sink-

* At the time, the Admiralty erroneously credited a B-24 of Squadron 86 with this kill. Including his role in sinking *U-563,* this was Oulton's second kill in May.

ing the 7,200-ton British Liberty ship *Fort Concord.* To get into shooting position, Clausen in *U-403* fought it out with a Swordfish. The new *Ritterkreuz* holder Hans Trojer, age twenty-seven, in the newly sailed VII *U-221* (of *Drossel*) sank the 9,400-ton Norwegian tanker *Sandanger,* which was straggling. Rudolf Baltz, merely twenty-two years old, the new skipper of the newly sailed veteran VII *U-603* (also of *Drossel*), sank another straggler, the 4,800-ton Norwegian *Brand.*

In retaliation, the escorts of Halifax 237 sank three veteran U-boats, all from the doomed group *Drossel.*

• The VII *U-89,* commanded by Dietrich Lohmann, age thirty-three. She had been in the Battle of the Atlantic for a full year. She was sunk by British warships: the four-stack destroyer *Broadway* and the frigate *Lagan,* drawn to the site by a Swordfish from *Biter.*

• The VII *U-456,* commanded by Max-Martin Teichert, which had been at the Arctic or Atlantic fronts for a year and a half. She was damaged by a B-24 of British Squadron 86, piloted by John Wright, who dropped a Fido homing torpedo. Teichert surfaced, radioed for assistance from any boats nearby, and held the B-24 off with his flak guns and survived the night. On the following morning, May 13, the British destroyer *Opportune,* commanded by J. Lee-Barber, bore down on *U-456* and Teichert dived, never to be heard from again. The VII *U-448* (of *Elbe*), commanded by Helmut Dauter, age twenty-three, came upon the bodies of two *U-456* crewmen and gave them a proper burial at sea. Teichert was awarded a *Ritterkreuz* posthumously.*

• The newly sailed *U-753,* commanded by Alfred Manhardt von Mannstein, age thirty-five. She had been in the Atlantic for a year and a half. A Sunderland of Canadian Squadron 423, piloted by John Musgrave, attacked *U-753* with depth charges in the face of heavy 20mm flak. Two frigates, the Canadian *Drumheller* and the British *Lagan,* finished off *U-753* with depth charges. Nothing further was ever heard from this boat.†

Helmut Dauter in the *Elbe* VII *U-448* joined a dozen other boats at the tanker *U-459* on May 16. He refueled the next day, but he was unable to repair a disabled radio and was forced to abort. He reached France on May 26, completing a patrol of forty days. Like the overwhelming majority of boats that sailed in April 1943, this cruise was unproductive.‡

Several *Drossel* boats continued to hold contact with Halifax 237. These included Paul Siegmann in *U-230.* In his book *Iron Coffins,* her first watch officer, Herbert Werner, claims that he, Werner, shot down a Swordfish. The biplane crashed very close to *U-230,* Werner wrote, and its armed depth charges exploded, atomizing the wrecked plane and the aircrew. The depth charges "kicked into

---

* His score in the Arctic and Atlantic was five confirmed ships (two tankers) sunk for about 54,000 tons; mortal damage to the 11,500-ton British cruiser *Edinburgh;* damage to a 7,200-ton British Liberty, *Fort Concord,* finished off by *U-403.*

† Account according to Franks (1995), reconfirmed by Niestlé. Originally the Admiralty listed the cause of the loss of *U-753* as "unknown."

‡ See Appendix 2.

our starboard side astern," Werner continued, "but we left the horrible scene unharmed."

The loss of this vulnerable Swordfish and the near-loss of others to U-boat flak in the battle with Halifax 237 led the British to put restrictions on Swordfish tactics. Whenever possible they were to patrol in pairs. A single Swordfish was never to attack a U-boat, but rather shadow it until air and/or surface reinforcements arrived.

Meanwhile, about two hundred miles farther south, group *Elbe* hunted for Slow Convoy 129. Consisting of twenty-six ships, this convoy was guarded by Donald Macintyre's British Escort Group B-2, comprised of seven warships: two destroyers, *Hesperus* and *Whitehall,* and five corvettes. In the event the convoy became threatened, Macintyre had authority to request assistance from the *Biter* support group.

Six *Elbe* boats, including the new but damaged IXC40 *U-533,* had left the group by May 11 due to fuel shortages or for other reasons. These departures left *Elbe* with twenty-one boats (six of them IXCs), which U-boat Control divided into two sections. That day the veteran IXC *U-504,* commanded by a new skipper, Wilhelm Luis, age twenty-seven, found Slow Convoy 129. His report brought up about a dozen boats, chattering away on radios. Since the heavy U-boat traffic and Enigma decrypts indicated that Slow Convoy 129 was at risk and Halifax 237 had reached the protection of land-based Coastal Command aircraft and was outrunning groups *Rhein* and *Drossel,* Western Approaches ordered *Biter* and her screen to rush two hundred miles south to reinforce Slow Convoy 129.

In the nine months that he had commanded Escort Group B-2, Macintyre had not lost a ship in convoy. He was therefore humiliated and furious when a veteran *Elbe* boat, *U-402,* commanded by the *Ritterkreuz* holder Siegfried von Forstner, age thirty-two, slipped past his escorts submerged and in broad daylight sank two freighters by periscope attack: the 4,500-ton British *Antigone* and the 3,100-ton Norwegian *Grado.* However, the corvette *Gentian* got *U-402* on sonar and pounded her with depth charges, inflicting so much damage that von Forstner was forced to join the parade of U-boats aborting to France. The *U-402* did not sail again until September.

Later in the day, Macintyre in *Hesperus* got a radar contact at five miles dead ahead of the convoy. This was the *Elbe* VII *U-223,* commanded by Karl-Jürgen Wächter, age twenty-seven, making his second patrol. Macintyre put on flank speed and soon saw a wake. Too late, Wächter crash-dived. Racing over the swirl, Macintyre fired a salvo of depth charges, plus one of the experimental 2,000-pound depth charges from a torpedo tube. These missiles exploded close to *U-223,* causing heavy external and internal damage and flooding, and drove the boat out of control to seven hundred feet. When the engineer reported that one of the electric motors was on fire, Wächter decided to surface and run.

Macintyre heard Wächter blow his ballast tanks and was fully alert when *U-223* popped up. He shot at the U-boat with his 4.7" main battery and all other guns that would bear. To Macintyre's astonishment, Wächter counterattacked. The Germans fired five torpedoes, all of which missed, and then attempted to ram the destroyer. Macintyre maneuvered out of the way and turned about to "gently" ram *U-223,* nuzzling the boat over on her beam ends. Believing that *U-223* was doomed, he then raced ahead to rejoin the convoy, which was thirty miles to eastward.

Wächter was by no means ready to concede defeat. When he broadcast an urgent plea for help, the VII *U-359,* commanded by Heinz Förster, responded. By great luck—some said a miracle—Förster found one of two crewmen of *U-223* who had fallen or had jumped overboard when *Hesperus* pushed the boat on beam ends. When *U-359* finally found *U-223,* Förster returned the crewman, causing a minor sensation. Förster then aborted to escort to France the wrecked *U-223,* which did not sail again until September.

Upon rejoining the convoy that night, *Hesperus* detected by Huff Duff another U-boat about ten miles dead ahead. This was the IXC40 *U-186,* commanded by Siegfried Hesemann, age thirty, on her second patrol. Macintyre raced ahead at flank speed. Too late, Hesemann in *U-186* saw *Hesperus* and crash-dived. Macintyre got a good sonar contact and let go several depth-charge salvos, which fell close and destroyed *U-186* with all hands. After listening to her implode and break up, Macintyre picked up some wooden debris that rose to the surface. He wrote that his men found "a gruesome piece of flesh" clinging to one piece of wood. *Hesperus* received sole credit for the killing of *U-186.*

During the next twenty-four hours, the destroyers *Hesperus*—low on depth charges—and *Whitehall* and the five corvettes raced hither and yon near Slow Convoy 129, driving off the dozen U-boats. In the face of this aggressive protection, no other *Elbe* boat could get into position to shoot. When *Biter* and her screen joined on May 13, Macintyre refueled B-2 and loaded up with depth charges from a tanker in the convoy assigned for that purpose. Swordfish from *Biter* augmented the escort, flying continuous patrols around the convoy, forcing U-boat Control to cancel operations.

These massive U-boat attacks on Halifax 237 and Slow Convoy 129, which, in aggregate, comprised seventy-two merchant ships, yielded the Germans little. Four boats of groups *Rhein* and *Drossel* sank three confirmed ships for about 22,000 tons from Halifax 237. One boat, von Forstner in the *Elbe U-402,* sank two ships for about 7,600 tons from Slow Convoy 129. Total for the three groups: five confirmed ships for about 30,000 tons sunk. In return, the two convoy close escort groups, B-2 and C-2, *Biter*'s Swordfish, and long-range aircraft sank five U-boats and severely damaged several others.*

Most of the surviving *Rhein, Elbe,* and *Drossel* boats returned to France. There was little to celebrate, nor was there grist for the propaganda mills. Most skippers and crews were grateful to have escaped death, especially those of group *Drossel.* Of its original twelve boats and two later reinforcements (*U-221* and *U-753*), seven

* Sunk were *U-89, U-186, U-456, U-753,* and the *Elbe* boat *U-266,* which, as related, had pulled out to refuel. There were no survivors from any of the lost U-boats. The *U-223* and *U-402* were among the most heavily damaged.

boats had been sunk and four had aborted to France early in their patrols. Only four of its fourteen boats (*U-221, U-230, U-436, U-607*) carried out full patrols.

Nor was that all the bad news from group *Drossel.* While homebound, *Ritterkreuz* holder Günter Seibicke, age thirty-one, in *U-436,* who had sunk no ships, came upon a big (sixty-ship) convoy, southbound to Gibraltar. There is no indication in the U-boat Control war diary that he reported the convoy, but he got very close submerged, apparently in an attempt to attack alone. Two of the British escorts, the frigate *Test* and the corvette *Hyderabad,* detected and attacked *U-436* with accurate depth charges on May 26, destroying the boat. There were no survivors. This kill brought the losses of group *Drossel* to eight out of the fourteen boats assigned.

Action in the North Atlantic in May: II

The various U-boat actions of late April and early May left no group directly south of Greenland to intercept the oncoming Outbound North and Outbound North (Slow) convoys. However, on May 6, U-boat Control began filling the gap with a new group of what it believed to be twenty-five boats, about half veteran or experienced ones from France and half new ones from Germany. Initially the group was to include three IXs, two of which were veterans (*U-66* and *U-109*) and one (*U-190*) on its second patrol. However, as related, *U-109* had been lost on May 7. The *U-66* and *U-190* were soon detached and went on to the Americas, replaced by VIIs. One of the new VIIs was the *U-954,* on which Dönitz's son Peter, age twenty-four, was a watch officer.

As the supposed twenty-five boats were assembling, Control divided the group into smaller task forces, as it had divided group *Amsel* earlier. The result was five subgroups, named for German rivers: *Isar* (five new VIIs), *Lech* (the lost *U-109* and three VIIs, all veterans), *Inn* (four VIIs, two of them veterans), *Iller* (six new VIIs), and *Naab* (six VIIs, one new and five veterans, including the VIID minelayer *U-218*).

The new VII *U-640,* commanded by Karl-Heinz Nagel, age twenty-six, outbound from Germany to join group *Iller,* spotted a westbound convoy on May 13. This was Outbound North (Slow) 7, composed of forty merchant ships, guarded by British Escort Group B-5. Commanded by Richard C. Boyle, B-5 consisted of eight warships: the frigates *Swale* and *Nene,* the sloop *Wren,* and five corvettes. Inasmuch as there were no other U-boats in the immediate vicinity, Control authorized Nagel to attack. At the same time, Control ordered the five other outbound boats of the still-forming group *Iller* to join Nagel as rapidly as possible. It also repositioned and combined the four groups west of *Iller* to promising locations to intercept the convoy. These were groups *Isar* and *Inn* (nine boats), renamed *Donau* (Danube) 1, and groups *Lech* and *Naab* (nine boats), renamed *Donau* 2.

Nagel in the VII *U-640* attacked the convoy after dark, firing four torpedoes at two different ships. He presumed both had sunk, but in fact, no hits were confirmed. Aircraft from Iceland bombed *U-640,* forcing the boat to crash-dive and lose contact with the convoy. Another *Iller* boat, the new VII *U-657,* commanded by Heinrich Göllnitz, age thirty-three, assisted *U-640* in the hunt; the other four *Iller* boats joined the north end of the *Donau* 1 and *Donau* 2 line, extending southeast from Greenland.

A Catalina of the Iceland-based U.S. Navy Squadron VP 84, piloted by P. A. Bodinet, hit and destroyed Nagel in *U-640* with a Fido homing torpedo on May 14, presumably the first success with that new weapon. Three days later, Göllnitz in *U-657,* a former Arctic boat, found the convoy and sank the 5,200-ton British freighter *Aymeric.* Boyle's close escort group counterattacked with twenty depth charges and two Hedgehog salvos and the frigate *Swale* sank *U-657.* There were no survivors from either of these U-boats.*

Two other VIIs outbound from Norway and Germany to join the boats hunting this convoy were themselves sunk by Hudsons of British Squadron 269 from Iceland. The first, on May 17, was *U-646,* commanded by Heinrich Wulff, age thirty-four, who had made one patrol in Arctic waters before his boat was transferred to the Atlantic force. The pilot, Francis H. W. James, destroyed *U-646* with four Torpex depth charges. The second, on May 19, was the new *U-273,* commanded by Hermann Rossmann, age twenty-four, merely twelve days out from Kiel. The pilot, J.N.P. Bell, sank the boat with four Torpex depth charges. There were no survivors from either U-boat.

Three destroyers of J. W. McCoy's Support Group 3 arrived from St. John's on May 18 to reinforce Boyle's Escort Group B-5. These and aircraft from Nova Scotia and Newfoundland helped shepherd Outbound North (Slow) 7 to a rendezvous with the local Canadian escort without further damage from U-boats. Allied decrypts of naval Enigma and use of Huff Duff had enabled the convoy to evade groups *Iller* and *Donau* 1 and *Donau* 2.

If the early sinking of the IXB *U-109* of group *Lech* is included, to this point the chase and sinking of one merchant ship from Outbound North (Slow) 7 cost the Germans five U-boats: *U-109, U-273, U-640, U-646,* and *U-657.* There were no survivors from the approximately 250 crew of these boats.

The next eastbound convoys were Halifax 238 and Slow Convoy 130. Relying on good information from *B-dienst,* Control established a new patrol line running southeast from Greenland comprised (north to south) of twenty-two boats: group *Iller* (four new boats), group *Donau* 1 (seven boats, five new), and group *Donau* 2 (eleven boats, three new). A fourth group, *Oder* (eight veteran boats), backstopped the *Iller* and the two *Donau* groups.

Acting on Enigma decrypts and Huff Duff information, Allied authorities diverted Halifax 238 to the south of the *Iller-Donau* patrol line. Guarded by Canadian Escort Group C-3 (the destroyers *Skeena,* the ex-American four-stack

* At the time, the Admiralty erroneously credited *Swale* with sinking *U-640* and another American Catalina of VP 84 with sinking *U-657.* In several postwar reappraisals, the credits were finally established as written. See Franks (1995), Milford (1997), and Niestlé (1998).

Burnham, and five corvettes), Halifax 238 (forty-five merchant ships) reached the British Isles undetected by the Germans. The other, Slow Convoy 130 (thirty-nine merchant ships), guarded by Peter Gretton's British Escort Group B-7 (nine warships), was not so fortunate.

A new VII of *Donau* 1, *U-304,* commanded by Heinz Koch, age twenty-eight, found Slow Convoy 130 on May 18 sailing under a full moon, and gave the alarm. Control ordered the twenty-one surviving boats of groups *Iller* and *Donau* 1 and 2 to join *U-304* at highest speed. By that time, two merchant ships of the convoy had aborted, one escorted back to port by the ASW trawler *Northern Spray.* That left thirty-seven merchant ships guarded by Gretton's Escort Group B-7, reduced to eight warships: two destroyers, *Duncan* and *Vidette,* the frigate *Tay,* and five corvettes. By prearrangement, later on the following day, Godfrey Brewer's British Support Group 1 (three frigates, *Jed, Wear, Spey,* and the former Coast Guard cutter *Sennen*) from Newfoundland was to reinforce the convoy, raising the number of warships to a formidable twelve: two destroyers, four frigates, one cutter, and five corvettes. The rescue ship *Zamalek,* the *Sennen,* and two other warships had Huff Duff. Most warships had Type 271 centimetric-wavelength radar.

The convoy and Allied authorities ashore DFed the U-boat beacons and radio chatter and quickly realized that Slow Convoy 130 was in peril. During the night of May 18–19, Gretton in *Duncan* and some other escorts chased off U-boats or forced them to dive and lose contact, but other U-boats replaced them. However, none of the gathering Germans attempted to attack that night.

In the early hours of May 19, the first of five B-24s of British Squadron 120, based in Iceland, arrived to provide air escort. The pilot, W. Stoves, saw a U-boat crash-dive. He descended and launched two Fido homing torpedoes and three 250-pound depth charges at the swirl. The airmen saw two "small upheavals" in the water but no debris that would confirm a kill.*

During that day several B-24s provided nearly continuous coverage to the convoy. Stoves's B-24, or others, attacked several more U-boats with depth charges and Fidos and drove them off and marked the sites with smoke flares. The destroyer *Vidette,* the frigate *Tay,* and the corvette *Pink* raced separately to the flares and hunted. The corvette *Sunflower* loosely cooperated with a B-24 to drive a U-boat under, but neither the corvette nor the B-24 had any luck. Peter Gretton later wrote that with better communications between aircraft and ships, he believed both could have carried out additional kills.

Some of the twenty-one remaining *Donau* U-boats near the convoy attempted to make submerged daylight attacks. Adolf Oelrich, age twenty-seven, in *U-92,* embarked on his fourth patrol, later reported that he sank one 6,500-ton freighter and hit another, but no sinkings or hits were confirmed. The approach of Gustav Poel, age twenty-five, in *U-413,* embarked on his third patrol, was spoiled when, as

---

* At first Allied authorities believed that in this attack Stoves sank *U-954,* commanded by Odo Loewe, age twenty-eight, on which Peter Dönitz was serving. There were no survivors. However, in postwar years the Admiralty credited the kill to two British warships of Brewer's Support Group 1: frigate *Jed* (R. C. Freaker) and the ex–American Coast Guard cutter *Sennen* (F. H. Thornton).

he later reported, the convoy made a sudden change of course. Three boats—the new *U-645,* commanded by Otto Ferro, age thirty-two; the new *U-952,* commanded by Oskar Curio, age twenty-five; and the *U-707,* commanded by Günter Gretschel, age twenty-eight, on his second patrol—reported that they were continually driven down by aircraft and destroyers and therefore could not attack.

The corvette *Snowflake* saw a periscope not fifty yards away. Her captain, the Australian Harold G. Chesterman, notified Gretton in *Duncan* and simultaneously launched a depth-charge attack. The target was thought to be the *U-381* on its third patrol under the command of Wilhelm-Heinrich von Pückler und Limpurg, age thirty. Gretton in *Duncan* hurried over, got a solid sonar contact, and fired a salvo of ten depth charges, followed by three separate Hedgehog attacks. The first Hedgehog salvo fell wide, but the second and third might have caused severe damage to *U-381.* There were no survivors. The Admiralty divided credit for the kill between Chesterman in *Snowflake* and Gretton in *Duncan* but in a postwar reassessment declared *U-381* to have been lost to unknown causes.

Later in the day, the four warships of Brewer's Support Group 1 from St. John's came up close astern of the convoy. Upon establishing contact with this group, Gretton, as planned, detached the Canadian corvette *Kitchener* to join the escort of convoy Outbound North 184, passing nearby. The three frigates of Brewer's support group, *Jed, Wear,* and *Spey,* and the cutter *Sennen* all saw, chased, and depth-charged U-boats that were trailing Slow Convoy 130 or attempting to circle ahead for a better shooting position. Cooperating in one furious depth-charge attack, *Jed* and *Sennen* afterward found a pool of oil and debris (splintered wood, some of it painted white, a twenty-pound lump of tallow or fat, a piece of blue paper or cloth) and claimed a kill, which the Admiralty credited.*

After the four warships of Support Group 1 joined, the escort of Slow Convoy 130 increased to eleven warships plus the B-24s. In the very late evening of May 19, the frigate *Tay,* commanded by R. E. Sherwood, carried out an aggressive attack on the new *U-952,* commanded by Oskar Curio. For the second time in as many patrols, the boat was heavily damaged, but it survived and limped into France on May 31, and did not sail again until September. No other boat got near the convoy that night.

The B-24s returned at dawn on May 20. One, from Squadron 120 based in Iceland and piloted by J.R.E. Proctor, dived out of low-hanging clouds and caught the experienced *U-258,* commanded by Wilhelm von Mässenhausen, age twenty-eight, on the surface. Too late, Mässenhausen crash-dived. Proctor raked the boat with machine-gun fire, then dropped four shallow-set depth charges that destroyed *U-258.* There were no survivors.

Proctor in his B-24 and other B-24s from Iceland and Northern Ireland chased and attacked U-boats during the forenoon. Whenever possible, the surface escorts cooperated, but the communications between ships and aircraft remained poor,

* The Admiralty believed the U-boat was *U-209,* which actually was sunk earlier (May 7) by an aircraft during the battle with Outbound North (Slow) 5. In the postwar reappraisal, the Admiralty did not withdraw the credit for the kill from *Jed* and *Sennen* but changed *U-209* to an "unknown" U-boat, in reality *U-954.*

Gretton wrote. Owing to the heavy air and surface escorts, at noon that day U-boat Control canceled operations against Slow Convoy 130. Control believed that group *Donau,* which opened the battle with twenty-two U-boats, had sunk only one freighter, but, in fact, the Germans had sunk no ships whatsoever.

The Admiralty credited four or five U-boat kills but the official records confirmed only three U-boats sunk attacking the convoy: von Mässenhausen's *U-258;* von Limpurg's *U-381;* and Odo Loewe's *U-954.* As related, there were no survivors from any of the U-boats. The loss of Peter Dönitz on *U-954* weighed heavily on the Dönitz family and on U-boat Control as well.

While group *Donau* was mounting its costly and futile attack on Slow Convoy 130, *B-dienst* provided information on two fast convoys: the eastbound Halifax 239 and the opposite-sailing Outbound North 184.

U-boat Control had by then created a new group on a line running southeast from Greenland, *Mosel,* composed of twenty-three boats. These included the eight boats of group *Oder,* which had backstopped the *Iller-Donau* line, and fifteen others arriving from U-tankers or from France or Germany. Group *Mosel* included two *Ritterkreuz* holders: twenty-seven-year-old Hans Trojer in *U-221* and the old hand Günther Krech, age twenty-eight, in *U-558.*

As *Mosel* was assembling, three of its assigned boats were bombed by Allied aircraft or depth-charged by warships. The first was the veteran Type VIID minelayer *U-218,* commanded by Richard Becker, age thirty-two. Although the *U-218* was badly damaged by surface ships, Control directed Becker to stay put with *Mosel* until the next convoy came along. Second, a Catalina of the Faeroes-based British Squadron 190, piloted by F. J. Gosling, hit *U-229,* commanded by Robert Schetelig, age twenty-four. Bombs from another aircraft (as yet unidentified) flooded the conning tower of *U-231,* commanded by Wolfgang Wenzel, age thirty-three, who was merely ten days out from Kiel. In the crash dive a man was left topside and drowned. The *U-229* and the *U-231* were so badly damaged that they were forced to abort to France. Schetelig in *U-229* gave some of his reserve fuel to the damaged, homebound *U-377,* commanded by Otto Köhler, and to the tanker *U-461.* Although Wenzel in *U-231* was hit by another (unidentified) aircraft, he reached France on May 30. Schetelig and Köhler got in on June 7. The aborts of *U-229* and *U-231* reduced *Mosel* to twenty-one boats.

Convoy Outbound North 184, composed of thirty-nine merchant ships, was guarded by Canadian Escort Group C-1. The group consisted of six warships: two Canadian destroyers, *St. Laurent* and the ex-American four-stack *St. Croix,* the British frigate *Itchen,* and three Canadian corvettes. The convoy and the escort group were backed up by American Support Group 6, the "jeep" carrier *Bogue* and her screen of destroyers, fresh from a crash course at the British ASW school. *Bogue,* newly outfitted with Huff Duff, had her normal complement of twenty-one aircraft, nine Wildcat fighters and twelve Avenger torpedo bombers. The big, tough Avengers could carry four 250-pound depth charges or two depth charges and a Fido.

In the early hours of May 22, *Bogue* routinely launched a radar-equipped

Avenger, piloted by Roger C. Kuhn. About fifty-five miles out from *Bogue,* Kuhn sighted a U-boat on the surface. She was the *Mosel* VII *U-468,* commanded by Klemens Schamong, age twenty-six, making his second patrol. American naval records suggest that Kuhn muffed his attack on *U-468* and gave *Bogue* a wrong position report, hence a relief plane and surface warships could find nothing. Contrarily, Schamong reported to U-boat Control that he had been bombed by aircraft both in the morning and the afternoon and was then pursued and depth-charged by surface escorts for hours. The damage incurred was so severe that he was forced to abort to France, arriving on May 29. His departure reduced *Mosel* to twenty boats.

Later that morning, another Avenger from *Bogue,* piloted by Stewart E. Doty, also found a surfaced U-boat. She was the *Mosel* VII *U-305,* commanded by Rudolf Bahr, age twenty-seven, also making his second patrol. Doty dropped four depth charges close to *U-305,* causing extensive damage. Bahr dived to carry out repairs and resurfaced about noon. Waiting overhead was yet another Avenger from *Bogue,* piloted by Robert L. Stearns, who attacked immediately, dropping four depth charges. Bahr crash-dived and got away from the aircraft and later, from two warships, but *U-305* was so badly damaged that Bahr, too, was forced to abort to France, arriving on June 1. His departure reduced *Mosel* to nineteen boats.

In the afternoon of that same day, May 22, still another Avenger from *Bogue,* piloted by William F. Chamberlain, sighted a U-boat. She was the VII *U-569,* commanded by Hans Johannsen, age thirty-two, who was also making his second patrol. Chamberlain attacked, dropping four depth charges in a "perfect" straddle that caused severe damage. A relief Avenger, piloted by Howard S. Roberts, was waiting overhead when Johannsen resurfaced. Roberts dropped four more depth charges in a good straddle and machine-gunned the bridge to prevent the Germans from manning the flak guns.

Johannsen had no intention of fighting back. According to American records, he shamefully ordered the crew to raise a white flag of surrender on the periscope. Working in a hurricane of machine-gun fire, the frenetic crewmen first tied a handkerchief to the periscope, but when it was realized that the handkerchief was too small to be noticed, they substituted a white sheet. Upon seeing this sheet, Roberts withheld fire and guided the Canadian destroyer *St. Laurent,* commanded by G. H. Stephen, to the scene. As the destroyer approached *U-569,* Johannsen ordered his crew to scuttle and jump overboard. *St. Laurent* fished out Johannsen and twenty-four of his crew of forty-six. One injured survivor was sent to a Canadian hospital, the other twenty-four to Washington for interrogation.

Like many Allied warships, *Bogue* (and her aircraft) had earlier been too loosely credited with U-boat kills. The *U-569* was the first kill by *Bogue* to be confirmed and by the aircraft of any Allied "jeep" carrier unassisted by surface craft. The first Avenger pilot to see *U-569,* Chamberlain, was awarded a Silver Star. The second Avenger pilot, Roberts, was awarded the DFC.

Richard Becker in the damaged VIID minelayer *U-218* avoided attacks by *Bogue* aircraft, but he did not get away entirely unscathed. One or several surface ships came out of a rain squall, pounced on *U-218,* and let fly salvos of depth charges. Damaged yet again, Becker spotted and reported the "expected" convoy, then aborted to France. He arrived on June 2, completing a luckless patrol of forty-four days. This departure reduced *Mosel* to eighteen boats.

The fast convoy Outbound North 184 passed close to the fast eastbound convoy Halifax 239 on May 21–22. The latter was composed of forty-two merchant ships guarded by British Escort Group B-3, commanded by M. J. Evans. The group consisted of eight warships: two destroyers, *Keppel* and *Escapade,* the frigate *Towy,* and five corvettes, three manned by Free French crews. The warships were backed up by British Support Group 4, the "jeep" carrier *Archer* and her screen of four destroyers.*

Apparently U-boat Control was unaware that these two opposite-sailing convoys, each supported by a "jeep" carrier group, were passing so close. At first the contact reports from the various boats caused confusion. When Control finally sorted out the situation, it decided to concentrate all available strength on the eastbound Halifax 239, heavily laden with war matériel. Control committed twenty-seven U-boats to this attack: the nine southernmost boats of *Mosel* and the eighteen remaining boats of the *Donau* groups, which were breaking off the futile and costly fight with Slow Convoy 130.

Dönitz exhorted the *Mosel* boats with a challenging personal message:

> With the last two North Atlantic convoys we have gotten nowhere. . . . Now if there is anyone who thinks that fighting convoys is therefore no longer possible, he is a weakling and no true submarine captain. The battle in the Atlantic is getting harder but it is the determining element in the waging of war.
>
> Keep yourselves aware of your high responsibility and do not fail to understand that you must answer for your actions. Do your best with this convoy. We must smash it to bits!
>
> If the circumstances permit, do not submerge from aircraft. Shoot and ward them off. Make surface escape from destroyers whenever possible. Be tough! Get ahead and attack. I believe in you.

The veteran VII *U-752,* commanded by the old hand Karl-Ernst Schroeter, age thirty, making his eighth patrol, got on the trail of Halifax 239 on the morning of May 23. His report was DFed by the destroyer *Keppel,* flagship of British Escort Group B-3. The supporting "jeep" carrier *Archer* launched a Swordfish biplane to run out the Huff Duff bearing. The plane found the *U-752* (or another U-boat) but its depth-charge attack apparently failed. *Archer* then launched a second Swordfish, armed with eight rockets fitted with 25-pound warheads.† The pilot, Harry Horrocks, astonished to find *U-752* running on the surface, dived out of a low-hanging cloud and in quick succession fired four pairs of rockets. The first three

---

* The *Archer* group had come across to Newfoundland in mid-May, escorting alternately Outbound North (Slow) 6 (thirty-one merchant ships) and the fast Outbound North 182 (fifty-six merchant ships) without the loss of a single vessel.

† Designed originally as an antitank weapon but hurriedly adapted for ASW aircraft.

pairs were close misses, but the fourth pair hit and penetrated *U-752*'s pressure hull forward of the conning tower near the radio room and captain's cabin.

The two hits severely damaged *U-752,* externally and internally, and caused heavy flooding. Schroeter was therefore forced to stop his crash dive and fight it out on the surface with flak guns. By the time he and his gunners got to the bridge, a Martlet from *Archer* attacked with machine guns. That fire hit Schroeter in the head and killed him instantly and also killed several other crew members. Thereupon, the chief engineer assumed command and ordered the crew to scuttle and abandon ship. As the boat went down bow first, the first watch officer refused to leave the bridge. He called for three cheers to honor the boat and disappeared with her.

The aircraft led the destroyer *Escapade* of Escort Group B-3 to the scene. She fished out thirteen of *U-752*'s forty-six-man crew, including one junior officer. Later that day the *U-91,* commanded by Heinz Hungershausen, age twenty-six, rescued four other lucky German survivors and eventually returned them to France. The *U-752* was the first U-boat to be sunk by aircraft from a British "jeep" carrier unassisted by surface ships or land-based aircraft, and the first to be sunk by rockets.

The returns from the dozens of U-boats deployed to the North Atlantic run in the two-week period from May 9 to May 23 were abysmal. Assisted by *B-dienst* information, they had found six out of seven eastbound and westbound convoys comprising about 277 merchant ships, outwitted only by Halifax 238. From the six convoys found, the U-boats sank only six ships for about 35,000 tons.

In return, Allied forces sank fifteen U-boats in these convoy battles: seven by land-based aircraft unassisted by surface ships, five by surface ships, two by "jeep" carrier aircraft, and one by a land-based aircraft teamed with a surface ship. No less important, in that same period, Allied forces so badly damaged eight other U-boats that they were forced to abort, one of them escorted by an undamaged boat (*U-359*) that must be counted as a ninth abort. Total U-boat casualties in this two-week period on the North Atlantic run: a ruinous twenty-four boats.

When the five losses and six aborts of the boats outbound in May are added to casualties on the North Atlantic run, the German "losses" from May 1 to May 23 were fifteen sunk and fifteen aborts, a total of thirty, or about 16 percent of the existing 186 boats of the Atlantic U-boat force. Of the approximately 750 German submariners serving on the fifteen lost boats, only thirty-eight survived to become POWs, twenty-five from *U-569* and thirteen from *U-752.* About seven hundred men, fourteen skippers, and Dönitz's son, Peter, perished at sea.

Withdrawal from the North Atlantic

Dönitz and Control were shocked and grieved over the catastrophic U-boat losses and aborts on the North Atlantic run. The losses, aborts, and failed opportunities, particularly against Slow Convoy 130 by the *Donau* groups, and against Halifax

239 by the *Mosel* group, weighed heavily. Control estimated that as of May 23, about thirty-one U-boats (manned by about 1,500 men) had been lost in May alone.* This was well over twice the rate of U-boat losses for the next worst month of the war.

The heavy losses led Dönitz and Control to conclude that the U-boat campaign against the North Atlantic run could not be continued until the interim upgrades on the VIIs (heavier flak guns, T-5 antiescort homing torpedoes, *Wanze* radar detector, and so on) had been completed. In the meantime, U-boats, including Type VIIs, were to patrol areas where it was believed Allied airpower was less strong: the Caribbean Sea, the areas east of Trinidad and Brazil, and the west coast of Africa from Dakar to Freetown and southward.

In a "Heil Hitler" message on May 24, Dönitz announced his decision and exhorted the skippers to do everything possible to prevent a collapse of morale among the crews, stressing that the withdrawal from the North Atlantic run was merely a temporary defensive measure and that in the end the Germans would win the naval war.

One of the withdrawing VIIs was the new *U-418,* commanded by Gerhard Lange, age twenty-two. He had sailed from Kiel on April 24 and joined the *Isar* and *Donau* 1 groups and, like most boats of those groups, he had no success. While *U-418* was homebound in Biscay on June 1, a Beaufighter of British Squadron 236, piloted by Mark C. Bateman and W. G. Easterbrook, was over the bay on a special mission. Their "observer" was a visiting Admiralty ASW expert, Francis J. Brookes, who spotted *U-418* with binoculars at ten miles. Bateman attacked, firing four 25-pound rockets. These hit and destroyed *U-418* with the loss of all hands.† Two days later, a flight of JU-88s jumped another Beaufighter, piloted by Michael Shannon and I. S. Walters. Their observer was the same Admiralty visitor, Francis Brookes. The Germans badly shot up the Beaufighter and mortally wounded Brookes. Shannon limped home and crash-landed at his home base in Cornwall.

In an attempt to disguise the U-boat withdrawal from the Allies, Dönitz directed thirteen VIIs (five from the disbanded group *Mosel*) to remain in the North Atlantic area as long as possible and broadcast a series of dummy radio messages simulating the operations of several groups. The Allies learned of this deception through timely breaks into naval Enigma, and sank three of the assigned decoys:

- On May 25, a Catalina of U.S. Iceland-based Navy Squadron VP 84, piloted by Robert C. Millard, sank the *U-467,* en route from the Arctic to the Atlantic. It was the twenty-eighth birthday of the U-boat skipper, Heinz Kummer. There were no survivors.

---

* The actual figures to that date were thirty-three boats and about 1,600 men lost: one Type XIV U-tanker, *U-463;* nine Type IXs; and twenty-three Type VIIs. The losses in all of May were a record forty boats (often and erroneously stated to be forty-one boats). These included three *Ritterkreuz* holders: Ulrich Folkers in *U-125,* Günter Seibicke in *U-436,* and Max-Martin Teichert in *U-456.* As related, the latter was awarded the medal posthumously. See Appendix 2.

† The rockets were still top secret, so he was required to say he used "depth charges" in the attack. See Franks, *Search, Find and Kill* (1995).

• On May 28, a B-24 of Iceland-based British Squadron 120, piloted by D. C. Fleming-Williams, sank the new *U-304,* commanded by Heinz Koch, age twenty-eight. There were no survivors of this boat either.

• On June 2, Johnny Walker's Support Group 2,* which was en route to reinforce convoy Halifax 241, found and hunted the veteran *U-202,* commanded by Günter Poser, age twenty-six. He was the skipper who had landed four German agents on Long Island the year before. After firing off 250 depth charges over fifteen hours, Walker's group forced *U-202* to the surface, then sank her with twenty-seven rounds of 4" shells. Four sloops of Walker's group, *Kite, Starling, Wild Goose,* and *Woodpecker,* participated in this attack, but sole credit for the kill went to Walker's flagship, *Starling.* The British rescued Poser and twenty-nine other Germans, most of them wounded.

Another of the *Mosel* boats assigned to decoy duty was Erich Topp's famous boat, *U-552,* commanded by Klaus Popp. She had sailed from Brest to the North Atlantic on April 4 but, like most U-boats, had achieved no successes. On May 27, while she was homebound, a B-24 of British Squadron 59, piloted by an Australian, H.A.L. (Tim) Moran, found *U-552.* In two attacks, Moran dropped eight depth charges. The U-boat survived but was severely damaged, Popp reported to Control. She could dive only to ninety-eight feet, and all her flak guns were destroyed. Control diverted Kurt Lange in the outbound *U-455* to provide "fuel and material" to *U-552,* then proceed on patrol. This rendezvous took place on June 7 and, as a consequence, Popp was able to limp into St. Nazaire on June 13. The boat did not sail again until early October.

Another of the returning decoys was the VII *U-650,* commanded by Ernst von Witzendorff. On June 23, a B-24 of British Squadron 86, piloted by John Wright, who had earlier damaged the VII *U-456,* found and attacked von Witzendorff. Wright dropped a 600-pound bomb that exploded, but Wright saw no solid evidence of a sinking. In fact, *U-650* was severely damaged and limped into St. Nazaire with *Luftwaffe* escort. The boat did not go on patrol again until January 1944.

Yet another of the returning decoys was the veteran *U-575,* commanded by Günther Heydemann, age twenty-six, completing his eighth patrol. The boat had left France in late April and had joined groups *Amsel* and *Elbe* in attacks against convoys Outbound North (Slow) 5 and Slow Convoy 129. In neither of these two battles had *U-575* shadowed well nor fired any torpedoes. Upon her return to France on June 11, Heydemann left the boat for other duty. On July 3, Dönitz awarded him a *Ritterkreuz.*†

All other decoys soon returned to France, replaced by new boats from Germany on maiden patrols or transfers from the Arctic. Control forbade the green but eager skippers of the new decoys to carry out any attacks on shipping until the period of the new moon in early July. All boats were to be especially alert to repel Al-

---

* Not to be confused with Macintyre's Escort Group 2.

† At the time of the award, his credited score was 85,676 tons sunk. His confirmed score was six big merchant ships sunk for 36,000 tons, including the British troopship *Abosso,* plus two sailing ships for 240 tons, and damage to three tankers for about 30,000 tons.

lied air attacks, running on electric motors when surfaced at night rather than diesels, so the bridge watch could better hear approaching planes.

Although the waters in the Gibraltar-Azores area had become quite perilous because of increased numbers of British and American B-24s and Catalinas based at Gibraltar and Port Lyautey, Morocco, political considerations in Berlin apparently demanded that Dönitz do all he could to redress the Axis setback in North Africa and to help prevent or at least interfere with an expected Allied invasion of Sardinia, Sicily, or Italy. Therefore on the same day that Dönitz ordered the U-boats to withdraw from the North Atlantic run, May 24, he directed Control to form a new group by May 31 to attack UG and GU convoys. More specifically, Control logged, the group was to attack convoy UGS 9, apparently put onto this target by *B-dienst* or other intelligence sources.

This new group, *Trutz* (Defiant), was initially composed of sixteen VIIs, eight from the disbanded group *Mosel* and eight newly sailed from Germany or France. The group was to include three *Ritterkreuz* holders: Hans Trojer in *U-221,* Siegfried Strelow in *U-435,* and Günther Krech in *U-558.* Apparently unknown to the Germans, the Allies assigned American Support Group 6 (the "jeep" carrier *Bogue* and four four-stack destroyers) to reinforce the escort of UGS 9. In a change of tactics, for the first time *Bogue*'s skipper, Giles E. Short, was permitted to operate independently of the convoy close escort—to range afield and run down nearby Huff Duff contacts.

Southbound to join the *Trutz* patrol line on May 25, *Ritterkreuz* holder Günther Krech in *U-558* happened upon the eastbound Slow Convoy 131. This was comprised of thirty-one merchant ships guarded by British Escort Group 6, commanded by R. Heathcote in the destroyer *Viscount,* and also by J. W. McCoy's Support Group 3. Inasmuch as "all available" U-boats were en route to *Trutz* by different routes, Control logged, none could immediately join Krech to attack this target. Control therefore authorized Krech to attack alone until Allied aircraft appeared, in which case, Krech was to break off operations.

Other U-boats heard these reports. Four inbound VIIs and another southbound *Trutz* VII, the new *U-951,* commanded by Kurt Pressel, age thirty-two, attempted to join the attack, but none succeeded. While boldly maneuvering close for a daylight submerged attack, Krech in *U-558* was detected by the numerous escorts and severely depth-charged. Later in the day, while making a second submerged attack, he was again detected and attacked by aircraft and surface escorts. Krech escaped but was forced to haul off to make repairs. He lost contact with Slow Convoy 131, which continued its voyage to the British Isles without further threats from U-boats.

At that specific time, Allied codebreakers could not read naval Enigma effectively, but DFs of the U-boat radio chatter gave Giles Short in *Bogue* a good idea of the *Trutz* assembly area. He maneuvered *Bogue* and her screen to that general area in such manner as to provide cover not only for UGS 9 but also for two other convoys passing east and west close by, UGS 7A and Flight 10, a special formation of nineteen eastbound British Landing Craft Infantry (LCI). On June 4, *Bogue*'s aircraft saw and attacked three *Trutz* VIIs on the surface, all formerly of group *Mosel* on second patrols: Erwin Christophersen, age twenty-eight, in *U-228;* Rudolf Baltz in *U-603;* and Horst Rendtel, age twenty-six, in *U-641.* Baltz and Rendtel fought back with flak guns, fouling the aim of the bombardiers, and all three boats escaped with only slight damage.

On the day following, June 5, two *Bogue* aircraft on patrol found another *Trutz* boat on the surface. She was the clumsy VIID minelayer *U-217,* commanded by Kurt Reichenbach-Klinke, age twenty- six. Pilot Richard S. Rogers, flying a Wildcat, dived and strafed the boat, knocking six Germans into the sea. After Rogers had made two more strafing runs, pilot Alexander C. McAuslan in an Avenger dropped four depth charges on *U-217* from an altitude of one hundred feet. The U-boat disappeared with the loss of all hands.*

Control was not pleased with the performance of group *Trutz,* the sole remaining U-boat group in the Atlantic Ocean. In view of the carrier aircraft in the vicinity of the convoys and fuel shortages, Control ordered *Trutz* to break off operations and go northward to refuel from the new Type XIV "Milk Cow" U-tanker, *U-488,* commanded by Erwin Bartke, age thirty-four. Afterward the group, less *U-92,* which was to go home by way of the Azores, but reinforced by the new IXC40 *U-193,* commanded by Hans Pauckstadt, age thirty-six, was to return to the United States–Gibraltar convoy route to look for other UG convoys and/or the opposite-sailing homebound GU convoys.

Meanwhile, in compliance with orders from Dönitz, a number of VIIs and IXs sailed for the Caribbean Sea, South America, and the areas near Freetown, as will be described later. With these sailed the big Type XB minelayer *U-118,* commanded by Werner Czygan, age thirty-eight, which was serving provisionally as a U-tanker. She was assigned to refuel about nine boats.

One of the VIIs scheduled for refueling by *U-118* was the *U-758,* commanded by Helmut Manseck, age twenty-eight, outbound to Trinidad on the boat's second patrol. She was the first U-boat to enter combat with a quad 20mm mounted on a bandstand aft of the bridge. While proceeding to the rendezvous with *U-118* on June 8, Manseck came upon convoy UGS 9, which group *Trutz* had failed to locate.

Unknown to Manseck, the *Bogue* support group was still in the vicinity. Running down a Huff Duff contact, two of *Bogue*'s Avengers found *U-758* on the surface. The first plane, piloted by Letson S. Balliett, dropped four close depth charges. The second, piloted by W. S. Fowler, dropped three. The seven explosions utterly savaged *U-758* and injured eleven men, four gravely. In keeping with the new "fight back" policy, Manseck remained on the surface, blazing away. Praising the quad 20mm, he later claimed eight *Bogue* aircraft attacked him and that he shot down one and damaged four, but in fact only four aircraft attacked him and only one was damaged.

---

* *U-217* was the fourth of six Type VIID minelayers (*U-213* to *U-218*) to be lost. While awaiting approval to plant SMA moored mines, all six conducted torpedo patrols, sinking altogether four ships for 22,800 tons by torpedo and one 75-ton sailing vessel by gun.

By dint of sharp seamanship and great luck, Manseck got away and that night reported his desperate situation to Control. Believing the smashed-up *U-758* might very well sink, Control directed two nearby boats to proceed to Manseck's position at maximum speed: the nearly dry XIV U-tanker *U-460,* commanded by Ebe Schnoor, and Werner Czygan's provisional tanker *U-118.* Both tankers reached *U-758* the following day. The doctor on *U-118* attended Manseck's wounded, transferring several of the men to *U-118* for close attention. Schnoor in *U-460* gave Czygan in *U-118* a few tons of surplus fuel then escorted *U-758* back to France, where both boats arrived on June 25. The *U-758* was in repair and further modification until September. To help build confidence in the new quad 20mm, U-boat Control passed along to all boats Manseck's exaggerated claims.

The Allies DFed numerous naval Enigma messages concerning the rescue of *U-758* and refueling instructions to *U-118.* This Huff Duff information led Short in *Bogue* to think another group was forming up. Proceeding to the area on June 12, *Bogue* aircraft found *U-118.* About eight planes attacked *U-118,* dropping fourteen close depth charges and firing over five thousand rounds from machine guns. This massive aerial assault destroyed *U-118.* Upon reaching the scene, one of *Bogue*'s screen, the four-stack destroyer *Osmond Ingram,* found twenty-one Germans in the water, four of them dead. The destroyermen fished out the seventeen living German survivors—all enlisted men—but one subsequently died of his wounds. Thirty-eight other crew and/or the retained wounded from *U-758* died in the attack or the sinking. The loss left only the new XIV tanker *U-488* at sea to supply the boats bound for distant southern Atlantic and Caribbean waters.* Low on fuel and again bedeviled by a faulty catapult, *Bogue* and screen returned to Norfolk on June 14 when U.S. Army Air Forces B-24s the 480th Group from Morocco arrived to escort the convoy.

While the fifteen boats of group *Trutz* were refueling from *U-488,* Control worked out a plan to attack the next slow United States–Gibraltar convoy, UGS 10. The plan was that *Trutz* was to go well to the west to a point in mid-ocean (about nine hundred miles east of Bermuda) to intercept this convoy. Allied codebreakers decrypted these orders or DFed the assembly and diverted UGS 10 (seventy merchant ships, nine close escorts, and a support group built around the light carrier *Santee*) farther to the south than had been intended, and ordered the convoy to maintain continuous air patrols from *Santee.* Thus the Allies again outwitted group *Trutz.*

By chance, another U-boat en route to the Trinidad area, the veteran VII *U-572,* commanded by Heinz Kummetat, age twenty-four, happened upon UGS 10 on June 22. Kummetat reported the contact and requested permission to attack. After

---

* In his book about World War II German POWs in United States camps, *The Faustball Tunnel* (1978), John H. Moore wrote that one of the sixteen survivors of *U-118,* seaman Werner Dreschler (a.k.a. "Limmer"), became a stool pigeon and when this was discovered by other German POWs, they murdered him at a camp in Papago Park, Arizona, on March 13, 1944. American authorities tried, found guilty, and on August 25, 1945, hanged seven German POWs for the murder, Moore wrote. ("Faustball" means a clenched fist.)

Control calculated that group *Trutz* was beyond the range of Allied land-based air from Morocco, it granted *U-572*'s request. Kummetat boldly slipped submerged by the American aircraft from *Santee* and nine unalert warships of the close escort (seven destroyers, two minesweepers) and sank the 4,200-ton Free French tanker *Lot.* Belatedly, the escort woke up and counterattacked *U-572,* but Kummetat evaded and continued his voyage to Trinidad.

Control then directed group *Trutz* to reverse course and sail east at economical speed. The group was reinforced to sixteen boats by the veteran VII *U-135,* commanded by a new skipper, Otto Luther, age twenty-four. Aware of this new formation and its orders from Enigma decrypts and Huff Duff, Allied authorities diverted two westbound convoys around *Trutz.* These were GUS 8, protected by a new American support group built around the "jeep" carrier *Card,* which had come over to Morocco in the role of aircraft ferry, and GUS 9, protected at first by the returning *Santee* group, then by another new support group built around the "jeep" carrier *Core,* that had come east with UGS 11.*

Outwitted and frustrated, Control dissolved group *Trutz* at the end of June. Low on fuel, the *U-666,* commanded by Herbert Engel, age thirty-one, returned to France, leaving fifteen boats. Control assigned two veteran VIIs commanded by the *Ritterkreuz* holders Hans Trojer in *U-221* and Günther Krech in *U-558* to patrol the very dangerous waters close to the mouth of Gibraltar Strait and two of the last to join the group, the VII *U-135* and the IXC40 *U-193,* both commanded by green skippers, to patrol west of Morocco. The other eleven *Trutz* boats, including *Ritterkreuz* holder Siegfried Strelow in the veteran *U-435,* were divided into three small subgroups (*Geier,* or Vulture, 1, 2, and 3) and directed to work slowly toward an area west of Lisbon. It was believed that most of these former *Trutz* boats were operating close enough to support one another, should one find a convoy.

Five of these ex-*Trutz* boats were promptly sunk, four by Allied land-based ASW bombers.

- The new VII *U-951,* commanded by Kurt Pressel, age thirty-two, making his first patrol. A B-24 of U.S. Army Air Forces ASW Squadron 1, based in Morocco and piloted by Walter S. McDonell, spotted her on July 7. Attacking into flak, McDonell toggled seven depth charges that destroyed *U-951* and all forty-six crew. The flak smashed into the cockpit area of the B-24, wounding four airmen, all of whom recovered.†
- The new VII *U-232,* commanded by Ernst Ziehm, age twenty-eight, also on his first patrol. A B-24 of U.S. Army Air Forces ASW Squadron 2, based in Morocco and piloted by James H. Darden, spotted her on July 8. In three attacks into

---

* To further relieve congestion in New York harbor, beginning with UGS 11, slow Torch convoys sailed from Norfolk every fifteen days to July 27, then every ten days.

† At Port Lyautey, Morocco, the war diary of U.S. Navy Fairwing 15 (including Army Air Forces B-24s and Navy Catalinas) noted sixteen attacks on U-boats from July 5 to July 15: seven attacks by USAAF Squadron 1, six by USAAF Squadron 2, two by USN Squadron VP 92, and one by USN Squadron VP 73. These planes sank two U-boats, *U-506* and *U-951.* One B-24 was "lost at sea," cause unknown.

heavy flak, Darden dropped six depth charges that destroyed *U-232* with the loss of all forty-six crew. The flak severely damaged the B-24 and slightly injured one gunner.

• The veteran VII *U-435,* commanded by *Ritterkreuz* holder Siegfried Strelow. A Leigh Light–equipped Wellington of Gibraltar-based British Squadron 179, piloted by E. J. Fisher, sank her with four depth charges on July 9. There were no survivors.

• The veteran VII *U-135,* commanded by the new skipper Otto Luther. Patrolling in the narrow waters between the Canaries and Morocco, Luther found a convoy, Outbound South 51. He attacked on July 15, damaging the 4,800-ton British freighter *Twickenham.* The convoy escorts counterattacked and forced the boat to scuttle. The Admiralty credited the veteran British sloop *Rochester* and the British corvettes *Balsam* and *Mignonette* with the kill. The British rescued Luther and forty other Germans.

• The veteran VII *U-558,* commanded by *Ritterkreuz* holder Günther Krech. Piloted by Charles F. Gallmeier, a B-24 of USAAF ASW Squadron 19 of the 479th Group, recently arrived in southwest England, devastated the boat with a salvo of seven depth charges on July 20. Flak from *U-558* hit one of Gallmeier's inboard engines, forcing him to abort. Fortuitously for the Allies, a British Halifax of Squadron 58, piloted by Geoffrey R. Sawtell, was also at the scene. Although the Germans were attempting to scuttle and to abandon ship, Sawtell in the Halifax attacked *U-558* with eight depth charges, slaughtering the Germans on deck and in the water with machine guns and depth charges. Five of the forty-six Germans, including Krech, who was badly wounded in the spine and upper thigh, escaped in a raft and lived to tell the tale. They were rescued on July 24 by a passing vessel, the British (later Canadian) destroyer *Athabaskan.* All others perished.

Six other ex-*Trutz/Geier* boats had close calls.

• On July 5 an unidentified aircraft attacked the VII *U-608,* commanded by the experienced Rolf Struckmeier. He reported to Control that he "dived away" and avoided damage or casualties. While homebound in Biscay on July 14, he sighted an enemy submarine, but no attack occurred and the *U-608* reached St. Nazaire on July 18, completing an unsuccessful patrol of sixty-five days. The boat did not sail again until October.

• On July 6, an unidentified Allied aircraft hit the new IXC40 *U-193,* skippered by the old hand Hans Pauckstadt, age thirty-six, who had commanded a duck and two VIIs before the war. The damage included two men wounded and the loss of the Metox equipment. Pauckstadt linked up with the failed IXD1 U-cruiser *U-195* returning from Cape Town, which had its Metox operational, and reached Bordeaux on July 23. He also did not resail until October.

• On July 8, a Catalina of British Squadron 202, piloted by G. Powell, spotted the VII *U-603,* commanded by Rudolf Baltz, who had refueled from the XB *U-119* and was still on his first patrol as skipper. Pilot Powell attacked with machine guns blazing and dropped depth charges that damaged the boat. Upon receiving Baltz's report (bombed by a "Sunderland," Control logged), Control authorized all *Geier* skippers that they could elect to come home if in their judgment Allied air was too intense. The *U-603* reached Brest on July 16, concluding a patrol of seventy-three days, during which Baltz sank one ship, the 4,800-ton Dutchman *Brand.* He sailed again in September.

• On July 9, an unidentified Allied aircraft attacked the new VII *U-953,* commanded by Karl-Heinz Marbach, who had celebrated his twenty-fourth birthday on July 5. He fought off the aircraft with flak guns, but one of his men was killed and two were wounded. Upon arrival in La Pallice, the boat underwent conversion to a "flak boat," and it did not sail again until October.

• That same day, July 9, an unidentified aircraft attempted to attack the *U-228,* commanded by Erwin Christophersen. He reported "no damage," but by July 12, he too was homebound. He arrived in Lorient on July 19, completing a patrol of seventy-seven days. He did not sail again until the last days of October.

• On July 10, an unidentified aircraft hit the *U-336,* commanded by Hans Hunger. Control logged that the aircraft was a "Sunderland" that caused only "slight damage." Hunger sailed again in September.

So ended the checkered story of group *Trutz/Geier,* the last and only group to operate in the Atlantic Ocean in the summer of 1943. Altogether, eighteen U-boats had been assigned to the group. Its only success was *U-603*'s freighter *Brand* and *U-135*'s damage to freighter *Twickenham.* Six of the eighteen boats were lost, along with about 250 men, plus forty-six captured. Owing to the assignment of four carrier support groups to the Middle Atlantic UG and GU convoys (*Bogue, Card, Core, Santee*), the extended coverage on both ends of the route by ever increasing numbers of land-based Allied ASW aircraft, and to the vast sea room available for evasive convoy routing, Dönitz decreed that no more groups were to operate against convoys in this Gibraltar-Azores zone until the boats had been upgraded with the new offensive and defensive weapons.

May Patrols to the Americas

Nine Type IXs sailed to American waters in May, including the new IXD2 cruiser *U-199.** As related, an aircraft hit one IXC, the *U-523,* in Biscay, forcing her to abort. Five of the eight that reached American waters were commanded by *Ritterkreuz* holders. One of these, Friedrich Guggenberger, age twenty-eight, in *U-513,* who had sunk the carrier *Ark Royal* in the Mediterranean, wore Oak Leaves. Five boats were to patrol the waters of the United States East Coast, the Gulf of Mexico, and the Caribbean; the other three were to patrol off Brazil.

Three of the first IXs to sail went to the Cape Hatteras area: Friedrich Markworth, age twenty-eight, in *U-66;* Max Wintermeyer, age twenty-nine, in the IXC40 *U-190;* and *Ritterkreuz* holder Klaus Bargsten, age thirty-five, in *U-521,*

* These nine included the *U-66,* which left France on April 29.

who had sunk the British destroyer *Cossack* earlier in the war while commanding *U-563.* Wintermeyer in *U-190* was first to arrive, and the reception was rude. On May 28 a radar-equipped U.S. Army Air Forces B-24, piloted by J. M. Vivian, caught and bombed *U-190,* causing severe damage. Although the damage was repaired, thereafter Wintermeyer patrolled with extreme caution and sank no ships in a cruise of 111 days.

Next on the Hatteras scene was *Ritterkreuz* holder Klaus Bargsten in the *U-521.* On May 30, he saw aircraft and two "destroyers" but was not himself seen, he reported. Three days later, on June 2, Bargsten cruised farther north to a position about ninety miles east of Chincoteague Bay, Virginia. Shortly after noon that day, one of the 173-foot American patrol craft, *PC-565,** commanded by a lawyer, Walter T. Flynn, which was escorting a large convoy from New York to Guantánamo (NG 365) got a good sonar contact on *U-521* and immediately attacked with five shallow-set depth charges. These exploded close to the unalert U-boat that was cruising at a depth of about one hundred feet. Leaping from his bunk, Bargsten ran to the control room to assess the damage. In his judgment, it was so severe that he ordered the boat to surface. Upon breaking water Bargsten hurried to the bridge alone, to find *PC-565* and another escort, the corvette *Brisk* (ex-*Flax* of the Royal Canadian Navy, designated U.S. Navy Gunboat 89), close by.

Boldly turning the little *PC-565* to ram, Flynn gave orders for his two main guns to open fire. Both failed. Number 1 gun misfired; the crew of number 2 was blinded by the PC's own exhaust smoke. However, the starboard 20mm gun fired fifty-five rounds, scoring several hits on *U-521*'s conning tower. The corvette *Brisk* got off one wild round from her 4" gun but had to cease shooting when the PC cruised into her line of fire.

Hopelessly hemmed in, Bargsten gave the order to scuttle and abandon ship. Inexplicably, *U-521* suddenly sank beneath his feet, leaving him alone in the water. He did not know whether or not the boat had survived. Nor did Flynn in *PC-565,* who threw over one more depth charge for good luck, then picked up Bargsten, splinters of freshly broken wood, and "a large piece of human flesh," which, in his mind, confirmed the kill. Less certain, the Eastern Sea Frontier sent the minesweeper *Chickadee* to the scene (in 7,200 feet of water) to mount another search, but other than an oil slick, no sign of *U-521* was ever found.

Markworth in the aging *U-66* had better luck. He gave the hostile Cape Hatteras area a quick once-over, then proceeded farther south toward Savannah, keeping well off the coast. On June 10, he hit the fully loaded 10,200-ton American tanker *Esso Gettysburg* with two torpedoes, and she burst into flames and sank. Nearly twenty-four hours elapsed before an Army Air Forces B-25 on convoy escort saw fifteen wretched survivors who were subsequently rescued. About three weeks later, on July 2, Markworth attacked with torpedoes and his deck gun another big American tanker, the empty 10,200-ton *Bloody Marsh,*

* Commissioned on May 25, 1942. The *PC-565* was one of seventeen such vessels on convoy duty in the Eastern Sea Frontier in May–June 1943. See photo insert.

about forty miles from the scene of his first success. The *Bloody Marsh* returned gunfire, but *U-66* carried the day and the tanker went down. Several days later, while making a submerged attack on a freighter, *U-66* was rammed but sustained only slight damage. Upon receiving Markworth's report, Dönitz awarded him a *Ritterkreuz.**

Homebound on July 22, Markworth encountered a third big American tanker, the 10,200-ton *Cherry Valley,* sailing in ballast. In his initial attack, Markworth claimed he saw two torpedo hits. In a second attack, he reported, he missed with three torpedoes, then attacked *Cherry Valley* with his 4.1" deck gun. However, the tanker's Armed Guard crew drove *U-66* off and saved the ship, which was repaired and returned to service. Resuming his homeward voyage by the "southern route," where he was to meet a U-tanker, the newly decorated Markworth was to run into difficulties, as will be described later.

The next two IXs to sail to American waters were *Ritterkreuz* holder Günther Müller-Stöckheim, age twenty-nine, in the IXC *U-67* and Herbert Uhlig, age twenty-seven, in the IXC40 *U-527.* While leaving the Bay of Biscay on May 13, Uhlig in *U-527* came upon a large storm-damaged freighter under tow by two tugs. He carried out a submerged attack on the freighter, but it failed. The attack drew a corvette escort, which counterattacked *U-527* with about fifteen depth charges and drove the boat away.

U-boat Control ordered these two IXs to patrol the Caribbean Sea. The *U-67* was to go by way of the Old Bahama Channel and Windward Passage to an area near Jamaica. The *U-527* was to go via the Straits of Florida into the Gulf of Mexico to the Yucatan Channel. On May 27, Müller-Stöckheim in *U-67* reported that his Metox was out of commission and irreparable. U-boat Control therefore held *U-67* in an open-ocean area between Bermuda and Puerto Rico until she could get a Metox from another U-boat.

While marking time in this remote area, Müller-Stöckheim came upon a big, fast freighter on June 8 and another on June 24. The first outran him, but he shot six torpedoes at the second. One torpedo prematured merely one hundred yards from the U-boat, the other five missed. Müller-Stöckheim then surfaced for a gun chase, but the gunners on the freighter beat him off. In late June, per plan, he received a Metox from an outbound boat (the VII *U-572*), but he never entered the Caribbean as originally intended. While homebound, *U-67* also ran into great trouble, as will be described.

Westbound near Bermuda, Herbert Uhlig in *U-527* came upon a big, fast freighter, at which he fired two torpedoes that missed. He then proceeded via the Straits of Florida across the Gulf of Mexico to the Yucatan Channel. He reported "heavy" air and surface-ship ASW patrols that inhibited his reconnaissance. He attacked one lone freighter with four torpedoes, but these also missed. About July 1

* At the time of the award, on July 8, his score was thirteen confirmed ships sunk for about 74,000 tons, plus two 32-ton motor launches sunk by his minefield at Port Castries, St. Lucia.

he commenced his homeward voyage via the Straits of Florida and Bermuda. Near that island, he reported, he was attacked by several aircraft, including one land-based plane that dived out of cloud cover. He survived these attacks and continued easterly to a rendezvous with a U-tanker. The *U-527* was also to encounter severe problems, as will be described.

This foray into United States and Caribbean waters was the least productive in the war to date. Of the five IXs which participated, only one, Markworth's *U-66,* inflicted any damage on Allied shipping: two tankers for about 20,400 tons sunk and a third tanker damaged. One boat, Bargsten's *U-521,* had been lost with all hands except Bargsten. The foray was thus useful only to foster the impression that the U-boat menace was still quite real and widespread, thus tying down a very great number of ASW resources in American waters and slowing down the movement of war matériel to the British Isles by convoying.

The three boats assigned to patrol Brazilian waters, all commanded by *Ritterkreuz* holders, were Carl Emmermann in the IXC *U-172;* Friedrich Guggenberger, new skipper of the IXC *U-513;* and the new IXD2 U-cruiser *U-199,* commanded by Hans-Werner Kraus, age twenty-seven.

These boats had troublesome and arduous patrols. Guggenberger in *U-513* and Emmermann in *U-172* refueled en route, Guggenberger from Ebe Schnoor's XIV U-tanker *U-460.** Owing to the loss of *U-118,* and to the loss of the XIV tanker *U-463* outbound in Biscay, U-boat Control was compelled to utilize several newly sailing IXC40s as provisional U-tankers. One of these, Kurt Lange in *U-530,* furious at his diversion to be a supply boat, refueled Emmermann's *U-172* on June 19. For these reasons Emmermann was to reach Brazilian waters well behind the other boats.

En route to Brazil, Guggenberger, a tough and demanding skipper, conducted so many drills that the crew felt they were back in Baltic workup. On the last day of May, Guggenberger got his first opportunity to lead the crew in the real thing. He found a large (10,000- to 12,000-ton) freighter sailing alone at about 16 knots. He chased her on the surface for several hours, but could not overtake her or get close enough for an effective attack. Finally, in desperation, he shot three torpedoes from very long range. All missed, leaving him with eighteen torpedoes, twelve below (one defective) and, in keeping with the new policy, only six air torpedoes in topside canisters.

A new U.S. Navy Fleet Air Wing (Fairwing), 16, commanded by Rossmore D. Lyon, was in the process of deploying to Brazil. It established its headquarters at Recife, adjacent to that of Admiral Jonas H. Ingram, Commander in Chief, Fourth Fleet, the U.S. naval presence in the southwest Atlantic. Initially Fairwing 16 consisted of the following units:

---

* Emmermann was scheduled to refuel from the XB minelayer *U-118,* commanded by Werner Czygan, but, as related, planes from the "jeep" carrier *Bogue* had sunk her on June 12.

VP 74	Mariners at Bahia*
VP 94	Catalinas at Natal†
VB 107	B-24s at Natal (ex-VP 83)‡
VB 127	Venturas at Natal
VB 129	Venturas at Recife§

Entering Brazilian waters first, Guggenberger promptly found targets. On June 21, he sank a 1,700-ton Swedish neutral, deemed to be carrying contraband. Four days later, on June 25, he shot three torpedoes at the 6,000-ton American tanker *Eagle.* One hit, but she got away and limped into Rio de Janeiro. In due course she was repaired and returned to service. Guggenberger downloaded four air torpedoes and stored the defective electric topside. This rearrangement gave him twelve torpedoes below and two good air torpedoes topside.

Kraus in the U-cruiser *U-199* was next to arrive in Brazilian waters. If he found these waters to be fallow, Kraus had authority to leave the area, cross the South Atlantic, and patrol off Cape Town. On June 27, he attacked the American Liberty ship *Charles Willson Peale* with three torpedoes. One or more hit, but she survived and her Armed Guard gun crew counterattacked *U-199.* Kraus returned fire with a new 37mm flak gun and his 4.1" forward deck gun to little effect. With enemy shells falling close, Kraus dived his big, clumsy boat and withdrew. The damaged *Peale* ran into Rio. Eventually she, too, was returned to service.

Emmermann in *U-172* reached Brazilian waters in the last week of June. With customary skill, he and his crew promptly found and sank the 4,700-ton British freighter *Vernon City.* Upon receiving the report of this sinking, Dönitz awarded Emmermann Oak Leaves to his *Ritterkreuz,*# placing him on a par in decorations with Guggenberger in *U-513.* Later, as was the custom, Hitler personally presented the award to Emmermann. A war correspondent, Helmut Brendt, sailing with Emmermann on this trip, joined in the improvised shipboard celebration.

Guggenberger was next to score. On the night of June 30, he found and chased a big freighter that escaped into a rain squall. Relentlessly pursuing on the estimated course of the enemy, Guggenberger came upon a ship, but it was not the same ship. Rather, it was a 1,100-ton Brazilian coaster, *Tutóla,* with a load of coffee. Guggenberger sank her with a single torpedo. Two days later, on July 3, he met a convoy of six ships, escorted by a single aircraft. With a risky, battery-draining

* PBM-3 Mariners. These were the troublesome models that, as related, had to be "stripped" to become PBM-3S. By the end of 1943, two more squadrons of PBM-3 Mariners, 203 and 211, at Bahia and Rio de Janeiro, respectively, were operating over Brazilian waters.

† Arrived in Natal on January 21, 1943.

‡ VP 83, an amphibious Catalina squadron, arrived in Natal on April 1, 1942, to relieve VP 52. VP 83 returned to Norfolk in May 1943, where it converted to B-24s and was renamed VB 107. As such, it returned to Natal and began operations on July 5, 1943. The B-24s (USN PB4Ys) could fly 1,200 miles eastward from Natal to Ascension Island and, of course, vice versa.

§ In addition, three more Ventura squadrons, 130, 143, and 145, at Fortaleza, Recife, and Natal, respectively, were assigned.

At the time of the award, he was credited with sinking 169,102 tons. His confirmed score was twenty-four ships for 134,706 tons sunk, ranging in size from a 35-ton sailing ship to the 23,400-ton troopship *Orcades.*

burst of underwater speed into merely one hundred feet of water, Guggenberger got close enough to shoot submerged. He fired five torpedoes into the formation at several targets but hit only one, the 7,200-ton American Liberty ship *Elihu B. Washburne,* which sank.

Nearby, Kraus in the IXD2 U-cruiser *U-199* had a close call. Two Brazilian aircraft found and pinned him down in shallow coastal waters. Later in the afternoon, a U.S. Navy Mariner of Squadron VP 74, piloted by Harold C. Carey, attacked *U-199.* Boldly standing his ground, Kraus counterattacked with a furious burst of flak that brought down the Mariner with the loss of all hands. On the day following, July 4, Kraus sank with his deck gun a sailing vessel that has not been identified.

Having received Oak Leaves, Emmermann in *U-172* might well have rested on his laurels but that would not have been in character. He continued to hunt aggressively, sinking three more ships: the 6,500-ton American freighter *African Star* on July 12, the 4,600-ton British freighter *Harmonic* on July 15, and the 7,200-ton British Liberty ship *Fort Chilcotin* on July 24. With a bag of four ships for about 23,000 tons, Emmermann soon commenced the voyage home. As will be seen, he, too, had a rough time reaching France.

Contemptuous of Allied ASW measures in Brazilian waters, Guggenberger in *U-513* continued to hunt boldly on the surface. On July 16, he torpedoed and sank his third ship, the 7,200-ton American Liberty ship *Richard Caswell,* sailing alone about four hundred miles south of Rio de Janeiro. The American Navy's small (1,800-ton) seaplane tender *Barnegat,* supporting the Mariners of Squadron VP 74 based at Florianópolis, rescued the survivors. This sinking persuaded the Mariners to patrol that area with greater diligence.

Three days later, a Mariner of that squadron, piloted by Roy S. Whitcomb, found Guggenberger's *U-513* on the surface not far from the scene of the *Caswell* sinking. Guggenberger saw the plane, but dismissed it as probably an "old crate" flown by Brazilians and manned his single 37mm and 20mm guns. After a few rounds, the 20mm jammed, but Guggenberger remained calmly confident as Whitcomb bore in boldly and dropped four depth charges. Two charges hit very close, utterly destroying *U-513,* which sank instantly.

The blasts threw a number of Germans, including Guggenberger, into the sea. Seeing them, Whitcomb made a low pass and dropped two rafts and life jackets. He then notified the tender *Barnegat,* which, after an unavoidable delay, got under way. When she reached the scene about dusk, she could find only one raft containing Guggenberger and six enlisted men. Forty-six other Germans perished. After extensive interrogation, Guggenberger was incarcerated at a POW camp, Papago Park, on an Indian reservation in Arizona.*

Patrolling farther to the north, near Rio de Janeiro, Kraus in the U-cruiser *U-199* attacked his first noteworthy ship on July 24, the 4,200-ton British freighter *Henzada.* The first three torpedoes missed, but one of two stern shots hit and the ship broke in half and sank in twenty minutes. A week later, sixty miles off Rio,

---

* Guggenberger's score on *U-81* and *U-513* was nine ships for about 57,500 tons, including the fleet carrier *Ark Royal* and four sailing vessels.

Kraus chased a lone ship until dawn on July 31. Responding to the alarm, a Mariner of Squadron VP 74, piloted by William F. Smith, found *U-199* on the surface. Boldly flying into the 20mm and 37mm flak, Smith attacked, dropping six depth charges in his first run and two more in a second run. These explosions badly damaged *U-199,* but Kraus kept up the flak and ran west toward shallow water, where he intended to bottom and make repairs.

Holding firmly to his target, Smith raked *U-199* with machine guns and radioed for help. Two Brazilian planes promptly responded, a Hudson and a Catalina. The Hudson dropped two depth charges that fell wide. While the Hudson, piloted by S. C. Schnoor, strafed the U-boat, the Catalina, piloted by Alberto M. Torres, finally sank *U-199* with four depth charges. Twelve of *U-199*'s sixty-one-man crew, including Kraus, the first and second watch officers, a midshipman, and a warrant quartermaster survived and were rescued by the tender *Barnegat,* and all eventually wound up in a POW camp.

This three-boat foray into Brazilian waters resulted in nine merchant ships sunk for about 44,000 tons and two ships damaged. It was a far better return than the concurrent five-boat foray into United States waters that resulted in only two ships sunk for about 20,000 tons and one ship damaged. But the price was a shock: two of the three boats sunk, one a valuable U-cruiser.

The combined results of the nine IXs that reached American waters in May was eleven ships for 64,000 tons sunk in return for three U-boats lost (*U-199, U-513, U-521*), commanded by the *Ritterkreuz* holders Kraus, Guggenberger, and Bargsten, all of whom survived. That was an unacceptable exchange rate of 3.6 ships per U-boat sunk and a miserable average return of 1.4 ships sunk per boat per patrol.

The homebound voyages of the surviving six IXs coincided with the American decision to allow the "jeep" carrier support groups with UG and GU convoys greater freedom of action. Although the Allies "lost" naval Enigma at about this same time (July 1 to July 21) due to a modification to the machine (a new rotor or reflector, Gamma), the land-based and shipboard Huff Duff stations were operating at peak efficiency. Hence the four carriers (*Bogue, Card, Core, Santee*) patrolling the "southern route" were able to capitalize on the radio chatter of inbound and outbound boats that were attempting a rendezvous to refuel.

Aircraft from the "jeep" carrier *Core,* making her first combat patrol in support of westbound convoy GUS 9, found the *Ritterkreuz* holder Müller-Stöckheim in the homebound *U-67* on July 16. The pilot of an Avenger, Robert P. Williams, attacked. Unalert, the men standing watch on *U-67,* including the young first watch officer, Walter Otto, failed to man the flak guns in time. Williams was thus able to drop four depth charges in a textbook attack. The explosions blew the four sailors on watch into the sea and destroyed *U-67,* which sank instantly.* Later that day,

* Having sunk no ships on this patrol, Müller-Stöckheim's score in the two full years he commanded *U-67* was thirteen confirmed ships (six tankers) sunk for about 72,000 tons, plus damage to three tankers.

one of *Core*'s screen, the four-stack destroyer *McCormick,* fished out three lucky survivors: Otto and two enlisted men. Pilot Williams was awarded the Navy Cross.

The sinking of the homebound *U-67* raised the losses in the group of eight Type IXs that reached American waters in May to four (50 percent). The four surviving boats were Markworth in *U-66,* Wintermeyer in the damaged *U-190* (who sank no ships), Emmermann in *U-172,* and Uhlig in *U-527.* All had yet to run the gauntlet of land- and carrier-based aircraft in order to reach France.

Thus it was that due in part to hazards involved in refueling in the "southern" area, and to the deployment of Fairwing 16 to Recife, U-boat patrols to American waters were no safer than patrols to the North Atlantic run. However, U-boat Control either did not yet realize this or chose to ignore it, for in June twenty-two more boats were to sail to the Americas.

"No Option But to Fight On"

In the months of April and May 1943, Allied forces sank fifty-eight U-boats at the battlefronts: fifty-three in the Atlantic, four in the Mediterranean, and one in the Arctic. The fifty-three losses in the Atlantic comprised almost one-third of that force: thirty-five Type VIIs, seventeen Type IXs, and one Type XIV U-tanker, *U-463.**

Throughout the U-boat officer corps a debate arose as to whether or not the "tonnage war" against Allied shipping should continue. Two of the most highly decorated skippers, Reinhard Suhren and Erich Topp, argued against it because of the anticipated "immense losses" and the lack of even "slightest prospect of success," as Topp put it later in his memoir. On the other hand, the even more highly decorated skippers Albrecht Brandi and Wolfgang Lüth thought the campaign should continue with the greatest intensity possible.

Even Dönitz was torn. He wrote in his memoir:

> In June 1943 I was faced with the most difficult decision of the whole war. I had to make up my mind whether to withdraw the boats from all areas and call off the U-boat war, or to let them continue operations in some suitably modified form, regardless of the enemy's superiority.

Dönitz correctly foresaw that if the U-boat campaign was to be continued, "losses would rise to an appalling height" and would "involve certain and deliberate self-sacrifice" on the part of the skippers and crews. That is, any attempts would be suicide missions. Nonetheless, after a meeting with the Senior Officer, Submarines (West), Hans-Rudolf Rösing, and the commanders of Combat Flotillas 3, 7, 9, and

---

* In addition, three boats were retired to the Training Command: the IXB *U-108,* and the VIICs *U-71* and *U-704.*

10,* Dönitz wrote, he came to the "bitter conclusion" that "we had no option but to fight on." A continuation of the submarine campaign would:

• Comply with Hitler's insistence that the U-boat war be carried forward at the highest possible intensity.

• Maintain the momentum and morale of the submarine force, avoiding a crippling hiatus followed by a difficult restart.

• Compel the Allies to continue convoying in all waters, reducing by one-quarter to one-third the movement of men and supplies to the various battlefronts.

• Tie down what Dönitz estimated to be 1,300 Allied aircraft and 3,300 ships assigned to ASW roles that might be deployed in other tasks against the Axis.

• Train under combat conditions the new generation of submariners required to man the new Type XXI and Type XXIII "electro boats."

• Enable the Germans to ferret out new Allied ASW technology so that countermeasures and tactics could be evolved for the "electro boats."

Theretofore Dönitz, "the Lion," had enjoyed nearly divine status among the men in the U-boat force. All German submariners had believed in his ability and judgment and had worshipped him faithfully. However, his order to fight on with such patently inferior weapons was seen by an embittered few as a cold-blooded decision to send his loyal corps to a certain death. Some thought that with his promotion to grand admiral and commander in chief of the *Kriegsmarine,* Dönitz had become much too closely involved with Hitler and his inner circle in Berlin. Others thought that given the colossal failures on battlefields in the Soviet Union and North Africa, the plan to produce a new fleet of war-decisive "electro boats" and "snort boats" in time to defeat the Allies was delusional.

U-boat Control mounted forty-eight patrols by attack boats in June. These comprised thirty-five VIIs, twelve IXs, and one new IXD2 U-cruiser, *U-200.* As in prior months, the number of Type XIV ("Milk Cow") U-tankers was not adequate to serve the needs of so many VIIs. Only two XIV U-tankers sailed in June: *U-462* and *U-487.* As will be described, an aircraft hit *U-462* in Biscay, forcing her to abort; however, she made repairs and resailed in the last days of the month. Carrier aircraft sank the *U-487,* setting in motion yet another refueling crisis.

The patrol areas assigned to thirty-three of these forty-eight attack boats reflected the continuing German belief that Allied ASW measures were less intense in distant waters. The fifteen patrols mounted in the North and Middle Atlantic included six boats on maiden parols from Germany and nine from France on decoy missions.

* At that time, Richard Zapp, Herbert Sohler, Heinrich Lehmann-Willenbrock, and Günter Kuhnke, respectively.

	North and Middle Atlantic	*South Atlantic*	*Americas*	*Totals*
Type VIIs	10	8	17	35
Type IXs	5	3*	5	13
Totals	15†	11	22	48

The seven new boats from Germany and the one from the Arctic force joining the Atlantic force incurred catastrophic losses. Six were sunk, one was so badly damaged that she had to abort to France, and the other, an IXC40, had to be diverted to a refueling mission. These were:

- The new VII *U-417,* commanded by Wolfgang Schreiner, age twenty-six. She was sunk on June 11 in the Iceland-Faeroes gap, merely nine days out from Kiel by a B-17 of British Squadron 206. Piloted by R. B. Thompson, the plane dropped four shallow-set depth charges. Before she sank, the *U-417* hit the B-17 with flak guns, inflicting such serious damage that the plane was forced to ditch.

Sighting the British airmen in a dinghy, an American Catalina of the Iceland-based Squadron VP 84 attempted to rescue them but crashed, forcing the Americans to scramble into their life raft. On June 14, a Catalina of the Faeroes-based British Squadron 190, piloted by J. A. Holmes, rescued the British aircrew but the American raft was not found until June 16, by which time only one airman was still alive. After rescue, the surviving British B-17 aircrew reported seeing "twenty to thirty" Germans in the water where *U-417* went down, "some covered in oil, some shaking their fists at the aircraft, but the majority prone." There were no survivors of *U-417.*

- The Arctic veteran VII *U-334,* commanded by a new skipper, Heinz Ehrich, age twenty-three. She was sunk ten days out from Norway on June 14 southwest of Iceland by the frigate *Jed* and sloop *Pelican,* which were escorting convoy Outbound North (Slow) 10. In six attacks the two escorts dropped forty depth charges and fired two Hedgehog salvos. The *U-334* surfaced twice during the attacks, but was destroyed with all hands. The Admiralty assessment committee wrote that the "terrible assortment of wreckage and fresh human remains, oil and bubbles [that] rose to the surface" was adequate proof of a kill.

- The new VII *U-388,* commanded by Peter Sues, age twenty-three. She was sunk on June 20, merely thirteen days out from Kiel, by an Iceland-based Catalina of U.S. Navy Squadron VP 84, piloted by E. W. Wood, which was escorting convoy Outbound North 189. Wood drove the *U-388* under with depth charges and machine-gun fire, then launched a Fido homing torpedo at the swirl. Wood reported that wreckage surfaced along with bubbles and oil and that he could see that the U-boat stern was split open and that a "10 to 15 foot" section of the after com-

* Including the IXC40 *U-188* and the IXD2 U-cruiser *U-200,* assigned to group *Monsun.*

† Including the Arctic transfer *U-334,* two new IXC40s, and four new VIIs from Kiel. Many other new VIIs and IXs were held back in the Baltic for upgrades and some others were delayed to reduce congestion at the overcrowded French bases, where slips inside the pens could not accommodate the number of boats already on hand.

PLATE 7

GERMAN U-TANKER ABORTS, LOSSES, AND DAMAGE

MAY–AUGUST 1943

Many historians of the Battle of the Atlantic write that the Allies, acting on naval Enigma decrypts, wiped out the U-boat tanker force in the summer of 1943, thererby crippling the operations of the Type VIIs. This is a myth. The Allies did indeed virtually wipe out the U-tanker force that summer, sinking nine of twelve boats at the front (including XB minelayers).[1] However, according to a recently declassified top-secret postwar American study, only two of the nine U-tankers were sunk with the help of Enigma decrypts. Most boats were sunk or forced to abort by Commonwealth and American aircraft engaged in the intense Bay of Biscay anti–U-boat campaign (Derange/Musketry/Seaslug) and by American "jeep" carriers, mostly as a result of ill-advised personal orders from Karl Dönitz for all U-boats to remain surfaced and fight back if detected and attacked by aircraft.

BOAT	TYPE	SAILED	SUNK/ABORT	ENIGMA HELP[2]	AGENCY
U-463	XIV	5/8	Sunk 5/15	No	RAF aircraft
U-118	XB	5/25	Sunk 6/12	Very good	*Bogue* aircraft
U-462	XIV	6/19	Abort #1	No	RAF aircraft
U-119	XB	4/25	Sunk 6/24	No	British warships
U-462	XIV	6/28	Abort #2	No	RAF aircraft
U-487	XIV	6/15	Sunk 7/13	No	*Core* aircraft
U-461	XIV	7/22	Abort #1	No	RAF aircraft
U-459	XIV	7/22	Sunk 7/24	No	RAF aircraft
U-461	XIV	7/27	Sunk 7/30	No	RAAF aircraft
U-462	XIV	7/27	Sunk 7/30	No	RAF aircraft
U-489	XIV	7/22	Sunk 8/4	No	RCAF aircraft
U-117	XB	7/22	Sunk 8/7	Good	*Card* aircraft

Totals: 9 XIV or XB sunk[3] (6 by Commonwealth forces, 3 by U.S. "jeep" carrier aircraft)

1. Surviving: the XB *U-220;* the XIVs *U-460* and *U-488.*

2. Extracted from SRH 368, RG 457, NARA. This 1952 study appears to contradict statements in the earlier SRH 008 and SRH 009 to the effect that signals intelligence played a role in the destruction of eight of sixteen refuelers between May 1943 and July 1944.

3. In addition, the XIV *U-490* accidentally sank on July 15, 1943, during Baltic workup. Salvaged and repaired, she reached the Atlantic force in May 1944, but was sunk on June 11, 1944, by ships and aircraft of the American "jeep" carrier *Croatan* hunter-killer group.

partment was visible. There were no survivors. The Admiralty awarded Wood a British DFC. The U.S. Navy gave him an Air Medal.

• The new IXD2 *U-200,* a U-cruiser assigned to a special mission, commanded by Heinrich Schonder, age thirty-two, who had won a *Ritterkreuz* while commanding the VII *U-77* in the Mediterranean. After embarking a small contingent of "coastal troops" (*Küstentruppe*)* of the Brandenburg Division, the *U-200*

* These troops were bound for South Africa to carry out a harebrained scheme to incite Boers against the British.

sailed from Kiel on June 12. Thirteen days out, as she was entering the Atlantic, a B-24 of the Iceland-based British Squadron 120, piloted by the Australian A. W. Fraser, sank her with the loss of all hands.

• The new VII *U-449,* commanded by Hermann Otto, age twenty-nine. On June 14, a B-24 of British Squadron 120, piloted by Samuel E. Esler, which was escorting Outbound North (Slow) 10, inflicted "slight damage" to the boat. When Otto reported that he urgently required a doctor to tend his wounded, U-boat Control directed the veteran VII *U-592,* commanded by Carl Borm, age thirty-two, which, as related, had sailed from France in the last days of May with a doctor, to close *U-449*'s position at maximum speed. On the chance that this meeting might fail, Control ordered Otto in *U-449* to abort to France at maximum speed and to join two other boats inbound to France, including the big Type XB minelayer *U-119,* commanded by Horst-Tessen von Kameke, age twenty-seven, who was returning from a mine-laying mission off Halifax and also had a doctor on board. The *U-119* had just given the new tanker *U-488,* commanded by Erwin Bartke, all possible spare fuel and Otto in *U-449* found *U-119* before *U-592* found him. Otto obtained the necessary medical assistance from *U-119,* then commenced a crossing of Biscay in company with her.

As part of the saturation ASW campaign in the Bay of Biscay, the Admiralty had assigned Johnny Walker's Support Group 2 to patrol the western edge of the Bay of Biscay, in cooperation with Coastal Command aircraft. Early on the morning of June 24, Walker in the sloop *Starling* got sonar contacts on *U-119,* while some other ships of the group got sonar contacts on *U-449.* Walker immediately attacked *U-119,* dropping ten depth charges that brought the U-boat to the surface with "dramatic suddenness."

All warships that could bring guns to bear opened fire, but after one friendly shell hit *Starling* in the bow, Walker ordered the others to cease fire while he rammed. He smashed into von Kameke's *U-119* solidly, riding up over her forward deck and capsizing her. The impact bent *Starling*'s bow 30 degrees off kilter, wiped off the sonar dome, and flooded the forward ammo magazine. For added insurance, *Starling* and the sloop *Woodpecker* each fired another salvo of depth charges. For proof of a kill, *Starling*'s whaleboat collected "locker doors and other floating wreckage marked in German, a burst tin of coffee and some walnuts." There were no survivors of *U-119.*

Thereafter four sloops of this group, *Kite, Wild Goose, Woodpecker,* and *Wren,* ganged up on Otto in *U-449.* Exchanging commands with D.E.G. (Dickie) Wemyss in *Wild Goose,* Walker led these four warships in renewed attacks. They hunted and depth-charged *U-449* for six hours before wreckage and oil rose to the surface, giving proof of a kill. There were no survivors of *U-449* either.

Having sunk two confirmed U-boats in one day, Walker's group followed the damaged *Starling* into Plymouth, where there was a stack of congratulatory letters from First Sea Lord Pound, Max Horton at Western Approaches, and others down the chain of command. For his part, Walker—undisputed king of the U-boat killers—sharply criticized the lack of cooperation the Coastal Command aircraft had shown his ships.

• The new VII *U-420,* commanded by Hans-Jürgen Reese, age twenty-five. On July 3, one of the newly acquired, Newfoundland-based B-24s of Canadian Squadron 10 escorting Slow Convoy 135* found *U-420* on the surface. In three low-level attacks, the pilot, R. R. Stevenson, dropped his entire load of ten depth charges close to *U-420.* The machine-gun fire and depth charges in these attacks killed two Germans, badly wounded a third, and savaged the boat, but Reese dived and escaped. Upon receipt of his SOS, U-boat Control directed three inbound VIIs that had sailed to the North Atlantic in late May to assist *U-420: U-271,* commanded by Kurt Barleben, age thirty-four; *U-669,* commanded by Kurt Köhl, age thirty-one; and Carl Borm in *U-592,* who still had the doctor on board. Although a British submarine fired six torpedoes at *U-592,* all missed and the four boats reached France from July 14 to July 16.

• The new IXC40 *U-194,* commanded by Hermann Hesse, age thirty-four. She was assigned to plant weather balloons in the Atlantic before proceeding to antiship operations near the Azores. On June 24, a veteran Iceland-based Catalina of U.S. Navy Squadron VP 84, piloted by J. W. Beach, spotted *U-194* on the surface. Beach attacked immediately into flak, but his depth charges failed to release. In a second run, the aircrew dropped two depth charges manually. One fell wide, one fell close. Nothing further was heard from *U-194.*

This was the fourth attack on a U-boat in which Beach had participated in one capacity or another. The Navy awarded the Air Medal to him and to his copilot, E. T. Allen, who was usually a first pilot and who had also participated in four attacks on U-boats. The Admiralty awarded both men the DFC.

• The new IXC40 *U-536,* commanded by Rolf Schauenburg, age thirty. Owing to the loss or aborts of U-tankers, U-boat Control was compelled to assign *U-536* to a provisional refueling role, along with two other new IXC40s that had sailed from Kiel in late May: the *U-170,* commanded by Günther Pfeffer, age twenty-eight, and *U-535,* commanded by Helmut Ellmenreich, age twenty-nine.

The skippers of these three new IXC40s were directed to abort war patrols and to give all possible fuel to Erwin Bartke's new Type XIV tanker *U-488.* This added fuel enabled Bartke to refuel ten more VIIs near the Azores.

After giving *U-488* as much fuel as they could, the three new IXC40s set off for France in company. While they were crossing the Bay of Biscay on July 5 with flak guns manned, a B-24 of British Squadron 53, piloted by the New Zealander W. Anderson on Musketry/Seaslug patrol, found and attacked all three boats. On the plane's first attach run, the boats put up a wall of flak, dodged wildly, and escaped undamaged. On the second attack in the face of more heavy flak, the depth charges failed to release, but the plane machine-gunned Schauenburg's *U-536.* On the third run, all three boats dived and Anderson dropped eight shallow-set depth charges on Ellmenreich's *U-535,* which sank with the loss of all hands. Anderson nursed the badly damaged B-24 back to base.

• • •

* Slow Convoy 135 was "massively escorted" by the RCAF. Her surface escort included the *Biter* support group and the first British MAC ship, the 8,200-ton *Empire MacAlpine,* with four Swordfish, which came across to Canada with convoy Outbound North (Slow) 9.

Partly as a result of the new orders to stay on the surface and fight enemy aircraft with flak guns, the boats sailing from France in June into the Bay of Biscay also incurred heavy losses and battle damage. Some others were crippled with mechanical problems. The outbound boats also sailed in small groups where possible, in order to increase flak firepower. Four newly sailed boats, including, as related, the veteran VII *U-135,* which joined group *Trutz,* were sunk and eight were forced to abort. Less *U-135,* these eleven boats were:

• A Type XIV ("Milk Cow") tanker, *U-462,* commanded by Bruno Vowe, age thirty-eight, which sailed from Bordeaux on June 19. When she was three days out, four twin-engine Mosquitos of British Squadrons 151 and 456 on anti–JU-88 patrol attacked her, killing one flak gunner and wounding four. Compelled to abort, Vowe returned to Bordeaux on June 23. The slight structural damage to *U-462* was quickly repaired and Vowe resailed on June 28. In a near replication of her prior aborted patrol, *U-462* again incurred damage from an aircraft that forced the tanker to return to Bordeaux on July 6. This plane was a B-24 of British Squadron 224, piloted by E.J.J. Spiller. The U-tanker did not resail until late July, another serious setback to U-boat operations that forced Control to divert more Type IXs to refueling roles.

• The veteran VII *U-564,* made famous by Reinhard Suhren, which sailed from Bordeaux on June 9 on her third patrol under command of Hans Fiedler, age twenty-eight, who had yet to sink a ship. In keeping with the new policy, Fiedler linked up with four other boats for the trip across the Bay of Biscay. On the evening of June 13, a Sunderland of British Squadron 228, piloted by Leonard Bertrand Lee, found the group and attacked *U-564* with depth charges. The group shot back en masse and brought down the plane with the loss of all hands, but *U-564* was severely damaged. U-boat Control directed another boat of the group, the IXC40 *U-185,* commanded by August Maus, age twenty-eight, to escort *U-564* to a port on the north coast of Spain where the boat could make repairs.

On the next morning, June 14, one of nine Whitleys of OTU 10 on patrol spotted the two U-boats. The pilot and copilot, Australians Arthur J. Benson and Robert L. Rennick, shadowed and radioed for reinforcements, to no avail. After two long hours, Benson attacked the two boats, concentrating his depth charges on the damaged *U-564,* which sank. But Maus in *U-185* had riddled the Whitley with flak and it had to ditch. Maus rescued Fiedler and seventeen other Germans from *U-564;* twenty-eight other crew died in the sinking. Maus transferred the survivors to the German destroyer *Z-24,* then continued his outward voyage to the Americas. Fiedler returned to Germany to commission a new VII. A French fishing trawler, *Jazz Band,* rescued the five Allied airmen of the Whitley and landed them in France, where they were captured.

• The veteran IXC *U-68,* commanded by Albert Lauzemis, age twenty-five, which sailed from Lorient on June 12 with two other IXs, *U-155* and *U-159.* On June 14 a flight of four Coastal Command Mosquito aircraft, three from Polish Squadron 307 and one from British Squadron 410, found the three boats. Fire from a Mosquito, piloted by Stanislaw Szablowski, killed one man and wounded four others on *U-68:* Lauzemis, the second watch officer, the quartermaster, and a seaman. Hit in the jaw and unable to carry on, Lauzemis aborted to Lorient, where he was hospitalized but retained command of *U-68*.

• The IXC *U-155*, commanded by *Ritterkreuz* holder Adolf-Cornelius Piening, age thirty-two, which sailed from Lorient with *U-68* on June 12. Also hit by Szablowski's fire, five men on *U-155* incurred serious wounds. As a result, Piening aborted and returned to Lorient in company with *U-68*. Upon completion of repairs and after obtaining crew replacements, Piening resailed for the Americas on June 30. However, owing to the acute U-tanker shortage, U-boat Control directed *U-155* to cancel the voyage to the Americas and to replenish several other boats.*

• The VII *U-338*, commanded by Manfred Kinzel, age twenty-eight, which sailed from Bordeaux on June 15 on his second patrol. On the first, from Kiel, Kinzel had shot down an attacking Halifax and captured one survivor. This time a B-17 of British Squadron 206, piloted by Leslie G. Clark on Musketry patrol, attacked *U-338* with seven depth charges on June 17. The attack killed one man and wounded three, and severely damaged the boat. Kinzel aborted and reached St. Nazaire on June 22. He did not sail again until late August. Earlier, pilot Les Clark and five of this aircrew had sunk *U-384* and had been erroneously credited with sinking *U-337*.

• The veteran IXC *U-518*, commanded by Friedrich-Wilhelm Wissmann, age twenty-seven, which sailed from Lorient on June 24 for the Americas. Four days later, on June 27, a Sunderland of British Squadron 201 on Seaslug patrol, piloted by the New Zealander Brian E. H. Layne, hit her, inflicting "heavy" damage and forcing Wissmann to abort. He put about for France but on June 30, a Sunderland of Australian Squadron 10, piloted by H. W. Skinner, hit the *U-518* again. She finally arrived in Bordeaux on July 2, in company with Werner Musenberg in the defective IXD1 U-cruiser *U-180* (which, as related, was carrying some Japanese officers and a cargo of gold) and Kurt Lange in the IXC40 *U-530*, a provisional refueler. After repairs, Wissmann resailed *U-518* in August.

• The VII *U-270*, commanded by Paul-Friedrich Otto, age twenty-six, which sailed from St. Nazaire on June 26 for a mission off the Iberian Peninsula with four other newly sailed VIIs. Owing to "damage to the oil-pressure leads," she was forced to abort. Having been out only seven days, she returned to St. Nazaire on July 2 and did not sail again until September.

• The VII *U-386*, which sailed from St. Nazaire on June 29, commanded by a new skipper, Fritz Albrecht, age twenty-three, who came from a year of service on the IX *U-43*. For reasons that are not noted in the war diary of U-boat Control, Albrecht aborted the patrol and returned to St. Nazaire on July 8, after a voyage of merely ten days.

• The veteran, battle-scarred IXC *U-505*, still commanded by twenty-four-year-old Peter Zschech, which had been undergoing battle-damage repairs and

* Because of a lack of suitable defensive armor, Mosquito pilots were not to attack U-boats. Another Polish pilot also attacked the U-boats but his guns jammed. Damaged by flak, Szablowski limped five hundred miles back to base and crash-landed. He survived but was killed in action in 1944.

modifications for a full six months. She sailed from Lorient on June 30, but, it was discovered, she was still not yet combat-ready and had to return immediately to Lorient.

In summary, of the forty-eight U-boats that sailed in June from Germany, Norway, and France, nineteen failed to carry out missions. Including *U-135* (with *Trutz*), nine were sunk, eight aborted, and two, *U-155* (which aborted but resailed) and *U-536*, carried out provisional refueling missions. All too many boats were knocked out as a result of the order to cross the Bay of Biscay in groups and remain on the surface and fight back if attacked by enemy aircraft.

June Patrols to Distant Waters

Of the boats that sailed in June, U-boat Control sent thirty-two to the Americas or the Freetown area, where Allied ASW measures were believed to be less threatening. Twenty-three sailed for the Americas. As related, three IXs did not get far: Piening in the *U-155*, who aborted, resailed, and was diverted to be a provisional tanker; Wissmann in the *U-518*, who was forced to abort with battle damage; and Zschech in *U-505*, who aborted on the second day with mechanical defects. These deletions reduced the foray to the Americas to twenty boats: seventeen VIIs and three IXs. Thirteen of these patrolled in the Caribbean or its approaches and seven went to Brazilian waters.

All seventeen of the VIIs going to American waters refueled on the outbound leg from the XIV U-tankers *U-487* and *U-488* or a provisional tanker, the IXC40 *U-530*. The plan was to refuel these seventeen VIIs a second time on the homebound leg. Even so, Dönitz issued explicit instructions that all boats were "duty bound" to conserve fuel for the operational areas. Hence the outbound VIIs ran on one diesel engine, making good only about 6 knots, a tedious, slow voyage in the nearly unbearable June and July heat of the southern waters.

Although the flow of naval Enigma decrypts was irregular and thin in June and July, the submarine tracking rooms in London, Washington, and Ottawa, relying on all available sources, were able to give timely warning of this large U-boat foray to the Americas. Hence Allied DF stations and ASW forces, air squadrons in particular, in Caribbean and South American waters were on red alert. As a consequence they were able to sink half of the twenty boats in American waters, a terrible slaughter.

The thirteen boats assigned to the Caribbean or its approaches consisted of one IXC, the *U-159*, commanded by a new skipper, Heinz Beckmann, who celebrated his thirtieth birthday en route, and twelve VIIs.

All U.S. ASW aircraft patrolling the Caribbean Sea came under control of Fleet Air Wing (Fairwing) 11. Commanded by Adrian O. Rule, its headquarters was in San Juan, Puerto Rico, adjacent to that of Admiral John H. Hoover, commander of the Caribbean Sea Frontier. Aircraft of Fairwing 11 also patrolled from

Trinidad southward to a line near the Amazon River, where the aircraft of the newly established Fairwing 16, headquartered at Recife, took over.*

Beckmann in *U-159* was to patrol the Panama Canal area, but he did not get there. He entered the Caribbean via the Anegada Passage. On July 28, while southeast of Haiti, a Mariner of U.S. Navy Squadron VP 32, piloted by D. C. Pinholster, caught *U-159* on the surface. Pinholster dropped his depth charges from wavetop level, and the *U-159* sank with the loss of all hands. U-boat Control had no clue to her loss, which the Navy incorrectly credited to another Mariner of VP 32, piloted by Robert C. Mayo.

Seven VIIs patrolled "inside" the Caribbean.

The VII *U-759,* commanded by Rudolf Friedrich, who celebrated his twenty-ninth birthday en route, entered via the Mona Passage on June 29. From a position south of the Windward Passage, he patrolled the Key West–Trinidad convoy route. On June 30 he imprudently sank a sailing vessel with his deck gun, but fortunately for *U-759* this victim was unable to alert Allied forces. On July 5, Friedrich sank the 3,500-ton American freighter *Maltran* from a small convoy. Two days later he found convoy TAG 70† (eight freighters, six escorts) from which he sank the 9,300-ton Dutch cargo vessel *Peolau Roebiah.* An escort, the American four-stack destroyer *Tattnall,* counterattacked *U-759,* but Friedrich evaded and slipped away. A Navy scout plane found him again on July 8 and dropped depth charges and summoned surface ships, but in a seven-hour cat-and-mouse game, Friedrich eluded these warships as well.

Friedrich reported this long chase to U-boat Control on July 10, adding "no casualties." It was to be the last communication from *U-759.* According to a reassessment by Alex Niestlé, in the early hours of July 15, another Mariner of Navy Squadron VP 32, piloted by Robert C. Mayo, which was escorting yet another convoy, TAG 74, found *U-759* on the surface. Mayo's depth charges sent *U-759* to the bottom with the loss of all hands. Friedrich was one of only two VIIs of this foray to sink ships inside the Caribbean. His total of two for 12,800 tons and a sailing vessel made him the top scorer.

The *U-359,* commanded by Heinz Förster, age thirty-four, who with the *U-466* had repelled an aircraft in Biscay and may have shot it down, patrolled inside the Caribbean south of the island of Hispaniola. On July 26, yet another Mariner of Navy Squadron VP 32, piloted by Ralph W. Rawson, found *U-359* and attacked through heavy flak, dropping four depth charges.

When Rawson returned to Puerto Rico, authorities merely credited him with "probable damage" to a U-boat. But in fact, *U-359* did not survive this attack. She was the third U-boat to be sunk within two weeks by the unsatisfactory PBM-3 Mariners of Navy Squadron VP 32, a record not exceeded by any other land-based ASW squadron in the war and a tribute to the courage of the aircrews.

---

* There were about twenty-five Army Air Forces and Navy ASW squadrons composed of B-18s, B-25s, Catalinas, Mariners, Hudsons, Venturas, and soon in the Caribbean and along the "bauxite route" to Brazil. In his *The U-boat War in the Caribbean* (1994), Gaylord T. M. Kelshall provides many details of the air order of battle and activity.

† TAG convoys: Trinidad, Aruba, Guantánamo Bay.

On the night before she sailed from France, the *U-615,* commanded by Ralph Kapitzky, who was to celebrate his twenty-seventh birthday en route, took aboard secret cargo and received special orders. The secret cargo was alleged to be a new ship-detection device, *Nachtfernrohr* (Night Telescope), which only Kapitzky was permitted to remove from its locked box. Having gained a reputation for excellent convoy shadowing, his orders were to lie south of the Windward Passage and, presumably, to find and track convoys for other boats, with the help of the secret telescope. He was not to attack ships unless the "circumstances were entirely favorable."

Kapitzky sailed from Brest on June 12 and crossed the Bay of Biscay with five other boats. Allied aircraft attacked the group on June 14. One plane hit Kapitzky's *U-615,* killing one of his 20mm gunners. In return, he claimed he shot down a plane, but the kill was also claimed by Bernhard Zurmühlen in the outbound *U-600.* Kapitzky (and six other VIIs sailing to American waters) refueled on June 28 from the Type XIV ("Milk Cow") U-tanker, Erwin Bartke's *U-488.*

Kapitzky entered the Caribbean via the Anegada Passage and patrolled for many days and nights carrying out his secret orders, apparently to no purpose. Finally released from this assignment, he cruised southwest to the islands of Curaçao and Aruba. On July 12 he found and chased a "tanker" but lost it. Two and a half weeks later, on July 28, he sank with two torpedoes the 3,200-ton Dutch tanker *Rosalia,* en route from Lake Maracaibo. The sinking—and DFing of Kapitzky's report to Control—set in motion one of the most relentless U-boat hunts of the war.

An Army B-18, based at Aruba and flown by T. L. Merrill, first found and attacked *U-615* on July 29. During the ensuing week, as Kapitzky limped toward the Atlantic, Army and Navy aircraft and an ASW blimp, K-68, based at Curaçao, Trinidad, and other islands, as well as submarine chasers (SCs) and patrol craft (PCs), joined in the hunt. Kapitzky fought off the swarms of aircraft with his flak guns. He shot down a PBM-3 Mariner of U.S. Navy Squadron VP 205, piloted by A. R. Matuski, killing all eleven men aboard. His flak killed the pilot of another Mariner of Navy Squadron VP 204, John W. Dresbach, and wounded four other crew. The copilot, Oren R. Christian, nursed the wrecked plane back to base. While tracking *U-615,* the blimp K-68, piloted by Wallace A. Wydeen, ran low on fuel and had to abort. Unable to reach Trinidad, Wydeen put down on the desolate island of Blanquilla. On the following day, high winds tore K-68 from her makeshift moorings and destroyed her, but the crew survived.*

The Navy and Army aircraft carried out at least a dozen depth-charge, bomb, and strafing attacks that wrecked *U-615.* Although Kapitzky was mortally wounded, he insisted that his flak gunners keep up defensive fire in order to buy time so the crew could make repairs. Finally, on August 6–7, six Mariners, a Navy Harpoon (a souped-up Ventura), and an Army B-18 delivered the coup de grace. A new American destroyer, *Walker,* which was near Trinidad on workup, rescued

---

* Wydeen was lost while piloting another blimp, K-94, on the night of October 30, 1943. The craft inexplicably burst into flames and sank in the sea near San Juan, Puerto Rico. No survivors were ever found.

forty-three Germans. American authorities credited Venturas and Mariners of Navy Squadrons 130, 204, 205, and Army Squadron 10 with the kill. Navy pilots Crockett, Christian, and Dresbach won the DFC, the last named posthumously.

Oddly, U-boat Control directed the oldest VII with the least range to the most distant area in the Caribbean. She was the *U-84,* a Type VIIB, commanded by Horst Uphoff, age twenty-six, who had commissioned the boat in April 1941 at age twenty-four and had commanded her ever since. In two years of combat Uphoff had sunk six ships for about 30,000 tons, two of them in the Straits of Florida exactly one year earlier.

Uphoff entered the Caribbean on July 10 via the Windward Passage in company with Claus-Peter Carlsen, age twenty-three, in *U-732,* who was making his second patrol. Uphoff followed a course along the south coast of Cuba westward to the Yucatan Channel. On July 16 he claimed hits on a 6,000-ton freighter that he "left burning" but the encounter has not been confirmed in Allied records. About ten days later, while withdrawing through the Straits of Florida, he reported a single and a double miss on a 7,000-ton ship and, on July 28, the futile chase of a tanker owing to a diesel-engine failure. Low on fuel, Uphoff welcomed an order from Control to return to France, but, as shall be told, he did not make it there.

Carlsen in *U-732* first patrolled in the area immediately south of the Windward Passage and east of Jamaica. On July 12, two Navy OS2U Kingfisher scout planes attacked Carlsen, but the boat survived with only slight damage. Two weeks later on July 28, while off the eastern tip of Cuba, Cape Maisi, Carlsen found three naval repair ships escorted by three destroyers, but the destroyers thwarted an attack with a persistent depth-charge hunt.

Going north through the Windward Passage, Carlsen loitered in the Old Bahama Channel. On August 1 he came upon a prime target: the New York to Guantánamo convoy NG 376, consisting of twenty-seven merchant ships and five escorts. Carlsen boldly attacked this formation all alone on the night of August 1–2. He claimed one 7,000-ton freighter sunk, another hit, and thought he heard two other hits. One of the escorts, Navy gunboat *89* (*Brisk*), thwarted any further attacks. The sinkings and hits could not be confirmed in Allied records. After a protracted voyage home, *U-732* reached France on the last day of August.

Inbound to the Caribbean on July 8, the second oldest of the VIIs, the *U-134,* commanded by Hans-Günther Brosin, age twenty-six, was hit by a Bermuda-based aircraft of U.S. Navy Squadron VP 201 southeast of the island. The plane, piloted by John T. Hitchcock, strafed and dropped "6 to 8" depth charges but, Brosin reported, *U-134* survived. Embarked on his second patrol, Brosin hunted in the Straits of Florida near Havana. While carrying out this mission, near midnight on July 18 the radar operator on Navy blimp K-74, commanded by Nelson G. Grills, which was patrolling near two big ships, spotted *U-134.* It was against Navy doctrine for lone blimps to attack U-boats, but two weeks earlier Grills's commander had exhorted his blimp pilots to take "more aggressive" action versus U-boats in order to prove his belief that blimps were good for something besides escort, reconnaissance, and rescue.

Accordingly, Grills headed directly for *U-134* at forty-seven knots to attack with depth charges. Doubtless astonished, Brosin manned his flak guns and hurled a barrage at this huge target. The bullets punctured the balloon and lit a fire in the gondola, but onward Grills came. Before the blimp dropped into the sea with the loss of one of the eleven-man aircrew,* Brills toggled the depth-charge release. Long unused, the release failed and no charges fell; the *U-134* dived and escaped. The four-stack destroyer *Dahlgren* and the *SC 657* rescued ten survivors of the blimp.

American authorities in the Florida area closed the straits to shipping and mounted an all-out hunt for *U-134.* On the night following, July 19, a Ventura piloted by John C. Lawrence found the U-boat and dropped three depth charges that caused extensive damage to *U-134*'s forward battery. Brosin notified U-boat Control of his victory over the blimp—another submarine "first"—and of his heavy damage from the Ventura's attack. In response, Control directed *U-134* to withdraw from the strait and retreat one thousand miles to the east to effect repairs. Brosin was proceeding to that remote area, low on fuel, when he received orders to return to France at once due to the acute refueling difficulties. He did not make it either.

While outbound in the Bay of Biscay, an unidentified Leigh Light–equipped Wellington drove under the *U-634,* commanded by Eberhard Dahlhaus, age twenty-three, who had made several patrols to American waters on another boat. He was originally assigned to patrol off Aruba and Curaçao, but after refueling, the boat was diverted to hunt for convoys between Bermuda and Hispaniola. The hunt produced no sinkings and because of this long diversion, her orders to patrol Aruba and Curaçao had to be canceled. In late July, Dahlhaus entered the Caribbean via the Windward Passage to patrol just south of Hispaniola and Puerto Rico, in effect replacing *U-615,* which, as related, went on to Aruba and Curaçao—and destruction. Dahlhaus had scarcely arrived at his area when he received orders to return to France. Thus he had no opportunity to shoot at shipping in Caribbean waters. After refueling on the homebound voyage, *U-634* came to grief in the Bay of Biscay.

Thus it was that in addition to the IXC *U-159,* three of the seven Type VIIs (*U-359, U-615, U-759*) that entered the Caribbean were sunk there. As will be related, three other VIIs of this group (*U-84, U-134, U-634*) were sunk en route home. Only one of these seven VIIs, *U-732,* got back to France.

Five of the twelve VIIs assigned to the Caribbean offensive were held "outside" to patrol the area east of Trinidad and south to French Guiana on the "bauxite route."

As related, while en route to this area, one of these four boats, the *U-572,* commanded by Heinz Kummetat, age twenty-four, sank the 4,200-ton French tanker *Lot* from convoy UGS 10. After refueling, Kummetat proceeded to the Americas, where on June 29, he met Müller-Stöckheim in the homebound IXC *U-67* and gave

* He was twenty-eight-year-old bombardier Isadore Stessel of Brooklyn, New York, killed by a shark. His posthumous Purple Heart went astray in the mail. However, a story in *The Miami Herald* in 1997 alerted relatives, to whom the Navy presented the medal and other awards on May 17, 1997.

him a Metox. He then patrolled an area east of Barbados and Trinidad. On July 14 and 15, he sank by gun two British sailing vessels southeast of the latter place, the 114-ton *Harvard* and the 176-ton *Gilbert B. Walters.* Returning to an area well to the east of Trinidad, Kummetat sought enemy shipping in vain. On July 31, he reported to Control "heavy air" and that *U-572* had repelled an aircraft east of Trinidad.

About that same time, two of the other three "outside" boats that were also patrolling from Trinidad southward to French Guiana tangled with Allied aircraft: the *U-406,* commanded by Horst Dieterichs, age thirty-one, and the veteran *U-653,* commanded by Gerhard Feiler, age thirty-three. Both expended a great deal of ammo in these engagements. As a result, Dieterichs in *U-406* requested a rendezvous with Kummetat in *U-572* farther north, to take on ammo and gun grease.

The Allies learned of the proposed rendezvous from intelligence sources. On August 3, a PBM-3 Mariner of U.S. Navy Squadron VP 205, piloted by Clifford C. Cox, arrived at the rendezvous and attacked a U-boat, doubtless Kummetat in *U-572.* Apparently Cox sank *U-572* and Kummetat shot down the Mariner because neither was heard from again. Dieterichs in *U-406* reported to Control on August 5 that *U-572* had failed to keep the rendezvous. When *U-572* did not respond to repeated queries, Control presumed correctly that she was lost. Owing to the crash of the Mariner, a minor mystery remained and the details of *U-572*'s last hours will never be known. It seemed somehow fitting that the U-boat upon which Heinz Hirsacker had brought so much disgrace—and his own condemnation to death—should disappear with no final history. Cox won a posthumous DFC.

Dieterichs in *U-406* patrolled east of Trinidad for about two more weeks in vain. He then commenced a protracted voyage to France, seeing no targets worthy of a torpedo. On August 23, an unidentified aircraft found and attacked *U-406,* killing two men and wounding three, but the boat sustained only slight damage. She arrived in St. Nazaire on September 15 and did not sail again until January 1944.

A Navy B-24 and an Army Air Forces B-18 found and attacked the *U-466,* commanded by Gerhard Thäter, age twenty-six, on July 23. The next day an Army Air Forces B-24 hit *U-466* with machine-gun fire and four depth charges. This attack "badly" wounded the first watch officer and a lookout and "slightly" wounded Thäter, the second watch officer, and a warrant quartermaster, and severely damaged the boat. Upon receiving Thäter's report, U-boat Control directed him to return to France as quickly as possible and to report his location day and night so that Control might arrange a rendezvous with another U-boat that carried a doctor. Thäter reached France on August 16 without assistance, completing a fruitless and frustrating patrol of forty-nine days. The *U-466* did not sail again until late October.

Kurt Neide in the *U-415* patrolled an area east of Martinique south to Trinidad. He too had a frustrating time in the tropical heat and with ASW aircraft. He found two convoys off Trinidad. The first, located on July 24, was heavily escorted by surface ships as well as by "continuous land-based four-engine" aircraft (apparently B-24s). In spite of the heavy escort, Neide attacked the convoy, but the assault failed and prompted an intense ASW hunt. While attempting to mount a submerged attack on the second convoy on August 2, a "corvette" counterattacked with a barrage of depth charges that drove Neide off. As a result Neide sank no ships.

Like most of the other VIIs in American waters, Neide ran critically low on fuel and had to find a fuel source on the way home. Control directed him to refuel from a provisional tanker, the XB (minelayer) *U-117.* When it became evident that the latter was sunk on August 7, Control told Neide to refuel from a backup provisional tanker, the IXC40 *U-525.* Neide waited at the rendezvous for five days before he was told or realized that *U-525* had been sunk as well. On August 14, Control assigned Neide to refuel from yet another provisional U-tanker, the IXD2 U-cruiser *U-847,* and he did so on about August 24. He reached France on September 8, after a nerve-racking homeward voyage of thirty-seven days.

Feiler in *U-653* had commanded that boat for two full years. In all that time and on many patrols, he had sunk but four confirmed ships for about 12,000 tons. Suffering from "tropical fever," as were many of his crew, Feiler found no targets. While east of Trinidad on August 2, a B-24 attacked *U-653,* Feiler reported, and he shot back and hit the aircraft and escaped. Homebound, Feiler, like Neide, was to refuel from the provisional tanker *U-117,* and when she was lost, the backup provisional tanker *U-525.* When she, too, was lost, Feiler joined Neide at the refueling rendezvous with the IXD2 *U-847.* After a full two weeks in the refueling area, Feiler, like Neide, finally got enough oil to reach France on September 11. Upon arrival, Feiler went on to other duty.

These five VIIs that patrolled "outside" the Caribbean achieved almost nothing: two sailing vessels for about 300 tons sunk and probably a Mariner shot down by Kummetat in *U-572.* Aircraft of Fairwing 11 relentlessly hounded all five boats in their patrol zones, sinking *U-572* and forcing *U-466* to abort early in the patrol. The other three boats (*U-406, U-415, U-653*) sank no ships either, but like *U-466,* they managed to survive.

Altogether, one IX and twelve VIIs of the June group patrolled "inside" and "outside" the Caribbean. Five were sunk in patrol areas. Three were sunk on the way home. In return for the catastrophic loss of eight of their number, these thirteen boats sank in these distant waters two ships for 12,800 tons and three sailing vessels, plus one ship of 4,200 tons from convoy UGS 10.

U-boat Patrols to or Beyond the Equator

Seven June boats sailed to Brazilian waters: two IXC40s and five VIIs. One of the IXs and two of the VIIs were commanded by new skippers. The VIIs refueled from the XIV ("Milk Cow") tanker *U-487.* As directed, all boats cruised to Brazil on one diesel in order to husband fuel for the operating area. The equatorial heat and humidity made life unspeakably miserable on all seven boats.

The IXC40 *U-185* and the IXC *U-510* sailed early in the month and went directly to South America without refueling. Within a period of about twenty-four hours, both found convoys and sank ships.

Commanded by August Maus, age twenty-eight, the *U-185* crossed the equator and traveled about 250 miles south to an area between Fortaleza and Natal. On July 7, Maus came upon a convoy en route from Bahia to Trinidad, BT 18. It was comprised of twenty merchant ships, thinly escorted by three gunboats and a patrol craft. In a classic attack, Maus hit four American merchant ships: the 7,000-ton tanker *William Boyce Thompson,* the 6,800-ton tanker *S. B. Hunt,* and the 7,200-ton Liberty ships *James Robertson* and *Thomas Sinnickson.* Three of these ships sank or had to be sunk. The fourth, the tanker *S. B. Hunt,* limped into port and was later repaired and returned to service.

Maus then sailed farther southward to an area below Recife. On the night of July 12, a radar-equipped Catalina found *U-185* on the surface and attacked with her landing lights turned on. Maus's gunners returned fire and he claimed an aircraft kill, but according to American records the damaged aircraft limped back to its base.

The IXC *U-510* was commanded by a new skipper, Alfred Eick, age twenty-seven. Eick had made a prior patrol to American waters as first watch officer of the IXC *U-176,* which was sunk in the Straits of Florida on May 15 on her next patrol. Eick believed her skipper, Reiner Dierksen, was simply "too aggressive" and that he, Eick, would be less so and survive.

En route to northern Brazil, Eick came upon southbound convoy TJ 1 off French Guiana, near Devils Island, on July 8. En route from Trinidad to Rio de Janeiro, it was comprised of twenty merchant ships, escorted by the modern (1937) American destroyer *Somers,* four patrol craft, and a Brazilian submarine chaser. Favored by rain and clouds that obscured the moon, Eick carried out two night surface attacks. In the first, he fired three torpedoes and claimed hits on a tanker and two freighters. In the second, he claimed hits on two freighters. Allied records confirmed two sinkings (10,300-ton Norwegian tanker *B. P. Newton,* 7,000-ton American freighter *Eldena*) and damage to the freighter *Everaga,* which was towed to Trinidad. Two days later, farther offshore, Eick sank by demolition the 1,600-ton Swede *Scandinavia,* which he stopped, boarded, and deemed to be carrying contraband. Homebound, Eick was to refuel from a provisional tanker, but it was sunk and he went on to France, arriving on August 29, completing a voyage of eighty-eight days.

These attacks on two major convoys off the South American coast, northbound BT 18 and southbound TJ 1, within the space of about twenty-four hours, caused great consternation in Allied ASW headquarters in that area. Reacting to what was perceived to be a massive U-boat onslaught, Fourth Fleet commander Admiral Jonas Ingram beefed up the air and surface escorts of the convoys in those waters and greatly increased aircraft hunter-killer patrols.

The result was that the five Type VIIs of the foray to Brazil had a ghastly time. In addition to the nearly unbearable tropical heat and constant worry about fuel replenishment, the VIIs were almost continuously harassed by aircraft. One skipper tersely described the intense hunter-killer activity to Control as: "Air like Biscay, day and night."

Only one of these VIIs sank a ship. She was the veteran *U-590,* with a new skipper, Werner Krüer, age twenty-eight. In a daring attack near the mouth of the Amazon River on July 4, Krüer got the 5,300-ton Brazilian freighter *Pelotaslóide,* which was escorted by two Brazilian sub chasers. When Krüer reported this sinking, it prompted a saturation U-boat search by Catalinas of U.S. Navy Squadron VP 94, based at Amapá, an airstrip just north of the mouth of the Amazon River.

One of the Catalinas found and attacked *U-590* on July 9. Krüer's 20mm gunners returned fire and hit the cockpit of the aircraft, killing the pilot, Frank F. Hare, and wounding the radioman. The copilot, J. P. Phelps, attempted a second attack but was repelled and aborted to Belém. Responding to this alert, another Catalina of Navy Squadron VP 94, piloted by Stanley E. Auslander, attacked *U-590* and sank her with a salvo of six depth charges. There were no survivors. The Navy awarded pilots Hare and Auslander DFCs, Hare's posthumously.

In a period of about ten days, Allied air patrols sank three more VIIs of the Brazil foray and so severely damaged another that it was compelled to abort.

- On July 19, an Army Air Forces B-24 of Squadron 35, based at Zandery Field, Dutch Guiana (Surinam), found the *U-662,* commanded by Heinz-Eberhard Müller, age twenty-seven. The aircraft attacked, dropping four depth charges, but they fell wide and Müller's 20mm gunners repelled a second attack, causing the damaged plane to break off and limp back to base. Later that day, an Army Air Forces B-18 based in French Guinea attacked *U-662,* but its five depth charges also fell wide. Müller claimed he shot down this plane but he was wrong; she limped home. The next day, July 20, a Catalina of Navy Squadron VP 94 attacked *U-662* and it, too, failed to achieve a kill, but the pilot circled out of flak range and called in other forces. These, too, also failed, but on July 21, another Catalina of Squadron VP 94, piloted by R. H. Howland, hit *U-662* with machine-gun fire and depth charges. Howland's gunfire killed the entire bridge watch and the depth charges wrecked the boat.

Müller ran to the bridge to take over the flak guns. Seconds later the depth charges exploded. The force of the blasts severely wounded Müller and threw him overboard, along with four other men, one of whom soon died. The U-boat appeared to have broken in half; no other men got out. Müller and the three other survivors climbed into one of the two life rafts that the Catalina had dropped and pulled the other raft atop them. Circled by sharks, the four men drifted for sixteen days until they were found by a B-24 and the former luxury yacht *Siren,* a U.S. Navy vessel that was escorting convoy TJ 4. One of the four Germans died on board *Siren,* leaving only Müller and two other survivors.*

In response to an earlier urgent request from Müller for ammo replenishment and unaware of the loss of *U-662,* Control directed him to rendezvous with a provisional refueler, the IXC *U-516,* in mid-Atlantic. On July 31, when *U-516* reported no sign of *U-662* at the meeting place, Control presumed correctly that she was lost.

---

* Still recovering from his wounds and no longer capable of combat, the disabled Müller was repatriated to Germany in March 1944. After further hospitalization, he joined the staff of U-boat Control to serve as "liaison officer for German prisoners of war."

• Off Natal on July 22, pilot Renfro Turner, Jr., in a B-24 of Navy Squadron VB 107, found the *U-598,* commanded by Gottfried Holtorf, age thirty-one. Turner attacked, dropping six depth charges. His alarm brought two other B-24s of VB 107 from Natal. One of these, piloted by John T. Burton, attacked the U-boat but owing to a "personnel error," the depth charges failed to drop. After that, Renfro Turner made a second attack, dropping his remaining three depth charges. These "appeared to straddle the conning tower" as the U-boat dived.

Turner returned to Natal, but Burton and the other B-24 established a U-boat "hold down," circling the area. Shortly after midnight on July 23, yet another B-24 of VB 107, piloted by Charles A. Baldwin, took off from Natal. At dawn, Baldwin spotted *U-598* and attacked, inflicting such damage that the U-boat could not dive. About two hours later, two more B-24s of VB 107, piloted by Goree E. Waugh and William R. Ford (who had earlier sunk *U-164*), attacked jointly at very low altitude. During his attack, Waugh, possibly disabled by the blast of his own depth charges, crashed into the sea. All twelve aircrew were lost. Waugh and his copilot, Robert S. Swan, won posthumous DFCs; the other ten men, Air Medals. Ford in the second plane hit the *U-598* with a salvo of depth charges and sank her.

The German survivors launched two life rafts, and six or seven men got into each. One raft capsized, but two of the men in it survived, the first watch officer, Heinrich Luschin, age twenty-three, and one engine-room petty officer. After about thirteen hours in the water, another aircraft saw the survivors and dropped yet another inflatable raft. Shortly thereafter, the Navy tug *Seneca,* out searching for survivors, rescued the two Germans. The other raft drifted away and was never seen again. Pilot Ford was awarded a DFC.

• When *U-598* was sunk on July 23, the veteran *U-591* was close by. The latter was commanded by a new skipper, Reimar Ziesmer, age twenty-five, replacing Hans-Jürgen Zetzsche, who had been wounded on the boat's prior patrol. Ziesmer became available when, as related, his new VII, *U-236,* was wrecked at the building yard in Kiel in an Allied air raid on May 14. The Navy B-24 of Squadron VB 107 that sank *U-598* twice attacked Ziesmer in *U-591,* but each time, rather than shoot it out, he dived and escaped.

One week later, on July 30, when Ziesmer was farther south off Recife, Navy pilot Walter C. Young, flying a Ventura of the newly arrived Navy Squadron VB 127, found the boat and attacked. In a straight-in run, Young caught *U-591* unalert and dropped six depth charges. Too late, Ziesmer ordered the flak guns manned. The depth charges holed *U-591* in several places, and she began to sink almost immediately. Ziesmer and twenty-seven other Germans got out of the boat and climbed into life rafts that Young dropped to them. One of the escorts of convoy TJ 2, en route from Trinidad to Rio de Janeiro, which Young had been escorting, rescued the twenty-eight Germans. Apart from Ziesmer, the survivors included two officers, a warrant quartermaster, and a doctor, Günther Feigs.

• That same day, July 30, another Ventura of another newly arrived Navy squadron, VB 129, was also escorting convoy TJ 2. The pilot, Thomas D. Davies, found the veteran but unalert *U-604,* commanded by Horst Höltring, age thirty, about one hundred miles east of Maceió. Davies attacked with machine guns and four depth charges, which fell very close. The machine-gun fire mortally wounded the first watch officer and a lookout, and wounded Höltring in his left shoulder and chest. The depth charges wrecked *U-604* so badly that there was no chance of getting her back to France. Pilot Davies returned to base claiming a kill. That was close to the truth, but, in fact, *U-604*'s crew managed to limp away from the scene submerged and later send out a desperate SOS.

At that time, August Maus in the IXC40 *U-185* and Carl Emmermann in the IXC *U-172* were the only U-boats left in Brazilian waters. U-boat Control therefore directed Maus and Emmermann to meet *U-604* as far off the coast as the latter could get by August 3, remove the crew, and scuttle the boat. En route to the rendezvous on August 1, Maus in *U-185* came upon the same convoy, TJ 2, and sank the impressive 8,200-ton Brazilian freighter *Bagé*.

Allied intelligence decrypted and DFed the radio chatter concerning the *U-604* rendezvous and realized that she had not been sunk after all. Therefore American ASW forces remounted a relentless hunt for her. On August 3, the commander of VB 107, Bertram J. Prueher, found *U-604,* gave the alarm, and attacked with depth charges, but again the U-boat dived to safety. While another Navy B-24 of VB 107 circled the area holding *U-604* down, Prueher refueled and rearmed his plane and returned and found August Maus in *U-185* nearby. Flying into flak, Prueher attacked Maus with four depth charges and machine-gun fire that seriously wounded a man on *U-185.* Maus escaped; Prueher returned to base with one engine shot out and other flak damage. Two modern destroyers, *Moffett* (1936) and *Jouett* (1939), raced out to polish off *U-604. Moffett,* commanded by Gilbert H. Richards, Jr., got a sonar contact and carried out two depth-charge attacks, but Höltring fooled Richards and a cooperating Navy B-24 with an *Aphrodite* radar decoy and got away yet again.

U-boat Control set up a new rendezvous for *U-604, U-172,* and *U-185* farther east on August 11. On the way there, Maus in *U-185* met and sank yet another ship, the 7,200-ton British Liberty ship *Fort Halkett.* This victory raised Maus's bag for this patrol to an impressive five confirmed ships sunk for 36,781 tons, plus damage to the American tanker *S. B. Hunt.*

Per plan, the crippled *U-604,* the *U-172,* and the *U-185* met on the morning of August 11, about nine hundred miles due east of Natal. Maus in *U-185* got there first and took all the fuel oil, ammo, and provisions from the doomed *U-604.* Since he was to embark half the crew of *U-604* when Emmermann arrived, he also took extra mattresses from her. As final arrangements were being set in motion to scuttle the *U-604,* a four-engine, land-based bomber suddenly appeared out of the overcast.

This was a B-24 of the U.S. Navy's Natal-based VB 107, piloted by the squadron commander, Bertram Prueher, who had attacked *U-604* on August 3. The beneficiary of naval Enigma decrypts and/or DFing that disclosed the new rendezvous, Prueher had flown the B-24 almost to the limit of its effective combat range. He made two low-level runs at the cluster of U-boats, dropping four depth charges, all of which fell wide. Emmermann in *U-172* dived; Maus in *U-185* stayed on the surface and shot back. Some of his flak hit Prueher's B-24, which crashed into the sea, killing all ten on board.

The loss of Prueher and his aircrew came as a harsh blow to VB 107. For the next three weeks the second in command, Renfro Turner, Jr., who replaced Prueher, mounted an intense search for possible survivors, sending out three to six B-24s per day. Later, in a remarkable gesture of respect for this daring but fatal mission, the commander of Fleet Air Wing 16, Rossmore Lyon, awarded posthumous DFCs to all ten airmen (four officers and six enlisted men).*

After the B-24 attack, Höltring and the surviving crewmen of *U-604* scuttled their wrecked boat and transferred to *U-185* as planned. Five days later, on August 16, *U-172* and *U-185* met and, per the original plan, Emmermann took on board about half (twenty-three) of the crew of *U-604*. Höltring and the other half of the crew remained on *U-185*. In response to questions about why he had earlier dived during the B-24 attack and abruptly left the scene, Emmermann replied that the plane had strafed *U-172,* killing one man and injuring another, that his flak guns were "out of order," and that he was unable to fight back and had to submerge. Emmermann and Maus continued homeward in search of a provisional refueler.

In all, the foray to American waters by the twenty boats that sailed in June produced thirteen confirmed sinkings for about 81,000 tons plus three sailing vessels. Credited with over a third of the ships (five) for almost half the tonnage (36,800), Maus in *U-185,* who had patrolled Brazilian waters, was the clear leader. Fourteen of the twenty boats that reached American waters sank no ships, a devastating failure. Of the twenty boats, ten (50 percent) were sunk in American waters. Most of the ten returning boats had great difficulty obtaining sufficient fuel to get home and four more were to be sunk before reaching France. Hence the outcome of this twenty-boat foray to American waters was an appalling fourteen boats and seven hundred men lost to sink thirteen Allied ships.

At this same time, U-boat Control sailed eleven June boats to the Freetown area and beyond to the Indian Ocean. Nine boats patrolled the Freetown area. Two were ordered to the Indian Ocean: the new IXD2 U-cruiser *U-200,* which, as related, was sunk two weeks out from Kiel as she entered the Atlantic; and the IXC40 *U-188,* which was to join a new foray to Cape Town and the Indian Ocean, group *Monsun.*

The nine boats that patrolled the Freetown area included one Type IXC, *U-508,* and eight Type VIIs. Commanded by Georg Staats, age twenty-seven, who had made a pioneering patrol to the Gulf of Mexico in May 1942, *U-508* went beyond Freetown to the Gulf of Guinea, between Accra, Ghana, and Lagos, Nigeria. Staats sank two ships on July 7: the 8,400-ton French *De la Salle* and the 5,300-ton British *Manchester Citizen.* These two sinkings earned Staats a *Ritterkreuz.*† He sank one other large ship in this area on July 18, the 7,400-ton British *Incomati.* After refueling from the IXD2 U-cruiser *U-847,* serving as a provisional tanker, Staats returned to France on September 14.

---

* At the time, Prueher's attack on *U-604* was assessed as a "definite kill."

† At the time of the award, his confirmed score was thirteen ships for 66,700 tons.

The eight VIIs included Claus von Trotha, age twenty-nine, in *U-306* and *Ritterkreuz* holder Peter Cremer, age thirty-two, returning to his old command, *U-333,* after a stint on the staff of U-boat Control while he recovered from battle wounds.

Ordered to patrol American waters, von Trotha in *U-306* apparently had made a mistake in decoding the Enigma message assigning his area. Therefore, on July 16, entirely unknown to Control, he was in the waters off Dakar, where he *thought* he should be. That day he encountered a southbound convoy and chased it for two days toward Freetown. In a series of lone attacks in the face of "heavy" land-based air escort, he claimed he sank four ships for 27,000 tons and that he probably sank another of 5,000 tons. Allied records showed that one British cargo ship, the 5,900-ton *Kaipara,* was damaged, but no sinkings could be confirmed.

Peter Cremer in the VII *U-333* had a miserable patrol. Apart from the heat, he had not yet fully recovered from his wounds. "In volunteering for service again, I had taken on too much," he wrote in his memoir. "I was in no way as fit as I had tried to persuade myself and often, when I had to leave the boat for the bridge, I hardly had the strength to dress without help."

Besides that, the battle-ravaged *U-333* developed numerous mechanical problems. The most serious was the breakdown of both air compressors, the main Junkers and the backup. At about the same time, Kurt Baberg, age twenty-six, in the VII *U-618,* who had sunk the 5,200-ton British freighter *Empire Kohinoor* off Freetown, also had compressor problems. At the suggestion of U-boat Control, both boats hauled away from the coast and rendezvoused to exchange various spare parts. The exchanges and cannibalizations produced sufficient parts for both Cremer and Baberg to reconstruct one main air compressor and to stay on patrol in the Freetown area. Cremer's compressor was jury-rigged and was thus a source of "constant anxiety," not to be relieved until he obtained more spare parts and gear from the new skipper of the veteran *U-571,* Gustav Lüssow, age twenty-five, and Bernhard Zurmühlen, age thirty-four, in *U-600.*

Perhaps encouraged by the successes of Staats in the IXC *U-508,* U-boat Control concentrated the eight VIIs in the Gulf of Guinea to intercept Allied convoys. None had any luck. Rolf Manke, age twenty-seven, in the *U-358,* reported that his Metox was out and requested detachment from the group to conduct a lone hunt, but Control told him to stay put—and stay off the air. Cremer in *U-333* reported a convoy off Freetown on July 25, but a "destroyer" thwarted his approach. The *U-257,* commanded by Heinz Rahe, age twenty-seven, and the *U-382,* commanded by Leopold Koch, age twenty-five, achieved nothing.

All nine boats soon turned homeward, only to encounter great difficulties in obtaining sufficient fuel to reach France. Control ordered six of the nine to refuel from the provisional tanker *U-117,* and when she was sunk, her backup, the IXC40 *U-525.* When she, too, was sunk, six boats refueled from yet another provisional tanker, the veteran IXC *U-129,* and three boats (*U-257, U-358, U-508*) refueled from the IXD2 U-cruiser *U-847.*

Inbound to France, Cremer wrote, he encountered a "strange" submarine. This turned out to be the big (2,600-ton) Japanese U-cruiser *I-8* (code-named *"Flieder"* or "Lilac"), arriving from the Far East with wolfram and other scarce cargo. She put into Brest on August 31, carrying an extra fifty submariners who were to train for and man another gift from Hitler to Tojo, the new IXC40 *U-1224* ("Marco Polo II").*

In all, the nine boats sent to Freetown and the Gulf of Guinea in June sank four ships for about 26,300 tons and damaged one for 5,900 tons, yet another disappointing foray. Staats in the IXC *U-508* sank most of the ships: three for about 21,000 tons. Remarkable for that period, no boat was lost. Whether the absence of losses was owing to the ineptitude of Allied ASW forces in that area or to excessive caution by the skippers or both remains moot. Upon return to France, Koch left *U-382* for other duty. In the last days of the war he was killed in Germany.

In aggregate, twenty-nine June boats actually reached patrol areas in distant waters of the Americas and West Africa: four Type IXs and twenty-five Type VIIs. These boats sank seventeen merchant ships for 107,300 tons and three sailing vessels, against the disastrous loss of fifteen U-boats, including the new IXD2 U-cruiser *U-200.* Three experienced skippers of IXs, Maus in *U-185,* Staats in *U-508,* and Eick in *U-510,* sank two-thirds of the total: eleven ships for about 77,000 tons. Twenty of the twenty-nine boats sank no ships; von Trotha in *U-306* damaged one. However, as intended, these twenty-nine boats tied down a very large number of Allied forces over a huge area of the Atlantic, assured that the Allies would continue convoying, provided experience in the combat zones for the fourteen crews that survived, and relieved the congestion in the five overburdened U-boat bases in France.

---

* The *I-8* left Brest on October 6 and arrived in Penang on December 5. Redesignated *RO-501,* the *U-1224* sailed from Kiel on March 30, 1944, with a Japanese crew. She was sunk on May 13 near the Cape Verde Islands by the new American destroyer escort *Francis M. Robinson,* part of the screen for the "jeep" carrier *Bogue.*

SIX

Husky

The Allied plan for Husky, the invasion of Sicily, underwent several last minute changes. The upshot was as follows. On the heels of a massive bombing campaign against Italy, American and British airborne forces would lead the assault on Sicily in the early hours of July 10 when the moon was new, or completely dark. Near dawn, the British Eighth Army (115,000 troops), commanded by Bernard Montgomery, would land on the southeast coast of the island near Syracuse. At the same time, the American Seventh Army (66,000 troops), commanded by George Patton, would land nearby on the south coast, near Gela and Scoglitti. The British and American navies would provide sea lift and escort for these amphibious assaults. Inasmuch as the Italian Navy was still capable of posing a threat,* the British would deploy powerful covering forces comprised of six battleships,

* According to the official British historian: six battleships, seven cruisers, thirty-two destroyers, forty-eight submarines, and so on. The official Italian naval historian, Marc' Antonio Bragadin, wrote that of the six battleships, the old *Cesare* had been converted to a "barracks ship"; the *Vittorio Veneto* was in dry dock for battle-damage repairs; and the old, smaller *Doria* and *Duilio* were in the yards being modernized. Hence only the first-line battleships *Littorio* and *Roma* were combat ready. Ten heavy and light cruisers were left, Bragadin wrote, but only five light cruisers were available for fleet operations. Twenty destroyers "remained afloat," but only eight to ten were available for fleet operations. Of about forty Italian submarines in the Mediterranean, Bragadin asserted, only one 1,000-ton large and eleven 600-ton mediums could be deployed for the defense of Sicily.

two fleet carriers, six cruisers, and eighteen destroyers.* In all: 2,590 Allied vessels.

Unlike Torch, the surprise Allied invasion of French Northwest Africa, the Axis high commands were expecting an invasion of Sicily. In June, the senior German commander in the Mediterranean, Albert Kesselring, had obtained authority from Hitler to send two Panzer divisions (about 30,000 men) to Sicily to reinforce Alfredo Guzzoni's uncertain Italian Army garrison. In addition, Hitler had directed the *Luftwaffe* to place the German 1st Parachute Division (based in the south of France) on standby for possible insertion into Sicily. Berlin deemed these German forces and supporting troops plus the Italians to be sufficient to defend the island, provided they took full advantage of its awesomely rugged terrain.

Although the Allied airborne operations were a deplorable fiasco, the amphibious assaults by the British Eighth Army and the American Seventh Army overwhelmed the slovenly, dispirited Italian garrison troops and Allied forces got ashore, more or less as planned. German Panzer forces counterattacked but the Allies held fast. Notwithstanding the standard inane order from Hitler forbidding retreat, the Germans gradually withdrew into a defensive enclave on the northeast shoulder of the island near Messina. Meanwhile, in accordance with a plan conceived by Admiral Dönitz on a recent visit to Rome, the senior *Kriegsmarine* officer in Italy, Friedrich Ruge (later a historian), secretly prepared to circumvent Hitler's order and evacuate all German forces from Sicily, utilizing an effective ferry service that a *Kriegsmarine* landing-craft expert, Gustav von Liebenstein, had put into place.

The Allied invasion of Sicily coincided with Hitler's last massive attempt to overwhelm the Red Army in the Ukraine (Citadel). The Germans launched that huge offensive on July 5 against what was viewed as a vulnerable Soviet salient at Kursk. In one of the decisive battles of World War II, the Red Army held, then repulsed the Germans, inflicting catastrophic losses. Rolling over the reeling Germans, Soviet forces then recaptured Orel and Kharkov. Blaming the *Wehrmacht* generals rather than admitting error for these colossal defeats, Hitler canceled all further offensive actions in that area and directed German forces to go over to the defensive. There was no longer any possibility that the Germans could conquer the Soviet Union. Henceforth the German "Eastern Front" became a titanic Soviet killing ground, draining the Third Reich of its manpower and matériel.

The fighting on Sicily also coincided with a massive Allied air attack on Hamburg, Germany (Gomorrah). Commencing on the night of July 24–25, RAF Bomber Command hit Hamburg with about three thousand sorties, including that

---

* Battleships *Howe, King George V, Nelson, Rodney, Valiant,* and *Warspite;* carriers *Indomitable* and *Formidable.* Since some of these warships came from the Home Fleet and *Tirpitz* was still in Norway, Admiral King sent seven warships to Scapa Flow for the months of June and July: two new (1942) battleships (*Alabama* and *South Dakota*) and five new (1941–42) destroyers (*Ellyson, Emmons, Fitch, Macomb,* and *Rodman*). In August the old carrier *Ranger* and the heavy cruisers *Augusta* and *Tuscaloosa* replaced the American battleships in the Home Fleet and, to distantly reinforce Home Fleet, the new American battleship *Iowa* moored in Argentia, Newfoundland, until late October.

night and the nights of July 27–28, July 29–30, and August 2–3. In all, about 2,600 RAF heavy bombers dropped about 8,300 tons of bombs. The American Eighth Air Force carried out two daylight raids on Hamburg on July 25 and July 26, deploying about 250 B-17s, of which about 150 dropped about three hundred tons of bombs.

The purpose of this saturation air attack was to destroy the numerous U-boat building yards in Hamburg. The bombs inflicted only modest damage on the U-boat yards* but generated a lethal firestorm. The air raids killed about 45,000 civilians, wounded or injured about 37,000, and destroyed 253,400 of 450,000 dwelling units, leaving 900,000 people homeless. The raids enraged the many German submariners who came from Hamburg and/or had relatives, loved ones, or friends who were killed, wounded, or displaced.

When the Allies invaded Sicily, the Mediterranean U-boat force numbered seventeen VIIs, including Hans-Ferdinand Massmann, age twenty-five, in *U-409,* who had slipped through the Strait of Gibraltar on June 8. The force was in the process of shifting its main base of operations from La Spezia to Toulon, but a number of boats were conducting patrols.

Seven U-boats in Mediterranean waters reported successes in June, during the Allied run-up to Husky.

- The veteran *U-97,* commanded by Hans-Georg Trox, age twenty-seven, patrolling the eastern Mediterranean near Haifa, sank two ships: the 9,000-ton British tanker *Athelmonarch* and the 1,200-ton Dutch freighter *Palima.* Trox did not live long enough to celebrate.

British forces in the eastern Mediterranean converged on the site of these sinkings to hunt down *U-97.* In the afternoon of June 16, a Hudson of Australian Squadron 459, piloted by David T. Barnard, spotted *U-97* on the surface and straddled her from very low altitude with four depth charges. The explosion of one missile, a direct hit, battered the Hudson, damaging both wings, the fuselage (over one hundred holes), and the tail. Barnard took photos of the sinking U-boat, then limped to base. British ships rescued twenty-one Germans, but Trox and about twenty-six others perished.

- Also patrolling in the eastern Mediterranean, the famous veteran *U-81,* commanded by Johann-Otto Krieg, age twenty-four, sank two confirmed vessels on June 26: the 3,700-ton Greek freighter *Michalios* and a Syrian sailing vessel. He claimed to have destroyed two other sailing vessels.

- In the western Mediterranean off Oran on June 21, the veteran *U-73,* commanded by Horst Deckert, age twenty-four, sank the 1,600-ton British cargo vessel

---

* The Type VIIC41s *U-996, U-1011,* and *U-1012* were damaged beyond repair. Two small (300-ton) Type XVIIIA Walter hydrogen-peroxide boats, *U-792* and *U-793,* were damaged, another setback to that futile program. It was estimated that the dislocation of shipyard workers at the Blohm & Voss plant caused a loss in production of twenty-five to thirty Type VIICs. Owing to the obsolescence of this U-boat type and the shift to construction of "electro boats," the practical effects of the air raids on the U-boat force were insignificant.

Brinkburn. A week later Deckert damaged the 8,300-ton Royal Navy tanker *Abbeydale.*

• Also off Oran on June 22, the *U-593,* commanded by Gerd Kelbling, sank two 1,600-ton LSTs (British *333* and American *387).* On July 5, in the same area, he got the 6,100-ton British freighter *Devis.* Prior claims and credits and these three sinkings earned Kelbling a *Ritterkreuz.**

• On the last day of June, the veteran *U-453,* commanded by *Ritterkreuz* holder Egon-Reiner von Schlippenbach, hit and damaged the British freighter *Oligarch* west of Tobruk. In the same area a week later, July 6, von Schlippenbach sank the 5,500-ton British freighter *Shajeban* from convoy MWS 36, en route from Alexandria to Gibraltar.

The confirmed June successes by these seven boats came to seven ships (including one tanker) sunk for 27,000 tons, one sailing vessel (possibly three) sunk, and one big tanker and one big freighter damaged for an aggregate 15,200 tons. Albrecht Brandi in *U-617* claimed sinking another destroyer, but this third claimed destroyer kill could not be confirmed either. Allied forces sank one boat in June, *U-97.*

Apart from the sinkings in July just described, in the days immediately preceding the invasion of Sicily, when hundreds of Allied ships were forming into assault and backup convoys and covering forces, two other U-boats had successes. From convoy KMS 18B, off the coast of North Africa between Oran and Algiers, Jürgen Könenkamp, age twenty-nine, in the veteran *U-375,* got two British freighters: the 5,600-ton *St. Essylt* and the 8,800-ton *City of Venice.* On Husky D day, July 10, Waldemar Mehl, age twenty-eight, in the veteran *U-371* damaged two American ships off Algiers: the 7,200-ton Liberty ship *Matthew Maury* and the 6,600-ton tanker *Gulfprince.*

During the tough battles ashore, several U-boats attacked Allied maritime forces near Sicily. Off the southeast coast on July 21–22, Johann-Otto Krieg in *U-81* damaged the 7,500-ton British freighter *Empire Moon.* Nearby on the following day, Ernst-Ulrich Brüller, age twenty-five, in *U-407* damaged the 8,800-ton British cruiser *Newfoundland,* flagship of a support force. On August 7, Waldemar Mehl in *U-371* sank the 6,000-ton British freighter *Contractor* off the coast of Tunisia. On August 23, Josef Röther, age thirty-five, in *U-380* damaged the 7,200-ton American Liberty ship *Pierre Soulé.* On August 26, Horst-Arno Fenski, age twenty-four, in *U-410,* sank two American Liberty ships off the southwest coast of Sardinia for an aggregate 14,400 tons: *John Bell* and *Richard Henderson.* Several other German claims of damage to Allied warships and merchantmen could not be confirmed.

Thus, during the fight for Sicily in July and August, the Mediterranean U-boat force sank seven Allied ships for about 45,000 tons and damaged five for 37,900 tons, including, notably, the British cruiser *Newfoundland.*

During this same period, Allied forces sank four U-boats, reducing the Mediterranean force to thirteen.

---

* At the time of the award, his confirmed sinkings were nine ships for about 33,000 tons and damage to several others.

• On the morning of July 12, the British destroyer *Inconstant,* part of the escort for a convoy of troopships, MKF 19, returning empty to Algeria, got Massmann in the *U-409,* the latest arrival in the Mediterranean, on sonar and attacked. Over a period of two and a half hours, *Inconstant* fired forty-six depth charges, the last salvo of five set for a depth of about seven hundred feet. These apparently holed *U-409*'s pressure hull aft and caused heavy flooding.

To stop the descent of the boat, Massmann blew all ballast tanks and *U-409* shot up "almost vertically" and completely out of control. When she reached the surface, she leveled off but sank almost at once. Before she disappeared, *Inconstant* hit the boat topside with shells from her main 4.7" battery, killing fourteen and seriously wounding six Germans who were attempting to abandon ship. *Inconstant* picked up Massmann and thirty-eight other Germans, including two other officers and a midshipman.

• That same night, a British *MTB-81* came upon a U-boat in the narrow Strait of Messina, separating Sicily and the "toe" of Italy. This was the outbound veteran *U-561,* commanded by a new skipper, Fritz Henning, age twenty-six. The British craft attacked the unalert *U-561* with torpedoes at very close range and sank her. Henning and four other crewmen were rescued by Axis small craft. Later, Henning was named commander of another veteran Mediterranean boat, *U-565,* replacing *Ritterkreuz* holder Wilhelm Franken, age twenty-six, who returned to Germany for duty in the Training Command and was later killed in an "unlucky accident."

• On July 30, the American patrol craft *PC-624*, commanded by Robert D. Lowther, found and sank the veteran *U-375,* commanded by Jürgen Könenkamp, off the island of Pantelleria, between Tunisia and Sicily. There were no survivors.

• On the night of August 22, the British destroyer *Easton* and the Greek destroyer *Pindos* (ex-*Bolebroke*), escorting convoy MKF 22, found the *U-458,* commanded by Kurt Diggins, age twenty-nine, near the island of Pantelleria. The warships blew *U-458* to the surface with thirty depth charges and hit her with gunfire, then *Easton* rammed her. Twelve Germans were killed in this action; the warships fished out thirty-nine of the *U-458* crew, including Diggins.

When some of these losses became known, on July 24 the OKM directed U-boat Control to send three more "experienced" VIIs from the Atlantic force to the Mediterranean force. All three sailed in late July, but none got there.

• The *U-614,* commanded by Wolfgang Sträter, age twenty-seven, sailed from St. Nazaire on July 25. On the fifth day out while still in Biscay, a Wellington of British Squadron 172, piloted by Rowland G. Musson, found and attacked *U-614,* dropping six depth charges. In accordance with policy, Sträter remained on the surface to fight it out with his new quad 20mm and other flak guns, but the depth charges blew the boat to pieces. The Wellington aircrew saw survivors in the water, "some wearing life jackets and yellow skull caps." All waved or defiantly shook fists, but no German survived. About a month later, Musson was killed in the crash of another Wellington.

• The *U-454* and *U-706* sailed in company from La Pallice on July 29. It was the fourth start in July for the *U-706,* commanded by Alexander von Zitzewitz, who had been bedeviled by a series of mechanical failures.

On July 30, von Zitzewitz in *U-706* and the *U-454,* commanded by Burkhard Hackländer, joined two boats from Brest for the Biscay crossing. The next afternoon, August 1, a Sunderland of Australian Squadron 10, piloted by Kenneth G. Fry on Musketry patrol, spotted the four U-boats on the surface. Fry gave the alarm and attacked Hackländer's veteran *U-454.* Flying into heavy flak, he dropped six depth charges. These missiles destroyed *U-454* but the flak so badly damaged the Sunderland that it crashed in flames. Fry and five other Australian aircrew died; six survived and were rescued by the sloop *Wren* of Johnny Walker's Support Group 2. Another sloop of that group, *Kite,* rescued Hackländer, his second watch officer Gerhard Braun, and twelve enlisted men.

On the morning of August 2, a Hampden of Canadian Squadron 415, piloted by Charles G. Ruttan, found Zitzewitz in *U-706* by radar and attacked with six depth charges in the face of heavy flak, results that were never undetermined. Responding to the alarm, a B-24 of Army Air Forces ASW Squadron 4, piloted by Joseph L. Hamilton, boldly flew into flak and dropped twelve depth charges in a close straddle from an altitude of fifty feet. These destroyed *U-706,* which sank in mere seconds. Hamilton reported "at least fifteen men" in the water. He dropped them a dinghy, but only the second watch officer, Henner Lappe, and three enlisted men survived. A Catalina of British Squadron 210 guided the frigate *Waveney* of the British 40th Support Group to the scene and she rescued the four Germans.

The loss of all three U-boats assigned to reinforce the Mediterranean force left that command at thirteen boats, most of them based at Toulon, France.

The official Italian naval historian, Marc' Antonio Bragadin, wrote that his Navy correctly anticipated an Allied landing in Sicily, but that owing to the paucity of combat-ready warships, Allied air supremacy, and a shortage of fuel oil, the surface forces were incapable of attacking the vast Allied armada. Two pairs of Italian cruisers sailed to conduct nuisance raids on Allied forces at Palermo, but when both pairs were discovered by Allied forces, they were recalled.

Bragadin went on to write that about one dozen Italian submarines sailed against Allied maritime forces. Seven of these claimed sinking or damaging Allied warships, but only one claim was ever confirmed: On July 16, Aldo Turcio in *Dandolo* hit and damaged the 5,500-ton British light cruiser *Cleopatra.* Allied air, surface, and submarine forces sank five of the twelve boats.* In addition, on July 12, the British minesweeper *Seaham,* commanded by Robert E. Brett, captured another, the medium *Bronzo,* commanded by A. Gherardi. Nine of her crew, including Gherardi, were killed in the action and thirty-six survived to become POWs. *Seaham* towed *Bronzo* to port.†

During the fighting on Sicily, the Fascist government of Benito Mussolini fell

---

* The 1,000-ton *Flutto,* and the 600-ton mediums *Nereide, Acciaio, Ascianghi,* and *Argento.* In addition, Allied forces sank three large Italian submarines that were transferring from Taranto to safer bases: the 1,600-ton minelayer *Pietro Micca* and the new 2,200-ton cargo carriers *Romolo* and *Remo.*

† Thus Italian submarine losses during Husky were nine.

on July 25. To replace Mussolini, King Victor Emmanuel III appointed seventy-two-year-old Pietro Badoglio, who immediately entered into secret negotiations with the Allies to surrender Italy. Suspecting this defection, Hitler issued orders for German forces to prepare to occupy and hold Italy by armed force and to capture Italian naval forces for the *Kriegsmarine*. Both were exceedingly complex undertakings.

July Patrols to the Americas

Owing to the diversion of five new VIIs to the Arctic* in order to maintain that force at twenty or more boats in the daylight summer months and to the usual mishaps in the Baltic,† only one—repeat one—new VII came out from Germany to the North Atlantic in July, *U-647*. Barred from attacking convoys, she was to serve as a radio decoy, simulating the operations of a group.

In July, U-boat Control sailed forty-eight U-boats, including U-tankers and other types. The majority embarked to distant waters where Allied ASW was assumed to be less effective. Here are the July deployments as they evolved:

	North and Middle Atlantic	*South Atlantic/Indian Ocean*	*Americas*	*Totals*
Type VII	9	7	10	26
Type IX	4	9	2	15
Type IXD2	0	2	0	2
Type XB	0	0	1	1
Type XIV	4	0	0	4
Totals	17‡	18§	13	48

The U-tanker force was still inadequate, especially since the many boats sailing to distant waters required one or more refuelings. Six of the eight Type XIV "Milk Cow" U-tankers of the Atlantic force remained. On July 1, half of this number, *U-459, U-460,* and *U-461,* were in French ports. The *U-460* had only just returned

* *U-277, U-307, U-387, U-713, U-737.*

† The new VIIC *U-670,* commanded by Guido Hyronimus, age twenty-four, was rammed and sunk in tactical exercises by the target ship *Bolkoburg*. Twenty-two men, including Hyronimus, were rescued; twenty-one were killed. The aged school VII *U-34,* commanded by Eduard Aust, age twenty-two, was rammed and sunk by the tender *Lech,* with the loss of four men. The new VIIC *U-977,* commanded by Hans Leilich, age twenty-five, was disabled in a collision and relegated to the Training Command. The new VIIC *U-474,* damaged in an Allied air raid on Kiel, had to be scrapped. The IXD2 U-cruiser *U-859,* commanded by Johann Jebsen, age twenty-seven (from the VIIC *U-565* in the Mediterranean), was severely damaged in an air raid at Bremen. The VIIC *U-736* and the IXC *U-845* were also delayed by various command or technical problems.

‡ Of the seventeen boats that sailed to the North and Middle Atlantic, four were Type XIV "Milk Cow" U-tankers; three were Mediterranean-bound; one, *U-441,* was a flak trap in Biscay; one was a VII assigned to a mine-laying mission off Morocco. Four other boats sailing to the North Atlantic were pressed into service as provisional tankers. Thirteen of the seventeen (76 percent) were caught in the RAF Biscay offensive, Musketry, and sunk.

§ Including ten boats of group *Monsun* assigned to the Indian Ocean.

and did not sail again until late August. The *U-459* and *U-461* were scheduled to sail later in the month. Two others, *U-462* (aborting) and *U-488* (empty) were returning to French bases. The *U-462* might make repairs and resail before the end of July, but *U-488* could not sail until early September. Another new Type XIV, *U-489,* was scheduled to leave Kiel in late July but she could not reach the Atlantic before early August. Hence only one Type XIV U-tanker was available for the month of July, the *U-487,* which had sailed from France on June 15.

All U-boats putting out from France were to confront Musketry/Seaslug, the most intense phase of the British ASW campaign in the Bay of Biscay. In compliance with the new doctrine, no boat was to sail without the new flak array and all were to cross Biscay in groups of three to five and remain on the surface and fight it out with enemy aircraft. Where possible, inbound and outbound U-boats in Biscay were to be escorted by *Luftwaffe* JU-88s and other planes. In an attempt to hide in the radar clutter of the shoreline, a great many boats would closely hug the coast of France and, in violation of international law, that of "neutral" Spain.

During July, thirteen boats set sail from France for the Americas. Owing to the scarcity of lone ships and to the risks incurred in attacking American convoys, seven of the thirteen were to plant minefields, a less satisfying but, in the summer of 1943, a less dangerous task. The other six boats that were not qualified in minelaying were to carry out torpedo patrols on the supposedly safer "bauxite route" between Trinidad and Brazil.

All the boats bound to the Americas had a difficult time. On the outbound leg, six were lost and three aborted:

- The *U-628* and *U-648,* commanded by Heinz Hasenschar, age twenty-six, and Peter-Arthur Stahl, age twenty-nine, respectively, sailed in company from Brest on July 1. On the afternoon of July 3, a B-24 of British Squadron 224, piloted by Peter J. Cundy, sighted Hasenschar in *U-628* on the surface in Biscay. This aircraft carried a load of experimental thirty-five-pound ASW contact bombs (to be dropped in one stick of eighteen) and, consequently, only four depth charges. On the first attack into heavy flak, Cundy dropped the stick of bombs and one depth charge. The bombs fell wide; the depth charge "bounced off the conning tower" into the sea.

Although his plane was riddled with flak and his gas tanks were leaking dangerously, Cundy made a second pass and dropped the remaining three depth charges. These fell nearby, exploding simultaneously, engulfing *U-628* in a "gigantic fountain" of water. The boat was destroyed and sank quickly. Cundy's aircrew reported thirteen Germans in the water and "several bodies" but only one of the swimmers had a life jacket. There were no survivors.

Stahl in the *U-648* was apparently unable to assist the *U-628* survivors and proceeded onward to a refueler and the Americas. However, owing to the U-tanker shortage, he was diverted to be a provisional refueler and never came close to American waters.

- The IXC *U-505,* commanded by Peter Zschech, age twenty-four, which had aborted in late June, resailed from Lorient on July 3 in company with five other boats. On the sixth day out, July 8, three British destroyers of a hunter-killer group caught and attacked *U-505* off Cape Finisterre. The close depth charges split an external fuel-oil tank. Following the trail of oil, the warships hunted and blasted *U-505* for thirty-six hours, a terrifying ordeal for the Germans. After finally shaking the hunters, *U-505* returned to Lorient on July 13, once again for extended repairs.

• The VII *U-607,* commanded by young Wolf Jeschonnek, which embarked from St. Nazaire on July 10 to plant eight big TMC mines in the harbor at Kingston, Jamaica. For the Biscay crossing, Jeschonnek teamed up with two other outbound VIIs, the *U-613,* commanded by Helmut Köppe, age thirty-four, who was to lay eight TMC mines off Jacksonville, Florida, and the *U-455,* commanded by Hans-Martin Scheibe.

On Jeschonnek's twenty-fourth birthday, July 13, which he celebrated with a bottle of champagne, a Halifax of British Squadron 58, piloted by Arthur R. D. Clutterbuck on Musketry patrol, sighted the three boats and gave the alarm. A Sunderland of British Squadron 228, piloted by Reader D. Hanbury, joined the Halifax to attack the *U-607.* Confident of his new quad 20mm and twin 20mm guns and coolly smoking a cigarette, Jeschonnek directed his gunners to repel the Sunderland. According to crewmen of *U-607,* contrary to policy, Scheibe in *U-455* and Köppe in *U-613* then dived, leaving *U-607* to fight it out alone. She did so until the 20mm guns jammed, leaving her completely vulnerable. The Sunderland killed the quad 20mm gun crew, then dropped a string of seven shallow-set depth charges that utterly destroyed *U-607.*

The force of the explosions, which may have included some of the TMC mines, blew seven men into the sea: Jeschonnek; his first watch officer, Egon Horsmann, age twenty-one; the twenty-two-year-old second watch officer; a nineteen-year-old midshipman; and three enlisted men. Hanbury in the Sunderland dropped them a life raft, then remained overhead with the Halifax to direct surface ships to the scene. In due course the sloop *Wren* of Johnny Walker's Support Group 2 found the raft and rescued the seven men.

Köppe in *U-613* survived only eleven more days. On July 23, the four-stack American destroyer *George E. Badger,* commanded by Thomas H. Byrd, which was part of the screen for the "jeep" carrier *Bogue* and was loosely escorting convoy UGS 12, got *U-613* on sonar. In three skilled attacks, Byrd hit *U-613* with depth charges and destroyed her, possibly detonating the TMC mines. Shattered wood, mattresses, clothing, mutilated bodies, and a German translation of Poe's *Murders in the Rue Morgue* rose to the surface, but no living Germans.

• The big XB minelayer *U-117,* commanded by Hans-Werner Neumann, age thirty-six, which sailed from Bordeaux on July 22 to plant sixty-six SMA moored mines off New York harbor. Five days later, on July 27, Control directed *U-117,* which was following a "southern route," to divert temporarily and provide fuel to the IXC *U-66,* commanded by Friedrich Markworth, inbound from the Americas.

Alerted by a "good" Enigma decrypt, two aircraft from the "jeep" carrier *Card,* which was supporting convoy UGS 13, launched a Wildcat-Avenger team. They found the *U-66* inattentive on the surface on August 3. While a Wildcat, piloted by Arne S. Paulson, bore in, strafed the boat, and drove her under, Richard L.

Cormier, piloting an Avenger, came up from behind, but his depth charges and Fido homing torpedo failed to release. In a second pass, Cormier was finally able to drop two depth charges and a Fido, but *U-66,* although badly wrecked, escaped.

The strafing by Paulson in the Wildcat caused heavy casualties on *U-66.* The bullets killed the second watch officer and an enlisted man and fatally wounded another enlisted man. They hit Markworth in the stomach, his first watch officer, Klaus Herbig, age twenty-one, in the knees, a midshipman in the chest, and an enlisted man in the heel. Four others were also slightly wounded. The survivors radioed U-boat Control for immediate help, stating that it was unlikely that *U-66* could reach France and suggested an emergency stop at El Ferrol, Spain. In response, U-boat Control directed *U-66* to continue the rendezvous with Neumann's outbound *U-117.*

The two U-boats met in the early hours of August 7. Neumann in *U-117* sent over his doctor and his first watch officer, Paul Frerks, age thirty-five, who was to take temporary command of *U-66* from the badly wounded Markworth. At daylight, as the doctor attended to Markworth and the other wounded, *U-117* commenced pumping fuel to *U-66.* Minutes later an Avenger from *Card,* piloted by Asbury H. Sallenger, came upon the scene and attacked. Both boats opened up with flak guns but Sallenger and his crew were not to be denied. They dropped two depth charges close to *U-117* and climbed out of flak range. The boats hurriedly separated and *U-66* dived. The *U-117* apparently tried to dive but could not, or stayed up to fight it out. Pilot Sallenger went after *U-66* with a Fido but it missed, and for the second time in a week *U-66* escaped from intense aircraft assaults.

Sallenger circled out of range of *U-117*'s flak guns and radioed *Card* for help. Twenty minutes later two Wildcats and two Avengers arrived at the scene. The Wildcat pilots, Norman D. Hodson and Ernest E. Jackson, strafed *U-117* "unmercifully." Then the Avenger pilots, Charles R. Stapler and R. H. Forney, bore in with depth charges and Fidos. These destroyed *U-117* with the loss of all hands, and possibly detonated her mines. For his heroism in attacking two U-boats alone, Sallenger was awarded a Navy Cross. The other pilots won Silver Stars.

Unaware of the loss of *U-117,* Control directed her skipper, Hans-Werner Neumann, to cancel his New York mine-laying mission and to serve as a provisional tanker at locations west of the Canaries. As related, a number of boats returning from the Americas and Freetown sought to refuel from *U-117,* but in vain.

• The Type VIIs *U-262* and *U-760,* commanded by Heinz Franke and Otto-Ulrich Blum, respectively, which sailed from La Pallice on July 24. Owing to the shortage of tankers, Control ordered another Type VII outbound to the Americas, *U-664,* commanded by Adolf Graef, which sailed from Brest on July 21, to refuel *U-262* and *U-760,* then return to France. On the first day at sea, Franke in *U-262* reported that an Allied aircraft had hit and damaged the boat, but that he could make repairs and continue.

Chattering away on radio transmitters, which the allies DFed, these three VIIs met near the equally talky *U-66* and *U-117* on August 6. As ordered, the *U-664* transferred oil to *U-262* (by means of a water hose!) in about four hours, not without difficulties. On the morning of August 7, Graef heard—and imprudently reported—distant explosions that he assumed, correctly, to be aimed at *U-66* and *U-117.* In view of all the carrier aircraft present, he postponed his meet with Blum in *U-760* by about twenty-four hours, to the morning of August 8. When they did meet, Graef's men passed the water hose to Blum in *U-760,* while *U-262* lay to a short distance away.

In the midst of this fuel transfer, a Wildcat-Avenger team from *Card* appeared out of the clouds and attacked all three U-boats. John F. Sprague in the Wildcat dived to rake the boats with machine-gun fire. All three skippers remained on the surface and manned their new quad and twin 20mm and other flak guns. The heavy flak riddled the Wildcat, which crashed into the sea, killing Sprague. However, his fire had killed *U-664*'s second watch officer, Heinz Böhme, and a coxswain, Helmut Jendeleit, who had run on deck to disconnect the hose, and wounded three others. The Avenger, piloted by Asbury Sallenger, who had helped sink *U-117* the day before, braved the flak to drop two depth charges, but the fire from the U-boats riddled his aircraft as well (killing his radioman) and he was forced to ditch. Later in the day *Card* arrived in the area and one of her screen, the four-stack destroyer *Barry,* rescued Sallenger and his gunner.

Some confusion was to arise as to who did what in this dramatic shoot-out. Franke in *U-262* claimed that he shot down one of the two aircraft, but these or perhaps other aircraft damaged *U-262* so severely that Franke was compelled to cancel his patrol to the Americas and abort to France. U-boat Control therefore directed Franke to give his newly acquired fuel back to Graef in *U-664* and also to Blum in *U-760,* who were then to resume their patrols to the Americas.

Later that night, August 8, while running on the surface to charge batteries, the bridge watch of Graef's *U-664* spotted a very large ship in the darkness. Graef pronounced it to be a tanker; the first watch officer, Herbert Stahn, age thirty-four, thought it was a "jeep" carrier. Stahn was right; it was *Card* and her screen, inexplicably and scandalously unalert. In a botched night surface attack, Graef fired two FATs from forward tubes I and III. The torpedo from Tube I missed; the torpedo in III misfired and had to be ejected. Swinging around, Graef fired a slow T-3 *Falke* homing torpedo from his stern tube but it, too, missed. Belatedly, one of *Card*'s screen, a four-stack destroyer, got *U-664* on radar, but Graef dived deep and evaded the desultory depth-charge attack.

At noon on August 9, Graef surfaced to air the boat and charge batteries. At that time an air patrol from *Card* consisting of a Wildcat, flown by Norman D. Hodson, and two Avengers, flown by Gerald G. Hogan and R. H. Forney, came upon *U-664.* In the first attack, Hodson in the Wildcat strafed, Hogan dropped a 500-pound bomb, and Forney dropped two depth charges. Graef had intended to fight back but inasmuch as only one of his six 20mm guns would fire, he dived. However, crewmen said later, the green first watch officer, Stahn, was too slow in dogging the hatch and the powerful explosions caught *U-664* at periscope depth and blew her back to the surface.

Confusion ensued on *U-664.* Some of the green crewmen misinterpreted the boat's return to the surface as a preliminary to abandon ship and rushed topside. Intense fire from the aircraft killed five of these men. Nine others jumped into the water as Graef was giving the order to redive, and these nine were left in the sea. Leaking badly, *U-664* submerged a second time, but the damage was so severe that Graef was compelled to resurface at once and abandon ship. Carrying water, provisions, and a profusion of life jackets, the surviving crew jumped overboard. About seven hours later another of *Card*'s screen, the four-stack destroyer *Borie,* fished out Graef and forty-three other Germans and took them on to Casablanca.

Unaware that *U-664* was lost, Franke in the aborting *U-262* proceeded to the proposed rendezvous to give her and also Blum in *U-760* spare fuel for their patrols to the Americas. On August 12, an unidentified aircraft caught Blum on the surface. Blum repelled the aircraft with his new quad 20mm and other flak guns but not before the B-24 had dropped three depth charges close to his bow. As a result of the damage from these explosions, Blum, too, was compelled to abort his patrol to the Americas and return to France. U-boat Control therefore directed Blum to give his spare fuel to Horst Uphoff in the VIIB *U-84,* which was returning from a barren patrol in the Gulf of Mexico and Yucatan Channel and, like a dozen other boats, had planned to refuel from Neumann's lost XB *U-117.*

Both severely damaged boats, *U-262* and *U-760,* proceeded to rendezvous with *U-664* and the homebound *U-84,* respectively, to give spare fuel. Blum in *U-760* reported on August 20 that he had waited at the site for Graef in *U-664* for ten days and that Graef must be presumed lost. U-boat Control agreed and told Franke in *U-262* to return home hugging the coast of Portugal and the north coast of Spain. In the unlikely event that Graef was not lost, Control directed him to abort his patrol to the Americas and to come home the same way, in company with Franke in *U-262,* if a meet could be arranged.

Blum in *U-760* also reported that Uphoff in the homebound *U-84* did not appear at the rendezvous but that several Allied "destroyers" did and these worked him over with depth charges, inflicting more damage. Believing he could not make it to France, Blum requested authority to take *U-760* into Spain to get medical assistance and to make repairs. Control was reluctant to grant Blum's request, but authorized a one-day stopover.

Shortly after midnight on September 6, a Leigh Light–equipped Wellington of British Squadron 179, piloted by a Canadian, Donald F. McRae, picked up *U-760* on radar. McRae attacked from an altitude of one hundred feet, straddling the boat with six depth charges. Although the *U-760* was badly wrecked, Blum limped into Vigo, Spain, on September 8. Unable to repair his boat, he interned himself and his crew, but all hands soon reached Germany. While returning to base, the Wellington lost both engines and McRae had to make a crash landing. The plane was badly wrecked but McRae and all hands survived.

By luck and good seamanship, Franke got *U-262* back to La Pallice on September 2. With the loss of *U-664* and internment of the wrecked *U-760,* she was thus the only survivor of these three Americas-bound VIIs. Uphoff in the *U-84,* homebound from the Americas, who was to meet these three but did not, was also lost, as will be described.

- The Type VIID minelayer *U-218,* commanded by Richard Becker, who sailed from Brest on July 29. Becker's task was to lay mines off Trinidad. On August 1, a Wellington of British Squadron 547, piloted by a Canadian, James W. Hermiston, attacked *U-218,* strafing and depth-charging. The charges fell wide but the strafing wounded six men, forcing Becker to abort to Brest, where he arrived on August 6.

The three (of thirteen) boats that sailed to American waters in July and actually got there laid minefields. All three survived to tell the tale.

• The VIIs *U-230* and *U-566,* commanded by Paul Siegmann and Hans Hornkohl, respectively, which sailed on July 5, laid minefields off Norfolk to foul the approaches to Chesapeake Bay and Hampton Roads. Siegmann planted eight big TMC mines on the night of July 26–27; Hornkohl planted twelve TMB mines on the night of July 30. Neither field produced any sinkings.

After laying his field, Hornkohl in *U-566* sank by torpedo an American warship, the 1,500-ton gunboat *PG-57,* on August 5. Built at the Krupp works in Kiel in 1931, she was originally a luxurious steel yacht, *Alva,* owned by W. K. Vanderbilt, who turned her over to the Navy in 1941, rechristened USS *Plymouth.* When Hornkohl sank her, ninety miles off the New Jersey coast, she was escorting a New York to Guantánamo convoy. Her captain, Ormsby M. Mitchel, Jr., who lost a leg in the sinking, another officer who was killed, Rubin Keltch, and a petty officer, Franklin A. McGinty, who was also killed, were awarded the Navy Cross for extraordinary heroism. The 165-foot Coast Guard cutter *Calypso,* assisted by an American-built British tugboat,* rescued ninety-two of *Plymouth*'s 183-man crew.

These U-boats provoked a massive but thoroughly botched hunt by green ASW forces directed by the newly created Tenth Fleet. During it, Hornkohl in *U-566* shot up one Navy Ventura, and it crash-landed in the sea. Another Ventura of the unit simply disappeared. Both *U-230* and *U-566* returned to France, but they encountered great difficulty in finding enough fuel to complete the voyage.

• The veteran IXB *U-107,* commanded by yet another new skipper, Volker von Simmermacher, age twenty-four, who had served as a watch officer on the boat since November 1941. He sailed from Lorient on July 28 in company with another boat. On the first day at sea, von Simmermacher reported later, aircraft attacked the boats, but the Germans repelled them and *U-107* continued onward to the Americas on one engine to conserve fuel.

A full month after leaving France, on August 28, the *U-107* successfully planted twelve TMB mines off Charleston, South Carolina. The minefield produced no sinkings but von Simmermacher probably attacked two American ships by torpedo near Savannah, the Liberty ship *Albert Gallatin* and the Navy tanker *Rapidan.* In neither instance did the torpedoes cause any damage. Owing to intense ASW measures that *U-566* had provoked, von Simmermacher said he was unable to radio a report of the mining mission until September 11, by which time Control assumed the boat was lost. She finally reached France on October 3, completing a fruitless voyage of sixty-eight days.

---

* Commanded by a retired British admiral, the Honorable Sir H. Meade-Fetherstonhaugh, who was recalled to service as a lieutenant to assist in sailing American-built ships for the Royal Navy to England.

Further German Losses

Apart from the boats that sailed in July to the Mediterranean, the Americas, and to the Indian Ocean (group *Monsun*), about twenty-two others sailed from Germany or France on various missions in the Atlantic. Musketry/Seaslug ASW forces harassed these boats relentlessly, sinking about half their number, including four more Type XIV "Milk Cow" U-tankers. The loss of these U-tankers was a catastrophic blow that all but shut down Type VII patrols to distant waters and caused the diversion of a half dozen attack boats to emergency refueling tasks in order to bring home the boats already in distant waters.

• The veteran VII *U-267,* commanded by Otto Tinschert, age twenty-eight, which sailed from St. Nazaire on July 4. Four days later, on July 7, while off Cape Finisterre, a Catalina of British Squadron 210, piloted by the gallant John A. Cruickshank (who won a Victoria Cross in 1944), found *U-267* running unalertly on the surface. Cruickshank attacked, strafing and dropping depth charges. Contrary to doctrine, Tinschert did not shoot back but dived. Later he surfaced, reported heavy damage, and requested assistance. Since there were no other U-boats near him that day, Control authorized Tinschert to put into the port of El Ferrol, Spain, if necessary.

Allied intelligence provided helpful information on *U-267*'s distress. Air and surface vessels converged on Cape Finisterre and El Ferrol, but Tinschert made repairs and eluded the pursuers. He reached St. Nazaire on July 13, completing a hair-raising voyage of ten days. Tinschert, who was ill, left the boat for a rest. She finally resailed in October for one patrol under another skipper; Tinschert returned to command her in November.

• The veteran VII *U-373,* commanded by Paul-Karl Loeser, age twenty-eight, which sailed from La Pallice on July 7. His task was to lay twelve TMB mines off the mouth of the Sebou River leading to Port Lyautey, Morocco. While Loeser was on the surface near Madeira on July 24, a Wildcat-Avenger team from the carrier *Santee* strafed the boat, drove her under, and dropped a Fido. The strafing killed two men, wounded several others, and caused so much damage that Loeser was compelled to abort and call for assistance. The four-stack destroyer *Bainbridge* and other *Santee* aircraft mounted an intense hunt for *U-373,* but Loeser slipped away.

To assist with manpower and medical supplies, U-boat Control arranged for *U-373* to rendezvous on August 5 with the IXC40 *U-190,* a May boat commanded by Max Wintermeyer, returning from the Americas. However, the meeting failed and both boats returned to France independently. When the *U-373* reached La Pallice on August 16, Loeser left the boat for other duty. She did not sail again until October.

• The VII flak boat *U-441,* commanded by Götz von Hartmann, age twenty-nine, which sailed from Brest on July 8. While patrolling in Biscay on the afternoon of July 12, a flight of three twin-engine Beaufighters of British Squadron 248 found and attacked *U-441* with machine guns and 20mm cannons. This intense fire, directed by the three pilots, C.R.B. Schofield, P.A.S. Payne, and G. C. Newman, and mounted through an astonishing wall of flak from *U-441,* killed ten Germans and wounded thirteen others, including von Hartmann and all of his officers. The boat's doctor, a "keen and efficient amateur yachtsman," assumed command of *U-441,* got the injured below, dived, and took the boat back to Brest, arriving on July 13. Confusingly, the wounded skipper, Götz von Hartmann, was relieved by the boat's former skipper, Klaus Hartmann. Although the experiences of *U-441* indicated that the flak boat was a very bad concept, the conversion of the other seven VIIs to flak configuration continued and the next one, *U-621,* sailed in August.

• The veteran XIV U-tanker *U-459,* commanded by Georg von Wilamowitz-Möllendorf, age forty-nine, which sailed from Bordeaux on July 22 in company with a sister-ship tanker, the *U-461,* and another boat. On the first day, the *U-461* developed a bad leak and aborted; her sister ship, *U-459,* and the other boat continued to sea, separating. Three days out from Bordeaux on July 24, a Wellington of British Squadron 172, piloted by W.H.T. Jennings, found *U-459* late in the day and attacked out of low clouds. Wilamowitz-Möllendorf remained on the surface and manned his new quad 20mm and twin 20mm guns and opened fire. Jennings boldly flew into this very heavy flak barrage and crashed into the starboard side of *U-459,* demolishing the quad 20mm and other guns and killing or wounding half a dozen of *U-459*'s crew.

Utter chaos ensued. The Germans cut away the wreckage of the Wellington fuselage and pushed it into the sea. Upon doing so, they found three unexploded depth charges, two on the bridge and one on the afterdeck. Apparently unaware that the depth charges were fitted with shallow-set pistols, Wilamowitz-Möllendorf rang up full speed and ordered his men to roll them overboard. One or more of the charges exploded as designed beneath the stern of *U-459,* inflicting horrendous damage.

A second aircraft appeared on the scene, a Wellington of British Squadron 547, piloted by J. Whyte. Upon seeing *U-459,* which was slowly circling out of control stern down, he attacked, dropping eight depth charges at wave-top level in a close straddle. These explosions dashed any hopes the *U-459* crew may have had of limping home. In a second attack run, Whyte dropped several more depth charges and raked the topside with machine-gun fire, killing and wounding more Germans and destroying some of the dinghies.

Following this attack, Wilamowitz-Möllendorf ordered his men to abandon ship and scuttle. As the dinghies pulled away, he saluted his men, then went below and opened the vents. Observed by Whyte and his aircrew, the *U-459* sank swiftly by the stern. This second Wellington and other aircraft directed the Polish-manned destroyer *Orkan* to the scene. Seven to eight hours after the first Wellington attacked, the Poles picked up forty-one Germans and one British airman, A. A. Turner, who had been blown out of the crashed Wellington and had climbed into his own dinghy. The Admiralty assessment committee gave credit for the kill to the first Wellington and in view of his "high degree of courage" recommended Jennings for a posthumous Victoria Cross. The loss of this valuable U-tanker was another severe blow to the Atlantic U-tanker force.

• The new XIV tanker *U-489,* commanded by Adalbert Schmandt, age thirty-three, which sailed from Kiel on July 22 in company with a new VII, *U-647,* commanded by Willi Hertin, age twenty-nine. Off Norway on July 29, Control notified

Schmandt and Hertin to search for a German aircrew that had ditched after a losing match with a Beaufighter of Canadian Squadron 404. Schmandt found the three Germans, took them on board, and proceeded to the Atlantic, still in company with the *U-647.*

A few days later, on August 3, a Hudson of British Squadron 269, flown by E.L.J. Brame, found the tanker *U-489* in a position south of Iceland and mounted two attacks with 100-pound ASW bombs in the face of the U-boat's quad 20mm and other flak guns. The first bomb missed, but the second fell close. When two other aircraft appeared (a B-17 and a Catalina), Schmandt dived deep (656 feet) and escaped. But the single bomb caused a leak of seawater into the after battery, posing the possibility of chlorine gas. Schmandt surfaced to radio U-boat Control of the mishap and to request orders, drawing in "several destroyers" that drove the boat under again. Schmandt's men fixed the leak, but the warships mounted a dogged hunt, dropping depth charges. None fell close; however, the destroyers held *U-489* down until her batteries were exhausted, and she was forced to surface the next morning.

When *U-489* came up on August 4, a Sunderland of Canadian Squadron 423, piloted by A. A. Bishop, son of a World War I ace, spotted her almost immediately and notified the destroyers and others. Bishop then attacked *U-489* from the stern, flying straight into the flak from the quad 20mm, which set the aircraft on fire. Bishop dropped six accurate shallow-set depth charges, then crash-landed into the sea. Six of the plane's eleven-man crew survived, including Bishop.

When three British destroyers, including *Castleton* and *Orwell,* appeared, Schmandt ordered his crew to abandon ship and scuttle. As she went down, there was an unexplained but "terrific" explosion in the aft section that mortally wounded the chief engineer. About twenty minutes later, *Castleton* picked up Schmandt and the other fifty-three members of the crew, including the chief engineer, who later died aboard *Castleton,* plus the three German airmen who had been rescued by *U-489.* The *Castleton* then picked up pilot Bishop and five of his aircrew who were less than one hundred yards away. Although numerous aircraft and ships had participated in the destruction of *U-489,* the Admiralty assessment committee gave sole credit for the kill to Bishop and his Canadian aircrew and awarded Bishop a DFC for killing this valuable German U-tanker, yet another big setback to the Atlantic force.

The *U-647,* commanded by Willi Hertin, the new VII that sailed from Kiel in company with *U-489,* had orders to serve as a radio decoy off Greenland and to report when it had passed a particular position south of Iceland. Hertin must have been close by when *U-489* went down, but he did not speak up then or later and the loss of *U-647* remains a mystery. Possibly Hertin was sunk by the Allied aircraft and/or surface ships that attacked *U-489* at this time or possibly he hit a British mine in the Iceland-Faeroes gap. On August 11, Control noted that neither *U-647* nor the tanker *U-489* had been heard from and therefore both were presumed to be lost.

• The veteran VII *U-404,* commanded by a new skipper, Adolf Schönberg, age twenty-four, which sailed from St. Nazaire on July 24 with *U-614,* one of the three boats assigned to the Mediterranean that was sunk.

The *U-404* had achieved fame under Otto von Bülow, who won a *Ritterkreuz* with Oak Leaves. He was all set to take her on this patrol but on the day before the scheduled sailing, he received orders from Viktor Schütze to leave *U-404* at once and take command of the new 23rd Training Flotilla in the Baltic. It was wrenching to leave his veteran crew, von Bülow remembered, but as it turned out, the last-minute transfer was lifesaving. The new skipper, Schönberg, had earlier served on *U-404* for a year as first watch officer before commanding a school duck.

In late afternoon of the fifth day out, July 28, two B-24s of U.S. Army Air Forces Squadron 4, piloted by this unit's commander, Stephen D. McElroy, and Arthur J. Hammer, found and attacked *U-404* in the face of very heavy flak. McElroy dropped eight depth charges, but these only damaged *U-404.* In turn, *U-404* hit one of McElroy's engines, forcing him to abort. Responding to McElroy's alert, Hammer made two runs, strafing and dropping twelve depth charges. With his plane badly riddled, he too had to break off, and he returned to a base in southwest England.

During Hammer's attack, a B-24 of British Squadron 224, piloted by Robert V. Sweeny, arrived on the scene. Sweeny attacked "straight in," accurately dropping seven depth charges from nearly wave-top level. These destroyed *U-404* with all hands. Sweeny reported seeing "about ten bodies" in the water, but he could not tarry because one of his engines was on fire and his B-24 was also riddled by flak. He made an emergency landing in southwest England and all aboard lived to tell the tale. The Admiralty credited both Hammer and Sweeny with the kill of *U-404.* Sweeny and a crewman were awarded DFCs.

• The VII *U-383,* commanded by Horst Kremser, age twenty-five, which sailed from Brest on July 29. On August 1, a Sunderland of British Squadron 228, piloted by Stanley White, found and attacked *U-383.* On the first run German gunners riddled the Sunderland, inflicting heavy damage on the starboard wing. On a second run White dropped seven depth charges that destroyed the U-boat. He reported that he saw Germans jumping into the water, but owing to his own damage, could not stay. Kremser had time to radio an *SOS* to Control stating he was "unable to dive" and "out of control." In response, German aircraft, three torpedo boats, and three U-boats looked for survivors of *U-383* the next day, but found none.

• Seven U-boats sailed from Lorient and Bordeaux on July 27 and July 28: one VII, four IXs, and two Type XIV U-tankers, *U-461* and *U-462.* On her routine deep-dive test, the VII, *U-231,* commanded by thirty-three-year-old Wolfgang Wenzel, developed leaks and he aborted. Inbound to La Pallice, the boat triggered a British mine that exploded six feet from the hull, Wenzel reported. He reached La Pallice, but repairs kept *U-231* in port until late September.

The other six boats of this group proceeded onward into Biscay only to meet intense Allied air and surface hunter-killer patrols. In one memorable day, July 30, British aircraft sank three of the six, including the two valuable XIV U-tankers, yet another crippling blow to the Atlantic U-boat force.

The action began in the morning when a B-24 of British Squadron 53, piloted by W. Irving, found the three boats and gave the alarm. This brought in six other aircraft: a Sunderland of British Squadron 228, a Catalina of British Squadron 210, a B-24 of American Army ASW Squadron 19, two Halifaxes of British Squadron

502, and a Sunderland of Australian Squadron 461. The aircraft also homed in the five sloops of Johnny Walker's 2nd Support Group.

Wary of the nests of flak guns on the group of U-boats, the bombers circled beyond range, plotting an attack scheme. A Halifax of British Squadron 502 made the first attack and dropped three of the new 600-pound ASW bombs from an altitude of 1,600 feet using a special bombsight. The bombs fell wide; the German gunners damaged the Halifax. A second Halifax of 502 Squadron followed with three separate attack runs, each time dropping a single 600-pound bomb from three thousand feet. One of these bombs hit and crippled Bruno Vowe's tanker, *U-462,* which slowed, then stopped dead in the water.

Three or four aircraft attacked Vowe's crippled *U-462* and Wolf-Harro Stiebler's undamaged tanker, *U-461.* In the lead of this group was a B-24 of British Squadron 53, flown by W. Irving. Next came a B-24 of Army Air Forces ASW Squadron 19, piloted by A. L. Leal, followed by a slower Sunderland of Australian Squadron 461, piloted by Dudley Marrows. Pilot Irving in the British B-24 dropped eight depth charges close to the *U-462.* Pilot Leal in the American B-24 did no damage because his depth-charge release gear, damaged by flak, would not function. Credit for the kill of the valuable XIV *U-462* went to a Halifax of British Squadron 502 flown by a Dutchman, A. van Rossum, who later won a DFC. One German gunner on *U-462* was killed. Vowe and sixty-three other survivors scuttled ship and got into dinghies.

The Australian Sunderland, piloted by Marrows, peeled off to attack the other XIV tanker, Stiebler's *U-461.* During his attack run, the plane's machine-gun fire killed the two loaders on the quad 20mm and severely wounded two officers. Consequently, the flak from *U-461* was less intense and Marrows was able to drop seven shallow-set depth charges from an altitude of fifty feet. Four missiles fell close to port and starboard of *U-461* and smashed her to pieces. Stiebler and fourteen other survivors of his sixty-man crew climbed into dinghies. Forty-five Germans perished in the sinking. The Admiralty gave Marrows sole credit for the kill of *U-461.*

At about that time, Johnny Walker's five sloops arrived on the scene. All five warships opened fire with main batteries on the flooding *U-462* and on Wilhelm Luis's IXC *U-504.* In a desperate attempt to escape, Luis dived *U-504.* Walker, in the sloop *Kite,* got a sonar contact and made the first depth-charge attack. The *Wren* followed up. Then *Kite* attacked a second time, followed by *Woodpecker,* which dropped thirty-two depth charges under Walker's supervision. Lastly, *Woodcock* and *Wild Goose* made similar attacks. These assaults brought to the surface a German "uniform jacket, a human lung, and some well-cured bacon," the last sign of *U-504,* which perished with all hands. The Admiralty gave credit for the kill to all five of the sloops, which also shared credit for *U-462.*

Later, Walker led his sloops back to the scene of the sinking of the tankers *U-461* and *U-462.* The sloops rescued seventy-nine Germans from the two U-tankers. Still later in the day, Walker's sloops picked up the crew of a Focke-Wulf Condor that had been shot down by a British Beaufighter the day before.

Combined with the loss of three other Type XIV "Milk Cow" tankers, *U-459, U-487,* and *U-489,* these additional two U-tanker losses—and the accident that befell the new XIV tanker *U-490* in the Baltic—reduced the operational tanker force to two XIVs: *U-460* and *U-488.* One consequence was that Control had to divert the other three boats of this newly sailed group, the IXs *U-106, U-129,* and *U-525,* to be provisional refuelers. Two of these did not get far:

• The veteran IXB *U-106,* commanded by a new skipper, Wolf-Dietrich Damerow, age twenty-four, who had served on the boat as a watch officer for almost two years. He sailed from Lorient in company with a sister ship, *U-107,* which, as related, planted a minefield in American waters.

On the fifth day out, August 1, Damerow reported that he had repelled an aircraft, but that it or another was shadowing the boat, doubtless calling in other planes. The shadower was a Wellington of the new Canadian Squadron 407, piloted by a British officer, J. C. Archer, who had dropped six depth charges and had indeed given the alarm.

Two Sunderlands responded on August 2: one from British Squadron 228, piloted by Reader D. Hanbury, and one from Australian Squadron 461, piloted by Irwin A. F. Clarke. Both aircraft strafed and dropped six depth charges that wrecked *U-106.* In reaction to Damerow's SOS, U-boat Control sent four JU-88s and three torpedo boats. The aircraft arrived too late, but the torpedo boats rescued Damerow, his log book, and thirty-five other Germans. Damerow, however, did not survive the war.

• The IXC40 *U-525,* commanded by the old hand Hans-Joachim Drewitz, age thirty-five. Control directed Drewitz to refuel VIIs returning from the Americas and Freetown. He was unable to carry out the mission. On August 11, a Wildcat-Avenger team from the "jeep" carrier *Card* found *U-525* on the surface. Jack H. Stewart in the Wildcat strafed and drove the boat under. The Avenger, piloted by Charles G. Hewitt, dropped depth charges and a Fido, which sank the boat with the loss of all hands. As related, six days later, on August 17, when Gerhard Feiler in the *U-653,* returning from a barren patrol off French Guiana, reported that he had waited in vain for three days at the rendezvous for Drewitz, Control correctly presumed *U-525* had been lost.

The other IX, von Harpe in the IXC *U-129,* carried out his new mission. He refueled four VIIs returning from Freetown: *Ritterkreuz* holder Peter Cremer in *U-333,* adrift with no oil and a sea anchor deployed; Gustav Lüssow in *U-571;* Bernhard Zurmühlen in *U-600;* and Kurt Baberg in *U-618.* On August 20, when von Harpe reported he had completed these refuelings and could spare no more fuel, U-boat Control directed him to return to France. He arrived safely at Lorient on September 5, completing a patrol of forty-one days.

The loss of U-tankers also led to the deletion of a Type IXD2 U-cruiser from group *Monsun,* the new foray to the Indian Ocean. This was the *U-847,* commanded by *Ritterkreuz* holder Herbert Kuppisch, who sailed from Kiel on July 6, struck ice in the Denmark Strait, and aborted to Norway, arriving on July 20. After repairs, Kuppisch resailed on July 29, but Control reassigned him to serve as a provisional tanker for the boats returning from the Americas and West Africa.

Kuppisch reached his refueling area in mid-August. His first task was to replenish some inbound boats from the Americas that had been assigned to refuel from the XB minelayer *U-117,* herself a provisional tanker that, as related, was sunk on August 7.

The first homebound boat to find Kuppisch was the wrecked IXC *U-66,* temporarily commanded by Paul Frerks from *U-117,* relieving the badly wounded Friedrich Markworth. The rendezvous took place on August 16. In return for a water purifier and lube oil, Kuppisch gave *U-66* food and sufficient fuel to get to France. When the *U-66* reached Lorient on September 1, Markworth left the boat for hospitalization, and later, other duty. In due course, the chief engineer of *U-66,* Georg Olschewski, was awarded a *Ritterkreuz* for his role in saving the boat. Frerks returned to the Training Command as captain of the new VII *U-975,* which was assigned to the submarine school.

At least three homebound boats approached Kuppisch in *U-847* on August 24. These were Carl Emmermann in the IXC *U-172,* who had been awarded Oak Leaves to his *Ritterkreuz;* August Maus in the IXC40 *U-185;* and Horst Uphoff in the VIIB *U-84.* As related, Emmermann and Maus were returning from Brazilian waters, each carrying one-half of the crew of Höltring's VIIC *U-604,* which had been scuttled, and Uphoff was returning from a barren patrol in the Gulf of Mexico.

Emmermann in *U-172* was first to make contact with Kuppisch. He surfaced close aboard with double lookouts posted and all flak guns manned. He was dismayed to find Kuppisch and his crew casually disposed. He requested that Kuppisch man his flak guns and double-time the refueling process. "He was from the earlier times when aircraft were not a great threat," Emmermann said later. "He had not been to sea in almost two full years." In two hours flat, Emmermann replenished and departed.

Later that morning, as Maus in *U-185* was approaching *U-847* to refuel, aircraft from the "jeep" carrier *Core,* loosely escorting convoy UGS 15, were out searching for U-boats. A Wildcat-Avenger team, piloted by Martin G. O'Neill and Robert P. Williams, respectively, found *U-185* and attacked. Diving out of cloud cover, O'Neill in the Wildcat strafed the bridge, wounding the entire watch, the second watch officer fatally. Williams came next and accurately dropped two depth charges. The explosions wrecked and almost instantly flooded *U-185,* and chlorine gas seeped through the boat.

A bizarre drama unfolded in the forward section of the boat. The skipper of the scuttled VII *U-604,* thirty-year-old Horst Höltring, still recovering from his wounds, leaped from his bunk, pistol in hand, and ran to the forward torpedo room, where two badly wounded men of his crew were confined to bunks. As the room filled with chlorine gas, the two crewmen begged Höltring to shoot them. He obliged, then killed himself with a shot to the head, survivors reported.

After *U-185* had been riddled by two more aircraft from *Core,* Maus ordered the crew to abandon ship and scuttle. When one of *Core*'s screen, the four-stack destroyer *Barker,* arrived at the scene a little later, she fished thirty-six Germans from the water, including Maus and his first watch officer, Hans Otto Rieve, age twenty-two. Nine of the men were survivors from Höltring's *U-604.* Two Germans from *U-185* died on *Barker* from the effects of chlorine gas: the engineer, Herbert Ackermann, and the ship's doctor, Georg Rammler.

On the voyage to France, Emmermann in *U-172* was hobbled by an epidemic of dysentery and was glad to have twenty-three men of *U-604* as replacements for his own sick. After he arrived, on September 7—completing a miserable voyage of 102 days—he received his Oak Leaves from Hitler, then returned to France to command Combat Flotilla 6 in St. Nazaire.* Upon review of Maus's arduous and outstanding patrol and hearing the stories from *U-604* crewmen of Maus's rescue of them, Dönitz awarded Maus a *Ritterkreuz* in abstentia.†

Eventually Maus wound up in the POW camp in Papago Park, Arizona. On about September 1, 1944, he joined in an escape scheme with four other U-boat skippers: Fritz Guggenberger (from *U-513*), who wore a *Ritterkreuz* with Oak Leaves; Hans-Werner Kraus (from *U-199*), who wore the *Ritterkreuz;* Jürgen Quaet-Faslem (from *U-595*); and Jürgen Wattenberg (from *U-162*). As recounted by the American writer John H. Moore, Maus and these skippers and two dozen other U-boat POWs dug a 178-foot escape tunnel, part of it through rock. On December 23, two days after the tunnel was completed, twelve officers and thirteen enlisted men escaped, but not Maus, who developed a hernia and had to drop out. All twenty-five men were soon caught—the last, Jürgen Wattenberg on January 28, 1945, in Phoenix.

Uphoff in the VIIB *U-84,* who had orders to refuel from the ill-fated *U-117,* then *U-262* and/or *U-760,* then *U-847,* did not establish contact with Kuppisch in *U-847* on that fateful August 24. It was believed that later that same day, an Avenger from *Core,* piloted by William A. Felter, found *U-84* unalert on the surface about ten miles from the place *U-185* had been sunk. Upon seeing Felter diving to attack, Uphoff unwisely dived himself. Realizing he had an excellent opportunity to use a Fido homing torpedo, Felter coolly dropped one in *U-84*'s swirl. Nothing further was ever heard from *U-84.* However, Niestlé doubts this kill and has listed *U-84* as lost to unknown causes.

Another VII returning from American waters, the *U-134,* commanded by Hans-Günther Brosin, who had shot down a blimp in the Florida Straits, also ran into fatal trouble. On August 21, a Wildcat-Avenger team from the "jeep" carrier *Croatan,* escorting convoy UGS 14, attacked *U-134* but Brosin escaped. Three nights later, on August 24, a Leigh Light–equipped Wellington of British Squadron 179, piloted by a Canadian, Donald F. McRae, found and attacked *U-134* in the face of heavy flak. McRae dropped six depth charges that destroyed *U-134,* but he was unable to provide positive evidence of a kill.

On the morning of August 27, Kuppisch in the IXC40 *U-847* refueled six more homebound boats. These were Paul Siegmann in the VII *U-230,* returning from a mine-laying mission off Norfolk; Kurt Neide in the VII *U-415,* returning from a barren patrol in the Trinidad area; Eberhard Dahlhaus in the VII *U-634,* returning from a fruitless patrol in the Caribbean; Gerhard Feiler in the VII *U-653,*

---

* With a score of twenty-seven confirmed ships for 152,904 tons sunk, Emmermann ranked fourteenth among all U-boat skippers in the war.

† At the time of the award, his score was nine confirmed ships sunk for about 63,000 tons.

also returning from a luckless patrol in the Caribbean; Heinz Rahe in the VII *U-257,* returning from a barren patrol to the Freetown area; and the new *Ritterkreuz* winner Georg Staats in the IXC *U-508,* returning from the Freetown and Gulf of Guinea areas. Like Emmermann in *U-172,* the first watch officer on *U-230,* Herbert Werner, believed that Kuppisch was insufficiently prepared to cope with enemy air.

Several days later, the "jeep" carrier *Card* relieved the "jeep" carrier *Core,* which had developed turbine-vibration problems. On the morning of August 27, two Wildcats and an Avenger from *Card* found Kuppisch in *U-847.* The two Wildcats, piloted by Jack H. Stewart and Frederick M. Rountree, strafed and forced the boat to dive. Pilot Ralph W. Long in the Avenger dropped a Fido just ahead of the swirl. Nothing further was ever heard from *U-847.* She was the sixth IXD2 U-cruiser to be lost, the fifth within the 104-day period from May 16 to August 27.*

One of the six boats that Kuppisch refueled on August 27 did not make it home. She was the VII *U-634,* commanded by Eberhard Dahlhaus. On August 30, while *U-634* was sailing north in company with Siegmann in *U-230,* she found a convoy, Sierra Leone 135, and maneuvered close to shoot. Two British escorts of the convoy, the sloop *Stork* (G.W.E. Casteus) and the corvette *Stonecrop* (J. Patrick Smythe), sank *U-634* with the loss of all hands.

One of the myths of the Battle of the Atlantic is that when the Allies finally broke into four-rotor Enigma in the summer of 1943, they then launched a concerted attack on the German U-tanker force and wiped it out, thereby crippling the operations of the Type VIIs. As related, the Allies did indeed inflict a heavy blow on the U-tanker force in the summer of 1943, sinking nine of twelve refuelers at the front (including three XBs), but apparently Enigma decrypts relating to refueling rendezvous played only a modest role in this slaughter.

According to a top-secret postwar study,† Enigma decrypts were useful in only two of the nine sinkings. Both of these were Type XB minelayers serving as provisional refuelers. The "very good" Enigma decrypts enabled aircraft of the American "jeep" carrier *Bogue* to sink *U-118* on May 25. The "good" Enigma decrypts enabled aircraft of the American "jeep" carrier *Card* to sink *U-117* on August 7. Enigma decrypts were of no help in the sinking of the other seven U-tankers, the XB *U-119* and six Type XIV "Milk Cows."‡

Six of the seven U-tanker sinkings carried out with no help from Engima decrypts were accounted for by Commonwealth aircraft and surface forces engaged in the Bay of Biscay offensive. The American "jeep" carrier *Core* got the seventh, *U-487.* Many of the U-tanker losses resulted from the ill-advised German decision to sail U-boats in groups on the surface and to fight enemy aircraft with flak guns.

* *U-179, U-182, U-197, U-199, U-200, U-847.* Two other failed IXD1 U-cruiser designs, *U-180* and *U-195,* were undergoing conversion to cargo carriers.

† See Plate 7.

‡ *U-459, U-461, U-462, U-463, U-487, U-489.*

Patrols to West Africa

Eight boats sailed from France to West Africa in July. All confronted the fury of the Allied Biscay ASW offensive, Musketry/Seaslug. Half of the number did not reach West Africa: One aborted, three were sunk. Owing to the inability to refuel, the other four (all VIIs) conducted inconsequential patrols.

• The VII *U-709,* commanded by Karl-Otto Weber, age twenty-eight, which sailed on July 5 from Brest. It was Weber's third patrol. Eight days out, on July 12, excessive hydrogen accumulated and exploded in the forward battery, killing two men and severely injuring a third. Weber aborted and limped back to Brest, arriving on July 20. The boat did not sail again until October.

• The VII *U-468,* commanded by Klemens Schamong, age twenty-six, which sailed from La Pallice on July 7. Alerted by a Catalina, a B-24 of British Squadron 200, flown by Lloyd Allan Trigg, found *U-468* on August 11 and attacked. In response, Schamong threw up a heavy curtain of flak with his new quad 20mm and other weapons. The flak hit and set the B-24 on fire but Trigg pressed on to drop about six shallow-set depth charges in a near-perfect straddle.

The explosions mortally holed *U-468* and caused chlorine gas and panic belowdecks, but Schamong and six other Germans launched a raft and survived. The B-24 crashed in flames with no survivors. Two days later, a Sunderland spotted the seven Germans in the raft, dropped another raft, and directed the British corvette *Clarkia* to the rescue. Based on the laudatory testimony of Schamong and his first watch officer, the Admiralty awarded pilot Trigg a posthumous Victoria Cross, the first such high honor to be bestowed on a British ASW pilot.

• The venerable IX *U-43*—the oldest boat in the Atlantic force—commanded by Hans-Joachim Schwantke, age twenty-four, which left Lorient on July 13. Her assignment was to lay twelve TMB mines off Lagos, Nigeria, in the Gulf of Guinea. She negotiated the Bay of Biscay, where Schwantke claimed he probably shot down an aircraft, but she did not get far beyond. On July 30, a Wildcat-Avenger team from the carrier *Santee,* which was loosely escorting convoy GUS 10, found *U-43* on the surface, preparing to give some fuel oil to the VII *U-403,* commanded by a new skipper, Karl-Franz Heine, age twenty-seven, who was also bound for West Africa.

The two aircraft attacked the two U-boats. Piloted by Edward Van Vranken, the Wildcat came first, strafing. Immediately behind came R. F. Richmond in the Avenger. Contrary to policy, both U-boats dived. Richmond dropped two shallow-set depth charges close to *U-403* and a Fido near *U-43.* The *U-403* escaped, but apparently the Fido worked as designed and destroyed *U-43.* Nothing further was ever heard from her.

Two and a half weeks later, on August 17, while *U-403* patrolled directly off Dakar, Senegal, searching for convoy Sierra Leone 135, a Wellington of Free French Squadron 697 from Dakar teamed up and attacked her with machine guns and depth charges. In September, when *U-403* failed to report in, U-boat Control assumed correctly that she was lost. There were no survivors.

Four VIIs sailing in July reached the Freetown area but achieved little. Only one sank a ship: Friedrich Deetz, age twenty-six, in *U-757,* who torpedoed the 4,116-ton Norwegian freighter *Fernhill* west of Freetown on August 7 and took one prisoner. On August 11, Heinz-Konrad Fenn in the *U-445,* who had celebrated his twenty-fifth birthday on July 20, reported ironically that the physician he carried was desperately ill. U-boat Control directed Fenn to rendezvous with Walter Schug, age thirty-two, in the aged VIIB *U-86,* who also had a doctor on board. Before the boats met, however, Fenn signaled that the doctor on *U-445* had died.

On the return to France, all four boats had a difficult time obtaining enough fuel to complete the voyage, but all got home. While hugging the coast of Portugal, the *U-340,* commanded by Hans-Joachim Klaus, age twenty-five, rescued five German airmen but was hit by Allied aircraft and sustained "several" casualties. However, Klaus reached France on September 2, completing a patrol of fifty-nine days. The other three VIIs returned to France from September 4 to 15, completing patrols of sixty to sixty-six days.

Excluding the ten big U-boats assigned to the Indian Ocean foray, group *Monsun,* the thirty-eight U-boats that sailed in July achieved almost nothing. The attack boats of this group sank two ships; one convoy escort, the 1,500-ton American yacht *Plymouth* in American waters, and the 4,116-ton Norwegian motorship *Fernhill* off Freetown. In return, a ruinous twenty-one U-boats of those sailing in July were lost, including the three VIIs sunk en route to the Mediterranean.*

The *Luftwaffe* aircraft based in France achieved better results against Allied shipping in July than the U-boats. The most notable success occurred on July 11 when a flight of HE-177 four-engine bombers, armed with a new type of radio-controlled bomb, the HS 293, found and attacked a British troopship convoy three hundred miles west of Portugal. These "smart bombs" sank the 22,000-ton liner *Duchess of York,* the 16,792-ton liner *California,* and damaged the 8,337-ton liner *Port Fairy,* which limped into Casablanca. Owing to excellent seamanship on the part of three escorts (the Canadian destroyer *Iroquois,* British destroyer *Douglas,* and British frigate *Moyola*) only fifty-seven troops perished in this little-known British troopship disaster. Returning to England with 628 Allied survivors, the *Iroquois* found and rescued three survivors of the *U-506,* which was sunk July 12, as related.

Group *Monsun*

The most ambitious U-boat operation undertaken by the Atlantic force in July was a new foray to the Indian Ocean, *Monsun,* so named because the boats were to arrive in the Indian Ocean toward the end of the rainy summer monsoon season. As originally planned, the foray was to consist of eleven boats, two IXD2 U-cruisers

---

* In the month of July 1943, Allied shipyards produced about two hundred new vessels for about 1.3 million gross tons. American yards produced 165 ships for 1.13 million gross tons, British and Canadian yards thirty-six ships for 183,000 gross tons. (Commonwealth figures are based on a total production of 2.2 million gross tons in 1943 divided by twelve months and assuming an average ship displacement of about 5,000 gross tons.)

on maiden patrols from Kiel, six Type IXC40s, and three Type IXCs. As related, Allied forces sank one of the U-cruisers in the Iceland-Faeroes gap, *U-200,* which was supposed to land "coastal troops" in South Africa to foment trouble. The other, *U-847,* sailed from Kiel on July 6 via the Denmark Strait, where she struck an iceberg and aborted to Norway, resailed later, was diverted to be a provisional tanker, and was lost.

Owing to the inclusion of nine Type IXs in such distant waters, the *Monsun* foray had a complex refueling plan. First, the IXC40s and IXCs were to refuel on the outbound leg from the Type XIV U-tanker *U-462,* which sailed from France on June 19. Second, all boats, including the two U-cruisers, were to replenish from the German tanker *Brake* in the Indian Ocean on September 8, then proceed to patrol areas. On the return voyage, the boats were to refuel again from *Brake* in the Indian Ocean and from another XIV U-tanker near the Azores on the final leg.

As related, the Type XIV U-tanker *U-462,* commanded by Bruno Vowe, was twice forced to abort in June with battle damage and therefore could not refuel the *Monsun* boats. Instead that vital task was reassigned to the Type XIV U-tanker *U-487,* commanded by Helmut Metz, which sailed from France on June 15 on her second combat mission.

The nine Type IXs of group *Monsun* sailed from France in the first week of July. All were fitted with new, heavy flak arrays and all remained on the surface in groups. Three of these nine were lost shortly after sailing:

- The IXC *U-514,* commanded by Hans-Jürgen Auffermann, age twenty-eight, which sailed from Lorient on July 3. On the sixth day out, July 8, a B-24 piloted by the renowned U-boat slayer Terence Bulloch, temporarily attached to British Squadron 224, sighted *U-514* on the surface amid a flotilla of Spanish fishing vessels near Cape Finisterre. Bulloch fired three rocket salvos. Contrary to doctrine, Auffermann dived, whereupon Bulloch dropped a Fido homing torpedo that apparently went astray. Looking down at the roiled water, Bulloch thought the U-boat might be surfacing and dropped a brace of shallow-set depth charges. These may have hit the errant Fido or the U-boat or both. In the event, nothing further was ever heard from *U-514.*
- The IXC *U-506,* commanded by *Ritterkreuz* holder Erich Würdemann, age twenty-nine, which sailed from Lorient on July 6. Six days later, on July 12, a B-24 of U.S. Army Air Forces ASW Squadron 1 from Port Lyautey, piloted by Ernest Salm on his first mission as aircraft commander, found *U-506* on radar about three hundred miles west of Cape Finisterre. Diving out of a low cloud cover, Salm toggled seven depth charges and destroyed the boat. Würdemann and forty-eight other Germans perished in the sinking. British destroyers rescued and captured six other Germans on a raft on July 15.
- The IXC *U-509,* commanded by Werner Witte, age twenty-eight, which sailed from Lorient on July 3. Twelve days out, on July 15, a Wildcat-Avenger team from the carrier *Santee* found *U-509* near the Madeira Islands. Pilot Jack D. Anderson in the Wildcat strafed and when *U-509* dived, pilot Claude N. Barton in the Avenger dropped a Fido. The Fido apparently worked as designed. Nothing further was heard from *U-509.*

The Type XIV U-tanker *U-487,* commanded by Helmut Metz, assigned to refuel the *Monsun* boats, first refueled seven Type VIIs that sailed in June to American waters* and the aborting IXD1 U-cruiser *U-195,* inbound from Cape Town. On July 12, Control directed Metz to shift two hundred miles southeast to refuel the VII *U-648,* outbound to American waters and the IXC40 *U-527,* inbound from American waters. Thereafter, Metz was to refuel the six surviving IXC40s of outbound group *Monsun* on July 23, about 350 miles farther south yet, then come home.

Metz was unable to carry out these orders. About noon on July 13, two aircraft from the "jeep" carrier *Core,* a Wildcat piloted by Earl H. Steiger and an Avenger flown by Robert P. Williams, spotted *U-487* on the surface with some crew topside sunbathing and some playing with a bale of cotton found in the water. Steiger attacked, strafing *U-487.* Williams followed, dropping four Torpex depth charges that fell close.

In response to a call for help, *Core* sent six more aircraft, two Wildcats and four Avengers. By the time they arrived, Metz on *U-487* had manned his quad 20mm and other flak guns and his gunners shot down and killed Steiger in his Wildcat. The other six planes strafed and depth-charged *U-487* until, finally, she sank steeply by the bow. One of *Core*'s screen, the four-stack destroyer *Barker,* fished out three officers and thirty men, but not Metz, who was killed by one of the strafing Wildcats. Twenty-six other Germans perished in the sinking. Williams, Steiger, and another Wildcat pilot, Charles W. Brewer, were credited with the kill.

Owing to the weight of the tasks assigned to Metz's tanker, *U-487,* Control directed the IXC *U-160,* which sailed from Bordeaux on June 28, commanded by a new skipper, Gerd von Pommer-Esche, age twenty-five, to "help out" the *U-487.* Therefore the *U-160* was en route to meet *U-487* when the latter was sunk.

While *U-160* was still well to the north of *U-487*'s position, a Wildcat-Avenger team from the *Santee* spotted her on the morning of July 14. H. Brinkley Bass in the Wildcat dived to strafe. John H. Ballentine in the Avenger came behind with depth charges and a Fido. In violation of the new standing orders, von Pommer-Esche dived, presenting a Fido target. Ballentine let go the Fido and it was assumed to have hit *U-160,* which was never heard from again. Her loss further complicated the excruciatingly tight refueling situation.

By this time, eight boats had arrived at the rendezvous site, expecting to meet *U-487* and/or her backup, *U-160.* Some boats had been at the site several days. One or more boats notified Control of the missing *U-487* and *U-160* and Control queried the *U-487.* When it received no reply from *U-487,* Control assumed she (but not *U-160*) was lost and issued a new refueling plan, designed to favor boats of the important group *Monsun.* The (lost) backup *U-160* was to refuel four *Monsun* boats (*U-516, U-532, U-533,* and the lost *U-509*). The IXC *U-155,* outbound to the Americas, was to refuel the other three *Monsun* boats (*U-168, U-183, U-188*) then come home. The VII *U-648,* outbound to the Americas, was to cancel her mission, refuel the IXC40 *U-527,* inbound from the Americas, then come home in company with *U-155.*

---

* *U-359, U-406, U-466, U-591, U-598, U-604, U-662.*

The three *Monsun* boats that were to resupply from the lost backup *U-160* reported her missing on July 19–20. Control correctly assumed she had been lost and assigned one of those four *Monsun* boats, *U-516,* which had reported irreparable mechanical difficulties, to refuel the other three on July 26: the lost *U-509, U-532,* and *U-533.* Then, as related, she was to go farther south to give the Americas-bound boat, *U-662,* ammo and a Metox. The *U-516* refueled the *U-532* and *U-533* but, of course, never found *U-662,* which, as related, was sunk on July 21. The *U-516* returned to France on August 23.

As directed, the IXC backup refueler *U-155,* commanded by *Ritterkreuz* holder Adolf-Cornelius Piening, who was diverted from a patrol to the Americas, met and refueled the other three *Monsun* boats (*U-168, U-183, U-188*) on July 23. The next day Piening made contact with von Trotha in *U-306,* homebound from Freetown. Piening gave von Trotha some fuel and the two boats returned to Lorient on August 11.

Per orders, the outbound VII *U-648,* commanded by Peter-Arthur Stahl, met the *U-527,* commanded by Herbert Uhlig, inbound from the Americas and transferred fuel on July 20. Control directed both boats to proceed in company to France.

Alerted to this rendezvous by Enigma decrypts and Huff Duff, aircraft from the "jeep" carrier *Bogue,* which was supporting eastbound convoy UGS 12, found *U-527* and *U-648* sailing side by side on the morning of July 23. An Avenger pilot, Robert L. Stearns, attacked the two boats. In violation of doctrine, Stahl crash-dived *U-648,* went deep, and escaped, returning to St. Nazaire on August 10. Uhlig in *U-527* remained on the surface, racing for a patch of fog and firing at the aircraft with 20mm flak guns. Stearns dropped four shallow-set depth charges that straddled the boat and blew open the pressure hull aft. The boat sank instantly, leaving Uhlig and a dozen other Germans in the water. Later, one of *Bogue*'s screen, the four-stack destroyer *Clemson,* fished the thirteen Germans from the water. Stearns, who helped sink the XB *U-118,* won a Navy Cross for this kill.

Assigned to *Monsun,* the new IXD2 U-cruiser *U-847,* which had incurred ice damage in the Denmark Strait and had aborted to Norway for repairs, was too far behind the surviving group to patrol with them and, as related, was assigned to be a refueler and was lost. Thus group *Monsun,* originally eleven boats, was reduced to the five Type IXC40s that had been lucky enough to escape from Biscay and to obtain fuel from provisional tankers *U-155* and *U-516.*

These five *Monsun* boats rounded the Cape of Good Hope into the Indian Ocean. On September 8, the day Italy capitulated, they met the German tanker *Brake.* As a precaution against the possibility that the Italians might reveal the rendezvous to the Allies, U-boat Control directed all German vessels to leave that area at once and proceed to a new rendezvous several hundred miles south. On September 12, *Brake* replenished the five *Monsun* boats and Control issued them patrol areas.

By that time American codebreakers had mastered naval Enigma by the use of the new four-rotor bombes, mathematical theory, and intuition. One result was that Allied authorities were able to keep track of the five *Monsun* IXC40s and to avoid them, minimizing merchant-shipping losses. The other results:

• Assigned to the Gulf of Cambay (near Bombay, India), Helmut Pich, age twenty-nine, in *U-168* sank the 2,200-ton British freighter *Haiching* by torpedo, and six cargo sailing vessels by deck gun. On the night of November 4, an as yet unidentified Catalina bombed *U-168,* thwarting an attack on a convoy.

• Patrolling off Mombasa, Kenya, Heinrich Schäfer, age thirty-six, in *U-183* sank no ships whatsoever. In extenuation, he reported that in the period from October 19 to October 24, he fired eight electric torpedoes at targets but all missed or malfunctioned.

• In the Gulf of Oman, Siegfried Lüdden, age twenty-seven, in *U-188* sank the 7,200-ton American Liberty ship *Cornelia P. Spencer* and damaged the 10,000-ton Norwegian tanker *Britannia.*

• Near the southern tip of India, Otto-Heinrich Junker, age thirty-eight, in *U-532* sank by torpedo and deck gun four freighters (two British, one Norwegian, one Indian) for about 24,500 tons.

• Assigned to the Gulf of Aden, Helmut Hennig, age twenty-nine, in *U-533* sank no ships. On October 16, a twin-engine Bisley light bomber of British Squadron 244, piloted by L. Chapman, sank *U-533* in the Gulf of Oman. Of the fifty-three crew, only one man survived: seaman Günther Schmidt, who washed ashore after twenty-eight hours in the water. Arabs found him and turned him over to a British patrol from Squadron 244.

The four surviving *Monsun* IXC40s went on to the new German-Japanese base on the island of Penang, Malaya. In aggregate they had sunk only six ships (and six sailing vessels) for about 33,800 tons, yet another humiliating U-boat failure, and another victory for Allied codebreakers. In Penang, Heinrich Schäfer in *U-183,* who had sunk no ships, was replaced by Fritz Schneewind, age twenty-six, who had earlier delivered the IXC *U-511* ("Marco Polo I") to Japan. Only two of these IXC40s (*U-188, U-532*) were to return to European waters. The other two (*U-168, U-183*) were to be sunk in the Far East by Allied forces.

The U-boat Stand-down of August

Partly as a result of Coastal Command's intense air offensive in the Bay of Biscay, the loss of U-boats in all waters had reached a catastrophic level by August 1. To repeat the Allied monthly kills:

April	15	(2 in Biscay)
May	40	(7 in Biscay)
June	17	(4 in Biscay*)
July	37	(12 in Biscay†)
Totals	109‡	(25 in Biscay)

* Two, *U-119* and *U-449,* by Support Group 2. See Plate 6.

† One, *U-504,* by Support Group 2. See Plate 6.

‡ At fifty men per boat, personnel losses would be 5,450. Allied records show that 733 of these were rescued and captured.

U-boat Control intended to maintain the tempo of patrols to distant waters in August, but the loss in late July of four Type XIV U-tankers (*U-459, U-461, U-462, U-487*) and another (*U-489*) on August 4, as well as a Type XB provisional tanker (*U-117*) on August 7, forced the Germans to revise plans and tactics drastically. As a first emergency step, Control recalled four boats that sailed from France on August 1.* Only one boat sailed to distant waters from France between August 1 and August 16, the *U-161,* which had first to carry out an urgent special mission. Eight more boats then sailed to distant waters in the ensuing days of the month.

As a second step, Control issued three important changes, two doctrinal and one technical.

- Commencing on August 2, U-boats were no longer to cross the Bay of Biscay in groups and/or to remain on the surface and fight it out with enemy aircraft. Both inbound and outbound boats were to travel singly, remain submerged, and surface to charge batteries only at night. The one exception to this rule was the new flak boat *U-621,* which put out on August 22 and was, of course, to remain on the surface in the Bay of Biscay deliberately to trap unsuspecting Allied aircraft.
- Commencing on August 12, all new boats sailing from Germany to join the Atlantic force were to stop at U-boat bases in Norway and top off fuel tanks. This was one measure to compensate for the heavy loss of U-tankers. Although a seemingly simple operation, it was not. The Germans had to ship precious fuel oil from German refineries to Norway by tanker, arrange for air and surface escorts in and out of Norway, and provide protection from air attacks while the boats were in Norwegian ports. Moreover, Norway gradually became a place where U-boats conducted final training, machinery and electronics retrofits, and voyage repairs, theretofore carried out in the Baltic. This practice overcrowded the Norwegian bases and led to delays in sailings.

Of the nine U-boats that sailed from Kiel to Norway from August 12 to August 31, none continued on in August. Six laid over in Norway for nearly a month. One got away after merely two weeks, but the average layover for the nine boats was 26.4 days. Control delayed the sailing of some of these boats for tactical reasons, but most simply became ensnared in the red tape of the new procedures and some were damaged during the layover. The layovers, of course, delayed considerably the reinforcement of the Atlantic force that had been savaged during the summer months.

- Commencing on August 15, all boats were to cease using the Metox radar detector, or FuMB. Experiments had convinced the Germans that Metox did indeed radiate a signal—albeit a very weak one—on which Allied aircraft might be able to home. All outbound boats were to be equipped with a new radar detector, W Anz Gi, dubbed *Wanze* (Bed Bug), built by the German firm Hagenuk.

There was, however, a flaw in the substitution of *Wanze* for Metox, yet another technical mistake and commentary on the sad state of German science and engineering under Hitler. Unlike Metox, *Wanze* was not supposed to give off electronic emissions, which the Germans believed the Allies were able to detect on their radar. But *Wanze* did in fact give off the same (weak) level of emissions as Metox. More

* *U-68, U-437, U-448, U-505.*

important, *Wanze,* like Metox, could only search in the broader, meter-wavelength bands, not in the centimetric-wavelength range. German scientists and engineers still did not believe that miniaturized centimetric-wavelength radar was possible!*

The weakness in German science and engineering was vividly revealed in a meeting between Dönitz and Hitler on August 19. According to the stenographer, Dönitz told Hitler that Metox emanations "may explain all the uncanny and unsolved mysteries of the past, such as the enemy avoiding traps set for him, and losses on the open seas." Hitler listened with "utmost interest to these explanations," the stenographer noted, then replied that "he believes that the [Metox-radiation] theory just advanced does account for many baffling facts, such as the ability of the enemy frequently to determine the exact number of [U-boats] in a patrol [line]." The "discovery" of Metox emanations, Hitler gushed, was "a great step forward" for the Germans.

During the August hiatus, U-boat Control, spurred by Admiral Dönitz, prepared to renew the U-boat war on the North Atlantic run that had been allowed to lapse since the previous May 24. The return to that decisive battleground in mid-September was to be a sudden dramatic blow, designed to create maximum psychological terror. An entire group, *Leuthen,* composed of twenty-one boats supported by the Type XIV tanker *U-460,* would sail secretly, assemble, and attack a convoy simultaneously. In a radical reversal in tactics, the boats were to first attack and destroy the surface escorts, then, secondly, the merchant ships.

To carry out this new tactical scheme with the greatest possible success, the twenty-one *Leuthen* boats (all Type VIIs) were to be equipped with the very best gear the Germans could provide. This package was to include:

- The new, somewhat faster, battery-powered T-5 *Zaunkönig* (Wren) homing torpedo, which the Allies called GNAT, an acronym for German Naval Acoustic Torpedo. U-boat skippers were to fire T-5s at the Allied escorts and wipe them out, then if any T-5s were left over, they could be used against the merchant ships, along with the regular air and electric and FAT looping and circling torpedoes with and without magnetic pistols.
- The new *Wanze* radar detector, replacing Metox.
- The *Aphrodite* radar decoy.
- The *Bolde* noisemaking sonar decoy.
- The quad 20mm and twin 20mm flak arrays for defense against Allied aircraft, mounted on improved bridge platforms.
- More sensitive passive-sonar arrays to enhance the ability of the boats to "hear" a convoy while submerged.

In its final configuration, group *Leuthen* was composed of eighteen experienced Type VIIs from France and three new Type VIIs from Germany. Nine VIIs and Ebe Schnoor's supporting tanker *U-460* sailed from France from August 23 to

* Nor that Enigma could be broken, nor that high-frequency direction finding (Huff Duff) was an effective U-boat locator.

August 31, the other nine VIIs from September 1 to September 9. The three new VIIs from Germany that in accordance with new procedure had laid over in Norway (for almost a month) sailed from Bergen and Trondheim from September 5 to September 9. The operations of group *Leuthen* in September are described later in this narrative.

Apart from the new flak boat *U-621,* which remained in the Bay of Biscay, and the boats of group *Leuthen,* nine U-boats sailed from France in August, all to distant waters.

To get out of Biscay without attacks from the air, some of these boats closely hugged the coast of France and northern Spain as far as Cape Finisterre. Aware of this routing from naval Enigma decrypts, the Admiralty deployed two support groups in areas near the Cape. These were the 40th, commanded by John S. Dallison (frigate *Exe* and five sloops and corvettes, backed up by British cruiser *Bermuda*), and the newly created Canadian Support Group 5, commanded by the Britisher J. D. Birch (British frigates *Nene* and *Tweed,* five upgraded Canadian corvettes and a British corvette).

The Germans reacted to this bold gathering of surface ships by deploying special *Luftwaffe* attack forces. On August 25, a flight of fourteen Dornier DO-217s fitted with HS 293 radio-controlled "smart bombs" and protected by seven JU-88s, attacked Dallison's Support Group 40. All the bombs missed but four near-misses heavily damaged the British sloop *Languard,* one of the ex-American Coast Guard cutters.

The British Support Group 1, commanded by Godfrey Brewer (sloop *Egret,* frigates *Jed* and *Rother,* backed up by destroyers *Athabaskan* and *Grenville*) relieved Dallison's Support Group 40. On August 28, a flight of eighteen DO-217s fitted with smart bombs and protected by JU-88s, attacked Brewer's Support Group 1. Most of the bombs missed the wildly dodging ships, but one hit and blew up the sloop *Egret,* Brewer's flagship, with the loss of two hundred of her 225-man crew. Another hit and damaged the *Tribal*-class destroyer *Athabaskan,* which, after about two months of repairs, was recommissioned in the Royal Canadian Navy.

• The IXC *U-161,* commanded by *Ritterkreuz* holder Albrecht Achilles, sailed from Lorient to Brazil on August 8. As directed, Achilles met the France-bound Japanese U-cruiser *I-8* (code-named *"Flieder,"* or Lilac) near the Azores on August 20. He handed over a German navigator/pilot, a new *Wanze* radar detector, radio personnel, and routing instructions for a rendezvous in Biscay with JU-88s and German destroyers.* This done, Achilles met Werner Hartmann in the homebound U-cruiser *U-198* in the middle of the South Atlantic on September 6, gave Hartmann a *Wanze,* obtained fuel, then proceeded to Brazilian waters.

Upon reaching his patrol area, Achilles sank two freighters in the week of Sep-

* The *I-8* reached Lorient on September 8. She had on board an extra fifty Japanese submariners to bring back another gift from Hitler to Tojo, "Marco Polo II," the IXC40 *U-1224.* The *I-8* sailed home about October 1 and reached the Far East in December.

tember 20 to 26. The first victim was the 5,500-ton British *St. Usk;* the second, the 5,000-ton Brazilian *Itapagé.* On the day after he sank the second ship, September 27, a Mariner of U.S. Navy Squadron VP 74, piloted by Harry B. Patterson, found *U-161* and attacked with machine guns and depth charges. Nothing further was heard from *U-161.*

• Two boats that had sailed on August 1 but returned to France, resailed in company to American waters on August 16. These were the famous old Drumbeat boat, the IXB *U-123,* and the IXC *U-523,* commanded by Horst von Schroeter and Werner Pietzsch, respectively.

In the dark early hours of the seventh day out, August 22, a Leigh Light–equipped Wellington of British Squadron 179 caught and bombed *U-523.* Pietzsch dived and escaped, but the Wellington's report alerted surface ships passing in the vicinity, including the British close escort of a convoy en route from the British Isles to Gibraltar. Unaware of the proximity of enemy surface ships, on the night of August 24–25 Pietzsch ran on the surface.

The destroyer *Wanderer* and the corvette *Wallflower* of the convoy escort got *U-523* on radar and caught her by complete surprise. Shaken, Pietzsch dived to elude, but *Wanderer,* commanded by Reginald F. (Bob) Whinney, immediately found the boat on sonar and commenced a dogged depth-charge attack, which *Wallflower* soon joined. Pietzsch went so deep (to 880 feet, some crewmen asserted) that the hull "groaned" and the interior wood trim "splintered" from the immense sea pressure. Finally Pietzsch gave up and surfaced to scuttle, taking gunfire from both warships. That fire killed about a dozen Germans before they could jump from the sinking boat. The destroyers *Wanderer* and *Hurricane,* the corvette *Wallflower,* and the convoy rescue ship *Zamalek* fished thirty-seven Germans from the water, including Pietzsch.

Near Cape Finisterre, Allied surface ships also found and depth-charged von Schroeter in *U-123* but he got away. Control assigned the boat to patrol the Trinidad area, but later modified the orders to include the "bauxite route" farther south, if von Schroeter chose to go there. He did and on September 21, he found and attacked a convoy of tankers and Liberty ships off French Guiana that had a powerful sea and air escort. He claimed two definite hits and three maybes, but these have not been confirmed in Allied records.

Due to the lack of refuelers, on October 11 Control ordered von Schroeter to come home. While the boat was approaching St. Nazaire on November 7, a Mosquito flying with British Squadron 248 (on detachment from Squadron 618) attacked *U-123.* Piloted by a Canadian, A.J.L. Bonnett, the Mosquito was fitted with a powerful new 57mm (six pounder) cannon called a "Tsetse." On the first run in, Bonnett fired eight 57mm rounds that struck *U-123* on or near the bridge. On the second run, the "Tsetse" jammed and Bonnett could only fire machine guns. Reporting the attack, von Schroeter said he had a hole in the conning tower that precluded diving and requested air support. He reached St. Nazaire that day, completing an arduous but fruitless patrol of eighty-four days.

• The IXC *U-518,* commanded by Friedrich-Wilhelm Wissmann, which sailed from Bordeaux on August 18. Wissmann patrolled the Old Bahama Channel to the waters off Florida. He then entered the Gulf of Mexico and patrolled westward to the Yucatan Channel. He sank no ships either. Also recalled by Control on October 11, the *U-518* finally reached France on December 1, completing a barren cruise of 106 days. At this time Wissmann left the boat for other duty.

• The veteran VIID (minelayer) *U-214,* commanded by Rupprecht Stock, which sailed on August 22. His assignment was to lay mines off Colón, Panama. While outbound on September 14, Stock also met Werner Hartmann in the homebound U-cruiser *U-198.* He transferred an engineer to *U-198,* obtained some fuel, then proceeded to Panama, where he laid the mines on October 10. None sank a ship.

Thereafter, Stock patrolled the Caribbean but had no luck. Control directed him to lay any remaining mines inside his exit passage from the Caribbean. After leaving that area, Stock claimed to have sunk a 7,000-ton freighter by torpedoes on October 21, but the sinking was never confirmed. On the homebound voyage, Stock was to refuel from one of the two remaining Type XIV tankers, *U-488,* but when an American "jeep" carrier crashed that party, Control ordered him to refuel from a provisional refueler, the IXC40 *U-193.* That worked out on November 7 and Stock finally reached France on November 30.

• The IXC40 *U-170,* commanded by Günther Pfeffer, which sailed from Lorient on August 29. For reasons that are not clear, Pfeffer had to rendezvous in Biscay with the new flak boat *U-621* on September 6 to pick up a *Wanze* radar detector. About a week later, on September 14, Pfeffer met the Type XIV tanker *U-460* and refueled. Control then sent *U-170* to Brazil to join Achilles in the *U-161,* which, however, was soon lost.

Pfeffer reached Brazilian waters in the first week of October. Merely a week later, on October 11, Control warned him that refueling on the return leg might be iffy owing to the shortage of refuelers. However, Pfeffer remained off Rio de Janeiro where, on October 23, he sank one freighter, the 5,700-ton Brazilian *Campos.*

While still in that area on November 5, Control directed Pfeffer to go at maximum speed to the assistance of the new, outbound IXD2 U-cruiser *U-848,* which was under heavy air attack in mid-Atlantic about one thousand miles to the northeast of *U-170.* Unknown to the Germans, *U-848* had been sunk in this attack but Pfeffer in *U-170* pressed on to the scene to pick up survivors, if any. Pfeffer combed the area of the sinking until November 12 but found no sign of *U-848* or survivors and headed home, low on fuel. On November 30, he met the Type XB minelayer *U-219,* serving as a provisional tanker, replenished, and finally reached Lorient on December 23, completing a largely fruitless patrol of 117 days.

• The VII *U-669,* commanded by Kurt Köhl, age thirty, which sailed from St. Nazaire on August 29. Control assigned Köhl to a special mission, *Kiebitz* (Lapwing). The task was to pick up the hero Otto Kretschmer and other U-boat POWs* who were to tunnel out of Canadian Camp 30 at Bowmanville on Lake Ontario,

* Hans Ey and Horst Elfe, ex-skippers of *U-433* and *U-93,* respectively; Kretschmer's first watch officer on *U-99,* Hans-Joachim von Knebel-Döberitz, and others.

twenty-five miles east of Toronto, then proceed to New Brunswick on the Gulf of St. Lawrence by various means.

On the night of September 7, a Leigh Light–equipped Wellington of Canadian Squadron 407, piloted by E. M. O'Donnell, found a U-boat, thought to be *U-669,* by radar and attacked her, dropping five depth charges. These supposedly destroyed *U-669* with the loss of all hands, but Alex Niestlé has attributed her loss to unknown causes. Six months later O'Donnell and most of this aircrew perished in another Wellington.

- The IXC40 *U-536,* commanded by Rolf Schauenburg, age thirty, which sailed from Lorient on August 29. When Control assumed correctly that Köhl in *U-669* had been lost, it assigned *U-536* to carry out the POW rescue mission, *Kiebitz.* After reaching the Gulf of St. Lawrence, Schauenburg lay off the appointed site, Pointe de Maisonette, New Brunswick, from September 24. However, Kretschmer and his cohorts were nowhere to be found.

Allied authorities had learned of the planned escape by decrypting the simple codes embedded in POW mail and intercepting materials (maps and so on) that were mailed to the would-be escapees concealed in gift packages. At this same time, POW Wolfgang Heyda, ex-skipper of *U-434,* escaped independently "over the wire" and made his way to New Brunswick, but he was recaptured there by Canadian authorities. An elaborate Allied plan to seize *U-536* in the Gulf of St. Lawrence miscarried.

After doing his utmost to complete this special mission, Rolf Schauenburg in *U-536* patrolled off Halifax, where he claimed sinking an American or British Liberty ship which, however, could not be confirmed. While on his homeward voyage, U-boat Control directed Schauenburg to join other U-boats that were attacking a large northbound convoy, Sierra Leone 139 combined with MKS 30, en route from the Mediterranean and Gibraltar to the British Isles (sixty-six merchant ships, massively escorted by nineteen surface escorts as well as by land-based aircraft).

The British frigate *Nene* and the Canadian corvettes *Calgary* and *Snowberry* of the close escort found *U-536* on November 20, blew her to the surface, and then sank her with concentrated gunfire. Thirty-eight of fifty-five crew on *U-536* were lost. Ironically, Schauenburg and sixteen other German survivors eventually wound up in another POW camp in Canada.

- The IXC *U-515,* commanded by Werner Henke, age thirty-five, who wore Oak Leaves on his *Ritterkreuz* that had been presented to him by Hitler on July 4 at his headquarters, *Wolfschanze,* in East Prussia. He sailed from Lorient on August 29 to patrol the Freetown area, where he had done so well the previous April and May. As the American archivist/historian Timothy Mulligan has related in his biography of Henke,* during his R&R at Innsbruck, Tyrol, Henke had had a run-in with the Gestapo. The cause was not earthshaking, but the Gestapo had inflated the incident to the point that Henke had sailed under a cloud.

The *U-515* had all the latest U-boat improvements: four of the faster T-5 *Zaunkönig* homing torpedoes, quad and twin 20mm flak arrays on a modified bridge

---

* *Lone Wolf* (1993).

structure, *Wanze,* and *Aphrodite.* The boat also had a new flak gun, the rapid-fire 37mm, which Hitler had encouraged. It was mounted on the main deck forward of the bridge in place of the standard 4.1" gun. In addition to all that, Henke carried six extra G7a torpedoes in topside canisters.

Control directed Henke to top off his fuel tanks from the Type XIV tanker *U-460* on September 4. While proceeding to that rendezvous the following day, Henke came upon a large convoy. This was Outbound South 54 combined with KMS 25: fifty-four merchant ships and about fifteen surface escorts plus heavy aircraft patrols. Henke shadowed during the day, and that night he came up on the rear of the convoy to mount a surface attack by the dim light of a first-quarter moon.

As Henke closed to one thousand yards, lookouts on one of the merchant ships, *Gascony,* spotted the U-boat. That vessel gave the alarm and opened up with her 4" gun, forcing Henke to dive. One of the escorts, the new British frigate *Tavy,* got the boat on sonar and commenced a close and accurate depth-charge attack that drove Henke to 820 feet. The explosion tore open an aft ballast tank, cracked most of the storage-battery cells, and smashed in all six topside torpedo canisters. Henke got *U-515* back to the surface, eluded the escorts, and aborted the patrol, reaching Lorient on September 12.

Henke's minor altercation with the Gestapo had by that time inflated to the point that Dönitz and Admiral Hans-Georg von Friedeburg had to personally come to his defense. In a letter of apology to Heinrich Himmler on October 19, von Friedeburg stated that owing to the heavy stress of U-boat warfare, skippers such as Henke were more apt to blow off steam than other German officers. Nevertheless he and Dönitz had sharply rebuked Henke, who acknowledged and regretted his inappropriate behavior.* As biographer Mulligan wrote, Himmler accepted the apology and closed the case.

The nine patrols Control mounted to distant waters in August resulted in the sinking of merely three Allied merchant ships for about 17,700 tons. In return, four U-boats were lost: three Type IXs (*U-161, U-523, U-536*) and one Type VII (*U-669*). Henke in the Type IX *U-515* was very nearly lost.

Quadrant, Baytown, and Avalanche

The invasion of Sicily and the ensuing tough fight with the Germans on that rugged Mediterranean island raised anew the issue of just how much effort the Allies were to expend in the Mediterranean. Although the military chiefs had agreed on the next steps, a rapid invasion of Calabria (Baytown), the "toe" of Italy, together with a landing up the "boot" at Salerno (Avalanche), the long-term plans for the Mediterranean remained unsettled. The British had again proposed a sustained campaign in Italy to at least liberate Rome, plus an invasion of the Balkan Peninsula, what Churchill called the "soft underbelly" of the Third Reich. Secretary of

---

* On a skiing trip to the Tyrol between war patrols, Henke had leaped to the defense of a local Innsbruk family that was under heavy-handed attack by the Gestapo.

War Stimson, George Marshall, Hap Arnold, and Admiral King vigorously opposed the British plan, urging instead that all the Allied effort be put behind Overlord, the invasion of Occupied France.

Returning from a visit to the British Isles, Stimson pleaded with Roosevelt to renew his support of Overlord in the strongest possible terms. As a first step, Stimson said, the President should insist on an American rather than a British commander. As he wrote:

> We cannot now rationally hope to be able to cross the Channel and come to grips with our German enemy under a British commander. His Prime Minister and his Chief of Imperial Staff are frankly at variance with such a proposal [Overlord]. The shadows of Passchendaele and Dunkerque still hang too heavily over the imaginations of these leaders of government. Though they have rendered lip service to the [Overlord] operation, their hearts are not in it and it will require more independence, more faith, and more vigor than it is reasonable to expect we can find in any British commander to overcome the natural difficulties of such an operation carried on in such an atmosphere of his government.*

At the suggestion of Prime Minister Churchill, he and President Roosevelt and their respective military advisers met yet again, this time in the city of Quebec. Churchill and party again crossed the Atlantic on the monster liner *Queen Mary,*† arriving at Halifax, Nova Scotia, on August 9. From there, Churchill went by train to visit Roosevelt at his home in Hyde Park, New York, from August 12 to 14, and returned to Quebec on August 15. Roosevelt arrived in Quebec by train on August 17, mere hours after the last Axis forces evacuated Sicily.

The conferees at this meeting—code-named Quadrant—reaffirmed previous strategic decisions and added others. The main decisions regarding Europe were:

- All hands, British and American alike, agreed that preparations for the cross-channel invasion of Occupied France, Overlord, were to receive the highest priority and that the invasion was to be carried out on approximately May 1, 1944. An American, probably Army Chief of Staff George C. Marshall, was to be named commander in chief. The Americans, however, were still not certain that the British fully supported Overlord.
- The newly launched combined heavy-bomber offensive against Germany (Sickle/Pointblank) was to receive the highest priority as well. The British were unflagging in support of the strategic bombing of Germany.
- Contingency plans for Allied invasions of Sardinia, Corsica, and/or the Balkans were tabled. A plan for an Allied invasion of southern France between Toulon and Marseilles (Anvil, later renamed Dragoon) to coincide with Overlord gained favor.
- At the urging of Churchill and the British contingent, Roosevelt overrode the objections of American scientific and military advisers and entered into an extraordinary formal agreement to share all the secrets of the atomic bomb with the British.

---

* From Matloff, *Strategic Planning* (1959).

† Escorted by the British carrier *Illustrious,* the American carrier *Ranger,* three heavy cruisers, destroyers, and land-based aircraft.

During the Quadrant conference, First Sea Lord Dudley Pound suffered a severe stroke that left him weak and partly paralyzed. When he and Churchill arrived in Washington by train on September 1 for further conferences at the White House, Pound informed Churchill that he could not go on and resigned his post. Pending the appointment of Mediterranean naval commander Andrew Cunningham to replace Pound, Edward Syfret held down the job.

Churchill remained in the United States and Canada another two weeks. On September 14, he arrived in Halifax, Nova Scotia, by train and sailed home on the old battlecruiser *Renown.* For Churchill, it had been quite a lengthy sojourn: August 4 to September 20, forty-eight days away from London. Dudley Pound returned with the Churchill party on *Renown.* In London, he suffered two more severe strokes and died on Trafalgar Day, October 21.

Meanwhile, the invasions of Italy proceeded. On September 2, Bernard Montgomery's Eighth Army crossed the narrow Strait of Messina (Operation Baytown) and landed unopposed in Calabria. It was noted that British ground forces had thus "returned to the European mainland," one day shy of the fourth anniversary of Britain's declaration of war against Germany. As secretly arranged, Italy surrendered on September 8, one day before the Anglo-American invasion at Salerno (Avalanche). These operations, and Hitler's determination to hold Italy at all costs, mired Allied forces in a prolonged and bloody campaign in the mountains of Italy that few senior American officials considered to be worthwhile.

As with the French fleet, Churchill was eager to capture the Italian fleet and to turn these assets against the *Kriegsmarine.* In compliance with the secret arrangements, the Italians forswore a beau geste "fight to the last" or scuttling. On September 9, the first-line battleships *Roma, Vittorio Veneto,* and *Littorio* (renamed *Italia*), together with six light cruisers and eight destroyers, sailed from Genoa and La Spezia to surrender in Malta. While en route, *Luftwaffe* aircraft, employing HS 293 radio-controlled smart bombs, sank *Roma* with heavy loss of life and slightly damaged *Littorio* (*Italia*). All the other Italian ships reached Malta, a parade that vastly cheered the long-besieged citizenry of that island. In due course, the old battleship *Cesare* and the small, old, but upgraded battleships *Doria* and *Duilio* also reached Malta.* The festivities were dampened considerably on the afternoon of September 16 when *Luftwaffe* aircraft hit the British battleship *Warspite* with a "smart bomb."

The Italian surrender led to awkward complications in the Axis submarine commands. At home in the Baltic, the Germans took back the ten Type VIIs that had been given to Italy in exchange for the conversion of big Italian submarines to cargo carriers. The Germans interned the Italian crews that were in training on those boats. The Germans also seized the five remaining Italian cargo submarines and their crews: *Finzi* and *Bagnolini* in Bordeaux; *Torelli, Cappellini,* and *Giuliani*

---

* Two more medium-size Italian submarines, *Velella* and *Topazio,* were sunk by British forces in the Mediterranean on September 7 and 12, respectively. The big U-cruiser *Cagni,* on patrol in the Indian Ocean, put into Durban, South Africa, on September 21 to surrender and from there proceeded to the Mediterranean, where she became a training ship for Allied ASW forces.

in the Far East. These were commissioned in the *Kriegsmarine* as *U-IT21* to *U-IT25,* but not one completed a successful voyage under German command. In due course three were sunk or destroyed. The remaining two, *Cappellini* (*U-IT24*) and *Torelli* (*U-IT25*), ultimately fell into Japanese hands in the Far East and were redesignated *I-503* and *I-504,* respectively.

The rapid Allied advances into Sicily and Italy imperiled the German Mediterranean U-boat force, reduced to thirteen U-boats. Operations in the Mediterranean, teeming with Allied ships and aircraft, which had always been hazardous, now became almost impossibly so. Besides that, the German submariners were harassed by sporadic Allied air bombardment of the flotilla headquarters in Toulon. Even so, Hitler insisted that this German U-boat flotilla be reinforced. In response, on September 17, Control ordered seven VIIs to slip through the Strait of Gibraltar as soon as possible.

Four VIIs led the way. The *U-223,* commanded by Karl-Jürgen Wächter, age twenty-seven, which had sailed from France three days before the order was issued, got through the strait in spite of heavy air attacks on the night of September 26, a dark period of new moon. Radar-equipped Allied ASW forces thwarted the other three: *U-264, U-455,* and *U-667.* After breaking off the attempts to get through the strait, the *U-455* and *U-264* sailed to the North Atlantic run; the *U-667* aborted to France with battle damage.

The return of the last named, *U-667,* commanded by Heinrich Schroeteler, age twenty-seven, was a memorable saga. On the night of September 24–25, two Leigh Light–equipped Wellingtons of Gibraltar-based British Squadron 179, piloted by A. Chiltern and D. J. McMahon, found and attacked *U-667,* each dropping six depth charges. The next day another Wellington of that squadron, piloted by S. H. Nicholson, attacked the damaged boat, dropping six more depth charges. Thereafter a Hudson of British Squadron 233, piloted by A. G. Frandson, and another Hudson of British Squadron 48 arrived at the scene. Each Hudson fired eight rockets at the boat in salvos of two, two, and four.

Somehow Schroeteler escaped these five (possibly six) aircraft. On September 29, he reported that he had withstood altogether eight separate aircraft attacks but had incurred "extensive damage" and was aborting. He added—significantly—that his *Wanze* radar detector had not warned of radar use in any of these aircraft. Finally he reached France on October 11.

By that time the Germans were finally persuaded that the Allies had developed miniaturized centimetric-wavelength radar for aircraft. Therefore, as Control logged with the greatest restraint on September 26, the new FuMB, or *Wanze* radar detector, was useless and the difficulty experienced by the boats attempting the Strait of Gibraltar was ample proof of that. Fortunately, Control went on, German engineers had already developed a centimetric-wavelength radar detector known as *Naxos.* It was "shortly" to be installed on all U-boats in place of *Wanze,* Control concluded. Until then no boat should attempt to pass through the Strait of Gibraltar.

During the Allied invasion of Calabria (Baytown) and Salerno (Avalanche) in early September, the Mediterranean U-boat force, thirteen boats, failed to inflict any decisive setback to Allied naval forces. The notable overclaimer Albrecht Brandi in *U-617,* who wore Oak Leaves on his *Ritterkreuz,* actually sank a British warship, confirmed in Allied records, on September 6. She was the 1,000-ton British *Hunt*-class destroyer *Puckeridge,* which went down forty miles east of Gibraltar. Brandi claimed sinking another "destroyer" in the same area on September 11, but it was never confirmed. Off the Salerno-Naples battleground, *Ritterkreuz* holder Gerd Kelbling in *U-593* sank two American vessels. The first, on September 21, was the 7,200-ton Liberty ship *William W. Gerhard.* The other, on September 25, was the 800-ton Navy minesweeper *Skill.* Off the coast of Algeria, near Bône, Horst-Arno Fenski in the *U-410* sank two more 7,200-ton Liberty ships, the British *Fort Howe* and the Norwegian *Christian Michelsen,* plus the 3,700-ton British tanker *Empire Commerce.* For these and past successes and claims, Fenski won a *Ritterkreuz.**

In follow-up operations against the Allied forces engaged in the invasion of Italy, five boats achieved successes in October.

- Waldemar Mehl in the *U-371* sank three confirmed vessels: the 7,200-ton American Liberty ship *James R. Lowell;* the 700-ton British minecraft *Hythe* and—most notably—the new (1941) American fleet destroyer *Bristol,* which was escorting a convoy near the Algerian coast and went down in ten minutes. The American destroyers *Trippe* and *Wainwright* rescued fifty-two men from *Bristol,* but 241 others perished, a terrible American tragedy.
- No less significantly, off Naples, Siegfried Koitschka in *U-616* sank the new (1940) American destroyer *Buck,* which two months earlier had sunk the Italian submarine *Argento.* The American destroyer *Gleaves* and a British LCT rescued ninety-seven crew, but about 150 others perished, yet another American tragedy.
- Victor-Wilhelm Nonn, age twenty-six, new skipper of *U-596,* sank a 5,500-ton Norwegian tanker near Tobruk.
- Karl-Jürgen Wächter in the newly arrived *U-223* sank a 5,000-ton British freighter off the coast of Algeria.
- Dietrich Schöneboom, age twenty-five, in *U-431,* claimed sinking three freighters for 26,000 tons, the probable sinking of another freighter of 10,000 tons, and damage to yet another of 12,000 tons. Although none of these claimed hits could be confirmed, Schöneboom won a *Ritterkreuz* for these and other alleged successes.†

During these operations, another U-boat was lost inside the Mediterranean.

On the night of September 10, a Leigh Light–equipped Wellington of British Squadron 179, piloted by a Canadian, D. B. Hodgkinson, found the highly decorated Albrecht Brandi in *U-617* about one hundred miles east of Gibraltar near the coast of Spanish Morocco. Attacking into "heavy" flak, Hodgkinson dropped six depth charges that disabled *U-617.* Three hours later, in the early hours of Septem-

---

* At the time of the award, his score was six confirmed ships sunk for 39,650 tons and one 7,200-ton Liberty ship damaged.

† At the time of the award, his confirmed score was one freighter of 6,415 tons and four sailing vessels.

ber 11, another Wellington from that squadron, piloted by W. H. Brunini, arrived and, in the face of "intense" flak, dropped six more depth charges.

These attacks so badly damaged *U-617* that Brandi could not dive. To avoid certain capture, he drove the boat into shallow water offshore and abandoned ship. After he and the crew reached the beach, Spanish troops took the Germans into custody. However, they were soon released and returned, via Spain, to Toulon, where Brandi, who had added to his laurels with this "escape," was given command of another boat, *U-380.*

After dawn on September 11, swarms of Hudsons and Swordfish of British Squadrons 48, 233, 833, and 886 (based at Gibraltar) located the abandoned hulk of *U-617* and attacked with bombs and rockets. Three warships (British corvette *Hyacinth,* British trawler *Haarlem,* Australian minesweeper *Woollongong*) then arrived to shell *U-617* into smithereens. Pilot Hodgkinson, the Canadian who originally found and disabled *U-617,* won a DFC.

"Cain," "Abel," and Other Siblings

At the National Cash Register Company in Dayton, Ohio, the Naval Computing Machine Laboratory (NCML) completed two more Model 530 four-rotor prototype bombes, "Cain" and "Abel." These embodied improvements suggested by the first two prototypes, "Adam" and "Eve." The first "formal" (or production) Model 530 was delivered on July 4 and had its first test run at the lab on July 23. According to the historian Colin Burke, by the end of July 1943, fifteen Model 530s had been completed, "but none would work!"

As Burke recounted the story, the main technical defect lay in the "Bakelite code wheels." As before, when run at the required extremely high speeds, the wheels distorted and failed to make proper electrical contacts. By July 26, Burke wrote, the chief electrical engineer at NCR, Joe Desch, as well as the Navy lab chief, Ralph Meader, and others "feared the American bombe might never be made operational." These men, Burke wrote, "almost declared" that a year of frenetic work had been wasted and "the American bombe came near to being abandoned."

Whether or not this Burke version of events is fair, accurate, and sufficiently complete cannot be judged until the National Security Agency releases the "RAM File" documents to which the agency gave Burke exclusive access for his book. As related, in his understandable eagerness to credit the genius of Joe Desch, Burke apparently found it necessary to depict Desch and Howard Engstrom as technical antagonists, usually resulting in victory for Desch and defeat for Engstrom.

Whatever the truth of the matter, Burke wrote that it was Joe Desch who saved the day. "Desch predicted that careful storage, handling, and refurbishing would solve the problem." "Again his judgment was trusted," Burke continued. "The wheels were reworked and production was resumed based on his hope that last-minute modifications would provide a permanent cure." Apparently his solution worked. "Desch's bombes proved to be very, very reliable," Burke concluded. "After their first shakedown runs, they could be used twenty-four hours a day."

According to the previously described Engstrom "Bombe History," NCR turned out about four bombes per week over the summer of 1943. In early August, OP20G directed Dayton to prepare to ship bombes to Washington as soon as the new two-story building at the Nebraska Avenue facility was ready to receive them. Dayton shipped four bombes on September 1 in heavily guarded railway cars. Seventy-three men and women from Dayton reported to Nebraska Avenue to run and repair these machines: thirteen officers (three Waves) and sixty enlisted persons (fifteen Waves). This unit, which expanded quickly to hundreds, was designated OP20G4E.

By the end of September 1943, there were seventeen Model 530 bombes in operation at Nebraska Avenue. Eleven other machines had arrived but were "not set up." However, by October 15, thirty-nine bombes were running and by November 1, forty-four. By January 1944, eighty-four bombes were on line.

Concluding his history, Engstrom wrote generously in April 1944:

> From a position of subordination in the [U-boat Enigma] problem, we have, by superior performance, gradually assumed a dominating position in the submarine problem. The part played by the British in the success of our work should not, however, be minimized. While it is possible that we might have been able to proceed independently, they have supplied elements, such as wheel wirings, absolutely essential to an early solution of the problem.
>
> Their coverage of the entire Enigma field and their resulting strong position with regard to cross-cribbing, as well as their ability to obtain physical possession of German cryptographic equipment and documents, make it highly advisable that we endeavor to maintain our present relations in this problem, despite their failure to carry out their obligations along certain lines.

The Americans concerned pledged never to reveal the secrets of breaking Enigma. The Britons concerned likewise pledged, but beginning in 1974* they began to leak the secret at such a fast rate that both London and Washington were finally compelled to declassify and release official documents. In the Niagara of British books about breaking Enigma, however, the fact that the British were unable to cope with four-rotor *Triton* and that from the fall of 1943 onward the Americans took over the job is almost never mentioned. If it is, the reference is so slight as to have no impact whatsoever.

Another reason historians and writers have ignored the American contribution to breaking U-boat Enigma is the belief that by the summer of 1943, the U-boat force was utterly defeated and therefore the information from the American decrypts was of little value. This, of course, is wildly untrue. As related, in March 1943, the Allies had projected a huge net increase of the U-boat force to 613 boats by year's end. In addition, they were aware from Enigma decrypts of the upgrades planned or in progress on the old boats (snorkels, microwave radar detectors, more powerful flak arrays, T-5 homing torpedoes, and so on) and the ongoing German crash program to build the high sprint-speed Type XXI and Type XXIII "electro

* See Winterbotham, *The Ultra Secret* (1974).

boats" and the even faster hydrogen-peroxide Walter U-boats. Therefore, every scrap of information on German U-boats then and to the end of the war was of vital importance to those charged with countering the menace they posed.

The Allies also faced daily the possibility that the Germans might increase the complexity of naval Enigma or even adopt an altogether new cryptographic system. Therefore the R&D work of Howard Engstrom's OP20G section continued at a relentless pace to the end of the war. He and his men produced a substantial number of exotic new devices that kept the Allies one step ahead of the Germans. Other projects proved to be important contributions to the birth of the computer age.

On the other side of the Atlantic, German codebreakers at *B-dienst* faced grave difficulties. When on June 10 the Allies began the shift from the compromised Naval Cypher Number 3 to Naval Cypher Number 5, the Germans lost the great flow of specific information on Allied convoy cycles.

B-dienst, however, was able to keep track of the convoy cycles on the North Atlantic run by other means. These included sporadic breaks in a low-level British naval code and the Allied merchant-ship code, describing "straggler routes"* and by traffic analysis and, occasionally, radio-direction finding. In early September, *B-dienst* proudly reported to the OKM that of the forty-nine loaded convoys on the North Atlantic run eastbound from the Americas to the British Isles that sailed between May 25 and September 3, it had obtained information from "radio sources" on all but five.

This information, plus past experience and intuition, enabled *B-dienst* to figure out convoy cycles on the North Atlantic run through much of September and October 1943. The Germans concerned knew that the information derived from "a secondary cypher" (as Dönitz put it), and they were aware that this source was likely to dry up at any hour. However, *B-dienst* codebreakers assured Dönitz and Godt that by mid-October the Germans would crack Naval Cypher Number 5, thus restoring German codebreaking supremacy and again providing U-boats with precise convoy information. As will be seen, this did not come to pass; the Germans never broke Naval Cypher Number 5.

Meanwhile, yet another report that the Allies were reading naval Enigma arrived in Berlin. This one came from the *Kriegsmarine* organization in Switzerland. The report stated quite accurately: "For some months German Naval codes giving orders to operational U-boats have been successfully broken. All orders are read currently." The report named the source as a "Swiss American in an important secretarial position in the U.S. Navy Department."†

---

* As the name implies, these were routes to be followed by vessels that fell behind the convoy to which they were assigned. Succeeding convoys would follow those same routes and pick up and incorporate the stragglers.

† Document courtesy of Dr. Timothy P. Mulligan, NARA. Found in Box 1279, "U-boat Logs," NSA History Collection, RG 457. Other NSA documents relating to this agent report are in Boxes 192 and 1276.

This report initiated yet another urgent reexamination of Enigma security. The chief of naval communications, Erhard Maertens, oversaw the investigation personally. Inasmuch as there had been no North Atlantic convoy battles since the U-boat withdrawal on May 24, his men focused on U-boat refueling rendezvous. They found that between June 6 and August 1, there had been twenty-one such meetings and that eight (or about one-third) had been "disturbed" by enemy aircraft. Maertens glibly dismissed these "interruptions" as lucky finds by land-based reconnaissance aircraft and/or carrier-based aircraft passing close by.

One reason at this time for the very high confidence in Enigma security was the incorporation of a top-secret procedure believed to thwart any possibility of an enemy cracking the code. This was a *Stichwort* permutation that completely altered the Enigma inner and outer key settings. A permutation of keys by the *Stichwort* procedure had taken place nearly every fortnight, on June 20, July 6, and July 23.*

Details of the *Stichwort* procedure were very closely held in German inner circles. A German document explained:

> At U-boat Control's radio station, the changing of the *Stichwort* is always undertaken by one and the same officer. Apart from him no one knows the key to the *Stichwort* procedure. The *Stichwort,* followed by a number, is transmitted [to the U-boats] by signal. On board [the U-boat] also the permutation may only be made by an officer. The key to the *Stichwort* procedures is never kept in writing on board [the U-boats] but the officer whose business it is makes an inconspicuous note of it and has to keep the details of the procedure in his head. On board [the U-boats] the radio room is given [only] the results of the *Stichwort* calculation and sets up [the Enigma] machine accordingly. The use of a *Stichwort* excludes the possibility of the enemy reading our traffic by cryptographic means.

Further investigation by the communications department revealed that between August 3 and August 8, when the July 23 *Stichwort* procedure was still in effect, U-boat Control arranged ten more refueling rendezvous. Allied aircraft interrupted nine of these meetings and Allied surface ships the tenth. That, Maertens said, certainly indicated foreknowledge on the part of the Allies for this *Stichwort* period, perhaps an Enigma capture. Against that, however, was the fact that several homebound U-boats utilized the route close along the north coast of Spain and were not molested. In any case, the *Stichwort* was changed on August 11, the day after the report from Switzerland. Moreover, Maertens reported, henceforth the *Stichwort*

---

* Basically, *Stichwort* was an additive procedure. Enigma historian Ralph Erskine has given the following example in three-rotor Enigma. The communications officer at Control radioed to the U-boats a single word, say *"baden."* The simple numerical substitutions for the letters in "baden" are 2 (for "b"), 1, 4, 5, and 14. Each of those numbers was to be used as an additive to the Enigma daily keys. For example, if the rotors for the day were II, V, and IV, the U-boat officer would add the "b" (or 2) in *"baden"* and chose rotors IV (II plus 2), VII, and VI. The numerical equivalents of the other letters in *"baden"* were used as additives to the daily ring and plug-board settings. See Erskine article "Ultra and Some U.S. Navy Carrier Operations."

would be changed weekly, beginning on August 16, and a "different method" would be employed.

In conclusion, Maertens wrote,

> The Chief of Naval Communications Department holds to the opinion he expressed in the spring of this year when there had been grounds for suspecting compromise or betrayal of keys. That is: The Chief of Naval Communications Department considers that continuous current reading of our radio traffic by the enemy is out of the question.*

RETURN TO THE NORTH ATLANTIC: GROUP *LEUTHEN*

In September 1943, the beginning of the fifth year of the war, the Atlantic U-boat force was hard-pressed to carry on. The ASW campaign in the Bay of Biscay during the summer by RAF Coastal Command and supporting naval forces had inflicted horrendous losses on the attack boats and U-tankers alike. Hitler had further reduced the strength of the Atlantic force by his orders to divert eight new Type VIIs to the Arctic in July and August, and to transfer seven Type VIIs from the Atlantic to the Mediterranean. In addition, eight Type VIIs of the Atlantic force had been converted to flak boats. The usual modifications, accidents, and losses in the Baltic† had delayed the arrival of other attack boats.

Taking into account new arrivals and loses, and transfers to and from the Arctic and to the Mediterranean, in the fall of 1943 the strength of the Atlantic force remained modest and virtually static.

	9/1	*10/1*	*11/1*	*12/1*	*12/31*
Type VII	93	99	89	90	90
Type IX	30	34	33	32	34
Totals	123‡	133	122	122	124

Reflecting the decision of Admiral Dönitz to reopen the U-boat campaign on the

* The identity of the "Swiss American" in the U.S. Navy Department has not come to light. Nor has his or her fate.

† The VII *U-988,* commanded by Erich Dobberstein, rammed and sank the VII *U-983,* commanded by Hans-Heinrich Reimers. Five crew of *U-983* were killed. The VII *U-346,* commanded by Arno Leisten, was sunk in an accident with the loss of thirty-seven hands. The VIIs *U-476,* commanded by Otto Niethmann, and *U-718,* commanded by Helmut Wieduwilt, collided. The *U-718* sank with the loss of forty-three hands. The VII *U-745,* commanded by Wilhelm von Trotha, rammed and sank the VII U-768, commanded by Johann Buttjer, but all hands survived. A raid by Allied aircraft on a Kiel shipyard on December 13 destroyed the VII *U-345,* commanded by Ulrich Knackfuss. Accidents or command changes delayed the VIIs *U-712* and *U-761,* the VIIF (cargo) *U-1059,* the IXC40 *U-845,* and the XB minelayer *U-233.*

‡ Not counting the XB minelayers, XIV U-tankers, or IXD1 and IXD2 U-cruisers, but including the eight Type VII flak boats and all other attack boats in France undergoing battle-damage repairs or modifications.

North Atlantic run that fall, U-boat Control sent the great majority of the available boats to that area.

	September	*October*	*November*	*December*	*Totals*
North Atlantic	33	28	20	20	101
Middle Atlantic	0	20	9	8	37
South Atlantic	3	2	5	1	11
Americas	5	7	1	0	13
Totals	41	57	35	29	162

The U-boats deployed in the North Atlantic were to confront ever-increasing numbers of radar-equipped land-based and carrier aircraft, as well as experienced escort and support groups composed of destroyers, sloops, frigates, and corvettes.

Owing to the U-boat stand-down in August, the weariness of Allied aircrews, and aircraft maintenance requirements, the ASW air offensive in the Bay of Biscay mounted by John Slessor's Coastal Command diminished in intensity. From about September 1, the newly arrived U.S. Navy Fleet Air Wing 7* began to assume greater and greater responsibility for air patrols over the Bay of Biscay. By October, according to its historian, the wing flew about half of all daylight missions mounted by the Allies.

This fairly powerful but seldom mentioned U.S. Navy land-based air unit performed yeoman ASW service over the Bay of Biscay in the fall of 1943. In September, the wing flew 1,888 hours of ASW patrols; in October, 2,109 hours; and in November, 2,521 hours. In that period the wing lost nine B-24s in combat† or in accidents or to unknown causes. On these long, arduous Biscay patrols the Americans rarely spotted a U-boat and probably attacked only two or three, splitting credit for one kill with RAF aircraft.

The diminished intensity of the land-based air offensive in Biscay was offset in part by the Allied naval airpower based at sea. It emerged that fall as a significant ASW force. Twenty-three American-built "jeep" carriers had been commissioned in the Royal Navy. Of the original five *Archer*-class, *Avenger* had been sunk by a U-boat; *Dasher* had blown up in the Firth of Clyde; and *Archer,* plagued by chronic engine failure, had been withdrawn from combat to serve as a barracks and stores ship. That left *Biter* and the much-delayed *Tracker* of that group for escort duty on the North Atlantic convoy run. Of the larger *Bogue*-class, ten had arrived in the British Isles. After modifications, *Battler* went to the Indian Ocean; *Attacker, Stalker,* and *Hunter* went to the KM and MK convoy routes; and *Fencer* was placed

---

* As related, Fairwing 7 was initially composed of four squadrons in the ETO: VP 63 (12 Catalinas based in Wales) and VB 103, VB 105, and VB 110 (36 B-24s based at St. Eval, southwest England). Lacking Leigh Lights, the B-24s were not yet properly equipped to fly patrols at night, and when they did they had to employ flares, an unsatisfactory stopgap. A fourth squadron, VB 111 (12 B-24s), arrived on October 1 for training, but a month later it was transferred to Fairwing 15 in Port Lyautey, Morocco.

† On September 4, six JU-88s—a constant hazard—damaged and forced a B-24 of VB 103, commanded by J. H. Alexander, to ditch. After thirty-six hours in a life raft, all ten aircrew were rescued by a vessel that delivered them to Spain, where they were briefly interned but soon repatriated.

on standby for the British occupation of the Azores (Operation Alacrity). Five other *Bogue*-class carriers, commissioned in April or June 1943,* were in British yards for modification. Eight *Long Island* class (British *"Ruler"*-class) were still in workup in American waters.†

As related, U-boat Control formed group *Leuthen,* composed of twenty-one upgraded Type VII boats, to reopen the campaign in the North Atlantic. From August 23 to September 9, eighteen experienced boats sailed from France and three new boats from layovers in Norway. The group was to be supported by one of the two remaining Type XIV "Milk Cow" U-tankers, *U-460,* commanded by Ebe Schnoor.

To cope with Allied aircraft, which had thwarted the assembling and attacks by U-boat groups on convoys in prior engagements, the *Leuthen* boats were to employ a revised tactical doctrine. Like the boats crossing the Bay of Biscay in June and July, the *Leuthen* boats were to remain on the surface and fight back when detected by enemy aircraft. The new *Wanze* radar detector, which searched only in the meter-wavelength band and supposedly did not give off detectable emissions (as did Metox), would alert the U-boats to the approach of enemy aircraft in time to fully man flak arrays. The newly installed quad and twin 20mm flak guns were supposed to give the U-boats sufficient firepower to repel even the most formidable aircraft, including B-17s, B-24s, and Halifaxes. When challenged by an enemy aircraft, a U-boat was to broadcast to Control and to other U-boats a special short-signal ("A/A defense") so that whenever possible the other U-boats could come up and add the support of more flak guns.

Outbound from France, three of the *Leuthen* boats were detected and attacked by Allied aircraft at night in the Bay of Biscay. The first was Fritz Albrecht, age twenty-three, in *U-386.* On September 6, he reported—significantly—that his "*Wanze* failed" to warn of radar-equipped aircraft approaching in the dark. The second was Joachim Deecke in *U-584.* He also reported that his *Wanze* gear had failed. However, both Albrecht and Deecke managed to repel the attacking aircraft with flak. *Ritterkreuz* holder Siegfried von Forstner in *U-402* shot down the aircraft attacking him, he reported. None of these attacking aircraft has been identified.

While still outbound, Albrecht in *U-386* came upon seven British airmen in a life raft. He considered picking them up but did not because he was outbound on a vital mission and because he suspected that the raft might well be "bait" to make him a target of air attack. Upon his return to France, his flotilla commander, Hans Witt, wrote that Albrecht's decision to abandon the airmen "was not correct" for he could have later transferred them to an inbound boat. Information about enemy ASW was "so scarce," Witt continued, "that every opportunity to bring in prisoners must be exploited."‡

---

* *Chaser, Pursuer, Searcher, Striker, Ravager.*

† As related, at this time the U. S. Navy had five *Bogue*-class "jeep" carriers on Atlantic convoy-escort duty (*Bogue, Block Island, Card, Core, Croatan*), as well as the larger *Sangamon*-class *Santee.*

‡ At Nuremberg, in a somewhat far-fetched refutation of the Allied charge that he had ordered U-boat skippers to shoot shipwrecked survivors, Dönitz introduced Witt's comment on Albrecht's pa-

Three boats aborted for various mechanical reasons. Two more reported "*Wanze* failures." These were the *Leuthen* VII *U-666,* commanded by Herbert Engel, and the VII *U-610,* commanded by Walter von Freyberg-Eisenberg-Allmendingen, age twenty-seven. Both boats aborted to France, but both resailed quickly, the *U-666* on September 6, the *U-610* on September 12. The third abort was the VII *U-413,* commanded by Gustav Poel, which carried a special direction-finding team.

Two other new VIIs sailing from Norway that had been directed to enter the Atlantic via the Denmark Strait incurred heavy damage from striking ice and were compelled to abort. These were the *U-274,* commanded by Günther Jordan, age twenty-four, and the *U-963,* commanded by Karl Boddenberg, age twenty-nine. Jordan reached Trondheim on September 13. Owing to overcrowded repair facilities, he could not resail until October 13. As a result of these accidents, Control prohibited further use of the Denmark Strait. All new boats were to sail for the Atlantic via the Iceland-Faeroes gap, where, owing to heavy Allied air patrols, the passage was to be made submerged regardless of time lost.

As also related, *B-dienst* had lost the main Allied convoy codes, but during the summer it had kept track of the convoy cycles by other means. In mid-September, *B-dienst* was still tracking the cycles by these other means, including straggler routes, and could yet provide useful data to U-boat Control.

There was still little to no help from the *Luftwaffe.* The Focke-Wulf Condors had never lived up to their fearsome propaganda image. The German airmen assigned to those aircraft remained undertrained and inept at finding convoys. When they did find one, the position they reported was usually wrong, setting in motion U-boat hunts for convoys that were doomed to failure. Berlin sent a few radar-equipped four-engine HE-177s and JU-290s and several six-engine BV-222s, but as the war diary at U-boat Control noted in the fall of 1943, electronic or mechanical failures grounded many planes or rendered them ineffective.

U-boat Control directed group *Leuthen* toward the old battleground in the Greenland Air Gap. It was to first attack empty *westbound* convoys (Outbound North, Outbound North Slow), that is, convoys that were moving away from the Iceland air bases rather than eastbound convoys (Halifax, Slow) that were moving toward air bases in Iceland and the British Isles. After refueling in the distant western Atlantic from *U-460,* the group would then attack eastbound convoys on the way homeward.

Dönitz radioed the group an exhortatory message: "The Führer is watching every phase of your struggle. Attack! Follow up! Sink!"

The *U-270,* commanded by Paul-Friedrich Otto, age twenty-six, who was in the center of the *Leuthen* patrol line, reported a westbound convoy on September 19. Control received his report with some reserve, Godt noted in the war diary, "Since dead reckoning on convoys is no longer accurate because data are lacking." Otto had found not one westbound convoy but two: Outbound North 202, plus Outbound North (Slow) 18, which Western Approaches had ordered to merge. Al-

---

trol report plus a confirming statement from Witt to argue that the German policy was to rescue shipwrecked survivors, not shoot them.

together there were sixty-eight merchant ships. They were protected by seven warships of Canadian Escort Group C-2 (the destroyers *Gatineau* and *Icarus,* frigate *Lagan,* three corvettes, and a trawler), commanded by P. W. Burnett of the Royal Navy; nine warships of British Escort Group B-3 (the destroyers *Escapade* and *Keppel,* frigate *Towey,* five corvettes, and an ASW trawler), commanded by M. B. Evans of the Royal Navy; and five warships of the new Canadian Support Group 9 (the destroyer *St. Croix,* frigate *Itchen,* and three corvettes), commanded by C. E. Bridgeman, also of the Royal Navy. Total: twenty-one escorts (five destroyers, three frigates, eleven corvettes, two trawlers) plus land-based aircraft and the experienced MAC ship *Empire MacAlpine.**

U-boat Control finally conceded that the convoy reported by Otto in *U-270* was probably the fast Outbound North 202. Accordingly, Control directed Otto to send beacon signals and authorized him to attack. In response, Otto fired a T-5 homing torpedo at an escort, the British frigate *Lagan.* He claimed only a hit for damage—the first confirmed T-5 hit of the war—but in fact *Lagan* was a wreck and twenty-nine of her crew were dead and one was missing. The tug *Destiny* towed *Lagan* to port, escorted by the trawler *Lancer,* but she was not repaired. Early in this confrontation, a Hedgehog exploded accidentally on the deck of the British destroyer *Escapade,* killing twenty-one men and forcing her to abort as well.

As the other twenty *Leuthen* boats raced toward Otto's contact position, radar-equipped B-24 and surface escorts sank two. These were the *U-341,* commanded by Dietrich Epp, age twenty-six, and the *U-338,* commanded by Manfred Kinzel, age twenty-eight. Pilot J. F. Fisher of the Newfoundland-based Canadian Squadron 10, newly equipped with very-long-range B-24s, was credited with sinking Epp's *U-341* with depth charges on September 19. Fisher and two other Canadian B-24 pilots of Squadron 10 had escorted Prime Minister Churchill and party returning from the Quadrant meetings on the battlecruiser *Renown,* and were on the way home to Canada. At the time, pilot John K. Moffatt of British Squadron 120, who had earlier sunk *U-189,* was credited with sinking Kinzel's *U-338* with depth charges and a Fido the next day, September 20, but in a postwar reappraisal, credit for the kill was withdrawn, and the cause of the loss of *U-338* remains unknown. There were no survivors from either U-boat.

Two other U-boats eluded the convoy screen and shot torpedoes. Hubertus Purkhold, age twenty-seven, in *U-260,* reported "two or three hits [but] without detonations," perhaps duds or very distant depth charges. Horst Hepp, age twenty-five, in the new *U-238,* who had survived the accidental sinking of his first command (*U-272*) in the Baltic, hit two 7,200-ton American Liberty ships in ballast, the *Theodore Dwight Weld,* which sank, and the *Frederick Douglass,* which was commanded by an African-American skipper, Adrian Richardson, and which had a net

* Merchant Aircraft Carriers (or MAC) ships—not to be confused with the catapult merchant (CAM) ships—were 8,000- or 9,000-ton grain ships or tankers fitted with flight decks 433 to 485 feet long. The grain ships carried four Swordfish; the tankers, three. Nineteen MAC ships (thirteen tankers, six grain ships) were commissioned and were attached to 217 convoys. None sank a U-boat, but the recoverable Swordfish in 4,177 sorties attacked and held down or drove off many U-boats.

defense streamed. When a torpedo ran through or around the net and hit *Douglass* in her after cargo hold, some of the crew panicked. The men failed to close the engine-room hatch and prematurely launched lifeboats. Had these cowards remained on the ship, as did the skipper, Richardson, it might have been saved, Samuel Eliot Morison wrote. But it fell behind the body of the convoy, and later that day Otto Ferro, age thirty-two, in *U-645,* sank her, to share credit with Hepp in *U-238.*

That night, September 20–21, a dozen boats closed the convoy and eight of them shot T-5 homing torpedoes at escorts.

- Rudolf Bahr, age twenty-seven, in *U-305,* claimed sinking two "destroyers" in two separate attacks. In reality he missed one escort but twice hit the Canadian destroyer *St. Croix* (ex-American four-stack *McCook*), which sank with the loss of sixty-six of 147 men.
- Oskar Curio, age twenty-five, in *U-952,* hit and sank the British corvette *Polyanthus.* Fourteen hours later the British frigate *Itchen* fished eighty-one survivors of *St. Croix* from the frigid waters and one from *Polyanthus.*
- Six other boats claimed sinking or probable sinkings of destroyers, but none of these claims were ever confirmed.

Much pleased by these aggressive attacks on the escorts—and the apparent success of the T-5 *Zaunkönig* "antidestroyer" homing torpedo—Control logged seven "destroyers" and three freighters for 15,500 tons sunk and three other "destroyers" probably sunk.*

Two boats of group *Leuthen* fell out. The first was the *U-386,* commanded by Fritz Albrecht, who had incurred "heavy damage" from depth charges. The second was the *U-603,* commanded by Rudolf Baltz, age twenty-three, who was last to sail from France and could not get to the battle scene in time. Control first instructed Baltz to refuel from the tanker *U-460* and get ready for action later, but when it received the abort notice from Albrecht in *U-386,* it told him to give his spare fuel to Baltz. However, this rendezvous was thwarted by Allied aircraft and *U-603* refueled from *U-460* as originally instructed, but was again delayed in joining *Leuthen.*

Several other U-boats braved the heavy escort screen to shoot on the second night, September 21–22. Gerhard Kluth, age twenty-five, new skipper of *U-377,* claimed damage to a "destroyer" and a freighter of 5,000 tons but neither report has been confirmed in postwar records. An as yet unidentified aircraft hit *U-377,* wounding Kluth in both arms. Upon receipt of his report, Control directed Kluth to abort and rendezvous with Albrecht's aborting *U-386,* which had a doctor on board, then return to France in company. Paul-Friedrich Otto in *U-270,* who had made first contact with the convoys, claimed sinking a "destroyer," but this success could not be confirmed either. An escort depth-charged *U-270* so closely that it cracked her hull, forcing Otto to abort as well. Control directed Otto to rendezvous with the aborting *U-386* and *U-377.* Kluth in *U-377* met *U-386* and got medical

---

* It was, of course, advantageous for the Germans to accept exaggerated claims for the debut of the T-5 torpedo. Postwar records showed that in these initial attacks U-boats had sunk two warships with T-5s only, the destroyer *St. Croix* and the corvette *Polyanthus,* and that they had wrecked the frigate *Lagan.*

assistance, but Otto in *U-270* found neither boat. However, all three eventually limped into France.

As the two convoys plodded westward with fifteen U-boats in pursuit, an Allied escort sank one more German in the early hours of September 22. She was the *U-229,* commanded by Robert Schetelig, age twenty-four. Credit for her kill went to the senior escort officer, M. J. Evans in the British destroyer *Keppel.* Catching sight of *U-229,* Evans opened fire and rammed her, crashing over the U-boat's aft deck. When the two vessels separated, Evans hurled ten shallow-set depth charges at *U-229* and the boat upended and sank. No German survived.

The next day, September 23, the new *U-422,* commanded by Wolfgang Poeschel, age twenty-three, was very nearly lost. The boat reported that a "Halifax" attacked it with depth charges and gunfire. The boat incurred damage, two men were seriously wounded, and one slightly wounded. When Poeschel requested medical assistance, Control set up a rendezvous with the tanker *U-460,* which finally took place on September 29.

As the convoys closed on the Newfoundland Bank, they entered dense fog, which grounded the land- and sea-based aircraft escort. Taking advantage of the absence of air escorts, several more U-boats got by the screen to shoot.

- Horst Hepp in the *U-238,* the most successful, claimed sinking four freighters for 19,000 tons. In fact, he sank three, two Norwegian* and one British, for 15,900 tons, bringing his confirmed bag for this first patrol to four and a half freighters for 26,636 tons, the best performance by any skipper on the North Atlantic run in many months.
- Herbert Engel in the *U-666* sank with a T-5 the frigate *Itchen,* which had on board the eighty-one survivors from *St. Croix* and the one survivor from *Polyanthus.* The explosion blew *Itchen* to pieces with a frightful loss of life. Only three men from the three warships survived, one from *St. Croix,* two from *Itchen.*
- Oskar Curio in *U-952* claimed sinking a "destroyer" with a T-5 and damage to two freighters for 16,000 tons. In fact, he sank the 6,200-ton American freighter *Steel Voyager* and hit another, the Liberty ship *James Gordon Bennett,* but that torpedo was a dud.
- Helmut Manseck in *U-758* claimed sinking a "destroyer" and a freighter but neither could be confirmed. Manseck was also badly depth-charged by escorts and had to haul away for repairs.

The dense fog, fuel shortages, and fatigue thwarted further U-boat attacks on the two convoys. In a detailed analysis of this battle, which was unearthed later by Allied intelligence,† Admiral Dönitz and U-boat Control declared a smashing victory for group *Leuthen.* As expected, the Germans wrote, the skippers, using the

---

* On one of these ships, *Oregon Express,* it was the third time the second mate radio operator, Birger Lunde, had been sunk in the war. His earlier lost ships were *Taranger* (1941) and *Blink* (1942). After the war he became an American citizen and was captain of several American merchantmen.

† Translated into English, this revealing sixteen-page, single-spaced, typed report, entitled "Convoy Operation NR5, *Zaunkönig* Convoy," was found at the Navy's Operational Archives, Box T-95, Folder 136.

T-5 *Zaunkönig* homing torpedo to great advantage, had destroyed the "outer" and "inner" rings of surface escorts, sinking twelve and probably sinking three more; in all, fifteen. Had it not been for the onset of heavy fog on the second and third days, the U-boat attack on the main body of merchant ships would have resulted in a massacre. As it was, the Germans went on, the U-boats sank nine merchant ships for 46,500 tons and damaged two others.

"This convoy operation, the first in months, brought a complete success," Dönitz wrote in the conclusion to the report. "The new weapons proved their worth in every respect. . . ." He went on to say that "special recognition is due to all U-boats that took part in this operation as pioneers in the renewed convoy war. Their readiness for and their coolness under stress has justified the confidence of all U-boat men in the new weapons and has pointed the way clearly onwards and upwards to the crown of the U-boat career, the convoy battle."

The confirmed sinkings and damage were much, much less: not fifteen escorts sunk but only three of twenty-two (the destroyer *St. Croix* and frigate *Itchen* of the new Canadian Support Group 9,* and the corvette *Polyanthus*); not nine but six of sixty-eight merchant ships sunk; not two but only one damaged. Total: ten vessels out of ninety in the two convoys sunk, hardly the "complete success" German propagandists, echoing Dönitz, proclaimed. The most remarkable aspect of this operation was that a green skipper, young Horst Hepp in the maiden patrol of *U-238,* accounted for four and a half of the six merchant ships sunk.

In achieving this alleged great victory, the Germans wrote, their own losses were "in no way proportionate to the losses of the enemy." Unaware as yet that the *U-341* had been lost during the assembly phase of group *Leuthen,* the Germans assumed that not three but only two U-boats had been sunk by the enemy (*U-229, U-338*) and two U-boats forced to abort; the true figure was three aborts (*U-270, U-377, U-386*). Assuming 130 Allied personnel on each of the fifteen escorts sunk, the Germans calculated, or about two thousand men as against one hundred personnel on the two lost U-boats, the ratio of casualties was twenty to one in favor of the Germans. "Added to this," the Germans gloated, "were the losses in merchant ship personnel who must be almost as valuable to the enemy as the personnel of the escort vessels."

As for tactics and equipment, Dönitz and U-boat Control had several important points to make.

- On the first day, a U-boat near the convoy attacked by an aircraft flashed "A/A defense," but too few U-boats remained on the surface to supply flak support. To avoid errors and the possibility of misjudgments, Control therefore ruled that in the future it and it alone would give the order "A/A defense." All boats were expected to comply expeditiously in order to hasten assemblies at the convoy.
- The new *Wanze* radar detector "stood the test [of battle] well," especially on the foggy days. However, it was apparent from the experiences of boats in group *Leuthen,* as well as the boats attempting the Strait of Gibraltar in September, that the enemy—contrary to predictions from German electronic engineers—had

---

* Accordingly, the British deactivated this new support group.

developed centimetric-wavelength radar that *Wanze* could not detect. The next generation of radar detectors (FuMBs), *Naxos,* which could detect centimetric-wavelength radar, had been successfully battle tested and all U-boats were to be fitted with it as soon as possible. Meanwhile, skippers were encouraged to use the *Aphrodite* radar decoy "as often as possible and above all in great numbers." Unknown to the Germans, the Allies had developed an even more powerful radar with a narrower beam that operated in the three centimeter range and was undetectable by *Naxos.*

- While the quad and twin 20mm flak arrays were great steps forward, Dönitz and Control recognized the need for improved, more powerful flak guns. Therefore, to replace the quad 20, the *Kriegsmarine* had ordered rush production of the new automatic 37mm naval flak gun that fired "a new and absolutely deadly type of ammunition," giving the gun twice the range and lethality of the quad 20 and a much greater possibility of destroying attacking aircraft. Beyond that, an even more powerful and deadly *twin* 37mm naval flak gun was under high-priority development.
- Inasmuch as "faultless navigation" and position reporting was absolutely essential for the massing of groups for a successful convoy battle, "new" navigational aids were being battle tested. One such device was the "gyro-sextant," which made it possible for a U-boat to determine its position (although not precisely) by stars at night, even when no horizon was visible. Meanwhile, "all possible means for improving the accuracy of a U-boat's position must therefore be utilized."
- Unimportant radio chatter by U-boats must be eliminated. Only matters of tactical importance should be transmitted on the convoy circuit. Above all, Control admonished, "do not afflict the morale of others with tales of terror."

While some of the material in this special analysis of group *Leuthen* might be dismissed as merely morale-building for the hard convoy battles to come, one matter is unequivocally clear. The Germans had wildly misjudged the effectiveness of the T-5 *Zaunkönig* homing torpedo against escorts. It was too slow, too sensitive, and still had too many bugs. The *confirmed* results—as opposed to the *claimed* results—were no better than what could have been achieved by an all-out attack on the escort forces with ordinary air or electric torpedoes with contact or magnetic pistols. Moreover, alerted to the deployment of the *Zaunkönig* from Enigma decrypts, the Allies had already developed a counterweapon. Dubbed the "Foxer," it was a simple but effective noisemaker towed well behind the escort to attract the homing torpedo.*

More German Failures on the North Atlantic Run

Twelve *Leuthen* boats, including *Ritterkreuz* holder Siegfried von Forstner in *U-402,* served as a cadre for a new group, *Rossbach* on the North Atlantic run. Five

---

* A similar device, developed by the Canadians, was dubbed "CAT Gear," an acronym for Canadian Anti-Torpedo.

boats from France and four new boats from home waters soon arrived, bringing the number in *Rossbach* to twenty-one, equal in size to group *Leuthen.*

In the last days of September, U-boat Control positioned *Rossbach* to intercept a westbound convoy, Outbound North 203. Allied codebreakers warned of this new group and land-based aircraft flew out to confirm its position. When one of the aircraft spotted the *U-448* and another boat newly arrived from France near the predicted position, Allied authorities diverted the convoy northward of the forming *Rossbach* patrol line. The convoy eluded the Germans and reached American waters with no losses.

Control next repositioned group *Rossbach* to intercept two other westbound convoys: Outbound North 204 and Outbound North (Slow) 19, which were expected about October 1. Inexplicably, Control directed one of the *Rossbach* boats, *U-631,* commanded by Jürgen Krüger, to send a weather report. Already aware of group *Rossbach* from Enigma decrypts, Allied authorities DFed *U-631*'s transmission and used it as a cover story to attack the *Rossbach* patrol line. Meanwhile, these two convoys, like the preceding convoy, Outbound North 203, went north of *Rossbach* and also reached American waters with no losses.

The swarms of Allied land-based aircraft that attacked *Rossbach* sank four Type VIIs with the loss of all hands:

• The *U-221,* commanded by *Ritterkreuz* holder Hans Trojer, age twenty-seven, which sailed from St. Nazaire on September 20. She was sunk in the late afternoon of September 27 by a Halifax of British Squadron 58, piloted by Eric L. Hartley, on patrol over the Bay of Biscay. Hartley dropped eight depth charges that destroyed *U-221,* but Trojer's flak set the Halifax on fire and Hartley had to crash-land in the sea. Two airmen perished in the crash, but Hartley, Group Captain R. C. Mead, and four other crew got into an inflatable life raft. Eleven harrowing days later, on October 8, the British destroyer *Mahratta* happened by and rescued the six airmen.

• The *U-336,* commanded by Hans Hunger, age twenty-eight, which sailed from Brest on September 14. She was sunk on the morning of October 4 by a Hudson of British Squadron 269 from Iceland, piloted by Gordon C. Allsop. He attacked into flak, firing eight rockets in salvos of two, two, and four. These hit and fatally holed *U-336.* Allsop saw momentarily "about fifteen" Germans in the heavy oil slick, but by the time he came around for a second pass, they had disappeared.

• The new *U-279,* commanded by Otto Finke, age twenty-eight, which sailed from Kiel on September 4. Finke landed an agent in Iceland on September 25, then proceeded south to join group *Rossbach.* On October 4, a Ventura of the U.S. Navy's newly arrived Iceland-based Squadron VB 128,* piloted by Charles L. Westhofen, found a U-boat (probably *U-305*) on the surface and drove her under. Westhofen hauled off to trick the U-boat into believing that he was gone for good. However, before he could return, he spotted a second U-boat and attacked into flak with machine guns and depth charges. This was Finke's *U-279,* mortally wounded.

---

* Replacing Catalina Squadron VP 84, which returned to the United States.

Westhofen saw the U-boat crew abandon ship and some men in "four or five" rafts. Nothing further was heard from this boat or the crew.

- The new *U-389,* commanded by Siegfried Heilmann, age twenty-six, which sailed from Trondheim on September 18. On October 4, a B-24 of the Iceland-based British Squadron 120, piloted by W.J.F. McEwen, found *U-389* on the surface. McEwen attacked with depth charges and *U-389* "split open like a pea pod," the plane's engineer Robert Fallon wrote. The aircrew counted "nine to eleven" Germans in the water. McEwen dropped three one-man inflatable dinghies and two emergency kits containing food, medicine, and so on), but nothing further was heard from *U-389* or her crew.

Harassed by ASW aircraft and surface ships, four boats of *Rossbach* aborted to France:

- A Hudson of British Squadron 269, piloted by H. M. Smith, hit the *U-731,* commanded by Werner Techand, age twenty-four, wounding him and five other crewmen.
- A "destroyer" caught and depth-charged the *U-666,* commanded by Herbert Engel, inflicting "severe damage."
- Rudolf Bahr in *U-305* reported serious damage from an aircraft. He was probably hit by U.S. Navy Ventura pilot Charles Westhofen, who afterward sank *U-279.*
- Hubertus Purkhold in the *U-260* reported that two men, including the chief engineer, were critically ill.

Allied aircraft attacked three other U-boats in early October, but all escaped serious damage. One was the new IXC40 *U-539,* commanded by Hans-Jürgen Lauterbach-Emden, age twenty-four, which sailed from Bergen on September 14. While traveling on the surface contrary to orders in the Iceland-Faeroes gap on September 21, the *U-539* had been attacked by an RAF Hudson that dropped three depth charges, but all missed. In the second air attack, on October 4, Lauterbach-Emden reported that he shot down a four-engine "Lancaster" bomber and repelled a "Hudson." The *U-610* reported that she had been attacked by "two or more" aircraft. The new *U-275,* commanded by Helmut Bork, age thirty-three, reported an unsuccessful attack by a Hudson.

Nine hundred miles to the south of *Rossbach,* the Type XIV tanker *U-460* was under orders to refuel and/or provide medical attention to several boats. As related, these included the new but damaged ex-*Leuthen* VII *U-422,* commanded by Wolfgang Poeschel, and two VIIs, *U-455* and *U-264,* that had attempted but failed to enter the Mediterranean via the Strait of Gibraltar. Upon completion of the refuelings, these three boats (as well as the tanker) were to move north to backstop *Rossbach.*

On the morning of October 4, the American "jeep" carrier *Card* and her screen, loosely escorting the Gibraltar-bound convoy UGS 19, received intelligence on the proposed *U-460* refueling operation. Avenger pilot Robert L. Stearns, who had earlier won a Navy Cross for his roles in sinking the XB minelayer *U-118* and *U-537,* spotted *U-460* and the three VIIs, refueling or waiting to refuel. After calling *Card* for reinforcements, Stearns boldly attacked the four U-boats, dropping a 500-pound bomb. It fell between the tanker *U-460* and *U-264,* commanded by Hartwig Looks, who was in the process of refueling, but it caused no damage.

Three other *Card* aircraft—two Wildcats and an Avenger—soon arrived. Diving into the heavy flak, the two Wildcats, piloted by Elbert S. Heim and David O. Puckett, attacked the clutch of U-boats, driving under the three VIIs (*U-264, U-422, U-455*) but Ebe Schnoor in the tanker *U-460* remained on the surface, returning fire. After Puckett raked the boat, inflicting heavy casualties, Schnoor dived. When he did, Stearns in the Avenger dropped a Fido and sank *U-460* with the loss of all hands. Stearns, Heim, and Puckett each won a Navy Cross for this important kill, which left only one Type XIV tanker in the devastated Atlantic refueler force, *U-488.*

Later that day, *Card* aircraft found and attacked Looks in *U-264* and Poeschel in *U-422.* Looks escaped but he had incurred heavy damage and was compelled to abort to France. Wildcat pilots Elbert S. Heim and David O. Puckett and Avenger pilot Robert L. Stearns sank *U-422* with machine-gun fire and a Fido. There were no survivors.

The loss of the XIV U-tanker *U-460,* which was to have gone north to directly support *Rossbach,* was yet another severe setback for the U-boats on the North Atlantic run. Four *Rossbach* VIIs, very low on fuel, were left virtually stranded. As a result, the remaining U-tanker, *U-488,* commanded by Erwin Bartke, who was en route to a position south of the Azores to refuel U-boats going to and from remote areas, was recalled and sent north to support *Rossbach.* Two of the four stranded VIIs, Manseck in the *U-758* and Curio in *U-952,* could not wait for the tanker and headed for France. The other two, *Ritterkreuz* holder von Forstner in *U-402* and Joachim Deecke in *U-584,* arranged a rendezvous.

Reinforced to fourteen boats by the arrival of two VIIs from France, *U-91* and *U-437,* on October 6 *Rossbach* redeployed to intercept two convoys eastbound to the British Isles: Halifax 259 and Slow Convoy 143. Fully aware of the threat posed by *Rossbach,* Allied authorities diverted Halifax 259 far to the south. Slow Convoy 143, comprised of thirty-nine merchant ships, was guarded by the reinforced Canadian Escort Group C-2, consisting of nine warships (the destroyer, *Icarus,* frigate *Duckworth,* five corvettes, one minesweeper, one ASW trawler) and the Merchant Aircraft Carrier (MAC ship) *Rapana.* Further reinforced by four destroyers of the British Support Group 10 (*Musketeer, Oribi, Orkan, Orwell*), the convoy, serving as "bait," was deliberately allowed to proceed directly at *Rossbach.*

The wounded Werner Techand in the aborting *U-731* was the first skipper to sight elements of Slow Convoy 143. His contact report—an eastbound "destroyer"—brought up seven other boats during the night of October 8–9. Two U-boats sank ships: Erich Mäder in *U-378* got the Polish destroyer *Orkan,* commanded by Stanislaw Hryniewiecki of Support Group 10, and Otto Ferro in the homebound *U-645* sank the 5,600-ton American freighter *Yorkmar.* Only forty-three of about two hundred crew survived the sinking of *Orkan.*

Rossbach paid a heavy price for these two sinkings. British Swordfish from the

MAC ship *Rapana* and land-based aircraft drove the U-boats off and down and sank three on October 8.

• A B-24 of British Squadron 86, based in Northern Ireland and piloted by John Wright, who had earlier sunk the VII *U-456,* found and attacked the new VII *U-419,* commanded by Dietrich Giersberg, age twenty-five. Wright dropped two close shallow-set Torpex depth charges. He reported that *U-419* upended and sank stern first and that he saw "fifteen" Germans in the water, but only one survived, the skipper Giersberg who suffered a broken leg but was rescued by the destroyer *Orwell* of Support Group 10. Forty-eight Germans perished in the sinking.

• Alerted by pilot Wright, another B-24 of British Squadron 86, piloted by Australian Cyril W. Burcher, as well as a B-24 from British Squadron 120, piloted by Dennis C. L. Webber, found and attacked the new VII *U-643,* commanded by Hans-Harald Speidel, age twenty-six. Burcher, who had earlier sunk the VII *U-632,* dropped four shallow-set depth charges but saw no firm evidence of a kill. Later, in two attacks, Webber dropped eight depth charges. Returning to the scene, Burcher dropped two more depth charges. These four depth-charge attacks together with machine-gun fire destroyed *U-643.* Racing to the site, the destroyers *Musketeer, Orwell,* and *Oribi* of Support Group 10 picked up the skipper, Speidel, and seventeen other Germans, including a doctor. Thirty Germans perished.

According to the recollection of an officer on *Orwell,* Ian Wedderburn,* skipper Speidel claimed that machine-gun bullets from one of the B-24s had hit German survivors in the water, and because of that, Speidel was "very bitter." In response to that published charge, the copilot of Webber's B-24, John Luker, replied: "It had been recorded that we fired at them [the German crewmen] in the water, but I can categorically deny any such suggestion."†

• A Sunderland of Canadian Squadron 423, piloted by Alfred H. Russell, found the VII *U-610,* commanded by Walter von Freyberg-Eisenberg-Allmendingen. In his initial attack, Russell toggled four depth charges, but only three fell. These closely straddled the boat near the conning tower, which, Russell said, "lifted fifteen to twenty feet." When the foam and swirl of the explosions subsided, Russell saw "fifteen" Germans in the water swimming amid oil and wreckage. None survived.

That same day, October 8, land-based aircraft hit two other boats:

• The new IXC40 *U-539,* commanded by Hans-Jürgen Lauterbach-Emden. He reported that an (unidentified) B-24 attacked him, dropping two depth charges nearby that caused heavy damage. This was the third air attack on *U-539* in eighteen days. It forced her to abort to France, where she arrived on October 20, completing a hazardous voyage of thirty-seven days.

• The new VII *U-762,* commanded by Wolfgang Hille, age twenty-five. This boat had sailed from Bergen eleven days before, on September 28, and was trying to join *Rossbach.* The plane was a B-24 of British Squadron 120, piloted by New Zealander Bryan W. Turnbull, who had earlier damaged and forced the abort of

---

* Recounted in G. Jones, *Autumn of the U-boats* (1984).

† In Franks, *Search, Find and Kill* (1995).

U-135. His attack drove *U-762* under and a destroyer came up to carry on. Allied authorities assessed the attacks as failures, but Hille had incurred two wounded and damage to a diesel engine, setbacks that took the boat out of action for several days. Control directed Hille to meet and transfer his wounded to Otto Ferro's homebound *U-645,* but Hille could not comply because of heavy seas. He hauled west for further operations and treated the wounded himself.

The departures of other boats for France with battle or mechanical damage or fuel shortages and of four VIIs to the arriving XIV tanker *U-488* to refuel reduced *Rossbach* to merely six combat-capable boats. However, the group was soon reinforced by seven boats from France and Norway and by the VII *U-455,* which came north from its abortive refueling rendezvous with the lost XIV tanker, *U-460.*

The operational orders (No. 59, dated October 7) for the newly sailed boats contained a new paragraph that to some Allies appeared to confirm in part Hitler's ruthless desire to destroy Allied merchant-marine crews to the fullest extent possible. It read:

> Rescue Ships: A so-called rescue ship is generally attached to every convoy, a special ship of up to 3,000 gross registered tons, which is intended for the picking up of survivors after U-boat attacks. These ships are for the most part equipped with a shipborne aircraft and large motorboats, are strongly armed with depth-charge throwers and are very maneuverable, so that they are often taken for U-boat traps by the [U-boat] commander. In view of the desired destruction of ships' crews, their sinking is of great value.*

U-boat Control redeployed these fourteen boats, designated group *Schlieffen,* to intercept the westbound convoys Outbound North 206 and Outbound North (Slow) 20. As this reorganization was taking place in mounting seas, Allied aircraft attacked five more U-boats, and two other boats collided.

• Aware from Enigma decrypts that the XIV tanker *U-488* was headed north to backstop the newly forming group *Schlieffen,* Allied authorities sent the "jeep" carrier *Card* and her screen to the new refueling rendezvous. On October 12, two Avenger pilots, Letson S. Balliett and W. S. Fowler, found and attacked *U-488* with Fidos. They claimed a sinking but the tanker was only badly rattled.

Nearby that same day, three Avengers from *Card,* piloted by Stewart E. Dory, Stewart B. Holt, and Edward R. Hodgson, found and attacked with bombs and guns the VII *U-731,* commanded by Werner Techand, who was aborting from an aircraft attack on October 4 and needed to refuel. Techand reported at first that he

---

* Prosecutors at Dönitz's Nuremberg trial introduced this paragraph and linked it to the so-called *Laconia* order of the year before to reinforce the charge that Dönitz ordered his U-boat skippers to deliberately murder shipwrecked crews. Dönitz rebutted that since rescue ships were "heavily armed" and carried "aircraft" and often served as "U-boat traps," they were legitimate targets and, in any case, the Germans were "justified" in "sinking such [merchant ship] crews" because they were not helpless civilians but combatants in every sense of the word. Rescue ships were not, of course, heavily armed nor did they carry aircraft, like the CAM and MAC ships. However, unknown to Dönitz, during the war and at the time of his trial, rescue ships were fitted with Huff Duff to help locate U-boat shadowers and for that reason alone could be considered legitimate targets.

was "heavily damaged" and "sinking," prompting Control to order all nearly boats to assist. Later he reported the boat was "fully serviceable," but he continued his abort to France.

• The next day, October 13, W. S. Fowler in his Avenger found and attacked with a homing torpedo the fuel-low *U-378,* commanded by Erich Mäder. The torpedo missed or malfunctioned, and Mäder got away.

The squadron commander on *Card,* Howard M. Avery, flying an Avenger, took off to assist Fowler in this attack. While proceeding to that area, he sighted *Ritterkreuz* holder Siegfried von Forstner in *U-402,* another of the VIIs looking for the tanker *U-488* in order to refuel. In response to Avery's alert, a second Avenger, piloted by Barton C. Sheela, arrived to assist. The two aircraft drove *U-402* under, whereupon Avery launched a Fido that destroyed the boat with all hands.*

• In the afternoon of that day, another Avenger from *Card,* piloted by Harry E. Fryatt, found and attacked with a Fido the *U-603,* commanded by Rudolf Baltz. The Germans, who survived this attack with no damage, reported that they had set a carrier aircraft "ablaze" but, in fact, they had only severed a hydraulic line. In any case, that proved to be a good hit for the Germans because Fryatt was unable to lower his right landing gear. He crash-landed on *Card* and hit another Avenger, piloted by Roger Kuhn, who had just landed, and knocked it into the sea. Luckily the four-stack destroyer *Barry* was able to pick up Kuhn, who was drenched and shaken, but only slightly injured.

• While searching for the U-tanker in heavy seas, the VII *U-455,* commanded by Hans-Martin Scheibe, collided with the VII *U-631,* commanded by Jürgen Krüger, age twenty-five. The *U-455* incurred such heavy damage that Scheibe was forced to abort to France. Krüger, who was most at fault, had smashed all four of his bow tubes so badly that he could not use them, but U-boat Control denied him permission to abort and held the boat in the patrol line as a lookout because he carried special direction-finding gear and operators. Those with long memories recalled that Krüger had rammed and sunk *U-71* in the Atlantic the previous April, giving rise to the macabre joke that Krüger had become highly effective at ASW.

Ten days out from a refueling stop in Norway, the new IXC *U-844,* commanded by Günther Möller, age twenty-five, found a convoy on October 15. This was either the expected Outbound North 206 or Outbound North (Slow) 20 or both, for these westbound formations were sailing in close proximity. Composed of sixty-five merchant ships, convoy ON 206 was protected by British Escort Group B-6, commanded by R. A. Currie, augmented by British Support Group 7, commanded by Peter Gretton. The two groups comprised thirteen warships: four destroyers (*Fame, Vanquisher, Duncan, Vidette*); one frigate (*Deveron*); seven corvettes, three of which were manned by Norwegians; and one trawler. Composed of fifty-two ships, convoy ONS 20 was protected by British Escort Group B-4, commanded by H. R. Paramor, made up of the first six frigates (destroyer escorts)

---

* In his two years of service in the Atlantic U-boat force, von Forstner sank fifteen confirmed ships for about 63,400 tons, and damaged three for 28,784 tons. Two of the latter for 16,700 tons were finished off by two other boats.

American yards had built for the Royal Navy, and two trawlers. Number of merchant ships in the two convoys: 117. Escorts: twenty-one.

In the mistaken belief that the T-5 *Zaunkönig* homing torpedo was a wonder weapon and the new flak arrays were deadly effective, U-boat Control became absolutely determined to massacre these convoys. In keeping with the new antiaircraft policy, Control issued a Hitlerian order: "Remain surfaced! Shoot your way to the convoy with flak!"

The U-boats complied with these orders, but only one boat managed to sink a ship. She was the new VII *U-426,* commanded by Christian Reich, age twenty-seven, ten days out from a fuel stop in Bergen. His victim was the 6,600-ton British freighter *Essex Lance,* a straggler from Outbound North (Slow) 20. After *Yorkmar,* she was the second and last confirmed freighter to be sunk by U-boats on the North Atlantic run in October.

The swarms of aircraft and surface vessels assigned to the two convoys sank six U-boats on October 16 and 17, one of the worst German naval calamities of the war.

- A B-24 of British Squadron 86, piloted by Eric A. Bland, found and attacked the new IXC40 *U-844,* commanded by Günther Möller, age twenty-five. Flying into heavy flak, Bland toggled four depth charges, but none released. The flak from *U-844* knocked out both port engines and damaged the port side of the fuselage.

Tenaciously circling *U-844* out of flak range on two engines, Bland radioed for help. A B-24 of British Squadron 59, based in Northern Ireland and piloted by W. J. Thomas, arrived and carried out two attacks on *U-844,* dropping eight depth charges. The flak from *U-844* knocked out Thomas's starboard inboard engine. Between Thomas's attacks, Bland boldly ran in, but again his depth charges failed to release and, moreover, his B-24 was so badly wrecked he had to ditch. *Pink,* a corvette of Gretton's group, rescued Bland and four others, but two airmen perished. *Pink* left the convoy and took the airmen to Halifax. Nothing more was ever heard from *U-844,* which had served merely eleven days in the Atlantic force. Bland received a DSO.

- Another B-24 of British Squadron 86, piloted by George D. Gamble, found and attacked the new VII *U-964,* commanded by Emmo Hummerjohann, age twenty-seven. Flying into intense flak, Gamble dropped four depth charges, then hauled out of flak range and called for a surface escort. This attempt at a coordinated attack could not be carried out, so Gamble attacked *U-964* a second time, dropping three depth charges. One hit close and destroyed the boat. Gamble reported thirty-five German survivors in the water, but the surface escorts rescued none. The *U-231,* commanded by Wolfgang Wenzel, came up and found four of the survivors, but one died during the rescue.
- A Sunderland of Canadian Squadron 422, piloted by Paul T. Sargent, found and attacked two surfaced U-boats, one of which was likely the new VII *U-470,* commanded by Günter Paul Grave, age twenty-six. Sargent attacked *U-470* in the face of heavy flak, dropping three depth charges, all of which fell wide. On a second attack, Sargent toggled three more depth charges, but only two released. These landed in "a perfect straddle" amidships. However, the flak from *U-470* and the other U-boat riddled the Sunderland and mortally wounded three crew.

Pilot Sargent radioed an SOS and steered the crippled plane toward convoy Outbound North (Slow) 20. He made contact with the frigate *Drury* of Escort Group B-4 and ditched near her. Sargent, who was killed in the crash, won a posthumous DFC. Two of the seven surviving airmen also won DFCs.

Two B-24s of British Squadron 120, piloted by Harold F. Kerrigan (a Canadian) and Barry E. Peck, who heard radio transmissions from a ditching aircraft, came up and found *U-470.* Kerrigan attacked first, dropping four depth charges while incurring flak damage. Nonetheless, he attacked a second time and dropped four more charges, one of which fell "very close" to the stern of *U-470.* Peck then carried out an attack into the face of "a hail of flak," dropping six depth charges ahead of the boat. On a second run into another "hail of flak," Peck dropped two depth charges that closely straddled the boat and blew it "clear of the water," Peck wrote. In between Peck's first and second attacks, a B-24 of British Squadron 59, piloted by Wesley G. Loney, attacked *U-470,* dropping four depth charge. These missiles and those of Kerrigan and Peck destroyed *U-470,* which sank stern first.

Peck notified Peter Gretton in the destroyer *Duncan* of this kill, reporting "fifteen to twenty survivors" in the water. He then homed Gretton to the scene. Owing to the presence of other U-boats, Gretton declined to mount a major rescue effort, Peck wrote. Instead, Gretton cruised *Duncan* through the German survivors at "moderate speed" with grapple nets streamed. Two crewmen of *U-470,* Gerhard Tacken and Heinz Knappe, caught a net and saved themselves. Forty-six Germans perished. The British divided credit for the kill of *U-470* among pilots Kerrigan, Peck, and Loney.

• Two aircraft returning from convoy escort to Iceland bases found the new IXC40 *U-540,* commanded by Lorenz Kasch, age twenty-nine. Pilot Eric Knowles in a B-24 of British Squadron 59 attacked first, dropping eight depth charges in two runs. The New Zealand pilot Bryan Turnbull, in a B-24 of British Squadron 120 (who had previously damaged *U-135* and *U-762*), attacked next, also dropping eight depth charges in two runs. Turnbull recalled that both of his salvos closely straddled the boat and broke it in half, and that Knowles in the other B-24 radioed: "You got him, good show!" The British divided the credit for the kill between Knowles and Turnbull and awarded Turnbull a DFC. Although Turnbull notified the surface escorts that he could see "about thirty" German survivors in the water, none was rescued. The *U-540,* which sailed from a fuel stop in Bergen, Norway, on October 4, had served only fourteen days in the Atlantic force.

• The corvette *Sunflower* of Gretton's Escort Group B-7, commanded by J. Plomer, who had earlier sunk *U-638,* attacked and sank the VII *U-631,* commanded by Jürgen Krüger. She was the boat that had rammed *U-455* and disabled her own four bow tubes, but had been refused permission to abort. There were no survivors of *U-631.*

• The new frigate *Byard* of British Escort Group B-4 found and sank the new Type IXC40 *U-841,* commanded by Werner Bender, age twenty-six. *Byard* fished out twenty-seven survivors of *U-841,* who revealed that shortly before sailing from Trondheim on October 4, popular second watch officer Ernst Huffmann (son of a general) had committed suicide when the Gestapo found "secret documents," including Enigma keys, left behind in his hotel room.

Like the new IXs *U-844* and *U-540,* which sailed from Norway and had been sunk, the *U-841* had served in the Atlantic force less than two weeks. The assignment to these North Atlantic convoy battles of Type IXs, which Control had earlier barred from such activity because they were not suitable, probably resulted from a desire to bring all possible flak arrays into play.

As a result of conflicting position reports, U-boat Control bollixed the follow-up attacks on convoys Outbound North 206 and Outbound North (Slow) 20. The veteran VII *U-91,* commanded by Heinz Hungershausen, correctly reported that the convoy had deviated to a *southwesterly* course. The new VII *U-413,* commanded by Gustav Poel, which also carried special direction-finding gear and an operating team, wrongly reported that Outbound North (Slow) 20 had deviated to a *northwesterly* course. Choosing Poel's report (deemed to be more reliable because of the direction-finding team) over Hungershausen's, Control sent group *Schlieffen* in the wrong direction.

Control later characterized the attack on these convoys as a "setback." Indeed so. The U-boats sank only one freighter, the straggler from Outbound North (Slow) 20. On the other side, the sinking of six U-boats was another smashing victory for the defense. To the German submariners at sea pursuing convoys, this battle made it quite clear that for a U-boat on the North Atlantic run to remain on the surface and fight it out with aircraft was as suicidal as it was in the Bay of Biscay.

Still More German Failures on the North Atlantic Run

At Control, the supposed successes of group *Leuthen* against surface and air escorts in September outweighed the disastrous failures of groups *Rossbach* and *Schlieffen* in October. Hence Control had not the slightest intention of scaling back or canceling operations on the North Atlantic run.

The loss of U-tankers, most recently *U-460,* seriously cramped operations in that area, especially in the distant western Atlantic near the Grand Banks. To carry on, Control was compelled to divert the two remaining XB minelayers in the Atlantic force to be provisional refuelers. These were the new *U-219* and *U-220,* commanded by the old hands Walter Burghagen, age fifty-two, who had entered the Imperial Navy in World War I, and Bruno Barber, age thirty-nine, respectively. Burghagen in *U-219* sailed from Norway on October 22 to back up the Type XIV tanker *U-488.* At about the same time, Barber in *U-220,* who had planted a minefield off St. John's, Newfoundland, on October 9, was also directed to assist *U-488,* either by giving her surplus fuel or taking on her surplus fuel so *U-488* could race to France, fill up, and return.

So valuable were these two Type XB provisional refuelers that Control directed two new flak boats, *U-256* and *U-271,* to protect them and the even more valuable Type XIV tanker, *U-488,* at the refueling rendezvous. In addition, Control restricted all future refueling operations to nighttime, and directed that in event of an Allied air attack, the tankers were to submerge while the U-boats waiting to refuel repelled the aircraft with flak guns.

Taking advantage of Enigma decrypts and DFs of U-boat radio chatter, the Allies continued to focus hunter-killer operations against the U-tankers. While pursuing *U-488,* Avengers and Wildcats of the "jeep" carrier *Core* tangled with two U-boats.

• On October 20, pilots Charles W. Brewer and Robert W. Hayman came upon the VII *U-378,* commanded by Erich Mäder, who had earlier sunk the Polish destroyer *Orkan.* The pilots attacked and sank *U-378.* There was one survivor, the quartermaster Karl-Heinz Brunkhorst, but he was lost when the ship that saved him went down.*

• On the next day, October 21, aircraft from *Core,* assisted by Catalinas, found and attacked the flak boat *U-271,* commanded by Kurt Barleben, age thirty-four, who was seeking the tanker *U-488* to offer protection. One German gunner was killed and others wounded, but *U-271* survived the attack. However, she was so badly smashed up that Barleben had to abort to France.

To replace the failed group *Schlieffen,* on October 24 U-boat Control directed the formation of a new group, *Siegfried.* In its final configuration, *Siegfried* was comprised of eighteen U-boats. Of these, eleven, or almost two-thirds, were commanded by green skippers; six in new boats from Norway and five in experienced boats from France. Owing to the absence of U-tankers, Control was compelled to order *Siegfried* to attack *eastbound* convoys, thereby bringing the fuel-low U-boats closer to French bases, but also closer to the most effective Allied land-based air.

From timely Enigma decrypts, the Allies were aware of group *Siegfried.* To avoid this line, they diverted all eastbound Halifax and Slow convoys—those with valuable cargoes—to a southerly course. At the same time, Allied authorities designated the empty ships of convoy Outbound North 207 a "bait convoy," and deliberately sent it directly at group *Siegfried* to seek a naval confrontation. For this purpose the Outbound North 207 was massively protected. The Canadian Escort Group C-1, the British "jeep" carrier *Biter,* which sailed inside the convoy, and a MAC ship provided close escort. The famous British Support Group B-2, commanded by Johnny Walker, to which the new British "jeep" carrier *Tracker* had been attached, patrolled nearby, as did Peter Gretton's Support Group, B-7. Land-based Coastal Command aircraft of all types lent added support.

The battle commenced on the morning of October 23. A B-24 of British Squadron 224, en route to Gretton's B-7 group to airdrop some radar spare parts, sighted a U-boat of group *Siegfried.* This was the new VII *U-274,* commanded by Günther Jordan, age twenty-four, ten days out from a fuel stop in Norway. The pilot, Edward Jacques (Billy) Wicht, a Swiss serving in the RAF, attacked with eight rockets, gave the alarm, and dropped a smoke float. Gretton in the destroyer *Duncan* accompanied by his other destroyer, *Vidette,* raced to the float, trailed by the slower corvettes. Meanwhile, Wicht drove the *U-274* under with gunfire and dropped two depth charges.

---

* According to Wise, *Sole Survivors of the Sea* (1994).

Upon gaining a sonar contact, *Duncan* twice attacked *U-274* with her Hedgehog and *Vidette* carried out a depth-charge run. These attacks destroyed the boat with the loss of all hands. The kill was confirmed by what Gretton described as "gruesome evidence" that rose to the surface. Johnny Walker, who had not yet got a U-boat kill this trip, radioed Gretton congratulations. "We were delighted to have wiped the eye for once of the leading expert in the Navy, who had forgotten more about 'pinging' than any of us had ever learnt," Gretton wrote with modesty in his memoir. The British divided credit for the kill among Wicht's B-24, *Duncan,* and *Vidette.*

Three days later, on October 26, one of eight B-24s of Canadian Squadron 10, based at Gander, Newfoundland, which came out to escort Outbound North 207, sighted another *Siegfried* boat. She was thought to be the VII *U-420,* commanded by Hans-Jürgen Reese, age twenty-five, which, in early July, had been badly damaged by aircraft of the same squadron. This second assault on the supposed *U-420* was mounted by pilot R. M. Aldwinkle. On the first pass, five of six depth charges failed to explode and the other fell wide. On the second pass, after a brief gun duel, the U-boat dived and Aldwinkle dropped a Fido homing torpedo (called "Zombie" by Canadians), but it probably missed or malfunctioned. On a third pass, Aldwinkle dropped two more depth charges that exploded close to the U-boat. The Admiralty credited him with the kill of *U-420,* but Niestlé has concluded that the boat was lost to unknown causes.

Into this great congregation of Allied ships and aircraft in mid-Atlantic came two more American "jeep" carrier groups. The first was the *Block Island,* newly assigned to Atlantic ASW operations and equipped with long-range, radar-equipped, night-flying Avengers. The *Block Island* group relieved the "jeep" carrier *Core* and her screen. The second "jeep" carrier was the *Card,* which had resupplied in North Africa. The main mission of the *Block Island* and *Card* carrier groups was to sink the tanker *U-488* and the XB provisional tankers *U-219* and *U-220.*

The *Block Island* group DFed a refueling rendezvous of *U-488,* and other boats on the night of October 25–26. Two four-stack destroyers of the screen, *Parrott* and *Paul Jones* (both veterans of the Asiatic Fleet of 1942), found *U-488,* but they botched the attack and the harassed tanker got away. However, the boats seeking fuel from *U-488* had to endure more days of anxiety.

That same day, October 26, a B-24 found and attacked the VII *U-91,* commanded by Heinz Hungershausen. Intercepting and decrypting a report of this attack by gunfire and depth charges, Allied codebreakers surmised that it probably was carried out by a B-24 of Canadian Squadron 10. The *U-91,* which had been out from France thirty-six days and was seeking the VII *U-584* to give her fuel, was not seriously damaged.

Two days later, on the morning of October 28, two aircraft from *Block Island* found the XB provisional tanker *U-220,* commanded by Bruno Barber, and her flak-boat escort, *U-256,* commanded by Wilhelm Brauel. It was believed that Avenger pilot Franklin M. Murray and Wildcat pilot Harold L. Handshuh sank *U-220* with the loss of all hands and so severely damaged *U-256* that Brauel, like Barleben in the other flak boat, *U-271,* was forced to abort to France. However,

Niestlé writes that Brauel in *U-256* logged an underwater telephone exchange with Barber eight hours later that day, which raises doubt about the kill of *U-220* that morning.

On the next day, October 29, Peter Gretton's Support Group B-7, which had switched from the "bait convoy" Outbound North 207 to the next convoy sailing west, Outbound North 208, found a shadower. She was the new VII *U-282,* commanded by Rudolf Müller, age twenty-six, who was merely ten days out from a fuel stop in Norway on his first patrol. The British destroyers *Duncan* and *Vidette* and corvette *Sunflower* of Gretton's group sank *U-282* by Hedgehog. "Even more gruesome and more numerous" evidence rose to the surface, Gretton wrote, confirming the kill, but there were no German survivors. After this victory—the group's third kill in as many weeks—Gretton returned to the British Isles with the fast eastbound convoy Halifax 263.* U-boat Control did not learn of the loss of *U-282* for weeks.

Hunting the XIV tanker *U-488* and/or the XB provisional tanker *U-219,* the *Card* group got good Huff Duff bearings on October 30–31. As it turned out, the prey was neither *U-488* nor *U-219,* both of which had run south to less hostile waters, but rather the VII *U-584,* commanded by Joachim Deecke (who had landed four saboteurs in Florida in June 1942) and the *U-91,* commanded by Heinz Hungershausen, which was to give *U-584* some fuel to get home.

Late on the afternoon of October 31, Avenger pilot Wilma S. Fowler from *Card* found *U-584* and *U-91.* In response to his alarm, two other *Card* Avengers, piloted by Letson S. Balliett and Alexander C. McAuslan, soon arrived. After putting up desultory flak, Hungershausen in *U-91* dived and escaped. Left alone, Deecke in *U-584* also dived, but too late. Avenger pilots Fowler and Balliett dropped Fidos that hit and destroyed *U-584* with the loss of all hands.

Wrongly assuming Hungershausen in *U-91* to be a U-tanker, the commander of the *Card* group, Arnold J. ("Buster") Isbell, was more than annoyed that she got away. He therefore sent one of his screen, the four-stack destroyer *Borie,* commanded by thirty-year-old Charles H. Hutchins, in pursuit. In the early hours of November 1, Hutchins got a radar contact. It was not *U-91* but rather a veteran of the Arctic, *U-405,* commanded by Rolf-Heinrich Hopmann, who was a ripe thirty-seven years old and thirsting for a fight.

The battle that ensued over the next hour and twelve minutes was one of the closest and most intense of the Atlantic naval war. When *Borie* closed, guns blazing, *U-405* dived. Owing to a defect in *Borie*'s depth-charge racks, Hutchins unintendedly unleashed a monstrous barrage on Hopmann. The impact of these close explosions blew *U-405* to the surface, whereupon *Borie* attempted to ram. However, the motion of the heavy seas thwarted *Borie* and she came down on *U-405*'s bow section very gently and hung up. Locked in a deadly V, the opposing crews shot at one another at extreme close quarters. The exposed Germans incurred very heavy casualties. The grinding of the vessels opened deep gashes in *Borie*'s hull but not that of *U-405.*

---

* Gretton logged that during twenty-five days at sea his group had steamed 6,700 miles and had refueled at various convoys six times. For Plomer in *Sunflower,* it was the third kill in six months.

When the two ships separated, they each shot a torpedo at the other, but both missed. Thereupon Hutchins outmaneuvered Hopmann and gained an advantageous position that enabled him to fire three shallow-set depth charges from his throwers in a good straddle. These explosions and two solid hits on *U-405*'s bridge by *Borie*'s 4" guns fatally holed the U-boat. About twenty surviving Germans threw dinghies over the side and jumped into the sea. In a maneuver reminiscent of that of the American destroyer *Roper*'s toward the survivors of *U-85,* Hutchins, believing *Borie* was threatened by another U-boat, plowed through the Germans in the water and hauled away, leaving the few who survived to fend for themselves. None lived.

The story was not yet over. The entanglement with *U-405* had flooded *Borie*'s engine rooms. In reporting his victory to Buster Isbell in *Card,* Hutchins added: "May have to abandon ship." However, this message was garbled and *Card* did not realize *Borie* was in serious trouble until Hutchins radioed: "Commenced sinking." Six hours later Hutchins ordered his crew to abandon ship. Bedeviled by fog, the *Card* group was slow to mount a rescue and twenty-seven of *Borie*'s crew died in the water. Finally, the four-stack destroyers *Barry* and *Goff* rescued 127 *Borie* survivors. The *Barry* and an Avenger sank the abandoned hulk on November 2. Hutchins, his senior engineer Morrison R. Brown, and a machinist, Irving R. Saum, Jr., each won a Navy Cross for this battle and for keeping the damaged *Borie* afloat for as long as possible.

The inability of *B-dienst* and the *Luftwaffe* to provide precise information on Allied convoys in October and the apparent ability of the Allies to locate and avoid U-boat patrol lines led Dönitz and U-boat Control to make several important tactical changes. Notwithstanding the upgrades, the standard group or "wolf pack" U-boat operations versus convoys were finally deemed to be no longer feasible. The U-boat campaign against the North Atlantic run was to continue but the boats waging it were to be much more widely deployed in a variety of experimental formations and to remain fully submerged in daytime to avoid detection. Owing to the inadequacy of the *Wanze* radar detector and the quad and twin 20mm flak guns, the "fight back" policy against Allied aircraft was rescinded until all boats could be fitted with the rapid-fire 37mm gun and the new *Naxos* radar detectors, which could detect centimetric-wavelength radar. On November 11, Control ordered that the eight flak U-boats be reconverted to normal boats. All U-boats were to remain submerged at all times in daytime to hide from enemy aircraft and attack enemy ships only at night.

The result was a dispersion of the boats on the North Atlantic run in November and thereafter. First, the boats of the luckless group *Siegfried* were divided into three subgroups (*Siegfried* 1 to 3), then into two large subgroups (*Jahn* and *Körner*), then into five subgroups (*Tirpitz* 1 to 5), and then, finally, into ten subgroups (*Eisenhart* 1 to 10). Aware from Enigma decrypts of these dispersions, Allied authorities routed convoys around the U-boats or took advantage of harsh winter weather and poor visibility to sail right through some of the thinly manned lines.

The destruction of U-boats on the North Atlantic run tapered off sharply in the month of November. On November 6, Johnny Walker's British Support Group 2—five sloops plus the "jeep" carrier *Tracker*—sank two:

- In the early hours of that day, the sloop *Kite,* commanded by W.E.R. Seagrave, got a radar contact on *U-226,* a VII of *Tirpitz* 4 from France, commanded by a new skipper, Albrecht Gänge, age twenty-four. *Kite* fired star shells and depth charges, forcing Gänge to dive. Meanwhile, Walker in the sloop *Starling* and C. Gwinner in the sloop *Woodcock* raced up to help *Kite.* In a dogged hunt, the three sloops trapped and sank *U-226.* There were no survivors.
- Responding to a Huff Duff contact a few hours later, a Swordfish from *Tracker* found and drove under the new IXC40 *U-842* of *Tirpitz* 5, commanded by Wolfgang Heller, age thirty-three, who, contrary to new and specific orders, was running on the surface in daylight. Walker in *Starling* raced to the scene with the sloops *Magpie* and *Wild Goose.* Directing the three sloops, Walker soon trapped and sank *U-842* with the loss of all hands. The kill was confirmed with the recovery of "human remains" and wreckage. *Starling* and *Wild Goose,* commanded by D.E.G. Wemyss, got credit for the kill.

Thereafter Walker's support group and *Tracker* encountered severe winter gales and mountainous seas. In such foul conditions, Walker deemed *Tracker* more trouble than she was worth. She could not launch aircraft, and Walker had constantly to screen her from U-boat attack. Furthermore, Walker reported on arrival in Argentia on November 12 that his sloops were not built stoutly enough. All had suffered heavy sea damage, *Woodcock* so much so that she had to return to England in noncombatant status with an eastbound convoy.

Walker's deep concerns about screening *Tracker* were not unfounded. On November 8, the *U-648,* a VII of subgroup *Tirpitz* 5 commanded by Peter-Arthur Stahl, came upon *Tracker* and fired three torpedoes at her from a range of two thousand yards. These torpedoes missed, as did a T-5 *Zaunkönig* (Wren) homing torpedo that Stahl fired at *Starling* or another of Walker's sloops. *Tracker* and her screen escaped behind a smoke screen and rain squalls, but the incident was too close for comfort.

Land-based aircraft accounted for three other boats in November:

- The new VII *U-966,* commanded by Eckehard Wolf, age twenty-five, which sailed from Trondheim on October 5. While inbound to France via the northern Spanish coast in the early hours of November 10, a Leigh Light–equipped Wellington of British Squadron 612, piloted by Ian D. Gunn, found and attacked *U-966,* dropping six depth charges, all of which fell short. After an exchange of gunfire, *U-966* dived.

Later that morning, a B-24 of American Navy Squadron VB 103, piloted by Kenneth L. Wright, found *U-966* near El Ferrol. Wright made two attacks, dropping six depth charges and killing some Germans by gunfire. A B-24 of U.S. Navy Squadron VB 105, piloted by Leonard E. Harmon, joined the attack. Soon there arrived yet another B-24 of American Navy Squadron VB 110 piloted by J. A. Parrish, who dropped six close depth charges in spite of the heavy flak. Lastly, a B-24 of Czech Squadron 311, piloted by Otakar Zanta, attacked *U-966* with rockets about three miles off the Spanish coast.

These attacks killed eight Germans and wrecked the boat. Wolf ran her aground off Punta Estaca, then blew her up. He and forty-one other Germans reached shore in dinghies. The Spanish authorities allowed nine crewmen to be repatriated to Germany but interned thirty-three others for the duration of the war.*

- The veteran IXC *U-508,* commanded by *Ritterkreuz* holder Georg Staats, which sailed from St. Nazaire to the North Atlantic on November 9. On the fourth day, November 12, Control logged, Staats reported that he was under attack by an aircraft. American naval authorities concluded that the attack had been carried out by a B-24 of American Navy Squadron VB 103, piloted by Ralph B. Brownell, who reported a U-boat contact at that time but failed to return to the new Fleet Air Wing 7 base in southwest England at Dunkeswell. It was assumed that while carrying out the attack, the *U-508* shot down Brownell's B-24 with the loss of all hands, then was herself sunk by the B-24's depth charges. The Navy awarded Brownell a posthumous Navy Cross, his copilot and navigator the DFC, and seven other crewmen the Air Medal.
- The new VII *U-280,* commanded by Walter Hungershausen, which had been assigned to the *Tirpitz* and *Eisenhart* groups. On November 16, a B-24 of British Squadron 86, piloted by an Australian, John H. Bookless, attacked *U-280* with depth charges through intense flak that knocked out the outer engine on the port wing. The depth charges fell wide but on a second run, the depth-charge salvo fell close and the B-24 nose gunner raked the German gunners on the bridge and bandstands. Hungershausen got off an attack report to Control, but nothing further was heard from the boat. She most likely sank with the loss of all hands as a result of this attack.

Allied aircraft hit three other U-boats on the North Atlantic run in November, but all survived.

- On November 5, an unidentified aircraft attacked the new VII *U-967,* commanded by Herbert Loeder, age twenty-four. While inbound in the Bay of Biscay on November 30, the boat was again hit by an aircraft, also unidentified. She did not sail again until January 20, 1944.
- On November 8, an unidentified aircraft attacked the new *U-714,* commanded by Hans-Joachim Schwebcke, age twenty-five. The boat reported "no damage" and went on to complete a full patrol of fifty-one days.
- On November 15, an unidentified aircraft attacked the experienced *U-709,* commanded by Karl-Otto Weber. He, too, reported no damage and completed a full patrol of fifty-four days.

By early December, eleven new boats from Germany and three from the Arctic† had reinforced the Atlantic force. Control formed these boats, plus three from

* Within a period of about two months, four U-boats disabled by Allied aircraft (*U-760, U-617, U-566,* and *U-966*) had scuttled or beached on Spanish territory. The British occupation of the Portuguese Azores and the Allied diplomatic pressure on Madrid hinting at invasion doubtless dampened the enthusiasm of Spanish officials to repatriate German U-boat crews. As a consequence, Dönitz ordered that all damaged boats making for Spanish territory be scuttled offshore so that the crews could claim they were "sunk" by the enemy and therefore entitled by international law to repatriation.

† *U-269, U-625,* and *U-629,* all veterans.

France and two others into group *Coronel,* which in turn was divided into three subgroups (*Coronel* 1, 2, and 3). Allied ASW forces hit one of the boats, the Arctic transfer *U-269,* commanded by Karl-Heinrich Harlfinger, age twenty-eight, inflicting such "extensive damage" that Harlfinger was forced to abort. That withdrawal left *Coronel* at a strength of eighteen boats.

Group *Coronel* represented in part a sort of "second wave" in the renewed campaign on the North Atlantic run. In conformity with orders from Dönitz, no boats could sail from France after December 1 or Germany after December 10 without the new 37mm flak gun and the new *Naxos* radar detector.* All boats carried T-5 homing torpedoes, but owing to lagging production of that weapon, boats of the Atlantic force were issued only four per patrol.†

At this time there was only one Type XIV U-tanker left in the Atlantic force, Bartke's *U-488.* One other Type XIV, *U-490,* had been built but owing to her accidental sinking during workup, she was still in the Baltic. Bartke in *U-488* was "sold out" and homebound to France for refit and Christmas leave. Therefore in the first half of December, only a provisional tanker, the XB minelayer *U-219,* was available to assist the VIIs of group *Coronel* and none at all in the second half of the month. As a result, *Coronel* was held to areas merely five hundred miles west of Ireland, well within range of Coastal Command's heaviest concentration of ASW aircraft.

The three *Coronel* groups took up positions in stormy winter weather, but the Allies knew their positions from Enigma decrypts and with great success diverted the convoys to avoid them. By German reckoning, three convoys that they had specifically targeted evaded the U-boats: Outbound North (Slow) 24, Outbound North 215, and the eastbound Halifax 268. Two *Coronel* boats incurred severe mechanical problems:

- On December 16, heavy seas caused so much damage to the VII *U-284,* commanded by Günther Scholz, age twenty-four, that he was forced to abort and call for help. When the Arctic transfer *U-629,* commanded by Hans-Helmut Bugs, answered the call on December 21, Scholz put his crew on *U-629* and scuttled the wrecked *U-284.* Inbound to France on December 29 with about one hundred men on board, Bugs came upon a "small" convoy and shot a T-5 at a "destroyer." He claimed it sank, but the claim was not confirmed.

---

* The standard flak array, which required a new bridge structure to accommodate it, was, at absolute minimum, two twin 20mm on the bridge and one 37mm with splinter shields on an aft bandstand. The VII *U-986* was fitted with thirty experimental antiaircraft rocket launchers around the tower, but the rocket gear was deemed "not promising" and therefore not adopted.

† An analysis of the T-5 results on December 1 concluded that of seventy-one fired by Atlantic and Mediterranean boats since about September 20, forty hit (56 percent), twenty-two misfired, and nine failed in the tube ("hot runners") or shortly after ejection from the tube ("prematures"). The supposed "hits" were said to have sunk thirty—repeat thirty—destroyers, probably two other destroyers, and one submarine. Confirmed results: four destroyers sunk (*Orkan, St. Croix, Bristol, Buck*) plus irreparable damage to another (*Quail*). One sloop (*Chanticleer*) was irreparably damaged. One frigate (*Itchen*) was sunk, plus irreparable damage to another (*Lagan*). One corvette (*Polyanthus*) was sunk. Three minecraft were sunk (*Skill, Hythe, Hebe*). Total: not thirty or thirty-two, but nine warships sunk and three damaged beyond repair.

• On December 17, the new VII *U-761,* commanded by Horst Geider,* age twenty-five, had an explosion in the forward battery. No one was seriously injured in the blast, but the new engineering officer, Karl Lendle, declared that battery unusable and *U-761* had to abort. She limped into Brest on December 26.

After two futile weeks, Control dissolved the three *Coronel* lines and replaced them with three other lines, each of six boats: *Sylt, Amrum,* and *Föhr.* Owing to the mountainous seas, the boats were unable to use flak arrays, so Control directed these boats to remain submerged in daytime. Thus immobilized, their search capability was vastly limited and they could not find convoys which, in any case, were diverted south to avoid the boats and the terrible weather.

Having achieved nothing with these three new patrol lines, on December 22, Control dispersed the boats even more widely. It divided the eighteen boats of the three groups into six groups of three boats each, *Rügen* 1 to 6. The next day, one of the *Rügen* boats, the new *U-471,* commanded by Friedrich Kloevekorn, age twenty-five, came upon a troop or military, convoy, TU 5, en route from the British Isles to the States. This convoy was massively escorted by the battleship *Nevada,* which had survived the Pearl Harbor attack, and other warships. Kloevekorn boldly attacked alone on December 23 and claimed a hit on an 8,000-ton freighter, but, in actuality, he missed. An unidentified British B-24 escorting the convoy sighted and bombed *U-471,* wounding three men and inflicting "serious damage," but Kloevekorn was able to doctor the wounded, make repairs, and continue the patrol.

Another *Rügen* boat, the new *U-392,* commanded by Henning Schümann, age twenty-four, found a convoy on the day after Christmas. It was Halifax 271 (fifty-four ships, eight escorts) partly scattered by heavy weather. Mistakenly reporting the formation as merely "three or four freighters" with a light escort, Schümann attacked with three FATs. One broached and prematured, he reported. One hit a destroyer "under the bridge," and the third may have hit a freighter. None of the hits was confirmed. The destroyers and other escorts of the convoy drove *U-392* down, and the convoy escaped with no damage.

On the penultimate day of December, two *Rügen* boats came upon separate elements of convoy Outbound North 217 (eighty ships, nine escorts) that had been scattered in a storm. Gert Mannesmann, age thirty-three, in the new IXC40 *U-545,* reported fifteen merchantmen. He fired four FATs and claimed four hits that sank one freighter, the 7,400-ton British *Empire Housman,* and damaged two freighters for 12,000 tons. However, he only damaged the *Empire Housman* and no other hits were confirmed. Heinz Blischke, age twenty-four, in the new VII *U-744,* came upon a single, straggling freighter and shot seven torpedoes at her, including one T-5, but all missed or malfunctioned. A few days later Blischke came upon the dam-

* Geider was the son-in-law of an Imperial Navy man who had served as a boatswain on Dönitz's U-boat in World War I. According to an American intelligence report, during the boat's thirty-six-day layover in Norway, the original engineering officer, Fritz Ammon, insulted Geider with "vituperative language." As a consequence, Geider had him arrested and court-martialed. According to the American reports, Ammon was sentenced to three months in jail and reduced in rank.

aged *Empire Housman* and sank her, to share credit with Mannesmann, who further claimed a "destroyer" and another freighter, but these were never confirmed. The Allies made an effort to salvage *Empire Housman,* but it was futile. She was the only merchant ship sunk by U-boats on the North Atlantic run in December.

Owing to a decision by Hitler to resume *Luftwaffe* raids on London at the end of December, Dönitz diverted two VIIs and a IX from *Rügen* to weather-reporting duties. Because of the great increase in Allied carrier and land-based air patrols, this special duty was extremely hazardous. All three boats survived this assignment, but the IXC40 *U-544* was later sunk while trying to refuel two boats inbound from the Americas, as will be described.

At the end of the year, Dönitz issued a new order (No. 34) that radically modified the way U-boats were to attack convoys. Inasmuch as the radar of Allied air and sonar of surface escorts had made convoy attacks so very difficult, U-boats, upon gaining contact with a convoy were henceforth to shoot FATS and T-5s "blind" from submerged positions without any use of the periscope. All five (or six) tubes were to be emptied in the attack. After firing, the U-boats were to descend at least to 131 feet to avoid the possibility of a looping FAT hitting the boat.

This order effectively ended the so-called wolf pack or group tactics whereby a U-boat in contact with a convoy would call up or home in other U-boats. By firing blind and going deep to evade looping FATS and to reload, the U-boat was almost certain to lose contact with the convoy fairly quickly, and especially so if the convoy made a radical course change upon detecting the torpedoes, as was customary. Under this set of circumstances, the U-boat could not report the convoy course and speed reliably and consistently enough for Control to send in other boats, which were already more widely scattered than ever.

The resumption of U-boat operations against Allied shipping on the North Atlantic run in the four months from September through December 1943 proved to be another futile gesture. In 101 patrols mounted to that area during those four months, U-boats caused the loss of only fourteen vessels: six escorts and eight freighters. In turn, forty-nine U-boats*—and about 2,450 men—had been lost and twenty-two other boats were compelled to abort, most of them with battle damage and casualties inflicted by aircraft.

All the new and supposedly war-decisive weapons—the *Wanze* and *Naxos* radar detectors, the *Aphrodite* radar decoy, surface-search radar (*Gema* and *Hohentwiel*) and direction-finding gear, the T-5 *Zaunkönig* (Wren) homing torpedo, the quad and twin 20mm flak guns—proved to be wanting, and in some cases, worthless. Except for *U-488* and *U-490* (still in the Baltic), the Type XIV U-tankers had been wiped out. The *Luftwaffe* had failed to find and report convoys. The price for continuing the U-boat campaign on the North Atlantic run was so high that Dönitz again ordered Control to cancel group operations and to scatter the boats at sea, singly, west of the British Isles and to shoot "blind," while submerged, as instructed.

* Including the XB *U-220,* returning from a mine-laying operation in the Americas, pressed into service as a provisional refueler.

At the close of 1943, Washington, London, and Ottawa happily agreed to a cautious statement, to be released early in 1944, that significantly degraded the U-boat threat:

> Total merchant shipping tonnage lost by U-boat action in December was again low.* Despite an extension of operating areas, fewer U-boats were destroyed during the month by our air and sea forces owing to several factors, including increased caution by the enemy. Our supply routes were, however, well secured against U-boat attack.
>
> In 1943 U-boats sank but 40 percent of the merchant ship tonnage that they sank in 1942. On the other hand, United Nations merchant ship tonnage constructed in 1943 approximately doubled the tonnage delivered in 1942. Nearly half of our tonnage lost for the year 1943 was during the first three months: 27 percent was lost during the second quarter of 1943, and only 26 percent was lost during the last six months.

Futile Operations Against Gibraltar Convoys

The Anglo-Portuguese Agreement of August 18, 1943, opened the way for the British to establish airfields in the Azores on Faial and Terceira islands. On October 3, a naval task force departed the British Isles to carry out Alacrity, the first phase of the mission. It included the "jeep" carrier *Fencer,* three destroyers, and the troopship *Franconia,* crowded with RAF ground crews. The commander of Coastal Command's 19 Group, Geoffrey Bromet, went along to make certain this delicate diplomatic maneuver proceeded according to plan.

The task force sighted Terceira Island on October 8. *Fencer* launched Seafire aircraft (a carrier version of the Spitfire) to patrol for hostile forces. The destroyers ran hither and yon searching for U-boats that might attempt to interfere. All went smoothly. Before nightfall, Bromet and other RAF personnel flew in Walrus seaplanes to the island capital, Angra do Heroísmo.

This smooth operation suddenly went haywire. Unfavorable weather in the British Isles grounded the land-based bomber squadrons that were to base in the Azores. As a temporary stopgap, the Admiralty directed the Seafires and Swordfish on *Fencer* to fly ashore to establish a British presence at Lagens airport. Finally, on October 18, the first British land-based bomber, a B-17 Flying Fortress, arrived at Lagens. On October 24, *Fencer* collected her Seafires and Swordfish and sailed back to the British Isles to escort KM and MK convoys.

Within the next week or two, about fifty British aircraft arrived in the Azores. These were thirty B-17s of British Squadrons 206 and 220, formerly based in the Hebrides, ten Hudsons of British Squadron 233 from Gibraltar, and six Leigh Light–equipped Wellingtons, part of British Squadron 179, also from Gibraltar. In

---

* In November and December 1943, 1,466 ships in thirty-seven convoys crossed the North Atlantic with no losses to U-boats. The *Empire Housman,* damaged on December 30, did not sink until January 3, 1944.

the ensuing months, more and more Allied aircraft arrived, necessitating another airfield.

The importance of these new Allied air bases to the Battle of the Atlantic cannot be overstressed. For the British (and later, the Americans), the Azores became in the Middle Atlantic what Iceland was to the North Atlantic. The land-based ASW aircraft operating from the Azores closed the Middle Atlantic "Air Gap," extending the convoy air umbrella eastward toward North Africa, westward toward Argentia and Bermuda, northward toward Iceland, and southward toward the Cape Verde Islands and Dakar.

Owing to the heavy Allied air cover provided to the KM-MK convoys proceeding between the British Isles and the Mediterranean, the Germans had not conducted group operations against them since June 1942. With the arrival in France of new *Luftwaffe* aircraft (JU-88s, HE-177s, JU-290s, BV-222s) and the loss of all but one U-tanker, Dönitz and Control deployed group *Schill* 1 against this convoy route. The group had what was considered to be the advantage of being close to French bases, thus reducing the need for refueling and profiting from the convoy-spotting by the *Luftwaffe.*

To avoid detection before its first strike, *Schill* 1 was deliberately kept small. It was composed initially of only eight boats, including the flak boats *U-211, U-441,* and *U-953.* Early in the deployment, unidentified Allied aircraft hit and severely damaged the *U-441,* commanded by Klaus Hartmann. Unable to make necessary repairs, Hartmann aborted to France.

The seven remaining boats of *Schill* 1 deployed west of Portugal to intercept the northbound convoy MKS 28, which was merged with the northbound convoy Sierra Leone 138, altogether sixty merchant ships. The two convoys were protected by British Escort Group 39, comprised of ten warships: two destroyers (*Whitehall, Wrestler*), three sloops (*Hastings, Rochester, Scarborough*), a frigate (*Tavy*), three corvettes, and, for protection against German aircraft, the antiaircraft light cruiser *Alynbank.*

A *Luftwaffe* BV-222 aircraft found and reported this large formation on October 27 but lost it over the next two days. However, Heinz Franke in *U-262* located and tracked the convoy on October 29 and 30 and brought up other boats, including *Ritterkreuz* holder Peter Cremer in *U-333.* Franke and Cremer attacked and both claimed a "destroyer" sunk, but neither claim has been confirmed. In addition, Franke claimed that he sank a 7,000-ton freighter, which proved to be the 3,000-ton Norwegian *Hallfried,* only the third freighter to be sunk by U-boats in the whole of the North Atlantic in the month of October.

During the action on October 31, two of the British escorts, the destroyer *Whitehall* and the corvette *Geranium,* found and sank by Hedgehog and depth charges one of the *Schill* 1 boats. She was the *U-306,* commanded by Claus von Trotha. The British confirmed the kill by fishing out "splintered woodwork" of the type known to be used in the interior of the VIIs. No survivors or bodies were found.

In order to maintain group *Schill* 1 at a strength of eight boats, U-boat Control directed two VIIs newly sailed from France to replace the lost *U-306* and the aborting flak boat, *U-441*. The group, which still included the flak boats *U-211* and *U-953*, then redeployed to intercept a KMS convoy southbound to Gibraltar.

Luftwaffe aircraft scouted for the convoy on November 2, 3, and 4, but they had no luck. However, on the night of November 4, *Ritterkreuz* holder Peter Cremer in *U-333* got a hydrophone contact and surfaced in "thick" fog. Suddenly, he wrote, "distorted by the shifting veil of the fog, disjointed and growing to gigantic size, hulls, masts and funnels came into view." But before he could prepare and send a contact report, a "destroyer" loomed out of the fog, bearing down on *U-333*. Cremer shot a T-5 at the "destroyer" by eye and dived to 590 feet, but the torpedo missed or malfunctioned and the "destroyer" pounded *U-333* with "a rain of depth charges."

The *U-333* survived, but Cremer remained submerged during the daylight hours, delaying his contact report for about eighteen hours. U-boat Control was furious. Not only had Cremer delayed his contact report, the diarist logged, but also he had failed to include a location. His lapses were "incomprehensible," the diarist admonished. Because of the delay, operations against this convoy could not be mounted.

Luftwaffe aircraft scouted for and found the expected northbound convoy, MKS 29, on November 7. U-boat Control shifted *Schill* 1 to intercept it but, as usual, the location given by the airmen was in error and the convoy sailed undetected through the U-boat line on the night of November 8. It was just like earlier days, the U-boat Control diarist complained. There were not enough aircraft in working order and the aircrews were not sufficiently trained in over-water navigation.

The luck of the *Luftwaffe* changed on November 9. Aircraft located northbound convoy MKS 29 in time to shift *Schill* 1, less the low on fuel, homebound flak boat *U-953*, to a promising position. After dark Heinz Franke in *U-262* reported "lights," brought up several of the boats, then attacked. Franke and another skipper, Gerhard Thäter in *U-466*, claimed hits on "destroyers" but none of the claims was confirmed. Erwin Christophersen in *U-228* claimed sinking a 5,000-ton freighter, but that claim was not confirmed either. The convoy escaped with no losses.

Allied ASW forces knocked out two of the remaining seven boats of *Schill* 1. Near dawn on November 9, a B-17 of British Squadron 220, newly arrived at the British base in the Azores, found the *U-707*, commanded by Günter Gretschel, age twenty-nine. Flying into "heavy and accurate" flak, pilot Roderick Patrick Drummond made two low-level passes and dropped seven shallow-set depth charges that destroyed the U-boat. Drummond reported that his crew saw "ten to fifteen" Germans in the water, swimming amid "wooden wreckage," and that he dropped them two dinghies and rations. Another B-17 of British Squadron 220, piloted by G. P. Robertson, arrived to find only one German in the water. Robertson dropped him supply packs and radios but the Allies recovered no one from *U-707*. In an unrelated action, surface-ship escorts of the convoy counterattacked Thäter in *U-466* and inflicted so much damage that he was forced to abort to France in the wake of the flak boat *U-953*.

At about this time, German intelligence reported the presence of a big northbound Allied formation. This was convoy MKS 30, merged with convoy Sierra Leone 139, altogether sixty-six merchant ships. Protection for these merged convoys was massive: twenty warships (two destroyers, five sloops, seven frigates, six corvettes) of escort groups 5, 7, and 40, plus the British armed merchant cruiser *Ranpura* and the Canadian antiaircraft merchant cruiser *Prince Robert.* In addition, Coastal Command B-24s and Wellingtons of British Squadrons 53 and 179, B-17s of British Squadrons 206 and 220 in the Azores, and Sunderlands of Canadian Squadron 422 provided saturation air cover.

The Germans were determined to strike a heavy blow at these convoys. To make certain of success, U-boat Control deployed three patrol lines from south to north, altogether about thirty U-boats.

• The southernmost line, *Schill* 1, was composed of seven boats, including the remaining flak boat, *U-211;* the *U-333,* commanded by *Ritterkreuz* holder Peter Cremer; and, temporarily, the newly sailed IXC *U-515,* commanded by Werner Henke, who wore Oak Leaves on his *Ritterkreuz.* Two other boats returning from operations on the North Atlantic run, *U-426* and *U-608,* were assigned to *Schill* 1, but they could not get that far south in time.

• The next line farther north, *Schill* 2, was composed of ten boats; six returning from the North Atlantic run,* including the *U-608;* one, the IXC40 *U-536,* returning from the aborted POW pickup in Canada; and three boats newly sailed from France. The *U-426,* returning from the North Atlantic run, was given freedom to operate independently near *Schill* 2.

• The third and most northerly line, *Schill* 3, was composed of twelve boats returning from the North Atlantic run. Two other boats low on fuel from the North Atlantic run, *U-91* and *U-552,* were encouraged to join *Schill* 3 if at all possible.

While en route to join *Schill* 3, the new IXC40 *U-542,* recently sailed from Norway, found a group of "destroyers" on November 16. The U-boat skipper, Christian-Brandt Coester, age twenty-four, boldly shot a T-5 homing torpedo at one of them, but it did not hit. The "destroyers" and a "Hudson" aircraft counterattacked *U-542* but Coester shot back with a second T-5. It prematured, but he eluded the hunters. When another new boat, the *U-969,* commanded by Max Dobbert, age thirty-three, en route to *Schill* 2, reported a "destroyer" from about the same area, Control speculated that these boats had probably encountered the screen of an eastbound convoy, perhaps Halifax 265 or Slow Convoy 146. However, the supposed convoy was already too close to the British Isles to mount a U-boat attack.

Luftwaffe aircraft found the merged northbound convoys MKS 30 and Sierra Leone 139 on November 16. U-boat Control shifted *Schill* 1 easterly to intercept it submerged at about midday on November 18. The dogged spotter and tracker Heinz Franke, in *U-262,* found the convoy. He and *Ritterkreuz* holders Cremer in *U-333* and Henke in *U-515* led the attack.

Cremer wrote in his memoir that "chance would have it that *U-333* was the first boat to intercept the enemy." The result was disastrous. The British frigate *Exe,* one

---

* Including the VII *U-343,* which had given *U-762* an emergency fuel supply on November 7.

other warship, and an aircraft spotted *U-333*'s periscope almost simultaneously and pounced. "A pattern of ten depth charges exploded with a deafening roar round the boat," Cremer continued, and "the effect was terrible . . . [and the] damage [was] very great." Moreover, *Exe*'s keel hit *U-333*'s periscope and broke it off. *Exe* and other escorts then depth-charged *U-333* for eight hours. By what was deemed a miracle, *U-333* survived her third collision with Allied vessels, aborted, and limped home.

Henke in *U-515* hit the 1,350-ton British sloop *Chanticleer* with a T-5 and blew off her stern. However, the sloop survived and a tug later towed her to the Azores. Other air and surface escorts, including notably the British sloop *Crane,* quickly found and aggressively attacked *U-515* and savaged the boat. The chief engineer, Georg Mahnken, urged Henke to return to France for repairs. Mahnken's understudy, Günther Alterburger, who had made twelve war patrols on other boats, believed the crew could repair the boat at sea. Always willing to "take a chance," as Allied intelligence put it, Henke proceeded to an isolated area in the Canary Islands. After rigging a camouflage net, the crew repaired the extensive topside damage and Henke took *U-515* on to Freetown.

Yet another *Schill* 1 boat was lost in this attack, the flak boat *U-211,* commanded by Karl Hause, age twenty-seven. A Leigh Light–equipped Wellington of the Azores-based British Squadron 179, piloted by the Canadian Donald F. McRae, who had earlier sunk *U-134* and forced *U-760* into internment in Spain, found *U-211* by radar and then by sight in the moonlight. In the belief that his chances of success were better if he did not use his Leigh Light, McRae achieved complete surprise and sank *U-211* with a nearly perfect straddle of four depth charges. There were no survivors.

The air and surface escorts of this convoy formation simply overwhelmed the U-boats of *Schill* 1. When it realized this, Control canceled the operations of *Schill* 1 and repositioned the next northerly line, *Schill* 2, for the second assault. Owing in large part to a massive air escort (seven Leigh Light–equipped Wellingtons the night of November 19–20, twelve B-17s and B-24s during the day on November 20), *Schill* 2 was unable to assemble and crack through. However, two boats of *Schill* 2 shot down Allied aircraft. The *U-618,* commanded by Kurt Baberg, got a Sunderland of Canadian Squadron 422. The *U-648,* commanded by Peter-Arthur Stahl, who had earlier shot at the "jeep" carrier *Tracker* but missed, and had been hit by an aircraft on November 18, got a B-24 of British Squadron 53.

Over the next several days, from November 20 to 23, boats of *Schill* 2 and *Schill* 3 attempted to break through the massive screen and attack the merchant ships, but none succeeded. The *Luftwaffe* inflicted the only damage to merchant ships of this convoy formation. That damage was slight, but the way it was done was innovative and startling.

Late on the afternoon of November 21, when it was likely that its air escorts had returned to bases, the *Luftwaffe* sent off a special force of twenty-five four-engine HE-177 bombers to attack the convoy. The Heinkel bombers were unsatisfactory planes, but each was armed with two HS 293 radio-controlled "smart bombs." At a range of about eight hundred miles from their base, twenty of the twenty-five HE-177s found the convoy and dropped (or "flew") forty bombs at various ships from an altitude of 1,300 to two thousand feet. Eleven bombs failed to detonate and almost all the others missed, but the Germans hit two merchant ships, *Marsa* and *Delius.* The former sank; the latter survived and reached port.

The *Kriegsmarine* concluded that this special *Luftwaffe* operation, mounted at high cost and with great expectations, was a flop. The "poor results," the OKM diarist logged, were due mainly to the lack of training of the aircrews. Of the five HE-177s (with ten glider-bombs) that failed to reach the convoy, three were lost and two developed engine problems and aborted. Following this fiasco, the OKM transferred the outfit to the Mediterranean theater.

Apart from continuing saturation air escort, the Allies reinforced the nineteen surface escorts of the convoy formation with British Support Group 4, which, as related, was comprised of six new, American-built frigates. This group increased the surface escort to twenty-five warships. The surface escorts sank three *Schill* U-boats:

- On November 20, the frigate *Nene* and two Canadian corvettes, *Calgary* and *Snowberry,* of Canadian Support Group 5 (commanded by a Britisher), found the IXC40 *U-536,* newly arrived from the failed POW pickup in Canada. The three warships attacked *U-536* and blew her to the surface with depth charges. *Nene* sent a boarding party to capture the boat or its secret documents, but she sank before anything could be done. *Nene* and another British frigate, *Tweed,* rescued the skipper, Rolf Schauenburg, and sixteen other Germans.
- On November 21, the sloop *Crane* and the frigate *Foley* of British Support Group 7 found the new IXC40 *U-538* of *Schill* 3, commanded by Hans-Egbert Gossler, age twenty-nine. In a notable display of teamwork, the two warships destroyed *U-538* with depth-charge salvos. There were no survivors.
- On November 23, three of the new frigates of British Support Group 4, *Bazely, Blackwood,* and *Drury,* found what was thought to be the *U-648,* commanded by Peter-Arthur Stahl. In another notable display of teamwork, the three warships trapped the U-boat and pummeled her with depth charges. In wartime, the Admiralty credited these ships with the kill of *U-648,* but Niestlé writes that the cause of her loss is unknown.

So ended operations of the three *Schill* groups. Of the approximately thirty U-boats that had been deployed against the two merged convoys, only one boat achieved anything: Henke in *U-515* blew off the stern of the British sloop *Chanticleer,* which made port in the Azores but was not repaired. In return, Allied forces had sunk six *Schill* boats (*U-211, U-306, U-536, U-538, U-648, U-707*) with the loss of about three hundred men (seventeen, from *U-536,* were captured). Three *Schill* boats (*U-333, U-441, U-466*) aborted to France with severe damage and/or personnel casualties.

Control reshuffled the three *Schill* groups into a new patrol line on November 23. This was *Weddigen,* to be composed of seventeen boats, or so it was believed. Actually, the Allies had sunk two of these (*U-538* and *U-648*), leaving only fifteen, and the IXC *U-515,* commanded by Werner Henke, had hauled away to repair damage and resumed her voyage to Freetown. Yet another, *U-586,* low on fuel, had to depart for home the following day, reducing group *Weddigen* to thirteen boats, several also quite low on fuel.

The *Weddigen* group included the bold and indefatigable Heinz Franke in *U-262* from the first *Schill* group, who continued to scout out and report convoys with exceptional valor and skill. On the late afternoon of November 26, when the *Luftwaffe* reported a big convoy—the merged MKS 31 and Sierra Leone 140—Franke put on full speed. Despite a radical course change by the convoy, the *Luftwaffe* relocated it on November 27. Thereupon Franke eluded depth-charging escorts, cannily positioned his boat, and surfaced at night in the middle of the convoy, like a latter-day Otto Kretschmer. He shot three T-5s and claimed that he sank three 5,000-ton freighters, but these sinkings were not confirmed.

Two other *Weddigen* boats got close enough to shoot T-5s at escorts. One was the new VII *U-764,* commanded by Hans-Kurt von Bremen, age twenty-five. The other was the aged IXB *U-107,* commanded by Volker von Simmermacher. Von Bremen claimed a sinking, von Simmermacher claimed a hit for damage, but neither hit was confirmed.

The recently arrived *U-238,* commanded by that fall's top scorer, Horst Hepp, saw two Allied aircraft crash in flames. Hepp rescued two British airmen and sent off a long (and useless) report on his interrogation of them, which the Allies DFed. Control ordered Hepp to rendezvous with von Bremen's homebound, low on fuel *U-764* on November 30 and turn over the airmen to that boat.

Allied codebreakers and Huff Duff experts provided good information on this rendezvous. Land-based aircraft and the *Bogue* hunter-killer group went out to break up the party and—hopefully—rescue the British airmen. On November 29, von Bremen reported that four land-based aircraft attacked the *U-764* and destroyers hunted him for sixteen hours before he escaped and continued to France. On November 30, Hepp reported that three (*Bogue*) aircraft hit the *U-238,* killing two men and wounding five others, including Hepp. Navy pilots James E. Ogle III, Carter E. Fetsch, and others carried out this attack; but Hepp, too, got away and aborted to France, still holding the two British airmen.

When Dönitz learned of the fine convoy shadowing carried out by Franke in *U-262* and of his attack in the middle of the merged convoys MKS 31 and SL 140, he immediately recommended to Hitler that Franke be awarded a *Ritterkreuz,* the only North Atlantic skipper to be so honored in the fall of 1943.* Dönitz then sent a pointed message to all U-boat commands and vessels:

> The Führer, acting on my suggestion, has awarded Lieutenant Franke a *Ritterkreuz.* One of the determining reasons was that Franke has repeatedly been the only one of those participating in an operation who has forced his way to the convoy against strongest air and sea defenses. In the present situation the prospects for sinkings are slight. In awarding distinctions I shall evaluate toughness and tenacity so much the more, even if they are not crowned with success.

---

* Credited with sinking three fleet destroyers and hits on another and shooting down a plane, at the time of the award Franke's confirmed score (all on *U-262*) was four ships for 13,935 tons, including the Norwegian-manned corvette *Montbretia.*

Allied forces sank three of the *Weddigen* boats:

- On November 25, the team of frigates *Bazely* and *Blackwood* of British Support Group 4 found the veteran *U-600,* commanded by Bernhard Zurmühlen, age thirty-four. In another well-executed attack with depth charges and Hedgehogs, the frigates destroyed *U-600.* There were no survivors.
- On the night of November 26, a Leigh Light–equipped Wellington of the Azores-based British Squadron 179 piloted by Donald M. Cornish found the new IXC40 *U-542,* commanded by Christian-Brandt Coester. As will be described, Cornish and his crew had earlier sunk *U-431* and forced *U-566* to scuttle. Flying into heavy flak, Cornish dropped six depth charges that destroyed *U-542,* his third U-boat kill. There were no survivors.
- On the afternoon of November 29, an Avenger from the "jeep" carrier *Bogue,* piloted by Bernard H. Volm, Jr., found what was thought to be the VIIB *U-86*—the oldest attack boat in the Atlantic force—commanded by the veteran Walter Schug. Volm radioed an alarm that brought in three more *Bogue* aircraft. An experienced Avenger pilot, Harold S. G. Bradshaw, led the attack. The *Bogue* aircraft got credit for the kill, but Niestlé writes that the cause of her loss is unknown.*

Like the *Schill* groups, *Weddingen* was a complete failure. No boat of *Weddigen* sank or even hit an Allied vessel. With the help of timely Enigma decrypts, the escorts of three convoys, Outbound South 59, KMS 33, and KMS 34, and two northbound convoys, Sierra Leone 140 and MKS 31, outfought and outwitted group *Weddigen.* In aggregate, Allied forces sank eight U-boats from the three *Schill* groups and the *Weddigen* group.

While crossing Biscay homebound on the night of December 13, another *Weddigen* boat, the new *U-391,* commanded by Gert Dültgen, was attacked by a Leigh Light–equipped B-24 of British Squadron 53. Flying into heavy flak, the pilot, Squadron Leader George Crawford, dropped six depth charges that destroyed *U-391* with the loss of all hands. Later in the war, Crawford and most of this crew failed to return from a mission.

Control dissolved group *Weddigen* on December 6 and replaced it with group *Borkum,* composed of thirteen boats. To maximize *Luftwaffe* assistance and reduce the threat posed by Allied air, newly based in Gibraltar, French Morocco, and the Azores, and to save fuel, U-boat Control deployed *Borkum* directly west of the Bay of Biscay. Its mission was like that of *Schill* and *Weddigen:* to intercept MKS and KMS convoys merged with convoys going to and from Sierra Leone. Control warned *Borkum* to stay clear of the blockade-runners *Osorno* and *Alsterufer,* which were to pass close by, inbound to France.

From Enigma decrypts, Allied authorities were aware of group *Borkum* and the

---

* In his two years in the Atlantic force, Schug had made eight war patrols in *U-86* and had sunk only two confirmed ships: a 342-ton sailing vessel by deck gun and a 4,300-ton Greek freighter by torpedo.

two inbound blockade-runners. Accordingly they rerouted the merged northbound convoys MKS 33 and Sierra Leone 142 to pass west of *Borkum,* and sent the merged southbound KMS 37 and Outbound South 63 east of *Borkum.* At the same time, they put in motion intricate plans to intercept and sink *Osorno* and *Alsterufer.* The upshot was a very busy time for both sides that, because of the secrecy imposed upon all Allied codebreaking activities, was to be confusing for historians.

The Allies ordered a hunter-killer group built around the "jeep" carrier *Card* to intercept the blockade-runners. Thereupon *Card* and her screen of three four-stack destroyers, westbound from Casablanca in company with convoy GUS 24, hauled out and ran north toward the likely area. As the hunter-killer group drew closer to the designated site in gale weather, a *Luftwaffe* aircraft saw and reported it and U-boat Control ordered group *Borkum* to rush southwest and to attack and sink the *Card.*

Shortly after midnight on December 24, the *U-305,* commanded by Rudolf Bahr, age twenty-seven, sighted the *Card.* Bahr got off a contact report, but it was DFed. One of the destroyers, *Schenck,* drove *U-305* off and down with gunfire and depth charges. Responding to Bahr's report, the *U-415,* commanded by Kurt Neide, age twenty-seven, came up, found *Card,* and shot three FATs, but all missed. Neide claimed that he sank a "destroyer" with a T-5, but that hit was never confirmed. Escorted by the detroyer *Decatur, Card* then withdrew, leaving *Schenck* and *Leary* to deal with the *Borkum* boats.

The *Schenck,* commanded by Earl W. Logsdon, got a radar contact on a U-boat and pursued. The quarry was thought to be the *U-645,* commanded by Otto Ferro, age thirty-two, who dived and possibly fired a T-5 at *Schenck.* When *Schenck*'s sonar reported a good contact, Logsdon carried out a systematic attack with depth charges. These evidently damaged *U-645* so badly that Ferro surfaced. *Schenck* again got the U-boat on radar and attacked with guns and drove her under and dropped more depth charges. It was believed that these destroyed *U-645* with all hands, but Niestlé doubts this and writes that the cause of the loss is unknown.

The *Leary,* commanded by James E. Kyes, also pursued a radar contact. Unwisely, Kyes fired star shells to illuminate the target, thereby exposing his own ship. The *U-275,* commanded by Helmut Bork, and the *U-382,* commanded by Rudolf Zorn, shot at *Leary* with T-5 torpedoes and sank her. Ninety-seven of *Leary*'s men, including Kyes, perished in the sinking or the water. *Schenck* rescued fifty-nine survivors and later transferred them to *Card.* After *Reuben James* and *Jacob Jones, Leary* was only the third American destroyer to be sunk by U-boats in the North Atlantic.*

Kurt Neide in *U-415,* who had missed *Card* with three FATs, had better luck that night, Christmas Eve. Neide got into favorable shooting position on the British destroyer *Hurricane,* which had left the merged southbound convoys KMS 36 and Outbound South 62 to reinforce the *Card* group. Neide hit and damaged *Hurri-*

---

* Not counting the four-stack destroyer *Borie,* which rammed and sank *U-405* and then sank from her own collision damage. As related, U-boats sank two other American destroyers in the Mediterranean: *Bristol* and *Buck.*

cane, but she did not sink. During the night the damage was found to be greater than originally estimated, and after daylight—on Christmas Day—the *Hurricane* crew transferred to the frigate *Glenarm* and British forces put *Hurricane* under.

Berlin was ecstatic. Based on flash reports from Bork, Neide, and Zorn, the OKM diarist logged that the U-boats of *Borkum* "had sunk four destroyers in two days." That was a 100 percent inflation. The confirmed number was two destroyers in two days.

A *Luftwaffe* aircraft sighted the blockade-runner *Osorno* in the extreme western waters of the Bay of Biscay. Upon receiving this report, the Germans sent out a flock of aircraft and six destroyers and six torpedo boats (Operation *Bernau*) to escort her and the other blockade-runner, *Alsterufer,* into France. Operating on Enigma decrypts, the British in turn sent out aircraft and two cruisers, *Glasgow* and *Enterprise,* to intercept and sink the blockade-runners, as well as the dozen would-be German escort vessels.

In a confused tangle of aircraft and surface ships, Allied forces humiliated the Germans, sinking the *Alsterufer,* the destroyer Z-27, and torpedo boats T-25 and T-26. Four Canadian corvettes rescued seventy-four Germans from *Alsterufer.* Two inbound and two outbound U-boats (group *Hela*) searched for survivors of Z-27 and the two torpedo boats. The "Hangar Queen" IXC *U-505,* outbound to distant waters, picked up thirty-four survivors of T-25 and returned to France. Kurt Baberg in the inbound *U-618* picked up twenty-one survivors of the destroyer Z-27 and landed them in France. The *Osorno* almost reached Bordeaux, but as she was going up the Gironde River, she hit a wreck and had to be beached.*

In the four months from September 1 to December 31, 1943, U-boat Control sailed thirty-seven upgraded VIIs and IXs to groups *Schill, Weddigen,* and *Borkum* operating in a Middle Atlantic triangle lying between Biscay, Gibraltar, and the Azores. In all, these boats sank one 3,000-ton merchant ship, the Norwegian *Hallfried,* two destroyers, the American *Leary* and British *Hurricane,* and wrecked the British sloop *Chanticleer* beyond repair. In return, nine of the thirty-seven U-boats were lost, plus two (*U-648* and *U-536*) that were shifted from North Atlantic to Middle Atlantic waters, a total loss of eleven U-boats and about 550 men. Moreover, as will be described, three other U-boats of this Middle Atlantic deployment were to be lost in January 1944. A half dozen other Middle Atlantic boats were forced to abort with battle damage.

The outcome of these operations demonstrated that with the Allied acquisition of air and naval bases in French Morocco and the Azores and the deployment of "jeep" carriers, the waters between Gibraltar and the Azores were as perilous to U-boat groups as were the waters between Iceland and the British Isles.

When the thirty-two losses on the North Atlantic run from September through

---

* Exploiting Enigma decrypts in the South Atlantic during the first week of January 1944, the old American light cruiser *Omaha* and modern destroyers *Somers* and *Jouett* sank or forced the scuttling of three other inbound blockade-runners: *Rio Grande, Weserland,* and *Burgenland.* After the loss of these six vessels, a colossal disaster, no other Axis surface ships in the Far East attempted to run the blockade to France.

December 1943 were added to the eleven losses in the Middle Atlantic in the same period, the result was forty-three U-boats. Two other VIIs returning from the Americas (*U-669* and *U-760*) were also lost in the Middle Atlantic or the Bay of Biscay, bringing the total losses for the period to a disastrous forty-five U-boats and about 2,200 men.

The Mediterranean: Further German Setbacks

The shrinking Mediterranean U-boat force, based at Toulon and still commanded by Leo Kreisch, suffered yet another loss on the night of October 21. This was the aforementioned *U-431,* sunk by the Canadian Donald M. Cornish, piloting a Leigh Light–equipped Wellington of British Squadron 179. Cornish attacked into heavy flak and dropped six depth charges. These destroyed *U-431* with the loss of all hands, including her skipper, Dietrich Schöneboom, but in the absence of positive evidence, the British did not credit Cornish and his aircrew with the kill. Instead, the Admiralty mistakenly gave the credit to the British submarine *Ultimatum,* commanded by the able and highly decorated W. Hedley Kett, who attacked a German U-boat off Toulon ten days later.*

In compliance with Hitler's oders, after the new *Naxos* radar detector had been installed, five more VIIs set sail from Atlantic bases for the Mediterranean in the second half of October. The result was even more setbacks for the Germans. Two boats, *U-450* and *U-642,* commanded by Kurt Böhme, age twenty-six, and Herbert Brünning, age twenty-eight, slipped through the Strait of Gibraltar, but Allied forces sank three others:

- In the early hours of October 24, a Leigh Light–equipped Wellington of British Squadron 179, piloted by the same Canadian, Donald Cornish (who had sunk *U-431* inside the Mediterranean just two days earlier), found Hans Hornkohl in the often bombed *U-566* off Vigo, on the northwest coast of Spain. Cornish attacked into heavy flak, dropping six depth charges that wrecked the boat beyond repair. Like Brandi in *U-617,* Hornkohl nursed his stricken boat into shallow water and scuttled. A Spanish fishing trawler, the *Fina,* rescued the Germans and put them ashore in Vigo. They were "interned" briefly by Spanish authorities but returned to Brest by train on October 31. Thereafter, Hornkohl and crew commissioned a new VII.
- On the afternoon of October 31, a British surface-ship patrol detected Claus-Peter Carlsen in *U-732* at the western mouth of the Gibraltar Strait. The big ASW trawler *Imperialist,* commanded by A.R.F. Pelling, attacked, dropping ten depth charges. These exploded directly below the keel of *U-732* and blew her to the surface. Before Carlsen could get the boat under water again, *Imperialist* opened fire with her main gun and scored several hits. When the boat dived, *Impe-*

* In a postwar reassessment, when it was discovered that Kett had unsuccessfully attacked *U-73,* the Admiralty credited pilot Cornish with the kill of *U-431.*

rialist dropped twenty-eight more depth charges that drove *U-732* to the bottom, where Carlsen lay doggo for about six hours.

After dark, Carlsen surfaced to escape at full speed on the diesels. One hour later an unidentified British aircraft got *U-732* on radar and flashed an alarm. Unable or unwilling to dive again, Carlsen gave orders to scuttle. As the men were jumping overboard, the British destroyer *Douglas,* commanded by K.H.J.L. Phibbs, attacked, dropping ten depth charges close to the sinking boat. *Douglas* rescued eight Germans; the British destroyer *Witherington* picked up another ten. A Red Cross ship found Carlsen, bringing the number of survivors to nineteen.

• Only a few hours later, in the early minutes of November 1, a Leigh Light–equipped Wellington of British Squadron 179, piloted by Arthur H. Ellis, found Hans-Joachim Klaus in *U-340* also at the mouth of Gibraltar Strait. Ellis attacked, dropping six depth charges, but an engine malfunctioned, forcing the Wellington to abort.

Later in the day another British surface patrol located *U-340* with sonar. Three British warships, the destroyers *Active* and *Witherington* and the sloop *Fleetwood,* pounded the boat with depth charges. Still later that day, Klaus elected to scuttle close to shore so the Germans could swim to Spanish soil. After the forty-eight Germans had been in the water about four hours, a Spanish fishing trawler came along and picked them up. The Germans celebrated their rescue, but, as it turned out, prematurely. The sloop *Fleetwood* came up and captured all the Germans.

Apparently some of the sixty-seven Germans captured from *U-732* and *U-340* talked freely. From them the British obtained detailed information about the T-5 Wren (or GNAT) "antidestroyer" homing torpedo, the ineffective *Wanze* and the new *Naxos* radar detectors, the *Aphrodite* radar decoy, and the quad 20mm and twin 20mm flak guns.

Allied ground forces in rugged Italy, inching northward up the "boot" toward Rome, liberated Naples, crossed the Volturno River, and finally bogged down at the so-called German Gustav Line above the Rapido River at the monastery of Monte Cassino. To crack this line and liberate Rome, Allied planners conceived Operation Shingle, a large-scale amphibious landing at Anzio, on the west coast of Italy behind the Gustav Line opposite Rome. To carry out this ambitious new task, in January 1944 a great many Allied naval assets (particularly LSTs) were retained temporarily in the Mediterranean, ultimately resulting in a postponement of Overlord.

The Mediterranean U-boat force contributed little to the campaign in Italy. The most significant strike was made by Egon-Reiner von Schlippenbach in *U-453.* On November 11, he planted minefields off Brindisi and Bari, seaports on the east coast of Italy. The British fleet destroyer *Quail* hit one of the mines and incurred such heavy damage that she had to be scrapped. Another of these mines destroyed the 800-ton fleet minesweeper *Hebe.* Second in importance during November was the work of Ernst-Ulrich Brüller in *U-407,* who late in the month damaged by torpedo the 9,100-ton British cruiser *Birmingham.* Two other veteran boats, *U-73* and *U-81,* each sank medium-size Allied freighters for an aggregate 7,400 tons.

The most notable German naval success in the Mediterranean in November was achieved by the *Luftwaffe.* The HE-177 squadron, equipped with HS 293 smart bombs, which had failed against Atlantic convoys, hit the 8,600-ton British troopship *Rohna* off Bougie on November 26. Jammed with Allied soldiers, she was en route from the British Isles in convoy KMF 26. Altogether 1,149 men perished. Of these, about one thousand were U.S. Army, the worst loss of American soldiers at sea in all of World War II. This appalling British troopship disaster was not revealed during the war, and the full dimensions of it have come to light only recently.*

Notwithstanding the urgent orders and exhortations from Berlin, only three U-boats had actually reached the Mediterranean in the fall of 1943: Wächter's *U-223,* Böhme's *U-450,* and Brünning's *U-642.* Inasmuch as two more U-boats had been lost (*U-617* and *U-431*) inside the Mediterranean during this period, the flotilla increased by only one boat to fourteen. Moreover, Allied forces sank two more Mediterranean boats in December.

• Off Algiers on December 11, Karl-Jürgen Wächter in *U-223* hit and wrecked beyond repair with a T-5 Wren homing torpedo the British frigate *Cuckmere,* which was escorting convoy KMS 34. The next day, a little farther east near Djidjelli, *Ritterkreuz* holder Gerd Kelbling in *U-593* sank with a T-5 Wren the British *Hunt*-class destroyer *Tynedale.* The loss of these two British warships in Algerian waters prompted Allied authorities to deploy a hunter-killer group of five surface ships. In the early hours of December 12, the group located *U-593,* but her skipper, Kelbling, sank yet another British *Hunt*-class destroyer, *Holcombe.*

Assisted by aircraft, the four remaining warships of the hunter-killer group carried out a relentless search for *U-593.* Late in the afternoon of December 13, the American destroyer *Wainwright* finally got an unambiguous sonar contact. She and another British *Hunt*-class destroyer, *Calpe,* conducted a brutal depth-charge attack that drove *U-593* to the surface, whereupon both warships opened fire with guns. Hopelessly trapped, Kelbling scuttled and abandoned ship. *Wainwright* and *Calpe* picked up all fifty-one of the *U-593* crew and took them to North Africa.

• Westward of that U-boat kill, near Oran, on the afternoon of December 16, Horst Deckert in *U-73* found convoy GUS 24 and hit the 7,200-ton American Liberty ship *John S. Copley,* which, however, limped into port. In response, a hunter-killer group, composed of three American destroyers, left Mers el-Kébir and raced to the scene. About an hour into the hunt, the *Woolsey* got a positive sonar contact and attacked with depth charges. The close explosions cracked the pressure hull of *U-73* and caused flooding that could not be stanched. Deckert surfaced to fight it out, whereupon *Woolsey* and *Trippe* opened fire with guns that killed many Germans, riddled the boat, and forced Deckert to scuttle and abandon ship. The *Woolsey* and the other destroyer, *Edison,* picked up Deckert and thirty-three other Germans, including two wounded men and a doctor, and took them to North Africa, where the crew of *U-593* was also temporarily imprisoned. Sixteen Germans perished in this sinking.

Both American and British warships were involved in the kills of *U-73* and *U-593.* As a consequence, Allied authorities fell into a minor bureaucratic spat

---

* See C. Jackson, *Forgotten Tragedy* (1996).

over where the POWs should be sent, Washington or London. During this delay, the second watch officers of both boats, Kurt Kinkele and Armin Weighardt, "hid in a closet" in Algiers, escaped to Spain, and ultimately reached Germany.

These two losses reduced the Mediterranean force to twelve U-boats, three of which had been damaged during a heavy Allied bomber raid on Toulon on November 24. On December 5, the experienced *U-230,* commanded by Paul Siegmann, got into the Mediterranean, raising that force once again to thirteen boats.

An astonishing event electrified the Mediterranean U-boat force that fall. The first of the force commanders, *Ritterkreuz* holder Viktor Oehrn (from November 28, 1941), reappeared, as if from the dead. He had a riveting story to tell. After Leo Kreisch had relieved Oehrn on February 1, 1942, Oehrn remained in various naval staff positions in Italy, all of them uninteresting and unimportant. On the night of July 13, 1942, while serving as a naval liaison to Erwin Rommel's *Afrika Korps* near El Alamein, Oehrn became lost in the desert, blundered into British Commonwealth positions, and was badly shot up and captured by Australian soldiers. Taken to a British hospital in Alexandria, Oehrn hovered on the edge of death for weeks. He never fully recovered from his wounds and, as a consequence, he was repatriated on November 3, 1943, having been a POW for almost sixteen months. Two weeks later, he reported for staff duty at U-boat Control in Berlin.

British naval intelligence was apparently unaware that the former first staff officer to Karl Dönitz, U-boat "ace," and former Mediterranean U-boat force commander was in British custody in Egypt all that time.

Patrols to or in Distant Areas

In the four months from September 1 to December 31, 1943, U-boat Control mounted twenty-four war patrols to or in distant areas: thirteen to the Americas and eleven to West Africa and the Indian Ocean.

Five boats sailed to the Americas in September:

- The new XB minelayer *U-220,* commanded by Bruno Barber, age thirty-nine, planted an SMA minefield off St. John's, Newfoundland, on October 9. About a week later these mines sank two medium-size freighters, the 3,400-ton American *Delisle* and the 3,700-ton British *Penolver.* Until the mines could be swept, the port was closed, with the usual shipping delays and confusion. As related, *U-220* then served as a provisional refueler in the North Atlantic and was sunk on October 28.
- The veteran IXC *U-155,* commanded by *Ritterkreuz* holder Adolf-Cornelius Piening, patrolled to Brazilian waters. In a cautious outing, Piening sank one freighter, the 5,400-ton Norwegian *Siranger.* Upon his return to France, Piening left the boat to command Combat Flotilla 7 in St. Nazaire.*

---

* While commanding *U-155,* from August 1941 to February 1944, Piening sank twenty-six confirmed ships for 141,521 tons, including the British "jeep" carrier *Avenger,* British troopship *Ettrick,* and five tankers. He ranked sixteenth among all U-boat skippers.

• The veteran VIID (minelayer) *U-218,* commanded by Richard Becker, planted an SMA minefield off Trinidad on October 27. The minefield produced no sinkings, but on November 4, Becker sank by gun a sailing vessel off the southeast coast of Trinidad. He returned to France on December 8.

• The "Hangar Queen," *U-505,* commanded by Peter Zschech, finally got away from Lorient on September 18. Two days later, while en route to top off her fuel tanks, one of *U-505*'s diesels "froze up tight." The crew fixed that problem, but on September 23, the important main trim pump broke and Zschech had no spare parts. He returned to Lorient on September 30, doubtless shamefaced.

• The new IXC40 *U-537,* commanded by Peter Schrewe, age twenty-nine, sailed to plant a sophisticated automatic weather station at Martin Bay, a bleak, deserted site on the east coast of Labrador. After Schrewe diverted temporarily to report weather himself and lost his flak gun in heavy seas, he reached Martin Bay on October 22. A scientist, Kurt Summermeyer, and Schrewe's crew placed the station on a 170-foot hill about four hundred yards inland. It functioned for several days but was then apparently jammed. Its remains were not discovered by Canadian officials until 1981.

Aware from Enigma decrypts of *U-537*'s special mission, commencing on October 29 Canadian ASW forces mounted a hunt to exhaustion (Salmon) for her. Although *U-537* had a *Naxos* radar detector, on October 31 a Hudson of Canadian Squadron 11, piloted by F. L. Burston, found her on the surface and attacked with eight rockets, none of which hit. Farther south, near Cape Race, a Canso (Catalina) of Canadian Squadron 5, escorting convoy Halifax 265, found *U-537* on November 10 and attacked through flak to drop four depth charges, which fell wide. The next day, another Canso of Squadron 5, piloted by R. Duncan, attacked *U-537* through flak to drop depth charges, which inflicted slight damage. The ex-American four-stack British destroyer *Montgomery,* an escort from convoy Halifax 265, and other Cansos came up, but again *U-537* slipped away. Senior Canadian authorities judged that this Salmon hunt had been thoroughly botched. After serving briefly as a radio decoy, *U-537* reached France on December 8.

Four boats sailed to West Africa or to the Indian Ocean in September and October.

• Wilhelm Rollmann, who won a *Ritterkreuz* on *U-34* in 1940, embarked for the Far East in the new IXD2 U-cruiser *U-848.* On November 2, he sank the lone 4,600-ton British freighter *Baron Semple.* This sinking alerted U.S. Army and Navy ASW aircraft on Ascension Island. These included, notably, a detachment of four B-24s of U.S. Navy Squadron VB 107 from Natal, Brazil.* While out searching about three hundred miles southwest of Ascension on November 5, the crew of a Navy B-24 piloted by Charles A. Baldwin found *U-848* on the surface and flashed a contact report. In two runs into massive flak, Baldwin dropped twelve depth charges and severely damaged the U-boat, which remained on the surface, trailing "a great amount" of fuel oil.

---

* The contingent had arrived on the island in early October.

Circling beyond flak range, Baldwin homed in two other Navy B-24s. These were piloted by William R. Ford (who had sunk *U-164* earlier in the year) and by William E. Hill. Supported by Baldwin, who strafed the boat, Ford made two runs into heavy flak. He dropped twelve depth charges, but both salvos fell short and he returned to Ascension. Also supported by Baldwin, who made another strafing run, Hill attacked the U-boat from behind, but Rollmann's gunners shot out one of Hill's engines, forcing him too to return to Ascension.

Baldwin continued to circle the damaged U-boat beyond flak range. Four hours after his crew had first spotted *U-848,* Baldwin homed in Ford's B-24, returning from Ascension with the same crew but a new pilot, Samuel K. Taylor. At about the same time, three Army Air Forces B-25s arrived from Ascension. These dropped 500-pound general-purpose bombs from 1,500 feet, but not surprisingly, the attacks were ineffective.

Taylor made two runs, dropping twelve depth charges. On this second attack, Taylor's aircrew performed with consummate skill. The depth charges fell close and "the enemy broke in half and sank." Taylor's crew counted "twenty-five or thirty" survivors in the water and dropped three life rafts, but only one German, chief boatswain Hans Schade, survived. A month later, on December 3, the American cruiser *Marblehead* rescued Schade from a raft, but he was delirious and died two days later in a hospital in Recife, Brazil, where he was buried with appropriate military ceremony.

- The veteran *U-68,* commanded by Albert Lauzemis, patrolled in the Gulf of Guinea and off Freetown. On October 22 Lauzemis found and attacked a convoy in the gulf. After misfiring seven torpedoes, he sank the British ASW trawler *Orfasay* and the 5,400-ton Norwegian tanker *Litiopa* with his deck gun. In subsequent weeks, Lauzemis sank by torpedo two more ships, the 6,600-ton British freighter *New Columbia* and the 5,200-ton Free French passenger-cargo vessel *Fort de Vaux.* These successes raised his bag for this 107-day patrol to four ships for 17,612 tons.
- The aging IXB *U-103,* commanded by Gustav-Adolf Janssen, age twenty-eight, laid a minefield at Takoradi on October 23. Thereafter Janssen cautiously hunted ships in the Gulf of Guinea and off Freetown. He had no luck with mines or torpedoes. On his return voyage, Janssen refueled from the Type XB minelayer *U-219,* serving as a provisional tanker, then retired *U-103* to the Baltic Training Command via Norway.
- *Ritterkreuz* holder Heinz-Otto Schultze in the new IXD2 U-cruiser *U-849* embarked from Kiel for the Far East on October 2. On November 25, another U.S. Navy B-24 of the Squadron VB 107 contingent staging at Ascension Island found *U-849* on the surface. The pilot, Marion Vance Dawkins, Jr., straddled *U-849* with six depth charges dropped from an altitude of merely twenty-five feet. The missiles sank *U-849,* but a ricocheting depth-charge warhead severely damaged the horizontal and vertical tail section of the B-24, which, however, limped back to Ascension. Dawkins reported "about thirty" survivors in the water to whom he dropped life rafts, but no Germans were ever recovered.

• • •

Seven boats sailed to the Americas in October.

Departing France on October 2, the IXC *U-154,* commanded by Oskar-Heinz Kusch, age twenty-five, patrolled via the Portuguese Azores, newly occupied by British ASW forces, then onward to northern Brazilian waters. Near the mouth of the Amazon on November 3, Kusch found a convoy but was prevented from attacking it by an unidentified Catalina, which he repelled, he reported. Kusch then moved north to the coast of French Guiana, where, he also reported, he was twice attacked by aircraft on the night of November 22. Low on fuel—and unable to refuel—Kusch returned to France on December 20.

During this patrol of *U-154,* the ideological and personality gulfs between Kusch and his first watch officer, Ulrich Abel (a doctor of laws who was six years older), widened drastically. On Christmas Day, when Kusch submitted an evaluation of Abel for commanding officer's school, he wrote that although Abel was an "inflexible, rigid, and one-sided officer" of "average talent," he was nonetheless suitable for U-boat command at the front.

This praising-with-faint-damnation endorsement evidently shocked and infuriated Abel, described as a die-hard Nazi. About three weeks later, on January 12, 1944, Abel filed a formal document accusing Kusch of sedition, and another on January 25 accusing Kusch of cowardice. The first document triggered formal legal proceedings that led to Kusch's arrest on January 20 and confinement at the Angers (France) Military Prison. Six days later, a military trial convened at Kiel to weigh the accusations against Kusch.

Abel's charges of sedition were backed up by two other watch officers on *U-154.* All three men swore that Kusch had ridiculed Hitler as insane, utopian, megalomaniacal, pathologically ambitious, and worse. Kusch had thrown out the standard wardroom photo of Hitler with the comment: "There will be no more idol worship on this boat." He had also predicted repeatedly that Germany would soon lose the war, one reason being that the U-boats were completely obsolescent. The constant flow of admonitions from U-boat Control to the skippers to fight on relentlessly was so much useless "whip-cracking" and "slave-driving." On top of all that, Kusch obsessively tuned in to BBC and other Allied news broadcasts, a grave crime in the Third Reich.

The court found Kusch guilty of sedition and listening to foreign radio stations. The prosecution recommended a sentence of ten years and six months imprisonment, but the court, which included U-boat skipper Otto Westphalen, ruled on January 29 that Kusch be executed. Later Westphalen said he would have supported a petition for clemency, with probation to a fighting unit, but Kusch filed no such petition. On May 12, a firing squad in Kiel carried out the sentence.

At no time before or during the trial did Karl Dönitz see Kusch or even allow his views of the situation to be known. However, numerous *Kriegsmarine* officers, including his former skippers on *U-103, Ritterkreuz* holder Werner Winter and Gustav-Adolf Janssen, and the *Ritterkreuz* holder Wilhelm Franken from *U-565* in the Mediterranean, leaped to defend Kusch. They and many others in the U-boat arm deeply resented the fact that neither Dönitz nor von Friedeburg nor Godt did anything at all to help this "comrade."

In his memoir, Erich Topp wrote:

> Whatever the political environment may have been, it would still have been in place here for Dönitz to speak to his commander at least once and to stand by him. Or was he so naive that he did not know what people were saying in the U-boat messes about the Party and the Gröfaz.* . . . If we comprehend tradition as being in touch with and continuing lofty intellectual currents, then Sub-Lieutenant Kusch undoubtedly fits into this pattern, whereas Admiral of the Fleet Dönitz does not.

In the postwar years, Topp, who became a ranking admiral in the *Bundesmarine,* the West German Navy, attempted to rehabilitate Kusch, but he encountered bitter opposition from Hans-Rudolf Rösing and Karl-Friedrich Merten, among others. Under an Allied occupation law that permitted the punishment of persons found guilty of war crimes, crimes against peace, or crimes against humanity, in 1949 and 1950 Kusch's father sued members of the court, including Westphalen, for the murder of his son. Jurors or judges in three different trials acquitted the defendants.†

The IXC *U-516,* commanded by Hans-Rutger Tillessen, age thirty, who departed France on October 4, also patrolled via the Azores to the Caribbean. Despite the debilitating heat and strong Allied ASW measures, Tillessen found fair hunting off Colón, Panama. In four weeks, from November 11 to December 8, he sank four ships (one tanker) for about 14,500 tons, plus a sailing vessel. On the return voyage through the Caribbean toward Trinidad, Tillessen added a big American tanker to his bag, the 10,200-ton *McDowell,* but he missed a destroyer. Total: five ships (two tankers) for 24,700 tons and the 39-ton Colombian sailing vessel *Ruby.* On December 19, near Trinidad, an unidentified Allied aircraft bombed *U-516,* causing "considerable damage," and Tillessen headed home, seeking fuel from any other attack boat that could provide it.

The IXC *U-505,* still commanded by Peter Zschech, age twenty-five, who had made countless attempts to carry out another war patrol in the ten months preceding, sailed for the Caribbean on October 9. This attempt also ended in an abort. In the midst of a depth-charge attack by unidentified Allied forces on October 24, Zschech, doubtless feeling intense pressure to perform or else, committed suicide with his pistol. The first watch officer, Paul Meyer, age twenty-six, assumed command, buried Zschech at sea, and returned *U-505* to France on November 7.

The IXC *U-129,* commanded by Richard von Harpe, age twenty-six, sailed on October 12 to patrol the United States East Coast from Cape Hatteras to Florida. En route, on October 26, von Harpe came upon the huge and fast ocean liner *Ac-*

---

* A scornful term for the Führer.

† The Kusch case still evokes heated debate among German U-boat veterans. The account here closely follows that of Heinrich Walle in Nicosia and Stokes (1991). See also Klenck (Luttitz).

quitania but was unable to get off a shot. On November 12, he met the Type XIV tanker *U-488* and refueled, along with the IXC40s *U-193* and *U-530,* bound for the Gulf of Mexico and Panama, respectively. The *U-193* had already given some fuel to the inbound VIID (minelayer) *U-214.*

The Tenth Fleet alerted Allied forces that were still pursuing *U-488* to this rendezvous. A hunter-killer group built around the "jeep" carrier *Core* arrived in the designated area on November 15. In the early hours of that day, von Harpe in *U-129* sighted *Core* and fired four torpedoes at her, but they missed. All ships in the *Core* group felt a "heavy shock wave" and "about six lighter shocks" on their hulls—probably end-of-run torpedo explosions. Von Harpe went deep, evaded the hunting destroyers, and continued his voyage to Cape Hatteras. The other two IXs and the tanker *U-488* also avoided detection. Upon learning of the presence of this carrier hunter-killer group, U-boat Control directed *U-488* to cease all refueling operations and to come home immediately.

Von Harpe in *U-129* found the hunting poor at Cape Hatteras. Patrolling to the southernmost limit of his zone on December 4, he came upon a convoy, KN 280, bound from Key West to Norfolk. He claimed sinking a freighter and a "destroyer" but only the freighter, the 5,400-ton Cuban *Libertad,* was confirmed. He had no further luck and commenced his homeward voyage, like Tillessen in *U-516,* seeking fuel.

In response to the urgent requests for fuel, U-boat Control directed the new IXC40 *U-544,* commanded by Willi Mattke, age thirty-four, to rendezvous with the homebound Tillessen in *U-516* and von Harpe in *U-129.* When Allied codebreakers learned of the proposed meeting from Enigma decrypts, a hunter-killer group built around the new "jeep" carrier *Guadalcanal,* which sailed from Norfolk on January 5, was directed to the scene.

Commanded by Daniel V. Gallery, *Guadalcanal* launched aircraft to search for the three U-boats about five hundred miles west of the Azores on January 16. Two aircraft, piloted by Bert J. Hudson and William M. McLane, found the three boats refueling and immediately launched an unorthodox attack, firing rockets and depth charges simultaneously. Some of these hit and sank the provisional refueler, Willi Mattke's *U-544.* The airmen saw "twenty to thirty-five" Germans in the water, but despite a diligent search, the *Guadalcanal*'s escort vessels could not find a single survivor. The *U-129* and *U-516* dived and escaped.*

Von Harpe in *U-129* went on to France, but Tillessen in *U-516,* desperate for fuel, could not. Therefore U-boat Control ordered the outbound IXC40 *U-539,* commanded by Hans-Jürgen Lauterbach-Emden, age twenty-four, to rendezvous with *U-516* and give her fuel.

The *U-539,* which had sailed from France for a patrol to the Caribbean on January 3, was the first boat of the Atlantic force to conduct a war patrol with a

---

* On this maiden voyage, *Guadalcanal* lost five airmen and fifteen of her twenty-one aircraft to wear and tear, accidents, or heavy weather. Her arrival in the Atlantic raised the number of American carriers primarily on ASW duty in that theater to eight: *Block Island, Bogue, Card, Core, Croatan, Guadalcanal, Santee,* and another new vessel, *Mission Bay.*

snorkel.* The two boats came within hailing distance on January 22, but owing to the foul weather—yet another ghastly winter storm in the North Atlantic—they were unable to carry out the refueling operations until February 5, when Tillessen in *U-516* finally got enough fuel to reach France. Delayed and low on fuel, Lauterbach-Emden in *U-539* patrolled to Canada rather than the distant Caribbean.

After obtaining fuel from the harassed tanker *U-488* on November 12, the IXC40 *U-193,* commanded by the old hand Hans Pauckstadt, age thirty-seven, patrolled to the Gulf of Mexico. West of the Florida Straits on December 3, Pauckstadt sank with three torpedoes his first—and only—ship, the new 10,200-ton American tanker *Touchet,* loaded with 150,000 barrels of heating oil. She blew up and burst into flames. Of the eighty crewmen, ten perished, and the rest were rescued from lifeboats.

Hans Pauckstadt in *U-193* was the last U-boat skipper to patrol the Gulf of Mexico in World War II. Altogether in this little-noted area, U-boats sank fifty-six ships (twenty-four tankers) and damaged fourteen other vessels.† Contrary to rumors that were rife during the war, no U-boat received any intelligence from Axis spies operating close to the seashore, nor did any boat refuel from secret supply ships in the Louisiana bayous or elsewhere, nor did any Germans go ashore in disguise to enjoy the delights of Mobile, New Orleans, Houston, or Galveston.

On the return voyage, Allied aircraft hit *U-193* off Cape Finisterre. She was "thrown on the rocks" and severely damaged, but she survived this mishap and limped into El Ferrol, Spain, on February 10. After extensive makeshift repairs, she sailed on February 20 and reached Lorient five days later.

After refueling from the tanker *U-488,* also on November 12, the IXC40 *U-530,* commanded by Kurt Lange, patrolled the Caribbean Sea to Panama. On the day after Christmas, Lange hit and damaged the 10,200-ton American tanker *Chapultepec* off Colón. Three days later, on December 29, he attacked another American tanker, *Esso Buffalo,* firing three torpedoes, but they missed. Unknowingly, this tanker rammed *U-530,* but Lange was able to make repairs and continue the patrol. He returned to France on February 22, completing an arduous voyage of 130 days, during which he sank no confirmed ships.

Unable to refuel on the outbound leg, Max Wintermeyer in the IXC40 *U-190* nevertheless patrolled to northern Brazilian waters. Cruising cautiously offshore between the mouth of the Amazon River and Fortaleza, Wintermeyer reported that he "saw nothing." Owing to the shortage of fuel—and the uncertainty of refueling—he commenced his homebound voyage on December 12. Control directed Wintermeyer to meet and obtain the newest *Naxos* radar detection gear from the *U-172,* which was outbound to Penang, but he could not find her and continued on

---

* In most accounts, the Type VII *U-264,* commanded by Hartwig Looks, is erroneously identified as the first boat to sail into combat with a snorkel. In a trial run off France with several flotilla commanders and chief engineers embarked, Looks had a disastrous snort failure that delayed his departure to February 2, a full month after the *U-539* sailed.

† See Wiggins, *Torpedoes in the Gulf* (1995), pp. 116–17 and Appendix 5.

to France. The boat arrived on January 15, completing a barren patrol of ninety-one days.

Owing to the absence of U-tankers and other factors, only one boat patrolled to the Americas in November 1943 and none in December.

The new IXC40 *U-543,* commanded by Hans-Jürgen Hellriegel, who had earlier commanded the *U-96* of the Atlantic force, sailed from Kiel to Newfoundland waters on November 9. En route, Hellriegel diverted temporarily to anticonvoy operations with group *Coronel.* Detached from *Coronel* on December 16, *U-543* proceeded toward Newfoundland with orders to hunt ships and also to broadcast weather reports twice daily. On December 27, Hellriegel reported that he had chased the big, fast, ocean liner *Acquitania* in vain. Alerted to the presence of this boat by Enigma decrypts and Huff Duff, Canadian authorities mounted a massive hunt for her three hundred miles east of the coast of Newfoundland.

This hunt, carried out from December 23 to January 6, entailed a great many Canadian forces, including aircraft, escorts of nearby convoys, and a hunter-killer group. The historian of the Royal Canadian Air Force, W.A.B. Douglas,* calculated that despite hideous flying weather, the Canadians completed twenty-one B-24 and seven Canso sorties. None, however, had any luck. Hellriegel shot T-5s at two "destroyers" hunting him on December 30 and January 3, and claimed both sank. Even though they could not be confirmed, Control credited these "sinkings," and Dönitz awarded Hellriegel a *Ritterkreuz* after his return to France.†

The thirteen patrols mounted to the Americas in September, October, and November sank eight merchant ships for 45,700 tons plus the sailing vessel *Ruby.* Tillessen in *U-516* accounted for about half of that number. Seven of the thirteen boats sank no ships. Probably as a result of better radio discipline in the patrol areas, the new *Naxos* centimetric-wavelength radar detector, and caution on the part of the skippers, no U-boats were lost.

Six attack boats sailed to West Africa and the Indian Ocean in November and December. As related, one boat, the outbound *U-505,* under a new skipper, Harald Lange, age thirty-nine, rescued survivors of the German torpedo boat *T-25* and returned to France. The others had various adventures.

Alfred Eick in the IXC *U-510,* embarked for Penang, refueled from the XB minelayer *U-219,* serving as a provisional tanker, on November 30. After rounding the Cape of Good Hope, Eick shot three torpedoes at a freighter off Durban on January 13 but missed. Per plan, on January 28 he met the German tanker *Charlotte Schliemann* about three hundred miles south of Mauritius and refueled.

Thereafter Eick patrolled aggressively but carefully the northernmost reaches of the Arabian Sea between Oman and India in "awful" heat and humidity. On Feb-

---

* In his magisterial *The Creation of a National Air Force,* vol. 2 (1986).

† At the time of the award, February 3, 1944, his confirmed score on the duck *U-140,* the VII *U-96,* and the *U-543* was five ships for 16,165 tons, including the 200-ton Soviet submarine *M-94* and a 416-ton Portuguese trawler, claimed (and credited) as an enemy submarine.

ruary 22, he found convoy PA 69 en route from the Persian Gulf to Aden. In two attacks, he claimed two tankers and a freighter sunk for 25,000 tons, one freighter of 7,000 tons left burning and probably sinking, and a hit on another freighter of 7,000 tons. Allied records show that in these two attacks, Eick sank the 7,400-ton British tanker *San Alvaro,* the 9,200-ton American freighter *E. G. Seubert,* and damaged the 10,000-ton Norwegian tanker *Erling Brovig.* In the month of March Eick claimed sinking three more freighters (two Norwegian, one American) for an aggregate of 18,000 tons plus a sailing vessel. Allied records confirmed three freighters of 14,700 tons sunk. Eick then proceeded to Penang, arriving on April 5. Two days later Berlin notified Eick that he had been awarded a *Ritterkreuz.**

The IXD2 U-cruiser *U-178* departed Penang on November 27 for France with about 153 tons of cargo: thirty tons of rubber, 121 tons of tin, and two tons of tungsten (wolfram). Inasmuch as *Ritterkreuz* holder Wilhelm Dommes, who had commanded the boat on its outward voyage, was still ill, he remained in Penang. The boat's first watch officer, Wilhelm Spahr, age thirty-nine, who had been Prien's quartermaster during the legendary sinking of the *Royal Oak* in Scapa Flow in 1939, moved up to command.

Near the Maldives, Spahr sank the 7,200-ton American Liberty ship *José Navarro,* then met Eick in *U-510* and the tanker *Charlotte Schliemann* south of Mauritius on January 28. He topped off his fuel tanks, took aboard nineteen more tons of rubber, got Enigma keys (for June) from *U-510,* then headed southwest for Cape Town.

Following his temporary attachment to group *Schill,* during which he hit the British sloop *Chanticleer* and was in turn heavily damaged, Werner Henke in the IXC *U-515,* who wore Oak Leaves on his *Ritterkreuz,* made repairs and patrolled to Freetown. In the week from December 17 to December 24, Henke sank three British freighters for 20,900 tons: *Kingswood, Phemius,* and *Dumana.* These together with the single freighter sunk in the Bahamas by von Harpe in *U-129* were the only successes by the Germans against merchant ships in the whole of the Atlantic Ocean in December.

While homebound, heavy seas and engine vibration opened up a temporary weld on one of *U-515*'s aft buoyancy tanks. For the second time on this patrol, Henke stopped off the deserted shore of a remote island to make repairs—this time in the Cape Verdes. Later, while approaching Lorient on January 16, he repelled two RAF twin-engine Mosquito bombers with his flak guns. He claimed sinking four ships for 22,000 tons (including the sloop *Chanticleer*), which closely matched the confirmed figures. Henke might well have requested a safe shore job, but in hopes of winning more fame and awards, he elected to retain command of *U-515.*

After an extensive overhaul and an upgrade in flak guns, the IXC *U-172* sailed from France to Penang on November 22 commanded by a new skipper, Hermann Hoffmann, her former second and first watch officer. Only twenty-two years old, Hoffmann was the youngest officer in the Atlantic U-boat force yet to be pro-

* At the time of the award, his confirmed score was eight ships sunk for 50,000 tons and the sailing vessel.

moted to command. While *U-172* was outbound in the Bay of Biscay, an unidentified Coastal Command land-based bomber detected her on the night of December 3, dropped six depth charges, then strafed the boat with machine-gun fire, but she escaped.

Hoffmann met the XB minelayer *U-219,* serving as a provisional tanker, on about December 10 and filled *U-172*'s fuel tanks. When Allied codebreakers provided reliable advanced information on this rendezvous, a hunter-killer group built around the "jeep" carrier *Bogue* left her convoy, GUS 23, and rushed to the area. The aircraft were unable to locate the U-boats during the meeting but shortly after sunrise on December 12, Avenger pilot Elisha C. Gaylord found *U-172* on the surface and drove her under. He summoned help and dropped a Fido that apparently missed, and Hoffmann went deep.

The skipper of *Bogue,* Joseph B. Dunn, ordered a "hunt to exhaustion." For the next twenty-seven hours, *Bogue*'s aircraft and her screen, the four-stackers *George E. Badger, Clemson, Du Pont,* and *Osmond Ingram,* hunted and blasted *U-172* with bombs, depth charges, Hedgehogs, and Fidos. Finally, at about 10 A.M. on December 13, the savaged *U-172* surfaced to fight it out. Manning a machine gun, Hoffmann killed one American and injured six others on *Osmond Ingram.* In return, *Badger, Clemson, Du Pont,* and *Osmond Ingram* raked *U-172* with intense fire of all kinds, killing thirteen Germans and forcing the survivors, including Hoffmann, to leap into the sea. The destroyers fished out Hoffmann and forty-five other Germans and took them on to Norfolk.

The new IXD2 U-cruiser *U-850* sailed from Kiel to Penang on November 18, commanded by the renowned submariner Klaus Ewerth, age thirty-six. A member of the crew of 1925, Ewerth had attended the first *Kriegsmarine* submarine-school class (1933) and was chosen to commission the first submarine, the duck *U-1,* in 1935. Subsequently he had commanded the Type VIIs *U-35* and *U-36,* and the Type 1 *U-26* that he took on two war patrols in the early months of the war. After a long stint in the Training Command, Ewerth had commissioned *U-850* in April 1943.

On the afternoon of December 20, U-boat Control signaled Ewerth the good news that his wife had given birth to their fifth child and all was well. A mere twenty minutes later, an Avenger from *Bogue,* piloted by Wallace A. LaFleur, sighted *U-850* running on the surface. LaFleur gave the alarm, then attacked. His depth charges failed to release on the first pass and fell short on the second. Four other aircraft (two Wildcats, two Avengers) arrived from *Bogue* to help. In the ensuing exchange of fire, the aircraft drove *U-850* under. Pilots LaFleur and Harold G. Bradshaw then launched Fidos that hit and sank *U-850.* The destroyers *Badger* and *Du Pont* picked up pieces of wood and clothing and "dismembered bodies" but could find no survivors.

The twenty-three patrols to the Americas, West Africa, and to or in the Indian Ocean mounted in the last four months of 1943 produced a bag of twenty-four Allied merchant ships (including four tankers) for about 134,500 tons, plus the sloop

Chanticleer and two sailing vessels. This made small impact on Allied maritime assets, but it was sufficient damage to ensure a continuation of convoying in those remote areas and the deployment of numerous Allied aircraft and surface ships on ASW patrols.

The Germans paid a stiff price for these twenty-four merchant-ship sinkings: four of the twenty-three U-boats sunk, including the famous IXC *U-172* and three new IXD2 U-cruisers, *U-848, U-849,* and *U-850*. The approximately 160 dead submariners included three of the four skippers: *Ritterkreuz* holders Wilhelm Rollmann and Heinz-Otto Schultze, and Klaus Ewerth.

The Arctic: *Tirpitz* Crippled, *Scharnhorst* Sunk

Midway between the Baywatch and Avalanche landings in Italy, on September 6 the German battleship *Tirpitz* and battle cruiser *Scharnhorst,* screened by ten destroyers, sailed from Altenfiord in northern Norway. This task force ran north in the Barents Sea to the island of Spitzbergen, bombarded the provisional British base there, then dashed back to Altenfiord. The official British naval historian noted that this minor operation was the only time in her twenty-one months in the Arctic that *Tirpitz* had fired her main battery at the enemy.

The British Home Fleet, reinforced by the old American carrier *Ranger,* two American cruisers, *Augusta* and *Tuscaloosa,* and five American destroyers, belatedly sailed to intercept the Germans but to no avail. *Tirpitz* and *Scharnhorst,* as well as the "pocket" battleship *Lützow,* remained moored in Altenfiord, serving in the role of "fleet in being" to tie down Allied warships and threaten Murmansk convoys.

The *Tirpitz* sortie rattled the Admiralty and persuaded it to approve a bold but chancy operation (Source), long in the making: a midget-submarine raid on the three big German warships in Altenfiord.

The British had built six midget subs specifically for this task. Known as "X-craft" (*X-5* to *X-10*), they were forty-eight feet long and displaced thirty-nine tons. Manned by four volunteers, each X-craft was armed with two 4, 000-pound Amatol detachable charges, designed to be released to the sea bottom beneath the hull of a moored vessel and triggered by a timed fuse. During extensive trials and drills, the X-craft had performed as designed, although they were not exempt from the inherent shortcomings of all midget submarines.

Six full-size "parent" submarines* sailed from Loch Cairnbawn, northwest Scotland, on September 11 and 12, each towing an X-craft. Three midgets (*X-5, X-6, X-7*) were to attack *Tirpitz,* two (*X-9, X-10*) were to attack *Scharnhorst,* and one (*X-8*) was to attack *Lützow.* However, two midgets (*X-8, X-9*) were lost or scuttled en route, leaving the three for *Tirpitz* but only one (*X-10*) for *Scharnhorst* and none for *Lützow.*

The parent submarines launched the four midgets on the evening of September

---

* *Sea Nymph, Sceptre, Stubborn, Syrtis, Thrasher,* and *Truculent.*

20 at a site about 150 miles from Altenfiord. One, *X-5,* was lost; another, *X-10,* could not find *Scharnhorst,* aborted to her parent submarine, and was lost while returning to Scotland. On September 22, two midgets, *X-6* and *X-7,* commanded by Donald Cameron and Basil Charles Godfrey Place, respectively, reached *Tirpitz* and released charges (four in all for 16,000 pounds), which blew up and damaged all three sets of the battleship's main turbines. This remarkable feat put *Tirpitz* completely out of action in Altenfiord until April 1944. Both midgets were lost in the operation; two of the eight crewmen of *X-6* and *X-7* were killed, six were captured.*

On the day after the British disabled *Tirpitz,* September 23, the "pocket" battleship *Lützow* sailed for the Baltic. Alerted to this departure, the British attempted to intercept *Lützow* with land-based RAF and fleet aircraft, but failed. She reached Danzig on October 1 and never again left the Baltic.

The damage to *Tirpitz* and the departure of *Lützow* left only the *Scharnhorst* and her screen in northern Norway to threaten Murmansk convoys. Therefore the commander in chief, Home Fleet,† Bruce Fraser, judged that these politically desirable convoys could resume sailing in the Arctic darkness of November. Churchill informed Stalin that the Admiralty intended to sail one convoy of forty merchant ships per month in November, December, January, and February, altogether 160 vessels plus escorts. However, when Fraser, like his predecessor John Tovey, objected strenuously to such large convoys, Churchill accepted Fraser's alternative plan to sail convoys of half that size (about twenty ships) every two weeks.

The Murmansk convoys recommenced sailing on November 1. On that day a return convoy, RA 54A (thirteen empty ships) left Kola Inlet and reached the British Isles with no losses. On November 15 and 22, eastbound convoys JW 54A (eighteen loaded ships) and JW 54B (fourteen loaded ships) left Loch Ewe for Kola Inlet. Both arrived with no losses. Another return convoy, RA 54B (eight empty ships) sailed from Kola Inlet on November 27 and also arrived in the British Isles with no losses.

During the hiatus in Murmansk convoys over the summer and into the fall of 1943, Dönitz allowed the Arctic U-boat force to remain at about a dozen boats. Except for a very few inconsequential Soviet ships, these U-boats sank nothing from March to November 1943, a waste of assets that Dönitz repeatedly deplored. However, U-boat losses in the Arctic area in this period were likewise inconsequential compared with other areas: only the *U-639* commanded by Walter Wichman, which was sunk by a Soviet submarine, *S-101,* in the Kara Sea while planting a minefield.

The Germans became aware belatedly that the Murmansk convoys had resumed in November. Humiliated by the X-craft attack on *Tirpitz* and the abject

---

* Cameron and Place, who survived, each won a Victoria Cross.

† Depleted to support naval operations in the Mediterranean and other distant waters, the Home Fleet then consisted of the old carrier *Furious,* the old battleship *Anson,* the new battleship *Duke of York,* five heavy cruisers, and smaller craft. The American carrier *Ranger,* the heavy cruisers *Augusta* and *Tuscaloosa,* and five destroyers remained with the Home Fleet until the end of November.

failure of the U-boats in the North and Middle Atlantic, Dönitz and his staff became determined to achieve a naval victory that would especially and directly help the embattled German forces in the Soviet Union. Therefore Dönitz directed his protégé, Oskar Kummetz, commander of the *Scharnhorst* task force, which included five destroyers, to prepare for a surface-ship assault on the Murmansk convoy that was to sail in December. At the same time, he directed the Arctic U-boat force to deploy patrol lines to intercept, shadow, and attack these convoys in conjunction with *Scharnhorst* and whatever *Luftwaffe* forces could be brought to bear.

British codebreakers provided exceptionally good information on the German plans and movements. When the next convoy, JW 55A (nineteen loaded ships), sailed from Loch Ewe for Kola Inlet on December 12, Fraser was very much alive to the possibility of a *Scharnhorst* sortie. He lent the convoy strong distant cover with two task forces that went all the way to Kola Inlet. One force consisted of his flagship, the new battleship *Duke of York,* the heavy cruiser *Jamaica,* and four destroyers. The other was made up of three cruisers, *Norfolk, Sheffield,* and the *Belfast,* the latter severely damaged early in the war by a mine planted by the duck *U-21.* Convoy JW 55A arrived in Kola Inlet with no losses. The *Duke of York* task force remained in Russia for two days, then sailed for home on December 18.

As Christmas approached, two more Murmansk convoys set sail. On December 20, JW 55B (nineteen loaded ships) left Loch Ewe for Kola Inlet. On December 23 a return convoy, RA 55A (twenty-two empty ships) left Kola Inlet, accompanied by the task force of three British heavy cruisers. By this time a U-boat patrol line, *Eisenbart,* consisting of eight boats, had taken up positions in the waters between Bear Island and northern Norway. The *Luftwaffe* provided a few reconnaissance aircraft, but all except a handful of the dive-bombers and torpedo-planes had been transferred from Norway to other theaters.

Admiral Dönitz met with Hitler at *Wolfschanze* on December 19 and 20. Among the topics discussed was the Arctic situation. According to the stenographer's notes, Dönitz said that the Allies possibly had resumed the Murmansk convoys and that "if a successful operation seems assured," *Scharnhorst* and five destroyers would attack the next one bound to Russia. The standing doctrine for big-ship sorties would be adhered to: If the enemy posed a threat to *Scharnhorst* with his big ships, she was to avoid an engagement and return to Altenfiord, thereby denying the enemy a propaganda as well as a material victory. Moreover, Dönitz said, he had diverted five more new U-boats to reinforce the diminished Arctic force* and if the Allies had indeed resumed Murmansk convoys on a regular basis, he would send yet more U-boats to the Arctic.

Dönitz returned to Berlin briefly, then set off for Brest to spend Christmas Eve with U-boat crews. While he was en route, a *Luftwaffe* aircraft sighted convoy JW 55B bound for Kola Inlet. Dönitz canceled his visit to Brest and stopped in Paris. He put the *Scharnhorst* task force on three-hour notice and persuaded the *Luftwaffe* to mount increased surveillance for the convoy and to look for distant covering forces. On Christmas Day, he returned to Berlin, where he authorized the

* *U-314, U-425, U-716, U-739, U-957.*

Scharnhorst task force commander, Erich Bey (temporarily replacing Oskar Kummetz, who was ill), to sail. Owing to very heavy seas that restricted movements of his five destroyers, and the lack of *Luftwaffe* support, Bey, hero of the battle of Narvik in April 1940, was reluctant to go, but go he did, that evening.

Based on information from British codebreakers, at 2:17 A.M., December 26, the Admiralty warned Bruce Fraser: "Emergency. *Scharnhorst* probably sailed at 1800, 25 December." At about this same time, *Luftwaffe* aircraft and three of the northernmost U-boats of the eight in the *Eisenbart* line* reported fleeting contact with the eastbound convoy JW 55B near Bear Island and attempted to pursue.

In foul weather and Arctic darkness, the opposing forces jockeyed for position. Using Enigma decrypts from the Admiralty and superior radar on his ships, Bruce Fraser quickly got the upper hand. While he put his task force (*Duke of York, Jamaica,* and four destroyers) on a course to cut *Scharnhorst* off from retreat to Altenfiord, he ordered the task force of three cruisers (*Belfast, Norfolk, Sheffield*) commanded by Robert Burnett, joined by four destroyers from the escort group of returning convoy RA 55A, commanded by R. L. Fisher, to close and attack *Scharnhorst* from the opposite direction. From Berlin, Dönitz exhorted German forces: "Strike a blow for the gallant troops on the Eastern Front by destroying the convoy."

In the early hours of December 26, Boxing Day, the *Belfast* found and reported *Scharnhorst* less her five destroyers, which had unaccountably separated. The four British destroyers from RA 55A joined *Belfast, Norfolk,* and *Sheffield,* but they could not get into position to fire torpedoes. The cruiser *Norfolk,* which had eight 8" guns, opened fire and scored two hits on *Scharnhorst,* which in turn twice hit *Norfolk* with her 11" guns. Suspecting correctly that Fraser's modern battleship *Duke of York* with 14" guns was part of the trap, Erich Bey ordered his five errant destroyers to attack convoy JW 55B, while he turned *Scharnhorst* south at thirty knots for Altenfiord, outrunning the three British cruisers and four destroyers.

Bruce Fraser's maneuver to cut off *Scharnhorst* worked perfectly. Late in the afternoon, his *Duke of York* got *Scharnhorst* on radar at a range of thirty miles. Fraser closed and opened fire with his 14" guns and achieved hits that slowed *Scharnhorst.* Thereupon, his cruiser *Jamaica* and Burnett's overtaking *Belfast* and *Sheffield* opened up with 6" guns. Then Fraser's four destroyers (*Saumarez, Savage, Scorpion, Stord*) and Fisher's four destroyers from convoy RA 55A (*Matchless, Musketeer, Opportune, Virago*) closed on *Scharnhorst* to shoot torpedoes and fire 4.7" guns.

Realizing the *Scharnhorst* was doomed, Erich Bey radioed Hitler and Dönitz that he would fight to the last shell. In a near replication of the slaughter of *Bismarck,* the British ships closed and destroyed *Scharnhorst* with guns and torpedoes. The destroyers *Scorpion* and *Matchless* fished out thirty-six enlisted men of her 1,943-man crew. All other Germans perished, yet another major defeat and humiliation for the *Kriegsmarine,* one which naturally infuriated Hitler.

---

* The veteran *U-601,* commanded by a new skipper, Otto Hansen, age twenty-five; the newly joined *U-716,* commanded by Hans Dunkelberg, age twenty-five; and the experienced *U-277,* commanded by Robert Lübsen, age twenty-seven.

The U-boat line *Eisenbart* played only a minor role in this Arctic naval battle. No other boats found convoy JW 55B; one boat aborted with mechanical defects. Upon learning of the loss of *Scharnhorst,* Dönitz directed the seven remaining *Eisenbart* boats to the scene to search for German survivors, but no boat found any. On December 28, the newly arrived *U-957,* commanded by Franz Saar, age twenty-four, found and shot two T-5 homing torpedoes at two "fast ships" but neither hit, extending the period of U-boat nonperformance against the Murmansk convoys into January 1944, a fallow and frustrating ten months for the Germans.

The loss of *Scharnhorst* left only the Arctic U-boat force to interdict the Murmansk convoys and repel the long-expected Allied invasion of Norway. Although Dönitz knew well that the U-boats were practically useless for either mission, politics demanded further reinforcements, again at the expense of the Atlantic U-boat force; on December 27, Dönitz directed that the Arctic/Norway U-boat force be increased immediately to twenty-four boats, all VIIs adapted for Arctic operations. Six more new boats arrived in the Arctic in January.*

The Arctic/Norway U-boat force was organized into two combat flotillas, the 11th in Bergen, commanded by Hans Cohausz, and the 13th in Trondheim, commanded by Rolf Rüggeberg. Both bases had concrete U-boat pens like those in France. However, refit and repair facilities were limited. New Type VIIFs (torpedo-supply boats), the *U-1060* and *U-1062,* ran back and forth with matériel for a modest advanced U-boat base in Narvik. On December 22, a flight of nine Beaufighters patrolling off southwest Norway found and attacked Karl Albrecht's *U-1062* with 20mm cannons and a torpedo, inflicting severe damage, but the boat reached Bergen the next day. The *U-1062* and her escorting surface ship shot down two Beaufighters.

* *U-278, U-312, U-313, U-472, U-965, U-990.*

SEVEN

Allied Plans: Sextant and Eureka

President Roosevelt for more than two years had sought a face-to-face talk with Joseph Stalin. He finally agreed to meet with Roosevelt and Churchill at Teheran, Iran, in late November 1943. This first meeting of the "Big Three" was one of the most important conferences of the war, and the preparations for it were immense and complex.

Encouraged by Roosevelt, China's Generalissimo Chiang Kai-shek sought a seat at the conference. However, this was easier said than done. China was formally at war with Japan, but not with Germany. The Soviet Union was formally at war with Germany but not Japan. For these and other reasons, both Stalin and Churchill opposed the inclusion of the Generalissimo. So it was arranged that Roosevelt and Churchill would first meet with Chiang Kai-shek in Cairo (Sextant), then meet with Stalin in Teheran (Eureka).

Churchill and a large British party, including the new First Sea Lord, Andrew Cunningham, boarded the battlecruiser *Renown* at Plymouth and sailed on November 12, a Friday. After a leisurely eight-day voyage, *Renown* arrived at Alexandria, Egypt, on November 21. The British party traveled overland to Cairo to await the arrival of the American delegation.

Roosevelt and party, which included Harry Hopkins and the Joint Chiefs of Staff, boarded the new battleship *Iowa* on the same day, November 12. Inasmuch as Roosevelt subscribed to the sailor's superstition that it was bad luck to sail on a Friday, *Iowa* waited to leave Norfolk until six minutes after midnight, Saturday, November 13. To avoid any possibility of a U-boat attack, *Iowa* cruised at a steady

25 knots. While matching that speed and carrying out escort duties, her screen of three destroyers burned fuel at a terrific rate. Since the Navy was loathe to slow down *Iowa* to refuel the escorts while under way, three groups of escorts (from the States, the Azores, and the Mediterranean) had to be employed in relays.

On the second day at sea, November 14, one of *Iowa*'s escorts very nearly achieved what the U-boats could not. During a battle drill, the new destroyer *William D. Porter* accidentally fired a live torpedo at *Iowa*. Luckily, *Iowa* was able to evade, and the torpedo exploded harmlessly in her wake. Thoroughly embarrassed, Admiral King moved to sack the destroyer skipper immediately, but, King remembered, "to his great amazement," Roosevelt told him to "forget it."*

The *Iowa* arrived at Mers el-Kébir, the seaport for Oran, on November 20. Welcomed by Dwight Eisenhower and others, the Roosevelt party boarded four C-54 transport aircraft (including Roosevelt's personal plane, the "Sacred Cow") and flew to Tunis, where Eisenhower had arranged special VIP quarters, dinner, and a sightseeing tour of the ruins of Carthage. By then, Admirals King and Leahy and General Hap Arnold of the Joint Chiefs of Staff had concluded that George Marshall was indispensable in Washington and that not he but Eisenhower should command Overlord. In a private (and awkward) meeting with Marshall and Eisenhower, King informed Eisenhower of his views. However, later, over dinner, Roosevelt told Eisenhower that Marshall was his choice for the job.

On the day following, November 21, the Roosevelt party reboarded the four aircraft and flew on to Cairo. Since that city was still very much a British area of responsibility, Churchill had arranged quarters for the Americans and, reluctantly, also for the Chinese. Over the next five days, from November 22 to November 26, Roosevelt and Churchill and the Combined Chiefs of Staff conferred, and from time to time invited the Chinese to join the discussions. The proceedings relaxed on Thanksgiving Day, Thursday, November 25, when, in another gesture of hospitality, the British arranged a special religious service at a cathedral in Cairo.

The American and British delegates met in a decidedly optimistic frame of mind. In the ten months since the Casablanca conference (Symbol), when the delegates had declared that the defeat of the U-boat had "first charge" on Allied resources, that goal had been achieved. The U-boats had sunk only three cargo ships in the North Atlantic in October; none in November and December. The massive Allied Atlantic convoy system, enhanced by the recent Allied occupation of the Azores,† now operated with scant to no fear of the enemy. Besides that (and partly owing to it), Allied forces were on the offensive against Axis forces in every part of the globe.

---

* Nonetheless, a court of inquiry convened later. The *William D. Porter* went to the Pacific with a new skipper. She was sunk by Japanese kamikazes on June 10, 1945, but her entire crew was saved.

† Besides providing a place for airfields to base ASW aircraft and facilities to refuel surface escorts, the Azores became a vital way station for the thousands of aircraft en route from the States to the British Isles and Mediterranean Basin. This new mid-Atlantic route, replacing the South Atlantic route (Puerto Rico–Brazil–Ascension–Dakar, and so on), saved much time and wear and tear on aircraft engines.

• Italy had been knocked out of the war. Although the Germans had occupied the northern half of the Italian peninsula, the Allies held the southern half, including the important seaports of Taranto and Naples. The Allies had approved plans to liberate Rome for political and psychological reasons, and to build a huge airfield complex at Foggia (on the Adriatic coast) to carry on the destruction of the German-held oil fields in Romania (Ploesti, in particular) and cities in middle and southern Germany.

• The Red Army, grown to a massive force of 6.5 million men and women, amply supplied with tanks, artillery, and other weapons, was on the offensive in almost every sector of its two-thousand-mile front. Stalin had prepared plans for a final, huge assault (Bagration) to coincide with Overlord. In a momentous shift in strategy and resources, on November 3 Hitler had secretly declared (in Führer Directive No. 51) that an Allied invasion of France and/or Norway appeared to be imminent and that therefore defenses in the western sector could no longer be neglected in favor of reinforcing the eastern sector.

• The Allied heavy-bomber attack on Germany (Sickle/Pointblank) had at last moved into high gear. As Roosevelt and Churchill conferred on the evening of November 22, RAF Bomber Command mounted the heaviest attack yet on Berlin. Among other damage, this raid destroyed the buildings housing Albert Speer's Ministry of Armaments and Munitions and that of the *Kriegsmarine.** On November 26, Allied bombers hit Frankfurt and Bremen. On November 29, the Allied target was again Bremen.

• In the Southwest Pacific, Allied forces in New Guinea and the Solomon Islands steadily closed on the Japanese stronghold of Rabaul. Highly effective carrier and land-based aircraft raids in November forced Japanese naval and air forces to abandon Rabaul and to withdraw a considerable distance to the islands of Truk and Palau, a stunning defeat that would enable the Allies in this sector to leapfrog Rabaul and recapture all Japanese bases on the north coast of New Guinea.

• At the same time, American naval and ground forces launched a second line of attack against the Japanese (Galvanic) in the Central Pacific. On the day the *Iowa* reached North Africa with the presidential party, November 20, these forces invaded the Gilbert Islands (Tarawa, Makin, Betio) and by November 23, that island area was firmly in American hands, another costly but electrifying Pacific victory.

The conferees at Cairo soon fell into acrimonious debate for several reasons. The most important bone of contention in American eyes was what appeared to be a slackening in British enthusiasm for Overlord. The primary cause in British eyes was Roosevelt's stubborn insistence that Washington and London provide Chiang Kai-shek increased military power to help eject the Japanese from Burma and

* The senior naval staffs moved into the emergency locations code-named "Tannenburg" and "Bismarck" (in Eberswalke), but communications were so inadequate that Dönitz had to direct *Kriegsmarine* headquarters in Kiel to temporarily take over. He established a temporary headquarters at U-boat Control in Steinplatz.

China, and greater political participation in grand strategy. Further complicating everything, Churchill renewed his campaign for major Allied operations in the Mediterranean, including an invasion of the Balkans, his "soft underbelly" strategy. Since the Americans believed Churchill's proposal would delay Overlord to 1945 or perhaps indefinitely and deny Chiang Kai-shek military assistance to carry out American proposals in the Far East, it increased tensions to the point that the usually cool and reticent George Marshall blew up and shouted down Churchill.

The Cairo meetings thus adjourned on November 27 with a number of important strategic issues unresolved. Chiang Kai-shek returned to China; the American and British delegations flew on to Teheran to meet with Stalin (Eureka) for a week, from November 27 to December 2. The American and British delegations then returned to Cairo for yet another round of strategy talks. One upshot of the Teheran and second Cairo conferences was a closer alignment of Washington and Moscow at the expense of London, which left Churchill in a black mood.

The second Cairo meeting concluded on December 7, the second anniversary of the Japanese attack on Pearl Harbor. Heavily influenced by Stalin at Teheran, the Allies agreed irrevocably that:

- Overlord was to take place in May or June 1944. Bowing to the advice of the American military chiefs (Stimson, Knox, Leahy, King, Arnold), Roosevelt reversed himself and named Eisenhower rather than Marshall to command Overlord, effective January 1944.
- Operations in Italy were to continue to the liberation of Rome, but the shift of ground troops and landing craft from the Mediterranean to the British Isles for Overlord was to proceed. At Churchill's urging, to break the German line at the Rapido River and facilitate the liberation of Rome, a limited Allied "end run" amphibious invasion (Shingle) farther up the "boot" at Anzio would be carried out in January 1944.
- Partly at the insistence of Stalin, Churchill's plan to invade the Balkans and the Dodecanese Islands with the hope of enticing Turkey into the war on the Allied side was shelved absolutely. Instead, Allied forces remaining in the Mediterranean after the liberation of Rome were to assist Overlord by a near-simultaneous invasion of southern France between Toulon and Nice (Anvil, renamed Dragoon).
- Also, partly at the insistence of Stalin, who promised to enter the war against Japan after the defeat of Germany, the Americans greatly scaled back plans to assist Chiang Kai-shek militarily. One result was that a tentative plan (Buccaneer) for the British to invade the Andaman Islands to cut the Japanese supply line to Burma, while other Allied ground forces struck into northern Burma from India (Tarzan), was also shelved, much to the relief of Churchill, who was still adamantly opposed to any aid for Chiang Kai-shek.
- Pacific operations were to be greatly intensified in 1944. Allied forces were to converge on the Japanese home islands by "two roads": a "southern route" through New Guinea to the Philippines and Formosa, and a mid-Pacific "island-hopping route" from the newly captured Gilberts to the Marshalls (Eniwetok, Kwajalein, Majuro), Marianas (Guam, Saipan, Tinian), Bonins (Iwo Jima), and Okinawa. Thereafter the "two roads" were to merge in an assault on the Japanese home islands. To facilitate that last huge undertaking, the Army Air Forces was to

establish massive air-base complexes on Guam and Tinian and Iwo Jima to accommodate the newest big heavy bomber, the Boeing B-29 Superfortress.

The Roosevelt party departed Cairo in its four C-54 aircraft on December 7 and returned to Tunis, where Roosevelt informed Eisenhower that he, not Marshall, was to command Overlord. Afterward Roosevelt visited Allied troops in Malta and Sicily, then flew to Dakar, where the battleship *Iowa* and her screen were waiting. Returning via Bahia, Brazil, Roosevelt reached Norfolk on December 17, concluding an absence of thirty-seven days from Washington, a period he called "a haven of rest" from the wartime toil and the toll on his deteriorating health. Marshall and Arnold returned to the States via the Pacific. King flew home by way of Accra, Brazil, and Puerto Rico.

Disconsolate and debilitated by a cold that developed into pneumonia, Churchill remained in the Mediterranean area, settling into a villa at Marrakesh, Morocco (near Casablanca), "a haven where I could regain my strength." On January 14, he left that "delectable asylum" and flew to Gibraltar, where the next day he boarded the battleship *King George V.* He returned to the British Isles on January 18, concluding an absence from London of well over two months.

Numerous important sea changes occurred or were set in motion during those two months. Not the least of these was the emergence of the United States as the dominant partner in the Allied alliance, the sudden ascendance of the Soviet Union, and the further decline of the power and prestige of Great Britain, which, like Churchill, was worn to the nub by four years and four months of all-out warfare.

Although the Canadians were partners in the Battle of the Atlantic, the Royal Canadian Navy was still regarded as an immature branch of the Royal Navy and therefore its views at Cairo and Teheran were not accorded the respect and discussion they deserved. Moreover, there was in Ottawa a major naval administrative wrangle afoot, blood spilling into the scuppers.

Facing important elections in the summer and fall of 1943, the Liberal government of Prime Minister William Mackenzie King was running a bit scared. King had announced that his party's strongest suit was its "splendid record" in the war effort. "There was only one thing that could undo it," King cautioned, and that was "a failure at some point on the Government's part to have anticipated the needs of the soldiers that had to be met."

In fact, the Mackenzie government had already failed in one respect. The Chief of Naval Staff, Percy Nelles, had not been sufficiently demanding of the Admiralty to provide the Canadians with the latest and best available warship designs and weaponry. As related, on every level (radar, sonar, Huff Duff, ASW weapons, and so on) the Canadian Navy lagged far behind the British. Even British ships manned by Norwegians and Poles had better equipment. Canadian sailors well knew these facts and morale had suffered. It was possible that if these shortcomings became known to the general public, the Mackenzie King government might well be toppled.

Whether politically inspired or not, in the fall of 1943 a number of official and unofficial reports of the insufficiency of Canadian warships compared to those of the other Allies had circulated in Ottawa. Thereupon, the naval minister of the

King government, Angus L. Macdonald, perhaps to protect himself, commenced bombarding Nelles with queries, asking, in effect, "What are the exact facts and why haven't I been kept informed of this disgrace?" In return, Nelles dissembled, excused, and waffled. The exchange became so tedious and acrimonious that by December 1943, Macdonald had concluded that he could no longer trust Nelles.

At the end of 1943, King and Macdonald sacked Nelles from the post he had held since 1934 (perhaps too long a tour for any man). They named his deputy, George C. ("Jetty") Jones, who may have conspired against Nelles, to replace him. They exiled Nelles to London and he retired in January 1945, before the war was over. Jetty Jones held the post of Chief of Naval Staff until February 1946, when he suddenly died.*

German Plans and Naval Resources

Inasmuch as the Allies had proclaimed a policy of "unconditional surrender" at the Casablanca conference, the leaders of the Third Reich believed that they had no choice other than to fight to the finish regardless of the cost and the consequences. Vital for his fight to the finish, Hitler believed, was the development of a large family of exotic new weapons. He therefore gave the highest priority to jet- and rocket-powered aircraft and land-based radar and radar detectors to counter Allied heavy bombers; a new heavy tank for the ground forces; the V-1 cruise and V-2 ballistic missiles; the small Type XXIII and big Type XXI "electro boats"; improved looping and homing submarine torpedoes with more powerful warheads; a "pressure" mine, activated by the wave action of surface vessels; and "midget" submarines that could attack Allied invasion forces with defensive mines or torpedoes.

Amid growing tension, shifting loyalties, and defections in the German high command, Admiral Dönitz assured Hitler and the German citizenry that, come what may, the *Kriegsmarine* would not waver in its support of the national government. Meeting with the Führer on two occasions in January 1944, at his command post in East Prussia, *Wolfschanze,* Dönitz and Hitler agreed to a number of important policy matters.

- Assuming that an Allied invasion of Norway or France or—more likely—both places was to occur in the spring, the U-boat force was to go over to the defensive at once to mass the greatest possible strength to repel these operations. By an order issued on January 10, the Arctic U-boat force was to be increased to a total of thirty boats. Another large group of U-boats (group *Mitte,* or Central), fresh from Germany, was to be held in readiness in southern Norway to repel an invasion of that area or Denmark. The Atlantic U-boat force was to accumulate a large ready force (group *Landwirt*) in Brest and in the Biscay ports to repel an invasion of France. Notwithstanding the general disappointment his U-boat crews had shown for snorts, Dönitz was to equip as many U-boats as possible with the device and hurry along the training of crews in its use.

* See Zimmerman, *The Great Naval Battle of Ottawa* (1989).

• U-boat operations against Allied convoys in the Atlantic were to be continued from French bases but on a sharply diminishing scale as the likely invasion date approached. The main purpose of these operations was not so much to sink ships as it was to give crews battle experience, test new electronics and flak guns, and free up space in the U-boat pens in France for snort upgrades. Fitted with the *Naxos* radar detector and the new 37mm automatic flak gun, the U-boats were to continue operations in scattered groups but were to stay in the eastern Atlantic so that if necessary they could be quickly redeployed against the expected invasion forces. In addition, certain boats were to broadcast twice-daily weather reports for the benefit of the *Luftwaffe* raids on London and for those German air and ground forces earmarked for anti-invasion duties.

• The Atlantic U-boat force was to provide the Mediterranean U-boat force with another dozen boats to ensure that the Allies were not relieved of convoying in that body of water. The forty-one-year-old Werner Hartmann, crew of 1921, who had won a *Ritterkreuz* on *U-37* in 1940 and had commanded the U-cruiser *U-198* on a two-hundred-day cruise to the Indian Ocean, was appointed to relieve Leo Kreisch as commander of the Mediterranean U-boat force, effective January 1944.

• Patrols to remote areas by long-range Type IXCs, IXC40s, and IXD2 U-cruisers were also to continue, albeit on a modest scale. The single remaining XIV "milk cow" tanker in the Atlantic force, *U-488,* was to provide replenishment services for the Type IXs of this group in what was believed to be relatively safe waters west of the Cape Verde Islands. The new rules governing the rendezvous with U-tankers were to be followed to the letter. The tenth—and last—Type XIV tanker, *U-490,* delayed by the aforementioned accident in the Baltic and the installation of a snort and experimental gear for submerged refueling, was to be brought to the Atlantic as soon as possible.

• Owing to the great—and possibly decisive—offensive capabilities they promised, the small Type XXIII and big Type XXI "electro boats" were to be rushed to completion with maximum priority. Setbacks to the production of electric motors and diesel engines caused by Allied air raids and labor shortages were to be compensated for by higher production goals, faster repair of bomb damage to the factories, and yet another set of new restrictions on drafting shipwrights into the German Army. Although the problem of providing exotic fuels had not been overcome, work on the "Walter boats," powered by a closed-cycle, hydrogen-peroxide engine, was also to continue at a high priority.

• In response to urgent requests from Dönitz, in order that the *Luftwaffe* could provide the oncoming "electro boats" with better information on Allied convoy movements, Hitler assured Dönitz that production of four-engine JU-290 aircraft was to be accelerated. However, Göring, citing priorities for other aircraft and shortages of materials, declared that an increase in JU-290 production was "impossible." By January 1944, only eight JU-290s were available to assist the Atlantic U-boat force in convoy locations and that number shrank rather than grew.

• The battleship *Tirpitz,* under repair in Altenfiord, was to remain in northern Norway as a "fleet in being" threat to tie down ships of the Home Fleet and to repel the expected Allied invasion of Norway. Consideration was given to moving the heavy cruiser *Prinz Eugen* from the Baltic to northern Norway for that purpose (and to prey on the Murmansk convoys), but finally she was held in the Baltic to fight Soviet forces advancing on Germany from the east.

• Owing to the heavy losses incurred while inbound and outbound to and from French ports, no more surface-ship blockade-runners were to sail to the Far East. All U-boats sailing to and from France and the Far East were to carry cargo. These included Japanese submarines,* the two failed IXD1 U-cruisers, and the several big Italian submarines that had been converted for that purpose.

Some historians of the Battle of the Atlantic write that on January 1, 1944, the German U-boat force reached a peak wartime strength of 436 or 456 boats.† Seen at a glance, these figures imply an enormous threat to Allied shipping, but nothing could be further from the truth. Although the personnel of the U-boat arm remained resolutely and famously defiant, its strategy, tactics, and weaponry had failed—indeed, had failed abysmally. The only hope for a comeback rested on the possibility—repeat possibility—of obtaining at the earliest feasible date an effective search radar and radar detector, improved sonar, a reliable, high-angle automatic 37mm antiaircraft gun, better T-5 homing and other torpedoes, small and big "electro boats," "Walter boats," and a big fleet of *Luftwaffe* JU-290s.

The gross inflation of the U-boat threat in early 1944 by many American and British historians, whether intended or unintended, doubtless arises from the picture presented in the war diary of U-boat Control. On January 1, 1944, it lists a total of 436 U-boats "in commission." Included is a breakdown by types, assignment, and location:

Type	*School*	*Workup*	*War fronts*
II (ducks)	33	0	6‡
VII	3	0	0
VIIB & C	48	140	120
VIIF (supply)	0	2	2
VIID	0	0	2
IXB & C	3	27	31
IXD2	0	8	5
XB (minelayer)	0	1	1
XIV (tanker)	0	1	1
XVII	0	2§	—
Totals	87	181	168

The 181 boats in "workup" included a few boats assigned to R&D and a great many being fitted with new flak guns and bridge configurations to accommodate them,

* The Japanese cruiser submarines *I-29* and *I-34* sailed to France from the Far East with cargo on November 12. Exploiting decrypts of enemy codes, the British submarine *Taurus,* commanded by Mervyn Wingfield, sank *I-34* on the day it sailed from Penang; the *I-29* reached Bordeaux on March 11, 1944.

† For example, see charts in *The War at Sea,* vol. 3, part 1, by Stephen W. Roskill (1960), p. 365; and *The U-boat Offensive* by V. E. Tarrant (1989), pp. 128 and 167.

‡ A token force of older ducks deployed in the Black Sea.

§ Two experimental Walter hydrogen-peroxide "ducks," *U-792* and *U-794,* commissioned in mid-November 1943.

snorts and new electronics (*Gema* and *Hohentwiel* search radar with retractable "mattress" antennae), new radar detectors (*Fliege* for ten and *Mücke* for three centimeter wavelengths), and other gear.* Therefore, the only real threat posed by the U-boat arm on January 1, 1944, was the 168 boats at the warfronts. Not counting the six ducks in the Black Sea and two Type VIIF torpedo-supply boats in the Atlantic or Norway, the remaining 160 warfront boats were distributed as follows:

	Atlantic	*Norway*	*Mediterranean*	*Total*
VIIB & C (attack)	88	19	13	120
VIID (minelayer)	2	0	0	2
IXB & C (attack)	31	0	0	31
IXD2 (cruiser)	5	0	0	5
XB (minelayer)	1	0	0	1
XIV (tanker)	1	0	0	1
Totals	128	19	13	160

Many of the 122 Type VIIs in the three main war zones were undergoing battle-damage repairs, modifications, or upgrades. For example, that figure includes in the Atlantic force the surviving seven Type VII flak boats (or would-be flak boats), which were reconverted to normal attack boats, and boats being fitted with snorts.

Owing to Hitler's orders to substantially increase the Arctic, Norway, and Mediterranean U-boat forces, and to heavy battle losses, the Atlantic U-boat force shrank sharply from January 1 to May 1. In this period, only twenty-five new attack boats (sixteen VIIs, nine IXs) joined the Atlantic force, while forty-nine attack boats were lost (forty VIIs and nine IXs) and eight VIIs went to the Mediterranean. The decline in strength of the Atlantic force month by month:

	1/1/44	*2/1*	*3/1*	*4/1*	*5/1*
VIIB, C, D	90	78	65	60	58
IXB, C	31	34	35	34	31
Totals	121†	112	100	94	89

* Accidents in the Baltic continued. The IXC40s *U-803* and *U-854,* commanded by Karl Schimpf and Horst Weiher, respectively, struck mines and sank. Schimpf and thirty-four crew survived; nine men perished. Schimpf went on to command a Type XXI "electro boat." Weiher and all but seven of his crew perished. A surface ship rammed and sank the VII *U-738,* commanded by Erich-Michael Hoffmann, with the loss of Hoffmann and twenty-one men; twenty-four men survived. The VII *U-286,* commanded by Willi Dietrich, and the VII *U-1013,* commanded by Gerhard Linck, collided and both sank. Dietrich and twenty-five men of *U-286* survived. Twenty-six of the crew of *U-1013* were saved, but Linck and twenty-four others perished. Later, the *U-286* was salvaged, rehabilitated, and returned to service. The VIIB *U-28,* a school boat commanded by Dieter Sachse, sank by accident at dockside in Newstadt. She was salvaged but retired in August. The school duck *U-7,* commanded by Günther Loeschke, sank in a diving accident with the loss of Loeschke and all twenty-eight others. The school duck *U-2,* commanded by Wolfgang Schwarzkopf, collided with a fishing steamer and sank. Eighteen men including Schwarzkopf survived; seventeen died. The VII *U-681,* commanded by Helmut Bach, who was "night blind," rammed three ships and a breakwater before Bach was finally relieved by another skipper.

† Not counting VIIF supply boats, IXD2 U-cruisers, one XB minelayer, and one XIV tanker.

As a consequence of this shrinkage and of the decision to recall and/or hold back boats to defend against the expected Allied invasion of France, the Atlantic force mounted an ever-shrinking number of patrols to its three principal areas of responsibility.

	January	*February*	*March*	*April*	*May*
North and Mid-Atlantic	28	21	18*	9†	2‡
South Atlantic and Indian Ocean	8	11	9	5	2
Americas	5	5	3	1	6
Totals	41§	37	30	15	10

It is clear from this analysis that the large number of U-boats listed as "in commission" on January 1, 1944, means little or nothing, and that the U-boat peril to the Allies was yet another glaring instance of "threat inflation." As a consequence of this inflation, the Allies continued to pour masses of new naval assets ("jeep" carriers, destroyers, destroyer escorts, frigates, sloops, corvettes, four-engine land-based aircraft, and so on) into the North Atlantic that might have been used to greater effect on other warfronts.

Historians generally omit or pass quickly over this phase of the U-boat war. It deserves greater attention, not so much for conventional reasons, but because it reveals a fascinating portrait of a once-proud naval force undergoing complete disintegration in the face of Allied ASW forces finally grown to maturity and to awesome size.

U-boat Actions in the North Atlantic: I

In mid-January 1944, Admiral Godt at U-boat Control sent a morale-boosting message to all U-boats. He gloated that from the onset of war to December 31, 1943, German U-boats had sunk 19 million gross tons of Allied shipping, including 184 warships. The true figure by *all* Axis submarines was about 14 million gross tons, including seventy-eight warships. Therefore, German overall claims exceeded actual results by about 25 percent and warship claims were inflated over 100 percent.#

Most of the twenty-eight attack boats sailing to the North and Middle Atlantic areas in January were to join the two organized groups that were already in operation, *Rügen* and *Borkum.* Owing to the absence of tankers and the mounting threat

---

* Seven of these were recalled to French bases.

† Four assigned to weather reporting.

‡ Does not include group *Dragoner.*

§ Includes U-cruisers, U-tankers, provisional U-tankers, U-cargo, and U-minelayers, but not U-boats en route to the Mediterranean.

\# Claims and the actuality: two battleships claimed (two sunk); fifteen heavy and light cruisers (four); five aircraft carriers (five); 111 destroyers (thirty-one); twenty corvettes (thirteen); and thirty-one other escorts (seventeen). In addition, U-boats sank one big Coast Guard cutter and five submarines.

PLATE 8

U-BOATS COMMISSIONED IN 1944

(BY TYPE PER MONTH)

	VII	IX	IXD2	OTHER	XXI	XXIII	TOTAL
January	16	3	1	—	—	—	20
February	15	3	1	—	—	—	19
March	18	3	1	XB	—	—	23
April	15	4	2	—	—	—	21
May	15	3	1	—	—	—	19
June	9	—	—	—	1	1	11
July	10	—	—	—	3	3	16
August	3	1	—	—	6	4	14
September	6	—	—	—	9	6	21
October	1	—	—	—	13	4	18
November	2	—	—	—	12	7	21
December	2	—	—	XVIIB[1]	17	6	26
Totals:	112	17	6	2	61	31	229

1. The *U-1405,* a high-speed duck-size (312-ton) "Walter boat," employing hydrogen-peroxide propulsion. She was commanded by Wilhelm Rex, age thirty-four. Two others of this type, *U-1406* and *U-1407,* were commissioned in February and March 1945, respectively. These "Walter boats" proved to be impractical curiosities.

of an Allied invasion, they, too, were held in the eastern Atlantic. The winter weather was ghastly. The captain of the old British destroyer *Warwick,* Denys Arthur Rayner, assigned to convoy escort, wrote that the weather was the "worst of the whole war" with "quite stupendous waves," which, in his opinion, rendered U-boat operations "impossible." *

The Allies enjoyed overwhelming intelligence and naval and air superiority in all areas. The four-rotor bombes of the U.S. Navy's OP20G continued to read Enigma fluently and currently, enabling Allied authorities to evade or to track and attack U-boats. Inasmuch as the boats operated close to air bases in Iceland, the British Isles, Gibraltar, Morocco, and the Azores, Coastal Command was able to provide saturation land-based air cover in most of the threatened areas. In addition, the Royal Navy finally had a sufficient number of "jeep" carriers and hunter-killer groups to reinforce the escort of almost all convoys, inbound or outbound, although sustained operations of aircraft from "jeep" carriers in the North Atlantic in winter were, as always, iffy.

Two VIIs outbound from France in January incurred mechanical or structural failures:

* *Warwick* and three other destroyers (*Havelock, Vimy, Volunteer*) of British close Escort Group B-5 aborted with heavy sea damage, Rayner wrote in his war memoir, *Escort* (1955). The convoy that B-5 was to escort was unable to form, Rayner explained. Its fifty-odd merchant ships were scattered far and wide.

The *U-714,* commanded by Hans-Joachim Schwebcke, which sailed from Lorient on January 11, reported a cracked exhaust manifold that could not be repaired. Schwebcke aborted to Lorient, but after repairs he was able to resail on January 20.

The ex–flak boat *U-263,* commanded by Kurt Nölke, which sailed from La Pallice on January 19, reported that "external fuel tank No. 2, portside, caved in during her deep dive test" and that the boat needed immediate help. Control rushed minecraft and aircraft into Biscay to assist, but they could find no sign of *U-263* or its crew. Control attributed her loss to "mechanical failure"; the Allies speculated that she hit a mine.

Of the twenty-eight boats that did sail to the North Atlantic in January, quite a few carried out special missions.

- In compliance with Hitler's orders, the VIIs *U-343* and *U-952,* which sailed in December, entered the Mediterranean from January 3 to 5, and three more VIIs sailed to the Mediterranean in January.*
- To assist in locating departing convoys, Control assigned three experienced VIIs to closely reconnoiter likely ports. The *U-260,* commanded by Hubertus Purkhold, laid off Reykjavik, Iceland. She accomplished nothing and finished out the patrol reporting weather. On return to St. Nazaire, Purkhold left the boat for other duty. The *U-386,* commanded by Fritz Albrecht, and the ex–flak boat *U-621,* commanded by Max Kruschka, laid off in areas close to the mouth of North Channel. On the morning of January 13, a B-24 of British Squadron 59, piloted by the Australian Wesley G. Loney, attacked *U-621* with eight depth charges and machine-gun fire that killed one man and wounded five. Forced to abort, Kruschka limped into Brest ten days later, on January 23.
- Apart from Purkhold in *U-260,* a half dozen boats fulfilled the urgent requirement for weather reporting.† Inasmuch as the twice-daily reports of these boats from the waters between Iceland and Greenland had been declared vital for the German anti-invasion forces in France, the patrols were maintained through the late winter and spring.
- The *U-257,* commanded by Heinz Rahe, sailed from St. Nazaire into Biscay to plant new *Thetis* radar decoys.‡ After completing this task, Control directed Rahe to meet the supposedly inbound (but actually lost) blockade-runner *Rio Grande* and give her updated charts.

When Control realized on January 27 that the *Rio Grande* was lost, it reassigned *U-257* to be a weather reporter. While homebound from that mission on February 24, Rahe came upon Slow Convoy 153, guarded by Canadian Escort Group C-5 and British Escort Groups 3 and 6. Two of the sixteen-odd escorts, the new Canadian frigate *Waskesiu* and the British frigate *Nene,* detected *U-260,* blew

---

* The *U-455,* commanded by Hans-Martin Scheibe; the *U-967,* commanded by Herbert Loeder; and the *U-969,* commanded by Max Dobbert.

† *U-544, U-549, U-763, U-846, U-960,* among others.

‡ Floating wooden poles sixteen feet tall (counterbalanced by a steel anchoring tube of equal length) to which dipoles were attached to simulate a U-boat on the surface to attract enemy radar.

her to the surface with depth charges, and *Waskesiu* sank her by gunfire. One of the nineteen German survivors who were rescued said that Rahe, who elected to go down with his ship, threw his life preserver into a dinghy to assist another man, then probably shot himself.

Notwithstanding the hostile winter weather, RAF Coastal Command maintained patrols in the Bay of Biscay and elsewhere in the eastern Atlantic. These operations included the thirty-six B-24s of the U.S. Navy's Fairwing 7 assigned to Bombing Squadrons 103, 105, and 110.* Although seldom mentioned in the histories of this period, the results in the first week of January were highly gratifying for the Allies. British aircraft over Biscay hit inbound and outbound boats.

Some air attacks on transiting boats:

- The VII *U-625,* commanded by Hans Benker, an Arctic transfer. When on January 2 a B-24 of British Squadron 224, piloted by J. E. Edwards, attacked, Benker damaged the plane and drove it off. When a second B-24 of Squadron 224, piloted by E. Allen attacked, Benker had the *Naxos* antenna on the bridge with its wire running to the control room through the conning-tower hatch. Under attack from Allen, Benker elected to dive but forgot to pull down the *Naxos* antenna wire. It caught in the hatch, prevented a seal, and caused flooding. Benker canceled the dive, and he and another German rushed to the bridge to unsnarl and reel in the wire. Benker's order to cancel the dive was not heard and the boat went deep, leaving Benker and the crewman topside. They were not recovered. The first watch officer, Kurt Sureth, brought the boat into Brest on January 6. Control promptly told all boats that this tragedy was wholly unnecessary; firm hatch pressure on the *Naxos* antenna wire would snip it.
- The VII *U-629,* another Arctic transfer, commanded by Hans-Helmut Bugs. This was the boat that had rescued the crew of *U-284,* so nearly one hundred men were crammed belowdecks. In the early hours of January 4, a Leigh Light–equipped Wellington of Polish Squadron 304, piloted by H. Czyzun, dropped six close depth charges and riddled the boat with 1,200 rounds of machine-gun fire. Heavily damaged, Bugs called for help and Control diverted two outbound boats, *U-426* and *U-539,* and sent two minesweepers to assist. Fortunately for the hundred-odd German submariners in his care, Bugs reached Brest on January 5.

One of Bugs's would-be assisters, the outbound *U-426,* commanded by Christian Reich, soon came to grief, hounded by enemy aircraft. On the morning of January 8, a Sunderland of Australian Squadron 10, piloted by J. P. Roberts, found the boat and during two runs into flak, dropped six depth charges and strafed. This

---

* The Catalinas of U.S. Navy Patrol Squadron VP 63, equipped with Magnetic Airborne Detector (MAD) gear, transferred from Wales to Morocco on December 14, 1943, replacing the Catalinas of Patrol Squadrons VP 73 and VP 92, which returned to the States. From Morocco, VP 63 established a MAD "barrier" across the Strait of Gibraltar consisting of two Catalinas (MADCATS) a day on ten-hour flights.

fusillade destroyed *U-426.* Roberts reported "about forty men in the water" amid debris, but none survived.

• The VII *U-415,* commanded by Kurt Neide, who had sunk the British destroyer *Hurricane* on Christmas Eve. On the night of January 5, a Halifax of British Squadron 58, piloted by I.J.M. Christie, found *U-415* and attacked with six near depth charges. Neide returned fire, then dived and escaped. He put into Brest the following day.

• The famous veteran IXB *U-107,* commanded by Volker von Simmermacher. On the night of January 5, an unidentified Allied aircraft attacked *U-107* in the Bay of Biscay. Von Simmermacher's gunners repulsed the aircraft, and the boat reached Lorient on January 8. She did not sail again until May.*

• The new VII *U-364,* commanded by Paul Heinrich Sass, age twenty-four. On the night of January 30, it is believed, a Leigh Light–equipped Wellington of British Squadron 172, piloted by Leighton D. Richards, attacked and sank *U-364,* with the loss of all hands. A further assumption is that flak from the doomed boat shot down the Wellington. However, Alex Niestlé believes that another boat, *U-608,* shot down the Wellington and that the cause of the loss of *U-364* is unknown.

Apart from *U-426,* which was sunk, two other outbound U-boats were forced back to France by Coastal Command aircraft in the first week of January:

• The VII *U-445,* commanded by Heinz-Konrad Fenn. In the early hours of January 2, a Halifax of British Squadron 58, piloted by T. A. Griffiths, dropped five depth charges. On return to St. Nazaire on January 10, Fenn went on to other duty. Commanded by a new skipper, the boat resailed on February 1.

• The VII *U-373,* commanded by Detlev von Lehsten, which sailed on January 1. In the early hours of January 3, a Leigh Light–equipped Wellington of British Squadron 612, flown by John B. Russell, hit *U-373* with depth charges. A B-24 of British Squadron 224, piloted by a Canadian, Harold R. Facey, came up to help and dropped eight more charges. Heavily damaged, von Lehsten limped into Brest on January 4, where he discovered two unexploded depth charges hung up in the superstructure. Authorities ordered *U-373* to clear out of the harbor immediately lest the depth charges explode inside the pens. Brave crewmen jettisoned the missiles, and *U-373* reentered port for repairs and a snorkel.†

The only U-boat group operating in North Atlantic waters in the first week of January 1944 was *Rügen.* Composed of eighteen boats (actually seventeen), it was divided into six subgroups of three each. On January 5, thirteen (actually twelve) of these boats were new ones from Germany or Norway commanded by green skippers, including three new Type IXs unsuitable for attacks on heavily escorted convoys but believed to be useful for flak support. A great many of the boats were

---

* In the first week of January, Allied aircraft hit three other inbound boats: the VII *U-275,* the new VII *U-421,* and the new IXC40 *U-541,* but all limped into French bases by January 11.

† Allied aircraft hit two other outbound boats on January 5, *U-650* and *U-666,* but they made repairs at sea and continued their patrols.

fitted with new 37mm flak guns; all boats had the *Naxos* radar detector. One VII, *U-972,* which sailed from Kiel on November 30, assigned initially to weather reporting, had not been heard from since her last report on December 15 and was assumed to be lost, as was the case, perhaps due to an air attack that has not been identified.

Another VII, outbound from France to *Rügen,* did not get there either. This was the *U-757,* commanded by Friedrich Deetz, who had an extra *Naxos* to give to *U-976,* which had sailed from Kiel on November 25. On January 8, Deetz happened upon the merged and heavily guarded convoys Outbound South 64 and KMS 38. Two of the fifteen-odd escorts, the British frigate *Bayntun* and Canadian corvette *Camrose,* got *U-757* on sonar and destroyed her with depth-charge and Hedgehog attacks. The Canadian historian Joseph Schull wrote that the only evidence of a kill was "a vast pool of oil, some bits of wreckage and a uniform cap," but a kill it was. The loss left the *U-976* of group *Rügen* without a *Naxos.*

One of the VIIs in *Rügen* had established another U-boat "record," of sorts. This was the new *U-283.* She had been commissioned on March 31, 1943, by Heinz-Günther Scholz. However, the boat sailed from Kiel on January 13, 1944, commanded by another skipper, Günter Ney, who had been a watch officer on the *U-431* in the Mediterranean for about six months. Born March 7, 1922, Ney was twenty-one years old in January 1944, the youngest officer yet to command a U-boat at the battlefronts.

Initially the *Luftwaffe* was to assist *Rügen* with convoy spotting. However, from spies, Control obtained information on the sailing from Gibraltar of a northbound convoy, MKS 35, and directed all its aircraft to assist the group in the Middle Atlantic, *Borkum,* as will be described. Therefore, in order that *Rügen* could enhance its chances of finding a convoy, on January 7 Control issued orders for the group to deploy, singly, in roughly north-to-south positions about two hundred miles off the coasts of Scotland and Ireland in the Northwest Approaches. Allied codebreakers decrypted these orders (and others) and thus diverted convoys to the Southwest Approaches and St. George's Channel into the Irish Sea.

At this time, one U-boat in the North Atlantic found and sank a freighter. She was the VII *U-960,* a weather reporter commanded by Günther Heinrich, which had sailed from Norway on December 4. His victim was the 7,200-ton American Liberty ship *Sumner I. Kimball,* a straggler in ballast from convoy Outbound North 219. Near dusk, in heavy seas, Heinrich fired six torpedoes at *Kimball* and claimed four hits. *Kimball* got off a distress report with her position but not her name, then she broke in half. In response to her SOS, the British destroyer *Forester* found the stern of the wreck but no survivors.

Control learned from *B-dienst* that *Kimball* had broken in half and that the halves were still afloat. Therefore it ordered Heinrich to return to the scene and sink both halves. Heinrich reported that he found both halves, took photographs, then sank the "largest half" with one torpedo and left the other half floating. He said nothing about survivors. Since none was ever found by the Allies, the loss of *Kimball* became something of a mystery in merchant-ship circles. After the British *Empire Housman,* she was only the second freighter lost to U-boats in January

1944. The *U-960* reached La Pallice on February 3, where she traded her ineffective quad 20mm flak gun for a 37mm.

Finally mounted at mid-month, *Luftwaffe* support for *Rügen* was again disappointing. Foul weather grounded many aircraft. Others incurred engine and radio failures. The searches conducted by those planes that did fly, Control logged, were "not thorough"; position reports on the few contacts made came too late or were in error.

During this cold, miserable, and fruitless deployment, five *Rügen* VIIs, operating more or less singly, came upon and attacked Allied escorts and freighters from January 14 to January 23. The experienced *U-271, U-281,* and *U-571,* commanded by Kurt Barleben, Heinz von Davidson, and Gustav Lüssow, respectively, each shot a T-5 at a "destroyer." The first, *U-271,* an ex–flak boat, most likely fired at *Vidette* or *Versatile,* escorting the eastbound convoy Halifax 275. The new *U-390* and *U-471,* commanded by Heinz Geissler and Friedrich Kloevekorn, respectively, each shot a three-fan plus a T-5 at freighters. Allied records do not show any hits corresponding to these attacks.

In addition to the aforementioned *U-757* and *U-972,* three other *Rügen* VIIs were lost in January, making a total of five, or about one-third of that group.

- On the afternoon of January 28, a Sunderland of Australian Squadron 461, escorting the inbound Slow Convoy 151 and Outbound North 221, came upon the *U-571,* commanded by Gustav Lüssow. In two runs into heavy flak, the pilot, Richard D. Lucas, dropped two salvos of depth charges. After the second salvo, the *U-571* blew up in a "huge explosion," which an airman caught on film. Lucas reported "thirty" Germans in the water, but none survived. He received a DFC for this certain kill.
- On the same day, a B-24 of U.S. Navy Squadron VB 103, providing escort for the same two convoys, found and attacked the ex–flak boat *U-271,* commanded by Kurt Barleben. The pilot, George A. Enloe, dropped six depth charges that destroyed the boat. There were no survivors.
- On the afternoon of January 29, a B-24 of U.S. Navy Squadron VB 110, commanded by H. H. Budd, found the *U-592,* commanded by Hans Jaschke. The copilot, who was flying the B-24, attacked into flak hurriedly, dropping depth charges that fell short. Budd then took the controls of the flak-damaged plane and called in two more American B-24s of his squadron. However, Jaschke crash-dived *U-592* and escaped.

Later he reported this attack to Control, which logged of this encounter: "Dive-bombed by [B-24] Liberator when surfacing. Eight bombs. Heavily hit in keel." In fact, the damage was so extensive that *U-592* had to abort. At that time, Johnny Walker's Support Group 2, composed of five sloops, was in that area. Exploiting Enigma and DF intelligence, Walker found and sank the aborting *U-592* on January 31. The Admiralty credited Walker in *Starling* plus *Wild Goose* and *Magpie* with the kill. There were no German survivors.

Group *Rügen* was another futile and humiliating German performance. Its boats had not hit a single Allied ship. Six of its number—about one-third—had been lost in January. On the few occasions the vaunted T-5 homing torpedo could be employed, it had malfunctioned or missed. The equally touted 37mm automatic rapid-fire flak gun, replacing the useless quad 20mm, appeared to be yet another failure.

Control dissolved *Rügen,* but before it was properly replaced, all U-boat operations in the North Atlantic were thrown into great confusion. On January 28, a *Luftwaffe* aircraft over the Bay of Biscay reported "200 to 300 landing craft" headed east toward Bordeaux. Although the Germans correctly believed an invasion to be highly unlikely at this time or place, the reports could not be ignored. Furthermore, a few hours later, a VII inbound to France from *Rügen,* the *U-302,* commanded by Herbert Sickel, seemed to "confirm" a possible invasion force. He reported "25 to 30 smoke trails" with "strong escort" zigzagging at sixteen knots on an easterly course.

U-boat Control took countermeasures at once. It diverted five VIIs* that were outbound from France to the location of the supposed invasion force. Next it directed all *Rügen* boats (then about eighteen) to cease anticonvoy operations and rush to the location at high speed on the surface "regardless of enemy aircraft." These steps were in motion when, eight hours after the *Luftwaffe* report, Sickel in *U-302* submitted a second report stating that the "smoke trails" were actually from "fishing trawlers." Thereupon Control canceled the invasion alert and released all U-boats involved to resume anticonvoy operations.

U-boat Actions in the Middle Atlantic

While group *Rügen* patrolled the North Atlantic in January, a smaller group, *Borkum,* hunted in the Middle Atlantic between Gibraltar and the Azores. Control believed that *Borkum* consisted of eleven boats on January 3, but one boat, *U-645,* had been sunk on Christmas Eve, leaving ten, and two were aborting: the *U-275,* whose skipper, Helmut Bork, claimed sinking two destroyers on January 1 (not confirmed) but had been felled by appendicitis, and the new IXC40 *U-541,* which had been damaged by an aircraft. The skipper of the latter, Kurt Petersen, claimed he had sunk a total of "five destroyers" on this patrol, a record. However, none was ever confirmed. While inbound to France on the night of January 6, unidentified Allied aircraft hit both *U-275* and *U-541,* but they reached French bases. Assigned to the anti-invasion group *Landwirt,* the *U-275* did not sail again until June.

Unaware of the loss of *U-645,* Control divided *Borkum* into three subgroups of three boats. Its task was to intercept the slow Mediterranean–British Isles northbound convoy MKS 35. As related, it was to be assisted by JU-290s on reconnaissance patrols. However, Control was not yet aware that MKS 35 had sailed two days earlier than expected, that it had merged at sea with convoy Sierra Leone 144, and that the combined formation was to be supported not only by land-based air but also by the "jeep" carrier *Block Island*'s hunter-killer group, which departed

---

* *U-91, U-238, U-256, U-709, U-963.*

Casablanca on January 8. The *Block Island* group was also to support the southbound convoys Outbound South 64 and KMS 38.

In compliance with standing orders, all *Borkum* boats had been fitted with the new 37mm flak guns. The impending convoy attack was to be a battle test for the gun, believed to be the perfect answer to Allied aircraft. "The development of the automatic 37mm flak gun was carried out with greatest rapidity," Control told *Borkum* on January 5. "Delivery on board was effected without the usual thorough tests, with a view to the quickest possible equipment of U-boats. It is therefore urgently necessary quickly to receive reports from the front on experiences with this weapon, so that if necessary the guns produced by serial [i.e., mass] manufacture, now running at full speed, may be improved." In clear weather with unrestricted visibility, the boats were to charge batteries in daytime, using the 37mm to repel Allied aircraft.

Like most U-boat groups that operated in the dangerous Middle Atlantic area, group *Borkum* was massacred. Its demise was a vivid example of Allied air and naval ASW maturity in the Atlantic in early 1944.

While proceeding to new positions, two *Borkum* boats had brief encounters with the enemy.

- On the night of January 3, the *U-305,* commanded by Rudolf Bahr, who had sunk the Canadian destroyer *St. Croix* on an earlier patrol, shot T-5s at the *Card* group on Christmas Eve, and fired a T-5 at a "destroyer" on January 2, repelled an aircraft attack. Three nights later, January 6, Bahr came upon several ships of British Escort Group 6, which were guarding convoys Outbound South 64 and KMS 38. He fired three torpedoes at the warships. One or more hit the British frigate *Tweed* on the starboard side and she sank in two minutes. The other warships rescued only forty-four crew of *Tweed.* Bahr lost one officer in this engagement.
- That same night, the *U-270,* commanded by Paul-Friedrich Otto, came under attack by a B-17 Flying Fortress of British Squadron 206, newly based in the Azores. In his bombing run, the pilot, A. J. Pinhorn, severely damaged *U-270,* but Otto shot down the B-17 with the loss of all hands. The damage forced Otto to abort. Assigned to *Landwirt,* the *U-270* did not sail again until June. His departure left *Borkum* with only seven U-boats to attack the oncoming merged convoys MKS 35 and Sierra Leone 144.

Control twice moved the *Borkum* lines southward and, based on reports from a JU-290, consolidated them into a single line of eight boats (actually seven) on January 9. In the late afternoon of January 11, the westernmost boat, Rudolf Bahr in *U-305,* found and reported the convoy. He attempted to shadow, but a "destroyer" drove him off and down and he lost contact.

Responding to Bahr's report, three other *Borkum* boats attempted to attack the convoy that night. The *U-641,* commanded by Horst Rendtel, heard explosions and chased but a diesel engine failed and she was forced to dive to make repairs. The *U-382,* commanded by a new skipper, Rudolf Zorn, who had sunk the American destroyer *Leary* on this patrol, shot a T-5 at a "destroyer" but missed. In return, escorts depth-charged *U-382* so badly that Zorn was forced to abort. The ex–flak boat *U-953,* commanded by Karl-Heinz Marbach, shot a T-5 at a corvette that missed. In return, escorts hunted him for thirteen harrowing hours with depth charges and Hedgehogs.*

That day, January 11, two Avengers from *Block Island,* piloted by Leonard L. McFord and Willis D. Seeley, found the *Borkum* boat *U-758,* commanded by Helmut Manseck. In addition to two depth charges each, the Avengers were fitted with new and powerful armament: eight 3.5" rockets.

Braving the heavy flak, McFord and Seeley attacked with the rockets and then with depth charges. These hits seriously damaged *U-758,* forcing Manseck to abort. He reached St. Nazaire on January 20, at which time he returned to Germany to commission a big "electro boat." Assigned to *Landwirt,* the *U-758* did not sail again until June. Her abort and that of *U-382* left *Borkum* with merely five boats.

In view of the losses and aborts, Control disbanded *Borkum.* Four of the remaining five boats went north to join group *Rügen* west of Ireland. The other, *U-953,* sailed south to conduct an individual patrol off Casablanca and returned to La Pallice on February 20. Remarkably, only one of the four *Borkum* boats reassigned to *Rügen* actually got there and Allied forces sank her as well as two others. A fourth disappeared from unknown causes. In brief:

- On January 13, destroyers of the *Block Island* group found and attacked the aborting *Borkum* VII *U-382,* commanded by Rudolf Zorn, who, as related, had sunk the American destroyer *Leary.* Zorn escaped and reached St. Nazaire on January 26, at which time he left the boat to command another. Assigned to *Landwirt,* the *U-382* did not sail again until June.
- On the night of January 13, a Wellington of British Squadron 172, based in the Azores and piloted by a Canadian, W. N. Armstrong, found the *U-231,* commanded by thirty-three-year-old Wolfgang Wenzel. In two runs into flak, Armstrong dropped six depth charges that wrecked the *U-231* beyond saving. The plane could not remain at the scene, however, because flak from the U-boat had badly wounded one of the airmen, B. W. Heard, whose leg had to be amputated.

With his boat flooding heavily aft, Wenzel ordered abandon ship. An American intelligence report stated the following: "Sometime during the abandoning of his boat, Wenzel, probably in a fit of despondence, attempted suicide by firing a revolver bullet into his mouth." Astonishingly that bullet "lodged harmlessly . . . in the back of the neck and most crew members were unaware of the event."

All fifty men on *U-231* escaped from the sinking boat in rafts and dinghies, but seven soon died of exposure. About thirteen hours later, on January 14, two aircraft from the *Block Island* found the survivors. Two four-stack destroyers of the *Block Island* screen, *Bulmer* and *Parrott,*† picked up the surviving forty-three Germans and transferred them to the carrier, which arrived in Norfolk on February 3. A doctor on *Block Island* removed the bullet in Wenzel's neck.

---

* American intelligence reports state that *U-953* actually tangled with escorts of the opposite-sailing, merged convoys Outbound South 64 and KMS 38, which were nearby.

† Later, on May 2, 1944, the freighter *John Morton* rammed *Parrott* off Norfolk. Although beached, *Parrott* was deemed too far gone for repairs.

These prisoners were the first to be captured from a U-boat fitted with the new 37mm high-angle automatic flak gun. The five-man gun crew criticized it severely, one gunner stating it was "useless" for operations on U-boats. It was too delicate, too prone to jam, and too likely to break down. In order to keep the gun battle-ready, it was necessary to surface and spend thirty minutes a day on maintenance (greasing and cleaning) and to carry out a "complete overhaul" once a week.*

• On January 14, the ex-*Borkum U-377,* commanded by Gerhard Kluth, reported to Control that he had been attacked by aircraft but apparently the damage was not crippling. The next day, Kluth said he had come upon a hunter-killer group and shot T-5s from his bow and stern tubes but probably achieved no hits. Nothing further was heard from *U-377.* It is possible that these as yet unidentified warships sank *U-377* or one of her own torpedoes circled back and destroyed the boat. On January 15, Control logged a fragmentary distress message: "Hit by torpedo, boat badly damaged, am sinking." However, Control doubted this message came from *U-377* or any other U-boat since it was believed that a torpedo hit would instantly destroy the boat, making it impossible to get off an SOS.

• On January 15, the ex-*Borkum U-305,* commanded by Rudolf Bahr, reported to Control that it could not join *Rügen* as ordered and was returning to France. Bahr gave no reason, but doubtless he was low on fuel and perhaps out of torpedoes. Control heard nothing more from *U-305* and did not know the cause of her loss.

In his war memoir,† Reginald ("Bob") Whinney, skipper of the old but upgraded British destroyer *Wanderer,* has described what he believed to be the last hours of *U-305.* He writes that *Wanderer* was assigned to a five-ship British hunter-killer group that had lost its senior vessel, *Hurricane,* on Christmas Eve, while supporting *Card.* Thereafter the outfit had been assigned to intercept surface blockade-runners and command of it had passed to the skipper of the British frigate *Glenarm.*

On the afternoon of January 17, Whinney continues, *Wanderer* got a weak sonar contact on *U-305* and he immediately attacked with his Hedgehog. Like many destroyer skippers, he "disliked and distrusted" these mortars, whose bombs exploded only on contact. However, in view of new Admiralty orders to proceed at slow speed (under eight knots) to avoid making sufficient noise to attract a T-5, the Hedgehog was preferable to depth charges, which if dropped at slow speed might blow off the ship's stern. Sonar reported a "possible" Hedgehog hit. The senior ship of the group, the frigate *Glenarm,* then came up and attacked two sonar contacts at slow speed with her Hedgehog. Presently, *Glenarm* concluded the "contacts" were fish, left the scene, and directed all ships of the group to resume lookout for blockade-runners, Whinney states.

* According to the war diary at Control, eight other U-boats reported specific 37mm gun failures at about this time: *U-382, U-547, U-592, U-621, U-641, U-764, U-845,* and *U-984.* Other failures certainly occurred, but they were not recorded in the diary. Some skippers also reported 37mm ammo failure, apparently a "rapid decay." In one case, ammunition exploded in the barrel.

† *The U-boat Peril* (1987).

Convinced he had trapped a U-boat, Whinney ignored the order to leave the scene and pursued the contact alone, an act of disobedience that could have ruined his naval career. In mounting seas and gale-force winds, he made another slow-speed Hedgehog attack, but this time there was no explosion. Unable to reload the Hedgehog because of the heavy seas, Whinney speeded up to 15 knots and carried out a risky depth-charge attack. This time sonar reported "breaking-up noises"—small explosions and the creaking of grinding metal. The Admiralty's assessment committee at first rated the U-boat as "probably slightly damaged" but later upgraded the rating to "known sunk." It divided credit for the kill between *Wanderer* and *Glenarm,* a success that Whinney believed probably saved his career.

• The ex-*Borkum U-641,* commanded by Horst Rendtel, who had reported a 37mm flak gun failure during an aircraft attack on January 14, joined the southernmost end of group *Rügen,* but was almost immediately lost. On January 17, a *Luftwaffe* aircraft on a meteorological sortie reported a southbound convoy west of North Channel. Control in response directed all *Rügen* boats to run at maximum speed even in daylight to intercept this formation, which was convoy Outbound South 65, merged with convoy KMS 39. Follow-up *Luftwaffe* flights failed to find the convoy, but *U-641* did on January 19, and on that day one of the convoy escorts, the British corvette *Violet,* commanded by C. N. Stewart, pounced on *U-641* and destroyed her with the loss of all hands.

Of the eight boats assigned to group *Borkum* on January 3, three (*U-231, U-305, U-641*) were positively sunk by Allied forces and one (*U-377*) was lost to unknown causes, perhaps Allied forces. Three (*U-270, U-382, U-758*) were compelled to abort with aircraft damage and none of these sailed again until June. Only one boat (*U-953*), which went south to Casablanca, completed a full patrol. When she returned, she was assigned to *Landwirt* and did not sail again until late May.

In return for heavy casualties, the *Borkum* boats had sunk one British frigate, *Tweed,* and shot down one British B-17.

U-Boat Actions in the North Atlantic: II

In compliance with Hitler's orders to reinforce the Arctic U-boat force to thirty boats, only one new VII came out to the Atlantic U-boat force in February 1944. She was the experimental *U-986,* fitted with an array of antiaircraft rockets that, so far, had not measured up. Since five more VIIs of the Atlantic force were ordered to the Mediterranean in February in compliance with another Hitler order, and battle losses continued to be heavy, the shrinkage of the Atlantic force accelerated rapidly.

The five VIIs that were ordered to the Mediterranean had an arduous time. Two, *U-421* and *U-586,* got inside, but two were sunk and one aborted with battle damage.

• On the afternoon of February 24, a swarm of aircraft patrolling the western mouth of Gibraltar Strait found the *U-761,* commanded by Horst Geider. Among others, these were a Ventura of U.S. Navy Squadron VB 127, piloted by Theodore M. Holmes; two Catalinas of U.S. Navy Squadron VP 63, piloted by T. Russell Woolley and Howard Jefferson ("Jeff") Baker; and a Catalina of British Squadron 202, piloted by John Finch.

The two American Catalinas were fitted with Magnetic Airborne Detector (MAD) gear and twenty-four Mark VI retrorockets that exploded only on contact. They attacked *U-761,* as did the U.S. Navy Ventura and the British Catalina. The latter developed a fuel leak and had to abort, but the two American Catalinas remained close by. Meanwhile, two British destroyers on ASW patrol, *Anthony* and *Wishart,* came up and threw over thirty depth charges, which savaged *U-761* and forced her to surface. When she popped up, the destroyers riddled her bridge with gunfire, which proved to be the coup de grace. The *U-761*'s chief engineer, Karl Lendle, and eight other Germans died in the sinking. *Anthony* and *Wishart* picked up Geider and forty-eight other Germans, one of whom died in a Gibraltar hospital. All the commanders of the American and British aircraft got DFCs; all the American enlisted men, Air Medals.

• In the early morning hours of March 16, a Catalina of U.S. Navy Squadron VP 63, piloted by Ralph C. Spears, found by MAD gear the *U-392,* commanded by Henning Schümann. Spears dropped floating flares and sonobuoys* and flashed an alarm to two other MADCATS of Squadron 63, then attacked with twenty-four contact retrorockets in three salvos of eight, per current doctrine. Two other Catalinas, piloted by Van A. T. Lingle and Matthias J. Vopatek, arrived to assist. Lingle attacked with thirty contact retrorockets in three salvos of ten; Vopatek stood by at a distance. Allied authorities credited Spears and Lingle with three and two hits, respectively, which damaged *U-392.* Two British warships, the destroyer *Vanoc* and frigate *Affleck,* rushed up and pounded *U-392* with depth charges and Hedgehogs, and finally destroyed her. There were no German survivors.

• During the week of March 19 to March 25, unidentified Allied air and surface ASW forces patrolling the western entrance to the strait hunted and harassed the *U-618,* commanded by Kurt Baberg. After incurring heavy damage, Baberg was compelled to abort, arriving at St. Nazaire on April 8. Having commanded *U-618* for two years and sunk three confirmed freighters for 15,788 tons, Baberg left the boat for other duty.

Apart from the boats on temporary weather reporting tasks, six VIIs sailing from France in February carried out special missions.

• Two boats went to Icelandic waters to report the sailing of Murmansk convoys or other naval forces and to sink shipping. These were the *U-448,* commanded by Helmut Dauter, age twenty-four, and the *U-744,* commanded by Heinz Blischke, also age twenty-four. Both were lost.

Six days out from Brest, on March 2, Blischke in *U-744* encountered the combined northbound convoys MKS 40 and Sierra Leone 149. He boldly attacked this big, heavily escorted formation, claiming a destroyer and three very small (1,000-

---

* Allied aircraft employed sonobuoys by the thousands. The hydrophonic tracking system was difficult to master and was seldom effective.

ton) "tankers" sunk. In reality, no destroyer was hit and the "tankers" turned out to be British 1,600-ton LSTs, shifting from the Mediterranean to England for Overlord. Allied records show that Blischke sank one, the *LST 362,* but missed the other two.

Having expended five of his eleven internal torpedoes, Blischke aborted his mission to Iceland and patrolled the main convoy routes. At first the decision appeared to be correct for on the morning of March 5, he came upon the fast convoy Halifax 280, guarded by a close escort group and also by C-2, a mixed group of Canadian and British warships under British command serving as a support group ahead of the convoy. Upon sighting a "destroyer," Blischke fired a T-5, but it missed and the noise of the attack alerted the warships of C-2.

The C-2 Support Group was composed of seven vessels: three destroyers (the veteran British *Icarus,* the Canadian *Chaudière* and *Gatineau*), a Canadian frigate (*St. Catherines*), two Canadian corvettes (*Chilliwack* and *Fennel*), and a British corvette (*Kenilworth Castle*). All seven vessels pounced on *U-744* for a relentless hunt. Over the next thirty-one hours the ships let loose about 350 depth charges, numerous Hedgehogs, and—for the first time against an enemy—three salvos from a British Squid forward-firing mortar* fitted on the new British corvette *Kenilworth Castle.* On the afternoon of March 6, Blischke was finally forced to surface into the waiting arms of five of the seven warships, all of which opened fire with all weapons that could safely bear. In the ensuing finale, Blischke was killed on the bridge, but forty of his crew survived.

The *U-744* did not sink right away. Sensing the possibility for a capture, the captains of the Canadian vessels *Chilliwack* and *St. Catherines,* C. R. Coughlin and H.C.R. Davis, respectively, put over boarding parties. The *Chilliwack* party got to *U-744* first. Signalman J. R. Starr ran up a white ensign, while lieutenants Atherton and Hearn and artificer Longbottom raced below. These three men, the Canadian naval historian Joseph Schull wrote, snatched up a "precious haul of code books, signal publications and mechanical equipment."† However, efforts to take *U-744* in tow failed and the *Icarus* finally had to sink her with a torpedo.

The other boat, Helmut Dauter in *U-448,* patrolled off the west coast of Iceland. He reported "no traffic" and concluded (somewhat rashly) that those waters were "of no importance for the enemy at the moment" and left for home. On April 14, Canadian Support Group 9 (three frigates, one upgraded corvette) and the British sloop *Pelican,* on ASW patrol west of the Bay of Biscay, found *U-448* and

---

* Squid, in effect an improved, much more powerful and sophisticated Hedgehog, automatically tracked its quarry from sonar bearings and depth recordings fed into a fire-control computer, thus in theory eliminating targeting guesswork. The Squid fired up to three 12", 390-pound projectiles with 207-pound Minol warheads. Unlike Hedgehog projectiles that required contact hits to detonate, the Squid projectiles were triggered by automated time fuses, good to a depth of nine hundred feet. The British gave the Americans a Squid that was installed on the U.S. Navy frigate *Asheville* on April 6, 1944, for testing, but the U.S. did not mass-produce this weapon for the Battle of the Atlantic.

† This "precious haul" (presumably an Enigma and keys and/or short-signal books) has not been described.

forced her to the surface with Hedgehogs and depth charges, then riddled her with gunfire. The warships rescued Dauter and forty-one other Germans. One of the ten Germans who died in the sinking was the ship's doctor, Martin Lange, an "elderly man" who had a fatal heart attack in the water, the British reported. The Admiralty gave credit for the kill to the Canadian frigate *Swansea* (C. A. King) and the sloop *Pelican* (John S. Dallison).

• Three VIIs patrolled very close to shore in waters off the British Isles, primarily to report news of departing convoys and to ferret out new Allied ASW gear but also to sink shipping when conditions appeared favorable. These were the *U-333,* commanded by *Ritterkreuz* holder Peter Cremer, and the *U-413* and *U-621,* commanded by Gustav Poel and Max Kruschka, respectively. Cremer was to patrol off the North Channel; Kruschka was to patrol North Channel to North Minch; Poel was to patrol near the Scillies.

Allied codebreakers supplied decrypts of the Enigma orders to these three boats. In response, British air and surface hunter-killer groups put to sea specifically to destroy them. On February 10, Poel in *U-413* reported a convoy but an unidentified aircraft escort drove him off. Denys A. Raynor in the 1,100-ton destroyer *Warwick* with another destroyer, *Scimitar,* in company, sailed from Plymouth to an area west of Land's End to hunt Poel. As it turned out, Poel saw *Warwick* first and hit her with a FAT (looping) torpedo that blew away her stern and sank her with heavy loss of life. When Poel returned to France on March 21, Dönitz awarded him a *Ritterkreuz.** It was the second of two such awards bestowed on U-boat skippers in the Atlantic force during the first five months of 1944.

Max Kruschka in *U-621* spent most of his time off North Minch. He claimed that in very poor visibility on March 20 he fired a T-5 at an unidentified target "with a searchlight" and assumed the torpedo hit and sank the ship, but it could not be confirmed. Owing to "the state of the battery," Kruschka reported on March 30, he set a course for France. He also reported that the automatic loading mechanism of his 37mm flak gun was broken.

All three of these boats got back to France. In his memoir, *Ritterkreuz* holder Peter Cremer wrote that after an aircraft spotted him on March 21, Johnny Walker's hunter-killer Support Group 2, en route from Liverpool to Scapa Flow (see below), hunted him relentlessly. Cremer escaped by lying doggo on a muddy bottom at 131 feet for ten hours. The boat stuck fast in the mud and it appeared to Cremer that he might not be able to break loose, but ten men sallied ship bow to stern and she finally rose. While inbound in Biscay on April 11, Kruschka in *U-621* came upon a hunter-killer group and shot a T-5 at a "destroyer," which missed. He then fired *Bolde* sonar decoys and escaped.

• One boat laid a minefield. She was the VIID *U-214,* commanded by Ruprecht Stock. In late March he planted SMA mines off Casablanca. Allied ships triggered four on April 3 and 12, but none caused any significant damage. The

* At the time of the award, his confirmed score—all on *U-413*—was four ships for 30,139 tons, including *Warwick.*

U-214 then proceeded to a rendezvous with the outbound *U-68* to get new Enigma keys, another disastrous meet, as will be described. On April 29, Stock returned *U-214* to Brest, where technicians commenced installation of a snort.

As in January, the primary task of the U-boats sailing in February was to man the single, loose group widely deployed in the eastern Atlantic, about two hundred miles off the west coast of the British Isles. Formerly named *Rügen,* that group was split in late January into two subgroups, *Hinein* and *Stürmer,* but only a few days later, on February 3, Control consolidated the subgroups into a new, loosely deployed, single group, *Igel* (Hedgehog).

Mere hours after *Igel* had been formed, one of the newly arrived boats, the VII *U-764,* commanded by Hans-Kurt von Bremen, came upon convoy Outbound North 222. It was composed of fifty-one merchant ships in ballast protected by eleven escorts, mostly Canadian: two destroyers, three frigates, five corvettes, and a MAC ship. Von Bremen reported the convoy, then dived. A section of it passed overhead but he did not shoot, then or later. The ex–flak boat VIIs *U-441* and *U-963,* plus four other VIIs, attempted to join *U-764,* but it was a case of too little too late and none of these seven boats was able to mount a proper attack.* An unidentified aircraft hit *U-953,* but the damage was not crippling.

Several boats that were low on fuel returned to France in early February. One was the new *U-763,* commanded by Ernst Cordes, age thirty. She was the first Atlantic boat to be fitted with *Hohentwiel* search radar.† Fearing that Allied aircraft might detect its radiation, Cordes did not use the gear in the two most dangerous areas, the Iceland-Faeroes gap and the Bay of Biscay. One result was that while he relied solely on the *Naxos* radar detector, three separate British aircraft hit the boat in Biscay on February 4 and 5.

Although Cordes shot down two of the aircraft,‡ officers at flotilla headquarters were incensed at his decision not to use *Hohentwiel* in danger areas. Enemy aircraft were *not* equipped with FuMB (radar detectors), Control emphasized in an admonition to all boats (citing Cordes by name), so they could *not* detect *Hohentwiel* radiations. Hence a U-boat fitted with *Hohentwiel* could safely detect an enemy plane at six or seven miles by radar before the plane detected the U-boat on its radar.

Aware from Enigma decrypts of *Igel* deployments, the Allies flooded the area west of the British Isles with an unprecedented number of ASW warships and air-

---

* A radioman on *U-764,* Heinz F. K. Guske, harshly criticized Bremen's failure to attack in his shrill book, *The War Diaries of U-764: Fact or Fiction?* Guske, in turn, has been denounced by his shipmates for manufacturing lies.

† Failure of the Germans to equip U-boats with search radar, such as *Hohentwiel,* until January 1944 was another example of the low state of science and engineering in Hitler's Germany, especially in electronics. American submarines patrolling Japanese waters had been fitted with war-decisive search radar eighteen months earlier, in the summer of 1942.

‡ A B-24 of Squadron 53, piloted by D. A. Bell, and a Halifax of Squadron 502, piloted by F. T. Culling-Mannix.

craft. Apart from the usual heavy close escorts for convoys, the Admiralty assigned "jeep" carriers* to all convoys as well as hunter-killer groups. The Americans provided the "jeep" carrier *Block Island.*

One of the British hunter-killer units operating in that area during February was Johnny Walker's famous Support Group 2, five sloops plus the "jeep" carriers *Nairana* and *Activity.* As related, this group had sunk the *U-592* on January 31 with all hands. In a remarkable series of actions from February 6 to February 19, the group sank by depth charges and Hedgehog five more U-boats, making a total of six kills in a single twenty-eight-day cruise. In brief:

- The sloops *Woodpecker* and *Wild Goose* sank the new *U-762,* commanded by Walter Pietschmann, age twenty-four, on February 6. There were no survivors.
- The sloops *Starling, Magpie,* and *Kite* got the *U-238,* commanded by Horst Hepp, age twenty-six, on February 9. No survivors.
- The sloops *Starling* and *Wild Goose* got the *U-734,* commanded by Hans-Jörg Blauert, age twenty-five, on February 9. No survivors.
- The sloops *Wild Goose* and *Woodpecker* got the *U-424,* commanded by Günter Lüders, age twenty-three, on February 11. No survivors.
- The sloops *Starling* and *Woodpecker* sank the *U-264,* commanded by Hartwig Looks, age twenty-six, on February 19.

This boat, merely fifteen days out from France, was embarked on the first war patrol of a Type VII equipped with a snort. Walker's sloops rescued Looks and fifty other Germans, some of whom revealed a great deal about snort technology, operations, limitations, and risks.

During Walker's attack on *U-264,* Wilhelm Brauel, age twenty-nine, in the ex–flak boat *U-256* came up and hit the sloop *Woodpecker* with a T-5. After rescuing the crew of *U-264,* Walker in *Starling* attempted to tow *Woodpecker* to England, but owing to inadequate gear and heavy seas, he turned over the task to the Royal Navy tug *Storm King.* On the seventh day, *Woodpecker* capsized and sank, but her salvage crew was saved. The other four sloops returned triumphantly to Liverpool on February 25 to well-deserved cheers from First Lord of the Admiralty Albert Alexander, Western Approaches commander Max Horton, and about two thousand others.

The badly damaged IXC *U-516,* homebound from the Caribbean, came upon the fast convoy Halifax 277 in mid-Atlantic on February 7. Owing to the damage to that U-boat, Control advised her skipper, Hans-Rutger Tillessen, not to attack or to shadow. At the same time, Control alerted the boats of group *Igel* to prepare to intercept this rich target on about February 10. For this purpose, Control organized *Igel* into two subgroups, *Igel* 1 and *Igel* 2, the former near Rockall Bank, the latter farther south, and directed the *Luftwaffe* to prepare for reconnaissance flights, weather permitting.

---

* British "jeep" carriers sailing to these waters in February included the British-built *Nairana* and *Activity* and the American-built *Fencer, Pursuer,* and *Striker.*

As it happened, the merged inbound convoys MKS 38 and Sierra Leone 147 were not far from Halifax 277. Some of the southernmost *Igel* boats mistook these formations for the intended target, Halifax 277, and attacked by a full moon. By that time, Johnny Walker's Support Group 2 had attached itself to these convoys. It was then—February 6 to 11—that, as related, the Walker group sank four *Igel* U-boats (*U-762, U-238, U-734,* and *U-424*).

Again, no boat of the *Igel* groups was able to mount a proper attack on a convoy. However, there was good news of sorts for the Germans from another sector. Off Iceland on February 8, the Arctic transfer *U-985,* commanded by Horst Kessler, age twenty-nine, which was three weeks out from Bergen, reported the sinking of a 6,000-ton freighter. The victim was really the lone 1,735-ton British cargo vessel *Margit* inbound to Loch Ewe in ballast from Murmansk convoy RA 56. This modest vessel was the only Allied merchant ship sunk by U-boats in the North Atlantic in February 1944.

During this period Coastal Command mounted saturation air coverage over those ocean convoys in the eastern Atlantic threatened by the *Igel* boats. Some unidentified aircraft had assisted Johnny Walker's Support Group 2 in the sinking of *U-238* and *U-762.* Other unidentified aircraft attacked the *U-283, U-413,* and *U-608* on February 10. Over the next two days, Coastal Command aircraft sank two boats.

- That same day, February 10, a Leigh Light–equipped Wellington of British Squadron 612, piloted by the Australian Max H. Painter, found by radar an *Igel* U-boat in the waters west of North Minch. She was another new IXC40, *U-545,* commanded by Gert Mannesmann. Painter attacked with depth charges by moonlight. These close explosions so badly damaged *U-545* that Mannesmann had to abandon ship and scuttle.*

In response to an SOS from Mannesmann, Control ordered three *Igel* boats of the northern subgroup to assist: another new IXC40, the *U-549;* and the VIIs *U-714* and *U-984.* One of the latter, *U-714,* commanded by Hans-Joachim Schwebcke, arrived in time and rescued all fifty-six men from *U-545.* Schwebcke then returned to France, arriving at St. Nazaire on February 25. Thereupon Mannesmann returned to Germany to command a big "electro boat."

- The next day, February 11, a Leigh Light–equipped Wellington of Canadian Squadron 407, piloted by P. W. Heron, found another *Igel* boat, the new VII *U-283,* commanded by the twenty-one-year-old Günter Ney, who had shot down a Wellington of British Squadron 612 the night before. In a snap attack, Heron dropped six depth charges and destroyed the boat with the loss of all hands. Ney earned a DFC.

Another new IXC40, *U-546,* commanded by Paul Just, had a very close call at this time. On February 16, an unidentified Sunderland attacked the boat, killing a

---

* The *U-545* was the tenth Type IX to be lost on operations in the North Atlantic in four months. The others were *U-508, U-536, U-538, U-540, U-542, U-544, U-841, U-842,* and *U-844.* All but *U-508* were new boats on maiden patrols from Germany. About five hundred men were lost (forty-four captured) in these sinkings.

gunner and inflicting diesel-engine damage. However, Just reported, he could make repairs "with his own resources" and continue his mission to report the weather. Homebound in Biscay from that task on April 17, the *U-546* survived three more air attacks and shot down a Mosquito.

The last action of group *Igel* took place on February 14. The *U-445,* commanded by a new skipper, Rupprecht Fischler von Treuberg, age twenty-four, shot a T-5 at a "destroyer." His target was probably a frigate of British Support Group 3. The T-5 missed and all warships of this group attacked and severely damaged *U-445,* but she got away. However, as a result of this punishing attack, Rupprecht Fischler von Treuberg was compelled to abort to France. He arrived in St. Nazaire on February 27 and did not sail again until June.

Although the groups in the North Atlantic had achieved almost nothing at ruinous cost in U-boats, Control continued these futile operations despite ever-mounting losses. When a *Luftwaffe* aircraft reported a large convoy outbound from North Channel on February 15, Control calculated its probable course and deployed the *Igel* boats in two tight patrol lines, *Hai* 1 and *Hai* 2, at a likely location for an "old style" convoy attack. The convoy in question was either Outbound North (Slow) 29 or the fast Outbound North 224, both heavily guarded by all manner of surface and air escorts.

Control exhorted these two patrol lines, composed of about twenty-six U-boats, to do their utmost to achieve a great naval victory. Because of Allied air in the area, carrier-based air in particular, the "main blow" had to be delivered the first night. "So that you reach the convoy no matter what," during this night attack the boats were not to dive from *Naxos* contacts, but remain on the surface with flak guns and a bow and stern T-5 homing torpedo ready to fire. If Control directed that the attack should continue into daytime, all boats except those with defective 37mm flak guns were to stay on the surface and, of course, go after the carriers first (with T-5s), then the destroyers of the escort or screen (again, with T-5s). "Do your best," Control exhorted, "this long-prepared operation *must* succeed."

This group operation, like those preceding it, failed utterly. The promised *Luftwaffe* reconnaissance did not happen, owing to mechanical defects in the planes. Allied carrier aircraft swarmed overhead. Too many U-boats had defective 37mm guns. It was in this would-be naval battle that Johnny Walker's hunter-killer unit, Support Group 2, sank the snort boat *U-264* and in return, the VII *U-256* fatally damaged Walker's sloop *Woodpecker.*

At this time, in the same area, the British frigate *Spey,* commanded by H. G. Boys-Smith, sank two *Hai* boats within twenty-four hours, a Royal Navy record of sorts. *Spey* was one of four frigates of the British Escort Group 10 attached to convoy Outbound North (Slow) 29.

- On the afternoon of February 18 *Spey* and another frigate, *Lossie,* found the VII *U-406,* commanded by Horst Dieterichs, and blew her to the surface with depth charges. As the first man to reach the bridge, Dieterichs encountered machine-gun fire from *Spey* that killed him. A boarding party from *Spey* got inside

U-406 and rounded up a heavy bag crammed with secret documents, but the boat sank before the documents could be removed. The boarding party scrambled to safety. *Spey* rescued forty-five Germans but four died, leaving forty-one, including an electronics engineer and his two assistants.

• The next afternoon, February 19, *Spey* found and attacked the veteran *U-386,* commanded by Fritz Albrecht, which had earlier conducted a special mission off North Channel. *Spey* blew *U-386* to the surface with depth charges, then closed, spraying the boat with 20mm fire to prevent the Germans from manning guns. As the German crew was leaping over the side, someone unintentionally engaged the boat's electric motors and she began to move off. Seeing that, *Spey* "opened up with everything she had," and sank the boat. *Spey* rescued Albrecht and fifteen other Germans who revealed that, as the Allies suspected, *U-386,* like *U-406,* carried electronic specialists.

Control dissolved the two *Hai* groups and established a new group, *Preussen,* on February 19. It was supposedly composed of seventeen boats, thirteen from the *Hai* groups plus four boats newly sailed from France. However, one of the *Hai* boats, the snort boat *U-264,* was already lost and another, *U-281,* was returning to France. That meant *Preussen* consisted of fifteen, not seventeen, boats. It was to be the last anticonvoy U-boat group or "wolf pack" of the war.

During this redeployment, one of the *Preussen* boats was sunk. She was one of the two oldest VIICs in the Atlantic force, *U-91,* commanded by Heinz Hungershausen, age twenty-seven, older brother of Walter Hungershausen, skipper of the *U-280,* which was lost with all hands the previous November 16. On the night of February 25, the British hunter-killer Support Group 1, composed of six frigates, found *U-91.* At that time Hungershausen got what he believed to be a *Naxos* aircraft contact and dived to two hundred feet. In actuality the *Naxos* contact had been made on radar from one of the frigates, *Gore,* which attacked with depth charges. As a devastating rain of missiles fell, Hungershausen dived deeper, to about 660 feet, but it was too late. Although the *U-91* was severely damaged, in desperation Hungershausen surfaced to run away on his diesels. When he popped up, *Gore* and two other frigates, *Gould* and *Affleck,* opened fire with all weapons that could bear and destroyed the boat. The frigates rescued Hungershausen and fifteen other Germans.

Another *Preussen* boat had a very close call. For reasons not clear, Control ordered the VII *U-212,* commanded by Helmut Vogler, to rendezvous with the new IXC40 *U-549,* commanded by Detlev Krankenhagen, and give her a *Naxos.* As Vogler attempted to carry out these orders, unidentified aircraft attacked the *U-212* on February 25 and again on February 27, when *U-212* lay alongside *U-549.* However, both boats survived and *U-212* reached France on March 12.

The expected target of group *Preussen* was convoy Outbound North 225. Believing it would take a southwesterly course like Outbound North 223 and 224, Control positioned *Preussen* accordingly for an attack on February 28. Aware of these positions from Enigma decrypts, Western Approaches diverted Outbound

North 225 to a westerly course along the Great Circle route and thereby outwitted Control.

Three more *Preussen* boats were lost on March 1, another appalling slaughter.

• The British Support Group 1, composed of six frigates, three of which had sunk *U-91* on February 25, found the veteran VII *U-358* on February 29. Commanded by Rolf Manke, she was two weeks out from St. Nazaire. The frigate *Garlies* and the three frigates that had sunk *U-91* (*Affleck, Gore,* and *Gould*) pounded *U-358* tenaciously with depth charges and Hedgehogs in a relentless hunt lasting over thirty hours. At the end of that time—the longest U-boat hunt of the war to then—the air in the boat was so foul the men could scarcely breathe. Finally, after dark on March 1, Manke had no choice but to surface and try to run away on his diesels.

By that time *Garlies* and *Gore* had departed for other duty, leaving *Affleck* and *Gould* to pursue *U-358.* When Manke reached periscope depth at 7:30 P.M., he set up quickly and fired a T-5 at the frigate *Gould,* commanded by D. W. Ungoed. As the T-5 hit and blew *Gould* apart, Manke surfaced to run. However, the frigate *Affleck,* merely 1,500 yards away, pounced on *U-358* and sank her with depth charges and the main gun battery. *Affleck* then turned about to rescue the crew of *Gould,* after which she returned to the site of the *U-358* sinking and found one survivor, an enlisted man. According to him, Allied fire hit and killed Manke on deck while he was waving a white flag of surrender.

• The American "jeep" carrier *Block Island,* which sailed from Norfolk on February 16 with a new screen of one destroyer (*Corry*) and four new destroyer escorts, reached the area of group *Preussen* on February 29. Late that afternoon, an Avenger team spotted a periscope trailing a feather in the water. The planes dropped sonobuoys and gave the alarm but were unable to attack.

Three destroyer escorts of the screen, *Bostwick, Bronstein,* and *Thomas,* raced to the site and found by radar the VII *U-709,* commanded by a new skipper, Rudolf Ites, age twenty-six. The *Bronstein,* commanded by Sheldon H. Kinney, fired a star shell to illuminate the scene and opened fire with her main battery (3"/50 caliber) and twin 40mms and drove the boat under. After firing two Hedgehog salvos, *Bronstein* moved aside as the *Bostwick,* commanded by John H. Church, Jr., and the *Thomas,* commanded by David M. Kellogg, came in with depth charges and more Hedgehogs. *Bostwick* and *Thomas* pounded *U-709* for about five hours. Finally, at about 3:30 A.M., March 1, they destroyed her with the loss of all hands. She was the first U-boat to be sunk solely by American destroyer escorts.

• In the meantime, shortly after midnight, March 1, Sheldon Kinney in *Bronstein* had found another quarry close by. She was the VII *U-603,* commanded by Hans-Joachim Bertelsmann. Kinney attacked immediately with a barrage of depth charges and Hedgehogs that destroyed *U-603.* She became the second U-boat to be destroyed by American destroyer escorts. There were no survivors of this boat either.

Another *Preussen* boat had a very close call. On March 2, an unidentified aircraft hit the ex–flak boat *U-441,* commanded by Klaus Hartmann. He reported "severe damage" and aborted. On March 14 he limped into Brest, where the boat was fitted with a snort and did not sail again until late May.

U-boat Actions in the North Atlantic: III

There was no longer the slightest possibility that U-boats could achieve anything of value on patrols in the eastern Atlantic close to the British Isles. Yet Dönitz insisted that such patrols should continue into March despite the heavy U-boat losses. After all, Hitler had proclaimed the U-boat arm to be his first line of defense against invasion in the west; the *Kriegsmarine* would not let him down. Besides that, the patrols provided a proving ground for information on the new weapons to be incorporated into the "electro boats," such as the latest version of the T-5 homing torpedo and yet another new looping torpedo, LUT; the 37mm automatic flak gun; the *Aphrodite* and *Thetis* radar decoys; the *Fliege, Tunis,* and *Naxos* radar detectors; and the *Gema* and *Hohentwiel* search radars.

Group *Preussen* was still at sea on March 7. Control believed it consisted of fifteen boats but four had been lost, leaving eleven, including the experimental VIIs *U-986* (antiaircraft rocket array) and *U-267* (snort). The group deployed close to the British Isles on a loose and widely spaced north-south line from Rockall Bank to the western approaches to the English Channel, somewhat like the U-boat deployment in the first days of the war. However, owing to the four losses, there were many "holes" in this line, all known to the Allies from Enigma decrypts and other intelligence sources.

One of the *Preussen* boats sank a ship. She was the VII *U-255,* commanded by Erich Harms, an Arctic transfer that had sailed from Bergen on February 26. On the evening of March 9, Harms happened upon a big tanker convoy, CU 16, inbound from the Caribbean via New York to the British Isles. The close escort group consisted of six new destroyer escorts, all manned by Coast Guard crews. Harms got off a contact report to Control and shadowed. However, one of the destroyer escorts, *Leopold,* commanded by Kenneth C. Phillips, perhaps assisted by a Huff Duff bearing, got *U-255* on radar, went to battle stations, and charged, firing star shells and her 3"/50-caliber main battery.

Harms dived and fired a T-5 at *Leopold* from extremely close range. After a run of merely twenty-seven seconds, he reported, the T-5 hit its target with a solid explosion. In fact, it broke *Leopold*'s back. She split in half and the stern sank. Armed depth charges rolled into the water, killing a great many of the crew. Another of the destroyer escorts, *Joyce,* commanded by Robert Wilcox, arrived at the scene, got *U-255* on sonar, and chased her for three hours, but Harms got away. *Joyce* returned to *Leopold*'s drifting bow section at dawn, rescued twenty-eight enlisted men, and sank the half hulk with guns and depth charges. Altogether, 171 Coast Guardsmen of *Leopold* perished in the sinking.

The next day, March 11, Harms reported, while he was attempting to overtake the convoy, an unidentified aircraft attacked *U-255*. Two men were wounded, one seriously. Upon receiving this report, Control directed Harms to rendezvous with another *Preussen* VII that had a doctor, *U-608,* commanded by a new skipper, Wolfgang Reisener, age twenty-five. When this meeting and another failed, Harms treated his own wounded and continued his patrol.

Control ordered five more VIIs to join group *Preussen.* The Allies handled this reinforcement roughly. In brief:

- The veteran *U-575,* the third VII to embark on a war patrol with a snort, which departed St. Nazaire on February 29. Ten days out, on March 9, the skipper, her former first watch officer, Wolfgang Boehmer, age twenty-three, attacked and sank with a T-5 the British corvette *Asphodel,* part of the escort of the merged inbound convoys Sierra Leone 150 and MKS 41. She was the first Allied ship to be lost to a snort boat, although that device played no direct part in the sinking.

Other British escorts, including *Baynton* and *Clover,* screening the "jeep" carrier *Striker,* hunted *U-575* with depth charges and Hedgehogs for eighteen hours, but Boehmer got away. When clear, he took advantage of the sinking and chase to report briefly on snort operations, as ordered. It was not advisable to snort in the vicinity of Allied surface ships, he said, because the noisy diesels drowned out the boat's own hydrophones and in daytime, despite all precautions, the snort intermittently emitted exhaust smoke that might be detected by the enemy vessels.

A Leigh Light–equipped Wellington of British Squadron 172, piloted by John P. Finnessey, providing escort for convoy Outbound North 227, came upon Boehmer in *U-575* in the early hours of March 13. Finnessey attacked with depth charges, dropped float flares, gave the alarm, and broadcast beacon signals. At dawn a B-17 Flying Fortress of British Squadron 206, piloted by A. David Beaty (later a well-known author), arrived at the scene and attacked into heavy flak and dropped four close depth charges. The automatic feed of the 37mm gun on *U-575* failed, and it had to be loaded by hand. In view of that fact, Boehmer submerged. Looking from above, it appeared to Beaty that she went down stern first, with her bow sticking up at a steep angle.

Beaty climbed, broadcast an alarm, and circled the site for five hours, sending beacons. A B-17 of British Squadron 220, piloted by Wilfred R. Travell, soon arrived. Seeing a large oil slick, Travell dived and dropped two depth charges into its middle. Travell then climbed and in response to orders, broadcast homing signals for the benefit of an American hunter-killer group built around the "jeep" carrier *Bogue,* which had sailed to this area from Norfolk on February 26.

An Avenger from *Bogue,* piloted by John F. Adams, came on the scene that morning, found the oil slick, and dropped sonobuoys. A destroyer of the escort, *Hobson,* also explored the area but found nothing. Later in the day, one of four new destroyer escorts of the screen, *Haverfield,* commanded by Jerry A. Matthews, Jr., arrived, got a sonar contact, and carried out depth-charge and Hedgehog attacks. While Matthews was so engaged, a Canadian frigate, *Prince Rupert,* commanded by R. W. Draney, happened along and, upon invitation, joined the attack. Another Avenger, piloted by Donald A. Pattie, circled overhead.

The destroyer *Hobson,* commanded by Kenneth Loveland, returned to join the hunt. Coached by *Haverfield,* she got a solid sonar contact and fired two massive, deep depth-charge salvos. These drove *U-575* to the surface, whereupon all three warships opened fire with main guns and Pattie in the Avenger attacked with rockets and bombs. These finally destroyed *U-575.* The *Prince Rupert* picked up fourteen Germans and took them to Newfoundland. The *Hobson* collected twenty-three survivors, including skipper Boehmer, and took them to Casablanca for eventual transfer to the States.

This was the second time the Allies had recovered prisoners from a snort boat. They learned many more technical details about the snort and its operation, including the fact that contrary to popular belief, U-boats *did not snort all the time,* but only for three or four hours at night to charge batteries. Based on these interviews, an American intelligence officer wrote:

> Prisoners' reactions to the *Schnorchel* were all of a pattern: Every one objected to its use and hoped that it would be discarded. Some feared the sudden creation of a vacuum in the U-boat if a wave should wash over the top of the intake mast; some complained of fumes in the diesel compartment, caused by insufficient exhaust; all feared that in a phosphorescent sea they could easily be detected by enemy aircraft and would rather proceed submerged. . . . A radio rating objected to the *Schnorchel* because, he said, it interfered with listening on the multi-unit hydrophones, especially aft. It was impossible to pick up sounds of any but greatest intensity at a safe distance.

Like the other lost VII snort boat *U-264,* the *U-575* had been at sea on her maiden snort patrol for merely two weeks. When the news of these two losses (of three snort VIIs) spread throughout the Atlantic U-boat force, it did nothing to build confidence in this clumsy and much-detested device.

• The next two VIIs sent to join group *Preussen* departed Brest on February 29.* These were the *U-625,* commanded by a new skipper, Siegfried Straub, age twenty-five, and the *U-741,* commanded by Gerhard Palmgren. While crossing the Bay of Biscay, the *U-741* was twice attacked by Allied aircraft at night, but neither attack was crippling.

On the eighth day out of Brest, Straub in *U-625* reported that a diesel engine had failed as well as his *Wanze* and *Naxos.* Control radioed instructions on how to make repairs and directed the *Preussen* boat *U-963,* commanded by Karl Boddenberg, to render assistance. Thereafter *U-625* proceeded to group *Preussen,* which had moved farther west.

A Sunderland of Canadian Squadron 422, manned by a new crew, spotted *U-625* on the surface on the afternoon of March 10. At that time, the controls were in the hands of an RAF check pilot, Sidney W. Butler. He attacked into very heavy flak and accurately dropped six depth charges. The *U-625* submerged, then resurfaced almost immediately. Moving beyond flak range, Butler circled the scene for ninety minutes, giving the alarm.

Skipper Straub in the *U-625* assessed the damage and decided to abandon ship. While preparing to do so, he got off an *SOS* to Control, which, in turn, directed two nearby *Preussen* boats, the ex–flak boat *U-256,* commanded by Wilhelm Brauel,

---

* 1944 was a leap year, adding one day to February.

and Palmgren in *U-741,* to rescue Straub and his crew. After the crew of *U-625* had abandoned ship in rafts and dinghies, Straub scuttled the boat.

While racing to locate and rescue the shipwrecked Germans, the *U-256* and *U-741* ran into difficulties. On March 11, a Leigh Light–equipped Wellington of Canadian Squadron 407, piloted by E. M. O'Donnel, found and attacked the boats. The inbound *U-256* incurred "severe" damage. British and Canadian sources state that *U-256* shot down the Wellington, but Brauel told Control that the plane "crashed 1500 meters off before own fire opened up." Palmgren in the outbound *U-741* also reported an air attack. When he later surfaced, he said, he was attacked again, this time by "four carrier aircraft and three destroyers," which pursued him for hours, but inflicted only "slight" damage.* Control ordered both boats to continue the search, but no trace of the *U-625* crew was ever found by friend or foe. The *U-256* reached Brest on March 22; the *U-741* continued her patrol.

• The *U-629,* commanded by Hans-Helmut Bugs, which sailed from Brest on March 4. The next day an aircraft of British Squadron 304 hit and damaged the boat, forcing Bugs to return to Brest on March 7. He resailed on March 9, but in the early hours of March 12, a Leigh Light–equipped Wellington of British Squadron 612, piloted by D. Bretherton, attacked into heavy flak and dropped four depth charges. These inflicted so much damage that Bugs was compelled to abort to Brest a second time, arriving on March 15. The boat did not resail until June.

• The *U-653,* commanded by Hans-Albrecht Kandler, which sailed from Brest on March 2. On March 15, as *U-653* was joining *Preussen,* a Swordfish from the new British "jeep" carrier *Vindex,* on her maiden combat mission, got *U-653* on radar and the pilot, P. Cumberland, marked the spot with flares as Kandler crash-dived. In response to this alarm, the sloops of Johnny Walker's Support Group 2, which, with the Canadian Escort Group 6, was providing escort for *Vindex,* raced to the scene. "Dickie" Wemyss in *Wild Goose* made sonar contact but deferred to Walker in *Starling.* Much to his chagrin, Walker sank *U-653* with a preliminary depth-charge run designed not to sink the boat, but to drive her deep for a main attack by *Wild Goose.*

In his account of Walker's wartime operations,† the British writer Terence Robertson stated that since it was customary in this group to allow the first ship to detect a U-boat to sink it, Walker signaled Wemyss: "I am guilty of flagrant poaching. Very much regret my unwarrantable intrusion into your game."

The Admiralty divided credit for the kill of *U-653* between *Wild Goose* and *Starling* of Walker's group and *Vindex.* There were no German survivors.

One of the newly arrived *Preussen* reinforcements, the VII *U-311,* commanded by Joachim Zander, found a convoy on March 16. This was another big, heavily guarded tanker formation, CU 17, en route from the Caribbean to the British Isles

---

* The carrier has not yet been identified. There were half a dozen "jeep" carriers in or near this area on March 10–11, so many, in fact, that they worked in pairs.

† *Escort Commander* (1956).

via New York. Zander gave the alarm and shot a T-5 at a "destroyer," but it missed. Four escorts hunted and depth-charged *U-311* for four hours, Zander reported, but he hung on tenaciously. In the early hours of the next day, the American destroyer escort *Daniel T. Griffin* got *U-311* on sonar, but Zander eluded her and shot two FAT (looping) torpedoes into the formation. These hit and wrecked the 10,300-ton American tanker *Seakay,* which was put under by the convoy escorts. She was only the fourth Allied merchant ship sunk by U-boats in the North Atlantic area in five months.*

During this convoy chase, the escorts found and heavily damaged another newly arrived *Preussen* boat. She was the *U-415,* commanded by Kurt Neide. For the second time in as many patrols, she was forced to abort because of aircraft damage. Neide limped into Brest on March 31. The next day, Neide, who had sunk the British destroyer *Hurricane* and two freighters for a total of 8,000 tons, left the boat for other duty. Her new skipper was Herbert Werner from the *U-230,* author of the 1969 best-seller *Iron Coffins.*

Control in mid-March logged that owing to the decision to concentrate U-boats in ports to defend southern Norway (group *Mitte*) and France (group *Landwirt*), the flow of new boats to the Atlantic force had virtually stopped. For that reason, and also because of the failure of *Luftwaffe* support, the ruinous battle losses in the North Atlantic, and the urgent need to upgrade the Atlantic boats with reliable 37mm flak guns and snorts and search radars, it was no longer possible to even pretend to mount anticonvoy warfare in the North Atlantic. Thus on March 22, Control dissolved *Preussen,* the last anticonvoy U-boat group of the war, and recalled to France eleven VIIs that were scheduled to reinforce that group: seven new VIIs from Norway and four VIIs from France.

Of the four boats that put out from France for *Preussen* and were recalled, one was lost. She was the *U-976,* commanded by Raimund Tiesler, who sailed from St. Nazaire on March 20. On the sixth day, when she was on the surface outside the port meeting her three German escort vessels, a flight of six Mosquitos attached to British Squadron 248 attacked the group. Two of these Mosquitos, piloted by Douglas J. Turner and Aubrey H. Hillard, were fitted with experimental 57mm cannons (code-named "Tsetse").† Turner attacked *U-976* four times with Tsetse, Hillard one time. These attacks destroyed the U-boat, killed four men, and badly wounded three others. The German surface escorts rescued Tiesler and forty-eight survivors and took them into St. Nazaire. Tiesler returned to Germany to command a big electro boat.

Another of these four recalled boats had a close call. She was the *U-960,* commanded by Günther Heinrich, which sailed from La Pallice on March 19. While inbound to La Pallice on March 27 with another U-boat and eight surface escorts,

---

* After the 7,400-ton *Empire Housman,* the 7,200-ton *Sumner I. Kimball,* and the 1,735-ton *Margit.*

† These hush-hush aircraft were on secret detached duty from British Squadron 618.

another flight of six Mosquitos, including Turner and Hillard with their 57mm Tsetse cannons, attacked *U-960,* wounding Heinrich and fourteen of his men, four seriously. Other Mosquitos attacked the surface escorts. The *U-960* survived this attack and limped into La Pallice that same day.

At the time Control issued the orders to dissolve group *Preussen,* it consisted of about a dozen boats. Eight continued independent patrols and returned to France in the period from March 27 to May 20.

One of these ex-*Preussen* boats, the *U-302,* commanded by Herbert Sickel, found a convoy on April 6. It was eastbound Slow Convoy 156. In a rare and notable success of this period of the Atlantic naval war, Sickel got around the escort and sank two Norwegian ships, the 6,200-ton tanker *South America* and the 3,500-ton freighter *Ruth I.* In the counterattack, the British frigate *Swale* of Escort Group B-5, commanded by Richard C. Boyle, sank *U-302* with depth charges and Hedgehogs, with the loss of all hands. Control knew nothing of this only successful attack by a U-boat in the North Atlantic in April, nor of the loss of the boat.

Three other ex-*Preussen* boats were lost, all to Allied surface ships using depth charges or Hedgehogs.

- On April 8, the sloops *Crane* and *Cygnet* of British Support Group 7, a hunter-killer unit, found and sank the *U-962,* commanded by Ernst Liesberg. There were no survivors.
- On April 17, two American warships, the minesweeper *Swift* and the *PC 619,* which were escorting a small coastal convoy in the approaches to the English Channel, sank the *U-986,* commanded by Karl-Ernst Kaiser, still on her maiden patrol and fitted with the antiaircraft rocket array. As a consequence of this loss, Control did not receive a comprehensive combat evaluation of the rockets, which in any case were not pursued.
- On April 22, the Canadian Support Group 9 (three frigates, one upgraded corvette) destroyed the *U-311,* commanded by Joachim Zander, who had sunk the tanker *Seakay* from convoy CU 17. At the time the British credited the kill of *U-311* to an aircraft of Canadian Squadron 423. However, in a postwar reassessment in 1986, it reassigned the credit to the Canadian frigates *Swansea* and *Matane.**

Two other ex-*Preussen* boats had close calls. Off Brest on March 26, unidentified Allied aircraft hit the inbound *U-963,* commanded by Karl Boddenberg, who had just met his escort. Boddenberg reported that nine men were wounded, two badly. The boat entered Brest the next day, March 27. Off Gibraltar that same day, unidentified Allied aircraft hit the *U-255,* commanded by Erich Harms, who had been ordered into the Mediterranean. Forced to abort, he reached the approaches to St. Nazaire on April 11, whereupon fifteen Mosquitos attacked the U-boat and her escort. Ten JU-88s in turn attacked the Mosquitos and claimed five destroyed for the loss of three German planes. *U-255* reached St. Nazaire with only slight damage.

---

* In the five months since November 20, 1943, this was the ninth U-boat kill in which Canadian forces played a sole, dominant, or conspicuous role: the VIIs *U-257, U-283, U-448, U-575, U-625,* and *U-744,* and the IXC40s *U-536* and *U-845* being the previous eight.

The Atlantic Convoy War Concluded

By early April 1944, the primary task of U-boat Control was to prepare three U-boat commands to repel Allied invaders. These were the Arctic force, the southern Norway force (group *Mitte,* or Central), and the Atlantic force (group *Landwirt).* The aim was to build to thirty ready boats in the Arctic, another thirty in group *Mitte,* and about fifty in group *Landwirt.*

In effect, these U-boats were to play strictly defensive roles. Although the experience of war had demonstrated time and again that U-boats were virtually useless against alert, strongly escorted amphibious forces,* the U-boat force had no option but to do the best job it could. It was still Hitler's "first line of defense" against invasion in the west. Equipped with snorts and the supposedly infallible T-5 torpedoes, the U-boats might delay and cause decisive damage to the invaders.

Only eleven U-boats sailed into the Atlantic in the month of April. Two were sent to the Mediterranean. Of the remaining nine, six were new boats from Norway that were to report weather, then put into France, five of these Type VIIs to reinforce group *Landwirt.* Three other boats sailed from France to serve as weather reporters, radio decoys to disguise the U-boat withdrawal from the North Atlantic, or for other purposes. These were to join about ten ex-*Preussen* boats still on patrols, including the two VII snort boats *U-267* and *U-667.*

All the boats on patrol in the North Atlantic in April confronted saturation air patrols mounted by land-based and "jeep" carrier aircraft. Control logged about twenty different reported aircraft attacks on U-boats in April. Two resulted in U-boat sinkings, as will be described. However, the few boats with the *Fliege* radar detector, which could operate in the centimetric-wavelength band, reported good results, doubtless averting several other aircraft attacks.

On the other hand, reports from the boats at sea about the automatic, rapid-fire 37mm flak gun continued to be negative. By April, the OKM had established that some elements of the gun's automatic-feed mechanism had been manufactured of nonrustproof metal, a striking stupidity. Until rustproof replacement parts could be made, tested, and distributed, the gun was not in the least reliable and, in almost all cases, had to be loaded by hand, an intolerable handicap while under enemy air attack. Besides that, more boats reported "rapid decay" of some of the gun's supposedly exotic ammunition.

Owing to the steady flow of Enigma decrypts, Allied intelligence on U-boat movements in April was exceptionally thorough. Ironically, the Germans unintentionally helped Allied codebreakers by adding a new *Stichwort* procedure to take effect on April 13. In order that recently sailed boats could supply the boats already at sea with material for the change, a dozen or more rendezvous had to take place,

---

* For example, the battle of Norway in the spring of 1940; North Africa in the fall of 1942; Sicily and Salerno in the summer of 1943; Anzio in early 1944. American submarines had failed in similar defensive roles in the Philippines in 1941–1942 and at Midway Island and the Aleutian chain in the summer of 1942.

arranged in the current Enigma. In one instance, the rendezvous failed owing to foul weather, and Control had to radio the new material to that boat in current Enigma, doubtless a windfall for Allied codebreakers.

The two boats that sailed to the Mediterranean in April were the *U-731* and *U-960,* commanded by Alexander von Keller and Günther Heinrich, respectively. Heinrich got through (see below) but von Keller, a new skipper, did not. On the afternoon of May 15, two Catalinas of U.S. Navy Squadron VP 63, fitted with MAD gear, detected von Keller in *U-731.* The pilots, Matthias J. Vopatek and H. L. Worrell, attacked with retrorockets and, per doctrine, summoned British surface craft. The sloop *Kilmarnock,* corvette *Aubrietia,* and ASW trawler *Black Fly* responded, and *Kilmarnock,* commanded by K. B. Brown, blasted *U-731* with depth charges and Hedgehogs that destroyed the boat. There were no survivors.

Apart from the attack of *U-302* on Slow Convoy 156 and by *U-621* on a destroyer, as related, three U-boats patrolling in the eastern North Atlantic had noteworthy encounters with enemy convoys or ships.

- The new VII *U-385,* commanded by Hans-Guido Valentiner, age twenty-three, which sailed from Norway on April 5 fitted with *Fliege* search radar. Southbound near Iceland on April 13, Valentiner attacked a "destroyer" of a small convoy with a T-5; it missed. Two days later he fired a three-torpedo salvo at what he described as an *"Empress"*-class ocean liner, but in fact it was the monster liner *Queen Mary.* He claimed "two hits" and "two boiler explosions," but *Queen Mary* was not hit. On that day and at that place she reported a heavy "underwater explosion," perhaps a premature or some other torpedo malfunction. On April 29, Valentiner shot a T-5 and reported a hit on a "destroyer" near the western mouth of North Channel, but it was not confirmed either.
- The VII snort boat *U-667,* formerly of group *Preussen,* commanded by Heinrich Schroeteler. On April 16, Schroeteler came upon a hunter-killer group and shot a T-5 at a "destroyer escort." It missed and the group chased *U-667* for twelve hours. The snort allowed Schroeteler to refresh the air in the boat during the chase and, finally, to escape. When he returned to France on May 19, he had high praise for the snort but cautioned that extensive drills were required to master snorting.
- The VII *U-473,* commanded by Heinz Sternberg, which sailed from Lorient on April 24, carrying a number of electronic specialists who were to test radars and radar detectors. On the night of April 28, a Halifax of British Squadron 58, fitted with a Leigh Light, found *U-473* on radar. The Halifax dropped seven depth charges but Sternberg repelled the plane and continued onward. The next day, April 29, a Wellington of British Squadron 304 attacked the boat with six depth charges, but still Sternberg did not turn back. On May 3, when he happened upon the eastbound tanker convoy CU 22, he attacked boldly and hit the 1,400-ton American destroyer escort *Donnell* with a T-5. The explosion blew off the stern of this ship, killing twenty-nine men and wounding another twenty-five. Two other destroyer escorts, *Reeves* and *Hopping,* towed *Donnell* to Londonderry, where she was converted to an accommodations (barracks) vessel. Sternberg erroneously reported a T-5 "miss."

Of the nine boats that sailed for patrols in the North Atlantic in April, five were lost in April and early May. In brief:

• The new VII *U-342,* commanded by Albert Hossenfelder, age thirty-six, which sailed from Bergen on April 3 for weather-reporting duties en route to France. On the morning of April 17, a Canso (Catalina) of the Iceland-based Canadian Squadron 162, piloted by Thomas Charles Cooke, spotted *U-342* on the surface and attacked out of the sun. Hossenfelder saw the Canso coming and put up heavy flak, but Cooke pressed on and dropped three close depth charges and riddled the superstructure with machine-gun fire. A few moments later, Cooke saw a "violent" explosion on the bow superstructure that destroyed the boat with the loss of all hands. The airmen reported that oil and all kinds of wreckage came to the surface (pieces of wood, cylindrical objects) but no bodies.

• The IXC40 *U-193,* which sailed from Lorient on April 23 to report weather and to serve as a provisional refueler if needed. This was the boat that had been driven into El Ferrol for repairs on February 10 at the end of her prior patrol, and finally reached Lorient on February 25. She had a new skipper, the lawyer Ulrich Abel, the former first watch officer of *U-154,* who had denounced his skipper, Oskar Kusch, for sedition and defeatism, resulting in a court-martial and death sentence.

In Biscay in the early hours of April 28, the sixth day out, the Admiralty believed, *U-193* came under air attack. A Leigh Light–equipped Wellington of British Squadron 612, piloted by the Australian C. G. (Max) Punter, a veteran of the U-boat wars, supposedly got *U-193* on radar and from wave-top level, dropped a salvo of depth charges that destroyed the boat. Punter reported "about ten small bluish lights in the water," evidently illuminants on the life jackets of the German survivors. However, Niestlé doubts this kill and lists the cause of the loss of *U-193* as unknown.

• The IXC40 *U-846,* commanded by Berthold Hashagen, which sailed on its second patrol from Lorient on April 29. On May 2, a Halifax of British Squadron 58 attacked *U-846* in Biscay, but Hashagen's gunners shot it down. Six days out, in the early hours of May 4, a Leigh Light–equipped Wellington of Canadian Squadron 407, piloted by L. J. Bateman, made radar contact with *U-846* in bright moonlight. Attacking into heavy flak, Bateman let go six depth charges. Nothing more was ever heard from the boat, which presumably was sunk at this time and place with the loss of all hands.

• The VII *U-473,* commanded by Heinz Sternberg, who hit and wrecked the American destroyer escort *Donnell* on May 3 with a T-5. As a result of this sinking, Western Approaches directed Johnny Walker's Support Group 2, recently returned from Kola Inlet, to hunt down *U-473.* In the early hours of May 5, one of the five warships of this unit, the sloop *Wild Goose,* got a solid sonar contact and dropped ten depth charges. Thereafter she and the other four ships, the sloops *Starling* and *Wren,* commanded by S.R.J. Woods, and the frigates *Bentley* and *Gore,* carried out a relentless hunt, dropping a grand total of 345 depth charges during the day, set at fifty to seven hundred feet. However, Sternberg went deep (656 feet), and none of these missiles did any harm.

Shortly after midnight on May 6, Sternberg surfaced to air the boat, charge the batteries, and run away on the diesels. The sloops *Starling, Wild Goose,* and *Wren,* which were waiting, opened fire with main batteries. Sternberg rang up full speed and shot a bow T-5 at *Wren,* which missed by about ten feet. From the bridge, Sternberg ordered the three other bow tubes made ready to be fired, but before he could shoot, Allied gunfire killed him. The other Germans abandoned ship and set scuttling charges. The sloops recovered thirty of fifty-three Germans. The prisoners alleged that the upper works of *U-473* were camouflaged with an exotic gray paint, "which was intended to absorb infrared."

- The VII *U-765,* commanded by Werner Wendt, who had sailed from Bergen on April 3. On May 3, the night *U-473* hit and wrecked *Donnell,* Wendt in *U-765,* a weather reporter, was not far away.* After DFing his transmissions, Western Approaches directed British Support Group 5, composed of the "jeep" carrier *Vindex* and a screen of six frigates, to the scene to mount a hunt to exhaustion. Swordfish from *Vindex* and four frigates, *Aylmer, Bickerton, Bligh,* and *Keats,* DFed *U-765*'s weather reports, closed, and engaged her.

Wendt fired a T-5 at *Bickerton* or *Bligh* but it missed. After dark he surfaced to run away but a Swordfish located the boat, illuminated it with a searchlight, and forced Wendt to dive again. When he resurfaced at dawn on May 6 to air the boat and charge batteries, the frigates and a Swordfish pounced, drove the boat under, and depth-charged it relentlessly. Again forced to the surface, Wendt abandoned ship and scuttled. The British rescued eleven of the forty-eight crew, including Wendt and his first watch officer, Alexander Gelhaus, age twenty-one. The prisoners revealed that owing to the acute scarcity of copper in the Third Reich, the torpedo tubes of *U-765* were made of steel, which rusted continually, and the diesels of this and all succeeding new U-boats had no reversing gear.

- The VII *U-955,* commanded by Hans-Heinrich Baden, which sailed from Bergen on April 15, in part to report weather. On April 29, Baden's radio receiver failed and therefore he did not get new orders from Control to join the Arctic force. Control was therefore surprised when on May 5, Baden reported that he had shot down an attacking B-24 in the Atlantic south of Iceland. At the conclusion of this patrol, the boat continued to France and destruction, as will be described.

Another boat had a close call at this time. She was the ex-*Preussen* weather reporter *U-672,* commanded by Ulf Lawaetz, who was planting *Thetis* radar decoys in the Bay of Biscay. Shortly after midnight on April 24, a Leigh Light–equipped B-24 of British Squadron 120, piloted by L. T. Taylor, found *U-672* on radar and attacked using the light, dropping six depth charges that evidently fell wide. About twelve hours later, near midday, a Sunderland of Canadian Squadron 423, piloted by F. G. Fellows, found the boat on the surface in the afternoon, and attacked into heavy flak. Fellows dropped six depth charges that hurt *U-672,* but the Sunderland incurred such severe damage from flak or her own depth charges that Fellows was forced to abort immediately. Lawaetz dived *U-672* and escaped, continued planting *Thetis,* and returned to St. Nazaire on May 12.

Only two U-boats sailed for patrols in the North Atlantic during May. Both were new Type IXs assigned to report weather. The IXC40 *U-534,* commanded by Herbert Nollau, age twenty-eight, left Bergen on May 8 and put into Bordeaux ninety-eight days later, August 13. The IXC40 *U-857,* commanded by Rudolf Pre-

* Some accounts erroneously credit the *U-765* with the hit on *Donnell.*

mauer, age twenty-five, left Kiel on May 9 and also put into Bordeaux on August 13. Neither sank any Allied ships.

All told, Control mounted seventy-eight U-boat patrols to the North and Middle Atlantic in the five months from January 1 to June 1, 1944. These boats sank or wrecked eleven Allied vessels, four merchant ships for 21,854 tons* and seven small warships.† Including three attempting to get into the Mediterranean, the Germans lost thirty-seven of the U-boats (47 percent) that sailed to the North and Middle Atlantic in this period, manned by about 1,900 submariners. Of these, 332 were captured from eleven different boats.‡

The Arctic

In compliance with Hitler's orders, in January and February 1944, Dönitz increased the Arctic U-boat force to thirty VIIs, basing mainly at Trondheim and Narvik. This force, still commanded by Rudolph Peters, was organized into Combat Flotillas 11 and 13.§ The veterans of these waters and some of the new arrivals achieved minor successes in the semidark Arctic "days" of late January 1944, but not much thereafter.

After the destruction of *Scharnhorst,* the Admiralty considered the Arctic to be relatively safe for Murmansk convoys. Therefore, when the first section of the January convoy JW 56A, composed of twenty merchant ships, sailed from Loch Ewe, Scotland, on February 12, the Home Fleet was not required to provide a battleship covering force, a welcome relief. That convoy ran into a brutal winter storm that forced it to abort into Akurey, Iceland. Less five damaged merchant ships, the convoy resailed on February 21, guarded by eleven escorts. The second section of this convoy, JW 56B, comprised of sixteen merchant ships with thirteen escorts, sailed from Loch Ewe at nearly the same time, January 22. A cruiser force (*Belfast, Kent, Norfolk*) of the Home Fleet provided distant cover for both sections.

The Germans deployed fifteen U-boats to intercept the first section of the convoy, JW 56A. All but three of the boats were newly arrived in the Arctic. They and the older boats were armed with T-5 homing torpedoes and twin 20mm and the unreliable automatic, rapid-fire 37mm flak guns. All had *Naxos* radar detectors and other new electronics, including improved passive sonar gear, capable of detecting a surface ship at a range of fifty miles. One boat, *U-957,* reported mechanical difficulties and requested dockyard facilities (in Trondheim) on her scheduled return.

* The IXD2 U-cruiser *U-859,* passing through the North Atlantic area, sank one other merchant ship for 6,300 tons, the Panamanian *Colin.*

† British *Asphodel, Gould, LST 362, Warwick, Woodpecker;* American *Donnell* and *Leopold.*

‡ *U-91, U-257,* snort boat *U-264, U-358, U-406, U-448, U-473,* snort boat *U-575, U-744, U-761, U-765.*

§ These flotillas were commanded by Hans Cohausz and Rolf Rüggeberg, respectively.

Fully aware of the U-boat deployments, the Admiralty diverted JW 56A to a northerly course to evade them. However, the northernmost boat in the line, *U-956,* commanded by Hans-Dieter Mohs, found JW 56A and gave the alarm. Running on the surface in Arctic darkness, other boats closed in for the kill on January 25 and 26.

In this group attack, eight U-boats shot ten T-5s as well as other torpedo types, such as FAT. They sank three 7,200-ton Liberty-type ships and damaged the British destroyer *Obdurate.* Joachim Franze in the new *U-278* got the American *Penelope Barker,* Klaus Becker in *U-360* hit the British *Fort Bellingham,* and Franz Saar in *U-957* finished her off to share credit. Hans Dunkelberg in the new *U-716* got the American *Andrew G. Curtin.* Becker in *U-360* also hit the *Obdurate,* which, however, survived and reached port.

The U-boats could not sustain the attack on JW 56A, but they were in position to strike the second section, JW 56B, on January 29 and 30. Nine boats shot twelve T-5s and other torpedoes at various ships. Only one boat had a success: Joachim France in the new *U-278,* who had sunk the Liberty ship *Penelope Barker* from JW 56A, hit and blew off the stern of the British destroyer *Hardy II* with a T-5. The British destroyer *Venus* rescued the crew and put down the wreck with a torpedo.

The U-boat skippers in these two attacks on JW 56 claimed many T-5 hits on destroyers and other sinkings that were not confirmed. Still confident that the T-5 was a war-decisive weapon, Control was only too willing to credit the claims. "That's a good job," Control radioed the boats on February 1, "keep it up!" Control credited a total of twenty-six hits or probable hits: seven destroyers and three merchant ships certainly sunk, three destroyers probably sunk, damage to six other merchant ships, and probable damage to six destroyers and one merchant ship. The confirmed results: the destroyers *Obdurate* and *Hardy II* hit, *Hardy II* fatally; three Liberty ships in JW 56A sunk.

One U-boat was lost in the second of these two battles. She was the new *U-314,* commanded by Georg-Wilhelm Basse. On January 30, the British destroyers *Meteor* and *Whitehall* in the escort of JW 56B destroyed her with depth charges and Hedgehogs. There were no German survivors.

The U-boat attacks on JW 56 rattled the Admiralty and concern for the safety of Murmansk convoys again mounted. That concern intensified when the British learned from Enigma decrypts that the German destroyers in Altenfiord had been put on two-hour notice. For these reasons and others, the Admiralty delayed the sailing of convoy RA 56, homebound from Kola Inlet, until the escorts of JW 56A were ready to return and could be added. That convoy, comprised of thirty-seven merchant ships and twenty-six escorts, sailed from Kola Inlet on February 2, evaded the U-boat lines, and reached Loch Ewe on February 11.

At the urging of Home Fleet commander Bruce Fraser, the Admiralty agreed to sail the next Murmansk convoy, JW 57, in one section and to provide it with a formidable escort. When it left Loch Ewe on February 23, JW 57 consisted of forty-two merchant ships. The close escort was comprised of the American-built British "jeep" carrier *Chaser,* light cruiser *Black Price,* and seventeen destroyers.

The British knew from Enigma decrypts that fourteen U-boats lay in wait for convoy JW 57. The Germans converged to attack on February 24. Six boats mounted assaults with T-5s. Only one got a hit: The new *U-990,* commanded by Hubert Nordheimer, sank the 2,000-ton British destroyer *Mahratta.* Other escorts rescued seventeen of her crew of about two hundred men; the rest perished in the sinking or in the frigid Arctic waters.

The escorts sank two U-boats during this encounter.

• On February 24, the old but skilled British destroyer *Keppel,* which had sunk *U-229* of group *Leuthen* the previous September, destroyed the *U-713,* commanded by Henri Gosejakob. There were no survivors.

• On the next day, February 25, an escorting Catalina of British Squadron 210, based in the Shetlands and piloted by Frank John French, found the *U-601,* commanded by Otto Hansen. French attacked into "inaccurate flak" and dropped two depth charges that destroyed the boat. French, who had been aloft for twelve hours, reported "eight to ten" Germans in the water and headed home. There were no survivors of this boat either.

The return convoy, RA 57, comprised of thirty-one merchant ships, sailed from Kola Inlet on March 2, protected by the "jeep" carrier *Chaser* and other escorts. As the British knew from Enigma decrypts, fifteen U-boats were deployed to intercept RA 57. The opposing forces met on March 4. Over the next forty-eight hours, five U-boats fired five T-5s and other torpedoes. Only one got a hit. The veteran *U-703,* commanded by Joachim Brünner, sank the empty 7,100-ton British freighter *Empire Tourist.*

In a notable performance during this Arctic encounter, Swordfish biplanes and Wildcats of Squadron 816 from the "jeep" carrier *Chaser* and a surface escort of the convoy sank three new U-boats in three days.

• On the first day, March 4, a *Chaser* Swordfish fitted with rockets found the *U-472,* commanded by Wolfgang-Friedrich von Forstner. The pilot, P. J. Beresford, damaged *U-472* with bombs and rockets and summoned help. The British destroyer *Onslaught,* commanded by A. Pleydell-Bouverie, destroyed the boat with gunfire. The *Onslaught* rescued von Forstner and twenty-nine of his men, who revealed that their flak guns were iced up and could not fire at the Swordfish and that they had shot a T-5 at *Onslaught* that missed.

• On the following day, March 5, *Chaser* launched Swordfish in spite of foul weather and heavy seas. One of these, piloted by J. F. Mason, found and sank the *U-366* commanded by Bruno Langenberg, the latest arrival in the Arctic. There were no survivors.

• On the third day, March 6, yet another Swordfish from *Chaser,* piloted by L.E.B. Bennett, sank a U-boat with depth charges and rockets. She was the *U-973,* commanded by Klaus Paepenmöller.* The British destroyer *Boadicea* recovered

---

* The *U-973* as well as *U-673* of the Arctic force were fitted with new Type VI conning towers that had a flat bandstand forward. Owing to the instability and displacement of fuel tanks in favor of greater ammo storage, the Type VI conning tower was declared unsatisfactory for the Atlantic U-boat force. The *U-362* of the same force had a similar conning tower, Type V.

the engineer, Franz Rudolf, and two enlisted men, but one of the latter died on board, leaving two prisoners. They asserted that most of the flak gunners and ammo passers had refused to carry out their duties. If true, it was a rare episode in the highly disciplined U-boat force.

Another boat was severely damaged. She was the *U-737,* commanded by Paul Brasack, age twenty-seven, who earlier had bombarded Allied facilities on Spitzbergen. On March 6, a B-24 of British Squadron 120, piloted by the Canadian Harold F. Kerrigan, found and attacked *U-737* in the face of intense and accurate flak. Kerrigan released six depth charges that damaged the U-boat, but the B-24 incurred two wounded and heavy damage, including the loss of two engines. Kerrigan limped home to a hero's reward, a DSO. Brasack aborted and limped into Hammerfest on March 12, terminating a voyage of fourteen days.

Enigma decrypts in mid-March revealed to the Allies that the battleship *Tirpitz,* apparently repaired, was undergoing trials in Altenfiord in northern Norway. Although other Enigma decrypts indicated that *Tirpitz* was probably not fully ready for combat, British authorities were compelled to take measures to protect the next Murmansk convoy, JW 58, against a possible *Tirpitz* raid.

That convoy of forty-nine merchant ships sailed from Loch Ewe on March 27. Its close escort was massive: the British-built "jeep" carrier *Activity* (seven Wildcats, three Swordfish), the American-built British "jeep" carrier *Tracker* (seven Wildcats, twelve Avengers), the British light cruiser *Diadem,* the old American light cruiser *Milwaukee* (in transit, a gift to Stalin in lieu of a share of the surrendered Italian fleet), twenty destroyers, four corvettes, and—in a radical change of mission—Johnny Walker's famous Support Group 2, consisting of five sloops. In total: thirty-three warships in the close escort.

In addition, the Admiralty deployed a huge British task force (Tungsten) to deal with *Tirpitz* during the passage of JW 58. This special force consisted of the battleships *Anson* and *Duke of York,* fleet carriers *Furious* (twenty-one Barracuda torpedo-bombers) and *Victorious* (twenty-one Barracudas), four American-built "jeep" carriers (*Emperor, Fencer, Pursuer, Searcher*), four cruisers (*Belfast, Jamaica, Royalist, Sheffield*), and fourteen destroyers.

From Enigma decrypts, the British knew that despite recent losses, the Arctic U-boat force numbered twenty-nine boats. Of these, sixteen were at sea to intercept JW 58 and thirteen were in port for voyage repairs, refits, or yard overhauls. In view of past successes with the "jeep" carriers in this area, the British welcomed an opportunity to deal the Arctic U-boat force a heavy setback.

The convoy escort delivered the first blow to the Germans on the night of March 29. Johnny Walker in the sloop *Starling* came upon the new *U-961,* commanded by Klaus Fischer, which had sailed from Bergen on March 25 to join the Atlantic U-boat force. It is possible that Fischer intended to attack Walker, but Walker's sonar operator picked up a solid contact and the ever-alert *Starling* attacked at once, firing two depth-charge salvos. These hit the mark, destroying *U-961* with all hands. A "stream" of wreckage and dead bodies rose to the surface to confirm yet another kill for this outstanding commander, warship, and crew.

Assisted by *Luftwaffe* spotters, twelve U-boats, organized into three four-boat groups (*Blitz, Hammer, Thor*), found JW 58 on April 1. Joined by five outbound boats—making a total of seventeen—these skippers carried out eighteen attacks over the next forty-eight hours, mostly firing T-5s. Not one attack succeeded. In return, British convoy escorts sank three more U-boats in three days.

- On April 1, Martlets and Avengers of British Squadron 846 from the "jeep" carrier *Tracker,* working with the destroyer *Beagle,* attacked a U-boat, thought to be the veteran *U-355,* commanded by Günter La Baume. Although these forces received wartime credit for a kill, Niestlé raises doubts and declares *U-355* lost to unknown causes.
- The next day, the destroyer *Keppel* sank the *U-360* with her Hedgehog. She was commanded by Klaus Becker, who had earlier damaged the British destroyer *Obdurate* and the Liberty ship *Fort Bellingham.* There were no German survivors.
- On the third day, April 3, a Swordfish of Squadron 819 from *Activity* and a Martlet-Avenger team of Squadron 846 from *Tracker* sank the new *U-288,* commanded by Willi Meyer. There were no survivors from this boat either.

Control was again generous in its assessments. Based on flash T-5 shooting reports, it calculated the Arctic U-boats had sunk "nine destroyers" and "probably" had sunk "four" others, a likely total of thirteen destroyers put down. In reality, no U-boat had sunk anything in convoy JW 58, which reached Kola Inlet on April 6. The escorts of this convoy had sunk four U-boats (*U-288, U-355, U-360, U-961*) and had shot down six German aircraft.

During the passage of JW 58, the big British task force struck at the *Tirpitz* in Altenfiord on April 3. The Barracuda torpedo-bombers from *Furious* and *Victorious* registered fourteen hits with 500- and 1,600-pound bombs. These bombs caused considerable damage to *Tirpitz*'s upper works and inflicted a total of 438 casualties (122 dead). As a result of this attack, *Tirpitz* was under repair—and out of action—for another three months.

Beginning in early April, the nearly constant Arctic daylight and the need to prepare for Overlord again forced the Admiralty to suspend Murmansk convoys. Two heavily escorted convoys, RA 58 (thirty-six empty merchant ships) and RA 59 (forty-five empty merchant ships), departed Kola Inlet on April 7 and 28. The U-boats attacked both convoys, shooting many torpedoes, but only one boat got a hit. She was the *U-711,* commanded by Hans-Günther Lange, who sank the American Liberty ship *William S. Thayer* in convoy RA 59 with a FAT on April 30.

The "jeep" carriers *Activity* and *Fencer* formed part of the heavy escort of the last homeward convoy, RA 59. Aircraft from *Fencer*'s Squadron 842 sank three more newly arrived Arctic U-boats on May 1 and 2. These were the new *U-277,* commanded by Robert Lübsen, age twenty-seven; the *U-674,* commanded by Harald Muhs, age twenty-four; and the new *U-959,* commanded by Friedrich Weitz, age twenty-four. There were no survivors of these boats.

Churchill had promised Stalin that the British would send 140 shiploads of armaments to Kola Inlet in the winter of 1943–44. In fact, the British sent 188 vessels, exceeding the pledge by forty-eight shiploads. In this campaign the U-boats sank only five merchant ships (three with cargoes and two returning empty), two British destroyers, *Hardy II* and *Mahratta,* and damaged British destroyer *Obdurate.*

At the peak, in the first five months of 1944, the Arctic U-boat force numbered thirty boats. In this campaign, British ASW forces sank twelve of these, plus the *U-961* en route from Norway to France.* Of the approximately 650 men on these thirteen boats, 311 survived, all to become POWs.

Throughout the war Dönitz repeatedly deplored the diversion of U-boats to the Arctic as a waste of naval assets. The outcome of those diversions in the winter of 1943–44 vividly proved his point. Moreover, to the ruinous U-boat losses must be added the loss of *Scharnhorst* and the second crippling of *Tirpitz.*

The Mediterranean

When he assumed command of the Mediterranean U-boat force in January 1944, *Ritterkreuz* holder Werner Hartmann established his headquarters in Château Costabelle, about fifteen miles outside of Toulon, France. The next man of importance in his chain of command was Gunter Jahn, crew of 1931, the chief of Combat Flotilla 29, who had won a *Ritterkreuz* while commanding *U-596.*

U-boat operations from Toulon, never less than hazardous, had become increasingly difficult. The possibility of Allied air raids staged from North Africa, Sicily, or Foggia, Italy, had compelled the Germans to draft plans for the construction of a bombproof U-boat pen like those at the five Atlantic bases. Pending the completion of this structure, the Germans had to refit the Mediterranean boats at open docks exposed to air attack. Moreover, the citizenry of Toulon was so hostile to the Germans that no U-boat men wore uniforms on liberty or leave in that area, according to one Allied intelligence report. The great increase of Allied air and surface-ship ASW patrols in 1944 made successful operations at sea almost impossible.

The Mediterranean U-boat force, consisting of thirteen boats, achieved nothing in January 1944. Army Air Forces bombers destroyed one boat, the *U-81,* commanded by Johann-Otto Krieg, during a raid on Pola on January 9. A new arrival, *U-343,* commanded by Wolfgang Rahn, was very nearly sunk two nights after getting through Gibraltar Strait.

Late in the evening of January 8, a Wellington of British Squadron 179, piloted by W.F.M. Davidson, found *U-343* by radar and a full moon. Attacking into heavy flak, Davidson dropped six depth charges. Riddled by flak, the Wellington crashed into the sea, throwing Davidson clear, but the rest of the airmen perished. Davidson found a raft, climbed in, and was later rescued by Allied forces.

---

* On April 19, the new Norwegian submarine *Ula* (British-built ex-*Varne*), commanded by R. M. Sars, sank Heinz Wolff in the new *U-974* as he was setting off from Bergen to France. German forces rescued Wolff and seven of his crew.

Attracted by the flak tracers, a Catalina of British Squadron 202, piloted by John Finch, arrived and also attacked *U-343,* flying into heavy flak. Finch dropped six depth charges, but his aircraft, too, was riddled by flak and he had to abort. The damage to *U-343* was sufficient that Rahn had to put into Toulon for repairs.

Three new boats, including *U-343,* had arrived in January and another three came in February. These arrivals increased the force to nineteen boats. However, on February 4, an Army Air Forces raid on Toulon damaged three boats, Rahn's newly arrived *U-343* and the *U-380* and *U-642.*

When the Allies landed an amphibious force at Anzio (Shingle) on January 22, 1944, all available U-boats put out on near-hopeless missions to repel the invaders. These boats were armed with T-5s and new electronics, such as the *Naxos* radar detector. Some of these boats had successes. In brief:

- The *Ritterkreuz* holder Horst-Arno Fenski in the experienced *U-410* sank three Allied vessels in February: the British light cruiser *Penelope,* the 1,600-ton American *LST 348,* and the 7,200-ton British Liberty ship *Fort St. Nicolas.*
- Paul Siegmann in the recently arrived *U-230* sank two 1,600-ton British warships in February: the *LST 305* and the *LST 418.*
- Max Dobbert in the newly arrived *U-969* hit two 7,200-ton American Liberty ships near Bône, Algeria, the *George Cleeve* and the *Peter Skene Ogden.* Although both vessels managed to beach, both were declared a total loss.
- The veteran *U-407,* commanded by a new skipper, Hubertus Korndörfer, age twenty-four, hit and damaged the 6,200-ton British tanker *Ensis.*

Remarkably, no Allied ASW unit sank a Mediterranean U-boat at sea in January or February 1944. Thus the force remained at a strength, on paper, of nineteen boats. Three more boats arrived from the Atlantic in March,* to raise the force to twenty-two.

Three U-boats achieved successes in March.

- Oskar Curio in the recently arrived *U-952* sank the 7,200-ton American Liberty ship *William B. Woods* off the southeast coast of Sicily.
- Waldemar Mehl, third skipper of the veteran *U-371* (the first VII to enter the Mediterranean), sank two ships off the coast of North Africa near Bougie from the fast convoy SNF 17, outbound from Naples. These were the 5,000-ton American freighter *Maiden Creek* and the 17,000-ton Dutch troopship *Dempo.* The last sank slowly and the loss of life was slight. For these and past successes Mehl earned a *Ritterkreuz.*†
- Peter Gerlach, new skipper of the veteran *U-223,* sank a British destroyer in a hunter-killer group searching north of Sicily. She was the 1,900-ton *Laforey,* which had attacked *U-223,* as will be described.

The Allies destroyed five U-boats in the Mediterranean in March:

---

* The *U-421,* commanded by Hans Kolbus; the *U-466,* commanded by Gerhard Thäter; the *U-471,* commanded by Friedrich Kloevekorn.

† At the time of the award, his confirmed score, all on *U-371* in the Mediterranean, was nine ships sunk for 41,317 tons, including the American destroyer *Bristol,* the British ASW trawler *Jura,* and the 700-ton British minecraft *Hythe,* plus damage to four ships for 28,072 tons.

• On March 10, off Cagliari, Sardinia, the British ASW trawler *Mull,* commanded by R. R. Simpson, sank the newly arrived *U-343,* commanded by Wolfgang Rahn. There were no survivors.

• On the same day, off Anzio, four British *Hunt*-class destroyers of a hunter-killer group found the recently arrived *U-450,* commanded by Kurt Böhme. Two of the warships, *Brecon* and *Exmoor,* attacked "doubtful" sonar contacts with depth charges. In fact, they were echoes from *U-450.* The missiles caused such heavy damage and flooding that Böhme was forced to surface.

When the boat popped up, *Brecon* and *Exmoor* opened fire with guns and Böhme abandoned ship and scuttled. *Brecon* and another British destroyer, *Urchin,* which joined the hunt late, fished out all fifty-one crew of *U-450.* The Admiralty credited the kill to this hunter-killer group, which also included *Blankney* and *Blencathra.*

• On the next day, March 11, the U.S. Army Air Forces mounted yet another raid on Toulon. The bombs demolished two U-boats: the *U-380,* commanded by Albrecht Brandi, who wore Oak Leaves on his *Ritterkreuz,* and the *U-410,* commanded by the *Ritterkreuz* holder Horst-Arno Fenski, who had only just sunk the British light cruiser *Penelope.* Both of these celebrity skippers elected to continue the fight at sea. Brandi took over the newly arrived *U-967* (his third command); Fenski got the veteran *U-371* from the latest *Ritterkreuz* winner, Waldemar Mehl, who returned to Germany.

• In the early hours of March 29, a three-ship British hunter-killer group searching north of Sicily found by sonar the *U-223,* commanded by Peter Gerlach. The three destroyers, *Laforey, Tumult,* and *Ulster,* commenced a relentless chase that lasted about twenty hours. During the day the group was reinforced by three other British destroyers (*Blencathra, Hambleton, Wilton*), two American destroyers (*Ericsson, Kearny*), and three American PCs *(264, 556, 558).* In this hunt, the various Allied warships carried out twenty-two separate depth-charge attacks, but Gerlach went very deep (722 feet) and the boat survived.

Among others, the biggest problems for Gerlach and his crew were the lack of oxygen and battery power. Finally, after about twenty-five hours submerged, Gerlach surfaced in darkness, aired the boat, and tried to creep away on his diesels, charging batteries. Four British destroyers (*Blencathra, Hambleton, Laforey, Tumult*) detected *U-223* and opened fire with guns. Thus trapped, Gerlach shot a T-5 at *Laforey,* which hit and blew it up. The other ships rescued only sixty-nine of *Laforey*'s crew; 189 men perished.

Concluding that *U-223* was doomed, Gerlach ordered the crew to assemble on deck in life jackets and abandon ship. The engineer, Ernst Sheid, age twenty-one, who set the scuttling charges, was the last man out of the boat. Skipper Gerlach told Sheid that he, Gerlach, was "no good without his boat" and elected to go down with her. While the boat was under way at full speed, Sheid and the others leaped over the side. As the destroyers hammered the boat with gunfire, it suddenly circled back through the men in the water. Her propellers and the gunfire probably killed many Germans. *Blencathra, Hambleton,* and *Tumult* found only twenty-seven of the fifty Germans, including engineer Sheid.

A senior British naval officer in the Mediterranean sent the following signal to all the ships which participated in this hunt:

> The destruction of *U-223* this morning was a magnificent example of skilful and determined hunting and reflects great credit on all who took part. I feel sure you will mourn with me the loss of H.M.S. *Laforey,* leader of the attack, at the moment of victory.

In April, the Mediterranean U-boat force was reinforced by one more boat from the Atlantic.* However, two more boats were lost in April, reducing the force to fifteen. One of the losses in April was the recent arrival *U-455,* commanded by Hans-Martin Scheibe. Some time after April 6, she disappeared without a trace and her loss remains a mystery.

The other U-boat loss in April was a recent arrival, the *U-421,* commanded by Hans Kolbus. On April 29, the Army Air Forces mounted another big raid on Toulon—480 bombers this time—which destroyed that boat, moored at a pier, and for the second time damaged the *U-642,* commanded by Herbert Brünning.

The Mediterranean boats achieved only two confirmed successes in April. Off Alexandria, the veteran *U-407,* commanded since January by Hubertus Korndörfer, attacked the heavily guarded inbound convoy UGS 37 (sixty merchant ships and six LSTs). He hit two 7,200-ton American Liberty ships. One, *Meyer London,* sank. The other, *Thomas G. Masaryk,* was towed into Alexandria, but was declared a total loss.

Among the many preparations to repel the Allied invasion of Occupied France, the Germans had initiated a little-known project to build "small battle units," developed by a German admiral, Hellmuth Heye. These armed craft included one-man "chariots," one-man "midget" submarines, two-man "midget" submarines, and little radio-controlled speedboats.

The Germans mass-produced two types of "chariots," *Neger*† and *Marder.* These consisted of two G7e (electric) torpedoes, mounted one atop the other. The operator "rode" the upper ("mother") torpedo, which had a cockpit with a plastic dome in place of a warhead and released the lower ("child") live torpedo at the target. The *Marder* (Marten) was a slightly larger version of the *Neger.* The Germans produced approximately two hundred *Neger*s and three hundred *Marder*s. A third prototype, *Hai* (Shark), was not put into production.

The one-man midget submarines *Biber* (Beaver) and *Molch* (Salamander) were infinitely more complex. Both carried two live torpedoes and both could dive like a U-boat and run surfaced or submerged. For surface cruising, the *Biber* had a gasoline engine. The *Molch* was all-electric. The Germans produced 324 *Biber*s and

---

* The *U-960,* commanded by Günter Heinrich.

† *Neger* (literally "nigger") was a racial slur and wordplay on the name of the designer, Richard Mohr, whose surname means "Moor."

383 *Molch*s, but these little craft proved to be too complex for one man to manage and they were not very seaworthy.

More sophisticated yet were the two-man midget submarines *Hecht* (Pike) and *Seehund* (Seal), which bore U-boat designations. The thirty-four-foot, 12-ton *Hecht* carried one torpedo or limpet mines. The Germans built fifty-three *Hecht*s (*U-2111* to *U-2113* and *U-2251* to *U-2300*), but all were relegated to school boats. The slightly larger thirty-nine-foot, 15-ton *Seehund* carried two torpedoes or mines. The Germans planned to produce one thousand *Seehund*s but completed only 285 (*U-5501* to *U-5786*) before the end of the war.

The least sophisticated of the "small battle units" was the little radio-controlled speedboat *Linse* (Lentil). About fifteen feet long, built of wood, these boats were armed with a 900-pound explosive charge. Working in pairs, volunteers steered these two flimsy boats close to the target, then dived overboard. A third "mother" or "pilot" speedboat picked up the drivers and steered the two pilotless boats onward to the target by means of radio controls.

The first combat use of "small battle units" took place in the Mediterranean on the morning of April 21, 1944. Thirty-seven one-man "mother-child" *Neger* "chariots" set off from a German-held beach in Italy near the besieged Allied enclave at Anzio to attack shipping off Nettuno. Fourteen *Neger*s beached on a sandbar and were abandoned. The other twenty-three mounted attacks but none had any success. Only thirteen of the thirty-seven returned to the launching beach. A British report on the interrogation of the captured German survivors stated:

> Prisoners were all young, their ages varying from 17 to 22 years. None of them exceeded 5 feet 8 inches in height* and all were very fit. They were found to be normally intelligent and security conscious. All had been volunteers for service in this new arm.

By May 1, the Mediterranean U-boat force was engaged in a losing fight for survival. Because of the urgent need to amass all available VIIs in Norway and France to repel Allied invaders, Berlin had decreed that no more were to go to the Mediterranean. Those boats of the remaining fifteen that were in shape to mount patrols confronted ever-greater ASW measures and, owing to the increased number of Allied ASW ships for hunter-killer groups, the probability of hunts to exhaustion, like that which destroyed *U-223*.

The veteran Mediterranean boat *U-371,* commanded by *Ritterkreuz* holder Horst-Arno Fenski (from the *U-410,* destroyed in an air raid), sailed from Toulon on April 23 to patrol the coast of Africa near Algiers. Like Fenski, most of the other fifty-two Germans of the crew were from *U-410.* However, first watch officer Mueller, who joined the boat for this patrol, was new. He had lived in California as a youth and had attended Los Angeles Junior High School.

While Fenski was on the surface charging batteries in the early hours of May 3

* Probably so chosen because they could fit inside the tiny cockpit with the rigid plastic dome.

near Bougie, he came upon a huge convoy bound for the States. This was GUS 38 (107 empty merchant ships) guarded by fourteen escorts. Fenski dived and fired a T-5 from his stern tube at a "destroyer." This hit a Coast Guard–manned American destroyer escort, *Menges,* killing thirty-one men, wounding twenty-five others, and wrecking the stern section. The British tug *Aspirant* and Free French tug *Bombardier* towed *Menges* into Bougie, and later the American Navy tug *Carib* towed her to New York.*

Fenski went deep and crept toward the coast. Other escorts got *U-371* on sonar and pounced, dropping countless depth charges that caused damage and flooding. The boat had dived without a full charge, so the battery power quickly seeped away. In spite of the heavy flooding, Fenski eased down to 757 feet and lay doggo on the bottom the whole day and late into the night. In the early hours of May 4, when the water inside *U-371* was "knee deep," Fenski broke the boat out of the mud and surfaced.

Six Allied warships by that time had gathered at the scene. These included two American destroyer escorts, *Joseph E. Campbell* and *Pride* (another Coast Guard–manned warship), the American minesweeper *Sustain,* the British destroyer *Blankney,* and two Free French destroyers, *L'Alcyon* and *Senegalais.* These vessels closed on the fleeing *U-371* in the dark with guns firing. In desperation, Fenski fired a stern T-5, which hit and damaged *Senegalais* and killed forty-nine of the 179 men on board. She survived, however, and her sister ship *L'Alcyon* towed her into Bougie.

With no hope of escape, Fenski ordered his crew to gather on deck, abandon ship, and scuttle. The engineer, Ferdnand Ritschel, and a rating went below to open ballast-tank vents and were never seen again. The American minesweeper *Sustain,* destroyer escort *Campbell,* and other American vessels picked up forty-six survivors, including Fenski, and took them to Algiers. *Senegalais* picked up three Germans and took them into Bougie. Three Germans perished.

The convoy, GUS 38, continued westward toward Gibraltar. In the early hours of May 5, the celebrity skipper Albrecht Brandi, in his newly acquired command, *U-967,* fired a T-5 and hit another of the warships, the American destroyer escort *Fechteler.* She blew up, broke amidships, and was gone in thirty minutes. The destroyer escort *Laning* and other vessels rescued 186 men (twenty-six wounded) from *Fechteler;* twenty-nine men perished.

When Brandi returned to Toulon from this patrol, he claimed he had sunk two "destroyers" and a 5,000-ton freighter. However, only the destroyer escort *Fechteler* was confirmed. Even so, Hitler and Dönitz bestowed yet another high honor on Brandi: Swords to his *Ritterkreuz* with Oak Leaves. This award placed Brandi in an elite circle of German submariners, consisting of Otto Kretschmer, Wolfgang Lüth, Reinhard Suhren, and Erich Topp.

At the time of this high award, Brandi's claims were impressive indeed:

---

* Remarkably, naval technicians grafted the stern of the destroyer escort *Holder,* which lost her bow in the Mediterranean in a fight with the *Luftwaffe,* to the bow of *Menges* to make one complete ship. *Menges* returned to Atlantic escort duty in November 1944.

twenty-six ships sunk for about 100,000 tons and thirteen ships for about 100,000 tons damaged. The claimed sunk included ten important warships: two light cruisers and eight destroyers. Inasmuch as ships and tonnage sunk in the Mediterranean were doubled for award purposes and warships sunk added bonus credits, Brandi easily qualified for the Swords. However, his actual (or confirmed) sinkings continued to be startlingly less: for the entire war a total of only twelve ships for about 32,000 tons. Of that dozen, only four were classified as warships: two destroyer escorts (the 1,050-ton British *Puckeridge* and the 1,300-ton American *Fechteler*), a minelayer (the 2,650-ton British *Welshman*), and an ocean tug (the 810-ton British *St. Issey*).

Nine days later, at about 4:00 A.M., May 14, the *Ritterkreuz* holder Siegfried Koitschka in the veteran *U-616* came upon the next westbound convoy, GUS 39, off Cape Tenez between Algiers and Oran. He shot T-5s and hit and damaged two British ships in ballast, the 10,600-ton tanker *G. S. Walden* and the 7,200-ton Liberty ship *Fort Fidler.*

Four modern American warships of the convoy escort fell out to hunt the U-boat. These were the destroyer *Hilary P. Jones* and the destroyer escorts *Bostwick, Bronstein,* and *Vance,* the last manned by a Coast Guard crew. After an eight-hour hunt, the *Hilary P. Jones* got a sonar contact (shortly after noon), but her two attacks produced no results.

During that afternoon, British naval authorities launched "Operation Swamp,"* a relentless hunt for *U-616.* For that purpose, *Hilary P. Jones* of the convoy remained at the scene. She was joined by two American hunter-killer groups, one of three destroyers (*Gleaves, Macomb, Nields*) and another of four destroyers (*Ellyson, Emmons, Hambleton, Rodman*), plus numerous Leigh Light–equipped Wellingtons of British Squadron 36.

That night, May 14, Koitschka surfaced at about 11:00 to charge batteries. Thereupon, a Wellington of British Squadron 36, piloted by J. M. Cooke, attacked into 20mm flak and drove the U-boat under with six depth charges, then alerted the eight destroyers. About an hour later, the nearest one, *Ellyson,* came up, got a solid sonar contact, and attacked *U-616* with more depth charges. The missiles of the Wellington and *Ellyson* damaged a fuel-oil tank of *U-616,* and she began to trail an oil slick that at dawn was quite visible.

While Allied ASW forces continued the hunt, Koitschka took *U-616* deep and remained virtually immobile during the daylight hours of May 15. By nightfall his battery was dangerously low and the air in the boat was foul, so he surfaced about midnight. Two more Leigh Light–equipped Wellingtons of British Squadron 36 got *U-616* on radar and drove her under again. Later, however, Koitschka was able to surface undetected and charge batteries.

During the daylight hours of May 16, Koitschka again went deep and remained virtually immobile. As a consequence, the Allied hunters lost contact. After dark, at about 9:00 P.M., Koitschka surfaced again to charge batteries but an hour later, another Wellington of Squadron 36, piloted by H. R. Swain, got a radar contact and drove the boat back under with depth charges.

---

* The U.S. Navy's designation was "Operation Monstrous."

On the heels of this Wellington attack, the destroyer groups (less *Hilary P. Jones*) raced to that position. Shortly after midnight, May 17, Koitschka surfaced again to charge batteries. The destroyer *Macomb* got the boat on radar, then illuminated her by searchlight and opened fire with her main battery. Koitschka crash-dived and evaded with violent maneuvers, but *Macomb* and *Gleaves* hung on and carried out depth-charge attacks. The other five destroyers joined in the depth-charging and finally, at about 8:00 A.M.—seventy-six hours after Koitschka hit and damaged the two British freighters of convoy GUS 39—the *Hambleton* loosed a salvo set for six hundred feet, and this drove *U-616* to the surface.

Those of the seven destroyers that could bring guns to bear opened fire. Koitschka scuttled and abandoned ship. *Ellyson* and *Rodman* rescued the entire German crew—six officers and forty-seven men—bringing to a conclusion the longest and most relentless U-boat hunt of the war.

As in the case of Albrecht Brandi, *Ritterkreuz* holder Koitschka had registered an impressive list of claims. He told his Allied interrogators that he had sunk "about 45,000 tons of shipping," which included "nine destroyers, two submarines and two landing ships." His claims listed in German records were likewise impressive: six destroyers, two LSTs, two Italian submarines, and seven freighters sunk or probably sunk. Like Brandi, Koitschka's confirmed score was startlingly less: one destroyer definitely sunk (the American *Buck*), one LST "probably sunk," and the damage to the two British freighters of GUS 39 that led directly to the loss of *U-616*.

As the seven destroyers of the Swamp/Monstrous operation were preparing to enter Mers-el-Kébir, the seaport of Oran, at about 1:00 P.M. on May 17, the destroyer *Ellyson,* which had most survivors of *U-616* on board, reported that three torpedoes had missed her astern. These were fired by the newest—and last—U-boat to enter the Mediterranean, the *U-960,* commanded by Günter Heinrich, who had passed through Gibraltar Strait on May 9. He dived to about six hundred feet and eased away toward Toulon.

Allied authorities immediately launched another Swamp/Monstrous operation. Five American destroyers (*Benson, Ludlow, Madison, Niblack, Woolsey*) steamed out of Mers-el-Kébir and Coastal Command aircraft of British Squadrons 36 and 500 saturated the area. After dark, Heinrich surfaced *U-960* and continued toward Toulon. One Wellington of the search group was forced to abort with mechanical defects, but another of Squadron 36 "chanced upon" *U-960* in the early hours of May 18 and drove her under.

The Allied forces converged on the Wellington's position report and hunted all day May 18, but found no trace of the U-boat. However, late in the evening of that day, another Wellington of British Squadron 36, piloted by the Canadian K.H.N. Bulmer, got a radar contact and gave the alarm. Heinrich dived but when he resurfaced three hours later at about 1:30 A.M. on May 19 to charge batteries, the Canadian crew of the Wellington was still circling. Bulmer again gave the alarm and this time dropped lighted marker buoys for the destroyers *Ludlow* and *Niblack,* which were not far away.

In a series of cool and deliberate attacks over four hours, *Ludlow* and *Niblack* pounded *U-960* with depth charges. These wrecked the boat and forced Heinrich to surface and scuttle. When he came up at about 7:00 A.M.—forty-two hours after shooting at *Ellyson*—*Ludlow* and *Niblack* opened fire with main batteries, and a Ventura of British Squadron 500, piloted by Canadian E.A.K. Munday, attacked with depth charges. Finally, *Niblack* closed the abandoned hulk of *U-960* and finished her off with a salvo of depth charges. She and *Ludlow* rescued twenty of the fifty-one Germans of *U-960,* including Heinrich, who was wounded, and three other officers.

The last U-boat success in the Mediterranean occurred at about noon that same day, May 19. Off the "toe" of Italy in the Ionian Sea, the veteran *U-453,* commanded by Dierk Lührs, sank from a local convoy, HA 43, the 7,200-ton British Liberty ship *Fort Missanabie* with a salvo of three torpedoes. Three British destroyers pounced with depth charges and Hedgehogs: *Liddesdale, Tenacious,* and *Termagant.* Lührs went to the bottom (590 feet) and lay doggo the night of May 19–20. Believing he could escape, at dawn the next day Lührs broke *U-453* loose from the bottom and attempted to flee. However, the British warships were waiting, and at noon they commenced a relentless depth-charge attack that went on for about twelve hours.

These missiles wrecked *U-453* and forced her to the surface to scuttle shortly after midnight on May 21. As the fifty-one Germans of the crew leaped over the side, the destroyers opened up with main batteries and achieved several hits before the U-boat disappeared. The gunfire killed one German. The *Tenacious* and *Termagant* picked up fifteen men and took them to Taranto; the *Liddesdale* recovered the other thirty-four Germans and took them to Palermo.

The sinking of the *Fort Missanabie* was the last confirmed success of the Mediterranean U-boat force. From June 1, the remaining eleven boats were mostly shipyard-bound for battle-damage repairs and installation of snorts. None survived. Army Air Forces raids on Toulon on July 5 and August 6 destroyed five boats (*U-471, U-586, U-642, U-952, U-969*). After the invasion of southern France (Dragoon) on August 15, three more U-boats were scuttled in or off Toulon (*U-230, U-466, U-967*). Allied forces destroyed the remaining three boats (*U-407, U-565, U-596,* all snort boats based at Salamis) in September.

Altogether, sixty-two Type VIIs passed through the Strait of Gibraltar into the Mediterranean Sea during the war and none survived. Operating under extremely hazardous conditions, these boats sank a confirmed total of thirty-seven warships and 137 merchant ships for about 503,000 gross tons. The confirmed warships:

1 battleship (HMS *Barham*)
2 aircraft carriers (HMS *Ark Royal* and *Eagle*)
4 cruisers (HMS *Galatea, Hermione, Naiad,* and *Penelope*)
1 large minelayer (HMS *Welshman*)
16 destroyers or destroyer escorts*
1 frigate (HMS *Cuckmere*)
1 sloop (HMS *Parramatta*)

* Twelve British: *Blean, Gurkha II, Grove, Heythrop, Holcombe, Jaguar, Laforey, Martin, Partridge, Puckeridge, Quail,* and *Tyndale.* Three American: *Bristol, Buck, Fechteler.* One Dutch: *Isaac Sweers.*

1 corvette (HMS *Silvia*)
3 minecraft (HMS *Hebe* and *Hythe;* USS *Skill*)
5 LSTs (four British, one American)
2 ASW trawlers (HMS *Vissiliki* and *Jura*)

Patrols to and from the Far East

During the period from January 1 to June 1, 1944, Control sailed sixteen boats *to* the Far East and eight boats *from* the Far East* to France. These carried supplies to the German U-boat base at Penang and scarce commodities, such as rubber, tin, wolfram (tungsten), quinine, and opium from Penang to France. Some conducted antiship patrols along the way, but only eight of the twenty-four completed their missions. In another great U-boat slaughter, Allied ASW forces sank eleven and compelled five to abort.

To facilitate the extraordinarily long voyages of these boats, as previously related Control directed the German surface tanker *Charlotte Schliemann* to a convenient position in the Indian Ocean. The Allies learned of these plans from Enigma decrypts and ordered a small British hunter-killer group, consisting of the light cruiser *Newcastle* and the destroyer *Relentless,* to the scene. Reinforced by seven British Catalinas from Mauritius, on the night of February 11–12, *Relentless* opened fire on *Charlotte Schliemann,* and the Germans scuttled and abandoned ship. The British ships picked up forty-one crew of the tanker.†

The loss of this tanker disrupted and confused German operations in the Indian Ocean. The first U-boat to feel the impact was the IXC40 *U-532,* commanded by Otto-Heinrich Junker. He had sailed from Penang to France on J anuary 4 with a load of tin, rubber, wolfram, quinine, and opium. Patrolling home via the coast of India, he had sunk the 7,200-ton American Liberty ship *Walter Camp* and damaged the 7,300-ton British freighter *Triona,* but to get home, he had to refuel.

Junker arrived at the rendezvous with *Charlotte Schliemann* on February 12. He reported to Control four days later that he had found no sign of the tanker but had seen two Catalinas. That led to the suspicion that the rendezvous had been compromised and that the *Charlotte Schliemann* was lost. Nonetheless Control directed *U-532* to a new rendezvous with the tanker on February 19. In case the tanker was lost, Control ordered Wilhelm Spahr in the IXD2 cruiser *U-178,* also returning to France with cargo, to go to the rendezvous prepared to give Junker fuel, after which Spahr could resume his voyage to France.

Junker reported on February 22 that he could not find *Charlotte Schliemann* and assumed she was lost. Control concurred and ordered the surface tanker *Brake*—the last German tanker in the Indian Ocean—to provide support for the

* Including the *U-178* that sailed from Penang to France on November 27, 1943.

† This was a flagrant British use of Enigma decrypts to achieve a tactical success. British historians have harshly criticized Admiral King for similar usages. Other examples of such usage by the British abound. See the British campaign versus *Bismarck*'s supply ships and the inbound German blockade-runners.

U-boats at a new rendezvous on or about March 11. Junker in *U-532,* who had received some fuel from Spahr in *U-178,* but not enough to reach France, was to meet *Brake* and refuel, along with three other IXC40s (*U-168, U-183, U-188*), also homebound from Penang to France with cargoes of tin, rubber, wolfram, quinine, and opium.

Commanded by Helmut Pich, the *U-168* had originally sailed from Penang on January 28. Five days out, the first watch officer, Hans-Georg Stenger, had come down with appendicitis and Pich had to return to Penang. He had resailed on February 7 with, as he remembered, a cargo consisting of about one hundred tons of tin, wolfram, quinine, and opium. Patrolling home via India, Pich had sunk two ships (the 1,400-ton British repair ship *Salviking,* and a 4,400-ton Greek freighter) and had damaged the 9,800-ton Norwegian tanker *Fenris.*

The *U-188,* commanded by Siegfried Lüdden, had sailed from Penang on January 9 with a similar cargo. Patrolling home via the Arabian Sea and Gulf of Aden, Lüdden had achieved astonishing results for this period of the war: seven confirmed British freighters for 42,500 tons sunk by torpedo, plus seven dhows (sailboats) with cargoes of cotton, sunk by flak guns and ramming.* Upon receiving Lüdden's report, Dönitz had immediately awarded him a *Ritterkreuz.*†

Commanded by Fritz Schneewind, the *U-183* had sailed from Penang on February 10 with the usual cargo. Patrolling home via the Maldives and Ceylon, Schneewind had mounted attacks on two British vessels. On February 29, he had sunk the 5,400-ton freighter *Palma.* On March 9 he had hit the 7,000-ton tanker *British Loyalty,* anchored off Addu Atoll in the Maldives. She burned and sank to the bottom. Efforts to salvage her failed, and she was scrapped.

The first boat to arrive at the rendezvous with *Brake* was Lüdden in *U-188.* He replenished and refueled on March 12 and left immediately for Bordeaux, France. Next on the scene that day was Junker in *U-532,* who had been dawdling around in the area for a full month. Last to arrive was Pich in *U-168.* Junker and Pich took on fuel, but Junker got no lube oil and Pich did not get a full load of either fuel or lube oil.

"The captain of *Brake* was very nervous and rushed," Pich remembered. "Before we finished up he broke off operations and instructed us to meet him at another rendezvous." Pich and his crew "had very bad feelings about all this" and were also "very nervous."

Not without reason. Allied codebreakers had also provided good information

---

* Several Japanese submarines in final forays to the Indian Ocean operated near Lüdden. On February 12, Toshiaki Fukumura in *I-27* sank the 7,500-ton British troopship *Khedive Ismail* from a thinly escorted convoy with the loss of one thousand persons, including Wrens and nurses. Too late to thwart this little-known tragedy, two of the three escorts, the destroyers *Petard* and *Paladin,* sank *I-27.* The Allies charged that Japanese skippers of this foray, Kazuro Ebato in *RO-111,* Tatsunosuke Ariizumi in *I-8,* Denshicki Nakagawa in *I-37,* and T. Kusaka in *I-26,* murdered scores of survivors from the British freighter *Daisy Moller,* the tanker *British Chivalry,* the Dutch freighter *Tjisalak,* and the American Liberty ship *Richard Hovey.*

† At the time of the award, his confirmed score was eight freighters for about 51,000 tons, the ex-American four-stack British destroyer *Beverley,* plus the seven dhows and damage to a 10,000-ton tanker.

on this rendezvous. Despite Churchill's warnings against using Enigma decrypts tactically, the Admiralty had sent out another hunter-killer group to spoil the party. It was composed of the "jeep" carrier *Battler,* the heavy cruiser *Suffolk,* the light cruiser *Newcastle,* and the destroyers *Roebuck* and *Quadrant.* As though on routine patrol, aircraft from *Battler* "spotted" *Brake* and the three U-boats. The British destroyer *Roebuck* raced up. Upon sighting the aircraft from *Battler,* the Germans realized they had been detected, took to the lifeboats, and scuttled *Brake.* Pich in *U-168* dived away but later rescued all 135 Germans from *Brake* (bringing the total personnel on *U-168* to 190) and returned to the Far East in company with Junker in *U-532.*

It was imprudent to use Enigma decrypts tactically to sink the last two German tankers, *Charlotte Schliemann* and *Brake,* at U-boat refueling meets in the vast reaches of the Indian Ocean within a period of one month. The German skippers and U-boat Control agreed that U-boat Enigma had been "systematically compromised." In a top-secret message, U-boat Control therefore immediately initiated an "emergency procedure" to outwit Allied codebreakers. Assuming that the Allies had somehow obtained current keys, on March 13 these settings were canceled. Until new keys could be distributed, every U-boat at sea was to set the four rotors and other keys to match the first letters of the given names and surnames and the home addresses of the radio-electrician and third watch officer, information known to U-boat Control from the crew sailing lists.

In this top-secret message, U-boat Control instructed all skippers to destroy the messages after committing the modifications to memory or "unobtrusively" making a private memo to be shown only to officers. Importantly, the message also informed skippers that "major changes in cipher settings" were to be made "shortly."

This news caused deepest concern and pessimism among Allied codebreakers at Bletchley Park and OP20G in Washington. The senior hands were furious that the Admiralty had acted so thoughtlessly against the tankers. Sheepishly the Admiralty got off a message on March 16 to all recipients of naval Enigma decrypts, informing them that the Germans had "modified" U-boat Enigma and that all commands were to steer clear of U-boat refueling meets until further notice.

Lüdden in *U-188* continued his voyage to France, but he needed help from other U-boats. Near Cape Town on March 22, he met the outbound VIIF supply boat *U-1062* and got the latest Enigma keys. One month later, on April 22, near St. Paul Rocks in the South Atlantic, he met Kurt Freiwald's outbound IXD2 cruiser *U-181,* got lube oil and took on board a sick engineer from *U-181.* Three hundred miles farther north, on April 26, Lüdden met the outbound IXC *U-129* and got a *Naxos* radar detector. On April 30, Control directed Lüdden to run at maximum speed to render assistance to a "stranded" IXC, *U-66,* near the Cape Verde Islands. Lüdden met that boat on May 2 and gave her some fuel and food, but he was attacked by carrier aircraft during the transfer. Lüdden's radio then failed and he was unable to notify Control of this meet—and of the presence of carrier aircraft—and inched onward to Bordeaux, where he arrived on June 19, to the surprise of Control, since it had assumed from Lüdden's radio silence that *U-188* had been sunk.

The loss of *Brake* placed two other U-boats in jeopardy. One was the homebound IXC40 *U-183,* commanded by Fritz Schneewind, loaded with the usual cargo. His batteries were in poor condition. He hoped to get help from *Brake* but he had to turn about and return to Penang. The other was the ex-Italian *Cappellini,* redesignated *U-IT24,* commanded by Heinrich Pahls, which was France-bound with the usual cargo of tin, rubber, tungsten, quinine, and opium. Pahls linked up with Junker in the IXC40 *U-532,* got fuel, and returned independently to Penang. Thus Enigma information enabled the Allies to thwart the sailing to France from the Far East of four out of six U-boats with cargoes and to sink the valuable German surface tankers *Charlotte Schliemann* and *Brake.**

In Penang, the commander of the IXD2 cruiser *U-183,* Fritz Schneewind, reported that all but 30 percent of his battery had disintegrated. Since he could not return *U-183* to France with only one-third of his battery operable, U-boat Control directed him to make a short patrol to Ceylon and the Maldives in the Indian Ocean, then take the boat to Japan, where the battery could be replaced or repaired, or so it was hoped.

In compliance with these orders, Schneewind sailed from Penang on May 17 and reached the western limit of his patrol area near the Maldives on June 5. That day he sank the 5,300-ton British freighter *Helen Moller.* Per further orders, on June 24 Schneewind met the IXC40 *U-843,* outbound from France to Penang under the command of Oskar Herwartz, and got two sets of new Enigma keys and *Naxos* gear. Schneewind was to meet and give one set of Enigma keys to Karl Albrecht in the VIIF supply boat *U-1062,* homebound to France. However, a broken air compressor compelled Albrecht to abort to Penang. The two boats canceled the rendezvous and returned to Penang, Albrecht on July 2, Schneewind on July 7.

Sixteen U-boats sailed from France, Norway, or Germany to the Far East during this same period, January 1 to June 1, 1944, most with supplies for the German base in Penang and the boats operating from there. Nine were U-cruisers, two were VIIF torpedo-supply boats, three were IXCs, including the second gift from Hitler to Tojo, the IXC40 *U-1224* or "Marco Polo II," and one was an ex-Italian cargo conversion.

---

* On February 14 in the Straits of Malacca, the British submarine *Tally-Ho,* commanded by a former enlisted torpedoman, L.W.A. Bennington, sank the ex-Italian *Giuliana,* redesignated *U-IT23,* temporarily commanded by Hans-Werner Striegler from the ex-Italian boat *Torelli,* redesignated *U-IT25.* Striegler and thirteen men were rescued by Japanese ships. Subsequently, Striegler returned to command *U-IT25,* which was assigned to transport duty between Singapore and Japan. In September 1944, Striegler was replaced by Alfred Meier, age thirty-six (from *U-183*). Striegler took command of the IXD2 U-cruiser *U-196,* which was thought to have been sunk in mid-November 1944, in the Sunda Strait, possibly by a mine planted by the British submarine *Porpoise.* Striegler and all hands were lost. When Germany surrendered in May 1945, the Japanese seized *U-IT25* and redesignated it *I-504,* but she made no further voyages.

These Far East boats sailed at a rate of four per month from January to May. The newest—and last—Type XIV "Milk Cow," *U-490,* long delayed in the Baltic, joined the parade with a load of supplies as well as fuel. Allied ASW forces sank ten of the sixteen boats; only six reached bases in the Far East. The long voyage of one of the U-cruisers was to become the most notorious of the war, the single, unequivocal German atrocity in the U-boat war.

The first of the four boats to sail was the veteran IXD2 cruiser *U-177,* commanded by Heinz Buchholz, age thirty-four, who left Bordeaux on January 2. About a month later, on February 6, a B-24 of U.S. Navy Bombing Squadron VB 107, based on Ascension Island, found and sank *U-177* with six depth charges. The aircrew, commanded by pilot C. I. Pinnell, reported "survivors in the water." Another Navy B-24 of VB 107 dropped a life raft and life jackets. About fifty-six hours later, the light cruiser *Omaha* rescued fourteen Germans who said Buchholz and about five other crew were killed in the water by three exploding depth charges during Pinnell's second attack. *U-177* sank no ships on this patrol.

The next to sail was the new VIIF torpedo-supply boat *U-1062,* commanded by Karl Albrecht, age thirty-nine. He left Bergen on January 3 with a load of forty torpedoes, including five in her tubes for self-defense. Albrecht was to refuel from *Charlotte Schliemann,* then *Brake,* but after those tankers were lost, he met Lüdden in the France-bound *U-188* on March 22, as related, and gave him new Enigma keys and got some fuel. Continuing on to Penang, on April 8, Albrecht linked up with Junker in the IXC40 *U-532,* who was aborting to Penang and took on some more fuel. The two boats entered Penang in company on April 19.

Then sailed the new IXD2 cruiser *U-852,* commanded by Wilhelm Eck, age twenty-seven, who left Kiel on January 18 to conduct what became the most notorious U-boat patrol of the war. Then a *Kapitänleutnant* (lieutenant commander), Eck was a member of the crew of 1934, who had commanded a minesweeper from the beginning of the war to May 1942. He then volunteered for U-boats and after the required specialized schooling for officers, he made one war patrol as a watch officer on the famous *U-124,* commanded by young Johann Mohr, who earned the *Ritterkreuz* with Oak Leaves before his death in the sinking of that boat.

Prior to Eck's departure from Kiel, Adalbert Schnee at U-boat Control, who had won a *Ritterkreuz* with Oak Leaves as well, briefed him. Schnee pointed out the ominous fact that four of five preceding U-cruisers in Eck's series—*U-847, U-848, U-849,* and *U-850*—commanded, respectively, by *Ritterkreuz* holders Herbert Kuppisch, Wilhelm Rollmann, Heinz-Otto Schultze, and the old hand Klaus Ewerth, had all been sunk on first cruises to the Indian Ocean,* most likely in the South Atlantic near the equator and/or Ascension Island, where the Allies had established an air base that worked in cooperation with Allied air bases in Freetown and elsewhere on the west coast of Africa, which included Navy B-24s of Squadron VB 107. Inasmuch as the U-cruisers were clumsy and slow divers,

* As will be described, the fifth boat of the series, *U-851,* was soon missing.

Eck was to be especially watchful, not only on the passage through the North Atlantic but also through the South Atlantic.

After an unusually stressful voyage—submerged most of the daylight hours—on March 13 Eck reached the South Atlantic waters near the site where Hartenstein in *U-156* had sunk the *Laconia.* Late that evening the bridge watch spotted a lone freighter, the 4,700-ton *Peleus,* a Greek under charter to Great Britain. Commanded by Minas Mavris, she was en route in ballast from Freetown to Buenos Aires, Argentina, with a total crew of thirty-five.*

Eck tracked *Peleus* until nightfall, then at about 7:50, while on the surface, he fired two torpedoes with magnetic pistols from close range. One or both hit and *Peleus* literally disintegrated. Except for the flotsam—and several life rafts—within three minutes there was no sign of *Peleus.* Probably half the crew survived the violent explosion and the rapid sinking and got in the life rafts or clung to debris. In order to ascertain the name and tonnage of his victim, Eck temporarily took on board *U-852* the Greek third officer, Agis Kefalas, and a "Russian" seaman, Pierre Neumann, from whom Eck got a life ring on which the ship's name was painted. After returning these men to their raft, Eck insisted that the lights on it and the other rafts be extinguished so that other Allied forces in the area would not find any trace of *Peleus* until *U-852* was well clear.

In the tension of the moment, Eck "lost his nerve," as Schnee aptly put it later. He decided that to absolutely conceal evidence of the sinking, the big pieces of debris—and the life rafts—should be destroyed, even though, as he said later, the acts of destruction might cost the lives of some survivors and, if successful, would certainly deprive the crewmen of their only means of survival.† He therefore ordered that machine guns, machine pistols, and hand grenades be brought to the bridge and that the twin 20mm and the 37mm flak guns be manned.

After summoning all officers topside, for about the next five hours—to about 1:00 A.M., March 14—Eck maneuvered *U-852* through the wreckage and lifeboats, firing away by the light of the signal lamps at close range, heedless of the survivors. The first watch officer, Gerhard Kolditz, and the experienced chief engineer, Hans Richard Lenz, age twenty-seven, "objected" to the carnage, Lenz strongly. And yet, Lenz said later, he grabbed a machine gun from an enlisted man, Wolfgang Schwender, and shot at the wreckage because "Schwender, long known to many as one of the most unsatisfactory ratings on our boat, was unworthy to carry out such an order." The second watch officer, August Hoffmann, age twenty-one, said later that he engaged in the slaughter only reluctantly—and on direct orders from Eck—because during his earlier interrogation of one of the two survivors, he felt "sorry" for him and "did not want to shoot at them." Eck even ordered the ship's physician and his close friend, Walter Weisspfenning, age thirty-three, to shoot.

---

* Including Mavris, eighteen Greeks; eight British; three Chinese; two Egyptians; and one man each from Aden, Chile, Poland, and the Soviet Union.

† Asked later if it was not clear to him "that through sinking the wreckage and rafts you would also sink the survivors," Eck responded: "It was clear to me that the possibility of saving their lives disappeared."

The life rafts proved to be very difficult to sink. Finally Eck called a halt and hauled away in the darkness. Informed that his crew was disgruntled and displeased, Eck went below and addressed his men on the ship's P.A. system. "I was under the impression that the mood on board was rather a depressing one," Eck recalled. "On account of that I said to the crew that with a heavy heart I had finally made that decision . . . to destroy the remainder of the sunk ship."

Four crewmen of *Peleus,* including the third officer, Agis Kefalas, who was badly wounded in the right arm, lived through the massacre, but Kefalas later died of his wounds. The other three men survived: two Greeks, chief officer Antonios Liossis and seaman Dimitrios Argiros, and a British stoker, Rocco Said. The Portuguese neutral *Alexandre Silva* found and rescued them on April 20, after forty-nine days on the raft. All three men later gave sworn affidavits to British naval authorities describing the *Peleus* atrocity.

Inasmuch as *Peleus* had been blown to bits, there had been no opportunity for her crew to broadcast a submarine alarm or an SOS. Allied forces therefore remained ignorant of her loss and mounted no special hunt for *U-852,* and thus she remained undetected. Continuing south, Eck reached the Cape Town area on April 1. While submerged that day, he found and sank another lone ship, the 5,300-ton British freighter *Dahomian.* Eck did not surface to determine the name and nationality of this vessel or to destroy wreckage or survivors. Well away from that area on April 4, he notified U-boat Control of his two sinkings, and Control in turn authorized him to "transfer to the Indian Ocean as commander sees fit."

Eck entered the Indian Ocean and patrolled northward through the Mozambique Channel toward Allied Somaliland (Somalia) and the Arabian Sea. Early on the morning of May 2, a Wellington of British Squadron 621 of the Aden Command, piloted by H. Roy Mitchell, sighted *U-852* on the surface near Ras Hafun, Somaliland, and attacked, dropping four well-aimed, shallow-set depth charges. Eck crash-dived, but the explosions damaged his main induction and his batteries and caused flooding, forcing him back to the surface. For the next twelve hours Eck fought off a half dozen Wellingtons of Squadron 621 and Squadron 8, incurring seven dead, including the first watch officer, Kolditz, and about fifteen wounded. Meanwhile, a British hunter-killer group (the destroyer *Raider,* sloop *Falmouth,* frigate *Parret*) hastened to the scene.

During the evening, Eck limped into a small bay to effect repairs. In so doing, he grounded fast in mud about 130 yards from shore. Concluding that he could no longer resist at sea, he gave orders to destroy secret papers, abandon ship, and blow up the boat. The survivors of *U-852* swam ashore, hoping to somehow escape overland. However, armed shore parties from the three British ships, assisted by the Somaliland Camel Corps, captured all fifty-nine Germans, including Eck, and landed them at Aden on May 6. Under interrogation, disaffected enlisted men revealed the *Peleus* atrocity and when Allied intelligence officers confronted the chief engineer, Lenz, he confirmed the story.

After the war, the British convened a military court in Hamburg on October 17, 1945, and charged five men of *U-852* with committing war crimes in the *Peleus* sinking. The accused were Heinz Eck, second watch officer August Hoffmann,

Chief Engineer Hans Richard Lenz, "helicopter" airman Wolfgang Schwender, and the physician Walter Weisspfenning. Finding all five men guilty, on November 8 the court sentenced Eck, Hoffmann, and Weisspfenning to death, Lenz to life imprisonment, and Schwender to fifteen years. At 8:40 A.M. on November 30, at Crossborsteler Chaussee in Hamburg, a British firing squad executed the three men. Subsequently British authorities reduced Lenz's sentence from life to twenty-one years and Schwender's from fifteen to ten years. Schwender was paroled on December 21, 1951, after seven and a half years of incarceration and Lenz on May 27, 1952, after eight years of incarceration.*

As stated, the *Peleus* atrocity proved to be an aberration, the single unequivocal instance of criminal conduct by a U-boat skipper in World War II. The evidence gathered for the trial of Eck et al. was introduced with telling effect at the trial of Dönitz at Nuremberg in an attempt to prove he waged criminal warfare. Furthermore, two *Kriegsmarine* officers, Karl-Heinz Moehle (commander of Training Flotilla 5) and Peter Josef Heisig, a close friend of Hoffmann's and a junior watch officer on *U-877,* came forward in Nuremberg to imply falsely under oath that Dönitz desired that U-boat skippers murder shipwrecked crews to prevent them from manning other ships and that Eck et al. were merely carrying out Dönitz's unspoken—and unordered—but clearly implied desires.†

The large, former Italian submarine *Bagnolini* left next with supplies for Penang.‡ Redesignated *U-IT22* and commanded by Karl Wunderlich, *Bagnolini* sailed from Bordeaux on January 19. Allied codebreakers tracked her southward. In mid–South Atlantic on February 12, a B-24 of American Navy Squadron VB 107, based on Ascension Island, attacked the boat, dropping six depth charges in three runs. Wunderlich reported that the missiles killed one man, wrecked a periscope and fuel tank, and caused other damage. He added that although he had lost thirty-two tons of fuel from the wrecked tank he could still reach Penang without refueling, luckily for him since the Allies destroyed the *Charlotte Schliemann* in the Indian Ocean this same day.

Wunderlich had on board a number of spare *Naxos* radar detectors, Enigma keys, and other electronics. Since Wilhelm Spahr's U-cruiser *U-178,* inbound from the Indian Ocean, had no *Naxos,* Control directed Wunderlich to rendezvous with Spahr south of the Cape of Good Hope on or about March 11. Again acting on Enigma decrypts, British authorities laid an air-sea trap for these two boats at

* The *Peleus* atrocity provided the basis for a 1967 novel, *An Operational Necessity,* by British author Gwyn Griffin. It was a best-seller in the United States. The German edition was entitled *Der letze Zeuge* [*The Last Witness*].

† Moehle's testimony to the effect that he briefed some new skippers in that vein, reflecting desired (but unspoken) policy at U-boat Control, led to charges against him. He was found guilty, but he served only five years in prison, probably a deal in return for his anti-Dönitz testimony. See Madsen (1998).

‡ The large, former Italian submarine *Fenzi,* redesignated *U-IT21,* had been declared unfit and was decommissioned in Bordeaux.

the meeting place. In successive depth-charge attacks on March 11, three Catalinas of British Squadron 262, piloted by the Canadian Frederick J. Roddick, E.S.S. Nash, and A. H. ("Oscar") Surridge, sank *U-IT22* with the loss of all hands. Spahr in *U-178* reported a big oil slick at the rendezvous and continued on to France without *Naxos*. Although he was bedeviled by serious engine problems, the canny Spahr escaped another Allied trap when he met the outbound IXC40 *U-843* on April 4 to get new Enigma keys and finally limped into Bordeaux on May 25, completing an unspeakably arduous and hazardous voyage of 181 days. The badly worn *U-178* did not sail again.

Next to sail was the new VIIF torpedo-supply boat *U-1059,* commanded by Günter Leupold. Loaded with forty torpedoes, she left Bergen on February 12, the day after Leupold's twenty-third birthday. She was to meet the XIV "Milk Cow" tanker *U-488,* commanded by a new skipper, Bruno Studt, age twenty-five, west of the Cape Verdes, top off all fuel bunkers, then proceed to Penang. The *U-488* sailed ten days later, on February 22, after seventy-three days of refit and upgrades at Brest.

At this time the American "jeep" carrier *Block Island* and her escorts were operating in the eastern Atlantic. As related, on March 1, the group sank the VIICs *U-603* and *U-709.* Thereafter, on March 8, the group put into Casablanca to refuel and replenish. American codebreakers provided information on the rendezvous of the XIV tanker *U-488* and the VIIF *U-1059,* which they described as the "first refueling operation in the Atlantic" area since the previous November, when *U-488,* the only "Milk Cow" then left in the Atlantic U-boat force, was last at sea.

After merely four days in port, the *Block Island* group sailed from Casablanca, commanded by a new skipper, Francis M. Hughes. Several days later, the Admiralty sent out the message prohibiting attacks on U-boats meeting to refuel.

The Americans either failed to receive this message or chose to ignore it, probably the latter. The *Block Island* group steamed west at best speed, determined to make every possible effort to sink the two valuable supply boats, the XIV tanker *U-488* and the VIIF *U-1059* torpedo carrier.

On the afternoon of March 16, a U-boat bound for West African waters surfaced to air the boat and to conduct much-needed gunnery practice. This was the IXC40 *U-801,* commanded by Hans-Joachim Brans, age twenty-eight, embarked on her second war patrol. By pure happenstance, *U-801* had surfaced in the air search path of the *Block Island* group. A Wildcat-Avenger team, piloted by Paul Sorenson and C. A. Wooddell, respectively, sighted and immediately attacked *U-801.* In two strafing runs, Sorenson in the Wildcat killed one German and wounded nine, including the skipper, Brans. As *U-801* crash-dived, Wooddell in the Avenger dropped two well-aimed depth charges and sonobuoys, but the U-boat got away.

Hughes in *Block Island* perhaps believed he had prematurely happened upon the rendezvous of *U-488* and *U-1059.* Whatever the case, he directed the group to hunt the U-boat to exhaustion. When Brans surfaced *U-801* that night to bury the dead crewman, he set up a rendezvous with the "Milk Cow" *U-488,* which had a doctor who could treat him and his wounded. The *Block Island* group DFed this transmission and sent out night-flying, MAD-equipped Avengers to track *U-801.* These planes and others, which arrived after dawn on March 17, dropped sonobuoys and depth charges, some of which severely damaged *U-801* and drove her down to 984 feet.

The *Block Island* aircraft homed in two ships of the hunter-killer group: the veteran destroyer *Corry* and the new but battle-tested destroyer escort *Bronstein,* which on March 1 had killed *U-603* and assisted in the kill of *U-709. Corry* and *Bronstein,* commanded by George D. Hoffmann and Sheldon H. Kinney, respectively, got sonar contacts and carried out eight depth-charge and Hedgehog attacks. These wrecked *U-801* and brought her to the surface to abandon ship and scuttle, whereupon *Corry* opened up with her four 4" guns and one 3" gun and *Bronstein* with her three 3" guns. The American intelligence report stated:

> A scene of the most appalling disorganization and devastation ensued. Within the boat the order to abandon ship never reached the bow compartment where members of the crew only realized that the end had come when they saw telegraphists destroying their secret equipment. Brans was the first on the bridge and after him were hoisted the wounded. The Quartermaster followed with two line officers after him. The surface craft immediately opened a very accurate fire and as the first of the men reached the bridge they saw Brans hanging like a corpse over the night firing stand. The Quartermaster, lying at his feet, was a ghastly headless figure.

The engineer, Franz Schumann, assumed command, scuttled, and elected to go down with the boat. Ten Germans perished; *Corry* and *Bronstein* recovered forty-seven.

Proceeding southwestward on March 19, another Wildcat-Avenger team from *Block Island* discovered Leupold's VIIF torpedo carrier *U-1059* on the surface. Like *U-801,* she was casually disposed. The pilots, William H. Cole and Norman T. Dowty, noted that about eighteen crewmen were in the water for a swim, a perfect setup for the Americans. Cole in the Wildcat strafed. Dowty in the Avenger dropped two perfectly aimed depth charges, which destroyed *U-1059* in mere seconds. At about the same time, flak damage forced Dowty to ditch. He and his radioman perished, but his rear gunner, Mark E. Fitzgerald (an ensign), got out. Eight Germans survived the sinking of *U-1059.* Three, including skipper Leupold, joined Fitzgerald in his and another life raft. About two hours later, the destroyer *Corry* of *Block Island*'s group rescued Fitzgerald, Leupold, and seven other Germans, all of whom were wounded or injured.

American intelligence officers who interrogated the garrulous anti-Nazi Leupold and some other Germans, wrote:

> Prior to the departure of *U-1059* from Kiel, Leupold had an interview with *Korvettenkapitän* Oskar Moehle, commanding officer of the 5th U-boat [training] Flotilla. In the course of issuing orders for the patrol, Moehle transmitted to

> Leupold specific oral orders from the admiral commanding U-boats [Godt] that if any ships were sunk all survivors were to be exterminated. When the commanding officer of *U-1059* expressed surprise and indignation at such an order, Moehle told him that this was a positive order from the commander-in-chief [Dönitz] and was a part of the total war that was now being waged. Before leaving, Leupold had occasion to discuss this order with other U-boat commanders, who all stated that, order or no order, they had no intention of complying.*

This episode led to a testy exchange of messages between Admiral King and First Sea Lord Cunningham. To protect to the extent possible the secret of having broken Enigma, the British again urged that the Americans refrain from attacking U-boats meeting to refuel. *Block Island* had intensified British worries inasmuch as she was operating in a U-boat rendezvous area, *after* the Germans had made the emergency modifications to Enigma keys (first letter of certain crewmen's first name, last name, plus home address, and so on) a fact that, if known to U-boat Control, might speed up its plan to make the forecasted "major changes" in Enigma.

King responded that the Americans *would not* conform to British requests. The kills of *Block Island* had not compromised the Allied codebreakers. The *Block Island* hunter-killer group was operating in an area derived from Enigma decrypts *before* the modifications had been made. Moreover, the Americans had been operating "jeep"-carrier groups in that area for quite some time. The *absence* of the hunter-killer groups at the refueling rendezvous might raise more suspicions among the Germans than their *presence.* The German suspicions that Enigma was compromised had not been caused by *Block Island,* but most likely by the British in routing convoys to evade U-boats and by sinking *Charlotte Schliemann* and *Brake.*

The next boat to sail to the Far East in February was the new IXC40 *U-843,* commanded by Oskar Herwartz, age twenty-nine, who left Lorient on February 19. She, too, was to refuel from Bruno Studt's XIV tanker *U-488* that sailed four days later. The two boats traveled south separately. On March 6 and 12, Herwartz in *U-843* stopped and searched neutral freighters, let them go, and then continued south. He met the XIV *U-488* west of the Cape Verde Islands on March 24 and topped off his fuel tanks, continuing southward.

As related, on April 4, he met Spahr in the homebound U-cruiser *U-178* to give him new Enigma keys. In the midst of the exchange, a B-24 of U.S. Navy Squadron VB 107 from Ascension Island, doubtless aided by Enigma decrypts, strafed *U-178* but dropped no bombs. In the South Atlantic on April 8, Herwartz found and sank the lone 8,300-ton British freighter *Nebraska.* Three days later, April 10, another B-24 of U.S. Navy Squadron VB 107, piloted by Edward A. Krug, attacked the boat, knocking out both stern tubes. As a result, Control directed Herwartz to cancel intended operations off Cape Town and refuel from a

* For reasons unclear, the Allies did not present Leupold's allegation at Eck's, Moehle's, or Dönitz's war-crimes trials.

Japanese submarine in the Indian Ocean. He did, and arrived in Jakarta on June 11, completing an arduous voyage of 114 days.

The next boat to sail in February was the new IXD2 cruiser *U-851,* commanded by Hannes Weingaertner, age thirty-five, who sailed from Kiel on February 26. He carried cargo, including 1,878 bottles of mercury and five hundred U-boat batteries. In compliance with ill-advised orders from Control, on March 27 Weingaertner broadcast a weather report from the North Atlantic for the benefit of the *Luftwaffe* and the anti-invasion forces in France. Nothing further was ever heard from him. In view of his large fuel supply, it was assumed at first that *U-851* reached the Indian Ocean, but on June 30, the 126th day after departure, Control declared the boat lost to "unknown causes." No trace of *U-851* has ever been found. She sank no ships on this patrol.

The last boat to sail in February was the IXC40 *U-537,* commanded by Peter Schrewe, which left Lorient on February 29. Six days out from France, on March 5, an unidentified Allied aircraft attacked the boat. The damage was so severe that Schrewe was forced to abort. He reached Lorient on March 6, and was under repair for the next twenty days.

Four boats sailed from France to the Far East in March.

First away was the veteran IXD2 cruiser *U-181,* commanded by a new skipper but a pioneer submariner, Kurt Freiwald, age thirty-eight, crew of 1925, who left La Pallice on March 16. In the middle of the South Atlantic on May 1, Freiwald sank his first ship, the lone 5,300-ton British freighter *Janeta.* Patrolling the Indian Ocean in June and July, *U-181* got three more freighters: the 7,100-ton Dutch *Garoet,* the 7,100-ton British *Tanda,* and the 5,300-ton British *King Frederick.* He arrived in Penang on August 8, completing a patrol of 146 days.

Next sailed the veteran IXD2 cruiser *U-196,* still commanded by *Ritterkreuz* holder Eitel-Friedrich Kentrat, age thirty-seven, crew of 1928, who left La Pallice on March 16. After reaching the Indian Ocean, Kentrat sank one ship in the Arabian Sea, the 5,500-ton British freighter *Shahzada.* He reached Penang on August 10, completing a voyage of 149 days. Thereafter he left the boat to command a small German naval unit in Japan.

The IXC40 *U-537,* commanded by Peter Schrewe, resailed from Lorient on March 25. He refueled in the Atlantic Ocean from the XIV tanker *U-488* on April 17 and proceeded to the Indian Ocean. Schrewe claimed sinking a destroyer off Ceylon on July 8, but the claim could not be confirmed. Inasmuch as Allied aircraft and submarines had mined the approaches to Penang and British submarines lurked off the port continuously, U-boat Control established new bases in Java. Schrewe arrived in Jakarta on August 2, completing a voyage of 131 days.

The last boat to sail for the Far East in March was the gift from Hitler to Tojo, "Marco Polo II," the new IXC40 *U-1224,* commanded by *Kriegsmarine* officer Georg Preuss, age twenty-seven, and redesignated *RO-501.* The boat sailed from Kiel on March 30 with a Japanese crew. Acting on information from Allied codebreakers, a hunter-killer group composed of *Bogue* and five new destroyer escorts searched for *U-1224* west of the Cape Verde Islands. At dusk on May 13, the destroyer escort *Francis M. Robinson,* commanded by John E. Johansen, got a sonar contact and attacked with depth charges and Hedgehogs. These apparently destroyed *U-1224.* No trace of her or Preuss or her Japanese crew was ever found.*

Four more new U-cruisers sailed to the Far East in April. None, of course, required refueling.

First out was the IXD2 *U-859,* commanded by Johann Jebsen, age twenty-seven. Fitted with a snort, she sailed from Kiel to Penang on April 4. While passing through the North Atlantic on April 26, Jebsen came upon several stragglers from Slow Convoy 157 and sank the 6,300-ton Panamanian freighter *Colin,* as related. He reported the sinking to Control and escaped detection by the swarms of Allied ASW forces in the area.

Jebsen rounded the Cape of Good Hope into the Indian Ocean in late June. In early July, an unidentified British Catalina attacked *U-859* southeast of Durban with machine-gun fire and depth charges, inflicting severe damage. One seaman was killed and three men were wounded, the second watch officer seriously. The explosions holed a fuel tank, smashed the snort elevating gear, and unseated two diesel engines or motors. Jebsen escaped the ensuing Allied ASW hunt, made repairs, and proceeded north to the mouth of the Gulf of Aden, where in late August he sank two freighters, the 7,200-ton American Liberty ship *John Berry* and the 7,400-ton British *Troilus.*

Jebsen then set a course for Penang, arriving off that port on September 23, the 173rd day of the patrol. The British submarine *Trenchant,* commanded by Arthur R. Hezlet, intercepted the U-boat as she was preparing to enter port with a Japanese escort. Hezlet fired three stern torpedoes at *U-859.* One hit the U-boat amidships and sank her. *Trenchant* rescued the junior engineer Horst Klatt, age twenty-two (who had survived the accidental sinking of the VII *U-612* in the Baltic), and ten enlisted men. The Japanese escorts rescued eight other enlisted men.†

Next to sail was the new IXD2 *U-860,* commanded by Paul Büchel, age thirty-six, crew of 1925, who sailed from Kiel on April 11. On June 9, while in the middle of the South Atlantic, Büchel reported to U-boat Control his position and the fact that he had lost two men overboard in the storm-tossed North Atlantic. Allied forces DFed this transmission, which confirmed Enigma tracking intelligence, and a hunter-killer group built around the American "jeep" carrier *Solomons,* newly arrived in the South Atlantic, commenced a search for *U-860.* On the morning of

---

* The Japanese U-cruiser *I-29* (German code designation *"U-Kiefer"*), which departed Japan on December 17, 1943, arrived at Bordeaux on March 11 with a cargo of rubber, wolfram, and two tons of gold bullion and twenty-five senior Japanese liaison officers. She sailed for Japan on April 16, with a cargo of the latest German radar and radar detectors and radar jammers, *Bolde,* ten Enigma machines, medicine, and so on. She embarked twelve officers and eight students for the homeward trip. She reached Penang but while en route to Japan, she was sunk on July 26, near the island of Luzon, by the American submarine *Sawfish.* As will be described, another Japanese U-cruiser, *I-52* (German code designation *"U-Tanne,"* or Fir Tree, later changed to *Föhre,* or Pine Tree), sailed from the Far East to Bordeaux with cargo, including two tons of gold, and fourteen passengers.

† Hezlet, who later sank the Japanese heavy cruiser *Ashigara,* rose to vice admiral, was commander of the British submarine force 1959–61, and published an influential book, *The Submarine and Sea Power.* An unconfirmed (and doubtful) media report in 1972 asserted that salvors had found *U-859* and had taken from her "thirty tons of mercury," valued at $17.7 million.

June 15, Avenger pilot George E. Edwards, Jr., found, reported, and attacked *U-860* four times in the face of intense flak, but his report was not discovered in the hunter-killer group until later. On the fourth run, Büchel's gunners shot down the Avenger. No trace of Edwards or his crew was ever found.

Toward sunset, another Avenger pilot, Howard M. Avery, found *U-860* on the surface. His contact report brought in two Wildcats and another Avenger. All four aircraft attacked *U-860* three times with rockets, machine guns, and depth charges. A depth charge from the low-flying Avenger exploded on the forward deck of the U-boat and engulfed the aircraft in flames. Neither the pilot, William F. Chamberlain, nor his crew was found.

Fatally damaged, *U-860* sank. Six hours later, the destroyer escorts *Herzog* and *Straub* of *Solomons*'s screen, searching in darkness, fished Büchel, his first watch officer Otto Wilhelm Carls, and nineteen other Germans from the water. One dead German was buried at sea. *Solomons* landed the other survivors in Recife, Brazil.

The third U-cruiser to sail in April was the veteran IXD2 *U-198*. Commanded by a new skipper, Burkhard Heusinger von Waldegg, age twenty-three, the boat left La Pallice on April 20. He was assigned to give Lüdden in the inbound *U-188* Enigma keys on May 14, but the rendezvous failed, probably because Lüdden's radios were out of commission. Seven days later, an Allied hunter-killer group detected and chased the *U-198* but she got away clean. Off Cape Town on June 16, von Waldegg sank the 3,300-ton South African freighter *Columbine*. After rounding the Cape of Good Hope into the Indian Ocean, two Venturas based in South Africa attacked *U-198* with depth charges on July 6, breaking loose a number of rubber dinghies stored under the topside decking. Cruising north in the Mozambique Channel, von Waldegg sank three British freighters: the 5,100-ton *Director,* the 7,300-ton *Empire City,* and the 7,200-ton *Empire Day.* Several other attacks on Allied shipping, including the ex-American Coast Guard cutter *Saranac,* renamed *Banff* by the Royal Navy, and the Australian motorship *Lismore,* failed.

On August 12, an Avenger from a British hunter-killer group built around the new American-built British "jeep" carriers *Begum* and *Shah* found and attacked *U-198* with depth charges. A British Catalina took up the tracking and homed in three ships of the screen: the British frigates *Findhorn* and *Parret* and the Indian sloop *Godavari. Findhorn* and *Godavari* teamed up to destroy *U-198* with depth charges and Hedgehogs. There were no survivors. The sixty-seven dead included the captain of *Empire Day,* whom Waldegg had taken prisoner.

The last U-cruiser to sail in April was the new IXD2 *U-861,* commanded by Jürgen Oesten, age thirty-one, which sailed from Kiel on April 20. Earlier in the war, Oesten had won a *Ritterkreuz* for sinking six ships while commanding the duck *U-61* and ten ships and a hit on the British battleship *Malaya* while commanding the IXB *U-106.* Subsequently, he had served as a staff officer at U-boat Control and as a chief adviser for submarine operations in the Arctic.

Oesten patrolled to the Indian Ocean by way of Brazil. Off Rio de Janeiro on July 20, he sank the 1,700-ton Brazilian freighter/troopship *Vital de Oliveira,* which was carrying about two hundred soldiers to Europe. Oesten also attempted to sink her single, small escort with a T-5, but the escort fled. The Brazilians reported that 101 men perished in the sinking. Four days later, Oesten sank the 7,200-ton American Liberty grainship *William Gaston.* The U.S. Navy had diverted her to avoid *U-861* but inadvertently put her exactly in Oesten's crosshairs.

There were sixty-seven men on *William Gaston,* including a twenty-six-man Armed Guard crew. All got away in three lifeboats and one raft. Following a horrible night in heavy seas, shortly after noon on July 24, a U.S. Navy Mariner of Squadron VP 203 spotted the survivors. The pilot, Charles Snyder, gave the alarm. Other U.S. Navy Mariners and Catalinas responded, but could not land in the heavy seas. They stood watch until the squadron's aviation tender *Matagorda,* based at Florianópolis, Brazil, arrived early on July 25 and rescued all sixty-seven survivors.*

After rounding the Cape of Good Hope on August 20, Oesten found and attacked a convoy, Durban North 68, composed of seven freighters, thinly escorted by three ASW trawlers. He claimed that he sank two ships for 16,465 tons from the convoy. Allied records confirmed the 7,500-ton British freighter *Berwickshire* but only damage to the 8,100-ton British tanker *Daronia.* Oesten sank a fourth confirmed ship on this patrol on September 5, the 5,700-ton Greek *Toannis Fafalios.* Thereafter, he proceeded to Penang, arriving on September 22, completing an exhausting summer voyage of 156 days. Of the four new U-cruisers sailing from Europe to the Far East in April, the *U-861* was the only one to complete the voyage.

Delayed seven to eight months by the aforementioned accident in the Baltic and the installation of a snort, the new XIV "Milk Cow" tanker *U-490,* commanded by thirty-nine-year-old Wilhelm Gerlach, sailed from Norway to the Far East on May 6. In addition to oil, she carried a large cargo of supplies, spare parts, and electronics. She made her way slowly south, running submerged in daylight hours, sometimes charging batteries submerged by use of the snort.

The Americans put a hunter-killer group, built around the "jeep" carrier *Croatan,* commanded by John P. W. Vest, which sailed from Norfolk on June 3, on the trail of *U-490.* In the early hours of June 11, when *U-490* got off a brief progress report to U-boat Control, the *Croatan* DFed the signal and Vest ordered the group to shape course to intercept her.

Shortly before 8:00 A.M. on June 11, *Frost,* one of the five destroyer escorts of the screen, got a sonar contact. The screen commander, Frank D. Giambattista in *Frost,* directed her skipper, John H. McWhorter, to attack. *Frost* fired her Hedgehog and got three hits. Another destroyer escort, *Huse,* commanded by James H. Batcheller, Jr., which hurried up to assist, threw over nine deep-set depth charges.

Caught unawares, Gerlach in *U-490* took the boat, which had a reinforced pressure hull, down to nearly one thousand feet. Since this was deeper than Allied depth charges could reach, Gerlach was confident he could escape. But Giambattista, determined not to lose this U-boat, brought up another destroyer escort, *Inch,* commanded by David A. Tufts, and the three ships stuck with *U-490* for over fif-

---

* For a vivid account of this sinking, see the memoir of the Armed Guard commander, McCormick, *Two Years Behind the Mast* (1991).

teen hours, carrying out twenty-five depth-charge attacks. Although these scores and scores of depth charges rattled the green German crew and the dozen-odd guinea pigs the ship's doctor had brought along for experiments, they caused no serious damage. Fearful that Allied sonar would hear the squealing pigs, Gerlach ordered the doctor, Herbert Stubbendorff, to kill them.

To encourage *U-490* to surface and attempt to escape in the dark, Giambattista at 11:00 P.M. put in motion a tactical trick. *Inch* and *Frost* pretended to give up the chase and exit to the north. *Snowden,* commanded by A. Jackson, Jr., which had relieved *Huse,* pretended to exit to the south. The trick worked. About thirty minutes after midnight on June 12, Gerlach surfaced *U-490* between *Frost* and *Snowden.* Thereupon the three destroyer escorts illuminated the U-boat with star shells and searchlights and raked her with gunfire.

Realizing he was trapped, Gerlach signaled in English, "SOS please take our crew," abandoned ship, and scuttled. The three warships continued to rake the valuable *U-490* until she sank, stern first. Thereafter the American vessels rescued all sixty German crewmen. According to the American intelligence report, in return for a promise from group commander Vest that he would not turn them over to the British, the Germans signed a statement agreeing to "answer all 'honorable questions.' " Among many other details, the prisoners revealed that German U-boats in the Baltic were experimenting with underwater refueling.

Although antiship operations by the twenty-four boats proceeding to and from the Far East in the first half of 1944 were in most cases secondary to the delivery of cargo, they nonetheless achieved some torpedo successes. The eight boats that set off from Penang for France (including *U-178*) sank fourteen ships for 77,500 tons. Lüdden in *U-188* sank half of these for 42,500 tons. The sixteen boats that set off from Europe for the Far East sank nineteen ships for 114,369 tons. Altogether: thirty-three ships for 191,860 tons.*

The cost to the Germans was ruinous: the tankers *Charlotte Schliemann* and *Brake* and eleven submarines sunk. These included six U-cruisers;† the last remaining Type XIV "Milk Cow" tanker, *U-490;* the Type VIIF torpedo-supply boat *U-1059;* Hitler's gift to Tojo, "Marco Polo II," the IXC40 *U-1224;* and two Italian cargo submarines, *U-IT22* and *U-IT23.* Of the approximately six hundred men serving on these eleven boats, 423 perished and 177 were captured by the Allies. Five boats bound from Penang to France were forced to abort.‡

Of the twenty-four boats sailing to and from the Far East in this period, only eight (33 percent) reached their intended destinations. Two, *U-178* and *U-188,* got to France with a combined total of about three hundred tons of rubber, tin, tungsten, quinine, and opium. Six§ got to the Far East, most loaded with supplies for the German U-boat base at Penang, including notably about sixty torpedoes and three U-boat propellers; and for the Japanese Navy, lead and mercury.

---

* In a patrol from Penang to the Indian Ocean and back to Penang in May and June, Fritz Schneewind in *U-183* sank one ship for 7,200 tons.

† *U-177, U-198, U-851, U-852, U-859, U-860.*

‡ *U-168, U-183, U-532, U-IT24, U-IT25.*

§ *U-181, U-196, U-537, U-843, U-861, U-1062.*

The Codebreakers

By April 1944, there were ninety-six four-rotor American bombes in continuous operation at the Nebraska Avenue facility in Washington, D.C. Two bombes had been combined to make a single "Double Unit #800 Bombe," a monster electromechanical machine that was sixteen feet long, seven feet high, and four feet wide. The other ninety-four bombes were the "standard" Model 530s. Hundreds of programmers and Waves assigned to three eight-hour watches operated the machines nonstop. Scores of enlisted men maintained the bombes in working order; other technicians set up experimental adaptations that emerged from Howard Engstrom's fecund Research Section.*

These American bombes produced about 1,400 naval Enigma decrypts a month, including all radio traffic to and from U-boat Control and the U-boat theater commanders and the flotilla commands as well as the U-boats at sea.† On April 24, Engstrom, Meader, and Wenger wrote that "the decryption of German naval traffic has been very successful during the past six months" (November 1943 through April 1944). They elaborated that during that period, each day "all units" [bombes] were first directed to produce the naval Enigma keys and when this had been accomplished, the bombes were used to solve "non-naval research problems carried out at the request of the British." Nearly half (45 percent) of all American bombe running time had been devoted to British problems, mostly concerning German Army and *Luftwaffe* networks.

The British had failed to produce a reliable four-rotor bombe, Engstrom wrote. "In the original discussions of this [4-wheel bombe project] with the British, the U.S. Navy was [only] to *assist* GC&CS in the German Naval problem. . . . British production of 4-wheel bombes has been extremely unsatisfactory. According to the latest information, eighteen (18) have been produced and continued operation of three (3) is the average performance. . . . At present the principal burden of the naval problem is carried by the U.S. Navy bombes." To buttress his estimates and assertions, Engstrom quoted from a message from GC&CS to OP20G on March 24, 1944:

> Performance of our machines is still poor and likely to remain so. In view of your 4-wheel capacity being more than adequate, priority is being given here [in England] to the production of new 3-wheel machines.‡

In February 1944, Hugh Alexander, who had succeeded Alan Turing in Hut 8, Bletchley Park, visited Washington and urged the U.S. Navy to build fifty more

---

* "Regular, Parallel, Slide, Cilly, Drag, Pluggable Series and Poly Grenades," "Inverted 530s," "Bulldozer," and so on.

† Ralph Erskine wrote that "there were almost 39,000 *Triton* decrypts in the 28 months between December 1942 and the end of the war."

‡ In another memo, dated April 1, 1944, Engstrom wrote that the British "have found their designs unsuccessful and the maintenance problem difficult so that the large proportion of their high speed equipment is out of commission most of the time. Probably for this reason and due to the volume of three-wheel non-Naval traffic, British production was shifted almost completely to three-wheel machines and the burden of the high speed problem has been shifted to us."

four-rotor bombes. "This was the first intimation that the U.S. Navy would be asked to extend its endeavor in this direction," Engstrom wrote. "Although a pessimistic outlook on the Atlantic situation can justify the additional equipment for Naval work, it is undoubtedly true that the prime impetus for the expansion lies in [American help in solving] the [German] Army and Air Force keys."

The case Alexander presented to Washington was persuasive. On February 25, Admiral King directed the contracting agent, the chief of the Bureau of Ships, to purchase the requested fifty improved production bombes, designated Model N-1530. "The operation of these additional bombes under [U.S.] Navy jurisdiction will, of course, speed up by one-third the recovery of Naval keys," Engstrom judged. "It will also increase by one-third the time devoted to non-Naval problems," such as German Army, *Luftwaffe,* and other networks.

The "pessimistic outlook" on the "Atlantic situation" to which Engstrom referred arose from the aforementioned discovery in March that the Germans intended to make a "major change" in Enigma to increase its complexity. As was soon learned, this was to be the inclusion of an internal reflector ("D") that could be rewired by the operator. The Germans had introduced this reflector on "certain air circuits" (i.e., *Luftwaffe* networks), causing "some concern," Engstrom wrote in vast understatement.

To deal with a possible inclusion of a "pluggable reflector" on naval Enigma machines, Engstrom stressed, a new type of decoding machine would be required. Engstrom and his R&D associates had anticipated the possibility of a "pluggable reflector" a year earlier (April 1943), he asserted, and the National Cash Register Company had almost completed a machine to cope with it. Called "Duenna," or N-1500, it was similar to a bombe but a completely "separate device." The Duenna under construction was twenty feet long, nine feet high, and four feet wide. It weighed eight thousand pounds (four tons). At Engstrom's insistence, the Duenna was awarded a higher priority than the fifty new model N-1530 production bombes, although there was no slack in either project.

Wenger and Engstrom explained their position in another document in April 1944:

> In our opinion there is serious question as to the necessity for building all of the [fifty] additional bombes. Certain important changes [pluggable reflectors] are apparently underway in the German Enigma machine which, if carried through as expected, will require use of a different type of machine [i.e., Duenna] designed by the Research Group of OP20G. The extent to which the [standard] bombe will be useful if these expected changes become extensive, is questionable.
>
> We are taking all reasonable steps to provide for eventualities. In order to insure meeting the problem when it arises, we are proceeding with the design and construction of ten (10) of these new units [Duennas] and may find it desirable to build, at most, only a portion of the additional [fifty standard] bombes [as requested by the British]. While the position as far as the Germans are concerned is not clear at the present time, we expect some clarification prior to the completion of the [standard] bombes, and, should it appear advisable, we shall recommend a reduction in the number to be built.

The overwhelming success of Overlord, the invasion of Occupied France that took place about ten weeks after Wenger and Engstrom wrote those words, evidently swept away the "pessimistic outlook" about codebreaking in the Atlantic sector. For one thing, the Germans soon lost the telephonic lines between U-boat Control in Berlin and the five U-boat bases on the Atlantic coast in France and were forced to use radio. For another, significantly more U-boats put to sea, generating naval traffic. These developments led to a sudden enormous increase in the flow of naval Enigma on various radio circuits and with it, an inevitable increase in procedural errors that produced a bountiful harvest of the cribs necessary to feed to the bombes. For another thing, the Allied invasion apparently caused the Germans to cancel plans for widespread distribution and introduction of the "pluggable reflector."

The upshot was that in September 1944, after the National Cash Register Company had completed half (twenty-five) of the new model N-1530 bombes requested by the British, Admiral King directed the Bureau of Ships to cancel the remainder. That left the number of American bombes built in the war at 121 (ninety-six plus twenty-five). The machines cost a total of about six million dollars, Engstrom estimated. By March 1945, shortly before the German surrender, only two giant Duennas (N-1500s) had been completed and put into operation and only three more were on order.

The U.S. Army's project to build Rapid Analytic Machines (RAMs), or three-rotor bombes, encountered as many setbacks as the British four-rotor bombe project. Bell Telephone Laboratories built only ten. By comparison to the U.S. Navy bombes, they were painfully slow: 910 "tries" of crib assumptions per second compared to the Navy's 20,280. In a typical day, a Navy bombe could therefore make 40,000 short three-wheel runs compared to the Army's 1,200. "The total U.S. Army installation can be considered equal to about one of our bombes," Joe Wenger wrote on February 16, 1945, comparing the two types. "To duplicate Navy production figures with bombes of the Army type would require a tremendous installation. . . . A rough estimate of the relative productive capacity of the complete U.S. Army and U.S. Navy installations is a factor of fifty in favor of the Navy."

Patrols to West Africa

Ten Type IXs patrolled to Freetown and the Gulf of Guinea in the period from January 1 to June 1, 1944. They were to be supported by the Type XIV "Milk Cow" U-tanker *U-488*. Five of this group and the U-tanker failed to return.

The famous IXB *U-123,* in which Reinhard Hardegen opened the Drumbeat campaign in United States waters, sailed on January 9, commanded by Horst von Schroeter, age twenty-four. The senior petty officer was Walter Kaeding, age twenty-eight, who had commissioned the boat in May 1940 and had made all thirteen of her war patrols under Moehle, Hardegen, and von Schroeter.

Von Schroeter found no targets off Freetown. On the return voyage, he met and refueled from the XIV tanker *U-488* on March 23. Reporting this meet, *U-488* said that the radio in *U-123* was out and unfixable and relayed von Schroeter's results: a triple miss on a troopship, a T-5 miss on a "destroyer," no hits or sinkings. Control then directed von Schroeter to rendezvous with the outbound *U-505* on April 7 and get new Enigma keys. When the boat arrived in Lorient on April 24, completing a fruitless voyage of 107 days, Control retired *U-123*. Admiral Dönitz awarded von Schroeter, Kaeding, and the chief engineer Reinhardt König the *Ritterkreuz*.* Von Schroeter and König returned to Germany to commission a big "electro boat." Promoted to officer rank, Kaeding briefly commanded a school duck, then a small "electro boat" that was never completed.

Next to sail was the no less famous IXC *U-66*, commanded by a new skipper, Gerhard Seehausen, age twenty-six. Passing Cape Finisterre, Seehausen saw a carrier and screen and boldly attempted an attack but he only managed to shoot one T-5 at a "destroyer," which missed. Off Freetown he missed another "destroyer" with a T-5. Proceeding east in the Gulf of Guinea, on February 26 he came upon a small convoy off Takoradi, STL 12, and sank the 5,300-ton British freighter *Silvermaple* and took her captain and another officer prisoner. He claimed another freighter from this convoy but it wasn't confirmed. In the week following, Seehausen sank two lone freighters: the 5,200-ton French *St. Louis* and the 5,000-ton British *John Holt*. Still later in March, he got the 4,300-ton British tanker *Matadian* in the shallow Bay of Nigeria. In return, British patrol craft savaged *U-66* with depth charges and forced her to bottom in tenacious mud at four hundred feet. Seehausen finally escaped by sallying ship fore and aft.

Having sunk what he believed to be an impressive five ships for 30,688 tons (actually, four ships for about 20,000 tons), Seehausen commenced the homeward voyage, low on fuel. Aware of his need for fuel, U-boat Control ordered Seehausen to rendezvous with the U-tanker *U-488* on April 26. Allied codebreakers decrypted Enigma messages about this rendezvous and American naval authorities put a hunter-killer group on the scent: the "jeep" carrier *Croatan* and five destroyer escorts. Upon reaching the rendezvous area, the Americans DFed signals between *U-66* and *U-488* and *Croatan* launched Avengers configured for prolonged night-search flights.

The night searchers found *U-488*, and in the early hours of April 26, all five destroyer escorts converged for an attack with depth charges and Hedgehogs: *Barber, Frost, Huse, Inch,* and *Snowden*. The attack was deadly. The U-tanker was never heard from again. Tenth Fleet credited four of the five ships (not *Inch*) with this important kill that left only one XIV tanker, the *U-490*, which, as described, was sent to the Far East and lost.

Nearby, Seehausen in *U-66* heard the attack on *U-488*. He hauled off and radioed Control: "Supplying impossible. . . . Noise of sinking heard. . . ." Upon receiving this message, U-boat Control repeatedly queried *U-488*. When she did not reply, Control correctly assumed the worst and attempted to rendezvous *U-66* with

* At the time of the award, von Schroeter's confirmed score— all on *U-123*—was six ships for about 28,000 tons, including the British submarine *P-615*, plus shared credit with *U-435* for the 7,100-ton British freighter *Empire Shackleton*. Kaeding was one of seven enlisted submariners to win the *Ritterkreuz*.

Lüdden's *U-188,* inbound from Penang, and the outbound *U-68.* Meanwhile, Control declared further refueling at sea to be "impossible" (until the development of submerged refueling) and warned the boats in distant areas to plan return voyages accordingly.

Seehausen in *U-66* proceeded to the rendezvous with *U-188* as related, but the Americans pursued him relentlessly. Two hunter-killer groups—the "jeep" carriers *Block Island* and *Bogue* with appropriate screens—relieved the *Croatan* group, which was low on fuel. Reporting the failure of the rendezvous, Seehausen added: "Supplying impossible since [we have been] DFed constantly since [April] 26th. . . . Mid-Atlantic worse than Biscay." On the night of May 5–6, a night-flying Avenger from *Block Island,* piloted by Jimmie J. Sellars, found *U-66* and homed in one of the destroyer escorts, *Buckley,* commanded by Brent M. Abel, a graduate of Harvard College and Harvard Law School, who that day celebrated his twenty-eighth birthday.*

Sighting *U-66* silhoutted against the moon, at four thousand yards, *Buckley* prepared to attack and ram. However, Seehausen saw *Buckley* first, possibly shot a T-5, and opened fire with his machine guns and flak guns. Abel returned fire from 2,100 yards with his three 3" guns, which knocked out *U-66*'s 4.1" deck gun, caused other damage, and probably killed or wounded some Germans. *Buckley* then rammed *U-66* forward and the two ships locked in a deadly embrace, reminiscent of the battle between *U-405* and the American destroyer *Borie.*

Seehausen feared that *Buckley*'s men were about to board *U-66* in an attempt to seize secret materials. Since that action would force him to scuttle with most of the crew belowdecks, he directed his first watch officer, Klaus Herbig, age twenty-two, and other men on the bridge to board *Buckley* and create a diversion while he broke away from *Buckley,* got the rest of the *U-66* crew topside, and scuttled. "Immediately," Herbig recalled, "I jumped over with eight men to where we could hang on to the rail of the destroyer."

When these Germans appeared on *Buckley*'s bow—to divert and/or to surrender—the Americans, believing they intended to capture *Buckley,* repelled them hand-to-hand as in days of yore. Abel described the counteraction in his official report:

> Men begin swarming out of submarine and up on *Buckley*'s forecastle. Machine gun, tommy gun and rifle fire knock off several. Ammunition expended at this time included several general mess coffee cups, which were on hand at ready gun station. Two of the enemy were hit in the head with those. Empty shell cases were also used by crew of 3" gun Number 2 to repel boarders. . . . *Buckley* suffers only casualty of engagement when man bruises fist knocking one enemy over the side. . . . The boatswain's mate in charge of forward ammunition party kills a man attempting to board with .45 pistol. Man falls back over side. Midships repair party equipped with

* Abel's Harvard College classmate (1937), writer/journalist E. J. Kahn, Jr., recounted the events that followed in a long piece in *The New Yorker* magazine on February 8, 1988, condensed and republished in *Naval History* magazine, Summer 1988.

> rifles mans lifelines on starboard side . . . and picks off several men on deck of submarine. Chief Fire Controlman uses tommy gun from bridge with excellent results.

The *Buckley* crew killed or fatally wounded an unknown number of Germans and captured five, including Herbig. Meanwhile, Seehausen broke *U-66* loose from *Buckley* and sped off in the darkness at maximum speed, leaving a string of Germans who were jumping into the sea. Notwithstanding a distended bow and other collision damage forward, Abel in *Buckley* chased with guns blazing, caught up, and prepared to ram *U-66* a second time. In the chaos of this close encounter, *U-66* swung around and rammed *Buckley* aft, wiping off her starboard propeller shaft and holing her plates. Thereupon the *U-66* chief engineer, Georg Olschewski, who had been awarded a *Ritterkreuz* by radio three days earlier, scuttled *U-66*. In the next three hours, Abel fished out and captured thirty-one more Germans, including *Ritterkreuz* holder Olschewski, but not Seehausen or his two British POWs. Altogether Abel captured and turned over to *Block Island* thirty-six Germans; twenty-four Germans perished.

Apart from the *U-801,* which as related was sunk by the *Block Island* group, in late February and during the month of March, five other Type IXs sailed to Freetown and the Gulf of Guinea. None sank a ship. Three were lost.

The veteran IXC *U-515,* commanded by the most highly decorated skipper still in Atlantic combat, Werner Henke, age thirty-five, who wore the *Ritterkreuz* with Oak Leaves, departed France on March 30. In addition to *Naxos,* the *U-515* was equipped with one of the first of the *Hohentwiel* search radars.* On that same day, the *Guadalcanal* hunter-killer group, commanded by Daniel V. Gallery, sailed from Casablanca to hunt down U-tankers and their customers west of the Cape Verde Islands.

Upon arrival in a likely area at sunset on April 8, Gallery launched four night-flying Avengers. Patrolling under a full moon, one of the pilots found *U-515* on the surface but his alarm was not heard in the hunter-killer group. After recovering these aircraft and learning of the contact, Gallery launched other Avengers and sent two of his five destroyer escorts, *Pope* and *Chatelain,* commanded by Edwin H. Headland, Jr., and James L. Foley, respectively, to chase down a possible radar contact. Believing they got sonar contacts, the ships dropped depth charges. When *Pope* reported seeing an oil slick rise to the surface, Gallery sent Avengers and two more destroyer escorts, *Pillsbury* and *Flaherty,* to the scene. Two Avengers positively sighted *U-515* and dropped depth charges, the second in the face of flak. None of these attacks caused any noteworthy damage to *U-515,* but Henke, who dived, was caught in a net he could not escape.

After dawn on April 9—Easter Sunday—Dan Gallery initiated a dogged hunt.

---

* The "mattress"-type antenna, stored in a bridge recess, could be raised and lowered hydraulically.

When Henke surfaced warily to charge batteries and air the boat, an Avenger, piloted by Douglas W. Brooks, dived to attack. Henke's automatic, rapid-fire 37mm flak gun jammed at the crucial moment, and Brooks dropped depth charges and forced Henke to dive deep (787 feet), by which time *Guadalcanal* and her screen were merely fifteen miles distant. Three of these warships, *Flaherty, Pillsbury,* and *Pope,* and other aircraft, closed rapidly on the scene and commenced a persistent and effective attack on *U-515* that went on for seven hours that Easter day.

The close explosions eventually caused flooding in the after torpedo compartment that could not be stanched. Henke abandoned and sealed off that area, but the weight of the flooding aft pulled the bow up at a steep angle of thirty degrees. Henke attempted to decrease the angle by sending crew to the forward torpedo compartment, blowing tanks, and speeding up, but these measures failed and *U-515* slid down backward to about 656 feet. There *U-515* went out of control and shot to the surface, stern first, with a down angle of 45 degrees.

When *U-515* popped up very close by, *Chatelain* and *Flaherty* opened fire with all guns that would bear, sweeping the U-boat's deck clean of men. In addition, *Chatelain* shot seven more shallow-set depth charges from her K guns and *Flaherty* shot a torpedo. The torpedo missed *U-515* and continued on toward the approaching *Pillsbury.* Astonishingly, an alert pilot saw the danger and sank the torpedo with machine-gun fire. He and other Wildcat and Avenger pilots then attacked *U-515* with machine guns and rockets. Finally, in mid-afternoon, Henke ordered abandon ship and scuttled. Sixteen Germans died; the destroyer escorts recovered Henke and forty-three others and turned them over to *Guadalcanal.*

In his colorful memoir of the U-boat war, Gallery asserted that he pressured Henke into signing a statement guaranteeing that he, Henke, would willingly give truthful information provided Gallery did not turn him and his crew over to the British authorities who had supposedly vowed to court-martial him and them for the "atrocity" of sinking the troopship/liner *Ceramic* (on December 7, 1942). In his book on the U-boat war,* the German journalist Hans Herlin, who interviewed three of Henke's officers, disputed this assertion. However, Henke's American biographer, Timothy P. Mulligan, has located in the National Archives and authenticated the document signed by Henke, as well as a similar document signed by forty enlisted men of *U-515.*

The *Guadalcanal* landed Henke and his men in Norfolk on April 26. After six days in an Army processing center, Camp Allen, American authorities divided the Germans into two groups. Henke and eighteen men went to Fort Hunt, an elaborate top-secret Army-Navy interrogation center near Mount Vernon about seventeen miles south of Washington, D.C.† The other twenty-five men went to Fort George C. Meade nearby in Maryland for onward transfer to POW camps at Papago, Arizona, and elsewhere.

During his interrogation at Fort Hunt from May 4 to 14, Henke recanted his

* *Verdammter Atlantik: Schicksale deutscher U-Boot-Fahrer* (1982).

† At the end of the war, Fort Hunt was dismantled and destroyed. Its function remained top secret and unknown until Mulligan found its records in the National Archives.

signed agreement to give truthful information and clammed up. The naval interrogators wrote:

> Henke proved extremely security-conscious. He professed preference for American captivity rather than British but this fact made him no more accessible. His interrogating officers found him sullen and embittered. His conceit was limitless although he somewhat grudgingly gave some credit for his success to his crew. . . . The feelings of *U-515*'s crew toward their commander were mixed. Some admired his personality; others held his extreme strictness against him. The surviving officers, although admitting his ability, acknowledged his frightful conceit. It seems that ashore Henke was particulary disliked and few in the 10th Flotilla and on the staff of the Admiral U-boats could forgive his boundless ambition and egotism. . . .

To punish Henke for his recantation of a signed pledge and to prevent him from bragging to his crew that he had defied the Americans and was therefore to be regarded as a POW hero, the Allied authorities concerned decided to make good on the original threat to turn Henke over to the British, ostensibly to stand trial for sinking the troopship *Ceramic*. Although there was never any intent to try Henke for that sinking, which was perfectly legal and proper, Henke did not know this and, as Mulligan writes, he must have viewed the proposed transfer to British control as "a death sentence," resulting in a "show trial" that "could only end on the scaffold."

Henke apparently decided that he would not allow himself to be subjected to that supposed humiliation and disgrace. During an exercise period on the evening of June 15, he suddenly bolted for the Fort Hunt security fence. An official report from Fort Hunt described the rest:

> At about 1855 . . . a guard saw Henke attempting to climb the enclosure wire fence. . . . In easily audible tones the guard twice called halt. Henke continued to climb and the guard called halt a third time just before subject reached the top of the fence. As Henke mounted the fence, the guard fired. The prisoner was hit and hung motionless on top of the fence. The officer of the guard, hearing the shot, went immediately to the scene and upon seeing Henke called the camp doctor. Injured prisoner was promptly placed in an ambulance and driven to [a] hospital, while the doctor administered first aid en route. Upon arrival at the hospital at approximately 2018, Henke was pronounced dead. A thorough investigation disclosed that the guard had acted properly and that death was due to prisoner's own misconduct.*

The sorriest U-boat in the Atlantic force, the IXC *U-505,* which had aborted at least a dozen starts since December 1942—one occasioned by the suicide of the

* Henke told his interrogators he had sunk a total of twenty-eight ships for 177,000 tons. U-boat Control credited him with sinking twenty-six ships for 166,000 tons and on August 1, 1944, declared that he was killed "while attempting to escape." His confirmed score—all on *U-515*—was twenty-five ships sunk for 142,636 tons, including the sloop *Chanticleer,* ranking him fifteenth among all U-boat skippers in the war.

skipper, Peter Zschech—finally sailed again on March 16. She was still commanded by Zschech's replacement, Harald Lange, age forty, the oldest captain of an attack U-boat on active service. Her first watch officer remained Paul Meyer, age twenty-six, who had brought the boat home when Zschech killed himself.

After he gave *U-123* new Enigma keys, Lange in *U-505* patrolled for about six weeks between Freetown and its neighboring seaport, Monrovia, Liberia. The Allies tracked his movements, diverted shipping, and in all that time he sank nothing. "The hex was still with us," the crewman Hans Decker wrote, unaware of the Allied break into Enigma. "It was maddening. Absolutely nothing turned up." The prolonged operations in the warm, humid tropics disgruntled and debilitated the crew and sapped the batteries. Low on fuel, Lange commenced the homeward voyage on May 27, electing to take a shortcut, hugging the Cape Verde Islands.

Allied codebreakers provided the approximate homeward track of *U-505.* Dan Gallery's hunter-killer group—the "jeep" carrier *Guadalcanal* and five destroyer escorts—attempted to locate *U-505* but failed. Low on fuel, on June 4 Gallery issued orders to steer for Casablanca.

One of the well-trained destroyer escorts, *Chatelain,* reported a possible sonar contact at 11:10 that same morning. Her new captain, Dudley S. Knox, a lawyer and son of the prominent naval historian Dudley Wright Knox, ran down the bearing, evaluated the contact as a "submarine," and fired a Hedgehog salvo that missed. Gallery promptly directed two airborne Wildcats and two destroyer escorts, *Jenks* and *Pillsbury,* to assist *Chatelain* and hauled *Guadalcanal* out of torpedo range, screened by the other two destroyer escorts, *Pope* and *Flaherty.* He then turned *Guadalcanal* into the wind and launched a Wildcat-Avenger "killer team."

The two airborne Wildcats, piloted by John W. Cadle, Jr., and Wolffe W. Roberts, provided cover for the destroyer escort *Chatelain.* When the pilots saw the outline of the submarine at periscope depth, Cadle radioed: "Ship that just fired Hedgehog reverse course." Thereupon Cadle twice "marked the spot" of the submarine with machine-gun bursts. Gallery later wrote that the "intelligent," "quick-thinking," and "courageous action" by Cadle and Roberts was decisive to the events that followed and was "one of the few cases in which an aircraft actually directed the attack" on a U-boat. Later, skipper Dudley Knox in *Chatelain* emphatically denied that was the case. He wrote that after his failed Hedgehog attack, he regained sonar contact on *U-505* at one hundred yards and never lost it. The observations and target marking by the Wildcats, Knox insisted, were "valuable" but only in that they enabled him to cut short standard procedure and commence a depth-charge attack at a range of five hundred yards rather than the prescribed one thousand yards.

Knox ran down the sonar bearing and at 11:21 commenced firing fourteen shallow-set depth charges. By that time Lange had discovered that *U-505* was in great peril and had ordered his engineer, Joseph Hanser, to take the boat deep. The depth charges shook *U-505* and caused some flooding, but they did not severely damage the main structure of the boat. However, it plunged "out of control" to about 755 feet, according to the account by crewman Decker. He went on to say that Lange then cried "his last organized order" to Hanser: "Take us up—take us up before it's too late!"

Merely twelve minutes after the original sonar contact, at 11:22, the *U-505* popped to the surface about seven hundred yards from *Chatelain.* Dudley Knox, who was on fullest alert, stopped and immediately opened fire with his 3"/50 caliber guns, shooting forty-eight rounds, some of which hit *U-505.* When it appeared that *U-505* was turning toward him—and a lookout shouted that a torpedo was coming toward *Chatelain*—Knox responded by shooting a single torpedo at *U-505,* but it missed, as did the German torpedo. Joining in the attack, *Jenks,* commanded by Julius F. Way, fired thirty-two rounds of 3"/50 caliber and *Pillsbury,* commanded by George W. Casselman, fired twenty-one rounds. At the same time, the two Wildcats ran in and strafed, drawing flak, the pilots reported (perhaps inaccurately). All this gunfire killed one of the fifty-nine Germans on *U-505* and wounded others, including skipper Lange and first watch officer Meyer.

The Wildcat pilots reported that the Germans were streaming topside with hands raised in surrender or jumping into the sea. Gallery, who had encouraged his captains to plan for a possible U-boat boarding, radioed all hands: "I would like to capture that bastard if possible." At 11:27, he ordered all elements to cease fire.

The subordinate commander of the five destroyer escorts, Frederick S. Hall, flying his flag in *Pillsbury,* reacted promptly. He directed *Pillsbury*'s captain, George Casselman, to close on the U-boat and lower away a whaleboat with a boarding party. At the same time, Knox in *Chatelain* and Way in *Jenks* were to launch whalers and recover survivors. *Pope,* commanded by Edwin H. Headland, was to continuously circle the scene at a range of two miles to thwart or kill any other U-boats that might be in the vicinity. *Flaherty,* commanded by Means Johnson, Jr., remained with *Guadalcanal* as plane guard and screen.

The *Pillsbury*'s boarding party, commanded by the ship's first lieutenant, Albert L. David, was composed of nine men. When the party boarded *U-505,* which was circling on electric motors slowly to starboard, David and two others, radioman Stanley E. Wdowiak and torpedoman Arthur W. Knispel, disregarding possible booby traps, demolition charges, or armed fanatical Germans, rushed below to the control room. It was deserted. Seeing a six- to eight-inch geyser of seawater spouting from an open strainer (one method of scuttling), the men found the valve cap nearby and shut off the flooding, a decisive measure in the capture of *U-505.* However, they were unable to immediately shut down the electric motors or unjam the rudder in the control room or at the emergency hand-steering station in the stern torpedo room, which they believed to be flooded and the watertight door to be booby-trapped. Instead, the three men, who thought the U-boat was on the verge of sinking, concentrated on salvaging secret "publications" (current Enigma keys, short-signal books, and so on) and "encoding machines" (Enigmas), which they passed topside to other members of the party. The haul was large—and priceless.*

Since *Guadalcanal* was no longer threatened by *U-505,* Gallery brought her and her screen, *Flaherty,* close to the U-boat. He then called away a ten-man

* For valor and resourcefulness, David was awarded a Congressional Medal of Honor; Wdowiak and Knispel the Navy Cross.

Guadalcanal boarding party, led by a veteran engineering hand, Earl Trosino, and, somewhat later, a second party of seventeen men. Lifted by a wave, Trosino's first boat crashed down on the forward deck of *U-505,* making a great noise, which terrified the three *Pillsbury* men belowdecks, who did not know *Guadalcanal* had sent a boarding party.

While this was going on, the three destroyer escorts were busy. In compliance with orders from Hall, Casselman in *Pillsbury* attempted to lash his ship to the circling *U-505.* His men got a line to *U-505,* but her rigged-out bow planes holed *Pillsbury* (flooding an engine room) and put her out of action temporarily, while another of her whalers captured seven German survivors. Knox in *Chatelain* captured forty-eight German survivors, including the wounded skipper Lange, the engineer Hanser, a photo-propagandist, Kurt Brey, and the ship's doctor, Karl-Friedrich Rosemeyer. *Jenks* captured the wounded first watch officer, Meyer. The first lieutenant of *Jenks,* John D. Lannon, who visited *U-505* in a whaler, returned with secret documents obtained from the *Pillsbury* and *Guadalcanal* parties and with two other German survivors. Later in the day, all fifty-eight Germans were put on board *Guadalcanal.*

Upon hearing from Trosino that *U-505* would sink unless she was towed, Gallery directed *Guadalcanal* to put a line on her. Not without considerable difficulty, Trosino and *Guadalcanal*'s men got a 1¼-inch steel cable through the U-boat's bullnose and tied it off. Thereupon Gallery went ahead with *Guadalcanal* gingerly, setting course north to Casablanca with three destroyer escorts, leaving *Pope* to stand by the stricken *Pillsbury* until her crew could complete emergency repairs. During the late evening, when engineers informed Gallery that they doubted the task group had sufficient fuel to reach Casablanca with *U-505* in tow, he changed course to the nearest Allied port, Dakar.

When Washington received news of the capture, it was thunderstruck and deeply concerned. Should Berlin learn of the capture of *U-505,* the Germans would doubtless go ahead with the promised "major changes" to improve U-boat Enigma security, perhaps temporarily blinding Allied codebreakers on the eve of the postponed Overlord invasion. Allan Rockwell McCann, a onetime submariner fresh from command of the new battleship *Iowa* who was to replace Francis "Frog" Low as Chief of Staff, Tenth Fleet, recalled that Admiral King was so furious at Gallery for possibly jeopardizing the Allied mastery of Enigma that he threatened to court-martial him.*

Cooler heads prevailed. In the belief that Dakar and Casablanca were crawling with Axis spies, Washington told Gallery that if possible, he should go west to the well-isolated British island of Bermuda. In furtherance of that plan, with which Gallery concurred, Washington immediately dispatched from Casablanca the big

---

* On the day of the capture, June 4, First Sea Lord Cunningham cabled Admiral King urgently: "In view of the importance at this time for preventing the Germans suspecting a compromise of their cyphers I am sure you will agree that all concerned should be ordered to maintain complete secrecy regarding the capture of *U-505.* I am instructing Flag Officer Commanding West Africa Forces and Flag Officer Gibraltar Mediterranean Approaches in this sense."

(20,000-ton) fleet oiler *Kennebec,* the seaplane tender *Humbolt,* which embarked an experienced submarine skipper, Colby G. Rucker, the destroyer escort *Durik,* and the 1,200-ton oceangoing tug *Abnaki.*

During the first night, June 4–5, the towline broke. The four American vessels circled *U-505* all night on a maximum U-boat watch. During the pause, the slow-moving *Pope* and patched-up *Pillsbury* had time to catch up to the main formation. After daylight, *Guadalcanal*'s men put over a 2¼-inch wire tow cable, but *U-505*'s rudder was still jammed full right and towing remained exceedingly difficult. Gallery himself boarded *U-505* and after a careful inspection, declared that the stern torpedo compartment was dry and that he could see no booby trap on the watertight door leading thereto. Holding their collective breath, Trosino and his men opened the door, gained access to the hand-steering station, and put the rudder amidships.

The supporting armada from Casablanca rendezvoused on June 7. *Kennebec* provided ample fuel for the onward voyage to Bermuda. The *Humbolt* delivered Colby Rucker, who assumed "command" of *U-505,* got her shipshape and dry with portable pumps, and jettisoned loose, unnecessary gear. *Abnaki* took the U-boat in tow with the 2¼-inch cable. *Jenks,* with "ten mail sacks" of secret documents (weighing about 1,100 pounds) and "the submarine's coding machines," raced ahead at maximum speed to Bermuda. All this material reached OP20G in Washington on June 12. Meanwhile, Washington and London ordered steps to keep absolutely secret the arrival of these ships in Bermuda. Aware of Gallery's overweening thirst for publicity,* Admiral King admonished him to lie low and to absolutely seal the lips of the three thousand sailors and airmen in the task group.

The *Guadalcanal* and other ships arrived in Bermuda under extraordinary security on June 19. Kenneth Knowles of the U.S. Submarine Tracking Room, the outgoing Chief of Staff, Tenth Fleet, Francis Low, and seven others flew to Bermuda to inspect the boat and to interrogate the prisoners of *U-505* (code-named "Nemo" or alternately, *U-606*).

Preoccupied with repulsing the Normandy invasion, the Germans assumed *U-505* had been sunk by Allied aircraft and made no major changes in naval Enigma. Except for two special complete copies to King and Ingersoll, Gallery's official patrol report mysteriously terminated on June 4, just prior to the capture. Remarkably, Allied personnel in the *Guadalcanal* hunter-killer group and the supporting armada and Bermuda kept their lips sealed until after the war. The IXC *U-505* was the second U-boat to be captured intact during the war after the VII *U-570,* and first foreign man-of-war to be captured by the U.S. Navy since 1815.†

---

* In postwar years, Gallery became one of the Navy's chief propagandists in its bureaucratic war with the Army and Air Force and published two colorful, self-serving books on the Atlantic war, *Clear the Decks!* (1951) and *Twenty Million Tons Under the Sea* (1956). He was also one of the first and most outspoken critics of the Allied decision to try and sentence Dönitz for war crimes.

† Largely through the efforts of Gallery, a Chicagoan, *U-505* wound up intact as a well-preserved and popular exhibit at the Chicago Museum of Science and Industry. Until 1993, when a salvage company raised the *U-534* from the Kattegat and transported her to Liverpool, England, for reconditioning and display, the *U-505* was the only existing Type IXC.

The intelligence haul from *U-505* matched—or perhaps exceeded—the hauls from *U-110* and *U-559*.* In a long memo of July 13, OP20G chief Joseph Wenger listed the cryptographic "benefits" from *U-505*. In summary:

• The Atlantic and Indian Ocean U-boat cipher keys for the month of June 1944. With these keys, the Americans were able to read that traffic as soon as the Germans did and, of course, no bombe time was required. The bombes that would have been used to find keys for that traffic were used to break Army and *Luftwaffe* keys, normally a British responsibility; four thousand extra hours on Mediterranean keys and nine thousand extra hours on other Army and *Luftwaffe* keys. Net gain: thirteen thousand bombe hours, as a result of which many new solutions "which would otherwise not have been possible," were obtained.

• The "extremely important" current grid-chart—or geographic location—cipher. In use by the Germans for about two years for position reporting, "this is the first time one has ever been physically compromised," Wenger wrote. It eliminated a lot of guesswork and enabled OP20G to "determine exactly all positions expressed in the text of U-boat messages."

• The "Reserve Short Signal" cipher, which was to go into effect on July 15, 1944. "This cipher," Wenger wrote, "prescribes the internal machine setting to be used for tactical signals from U-boats and surface craft."

• The "Reserve Bigram Tables," which were to go into effect on August 1, 1944, replacing those of July 1943, which OP20G had "reconstructed" cryptographically. "These tables determine the internal set-up for each message," Wenger wrote. "Hence, even though one message for the day can be read, all messages cannot be read until these Bigram Tables are available or reconstructed."

• The current "Short Weather" cipher for U-boats. This cipher enabled OP20G to determine accurately the position of weather-reporting U-boats. Prior to this capture, OP20G had only "partially reconstructed" this cipher.†

Another valuable discovery in the haul from *U-505* was a description of and operating instructions for a new German electronic-navigation system for ships and aircraft, *"Elektra-Sonne."* Similar in principle to Loran and the RAF "Gee" electronic systems, widely separated shore-based German radio transmitters projected a "fan" or "cross pattern" of beams over the Bay of Biscay and the Atlantic Ocean that could be utilized to obtain a fairly precise "fix."

In his memoir, the canny RAF scientist R. V. Jones‡ wrote that he learned (probably from Enigma) that to improve the *Elektra-Sonne* system, the Germans were building another land-based site at Lugo, in northwest "neutral" Spain. Jones asked Coastal Command whether it should be destroyed or saved for use by Allied aircraft. Coastal Command replied, in effect, "Save it." The British code-named the

---

* For the *U-110* capture on May 9, 1941, see Volume I, pp. 278–85; for the *U-559* capture on October 30, 1942, see this volume, p. 84.

† The complete top-secret Wenger memo and other declassified NSA documents were kindly provided by Keith Gill, director of the *U-505* exhibit at the Museum of Science and Industry in Chicago.

‡ *The Wizard War* (1978).

system "Consol" and, Jones wrote, "used it with much success." It was "beautifully simple," much superior to the British "Gee." In the postwar years, *Elektra-Sonne* replaced the British "Gee" system and spread all over the world.

After the interrogation process had been completed, the fifty-eight Germans from *U-505* were carefully segregated from other German POWs at a U.S. Army facility, Camp Ruston, Louisiana. The Army's Assistant Chief of Staff, G-2, Clayton Bissell, directed that "no reports of captures of members of this group of naval prisoners of war will be submitted either to the protecting power or to the International Red Cross." Günter Hessler wrote that U-boat Control did not learn of the capture until late 1944 or early 1945, when a German officer in a Canadian POW camp managed to warn of "the probable capture of a U-boat, intact and complete with signal publications."

Not described in the Wenger memo was mention of another communications item found in the secret papers of *U-505*. This was a reference (in a table of contents) to "Short-Signal Procedure *Kurier*." Of itself, this was not particularly alarming; Allied codebreakers had seen a prior reference to *Kurier* in late 1943. However, this new reference led the codebreakers to deduce that the Germans might be—or were—contemplating a new short-signal procedure. All hands involved with Enigma breaking kept a sharp lookout for further *Kurier* information or procedures.

Allied codebreakers had confirmed by August 26, 1944, that "a radically new communications system was being introduced into German U-boat operations." This was *Kurier*, which the Allies dubbed "Squash" and, later, "Turnip." It was a super-high-speed transmission device (*Geber*) for use by U-boats at sea. It could transmit a seven-letter message in a burst of about half a second. It was therefore not only extremely difficult for the Allies to intercept but also virtually impossible to DF. Adding to the complexity, the *Kurier* could be transmitted daily over four wavelengths of varying frequencies. Two of these were available in any given hour.

The Allied "*Kurier* watch" had a very tough time spotting test transmissions from U-boats and assembling useful data. It was not until December 18, 1944, that British and American communications specialists had learned the "essential elements" of *Kurier*. Fearing that the Germans might give the Japanese *Kurier* devices to copy, in January 1945 the Americans gave MIT and Bell Telephone Laboratories contracts to develop sophisticated devices to intercept and DF *Kurier* transmissions.* Fortunately for the Allies, before the use of *Kurier* became widespread, the Germans capitulated. No evidence has come to light that the Germans gave the Japanese *Kurier* technology.

The IXC40 snort boat *U-543*, commanded by Hans-Jürgen Hellriegel, who won a *Ritterkreuz* on his one prior patrol in this boat, sailed from France to the Caribbean on March 28. On April 9, Hellriegel came upon a "small convoy" but escorts drove

---

* The Allies had not solved the *Kurier* problems by the end of the Pacific war in August 1945. In case the Soviets had obtained *Kurier* technology from the Germans, American R&D work continued in postwar years on counterdevices renamed "Spinach."

the boat off and depth-charged her, thwarting an attack. Ten days later Hellriegel refueled from the XIV tanker *U-488*. Aware of this rendezvous from Enigma decrypts, Allied authorities sent an American hunter-killer group built around the newly arrived "jeep" carrier *Tripoli* to the area. An Avenger from *Tripoli,* piloted by C. B. Humphrey, found and attacked *U-543*. In three runs into heavy flak, Humphrey's depth charges hung up but he fired rockets, drove *U-543* under, and dropped a Fido. Hellriegel went deep and escaped.

Later, when U-boat Control assumed (correctly) that the XIV tanker *U-488* had been lost, it directed Hellriegel to abort his patrol to the Caribbean and reverse course to the area west of the Cape Verde Islands and serve as a provisional refueler. He was to supply Lüdden's *U-188,* inbound from the Indian Ocean and/or Seehausen's *U-66,* inbound from the Gulf of Guinea. On May 14, when Control assumed (wrongly) that *U-188* and (rightly) that *U-66* had been sunk, it released Hellriegel from refueling responsibilities and gave him a free hand. He elected to patrol off Freetown and in the Gulf of Guinea.

After several miserable weeks in tropical waters and no sinkings, Hellriegel headed north for France. Allied codebreakers calculated his homeward track from Enigma decrypts and, on June 28, a hunter-killer group built around another new American "jeep" carrier, *Wake Island,* got on the scent. On the evening of July 2, an Avenger, piloted by Frederick L. Moore, found *U-543* on radar and attacked, notwithstanding flak. When Hellriegel crash-dived, Moore dropped a Fido on the swirl. It apparently hit. Nothing further was ever heard from *U-543*.

The other three attack boats that patrolled to Freetown and the Gulf of Guinea in March and April also fared poorly. The veteran IXC *U-155,* commanded by a new skipper, Johannes Rudolph, who celebrated his twenty-eighth birthday en route, sank no ships. Nor did the IXC40 *U-190,* commanded by Max Wintermeyer, age thirty. The IXC40 snort boat *U-547,* commanded by a new skipper, Heinrich Niemeyer, age thirty-three, sank two freighters for 8,400 tons (the Dutch *Bodegraven,* the French *Saint Basile*) and the 750-ton British ASW trawler *Birdlip.* Wintermeyer and Rudolph returned to chaos in France on June 20 and 23, respectively; Niemeyer on August 11. The unpopular Wintermeyer left *U-190* for other duty. While *U-155* was joining her escort off Lorient, a Mosquito of British Squadron 248, piloted by Leslie Cook Doughty, attacked with Tsetse 57mm cannon, machine guns, and two depth charges, but the boat limped into port.

In return for one boat captured (*U-505*) and four sunk, including those of *Ritterkreuz* holders Henke (*U-515*) and Hellriegel (*U-543*), the ten boats patrolling to Freetown and the Gulf of Guinea from January through May 1944 sank seven confirmed ships for about 29,000 tons—Seehausen in *U-66,* four; Niemeyer in *U-547,* three. American codebreakers, hunter-killer groups, and the contingent of B-24s from U.S. Navy Squadron VB 107 on Ascension Island had made patrols to that area not only unprofitable but also as dangerous for U-boats as the Northwest Approaches to the British Isles and the Bay of Biscay.

Patrols to the Americas

U-boat Control mounted twenty-one patrols to American waters in the period from January 1 to June 1, 1944; including two by the snort boat *U-539*. As related, Control recalled *Ritterkreuz* holder Hans-Jürgen Hellriegel in the snort boat *U-543* to serve as a provisional tanker near the Cape Verde Islands, after which he elected to patrol in West African waters and was sunk on the return voyage.

Another of the boats of this group was sunk early on the outbound voyage. She was the famous IXC *U-68,* commanded by Albert Lauzemis, age twenty-six, who had commissioned the boat as a watch officer in February 1941. Except for a six-month stint as a skipper of two school boats, Lauzemis had made all of the patrols of *Ritterkreuz* holder Karl-Friedrich Merten and had himself commanded *U-68* for fourteen months.

Assigned to patrol off Panama, Lauzemis was first to meet the VIID minelayer *U-214* on April 9 to give her new Enigma keys. After that he was to refuel from the XIV "Milk Cow" tanker *U-488,* but he did not arrive at the rendezvous. Allied codebreakers decrypted Enigma instructions for this meet. In the early hours of April 10, the day after the *Guadalcanal* hunter-killer group sank *U-515* and captured the ranking ace, *Ritterkreuz* holder Werner Henke, one of the "jeep" carrier's Avengers, piloted by Eugene E. Wallace, came upon *U-68* close by. Wallace attacked twice, but *U-68* dived and got away.

In response to this alarm, three other aircraft from *Guadalcanal* joined Wallace. At about dawn, Squadron Commander Richard K. Gould in a Wildcat spotted the resurfaced *U-68* and strafed, drawing flak. Thereupon two Avengers, piloted by Samuel G. Parsons and Helmuth E. Hoerner, attacked with depth charges, rockets, and Fidos. These three attacks killed or wounded flak gunners and forced Lauzemis in *U-68* to crash-dive. Avenger pilot Wallace, who was out of ammo, circled and relayed a blow-by-blow account to Dan Gallery in *Guadalcanal.*

Gunner Hans Kastrup at the 37mm flak station aft headed for the conning-tower hatch and stumbled upon another gunner who was badly wounded and dragged him along. When Kastrup reached the hatch, he found it slammed shut. He shouted into the bridge voice tube, but it, too, had been sealed off for the dive. The *U-68* plunged beneath the sea, stranding Kastrup and the wounded man in the water. Kastrup and the wounded man survived the Avenger attacks, but *U-68* did not. Pilot Wallace reported "debris, oil, battery acid, torpedo air flasks, and several survivors. . . ." Spotting Kastrup and his wounded companion in the water, Wallace dropped them a life raft.

About three hours later, several destroyer escorts arrived at the scene. One of these, *Chatelain,* found and rescued Kastrup on the raft, but the wounded man he tried to save was dead. Other destroyer escorts recovered pieces of three torpedoes as well as "cork, cloth, food, a canvas bag, a sofa pillow, a leather jacket and human remains" to confirm the kill. The sole survivor, Kastrup was temporarily confined at Fort Hunt, Virginia, for interrogation and was the last German submariner to see Werner Henke alive.

• • •

As related, while outbound, the first snort boat into combat, the IXC40 *U-539,* commanded by Hans-Jürgen Lauterbach-Emden, age twenty-four, which sailed on January 3, was diverted to give fuel to the inbound IXC *U-516.* Consequently *U-539* could not safely patrol the Caribbean and with the fuel remaining went to frigid Canadian waters instead. Two other boats, both on maiden patrols, also went to the icy Canadian waters in January: the IXC40s *U-802* and *U-845,* commanded by Helmut Schmoeckel, age twenty-six, and Werner Weber, age thirty-six, respectively.

Canadian ASW forces were on full alert for these three boats. In spite of foul February weather, aircraft harassed *U-539* and *U-845.* The snort in *U-539* helped Lauterbach-Emden to escape detection, but he worried about his dwindling fuel supply. On March 1, he sighted and attacked "part of a convoy," but his torpedoes missed and he got nothing. He returned to France on March 21, completing a patrol of seventy-nine days that profited him nothing except snort experience.

Fresh from Kiel, Weber in the new *U-845* was recklessly brave. Off St. John's on February 1, he attempted to follow the British corvette *Hardleigh Castle* into the inner harbor but ran on a rock at Cape Spear and stuck fast. He finally broke loose, but the damage was severe: two ruptured tanks, both rudders, and two bow torpedo-tube outer doors jammed. When he saw the extent of the damage, Weber wanted to abandon ship and scuttle, but the thirty-seven-year-old engineer, Otto Strunk, who had served on Prien's *U-47* at Scapa Flow, dissuaded him.

After makeshift repairs, Weber returned to the hunting grounds. On February 9, he fired five torpedoes at the 7,000-ton British freighter *Kelmscott,* which was en route to join fast convoy Halifax 278. At least two torpedoes hit and Weber claimed a sinking, but it was not so. Other ships towed *Kelmscott* into St. John's, where she was repaired and eventually reentered service.

This attack drew an intense response from Canadian aircraft. On February 14, a B-24 of Squadron 10, piloted by A.P.V. Cheater, found and attacked *U-845,* notwithstanding "intense" flak. In two runs, Cheater dropped eight depth charges and strafed, killing one German gunner and slightly wounding another two. Weber dived and escaped and, on the following day, shot at but missed the 6,100-ton freighter *Pachesham.*

Also low on fuel, Weber departed Canadian waters on about March 1, coincidentally near the track of the returning Lauterbach-Emden in *U-539.* About ten days later, on March 10, Weber came upon Slow Convoy 154. Although *U-539* was close by, U-boat Control apparently did not want Lauterbach-Emden to join, and advised Weber that he was all alone and directed him not to attack the convoy unless conditions were entirely favorable.

Slow Convoy 154 was escorted by Canadian group C-1, commanded by the Britisher J. A. Burnett in the British destroyer *Forester.* In addition to that ship, the group consisted of eight Canadian vessels: the destroyers *St. Laurent* and *Assiniboine,* the frigates *Swansea* and *Valleyfield,* and four corvettes. Having dropped back to assist a burning freighter, George H. Stephen in *St. Laurent* got a good Huff Duff bearing on Weber's contact and shadow reports. He and Burnett in

Forester, the frigate *Swansea,* and the corvette *Owen Sound,* commanded by J. M. Watson, hunted and hounded *U-845* for almost six hours, finally forcing her to the surface with an exhausted battery.

When Weber popped up, *St. Laurent, Forester,* and *Swansea* were close by. In a bold, dogged attack, Stephen in *St. Laurent* pumped 119 rounds of 4.7" shells at *U-845.* This and the 40mm and 20mm fire from all three vessels killed Weber, his first watch officer, and all others on the bridge. Engineer Strunk assumed command, abandoned ship, and scuttled. The escorts rescued forty-five survivors of the fifty-four men who sailed on this one and only patrol of *U-845.*

A diversion to weather reporting delayed the arrival of Schmoeckel in the new IXC40 *U-802.* Off Halifax on March 22, he attacked a convoy of small coasters (SH 125), claiming three sunk for 5,000 tons and one for 1,500 tons damaged. Allied records confirmed one sinking: the 1,600-ton British freighter *Watuka.* This attack—and Schmoeckel's report to Control that night—triggered another ASW hunt by Canadian forces, but Schmoeckel eluded his pursuers. On April 9, he intercepted and attacked the fast convoy Halifax 286 composed of fifty merchant ships. He claimed one 10,000-ton freighter sunk and another of 10,000 tons damaged, but Allied records did not confirm any sinkings or torpedo hits in that convoy. The *U-802* returned to Lorient on May 2, completing a voyage of ninety-five days. While the crew was on leave in Germany, shipfitters equipped her with a snort.

Two more boats sailed to Canadian waters in February. Both came to grief.

• The new IXC40 *U-550,* commanded by Klaus Hänert, age twenty-six, which relieved *U-802* as a weather reporter in mid-Atlantic. On February 22, a Canso (Catalina) of the Iceland-based Canadian Squadron 162 attacked *U-550* with machine guns and four depth charges. The machine-gun fire killed one gunner and severely wounded another. The close depth-charge explosions holed a starboard fuel-ballast tank and washed a man overboard. After reporting weather twice a day for two weeks, Hänert headed *U-550* for New York via Canadian waters.

Hänert reached an area east of New York and about seventy-five miles south of Nantucket Island by April 16. That day, while *U-550* was submerged, tanker convoy CU 21, about twenty vessels en route from the Caribbean via New York to Northern Ireland, passed overhead. Hänert boldly rose to periscope depth and fired a salvo of three torpedoes at the 11,000-ton American tanker *Pan Pennsylvania,* which was loaded with 140,000 barrels of gasoline and had seven aircraft lashed on deck. Some torpedoes hit, and the tanker burst into flames and eventually sank.

The destroyer escorts *Joyce* and *Peterson,* commanded by Coast Guardsmen, Robert Wilcox and S. M. Hay, respectively, hurried to the scene to pick up survivors of the tanker. As they were doing so, *Joyce* got a sonar contact on *U-550* and her captain, Robert Wilcox, carried out a depth-charge attack, firing eleven missiles. Hänert bottomed *U-550* at about three hundred feet, but some of the depth charges ruptured air and fuel lines, causing serious flooding and other damage. Wrongly believing that he was being hunted by only one warship, Hänert decided to surface in broad daylight and fight it out.

When *U-550* came up, Hänert had T-5s in two bow tubes ready. By that time, a third destroyer escort of the convoy, *Gandy,* manned by a Navy crew, had come on the scene to assist *Joyce* and *Peterson.* Shaken by the number of warships converging on him, Hänert nonetheless attempted to fire the T-5s. However, the torpedo tube outer doors were jammed shut and he could not shoot.

All three ships opened fire on *U-550* with all guns that would bear. Seeing that his was the closest ship, W. A. Sessions in *Gandy* put on speed to ram. Owing to a last-second maneuver by Hänert, *Gandy* struck the submarine well aft, incurring four wounded and damage to her own bow. When *Gandy* hauled clear, all three escorts resumed the punishing fire from 3"/50 caliber guns and 40mm and 20mm cannons. Overwhelmed, Hänert gave orders to abandon ship and scuttle, thwarting a boarding party from *Joyce,* which picked up twelve German survivors, including Hänert, who was wounded. Wilcox in *Joyce* transported these prisoners to Northern Ireland, where he turned them over to British authorities.

• After duty as a weather boat, the new IXC40 *U-856,* commanded by Friedrich Wittenberg, age twenty-five, followed *U-550* into Canadian waters. Forewarned by Allied codebreakers, Canadian ASW forces hunted for Wittenberg, but they had no immediate luck.

Upon learning from the codebreakers that *U-856* intended to follow *U-550* into the area off New York, American authorities mounted an all-out hunt for her by the "jeep" carrier *Croatan* and her five destroyer escorts plus two American hunter-killer groups comprising a total of seven destroyers.

In the early hours of April 7, one of two Avengers from *Croatan,* piloted by Wilburt A. Lyons, got *U-856* on radar but could see nothing by eye. As the Avenger approached, Wittenberg made the mistake of firing at it with flak guns, giving away his position. In excited response, Lyons dropped a Fido rather than a flare, but *U-856* was moving too fast for the Fido to home and Wittenberg escaped and went deep.

Other aircraft from *Croatan* and the armada of destroyers and destroyer escorts mounted a U-boat hunt to exhaustion. The destroyer *Boyle* got a sonar contact on *U-856* and attacked with thirteen depth charges, but Wittenberg escaped again. Ten hours later, the veteran destroyer *Champlin,* which had sunk the IXC *U-130* a year earlier, again found *U-856.* Assisted by the destroyer escort *Huse,* commanded by R. H. Wanless, who attacked with Hedgehogs, *Champlin* dropped twenty-one depth charges. These savaged *U-856* and forced her to the surface.

Wittenberg ordered his crew to abandon ship and scuttle, but the conning-tower hatch was jammed shut and had to be pried open with a crowbar. While the Germans coped with this blockage, *Champlin* and *Huse* opened up with 5" and 3"/50 caliber guns. The captain of *Champlin,* John J. Schaffer III, then rammed *U-856* solidly in the stern. Not to be outdone, *Huse* also steamed in to ram, but she missed. Presently *U-856* upended and sank. Tragically, an errant 20mm on *Champlin* wounded four of her own men, skipper Schaffer mortally. The destroyers *Nields* and *Ordronaux* fished out eleven and seventeen Germans, respectively. The twenty-eight survivors of *U-856* included Wittenberg and his first watch officer.

• • •

After a stint as a weather boat, the new IXC40 *U-548,* commanded by Eberhard Zimmermann, age twenty-seven, which sailed on March 21, was next to enter Canadian waters. Patrolling near St. John's, Newfoundland, on the night of May 3, Zimmermann came upon the new British destroyer escort *Hargood* assisting the damaged freighter *Baltrover* of convoy Outbound North (Slow) 236. Zimmermann fired a T-5 at *Hargood* but missed. At that moment, a B-24 of Canadian Squadron 10 arrived, illuminated *Hargood* with a Leigh Light, and fired a recognition flare that failed. Convinced that he was the intended target, Zimmermann opened up with flak guns, then dived to the bottom and lay doggo. Believing *Hargood* had shot at the plane in error, the B-24 crew, justifiably miffed, hauled out of danger. Allied forces remained mystified by this encounter.

On the evening of May 6, Zimmermann lay submerged at periscope depth amid ice clutter. Control that night told him that his wife had given birth to a daughter and that all was well. Toward midnight the periscope watch caught sight of what appeared to be the shadow of a ship. Zimmermann shot a T-5 at a range of 1,500 yards and went deep.

This ship was the Canadian frigate *Valleyfield,* commanded by D. T. English. She was the senior of the five escorts of Canadian Escort Group C-1, which had detached from convoy Outbound North (Slow) 234 and were headed, line abreast, for refits and crew rest at St. John's. Owing to the scattered ice, none of the ships was zigzagging or streaming anti–homing torpedo noisemakers, known as Cat Gear or Foxers. Moreover, *Valleyfield*'s radar was down. The officer of the deck, Ian Tate, was keeping station with the other ships by a bright moon. At 11:35 P.M., the T-5 hit *Valleyfield,* blowing her in half. The bow sank in ninety seconds, the stern in six minutes. Three enlisted men on the stern bravely defused the depth charges, but it was an unnecessary action because the fuses were set to explode the charges deep. These men were among 125 crew of *Valleyfield* who perished that night.

The other four ships—all Canadian corvettes—did not at first realize what had happened. By the time they did, considerable time had elapsed, but they reversed course and carried out a submarine hunt. Zimmermann bottomed *U-548* at 335 feet and lay doggo, again outwitting Canadian ASW forces. The corvette *Giffard,* commanded by C. Peterson, rescued thirty-eight frozen, oil-soaked men of *Valleyfield* (but not her skipper, English) and took them on to St. John's. An official investigation faulted Escort Group C-1 for its failure to follow proper steaming procedures. Zimmermann in *U-548* returned to the chaos in France on June 24, where technicians hurriedly grafted a snort to the boat.

The last two boats to enter Canadian waters in the spring of 1944 both had snorts: the venerable IXB *U-107* and the new IXC40 *U-1222.* They were commanded by the new skipper Volker von Simmermacher, age twenty-three, and by Heinz Bielfeld, age twenty-seven, respectively. Bielfeld in *U-1222* came upon the eastbound fast convoy Halifax 292 on May 22. He shot two torpedoes at the big American tanker *Bulkoil* but missed. On June 8, Bielfeld fired a three-fan at a 12,000-ton "troopship" and two Liberty ships in the westbound convoy UC 24, but the torpedoes missed. Near Cape Sable, von Simmermacher in *U-107* attacked a large American fishing schooner, *Lark,* on June 13. After missing with two torpedoes, he riddled her with his 4.1" deck gun. The crew abandoned ship but reboarded and limped on to Boston.

A massive Allied task group, comprised of the "jeep" carrier *Wake Island* hunter-killer group and several Canadian ships and numerous land-based aircraft, mounted an intense hunt for *U-107,* but von Simmermacher escaped and returned to France on July 22. Bielfeld did not reach France. While he was inbound in the Bay of Biscay on July 11, a Sunderland of British Squadron 201, piloted by the veteran U-boat hunter I.F.B. (Wally) Walters, spotted *U-1222*'s snort, attacked with depth charges, and sank her with the loss of all hands. Walters received a second DFC for this success, the first kill of a snort boat in daylight.*

The returns from these seven Type IX patrols to Canadian and American waters were less than satisfactory. Only four had any luck and it was minimal from the German viewpoint: Hänert in *U-550* sank the 11,000-ton American tanker *Pan Pennsylvania,* Schmoeckel in *U-802* sank the 1,600-ton Canadian freighter *Watuka,* Zimmermann in *U-548* sank the 1,400-ton Canadian frigate *Valleyfield,* and Weber in *U-845* damaged the 7,000-ton British freighter *Kelmscott.* In return, four of the seven boats were lost: *U-550, U-845, U-856,* and *U-1222.*

Besides Hänert in *U-550,* two other IXC40s that sailed in March entered waters of the United States East Coast about twenty days apart. These were first the veteran *U-170,* commanded by Günther Pfeffer, age twenty-nine, and then the *U-541,* commanded by Kurt Petersen, age twenty-seven. Both cruised south down the East Coast from New York to Florida. Pfeffer shot six torpedoes at two different Liberty ships but he inflicted no damage. The newly arrived *U-541* was to meet the homebound *U-170* and give her new Enigma keys on April 10, but Petersen told Control that the Allies had fouled the rendezvous, so he canceled it and sent *U-170* the new keys by radio, doubtless a breach of communications security from which Allied codebreakers profited. Pfeffer returned *U-170* to France on May 27, completing a useless voyage of 109 days, at which time he left the boat for other duties. Petersen in *U-541* found a convoy off Florida on May 14 and shot seven torpedoes but none hit. On May 26, he stopped a Portuguese neutral, *Serpa Pinto,* and seized two American passengers and took them on board. He arrived in France on June 22, after an equally useless voyage of 115 days.

The *Pan Pennsylvania* was the only confirmed ship sunk by U-boats in United States waters in the spring of 1944.

Five boats sailed to the Caribbean Sea in the period from January 1 to June 1, 1944.

The IXC *U-154,* commanded by a new skipper, Gerth Gemeiner, age twenty-five, replacing the disgraced skipper Oskar-Heinz Kusch, left France on the last day of January, mere hours after a court had condemned Kusch to death. The boat

---

* The Allied three-centimeter-wavelength radar could detect a raised snort. Aware of this, the Germans had initiated an R&D program, *Schornsteinfeger* (Chimney Sweep), to coat the snorts with various radar-absorbent (or stealth) materials, such as laminated paper, rubber, and sisal.

patrolled all the way to Panama. On March 13, Gemeiner found a convoy and shot torpedoes at two tankers, but missed both. An escort—probably the American patrol boat *PC-469*—attacked the U-boat with depth charges, but she escaped with slight damage. Gemeiner sank no ships and returned to France on April 28, completing a barren voyage of eighty-nine days.

The veteran IXC *U-518,* also commanded by a new skipper, Hans-Werner Offermann, age twenty-two, left France on January 23. Per orders, while outbound, Offermann rendezvoused with the big inbound Japanese submarine *I-29,* (code-named *"U-Kiefer"* or "Pine Tree") to transfer to her a German navigator, *Naxos* gear, and *Naxos* operators. As Offermann approached the meeting point on February 12, he saw what he reported to be a seaplane tender escorted by four "destroyers." Actually it was a hunter-killer group built around the "jeep" carrier *Croatan* that was assigned to foul this meeting. Offermann fired torpedoes at *Croatan*—and reported three hits—but in actuality all missed.

After her meeting with the Japanese submarine, Offermann took *U-518* west and entered the Caribbean via the Mona Passage where, on March 3, he shot at a 4,000-ton freighter but missed. Near Aruba on March 7, he sank the 3,400-ton Panamanian tanker *Valera,* and on March 13 at Colón, he "thrust unseen into main harbor" (as he put it), then lay outside, harassed by air and surface patrols. Homebound a month later, on April 2, he claimed sinking a 7,000-ton tanker, but it was not confirmed. Offermann returned to Lorient on May 7, completing a voyage of 106 days. While the crew rested, technicians installed a snort. Control inquired sharply into the reasons for Offermann's failure to sink more shipping.

The VIID minelayer *U-218,* commanded by the old hand Richard Becker, age thirty-three, sailed from Brest on February 12 to lay a field off Trinidad. Owing to intense ASW measures, Becker was forced to cancel operations at Trinidad. Instead, he laid fields off Port Castries, St. Lucia, on March 23, and San Juan, Puerto Rico, on April 1. Neither field sank any ships. Becker returned to Lorient on May 7, yet another useless voyage, this one of eighty-six days.

The IXC40 snort boat *U-539,* commanded by Hans-Jürgen Lauterbach-Emden, departed France on May 1 for her second patrol to the Americas in 1944. Entering the Caribbean via the Mona Passage on June 5, Lauterbach-Emden sank in those waters the 1,500-ton Panamanian freighter *Pillory.* En route to Panama on June 11, he attacked two medium Dutch tankers with T-5s off Curaçao. When neither hit, he surfaced and attacked the 2,700-ton *Casandra* with his deck gun. The tanker returned fire, inflicting slight damage on *U-539,* which broke off the action. On the next day, a U.S. Navy Mariner found and, notwithstanding intense flak, attacked *U-539,* but the U-boat got away. Off Panama on July 4, Lauterbach-Emden shot at a convoy of tankers and claimed hits on four for 26,000 tons. Allied records confirmed slight damage to one tanker, the 10,200-ton American *Kittanning,* which entered Cristobal on July 6, assisted by a Coast Guard cutter.

The IXC *U-516,* commanded by Hans-Rutger Tillessen, age thirty-one, patrolled the Caribbean between Aruba and Panama. Near Aruba on July 7 and 8, Tillessen attacked two American tankers, the 9,900-ton *Esso Harrisburg* and the 4,800-ton *Point Breeze.* He sank the first with three torpedoes but *Point Breeze* evaded four torpedoes and got away.

Allied codebreakers provided good information on the return voyages of Lauterbach-Emden in *U-539* and Tillessen in *U-516*. Tenth Fleet ordered the *Card* and *Guadalcanal* hunter-killer groups to hunt them down. Both groups found and attacked *U-539* in the Mona Passage but she got away and reached Norway on September 17. The *U-516* reached Norway on October 1. During the attack on *U-539, Card* suffered an engine breakdown that left her dangerously dead in the water for several hours. Forced to abort, she went into Puerto Rico.

The five boats patrolling the Caribbean Sea through July 1944 sank three merchant ships: the 1,500-ton freighter *Pillory* and two tankers, the 3,400-ton *Valera* and the 9,900-ton *Esso Harrisburg*. Although all five boats had achieved the primary mission of tying down massive Allied forces and all got back to Europe, owing to the impossibility of refueling at sea and other factors, U-boat Control sent no more boats to the Caribbean.

Two boats sailed to Brazilian waters.

The venerable IXC *U-129,* commanded by Richard von Harpe, age twenty-six, left France on March 22. En route, he refueled from the tanker *U-488* before she was sunk and gave *Naxos* gear to Lüdden in *U-188,* inbound from Penang. Although Tenth Fleet alerted Allied forces to *U-129*'s arrival and patrol area, she remained undetected during her entire cruise. Against this desultory ASW, von Harpe had the best luck of all the boats patrolling to American waters in 1944. Off the southern Brazilian coast, he sank two British freighters: the 5,300-ton *Anadyr* on May 6 and the 6,600-ton *Empire Heath* on May 11. He returned to France on July 18, completing an arduous voyage of 119 days. Deemed to be too old and infirm for a snort, the boat was decommissioned in Lorient a month later. Von Harpe returned to Germany to commission a Type XXI "electro boat."

The IXC40 snort boat *U-549,* commanded by Detlev Krankenhagen, age twenty-six, sailed from France on May 14. American codebreakers speculated that she might be going to Argentina "to deliver agents and clandestine radio equipment," but German records listed no special mission, merely her assigned patrol area, Brazil. Acting on decrypted Enigma traffic, Tenth Fleet put the *Block Island* hunter-killer group, which sailed from Casablanca on May 23, on her trail near the Madeira Islands.

The *Block Island* group made contact with *U-549* on May 28, but she dived and escaped. In the early hours of the next day, May 29, an unarmed night-flying Avenger got a "strong" radar contact. Two other Avengers flew out for the kill, but the attack failed and *U-549* again dived to safety. Determined to hunt this boat to the death, the hunter-killer group commander, Francis M. Hughes, mounted searches all day long on May 29. The search peaked at 5:00 P.M. with the launch of six Wildcats that were to be relieved about three hours later by six Avengers and another Wildcat.

About 8:00 P.M., one hour before dark, Krankenhagen in *U-549* hit the 8,600-ton *Block Island* with three torpedoes. One of the four destroyer escorts of the screen, *Barr,* commanded by Henry H. Love, saw a periscope and attacked, dropping thirteen depth charges, but all fell wide. Thereupon Krankenhagen fired a T-5 at *Barr.* It hit her solidly in the stern, killing twelve men, wounding sixteen, and knocking the ship out of action.

Mortally holed, *Block Island* sank slowly. At 9:00 P.M., Hughes ordered the 957 men on the carrier to abandon ship. The six airborne Wildcats flew toward the Spanish Canary Islands but all had to ditch in the dark and only two of the six pilots survived. The destroyer escorts *Ahrens,* commanded by Morgan H. Harris, and *Robert I. Paine,* commanded by Drayton Cochran, came in slowly to rescue survivors of *Block Island. Ahrens* picked up 674 men; *Paine* 277. Amazingly, only six men of the "jeep" carrier perished.

While engaged in the rescue, *Ahrens,* commanded by Morgan H. Harris, got a sonar contact. Unable to pursue, Harris coached the fourth destroyer escort, *Eugene E. Elmore,* commanded by George L. Conkey, into an attack. Picking up the sonar contact, Conkey fired three successive Hedgehog salvos. He reported three explosions and heavy "crumbling" noises. That was apparently the end of *U-549.* She was never heard from again.

Two of the three operable destroyer escorts scoured the area for U-boats during the night of May 29–30, while Conkey in *Elmore* tended the stricken *Barr. Elmore* helped bury *Barr*'s dead and took on board fourteen wounded and other "excess" personnel, leaving only her captain, Henry Love, and the damage-control and salvage parties. She then took *Barr* in tow and headed for Casablanca. The American seaplane tender *Humbolt,* destroyer escort *Wilhoite,* and the Dutch tug *Antic* left that port to take over the towing. *Ahrens* and *Paine* reached Casablanca on June 2 with 951 survivors of *Block Island; Elmore,* with *Barr*'s wounded and much of her crew, and *Barr* (under tow) reached Casablanca three days later.*

After the British *Audacity* and *Avenger,* the *Block Island* was the third Allied "jeep" carrier to be lost to U-boats in the Atlantic to that point. Remarkably, she and her screen had sunk seven U-boats, including her nemesis *U-549.* In her honor, the "jeep" carrier *Sunset Bay* was renamed and commissioned as *Block Island* on December 30, 1944. She was manned by many crew of her namesake who took her to the Pacific.

Two boats sailed for the Americas in May.

The IXC40 snort boat *U-530,* commanded by Kurt Lange, age forty, left Lorient for the Trinidad area on May 22. Lange was to rendezvous en route with an inbound Japanese U-cruiser, *I-52* (code-named *"U-Föhre,"* formerly *"Tanne"*), and provide her with *Naxos,* a *Naxos* operator, and a German navigator. Allied codebreakers, decrypting both Japanese and German traffic, tracked both boats. On June 2, the *Bogue* hunter-killer group, under a new commander, Aurelius B. Vosseller, sailed from Casablanca to foul the meeting.

The huge *I-52* (356 feet, 2,600 tons) had sailed from Singapore on April 23. She carried ninety-five crew and fourteen German-bound passengers, two tons of

* Patched up, *Barr* was towed to Boston and fully repaired, then sent back into combat in the Pacific.

gold in the form of 146 bars, and a cargo of tin, rubber, wolfram, quinine, opium, and molybdenum. On June 23, she and *U-530* met, as planned, about 850 miles west of the Cape Verde Islands. Lange did not linger. In compliance with orders from U-boat Control, he cruised to the western Atlantic near Trinidad and southward along the "bauxite route." He sank no ships and returned to Norway on October 1, completing a fruitless patrol of 133 days.

The *Bogue* group DFed the exchanges of messages between *U-530* and *I-52.* On the evening of June 23, Vosseller launched Avengers to hunt down both submarines. Two separate aircraft, piloted by A. L. Hirsbrunner and Jesse D. Taylor, got radar contacts and dropped sonobuoys. Upon picking up propeller noises, Taylor attacked, dropping two depth charges and a Fido. Three minutes later, Taylor and his crew heard sounds that they likened to a tin can being crushed or twigs snapping.

When Taylor reported, "We got that sonofabitch," Vosseller launched another Avenger to get the "other" submarine. Homed to the likely site by Hirsbrunner, this third Avenger, piloted by William D. ("Flash") Gordon, dropped sonobuoys, got a contact, and attacked with a Fido. Gordon reported that he missed, but eighteen minutes later he heard a "loud, rolling explosion" that lasted almost a full minute.

Vosseller believed his aircraft had killed two submarines, but he was mistaken. One possibility is that Taylor's Fido fatally damaged *I-52* and Gordon's Fido hit a remnant of that submarine. In any case, the next day destroyer escorts of *Bogue*'s screen recovered 115 blocks of crude rubber, bolts of silk, a Japanese sandal, and numerous pieces of mahogany lumber. That appeared to be positive evidence of the kill of *I-52,* but the kill was to be clouded by a decrypted Japanese radio message. On July 31, the Japanese naval attaché in Berlin told Tokyo that he had established communications with *I-52* on the previous day, July 30, that the *I-52* would arrive in Lorient on August 4, and that a Japanese "reception party" had already left Berlin. German escort vessels reached the rendezvous on August 1 and remained until August 4, but found no sign of *I-52.* On August 6, the attaché radioed *I-52* that the German escorts had returned and requested her estimated time of arrival, but there was no response.

An American salvor, Paul Tidwell, and a team of experts equipped with state-of-the-art search gear claimed to have located *I-52* in 1995. According to Tidwell, she lay 1,200 miles west of the Cape Verdes, in seventeen thousand feet of water (about 3.2 miles deep). Working remote-control sonars and cameras from a leased Russian research vessel, the team allegedly got fairly good images of *I-52* and an adjacent "debris field." She appeared to be "upright and intact" except for a "torpedo hole" on her starboard side, Tidwell stated to the media. A shortage of money, legal entanglements, and other problems thwarted further confirmation and salvage efforts through 1998.

The new XB minelayer *U-233,* commanded by Hans Steen, age thirty-six, sailed from Kiel on May 27. Steen's mission was to lay sixty-six SMA (moored) mines off Halifax, Nova Scotia. Although his crew was green, Steen had served as a watch officer on the sister ship *U-117* for sixteen months and had scored well in practice minelaying in the Baltic.

After topping off her large fuel tanks in Norway, *U-223* put out for Halifax. Since she had no snort, she was frequently detected and attacked by Allied aircraft. Steen thwarted these ASW hunts by remaining submerged about twenty hours each day and crept across the Atlantic very slowly. On the fortieth day out, July 5, he finally reached Canadian waters, about 250 miles southeast of Cape Sable.

Allied codebreakers alerted Tenth Fleet to this oncoming menace. On June 25, the *Card* hunter-killer group, commanded by Rufus C. Young, sailed from Norfolk via Bermuda to Canadian waters to sink her. On the evening of the day *U-233* arrived there, July 5, one of the five destroyer escorts, *Baker,* commanded by Norman C. Hoffman, got *U-233* on sonar. Hoffmann gave the alarm and went to battle stations. While Young took *Card* out of torpedo range, protected by *Bostwick, Breeman,* and *Bronstein,* the *Thomas,* commanded by David M. Kellogg, raced up to assist *Baker.*

Hoffman in *Baker* carried out two depth-charge attacks, the first astonishingly accurate, the second wide. The charges savaged the stern of *U-233,* flooding some compartments. She plunged to four hundred feet, out of control and heavy aft. Unable to communicate with the aft section or stabilize the boat, Steen blew all ballast tanks and surfaced to abandon ship and scuttle.

When the U-boat popped up, Hoffman in *Baker* opened fire with all guns that could bear. The heavy fire decapitated the chief engineer, Wilhelm Bartling, and wounded numerous other Germans who were trying to abandon ship, including the skipper, Steen. The screen commander, George A. Parkinson in *Thomas,* ordered her skipper, David Kellogg, to ram. Guns blazing, *Thomas* smashed into *U-233* aft of the conning tower, and the U-boat sank swiftly by the stern.

Baker and *Thomas* fished about half the U-boat crew from the water. *Baker* picked up ten Germans; *Thomas,* twenty. The destroyer escorts then transferred the prisoners to *Card.* Mortally wounded, Steen died and was buried the following day with military ceremony. On July 7, the hunter-killer group put into Boston, its quite specific task accomplished.*

The nineteen patrols (two by *U-539*) in American waters from January 1 to June 1, 1944, accomplished little beyond tying down Allied forces. Including the "jeep" carrier *Block Island,* sunk by Krankenhagen in *U-549* near Madeira while he was en route to Brazil, these boats destroyed nine ships for about 50,000 tons. In return, seven U-boats failed to return. About 350 submariners manning these boats were lost, eighty-seven of them captured.

---

* Reporter Royal Ford of *The Boston Sunday Globe* suggests in a 1997 article that U.S. Navy blimp K-14 tangled with *U-233* on the night of July 2 and, as a result, the blimp crashed into the sea. Based on an official naval court of inquiry, J. Gordon Vaeth in his book *Blimps and U-boats* (1992) wrote that K-14 flew into the sea, owing to crew error. Seven aircrew died; four survived. During interrogations, none of the thirty German POWs mentioned a fight with a blimp.

Family Grief

It will be recalled that Peter Dönitz, the youngest son of Karl Dönitz, was lost in combat in May of 1943 while serving as a watch officer on the new Type VIIC *U-954.* Hitler had issued a policy stating that if a senior officer such as Dönitz lost a son in battle and had other sons in the military, the latter could withdraw from combat and return to civilian life.* Therefore, Dönitz's older son, Klaus, a naval officer, entered Tübingen University to pursue studies to qualify as a naval doctor, considered to be a noncombatant position by all nations at war.

Klaus nonetheless kept in close touch with his friends serving in the military. On the eve of his twenty-fourth birthday, May 13, 1944, he visited chums in the 5th Schnell Flotilla at Cherbourg, France. Purely for the adventure, that night he inveigled a ride on the motor torpedo boat *S-141,* which was to carry out a mission at Selsey, on the English coast.

Two Allied warships intercepted and destroyed *S-141.* These were the British frigate *Stayner* and the Free French destroyer *La Combattante.* The Allies rescued six German survivors, not including Klaus Dönitz. Eventually his body washed ashore in France and it was buried near Amiens.

The loss of this second son doubtless shattered the Dönitz family: Dönitz; his wife, Ingebord; his daughter, Ursula; and her husband, Günther Hessler,† serving as first staff officer at U-boat Control. It was all the more painful inasmuch as Klaus was killed on a lark, rather than on an important combat assignment.

* See Padfield, *The Last Führer* (1984).

† For Dönitz family history, see Volume I.

EIGHT

The German Run-up to Overlord

Adolf Hitler and his military advisers correctly anticipated that the Allied invasion of France would occur in May or early June, but they could not agree on exactly where the landings would come. Fooled by clever Allied deceptions, Hitler and the chiefs of the German Army and Air Force believed that the Allies would strike at the mouth of the Somme River, near Abbeville, about ninety miles north of Paris. Dönitz and other naval strategists believed correctly that the Allied forces would strike farther west in the Bay of the Seine, near Le Havre, a large, well-sheltered seaport about eighty-five miles across the channel from Portsmouth.

The impending invasion of France was not the only major problem confronting Berlin. Likewise fooled by Allied deceptions, Hitler was convinced that the long-awaited invasion of Norway (and/or Denmark) was to take place at or about the same time, probably together with an all-out Soviet summer offensive westward toward Germany. In addition, Allied forces in Italy had at last broken through German defenses and were advancing on German-occupied Rome. This posed a grave threat to the northern industrial regions of German-occupied Italy, which were still working to supply Germany with weapons, including about twenty small (Type XXIII) electro boats under construction at Genoa, intended for operations in the Mediterranean and Black Sea.

Hitler had long insisted that the Arctic and Atlantic U-boat forces were his first line of defense against an Allied invasion in the west. He still held that view in May of 1944. Presumably the large-scale minefields that the Germans had planted in the English Channel constituted the second line of defense and the stout beach defenses (the "Atlantic Wall") made up the third line of defense. The main line of defense, of course, consisted of the many armored and infantry divisions positioned behind the beaches.

Admiral Dönitz and five of his most loyal senior aides drew the plans for the creation and disposition of this "first line of defense," the U-boat forces. These men were Hans-Georg von Friedburg, commander in chief, U-boats; Eberhard Godt, commanding U-boat Control; Günter Hessler, Dönitz's son-in-law; Reinhard Suhren, named commander of U-boats, North (Arctic/Norway), replacing Rudolph Peters; and Hans-Rudolf Rösing, named commander of U-boats, West (France).

The main elements of the plan were as follows:

- Commencing on or about April 1, most of the fifty-odd Type VIIs based in four of the five U-boat bases in France (Brest, St. Nazaire, Lorient, La Pallice) were to cease war patrols. While berthed in protective pens, they were to be fitted with snorkels, search radar, new antiaircraft guns, the latest torpedoes, and other upgrades. When deemed combat ready by Hans Rösing, they were to be assigned to the designated anti-invasion U-boat force, group *Landwirt,* and be ready in all respects to sail on six hours notice.
- At about the same time, Reinhard Suhren was to create a second anti-invasion force to be berthed in Bergen, where there was a pen, and in small ports in southern Norway. Designated group *Mitte* (or Central), it was to grow to twenty Type VII U-boats fresh from the building yards in the Baltic. This group, also to be held at six hours notice, would deploy to the North Sea to serve as the first line of defense against an Allied invasion of southern Norway or Denmark. It was commanded by Viktor Schütze, who wore the *Ritterkreuz* with Oak Leaves.
- Also on about April 1, the Arctic U-boat force, consisting of about thirty Type VIIs deployed in groups on the Murmansk run or in refit, was to prepare to serve as a third anti-invasion force. It was to be berthed in Trondheim, where there was also a pen, Narvik, and in other small ports in northern Norway, all on six-hours notice.

These three anti-invasion forces would comprise about one hundred Type VII U-boats. They could be reinforced rapidly by another twenty or thirty Type VIIs from the Baltic.

Combat experience in 1943 and 1944 had demonstrated beyond doubt that only Type VIIs fitted with snorts could survive against the aircraft and surface ships of the Allied ASW forces. Hence Dönitz decreed that all available snort-equipped VIIs should be posted to France (for group *Landwirt*) and that as many nonsnort VIIs as possible should be fitted with snorts in Germany, Norway, and France. However, the intense Allied bombing campaigns against U-boat yards in Germany and the French rail system severely disrupted the production of snorts at the source and the flow of snorts to the U-boat bases in France and Norway.

Partly as a consequence of the Allied bombing campaigns, on D day, June 6, 1944, only about one-third of the approximately one hundred Type VII U-boats in Norway and France were equipped with snorts and were combat ready or nearly combat ready: sixteen in France,* eight en route from Norway to France, five in southern Norway, and three in Kiel. Nine VIIs were en route from Norway to

* Including two, *U-267* and *U-667,* that had just returned to St. Nazaire from prolonged war patrols in the Atlantic and were in extended refit.

France to be fitted with snorts at the Atlantic U-boat bases, but, as will be seen, none of these got there.

Some authors have greatly exaggerated the threat posed to the Allies by these thirty-two combat-ready or nearly combat-ready snort boats. Therefore the limitations of the snort boats of that era bear repeating.

- Most snorts were technically primitive and newly fitted, and not yet fully debugged. Catastrophic breakdowns in the raising and lowering systems and the exhaust and intake mechanisms were more the rule than the exception.
- Contrary to the general impression, snort boats were not "true submersibles." They did not snort continuously. Most skippers snorted only about four hours each day, principally to charge the batteries. The rest of the time they cruised at 1 to 3 knots on battery power. Hence the average snort boat en route to and from the operating area could only cover about fifty or sixty miles a day. It took a snort boat nearly three weeks to travel one thousand sea miles.
- A snorting U-boat could not use its radio receivers or hydrophones (passive sonar array), and therefore it was "deaf." Enemy aircraft employing sonobuoys and surface ships with active sonar ("pinging") could "hear" a snorting U-boat at a time when the "deaf" U-boat could not "hear" the enemy.
- A snorting U-boat could rarely use its periscopes. At a snort speed of 5 knots, periscopes tended to vibrate radically, causing the optics to slip out of alignment and, of course, increasing the boat's visible wake. Except while stopped or making only 1 or 2 knots, a snorting boat was therefore also "blind."
- Snorts were prone to emit exhaust smoke, visible to the enemy in twilight and daylight.
- Snorts often leaked carbon monoxide into the pressure hull, killing or sickening crewmen.
- When waves dunked the snort, the diesel engines sucked air from inside the pressure hull, causing painful headaches, eye strain, earaches, and other health problems.
- On extended operations, a boat dared not raise its snort merely to ventilate the boat and it had no means of disposing of waste. Hence (as Günter Hessler wrote), "The atmosphere, which was always pretty foul in a snorkel boat, was further polluted by the stench of decaying waste food and other refuse." The odor was so repulsive that dockyard workers "recoiled from the open hatch" of a returning snort boat.
- Almost without exception, U-boat crews distrusted snorts and hated to use them.

Inasmuch as the Germans had so few combat-ready snort boats and there were disagreements about where the Allies might attempt to land, it was not possible to position them in advance to meet the Allies head on. Hence, upon orders, the boats would have to sail from Biscay ports to the Allied landing area. To cut the reaction time, eleven of the fourteen combat-ready snort boats of *Landwirt* were positioned at Brest, the U-boat base closest to the English Channel. However, even by the most direct route (roundabout the island of Ushant), it was at least four hundred miles to the Normandy beaches, a snort trip from Brest of seven or eight days.

Once under way, the snort boats would have to deal with Allied amphibious forces protected by heavy ASW forces on extraordinary alert.

Another very serious handicap was the shallow water of the English Channel. Traditionally, of course, submarines shied clear of shallow water inasmuch as it was believed that detection there could be quick and fatal. On the eve of the invasion, however, Dönitz attempted to persuade his skippers of the reverse: that operations in shallow waters might be safer. In shallow waters, he said, enemy sonar was apt to be less efficient due to the distortions in active sonar caused by the nearness of the ocean floor and the inflow of fresh water from rivers, which created thermoclines and variable salinity levels, and to the fact that it was difficult for sonar operators to distinguish between U-boats and the many shipwrecks and the metallic debris littering the channel floor. This was not an easy sell, but German submariners could console themselves with the thought that escape and survival from a submarine wrecked in shallow water might be easier. It might also be possible to swim or paddle a dinghy or life raft to a friendly beach.

No matter how one viewed it, the German plan for employing U-boats as the "first line of defense" against Allied invaders was futile. The snort boats might survive; conceivably some might inflict some minor damage. For the nonsnorts, operations in the channel would be nearly suicidal.

There were no electro boats available to throw against the Allied invaders. Not surprisingly, the production schedule had slipped badly. The first oceangoing Type XXI, *U-2501,* was commissioned at Blohm & Voss, Hamburg, on June 27; the first small "duck" Type XXIII, *U-2321,* at Deutsche Werft, Hamburg, on June 12. The OKM diarist logged on July 30 that "six" Type XXIs had been "delivered" (i.e., commissioned) and that it was hoped a total of 144 would be delivered by the end of 1944. It was also noted that the expected delivery of Type XXIIIs by October 1 had been reduced from forty-three to twenty-three boats and that, owing in part to the loss of eighteen boats under construction in Genoa, it would not be possible to complete eighty-seven Type XXIIIs by the end of 1944.

Delays continued to mount. Actual deliveries of electro boats by the end of 1944: sixty-one Type XXIs and thirty-one Type XXIIIs, all with flaws, none combat ready.*

The Allied Run-up to Overlord

On the opposite shores, Allied planners completed final details for Neptune, the amphibious assault phase of Overlord. Responsibility for getting troops safely across the English Channel fell indirectly on the broad back of First Sea Lord Andrew B. Cunningham and directly on the senior Allied naval commander under Eisenhower, Bertram H. Ramsay of the Royal Navy, and his two subordinate admirals, a famous (Victoria Cross) Briton, Philip L. Vian, and an obscure American, Alan G. Kirk, who had been the naval attaché in London under

---

* See Plate 8.

Ambassador Joseph P. Kennedy in the early days of the war and a task force commander in Torch.*

The planners assumed that the most formidable opposition to the landings would be mounted by U-boats. Fortunately for the planners, American and British codebreakers had mastered almost every relevant naval Enigma network and were able to provide remarkably accurate estimates of the numbers of U-boats Neptune might face. These estimates were reflected in the weekly summaries emanating from Rodger Winn's Submarine Tracking Room during April and May 1944.

Winn's estimate of Type VIIs, dated May 15, was typical:

45	VIIs in various Biscay ports (group *Landwirt*)
16	VIIs in southern Norway ports (group *Mitte*)
30	VIIs in northern Norway ports and Arctic waters
91	VIIs total

There were some unknowns and miscalculations:

• The exact number of Type VIIs in France and Norway fitted with snorts was not known and was underestimated.

• The number of new or upgraded Type VIIs (both snorts and nonsnorts) that were ready or nearly ready to sail from the Baltic Sea to Norway or onward to France was not known and was overestimated.

• The number of Type VIIs of the Arctic and Norway forces that were earmarked for transfer to France was not known. Conceivably most of the forty-six VIIs located in the Arctic/Norway area in the May 15 estimate could rush to waters of the British Isles or France to attack the invaders.

The Allies therefore planned for a "worst case" U-boat offensive. They envisioned a total threat of 120 U-boats, with possibly ninety actually in the "invasion area" by June 1. That threat might well include as many as fifty 250-ton "high speed" (40 to 50 knots) "Walter boats," powered by closed-cycle engines.† In sum, as the Canadian naval historian Marc Milner put it, the Germans might throw every possible U-boat into the battle in a kind of Wagnerian "Götterdämmerung."

The Allied plan to counter the U-boat threat to Neptune was straightforward and simple in concept. It had two strategic and tactical goals. First, to keep all

---

* Vian and Kirk commanded the Eastern Task Force and Western Task Force, respectively. Their subordinate commanders were Cyril E. Douglas-Pennanat, Geoffrey N. Oliver, and A. G. Talbot of the Royal Navy, and Don P. Moon and John L. Hall, Jr., of the U.S. Navy.

† In April and May 1944, the Allies knew virtually nothing about the electro boat or the "Walter boat" programs. The first hints were found on May 1, 1944, when the Allies decrypted a December 1943 message from the Japanese naval authorities in Berlin to Tokyo. This message referred to the German crash program to produce "high speed" U-boats (i.e., Types XXI and XXIII), but the author of the message incorrectly described these as "Walter boats" with closed-cycle propulsion systems, rather than as the electro boats that they were. From this message and from incorrect German POW assertions that "Walter boats" would be shipped to France by rail and be employed against the invasion forces, the Allies at first had to assume that they would face this ominous added threat. However, at the very last minute, on May 30, the Allies decrypted another Japanese message from Berlin to Tokyo, dated April 24, that clarified the types and led the British to conclude by "negative implication" that "Walter boats" had not yet reached a "practical stage" and that only two small Type XXIII electro boats had been launched in Baltic yards and they were far from combat ready.

U-boats out of the English Channel and St. George's Channel where Allied forces and logistical backup were to cross from southern England to France, and second, to block the transfer of U-boats from Norway to France. In pursuing these goals, of course, the forces earmarked to carry them out were urged to act offensively and kill as many U-boats as possible.

As to the first task of sealing off the English Channel, it will be recalled that since the beginning of the war the British had maintained a massive minefield across the narrowest area of the channel at Dover–Cape Gris. This strong and well-tended field in shallow water completely blocked the eastern ingress to the channel. Should a suicidal force of the remaining big German surface warships* (and/or U-boats) attempt to smash through this wall of mines in narrow waters, it would fail absolutely.

The main task for Neptune ASW forces was therefore to tightly seal off the western ingresses to the English Channel and to St. George's Channel. Anticipating a massive U-boat assault, the Allied planners devoted vast resources to these tasks.

First, air.

The responsibility for putting in place saturation offensive airborne ASW forces in the U-boat blocking areas fell on the shoulders of Sholto Douglas, who had replaced John Slessor as chief of RAF Coastal Command in January 1944. The 19 Group would carry the main air burden.

William Brian Baker's 19 Group, based mostly in southern England, was increased to twenty-five squadrons. These included four squadrons of the Royal Navy's Fleet Air Arm and four B-24 squadrons of the U.S. Navy's Fleet Air Wing 7.† The rest were RAF squadrons comprised of B-24s, B-17s, Halifaxes, Sunderlands, Wellingtons, Mosquitos, and Beaufighters. Usually an aircraft squadron was composed of fifteen aircraft: twelve combat ready and three in reserve. Thus Baker commanded about 375 aircraft. Most of those planes were fitted with ten or the new, more powerful three-centimeter-wavelength radar. Most carried depth charges or ASW bombs. All had .50 caliber machine guns, many had 20mm cannons, a few had 57mm Tsetse cannons, and some had rockets. Many larger planes carried sonobuoys.

In Baker's plan, the area to be saturated covered twenty thousand square miles. He divided this space into twelve rectangles, A to K plus Z. The long-range aircraft patrolled an outer barrier (B, E, and F) reaching from the southern coast of Ireland southeastward to the latitude of St. Nazaire (47 degrees, 15 minutes north). The short-range aircraft patrolled two other contiguous and continuous barrier lines (C–D and G–H), east of the outer barrier. The other four zones (I, J, K, and Z) were directly over the English Channel in the invasion area.

The Baker plan called for aircraft to be covering these dozen rectangles at all

---

* The Baltic-based "pocket" battleships *Lützow* and *Admiral Scheer;* heavy cruisers *Hipper* and *Prinz Eugen;* light cruisers *Emden, Köln, Leipzig,* and *Nürnberg.*

† USN Bombing Squadrons VB 103, VB 105, and VB 110. Eight B-24s of Squadron VB 114, equipped with searchlights, were temporarily transferred from Port Lyautey to Dunkeswell, Devon, on June 18. Four other B-24s of VB 111 based at Port Lyautey were also transferred to the U.K. Total USN B-24s in Neptune: fifty-seven.

times. They were to fly singly around the legs of the rectangles on the same flight paths at preset intervals. In this way, Baker would cover the entire twenty thousand square miles of water every thirty minutes. This dense coverage would almost certainly prevent most U-boats from surfacing to charge batteries or to refresh the air in the boat and would catch any U-boat on the surface attempting to carry out these routines.

The historian of U.S. Navy Fleet Air Wing 7 wrote that by D day the wing's areas of responsibility were substantial. The wing flew seven B-24 missions daily per squadron. With three squadrons participating, that came to twenty-one missions each day. Including the temporarily assigned VB 114, the total increased to twenty-eight missions daily. On about July 1, VB 114 returned to Port Lyautey for further transfer to ASW duty in the Azores, augmenting the British B-17s and Wellingtons already based there. On July 15, owing to the absence of U-boats, the daily missions of Fairwing 7 were reduced to five per squadron, or fifteen aircraft per day.

Second, surface ships.

First Sea Lord Cunningham and Bertram Ramsay earmarked ten special task forces, or support groups, to form naval blockade lines running beneath the outer aircraft barriers more or less south from Ireland to Ushant. The task forces, or hunter-killer groups, were comprised of destroyers and frigates. Six groups were Royal Navy; four were Royal Canadian Navy, fulfilling a long-held Canadian desire for offensive action, as opposed to defensive convoy escort. The British groups (numbers 1, 2, 3, 5, 14, and 15) were composed of destroyers. The Canadian groups (6, 9, 11, and 12) were composed of five destroyers each (11 and 12), and six frigates each (6 and 9). All ships in these ten groups were fitted with ten centimeter-wavelength search radar, upgraded active ("pinging") sonar, Hedgehogs, and depth charges, as well as guns ranging in size from 20mm to 4.7 inches.

Six of these groups (1, 2, 5, 6, 9, and 15), reinforced by three American-built British "jeep" carriers (*Emperor, Pursuer, Tracker*), formed a north-south "outer naval barrier" 130 miles west of Land's End. The other four groups (3, 11, 12, and 14), all destroyers, formed a "middle naval barrier" to the east of the outer naval barrier. Including the screens of the three "jeep" carriers, these naval barriers comprised in all about sixty destroyer- or frigate-class warships. Eastward of these lines in the English Channel, other Allied destroyers and frigates formed similar north-south barriers to directly protect the streams of landing forces from any and all German warships (destroyers, torpedo boats, U-boats, midget submarines, and so on).*

Inasmuch as the Type VII U-boats in French ports were immobile, safely housed in bombproof pens, the best opportunities for kills in the period preceding Neptune

* On D-plus four, June 10, the British "jeep" carrier *Tracker* of the outer barrier smashed into the Canadian frigate *Teme* of Support Group 6 and wrecked her with the loss of four men killed. Another Canadian frigate, *Outremont,* towed *Teme* two hundred miles to Cardiff. The next day, June 11, the three "jeep" carriers were withdrawn, having achieved little or nothing. Hence they will not be discussed further in this account.

lay in Norwegian waters, to be covered by aircraft of 18 Group, and to a lesser extent by 15 Group, based mainly in northern England, Scotland, and islands to the immediate north. Theretofore Coastal Command had been barred from attacking U-boats in Norwegian waters lest its planes hit British-controlled submarines operating there. Hence Coastal Command's sudden aerial onslaught caught the German U-boats by surprise and resulted in a substantial but largely unheralded victory. From May 1 to D day, aircraft of 15 Group and 18 Group hit twelve U-boats in Norwegian waters, sinking seven and damaging five.

The stories of the seven U-boats sunk, in brief:

- On May 16 off Trondheim, a Sunderland of Norwegian Squadron 330 of 18 Group, piloted by C. T. Johnsen, attacked a U-boat thought to be the new VIIC *U-240,* commanded by Günter Link, age twenty-six. Flak killed one airman, wounded two, and heavily damaged the aircraft, which barely made it back to base.* Niestlé discounts this kill, listing *U-240* as lost to unknown causes.
- In the early hours of May 18 off Stadtlandet, a Catalina of British Squadron 210, also of 18 Group, piloted by B. Bastable, sank the new VIIC *U-241,* commanded by Arno Werr, age twenty-three. Bastable saw "many survivors" in the water, but all hands were lost.
- On May 24 off Namsos, another Catalina of British Squadron 210 of 18 Group, piloted by a South African, F.W.L. Maxwell, fatally damaged the new VIIC *U-476,* commanded by Otto Niethmann, age twenty-four. The VIIC *U-990,* commanded by Hubert Nordheimer, raced to rescue the crew of *U-476.* Nordheimer took aboard twenty-one Germans, including Niethmann—ten from a raft and eleven from the wrecked hulk—and then sank the abandoned *U-476* with a torpedo. Thirty-four other men of *U-476* perished.
- On the following day, May 25, while rescuer Nordheimer in *U-990* was preparing to enter Trondheim with an escort, a B-24 of British Squadron 59 of 15 Group, piloted by B. A. Sisson, attacked the formation. Nordheimer and the escort hurled flak at the plane, but *U-990*'s 37mm flak gun failed and the B-24 dropped six depth charges, which sank the boat. The escort, Patrol Boat *V-5901,* rescued fifty-two Germans of *U-476* and *U-990,* including Niethmann and Nordheimer. They returned to Germany to command big electro boats.
- On May 24, a Sunderland of a British training squadron, OTU 4, piloted by an Australian, T. F. Peter Frizell, attacked the new *U-675,* commanded by Karl-Heinz Sammler, age twenty-five. Frizell dropped five depth charges, one of which hit and bounced off the forward deck and exploded. There were no German survivors. Frizell, an instructor, reported that bodies and wreckage ("oil drums and planking") rose to the surface.
- On May 27 off Trondheim, a B-24 of British Squadron 59 of 15 Group, piloted by a lawyer serving in the Canadian Air Force, V. E. Camacho, sank with six depth charges the new VIIC41 *U-292,* commanded by Werner Schmidt, age twenty-three. There were no survivors.†

---

* The copilot, Fredrik Meyer, wrote a history of the Norwegian Air Force in World War II.

† In Arctic waters on May 30, the British destroyer *Milne* sank the VIIC *U-289,* commanded by Alexander Hellwig, age twenty-eight. There were no survivors.

• In the early hours of June 3, a Canso (Catalina) of Canadian Squadron 162 of 18 Group, which had only just transferred to northern Scotland, braved heavy flak and sank with four depth charges the new snort boat *U-477,* commanded by Karl-Joachim Jenssen, age twenty-three. The pilot, Canadian R. E. MacBride, who circled the site for four hours, reported "at least five" survivors in the water, but they perished as well. The *U-477* was the second snort boat (after *U-575*) to be sunk by Allied aircraft, the first by a land-based plane of Coastal Command.

The five boats damaged by aircraft of 18 Group were, in brief:

• On May 17 off Trondheim, a Catalina of Norwegian Squadron 333, piloted by Harald E. Hartmann, hit the newly arrived Arctic VII *U-668,* commanded by Wolfgang von Eickstedt, age twenty-eight. The Germans shot back and riddled the Catalina, killing one crewman. The damaged *U-668* aborted to Trondheim for repairs. Pilot Hartmann limped back to base and landed the Catalina safely.

• In the same area off Trondheim on May 21, a Sunderland of British training squadron OTU 4, piloted by E. T. King, hit the new Arctic VIIC41 *U-995,* commanded by Walter Köhntopp. King dropped six depth charges and strafed the boat, wounding five Germans. Köhntopp aborted to Trondheim for repairs and to replenish his crew.

• On May 24 off Namsos, a Sunderland of Canadian Squadron 423, piloted by R. H. Nesbitt, attacked the VII *U-921,* commanded by Wolfgang Leu, age twenty-six, who was en route to search for survivors of the lost *U-476.* When the U-boat's 37mm flak gun failed, Leu, who was wounded on the bridge, dived the boat, but he could not get below and he perished. His first watch officer, Rainor Lang, who was also wounded, took the boat into Trondheim. A wounded seaman died later. After repairs in Norway, the boat joined the Arctic force, commanded by a new skipper.

• On May 25, an unidentified aircraft hit the *U-276,* commanded by Rolf Borchers, age thirty, while she was attempting to assist in the rescue of survivors from the sinking *U-476.* The *U-276* incurred three casualties and such severe damage that she was retired to the Baltic for R&D experiments.

• On May 26 off Trondheim, two Mosquitos of Norwegian Squadron 333, piloted by Jacob M. Jacobsen and Hans Engebrigsten, hit the new nonsnort VII *U-958,* commanded by Gerhard Groth, age twenty-seven. The 57mm Tsetse cannon fire killed one German crewman and wounded two others. After repairs in Bergen and Kiel, the boat was transferred to the eastern Baltic.*

These British air attacks in Norwegian waters significantly disrupted U-boat operations on the eve of Overlord. Owing to the massive number of air-dropped British offensive mines fouling the Baltic, the Germans had transferred most workup and training exercises to southern Norway, in particular snort familiarization and acclimation. This training could no longer be conducted without the likelihood of British air attacks, which could be especially lethal because most of the U-boat crews were green and the 37mm flak gun was still unreliable and unsafe.

* RAF Spitfires accidentally shot down Engebrigsten's Mosquito on June 11. He was rescued, but his navigator-copilot, Odd G. Jonassen, perished.

Moreover, frontline boats of the Arctic force and group *Mitte* and those transferring to group *Landwirt* in France were likewise vulnerable. Finally, the loss of about 350 submariners on the seven boats sunk and five boats damaged would have been sufficient to cadre at least eight big electro boats under construction, another setback to that program.

Brian Baker's 19 Group, dutifully patrolling the dozen rectangular subdivisions of the western English Channel area throughout the month of May, achieved only minor successes. Baker's aircraft detected and harassed the five snort boats of group *Dragoner* carrying out test patrols in the English Channel from May 18 to May 27, and severely damaged the new Type VII nonsnort *U-736,* commanded by Reinhard Reff, age thirty, which sailed from Norway to Brest on April 1 to reinforce *Landwirt.*

The credit for the hit on *U-736* in the western area of the English Channel on the night of May 24 is still uncertain. Possibly it was inflicted by a Leigh Light–equipped Wellington of British Squadron 612, piloted by a Canadian, Kenneth H. Davies, who did not return from this, his first mission. Or possibly it was inflicted by a Leigh Light–equipped B-24 of British Squadron 224, piloted by E. W. Lindsay, who dropped fourteen depth charges on or near a surfaced U-boat in two runs. Whatever the case, the *U-736* limped into Brest under surface-ship escort the next night, May 25, but she did not sail again until August 5.

U-boats Deployed from France in June Versus Neptune

The Allied maritime forces and aircraft assigned to the Neptune phase of Overlord were enormous beyond imagining: 1,213 warships and 4,126 transports and landing craft, a total of 5,339 vessels. The warships included about two hundred destroyers (thirty-four American), destroyer escorts or frigates, sloops, and corvettes. Covering and backing up the maritime forces were 5,886 Allied bombers and fighters (3,612 American).

In the early hours of June 6, when the Germans became aware of Neptune, Hans-Rudolf Rösing, chief of U-boats, West, directed group *Landwirt* to put to sea. Thirty-six Type VIICs responded immediately: eight snort boats (seven from Brest; one from La Pallice) and twenty-eight nonsnorts (nine from Brest; nineteen from Lorient, St. Nazaire, and La Pallice). In subsequent days, seven other snort boats put out, bringing the number of U-boats deployed from France in June to repel Allied invaders to forty-three (fifteen snort boats and twenty-eight nonsnorts) manned by about two thousand German submariners.*

Fully aware that anti-invasion U-boat operations were to be hazardous in the extreme, upon receiving early word of the landings in the Bay of the Seine, Dönitz exhorted his submarine skippers to throw caution to the winds and make ever greater sacrifices:

---

* See Plate 9 and Appendix 2.

PLATE 9

TYPE VII U-BOATS IN FRENCH BASES

JUNE 4, 1944[1]

BOAT	LAST ARRIVED	DAYS IN PORT	NEXT SAILED	FATE
U-92	5/10	99	8/16	Norway
U-212/S[2]	3/12	87	6/6	Lost 7/21
U-214/S	4/29	44	6/11	Lost 7/26
U-218/S	5/7	38	6/13	Norway
U-228	3/26	73	6/6	Norway
U-255	4/11	76	6/6	Decommissioned
U-256	3/22	77	6/6	Norway
U-260	3/27	72	6/6	Norway
U-262	4/29	39	6/6	Norway
U-267/S	5/20 (patrol)	127	9/23	Norway
U-269/S	5/27 (Dragoner)	11	6/6	Lost 6/27
U-270	1/17	142	6/6	Lost 8/12
U-275/S	1/11	148	6/6	Norway
U-281	3/5	94	6/6	Norway
U-309/S	2/14	129	6/21	Norway
U-333	4/20	48	6/6	Lost 7/31
U-373	11/26	195	6/7	Lost 6/8
U-382	1/26	133	6/6	Norway
U-385	6/4	67	8/9	Lost 8/11
U-390/S	2/13	130	6/21	Lost 7/5
U-413	3/27	72	6/6	Lost 8/20
U-415	3/31	68	6/6	Mined 7/14
U-437	4/1	67	6/6	Norway
U-441/S	5/27 (Dragoner)	11	6/6	Lost 6/18
U-445	2/27	101	6/6	Lost 8/24
U-608	4/3	65	6/6	Lost 8/10
U-618	4/8	110	7/26	Lost 8/18
U-621/S	4/19	49	6/6	Lost 8/18
U-629	3/15	84	6/6	Lost 6/8
U-650	3/2	97	6/6	Norway
U-667/S	5/19 (patrol)	65	7/22	Lost 8/25
U-672	5/12	56	7/6	Lost 7/18
U-714	2/25	103	6/6	Norway
U-736	5/26 (patrol)	72	8/5	Lost 8/6
U-740	4/21	47	6/6	Lost 6/9
U-741/S	5/3	49	6/20	Lost 8/15
U-758	1/20	139	6/6	Norway
U-763/S	3/27	72	6/11	Norway
U-764/S	5/27 (Dragoner)	11	6/6	Norway
U-766	4/16	52	6/6	Decommissioned
U-821	4/12	56	6/6	Lost 6/10
U-953/S	5/27 (Dragoner)	11	6/6	Norway
U-963	3/27	72	6/6	Norway
U-970	4/22	46	6/6	Lost 6/7
U-981	1/30	129	6/6	Lost 8/12
U-984/S	5/27 (Dragoner)	11	6/6	Lost 8/20
U-985	3/12	87	6/6	Norway
U-989	3/4	95	6/6	Norway
U-993	4/22	46	6/6	Norway

TYPE VIIS ARRIVING AFTER JUNE 4, 1944

U-247/S	7/27	31	8/3	Lost 9/1
U-480/S	7/6	29	8/3	Norway
U-671	7/5	31	8/4	Lost 8/4
U-673/S	7/23	54	9/14	Norway

1. Source: U-boat Control War Diary (KTB, BdU).
2. S = snorkel.

> The enemy has started his invasion of Europe. The war has thus entered its decisive phase. If the Anglo-American landing succeeds, it would mean for us the loss of large territories vital to our war economy and an immediate threat to our most important industrial regions without which the war cannot be continued.
>
> The enemy is at his weakest at the very moment of landing. Everything must be done to hit him at this moment and to inflict such losses on him that he will have no desire ever to try any landings again. Only then, furthermore, can the forces lacking on the Eastern Front be sent there.
>
> Men of the U-boat arm! On you too the future of our German people depends, now more than at any other time. I therefore require of you the most unstinting action, and no consideration for otherwise valid precautionary measures. Each enemy vessel useful to him for landing is to be subjected to all-out attack, even when there is danger of losing your own U-boat. Every enemy man and enemy weapon destroyed before landing diminishes the enemy's prospect for success. In this crisis I know that you men of the U-boat arm—who have been tried in the toughest battles—are men on whom I can rely.*

The Neptune phase of Overlord provided Allied codebreakers with an unforeseen windfall. American and British airborne troops and others in Normandy had been ordered to cut all German communications lines they could find and they did a very good job. At Rösing's headquarters in Angers on June 8, the communications officer informed U-boat Control in Berlin by "emergency radio circuit" that "all land-line connections with Berlin, Kiel, Wilhelmshaven, Paris, Brest, Aix and La Rochelle were out of order due to enemy action." In a summary of Overlord operations, American codebreakers wrote,

> With this wholesale breakdown of land-line communications, emergency radio circuits . . . were put into operation for traffic between Control [and the U-boat] flotillas and other shore authorities. As a result [Enigma] traffic to be processed . . . fully tripled in volume. The inner workings of the administrative, supply and command structures of the U-boat force were opened [to the Allies] for direct and current inspection. It became possible to follow U-boat operational orders, reports, controversies, confusions, and troubles of all sorts from one end of the *Kriegsmarine* hierarchy to the other and back again.

The thirty-six *Landwirt* boats that sailed on D day to block Neptune had to contend with Coastal Command's saturation ASW campaign, Cork (as in corking a bottle), mounted by Brian Baker's 19 Group with an assist from 15 Group. The twenty-eight nonsnorts were especially vulnerable. Within the first ninety-six hours, British aircraft knocked out over one-third of that group: five sunk, five forced to abort.†

The stories of the five nonsnorts that were sunk, in brief:

---

* See NARA, RG 457, SRMN 043.

† Per Franks (1995) and Niestlé (1998).

• On June 7 in the Bay of Biscay, a Sunderland of British Squadron 228, piloted by Charles Gordon Drake Lancaster, got the VII *U-970,* commanded by Hans-Heinrich Ketels, age twenty-six. German seaplanes rescued Ketels and thirteen others of the crew after twenty-three hours in the water. About thirty other Germans perished. Ketels returned to Germany to command a Type XXI electro boat.*

• In the early hours of June 7, west of Brest, a B-24 of British Squadron 53, piloted by John W. Carmichael, sank the VII *U-629,* a transfer from the Arctic force, commanded by Hans-Helmut Bugs, age twenty-seven. There were no survivors; three bodies were recovered.

• Also west of Brest on June 8, a B-24 of Bristish Squadron 224, piloted by Canadian Kenneth Owen Moore, got the veteran *U-373,* commanded by Detlev von Lehsten, age twenty-six. A fishing smack rescued von Lehsten and forty-six others (who claimed they shot down the B-24) and landed them in France. Two German crewmen perished. Von Lehsten returned to Germany to fit out a big electro boat. Inasmuch as the Admiralty believed—wrongly—that Moore had unprecedentedly sunk *U-373* and *U-629* in a single sortie, it awarded him a DSO and the crewmen DFCs.

• On June 9, near the western mouth of the English Channel, a B-24 of British Squadron 120 of 15 Group, on "Cork" patrol, piloted by Alfred Kenneth Sherwood, supposedly sank what was thought to be the new *U-740,* commanded by Günther Stark, age twenty-seven. However, Niestlé lists *U-740* as lost to unknown causes.

• At midday on June 10, off Ushant, four Mosquitos of British Squadron 248, led by Stanley G. Nunn, and a B-24 of British Squadron 206, piloted by Alexander D. S. Dundas, teamed up to get the *U-821,* commanded by Ulrich Knackfuss, age twenty-three. German launches rescued a number of the crew but another flight of Mosquitos of Squadron 248, commanded by Max Geudj, shot up the launches. Other German launches finally rescued one wounded chief petty officer. All other crew of *U-821* perished.

The stories of the five nonsnorts that were forced to abort, in brief:

• In the early hours of June 7, a B-24 of British Squadron 53 on Cork patrol, piloted by John William Carmichael, hit and damaged the *U-963,* commanded by Karl Boddenberg, age thirty. Damaged, Boddenberg returned to Brest within twenty-four hours of sailing and dry-docked for emergency repairs.

• An hour later, pilot Carmichael hit the veteran (ex–flak boat) *U-256,* commanded by Wilhelm Brauel, age twenty-nine. Damaged, she limped into Brest on June 7. The Germans deemed this oft-battered boat unfit for further combat and decommissioned her. Thereafter Brauel took command of the aged VII *U-92,* whose skipper, Horst-Thilo Queck, returned to Germany to command a big electro boat.

Decorated and promoted to Squadron Leader, Carmichael attacked another

---

* That same day, nearby, a Sunderland of British Squadron 201, piloted by Leslie H. Baveystock, sank the new nonsnort VII *U-955,* which was inbound to Lorient from a fifty-four-day weather patrol. Her skipper, Hans-Heinrich Baden, age twenty-nine, and all others perished.

U-boat on June 13–14, but the boat (*U-270*?) shot down the B-24 with the loss of all hands.

• In the early hours of June 7, a Leigh Light–equipped Wellington and/or a B-24, and perhaps other aircraft as well, hit the *U-415,* newly commanded by the future author of *Iron Coffins,* Herbert Werner, age twenty-four. Werner claimed shooting down the Wellington and another aircraft (possibly a B-24) with his 37mm flak gun.* He rightly wrote that, in view of the density of Allied airpower engaged in Cork, he considered his patrol a "suicide" mission and he limped back to Brest with several wounded and severe battle damage. He dry-docked *U-415* for emergency repairs, he stated, and went to a hospital to have a slight head wound dressed.

• In Biscay on the early hours of June 7, several aircraft of 19 Group attacked Hardo Rodler von Roithberg in the VII *U-989.* Coastal Command gave credit for the damage to a Leigh Light–equipped Wellington of British Squadron 179, piloted by W. J. Hill. A B-24 and a flight of Mosquitos that participated in the attack have not been positively identified. Wounded in the thigh by Mosquito gunfire, Rodler von Roithberg aborted to Brest for medical attention.

• In the early hours of June 8, a Halifax of British Squadron 502, piloted by J. Spurgeon, found the VII *U-413,* commanded by a new skipper, Dieter Sachse, age twenty-six. Attacking into heavy flak, which badly riddled the Halifax, Spurgeon dropped a stick of four 600-pound bombs. The damage forced Sachse to abort to Brest for repairs.

In view of these ten nonsnort-boat losses and aborts, on June 10 Control ordered that no more were to sail from any French base to repel Allied invaders, except for last-ditch port defense. At the same time, Control directed Rösing to pull back the eighteen surviving nonsnort boats deployed into the Bay of Biscay to static positions on a defensive line running roughly along the hundred fathom (six-hundred-foot) curve.

From Enigma decrypts, the Allies learned of this defensive line of nonsnort boats in Biscay and sent ASW aircraft to attack it, driving the boats down. These saturation Allied air attacks caused considerable damage but sank no boats. The results were as follows:

• On June 10, a Sunderland of Australian Squadron 10, piloted by H. A. McGregor, hit the *U-333,* commanded by *Ritterkreuz* holder Peter Cremer. His 37mm jammed after the first round, but the German 20mm gunners repelled the Sunderland. Even so, the boat incurred heavy damage. On the following day, June 11, a Sunderland of British Squadron 228, piloted by a Canadian, M. E. Slaughter, hit *U-333.* Cremer's gunners shot down this Sunderland with the loss of all hands, but *U-333* was so badly damaged that Cremer had to abort to La Pallice. Upon ar-

* Many U-boats and Allied aircraft tangled in the channel on the night of June 6–7. Per Franks, Coastal Command reported the loss of three B-24s and a Wellington, but it is impossible to say with exactitude which boats made which kills.

rival at that place, Cremer left the boat and returned to Germany to command a big electro boat, taking along about half of his crew. When Rösing informed Cremer of this new assignment, Cremer wrote in his memoir, he said: "Cremer, old friend, you're a lucky fellow." Indeed.

• On June 13, a B-24 of British Squadron 53 hit the *U-270,* commanded by Paul-Friedrich Otto. The German gunners, who had earlier destroyed a B-17 of British Squadron 206, shot down this aircraft as well. On June 13, a Leigh Light–equipped Wellington of British Squadron 172, piloted by L. Harris, hit *U-270* and caused such damage that Otto aborted to Lorient. Thereupon the lucky Otto also left for Germany to command a big electro boat.

The Allied air attacks on nonsnort boats in Biscay were so intense that it was almost impossible for the boats to charge batteries.* Therefore, on June 13, Control directed Rösing to recall the boats of this defensive line to Lorient, St. Nazaire, and La Pallice. Thenceforth, these eighteen boats were to be kept in "ready" status, to sail from those places on the briefest notice to repel an Allied invasion of Brittany. Two of the Biscay nonsnort boats, *U-608* and *U-993,* put into Brest, joining the five others that had sailed from Brest and survived and had aborted to that place.

Like the nine nonsnort boats that sailed from Brest, the nineteen that sailed from Biscay ports following June 6 sank no Allied ships. During this nerve-racking and fruitless week in Biscay, one nonsnort boat, *U-970,* had been lost, as well as the *U-955,* inbound in Biscay from weather patrol.

The "Sunday Punch"

The fourteen snort boats that sailed from France in June to repel the Allied invaders were, in a phrase of the times, the German "Sunday Punch." Much was expected of these boats, but all fourteen had an arduous time and achieved almost nothing. Three were lost. The stories of the first anti-Neptune snort-boat war patrols from France:

• The veteran *U-212,* commissioned and commanded for two years by Helmut Vogler, age twenty-seven, sailed from La Pallice on June 6. While northbound in the Bay of Biscay the next day, two experienced Mosquitos of British Squadron 248, piloted by Douglas J. Turner and a Canadian, A.J.L. Bonnett, hit the boat with 57mm Tsetse cannon fire. Damaged, Vogler aborted to La Pallice for repairs. Two days later, pilot Bonnett and his copilot-navigator, A. McD. McNicol, were killed in a midair collision.

Vogler resailed *U-212* on June 12, but he was beset by mechanical problems and aborted to La Pallice for the second time on June 16. Thereafter, Berlin directed Rösing to load four snort boats with ammo and rush them to German ground forces that were cut off in Cherbourg. Assigned to this dangerous mission, the *U-*

* Eight other nonsnort VIIs in Biscay that reported air attacks from June 6 to June 14, according to the war diary at Control: *U-382, U-437, U-445, U-608, U-766, U-981, U-985,* and *U-993.* Doubtless there were other unreported attacks.

212 loaded and sailed from La Pallice for the third time on June 22. The next day, when Berlin learned that the Allies were already at the gates of Cherbourg, Control canceled the mission and *U-212* again returned to La Pallice. Vogler unloaded the ammo and resailed on June 28 from La Pallice to Brest to stage for a torpedo patrol to the Allied landing area in the Bay of the Seine. He arrived in Brest on July 4.

• The veteran *U-275,* commissioned and commanded for twenty months by Helmut Bork, age thirty-four, sailed from Brest on June 6. Hounded by unidentified Allied air and surface ASW forces, Bork shot a T-5 at a "destroyer" but missed. Unable to snort long enough to charge batteries in the combat zone, after one miserable week Bork put into St. Peter Port on the German-occupied island of Guernsey. While charging batteries there, he filed a lugubrious and defeatist report stating that Allied sonar could easily detect a snorting boat and that therefore the use of the snort to recharge batteries in the English Channel was "extremely hazardous." Bork resailed *U-275* on June 14. A week later Rösing directed him and some other snort boats to close Cherbourg to attack Allied heavy units that were shelling the port. Unable to offer any help there, Bork returned to Brest on June 24, at which time he went on to other duty.

• The veteran *U-269,* newly commanded by Georg Uhl, age twenty-nine, sailed from Brest on June 6. Likewise harassed by unidentified Allied air and surface ASW forces, Uhl made no attacks and put into to St. Peter Port on June 14 to charge batteries and resailed on June 16. Also directed to Cherbourg, Uhl was unable to offer any help either. While *U-269* was returning again to St. Peter Port on June 25 to charge batteries, the frigate *Bickerton* of British Support Group 5 detected *U-269* and blasted her to the surface with depth charges. After Uhl gave the order to scuttle and abandon ship, he became entangled in the propellers of *Bickerton* and was chopped to pieces, German survivors said later. *Bickerton,* commanded by E. M. Thorpe, rescued thirty-nine other Germans, including two men who were trapped inside the conning tower but got out and reached the surface from a depth of about two hundred feet without escape apparatus.

• The veteran (ex-flak) boat *U-441,* commanded by Klaus Hartmann, age thirty-one, sailed from Brest on June 6. Nothing further was ever heard from the boat. U-boat Control ordered *U-441* to the landing area in the Bay of the Seine. In wartime, the Admiralty credited a Wellington of Polish Squadron 304 with the kill of *U-441.* However, in a recent reassessment, the Admiralty credited a B-24 of British Squadron 224, piloted by Canadian Kenneth Owen Moore, with the kill on the night of June 8, restoring his unprecedented claim of two sinkings in a single sortie, justifying the DSO.

• The veteran (ex-flak) boat *U-621,* newly commanded by Hermann Stuckmann, age twenty-three, sailed from Brest on June 6. En route to the Bay of the Seine the next day, Stuckmann shot a T-5 at a "destroyer" but missed. On June 9 he aborted to Brest with bomb damage incurred during an attack by an unidentified aircraft and, after hurried repairs, resailed on June 12. Reaching the Allied invasion area on June 15, Stuckmann shot a T-5 at the 1,500-ton American *LST 280* and sank her, the first confirmed Allied vessel to be lost to a U-boat in the Neptune phase of Overlord. Three days later, Stuckmann came upon—and shot at—two

British battleships of a support force. However, all torpedoes missed and on June 21, Stuckmann returned *U-621* to Brest.

• The *U-764,* commanded by Hans-Kurt von Bremen, age twenty-five, sailed from Brest on June 6. In the invasion area on June 15, von Bremen hit and severely damaged the British frigate *Blackwood* with a T-5, and she sank under tow the following day. In the ensuing counterattack, von Bremen shot all the rest of his torpedoes, to no avail. In return, British warships severely damaged *U-764* and forced von Bremen to abort to St. Peter Port with a broken snort. Owing to a "navigational error," however, he entered Brest on June 21.

• The *U-984,* commanded by Heinz Sieder, age twenty-three, sailed from Brest on June 6. En route to the Allied landing area, Sieder shot three T-5s at three "destroyers," including the Canadian *Saskatchewan.* One torpedo prematured, one missed, and one hit the Cat Gear (towed noisemaker decoy) of *Saskatchewan* and exploded. Thereafter Sieder was forced back to Brest on June 9 with bomb damage from an unidentified aircraft.

Sieder resailed from Brest to the Bay of the Seine on June 12. Two days later he encountered a hunter-killer group and fired two T-5s at the formation. One torpedo failed to leave the tube; the other missed. Unable to get in a battery charge, on June 19 Sieder also put into St. Peter Port. Allied air was so heavy that he was not able to get a full charge in that port; nonetheless, he resailed on June 19. Once again en route to the Bay of the Seine on June 25, Sieder encountered another hunter-killer group and shot two T-5s at the formation. One missed but the other hit the 1,300-ton British frigate *Goodson* in the stern. Another British frigate, *Bligh,* towed the wrecked *Goodson* into Portland.

Four days later, on June 29, Sieder came upon a loaded Allied convoy, EMC 17, and shot two torpedoes at the port column. One hit and damaged an 8,000-ton freighter that Sieder later thought he put under with a finishing shot. The other missed the port column but hit in the starboard column a 7,000-ton freighter that sank slowly, Sieder claimed. He then shot a T-5 at another freighter of 9,000 tons and got a hit in the stern. A finishing shot at this vessel missed, Sieder reported.

Allied records showed that Sieder did better than his claims and in so doing, delivered the only really significant blow to the Neptune invasion forces in June. Apart from the damage to the frigate *Goodson,* his torpedoes hit four 7,200-ton American Liberty ships, some carrying troops. One, *Edward M. House,* reached England and was repaired. The other three, *Henry G. Blaisdel, James A. Farrell,* and *John A. Treutlen,* had to be scrapped. Seventy-six American soldiers were lost on *Blaisdel,* manned by Coast Guard personnel.

Upon the arrival of *U-984* in Brest on July 4, Dönitz awarded Sieder a *Ritterkreuz,* the first of four such awards presented to U-boat skippers engaged in attacking Neptune invasion forces.

• The veteran (ex-flak) *U-953,* commanded by the experienced Karl-Heinz Marbach, age twenty-four, sailed from Brest on June 6. En route to the invasion area, Marbach shot four T-5s at four destroyers of the Canadian hunter-killer Support Group 12, which included *Ou'Appelle, Restigouche, Saskatchewan,* and *Skeena.* He claimed—and was credited with—sinking three destroyers, but Allied records revealed that his torpedoes exploded harmlessly in the wakes of the ships, probably on Cat Gear decoys. Before reaching the invasion area, Marbach had a serious mechanical breakdown that forced him to abort to Brest, where he arrived on June 18.

After hurried repairs, Marbach resailed *U-953* to the Bay of the Seine on June 24. Snorting and making good about forty miles a day, he reached the Allied landing area on July 5, where he sighted three large convoys. He attacked one, firing three torpedoes. He claimed two freighters for 11,000 tons sunk, but Allied records confirmed only the sinking of one small freighter, the 1,927-ton Britisher *Glendinning.*

A week later, on July 11, Marbach attacked another big convoy and shot five torpedoes into the rows of overlapping ships. He claimed sinking another "destroyer" and a 9,000-ton freighter, both of which "hit bottom with a wallop," but Allied records do not substantiate either of these sinkings. Generously credited with sinking four "destroyers" and three freighters for 20,000 tons in two brief patrols, upon the return of *U-953* to Brest on July 21, Dönitz awarded Marbach a *Ritterkreuz,* the second such award to U-boat skippers engaged against Neptune forces. Marbach then left *U-953* and returned to Germany to command a big electro boat.

- The *U-763,* commanded by Ernst Cordes, age thirty, sailed from La Pallice on June 11, but on June 16 he aborted to Brest, reporting a broken periscope. After repairs he resailed but on June 18, he again aborted to Brest with mechanical problems.

Cordes resailed from Brest to the Bay of the Seine yet again on June 20. En route, air and surface forces continually hounded, bombed, and depth-charged the boat. Cordes counterattacked "destroyers" on two separate occasions with T-5s, but both torpedoes missed.

In the Allied landing area on July 5, Cordes found and attacked convoy ETC 26. He shot five torpedoes: three at the mass of overlapping ships, one T-5 at a 4,000-ton freighter and one T-5 at a "destroyer." A hunter-killer group pounced on *U-763,* Cordes reported, and chased the boat for thirty hours, dropping an astonishing total of 550 depth charges, according to the German count.

Cordes escaped this hunt to exhaustion but lost track of his position. On July 7, when he saw land in the periscope and touched bottom at fifty-two feet, he assumed he had drifted close to the French coast. In fact, he had drifted in the opposite direction (north) and was on the south coast of England in the Portsmouth roadstead—Spithead, gateway to the home of the Royal Navy! He lay doggo and undetected off Nab Light, then escaped south to deeper water.

Approaching Brest on July 11, Cordes shot two torpedoes at warships of a hunter-killer group. Upon his arrival, Cordes was credited with hits on two freighters and a "destroyer," probably sinking one freighter and a probable hit on another "destroyer." Allied records confirmed only the sinking of the 1,500-ton Norwegian freighter *Ringen.* Cordes turned over command of *U-763* to another skipper and returned to the Baltic to command a new VII, attached to the Training Command.

• The *U-390,* only recently fitted with a snort and commanded by Heinz Geissler, sailed on June 21 from St. Nazaire to deliver a load of ammo to Cherbourg. When that mission was canceled, Geissler put into Brest on June 24 to take on torpedoes, and resailed for the Bay of the Seine on June 27. In the early hours of July 5, Geissler came upon a convoy and fired two torpedoes at two vessels. It is believed that torpedoes hit both targets, sinking the British ASW trawler *Ganilly* and inflicting damage on the 7,900-ton American ship *Sea Porpoise.*

One of the convoy close escorts, the British frigate *Tavy,* commanded by F. Arden, got *U-390* on sonar and attacked immediately with depth charges. Geissler may have counterattacked with a T-5 that malfunctioned or missed. *Tavy* then carried out three Hedgehog attacks that severely damaged *U-390* and drove her to the bottom. Another escort, the old British destroyer *Wanderer,* commanded by Reginald ("Bob") Whinney, who had earlier sunk the VII *U-305* and had shared credit for sinking the IXC *U-523,* joined the hunt and carried out two Hedgehog and one depth-charge attack.

Below in *U-390,* all was chaos. Fuel oil and seawater flooded the boat. Men gathered in the control room with escape gear. However, only one man, chief engineer Erich Tein, got out. When he popped to the surface unconscious, *Tavy* fished him out and medics revived him. He was the lone survivor of *U-390*'s forty-eight-man crew.

• The *U-309,* also recently fitted with a snort and commanded by Hans-Gert Mahrholz, sailed from La Pallice on June 21 to deliver ammo to Cherbourg. When that mission was canceled, Mahrholz also put into Brest on June 25 to unload the ammo and take on torpedoes. He resailed for the Bay of the Seine on June 29.

Owing to the absence of reports from the first wave of snort boats and to a British propaganda claim of sinking ten U-boats in the English Channel, on July 2 Rösing recalled *U-309* and other newly sailed snort boats to Brest until the situation clarified. Rösing rescinded these orders the very next day. By that time Mahrholz had encountered a hunter-killer group of four "destroyers." He shot two torpedoes at two "destroyers," claiming he sank one and missed the other, but the sinking could not be confirmed in Allied records. Ignoring orders to continue on to the Bay of the Seine, Mahrholz put into Brest to replenish his torpedo supply on July 6.

• The *U-741,* commanded by Gerhard Palmgren, took on a load of ammo for Cherbourg and sailed from Brest on June 20. When that mission was canceled, Palmgren returned to Brest on June 27 to unload the ammo and take on torpedoes and sail to the Bay of the Seine.

In addition to these attack snort boats, the two remaining Type VIID (minelayers), *U-214* and *U-218,* both fitted with snorts, were ordered to plant minefields off the southwest coast of England.

• The *U-214,* commanded by Rupprecht Stock, age twenty-eight, sailed on June 11 from Brest to lay fifteen SMA mines in the western English Channel off Plymouth. Unidentified Allied aircraft hit *U-214* and forced Stock to abort to Brest on June 14. He resailed on June 16, planted the mines on June 26, and returned on July 1, but the minefield produced no sinkings.

• The *U-218,* commanded by Richard Becker, age thirty-three, sailed from Brest on June 13 to lay fifteen SMA mines in the western English Channel off Falmouth. While en route, Allied surface ships hunted and depth-charged *U-218* for sixty hours. The snort exhaust backed up and carbon monoxide felled Becker and about two-thirds of his crew. After planting the mines on July 1, Becker returned to Brest on July 9. At that time Rupprecht Stock from *U-214* relieved Becker, who returned to Germany to command a big electro boat. Becker's minefield at Falmouth damaged one ship, the 7,200-ton British *Empire Halberd* on July 6.

So much for the German "Sunday Punch." In these first forays, the fourteen snort boats (including the minelayers *U-214* and *U-218*) sailing from France in June to repel Allied invaders sank or destroyed only eight ships: three warships for 3,100 tons (*LST 280;* frigate *Blackwood;* ASW trawler *Ganilly*) and five freighters for 25,000 tons (*Blaisdel, Treutlen, Farrell, Glendinning, Ringen*). The U-boats also damaged one warship for 1,300 tons (frigate *Goodson*) and two freighters for 15,000 tons (*Sea Porpoise* and *Empire Halberd*). In return for these slight successes, three snort boats (*U-269, U-390, U-441*) were lost with about 150 submariners (forty captured).

U-boat Reinforcements Sailing from Norway to France

Eleven Type VII snort boats survived the intense preinvasion Allied ASW campaign in Norwegian waters and sailed to join the Atlantic U-boat force in June.

U-boat Control radioed these reinforcements Hitlerian orders:

> Attack the invasion fleet without consideration for anything else whatsoever. Each enemy vessel which serves his landing, even if it delivers, say, 50 troops or 1 tank, is a target demanding all-out U-boat attack. It is to be attacked even at risk of losing your own U-boat. When it is a matter of getting at the enemy invasion fleet, have no regard for danger from shallow water, or possible minefields or any misgivings at all. Each enemy man and each enemy weapon destroyed before landing diminishes the enemy's prospects of success. But the U-boat which inflicts losses on the enemy during his landing has fulfilled its supreme task and has justified its existence, even if it accomplishes nothing more.*

Allied forces sank seven of the eleven before they completed these transit patrols. Therefore only four snort boats reached France from Norway and one, *U-673,* came there by mistake. The stories of the seven lost snort boats, in brief:

• While approaching the western end of the English Channel, the *U-767,* commanded by Walter Dankleff, age thirty-seven, sank the 1,370-ton British frigate *Mourne* on June 15. Three days later, on June 18, British Support Group 14, composed of five veteran destroyers (*Fame, Havelock, Hotspur, Icarus, Inconstant*), detected *U-767.* Attacking with her Hedgehog, *Fame* reported "two or three hits at ninety-five feet." *Fame, Havelock,* and *Inconstant* then carried out three deliberate depth-charge attacks in the next hour.

These attacks wrecked *U-767* and drove her to the bottom at a depth of 240 feet. Remarkably, one of the fifty-man crew, a stoker, Walter Schmietenknop, es-

---

* See NARA, RG 457, SRMN 043.

caped through a torpedo tube amid the depth charges and rose to the surface to be rescued by *Fame.* All other Germans perished.

• While passing near the Faeroes on the night of June 15, the *U-971,* commanded by Walter Zeplien, age twenty-five, repelled an attack by a Sunderland of British training squadron OTU 4. Five nights later, on June 20, as Zeplien approached the western mouth of the English Channel, a Leigh Light–equipped Wellington of Canadian Squadron 407, piloted by F. H. Foster, attacked with depth charges and damaged three of *U-971*'s four bow tubes. On June 21, two other Coastal Command aircraft hit the boat: a Sunderland of British Squadron 228 and a Halifax of British Squadron 502. Although several of his torpedo tubes were wrecked, Zeplien attempted but was unable to comply with orders from Hans-Rudolf Rösing to proceed to Cherbourg to attack big ships shelling that place.

Hounded by Allied air and surface ASW forces, on June 24 Zeplien aborted his patrol and headed for Brest. However, a B-24 of Czechoslovak Squadron 311, piloted by Jan Vella, sighted *U-971,* attacked with rockets and depth charges, and homed in two destroyers, the British *Eskimo* and the Canadian *Haida.* When depth charges from the two ships wrecked and flooded the boat knee deep, Zeplien issued a round of beer, thanked the men for their loyalty, then ordered them to surface and scuttle. The Allied destroyers rescued Zeplien and fifty-one others of *U-971;* one German perished.

• The *U-988,* commanded by Erich Dobberstein, age twenty-four. Very little is known with certainty about the loss of this boat. She made her "passage report" (upon reaching the North Atlantic) on D day, June 6. Two days later, Control ordered her (and three other snort boats from Norway) to the Allied landing area in the Bay of the Seine at maximum speed, cruising on the surface when possible. On June 16, Control assumed she had reached the English Channel and so logged. Two nights later, on June 18, *U-988* reported that she had been attacked by an aircraft. Although Control assumed she reached the landing area and subsequently ordered her to Lorient, nothing further was ever heard from *U-988.**

• The *U-1191,* commanded by Peter Grau, age twenty-four, reached the western entrance of the English Channel, but apparently had no opportunity to attack Allied forces. In wartime, the Admiralty credited two British frigates, *Affleck* and *Balfour,* with the kill of *U-1191* on June 25 but recently declared the cause to be unknown. There were no survivors.

• The *U-678,* commanded by Guido Hyronimus, age twenty-five, who had lost his first command, *U-670,* in a Baltic collision, reached the Bay of the Seine in late June. On the night of July 5–6, Hyronimus attacked a convoy but had no success. Three warships, the Canadian destroyers *Ottawa* and *Kootenay* of Support Group 11 and the British corvette *Statice* of the convoy escort, pounced on and sank the *U-678* with the loss of all hands.

---

* Niestlé writes that *U-988* was sunk by a B-24 of British Squadron 224 (piloted by John W. Barling) and four British frigates on June 30. If that is the case, the assumption by Jürgen Rohwer that *U-988* wrecked or sank on June 27, 28, and 29 the British corvette *Pink* and two British freighters, the 2,400-ton *Maid of Orleans* and 7,200-ton *Empire Portia,* is probably correct. See Franks (1995), p. 166, Rohwer, *Axis Submarine Successes,* p. 182, and Niestlé, p. 95.

• The *U-243,* commanded by Hans Märtens, age twenty-six, shot down a JU-88 by mistake on the night of June 9–10 and almost torpedoed a recalled non-snort boat, *U-1000.* Five days later, Märtens aborted to Bergen with a badly damaged diesel engine and resailed to the English Channel on June 20. En route, Control diverted the *U-243* to Brest.

On the afternoon of July 8, a Sunderland of Australian Squadron 10 of 19 Group, piloted by William Boris Tilley, found *U-243* on the surface about ninety miles from Brest and attacked with machine guns and depth charges. Another Sunderland of that squadron and a U.S. Navy B-24 of Squadron VB 105, piloted by Aurelian H. Cooledge, joined the attack and both dropped depth charges. These attacks mortally wounded Märtens and flak gunners topside. Belowdecks, the engineer, Wolfgang Heinze, scuttled and went down with the boat. British destroyers of hunter-killer Support Group 14 rescued thirty-eight of the fifty-man crew.

• The *U-719,* commanded by Klaus-Dietrich Steffens, age twenty-six, was directed to patrol the mouth of North Channel. On June 26, British forces detected the boat and launched an intense air and surface hunt. The British destroyer *Bulldog,* commanded by J. H. Pennell, delivered the coup de grace to *U-719* west of Bloody Foreland. There were no German survivors.

The four snort boats from Norway that ultimately reached France did so with difficulties. In brief:

• The *U-480,* commanded by Hans-Joachim Förster, age twenty-four, sailed from Norway on June 10 to the Bay of the Seine. The outer hull of this boat had a coating of antisonar material (*Alberich*). Four days out, on June 13, a Canso of Canadian Squadron 162, piloted by Laurance Sherman, attacked *U-480.* The German flak gunners riddled the Canso, forcing Sherman to ditch. Three of the eight airmen, including Sherman, died in the crash; five got into an inflatable raft. Four of the five survivors died on the raft. On the tenth day after the crash, June 22, a Norwegian whaler rescued the lone survivor, J. E. Roberts, and turned him over to the Germans. Hans-Rudolf Rösing directed Förster in *U-480* to abort his voyage to the Bay of the Seine and to put into Brest. The *U-480* arrived there on July 6 but did not resail for a month.

• The *U-671,* commanded by Wolfgang Hegewald, age twenty-six, reached the Bay of the Seine on June 25. During the following week, enemy warships hounded and harassed *U-671,* thwarting any attacks on enemy vessels, except a single T-5 that malfunctioned and missed a "destroyer." While the boat was bottomed at 203 feet on July 2, a group of "destroyers" detected her and attacked with depth charges. Hegewald fired two T-5s at these ships but both torpedoes failed. After finally shaking the hunters, Hegewald realized that *U-671* was badly damaged and he aborted to Boulogne, arriving on July 5 with a completely dead battery. Inasmuch as there were no submarine technicians in that place, Rösing ordered thirty from St. Nazaire to repair *U-671* in Boulogne.

• The *U-247,* commanded by Gerhard Matschulat, age twenty-four, was directed to patrol off northwest Scotland near the mouth of North Minch, between the Butt of Lewis and Cape Wrath. In the late daylight hours of July 5, Matschulat came upon a half dozen armed fishing trawlers about eighteen miles west of Cape Wrath. He chose one, the 207-ton *Noreen Mary,* for a target and shot three torpedoes at her.

All missiles malfunctioned or missed, a frustrating outcome that prompted Matschulat to surface and sink the trawler with his flak guns. The gunfire killed six of the ten men on the trawler, including the skipper, John Flockhart. Two other men perished in the water. Another trawler, *Lady Madeleine,* rescued two survivors, William Pryde, who said he had forty-eight shrapnel wounds, and James MacAlister, who reported fourteen wounds. Later, in a sworn affidavit, MacAlister accused Matschulat of shooting at him while he clung to the wreckage of a lifeboat.*

Matschulat patrolled North Minch for another week without further success. He then set sail for Brest, arriving on July 27. In his postpatrol debriefing, he reported that *U-247* had neither seen by periscope nor heard by hydrophones any convoys. His flotilla commander approved the sinking of the trawler and praised Matschulat for his "great offensive spirit and verve."

• The *U-673,* commanded by Heinz-Gerd Sauer, age twenty-nine, carried out a weather-reporting patrol south of Iceland partly to battle test his experimental Type VI bridge configuration. Control directed Sauer to return *U-673* to Norway, but he did not get this message and proceeded to France. Surprised by the arrival of the boat off Lorient on July 21, Rösing directed Sauer to put into St. Nazaire. Upon his arrival there on July 23, Sauer went on to other duty.

Eleven new snort boats survived the surprise Allied air assault off Norway in May and early June and sailed to reinforce the Atlantic U-boat force. Seven of these were lost. About 350 more submariners in those boats failed to return (eighty-seven were captured), enough to cadre another eight big electro boats. The other four positively sank two ships: the 1,370-ton British frigate *Mourne* and the 207-ton fishing trawler *Noreen Mary.*

All told, between June 3 and July 8, the Allies sank fourteen snort boats opposing Neptune, three operating from France and eleven en route from Norway to France. The figure includes another four snort boats lost in Norwegian waters, as will be described: the VIICs *U-423, U-478,* and *U-715,* and the IXC40 *U-1225.* About six hundred Germans serving on these boats were lost, 105 captured.†

Further Allied Attacks on U-boats in Norwegian Waters

Group *Mitte* (Central), the twenty-odd VIIs based in southern Norway being held on six hours notice to repel an Allied invasion of that area or Denmark, was not a model of the legendary German efficiency on D day, June 6. Rather, it was a ragtag group composed of nonsnort VIIs recalled from transfer to France, and other VIIs, some still in workup, which sailed from ports in southern Norway and Kiel. On

* The affidavit was introduced by the British at Dönitz's trial at Nuremberg as another example of U-boat barbarism. Dönitz denied the accusation with the convincing explanation that many such survivors who were in or near the line of gunfire directed at their vessels mistook this fire to be aimed at them.

† From *U-269, U-390, U-715, U-767,* and *U-971.*

June 8, only ten VIIs of *Mitte* were in place at sea. Including the recalled VIIs, on June 9 *Mitte* at sea increased to twelve boats and on June 11, to sixteen, its peak strength. Inasmuch as the Allies showed no signs of invading Norway or Denmark, on June 24 Dönitz directed that the *Mitte* group at sea be reduced to six boats and transferred the surplus boats to the Arctic or to the Baltic Sea to help repel Soviet forces advancing from the east.

While the land battles raged on the Normandy beachhead, the Allies continued the vigorous campaign against U-boats in Norwegian waters. In the three weeks from June 11 to July 3, Allied forces knocked out another thirteen U-boats: six sunk, seven forced to abort to Norway, one of the latter so badly damaged that she was retired. The stories of the seven lost boats, in brief:

• North of the Shetlands on the afternoon of June 11, a Canso of Canadian Squadron 162 of 18 Group, piloted by Laurance Sherman, attacked the new nonsnort VII *U-980,* commanded by Herman Dahms, age twenty-eight. The German flak gunners threw up heavy fire but Sherman bore through to drop four depth charges that sank *U-980.* Sherman reported wreckage and "about thirty-five men" in the water. None of these Germans survived. As related, three days later pilot Sherman attacked the France-bound snort boat *U-480,* only to be shot up and forced to ditch, resulting in his death and the loss of six of his seven crew.

• Off Trondheim on June 13, yet another Canso of the Iceland-based Canadian Squadron 162, piloted by Wing Commander Cecil St. George William Chapman, sighted the periscope and snort of the new *U-715,* commanded by Helmut Röttger, age twenty-five. Chapman forced *U-715* to the surface with four depth charges, then killed three of her crew on deck with machine-gun fire. Röttger, in turn, raked the Canso with his 37mm flak gun and Chapman was forced to ditch. Three of the eight crewmen of the Canso perished; five were picked up by a British air-sea rescue launch after eight hours adrift in the water. Wing Commander Chapman received an immediate DSO. The second pilot, J. M. McRae, and the three others also won high awards.

The *U-715* sank in this action. British air-sea rescue launches picked up sixteen of the forty-five Germans, but Röttger was not among them. The German survivors told British interrogators that Röttger had "lost control of himself during the air attack" and "shot himself during the sinking."

• Off Narvik on June 15, the British submarine *Satyr,* commanded by T. S. Weston, sank the Arctic-bound nonsnort *U-987,* commanded by Hilmer Karl Schreyer, age twenty-eight, onetime enlisted quartermaster on Günther Krech's highly successful *U-558.* In his attack, Weston fired a full bow salvo of six torpedoes. Two fouled and prematured, but two hit *U-987,* Weston thought. There were no German survivors.

• Off Stadtlandet on June 17, a Catalina of Norwegian Squadron 333 of 18 Group, piloted by Carl Fredrik Krafft, sank the new snort boat *U-423,* commanded by Klaus Hackländer, age twenty-seven. The *U-423* had sailed from Kiel on June 9 and was en route from Norway to France. There were no survivors.

• Off Trondheim on June 24, yet another Canso of Canadian Squadron 162, piloted by David E. Hornell, found the new Type IXC40 snort boat *U-1225,* commanded by Ernst Sauerberg, age thirty, who was outbound for a weather-reporting patrol. As airman Hornell began his attack, Sauerberg stayed on the surface and threw up heavy flak that blew off the starboard engine of the Canso and set the wing on fire.

Heroically carrying out his attack plan, Hornell sank *U-1225* with depth charges and then ditched. He and his copilot, Bernard C. Denomy, and six other airmen piled into a single life raft. Two enlisted men died in the raft. Eventually a Catalina of Norwegian Squadron 333, piloted by the aforementioned Carl Krafft, and a Warwich of British Squadron 281 found the six survivors and directed an air-sea rescue launch to the scene. Hornell died on board the launch, but five Canadian airmen lived.

British authorities awarded Hornell a posthumous Victoria Cross, the first such high honor to be earned by a Canadian airman and the first for Coastal Command. Second pilot Denomy got a DSO and the other four men received high awards. The Norwegian airmen reported "thirty-five to forty" Germans of *U-1225* in the water, but none survived.

- Off Trondheim on June 26, a B-24 of British Squadron 86 of 18 Group, piloted by Geoffrey William Tyndall Parker, sank the *Mitte* boat *U-317,* a nonsnort VIIC41, commanded by Peter Rahlf, age thirty-five, making his first war patrol. There were no survivors. Although badly damaged by flak, Parker was able to fly the B-24 to an alternate base, after which the plane was scrapped.
- On June 30, another Canso of Canadian Squadron 162, flown by R. E. McBride (who, as related, had sunk *U-477* on June 3), sighted the periscope of the new snort boat *U-478,* commanded by Rudolf Rademacher, age twenty-five. Circling the area near the submerged U-boat, McBride homed in a Sunderland and two B-24s of British Squadron 86 and set up an aerial hunt to exhaustion. Already low on fuel, the Sunderland soon had to leave; but three hours later, when *U-478* surfaced, McBride in the Canso and the two B-24s were still circling nearby.

Flying into heavy flak that damaged his Canso, McBride attempted to depth-charge *U-478,* but the charges failed to release. Thereupon he homed in one of the B-24s, piloted by N.E.M. Smith, which sank *U-478* with six depth charges. There were no German survivors.

The stories of the six U-boats that aborted, in brief:

- The snort boat VIIC *U-290,* commanded by Helmut Herglotz, age twenty-six. On the afternoon of June 14, a Mosquito of Norwegian Squadron 333, crewed by Erling U. Johansen and Lauritz Humlen, attacked *U-290* with the 57mm Tsetse cannon and a single depth charge. Herglotz claimed he shot down an Allied aircraft, but that assertion has not been confirmed in postwar records. Having incurred eight wounded, he aborted to Egersund. After repairs and remanning, the boat went to the eastern Baltic in August.
- The new Type VIIC41 snort boat *U-998,* commanded by the ill-starred old hand Hans Fiedler, age twenty-nine, second skipper of Reinhard Suhren's famous VII *U-564,* which was forced to scuttle off Spain with aircraft damage. On the afternoon of June 16, the same Norwegian Mosquito, crewed by Johansen and Humlen, attacked *U-998* with 57mm cannon fire and two depth charges. Fiedler incurred "se-

vere" damage, called for help, and aborted. Upon limping into Bergen, this severely damaged boat was retired,* and Fiedler went to France to command a third boat.

- The new IXC40 snort boat *U-804,* commanded by Herbert Meyer, age thirty-three, outbound for a weather patrol. While attempting to assist Hans Fiedler in the damaged *U-998* on the evening of June 16, another Mosquito of Norwegian Squadron 333, crewed by Jacob M. Jacobsen and Per C. Hansen, hit *U-804.* Meyer shot down the Mosquito but incurred eight wounded (three serious) and also aborted to Bergen. Another of the France-bound recalled nonsnort boats, *U-1000,* commanded by Willi Müller, age thirty-two, rescued Jacobsen and Hansen, and aborted to Norway. After repairs and remanning in Norway, on June 19 Meyer in *U-804* resailed to the Atlantic for a weather patrol. Subsequently, Müller took the *U-1000* to the eastern Baltic.

When Allied intelligence DFed the weather reports from Meyer in *U-804,* the American Tenth Fleet diverted a homebound hunter-killer group, built around the "jeep" carrier *Wake Island,* to kill the boat. On August 2, the American destroyer escorts *Fiske* and *Douglas L. Howard* of this group spotted *U-804* on the surface and attacked. Meyer dived and fired three T-5s at his pursuers. One hit the *Fiske,* which broke in half and sank in ten minutes. Thirty men perished and fifty were wounded. Another American destroyer escort of the group, *Farquhar,* rescued 186 men of *Fiske* (including the fifty wounded) and sped west to Argentia.

Meyer in *U-804* continued his weather-reporting patrol and returned safely to Norway on October 7, completing a voyage of 111 days.

- The new VII snort boat *U-743,* commanded by Helmut Kandzior, age twenty-four, outbound from Kiel to Norway. On June 20, a B-24 of British Squadron 86 of 18 Group, piloted by an Australian, E. D. Moffit, hit the *U-743* with eight depth charges. In this attack, which damaged the boat, one German gunner was killed and two were wounded and Kandzior aborted to Bergen. After repairs in Norway, the boat resailed to the Atlantic in late August. While on a mission in another B-24 on June 26, Moffit and his aircrew disappeared.
- The new VIIC snort boat *U-396,* commanded by Ernst-Günther Unterhorst, age twenty-five, en route from Kiel to Norway. On the afternoon of June 28, a Catalina of British Squadron 210, piloted by J. C. Campbell, hit and damaged the *U-396.* Forced to abort on July 1 owing to carbon-monoxide leakage from her snort, which was damaged in the air attack, the boat reached Bergen on July 3 with several crewmen ill. She did not resail until October.
- The new Type IXC40 snort boat *U-865,* commanded by Dietrich Stellmacher, age twenty-nine, en route to the Atlantic for a weather patrol. Hit by an unidentified aircraft, Stellmacher was forced to abort to Norway on July 5. After repairs, the boat resailed at the end of the month.

When the thirteen U-boats knocked out in June in Norwegian waters (seven sunk, six forced to abort) are added to the twelve boats hit in these waters in May (seven

---

* In the postwar reassessment, this Mosquito was, of course, rightly credited with a "kill."

sunk, five forced to abort), the totals were impressive indeed: twenty-five boats hit; fourteen sunk, eleven forced to abort. In the June sinkings, another 350 experienced German submariners perished or were captured, bringing German personnel losses on U-boats in Norwegian waters during May and June to about seven hundred. The loss of trained personnel was sufficient to cadre fourteen big electro boats, another setback to that program.

The Arctic

On D day in Normandy, there were thirty-two VIIs in the Arctic force. Seventeen were at sea, hunting futilely for Murmansk convoys, which the Allies had suspended temporarily. These boats were organized into two attack groups: *Grimm* (ten boats) and *Trutz* (seven boats). The other fifteen were in northern ports from Trondheim to Narvik on standby or in refit.

Upon learning of the Allied invasion, per plan, the chief of U-boats North, Reinhard Suhren, recalled seven of the boats in the *Grimm* and *Trutz* groups. They were to proceed "at maximum speed" to Narvik, where they were to refuel and replenish and then standby "in immediate readiness." The other ten boats of *Grimm-Trutz* were to remain at sea in a line northeast of Jan Mayen Island to repel putative Allied invaders of northern Norway or to attack Murmansk convoys. Redesignated group *Trutz,* this line remained in place (with alternating U-boats) until July 1.

After the success of Neptune, the naval phase of Overlord, was assured, Churchill proposed to Roosevelt that the Murmansk convoys be resumed to provide all possible supplies for Stalin's massive summer offensive (Bagration), which began on June 22. Roosevelt agreed readily.

This decision raised anew the threat posed by *Tirpitz* to those convoys. Accordingly, the new commander of the Home Fleet, Henry Moore (succeeding Bruce Fraser), drew plans for yet another attack on *Tirpitz* in mid-July. From Scapa Flow sailed a task force consisting of the battleship *Duke of York,* three fleet carriers (*Formidable, Furious,* and the new *Indefatigable*), four cruisers, and twelve destroyers. Barracuda aircraft from the carriers twice attempted to hit *Tirpitz* on July 17, but they were thwarted, first by a smoke screen, then by fog.

During these naval actions in July, aircraft of Coastal Command's 18 Group provided support. They knocked out ten more U-boats: four sunk, six forced to abort. These further losses led Control to abolish the at-sea section of group *Mitte* and to recall those boats to various ports. In brief:

- In the North Sea on July 15, a B-24 of British Squadron 206, piloted by D. W. Thynne, sank the *Mitte* VIIC41 *U-319,* commanded by Johannes Clemens, age thirty-three. There were no German survivors. Apparently Clemens shot down the B-24 during this attack. Near that place on July 16, a British launch recovered the body of one crew member of the B-24 from a dinghy.
- Off Narvik on July 17, a Catalina of British Squadron 210, piloted by John A. Cruickshank, attacked the Arctic VII *U-361,* commanded by Hans Seidel, age

twenty-six. On the first pass, the depth charges failed to release. On the second, the depth charges fell and sank the boat, but the Germans riddled the Catalina with flak. This fire killed the navigator, gravely wounded the command pilot, Cruickshank, who was placed in a bunk, and seriously wounded three other crew, including the copilot, Jack Garnett, who remained at the controls, assisted by a third pilot, S. I. Fiddler, who was flying his first combat mission.

As the plane approached its home base, Cruickshank insisted that he be carried forward to assist in the landing. He and Garnett put the damaged plane down on the water and then ran it up on the beach. Thereupon Cruickshank, still at the controls, died of his wounds. For this heroic performance, the British awarded Cruickshank a posthumous Victoria Cross, the second of only two such awards to personnel of Coastal Command in the war.

- Off Narvik on July 17, a B-24 of British Squadron 86, piloted by Michael George Moseley, sank the newly arrived Arctic VII *U-347,* commanded by Johann de Buhr, age thirty-two. Although the B-24 was hit by flak, Moseley circled the area for ninety minutes, reporting wreckage and "at least six survivors" in the water. No Germans survived.
- Off Narvik in the same area on July 18, a Catalina of British Squadron 210, piloted by Ronald William George Vaughan, sank the new Arctic boat *U-742,* commanded by Heinz Schwassmann, age twenty-eight. During this attack, German gunners hit the Catalina with flak, wounding two men and puncturing oil and gasoline tanks, which forced Vaughan to abort and to shut down one engine. He made an emergency landing on friendly waters and beached the aircraft. Vaughan reported "thirty-five to forty" German survivors in the water, but none was ever found.

The stories of the six U-boats damaged by aircraft of Coastal Command's 18 Group in Norwegian waters in the last two weeks of July are as follows:

- Off Narvik on July 19, a B-24 of British Squadron 86, piloted by W.F.J. Harwood, hit the newly arrived Arctic boat *U-968,* commanded by Otto Westphalen, age twenty-four. As related, Westphalen was one of the prosecution's technical consultants in the sedition trial of Oskar Kusch, but he had opposed the death sentence and had recommended a limited form of clemency. Having incurred one killed and six wounded in this attack, Westphalen aborted to Narvik for repairs and remanning.
- Off Hammerfest on July 19, a B-24 of British Squadron 59, piloted by R. C. Penning, attacked the Arctic boat *U-716,* commanded by Hans Dunkelberg. The eight depth charges seriously damaged *U-716* and she aborted to Hammerfest for repairs.
- Off Narvik on July 19, a Sunderland of Norwegian Squadron 330, piloted by Bredo Thurmann-Nielsen, hit the Arctic boat *U-387,* commanded by Rudolf Büchler. He aborted to Trondheim for repairs.
- Off Bergen on July 20, a Mosquito of Norwegian Squadron 333, piloted by Rolf Leithe, attacked the new IXD2 snort boat U-cruiser *U-863,* commanded by Dietrich von der Esch, who was setting off to the Far East with cargo. Leithe fired his 57mm Tsetse cannon and machine guns and dropped two depth charges, which

damaged the U-boat. Von der Esch aborted to Bergen for repairs and resailed to the Far East on July 26, via Brazil.

• Off Kristiansund on July 25, two Mosquitos of Norwegian Squadron 333 found the VII snort boat *U-244,* commanded by Ruprecht Fischer, age twenty-seven, who was en route to reconnoiter Iceland and also to report weather. The pilots, Sigmund Breck and J. A. Stiff, hit the boat with 57mm Tsetse cannon fire that killed one German and wounded eight others. Fischer aborted to Kristiansund for repairs and remanning and resailed on August 23. Pilot Breck was killed in action in December 1944.

• Off Trondheim on July 27, a B-24 of British Squadron 86, commanded by G. G. Gates, hit the new IXC40 snort boat *U-865,* commanded by Dietrich Stellmacher, age twenty-nine. Heavy flak set on fire two engines of the B-24 and caused other damage, but Gates extinguished the fires and limped home. Stellmacher returned to Trondheim for repairs. He resailed twice in early August, but aborted each time. He finally sailed again on September 8, only to be sunk ten days later, as will be described.

Coastal Command had every reason to walk tall. During seventy-seven days in May, June, and July, it knocked out thirty-seven U-boats in Norwegian waters: seventeen sunk and twenty forced to abort. The British destroyer *Milne* and submarine *Satyr* had sunk two other U-boats (*U-289, U-987*) in this period for a total of nineteen U-boat kills. These Allied successes further imperiled and disorganized U-boat operations in that area and, of course, prevented the transfer of many U-boats to the English Channel to attack Neptune forces.

The first of the renewed series of Murmansk convoys, JW 59 (thirty-three ships), sailed from Loch Ewe on August 15. Owing to the possibility that the *Luftwaffe* might take advantage of the long daylight hours and to the certainty of U-boat attacks, Home Fleet commander Henry Moore provided the convoy with a massive British close escort: the "jeep" carriers *Vindex* and the American-built *Striker,* cruiser *Jamaica,* seven destroyers, four sloops, two frigates, and five corvettes.*

To assure that *Tirpitz* could not sail against this convoy, Moore mounted yet another air strike at her in mid-August. This task force consisted of the battleship *Duke of York,* three fleet carriers (*Formidable, Furious, Indefatigable*), two American-built "jeep" carriers (the Canadian *Nabob* and British *Trumpeter*), three cruisers, fourteen destroyers, and several frigates. Two fleet tankers, escorted by four corvettes, sailed separately in support.

While convoy JW 59 was traversing the Arctic seas, Moore launched the attack on *Tirpitz* on August 22. Again the aircraft encountered dense fog and again the at-

---

* The British naval contribution to Stalin, in lieu of sharing vessels of the Italian fleet, sailed in conjunction with JW 59, manned by Soviet crews: the British battleship *Royal Sovereign (Archangelsk),* recently refurbished in America; and eight destroyers, all of them ex-American four-stackers that had been transferred to the Royal Navy in 1940–41. (See Volume I, Appendix 9, pp. 741–745.) A ninth ex-American four-stacker sailed with JW 60. The British also gave the Soviets four submarines: *Sunfish, Unbroken, Unison,* and *Ursula.*

tack failed. Moore then hauled away westward to refuel so that a second attack could be mounted on August 23 or 24, weather permitting.

That day, August 22, the veteran Arctic boat *U-354,* commanded by Hans-Jürgen Sthamer, sailed from Narvik and came upon a section of Moore's task force. Sthamer fired a FAT spread and a T-5 quickly, then dived. A FAT hit and wrecked the Canadian "jeep" carrier *Nabob,* and the T-5 blew off the stern of the 1,300-ton British frigate *Bickerton,* killing more than forty men. *Nabob* limped to Scapa Flow but did not sail again as a warship; the British destroyer *Vigilant* sank the stricken *Bickerton.* Had the Germans been fully aware of these successes at that time, doubtless they would have awarded Sthamer a *Ritterkreuz,* but he did not live to amplify his flash report.

In the meantime, a half dozen U-boats had converged on convoy JW 59. The first to shoot was Ulrich Pietsch in *U-344.* He fired a FAT spread and claimed he sank a 5,500-ton *Dido*-class British light cruiser. In actuality, he hit and sank the sloop *Kite,* formerly of Johnny Walker's famous Support Group 2. Other British warships recovered only six of *Kite*'s gallant two-hundred-man crew.

Pietsch in *U-344* continued to dog convoy JW 59. On August 24, a Swordfish from *Vindex,* piloted by G. Bennett, sank *U-344* with the loss of all hands. Having hit and wrecked *Nabob* and *Bickerton,* Sthamer in *U-354* raced farther north and joined the attack on JW 59. Four warships of the convoy close escort trapped and sank *U-354* with the loss of all hands. The Admiralty credited this kill to the destroyer *Keppel,* the sloops *Mermaid* and *Peacock,* and the frigate *Loch Dunvagen.**

Among the several other Arctic U-boats that shot at convoy JW 59, none made greater claims than Hans-Günther Lange in *U-711.* He reported he had hit the Soviet battleship for damage, sunk one of the Soviet destroyers, damaged a Soviet submarine, and sunk a British destroyer. U-boat Control accepted these claims and Dönitz awarded Lange a *Ritterkreuz* on August 26 while the boat was still at sea. However, Allied records do not confirm any of these claims.

Home Fleet commander Moore's task force struck again at *Tirpitz* on August 24 and 29. One armor-piercing 1,600-pound bomb from a Barracuda aircraft penetrated eight decks, but it failed to detonate. Having done no further harm to *Tirpitz,* Moore returned his task force to Scapa Flow in a glum mood. Thereafter London gave RAF Bomber Command responsibility for destroying *Tirpitz.* A special force of twenty-seven Lancaster four-engine heavy bombers, each with one 12,000-pound "Tallboy" bomb, attacked *Tirpitz* on September 15. One bomb hit in her forward section, flooding that area and putting an end to *Tirpitz* as a warship. The Lancasters attacked her again on October 19, but failed to do any damage. Finally on November 12, Lancaster bombers with Tallboy bombs got two or three direct hits. The great ship turned turtle. In this brief finale, 950 of the crew of 1,630 perished.

Convoy JW 59 reached Kola Inlet on August 28, without the loss of any merchant ships. That same day the return convoy, RA 59A (nine merchant ships) left

---

* At this time, another Arctic boat, *U-362,* was lost with all hands to "unknown causes" in the Kara Sea.

Kola Inlet, guarded by the massive returning escort of JW 59. The Arctic U-boats attempted to attack this formation but none had any luck. On September 2, a Swordfish from *Vindex,* piloted by F.G.B. Sheffield, teamed up with the veteran destroyers *Keppel* and *Whitehall* and the sloops *Mermaid* and *Peacock,* and sank the new *U-394,* commanded by Wolfgang Borger. There were no survivors of this boat.

The next Murmansk convoy, JW 60 (thirty merchant ships) sailed from Loch Ewe on September 15. Its close escort included the British "jeep" carriers *Striker* and *Campania.* The convoy reached Kola Inlet on September 23 without loss. On September 25, some of the escort forces returned with the reverse convoy, RA 60. By chance, the convoy overran the Arctic boat *U-310,* commanded by Wolfgang Ley, who gave the alarm and sank the empty American Liberty ship *Edward H. Crockett* and the empty British Liberty ship *Samsuva.* In turn, it was thought that Swordfish from the *Campania* sank with the loss of all hands the VII *U-921,* commanded by Alfred Werner. However, in a recent reassessment, the Admiralty declared the loss of *U-921* was due to unknown causes.

The next pair of Murmansk convoys got through with minor damage. Convoy JW 61 (thirty merchant ships) left Loch Ewe on October 20 under heavy escort, including the British "jeep" carriers *Nairana, Tracker,* and *Vindex.* The Arctic U-boats attacked the convoy on October 26–27 and claimed one "destroyer" sunk and four "destroyers" damaged with T-5s. However, no hits were confirmed and the convoy arrived at Kola Inlet without loss on October 28. The reverse convoy, RA 61 (thirty-three merchant ships), sailed on November 2. The Arctic boat *U-295,* commanded by Günter Wieboldt, hit and damaged the British frigate *Mounsey* with a T-5. She limped back into Kola Inlet. The rest of the convoy reached Loch Ewe on November 9 without loss.

To keep the Arctic boats supplied with T-5s, FATs, and other arms, two VIIF torpedo-supply boats, *U-1060* and *U-1061,* plied between Germany and Norway. On October 19, while *U-1060,* commanded by Herbert Brammer, was in Narvik, an inbound Arctic boat, the veteran *U-957,* commanded by Gerd Schaar, who had just won a *Ritterkreuz,** collided with a German freighter and had to be decommissioned in Narvik. Schaar and the crew of *U-957* boarded the *U-1060* to return to Germany.

While *U-1060* was southbound on October 27, a swarm of aircraft from the new British fleet carrier *Implacable* attacked her and her minesweeper escort. One bomb sank the minesweeper. Another fell precisely through the conning-tower hatch of *U-1060,* killing her skipper, Brammer, and eleven other crew and causing so much damage that the boat had to be beached in Fleina. Control logged that of the total of 144 men on *U-1060,* seventy-one had been rescued, including Schaar and twenty-seven of the crew of *U-957,* but that sixty-one men of the two crews were still "missing."

Aware of this sitting duck, Coastal Command dispatched aircraft to demolish her on November 4. The aircraft were two B-24s of Czechoslovak Squadron 311 of 18 Group, piloted by F. Pavelka and A. Sedivý, and two Halifaxes of British

* For past claims and successes and for a patrol to the Kara Sea, during which he sank two small Soviet vessels and destroyed a Soviet weather station on the island of Sterligova.

Squadron 502, piloted by W. G. Powell and H.H.C. Holderness. The attacks by these planes finished *U-1060.*

At about this same time off Bergen, Allied aircraft of 18 Group disabled the other VIIF torpedo-supply boat, *U-1061,* commanded by Otto Hinrichs. On the night of October 30, a Leigh Light–equipped Wellington of Canadian Squadron 407, piloted by J. E. Neelin, and a B-24 of British Squadron 224, piloted by W. S. Blackden, converged on *U-1061* and "heavily damaged" her with depth charges, but she limped into Malöy. U-boat Control logged that "attempts will be made to repair her as she is particularly valuable."

U-boats Deployed from France in July

Overlord ground forces in Normandy consolidated the beachhead in June but were unable to "break out" as planned, owing to the fierce resistance of the Germans in the *bocage* (hedgerow) country. This intense ground warfare and the relentless Allied air attacks on French railroads, highways, and bridges crippled the logistical pipeline between Germany and the U-boat bases on the French Atlantic coast.

During that same time, the surviving U-boats of the defensive group in France, *Landwirt,* were unable to interdict significantly the massive flow of Allied men and matériel across the English Channel. Owing to the effectiveness of Allied air and surface ASW forces—especially Coastal Command aircraft—even the "Sunday Punch" snort boats continued to fail.

The experience of June had demonstrated anew that submarines were useless against alert invasion forces. Indeed, as Herbert Werner in *U-415* wrote, these U-boat sorties from French bases were virtually "suicide" missions with no prospect of success, despite the repeated exhortations from Dönitz and Godt. Moreover, the continuing loss of battle-experienced submarine personnel needed to cadre the new electro boats could not be tolerated much longer.

Nevertheless, under the circumstances, the U-boat arm could not simply quit. Despite losses, an effort to assist the ground forces had to be made for as long as possible. Herbert Werner notwithstanding, there were many U-boat skippers and crews who actually demanded the authority to sail against the Allies.

The production of "small battle" fleet units ("chariots," "midget" submarines, explosive-filled motor boats, and so on) had lagged badly.

The most important of these vehicles, the *Biber* and *Molch,* were far from ready on D day. However, the Germans launched one-man *Neger* and *Marder* "chariots" against Overlord forces from the French channel port Villers-sur-Mer on the nights of July 5–6, July 7–8, July 20–21, and August 3–4, and perhaps other nights. These craft completely wrecked the old Polish-manned British light cruiser *Dragon;* sank the British destroyers *Isis* and *Quorn;* the British minesweepers *Cato, Magic,* and *Pylades;* the British ASW trawlers *Gairsay* and *Colsay;* and the 800-ton British auxiliary *Fratton. Neger* and *Marder* losses were very high.*

---

* An exact account of German explosive motor boats and midget submarines' successes and losses is beyond the scope of this work.

• • •

The chief of U-boat Forces West, Hans-Rudolf Rösing, mounted eleven war patrols from France in the month of July to attack Allied invasion forces: ten by snort boats and one by the nonsnort *U-333.* One of the snort boats, the VIID *U-214,* was to lay a second minefield, this one off the south coast of England. The result was yet another catastrophe: Seven of the eleven U-boats were lost and two were forced to abort* to French ports in the English Channel. The stories of these boats, in brief:

• The snort boat *U-741,* commanded by Gerhard Palmgren, returned from the aborted ammo mission to Cherbourg and resailed from Brest to the Bay of the Seine on July 5. A few hours after leaving port, three Allied "destroyers" attacked *U-741* and her escorts. Palmgren crash-dived and escaped, but the gunfire damaged his forward periscope. Nonetheless, he continued to the Allied landing area, hugging the south coast of England where, he reported, ASW measures were less intense.

While cruising on electric motors at 131 feet on July 12, the gear of an Allied minesweeper caught in the top hamper of *U-741.* This mishap carried away the U-boat's forward and aft radio antenna lines and one tangled in the port propeller. Later that night Palmgren surfaced and cut away the line, but still later, while he was snorting to charge batteries, an Allied vessel rammed the boat and severely damaged the snort and the main periscope.

Palmgren aborted and set a course for Le Havre, where his father served in the minesweeper force. When Rösing got the word, he radioed Palmgren that Allied aircraft had demolished the dockyards at Le Havre and since the place was imperiled by further air attacks, Palmgren was to return to Brest or, failing that, put into Boulogne. The message did not arrive in time; Palmgren put into Le Havre on July 15.

• The snort boat *U-212,* commanded by Helmut Vogler, also returned from the aborted ammo supply mission to Cherbourg, resailed from Brest to the landing area on July 5 with *U-741.* When the British "destroyers" attacked the two U-boats and the escorts, the *U-212* also avoided destruction.† But nothing further was ever heard from Vogler in *U-212.* It is believed that he reached the Allied landing area on about July 13. According to the Allied reckoning, on July 21 the British frigates *Curzon* and *Ekins* teamed up to sink *U-212* with Hedgehogs and depth charges near Beachy Head on the south coast of England. There were no German survivors.

---

* *U-275, U-741,* as will be described.

† This attack so close to home persuaded Rösing to sail in July some of the remaining nonsnort boats in Brest specifically to defend the approaches to that place for the benefit of the outgoing and incoming snort boats. The *U-92* and *U-989* (group *Räuber*) pioneered this defensive patrol on July 6. After seventy-two hours, they returned to Brest. The *U-415* and *U-963* (group *Pirat*) replaced them on July 11. About a dozen Allied fighter-bomber aircraft attacked these boats, but inflicted no damage. After futile attempts to vector them to Allied warships by land-based radar, the Germans recalled the boats. On a second sortie on July 13, the *U-415,* commanded by Herbert Werner, hit a British mine in the early hours of the next day and wrecked, but the crew survived. The *U-963* and *U-993* (group *Flibustier*) sailed on July 17 and returned in forty-eight hours. The *U-260* and *U-608* (group *Marder*) sailed on July 22 and put into Lorient the next day. In these nine defensive sorties, no skipper encountered a target worth a torpedo. In the last days of July, the *U-618* and *U-766* sailed from St. Nazaire to Brest for defensive patrols but these too were canceled.

• The *U-672,* newly fitted with a snort and commanded by Ulf Lawaetz, age twenty-seven, sailed from St. Nazaire to the Bay of the Seine on July 6. While approaching the mouth of the English Channel a week later, on July 13, an Allied aircraft detected the submerged *U-672* and dropped four depth charges. They missed and caused no damage, but the pilots alerted Allied surface forces. Later that afternoon, Lawaetz sighted what he took to be an American hunter-killer group comprised of four "destroyers" and "one light cruiser." He boldly shot a T-5 at the "light cruiser" and another at a "destroyer" but both torpedoes malfunctioned or missed.

Upon learning of this action and the *U-672*'s position, Rösing ordered Lawaetz to patrol off the Isle of Wight. The *U-672* reached that area on July 18 and lay doggo on the bottom. That same afternoon, the British frigate *Balfour,* commanded by C.D.B. Coventry, detected *U-672* and attacked with Hedgehogs. These accurate attacks wrecked and flooded *U-672.*

Lawaetz soon concluded his situation was hopeless, and in the early hours of July 19 he ordered the crew to surface and scuttle. After his men had destroyed all secret papers and the Enigma, and abandoned ship in individual rubber dinghies, Lawaetz and his chief engineer, Georg Käseberg, scuttled and left the ship last. About twelve hours after the sinking, two British Spitfires reported sighting the survivors in the water. In response, air-sea rescue launches and PT boats sailed from Dartmouth and picked up all fifty-two men of the crew.

• The snort boat *U-309,* commanded by Hans-Gert Mahrholz, sailed from Brest for the second time to the Bay of the Seine on July 13. After reaching the Allied landing area, he attacked two convoys. From the first, on July 20, he claimed a hit on a 6,800-ton freighter. From the second, on July 24, he claimed sinking two freighters for 14,000 tons. Allied records confirmed only damage to the 7,000-ton British freighter *Samneva* in the second convoy. Mahrholz returned to Brest on August 2 and, owing to the chaos and lack of berths in that place, he left for La Pallice on August 7.

• The (ex-flak) snort boat *U-621,* commanded by Hermann Stuckmann, who sank *LST 280* on his first patrol, resailed from Brest to the Bay of the Seine on July 15 and reached the Allied landing area on July 23. Two days later he found a convoy and fired two torpedoes. One misfired; the other missed. The next day Stuckmann incurred a snort breakdown that felled many of the crew and partially flooded the boat.

After repairs at sea, Stuckmann resumed his patrol and attacked two more convoys. From the first, on the night of July 29–30, he claimed sinking two freighters for 10,000 tons. Allied records confirmed the sinking of the 2,938-ton British Landing Ship Infantry (LSI) *Prince Leopold* and damage to the 10,000-ton British troop transport *Ascanius.* From the second convoy, on August 3, Stuckmann claimed sinking two freighters for 13,000 tons and reported a T-5 miss on a "destroyer." Allied records do not confirm the sinkings.

Leaving the landing area on August 3, Stuckmann reached Brest eight days later. Generously credited with sinking five freighters for 32,000 tons on this patrol, Stuckmann was awarded a *Ritterkreuz,* the third to a skipper opposing Neptune forces. His confirmed score for his two patrols into the Allied landing area was two ships sunk (*LST 280, LSI Prince Leopold*) and one damaged (troop transport *Ascanius*).

• The snort boat *U-275,* commanded by a new skipper, Helmut Wehrkamp, age twenty-three, sailed from Brest on July 16 to patrol the waters off Plymouth. On July 22, when Wehrkamp rose to periscope depth to take a navigational bearing on the Eddystone Lighthouse, an aircraft spotted him and alerted a British hunter-killer group. The group hounded *U-275* for seven hours, but Wehrkamp got away.

Having been detected, Wehrkamp left the Plymouth area to patrol the Allied landing area in the Bay of the Seine. Almost immediately upon arrival there, a hunter-killer group found *U-275* and chased and depth-charged her for eight hours. The resulting damage to *U-275* was severe. Thereafter, each time Wehrkamp attempted to snort, Allied "destroyers" pounced and depth-charged the boat. Unable to charge batteries, he let *U-275* drift with the currents for about forty-eight hours. When finally the battery was completely exhausted, he surfaced and ran into Boulogne on diesels, arriving on August 1.

• The VIID (minelayer) snort boat *U-214,* commanded by a new skipper, Gerhard Conrad, age twenty-three, sailed from Brest on July 22 to plant a field of fifteen SMA mines off the southwest coast of England. Four days later, on July 26, the British frigate *Cooke,* commanded by L. C. Hill, sank *U-214* with the loss of all hands.

• The veteran snort boat *U-667,* which had earlier made a seventy-three-day patrol to the Atlantic in March and April, sailed from St. Nazaire to the English Channel on July 22. She was commanded by a new skipper, Karl-Heinz Lange, age twenty-six. Rösing directed the boat to patrol the mouth of the Bristol Channel.

The salty crew of *U-667* supported well its green commander. On August 8, Lange found and attacked convoy EBC 66. His first torpedoes hit the 7,200-ton American Liberty ship *Ezra Weston.* A convoy escort, the Canadian corvette *Regina,* rushed to cover the damaged American ship and directed an American LST to remove her crew and take her in tow. While this was going on, Lange torpedoed *Regina,* which sank "in a matter of seconds." The American LST rescued about half the crew of *Regina*—sixty-six men. The damaged *Ezra Weston* did not reach port.

A week later on August 14, *U-667* found another convoy, EBC 72, and Lange attacked, sinking what he thought were two 4,000-ton tankers or freighters. In fact, these confirmed American victims were two landing craft: the 1,653-ton *LST 921* and the 246-ton *LCI 99.*

On August 16, Rösing ordered *U-667* to return to a Biscay port. Five days later, Lange reported that he was forty-eight hours out from La Pallice and required an escort and that he had sunk one "destroyer" and 15,000 tons of merchant shipping. Nothing further was ever heard from *U-667.* Allied and German authorities presumed she hit a mine off La Pallice on or about August 25 and sank with all hands.

• After her brief sortie into the Bay of Biscay on D day under the command of *Ritterkreuz* holder Peter Cremer, the famous old nonsnort *U-333* had aborted to Lorient, and, as related, Cremer returned to Germany to commission a big electro boat, taking about half the *U-333* crew. The ill-starred Hans Fiedler, who had lost *U-564* and, more recently, *U-998* to Allied air attacks, arrived from Norway to take command of *U-333*.

Deemed too old and battered to warrant a snort, *U-333* finally sailed from Lorient on July 23 to patrol off Land's End near the Scillies. Nothing further was ever heard from this boat. After the war, Cremer learned that on or about the day Fiedler arrived in his patrol area, July 31, the famous British Support Group 2 detected, attacked, and sank *U-333,* with the loss of all hands. It was Fiedler's third—and final—command, all destroyed by Allied forces.

The sloop *Starling* and frigate *Loch Killin,* which was fitted with the powerful new Squid forward-firing ASW mortar, carried out the attack and received joint credit for the kill, the first by Squid. The much-decorated commander of Support Group 2, forty-eight-year-old Johnny Walker in the sloop *Starling,* was not present to celebrate this victory. In Liverpool on July 9 he had died of a stroke, thought to have been brought on by overwork and stress.

• After its emergency abort to Boulogne on July 5, the new snort boat *U-671,* commanded by Wolfgang Hegewald, sailed on July 26 to patrol the Isle of Wight. Merely one day out, the snort broke, flooding the boat and forcing Hegewald back into Boulogne for repairs. He resailed in the early hours of August 1, but the snort again malfunctioned. When the chief engineer, Robert Schröter, age twenty-three, advised Hegewald that the snort could not be repaired at sea—and that four tons of seawater would enter the boat each time the snort was raised—Hegewald aborted the patrol and once again shaped course for Boulogne.

In the late hours of August 4, two British warships, the destroyer *Wensleydale* and the frigate *Stayner,* which were escorting four PT boats on patrol off Le Havre, detected the submerged *U-671.* Gaining sonar contact first, *Stayner* carried out five depth-charge and three Hedgehog attacks. Hegewald counterattacked with two T-5s, but they malfunctioned or missed. After *Wensleydale* came up to assist, *Stayner* conducted three more attacks and *Wensleydale* four.

These fifteen attacks wrecked and bottomed *U-671.* Twenty of her fifty-two-man crew, including Hegewald and engineer Schröter, gathered in the conning tower and escaped with breathing apparatus. The British fished out six of these twenty Germans, but one died. The five survivors included engineer Schröter; a watch officer, Hans Schaefer, age twenty-two; and three enlisted men, but not Hegewald.

• The *U-984,* commanded by the newest *Ritterkreuz* holder, Heinz Sieder, sailed from Brest for the second time to the Bay of the Seine on July 26. On August 16, Control ordered her to abort her patrol and return to a Biscay port. The boat was never heard from again. Allied authorities credited her kill to three destroyers of Canadian Support Group 11 in the Bay of Biscay, *Chaudière, Kootenay,* and *Ottawa II,* on August 20. There were no German survivors.

The eleven U-boat patrols mounted in July from French bases* against the Allied invasion forces resulted in the sinking of four Allied warships and one

---

* Not counting the nine brief "port defense" sorties per footnote on p. 602.

freighter for about 14,000 tons (four ships by Lange in the *U-667*) and damage to two freighters for 17,000 tons. In return, Allied forces sank six snort boats and the nonsnort *U-333.* They forced two snort boats, *U-275* and *U-741,* to abort. About 350 more German submariners were lost (fifty-one captured), enough to man another eight big electro boats.

The convoys on the North Atlantic run supporting Overlord continued to grow in size and complexity and met no opposition from U-boats. The largest convoy of the war, Halifax Slow 300, sailed from New York on July 17. Initially it consisted of 109 merchant ships. Proceeding northeastward, it was joined by thirty-one ships from Halifax, twenty-four from Sydney, and three from St. John's, Newfoundland, for a total of 167 vessels* plus a Canadian escort group consisting of one frigate and six corvettes. Three of the merchant vessels were operational MAC ships that launched ASW aircraft, but they saw nothing during the crossing.

All but one ship, a straggler, of Halifax Slow 300 reached the British Isles by August 3. Altogether the ships delivered one million tons of weaponry, war matériel, and food. The tonnage by category:†

Oil	307,874
Food and Foodstuffs	254,176
Military Equipment	251,297
General Cargo	80,699
Vehicles and Tanks	53,490
Iron and Steel	36,705
Lumber	35,588
	1,019,829

The Allied Breakout in France

For months a cabal of dissident German Army officers sought to overthrow the Nazi regime by assassinating Hitler, Göring, and SS chief Heinrich Himmler. On July 20, one of the conspirators, a thirty-seven-year-old lieutenant colonel, Count Claus von Stauffenberg, planted a time bomb in Hitler's war room at *Wolfschanze* (Wolf's Lair) at Rastenberg, East Prussia. The bomb exploded, killing or fatally wounding four men, but Hitler survived the blast and immediately initiated a roundup of the plotters.

That same day, Admiral Dönitz flew to *Wolfschanze* where, by coincidence, Benito Mussolini had arrived for a conference. In a meeting with Hitler and Mussolini that afternoon, Dönitz pledged his loyalty to Hitler, as did retired Admiral Raeder later. In the early evening, Dönitz issued a statement to all hands in the *Kriegsmarine:*

> The treacherous attempt to assassinate the Führer fills each and everyone of us with holy wrath and bitter rage toward our criminal enemies and their hirelings. Di-

---

* Seventy-five U.S., fifty British, thirty-nine other Allies, and three "neutral."

† Source: Tucker, vol. 2 (1952), Plate 15.

vine providence spared the German people and its Armed Forces this inconceivable misfortune. In the miraculous escape of our Führer we see additional proof of the righteousness of our cause. Let us now more than ever rally around our Führer and fight with all our strength until victory is ours.

About an hour later, Dönitz issued an amplifying message to all commands of the *Kriegsmarine:*

The attempt on the Führer's life was brought about by the clique of generals who were undertaking a military coup. The heads of this clique are General Fromm, General Hoepner, and Field Marshal General von Witzleben.

In place of General Fromm, Reich Führer of the Elite Guard [SS] Himmler will take over the Reserve Army as Commander in Chief. The Navy will institute a state of readiness at once. In this connection, orders to the Navy will come only from the Commander in Chief of the Navy. Orders from Army officers are not to be followed. Orders and instructions of the Reich Führer of the Elite Guard are to be obeyed. See that all Navy officers are informed at once.

Long live the *Führer*!

Later that same night, Hitler went on the radio to tell the German people about the conspiracy and its failure and to promise revenge in the manner to which the Nazis were accustomed, as he put it. Admiral Dönitz followed the Führer on the air to give the widest possible circulation of his pledge of loyalty to Hitler and to repeat his earlier message to the *Kriegsmarine.* Historian William L. Shirer wrote that as a result of this failed revolt, the Nazi regime probably executed about five thousand men, most of them German army officers. Among the victims were three senior generals in France who were encouraged to commit suicide: Erwin Rommel, Günther Hans Kluge, and Karl von Stülpnagel. In due course, Admiral Wilhelm Canaris, onetime chief of the *Abwehr,* was among those hanged.

Five days after the failed assassination, General Omar N. Bradley's First Army achieved its famous breakout (Cobra) through German defenses at Saint-Lô. Several days thereafter, General George S. Patton's Third Army raced through the Saint-Lô gap to Avranches, posing a threat to all of German-occupied Brittany, which had been stripped of most German Army units to fight the battles in Normandy.

Promoted to command the 12th Army Group, composed of the American First, Third, and Ninth Armies, Bradley directed Patton to wheel west and capture St. Malo, Brest, Lorient, and St. Nazaire. Inasmuch as the restoration of Cherbourg as a major Allied unloading facility was badly lagging and Bradley was concerned that a storm might wreck the temporary facilities in the Normandy beachhead, he needed to capture those Brittany ports so men and matériel could be shipped directly from the States to his armies. Depriving the Germans of U-boat bases in France figured in Bradley's thinking, but only to a minor degree.

Sensing the possibility of capturing all German forces in Normandy west of the Seine River in a giant wheeling maneuver, Bradley soon canceled his orders to Patton to clear Brittany and directed him to rush the majority of his forces to the east. In this revised plan, only the VIII Corps (three divisions) of the Third Army, commanded by Troy H. Middleton, was to lay siege to the Brittany ports.

When Middleton's VIII Corps arrived in Brittany in early August, the thin German forces there fell back on the seaports and constructed strong defensive networks. To save the *Kriegsmarine* bases for as long as possible so that an orderly evacuation of the U-boats, the technicians, and some U-boat gear could be mounted, Hitler ordered the German soldiers to yield no ground and fight to the last man. However, there were not enough German troops to hold all five U-boat bases. Therefore, when the Allies invaded southern France on August 15 (Dragoon), posing an imminent threat to Bordeaux, that southernmost base had to be abandoned by August 25. Nearly four weeks later, on September 19, the northernmost base, Brest, was likewise abandoned.*

The Germans thus consolidated defenses at the three center naval bases: Lorient, St. Nazaire, and La Pallice. Due to the need to press eastward at the utmost speed with all possible ground forces, Eisenhower informed Bradley on September 9 that it was unnecessary to capture those three ports. The German garrisons at those places were therefore to be bypassed, isolated, and contained. Remarkably, these three seaports remained in German hands until the end of the war in Europe.

The Allied pressure on the U-boat bases in August triggered sixteen U-boat transfers among the bases. From Brest, six U-boats retreated to La Pallice and one, *U-766,* to Bordeaux; the latter then went from Bordeaux to La Pallice. From Lorient, five U-boats shifted to La Pallice. From St. Nazaire, two U-boats went to La Pallice. Two Type VIIs carried ammo from La Pallice to Lorient.†

The Allies sank or caused the loss of seven of the sixteen boats engaged in these interbase transfers. In brief:

- On the afternoon of August 9, a B-24 of British Squadron 53 of 19 Group, piloted by R.T.F. Gates, spotted a mile-long oil slick in the Bay of Biscay and then a submerged U-boat at the apex of the slick. This was the nonsnort *U-608,* commanded by Wolfgang Reisener, age twenty-five, en route from Lorient to La Pallice. Gates dropped a marker and six depth charges, then alerted British Support Group 2, composed of the sloops *Starling* and *Wren* and the Squid-equipped frigate *Loch Killin.*

About an hour and a half later, the British hunter-killer group arrived at the scene, guided by a Sunderland. The ships found scraps of wood believed to be from the decking of a U-boat. However, the group could not get a sonar contact. Assuming the U-boat lay damaged on the bottom, *Starling* departed, leaving *Wren,* commanded by S.R.J. Woods, and *Loch Killin* to continue the search. Finally, at

---

* In three raids, on August 5, 12, and 13, thirty-three Lancasters of RAF Bomber Command devastated Brest. The bombs they dropped included twenty-six 12,000-pound Tallboys aimed at the U-boat pens. Nine of the Tallboy bombs hit the sixteen-foot-thick roof of the pen. These penetrated six or seven feet but failed to pierce the ceiling.

† See Appendix 2.

In World War I, Allied aircraft sank only one confirmed U-boat. In World War II, land- and sea-based Allied aircraft, which proved to be the most effective U-boat killers, were involved in the sinking or destruction of 324 U-boats. Photos of some of the Allied anti-submarine aircraft may be found in Volume I. Others follow here.

National Archives 80G25435

Indisputably the most effective anti–U-boat aircraft in World War II was the American-built Consolidated B-24 Liberator bomber, shown here with British markings.

National Archives 80G464013

Another effective anti–U-boat aircraft was the American-built Boeing B-17 Flying Fortress.

National Archives 80G25025

Yet another was the British-built Handley Page Halifax.

National Archives 80G16447

The American-built Martin Mariner flying boat was designed to supplement or replace Catalinas and Sunderlands. However, owing to defects, the plane was a marginal anti–U-boat weapon.

National Archives 80G25005

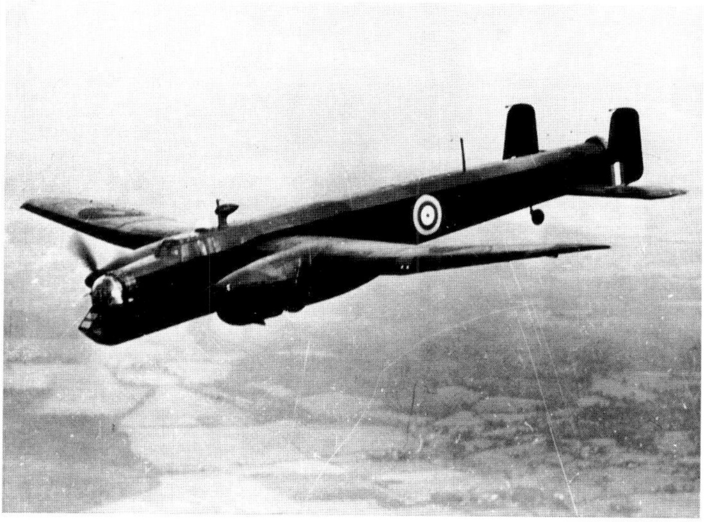

The British-built Armstrong-Whitworth Whitley was employed extensively on anti–U-boat patrols in the earlier years of the war, but it was ultimately downgraded to a trainer.

National Archives 80G25087

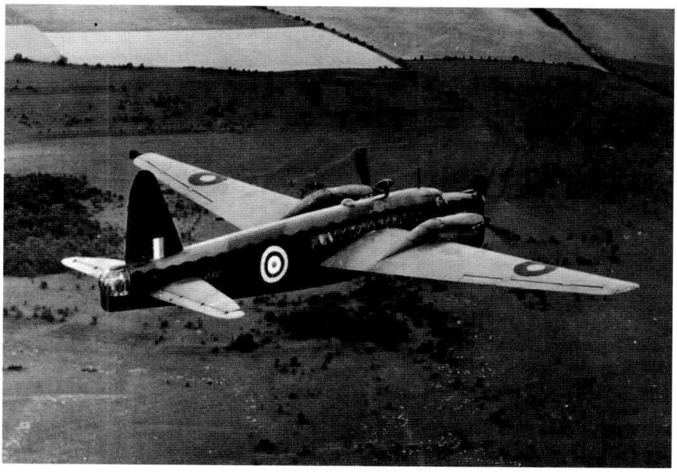

The British-built Vickers-Armstrong Wellington, fitted with radar and a powerful searchlight, proved to be a highly effective, medium-range antisubmarine workhorse, especially at night over the Bay of Biscay.

National Archives 80G254119

Another workhorse anti–U-boat aircraft was the American-designed Lockheed Hudson, first cousin of the U.S. Navy's Lockheed PV Ventura and the U.S.A.A.F.'s B-34.

National Archives 80G360922

The long-range German Focke-Wulf Condor 200, military version of a civilian airliner, was pressed into service to hunt down convoys for the benefit of the U-boats and to attack Allied aircraft protecting the convoys. However, the plane and the aircrews were not suited to these tasks and failed.

National Archives RG18-WP-194884

Medium-range Junkers 88 (JU-88s) were deployed to western France to repel Allied air attacks on U-boats in the Bay of Biscay. The planes were suitable for that task but were always in short supply.

National Archives 80G25079

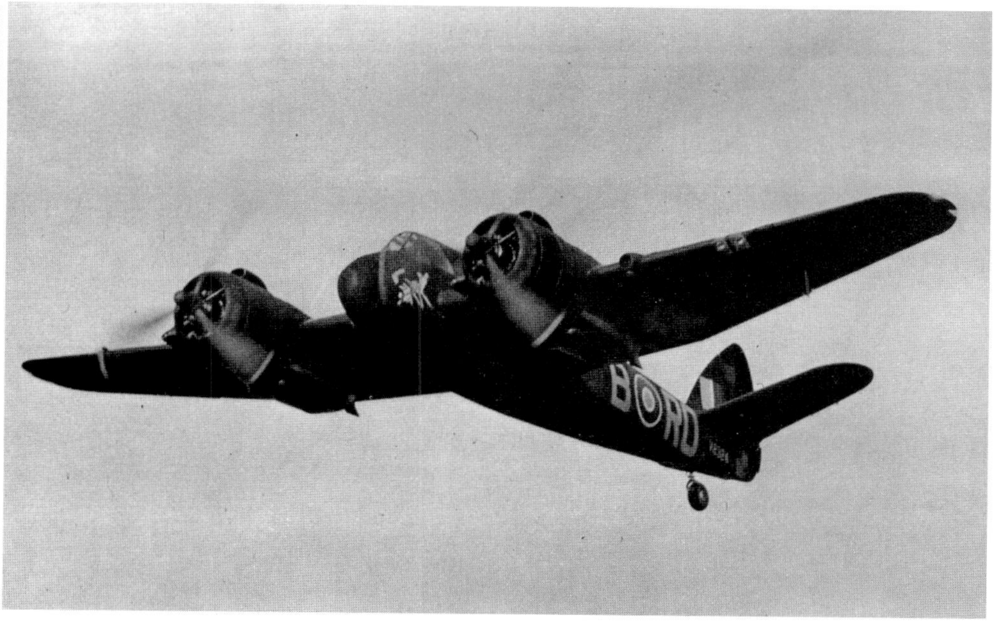

RAF Coastal Command deployed two types of fighter-interceptors over the Bay of Biscay and elsewhere to deal with the Focke-Wulf Condors and JU-88s. The first was a prewar British design, the Bristol Beaufighter.

National Archives 80G25068

The second was the DeHavilland Mosquito, some of which were armed with 57mm nose cannons and were thus capable of attacking U-boats beyond the range of the German 20mm and 37mm antiaircraft arrays.

National Archives 80G74764

From 1943, Allied escort carriers, such as the *Santee* shown here, were stationed in or near convoys to provide additional protection from U-boats. The carriers, in turn, were protected by several extra destroyers, frigates, or destroyer escorts.

National Archives 80G469849

Carrier aircraft attacked U-boats in teams. The pilot of this Grumman F4F Wildcat fighter (British Martlet) attacked first, strafing the U-boat with machine guns to knock out the exposed German anti-aircraft gunners on the bridgeworks.

National Archives 80G13079

The second attack was mounted by the crew of this Grumman TBF Avenger. Conceived originally as an antiwarship torpedo bomber, the Avenger, armed with depth charges or Mark XXIV "Fido" homing torpedoes, was a rugged and highly effective anti–U-boat weapon.

All convoy surface escorts and warships of hunter-killer groups grew in size and firepower as the war progressed through 1942 to 1945. In addition to the three antisubmarine warships pictured in Volume I, the following warships were produced in very large quantities by Allied shipyards.

National Archives 80G472212

The 110-foot U.S. Navy submarine chaser (SC) *642*. American shipyards turned out hundreds of these small warships. They were useful as training vessels or for convoy escort in relatively calm waters, such as the Gulf of Mexico, where no enemy aircraft were present.

National Archives 80G78408

The 173-foot U.S. Navy patrol craft (PC) *565*. American yards produced 417 of these small warships. They were also useful as training vessels and as convoy escorts in relatively calm waters where no enemy aircraft were present.

National Archives RG8066993

The 306-foot U.S. Navy destroyer escort (DE) *Levy*. American shipyards built 573 warships of this or similar classes. They were not fast, but with at-sea refueling, they were perfectly suited for convoy escort.

National Archives 80G450373

The 304-foot British-designed *River*-class frigate (PF) U.S.S. *Natchez*. The frigate was similar to the destroyer escort in size, characteristics, and armament. American yards turned out ninety-eight frigates and gave twenty-one of them to the Royal Navy. The *Natchez* (PF 2) was built in a Canadian shipyard and lent to the U.S. Navy.

National Archives 80G450253

The 310-foot U.S. Navy fleet destroyer (DD) *Harding*. Fast and heavily armed, this destroyer type was the most formidable and effective of the blue-water convoy escorts and suited for operations where enemy aircraft were present.

National Archives 80G84360

The heavily laden Liberty ship *Mark Twain* en route to a slot in a convoy column. U.S. shipyards mass-produced 2,700 Liberty ships in World War II, far outstripping U-boat successes against Allied merchant ships.

National Archives 357G6990

The Oregon Shipbuilding Corporation, Portland, Oregon, one of dozens of wartime yards that produced Liberty ships.

UPI/Corbis-Bettmann

Nine Liberty ships lined up at the California Shipbuilding Corporation in Los Angeles give an idea of the magnitude of the work turned out by this wartime shipyard.

National Archives 26G2556

Allied surface ships and aircraft relentlessly hunted down U-boats at sea. Here, three American destroyer escorts, *Gandy, Joyce,* and *Peterson,* manned by Coast Guard crews, destroy the Type IXC40 *U-550* on April 16, 1944. The ships rescued twelve German survivors.

National Archives 80G79388

Aircraft from the American hunter-killer group built around the "jeep" carrier *Card* attacked and sank this Type VIIC *U-664* on August 9, 1943. The *Card* group rescued forty-four German crewmen.

National Archives 80G324787

An American hunter-killer group built around the "jeep" carrier *Guadalcanal* captured the Type IXC *U-505* on June 4, 1944. Secretly towed to Bermuda Island, she yielded intelligence of great value to the Allies. Fully intact, in the postwar years she became a prime exhibit at the Chicago Museum of Science and Industry.

AP/Wide World Photos

In 1996, salvors raised the Type IXC40 *U-534*, sunk off Denmark by RAF aircraft in the closing days of the war. She was barged to Liverpool, England, to become an exhibit in nearby Birkenhead.

National Archives 306-NT-3587

In the last few months of the war, the Germans commissioned two types of electro boats, one small and one large, capable of high sprint speed. This is a small Type XXIII, *U-2361,* which put in to England after the war for demolition. Armed with merely two torpedoes and too small for blue-water operations, these tiny U-boats were all but useless.

National Archives 80G705573

The larger Type XXI electro boat was developed too late in the war to influence the outcome. Bombing attacks by Allied aircraft destroyed many under construction in shipyards like this. None saw combat.

National Archives 80G705562

The U.S. Navy was allotted several Type XXI electro boats for evaluation purposes. The *U-2513* shown here had been commanded briefly by one of the leading German U-boat aces, Erich Topp. As described in the Foreword of Volume I, the author boarded and inspected *U-2513,* which moored alongside his own submarine, U.S.S. *Guardfish,* at the U.S.N. Submarine Base, New London, Connecticut.

National Archives 208PU52P1

National Archives 238NT727

Grand Admiral Karl Dönitz as he appeared in German propaganda photos (left) and as he appeared on trial at Nuremberg. He conducted a hard and tough but clean naval war. Of the senior Nazis tried at Nuremberg, Dönitz received the lightest sentence: ten years and twenty days in Spandau prison.

Theodore M. Hannah

A number of dead or captured German submariners were buried on U.S. soil during the war. This is the grave of a leading U-boat ace, Werner Henke, skipper of the IXC *U-515,* which was sunk April 9, 1944. Henke committed suicide at a secret POW interrogation center, Fort Hunt, Virginia, and was buried at Fort Meade, Maryland, now the home of the National Security Agency. Secret admirers frequently decorate Henke's grave with flowers or a German flag.

about ten o'clock that evening, *Wren* detected *U-608* and dropped a salvo of depth charges that utterly wrecked the boat. In the early hours of August 10, Reisener surfaced and scuttled. *Wren* rescued all fifty-one men from *U-608.* Wing Commander Gates was awarded a DFC and promoted to Group Captain.

• In the early hours of August 12, the nonsnort *U-981,* temporarily commanded by Günther Keller, age twenty-five, en route from Lorient to La Pallice, hit a British mine. A Halifax of British Squadron 502 of 19 Group, piloted by J. Capey, saw and attacked the disabled boat with five 600-pound bombs. Soon other British aircraft converged on the scene. The mine and the bombs destroyed *U-981.* Twelve Germans were killed in the sinking, but forty men survived.

Luckily for the survivors, the snort boat *U-309,* commanded by Hans-Gert Mahrholz, en route from Brest to La Pallice with about fifty crew and fifty passengers, was close by. Mahrholz rescued the forty men, including Keller, and took them into La Pallice. Owing to "nervous exhaustion," Mahrholz was declared too ill for command and went on to other duty. Keller returned to Germany to command a new snort boat. The journalist-photographer Lothar-Günther Buchheim (author of the novel *Das Boot*) was on board *U-309* for this transfer voyage and after daylight, he was able to take dramatic pictures* of the forty survivors huddled in blankets topside on *U-309.*

• Six unidentified twin-engine British aircraft detected, hit, and damaged the nonsnort *U-766,* commanded by Hans-Dietrich Wilke, age thirty-two, while the boat was en route from Brest to Bordeaux, from August 8 to 18. On the eleventh day of this harrowing voyage, Wilke reached the mouth of the Gironde, but due to enemy mines, Rösing redirected the boat to La Pallice. Upon arrival there on August 20, the *U-766* was declared unfit for further war service and decommissioned. To deter her capture, on September 15 the Germans disabled the boat. Wilke went on to command of another VII, *U-382,* earmarked for evacuation from La Pallice to Norway. The *U-766,* a French war prize, was recommissioned *Laubie.*

• Shortly after midnight on August 12, a Leigh Light–equipped Sunderland of Australian Squadron 461 of 19 Group, piloted by Donald A. Little, detected a surfaced U-boat off Lorient. This was the veteran nonsnort *U-270,* en route from Lorient to La Pallice. As related, this boat had been declared unfit for combat and her skipper, Paul-Friedrich Otto, and the entire crew had returned to Germany to commission a big electro boat. She was manned by a scratch crew from Lorient, commanded by Heinrich Schreiber, age twenty-seven, and also had on board about thirty other submariners, a total of eighty-one men. She carried two snorts lashed flat to the topside deck and snort spare parts below.

When the Sunderland commenced its attack, Schreiber remained on the surface and opened fire with his flak guns. Nonetheless, the pilot held his course and dropped six depth charges, which closely straddled *U-270.* Seeing that these had

---

* Published in Buchheim's unpaginated, nonfiction work, *U-boat War* (1979). However, the two U-boats and crews involved are not identified. Doubtless this pathetic episode was a shock to propagandist Buchheim and may well have contributed to the untimely and incongruous defeatist tone of his novel *Das Boot,* which was based on his 1941 voyage in *U-96,* when morale in the U-boat force was highest.

wrecked the boat beyond repair, Schreiber ordered abandon ship and opened the bow torpedo-room loading hatch to speed the sinking. The Canadian destroyers *Ottawa II* and *St. Laurent* of Support Group 11, boldly operating in the Bay of Biscay, recovered seventy-one of the eighty-one Germans, including Schreiber.

- On August 14, a B-24 of British Squadron 53 of 19 Group, piloted by Gilbert G. Potier, detected and attacked the nonsnort *U-618,* commanded by Erich Faust, age twenty-three, en route from Brest to La Pallice. Two British frigates of Support Group 3, *Duckworth* and *Essington,* came up to assist in the kill. There were no survivors of *U-618.* The British awarded pilot Potier a second DFC.
- On August 18, Canadian Support Group 11, composed of four destroyers,* detected and attacked the snort boat *U-621,* commanded by a hero of the channel battles, *Ritterkreuz* holder Hermann Stuckmann, who was en route from Brest to La Pallice. The Admiralty doubted that this attack resulted in a kill, but in a postwar reassessment, it credited the three remaining Canadian destroyers, *Chaudière, Kootenay,* and *Ottawa II.* There were no German survivors. Stuckmann had enjoyed the prestige of his *Ritterkreuz* for only eight days.
- On the same day, August 18, a Sunderland of British Squadron 201 of 19 Group, piloted by Leslie H. Baveystock, who had sunk the VII *U-955* on D day plus one, detected and attacked the famous old IXB *U-107,* en route from Lorient to La Pallice. Commanded by Karl-Heinz Fritz, age twenty-three, the *U-107* had recently been fitted with a snort and was earmarked for evacuation to Norway, thence to Germany and retirement. There were no survivors. For this second confirmed U-boat kill, the British awarded Baveystock a DSO.

Apart from Mahrholz in the snort boat *U-309,* eight other U-boats that embarked on interbase transfers reached their destinations. These were: *U-763, U-953,* and *U-963* from Brest to La Pallice, Bordeaux, and La Pallice, respectively; the *U-260* from Lorient to La Pallice; the *U-281* and *U-437* from St. Nazaire to La Pallice; and the *U-445* and *U-650* from La Pallice to Lorient, each of the latter with about seventy-five tons of ammo. Upon arrival at their destinations, all of these boats, as well as *U-309,* were ordered to prepare for evacuation to Norway.

Evacuation of the Type VIIs from France

From early August when Allied forces wheeled into Brittany, Dönitz assumed that the U-boat bases could not be held. The Allied invasion of southern France on Au-

---

* *Chaudière, Kootenay, Ottawa II,* and *Restigouche.* The last came from Canadian Support Group 12, which had been operating in Biscay also but was temporarily sent to shipyards because of accidents and mechanical breakdowns. *Saskatchewan* went to Canada for refit; *Skeena* and *Ou'Appelle* to England for extended repairs after a collision; *Assiniboine,* fresh from refit, to England after being "seriously damaged" by a "premature depth-charge explosion." Some of these problems could be attributed to the thirst of the Canadian destroyer crews for *offensive* action. *Restigouche* remained with Support Group 11 only a week before she, too, aborted to England with "defects."

gust 15 (Dragoon) reinforced that assumption. Dönitz therefore directed the Chief, U-boats West, Hans-Rudolf Rösing, to prepare to evacuate to Norway all U-boats deemed fit to make the long (two-thousand-mile) and dangerous voyage, taking along certain key personnel, as much fuel oil as possible, and some valuable gear, such as spare radar and radar-detector sets, T-5 homing torpedoes, and the like. U-boats deemed unfit for the voyage were to be decommissioned and demolished.* All German personnel left at the deactivated bases, including submariners and submarine technicians, were to join the ground forces defending those places.

The evacuation orders set in motion a reorganization or disbandment of the flotilla commands and a frenetic effort to equip all remaining VIIs with snorts and appoint temporary skippers and crews to man those boats whose captains and crew were unable to get back to the French bases from leave in Germany.

In Brest, in compliance with orders from Dönitz, the commander of Combat Flotilla 9, Heinrich Lehmann-Willenbrock (who had served on *U-96,* portrayed in Buchheim's novel *Das Boot*), made plans to evacuate to Norway on a Type VII. Dönitz named *Ritterkreuz* holder Werner Winter (formerly of *U-103*), who was commander of Combat Flotilla 1 at Brest, temporary commander of naval defenses at this besieged and battered base.

In Lorient, in compliance with orders from Dönitz, *Ritterkreuz* holder Günter Kuhnke (formerly of *U-28* and *U-125*), commander of Combat Flotilla 10, also prepared to evacuate by U-boat. Dönitz merged Combat Flotilla 10 with Combat Flotilla 2 at Lorient, commanded by *Ritterkreuz* holder Ernst Kals (formerly of *U-130*). Kals reorganized the personnel of the two merged flotillas as *Stützpunkt Lorient* to defend that place.

At St. Nazaire, Dönitz ordered the commander of Combat Flotilla 6, Carl Emmermann (formerly of *U-172*), who wore the *Ritterkreuz* with Oak Leaves, to return to Germany (by auto, a wild ride) to command Training Flotilla 31, which was to develop tactics for the big Type XXI electro boat. Dönitz merged Combat Flotilla 6 with Combat Flotilla 7 at St. Nazaire, commanded by *Ritterkreuz* holder Adolf-Cornelius Piening (formerly of *U-155*). Piening reorganized the personnel of the two merged flotillas as *Stützpunkt St. Nazaire* to defend the city.

At La Pallice, which was to become the last redoubt of the operational U-boats in France, *Ritterkreuz* holder Richard Zapp (formerly of *U-66*) remained commander of Combat Flotilla 3. However, he was outranked on August 8 when Hans-Rudolf Rösing arrived with a special radio-communications truck and established the temporary headquarters of Chief U-boats, West, in that port.

At Bordeaux, the commander of Combat Flotilla 12, Klaus Scholtz (formerly of *U-108*), who wore Oak Leaves on his *Ritterkreuz,* came under intense pressure when Dragoon forces landed in southern France against slim German opposition on August 15. His operations were further handicapped when Allied aircraft heav-

* On August 6, Berlin directed Rösing at Angers, France: "Destroy *Kurier*-set apparatus completely or make sure of its salvage." At that time *Kurier* was still undergoing trials at sea. After Allied soldiers cut the land lines to Berlin, forcing U-boat bases to use radio, *Kurier* might have been employed between Angers and Berlin.

ily mined the Gironde River, the long waterway into Bordeaux. Owing to the rapid advances of Dragoon forces and to the infestation of Allied mines, Bordeaux was the first U-boat base in France to be closed down and completely evacuated of operational submarines and submarine personnel.

During the chaotic events of August and September, thirty Type VIIs were evacuated from France to Norway.* Perhaps owing to the catastrophic U-boat losses or to the collapse of German forces in Normandy, or both, Dönitz felt the need to issue another exhortation. He radioed all U-boat skippers engaged in the evacuation:

> In the stern battle against the enemy storming us from the west you are in the foremost line, now as before. Even now, when the enemy has succeeded in gaining a foothold on shore and pushing forward to the east, your full cooperation is necessary to relieve the land front.
>
> Always think how much fighting and expenditure of materials, and especially how much blood is necessary to destroy a shipload of men and materials in land fighting. You can do it with a single torpedo hit.
>
> I know what hardiness, toughness and endurance you must bring to bear in order to endure the hardships and unceasing attacks. But I also know that you, my U-boat warriors, carried on by the old spirit of attack, think only of destroying the enemy. Be assured that I follow your battle continually and that you are always in my thoughts.

All thirty of the evacuating VIIs had snorts. Some boats conducted war patrols; others went directly to Norway. Allied forces sank or destroyed ten of these. Three others of this group came to grief shortly after reaching Norwegian waters, making a total loss of thirteen, or 43 percent. The stories of those boats, in brief:

• The *U-736,* commanded by Reinhard Reff, age thirty, sailed from Lorient on August 5 to patrol the Allied landing area in the Bay of the Seine. When first activated, the snort failed and the boat filled with exhaust gases. Owing to the presence of Allied ASW forces, Reff was unable to surface and many men fell ill.

In the afternoon of the following day, August 6, Reff raised the snort to air the boat and was immediately detected by the British hunter-killer Support Group 2. Reff fired two T-5s at the warships, but both misfired, ran hot in the tubes, and had to be gingerly ejected. The British frigate *Loch Killin* fired her Squid at *U-736* and wrecked her. Reff blew all tanks, came up directly beneath *Loch Killin,* and hung up. In the battle that ensued, only nineteen of forty-seven Germans survived, including Reff, his chief engineer, Helmut Vater, and the first watch officer, Adalbert Kleinert, all rescued by *Loch Killin* and *Starling.*†

---

* The decommissioned VIIs *U-255* and *U-766* were left behind, the latter, as related, blown up.

† The Admiralty thought *U-736* was the first U-boat to be sunk by Squid, but as related, the *U-333,* sunk by *Loch Killin* and *Starling* on July 31, was the first.

• The *U-385,* commanded by Hans-Guido Valentiner, age twenty-five, sailed from St. Nazaire on August 9 to patrol the English Channel. Upon activation of the snort, it malfunctioned and filled the boat with exhaust gases, felling Valentiner and many crewmen. At about dusk on August 10, Valentiner surfaced the boat, merely seven thousand yards from the sloop *Starling,* flagship of British Support Group 2. Commanded by N. A. Duck, *Starling* opened fire, drawing counterfire from *U-385*'s flak guns. After about a half hour, Valentiner dived and attempted to escape submerged.

When Valentiner resurfaced three and a half hours later, in the early hours of August 11, a Leigh Light–equipped Sunderland of Australian Squadron 461, piloted by Ivan F. Southall, got the boat on radar. The aircraft attacked and dropped six depth charges, which blew off *U-385*'s rudder, damaged a hydroplane, and caused serious flooding through the stern torpedo tube. Valentiner dived, but foul air forced him to resurface about dawn. Still nearby, the sloop *Starling* again opened fire, this time at close range, killing the first watch officer and forcing Valentiner to abandon ship and scuttle. The sloop *Wren,* which had the survivors of *U-608* on board, rescued forty-one Germans, including Valentiner. In the postwar years, Southall wrote and published an account of Australian Squadron 461.*

• The *U-741,* commanded by Gerhard Palmgren, which had put into Le Havre with damage, resailed on the morning of August 8. To mislead Allied agents in that port into believing he was too badly damaged to conduct a patrol, that same day Palmgren put a heavy list on the boat and "limped" back into Le Havre. Then, under cover of darkness in the early hours of August 9, Palmgren resailed to an area off the Isle of Wight.

On the afternoon of August 15, Palmgren sighted a convoy, FTM 69. He fired two torpedoes and hit the *LST 404.* Remarkably, the LST survived and was towed to Spithead. Palmgren dived to 190 feet, but the British corvette *Orchis,* an escort of convoy FTC 68 nearby, raced over and commenced a skilled hunt for *U-741.* Gaining and holding sonar contact, *Orchis,* commanded by B. W. Harris, carried out four separate attacks on *U-741,* two with depth charges and two with the Hedgehog.

These attacks wrecked and flooded the U-boat and trapped about eleven men aft. Two of these, twenty-four-year-old leading stoker Leo Leuwer and another stoker, escaped via the aft torpedo-room hatch. Leuwer survived to be picked up by *Orchis* but the other stoker died. None of the other forty-seven Germans of the crew was found.

• The *U-413,* commanded by Dieter Sachse, age twenty-seven, sailed from Brest on August 2 to attack Allied invasion forces off the south coast of England between Portsmouth and Beachy Head. On August 19, Sachse found convoy ETC 72 and shot T-5s. He thought he sank two freighters for 8,000 tons, but only one victim could be confirmed, the 2,400-ton British *Saint Enogat.*

On the following morning, August 20, a British hunter-killer group comprised

---

* *They Shall Not Pass Unseen* (1956).

of the veteran destroyers *Forester, Vidette,* and *Wensleydale* detected *U-413* on sonar. *Forester* attacked with her last depth charges, but they fell wide. *Vidette,* the only one of the three warships with any charges remaining, carried out a Hedgehog attack. These well-aimed missiles wrecked and flooded *U-413* and drove her to the bottom.

The U-boat's chief engineer, Karl Hütterer, and others sealed themselves in the bow torpedo compartment and flooded it waist-deep. Per escape procedure, Hütterer opened the forward loading hatch. He reached the surface and was later rescued by *Wensleydale,* but no other Germans survived.

After recovering engineer Hütterer and some oil-soaked scraps of interior wood paneling, the skipper of *Wensleydale* called off the attack. Although they had no more depth charges, the skippers of *Forester* and *Vidette* believed the oil and scraps of wood—and perhaps even Hütterer—were likely released from the boat as a *ruse de guerre,* and wished to remain in the area until *U-413* was forced to surface for fresh air. Their protestations were ignored or dismissed and the hunter-killer group returned to port with Hütterer, who told his interrogators little except that submarine warfare in the English Channel was "lousy."

• The *U-445,* commanded by Rupprecht Fischler von Treuberg, and *U-650,* commanded by Rudolf Zorn, which had brought ammo to Lorient from La Pallice, resailed from Lorient on August 22, direct for Norway. The *U-650* reached Bergen on September 22, a miserable voyage of thirty-two days, but Fischler in *U-445* did not make it. On August 24, the British frigate *Louis,* commanded by L.A.B. Majendie, sank the boat in the Bay of Biscay, merely one hundred miles west of Lorient. There were no survivors.

• The *U-247,* commanded by Gerhard Matschulat, sailed from Brest on August 27 to patrol near the Scillies and Land's End. In the late evening of the fifth day, August 31, the frigates *St. John* and *Swansea* of the Canadian hunter-killer Support Group 9, on ASW patrol near Land's End, detected *U-247* on sonar and commenced a dogged hunt that lasted through the night and well into the next afternoon, September 1.

Attacking that afternoon on a strong sonar contact, *St. John* dropped five accurate depth charges. The Canadian naval historian Joseph Schull described the "satisfying" result: "There was a huge gush of oil, followed by a mass of letters and photographs, a certificate commemorating the ten-millionth engine revolution of *U-247,* log books, shirts, socks . . . [and other] clothing and German charts." There were no survivors.

The loss of these six boats cost the Germans about three hundred experienced crewmen (sixty-two captured), sufficient to man six big electro boats.

Aware of the concentration of U-boats in Bergen and the shortage of pens, RAF Bomber Command mounted a large-scale attack on that port on the night of October 4. The bombers scored seven direct hits on the U-boat pen, but no bombs penetrated the thick concrete roof. Other bombs, however, sank or destroyed four unprotected Type VIIs that had only just arrived from France, and knocked out the big dock cranes. The bomb damage reduced the capacity for major repairs at Bergen to four U-boats at one time, a devastating setback to future operations.

The four VIIs sunk or destroyed in this attack were:

• The aged *U-92,* commanded by the new skipper Wilhelm Brauel, age twenty-nine, which sailed from Brest on August 16. Brauel patrolled to Norway by way of the south coast of England near the Isle of Wight, where, on August 27, he fired a torpedo at an LST, but missed. He arrived in Norway on September 29, completing a voyage of forty-five days. After *U-92* was declared a total wreck at Bergen, Brauel and some of his crew returned to Germany to man a big electro boat.

• The *U-228,* commanded by a new skipper, Herbert Engel, age thirty-two, replacing Erwin Christophersen, age twenty-nine, who returned to Germany to command a big electro boat. The *U-228* sailed from St. Nazaire direct for Norway on August 12, skirting the British Isles well to the west. After a voyage of forty days, the *U-228* arrived in Bergen on September 20. Engel, who began his U-boat service in April 1940 as a quartermaster on the famous *U-48* and rose to command the *U-666* for sixteen months, did not command another boat after the destruction of *U-228.*

• The veteran *U-437,* commanded by Hermann Lamby, age twenty-eight, which sailed from Bordeaux direct for Norway on the night of August 24. Also skirting well to the west of the British Isles, Lamby reached Bergen on September 22, a voyage of nearly thirty days. Upon destruction of the boat at Bergen, Lamby and some of his crew went on to Germany to man a big electro boat.

• The *U-993,* commanded by a new skipper, Karl-Heinz Steinmetz, age twenty-three, replacing Kurt Hilbig, who had returned to Germany to command an electro boat, sailed from Brest on August 17. Also skirting well to the west of the British Isles, Steinmetz reached Bergen on September 18, after a voyage of thirty-three days, during which one crewman died of what was diagnosed as "yellow jaundice." After the destruction of *U-993* at Bergen, Steinmetz went to the Submarine School.

Three other VIIs came to grief in Norwegian waters shortly after leaving France. They were:

• The decommissioned veteran (ex-flak) *U-256,* which was recommissioned and sailed from Brest on September 3. Commanded by Heinrich Lehmann-Willenbrock, who wore Oak Leaves on his *Ritterkreuz,* the boat had a jerry-rigged snort that enabled her to evade Allied ASW forces. Cruising well to the west of the British Isles, Lehmann-Willenbrock arrived in Bergen on October 17, completing an arduous voyage of forty-five days, during which he maintained absolute radio silence, leading Control to assume that Allied forces had sunk the boat. Lehmann-Willenbrock declared *U-256* to be beyond saving and on October 23, she was once again decommissioned, this time in Norway.

• The *U-985,* commanded by Heinz Wolff, age twenty-six. Wolff sailed from La Pallice directly to Norway on August 30, also by a route which took him well to the west of the British Isles. While approaching the Norwegian coast on October 22, Wolff hit a German defensive mine that caused "immense" damage but no casualties. A German patrol boat towed *U-985* into Kristiansand on October 26.

Deemed unfit for further service, she was decommissioned and abandoned. Wolff and some crew went on to Germany to man a big electro boat.

- The *U-673,* commanded by a new skipper, Ernst-August Gerke, age twenty-three. She, with the decommissioned/recommissioned *U-382,* newly fitted with a snort and also commanded by a new skipper, Hans-Dietrich Wilke,* age thirty-two, sailed from St. Nazaire on September 14 and La Pallice on September 10, respectively. Both skippers set a course direct for Norway via waters well west of the British Isles, and both reached Bergen on October 19.

Owing to the air-raid damage and crowded conditions at Bergen, Control directed both boats to proceed to the U-boat base at Stavanger, Norway. While making this transit on October 24, Wilke in *U-382* rammed and severely damaged *U-673,* which flooded and beached in Nerstrandfiord. Wilke in *U-382* took off the crew of *U-673* and later the Germans destroyed the boat. Wilke then sailed *U-382* on to the Baltic, where she patrolled against Soviet forces under a new skipper.† Wilke and Gerke were assigned to command big electro boats.

The other sixteen Type VII snort boats that survived the evacuation from France to Norway did so not without difficulties. Twelve carried out brief patrols in the English Channel, Bristol Channel, and North Channel. Three sank ships. The stories of these boats in brief:

- The *U-480,* commanded by Hans-Joachim Förster, sailed from Brest on August 3 to patrol the south coast of England near the Isle of Wight. Conducting one of the most aggressive patrols of that time (perhaps emboldened by his *Alberich* antisonar coating), Förster attacked ships on August 18, 21, 22, 23, and 25 and sank or destroyed four. The sinkings included the Canadian corvette *Alberni* and the 850-ton British minesweeper *Loyalty. Alberni* plunged under within a few minutes with the loss of fifty-nine men. British PT boats rescued the thirty-one survivors. Förster's other two victims were freighters: the 5,700-ton British *Orminister,* and the 7,200-ton British Liberty ship *Fort Yale,* which beached, a total wreck.

Förster proceeded to Bergen, where he arrived on October 4 to high praise. On October 18, Dönitz presented him a *Ritterkreuz,* the fourth and last such award to skippers engaged in attacking Neptune forces.

- The *U-764,* commanded by Hans-Kurt von Bremen, sailed from Brest to the English Channel on August 6. Near Beachy Head on August 20, von Bremen sank the 638-ton British freighter *Coral* from convoy ETC 72. Thereafter he proceeded to Bergen, arriving on September 19, completing a patrol of forty-five days.
- The *U-989,* commanded by Hardo Rodler von Roithberg, sailed from Brest to the Bay of the Seine on August 9. He shot at ships on August 23 and 26 and sank the 1,791-ton British freighter *Ashmun J. Clough* and damaged the 7,200-ton

---

* Wilke came from the decommissioned *U-766,* replacing Rudolf Zorn, who replaced Ernst von Witzendorff in *U-650,* who returned to Germany to command a big electro boat. Gerke replaced Heinz-Gerd Sauer in *U-673.*

† Ironically, in January 1945, the *U-382* was rammed and sunk in the Baltic.

American Liberty ship *Louis Kossuth.* Proceeding to Norway, Rodler von Roithberg arrived on September 25 and then took *U-989* to the Baltic.

- The VIID (minelayer) *U-218* sailed from Brest on August 10 to lay her second minefield since D day. Newly commanded by Rupprecht Stock (from *U-214,* replacing Becker), the *U-218* planted her field off Start Point, near Plymouth in the western waters of the English Channel, on August 18. Thereafter Stock headed for Norway, arriving on September 23, completing a stressful voyage of forty-five days. His minefield inflicted no damage. From Norway, Stock sailed on to the Baltic.
- The *U-275,* commanded by Helmut Wehrkamp, age twenty-three, who had put into Boulogne on August 1, resailed on August 13. Owing to the heavy Allied ASW forces in the Bay of the Seine, Wehrkamp left that area "early" and "without orders," Control logged. West of Ireland on September 2, Wehrkamp shot a T-5 at what he reported to be a 12,000-ton ocean liner. Claiming a hit for damage, Wehrkamp asserted as proof that after the explosion, the ship had twice halted temporarily, then headed for the coast. The hit has not been confirmed in Allied records. After a brief pause off North Minch, Wehrkamp arrived at Bergen on September 18, completing a voyage of thirty-seven days.
- The *U-714,* commanded by Hans-Joachim Schwebcke, age twenty-six, sailed from La Pallice on August 27. Patrolling to Norway by way of the mouth of the Bristol Channel, Schwebcke found no targets. He arrived in Norway on October 24, completing an exhausting voyage of fifty-nine days. The following day he sailed on to the Baltic.
- The *U-309,* commanded by Hans-Gert Mahrholz, age twenty-five, sailed from La Pallice on August 29. He patrolled off North Channel for five days, but an unidentified aircraft bombed the boat, forcing Mahrholz to abort. He arrived "unannounced" in Bergen on October 9, completing a voyage of forty-two days, then sailed on to the Baltic.
- The *U-963,* commanded by the returning Karl Boddenberg, age thirty, sailed from La Pallice the same night, August 29, and also patrolled off North Channel. Boddenberg found no targets and went on to Norway, arriving in Bergen on October 7, completing an arduous voyage of forty days. He then sailed on to the Baltic.
- The *U-763,* commanded by a new skipper, Kurt Braun, age twenty-one, sailed from Bordeaux directly to Norway on August 23. Taking a course well to the west of the British Isles, Braun arrived in Norwegian waters on September 24, a voyage of thirty-three days. That night a Leigh Light–equipped B-24 of British Squadron 224 of 18 Group, piloted by John C. T. Downey, found, attacked, and damaged *U-763.* After repairs in Bergen and Kristiansund, Braun returned the boat to Germany.
- The *U-262,* which incurred bomb casualties (three killed, one wounded) and damage in La Pallice on August 18, sailed from there to Norway in company with *U-763* on August 23. Still commanded by Helmut Wieduwilt, age twenty-four, *U-262* patrolled the mouth of Bristol Channel and to the north of Land's End, but found no targets. Control speculated in the war log that "the boat did not approach close enough to the convoy routes." Wieduwilt arrived in Norway on No-

vember 1, completing the longest of the evacuation voyages: seventy-one days. He then took the boat onward to the Baltic.

- The *U-758,* still commanded by Hans-Arendt Feindt, age twenty-two, sailed from St. Nazaire on August 23. Feindt also patrolled the areas at the mouth of the Bristol Channel and north of Land's End. He found no targets either and after seven fruitless days in those areas, he went on to Norway, arriving at Bergen on October 10, completing a voyage of forty-nine days. From there, Feindt took the boat onward to the Baltic.
- The *U-953,* newly commanded by Herbert Werner from the *U-415,* which was mined and destroyed off Brest, sailed from La Pallice on August 31. Werner implied in his war memoir *Iron Coffins* that the *U-953* was the last boat to leave France, but that is not correct. Werner patrolled the mouth of North Channel but was forced to abort after seven days because he could not retract his snort, even by hand. "The Schnorkel routine had become a nightmare," he wrote. He arrived in Bergen "unannounced" on October 11, Control logged, completing a voyage of forty-two days. Werner then sailed *U-953* onward to the Baltic.
- The *U-260,* still commanded by Klaus Becker, age twenty-four, sailed from La Pallice on September 3. Bedeviled by a defective snort that leaked exhaust gases into the boat, felling many crewmen, Becker chose a course that skirted the British Isles well to the west. He arrived in Bergen on October 17, completing a voyage of forty-five days. Becker then took the boat onward to the Baltic.
- The *U-281,* commanded by Heinz von Davidson, age twenty-five, sailed from La Pallice the next night, September 4. Von Davidson patrolled off North Minch, but after seven days in that area his hydrophones malfunctioned and he aborted to Norway. On October 17, an unidentified aircraft hit *U-281,* wounding three crewmen. The boat arrived at Farsund, Norway, on October 28, a voyage of fifty-five days.

Brest fell to Allied forces on September 15. The senior submariner in Brest, flotilla commander Werner Winter, radioed Berlin:

> U-boat base and 9th Flotilla have been forced to capitulate after several days of brave fighting. . . . U-boat base going off the air. Hail our Führer!

In St. Nazaire, the base commander, Adolf-Cornelius Piening, judged that the *U-267,* which had been decommissioned, could be made seaworthy. He directed that the boat be recommissioned, and named Bernhard Knieper, age thirty-three, to command her. Using a temporary snort, Knieper sailed from St. Nazaire on September 23 direct to Norway. The *U-267* thus became the last U-boat to leave from a French Atlantic port, bringing to an end four years and two months of U-boat operations from those five bases. Knieper reached Norway on October 29, completing a voyage of thirty-seven days. He then took *U-267* onward to the Baltic.

Thus it was that only seventeen of the thirty Type VIIs that were evacuated from France in August and September survived in service. This was the bedraggled remnant of the once impressive Atlantic U-boat force that, at its peak, had attacked Allied convoys in groups numbering from twenty to forty Type VII boats.

Owing to the chaos and confusion in, over, and under the English Channel in the summer of 1944, it is not possible to give an exact accounting of the Type VII U-boat successes against Neptune forces from D day to their evacuation. The tally compiled by Professor Jürgen Rohwer is doubtless the most accurate. U-boats sailing from France and Norway in this period, he calculated, probably sank or destroyed twenty-six Allied vessels for about 73,000 tons: twelve smallish warships for about 13,000 tons* and fourteen merchantmen for about 60,000 tons, including six Liberty ships.

Dönitz and the OKM downplayed the loss of Type VIIs in the invasion period. In actuality, the loss of Type VIIs in or putting out from bases in France and Norway to repel Allied forces from May 16 to November 1, 1944, was horrific: seventy-two boats, manned by approximately 3,500 men.† British, Canadian, Australian, Norwegian, Polish, and Czech ASW aircraft and RAF bombers and British and Canadian surface ships accounted for the kills.

The United States air and surface forces patrolled relentlessly for U-boats but the rewards were few. The many B-24s of the U.S. Navy's Fleet Air Wing 7 could claim only one victory and, as related, that was shared with two Australian Sunderlands. This was the kill of the *U-243* in Biscay on July 8 by Aurelian H. Cooledge of Squadron VB 105, who received a British DFC.

Fairwing 7, meanwhile, had embarked on a highly dangerous secret project to destroy U-boats in a different way. On July 23, before the U-boat evacuation from France had commenced, it formed from Squadron VB 110 the Special Air Unit One. Its purpose was to bomb U-boat pens with radio-controlled B-24 drones jammed with twelve tons of Torpex explosives. This payload was twice the explosive power of the six-ton British Tallboy bombs that had failed to inflict any substantial damage on the pens in Brest.

The most difficult and sensitive part of the flight of the radio-controlled drone was the takeoff from base. The pretakeoff checklist and the starting of the four B-24 engines was too complicated to manage remotely. There was also the possibility that the drone might go out of control on takeoff and crash into a British town or city with unthinkable consequences. It was therefore decided that a pilot (or pilots) would man the controls of the drone during takeoff and climb to cruising altitude and then bail out through the retractable nose-wheel compartment, whereupon a "mother ship" would take over by radio controls the rest of the flight.

A number of pilots of VB 110, bored with the endless and fruitless ASW pa-

---

* The British frigates *Blackwood, Mourne,* and *Goodson;* British corvette *Pink;* Canadian corvettes *Alberni* and *Regina;* American *LST 280* and *LST 921;* British LSI *Prince Leopold;* British minesweeper *Loyalty;* British ASW trawler *Ganilly;* American *LCI 99.*

† Including eight boats that were unfit for combat, decommissioned, and/or scrapped in France or Norway (*U-255, U-256, U-276, U-673, U-766, U-957, U-985, U-998*) and four sunk in the Bergen air raid on October 4 (*U-92, U-228, U-437, U-993*). Eleven of the seventy-two losses were Arctic boats. Not included in the seventy-two losses were five *Mitte* boats that returned to the Submarine School in the Baltic (*U-397, U-677, U-982, U-999, U-1192*).

trols, volunteered for duty in the Special Air Unit One. Among them was Joseph P. Kennedy, Jr., eldest son of onetime Ambassador Kennedy and brother of the future president. During training on August 12, Kennedy and his copilot, Wilford J. Willy, took off in a B-24 drone, fully loaded with fused Torpex for a check ride. Minutes later the Torpex exploded, vaporizing the aircraft and the pilots. Undeterred, the Navy proceeded with the project and on September 3, pilot Ralph D. Spalding manning the controls of a similarly loaded B-24 drone, took off, climbed to altitude, and bailed out. Operators in a B-17 "mother plane" guided the drone to the German submarine pens on the island of Heligoland in the North Sea, but in the final approach, the drone strayed and the operators missed the pen.*

The forced evacuation of the Type VIIs from the U-boat bases in France was, of course, the most devastating setback possible for Dönitz and the *Kriegsmarine.* Yet he and the majority of German submariners, like their forebears in the Imperial Navy, defiantly soldiered on with no widespread diminution in fighting spirit. Almost to a man, German submariners believed that the big Type XXI and small Type XXIII electro boats were to usher in a new era in naval warfare, which the Germans were to dominate decisively.

One of the ironies of naval history is that the submarine, initially developed as a "coast defense" weapon, proved to be all but worthless in that role. As related, in World War II this fact was amply demonstrated in Norway in 1940, in the Philippines and at Midway Island in 1941 and 1942, in the Mediterranean from 1941 to 1944, and in France in 1944. Submarines performed most effectively in lone surprise attacks against merchant shipping, wherein the advantage of stealth could be used to the fullest.

Evacuation of the Type IXs from France

When the Allies invaded Normandy, there were thirty-seven Type IXs in the Atlantic U-boat force, including nine U-cruisers.† Excluding the latter and six conventional IXs in the Far East,‡ the other twenty-two IXs were disposed as follows: three newly sailed for weather-reporting patrols in the North Atlantic,§ eight in or returning from American waters, five in or returning from West African waters, and six in refit and modernization at French bases.

Fourteen of the twenty-two IXs that were on patrol on June 6 returned: three to

* Kennedy was recommended for the Medal of Honor, but higher authority reduced the decoration to a Navy Cross. His copilot, Wilford Willy, also received a Navy Cross, as did Ralph Spalding. Only one other pilot in Fairwing 7 earned a Navy Cross: James H. Alexander, Jr., whose B-24 was attacked over Biscay by six JU-88s. His aircrew shot down several enemy planes, but the wounded Alexander had to ditch the riddled B-24. All ten airmen survived thirty-six hours in a life raft and were rescued by the Spanish and ultimately repatriated.

† The IXD1 cargo conversions *U-180* and *U-195* and the IXD2 *U-178* at Bordeaux; the IXD2s *U-181, U-196, U-198, U-859, U-860,* and *U-861* in the Far East.

‡ *U-168, U-183, U-510, U-532, U-537, U-843.*

§ *U-534, U-853, U-857.*

Norway (*U-516, U-530, U-539*) and eleven to France, including the three newly sailed weather boats. As related, the *U-107* was lost while shifting bases in the Bay of Biscay. Three others, the famous Drumbeater *U-123,* the IXC *U-129,* and the IXC40 *U-188,* just back from the Far East, were deemed unfit for further service and scrapped in Lorient and Bordeaux.* Including those in refit and modernization, the remaining thirteen IXs in French bases were evacuated to Norway.

Six of these thirteen IXs received orders to sail to Norway via patrols in remote areas: two to West Africa and four to the Americas. Their stories in brief:

- The IXC40 snort boat *U-546,* commanded by Paul Just, age twenty-eight, sailed from Lorient on June 15 bound for the Gulf of Guinea, off West Africa. Attacked by unidentified Allied aircraft in the Bay of Biscay, Just exhausted his flak ammo in counterfire, put back to Lorient to reload on June 22, and resailed on June 25. Allied codebreakers decrypted traffic related to her voyage by July 13 and Tenth Fleet sent a "jeep" carrier hunter-killer group in pursuit. On July 20, Just logged, *U-546* sighted a "carrier" and attacked with one T-5, but it missed. The carrier escorts depth-charged *U-546* for three hours but Just slipped away.

Owing to the need to conserve fuel for the return to Norway, Just canceled the plan to sail to the Gulf of Guinea. Instead, he patrolled the west African coast from Dakar southward for about five weeks. During this time, Just found a convoy and attacked, firing three torpedoes, but these also missed. After she reported being homebound, Control assigned the *U-546* to weather reporting. Just finally reached Norway on November 6, completing an utterly fruitless voyage of 135 days.

- The IXC40 snort boat *U-170,* commanded by a new skipper, Hans-Gerold Hauber, age thirty, sailed from Lorient to the Dakar-Freetown area on August 4. Hauber patrolled his area for about a month without success. When he radioed his plan for returning to Norway, Allied codebreakers decrypted the message and located *U-170*'s position by direction finding. Tenth Fleet put the "jeep" *Guadalcanal* hunter-killer group athwart her track. On October 25, carrier aircraft found, attacked, and damaged, but did not sink, *U-170.* In the days following, Hauber attacked with T-5s two "destroyers"—probably destroyer escorts of the *Guadalcanal* group—but missed. On November 5, he reported "depth-charge damage, snort out of order, hauling off to repair." He finally reached Norway on November 30, completing an equally fruitless voyage of 119 days.

- The snort boat IXC *U-154,* commanded by Gerth Gemeiner, age twenty-five, sailed again to the Americas on June 20, this time by the southern route to Cape Hatteras. In response to Enigma decrypts relating to the track of this boat, Tenth Fleet sent the "jeep" carrier *Croatan* and her escorts from Casablanca on June 30 to stalk her near Madeira. On the morning of July 3, two warships of this group, the destroyer escorts *Inch* and *Frost,* got *U-154* on sonar and attacked. During this engagement, *Croatan*'s catapult failed and she could not launch aircraft,

---

* Allied guerrillas ambushed an auto convoy and killed the skipper of the *U-188,* Siegfried Lüdden, who was en route to Berlin to make his oral report. The guerrillas found valuable papers in his effects, including his patrol report with a special section containing the current U-boat approach routes to Penang, Jakarta, Singapore, and so on.

but as it turned out, they were not needed. Gemeiner fired two torpedoes at his attackers, but missed. *Inch* and *Frost* then hammered the boat with depth charges and destroyed it with the loss of all hands. The debris that rose to the surface included scraps of wood, German uniforms, and human remains.

• The IXC snort boat *U-518,* commanded by Hans-Werner Offermann, age twenty-three, sailed from Lorient on July 15 to again patrol the Caribbean, this time off Panama. Alerted to the boat's track by Enigma decrypts, Tenth Fleet diverted escorts of convoy UGS 50 to hunt *U-518.* These escorts attacked a sonar contact on August 9, which was likely *U-518,* but Offermann got away. When Control informed him that he must conserve fuel for a return to Norway rather than France, Offermann elected to patrol off Cape Hatteras rather than Panama.

The Allies decrypted and DFed this radio transmission and Tenth Fleet diverted escorts from the Trinidad-Freetown convoy TF 6 to hunt her, but Offermann again eluded his pursuers. Tenth Fleet next sailed the "jeep" carrier *Croatan* hunter-killer group from Norfolk, but it had no better luck. Nor did two other "jeep" carrier hunter-killer groups and ASW aircraft from Bermuda and the United States East Coast. On September 12, Offermann torpedoed the 7,200-ton American Liberty ship *George Ade* off Cape Fear. A salvage vessel, *Escape,* towed her into an anchorage, but a few hours later, on September 13, a hurricane struck, sinking her.* Offermann returned *U-518* to Norway on October 22, completing a voyage of one hundred days.

• The IXC40 snort boat *U-802,* commanded by Helmut Schmoeckel, age twenty-six, sailed from Lorient to Canadian waters for the second time on June 22. About ten days out, the snort broke and Schmoeckel aborted to France, arriving on July 8. After repairs, he resailed on July 16. Control directed Schmoeckel to enter the mouth of the St. Lawrence River, a high-risk area not patrolled by U-boats since 1942. In view of the surprise attainable and the heavy traffic and the concealment provided by the snort, Control exhorted Schmoeckel to "get right on in there" and seek "great success."

Alerted to the track of this boat by Enigma decrypts, Tenth Fleet sent the "jeep" carrier *Bogue* hunter-killer group in pursuit. On the night of August 19, a *Bogue* aircraft with radar and a searchlight straddled "a surfaced U-boat" with three depth charges about 150 miles southeast of the Grand Banks, but Schmoeckel escaped and snorted slowly to the Gulf of St. Lawrence via Cabot Strait. Aware of the approach of this boat and another, Allied ASW forces in or near the gulf deployed in strength. On the night of August 28, one of the ASW aircraft drove *U-802* under, Control logged, but the boat again escaped.

Schmoeckel snorted into the mouth of the St. Lawrence River, a bold stroke in view of the intense ASW measures. He lurked there in poor sonar conditions for about a week but found no worthwhile targets. Believing he had lost the element of surprise, he withdrew to safer waters in the gulf where, on September 14, he shot a T-5 at a "destroyer," later identified by the Canadian naval historian Michael

* The hurricane also sank four American warships with heavy loss of life: destroyer *Warrington,* the small harbor minesweeper *409,* and the Coast Guard cutters *Jackson* and *Bedloe.*

Hadley as the Canadian frigate *Stettler.* The torpedo missed. *Stettler* and other warships hunted *U-802,* but she slipped away. On November 12, the boat entered Bergen with a broken snort, completing an arduous, fruitless voyage of 120 days.

• The IXC40 snort boat *U-541,* commanded by Kurt Petersen, age twenty-seven, also sailed from Lorient for the St. Lawrence River three weeks later, on August 6. Taking advantage of the poor flying weather and an improved radar detector, Petersen cruised on the surface much of the time and actually reached the gulf a few days before *U-802.* Near Cabot Strait on September 3, he sank the 2,100-ton British freighter *Livingston.* This success greatly intensified ASW measures and doubtless contributed to the dearth of shipping in the St. Lawrence River that frustrated Schmoeckel in *U-802.*

Pressing on toward the river, Petersen found a target on the night of September 7–8, surfaced, and prepared to shoot a T-5. An escort, the Canadian corvette *Norsyd,* got *U-541* on radar and broke up the attack with a withering barrage of accurate gunfire. Forced under, Petersen shot the T-5 at *Norsyd* and claimed a "destroyer," but the torpedo missed. After eluding these attackers, Petersen boldly snorted into the St. Lawrence River, but he, too, found no targets and after a week, withdrew to safer waters. While exiting the gulf in late September, Michael Hadley wrote, Petersen shot five torpedoes at two freighters, but all missed.

Homebound to Norway, Petersen learned from Control that the Allies had deployed a heavy ASW screen in the Iceland-Faeroes gap. He therefore elected to return via the Denmark Strait and northabout Iceland. In those frigid northern waters, he encountered unusually heavy ice, but boldly cruised beneath it, surfacing occasionally to air the boat and charge batteries. He arrived in Norway on November 6, completing a nerve-racking voyage of ninety-three days.

Altogether, Schmoeckel in *U-802* and Petersen in *U-541* were at sea 213 days. The confirmed result was one small freighter (*Livingston*) sunk. The skippers were thwarted by Allied codebreakers and ASW forces. Despite this lack of success—and the sharply diminished traffic in the gulf with the onset of winter—Control was to mount many more IXC patrols to Canada. The mere presence of snort boats in the gulf caused consternation and embarrassment in Ottawa—and thus a propaganda victory of sorts in Berlin—and tied down Allied ASW forces and gave German submariners who were to cadre the electro boats combat and snort experience.

Seven Type IXs sailed directly from France to Norway:

• The IXC40 *U-548,* temporarily commanded by the old hand Günther Pfeffer, age twenty-nine, was the first big boat to evacuate. Commanded by Eberhard Zimmermann, age twenty-seven, she had made one ninety-six-day war patrol to Canada, arriving back in Lorient on June 24. During forty-nine days at Lorient, she was fitted with a snort, but due to the Allied invasion, Zimmermann and many crewmen were unable to get back to Lorient from leave in Germany. The boat sailed on August 11, manned by a scratch crew. In addition, she embarked about thirty other men, raising the sailing list to eighty-four, one of whom was lost overboard en route.

The boat arrived in Bergen on September 25. Four days later she sailed in company with other boats for Flensburg, Germany, reassigned to a new outfit, Combat

Flotilla 33, created especially to administer the operations of Type IX U-boats that could not be refitted at any base in Norway. Her permanent skipper, Eberhard Zimmermann, and the other crew rejoined the boat; Pfeffer went to other duty. The boat did not resail for a war patrol until March 7, 1945, commanded by yet another skipper.

• The next boat to sail directly from Lorient to Norway was the veteran IXC40 *U-190*. She, too, had a new snort and a new skipper, Hans-Edwin Reith, age twenty-four, replacing Max Wintermeyer, who had gone to other duty.

Reith left Lorient on August 22 and arrived in Norway forty days later, on October 1. He went on to Flensburg with other boats, reassigned to Combat Flotilla 33. Reith retained command, but the boat did not resail for a war patrol until February 21, 1945.

• The third to sail from Lorient directly to Norway was the IXC40 *U-853*, commanded by Helmut Sommer, age twenty-nine. This new boat had made one weather patrol of sixty-six days in the North Atlantic. Homing on her reports, Allied aircraft from a MAC ship and from the "jeep" carrier *Croatan* had attacked and killed two men and wounded twelve and damaged the boat, forcing Sommer to abort to Lorient on July 3. During fifty-six days in that port, the boat got a new snort, but Sommer and some crew were unable to return from leave in Germany.

Dönitz appointed longtime commander of Combat Flotilla 10, *Ritterkreuz* holder Günter Kuhnke, to command the new Combat Flotilla 33 at Flensburg. Authorized to travel to Flensburg by U-boat, Kuhnke assumed temporary command of the *U-853* and sailed on August 27, with nine extra passengers. After a voyage of forty-six days, he arrived in Norway on October 11. From there he went on to Flensburg and assumed command of Combat Flotilla 33 from its temporary commander, *Ritterkreuz* holder Georg Schewe. Commanded by yet another skipper, *U-853* did not resail for a combat patrol until February 23, 1945.

• The IXC40 snort boat *U-547*, commanded by Heinrich Niemeyer, was the first of three Type IXs to leave Bordeaux. The boat had only just returned (August 11) from a snort patrol of 104 days, at the end of which she had incurred heavy damage from British mines in the Gironde River. There had been neither time nor labor nor spare parts to carry out proper repairs and a refit.

Harassed by Allied aircraft, on August 24* Niemeyer sailed down the Gironde at night to open water, dodging mines. Most of the crew remained topside wearing life preservers, in case the boat hit a mine. Finally Niemeyer reached the open waters of the Bay of Biscay, rigged his snort, and headed for Norway by a safer route, far to westward. Along the way, the snort failed and exhaust gases felled many of the crew and passengers. After a miserable voyage of thirty-five days, Niemeyer

---

* At about the same time, the reengined IXD1 cargo U-cruisers *U-180* and *U-195* and the big Type XB minelayer *U-219* sailed from Bordeaux to the Far East with supplies for the U-boats basing at Penang, Jakarta, and elsewhere. Upon reaching the Bay of Biscay, the *U-180*, commanded by Rolf Riesen, age twenty-four, probably hit a British mine and sank with the loss of all hands. The *U-195*, commanded by a new skipper, Friedrich Steinfeldt, and *U-219*, commanded by Walter Burghagen, reached Jakarta in December.

reached Bergen on September 27. From there he joined other boats for the trip to Flensburg, where the boat also reported to Combat Flotilla 33, but she hit a British mine in the Baltic and made no more war patrols.

- The IXC40 *U-534,* commanded by Herbert Nollau, was next to sail from Bordeaux on the night of August 25. She, too, had only just completed her first war patrol—ninety-eight days in the North Atlantic as a weather boat—and had arrived on August 13. There had been no chance for a refit but remarkably, in the brief stop at Bordeaux, technicians had jerry-rigged a snort to *U-534,* a rigid pipe that could not be raised or lowered.

When Nollau sailed on the night of August 25, he also kept the crew on deck wearing life preservers. Dodging mines and/or detonating them with temporarily streamed noisemakers and diving to escape swarms of Allied aircraft, Nollau finally reached the open waters of the Bay of Biscay. When the snort was activated, it malfunctioned and filled the boat with exhaust gases, which felled Nollau and many crewmen. When Nollau surfaced to get fresh air, Allied aircraft attacked the boat. Nollau returned fire with his flak guns—claiming one aircraft destroyed—but was soon forced to make an emergency crash dive, during which the boat accidentally shipped about twenty-five tons of seawater and plunged to an extreme depth before Nollau and his engineer could regain control.

After this close call, *U-534* proceeded well westward to skirt the British Isles, all the while learning to snort on this temporary fixed apparatus. On the way, Control directed Nollau to serve as a provisional weather boat. After a sixty-one-day trip, the boat reached Norway on October 24 and sailed for Flensburg the next day. Nollau retained command, but the boat did not resail for a war patrol until May 3, 1945.*

- The IXC40 *U-857,* commanded by Rudolf Premauer, age twenty-five, sailed from Bordeaux the same night as *U-534,* August 25. She was the last of the big boats to leave that base for Norway.

This new boat also had just completed a ninety-seven-day weather patrol, arriving in Bordeaux on August 13. She, too, had been fitted with a temporary, rigid snort and also had to tediously negotiate the mined Gironde River, harassed by Allied aircraft. After the boat finally reached the open waters of the Atlantic, Control directed Premauer to carry out another weather-reporting task. Forty-four days later, on October 7, the boat arrived in Norway and sailed the next day for Flensburg. Premauer retained command but he did not leave for another war patrol until February 8, 1945.

The last of the seven Type IXs to leave France directly for Norway was the famous veteran IXC *U-155.* Commanded by Johannes Rudolph, age twenty-eight,

---

* Two days after sailing on this last patrol, on May 5, 1945, a B-24 of British Squadron 86, piloted by J. D. Nicol, sank *U-534* in the Kattegat. Three crewmen perished, but forty-nine Germans survived, including Nollau. On August 23, 1993, the boat broke into the news when a Dutch salvage company, Smit Tak of Rotterdam, raised *U-534* intact, while some of the B-24 aircrew and some of *U-534*'s wartime crew observed. At that time news accounts reported that Nollau had "committed suicide in 1976." The salvors said *U-534* would be refurbished and placed on exhibit in Liverpool.

she had made a patrol of 105 days to the Gulf of Guinea, arriving off Lorient on June 24, where, as related, Allied aircraft killed two men, wounded seven, and damaged the boat. When it was learned that Rudolph was unable to return to Lorient from leave in Germany, the first watch officer of the IXC40 *U-548,* Ludwig-Ferdinand von Friedeburg, age twenty, was given temporary command and he sailed on September 9, the youngest officer yet to command an oceangoing U-boat in the Atlantic war zone.

Von Friedeburg brought *U-155* into Norway on October 17, completing a harrowing voyage of thirty-nine days. From there he resailed to Flensburg, where Rudolph reassumed command and von Friedeburg went on to command a small Type XXIII electro boat. The *U-155* made no more war patrols.

The voyages of these last thirteen Type IXs to evacuate from French bases were designed principally to save the boats from capture, battle-harden the crews for duty in electro boats, and provide weather reports and transportation to Germany for flotilla commander Kuhnke. In 581 days at sea, the six snort boats in this group that mounted war patrols to the waters of West Africa and America sank or caused the destruction of only two ships, the 7,200-ton American Liberty ship *George Ade* and the 2,100-ton British freighter *Livingston.*

These minuscule results and those of the Type VIIs belie the rosy reports on the offensive effectiveness of snort boats emanating from Admiral Dönitz and U-boat Control. The only advantage the snort of that era gave a U-boat was the ability to avoid detection by radar-equipped Allied aircraft and survive—it did nothing to aid in successful attacks on Allied shipping.

Type VII Snort Boat Patrols from Norway: 1944

During the evacuation of the U-boat bases in France in August 1944, the Red Army summer offensive (Bagration) advanced steadily westward into Poland toward the Vistula River and Warsaw. On September 4, German-occupied Finland formally surrendered to the Russians. This "defection," as Berlin viewed it, deprived the Germans of naval bases that had been used to maintain the minefield sealing off the Gulf of Finland and to support a few Type VII U-boats operating in that area. On October 13, Riga fell to Soviet forces, forcing the Germans to evacuate Estonia and to reorganize farther south in Latvia and Lithuania.

The dominance of Soviet forces in the eastern Baltic and the intense Allied mining and bombing of the western Baltic severely hampered U-boat operations. All school boats and new combat boats in workup that sailed into the Baltic were vulnerable to Allied air attack and to acoustic and other types of offensive Allied mines.

Allied air raids on Hamburg, Bremen, and Kiel continued to retard new U-boat construction. Production of the big Type XXI and the small Type XXIII electro boats slipped ever further behind schedule. Subsections of the big Type XXIs—potentially the greatest threat to Allied maritime assets—were built in the interior of Germany and barged to three main locations for assembly: Hamburg, Bremen, and (to escape Allied air attacks), Danzig. In the summer of 1944, from June through August, the three main assembly areas commissioned only ten Type XXI boats: four at Hamburg (*U-2501* to *U-2504*), four at Bremen (*U-3001* to *U-3004*), and two at Danzig (*U-3501* and *U-3502*). Advancing Soviet forces in the eastern Baltic posed an especially grave threat to Danzig, which produced only twelve more Type XXIs in 1944.*

The fact that Albert Speer and German engineers were able to serially produce at numerous dispersed manufacturing sites a new oceangoing combat submarine type in about fourteen months awed Allied navalists. What seldom has been emphasized, however, is that the design was merely a modification of an oceangoing Walter boat and that the sea trials of the Type XXI boat revealed numerous design flaws. Since there had been no time to build a prototype for testing, flaws were to be expected, but at least two flaws in the Type XXI were crippling.

- To conserve battery power for operations, the Germans introduced a system of hydraulic power in place of the electrical motors theretofore used to control the periscope hoist, bow and stern planes, rudder, torpedo-tube doors, and other gear. Lacking experience with hydraulics on submarines, the Germans produced a system that was much too complicated and much too delicate. Besides that, too many of the hydraulic lines and pistons were placed *outside* the pressure hull, where they could not be repaired when submerged and were highly vulnerable to close explosions. Moreover, inasmuch as the external hydraulic piping and fittings could not be made entirely leakproof, seawater constantly contaminated the system and diluted its power and the boats left an oil trace. Although pieces of the hydraulic system were improved and retrofitted, the most serious flaws could not be eliminated.
- To offset the weight of and to make more space available for the huge (372-cell) battery, the Germans powered the XXIs with two newly developed six-cylinder, lightweight diesels, rated in design at 1,970 horsepower each with superchargers driven by the exhaust gases. The superchargers did not produce the design horsepower. Moreover, the temperature of the exhaust was far in excess of the safe operating limit of the metal in the exhaust valves (350 degrees above the limit imposed in American submarines). To assure safe and prudent operations, the superchargers had to be removed, thereby reducing the horsepower of each engine from almost 2,000 to 1,200. This necessary modification left the Type XXI vastly underpowered and increased the time required for a full battery charge from one hour to four hours. A maximum surface speed of 15.6 knots (less than the 16-knot corvette), inherent in the design, could not be improved.†

When the U-boats in France were preparing to evacuate in July 1944, Control conceived a "new U-boat war," which was to be waged by new snort boats sailing from Norwegian bases.

---

* The various production schedules called for thirty to thirty-three Type XXIs per month, commencing in August 1944. At that rate, the Germans were to produce 165 Type XXIs in 1944. But only sixty-one XXI boats were commissioned by the *Kriegsmarine* in that period: twenty-eight at Hamburg, nineteen at Bremen, and fourteen at Danzig. About one-third of the sixty-one Type XXIs commissioned in 1944 came into service in December. See Plate 8.

† For an official postwar evaluation of the Type XXI by the U.S. Navy, see Foreword to Volume I or Afterword to this volume.

Admiral Dönitz or a senior OKM staffer apparently felt the need to justify this new campaign (and possibly the impending campaign by Type XXI and XXIII electro boats) to all hands in the *Kriegsmarine* with yet another exhortation. From Berlin came a long propaganda screed entitled "Why the U-boat War?" Briefly repeating the familiar strategic arguments for isolating the British Isles (buttressed by incorrect and inflated numbers), the statement proclaimed that "a new U-boat war must and shall be our most important goal in the war against the Western Powers." Therefore the *Kriegsmarine* and industry "must work for that end with fanatical energy":

> This new war must have a decisive influence even in the current year of the war [1944]. If it does, success will not be denied our iron will and zealous labors. Thus every man in the *Kriegsmarine* can say with pride that his activity—his work in this war—is of an importance at least equal to that of the best armored defense or grenadier on the distant fronts. Yes, the final decision itself may depend upon the revived U-boat war.

Taking this propaganda proclamation at face value, some writers have asserted that in the fall of 1944, Germany launched a new and telling phase of the U-boat war with snort boats, which were a major step toward a "true submersible," as opposed to conventional but obsolete (and defeated) Type VIIs and Type IXs, dismissed as basically surface ships with the ability to submerge only briefly. It would be closer to the truth to describe the patrols of the new snort boats from Norway from July to December 1944 as a combination of propaganda strikes and advanced training exercises in combat snorting that it was vital to master if the Type XXI and Type XXIII electro boats were to be effective, when—or if—they ever reached readiness for combat.*

Owing to the absence of U-tankers and to the markedly increased distances from Norway to the convoy hunting grounds and to the dangers posed by the increased Allied ASW measures, it was not possible to mount group attacks versus

---

* Losses and accidents continued in the Baltic. Allied air raids on Kiel, Bremen, Danzig, and elsewhere sank Type VIICs *U-239* and *U-777,* the VIIC41 *U-1164,* and the IXD2 U-cruiser *U-872.* Allied aircraft damaged the Type XXI electro boat *U-3509,* the IXD2 U-cruiser *U-873,* the Type IXC40 *U-870,* the Type VIICs *U-773* and *U-901,* and the Type VIIC41s *U-1014, U-1109,* and *U-1273.* In the Gulf of Finland a Soviet patrol boat sank the VIIC *U-250,* commanded by Werner-Karl Schmidt, age twenty-nine, who was rescued with five other crewmen. The Soviets raised and salvaged *U-250,* obtaining an Enigma machine, T-5 homing torpedoes, and other arms and equipment. The new small Type XXIII electro boat *U-2323* hit a mine near Kiel and sank. Another, *U-2331,* sank during trials off Hela. The VIIC41 *U-1000* hit a mine near Pillau (Baltisk) and due to severe damage, had to be decommissioned. The IXC40 *U-1234* collided with a tugboat and sank. She was raised and salvaged, to become a school boat. Wrecked by an accidental torpedo explosion, the VIIC *U-1196* also became a school boat. Severely damaged in a collision, the VIIC *U-1054* was decommissioned. The IXD2 U-cruiser *U-874* collided with the IXC40 *U-1235,* as did the XB (minelayer) *U-234* and the VIIC41 *U-1301.* The latter became a school boat; the other three boats were in the yards for repairs for months. The VIIC41 *U-1018* was also delayed by a collision with another vessel. The Type VIIC school boat *U-80* was lost in an accident near Pillau. Fed up with the careless ship handling that had led to many collisions, Admiral Dönitz issued a stern warning that further U-boat losses due to carelessness would be "ruthlessly punished."

convoys by the Type VII snort boats or long-distance individual patrols to the Caribbean, the Gulf of Mexico, Latin America, or Freetown and the Gulf of Guinea by the Type IX snort boats. Excepting some weather-reporting patrols, which were deemed vital for Hitler's planned Ardennes counteroffensive against Allied forces that were closing in on Germany from the west, the VIIs mostly patrolled close to the British Isles as in 1939 and 1940 and the IXs in the less distant Canadian waters.

To carry out this "new U-boat war," Control mounted sixty-eight Type VII snort-boat patrols from Norway in the period of July through December 1944. Eighteen VIIs aborted; sixteen were lost.

The VII sailings by month:

*July**	*August†*	*September*	*October‡*	*November§*	*December#*	*Total*
1	15	1	14	15	22	68

The Type VIIs operated under difficult conditions. Refit facilities in Norway, which had to accommodate the thirty-odd boats of the Arctic force as well, were limited and often under heavy Allied air attack. Many of the new VIIs from Germany overlapped with the older VIIs evacuating from France, creating a traffic jam in the fjords and inshore leads used for interbase travel. All U-boats in northern waters in summer and early fall had to contend with the lack of darkness, the best time to snort to charge batteries and ventilate the boat.

It needs to be stressed yet again that the boats did not snort full time. They traveled on batteries for most of the day at about two or three knots. Once a day the boats snorted at five knots for four hours to recharge batteries, and surfaced for about a half hour to air the boat. Hence it was difficult for a snort boat to travel more than about fifty sea miles a day.

While the snorts afforded a welcome degree of protection from Allied aircraft, the VIIs deployed from Norway in the "new U-boat war" were greatly handicapped by the snail-like pace of the boat. Under the new tactical doctrines, it was to take a Type VII snort boat about twenty-five days each way to travel to and from Bergen to the English Channel, leaving only about ten days for operations in the assigned patrol zone. This was not unlike the limitations inherent in Type VII operations in the early days of the U-boat assault on America, Drumbeat. Snort imperfections and catastrophic failures made the travel to and from the patrol zone even more uncomfortable and often unbearable for the crews.

---

* The *U-300* aborted and resailed in October. See Appendix 2.

† The *U-285* aborted and resailed in December. The *U-396* aborted and resailed in October. The *U-680* aborted, resailed in October, aborted again, and resailed in November.

‡ The *U-246* aborted and resailed in February 1945. The *U-1200* aborted and resailed later in the month.

§ The *U-1009* aborted and resailed in December.

The *U-244* aborted and resailed in January 1945. The *U-275* aborted and also resailed in January. The *U-278* aborted and resailed later in the month. The *U-285* aborted and resailed in March 1945. The *U-312* and *U-739* aborted and returned to the Arctic force. The *U-905* aborted and resailed in March 1945.

Aware from Enigma decrypts that this "new U-boat war" was afoot, the Allies took several important steps to thwart it. In hopes of destroying U-boats before they reached the Atlantic, they increased air and surface ASW patrols in the Shetland-Faeroes and Faeroes-Iceland "gaps" and planted new minefields in those passages. They mounted heavy-bomber raids against the naval bases in Trondheim, Bergen, Stavanger, and Horten, and also attacks against U-boats at sea in the Norwegian training areas. They switched the convoy routes into and out of North Minch and North Channel to the much more distant St. George's Channel, going southabout Ireland, as in the early months of the war.

Four Type VII snort boats sailed to patrol North Minch, Scotland. Their stories in brief:

- The VIIC41 *U-300,* commanded by Fritz Hein, age twenty-four, the first and only Type VII snort boat to sail from Norway in the month of July, originally was to patrol the east coast of Iceland. On second thought, Control sent the *U-300* to North Minch. But she never got there. On August 4, an Iceland-based Canso of the highly effective Canadian Squadron 162, piloted by W. O. Marshall, attacked *U-300* with three depth charges. Contrary to policy—and good sense—Hein crash-dived. The explosions damaged both periscopes and cracked a ballast tank and a fuel tank, forcing Hein to surface and man flak guns. His 37mm gunners drove off the Canso, and Hein dived and got away. However, the damage forced Hein to abort to Bergen, arriving on August 28, and he did not resail until early October.
- Two other boats that patrolled to North Minch were also forced to abort. Commanded by Konrad Bornhaupt, age twenty-four, the *U-285* sailed from Norway on August 24, sank no ships, incurred heavy depth-charge damage, and returned to Bergen on September 18, after merely twenty-six days. Commanded by Erich Taschenmacher, age twenty-five, the *U-775* sailed from Norway on November 18, sank the 1,300-ton British frigate *Bullen,* but had an engine failure and returned to Bergen on December 22, after a voyage of thirty-five days.
- The fourth boat, the Type VIIC41 *U-296,* commanded by Karl-Heinz Rasch, age thirty, conducted two patrols off North Minch. Neither resulted in any sinkings. On the first, from August 16 to September 29, Rasch reported that he remained continuously submerged on his snort and batteries for thirty-four days of the forty-five. For the second, of fifty-two days, he sailed on November 4 and returned to Norway on Christmas Day.
- Nine boats set out for patrols two hundred miles farther south, off North Channel (separating Scotland and Ireland). In brief:

The first to arrive there was *U-482,* commanded by Hartmut von Matuschka, age twenty-nine, who sailed on August 14. In merely nine days, from August 30 to September 8, he carried out far and away the most productive patrol of *any* Type VII in 1944: five confirmed ships sunk for 32,671 tons. His victims (from three different convoys) were the British corvette *Hurst Castle,* two big, valuable tankers (the 10,400-ton American *Jacksonville* and the 15,702-ton British *Empire Heritage*), and two freighters (the 4,100-ton Norwegian *Fiordheim* and the 1,300-ton British *Pinto*).

On a second patrol to North Channel in *U-482* commencing on November 18, von Matuschka again found good hunting. On January 15, 1945, he damaged the 8,300-ton British "jeep" carrier *Thane* and the 7,400-ton Norwegian tanker *Spinanger.* Towed into Greenrock, the *Thane* was not repaired during the war. In wartime it was thought that on the following day, January 16, the British Support Group 22 (sloops *Starling, Peacock, Hart,* and *Amethyst;* frigate *Loch Craigge*) sank *U-482* with the loss of all hands. However, in a recent reassessment, the Admiralty declared that the cause of the loss of *U-482* was unknown, possibly sunk by a mine.

The other eight U-boats that set out for North Channel during this phase of the "new U-boat war" fared poorly.

- British surface ships or mines caused the loss of two with all hands on about September 9, while en route to the area: the *U-484,* commanded by Wolff-Axel Schaefer, age thirty-three, and *U-743,* commanded by Helmut Kandzior, age twenty-four, sunk by British frigate *Helmsdale* and British corvette *Portchester Castle,* Niestlé writes.
- The *U-1200,* commanded by Hinrich Mangels, age twenty-five, sailed on October 7 but aborted after one week with mechanical problems.
- Control berated and relieved the skipper of *U-398,* Johann Reckhoff, age thirty-three, for failing to act more aggressively and sent the boat back to the Baltic.
- The *U-248,* and the Type VII41s *U-1003* and *U-1004,* commanded by Bernhard Emde, age twenty-six, Werner Strübing, age thirty-seven, and Hartmuth Schimmelpfennig, age twenty-four, respectively, did not sink anything either. Emde left to command the nonsnort VIIC41 *U-299* of group *Mitte;* Schimmelpfennig left for other duty, but the oldster Strübing retained command of *U-1003.*

Only one of the eight boats hit a target: *U-483,* commanded by Hans-Joachim von Morstein, age thirty-five. He damaged the British frigate *Whitaker,* which was towed to port, a total loss, but he had to abort the patrol with a disabled hydroplane.

Four boats set out to patrol off Reykjavik, Iceland.

- The *U-396,* commanded by Ernst-Günther Unterhorst, age twenty-five, whose first command, *U-395,* was destroyed in Kiel by Allied aircraft, sailed from Trondheim on August 6. A week thereafter, the snort failed, forcing Unterhorst to return to Trondheim after eleven days at sea. He did not resail until late October.
- While en route from Kiel to Norway, the *U-244,* commanded by Ruprecht Fischer, age twenty-seven, came under Allied air attack on July 25, as related. In this fierce engagement, Fischer incurred one dead and eight wounded. After repairs and remanning, he sailed from Bergen to Iceland on August 23. He patrolled off Reykjavik where on September 22, he missed a "destroyer" with a T-5, then returned to Bergen on October 10, a fruitless patrol of sixty-three days.

Fischer resailed *U-244* from Bergen on December 12 to patrol off Reykjavik a second time. However, his snort failed, forcing him to abort. The boat returned to Bergen on December 23, where the crew celebrated Christmas and New Year's.

- The *U-979,* commanded by Johannes Meermeier, age twenty-seven, also made two patrols to Reykjavik. On September 22, he shot four torpedoes at the

5,700-ton U.S. Navy store ship *Yukon,* which was escorted by "corvettes and aircraft." One torpedo missed and two were duds, but one hit *Yukon* near the stern. However, she made port under her own power.

The next day, Meermeier attacked a small convoy, claiming a 3,000-ton freighter sunk, but it has not been confirmed in Allied records. A British patrol craft, *St. Kenan,* counterattacked *U-979* with depth charges and rammed her, knocking the periscope askew. Meermeier escaped, eluded his pursuers, and aborted to Bergen, arriving on October 10, a patrol of forty-three days, almost all of it spent going and coming. The second patrol to Reykjavik, from November 9 to January 16, produced no confirmed sinkings either.

- Fritz Hein in *U-300,* who was forced to abort his first patrol to North Minch because of battle damage, sailed for Iceland on October 4. Over a month later, on November 10, he intercepted elements of the disorganized convoy UR 142, which had been scattered by a gale en route from the British Isles, and which was merely two hours out from Reykjavik. Practically within sight of the city, Hein sank two British ships by torpedo: the 6,000-ton tanker *Shirvan* and the 260-ton tug *Empire World,* which was attempting to assist *Shirvan.* Shortly thereafter Iceland's largest passenger-freighter, the 1,500-ton *Godafoss,* came up to rescue survivors, and Hein sank her as well. He returned to Norway on December 2.

Two boats sailed to Moray Firth, northeastern Scotland, an area of the North Sea last patrolled by Type II ducks in 1941.

- The first to put out, the *U-680,* commanded by Max Ulber, age twenty-seven, left Horten on August 14. Shortly after arriving in the area, on August 27, Ulber reported he had been detected and depth-charged. The damage, he said, was severe: smashed snort, periscopes, hydrophones, tanks, and valves. Forced to abort, he reached Bergen on September 8, lucky to return from a patrol of twenty-six days.
- The second boat to that area was *U-1199,* commanded by Rolf Nollmann, age twenty-nine. Sailing from Bergen on September 14, Nollmann remained continuously submerged for fifty days—probably a snorting record at the time—and, contrary to most reports, had nothing but praise for the device. ("Proved its worth to the full; personnel are enthusiastic," he wrote.) Nollmann spent thirty-one days in North Sea waters between Peterhead and Aberdeen. He claimed and was credited with sinking one 8,000-ton freighter but it was never confirmed in Allied records. His patrol, Control logged, proved conclusively that the "old type" U-boats fitted with snorts "could operate close off the coast."

In its continuing effort to build confidence in the snort, Control circulated widely Nollmann's "enthusiastic" endorsement of the device. However, Control soon felt the need to temper that endorsement with a strong caution, also circulated widely.

> Improper servicing while *Schnorcheling* has on several occasions led to smoking up of the U-boat and resulting injury to members of the crew from carbon monoxide gas. Several commanding officers report that evidence of poisoning does not appear until several hours after ventilation has taken place. General weakened

> condition of the crew is then so pronounced that surfacing and opening of the [conning] tower hatch is possible only by exerting the greatest energy. The bridge watch was barely in a condition to stand on its feet. In the case of one U-boat, these conditions did not appear until the U-boat had been ventilated for a half an hour on the surface after smoking up.

In the fall and early winter, twenty-five VIIs set off on the long voyage from Norway southabout Ireland to the English Channel, Bristol Channel, or Irish Sea. Two more skippers won the *Ritterkreuz* but nine were lost, a casualty rate of 36 percent. The stories in brief:

• The *U-246,* commanded by Ernst Raabe, age thirty-one, sailed from Kristiansand on October 7. On the twentieth day at sea, October 26, an unidentified Allied aircraft hit *U-246,* causing so much damage to the periscope and other gear that Raabe was forced to abort. The boat reached Stavanger on November 11.

• The VIIC41 *U-1006,* commanded by Horst Voigt, age twenty-four, sailed from Bergen on October 9. Near the Shetland Islands seven days later, on October 16, the Canadian Support Group 6 (six frigates) discovered her. One warship, the *Annan,* commanded by C. P. Balfry, fired eight close depth charges that severely damaged the boat and brought her to the surface. Another frigate, *Loch Achanalt,* got her on radar, whereupon *Annan* illuminated and attacked her with her main battery and smaller armaments and bore in to ram. Voigt shot a T-5 at *Annan* from his stern tube and returned fire with 20mm flak guns. The T-5 missed *Annan,* which closed rapidly and scored hits with her 4" guns and threw over more depth charges, one of which landed on the deck of *U-1006.*

Hopelessly trapped by *Annan* and the five other frigates, Voigt abandoned ship and scuttled. *Annan* and other frigates rescued forty-four of the fifty-two-man crew, including Voigt and two other officers. British intelligence attempted to plant disinformation with a turned German agent who reported that *U-1006* had hit a new minefield off southwest Ireland. However, Berlin scoffed at this report, noting accurately that the agent had been in England three years and was probably working for the enemy.

• The *U-978,* commanded by Günther Pulst, age twenty-six, also sailed from Bergen on October 9. Pulst avoided detection by the Allied ASW forces that had sunk *U-1006* and reached the English Channel about November 3, a snort voyage of twenty-four days. He then proceeded to the Allied landing area in the Bay of the Seine. In the five-day period from November 19 to 23, he attacked three convoys and claimed sinking three freighters for 22,000 tons. Control credited all the claims and after his return on December 16, awarded Pulst a *Ritterkreuz.* Allied records positively confirmed only one sinking, the 7,200-ton American Liberty ship *William D. Burnham.**

• The *U-1200,* commanded by Hinrich Mangels, who earlier had aborted a patrol to North Minch, sailed from Bergen on October 17 to join Pulst in the Bay of

---

* At the time of the award, his confirmed score was one ship for 7,200 tons.

the Seine. He did not get there. On November 11, the British hunter-killer Support Group 30 (four *Castle*-class corvettes), commanded by Denys Arthur Rayner, who had earlier lost his destroyer *Warwick* to a U-boat, detected the surfaced *U-1200* on radar south of Ireland. Rayner deployed his four corvettes (*Pevensey, Launceston, Portchester, Kenilworth*) line abreast. Mangels in *U-1200* dived and bottomed, but the corvettes destroyed the boat with depth charges and Squids. Rayner wrote that one of the Squids, fired from his flagship *Pevensey,* brought to the surface a "tin of oil with a Hamburg address on it." There were no survivors. Control was unaware of this loss until the boat failed to return to Norway in December.

- The *U-991,* commanded by Diethelm Balke, age twenty-five, sailed from Bergen one day after *U-1200,* October 18. The boat reached the English Channel about November 12 with orders to relieve Pulst in *U-978.* Off Cherbourg on November 27, Balke shot three torpedoes at what he reported to be a 14,000-ton troopship or supply ship and believed he got two hits for damage, but the claim could not be confirmed in Allied records. While homebound near the southern tip of Ireland on December 15, Balke attacked what he described as a 7,200-ton "Liberty ship" in an inbound convoy "running for port" and claimed he sank her. That success was never confirmed either. After seventy days at sea, he arrived in Bergen on Christmas Day, bedeviled by a broken snort. He returned *U-991* to Flensburg for refit and did not make another war patrol.
- The *U-1202,* commanded by Rolf Thomsen, age twenty-nine, sailed from Kristiansand on October 30. Control directed Thomsen on November 19 to enter Bristol Channel and patrol off Milford Haven. In that area on December 10, Thomsen attacked a convoy. He claimed the probable sinking of four big freighters for 26,000 tons, but only one, the 7,200-ton American Liberty ship *Dan Beard* was confirmed. Afterward Thomsen boldly stuck his nose into the Irish Sea for a look-see. Upon his return to Bergen on New Year's Day (with serious mechanical problems), Control credited his claims, praised his reconnaissance of the Irish Sea, and Dönitz awarded him a *Ritterkreuz.**
- The *U-680,* commanded by Max Ulber, who had earlier aborted a patrol to Moray Firth with depth-charge damage, sailed from Bergen on October 26 to patrol North Minch. However, after two weeks at sea, mechanical failures forced Ulber back to Bergen on November 8. When he resailed on November 13, Control directed him to patrol the English Channel off Cherbourg. Ulber reached that dangerous area but sank no ships and returned to Bergen on January 18, a luckless voyage of sixty-seven days. The *U-680* made no more war patrols.
- The VIIC41 *U-322,* commanded by Gerhard Wysk, age twenty-four, sailed from Horten on November 15 to patrol off Cherbourg. He never got there. Ten days out, on November 25, near the Shetland Islands, a Sunderland of Norwegian Squadron 330 and the British frigate *Ascension* teamed up to sink *U-322* with the loss of all hands. Unaware of the kill until the boat failed to return to Norway, Control assumed that Wysk was patrolling off Cherbourg or, if he had found conditions there unfavorable, off Milford Haven in Bristol Channel.

---

* At the time of the award, his confirmed score was one ship for 7,200 tons.

• The *U-400,* commanded by Horst Creutz, age twenty-nine, sailed from Horten on November 15. Creutz was also to patrol off Cherbourg, or if conditions there were unfavorable, Milford Haven. On December 17, Creutz found an inbound convoy, guarded by British Escort Group 18. As Creutz was closing to shoot, a frigate of that group, *Nyasaland,* commanded by A. E. Selby, got a strong sonar contact at 2,500 yards and attacked with ten depth charges and a Hedgehog. These missiles hit and destroyed *U-400* with no survivors. Control was unaware of this loss as well, until the boat failed to return to Norway.

• The *U-772,* commanded by Ewald Rademacher, age twenty-six, who had taken the boat on one weather patrol from August 13 to October 6, sailed from Trondheim on November 19. Much was expected of Rademacher, who was directed to patrol off Cherbourg or, failing there, Milford Haven. Living up to Control's expectations, Rademacher attacked three separate convoys off Cherbourg. From these he sank or destroyed four confirmed ships for about 21,100 tons: the 7,200-ton British troopship (LSI) *Empire Javelin,* crammed with 1,500 soldiers;* the 7,200-ton American Liberty ship *Black Hawk,* beached, a total wreck; and two British freighters, the 5,100-ton *Dumfries* and the 1,500-ton *Slemish.* In addition, Rademacher damaged the 7,200-ton American Liberty ship *Arthur Sewall.*

Rademacher did not, however, survive to savor these considerable victories. On December 30, a Leigh Light–equipped Wellington of Canadian Squadron 407, piloted by its leader, C.J.W. Taylor, spotted *U-772*'s snort "on the calm sea in the moonlight," as the official Canadian historian W.A.B. Douglas put it, and straddled her with six depth charges. These destroyed *U-772* with the loss of all hands.

• The *U-1209,* commanded by Ewald Hülsenbeck, age twenty-four, sailed from Kristiansand on November 24. Control directed Hülsenbeck to patrol off Cherbourg, but he did not make it there.

While scouting the waters off Land's End on December 18, Hülsenbeck ran aground at Wolf Rock and wrecked the boat. The astonished lighthouse keeper flashed an alarm via radio and a "running commentary" en clair. Two Canadian frigates, *Montreal* and *Ribble,*† which arrived an hour and a half later, and some British motor launches rescued forty-four of the fifty-one-man crew. The survivors included Hülsenbeck and the chief engineer, Hans Claussen, but Hülsenbeck died (of a "heart attack," the British reported) on *Montreal* and Claussen died later in a hospital.

Assuming the Germans had intercepted the lighthouse keeper's uncoded alarm and commentary, London released news of the wreck and captures from *U-1209* at once. Washington immediately questioned the wisdom of the release on the basis

* Because of smart seamanship and rescue operations, only six soldiers on *Empire Javelin* perished.

† Of the new Canadian hunter-killer Group 26. That group and the new Canadian Group 25, in effect, replaced in British waters the deactivated Canadian Group 12 and Group 11, disbanded when a storm wrecked one of its destroyers, *Skeena,* on rocks near Reykjavik, Iceland, on October 25, 1944, with the loss of fifteen men.

that the Germans may have missed the lighthouse keeper's traffic but they were not likely to miss a BBC broadcast. Upon learning that *U-1209* went on the rocks, the Germans would assume that Allied salvagers might get Enigma keys from the wreck and would therefore change the current keys. This, in fact, did happen: The Germans made an emergency Enigma key change effective at noon on December 21.

Inasmuch as many U-boats were patrolling in shallow water, Control soon expressed anxiety over Enigma security to all U-boats:

> Loss of U-boats in shallow waters gives the enemy the possibility of diving for cipher material and data. Make sure that cipher data are so kept that [sea] water can actually come into contact with the red print [on water-soluble paper]. When the Enigma machine is not in use, disconnect the plugboard, take out the [rotor] wheels and disarrange them. Keep everything concealed in separate places. See to it that key word orders are known to three officers only. Destroy at once slips of paper on which settings are figured. Lack of attention to these points may have unforeseeable consequences for the U-boat war.

• The sister ships *U-485* and *U-486,* commanded by Friedrich Lutz, age thirty-three, and Gerhard Meyer, age twenty-nine, respectively, sailed from Bergen to the English Channel in the last days of November. Lutz in *U-485* missed a "destroyer" and other targets, but the boat survived and returned to Norway after sixty-six days at sea, having achieved nothing.

Meyer in *U-486* also survived, but he conducted a lively and successful patrol. Inbound to Cherbourg on December 18, he sank from a convoy the 6,100-ton British freighter *Silverlaurel.* Three days later he shot a T-5 at a "destroyer" and claimed a sinking, but it was not confirmed. In the same area on Christmas Eve, Meyer hit the 11,500-ton Belgian troopship *Leopoldville* (under British charter), which was inbound to Cherbourg with 2,237 soldiers of the American 66th Infantry Division and a ship's company of 237 men. The British destroyer *Brilliant* took off about 850 soldiers, but *Leopoldville*'s Belgian crew prematurely abandoned ship and left the other soldiers to fend for themselves. When *Leopoldville* suddenly sank only five miles off Cherbourg, 801 men perished (785 soldiers; sixteen crew, including the captain), most in the icy water. Although 1,673 men were saved, it was one of the worst troopship disasters of the war and yet another little-known scandalous episode in British naval history.

Meyer was not yet done. On the day after Christmas, he shot three T-5s at what he described as two destroyer escorts and a corvette. He claimed sinking the two destroyer escorts and damage to the corvette. Allied records show that Meyer hit two frigates that day: the 1,100-ton *Capel,* which sank, and the 1,100-ton *Affleck,* which was damaged but survived and reached port, a total wreck.

If any U-boat skipper of those days deserved a *Ritterkreuz,* it was Gerhard Meyer for this patrol. He sank or destroyed four confirmed ships for 21,053 tons: two frigates, the troopship *Leopoldville,* and the freighter *Silverlaurel.* However, London and Washington clamped a tight security lid on the *Leopoldville* scandal and put out the disinformation that a "hospital ship," the *Amsterdam,* had been sunk off Cherbourg. As designed, this broadcast confused U-boat Control, threw Meyer's claims into doubt, and put a cloud on the patrol.

• The *U-275,* commanded by Helmut Wehrkamp, sailed from Bergen on December 2. She was the first of the boats that had evacuated from France in August to complete a refit and reenter combat. She did not get far. Nine days out, on December 10, she reported irreparable damage to her blowers and aborted, returning to Bergen on December 12.

• The *U-650,* commanded by Rudolf Zorn, sailed from Bergen on December 9. She was the second of the boats that evacuated from France in August to reenter combat. Zorn had orders to patrol off Cherbourg, but the boat disappeared without a trace. Allied and German authorities assumed she went down near the mouth of the English Channel in January but listed the cause of her loss as "unknown."

• The VIIC41 *U-325,* commanded by Erwin Dohrn, age twenty-four, sailed from Kristiansand on December 11. He patrolled the English Channel off Cherbourg but had no success and returned to Norway on February 14, a luckless patrol of sixty-six days.

• The *U-905,* commanded by Bernhard Schwarting, age thirty-one, also sailed from Kristiansand on December 11. Control assigned the boat to patrol the English Channel near the Bay of the Seine, but she did not get there. Forced by mechanical problems to abort, Schwarting returned to Norway on February 1, a fruitless voyage of fifty-three days. He resailed on March 13.

• The VIIC41 *U-1009* also sailed from Kristiansand on December 11. Normally commanded by Claus Hilgendorf, age thirty-two, the boat had aborted a prior patrol after six days, owing to serious snort defects. This time she sailed under command of a temporary skipper, Dietrich Zehle, age twenty-three, who came from sixteen months' war service on another VII.

Initially, Control ordered Zehle to carry out weather-reporting duty but owing to a defective radio antenna, the reports did not get through. When Zehle described the problem on January 1, Control directed him to take *U-1009* into the Irish Sea via North Channel, hugging the north coast of Ireland near Londonderry. He was to go southward to waters off Anglesey, England (opposite Dublin), then withdraw via North Channel after two weeks.

However, when Control learned from a German "spy" on January 14 that the Allies had planted new minefields in North Channel, Zehle's orders to patrol the Irish Sea were rescinded. He returned via the longer route through the Faeroes-Iceland gap (rather than the Faeroes-Shetland gap) and reached Norway on February 8. Control "severely criticized" him for taking the longer route, and Zehle went on to other duty.

• The *U-1055,* commanded by Rudolf Meyer, age twenty-four, also sailed from Kristiansand on December 11. Control directed Meyer to go southabout Ireland and patrol Land's End and Milford Haven, and then go northward into the Irish Sea to Anglesey. While carrying out these orders, Meyer found plenty of action and claimed four, possibly five, sinkings for 21,000 tons plus. Allied records confirmed four sinkings for about 19,400 tons: the 8,200-ton British tanker *Maja,* the 7,200-ton American Liberty ship *Jonas Lie,* the 2,600-ton American freighter *Roanoke,* and the 1,400-ton British freighter *Normandy Coast.*

Meyer was to patrol home via the Irish Sea and North Channel, but these orders were rescinded when Control received the "spy" report of the new minefields. He reached Norway on February 8, completing a patrol of sixty days—one of the most successful of that time.

• The VIIC41 *U-1172,* commanded by Jürgen Kuhlmann, age twenty-four, sailed from Kristiansand on December 23. Control directed Kuhlmann to enter the Irish Sea via North Channel and patrol south to Anglesey, then return to Norway by the same route. When Control got the "spy" report of the minefields, it rescinded these orders and directed *U-1172* to go southabout Ireland into St. George's Channel, thence into the Irish Sea and return to Norway the same way.

Kuhlmann had a brief but lively patrol. On January 21 and 23, he sank two small Norwegian freighters off Anglesey: the 1,200-ton *Galatea* and the 1,600-ton *Vigsnes.* On January 27, British hunter-killer Support Group 5, composed of the American-built British destroyer escorts *Bligh, Keats,* and *Tyler,* found and sank *U-1172.* There were no survivors.

• The *U-285,* commanded by Konrad Bornhaupt, sailed from Bergen for her second patrol on December 20. Like Kuhlmann in *U-1172,* Bornhaupt had orders to go southabout Ireland to St. George's Channel, thence northward into the Irish Sea near Anglesey and to return to Norway via North Channel. After the "spy" report of new minefields in North Channel came in, Control rescinded the orders for *U-285* to return via North Channel and told Bornhaupt to come home southabout Ireland. Bornhaupt found no targets and reached Norway on January 31, a patrol of forty-three days.

• The *U-764,* commanded by Hans-Kurt von Bremen, sailed from Bergen on the day after Christmas. She was the third of the boats that had left France in August to return to combat. Control sent her to patrol in the English Channel off Cherbourg. Von Bremen had no success and returned to Norway on February 10, a fruitless cruise of forty-seven days. The boat did not sail again until May 1.

• The *U-825,* commanded by Gerhard Stoelker, age thirty-four, sailed from Kristiansand on December 29. Control directed Stoelker to go southabout Ireland and patrol through St. George's Channel to Anglesey in the Irish Sea. Although the record is not clear, it is likely that while in St. George's Channel, on January 27, he hit two ships of the inbound fast convoy Halifax 332, the 8,300-ton Norwegian tanker, *Solör,* which beached, a total wreck, and the 7,200-ton American Liberty *Ruben Dario,* which limped into port. Stoelker returned southabout Ireland to Norway on February 18, a patrol of fifty-two days. He resailed *U-825* on April 3, too late to achieve anything.

• The *U-1051,* commanded by Heinrich von Holleben, age twenty-five, also sailed from Kristiansand on December 29. Control likewise directed von Holleben to go southabout Ireland to St. George's Channel to the Irish Sea near Anglesey. It is just possible that von Holleben in *U-1051,* who was close by Stoelker in *U-825* on January 27, also hit *Solör* or *Ruben Dario* or both. The speculation cannot be resolved because warships of one of the six hunter-killer groups that the Admiralty deployed in this area of the Irish Sea sank *U-1051* that same day with the loss of all hands. In a postwar reassessment, the Admiralty credited this kill to the American-built British destroyer escorts *Alymer, Bentinck, Calder,* and *Manners.* During the fight, von Holleben hit *Manners* with a T-5, but she made port.

- The VIIC41 *U-1017,* commanded by a new skipper, Werner Riecken, age thirty-two, also sailed from Kristiansand on December 29. Control directed the boat to patrol the English Channel off Cherbourg and the Bay of the Seine. In a busy and effective cruise, Riecken claimed sinking four freighters for about 25,000 tons plus possibly a corvette. Allied records confirmed three freighters sunk off Portsmouth and Falmouth, respectively: the 7,200-ton British Liberty ship *Fort Douglas,* the 5,200-ton British *Everleigh,* and the 5,400-ton Belgian *Persier.* Riecken also may have sunk the 7,200-ton American Liberty ship *Sibert.* He returned to Norway on February 28, completing a quite successful patrol of sixty-two days.

Three Type VIIs preparing to sail on first war patrols from Norway in late 1944 did not make it. The new VIIC41 *U-1276,* commanded by Karl-Heinz Wendt, age twenty-four, hit a mine outside Kristiansand on November 16 and had to abort for repair. On the night of December 28–29, about two hundred aircraft of RAF Bomber Command raided Horten. Bombs hit the *U-682* and *U-735,* commanded by Sven Thienenmann, age thirty-two, and Hans-Joachim Börner, age twenty-six, respectively. The *U-682* was severely damaged and returned to Hamburg, where in March other Allied bombers destroyed her. The *U-735* was sunk with the loss of most of the crew, including skipper Börner.*

In order to deter—or eliminate—British aircraft-carrier attacks on the Norwegian naval bases and inshore waters, and possibly to add to the impact of Hitler's upcoming December 16 Ardennes offensive by sinking a carrier or two, Dönitz directed Control to blockade the British naval base at Scapa Flow. Eight snort boats were designated for this important "anticarrier" task, two from the Atlantic force and six from the Arctic. The upshot was another humiliating fiasco for the *Kriegsmarine.* In brief:

---

* Losses in the Baltic continued. On December 12, the VII *U-479,* commanded by Friedrich-Wilhelm Sons, age thirty-four, hit a mine in the Gulf of Finland and sank with the loss of all hands. On the same day, the school boat VII *U-416* collided with a German minesweeper and sank. Five crew survived, but not the skipper, Eberhard Rieger, age twenty-one. Late in the month, the Hamburg-built Type XXI electro boat *U-2508,* commanded by the youthful Uwe Christiansen, age twenty-four, sank in a diving accident during workup. The boat was raised in due course but too late in the war to be of any use. Christiansen went on to command of the small Type XXIII electro boat *U-2365.* Another small Type XXIII electro boat, *U-2342,* hit a mine and sank. Four men were rescued. Allied air raids on Hamburg on December 31 and January 17 destroyed the new, combat-ready Type VII *U-906,* and destroyed or badly damaged four Type XXI electro boats nearing completion: *U-2515, U-2530, U-2532,* and *U-2537.*

• The VIIC41 *U-1020* of the Atlantic force, commanded by Otto-Emil Eberlein, age thirty-one, sailed from Kristiansand on November 24. Eberlein loitered for twenty-five days in the vicinity of Scapa Flow but saw nothing to shoot. On December 30, Control directed him to leave Scapa Flow and patrol the North Sea off northeast Scotland in Moray Firth. The next day, December 31, Eberlein hit the 1,700-ton British destroyer *Zephyr* but she limped into port. The *U-1020* was never heard from again. Allied authorities listed the cause of her loss as "unknown." German authorities believed she hit a mine.

• The VIIC41 *U-297* of the Atlantic force, commanded by Wolfgang Aldegarmann, age twenty-four, sailed from Kristiansand on November 26. It was thought that eleven days later, on December 6, warships of British hunter-killer Support Group 19 and Sunderlands of British Squadron 201 teamed up and sank *U-297* with the loss of all hands. However, in a recent reassessment, the Admiralty declared her loss to unknown causes. Unaware of the loss, on December 30 Control directed Aldegarmann to leave Scapa Flow, enter North Minch, and patrol for carriers off the British naval base at Loch Ewe!

• The Arctic boat *U-739,* commanded by Ernst Mangold, age twenty-seven, sailed from Trondheim on December 16. En route to Scapa Flow, the boat's port diesel failed beyond repair, forcing Mangold to abort to Trondheim. He arrived on December 21, after merely five days at sea. He then returned the boat to the Baltic for refit and left for other duty. Refurbished, the *U-739* returned to the Arctic force commanded by a new skipper.

• The Arctic boat *U-312,* commanded by a new skipper, Friedrich-Georg Herrle, age thirty-four, sailed from Trondheim on December 13. Off Hoxa Sound, the main entrance to the Scapa Flow anchorage, strong currents forced *U-312* on the rocks and smashed her rudder. Skillfully steering the boat by her diesels and electric motors, Herrle returned *U-312* to Trondheim on January 3, and went to other duty. After repairs, the boat returned to the Arctic force, commanded by a new skipper.

• The Arctic boat *U-737,* commanded by a new skipper, Friedrich August Gréus, age twenty-three, who came from long service on the lost VIID (minelayers) *U-214* and *U-217.* He left Narvik on December 6 and entered Trondheim on December 10. Control relieved him of the assignment to Scapa Flow because of his inexperience in command, and directed Gréus to return *U-737* to Narvik. While entering that place on December 19, a German minesweeper accidentally rammed and sank *U-737.* Gréus and nineteen of the crew survived.

• The Arctic boat *U-315,* commanded by Herbert Zoller, age twenty-five, sailed from Trondheim on Christmas Day. While en route to Scapa Flow, Zoller's starboard diesel failed and he was forced to return to Trondheim on January 6. After repairs, this Arctic boat was transferred to the Atlantic force.

• The Arctic boat *U-278,* commanded by the veteran Joachim Franze, age twenty-six, sailed from Trondheim on December 12. Nine days later Franze entered Bergen with a defective periscope. After repairs, he resailed to Scapa Flow on Christmas Eve. On January 14, after two arduous and luckless weeks off Scapa Flow, Franze requested permission to shift to the North Sea off northeast Scotland as far south as the Firth of Forth. Concluding that the Scapa Flow operation was futile, Control granted the request.* Franze returned *U-278* to Norway on February 11.

• The Arctic boat *U-313,* commanded by Friedhelm Schweiger, age twenty-seven, sailed from Trondheim on December 23. After two stressful and fruitless weeks off Scapa Flow, Control also authorized Schweiger to shift to the North Sea off northeast Scotland, patrolling as far south as the Firth of Forth if he so desired. He sank no ships in these waters and put into Norway on February 15. After a refit he returned the boat to the Arctic force.

So ended the important Scapa Flow "anticarrier" operation. Both VIIC41s of the Atlantic force that participated (*U-297, U-1020*) were lost. One of the six boats transferred from the Arctic force was rammed and lost (*U-737,* returning to Narvik). Three Arctic boats (*U-312, U-315, U-739*) aborted with mechanical difficulties. Only two boats (*U-278, U-313*) carried out full patrols to Scapa Flow and northeast Scotland and returned to Norway. The total damage inflicted on the Allies by these boats was minuscule: the British destroyer *Zephyr* damaged by Eberlein in *U-1020;* possibly two freighters, *Bestik* and *Ashbury,* hit by Franze in *U-278.*†

Nine Type VII snort boats sailing from Norway carried out other special missions. In addition to the aforementioned *U-772* and *U-1009,* five VIIs conducted weather-reporting patrols for the benefit of the *Luftwaffe* and German Army. Three survived (*U-245, U-396, U-1053*), but two were lost:

• The new *U-925,* commanded by Helmut Knoke, age thirty-eight, which sailed from Kristiansand on August 24. The boat was never heard from again. German authorities believed she hit a mine on or about September 18 in the Iceland-Faeroes gap while attempting to enter the Atlantic.

• The *U-248,* commanded by a new skipper, Johann-Friedrich Loos, age twenty-three, which sailed from Trondheim on December 3. Initially Control directed Loos to patrol the English Channel but on December 20, it rescinded those orders and Loos went to an area northwest of the Azores to become the "south" weather reporter for the benefit of Hitler's December 16 Ardennes offensive. When Allied codebreakers provided information on this change of mission for *U-248,* the American hunter-killer Support Group 62 (four destroyer escorts) sailed from the Azores to hunt her down.

The group apparently found *U-248* on January 8. Loos reported that he shot at a "corvette" that day, then eluded his hunters. Stressing the vital importance of the weather reports to the *Luftwaffe* and German Army units in the Ardennes offensive,

---

* Although the record is unclear, it is possible that Franze torpedoed two freighters: the 2,700-ton Norwegian *Bestik* and the 3,900-ton British *Ashbury,* the latter a total loss.

† Irreparable damage to German radio security resulted from the Scapa Flow fiasco. American codebreakers reported in a memo that Control radioed one of the U-boats off northeast Scotland "instructions for deciphering a specially enciphered message" that had previously been sent to two other U-boats. That priceless information enabled the Americans "to read these two special ciphers," and, the codebreakers concluded at that time, "it now appears that others may soon be broken."

Control authorized Loos to shift two hundred miles to the north if the hunter-killer group remained persistent. Loos was unable to shake the group and on January 16, the warships sank *U-248* with the loss of all hands and fished out "clothing, books, flesh and debris" for proof of the kill. Allied authorities gave credit for the victory to all four American destroyer escorts: *Hayter, Hubbard, Otter,* and *Varian.*

Control diverted two other experienced VIIs to special missions. These were the *U-722,* commanded by Hans-Heinrich Reimers, age twenty-eight, and the *U-773,* commanded by Hugo Baldus, age twenty-three. Both sailed from Norway in mid-October with a load of antitank weapons and ammo for the German garrison holding out at St. Nazaire. Baldus in *U-773* reached that port on November 18; Reimers in *U-722* on November 20.

After each boat took on fuel, 3.2 tons of valuable cargo, and four dockyard specialists, they sailed from St. Nazaire on December 7. Both returned to Bergen: Reimers in *U-722* on December 29, Baldus in *U-773* on January 10.

The sixty-eight Type VII snort boats that sailed for war patrols from Norway in the "new U-boat war" from July to December 1944 achieved little in meaningful damage to Allied shipping. Sixteen boats were lost, thirteen on first patrols. Eighteen starts ended in aborts. Fourteen of the fifty-one boats sank or destroyed twenty Allied ships for 98,600 tons in the last six months of 1944 and eleven ships for 53,600 tons in the early weeks of 1945. This was a total of thirty ships for 147,895 tons sunk or destroyed, including seven warships.* Thirty-seven sank no confirmed ships.

When viewed in the larger prospective, the results of the VIIs in the "new U-boat war" were virtually negligible. However, the reappearance of U-boats close to their coasts rattled the ordinarily imperturbable British. These new snort boat operations led to exaggerated fears, unfounded threat inflations, and unreasonably dire forecasts about the probable effectiveness of the impending campaign by the Type XXI and Type XXIII electro boats. In fact, the chief contribution by these Type VII snort boats was to terrorize the Admiralty, punch-drunk from almost five and a half years of naval warfare.

Type IX Snort Boat Patrols from Norway: 1944

Seventeen Type IX snort boats sailed from Germany via Norway to the Atlantic to add impact to the "new U-boat war" from July to December 1944.† All were new

---

* The damaged British "jeep" carrier *Thane,* not repaired during the war; British frigates *Affleck, Bullen, Capel, Manners* (damaged and not repaired), and *Whitaker;* British corvette *Hurst Castle.*

† Not counting three new IXD2 U-cruisers, *U-862, U-863,* and *U-871,* bound for the Far East. The *U-862,* commanded by Heinrich Timm, age thirty-four, actually sailed from Norway on June 3, sank five ships for 28,000 tons, won a *Ritterkreuz* for its captain, and reached Penang on September 9. Near the Azores on September 26, a B-17 of British Squadron 220, commanded by Arthur Francis Wallace, sank the *U-871,* commanded by Erwin Ganzer, age thirty-five. There were no survivors. Off Brazil on September 29, two B-24s of U.S. Navy Squadron VB 107, piloted by John T. Burton and Edward A.

boats. Some stopped in Norway briefly to repair battle damage or to make voyage repairs or top off fuel tanks. Owing to the lack of facilities in Norway, returning IXs had to go on to Germany for refits.

Inasmuch as the Type IX snort boats were unsuitable for operations in British coastal waters and there were no more U-tankers to support patrols to remote waters, Control sent most of them to Canadian waters and several to the areas between Gibraltar and the Azores. One of the latter sailed only to report weather. Several reported weather while going to or returning from Canada. From September 12, Control authorized the use of the *Elektra-Sonne* "beam" navigational system, which employed seven shore-based transmitting stations, including one in "neutral" Spain.

These were arduous and stressful patrols, very hard on the crews. The boats had first to travel from Kiel to Wilhelmshaven to Norway, dodging enemy mines and enduring saturation Allied air coverage. As related, Allied aircraft damaged one of the seventeen IXs, *U-865,* which had aborted three times in July and August. The facilities in Norway were still limited, and all were the targets of Allied air raids. Another RAF Bomber Command raid on Bergen on the night of October 28–29 by fifty-one Lancasters left the dockyards "a total loss," Control logged. Some IXs had to conduct further snort training in Norwegian waters. Snort accidents and failures remained commonplace.

Upon leaving Norway for the North Atlantic, the IXs cruised on batteries and the snort for about 1,500 miles to an area south-southwest of Iceland that was safer from air attack. Generally during that leg, the skippers ran submerged on batteries during the twenty hours of "daytime" and snorted during the four hours of semi-darkness or darkness, making good about fifty or sixty miles a day. Hence the voyages to and from safer open Atlantic waters took three weeks or longer. Those boats proceeding to Canadian waters had to resume this crawling pace when they approached the Newfoundland Bank, so that the one-way four-thousand-mile transatlantic voyage from Bergen, Norway, to Halifax, Nova Scotia, might take six weeks or longer.

Later in the fall, those boats making the voyage to Canada bucked the usual hostile and stormy weather in the North Atlantic. By October it was again freezing cold not only topside but also belowdecks. The boats encountered ice and snow storms. Never reliable at best, the snorts in Canadian waters iced up severely, adding new challenges. Communications with Control were poor.

The seventeen patrols, in brief:

- The IXC40 *U-855,* commanded by Prosper Ohlsen, age twenty-six, sailed on July 3 to relieve a weather boat, the new IXC40 *U-858.* In addition to weather reports, both boats had orders to provide fuel to two Type IXs returning to Norway from the Caribbean, *U-516* and *U-539.* The Allies decrypted Enigma and DFed radio messages relating to the refueling rendezvous and put "jeep" carrier hunter-killer groups on the scent, but they had no luck. After refueling *U-539,* the returning weather boat *U-858,* commanded by Thilo Bode, age twenty-six, set a course for German waters to refit. On September 19, unidentified Allied aircraft hit her

---

Krug, sank the *U-863,* commanded by Dietrich von der Esch, age twenty-nine. The pilots dropped life rafts to the "fifteen or twenty" Germans, but none survived.

hard but she managed to limp into Flensburg on October 4. After refueling *U-516,* Ohlsen in *U-855* also set a course for home waters, but on about September 18, the boat possibly hit a mine and sank with the loss of all hands.

• The IXC40 *U-1229,* commanded by Armin Zinke, age thirty-six, sailed from Kiel on July 13. Zinke had embarked a forty-two-year-old *Abwehr* agent, Oskar Mantel, whom he was to land on the coast of the United States, probably in Maine or Massachusetts. After that "special task" had been completed, he was to conduct an antishipping patrol in Canadian waters. Zinke topped off his fuel tanks in Norway and sailed from there on July 17, but a serious snort failure forced the boat into Trondheim on July 20. A week later she finally snorted off for Canada.

Allied U-boat trackers DFed the position of *U-1229* on August 8 and put the "jeep" carrier *Bogue* hunter-killer group on her trail. About noon, on August 20, an Avenger from *Bogue,* piloted by Alex X. Brokas, found *U-1229* on the surface and attacked with rockets. These missed but Brokas dropped two close depth charges that hurled five flak gunners overboard and forced Zinke to crash dive. He remained submerged for two hours, but the explosions had wrecked thirty-five battery cells and he ran out of power and had to surface. Six aircraft from *Bogue* were waiting and attacked immediately with machine guns and depth charges, a wild melee that probably killed Zinke and his first watch officer. The engineer, Willy Büttner, scuttled the boat. *Bogue* escorts rescued forty-one of the fifty-nine Germans and took them to Argentia. One died en route.

The agent, Oskar Mantel, wearing a *Kriegsmarine* uniform and wounded in three places, was among the forty German survivors. When he was identified, the FBI found an old file on him and J. Edgar Hoover requested that the Navy turn him over to his agency so that his American "contacts" could be ascertained and arrested. Concerned that Hoover would publicize the capture of this "spy" and that American POWs might be turned over to the Gestapo in reprisal, the Navy kept Mantel unpublicized and treated him like other POWs until 1947, when he was repatriated. He was never tried for being a German "spy," and therefore the purposes of his mission so late in the war have never come to light.

• The IXC40 sister ships *U-1221* and *U-1223,* commanded by Paul Ackermann, age twenty-four, and Albert Kneip, age twenty-three, respectively, sailed on antishipping patrols to Canadian waters on August 20 and 28, respectively. When Allied codebreakers alerted Tenth Fleet to the threat, the "jeep" carrier *Core* hunter-killer group searched doggedly but failed to find either boat.

Control ordered Ackermann in *U-1221* to patrol off Halifax, Nova Scotia. While inbound to that place on September 24, a bizarre event occurred. A disgruntled troublemaker in the crew, Emil-Heinz Motyl, went up to the bridge and leaped overboard. Ackermann did not believe—or did not wish to admit—that Motyl was a suicide, but he offered no plausible explanation. In any event, the patrol of *U-1221* was a notable failure. Ackermann spotted numerous warships, troopships, and cargo vessels and attacked several from a distance, but hit none. Upon his return to Flensburg on November 26, completing a barren patrol of ninety-nine days, Control criticized Ackermann for his failure to close and attack more aggressively.

Control directed the other boat, Kneip in *U-1223,* to patrol the mouth of the St.

Lawrence River. Off Pointe des Monts on October 14, he hit the Canadian frigate *Magog* with one of two T-5s and blew off sixty feet of her stern, killing three men. Other warships and tugs towed *Magog* to Quebec City, where she was decommissioned and eventually sold for scrap. In the same area about three weeks later, on November 2, Kneip hit the 7,200-ton Canadian grain ship *Fort Thompson* with a torpedo, but she survived the blast, which the Canadians initially ascribed to a mine. Kneip returned to Flensburg on December 14, completing a patrol of 109 days.

• The IXC40 *U-865,* commanded by Dietrich Stellmacher, which, as related, had aborted three times in July and August, finally got away on September 8. It was thought that twelve days later, September 19, a B-24 of British Squadron 206 sank *U-865.* The aircrew reported seeing "about twenty" German survivors in dinghies, but none was ever recovered. In a postwar reassessment, the Admiralty withdrew credit for the kill and declared that *U-865* was lost to unknown causes.

• The IXC40 *U-867,* commanded by Arved von Mühlendahl, age thirty-nine, sailed from Norway on September 12. His mission was to plant another automatic weather station on Labrador. However, the boat came under air attack and also had severe mechanical failures. On the eighth day, von Mühlendahl radioed Control that both diesels were out, his battery was completely dead, and he needed a tow back to Norway.

Control mounted a rescue mission by other U-boats to get the crew of *U-867* and the weather station, but it failed. A B-24 of British Squadron 224, piloted by P. M. Hill, hit one of the rescue boats, the IXC40 *U-1228,* commanded by Friedrich-Wilhelm Marienfeld, age twenty-four. Limping into Norway, his snort failed and felled him and most of the crew. Meanwhile, another B-24 of British Squadron 224, piloted by H. J. Rayner, found and sank the helpless *U-867,* reporting "fifty survivors in dinghies." None was ever recovered.

• The IXC40 *U-1227,* commanded by Friedrich Altmeier, age twenty-four, sailed from Bergen on September 12. When the boat surfaced on September 30 south of Iceland, Control directed her to patrol in the area between Gibraltar and the Azores.

En route to that place on October 4, Altmeier came upon convoy Outbound North (Slow) 33, composed of fifty-two ships and six escorts. In an astonishing display of aggressiveness and boldness, he commenced a lone night surface attack on the convoy by the light of a full moon. Predictably, an escort detected *U-1227* and with several others pursued her for an hour, firing star shells. In defense, Altmeier shot a T-5 at one of the "destroyers," which was, in fact, the 1,400-ton Canadian frigate *Chebogue.* The T-5 hit and inflicted severe damage, but the Canadian frigate *Ribble* and Canadian corvettes *Arnprior* and *Chambly* and some British vessels came to her assistance and got her under tow. Seven days later, on October 10, a full gale struck the crippled ship in St. George's Channel near Swansea Bay. The *Chebogue* grounded at Port Talbot, Wales, and was not repaired.

Pressing southward, Altmeier in *U-1227* had a lively patrol. Aware of her mission from Enigma decrypts, Tenth Fleet put the *Card* hunter-killer group on her track. On October 12, two destroyer escorts of the *Card* group harassed *U-1227* with gunfire, depth charges, and Hedgehogs for three hours but Altmeier finally shook them. While snorting two hundred miles west of Gibraltar on October 31, Altmeier came upon "one large and one small warship" that may have been out hunting U-boats. He fired all four bow torpedoes, but two misfired and the other two missed.

Nine days later, the *U-1227* very nearly came to grief during an attempt to attack another convoy on November 8. While she was at periscope depth, escorts detected and pounced on the boat with depth charges. These inflicted such heavy damage that Altmeier had to withdraw westward to make repairs. Three days later, another hunter-killer group found *U-1227* snorting and attacked with depth charges. The additional damage forced Altmeier to abort to Norway. Near Rockall Bank the snort broke down, but the crew repaired it and *U-1227* reached Bergen on the day after Christmas, completing a stressful patrol of 106 days.

• The IXC40 *U-1230,* commanded by Hans Hilbig, age twenty-seven, sailed from Kiel on September 26. Her first task was to land two more *Abwehr* agents, William C. Colepaugh and Erich Gimpel, at a remote site on the coast of Maine. Thereafter she was to conduct an antishipping patrol off Halifax, Nova Scotia. En route to Norway, Hilbig incurred many snort malfunctions, causing nosebleeds and other discomforts. One snort failure knocked out eight men in the engine spaces and, unknown to Hilbig, popped open the entire canned milk supply, a calamity that was not discovered until much later at sea.

Hilbig sailed from Norway on October 8 and fifty-one days later, made a landfall on Cape Cod on November 27, and proceeded to Frenchman's Bay in the Gulf of Maine. In the late evening of November 29, two crewmen of *U-1230* rowed Colepaugh and Gimpel ashore in a rubber dinghy at Hancock Point. From there, the two agents trudged through snow to a road. A high school senior, Harvard Merrill Hodgkins, who was returning by car from a dance, noted these strangers and their unusually thin clothing considering the weather. The next day he told his father (a deputy sheriff of Hancock County) about the men and later, the FBI, which was aware from Enigma decrypts that *U-1230* was to carry out a "special task" and suspected another agent insertion.

Colepaugh and Gimpel eluded the manhunt and reached New York City by train with $60,000 in cash and ninety-nine small diamonds. They rented an apartment, bought new clothes, and partied. Apparently regretting his spying role, Colepaugh, who was born and raised in New England, revealed his mission to a childhood friend, then, on the evening of December 26, gave himself up to the FBI. Following leads provided by Colepaugh, FBI agents found and arrested Gimpel in New York City on the evening of December 30. Both agents were tried for espionage, found guilty, and sentenced to death, but in the postwar years, President Truman commuted the death sentences.

During the extensive interrogations of Colepaugh and Gimpel, the Americans got the impression that perhaps Germany had developed U-boats capable of firing big rockets and that a fleet of these U-boats might attack the United States in early 1945. This was not true and technically infeasible, but the Americans took the news seriously and laid elaborate plans to track and intercept the fleet, just in case. This disinformation, which caused the diversion of considerable numbers of American ships and manpower, was the only known service Colepaugh and Gimpel performed on behalf of the Third Reich.

After landing the two agents, Hilbig in *U-1230* sank the 5,500-ton Canadian steamship *Cornwallis.* American ASW forces, including the "jeep" carrier *Bogue* hunter-killer group, scoured the Gulf of Maine, but Hilbig took *U-1230* north to the waters off Nova Scotia and eluded his hunters. He returned to Flensburg in late January 1945 and did not sail on another war patrol.

• The IXC40 *U-1226,* commanded by August-Wilhelm Claussen, age twenty-five, sailed from Norway to Canada on September 30. However, when Claussen reported on October 22 that the snort lifting gear failed and he had to raise it by means of block and tackle, Control directed *U-1226* to cancel the trip to Canada and serve as a provisional weather boat in the area well south of Iceland from about October 27. He was to try to get the snort upright for the trip home but not to try to snort in his remote corner of the Atlantic.

Nothing further was ever heard from *U-1226.* In spite of repeated reminders from Control that weather reports were "urgently needed," she broadcast none. Finally it was presumed that the boat was lost by accident south of Iceland, probably due to the defective snort.*

• The IXC40 *U-1228,* which had been hit by a British B-24 in September during the futile attempt to rescue the crew of the lost IXC40 *U-867,* resailed from Norway for Canada on October 12. Having been badly bombed during trials in the Baltic as well, the skipper, Friedrich-Wilhelm Marienfeld, was properly respectful of Allied ASW aircraft and patrolled with due caution.

Control directed *U-1228* to operate in the mouth of the St. Lawrence River. Shortly after midnight on November 25, Marienfeld came upon the veteran Canadian corvette *Shawinigan* inside the Gulf of St. Lawrence, and hit her with a T-5. The warship blew up and sank with the loss of all eighty-five hands. Thereafter, Marienfeld, ignoring new orders to patrol off Halifax, reversed course and left the gulf through Cabot Strait to the open Atlantic, and on December 8, reported his success, as well as a snort and compass failure, and his decision to terminate the patrol. By radio to all U-boats, Control "publicly" rebuked Marienfeld for failing to reach the St. Lawrence River notwithstanding snort and other problems. This unhappy boat reached Flensburg on January 4, 1945, completing a patrol of eighty-five days. Marienfeld retained command.

• The IXC40 *U-1231,* commanded by Hermann Lessing, age forty-four, the oldest U-boat skipper on active service, sailed from Norway to Canadian waters on October 15 to continue the U-boat campaign in the mouth of the St. Lawrence River.

---

* In June 1993, two Bostonians, Edward Michaud and Paul Matthias, claimed with absolute certainty that they had found the wreck of *U-1226* in forty-one feet of water, four miles off Cape Cod. According to these men, the media reported, *U-1226* was "part of a four-submarine squadron on a spy mission," and was sunk by a single fifty-pound bomb from an aircraft based at Hyannis. Authorities in the United States, Germany, and Canada threw cold water on this "find," asserting that if the men had indeed found a U-boat, which was unlikely, it was certainly not *U-1226.*

Owing to winter weather and to the ice buildup and the curtailment of convoys between Quebec City and Sydney and vice versa, Lessing had a frustrating time. His snort "constantly iced up" and his "torpedoes malfunctioned." In the St. Lawrence River off Matone, he shot three torpedoes at a freighter and others at an escort, but all were duds, he reported.

Control, on December 2, gave *U-1231* freedom to leave the gulf and patrol off Halifax if Lessing so desired. He withdrew via Cabot Strait, but owing to an overly pessimistic miscalculation of the fuel supply by the chief engineer, he set a course for home. When the error was discovered, Lessing backtracked to Halifax, having lost six days. Patrolling off Halifax at Christmastime, Lessing chased ships in the freezing cold but had no luck at all. On January 3, he headed for home a second time and arrived in Norway on January 30, completing an utterly fruitless patrol of 108 days.

• The IXC40 *U-806,* commanded by Klaus Hornbostel, age twenty-eight, sailed from Norway on October 30 to patrol off Halifax. After a diversion to weather reporting, the boat arrived in the assigned area on December 13, a voyage of four thousand miles in forty-five days.

Hornbostel nudged *U-806* very close to the marked channels leading in and out of Halifax. He navigated by the glare of the city lights, the nearby lighthouses and lightships, and the channel buoys that the officers named for their spouses or girl friends. On the night of December 21, he fired a salvo of two torpedoes at a 7,200-ton British freighter, the *Samtucky.* These and a finishing shot missed but a T-5 hit. Although damaged, *Samtucky* was able to beach herself near Halifax and was later repaired and returned to service.

Hornbostel found plenty of action over the next seventy-two hours. On December 22, he shot three torpedoes at a freighter and her corvette escort, but all missiles malfunctioned or missed. On Christmas Eve, the *U-806* sighted two converging convoys. Hornbostel shot a T-5 at one of the convoy escorts, the 672-ton Canadian minesweeper *Clayoquot.* It hit and destroyed this small warship, which sank in nine minutes. Another torpedo aimed at a freighter exploded harmlessly on the Cat Gear of the Canadian minesweeper *Transcona,* which then pulled seventy-six of *Clayoquot*'s eighty-four-man crew from the frigid waters. Hornbostel eluded a massive ASW counterattack and slipped away submerged southeasterly to celebrate Christmas.

After that busy period, the *U-806*'s luck ran out. On January 4, her snort-lifting gear failed, making it impossible to lower the mast and forcing Hornbostel to abort. Eastward of Newfoundland Bank his men got the snort back in working order, but because of a diminishing fuel supply, the boat headed for Norway. Control again diverted the boat to weather reporting and, as a result, she did not reach Norway until February 22, completing an arduous voyage of 116 days, of which about ninety-three days were spent in transit and reporting weather.

• The IXC40 *U-1232,* commanded by Kurt Dobratz, age forty, sailed from Norway to Halifax on November 12. She was the last U-boat to reach the Nova Scotia area in 1944.

A onetime *Luftwaffe* pilot, Dobratz was an enthusiastic skipper with a great sense of humor. He arrived off Halifax after Christmas, when Hornbostel in *U-806* and Lessing in *U-1231* were still in the area. Determined to outdo all the U-boat skippers who had sailed to Canada in the fall of 1944, Dobratz took up a favorable shooting station in shallow water off Chebucto Head, practically athwart the main channel leading into Halifax.

He found no shortage of action. In the period from January 2 to 3, he shot a T-5 at a "destroyer" and three other torpedoes at the big Dutch troopship *Nieuw Amsterdam.* He claimed sinking the "destroyer," but it was not confirmed in Allied records. The torpedoes he shot at the *Nieuw Amsterdam* exploded harmlessly in her wake, leading Control to believe that she and other important Allied troopships towed a noisemaking decoy, but that could not be confirmed.

The next day, January 4, Dobratz found better shooting. A coastwise Canadian convoy, SH 194, en route from Sydney to Halifax, suddenly hove into view. It was composed of the small Canadian tanker *Nipiwan Park* and two small freighters, escorted by the corvette *Kentville* and an aircraft. Dobratz missed the lead freighter, *Perast,* but hit the 2,400-ton *Nipiwan Park* and the 1,600-ton Norwegian freighter *Polarland.* The tanker broke in half and the freighter went straight down. Dobratz claimed he saw both halves of the tanker sink, but, in fact, tugs salvaged her stern and towed it into Halifax. Dobratz claimed two ships for 13,500 tons, but in actuality he sank or destroyed two ships for 4,000 tons.

Allied ASW forces mounted a massive hunt for *U-1232,* but Dobratz slipped away and, as he said later, "laid on the bottom for ten days." During that nerve-racking, uncomfortable time, the 18,000-ton hospital ship *Llandovery Castle,* en route from Halifax to Naples, Italy, passed directly overhead. Dobratz rose to periscope depth to have a look, but upon establishing the identity of the ship, he let her pass unmolested.

Finally, on January 14, Dobratz crept back to the shooting grounds off Chebucto Head, bedeviled by the constant icing up of the snort and periscope. He was rewarded, however, almost immediately by the appearance of a convoy, BX 141, en route from Boston to Halifax, composed of nineteen merchant ships, plus escorts. Boldly closing this tempting formation, Dobratz shot torpedoes at four different ships, two tankers and two freighters. He claimed sinking all four for 30,400 tons, but in actuality he hit three. These were two British tankers, the 7,000-ton *British Freedom* and the 8,800-ton *Athelviking,* and one American Liberty ship, the 7,200-ton *Martin Van Buren.* The two tankers sank; the Liberty beached, a total wreck.

This attack very nearly led to the loss of *U-1232.* One of the escorts, the Canadian frigate *Ettrick,* counterattacked and ran down the U-boat. Before Dobratz could get deep, *Ettrick* rammed her upper works. The collision bent the periscope flat over, tore up the bridge, and carried away the radio-antenna wires. Allied ASW forces again mounted a massive hunt, but Dobratz slipped away and set a course for Norway.

When *U-1232* reached the open waters of the Newfoundland Bank, Dobratz reported his actions and damage to Control. Granting his claims (three tankers and three freighters for 43,900 tons plus a "destroyer"), Dönitz happily awarded him a

Ritterkreuz by radio on January 23. His confirmed score was five ships: three for 17,400 tons sunk (*Polarland, British Freedom, Athelviking*) and two for 9,500 tons wrecked. This was the best patrol of any Type IX sailing from Norway in the six months from July to December 1944, and far and away the best of the Type IX patrols to Canada. Dobratz reached Norway on February 14, completing a patrol of ninety-six days.

• The IXC40 *U-870,* commanded by Ernst Hechler, age thirty-seven, sailed from Kristiansand on November 12 to the Gibraltar-Azores area to report the weather for Hitler's December 16 Ardennes offensive. To avoid Allied ASW measures, Hechler remained well west of the French and Portuguese coasts. However, by the time he reached his assigned area, on December 17, weather reports were no longer vital and Control directed Hechler to close the Strait of Gibraltar and attack shipping.

Hechler, another onetime *Luftwaffe* pilot who had never made a war patrol, carried out an aggressive first cruise. West of Lisbon on December 20, he attacked a special convoy of American landing craft and escorts. He claimed a corvette and two LSTs for 6,000 tons sunk. Allied records confirmed the 1,400-ton *LST 359* sunk and a severely damaging hit on the American destroyer escort *Fogg,* which killed four men and wounded two. Subsequently, *Fogg*'s stern sheared off, but a skeleton crew got her into the Azores under tow. Still later, tugs towed her to Boston, where she was repaired. An aircraft of the Azores-based British Squadron 220 attacked *U-870,* but Hechler eluded the plane and two British hunter-killer groups.

Closing the western approaches to the Strait of Gibraltar, Hechler was not shy. On January 3 he attacked a convoy en route from Gibraltar to the United States, GUS 63, and damaged the 7,200-ton American Liberty ship *Henry Miller,* which, however, reached Gibraltar under tow. In the period from January 8 to 10, Hechler boldly attacked three more convoys. He claimed a corvette, a 6,000-ton tanker, and a 4,000-ton freighter sunk and damage to a 6,000-ton freighter. Allied records confirmed as sunk only a 335-ton ex-American patrol craft in service with the Free French, *L'Enjoue* (an escort of the Gibraltar-Casablanca convoy GC 107) and the 4,600-ton freighter *Blackheath* (in the British Isles–Mediterranean convoy KMS 76), which beached at Cape Spartel.

Control happily credited all of Hechler's claims and on January 21 Dönitz awarded him a *Ritterkreuz* by radio.* He reached Norway on February 20 and went on to Flensburg for refit. A month later, on March 30, American bombers destroyed *U-870* in Bremen.

• The IXC40 *U-877,* commanded by Eberhard Findeisen, age twenty-eight, sailed from Kristiansand on November 26 to relieve *U-870* as the "south" weather boat. While she was outbound from Norway on the surface with escorts, Beaufighters of British Squadron 489 attacked *U-877* and dropped two nearby depth charges. In the crash dive that ensued, the retractable "mattress" antenna of the boat's *Hohentwiel* radar was ruined, so the boat was handicapped for the entire patrol.

---

* At the time of the award, his confirmed sinkings, all on *U-870,* were three ships for 6,462 tons, including *LST 359,* the small French patrol craft *L'Enjoue,* and the freighter *Blackheath.* He also damaged two American ships, the destroyer escort *Fogg* and Liberty ship *Henry Miller.*

For the next three weeks, *U-877* crawled along, making no more than sixty to eighty miles per day. On about December 22, she reached her weather-reporting area. However, her radio failed; she could receive but could not transmit messages. It was believed she was lost, but in case she was not, Control released her from weather reporting and gave her complete freedom of movement. Upon receipt of these instructions, Findeisen chose to proceed west to the New York area.

Two days after Christmas, on December 27, the Canadian corvettes *Edmundston* and *St. Thomas,* commanded by L. P. Denny, got sonar contacts on *U-877. Edmundston* tracked but concluded the contact was not a U-boat. *St. Thomas* was of much the same mind, but persisted and finally fired her Squid. On a second deliberate pass on the contact, *St. Thomas* made another Squid attack. Some of these missiles hit *U-877* and she plunged nose-first out of control and flooding to almost one thousand feet. In a last-ditch effort to save her, Findeisen blew all ballast tanks, and the boat rose "violently" from that great depth to the surface.

When Findeisen opened the conning-tower hatch, the built-up internal air pressure blew him and the quartermaster through the hatch onto the bridge, and they both fell to the deck with severe head injuries. After the engineer scuttled, the two corvettes rescued all fifty-five Germans and took them to England. The Admiralty credited the Canadian *St. Thomas* with the kill.

- The IXC40 *U-869,* commanded by Helmut Neuerburg, age twenty-seven, sailed from Kristiansand on December 8. By the end of the third week, December 29, the boat should have reached the Atlantic via the Iceland-Faeroes gap, but Control had not received the customary signal ("passage report") indicating this to be the case. Several queries to the boat at the time went unanswered, causing worry at Control. Nonetheless, Control directed *U-869* to proceed west and conduct anti-shipping operations off New York. This message also went unanswered, causing "considerable anxiety" at Control, per the war diary of January 3.

The *U-869* was one of the boats fitted with the high-speed ("burst") radio transmitter *Kurier.* She had conducted *Kurier* trials in the Skaggerak from November 26 to December 1 with six other boats. These trials were technically difficult and not completely successful. However, Control directed *U-869,* which was to serve first as a weather boat (Number 3) for the Ardennes offensive, to transmit only by *Kurier.* It is possible that *U-869* sent her "passage report" by *Kurier* and Control did not receive it.

Having heard nothing from *U-869* by January 6, Control was almost certain that the boat was lost. That day, however, in response to repeated queries from Control to state her position, *U-869* responded that she was in grid square AK 63, about six hundred miles southwest of Iceland. This message caused further puzzlement at Control. Had the boat followed the usual route through the Iceland-Faeroes gap, the war diary stated, "she should have been considerably further southwest." Control concluded that on the basis of fifty-five miles per day, the boat must have proceeded to the Atlantic via the Denmark Strait, an unorthodox choice. Furthermore, the absence of weather reports from her for the Ardennes offensive was a grave matter indeed.

Control was in a quandary. Assuming the long passage to the Atlantic had consumed much fuel, Control doubted she had enough left to patrol New York. It directed *U-869* to report her fuel reserves immediately "so that a decision can be taken as to allocation of an operational area." Again there was no response from *U-869,* "in spite of continuous queries." Absent any messages, on January 8 Control directed *U-869* to carry out a snort patrol off Gibraltar, west of grid square CG 9592, but to go no closer to the strait. Either the boat did not respond to this change of orders or it did so by a *Kurier* message or by a conventional message that Control did not receive. Nothing further was ever heard positively from *U-869.*

Control *assumed* the boat had complied with this change in orders. On February 18, it logged that *U-869* had sent a B-bar convoy contact report and had sunk a ship off Gibraltar. Almost a month later, March 16, Control again logged that *U-869* had possibly sent another B-bar message from the Gibraltar area.

American codebreakers who decrypted these messages were likewise puzzled. Kenneth Knowles in the Submarine Tracking Room assumed from the December 29 orders from Control that *U-869,* identified by the bigram Oboe Item (OI), was headed for New York. The codebreakers intercepted the report of January 6 from *U-869* (Oboe Item) that she was in grid square AK 63, but they missed Control's message of January 8 redirecting the boat to Gibraltar. However, on January 19, the codebreakers decrypted a message from Control to *U-869* stating that she was to arrive about February 1 off the operational area of *U-870,* which they knew to be a boat that had been sent to Gibraltar earlier.

Knowles speculated from what he knew positively that "maybe" *U-869* "had missed" an "Ursula" signal* redirecting her to Gibraltar and that she was in fact still headed for New York. Accordingly, Tenth Fleet directed two "jeep" carrier hunter-killer groups built around *Core* and *Croatan* to hunt down *U-869.* Neither group had any success. Nor was there ever any indication that *U-869* had, in fact, reached the New York area.

Allied authorities finally concluded that *U-869* had indeed received the message and had patrolled off Gibraltar and never returned. Lacking any positive evidence of her demise, they speculated that she may have been sunk by the American destroyer escort *O'Toole* on February 26, about 175 miles northeast of the Madeira Islands. In the final reckoning, however, the Allies concluded that *U-869* had been lost while attempting to attack convoy GUS 74. The attack failed and five escorts pounced on what was later believed to be *U-869:* the American Coast Guard–manned frigate *Knoxville;* two American destroyer escorts, *Fowler* and *Francis M. Robinson;* and two ex-American patrol craft, the Free French *L'Indiscret* and *Le Résolu.* The Allied assessment committee officially credited this "kill" to *Fowler* and *L'Indiscret.*

This is where matters stood until September 2, 1991. That day, a group of amateur shipwreck divers, led by William Nagle and John Chatterton, dived on a wreck 230 feet down, sixty miles east of Point Pleasant, New Jersey. The wreck resembled a submarine. In two subsequent dives that fall, the divers recovered crockery bowls dated 1942 and marked with the eagle and swastika, and a dinner knife with

---

* Ursula, Knowles logged, was a "new type short signal" probably used to designate U-boat operational areas and was as yet unreadable by Allied codebreakers.

the name "Horenburg" carved in the wooden handle. Exploring the boat at this extreme depth, one of the scuba divers, Steve Feldman, apparently passed out and was swept away.

In subsequent years, John Chatterton led further diving expeditions to the U-boat. Two more divers died in these excursions, but Chatterton and his team recovered pieces of wreckage that identified the boat as a Type IXC, built at the Deschimag shipyard in Bremen (as was *U-869*), remains of a snorkel head, an escape lung tested April 15, 1944, and finally, in 1997, a box with a tag marked *U-869.* This last, together with a sailing list showing that the owner of the knife, Martin Horenburg, was chief radioman on *U-869,* was convincing proof that the U-boat was indeed *U-869.*

What had happened? As Kenneth Knowles initially speculated, *U-869* doubtless had missed Control's message redirecting her to Gibraltar and had continued westward to the New York area. From the condition of the wreck (port side amidships blown away) Chatterton believes that *U-869* shot a torpedo at a ship; the torpedo missed, malfunctioned, circled back, and struck the U-boat, not an uncommon mishap in the U-boat force. Of course, the fatal blow could have been delivered as a result of an Allied ASW ship or aircraft attack that has not yet come to light.*

• The last large snort boat to leave Norway in 1944 for war patrol was the IXC40 *U-1233,* commanded by Hans-Joachim Kuhn, age thirty-four. After two aborts, Kuhn finally got away to the Americas on Christmas Eve. He patrolled via Bermuda to the area between the Gulf of Maine and Nova Scotia. On March 4, he radioed Control a terse situation report, stated his intent to begin his homeward journey, but made no sinking claims.

Upon receipt of this message from *U-1233,* Control declared it to be "entirely insufficient" and demanded greater detail for the benefit of other Type IXs en route to that sector. Kuhn returned to Norway on March 28 and went on to Flensburg for refit. The boat did not sail again on war patrol.

These seventeen Type IX patrols from Norway in the last six months of 1944 accounted for fifteen confirmed Allied ships sunk or destroyed for 57,346 tons. The victims included six warships† and nine tankers or freighters. One skipper, *Ritterkreuz* winner Dobratz in *U-1232,* sank five of the nine merchant ships. Ten U-boats (59 percent) sank no ships.

Although the snort offered good concealment from Allied aircraft and all skippers used radio transmitters sparingly or the *Kurier* "burst" system, and some of the boats had *Hohentwiel* (Owl) search radar and *Fliege* and *Mücke* radar detectors,‡

---

* Chatterton reports that he and his teams have meticulously avoided the human remains inside the boat.

† The Canadian frigates *Chebogue* and *Magog,* Canadian corvette *Shawinigan,* Canadian minesweeper *Clayoquot,* American *LST 359,* and Free French patrol craft *L'Enjoue.*

‡ *Fliege* (Fly) covered the eight to two centimeter wavelengths out to thirty-seven miles; *Mücke* (Gnat), two to four centimeters. When the sets were combined in May 1944, the resulting detector was called *Tunis.*

German losses were no fewer. Seven of the seventeen boats failed to return, a casualty rate of 41 percent. British land-based aircraft got two (*U-865, U-867*); aircraft of the "jeep" carrier *Bogue* got one (*U-1229*); Canadian surface forces got one (*U-877*); one (*U-855*) probably hit a mine; and two were lost to unknown causes: *U-869* and *U-1226,* the last most likely to a catastrophic snort failure. There were seventy-three survivors from the approximately 350 men on these seven boats, all captured.

Altogether, in the "new U-boat war," from July to December 1944, Control mounted eighty-five war patrols from Norway: sixty-eight by VIIs, seventeen by IXs. Only about one-quarter of the patrols (twenty-two) produced sinkings or destruction of shipping: fourteen by VIIs, eight by IXs. The confirmed sinkings in these twenty-two successful patrols came to forty-six ships for 205,893 tons: thirteen warships and thirty-three merchantmen. In return, twenty-two U-boats were lost: sixteen VIIs and six IXs. This was an "exchange rate" of about one U-Boat lost for every two merchant ships sunk. About one thousand German submariners were lost in these boats; 169 were captured from four.*

Except for the terror and consternation they caused and the Allied forces they tied down, these snort boats had no significant impact on Allied maritime assets, which continued to swell at an awesome rate. During the same period, July to December 1944, American shipbuilders alone turned out 867 new vessels for about 6 million gross tons, or about thirty times more new tonnage than was lost to U-boats. In all of 1944, U-boats sank only sixteen of the 18,856 Allied-controlled ships that sailed in North and Middle Atlantic convoys.†

* *U-877, U-1006, U-1209, U-1229.*

† See Plates 12 and 13.

NINE

ARGONAUT

Hitler's Ardennes offensive, launched on December 16, split the American and British ground forces and threatened briefly to reach Antwerp, its first major geographical objective. Within thirty days, however, Allied forces recovered from the blow, counterattacked, and severed the German salient at Houffalize. Little more than one week later, on January 28, five American corps, comprising twenty-one divisions, launched a major offensive eastward toward Germany in freezing cold and deep snow. Despite the weather and other obstacles, by the early days of March, American forces had reached the Rhine River and captured a bridge at Remagen.

Meanwhile, on January 12, the Red Army launched a massive offensive westward toward Germany. By February 1, Soviet troops were firmly entrenched at the Oder River, merely fifty miles from Berlin. Behind them, German enclaves at Danzig and Königsberg held out in order to buy time to evacuate finished and partly finished Type XXI electro boats, other new U-boats in workup or older ones in school flotillas, as well as torpedoes, submarine personnel, and hundreds of thousands of German refugees.

Countless *Kriegsmarine* vessels of all sizes and types carried out the evacuation by sea. German naval records reveal that German ships evacuated 2,116,500 persons, 1,668,000 refugees and 448,500 military personnel. Owing to Allied air attacks, British aerial minelaying,* and Soviet submarine attacks, scores of German ships were damaged or sunk. Soviet submarines sank three big German troop transports loaded with troops and refugees. The loss of life was the worst of the war at sea: 6,200 on the 5,200-ton *Goya;* 5,500 on the 25,500-ton *Wilhelm Gustloff;* and 2,700 on the 15,000-ton *General Steuben.*

The war in Europe was rushing to a conclusion. The impending end of this unprecedented horror raised scores of military and political questions. Would the Soviet Union at last enter the war against Japan? If so, when and at what price? How would the Allies divide areas of responsibility and influence in postwar Europe?

As the Battle of the Bulge slowly and agonizingly turned in favor of the Allies, Prime Minister Winston Churchill urged another "Big Three" meeting (Argonaut) between President Roosevelt, Joseph Stalin, and himself to settle some of the many unresolved wartime and postwar issues. At Stalin's insistence, they agreed to meet in early February at Yalta, a Black Sea resort in the Crimea, where long ago the Czars had summered.

At Norfolk on January 23, President Roosevelt and his personal staff boarded the new (1943) heavy cruiser *Quincy,* which had participated with distinction in both the Neptune and Dragoon invasions. The sailing arrangements to Malta were personally supervised by the new commander of the Atlantic Fleet, fifty-eight-year-old Admiral Jonas Ingram, a close friend of Admiral King's. A football star at the Naval Academy (1907), Ingram had dutifully commanded the unglamorous but necessary U.S. Navy Fourth Fleet based in Natal, Brazil, for two years† and was in line for four stars. Among other tactful steps, Ingram included the old light cruiser *Savannah* in the presidential escort. Admiral King's son, Ernest Joseph, Jr., served on the *Savannah.*

It was agreed that Roosevelt and Churchill and their military staffs would first meet on the Mediterranean island of Malta (Cricket) to resolve any differences, so that at Yalta (Magneto), they could present Stalin with a united front. Admiral William D. Leahy, Chairman of the U. S. Joint Chiefs of Staff, accompanied Roosevelt on the *Quincy.*‡ Admiral King flew via Bermuda to Casablanca (where he met with Dan Gallery, who had captured *U-505*), thence by plane to Malta. General Marshall flew via the Azores to Marseilles, France, where he met with General Eisenhower on January 28, the day of the momentous Allied counterattack in the Battle of the Bulge. The next day Marshall flew on to Malta. The chief of the Army Air Forces, Hap Arnold, was ill and could not make the trip.

---

* According to Jürgen Rohwer and Gerd Hümmelchen *(Chronology),* in January, February, and March, RAF aircraft in 720 sorties planted 3,240 mines, a menace that sank 67 ships for 137,764 tons and damaged 32 ships for 71,224 tons and caused widespread evasive action and minesweeping.

† Ingram had officially relieved the sixty-one-year-old four-star admiral Royal Ingersoll on November 15, 1944. Ingersoll went on to a sinecure, the Western Sea Frontier. He retired on August 1, 1946, Ingram on April 1, 1947.

‡ While on board the *Quincy,* on January 30, Roosevelt celebrated his sixty-third birthday. He was the youngest of the senior American delegates. Leahy was sixty-nine, King sixty-six, Marshall sixty-four.

The Churchill party departed London on January 29 in three aircraft, Churchill in a plush four-engine, American-built Douglas C-54 Skymaster (the military version of the DC-4 airliner), a gift from Hap Arnold.* As the aircraft neared Malta, one of them developed serious problems and crashed near the island of Pantelleria. "Only three of the crew and two passengers survived," Churchill wrote. "Such are the strange ways of fate."

When the Americans and British delegates convened in Malta to discuss military operations, the main—and most contentious—subjects were Allied ground and air command and operations in the European and Mediterranean theaters and the Pacific. Nonetheless, the U-boat menace in the Atlantic Ocean was not neglected.

And with good reason. By January 1945, the Allies were deeply concerned about a renewed U-boat offensive that might seriously imperil the ground offensive toward Germany from the west. President Roosevelt in his State of the Union address on January 6 had stressed the possibility of a renewed U-boat offensive. Three days later, Roosevelt and Churchill issued a joint communiqué on the same theme. The media on both sides of the Atlantic had published and broadcast alarmist stories reflecting these dire forecasts.†

The lugubrious forecasts were based on faulty or incomplete Allied intelligence and—whether sincere or calculated—on a classic instance of threat inflation. Although the Allied intelligence failure did not appreciably influence the course of the war, as did the failures in the Pearl Harbor attack and Hitler's December 16 Ardennes offensive (the Battle of the Bulge), it is worth noting.

Some of the factors that led to the intelligence failure were:

- The assumption that on January 1, 1945, there were eighty-seven big Type XXI electro boats fitting out or in workup and another fifty-two under construction, and that by March 1, fifty Type XXIs were to be ready in all respects to launch the new offensive.

This estimate vastly overcredited the ability of the Germans to build, debug, and work up Type XXIs in the face of intensified Allied air raids on U-boat yards and bases, the heavy mining of training areas in the Baltic, adverse winter weather and ice in the Baltic, not to mention the widespread chaos throughout besieged Germany.‡ Moreover, Allied intelligence apparently failed altogether to discover promptly that the Type XXIs were crippled by the failures of the engine supercharger scheme, the hydraulic systems, and other defects.

In reality, no Type XXI was anywhere near ready for operations on March 1.

---

* The plane was a sister ship of Roosevelt's famous "Sacred Cow," on which Harry Hopkins had flown to London. In the Pacific, General Douglas MacArthur had another, "Bataan."

† Hadley, *U-boats Against Canada* (1985), cites newspaper articles depicting an oncoming wave of two hundred to three hundred "Nazi subs" that could remain submerged for up to thirty days at a speed of 10 knots.

‡ On January 12, American Army troops captured approximately twenty stern sections of Type XXI electro boats at a shipyard in Strasbourg on the upper Rhine River. These stern compartments could not be duplicated or replaced. This heretofore unrecorded capture was therefore as crippling to Type XXI production as were all the Allied air raids and the capture of the Danzig shipyards by Soviet troops.

PLATE 10

ALLIED BOMBER RAIDS ON ELECTRO BOAT ASSEMBLY YARDS IN HAMBURG, BREMEN, AND KIEL

DECEMBER 31, 1944–APRIL 14, 1945[1]

At the Malta/Yalta conferences in February 1945, the Allies, fearing a renewed U-boat campaign by snort boats and the Type XXI and Type XXIII electro boats, validated a plan for RAF Bomber Command and the U.S. Eighth Air Force to carry out heavy air raids on the electro boat assembly yards. Owing to the preference of the airmen to strike at other strategic targets, the need to support Allied forces engaged in the Battle of the Bulge, and poor flying weather, this campaign proceeded slowly.

These air raids are not to be dismissed as inconsequential. They resulted, finally, in the destruction of U-boat yards in Hamburg, Bremen, and Kiel. Nor should they be overrated. Germany was in chaos and collapsing and could not possibly mount and sustain a revitalized U-boat war. Moreover, the design of the Type XXI was so seriously flawed that it could not have played a role in a new, 1945, U-boat offensive and did not.

	TARGET	AGENCY	NUMBER OF AIRCRAFT	BOMBS (TONS)
DECEMBER 1944				
31	Hamburg	USAAF	72	187
JANUARY 1945				
17	Hamburg	USAAF	71	174
FEBRUARY				
17	Bremen[2]	RAF	6	12
18	Bremen	RAF	6	12
19	Bremen	RAF	5	10
21	Bremen	RAF	3	6
22	Bremen	RAF	6	12
24	Bremen	USAAF	195	576
25	Bremen	RAF	6	12
27	Bremen	RAF	6	10
MARCH				
4	Bremen	RAF	3	6
8	Hamburg	RAF	304	941
11	Bremen	USAAF	403	966
11	Hamburg	USAAF	466	1,089
11	Bremen	USAAF	403	965
11	Kiel	USAAF	340	850
20	Hamburg	USAAF	13	39
30	Bremen	USAAF	433	1,297
31	Hamburg	RAF	454	2,217
APRIL				
3	Kiel	USAAF	220	n/a
8	Hamburg	RAF	414	1,046
9	Hamburg	RAF	424	1,571
9	Kiel	RAF	359	n/a
13	Kiel	RAF	467	n/a
Totals	24 raids		5,079	11,998

1. Source: U.S. Strategic Bombing Survey, NARA, Record Group, 243, Box 47. U-Boat Control War Diary (KTB-BdU), 12/31/44.

2. The RAF attacks on Bremen with three to six aircraft were "precision" attacks by twin-engine, unarmored, very fast Mosquito bombers with 4,000-pound bombs.

Only one—repeat one—Type XXI was far enough along to leave the Baltic in March for further workup in Horten, Norway. That was the show boat *U-2511,* commanded by Adalbert Schnee, who wore Oak Leaves on his *Ritterkreuz,* and who had *Ritterkreuz* holder Gerhard Suhren for his chief engineer.* The boat sailed from Kiel on March 18 and arrived in Horten on March 23, at which time Schnee and Suhren requested that experts be sent there to fix the periscope, which oscillated badly, even at the slowest speed. The *U-2511* sailed from Bergen on April 18, but diesel-engine defects forced her to return on April 21. She finally resailed on April 30—about which more later.

• A similar miscalculation about the readiness of the duck-size Type XXIII electro boats. On January 1, 1945, Allied intelligence estimated there were forty-three Type XXIIIs fitting out or in workup and eighteen under construction in Kiel and Hamburg and that those yards had a combined production rate of ten boats per month. In reality, the commissioning rate of the Type XXIIIs from June to December 1944 averaged 4.4 boats per month. Less three losses during workup† by January 1, there were twenty-eight Type XXIIIs in commission. Only twenty more were to be commissioned by war's end, a total of fifty-one.

Four small Type XXIII electro boats carried out full war patrols by May 1. The first two, *U-2322* and *U-2324,* each made two patrols of about three weeks duration in the North Sea off the east coast of Scotland and England. The *U-2321* and *U-2329* each made one patrol to those same areas, the latter a cruise of merely fifteen days. A fifth boat, *U-2326,* attempted to carry out a patrol but had to abort a luckless cruise of ten days. In total, these five XXIIIs logged 178 patrol days. Altogether they sank five small British freighters for 8,542 tons and damaged the 7,200-ton Norwegian Liberty ship *Sverre Helmerson* and the British destroyer escort *Redmill.*

The Type XXIII electro boats also had numerous drawbacks and faults. The most severe drawback was their tiny size: 114 feet long, about 234 tons displacement. They were smaller even than the prewar and wartime Type II ducks. The XXIIIs had only two torpedo tubes—both forward—and no space for torpedo reloads, compared with three tubes forward and three reloads in the Type II ducks. The XXIIIs were so delicately balanced that after firing even one of the two torpedoes, they had a tendency to broach. The telescopic snorts on the XXIIIs, which were raised and lowered by a compressed-air system similar to that on the Type XXIs, were unreliable.

In sum, the Type XXIII electro boats were little better than useless. Their chief contribution to the German war effort was to confuse many in the Allied camp into thinking that they were more or less the equivalent of the larger Type XXI electro boats.

• A consistent tendency, even by some Allied submarine experts, to overvalue the snort and to underrate the severe immobility it imposed on the U-boat, and the snort failure rate of that era.

---

* Older brother of Reinhard Suhren, who wore Oak Leaves on his *Ritterkreuz* and commanded the Arctic and Central Group U-boat forces.

† *U-2323, U-2331, U-2342.*

Contrary to a widespread view in the Allied camp, U-boats did not snort continuously on diesel engines at speeds of 6 to 10 knots, making good 150 to 250 sea miles a day fully submerged. As related, they snorted at about 5 knots for only about four hours in twenty-four and they were lucky to make fifty or sixty miles a day. Therefore, it took a snort boat nearly eight weeks of a nine-week patrol to reach the English Channel from Norway and return, leaving barely one week for operations. Hence significantly larger numbers of snort boats were required to cover the sea areas and do the work that had been done in earlier and easier times by the nonsnort-equipped boats. Moreover, there was an acute shortage of upgraded, combat-ready Type VII and Type IX snort boats.

Foremost among the Allied submarine specialists who predicted that a very tough fight versus the new U-boats lay ahead in 1945 was the British admiral commanding Western Approaches, Max Horton. His deep but misplaced concern influenced seniors in the Admiralty to forecast extremely heavy Allied shipping losses in March 1945, perhaps heavier than the spike in the spring of 1943. If and when this occurred, First Sea Lord Andrew B. Cunningham warned the British Chiefs of Staff Committee that land operations on the Continent were bound to be adversely affected.

These overly pessimistic views greatly angered the Admiralty technocrats in charge of the anti–U-boat activities, particularly two senior division chiefs, N. A. Prichard and C. D. Howard-Johnston. They drafted a blistering attack on Max Horton. In part:

> At various meetings recently the Commander in Chief, Western Approaches, has made statements to the effect that he considers that we are worse off materially at the present moment, for means of locating and destroying U-boats, than we have been at any time during this war (and, he added on one occasion, "or the last war").
>
> These statements are, in our opinion, both untrue and misleading, and although the true state of affairs is no doubt appreciated by Their Lordships, we feel that such statements are bound to give a false impression when made in the presence of other senior officers and members of other services who may not be so well informed, and we feel it our duty to submit the true facts as they are known to us. . . .

At Malta, from January 30 to February 2, Roosevelt, Churchill, and the combined military staffs agreed to several important measures to deal with the renewed U-boat menace that they expected.

• A new strategic bombing directive that called for a significant increase in heavy-bomber air raids on U-boat construction and assembly factories, and shipyards and canals in Germany by RAF Bomber Command and the U.S. Eighth Air Force.*

• The doubling of the RAF mining of the U-boat workup areas in the Baltic, thereby driving more U-boat flotillas to abandon the eastern Baltic in favor of workup in the western Baltic, the Jade, and Norway, areas RAF aircraft could reach more easily.

---

* See Plate 10.

• Intensification of the RAF air campaign against U-boat bases in Norway and German surface shipping supplying those bases.

• The retention in home waters of about half of three hundred British destroyers and escort vessels that were earmarked for the Far East to support the war against Japan. Many of these vessels were deployed in new hunter-killer groups operating in the Minches, North Channel, Irish Sea, and English Channel.

• An increase in Coastal Command ASW squadrons from thirty-two to thirty-eight and a half, comprised of 528 aircraft, and the transfer of several Iceland-based squadrons to bases in Northern Ireland, Scotland, and England. These planes were to concentrate against likely U-boat routes to and from Norway to the British Isles and in the waters of the latter.*

• The laying by surface ships of seventeen thousand defensive mines in "deep" fields on the main Allied convoy routes, focal points in the Irish Sea, and on well-known "shallow patches," which it was assumed U-boats used for navigational purposes.

At first mystified by the public Allied forecasts of an intensification of the U-boat war, Admiral Dönitz finally concluded that these statements were part of a clever deception. He therefore informed Tokyo that

> [t]he sudden onset of a new U-boat war, as announced by the enemy, is not to be expected because we have already been in the new U-boat war since the equipping [of U-boats] with *Schnorchel*. . . . If the new U-boats fulfill our expectations of them, a gradual increase in the number of sinkings can be counted on, which will grow with the monthly sending of U-boats to the front. . . .
>
> The enemy continues to be afraid of the U-boat war and its intensification. By a tactical bluff—that is, repeated announcement of a new U-boat offensive—he is attempting, even though the offensive announced by him does not materialize, to give the impression that he has once again succeeded in becoming master of the U-boats.

The American and British parties, grown to about seven hundred persons (!), left Malta for Yalta on the night of February 2–3 in about twenty aircraft. President Roosevelt, Harry Hopkins, Averell Harriman, and others of the Roosevelt inner circle flew in his C-54, the "Sacred Cow." Churchill and his party flew in Churchill's C-54 sister ship. It was 1,400 miles to Saki airfield in the Crimea, a seven-hour flight. It took eight more hours to travel by auto the forty primitive and mountainous miles from Saki to Yalta, altogether a hideous trip that further eroded the health and spirits of Roosevelt, already gravely ill.†

This second and final meeting of Roosevelt, Churchill, and Stalin stretched over eight days from February 3 to February 10. The conferees agreed to a number

---

* Coastal Command still included U.S. Navy Fleet Air Wing 7. In January and February 1945, it consisted of five full B-24 squadrons: VB 103, VB 105, VB 107, VB 110, and VB 112; six "searchlight" B-24s of VB 114; and four MAD Catalinas of VP 63. Total aircraft: seventy. In 1944, the wing flew 7,732 ASW missions, covering six million statute miles in 35,580 hours of flight. During these missions, the aircraft attacked forty-five U-boats or presumed U-boats. A B-24 of VB 103 sank the VII *U-271*. A B-24 of VB 105 shared credit for the kill of the VII *U-243*.

† Churchill wrote that Roosevelt was "frail" and that he had only "a slender contact with life."

of fateful military and geopolitical decisions that had no bearing on the U-boat war and do not warrant extended discussion in this history. The most important of the military decisions was Stalin's pledge to enter the war against Japan "two or three months after Germany surrendered." The most important of the geopolitical decisions were Stalin's agreement to fully participate in the newly forming United Nations, the ratification of Soviet hegemony over Eastern Europe, including eastern Germany, which the Soviets had already overrun,* and the establishment of four Allied zones of occupation in postwar Germany.

At the conclusion of the conference, Roosevelt and Churchill traveled by auto on February 11 to Sevastopol, a three-hour trip over rough roads. Both spent the night on headquarters and communications ships: Roosevelt on *Catoctin,* Churchill on the liner *Franconia.* The next day, Roosevelt returned by car over more primitive roads to Saki airfield. There he boarded the "Sacred Cow" and flew to Egypt, where he reboarded the heavy cruiser *Quincy,* and on February 14 held brief conferences with three kings: Farouk of Egypt, Haile Selassie of Ethiopia, and Ibn Saud of Saudi Arabia. Churchill left Sevastopol by car for Saki on February 14, boarded his own C-54, and flew to Athens. The next day he flew on to Alexandria, Egypt, where he established quarters on the light cruiser *Aurora* and had a final meeting with Roosevelt on the *Quincy.* The next day the *Quincy* set sail for the States. After an overnight stop in Algiers on February 18, *Quincy* reached Norfolk on February 27. Roosevelt returned to Washington where, on March 1, he addressed a joint session of Congress from his wheelchair. Churchill flew back to England on February 19 and on February 27, addressed the House of Commons, which approved his decisions at Yalta, although not unanimously. Admiral King and General Marshall, who were not permitted to fly in the same aircraft, returned to Washington by various means and routes.

It was obvious to everyone who saw President Roosevelt—including all of Congress on March 1—that he was gravely ill. On March 29, aides lifted him aboard his private train and he traveled to his favorite hideaway and spa, "the Little White House" in Warm Springs, Georgia. There, on April 12, he died of a massive cerebral hemorrhage. Vice President Harry S Truman assumed the positions of president and commander in chief.

U-boat Patrols in British Waters: 1945

Displaced to Norway, Heligoland, the Jade, and to western Baltic ports, the U-boat force, like its World War I predecessor, dutifully carried on until Germany finally gave up and capitulated.

As commander in chief of the *Kriegsmarine* in a desperately crumbling Germany, Grand Admiral Karl Dönitz could no longer give the U-boat war his undi-

* As related, by the time of the Yalta meeting, Soviet armies were poised at the Oder River, fifty miles from Berlin.

vided personal attention. The construction and readiness of the U-boats remained the responsibility of Admiral Hans-Georg von Friedeburg. At U-boat Control, Admiral Eberhard Godt, assisted by Dönitz's son-in-law, Günter Hessler, continued to plan U-boat strategy and tactics.

The remaining Type VII snort boats designated to carry on the naval war in the Atlantic were based in Norway. Hans-Rudolf Rösing, commander in chief, U-boats West, retained that title after the withdrawal from France to Norway. Reinhard Suhren retained the title of captain, U-boats North (Norway, Arctic). The VIIs were assigned to three combat flotillas: the 11th at Bergen, commanded by Hans Cohausz; 13th at Trondheim, commanded by Rolf Rüggeberg; and 14th at Narvik, commanded by Helmut Möhlmann.

The situation in Norway made it difficult to mount the VII war patrols. Unlike the French, the Norwegians, virtual prisoners of the Germans for nearly five years, remained hostile. Emboldened by the Allied pincers closing tightly on Germany, Norwegian resistance groups stepped up acts of sabotage against the German occupiers and their infrastructure. Allied aircraft repeatedly attacked the U-boat pens and dockyards at Bergen and Trondheim and the German shipping attempting to supply forces in Norway via the Kattegat and the inshore leads. British submarines joined in the antishipping campaign. Further complicating and endangering German naval operations, the RAF planted thousands of mines off the naval bases and in the leads.

Under this continual Allied pressure, most of the VIIs were forced to disperse widely in protective fjords and primitive ports, where refits and replenishing were difficult and hazardous. There were shortages of fuel oil, food, torpedoes, electronics, and competent repair and replacement personnel. Warmed by the last fingers of the Gulf Stream, the seas were ice-free, but everything else was cold, cold, cold, and assaulted by snow and ice.

Remarkably, the Germans were able to mount 145 U-boat patrols from Norway and Germany in the four months from January 1 to April 30, 1945. The boats were assigned as follows:

Area	*January*	*February*	*March*	*April*	*Totals*
North Atlantic	21	30	30	38	119*
Far East	3†	1‡	0	2§	6
Americas	0	5	8	5	18
Totals	24	36	38	45	143#

* Includes round-trips of the IXC40s *U-868* and *U-878* to France, taking supplies to the cut-off U-boat bases at Lorient and La Pallice. Also, the IXC *U-516,* which embarked from Norway on a similar supply mission, but did not reach France before the war ended.

† All *from* the Far East.

‡ One *to* the Far East.

§ One *to* the Far East; one *from* the Far East.

Accidents, air raids, and other calamities continued to plague U-boats in the Baltic and in Danish and Norwegian waters. A Soviet patrol craft sank the VII *U-679* in the Baltic. The VIIs *U-676* and *U-745* hit mines and sank in the Gulf of Finland. The VII *U-923* hit a mine in the Baltic and sank. The

As can be seen, the preponderance of Type VII snort-boat patrols from January 1 to April 31, 1945, were conducted in waters of the British Isles via the Atlantic: 113 of 119. The other six shown in the chart were mounted by four different tiny Type XXIII electro boats via the North Sea.

These Type VII snort-boat patrols, constituting the so-called "renewed" U-boat war, were difficult and unrewarding. Of the 113 that sailed, nearly half, fifty-six, manned by about 2,800 men, were lost to Allied ASW forces. Those authors who have written exuberantly that the snorkel gave the Germans a decided edge in the naval war should ponder well these figures. It was another terrible U-boat slaughter.

Nineteen VIIs sailed in January, eleven of them new boats making first patrols. Seven of the latter were the deep-diving VIIC41s. Six of these were new. The boats sank ten Allied ships for 30,726 tons. Ten U-boats (53 percent) were lost with about five hundred crew, of which forty-three were captured.* For every Allied ship sunk, one U-boat was lost, a ruinous exchange rate.

Some of the VIIs patrolled off North Minch, some off North Channel, and nine went to the English Channel. It should be stressed once again that the snort voyage between Norway and the English Channel was a long ordeal, usually taking about twenty-eight days each way, leaving only a brief time to patrol the channel.

Because the U-boats remained submerged about twenty hours a day and raised the snort for only four hours to charge batteries and air the boat, sightings and kills by Allied aircraft fell off drastically. Aircraft killed only nine U-boats in the North Atlantic in the period January through April. Catalinas and B-24s of the U.S. Navy's Fairwing 7 got three of these and shared credit for a fourth kill with British surface ships.

Some January VII patrols, in brief:

• In early January, the *U-245,* commanded by Friedrich Schumann-Hindenberg, who had made a weather patrol in the fall of 1944, sailed from Norway to the island of Heligoland to carry out a special mission, *Brutus.* This directed him to sail across the lower North Sea to the mouth of the Thames River and sink shipping. Fighting strong currents in shallow water and mines, Schumann-Hindenberg did in fact sink a ship: the 2,600-ton Dutch tanker *Liseta.* He returned to Heligoland to prepare for a second *Brutus* patrol.

• The *U-1199,* commanded by Rolf Nollmann, making his second patrol, sailed on New Year's Day. Three weeks later, near Land's End, he found coastal convoy TBC 43 and hit the 7,200-ton American Liberty ship *George Hawley.* The tug *Allegiance* towed her into Falmouth, a complete wreck. Two British warships,

---

VII *U-1053* failed to surface after her prepatrol deep-dive test. Entering Horten, the new VIIC41 *U-1273* hit a mine and sank with the loss of fifty-seven of her sixty-five crew and passengers. The VII *U-367* hit a mine in the Baltic off Hela and sank. Thinking the VII *U-235* was a Soviet submarine, a German PT boat depth-charged and destroyed her. Allied aircraft at Kiel sank the VIIs *U-236* and *U-237.* The XXIII electro boat *U-2344* collided with the XXIII *U-2336* and sank. Allied aircraft destroyed the XXIIIs *U-2340* and *U-4708* at Hamburg and Kiel, respectively. The XXI electro boat *U-3520* hit a mine off Kiel and sank. Allied aircraft destroyed the XXIs *U-2509, U-2514, U-2515, U-2516, U-2523, U-2530, U-2532, U-2537, U-2542, U-3003, U-3007, U-3508, U-3512.* And so on.

* From *U-300, U-1018,* and *U-1199.*

the destroyer *Icarus* and corvette *Mignonette,* pounced on and sank *U-1199* on January 21. One of the crew of forty-seven survived: Chief Quartermaster Friedrich Claussen.

• The veteran *U-275,* commanded by Helmut Wehrkamp, sailed on January 13. He incurred snort problems and put into Lorient on February 10. After repairs he resailed from France on February 25. Off the south coast of England on March 8, Wehrkamp sank the 5,000-ton British freighter *Lornaston.* The Admiralty believes that *U-275* struck a mine off Beachy Head two days later, March 10, and sank with the loss of all hands.

• The new *U-1208,* commanded by Georg Hagene, sailed from Norway on January 14. Over a month later, in St. George's Channel on February 20, Hagene sank the British corvette *Vervain,* from convoy Halifax 337.

Off the Lizard in the twilight of February 27, three ships of the famous British hunter-killer Support Group 2, the frigates *Labaun* and *Loch Fada* and sloop *Wild Goose,* got *U-1208* on sonar and attacked with depth charges, Hedgehogs, and Squids. Nothing further was ever heard from *U-1208.* The Admiralty apportioned credit for the kill among the three ships.

• The experienced VIIC41 *U-300,* commanded by Fritz Hein, making his third patrol, sailed from Trondheim on January 21. Since there were too many U-boats in the English Channel, Hein got permission to patrol off Gibraltar Strait. On February 17, he attacked convoy UGS 72 and damaged two ships, the 7,200-ton American Liberty ship *Michael J. Stone* and the 9,551-ton British tanker *Regent Lion.* Salvage vessels towed the *Regent Lion* into Tangier on February 19, where she was declared a total loss.

A British hunter-killer group composed mostly of corvettes got *U-300* on sonar on February 19, just west of the mouth of the strait and attacked. The depth charges—in particular those from the British yacht *Evadna*—severely damaged *U-300* and flooded the forward end. Hein remained submerged for as long as possible without periscopes or sonar gear, all wrecked by the depth charges. Finally, on the morning of February 22, he was forced to surface and, quite by coincidence, he came up in the middle of a convoy. Two astonished escorts, the minesweepers *Pincher* and *Recruit,* opened fire with all guns that would bear, killing Hein, his second watch officer, his engineer, and six others. The German survivors scuttled and jumped overboard, and the British ships rescued forty-one.

• The new VIIC41 *U-1018,* commanded by Walter Burmeister, sailed from Horten for the English Channel on January 21. Over a month later, on February 27, the boat intercepted a coastal convoy, BTC 81, off the Lizard and sank the 1,317-ton Norwegian freighter *Corvus.* The convoy escort counterattacked promptly, dropping 150 depth charges. Finally the British frigate *Loch Fada,* commanded by B. A. Rogers, got a good contact on U-1018 at 164 feet—sixteen feet off the bottom. *Loch Fada* fired a Squid that hit and blew a huge hole in the U-boat's side, instantly flooding the bow and stern compartments and the control room and killing nearly all of the crew. Five Germans rose to the surface, but three drowned. *Loch Fada* rescued one officer and one enlisted man, who described a scene of the utmost horror inside the doomed U-boat.

• The new *U-927,* commanded by Jürgen Ebert, sailed from Kristiansand to the English Channel on the last day of January. Off the Lizard on the evening of February 24, a Leigh Light–equipped Warwick* of British Squadron 179, piloted by Antony G. Brownsill, got a radar contact on *U-927*'s snorkel. The plane attacked from an altitude of seventy feet, dropping six depth charges at the snort in a perfect straddle. Nothing further was heard from *U-927.* Brownsill was later awarded a DFC.

Twenty-nine VIIs sailed from Norway in February, fifteen of them new boats making first patrols. Twelve were deep-diving VIIC41s. These boats sank sixteen Allied ships for 50,000 tons. Sixteen boats (55 percent) were lost with about eight hundred crew, eighty-eight of whom were captured.† For the second month in 1945, the Germans lost one U-boat for every Allied ship sunk, continuing the ruinous exchange rate.

Some February VII patrols in brief:

• The new VIIC41 *U-1302,* commanded by Wolfgang Herwartz, sailed from Norway on February 6. The boat snorted southabout Ireland, thence northeast into St. George's Channel to an area off Milford Haven. There on February 28, Herwartz sank two small freighters, the 1,926-ton Panamanian *Soreldoc* and the 646-ton British *Norfolk Coast.* In the same area three days later, on March 2, he sank two larger freighters inbound from the transatlantic Slow Convoy 167, the 4,536-ton British *King Edgar* and the 3,204-ton Norwegian *Novasli.* Total: four ships for 10,312 tons.

In terms of numbers of ships sunk, this was the best VII war patrol of 1945. However, the crew of *U-1302* did not live to savor the achievement. Five nights later, on March 6, in the same area, the frigate *La Hulloise* of the Canadian hunter-killer Support Group 25, northbound in the Irish Sea, got a radar contact on *U-1302*'s snorkel and periscope. Her skipper, John Brock, fixed a spotlight on the snort and periscope, forcing the U-boat deep. Brock did not attack but her alarm brought up two other frigates of the group, *Strathadam* and *Thetford Mines.* While the other two frigates held sonar contact, Howard Quinn in *Strathadam* made a perfect Hedgehog attack that destroyed *U-1302.* German food, books, clothing, shoes, snapshots, and "numerous other small objects," including a harmonica, rose to the surface, but no German survivors or bodies.

• The new *U-681,* commanded by Werner Gebauer, sailed from Kristiansand on February 16. En route to the English Channel on March 6, Gebauer shot a T-5 at an ASW trawler, but it missed. Five days later, on March 11, while running submerged, the *U-681* smashed into a rock near Land's End and was so badly damaged that Gebauer surfaced to abandon ship and scuttle. As it happened, a B-24 of U.S. Navy Squadron VB 103, piloted by Norman R. Field, spotted the stranded *U-681* and attacked from an altitude of one hundred feet, dropping eight depth

---

* A new production aircraft replacing the Wellingtons.

† From *U-399, U-681, U-1003,* and *U-1195.*

charges that destroyed the boat. The crew jumped into the water, some with dinghies. In response to Field's alarm, ships of British Support Group 2 came up and the frigate *Loch Fada* rescued thirty-eight Germans, including Gebauer. Pilot Field received both a British and an American DFC.

• The VIIC41 *U-1003,* commanded by Werner Strübing, sailed from Bergen for his second patrol on February 19. Control initially directed the boat to the English Channel but later it shifted the target area to North Channel and, possibly, the Irish Sea via that entryway. About seventeen days out, the snort blocked and felled a number of crewmen, but others made repairs while *U-1003* lay in a remote bay on the west coast of Ireland. Strübing, who was dispirited and defeatist, according to some of his crewmen, reluctantly resumed the patrol.

While snorting off Loch Foyle, the waterway to the big Allied naval base at Londonderry, Northern Ireland, a few minutes before midnight on March 20, an undetected ship smashed into the upper works of *U-1003.* That ship was the Canadian frigate *New Glasgow,* outbound from Londonderry with three other frigates of Canadian hunter-killer Support Group 26. According to the Canadian naval historian Joseph Schull, when *New Glasgow* spotted *U-1003*'s snort, "she bore in at high speed" and hit the enemy vessel "with a grinding crash" and, although herself damaged badly, attacked with 600-pound depth charges and a Hedgehog.

Allied ASW doctrine of that time called for surface ships to hunt to exhaustion any possible U-boat contact, however uncertain, and to press all nearby warships into the chase. Thus while *New Glasgow,* commanded by Reader M. Hanbury, prepared to put back into Londonderry for repairs to her collision damage, three frigates of Canadian hunter-killer Support Group 25 raced out from Londonderry and six warships of Canadian Escort Group C-4 joined the four remaining frigates of Canadian Support Group 26. In all, fourteen Canadian warships (including *New Glasgow*) hunted *U-1003* for many, many hours without success.

The collision with and depth charges from *New Glasgow* severely damaged *U-1003.* The snort and attack periscope were bent flat back. The bridge rails, radar antennae, and one twin 20mm were carried away. Seawater flooded through a warped hatch into the conning tower and into the control room below. After slipping away, Strübing bottomed for about forty-eight hours to make repairs, but the damage was too great for the crew to overcome.

Shortly after midnight, March 23, Strübing surfaced to run to the coast of Ireland and beach. Some Canadian warships that were still in the vicinity got *U-1003* on radar. Seeing these approaching warships, Strübing gave up the fight and at 4:30 A.M., scuttled and abandoned ship. Sixteen Germans, including Strübing, perished in the sinking. Some hours later, the Canadian frigate *Thetford Mines* of Support Group 25, inbound to Londonderry, picked up thirty-three German survivors from life rafts or dinghies, but two died before the frigate reached port.

• The veteran *U-260,* commanded by Klaus Becker, one of the last boats to evacuate from France, sailed from Kristiansand on February 21. Three weeks later, on March 12, while going southabout Ireland into St. George's Channel, the *U-260* hit a mine off Fastnet. As a result of the damage, Becker could not dive *U-260* and reported that fact to Control, which ordered him to scuttle. When Becker and his crew struggled ashore, Irish authorities interned them.

• The *U-246,* commanded by Ernst Raabe, left Bergen on her second patrol on February 22, and snorted southabout Ireland into the English Channel. Near the Lizard on the night of March 29, Raabe found a convoy and shot a T-5 at one of the trailing escorts, the Canadian frigate *Teme.* It hit and blew off about sixty feet of the frigate's stern, but fortunately killed only four men. A Canadian sister ship, *New Waterford,* hunted for the U-boat while salvage vessels towed *Teme* into Falmouth, where she was declared a total wreck. That same night, it was thought another of the close escorts, the American-built British destroyer escort *Duckworth,* found, attacked, and sank *U-246* with the loss of all hands.* However, Alex Niestlé attributes her loss to unknown causes.

• The new *U-1195,* commanded by Ernst Cordes, sailed from Bergen on February 24. He was the skipper who had drifted his VII, *U-763,* into the British naval base at Spithead during Overlord. He was therefore well acquainted with the difficult currents and shallow water in the English Channel and there was every expectation that *U-1195* would survive. It took Cordes twenty-seven days to reach the English Channel. In St. George's Channel on March 21, he found coastal convoy BTC 103 off Milford Haven. He shot and probably hit the American Liberty ship *James Eagan Layne,*† which was so badly damaged that she had to be scrapped.

While bottomed off Portsmouth on the morning of April 6, Cordes heard the noise of ship propellers and rose to periscope depth to find an oncoming small coastal convoy, VWP 16. He fired T-5s at two different ships and sank the impressive 11,420-ton British freighter *Cuba.* She was by far the largest ship sunk by a U-boat in 1945.

Cordes bottomed *U-1195* at ninety-eight feet, but the escorts easily found her and depth charges began to fall. The British destroyer *Watchman,* commanded by J. R. Clarke, carried out a deadly Hedgehog attack. Holed, the bow compartment of *U-1195* flooded knee deep in two minutes and the men abandoned the room. When Cordes tried to surface, he found the boat was too heavily flooded and gave orders for a submerged escape from the control and after-torpedo rooms. The *Watchman* fished out eighteen Germans (of forty-nine), but Cordes was not among the survivors.

Twenty-nine VIIs sailed from Norway to British waters in March 1945. Fifteen were new boats on maiden patrols. In all, these U-boats sank nine ships for 20,000 tons, an average of one-third of a ship per boat per patrol. Seventeen of the twenty-

---

* Niestlé writes that on April 30, the famous British destroyers *Havelock* and *Hesperus* depth-charged the wreck of *U-246* and brought up the personal effects of the crew, which led to the mistaken belief that this ship sank the *U-242,* which, in fact, hit a British mine on April 5 and sank with all hands.

† As Rohwer points out (*Successes*), *U-246* and *U-399,* both subsequently lost on these patrols, were nearby that night and it is difficult to know which boat hit the ship.

eight (60 percent) that sailed were sunk, a loss of another eight hundred German submariners, fifty-four of whom were captured.*

Some March VII patrols, in brief:

• The new VIIC41 *U-1024,* commanded by Hans-Joachim Gutteck, sailed from Kristiansand on March 3. Control directed him to go southabout Ireland and up through St. George's Channel to the Irish Sea to an area near Anglesey.

While in St. George's Channel, Gutteck conducted an aggressive patrol. On about April 4, he shot two torpedoes at a "corvette" and claimed a sinking, but it was not confirmed in Allied records. Several days later off Holyhead, he came upon inbound transatlantic convoy Halifax 346 and fired two torpedoes into the huge formation. One missile misfired, but the other hit the 7,200-ton American Liberty ship *James W. Nesmith.* Gutteck claimed she sank, but although badly damaged, *Nesmith* made port. Convoy escorts counterattacked *U-1024,* but Gutteck eluded them and bottomed in a hollow until they canceled the hunt.

While still in the Holyhead area on the morning of April 12, *U-1024* sighted yet another formation of big ships: what Gutteck described as a 12,000-ton ocean liner and four other vessels of 8,000 to 12,000 tons. He shot three torpedoes at the formation and claimed sinking the 12,000-ton ocean liner, a freighter of 8,000 tons, and another of 6,000 tons, bringing his total claims for the patrol to one corvette and three merchantmen for 28,000 tons sunk and one 6,000-ton merchantman damaged. Allied records confirmed only one sinking in this third attack, the 7,200-ton American Liberty ship *Will Rogers,* making Gutteck's actual score one 7,200-ton Liberty ship sunk and one 7,200-ton Liberty ship damaged.

British hunter-killer Support Group 8, patrolling nearby, pounced on *U-1024.* That evening one of the frigates, *Loch Glendhu,* blew *U-1024* to the surface with a Squid attack. Two other frigates, *Loch Achray* and *Loch More,* joined in the hunt. Believing his U-boat to be doomed, Gutteck ordered the crew to abandon ship and scuttle, but the scuttling went awry and salvage parties from the frigates boarded and captured *U-1024* and obtained valuable gear and papers.† In this melee, eight Germans were killed, including Gutteck, who shot himself, or so the Germans asserted. The British held the other thirty-seven German crewmen belowdecks on *U-1024.* One frigate, *Loch More,* took the U-boat in tow, but a thick fog enveloped the formation and shortly after midnight on April 13, *U-1024* broke loose, swamped, and sank. The frigates rescued the thirty-seven German survivors.

• The *U-1202,* commanded by Rolf Thomsen, sailed from Bergen on her second patrol on March 4. Thomsen had won a *Ritterkreuz* for his bold, solo attack on a convoy in St. George's Channel on December 10 during his first patrol. He had claimed sinking four freighters for 26,000 tons, but only one, the American Liberty ship *Dan Beard,* was confirmed.

Thomsen conducted what Control believed to be another sensational patrol. On March 21, he claimed that he sank a destroyer and got two hits on a "jeep" carrier

---

* From *U-1024* and *U-1063.*

† Presumably useful Enigma documents and/or short-signal books, and so on. They have not yet been described.

that produced sinking noises, but neither claim was confirmed. Ten days later he claimed he hit two Liberty-size ships and sank both for a total of 14,000 tons. However, these sinkings could not be confirmed either. In the same area on the following day, April 1, Thomsen claimed that he sank two corvettes and damaged another 7,000-ton freighter. Again, none of these successes could be confirmed.

However, inasmuch as Thomsen's total claims in two patrols were a destroyer, two corvettes, and six freighters for 40,000 tons sunk, as well as damage to a carrier and another big freighter, Dönitz awarded Thomsen Oak Leaves to his *Ritterkreuz.* This was the first such high honor to be given an Atlantic skipper since the Oak Leaves awarded to Werner Henke, skipper of *U-515,* nearly two years earlier.*

Thomsen returned *U-1202* to Norway on April 27. He did not make another patrol. The *U-1202* was sunk in Bergen on May 10 and later salvaged by the Norwegian Navy, which rechristened her *Kynn.*

• The new VIIC41 *U-1023,* commanded by Heinrich Schroeteler, sailed from Norway on March 7. This was Schroeteler's second command. Earlier, he had been skipper of one of the first Type VII snort boats in the Atlantic, *U-667.* Almost alone he had praised the snort ("He who knows how to snorkel lives longer") in a long message that Dönitz distributed widely throughout the U-boat service to build confidence in the device. After four patrols on *U-667,* Schroeteler had left the boat to relieve Adalbert Schnee as first staff officer in U-boat Control, Berlin. There he met and married the daughter of Admiral Rolf von der Marwitz.

Schroeteler was a free spirit with an artistic temperament. He did not like desk duty in Berlin. He persuaded Dönitz's son-in-law, Günter Hessler, to send him back to sea. In Norway, Schnee gave him command of *U-1023,* replacing her first skipper. Merely to be different, he said later, Schroeteler did not wear the traditional captain's white cap.

Schroeteler conducted an aggressive patrol. Southbound off North Channel on April 9, he intercepted Slow Convoy 171 and fired three torpedoes into the formation, almost hitting the Canadian frigate *Capilano.* Ten days later, he came upon another convoy off the southern tip of Ireland. He shot three torpedoes into this formation and claimed sinking an 8,000-ton freighter, but it was not confirmed in Allied records. In the same area four days later, he came upon a coastal convoy, TBC 135, and shot two torpedoes at a 10,000-ton freighter. He claimed another possible sinking, but it was not so. Allied records showed that he hit—and damaged—the 7,300-ton British freighter *Riverton,* but she made port. Upon receiving word of Schroeteler's supposed three big successes for 26,000 tons, Dönitz presented him a *Ritterkreuz* by radio, the last such award to a U-boat skipper in the war.

Proceeding into the English Channel on May 6, near Portland, Schroeteler shot a T-5 at a "destroyer" or "corvette." It hit and sank the vessel, which proved to be the small (335-ton) British minesweeper *NYMS 382.* She was the last Allied warship to be sunk by a U-boat in the war. Upon receiving word of the German surrender, Schroeteler put into Portland on May 12, completing a forty-nine-day cruise.†

* At the time of the award, Thomsen's confirmed score was one ship for 7,200 tons.

† Schroeteler remained a POW until 1948. After his return to Germany, he graduated magna cum laude as a doctor of philosophy. A gifted sculptor, he remained close to the Dönitz family in the postwar

• The new VIIC41 *U-1063,* commanded by Karl-Heinz Stephan, sailed from Kristiansand on March 12 to patrol the mouth of the English Channel between Land's End and Brest. Stephan attempted to navigate submerged by means of an *Elektra-Sonne* antenna mounted on the snort, but the system was not yet reliable. Off Land's End shortly before midnight on April 15, Stephan rose to periscope depth to take a navigational bearing on the English coast, snort raised and ready.

British Support Group 17 got a radar contact on *U-1063*'s snort. The very capable frigate *Loch Killin* carried out three attacks, dropping twenty-one depth charges. German survivors said these attacks damaged *U-1063,* but not enough to justify Stephan's panicky order to surface and abandon ship. When the U-boat popped up, *Loch Killin* raked her with gunfire, killing several Germans. Others, including Stephan, the second watch officer, and a chief petty officer, drowned. The frigates rescued seventeen German survivors.

• The *U-396,* commanded by a new skipper, Hillmar Siemon, also sailed from Norway on March 13. His primary mission was to report weather, and secondarily to sink ships. It was thought that while the boat was homebound near the Orkneys, a B-24 of British Squadron 86, piloted by J. T. Laurence, attacked and sank the boat with the loss of all hands. However, Niestlé writes that *U-396* was lost to unknown causes.

• One of the newly arrived VIICs, *U-905,* commanded by Bernhard Schwarting, also sailed from Norway on March 13. It was believed that on March 20, a B-24 of British Squadron 86, piloted by N.E.M. Smith, possibly spotted *U-905* west of the Orkney Islands. The aircraft attacked with two Fido homing torpedoes. On March 31, Control directed Schwarting to patrol west of the English Channel, but nothing further was ever heard from *U-905.**

• Another newly arrived VIIC41, the *U-321,* commanded by Fritz Berends, sailed from Kristiansand on March 17. On April 2, a Leigh Light–equipped Wellington of Polish Squadron 304, piloted by R. Marczak, spotted her snort and periscope about 150 miles off Cape Clear, the southernmost tip of Ireland. The boat dipped under but Marczak attacked at an altitude of 120 feet with six depth charges which, it was assumed, destroyed *U-321.* Nothing further was ever heard from her.

• The new VIIC, *U-1106,* commanded by Erwin Bartke, age thirty-three, sailed from Kristiansand on March 23. Bartke had commissioned and commanded the "Milk Cow" tanker *U-488* from February 1943 to March 1944. On the seventh day out from Norway, the crew of a B-24 of British Squadron 224, piloted by M. A. Graham, spotted a snort and periscope. Graham attacked with depth charges, which blew the stern of the boat to the surface. He then dropped a pattern of sonobuoys that returned noises that sounded like a dying U-boat. Nothing further was heard from *U-1106.*

---

years. At the request of the family, Schroeteler sculpted monuments for the graves of Peter and Klaus Dönitz, who were killed in the war, and for their mother, Ingeborg Dönitz.

* Franks (1995) and Niestlé (1998) doubt that Smith sank *U-905.* He had earlier sunk *U-478* and won a DFC, but the evidence in the case of *U-905* is not conclusive. Niestlé attributes the loss of *U-905* to depth charges of the American-built British destroyer *Conn,* commanded by T. D. Williams on March 27 off North Minch.

• Another VIIC41, the *U-326,* commanded by Peter Matthes, sailed from Bergen on March 29. Nearly a month later, on April 25, while on patrol just southwest of Brest, a B-24 of U.S. Navy Squadron VB 103, piloted by Dwight D. Nott, sighted a snort and a periscope. Nott attacked with depth charges, reporting that the snort jumped out of the water. Later the aircrew saw a body floating on the surface. This was the end of *U-326* and all hands.

• The new VIIC41, *U-1107,* commanded by Fritz Parduhn, sailed from Horten on March 30. West of Brest on April 18, Parduhn came upon the transatlantic convoy Halifax 348 and boldly attacked. His torpedoes sank two valuable loaded ships: the 8,000-ton British tanker *Empire Gold* and the 7,200-ton American Liberty ship *Cyrus H. McCormick.* In terms of confirmed tonnage sunk (15,209), this was the third best patrol of any VII in 1945.

It was a victory not long celebrated by the Germans. On April 30 a Catalina of U.S. Navy Squadron VP 63, piloted by Frederick G. Lake, spotted the snort spray of *U-1107* near the western mouth of the English Channel. Lake carried out a textbook retrobomb attack on the snort, firing twenty-four retrorockets from an altitude of one hundred feet. Debris rose to the surface. Responding to Lake's alarms, British hunter-killer Group 1, sixty miles away, came up and got a bottom sonar contact and found oil.

This was the last U-boat kill by the U.S. Navy's Fairwing 7. Since its arrival in southwest England in the summer of 1943, the wing had sunk four U-boats and shared credit for two others.* From January 1 to April 30, 1945, the wing's aircraft flew 1,549 ASW missions, requiring 14,513 hours, almost all over water. These planes doubtless harassed many U-boats and forced many into evasive actions that thwarted attacks on Allied shipping. On May 17, Admiral King ordered the wing† to return to the States.

By April 1945, the American 12th and British 21st Army Groups, commanded by Omar Bradley and Bernard Montgomery, had crossed the Rhine River into Germany proper and were striking toward the prearranged stop line at the Elbe River. Soviet armies, commanded by Georgi Zhukov, were surrounding Berlin and fighting in the suburbs.

Notwithstanding this chaotic situation, what remained of the U-boat force carried on with loyalty and verve. Twenty-eight VIIs sailed from Norway in April to carry out war patrols in waters of the British Isles, eight in the last week of the month. Twelve were new boats or transfers from the submarine school. Four were commanded by new skippers. All told, these boats sank four ships for 20,000 tons. Ten of the twenty-eight boats, manned by about five hundred men, were lost, including forty-six captured (from *U-1206*) and one hundred interned (from *U-963* and *U-1277*) by the Portuguese. As ordered, eleven other VIIs of the April group manned by about six hundred men put into British naval bases to surrender.

---

* Sunk unassisted: *U-271, U-326, U-681,* and *U-1107.* Shared credit: *U-243,* and *U-966.*

† Squadrons VB 103, VB 105, VB 107, VB 110, VB 112, and VP 63.

Some April patrols in brief:

• The *U-1055,* commanded by Rudolf Meyer, making his second patrol, sailed from Norway on April 5. On April 23, the boat reported her position from the southwest tip of Ireland, but nothing further was ever heard from her. Niestlé writes that the cause of her loss is not known.

• The *U-486,* commanded by Gerhard Meyer, who sank the troopship *Leopoldville,* a big British freighter, and sank or wrecked two British destroyer escorts (*Capel, Affleck*) on his first patrol in December, sailed from Bergen for another patrol in the English Channel on April 7. The snort broke four days later and Meyer aborted the patrol.

At that time, the big new 1,300-ton British submarine *Tapir,* commanded by John C. Y. Roxburgh, who had earlier commanded the submarine *United* in the Mediterranean, was patrolling off Norway. In the early hours of April 12, *Tapir* detected *U-486* running on the surface, inbound to Bergen. Roxburgh fired a full salvo from his eight bow tubes. One or more torpedoes hit and blew the U-boat to pieces with the loss of all hands.

During his earlier action as commander of *United,* Roxburgh had sunk the Italian destroyer *Bomdadière* and the big Italian submarine *Remo,* plus a number of Italian and German freighters. Highly decorated for these successes and for sinking *U-486,* Roxburgh rose to lofty positions in the Royal Navy in the postwar years and retired with the rank of vice admiral.

• The new *U-1206,* commanded by Karl-Adolf Schlitte, left Kristiansand on April 7. Her task was to relieve *U-778* off the east coast of Scotland between Moray Firth and the Firth of Forth, concentrating on Peterhead.*

Schlitte navigated by *Elektra-Sonne.* Three days out, the supercharger on the port diesel failed. After the boat reached the area off Aberdeen on April 13, the starboard diesel failed. Forced to run on batteries while the crew worked feverishly to get the diesels back on line, Schlitte had to let pass what he described as an 8,000-ton freighter.

The next day, April 14, the *U-1206* suffered another mechanical failure, this one with devastating results. The outboard valve of the forward head (toilet) gave way and the bow torpedo compartment flooded. Because the main bilge pump and other auxiliary machinery also failed, Schlitte could not check the flooding. Faced with this calamity, he fired the torpedoes in the tubes and destroyed the others, as well as all secret materials, then surfaced to scuttle and abandon ship. Three men were lost but local small craft rescued thirty-six survivors and ten others reached the shore at Aberdeen in a raft. All forty-six Germans were promptly escorted to British POW interrogation centers.

• The *U-245,* commanded by Friedrich Schumann-Hindenberg, sailed on April 9 from Heligoland for a second hazardous (*Brutus*) patrol to the mouth of the Thames River. In shallow water off Harwich on April 17, he came upon coastal convoy TAM 142 and sank two freighters with new and experimental, extremely long-range acoustic torpedoes. The victims were the 4,900-ton British *Filleigh* and

---

* In 1945, four Type VII snort boats had preceded *U-1206* to this dangerous area: *U-309, U-714, U-778,* and VIIC41 *U-1274.* Only *U-778,* which had aborted when her sonar failed, survived.

the 5,000-ton Norwegian *Karmt.* A T-5 shot at a escorting corvette missed. When Germany collapsed, Schumann-Hindenberg returned *U-245* to Bergen.

• The VIIC41 *U-1017,* commanded by Werner Riecken, making his second patrol, sailed from Trondheim on April 14. Two weeks later, in the early afternoon of April 29, while snorting off Malin Head at the entrance to North Channel, an aircraft spotted the snort wake and smoke. This was a B-24 of the renowned British Squadron 120, piloted by H. J. ("Pop") Oliver, a protégé of the U-boat killer "ace" Bryan Turnbull. Oliver pounced promptly on the snort, dropping four depth charges. Per doctrine, he then laid out a pattern of sonobuoys at the site of his attack. These picked up "loud and long-drawn-out explosions" and transmitted the noise to the B-24, providing fair proof of a kill, confirmed later by Allied intelligence. There were no German survivors.

• The new VII, *U-1105,* commanded by Hans-Joachim Schwarz, sailed from Kristiansand on April 13. Two weeks later, close off the west coast of Ireland near Donegal Bay, Schwarz shot torpedoes at the American-built British destroyer escort *Redmill,* which, with American-built British sister ships *Byron* and *Fitzroy,* had sunk the VII snort boat *U-722.* The torpedo hit the stern of *Redmill,* leaving her a total wreck. Salvage vessels towed her into port, but she was never repaired. The British eventually returned the hulk to the U.S. Navy, as well as her sister ships *Byron* and *Fitzroy.* Per orders, Schwarz surrendered and concluded his brief patrol at Loch Eriboll, Scotland, on May 10.

• Among the last VIIs to sail from Norway were the new VIIC41, *U-1277,* commanded by Ehrenreich-Peter Stever, and the veteran VIIC, *U-963,* commanded by Rolf-Werner Wentz, making his second patrol as skipper. Stever was to patrol the English Channel and Wentz was to lay a minefield. Neither boat carried out its mission. Both scuttled off the Portuguese coast, Wentz on May 21, Stever on June 3. Portuguese authorities interned both crews and later turned them over to Allied authorities.

Soon to become somewhat famous (or infamous) and the cause of wild speculation in the tabloids, the *U-977,* commanded by a new skipper, Heinz Schäffer, age twenty-four, sailed from Kristiansand on May 2 to patrol in the English Channel. Commissioned on March 31, 1943, in Kiel by Hans Leilich, age twenty-five, she had not previously made a war patrol. During workup in the Baltic, according to Allied intelligence documents, *U-977* rammed (or was rammed by) other vessels three times. In the last incident, she incurred so much damage to the pressure hull that German authorities relegated her to school boat status.

In early 1945, Heinz Schäffer, crew of 1939, assumed command of the boat in Hamburg, where on February 20 she entered the yards to be fitted with a snort. Schäffer had made four war patrols, including one in the Gulf of Guinea, as a watch officer on the *U-445,* based in France. From December 1943 to December 1944, he had commanded the Type IID school duck *U-148.*

Schäffer said later that he regarded his new command as a "means of escape" from the Allies, rather than a combat vehicle. When Germany surrendered, the

U-977 was outbound in Norwegian waters. Schäffer thereupon decided to cruise to Argentina and surrender to what he believed might be more hospitable authorities. "One of my main reasons in deciding to proceed to the Argentine," he later said in an official statement to the Allies, "was based on German propaganda, which claimed that the American and British newspapers advocated . . . that all German men be enslaved and sterilized. . . . It was absolutely my intention to deliver the boat undamaged into Allied hands, while doing the best I could for my crew. I felt the ship's engines might be a valuable adjunct to the reconstruction of Europe."*

Having reached the decision to flee, Schäffer said, he then gave the married crewmen a choice of going ashore or going to Argentina. About a third of the crew—sixteen men—voted to go ashore. On May 10 Schäffer ran in close to the Norwegian coast at the island of Holsenöy, unintentionally grounded the boat on some rocks, and put over the sixteen men in dinghies. He then sallied the boat off the rocks and set off for Argentina, about seven thousand miles away. All three of his officers† and twenty-eight enlisted men remained on board. The sixteen men who left the boat were subsequently taken into custody by the British.

The voyage to Argentina was hideous. Schäffer remained completely submerged for a record sixty-six days—from May 10 to July 14—snorting for about four hours a day. The boat crawled southward into ever greater summer heat and many men, Schäffer remembered, were on the edge of nervous breakdowns. He stopped for four hours in the Cape Verdes for a swim call and then proceeded on the surface using one diesel to St. Paul's Rocks, making good about 150 miles a day. When the boat crossed the equator (July 23) Schäffer authorized the customary initiation ceremony. Finally, on August 17, after a patrol of 108 days and 7,644 nautical miles, Schäffer put into Mar del Plata.

Latin American newspapers soon published stories stating that *U-977* had secretly brought Adolf Hitler to Latin America to live out his life incognito. That false story spread to the tabloids worldwide, provoking a good deal of speculation as to whether or not it could be true.

It is improbable that Hitler—or any other high Nazi official—chose to escape on *U-977*. Given the high rate of loss of U-boats in the spring of 1945 (50 percent plus), the chances of survival on a fleeing submarine were extremely dim. Even if Hitler or some other high Nazi had chosen this risky means of escape, in all likelihood he would have demanded a bigger Type IX snort boat or an IXD2 U-cruiser snort boat, rather than a cramped VIIC. Moreover, young Heinz Schäffer was an unlikely choice of skipper for such an exalted mission. He had never made a war patrol in command of a U-boat and had not served in the Atlantic since October 1943. Furthermore, neither Schäffer nor his crew had any snort experience; *U-977* had only recently been fitted with one.

Even if Hitler, notoriously prone to seasickness, chose to flee in a Type VII and to endure the hideous voyage that entailed, he would not have picked this particu-

* Presumably by providing electrical power for bombed-out cities.

† Watch officers Karl Reiser and Albert Kahn, engineer Dietrich Wiese.

lar VII, which had been thrice rammed in the Baltic and, because of pressure-hull damage, reduced to school-boat status. Moreover, while the *U-977* was in the Hamburg shipyard to be fitted with a snort, Schäffer wrote later,* the batteries "were only running at 70 percent efficiency." He had requested new batteries, but "for want of material" his requests "had been rejected." None of the thirty-two men on *U-977* has come forward to confirm that Hitler (or his ashes), Martin Bormann, or other high-ranking Nazis traveled to Argentina in *U-977*. In the journalistic climate of the 1990s, an authentic story of that type would be worth millions.

After undergoing close interrogation by the Americans and British, in 1950 Schäffer returned to live in Argentina.

Toward April, a few of the big Type XXI electro boats began to sail from Kiel to Norway. As related, the first XXI, *U-2511,* commanded by Adalbert Schnee, arrived in Norway on March 23 with snort and periscope problems. Schnee also reported that the maximum safe diving depth of *U-2511* was 570 feet, about half of her designed depth limit. On April 18, Schnee sailed from Kristiansand, but his diesel engines were not working properly and he aborted and put into Bergen on April 21, after eluding a British submarine. He resailed on May 3, made a practice approach on a British cruiser, withheld fire, and returned to Bergen.

Several other Type XXIs sailed to Norway. Among them was the *U-2513,* commanded by Erich Topp, who wore a *Ritterkreuz* with Oak Leaves and Swords.† Yet another was the *U-2506,* commanded by *Ritterkreuz* holder Horst von Schroeter (from the Drumbeater *U-123*). On April 19, an as-yet-unidentified British aircraft hit the *U-2506* but von Schroeter took her on to Bergen and was there when the war ended. Still another was the *U-2529,* commanded by Fritz Kallipke, whose earlier Type XXI command, *U-2516,* had been destroyed by an air raid on Kiel.

British aircraft destroyed or damaged a number of Type XXIs in the Skagerrak and Kattegat en route to Norway. These included the *U-2502,* commanded by *Ritterkreuz* holder Heinz Franke, whose earlier XXI command, *U-3509,* had been abandoned in Bremen. Although damaged by RAF Mosquitos, Franke got the *U-2502* to Horten and was there when the war ended. Hans Hornkohl, the former skipper of *U-3512,* destroyed in an air raid on Hamburg, got his new XXI *U-3041* to Horten. Eleven British Beaufighters hit the *U-2503,* commanded by Karl Jürgen Wächter, in the Kattegat. Rockets and cannons savaged the boat and killed

---

* In a book, *U-boat 977* (1952). In part, Schäffer said, he published his book to refute the many newspaper stories and a book published in Argentina (*Hitler Is Alive*) alleging that *U-977* had brought Hitler to Argentina. The rumors continued. In the fictional *Adolf Hitler and the Secrets of the Holy Lance* (1988), Buechner and Bernhart state that *U-977* carried a "funeral urn" containing the ashes of Hitler and Eva Braun and other Nazi treasures to a prearranged site in an ice cave in Antarctica, which one of Dönitz's U-boat crews had built in 1943.

† Topp first commanded the XXI *U-3010,* but it was badly damaged in an air raid on Bremen. His engineer on *U-3010* and *U-2513* was Gerhard Bielig, who had won a *Ritterkreuz* on the IXD2 U-cruiser *U-177*. As related in the Foreword to Volume I, the *U-2513,* which did not sail on patrol, became a war prize of the United States.

Wächter. Others took charge and ran the boat onto a beach to save themselves. On the same day in the Kattegat, British Typhoon aircraft damaged the *U-3030* and sank the *U-3032,* commanded by twenty-four-year-old Bernhard Luttmann and twenty-two-year-old Horst Slevogt, respectively.

The Arctic

The Allies continued to sail Murmansk convoys to Kola Inlet in the dark and stormy winter months of 1944–45. The Commander, U-boats, Norway, Reinhard Suhren, maintained Combat Flotilla 14 at Narvik, commanded by Helmut Möhlmann, to attack these convoys.

As Dönitz had long pointed out, the returns from these Arctic boats were too small to justify the force. In the year 1944, the Allies sailed 243 loaded ships to Kola Inlet. The U-boats sank merely three, all from convoy JW 56A in January: two American Liberty ships, *Penelope Barker* and *Andrew G. Curtin,* and the British Liberty ship *Fort Bellingham.** Yet Hitler insisted that the Arctic force of about twenty U-boats keep patrolling.

These convoys in brief:

• JW 62 (thirty ships) sailed from Loch Ewe on November 29, 1944. By then Dönitz had persuaded Hitler to order the *Luftwaffe* to strengthen its forces at air bases in northern Norway to help the U-boats find the convoys. The German airmen located JW 62, but the convoy eluded the planes and the U-boats and there were no losses.

The return convoy, RA 62, had a tougher time. The *U-365,* commanded by Diether Todenhagen, fired a T-5 at the British destroyer *Cassandra* and blew off its bow. Salvage vessels towed *Cassandra* back into Murmansk. Twice during the voyage torpedo-equipped JU-88s attacked RA 62 but they failed to do any appreciable damage. Two Swordfish aircraft from the new (1944) "jeep" carrier *Campania,*† piloted by W. J. Hutchinson and M. W. Henley, sank Todenhagen's *U-365* with the loss of all hands on December 13.

• JW 63 (thirty-five ships) sailed from Loch Ewe in early January. The flagship was the carrier *Vindex,* sister ship of *Campania.* No U-boat or enemy aircraft attacked this convoy and it arrived safely at Murmansk. The return convoy, RA 63 (thirty ships), sailed from Kola Inlet on January 11. This convoy likewise eluded U-boats and *Luftwaffe* aircraft and arrived safely at Loch Ewe. After these ships proceeded to new destinations, the British closed Loch Ewe to save manpower.

---

* U-boats also sank four empty freighters returning from Kola Inlet to the British Isles, all in RA convoys: two American Liberty ships, *William S. Thayer* and *Edward H. Crockett,* and two British vessels, the Liberty ship *Samsuva* and the 7,000-ton freighter *Empire Tourist.*

† One of three 14,000-ton, 17-knot escort carriers built by the British. The others were *Nairana* (1943) and *Vindex* (1943). Each carried eighteen aircraft, usually American-built TBF Avengers and F4F Wildcats, which the British called Tartans and Martlets, respectively.

Inasmuch as the fleet carriers of the Home Fleet had sailed to the Far East to join in the attack on Japan, there was now room in the Firth of Clyde to assemble and sail Murmansk convoys.

• JW 64 (twenty-six ships) sailed from the Clyde on February 2. The escort carriers *Campania* and sister ship *Nairana;* a cruiser; and seventeen destroyers, sloops, and corvettes served as escort. The Germans found and shadowed JW 64, but the shadower's radio failed and forty-eight torpedo-equipped JU-88s that came out to attack the convoy on February 7 could not find it. Three days later, the *Luftwaffe* tried again with a massive flight of JU-88s. One of these, romping ahead of the main flights, fired a torpedo at the new (1944) Canadian destroyer *Sioux,* but missed. This action alerted all hands and when the JU-88s arrived, they met a murderous antiaircraft reception and achieved nothing noteworthy.*

The Germans deployed group *Rasmus,* composed of eight boats, on a line near Bear Island, but the convoy eluded the group. When the Germans realized this, these boats raced eastward to Kola Inlet, where four other U-boats, including Hess's *U-995,* were already waiting. One of the *Rasmus* boats, the *U-992,* commanded by Hans Falke, shot a T-5 at one of the convoy escorts and hit the British corvette *Denbigh Castle.* The British corvette *Bluebell* towed the severely damaged *Denbigh Castle* into Kola Inlet, but the British did not repair her. All other vessels arrived safely.

These fourteen U-boats loitered off Kola Inlet, waiting for the return convoy, RA 64, to sail. While waiting, four of the U-boats tore into a local Soviet convoy. All four claimed sinkings or hits on nine ships, but only two were confirmed: the American Liberty ship *Horace Gray,* sunk by the *Ritterkreuz* holder Hans-Günther Lange in *U-711,* and the 8,129-ton Norwegian tanker *Norfjell,* wrecked by Otto Westphalen in *U-968.*

RA 64 (thirty-four ships) sailed in the early hours of February 17. An advance ASW sweep off Kola Inlet found the veteran *U-425,* commanded by Heinz Bentzien, who had commissioned the boat on April 21, 1943. Fitted with a snorkel and *Hohentwiel* radar, *U-425* was out on its eighth patrol, but Bentzien had yet to sink a ship. The British sloop *Lark* and corvette *Alnwick Castle* savaged the U-boat with depth charges, Hedgehogs, and Squids. Fatally damaged, the boat sank out of control to 853 feet, then Bentzien blew ballast tanks to surface and scuttle.

The *U-425* came up between the sloop and corvette, with the crew scrambling on deck. Both ships opened fire, raking the boat from stem to stern. As the U-boat sank stern first, the crew jumped into the water. Although wounded, one very determined German, Herbert Lochner, survived. The *Alnwick Castle* rescued him after fifty minutes in the water.

---

* That night, the nonsnort *U-995,* commanded by Hans-Georg Hess, age twenty-one (the youngest skipper in the U-boat force), making his second Arctic patrol, slipped into the harbor at Kirkenes, then in Soviet hands. He set up and fired at the 6,000-ton Norwegian freighter *Idefjord,* which was moored at a pier. Hess claimed a sinking, but in actuality, he missed. For this bold stroke and later daring, Dönitz awarded Hess a *Ritterkreuz.*

Two U-boat skippers added to their laurels. Otto Westphalen in *U-968* wrecked the British sloop *Lark* with a T-5, mere hours after she had helped sink *U-425*. A salvage vessel towed *Lark* into Kola Inlet but the British did not repair her either. The Soviets did, however, renaming her *Neptun*. Westphalen then wrecked the American Liberty ship *Thomas Scott*, which Soviet vessels towed back into Kola Inlet. Westphalen also claimed a hit on a destroyer, but that could not be confirmed. Lange in *U-711* sank the British corvette *Bluebell*. All but one of the *Bluebell* crew perished in this sinking.

Proceeding toward the British Isles, convoy RA 64 sailed into the worst weather ever encountered by a Murmansk convoy. Between the violent storms, the *Luftwaffe* twice launched JU-88s. In spite of the adverse weather, the "jeep" carriers *Campania* and *Nairana* each got off ten Wildcats to fight off the Germans. One German plane torpedoed a straggler, the American Liberty ship *Henry Bacon*. A destroyer rescued all but twenty-two of the eighty-six-man crew and thirty-five Norwegian passengers. When the battered convoy reached the Clyde on March 1, a dozen destroyers had to be docked for hull repairs, damage caused by the hostile seas.

• JW 65 (twenty-four ships) sailed from the Clyde on March 11. It was escorted by two "jeep" carriers, *Campania* and the *Ruler*-class11,500-ton American-built *Trumpeter;* a cruiser; and nineteen sloops, corvettes, and other smaller craft. The convoy escaped hostile forces until March 20, when it approached Kola Inlet. Eleven U-boats were lying in wait. Five attacked ships in the convoy.

Otto Westphalen in the *U-968* sank two ships: the British sloop *Lapwing* and the American Liberty ship *Thomas Donaldson*. When Dönitz received Westphalen's action report, he awarded him a *Ritterkreuz*.*

The youthful Hans-Georg Hess in *U-995*, who had recently penetrated Kirkenes Harbor, hit the American Liberty ship *Horace Bushnell*. She beached and her cargo was saved, but so far as is known, she was never repaired and returned to service.† This was Hess's first and only confirmed sinking.‡

Jürgen Thimme in *U-716* reported sinking a 1,600-ton destroyer. However, this claim could not be confirmed.

Friedhelm Schweiger in *U-313* claimed probable hits on three Liberty ships for an aggregate 21,000 tons. None of these claims could be confirmed either.

The return convoy, RA 65 (twenty-six ships), sailed from Kola Inlet on March

---

* At the time of the award, his confirmed score was two sloops, *Lark* and *Lapwing*, a Norwegian tanker, and two American Liberty ships.

† The *Bushnell* popped into the news in December 1997, when the late American Ambassador to Switzerland, M. Larry Lawrence, was buried with full military honors in Arlington National Cemetery. Lawrence had earlier and falsely claimed that he was a crewman on the *Bushnell*, and as a result of the torpedo hit he had been "thrown overboard into frigid Arctic waters and suffered serious head injuries, which required many months of convalescence." When this false claim came to light, authorities ordered the removal of his body and tombstone, and he was reburied in less hallowed ground.

‡ After the war, the Allies allotted *U-995* to the Norwegian Navy, which renamed her *Kaura*. Owing to the untiring efforts of her last German commander, Hans-Georg Hess, she was returned to the *Bundesmarine* and on March 13, 1972, she was mounted on an outdoor cradle at the German Naval Memorial at Laboe, a suburb of Kiel. Preserved as a museum, the *U-995* is the only existing VIIC U-boat.

21. Nine U-boats were still waiting outside, but the convoy eluded all of them. The convoy reached the Clyde on April 1 with no losses.

• JW 66 (twenty-six ships), the last of the wartime convoys to Murmansk, sailed from the Clyde on April 16. The escort consisted of two "jeep" carriers, *Vindex* and the American-built *Ruler*-class *Premier;* a cruiser; twenty-two destroyers, frigates, and corvettes; and smaller craft. *Vindex* carried twelve Wildcats and eight Swordfish; *Premier,* twelve Avengers. Group *Faust,* composed of six U-boats, deployed in a search line west of Bear Island, but JW 66 slipped by undetected. When the Germans realized this, group *Faust* redeployed to Kola Inlet, where ten other U-boats gathered, making sixteen in all.

JW 66 incurred no losses and entered Kola Inlet. The U-boats remained outside, waiting. While marking time, *U-997,* commanded by Hans Lehmann, attacked a local Soviet convoy, PK 9. He missed two escorts but hit two freighters: the 4,300-ton Norwegian *Idefjord* (which Hess in *U-995* had missed in Kirkenes Harbor) and the 1,603-ton Soviet *Onega.* The former survived, the latter sank.

The return convoy, RA 66, sailed from Kola Inlet on April 29. Group *Faust,* reduced to fourteen U-boats, lay waiting. *Ritterkreuz* holder Otto Westphalen in *U-968* shot at what he described as two destroyers and claimed his torpedoes hit and sank these two warships. In reality, he missed the British corvette *Alnwick Castle* and sank the British destroyer escort *Goodall.* Only forty-four of *Goodall*'s crew were rescued.

The next—and last—shooter was Karl-Gabriel von Gudenus, commanding the snort boat *U-427* on her first war patrol. While cruising submerged in foggy twilight, a destroyer suddenly appeared. Already on keen alert, von Gudenus fired three torpedoes and claimed sinking that destroyer and another. Actually, he missed the big Canadian *Tribal*-class destroyers *Haida* and *Iroquois.*

In this last convoy battle of the war, British forces sank two U-boats off Murmansk, both during the battle on April 29. The frigate *Loch Insh,* commanded by E.W.C. Dempster, got sole credit for *U-307,* commanded by Erich Krüger. *Loch Insh* rescued Krüger and thirteen other Germans.* The frigates *Anguilla* and *Loch Shin* and the destroyer escort *Cotton* shared credit for *U-286,* commanded by Willi Dietrich. There were no German survivors.

RA 66 proceeded to the Clyde, arriving on the last day of the war, May 8, without incurring further losses. Von Gudenus in *U-427,* savaged by aerial bombs and hundreds of depth charges, could not dive. Otto Westphalen in *U-968* and Klaus Andersen in the snort boat *U-481* escorted von Gudenus back to northern Norway, where they arrived on May 3.

During several Arctic patrols, *Ritterkreuz* holder Hans-Günther Lange in *U-711* claimed sinking two "destroyers." One turned out to be the British corvette *Bluebell;* the other could not be confirmed. For these and other supposed successes, Dönitz awarded Lange Oak Leaves to his *Ritterkreuz* by radio on April 29. Five days later, on May 4, a British task force, including the American-built "jeep" carriers *Queen, Searcher,* and *Trumpeter,* launched forty-four Avengers against the

* These were the last German submariners captured at sea. Grand total: about 5,004.

U-boat base at Harstad, Kilbotn. They sank a submarine tender, a freighter, and Lange's *U-711*.

During 1945, four JW Murmansk convoys, composed of 111 loaded freighters, had sailed from the British Isles to Kola Inlet. From these, U-boats destroyed two American Liberty ships: *Horace Bushnell* and *Thomas Donaldson.** In return, Allied forces sank four U-boats with the loss of two hundred men, fifteen of whom were captured (from *U-425* and *U-307*).

In all, from 1941 to 1945, the Allies sailed forty convoys (PQ, JW) comprised of 811 merchant ships to northern Russia. Thirty-three ships aborted for various reasons. Fifty-eight were sunk and 720 arrived safely. As detailed by Professor Rohwer, the Arctic U-boat force sank twenty of these loaded eastbound ships.† The Allies sailed thirty-seven return convoys (QP, RA) comprised of 715 ships from northern Russia to the British Isles or Iceland. Twenty-nine of these merchant ships were lost, twenty-one to U-boats. In all, the Arctic U-boat force sank forty-one merchant ships and thirteen warships from these convoys.‡ In return, forty-three U-boats were lost, manned by about two thousand men, of whom ninety-nine were captured. That was an "exchange rate" of one U-boat sunk for every merchant ship sunk.

Including the routes in the Persian Gulf to Basra and the Sea of Japan to Vladivostok, the Americans and British delivered to the Soviet Union under Lend-Lease staggering quantities of goods, including the following:

376,000	Trucks
131,633	Submachine guns
51,500	Jeeps
35,000	Motorcycles
22,206	Aircraft
12,755	Tanks
8,218	Antiaircraft guns
5,000	Antitank guns
473 million	Projectiles
350,000	Tons of explosives§

The Murmansk convoys delivered less than a quarter (22.7 percent) of this vast tonnage to the Soviet Union. However, the dangers of the Arctic Ocean and seas

* U-boats in 1945 sank one empty American Liberty ship, *Thomas Scott,* from returning RA convoys.

† Assuming seven sinkings by U-boats in PQ 17. See B. B. Schofield (1964), pp. 215–21 and Appendix 1; Rohwer, *Axis Submarine Successes.*

‡ The heavy cruiser *Edinburg, Battle*-class or *Tribal*-class destroyers *Mahratta, Matabele, Somali,* fleet destroyer *Hardy,* sloops *Kite, Lapwing, Lark,* destroyer escorts *Bickerton* and *Goodall,* corvettes *Bluebell* and *Denbigh Castle,* minesweeper *Leda.*

§ See B. B. Schofield (1964), Appendix Z, which is based on official American and British Lend-Lease records.

from the enemy and no less from the elements captured imaginations far more so than did the more perilous North Atlantic run. Moreover, in part to assuage Stalin by highlighting the Arctic deliveries, the Allies propagandized the Murmansk convoys more than could be justified by the results achieved. Thus was left in some quarters the wrong impressions that not only were the Murmansk convoys the most hazardous and costly in terms of ships lost and seamen killed and missing, but also that the deliveries to Kola Inlet saved the Soviet Union from certain defeat.

Last Patrols to the Americas

During 1945, U-boat Control sailed nineteen Type IX snort boats to the Americas: five in February, eight in March, five in April, and one in early May. These included a new IXD2 U-cruiser, the *U-873,* and five new IXCs on maiden patrols. Four were more experienced boats with new skippers. Hence, ten skippers were untried as such in that role in battle.

These boats achieved almost nothing. In all, they sank six ships for 23,000 tons: three freighters and three small warships. Nine boats manned by five hundred men were lost; thirty-three men were captured.* Eight boats surrendered to U.S. Navy or Royal Canadian Navy forces. One fled to Argentina.

These boats confronted some of the worst winter-sailing conditions of the war: hurricane-force storms, raging blizzards, towering seas. It was no better off the North American coast. The official British oil historian wrote that

> [t]he winter of 1944–45 was the most severe for forty years in the eastern United States and weather conditions sharply cut down the amount of oil that could be moved overland. Many marshalling yards and junctions were almost put out of action; [railway] tank cars were immobilized. . . . The effects of the severe weather on rail and road transport made extra coastwise deliveries of oil by tanker unavoidable. All the main war theaters, even the Pacific, were dunned to release "Greyhounds" [big, fast tankers] to carry oil to the northeast United States. Shipments to the Mediterranean were held back and more vessels were withdrawn from the CU tanker squadrons.†

What makes the recounting of these futile patrols to America worthwhile is that many were featured in another embarrassing Allied intelligence failure. This was a preposterous belief that these boats intended to smash New York and Washington with V-1 cruise missiles and/or V-2 ballistic rockets.

Exactly how this belief took root has not been established absolutely. It may have begun with a secret OSS report of October 26, 1944, from Stockholm, in which that station telegraphed that reliable sources indicated a U-boat would "depart for New York harbor to use V-1" for propaganda purposes. OSS Stockholm

---

* From the IXC40 *U-546.*

† Payton-Smith, *Oil* (1971), p. 431.

followed this with similar reports on November 3, November 6 ("four U-boats will be used in operation against New York"), and December 22.*

The American naval historian Philip K. Lundeberg wrote recently† that the German agents recovered from *U-1229* and *U-1230* (Oscar Mantel, Erich Gimpel, and William C. Colepaugh) predicted a missile or rocket attack on New York mounted from U-boats. In response to a query from Bernard F. Roeder in OP20G, Harry H. Hinsley in the Naval Section, Bletchley Park, wrote on November 29, 1944:

> We have of course received the rumours to which you refer that the Germans plan to use a U-boat (or U-boats) to fire robot bombs on the East Coast of the United States and—because, as you say, the project is worthy of considerable attention—we have been in close touch with the Admiralty in an effort to discover whether these rumours have any foundation. To date, both Admiralty and G.C.&C.S. are quite happy that the rumours are mere propaganda, and that they are not corroborated by any reliable high-grade evidence. . . .‡

Two high-level American officials spoke publicly about German rocket attacks on New York City. On December 10, New York's Mayor, Fiorello La Guardia, caused a near panic when he raised the possibility. As Lundeberg wrote, a month later, on January 8, 1945, Admiral Jonas Ingram, commander in chief of the U.S. Navy's Atlantic Fleet, also raised the possibility, but stated that the U.S. Navy and the Army Air Forces were fully prepared with a secret plan (Bumblebee, later renamed Teardrop) to thwart any German U-boat missile attack on any shore of the United States.

Then, astonishingly, Hitler's chief of war production, Albert Speer, announced in a Berlin radio broadcast that V-1 missiles and V-2 rockets "would fall on New York by February 1, 1945." This caused renewed panic in the highest military levels in the United States. The Admiralty, however, remained calm, and on February 16, cabled this logical appreciation to Admiral King:

> A. There was no evidence from photographic reconnaissance to confirm preparations by the Germans to mount such attacks.
> B. The V-2 ballistic missile could not be launched from a U-boat.
> C. The winged V-1 "buzz bomb" (i.e., cruise missile) *could* be stored in a topside hangar in knocked-down condition, assembled, and fired from launch skids on a Type IX U-boat.
> D. The damage created by one V-1 (assuming it could hit a target) would be so negligible as to make the putative project not worthwhile.
> E. A missile attack from U-boats at this stage of the war was "highly unlikely."§

---

* OSS information from NARA documents, courtesy of Paul M. Cole.

† "Operation Teardrop Revisited," in Runyan and Copes (1994).

‡ NSA History Collection, NARA, RG 457, Box 625.

§ A paraphrase from documents at NARA: RG 457, SRH 008, p. 228 and SRMN 037, p. 597.

Nonetheless, the Americans remained fixated on the likelihood of a U-boat missile attack on the U.S. East Coast. The plan to thwart the attack, Teardrop, proceeded. It would mobilize massive American air and naval forces.

Some last patrols to the Americas, in brief.

- In the period from February 6 to 11, three IXC40s sailed from Norway for Canadian waters. These were the experienced *U-857,* commanded by Rudolf Premauer, age twenty-five; the *U-866,* an experienced boat commanded by a new skipper, Peter Rogowsky, age twenty-five; and the *U-879,* a new boat commanded by Erwin Manchen, age twenty-six.

As these boats crawled westward on snorts and batteries, U-boat Control directed them to radio daily weather reports, for what urgent reason it is difficult to imagine. These reports enabled Allied intelligence to determine the exact daily positions of the U-boats. Tenth Fleet directed a hunter-killer group of six American destroyer escorts, then refueling in Iceland, and two other destroyer-escort groups to track down these U-boats.

One of these groups sailed from New London, Connecticut, on February 23. It was comprised of four destroyer escorts, manned exclusively by Coast Guardsmen. A year earlier in the Mediterranean, *U-371* had blown off the stern of one of these vessels, the *Menges.* Towed to the States and repaired with a patched-on stern from a sister ship, the *Holder, Menges* was now back in action with sister ships *Lowe, Mosley,* and *Pride.*

Alerted by Tenth Fleet, this group deployed one hundred miles east of Halifax. On March 18, the *Lowe* got a positive sonar contact and the four ships attacked all day with Hedgehogs and depth charges. These destroyed the *U-866* with the loss of all hands. Thus were the hurts of *Holder* and *Menges* avenged.

Admiral Ingram and Tenth Fleet deployed massive ASW forces into the northwestern Atlantic to hunt down the other two IXs, *U-857* and *U-879.* These included the hunter-killer groups built around the "jeep" carriers *Mission Bay* and *Croatan,* as well as hunter-killer groups of destroyer escorts or frigates.

Directly off Cape Cod on April 5, Premauer in *U-857* hit and damaged the 8,500-ton American tanker *Atlantic States.* A hunter-killer group comprised of two frigates and two destroyer escorts raced to the scene to mount a dogged U-boat hunt. On April 7, the veteran U.S. Navy destroyer escort *Gustafson* found a U-boat and blasted her "all day" with Hedgehogs. It was thought that these destroyed the *U-857* with the loss of all hands. However, the Admiralty recently declared that *U-857* was lost to unknown causes.

Off Norfolk on April 14, Manchen in *U-879* sank the freighter *Belgian Airman.* On the night of April 29–30, Manchen attempted to attack a Key West–Norfolk convoy, KN382, but one of the escorts, the Canadian-built American frigate *Natchez,* drove *U-879* off with depth charges. A hunter-killer group comprised of three American destroyer escorts, *Bostwick, Coffman,* and *Thomas,* destroyed *U-879* with the loss of all hands.

- The veteran IXC40 *U-190,* commanded by Hans-Edwin Reith, sailed from Kristiansand on her sixth patrol February 22. Off Halifax in the period from April

12 to 16, Reith may have shot at several ships (the pages of the logbook for some days are missing and the record is not clear). On April 16, he definitely sank the Canadian minesweeper *Esquimalt* with a T-5 off the approaches to Halifax. She went down with sickening speed, so fast that the men could not launch lifeboats. The survivors climbed onto Carley floats, washed by icy seawater. A sister ship, *Sarnia,* happened along six hours later and rescued twenty-six of *Esquimalt*'s sixty-five-man crew.

The *U-190* was homebound when Germany capitulated. Reith returned to Canadian waters and jettisoned all torpedoes, ammo, and secret papers. Per instructions, he met two Canadian warships on May 12: the frigate *Victoriaville* and corvette *Thorlock.* The Canadians boarded the U-boat and obtained "a signed deed of surrender." Captors and captives then proceeded to Bay Bulls, Newfoundland.

• The IXC40 *U-853,* commanded by a new skipper, Helmut von Frömsdorf, age twenty-three, sailed from Stavanger on February 23. En route to the Americas on March 26, he celebrated his twenty-fourth birthday. Off Portland, Maine, on April 23, he probably sank the old 430-ton American patrol boat *Eagle 56.* Off Block Island on May 5, he definitely sank the 5,400-ton collier *Black Point,* en route to Boston with a load of soft coal. The explosion blew away forty feet of the ship's stern. In the blast or in the water, twelve of the crew of forty-six perished. The freighter *Kamen* rescued the thirty-four survivors and broadcast an alarm.

Four Boston-bound American warships, which had escorted ships of convoy GUS 84 to Norfolk, Philadelphia, and New York, heard the alarm. The senior vessel, the destroyer *Ericsson,* was already inside the Cape Cod Ship Canal, but the next senior vessel, the frigate *Moberly,* manned by a Coast Guard crew, and the destroyer escorts *Amick* and *Atherton* raced to the scene to carry out a determined hunt.

The *Atherton* got a strong sonar contact and attacked, dropping thirteen depth charges fitted with magnetic pistols. One missile may have hit. Meanwhile, an armada of powerful warships converged to hem in *U-853:* the destroyer *Ericsson,* which about-faced in the canal; the destroyers *Barney, Blakeley, Breckinridge;* the frigate *Newport;* two former Royal Navy corvettes, *Action* and *Restless;* and the auxiliary destroyer *Semmes.* Upon the arrival of these vessels, *Amick* left for a vital prior assignment.

The hunt continued through the night into May 6. *Atherton,* commanded by Lewis Iselin, attacked with Hedgehogs and depth charges, while *Moberly,* commanded by Leslie B. Tollaksen, held sonar contact, and other warships formed outer lines to block *U-853* from escaping to deep water. Owing to the shallow water (one hundred feet), back blasts from the depth charges damaged *Atherton*'s electronics. *Moberly* then carried out a high-speed depth-charge attack that damaged her own steering gear. When this had been repaired, *Moberly* made a second attack with Hedgehogs. These attacks probably destroyed *U-853,* for German escape lungs, life jackets, an officer's cap, and other gear rose to the surface amid leaking oil.

At dawn, two Navy blimps, *K-16* and *K-58,* from Lakehurst, New Jersey, arrived to assist in the kill. When *K-16* got a precise MAD contact, *Atherton, Ericsson,* and *Moberly* resumed attacks at that site with Hedgehogs and depth charges, perhaps on a dead U-boat. These explosions brought up more wreckage: a chart desk, life raft, foul-weather gear, and cork. Then the blimps attacked with 7.2" rockets. Thereafter, *Ericsson* declared the U-boat killed—the last U-boat sunk by U.S. forces in World War II—and marked the location with a buoyed line. Later that day, a diver from the Navy salvage vessel *Penguin* descended to 127 feet to the bottomed U-boat to confirm the kill, reporting massive damage and bodies strewn about inside the hull. He identified the boat by its number.*

Nine Type IXs sailed from Norway to the Americas in March. These included four new boats and two older boats with new skippers. On April 12, U-boat Control designated seven of these as group *Seewolf,* leaving out *U-530* and *U-548,* the older boats with new skippers. Group *Seewolf* was to attack shipping along the U.S. East Coast from New York southward; the two older boats were to attack shipping in waters of Canada and the northeast United States coast. Two of the chosen seven aborted with snort failures, but both resailed after a week of repairs, delayed but still elements of *Seewolf.*

Fully aware of these German plans from OP20G's Enigma decrypts and almost dead certain that the boats of group *Seewolf* were the long-anticipated V-1 launchers, Tenth Fleet and Admiral Ingram deployed massive naval and air forces to intercept them. These were two hunter-killer groups consisting of the "jeep" carriers *Mission Bay* and *Croatan* and twenty escorts in northern waters and two hunter-killer groups consisting of the "jeep" carriers *Core* and *Bogue* and twenty-two escorts in more southerly waters.

U-boat Control directed the seven boats of *Seewolf* to rake westward along the North Atlantic convoy routes and to ruthlessly pursue any contacts, because "we must sink ships!" Snorting slowly westward, making barely one hundred miles a day, these boats found no targets. To avoid this U-boat menace, as well as the hideous winter weather, Allied authorities routed North Atlantic convoys well to the south.

American naval forces sank five *Seewolf* boats. Owing to heavy storms that impeded air operations and to the difficulty of spotting snorts, surface warships got credit for almost all of the killing.

- On April 15, according to Tenth Fleet, two destroyer escorts of the *Croatan* group, *Stanton,* commanded by John C. Kiley, and *Frost,* commanded by Andrew E. Ritchie, sank the new IXC40 *U-1235,* commanded by Franz Barsch, age thirty-three. There were no survivors and no positive evidence of a kill.
- The next day, according to Tenth Fleet, these same two warships sank the new IXC40 *U-880,* commanded by Gerhard Schötzau, who celebrated his twenty-eighth birthday that day. There were no survivors or positive evidence of a kill from that boat either.
- On April 22, according to Tenth Fleet, while inbound to Argentia in "mountainous seas," two other destroyer escorts of the *Croatan* group, *Carter,* commanded by F.J.T. Baker, and the *Neal A. Scott,* commanded by P. D. Holden, sank

* Sport divers with scuba gear routinely visit the hulk of *U-853.*

the IXC *U-518,* commanded by Hans-Werner Offermann, age twenty-three. Again, there were no survivors or positive evidence of a kill.

• On April 23, the veteran IXC40 *U-546,* commanded by Paul Just, sailed into the zone guarded by the hunter-killer groups of the "jeep" carriers *Bogue* and *Core.* Spotting the *Core,* skipper Just boldly ran in to attack. However, a patrolling Avenger from *Bogue,* piloted by William W. South, spotted *U-546* and drove her under with depth charges.

This sighting, of course, set in motion a massive hunt. The next morning, one of *Core*'s destroyer escorts, *Frederick C. Davis,* commanded by James R. Crosby, got *U-546* on sonar. Moments later Paul Just fired a T-5 at *Davis* and it hit with a shattering blast. *Davis* sank quickly with the loss of 126 from her crew of 192, including her skipper.*

Nearby destroyer escorts of the *Core* group raced to the site of the *Davis* sinking to rescue survivors and find her killer. For ten hours eight determined destroyer escorts probed the seas with sonar and fired off Hedgehogs and depth charges. Finally, the noted veteran *Flaherty,* commanded by Howard C. Duff, a ship that a year earlier had helped kill Henke's *U-515* and capture the *U-505,* hit *U-546* with Hedgehogs and blew her to the surface. Four or five other warships nearby opened fire with guns and *U-546* sank swiftly.† Five warships rescued thirty-three of her crew of fifty-nine, including Just.

Allied authorities rushed the German survivors to Argentia to elicit what information they could about the supposed attack on American cities by V-1 or V-2 missiles. Paul Just charged in his memoir‡ that the Americans beat and tortured them. Seeming to confirm Just's charge, Samuel Eliot Morison wrote: "They were a bitter and truculent group of Nazis, who refused to talk until after they had been landed at Argentia and had enjoyed a little 'hospitality' in the Marine Corps brig."§ Of course, Just had no knowledge of the V-1 or V-2 attack.

• In the early hours of May 6, the veteran destroyer escort *Farquhar* of the *Mission Bay* hunter-killer group, returning to New York, got a close sonar contact. This was the IXC40 *U-881,* a *Seewolf* boat commanded by Heinz Frischke, which had aborted with snort problems and resailed on April 7 and was therefore lagging. *Farquhar*'s watch officer, Lloyd R. Borst, fired off a quick pattern of thirteen depth charges. These destroyed *U-881* with the loss of all hands. This kill occurred on the same day that other American warships got the *U-853* off Block Island.

The other two *Seewolf* boats, the IXC40 *U-805* and the IXC40 *U-858,* achieved nothing and surrendered at sea to U.S. naval forces. The destroyer escorts *Otter*

---

* One of the sixty-six survivors was Lieutenant Philip K. Lundeberg, who became an aide to and researcher for naval historian Samuel Eliot Morison on his Volume X, *The Atlantic Battle Won.* This research also earned Lundeberg a Ph.D. in history at Harvard University.

† Tenth Fleet split credit for the kill among eight warships: *Chatelain, Flaherty, Hubbard, Janssen, Keith, Neunzer, Pillsbury,* and *Varian.*

‡ *Vom Seeflieger zum Uboot-Fahrer* (1979), p. 192ff.

§ *Vol. X: The Atlantic Battle Won* (1956), p. 355. Morison, of course, meant the U.S. Navy brig. Philip Lundeberg believes that the beating and torture of Paul Just and his crewmen amounted to a singular POW atrocity arising from the acute desire of the Americans to get information on the supposed V-1 and V-2 attacks as quickly as possible.

and *Varian,* sailing from Argentia, took control of *U-805,* commanded by Richard Bernardelli, age thirty-six. The destroyer escorts *Carter* and *Muir,* also sailing from Argentia, took control of *U-858,* commanded by Thilo Bode, age twenty-seven. These warships and/or others escorted these boats to the Portsmouth Navy Yard in New Hampshire.

The seven boats assigned to group *Seewolf* sank only one ship, the destroyer escort *Frederick C. Davis.* In return, five of its seven boats were sunk, manned by about 250 men, thirty-three of whom were captured.

The two older boats with new skippers that patrolled to Canadian and northeastern American waters in March achieved slightly more than group *Seewolf.*

• The IXC40 *U-548,* commanded by Erich Krempl, age twenty-three, sailed from Norway on March 7. East of Norfolk on April 18, Krempl sank the unescorted 8,300-ton American tanker *Swiftscout.* Five days later, he torpedoed and damaged another tanker, the 7,345-ton Norwegian *Katy,* which was towed into Lynnhaven Bay, Virginia. A hunter-killer group that included the veteran destroyer escort *Buckley,* commanded by E. H. Headland, raced out to hunt *U-548* to exhaustion. Guided by Tenth Fleet, on April 19, *Buckley* and another destoyer escort with a famous pedigree, *Reuben James,* found and destroyed *U-548* with the loss of all hands.

• The IXC40 *U-530,* commanded by Otto Wermuth, age twenty-four, sailed from Kristiansand on March 4. Wermuth had made a number of patrols as watch officer on the earlier IXs *U-37* and *U-103,* but he had not yet commanded a U-boat in combat. In two years in the Atlantic, *U-530* under Kurt Lange had accomplished little or nothing. On this voyage, her crew and her skipper were mostly young new hands.

Wermuth had orders to patrol near Halifax. When he found no worthwhile targets there, Control directed him to go south to New York waters. In the period from May 4 to 7, Wermuth encountered ships of several convoys (probably of Halifax 354 and/or Outbound North 298) that had scattered in dense fog. He shot nine of his fourteen torpedoes at these vessels, but all missed or malfunctioned.

When Wermuth learned of Germany's surrender, he decided to flee to Argentina. After all hands except a few enlisted men approved of this idea, Wermuth jettisoned his five remaining good torpedoes, ammo, and secret papers and headed south. On July 10, the boat reached Mar del Plata and surrendered to the Argentine Navy.

Argentine and American intelligence officers thoroughly interrogated all fifty-four Germans of the crew, seized logbooks, and inspected the boat. Although none of these officials found anything exceptional to report, Latin American newspapers were soon ablaze with all sorts of nonsense, including the assertion that *U-530* had smuggled Adolf Hitler and Eva Braun (and/or Martin Bormann and others) out of Germany to Argentina.*

---

* "Wilhelm Bernhart," coauthor of a preposterous novel, *Adolf Hitler and the Secrets of the Holy Lance* (1988), self-described as a member of the *U-530* crew, wrote that before arriving in Argentina *U-530* carried "six bronze lead-lined boxes" containing "selected treasures" of the Third Reich, and

Had Hitler or Bormann elected to flee Germany by submarine, it is unlikely that he or they would have chosen the aging IXC40 *U-530,* commanded by a green skipper, twenty-four-year-old Otto Wermuth. There were plenty of big new IXCs, the XB *U-234,* and some new IXD2 U-cruisers on hand, as well as numerous battle-wise U-boat skippers beholden to Hitler for medals and other considerations, for example, Wolfgang Lüth, then commandant of the naval academy in Mürwick, who wore the *Ritterkreuz* with Oak Leaves, Swords, and Diamonds, and whose last command was the U-cruiser *U-181.* No other crewman of *U-530* has come forward to verify the assertions of Farago et al.

There is another point. Had the Allies put any credence in the stories that Hitler or Bormann had fled Germany in a submarine, they doubtless would have charged Dönitz and his underlings with the serious offense of aiding and abetting the escape of war criminals. Yet not even the slightest suggestion of this charge arose in the lengthy investigations for Dönitz's trial at Nuremberg or during the trial itself.

Apart from the resailing *U-881* of group *Seewolf,* four IXs sailed to the Americas in April to attack shipping.* Two were new boats. One was an experienced boat with a new skipper.

- The first to sail, on April 1, was the new IXD2 U-cruiser *U-873,* originally converted to a cargo boat. She was commanded by Friedrich Steinhoff, age thirty-five. Earlier in the war, Steinhoff had commanded for a full year the IXC *U-511,* the boat that Hitler gave Tojo ("Marco Polo I"). During that year, Steinhoff had been assigned briefly to R&D at Peenemünde, where German rocket scientists were developing the V-1 and V-2. They had fitted *U-511* with experimental topside antiaircraft rockets that could be fired from a submerged position, but the tests were not sufficiently encouraging to justify further work in that direction.

What has not come to light is whether or not the Allies had made the connection between Steinhoff's *U-511* and his *U-873* and his work with rockets. If they had, it might have lent credence to the suspicion that U-boats intended to hit New York with V-1 missiles. More likely, U-boat Control reconverted Steinhoff's *U-873* to an attack boat and sent her to America to serve as a provisional refueler and supply vessel with a doctor, Carl Wilhelm Reinke, on board.

When Germany capitulated, Steinhoff and several officers considered fleeing to South America. However, the crew objected and after jettisoning her T-5s, all secret papers, the *Tunis* radar detector, and *Kurier* radio transmitter the boat prepared to surrender. The American destroyer escort *Vance* took control of *U-873* and escorted her into Portsmouth on May 17. Apparently naval personnel (or Marines)

---

placed them in an ice cave in Antarctica. Supporting these assertions, the American author Ladislaus Farago (*Tenth Fleet, Patton,* etc.) stated in 1973 that Bormann had fled Germany "in a submarine" and was living in Argentina. The Farago claim is included in the otherwise quite responsible book *Hitler's Elite* (1989), by Louis Snyder, Distinguished Professor of History at Columbia and City College of New York.

* Two other IXC40s, *U-804* and *U-843,* were to join the westward voyages, but on April 9 they were caught and sunk in the Skagerrak by a swarm of RAF Mosquitos of Squadrons 143, 235, and 248. These Mosquitos also sank the VIIC41 *U-1065.*

handled Steinhoff and his crew roughly. An official Navy investigation followed. After transfer to Boston's Charles Street Prison, Steinhoff broke the glass of his watch and committed suicide by slashing his wrists.*

• Next to sail, on April 6, was the new IXC40 *U-889,* commanded by Friedrich Braeucker, age twenty-five. He snorted slowly across the Atlantic but saw no targets. When Germany capitulated, he surrendered to a local Canadian group escorting the outbound Slow Convoy 175: the corvette *Dunvegan* and three minesweepers. *Dunvegan* and the minesweeper *Rockcliffe* escorted *U-889* toward Shelburne, Nova Scotia. Two Canadian frigates, *Buckingham* and *Inch Arran,* took over escort near Sable Island and observed by swarms of journalists in an aircraft, entered Shelburne on May 14.

• The experienced IXC40 *U-1228,* commanded by Friedrich-Wilhelm Marienfeld, age twenty-five, defied superstitions and sailed from Kristiansand on her third patrol on Friday, April 13. He was to operate off New York. When the war ended, he kept going westward and jettisoned torpedoes, secret papers, the *Tunis* and *Kurier* receivers and transmitters, and other gear. On May 11 off the Grand Banks, the U.S Navy destroyer escort *Neal A. Scott* took control of *U-1228* and escorted her into the Portsmouth Navy Yard on May 17.

• The experienced IXC40 *U-1231,* commanded by a new skipper, Helmut Wicke, age twenty-four, sailed from Norway on April 27. When Germany capitulated, he surrendered to British forces and put into Loch Eriboll on May 14.

One boat sailed from Norway to the Americas in May. She was the veteran IXC40 *U-802,* commanded by Helmut Schmoeckel, age twenty-seven. He left Bergen on May 3 to patrol off New York. However, when Germany capitulated, he surrendered to British forces and put into Loch Eriboll on May 11.

Last Patrols to and from the Far East

Six U-boats sailed between Norway and the Far East in 1945: four *from* the Far East and two *to* the Far East.

Three boats in the Far East set off for Norway in January. Since there were no more surface tankers or U-tankers anywhere, the IXD1 cargo carrier *U-195,* commanded by Friedrich Steinfeldt, sailed to the Indian Ocean on January 26 to serve as a provisional refueler. The boat carried out this task and returned to the Far East on March 4. When Germany capitulated, the Japanese took control of *U-195* and renamed her *I-506.*

The patrols in brief:

• The IXC *U-510,* commanded by *Ritterkreuz* holder Alfred Eick, sailed from Jakarta, Java, on January 10. He had 150 tons of cargo: wolfram, tin, raw rubber, molybdenum, and caffeine. As arranged, he refueled from Steinfeldt in *U-195* in the Indian Ocean. After rounding the Cape of Good Hope on February 23, Eick

* Contrary to rumors, historian Lundeberg does not believe that the American jailers beat or tortured Steinhoff. They may have slapped his face once to snap him out of a deep depression.

sank the 7,100-ton Canadian freighter *Point Pleasant Park* which was sailing alone. Believing he could not survive without a snorkel, on April 24, he put into St. Nazaire to get one. He was still there when the war ended.

• The IXC40 *U-532,* commanded by Otto-Heinrich Junker, sailed from Jakarta on January 13. He also carried about 150 tons of cargo like that in *U-510.* A month later he met Steinfeldt in *U-195* and refueled. After rounding the Cape of Good Hope, Junker sank two ships sailing alone in the Atlantic: the 3,400-ton British freighter *Baron Jedburgh* and the 9,300-ton American tanker *Oklahoma.* When Germany capitulated, *U-532* was in the Iceland-Faeroes gap. Following Allied instructions, Junker surrendered and British ships escorted the boat into Loch Eriboll on May 10.

• The IXD2 U-cruiser *U-861,* commanded by *Ritterkreuz* holder Jürgen Oesten, sailed from Surabaya, Java, on January 14. He also carried about 150 tons of cargo similar to that in *U-510* and *U-532.* In the Indian Ocean, Oesten met those two and gave some fuel to Eick in *U-510.* The boat did not attempt to sink shipping and reached Trondheim on April 18.

• The last boat to sail was the IXC40 *U-183.* She was commanded by Fritz Schneewind, who had brought the *U-511* ("Marco Polo I") to the Far East in July 1943 and had been there ever since, well over a year and a half as skipper of *U-183.*

Allied codebreakers intercepted Japanese and German messages and predicted that *U-183* was to leave Surabaya on about April 12 for a war patrol off New Guinea. He actually left Surabaya on April 21 to cruise homeward.

The Americans, meanwhile, had directed the American fleet submarine *Besugo* to lie off Surabaya and sink *U-183.* On April 23, the commander of *Besugo,* Herman E. Miller, found *U-183* running on the surface and shot all six bow tubes. One or more torpedoes hit, and the U-boat sank instantly. There had been seven men on *U-183*'s bridge, including the officer of the deck, Karl Wisniewski, a warrant quartermaster. Although he suffered from a broken leg, collarbone, and ribs, he alone survived, and *Besugo* rescued him. Sixty Germans perished.*

Two boats sailed from Norway to Japan in 1945.

The first was the snort-equipped IXD2 U-cruiser *U-864,* commanded by Ralf-Reimar Wolfram, age thirty-two. He left Bergen on February 5 with cargo for the Japanese. This included plans and parts for the Messerschmitt ME-163 *Komet* rocket-powered interceptor and the ME-262 twin-jet fighter, as well as signed contracts authorizing the Japanese to legally manufacture these aircraft; plans for other aircraft (JU-1 to JU-6 and "Campini"); plans for *"Caproni-"* and a *"Satsuki"*-type submarines; plans for radar manufactured by the Siemans company; and 1,857 flasks of mercury. The passengers included a number of German and Japanese aircraft engineers.

Apparently the snort on *U-864* failed and Wolfram aborted to Bergen. One of the British submarines that maintained a continuous watch on Bergen, the small

---

* After *U-168* and *U-537,* the *U-183* was the third German U-boat sunk by Allied forces in the Far East, all off Surabaya. The Dutch submarine *Zwaardvisch* sank *U-168* and the American fleet submarine *Flounder* sank *U-537.*

(600-ton) *Venturer,* commanded by James S. Launders on his eleventh patrol, intercepted *U-864* on April 9, while both boats were submerged about thirty-five miles off Bergen. Launders, who won a DSO for sinking the VII *U-771* off northern Norway in November 1944, had sailed from Lerwick on February 2. The sonar watch on *Venturer* picked up loud sounds and shortly thereafter, the periscope watch sighted a "thin mast" and soon, two "masts" or periscopes. With uncanny skill, Launders set up and fired four torpedoes by passive sonar and guesswork at eighteen-second intervals from three thousand yards, their depth set at forty feet.

One or more torpedoes hit, destroying *U-864* with the loss of all hands and her valuable cargo. Launders inspected the site by periscope, seeing much oil and "wood" and what might have been a topside torpedo or storage canister. He then returned to Lerwick to well-deserved high praise. He was the only British skipper in the war to sink two German U-boats and the only skipper of any nation to sink another submarine while they were both submerged.

The second U-boat to sail from Norway to the Far East in 1945 was the big XB minelayer *U-234.* During her construction at the Krupp *Germania* yards in Kiel in May 1943, she had been severely damaged by an Allied air raid and was therefore much behind schedule. Commissioned on March 2, 1944, she was commanded by Johann-Heinrich Fehler, age thirty-four. After her trials and workup with snorkel, U-boat Control ordered that she be converted to a cargo carrier, removing some mine-launching shafts and using others for storage, as well as other areas and four topside containers. When she was completed, German technicians estimated that *U-234* could carry 250 tons of cargo and sufficient fuel and provisions for a six- to nine-month trip.*

According to Allied documents, the type and amount of cargo for *U-234* was determined by the *Marine Sonder Dienst Ausland,* headed by a Commander Becker. An officer of that agency—a Lieutenant Commander Longbein—served as loading officer. The second watch officer of *U-234,* Karl Ernst Pfaff, was Longbein's onboard counterpart. These and others stored the following cargo on *U-234:*

74	tons of lead
26	tons of mercury
12	tons of steel
7	tons of optical glass
43	tons of aircraft plans, instruments, arms, and medical supplies
5	tons of 20mm and 37mm ammo
6	tons of equipment for the U-boat bases
1	ton of mail, films, and courier post
1,232	pounds of uranium-oxide ore†
1	disassembled twin-jet ME-262

* Sufficient fuel bunkerage for such a journey was obtained by using the aft torpedo compartment (two tubes) for fuel storage. To compensate for that weight, a small bow compartment was flooded with water.

† The "uranium-oxide" ore was contained in ten cube-shaped metal cases about nine inches on a side. These were stored in the six vertical mine shafts forward.

The *U-234* embarked twelve passengers. Eleven boarded in Kiel. These were:

- Two Japanese officers: Air Force Colonel Genzo Shosi (an aeronautical engineer) and Navy Captain Hideo Tomonaga (a submarine architect).
- Three *Luftwaffe* officers: Colonel Fritz von Sandrath (antiaircraft), Colonel Erich Menzel (communications), and Lieutenant Colonel Kai Nieschling (a military judge).
- Four *Kriegsmarine* officers: Lieutenant Commander Heinrich Hellendorn (gunnery), Captain Heinz Schlicke (electronics), Captain Gerhard Falk (a naval architect), and Lieutenant Commander Richard Bulla (air-sea cooperation).
- Two civilians from Messerschmitt: August Bringewald (an engineer) and Franz Ruf (procurement).

The chief radioman on *U-234,* Wolfgang Hirschfeld, wrote* that his skipper, Fehler, was dissatisfied with his first watch officer. He prevailed on passenger Richard Bulla, a friend who had served with Fehler on the merchant-ship raider *Atlantis,* to take on that position.

Fehler left Kiel on March 25 for Norway. Two days later, the heavily laden boat arrived in Horten. During further snorkel trials, the new VIIC41 *U-1301* rammed *U-234* abaft the conning tower, tearing open a fuel-ballast tank, spilling sixteen tons of oil into the sea. Unable to dry-dock for repairs in Bergen, Fehler sailed into a quiet fjord near Kristiansand, flooded the boat forward (raising the stern), and his crew carried out repairs.

Finally, the last passenger boarded. He was the flamboyant *Luftwaffe* General Ulrich Kessler. A specialist in antiaircraft and antiship missiles, he was to be the new German air attaché in Tokyo. He shocked Fehler and others with his derogatory remarks about Hitler and his cronies, *Luftwaffe* chief Hermann Göring in particular.

The *U-234* left Kristiansand on April 15. Fehler was dubious about reaching Japan, but nonetheless he snorkeled on for sixteen days, until May 1, when he reached the Atlantic and a storm forced him to surface temporarily. He resumed submerged cruising day after day, surfacing for two hours at night to charge batteries and air the boat.

When Germany capitulated, Fehler was in mid-Atlantic and he chose to surrender to the Americans, so he surfaced and headed westward. After disposing of his *Tunis* radar detector, *Kurier* transmitter, and all Enigma and other secret papers, Fehler met the American destroyer *Sutton.* Rather than be captured, the two Japanese officers committed suicide, each swallowing a dozen Luminal sleeping pills. Fehler secretly buried the bodies in weighted seabags. *Sutton* took control of the boat and escorted *U-234* into Portsmouth to berth with *U-805, U-873,* and *U-1228.*

Like other U-boat prisoners, the Germans on *U-234* were jailed at Portsmouth. The Navy took the passengers and some officers to Fort Hunt, outside Washington, D.C., for extended interrogations. Hirschfeld wrote that the second watch officer, Karl Pfaff, returned to Portsmouth to advise the Americans about unloading the boxes of uranium-oxide ore. Scientists say this uranium ore would have yielded

---

* *The Story of a U-boat NCO, 1940–1946* (1996).

about 3.5 kilograms (7.7 pounds) of isotope U-235 (not a U-boat), about one-fifth of what was needed to make an atomic bomb.

Subsequently this uranium ore "disappeared." That is, up to 1998 researchers had not found a paper trail tracing its use and/or disposal. The most plausible speculation is that it was shipped to the Manhattan Project's diffusion factory in Oak Ridge, Tennessee, where in the postwar years it might have been processed into atomic-bomb material.

When Germany capitulated, there were four big German U-boats in the Far East. These were three IXD2 U-cruisers, and one XB minelayer, which, like *U-234,* had been converted to a cargo carrier. The Japanese took control of these four and commissioned them in the Imperial Japanese Navy. Thus the IXD1 *U-195* became *I-506,* the IXD2s *U-181* and *U-862* became *I-501* and *I-502,* and the XB *U-219* became *I-505.* The Japanese interned the German crews, but they were held in fairly comfortable circumstances.

Berlin: The Final Days

As the Third Reich crumbled and self-destructed, two of its most powerful Nazis, Hermann Göring and Heinrich Himmler, betrayed Hitler. Power mad and severely addicted to drugs, Göring telegraphed Hitler to propose that he, Göring, replace Hitler as Führer of the Third Reich. Himmler, no less power mad, secretly initiated surrender talks with the West through the Swedish consulate in Lübeck, in the person of Count Folke Bernadotte. When Hitler received Göring's telegram, he stripped him of all official posts, expelled him from the Nazi Party, and directed that Göring be arrested for high treason. When Hitler learned of Himmler's defection (via a BBC broadcast), he also stripped him of all official posts and expelled him from the Nazi Party.

Few of the senior officials in the Third Reich remained loyal to Hitler to the very end. One was Karl Dönitz. There are several possible reasons for his steadfastness.

- He had sworn a personal oath of loyalty to Hitler. His character was so rigidly fixed that he was unable to bend or break that oath.
- Mindful of the fact that defections in the Imperial Navy led to the overthrow of the Kaiser in 1918, Dönitz was determined in a knightly manner to prevent repetition of that betrayal, and thereby uphold the honor of the *Kriegsmarine.*
- That by retaining Hitler's confidence he might eventually gain sufficient power and authority to legally negotiate surrender terms with the West short of "unconditional," minimize the incursions and plundering by Soviet troops, and prevent the utter and complete dissolution of Germany as a sovereign nation.
- That his growing prominence and power with the German people might make him a logical appointee in the postwar years to the job of temporary head of state and put him in a favorable position to win a majority of votes for the presidency of a newly formed, democratic Germany.
- That although Dönitz was not an official Nazi Party member, he had in fact become a dedicated Nazi and was Hitler's most trusted military subordinate.

One thing is clear: Contrary to some speculation, Dönitz did not remain loyal to Hitler because he believed that the new electro boats and other secret weapons could turn the tide of battle or put Hitler in a more favorable bargaining position to negotiate a surrender. No one knew better than Dönitz that the new Type VII and Type IX snort boats and Type XXI electro boats could no longer make a noteworthy impact on Allied shipping; that, indeed, the vaunted Type XXIs were crippled by mechanical defects that could not be overcome in time.

Whatever his motivation, in the last months of the war Admiral Dönitz relentlessly exhorted the men of the *Kriegsmarine* to soldier on loyally for Hitler and the Third Reich. Often his language took on a threatening tone. Most of his exhortations were intercepted and decrypted by Allied codebreakers, who circulated and preserved them. Some excerpts from that source:*

• On January 31 in a message to "all Sea Defense Commandants," Dönitz conceded that the advance of the Red Army had brought on a "serious crisis." It could be overcome, Dönitz told his officer corps, "if every German wholeheartedly obeying the Führer's orders" performed his duty to the utmost. Everything possible was being done to meet the crisis. He had combed the *Kriegsmarine* for surplus manpower with which to create several infantry divisions. He had already ordered four naval regiments into action on the Eastern Front.

"Over and above this," Dönitz went on, "every one of us must prepare himself for this crisis. . . . We must grow harder. Wailing and complaining is unmanly and shortsighted. Nothing is accomplished by empty, negative talk. . . . I cannot rely on officers . . . who through too much talking, through an overbearing sense of knowledge, or through miserable feelings of fear express themselves negatively, thereby not only failing in the fulfillment of their duties in leadership but also harming our power of resistance. I will dismiss them and place them at the army's disposition, with no regard for rank or position."

• On March 1, Dönitz sent a message to "all U-boats." "We know," he said,

> that the life of our nation is at stake. . . . We must lose no time, must use every hour, every day. We fighting men must serve as the best examples. . . . It is a question of action. From nothing comes nothing. Nothing will be accomplished by mere speech making: "Carry on" or "We will soon throw the Russians out again." . . .
>
> Let us learn to improvise. In this sixth year of the war there are many things no longer at hand to which we were formerly accustomed. . . . Let us attack every task with resourceful spirit and initiative, however things may be going.
>
> Let us fly into the face of all those who want to give up, who adopt the silly motto "It is no longer any use." Those are the greatest weaklings. They are the ones who let themselves be led to the slaughter like patient cattle.
>
> Let us guard against being stifled by dogma in waging our war. The fortune of war is infinitely many-sided, and, especially in naval warfare, dependent on chance and the combination of so many circumstances that new situations and new combat situations are presented again and again. . . . A fighting service which is stifled by

---

* This and quotations following are distilled and/or excerpted from NSA Enigma decrypts in NARA: RG 457, SRMN-032, and SRMN 037.

dogma accomplishes nothing more. Many victorious battles have been waged contrary to all rules of the art of war.

Let us show our enemies that the destruction of Germany will cost them more in blood, treasure and time than they can withstand. Then they will have to give up that aim ... and we will have won the war. Therefore let us exert all our power to the utmost, for example by sinking as many ships as possible for the Anglo-Saxons in total disregard of risk. Then their doubts as to whether the unconditional defeat of Germany is practicable and not too costly will increase.

Let us fly into the face of any German who now becomes the least bit shaky in his loyalty to the National Socialist State and to the Führer. The motives for this are only fear, cowardice and weakness. We are the strong and faithful.

• On March 20, in a message to "all officers," Dönitz stated that "capitulation is suicide and signifies certain death" and would bring "the speedy or gradual destruction of millions of German people."

Our honor demands that we fight to the end. The same is required by our pride, which rebels against humbling ourselves before a people like the Russians, before Anglo-Saxon sanctimony, arrogance and lack of culture. Every thought rebels against the possibility of handing over cultivated German territory to Polish mismanagement. Thus stern necessity, duty, honor and pride bid us fight to the last if need be.

Let us not allow to exist ... dangers which may injure the fighting morale of the men. ... Trample them out ruthlessly at their first appearance. ... Be hard and strict rather than too soft. ... If circumstances demand making a quick, horrible example of someone, let us not shrink from the task.

For example, it was recently reported to me that discovery was made of an act of sabotage by a German member of the crew of a passenger steamer which was being used for military purposes under control of the Navy. If the captain of this ship had summarily strung this man upon the yardarm in order to quench such crimes once and for all on board his ship, I would have defended this act of the captain under any circumstances. It is thus better to act at once and vigorously than to let such things keep on smoldering. ...*

Let us make our troops fanatical. Let us sow hatred for our enemies ... fill our soldiers with passion, so they will feel superior to the enemy. ... The more fanatical and passionate the will to fight is in a soldier, the stronger he is. ...

Let no one brag about old deeds. Whoever fails now in his duty in this decisive hour of our people must be treated ruthlessly, without mercy in view of earlier achievements. The higher he is stationed as a soldier, the more must be demanded of him. In the present fight for life or death of our people, a flag officer as captain who is in a responsible position and fails decisively in his duty to the detriment of our people can atone for this crime only by death.

Let us trust the leadership of Adolf Hitler without reservation. Believe me, in the two years of my activity as Commander in Chief, I have always found that the Führer has always been right in his strategical and operational views. Our military

* This order to "trample" out "ruthlessly" and "summarily" the "dangers which may injure fighting morale" and presumed acts of sabotage without legal proceedings, such as a court-martial, was not introduced at Dönitz's trial at Nuremberg, perhaps because it came from a highly classified Enigma decrypt known to only a few.

situation would be better off today if all operational military commands had believed without reserve and had acted accordingly without delay. Very often the realization that the Führer was right again this time did not come for weeks but then it was mostly too late. Let us therefore strengthen our troops by faith in our Führer.

All in all: let us be proud of the fighting spirit of our Navy. Let us watch over it as our most precious possession. In whatever way the situation may yet develop, the Navy must stand like a belligerent block that cannot be diverted from its task. It will never bow under the hostile yoke.

• On April 7, Dönitz reiterated his demand for loyalty:

We soldiers of the *Kriegsmarine* know how we have to act. Our military duty, which we fulfill regardless of what may happen to right or left or around us, causes us to stand bold, hard and loyal as a rock of resistance. A scoundrel who does not behave so must be hanged and have a placard fastened to him: "Here hangs a traitor who by his low cowardice allows German women and children to die, instead of protecting them like a man. . . ."

• On April 11, in a long screed, Dönitz again rose to the defense of Hitler.

I turn against the irresponsible and shortsighted weaklings who say "If we had not had National Socialism, all this would not have happened." If we had not had National Socialism we would already have had Communism in Germany, further unemployment and political chaos. Without the rearmament which the Führer brought us, Germany would have been trampled over by the Russians in their expansionary push to the west. . . .

I turn against the clever people who say we should have avoided the war against Russia in 1941. Had the leadership done that, then the unweakened Russians would have rolled over us long since at a time that suited them. Then those same clever people would have said: "Yes, the leadership should have prevented it with a timely attack on Russia. . . ."

Alone for years the Führer clearly recognized the threat from Bolshevism. Therefore he did away with our disunity and monstrous unemployment, made us powerful in defense and attempted to enlighten Europe. On the other side stands this hate-blinded Churchill, the grave digger of English power, who entered the war in order to preserve the balance of power and to pledge himself to the freedom of small nations. What now remains of power and where has the freedom of the small nations gone? . . . [They] are provinces of Bolshevik Russia. . . .

Europe will learn that Adolf Hitler is the single statesman of stature in Europe. Therefore all negative brooding is unfruitful and objectively incorrect. Because it is born of weakness it cannot be anything else, since cowardice and weakness make one stupid and blind. . . .

Again he demanded that flag officers and captains of the *Kriegsmarine* "clearly and plainly tread the path of soldierly duty":

The honor of our flag on board is sacred to us. No one thinks of giving up his ship. Rather, go down in honor. . . . The *Kriegsmarine* will fight to the end. Some day its bearing in the severest crisis of this war will be judged by posterity. The same goes for each individual. . . .

• • •

In the last hours of the Third Reich, the fifty-six-year-old monster Adolf Hitler holed up in his Berlin *Führerbunker* and drew up a "last will and testament" in which he named Dönitz to succeed him as "President of the Reich and Supreme Commander of the Armed Forces." He then married his mistress, Eva Braun, and on the afternoon of April 30, while Eva died of self-inflicted poison, Hitler took poison and also shot himself in the mouth with a pistol. The next day, his ever faithful propagandist, Joseph Goebbels, had a doctor kill the six young Goebbels children (ages three to twelve) with lethal injections of poison. Then, at his orders, an SS orderly shot him and his wife, Magda. Designated aides burned the bodies of Hitler and Eva Braun and Goebbels and his wife. Per Hitler's orders, his "secretary," Martin Bormann, fled the bunker to carry Hitler's last will and testament to Dönitz and to seek a high position in the new German government.

All that remained of the Nazi hierarchy also fled Berlin. Dönitz shifted the naval staff from Koralle to Plön, a small city on an inland body of water midway between Kiel and Lübeck. The senior staff of the former military high command (OKW), including Wilhelm Keitel and Alfried Jodl, moved to the small town of Rheinsberg, north of Berlin, then farther northwest to a site near Krakow, closer to Plön. When the Red Army threatened to overrun those places, Dönitz moved to the naval academy at Mürwick, near Flensburg, and established the new German "government" on the large, modern passenger liner *Patria,* berthed in Flensburg harbor. He was joined there by SS chief Heinrich Himmler and former Foreign Minister Joachim von Ribbentrop (both futilely seeking jobs) and by munitions chief Albert Speer, OKW generals Keitel and Jodl, the new chief of the *Luftwaffe,* Robert Ritter von Greim, and the new commander in chief of the *Kriegsmarine,* Admiral Hans-Georg von Friedeburg, and others.*

On May 2, Admiral Dönitz assumed the position of chief of state and commander of all German military forces. He broadcast by radio his intentions to the military forces:

> My comrades!
>
> The Führer has fallen. True to his great purpose of saving the culture of Europe from Bolshevism, he dedicated his life and met a hero's death. In him we have lost one of the greatest heroes of German history. In awe and grief we lower the flag for him.
>
> The Führer designated me as his successor and Chief of State and Supreme Commander of the Armed Forces. I assume the Supreme Command over all branches of the German Armed Forces with the determination to continue the battle against Bolshevism until the fighting troops and the hundreds of thousands of families in Eastern Germany are saved from slavery or annihilation. I must continue the battle against the English and the Americans as long as they obstruct me in the prosecution of the battle against Bolshevism.
>
> The situation demands of you, who have already achieved such memorable deeds and who therefore are longing for the end of the war a continued and un-

* No indisputable evidence has come to light to substantiate the rumors that Martin Bormann survived his eleventh-hour escape from the *Führerbunker* in Berlin.

> abated effort. I demand discipline and obedience. Only through the unconditional execution of my orders will chaos and ruin be avoided. He is a coward and a traitor who now shirks his duty and thereby brings death and slavery to German women and children.
>
> The allegiance you pledged to the Führer is henceforth to be given by each one of you to me as the successor designated by the Führer. German soldiers do your duty. The life of our people is at stake.

In Eisenhower's view, British forces under Bernard Montgomery, which manned the left (or north) flank of the massive line of Anglo-American forces invading Germany, were not moving fast enough to beat the Red Army to Kiel and Lübeck. Wishing to deny those places to the Red Army and to "seal off" Denmark, on April 23, Eisenhower temporarily assigned to Montgomery the crack American XVIII Airborne Corps (four divisions) commanded by Matthew B. Ridgway. In a little-known operation, which Omar Bradley characterized as "remarkable" and George Marshall, not given to superlatives, described as "sensational," Ridgway's corps crossed the Elbe River on May 1 and dashed north-northeast to Wismar on the Baltic. There the corps "linked up" with the Red Army and blocked it from moving farther northwest to Lübeck and Kiel, or Denmark and Norway. Meanwhile, on May 3, Montgomery's slow-moving British XII Corps finally occupied Hamburg.

In the final hours of the Third Reich, Dönitz sought to hold the new German government together and to surrender as many German forces as possible to the Americans and British, rather than the more feared Red Army. In pursuit of the latter goal, he designated Admiral von Friedeburg as Special Emissary to negotiate terms. On May 3, von Friedeburg and another admiral, Gerhard Wagner, and the German Commander in Chief, Army Group Northwest, Ernst Busch, and subordinates arrived at Montgomery's tactical headquarters near Hamburg. The delegation proposed that the three German armies (Third Panzer, Twelfth, Twenty-first) facing the Red Army in that area surrender to Anglo-American forces. When queried by Montgomery, Eisenhower rejected the proposal, stating that any formal German surrender must be "unconditional and simultaneous" in all theaters. However, as a "tactical" matter, Eisenhower authorized Montgomery to accept the surrender of German forces in Denmark, the Netherlands, Heligoland, and Schleswig-Holstein and any individual German soldiers who so wished.

This agreement was to take effect at 8:00 A.M. on May 5. As part of the terms, Dönitz directed all U-boat skippers to cease fire and prepare to surrender per instructions to be issued at a later time. He had one final message for these warriors, almost all of whom were unswervingly loyal to him to the very end.

> My U-boat men!
>
> Six years of U-boat warfare lie behind us. You have fought like lions.
>
> A crushing material superiority has compressed us into a very narrow area. A continuation of the struggle is impossible from the bases that remain.
>
> U-boat men, unbroken in your warlike courage, you are laying down your arms after an heroic fight that knows no equal. In reverent memory we think of our comrades who have sealed their loyalty to the Führer and the Fatherland with their death.

> Comrades, maintain in the future your U-boat spirit with which you have fought at sea bravely and unflinchingly during long years for the welfare of the Fatherland.
>
> Long live Germany!

Earlier the U-boat force had conceived a plan to scuttle all boats à la the Pyrrhic triumph at Scapa Flow in 1919. According to some sources, the codeword *Regenbogen* (Rainbow), the directive to initiate scuttling, was transmitted from Flensburg at 1:34 A.M. on May 5, German time, but rescinded by Dönitz or an aide eight minutes later. Whether this is true or not, it is certain that ambiguous orders of some kind regarding scuttling reached the U-boats. As a result, some skippers or surrogates commenced scuttling on May 5, but others did not. According to Allied documents compiled in September 1945 and subsequently revised, German submariners scuttled 222 U-boats, while another 174 U-boats surrendered to Allied forces.*

Still determined to do his utmost to avoid German surrenders to the Red Army, on May 5 Dönitz sent von Friedeburg to Eisenhower's headquarters in Reims, France, to pursue negotiations. Eisenhower refused to see von Friedeburg or engage in any form of negotiations through surrogates. When von Friedeburg notified Dönitz of Eisenhower's implacability, Dönitz sent Alfried Jodl, also a fierce opponent of surrender to the Red Army, to Reims. Viewing these emissaries and their imprecations to negotiate as merely vehicles for buying time while German armies all along the front fled to American or British lines, Eisenhower held firmly to his position. Seeing that the situation was completely hopeless, von Friedeburg and Jodl finally obtained permission from Dönitz to sign a formal surrender of all German forces on all fronts simultaneously.

In the early hours of May 7, von Friedeburg and Jodl and other Germans of the delegation met with senior Allied authorities in the war room of SHAEF headquarters, located at the École Professionelle et Technique de Garçons, in Reims. The senior Germans signed the surrender document,† which was to take effect from midnight, May 8. Eisenhower then cabled Washington and London:

> The mission of this Allied force was fulfilled at 0241, local time, May 7th, 1945.

A Time of Reckoning

In a joint statement of October 30, 1943, which came to be known as the Moscow Declaration, the United States, Great Britain, and the Soviet Union pledged to hunt down and try all those Nazis suspected of committing atrocities and war crimes. At the Potsdam conference of the Big Three, from July 16 to August 1, 1945, the two new heads of state, Harry S. Truman and Clement R. Attlee, joined with Joseph Stalin to reaffirm the Moscow Declaration.

In retrospect, the Moscow Declaration on war criminals seems right and decent,

---

* See Appendices 18 and 19 for lists of U-boats that were scuttled or surrendered.

† When Allied authorities arrested Dönitz, von Friedeburg, and others on May 23, von Friedeburg committed suicide.

but at the time it was not held in universal favor. Many questioned the legal right of one nation or several to try enemy heads of state for waging war against them. (The Kaiser was not tried for his role in initiating and waging World War I.) Some believed that to allow representatives of the bloody Stalinist regime to sit in judgment on high figures of the bloody Nazi regime would be the height of hypocrisy. Others questioned whether it was possible in the climate of the times to give the Nazis a fair trial. The proceedings might go down in history as a farcical and embarrassing kangaroo court, conducted by victors demanding vengeance and retribution. Still others wondered at the difficulties and cost of amassing and properly presenting hard evidence against what might prove to be thousands of Germans.

The public revulsion at the revelations of ever more horrible atrocities committed by the Nazis became so intense that disputes over legal niceties were soon swept aside. The governments in Washington, London, and Moscow appointed judges and prosecutors to what was officially called the International Military Tribunal, which was to convene at the symbolic soul of Nazism, Nuremberg, on November 1, 1945.

British naval authorities firmly opposed suggestions that Admirals Erich Raeder and Karl Dönitz be indicted and tried. As reported by Ann and John Tusa,* historians of the Nuremberg proceedings, "The British Admiralty took the view that the German Navy had fought a pretty clean war . . . [and] they knew that the laws of naval warfare were notoriously vague and dangerously open to conflicting interpretations. . . ." The Tusas went on to say that in October 1945, a distinguished legal expert at the Admiralty, Humphrey Waldock, later president of the International Court at The Hague, drafted a paper, "warning of legal difficulties in a case against the German Navy," concluding, the Tusas wrote, that generally, the case against the *Kriegsmarine* was "shaky" and "weak."

Senior naval authorities in the United States were of like mind. No evidence had yet come to light indicating that on the whole Raeder and Dönitz had conducted anything other than a clean naval war. Harsh and hard, but clean. Moreover, from December 7, 1941, the United States had conducted harsh and hard unrestricted submarine warfare against Japan, a naval campaign that at times was more merciless than the German U-boat war. In their desire to avenge Pearl Harbor, American submariners shot at and sank Japanese merchant ships without warning, rarely attempted to assist survivors, and, on a few occasions, murdered Japanese survivors in lifeboats or the water.

Nonetheless, ranking government officials in Washington, Moscow, and London insisted that Raeder and Dönitz be tried. Not to do so would be politically and morally unacceptable. It would leave the heavy casualties in the Allied merchant-marine fleets and the ascendancy of Dönitz to the post of Führer of the Nazi Third Reich unredressed.

Ironically, British prosecutors drew the task of making the case against Raeder and Dönitz. The chief of the British team was a well-known barrister and MP, David Maxwell Fyfe. In pursuit of incriminating evidence, he and his team

* *The Nuremberg Trial* (1984).

combed through tens of thousands of pages of *Kriegsmarine* documents that a British combat intelligence team, assigned to George Patton's Third Army, had captured at Tambach Castle near Coburg.* In addition, British naval intelligence provided synopses of relevant Enigma messages, such as "Policy and Tactical Orders to Submarines," for background.

Apart from Dönitz's numerous exhortations of praise for Hitler and National Socialism and his denouncement of "the spreading poison of Jewry," the teams of British prosecutors found only a single document that could be interpreted as incriminating. This was the so-called Laconia Order of September 17, 1942, which Dönitz issued in the aftermath of the sinking of the British troopship *Laconia* by Werner Hartenstein in *U-156*. As related, due to the risks Hartenstein ran in the rescue of *Laconia* survivors, that order instructed U-boat skippers to "be harsh" and specifically *not* to assist the crews of torpedoed ships. One could argue that the language of the Laconia Order† was, per se, a violation of the laws of the Submarine Protocol, which Germany signed in 1936.

Owing to the ambiguity of the Laconia Order, the British prosecutors needed testimony from German submariners to the effect that it was a subtle instruction to kill the survivors of torpedoed ships. Astonishingly, the British obtained just such testimony from a prominent submariner, *Ritterkreuz* holder Karl-Heinz Moehle (from *U-123*), who commanded Training Flotilla 5 in the Baltic for four years, from 1941 to 1945. It happened that when Moehle was arrested at the end of the war, the British had accused him of issuing the Laconia Order. He swore in an affidavit, taken on July 21, 1945, that not only did he not issue the Laconia Order but he had in fact interpreted it to be a subtle order from Dönitz to kill survivors and, furthermore, that he had implied so to new skippers sailing to the war zones. Moehle agreed to testify in that vein if Dönitz were to be tried.‡

Another German submariner willing to testify against Dönitz on this issue also appeared. He was a young lieutenant, Peter Josef Heisig, who had been captured by the Canadians from *U-877* on December 27, 1944. Heisig was a close friend of August Hoffmann, a watch officer on Heinz Eck's *U-852*, whom a British court had condemned to death for shooting survivors of the Greek freighter *Peleus*. In a futile effort to save his friend Hoffmann from a firing squad, Heisig had given that British court an affidavit on November 27, 1945, asserting that in an address to his class of midshipmen in October 1942, soon after the Laconia Order was issued, Dönitz had left the impression that the killing of shipwrecked survivors was desirable. He, too, would testify against Dönitz.

---

* The documents, comprising the entire German naval archives dating to about 1850, had been removed from Berlin to Tambach Castle for safekeeping and, at the insistence of Dönitz, were not destroyed. The documents included the massive, meticulous daily war diaries of the OKM and U-boat Control and all U-boat patrol reports.

† "No attempt of any kind must be made at rescuing members of ships sunk and this includes picking up persons in the water and putting them in lifeboats, righting capsized lifeboats and handing over food and water. Rescue runs counter to the rudimentary demands of warfare for the destruction of enemy ships and crews."

‡ And, as related, Moehle was tried for war crimes and convicted, but served only five years in prison.

When the International Military Tribunal convened on November 1, 1945, prosecutors charged both Dönitz and Raeder on three counts:

1. Plotting to wage aggressive war
2. Waging aggressive war
3. War crimes

The tribunal commenced formal proceedings against Dönitz first, on May 7, 1946, one year after he surrendered Germany. The chief defense counsel was a brilliant naval officer, Otto Kranzbühler, who had held the post of Judge Advocate in the *Kriegsmarine.* He was particularly well prepared to deal with the Laconia Order and with the hostile witnesses Moehle and Heisig. In addition—and most important—with the assistance of one of the two American judges, Francis Biddle, he had obtained permission to interrogate by mail American Fleet Admiral Chester Nimitz on his conduct of the American submarine war against Japan in the Pacific.

The chief British prosecutor, David Maxwell Fyfe, laid the case against Dönitz before the tribunal. Inasmuch as Dönitz was a relatively junior captain when the war began in September 1939, Fyfe was unable to convince the judges that Dönitz was guilty on count one, plotting to wage aggressive war. At the end, the tribunal acquitted Dönitz of that specific charge. Since it was the responsibility of Dönitz as a naval officer to wage war in accordance with orders from Berlin—from Raeder and Hitler—to the best of his ability, Fyfe was also unable to make a convincing case that Donitz was criminally accountable on count two: waging aggressive war. Nonetheless, in a vague and confusing verdict, the tribunal found Dönitz guilty on count two.

It was on the third count, war crimes, that Fyfe mounted his most aggressive and telling attacks against Dönitz. He introduced the Laconia Order, argued that it was a subtle instruction to kill crews of torpedoed ships and, as foreseen, put Moehle and Heisig on the witness stand to buttress his case. Furthermore, he introduced the *Peleus* incident as one example of compliance with these instructions.

Defense counsel Kranzbühler counterattacked along three main lines.

- He showed the court that the Laconia Order prohibiting help to survivors of torpedoed ships was issued directly as a result of the Allied air attacks on *U-156,* and the other U-boats attempting to rescue *Laconia* survivors, which had asked in the name of humanity for a temporary cease-fire in that area. Furthermore, he argued that an order prohibiting assistance to survivors in no way carried with it an implication that survivors should be shot. To make the contrary case, he introduced another Dönitz order of May 20, 1943, in which he instructed U-boat skippers to capture whenever possible ship captains and engineers, stressing the point that the second order contravened any implication in the first to kill survivors. That is to say, it was not wise to rescue some survivors and to kill the rest because the captured German survivors could testify to the atrocity.
- He impugned the credibility of the hostile witnesses Moehle and Heisig. He brought out that each officer had had an axe to grind: Moehle to absolve himself of any blame for the issuance of the Laconia Order and his interpretation of it to the green skippers, and Heisig to save his friend Hoffmann from the firing squad. In

his cross-examination, he established that Moehle had completely misinterpreted another important Dönitz order, that neither officer had ever seen a specific and unequivocal order from Dönitz or Control to shoot survivors, and that in Moehle's twenty ship sinkings while in command of *U-123* he had never harmed a survivor. In addition, Kranzbühler introduced a deposition that he had obtained from Heinz Eck on November 21, 1945, just before Eck was executed, stating that he, Eck, had no orders to kill the survivors of the *Peleus,* that in fact, he acted in what he believed to be his own self-interest.

• He put Dönitz and his chief U-boat operations officers, *Ritterkreuz* holders Eberhard Godt and Günter Hessler, on the witness stand to vigorously deny that the Laconia Order was a subtle hint to kill survivors. He also introduced an affidavit, signed by sixty-seven U-boat skippers (then in British POW Camp 18), which stated, in effect, that the Laconia Order was not viewed as a subtle hint to kill survivors. "The undersigned declare that the German Navy was educated by their leaders to respect the written and unwritten law of the sea," the affidavit concluded. "We have always seen it as fitting our honor to keep these laws and to conduct the combat at sea in a chivalrous manner."

Finally, Kranzbühler was permitted to introduce the written interrogation of Fleet Admiral Chester Nimitz. In response to questions, Nimitz stated that with the exception of hospital ships and other vessels specifically granted safe passage, it was customary for American submarines to attack Japanese merchant ships without warning and, furthermore, that "on general principles the U.S. submarines did not rescue enemy survivors. . . ."

The Nimitz document had a decisive impact on the tribunal, the Tusas write. The American judge, Francis Biddle, who opened the door for Kranzbühler to obtain it, declared not inaccurately that "Germany waged a much cleaner [submarine] war than we did," and he voted to acquit Dönitz on count three, war crimes. However, the other seven judges did not believe Dönitz should get off scot-free and voted him guilty on count three as well as count two. The tribunal then sentenced Dönitz on October 1, 1946, to serve ten years in prison, the lightest penalty assessed of any of those found guilty at Nuremberg. He served the full sentence at Spandau Prison and was released in October 1956.*

The trial of Raeder followed. Inasmuch as he had held a high military post in the Third Reich at the beginning of the war, he was found guilty of count one—plotting aggressive war—as well as counts two and three, waging aggressive war and war crimes. The tribunal sentenced the seventy-year-old Raeder to life imprisonment, but owing to his ill health, he was released in September 1955, at the age of eighty, after serving nine years.

The conviction of Dönitz at Nuremberg outraged a large number of senior Allied naval officers. Over one hundred of them wrote Dönitz to deplore the verdict

---

* This synopsis of the complex Dönitz trial is limited to the main issues, the Laconia Order and the *Peleus* incident. As has been related in part, during the course of the trial, the prosecution team presented numerous other charges against Dönitz, but it did not pursue these as vigorously or with the same conviction.

and the sentence. Some American naval officers published their views. Typical of the comments on Dönitz of that era:

- Four-star Admiral and later U.S. Senator Thomas S. Hart wrote:

> I rate Admiral Dönitz as the best of all of . . . [German commanders], land or sea. He was unique in his handling of the German submarines and they were our most dangerous enemy. His performance with them—and he did most of it himself—was the most outstanding Axis performance of the war. Then he succeeded to command all German naval forces. It was too late for real accomplishments but he made no mistakes and no one could have done better. Then he succeeded the Führer himself, and his performance from there on seems to me to have been perfect. So I think Dönitz was the best.

- Postwar naval propagandist Rear Admiral Daniel V. Gallery, wartime commander of the hunter-killer group built around the "jeep" carrier *Guadalcanal,* which sank Werner Henke in *U-515* and captured him and captured *U-505* intact, wrote in the epilogue of his 1957 war memoir, *Twenty Million Tons Under the Sea:*

> Nuremberg was a kangaroo court and a travesty on justice. The trial of Dönitz was an outstanding example of barefaced hypocrisy. His conviction was an insult to our own submariners in the Pacific who waged unrestricted warfare the same as the Germans did in the Atlantic.

In the years since, journalists and scholars have diligently sifted the mass of records of the Third Reich seeking proof that subtly or otherwise Karl Dönitz encouraged a dirty naval war and crimes against humanity at sea. Beyond the allegations produced by the British team at Nuremberg, no evidence to support that view has come to light. Notwithstanding shrill attacks on Dönitz in recent years, the preponderance of existing evidence supports the judgment of the International Military Tribunal at Nuremberg and the sentence imposed on Dönitz.

Dönitz was deeply loyal to Hitler and the Third Reich. He waged a hard, harsh naval war, but a clean war. Moreover, the thousands of Allied seamen his operations caused to be killed or wounded at sea were not innocent civilian bystanders, like the tens upon tens of thousands of women and children who were killed by Allied bombers in Hamburg, Dresden, Berlin, Bremen, Kiel, and elsewhere. Allied seamen manning merchant ships were as much warriors as were the German submariners.

The U-boat war was not a close-run thing, but rather one more suicidal enterprise foisted on the Germans by Adolf Hitler. According to Alex Niestlé, of 859 U-boats that set off on war patrols, 648 were lost (75 percent). Of these, 429 yielded no survivors. Most shocking of all, 215 U-boats (33 percent) were lost on *first patrols,* usually before the green crews had learned the ropes or inflicted any damage on Allied shipping.

True, Karl Dönitz fought a clean, hard naval war, yet this begs the question. He knowingly and willingly sent tens of thousands of German sailors to absolutely certain death. While not a war crime per se, the fact that he aided and abetted Hitler in this suicidal naval enterprise demands a reevaluation of his unusually high standing in the Hall of Warriors.

AFTERWORD

In the preceding pages of this volume, we have from time to time assessed the results of the various phases of the U-boat war from September 1942 to May 1945.

We recognize that those assessments are too much for anyone to hold in mind through so many pages. Therefore it is appropriate at this ending point to repeat the gist of those assessments, to provide a final summing up.

First, it may be useful to recount the phases of the naval war in this volume. We arbitrarily put them at seven.

- September 1942 to November 1942, when the main weight of the U-boat force was shifted from the all-out assault in American waters back to the North Atlantic run, the vital lifeline between the Americas and the British Isles. This renewed North Atlantic campaign was again interrupted, this time by Torch, the Allied invasion of Northwest Africa, on November 8. At that time, almost all available Atlantic-force boats were withdrawn and shifted to the Gibraltar/Morocco or Mediterranean area to counterattack Torch maritime forces.
- December 1942 to April 1943, when the bulk of the U-boat force was again deployed against the North Atlantic run to the British Isles. Owing to ruinous U-boat losses, this campaign was interrupted yet again, in May 1943, to upgrade the inadequate and vulnerable Type VIIs and IXs.
- May 1943 to August 1943, when the Allies mounted a punishing antisubmarine air campaign in the Bay of Biscay, a so-called choke point that U-boats had to negotiate while transiting between their bases in western France and their mid-ocean hunting grounds. In response, Dönitz directed the U-boats to cross this danger area in clutches of three or more boats on the surface, shooting back at the Allied aircraft with an increased array of flak guns, including quad 20mm and rapid-fire 37mm weapons.
- September 1943 to December 1943, when the U-boats again returned to the vital North Atlantic lifeline. By this time, the U-boats had been upgraded, to little effect, with, in addition to the quad 20mm and 37mm flak guns, new radar detectors and improved battery-powered T-5 torpedoes, which could "home" on the acoustic "signatures" of escorts and, to a lesser extent, merchant ships. This renewed campaign on the North Atlantic run was terminated yet again in December 1943, because of heavy U-boat losses, hideous weather, and the perceived need to husband U-boats to counterattack the maritime forces supporting Overlord, the impending Allied invasion of Occupied France.

• January 1944 to D day, June 6, 1944, when the U-boats were withdrawn entirely from the Battle of the Atlantic to be further upgraded (or so it was thought) and to man, commission, fit out, and work up a new generation of U-boats, the supposedly war-decisive Type XXI electro boats.

• June 1944 to September 1944, the first three months of the Allied invasion of Western Europe, when U-boats attempted to operate against Overlord maritime forces but failed and were forced to abandon all five Atlantic bases in France and flee to Norway or to Germany.

• September 1944 to May 1945, the period of the so-called "renewed" U-boat war, when the U-boats, now equipped with snorkels and based in Norway and Germany, were again thrown against Allied convoys and merchant shipping on the North Atlantic run and in the Irish Sea and English Channel. This final phase of the Battle of the Atlantic was brought to an end when Dönitz, replacing Hitler as chief of state, directed all U-boats to cease fire and surrendered Germany to the Allies.

As we have previously noted in our running assessments, each of the seven phases listed above resulted in a German failure. Contrary to the accepted wisdom or mythology:

• U-boats never even came close at any time to cutting the vital North Atlantic lifeline to the British Isles.

• There was not the slightest possibility that, had they only come into play earlier, U-boats equipped with snorkels or the new Type XXI and XXIII electro boats, with their high sprint speed, could have won the Battle of the Atlantic or significantly intervened against Allied shipping.

Figures support the first contention. During the period under examination, from September 1942 to May 1945, according to American and British sources,* the Allies sailed 953 convoys east and west on the North and Middle Atlantic runs. These convoys were composed of 43,526 merchant ships. Of these, 272 were sunk by U-boats. Ninety-nine point four (99.4) percent of all Allied merchant ships sailing in North Atlantic convoys in this period reached their destinations intact.

These figures so completely turn on its ear the accepted wisdom that U-boats came very close to cutting the strategically critical lifeline between the Americas and the British Isles that they warrant restating, elaboration, and a breakdown by year.

First, a list of *all* transatlantic convoys sailing between the Americas and the British Isles and between the Americas and Gibraltar and the reverse:

* See Plates 12 and 13, and Appendices 3, 9, and 20.

	1942*	1943	1944	1945†	TOTALS
Convoys	72	299	380	202	953
Ships	3,402	12,754	18,856	8,514	43,526
Losses ‡	89	158	18	7	272 (less than 1 percent)

Second, a list of convoys on the North Atlantic run only (HX, SC, ON, ONS, UT, TU, CU, UC):

	1942 §	1943	1944	1945 #	TOTALS
Convoys	65	193	266	133	657
Ships	3,250	9,097	12,907	5,857	31,111
Losses **	89	139	13	6	247 (less than 1 percent)

Third, only loaded *eastbound* convoys on the North Atlantic run—from the Americas to the British Isles (HX and SC):

	1942 ††	1943	1944	1945 ‡‡	TOTALS
Convoys	33	89	69	40	231
Ships	1,650	4,656	4,859	2,122	13,287
Losses §§	39	76	5	5	125 (less than 1 percent)

During this same period, American shipbuilding yards alone turned out the following new ships and their gross registered tonnage:

	1942 ##	1943	1944	1945 ***	TOTALS
Ships	391	1,949	1,786	590	4,716 †††
G.R.T. ‡‡‡	2.67	13.00	12.26	4.30	32.23

* September through December inclusive. Assuming an average fifty ships per convoy. Source: Metcalf (1949); Rohwer, *Critical Convoy Battles and Successes;* British Monthly Anti Submarine Reports.

† January through May, inclusive.

‡ Merchant ships in convoy or straggling.

§ September through December, inclusive. Source: Metcalf (1949); Rohwer and British Monthly Anti Submarine Reports.

\# January through May, inclusive.

** Merchant ships in convoy or straggling.

†† September through December, inclusive. Source: As above.

‡‡ January through May, inclusive.

§§ Merchant ships in convoy or straggling.

\## September through December, inclusive. Source: Fisher.

*** January through May, inclusive.

††† Seventeen times the losses (272) on the combined North Atlantic and Middle Atlantic runs, both eastbound and westbound.

‡‡‡ In millions.

The German U-boat and crew losses in the same period were devastating:

	1942*	1943	1944	1945†	TOTALS
Boats	46	241	254	172	713
Men‡	2,070	10,845	11,430	7,740	32,085§
Captured	295	1,278	1,503	280	3,356

As for the much-vaunted German snorkel of the wartime era, we have noted repeatedly in the narrative of this volume what an abject failure this device turned out to be. Several of its major shortcomings bear repeating:

• It was a fallacy that the snorkel of that era allowed the U-boat to operate effectively while submerged. Contrary to the general belief, the Germans did not snort continuously, but rather for only about four hours in twenty-four, mainly to charge the main propulsion batteries. During the other twenty hours, the snort was retracted and shut down and the U-boat proceeded at 2 or 3 knots on battery power. Inasmuch as vibration problems restricted snort speed to about 5 knots and contrary currents often slowed or deflected a U-boat proceeding on battery power, a U-boat could rarely make good more than fifty or sixty miles per day. Hence, a snorting U-boat spent the bulk of its patrol time reaching its operating area and returning to base. These considerations therefore limited the boat's hunting time to merely a few days, all the while virtually immobile.

• Snorkels repeatedly broke down or dunked and flooded, causing extreme discomfort—or illness or death—inside the pressure hulls and probably, in some cases, caused the loss of the boat.

• A snorting U-boat was usually rendered virtually "deaf" and "blind" because the diesel engines made a terrific racket and the periscopes could not be raised because of vibration and other problems. By sonar and eyesight, Allied antisubmarine forces detected U-boats by the noise and the leaking exhaust smoke of the snorkel. In the last year of the war, the Allies perfected a powerful radar of three-centimeter wavelength that could detect a snorkel head despite German efforts to camouflage it with radar-absorbing (stealth) coats of various materials.

As for the even more vaunted Type XXI electro boat, designed to provide high sprint speed submerged, its crippling faults bear repeating in detail.#

• **Poor Structural Integrity.** Hurriedly prefabricated in thirty-two different factories that had little or no experience in submarine building, the eight major hull sections of the Type XXI were crudely made and did not fit together properly.

* September through December, inclusive; all classes in all areas. Sources for lost U-boats: *German, Japanese and Italian Submarine Losses* [in] *World War II* (U.S. Navy Dept., 1946), Tarrant (1989), and Niestlé (1998); number of men captured: NAVOPARCH, GNR, Box T-76.

† January through May, inclusive. All classes in all areas, but not counting U-boats scuttled or surrendered. For those figures, see Appendices 18 and 19.

‡ Assuming 45 men per boat.

§ Apart from those captured. A few of these men were rescued by German forces, but exact figures have not been calculated.

\# Excerpted from the Foreword of Volume I, pp. x–xi.

Therefore the pressure hull was weak and not capable of withstanding sea pressure at great depths or the explosions of close depth charges. The Germans reported that in their structural tests the hull failed at a simulated depth of nine hundred feet. The British reported failure at eight hundred feet, less than the failure depth of the conventional German U-boats. In reality the failure depth was much less.

- **Underpowered Diesel Engines.** The new model six-cylinder diesels fitted to the Type XXI were equipped with superchargers to generate the required horsepower. The system was so poorly designed and manufactured that the superchargers could not be used. This failure reduced the generated horsepower by almost half: from 2,000 to 1,200, leaving the Type XXI ruinously underpowered. Consequently, the maximum surface speed was only 15.6 knots, less than any oceangoing U-boat built during the war and slightly slower than the corvette convoy-escort vessel. The reduction in horsepower also substantially increased the time required to carry out a full battery charge.
- **Impractical Hydraulic System.** The main lines, accumulators, cylinders, and pistons of the hydraulic gear for operating the diving planes, rudders, torpedo-tube outer doors, and antiaircraft gun turrets on the bridge were too complex and delicate and were located *outside* the pressure hull. This gear was therefore subject to saltwater leakage, corrosion, and enemy weaponry. It could not be repaired from inside the pressure hull.
- **Poor Habitability and Sanitation.** As with the Types VII and IX, the facilities and amenities provided for the comfort and feeding of the crew did not even meet "minimum" standards of the U.S. Navy. Owing to interconnections of washing and drinking water, the sanitation was deemed to be "inadequate" and "unsafe."

Finally, a few words about the aircraft as a U-boat killer.

In World War I, when the German U-boat rose to front rank as a naval weapons system, Allied airpower, then also in its infancy, positively sank only one U-boat in four years of the war at sea. The extent to which Allied air patrols harassed and/or drove U-boats off and under, thwarting attacks on shipping, is not known, but it could have been very great.

In preparing his U-boats and crews for warfare in the 1930s, Karl Dönitz, a U-boat skipper in World War I, consistently sneered at the aircraft as a possible U-boat killer. Bridge lookouts on the U-boat, he proclaimed, could see and hear an Allied aircraft before it saw the U-boat, giving it time to dive safely out of sight beneath the sea. Doubtless this mind-set powerfully influenced Dönitz's failure to demand microwave search-radar and radar-detector technology for U-boats, an enormous lapse, for which the Germans paid a huge price.

At first, it appeared that Dönitz was right. Until the latter months of 1942, Allied aircraft sank very few U-boats unassisted by surface ships. But with the perfection of centimetric-wavelength radar, which was installed in big four-engine long-range bombers such as the B-24 Liberator, the B-17 Flying Fortress, and the British Halifax, land-based aircraft vaulted to top rank as U-boat killers. According to Alex

Niestlé, they sank unassisted 204 U-boats and 30 more in cooperation with surface ships, a grand total of 234, nearly a third of all German losses at battlefronts.

Less impressive but nonetheless significant was the contribution of the smaller Allied aircraft based on "jeep" carriers. According to Niestlé these aircraft sank unassisted 39 U-boats and another 12 in cooperation with surface ships. Including land- and sea-based aircraft, Allied air forces were involved in the kill of 285 U-boats at sea. Allied aircraft killed another 39 in bombing raids on bases and shipyards and as a result of aerial mining. All told, Allied aircraft were involved in 324 U-boat kills.

This emphasis on aircraft kills is by no means intended to deprecate the immensely effective work of the warships in convoy escort groups and in hunter-killer support groups or warships operating independently. Altogether, Niestlé writes, Allied warships sank 240 U-boats and shared credit with land- and sea-based aircraft for 42 others. All told, Allied warships were involved in 282 U-boat kills.

PLATE II

SUMMARY OF NORTH ATLANTIC CONVOY ARRIVALS

1942–1945

(As calculated by USN Tenth Fleet[1])

Numbers of ships and losses ( )

TYPE	1942	1943	1944	1945 (THROUGH MAY)	TOTALS
HX	1,899 (14)	3,010 (38)	4,169 (2)	1,776 (3)	10,854 (57)
SC	2,021 (52)	1,646 (38)	690 (2)	346 (2)	4,703 (94)
ON ONS	3,660 (99)	4,110 (63)	4,595 (3)	2,408 (1)	14,773 (166)
RB	8 (4)	—	—	—	8 (4)
CU UC	—	133	2,842 (4)	1,325	4,300 (4)
UT TU	—	198	286	—	484
Special	—	—	325	2	327
Totals	7,558 (169)	9,097 (139)	12,907 (11)	5,857 (6)	35,449 (325)

COMBINED TOTALS: 1942–1945 (MAY)

Number of:	
Convoys	838
Ships	35,449
Losses	325 (.009 percent)

1. Extracted from Metcalf, unpublished document, "History of Convoys and Routing," NHC. Losses do not include escorts.

PLATE 12

SUMMARY OF MIDDLE ATLANTIC CONVOY ARRIVALS

1942–1945
(As calculated by USN Tenth Fleet[1])
Numbers of Ships and Losses ()

TYPE	1942	1943	1944	1945 (May)	TOTALS
UGS[2]	83	1,728 (9)	2,936 (4)	1,289 (1)	6,036 (14)
GUS	—	1,251	2,555 (1)	1,277	5,083 (1)
UGF	39	176	134	17	366
GUF	30	157	93	30	310
CU[3]	—	73	—	—	73
UC	—	60 (3)	—	—	60 (3)
TM/OT[4]	—	90 (7)	36	—	126 (7)
TO	—	63	31	—	94
Special	—	—	164	44	208
Totals	152	3,598 (19)	5,949 (5)	2,657 (1)	12,356 (25)[5]

COMBINED TOTALS: 1942–1945 (MAY)

Number of:	
Convoys	296
Ships	12,356
Losses	25 (.002 percent)

1. Extracted from Metcalf, History of Convoys and Routing.

2. Cargo convoys: UGS = U.S.A.–Gib., Slow. GUS = Gib.–U.S.A., Slow. Mixed troopship and cargo convoys: UGF = U.S.A.–Gib., Fast. GUF = Gib.–U.S.A., Fast. Escorts were strictly USN.

3. CU UC were Caribbean–U.K. tanker convoys and reverse. From November 1943, these sailed via New York. Escorts were strictly USN.

4. TM 1 and TMF 2 were British tanker convoys between Trinidad and the Mediterranean, with British escorts. OT TOs were American convoys between the Caribbean and the Mediterranean with USN escorts.

5. Does not include a few escorts lost.

PLATE 13

ALLIED CONVOYS THAT LOST SIX OR MORE SHIPS

JANUARY 1942–MAY 1945[1]

DATE	CONVOY	SHIPS SUNK	G.R. TONS
2/11/42	Outbound North 67	8	54,750
5/12/42	Outbound North(S) 92	7	36,284
7/4/42	PQ 17	24[2]	102,296
8/5/42	Slow Convoy 94	11	53,421
9/42	PQ 18-QP 14	19[3]	98,376
9/10/42	Outbound North 127	8[4]	51,562
10/12/42	Slow Convoy 104	8	43,970
10/26/42	Sierra Leone 125	12	80,005
10/27/42	Halifax 212	6	51,997
11/2/42	Slow Convoy 107	15	82,817
11/15/42	Outbound North(S) 144	6[5]	26,321
12/27/42	Outbound North(S) 154	14[6]	69,378
1/3/43	TM 1[7]	7	56,453
2/4/43	Slow Convoy 118	11[8]	59,765
2/21/43	Outbound North 166	14	78,653[9]
3/7/43	Slow Convoy 121	12[10]	55,651
3/11/43	Slow Convoy 122	9	53,094
3/16/43	Halifax 229	13	93,502
4/1/43	Halifax 231	6	41,500
4/29/43	Outbound North(S) 5	13	61,958
9/20/43	Outbound North 202	10	41,277
Totals	21 convoys	233[11]	1,293,030[12]

1. For earlier years, 1939–1941, see Plate 11, Volume I, p. 425.

2. U-boats sank seven ships unassisted. Aircraft sank eight ships unassisted. U-boats and aircraft shared credit for nine ships.

3. U-boats sank nine ships for 43,216 tons unassisted, including two British escorts, destroyer *Somali* and minesweeper *Leda.* Aircraft sank the other ten ships for 55,160 tons.

4. Includes Canadian destroyer *Ottawa.*

5. Includes Norwegian-manned corvette *Montbretia.*

6. Plus two 10-ton LCV landing craft.

7. Nine-ship British Middle Atlantic tanker convoy, Trinidad to Mediterranean.

8. Plus one British 143-ton LCT landing craft.

9. Plus damage to two tankers for 18,730 tons.

10. Plus two British 143-ton LCT landing craft.

11. From North Atlantic convoys, 166 ships, of which 86 were inbound to the British Isles and 80 outbound.

12. In the nearly six years of World War II naval warfare, U-boat "wolf packs" carried out attacks on forty convoys in which six or more ships were confirmed sunk. Total ships sunk in these forty convoys, including those sunk solely by aircraft or shared jointly by U-boats and aircraft: 420 for 2,164,863 gross tons.

APPENDIX 1

(Note: Ships in the appendices are neither italicized nor listed in the index.)

OCEANGOING U-BOATS ASSIGNED TO COMBAT

THE FINAL YEARS: SEPTEMBER 1942–MAY 1945[1]

BOAT	TYPE	SKIPPER	CREW	D.O.B.	LOST/ RETIRED
IN COMBAT UNITS 9/1/42:					
U-A	Turk	Friedrich Schäfer	1914IV	2/1893	3/15/43 R
U-43	IX	Hans-Joachim Schwantke	1936	8/18	7/30/43
U-66	IXC	Friedrich Markworth	1934	2/15	
		Gerhard Seehausen	1937	7/17	5/6/44
U-67	IXC	Günther Müller-Stöckheim	1934	12/13	7/16/43
U-68	IXC	Karl-Friedrich Merten	1926	8/05	
		Albert Lauzemis	1937A	3/18	4/10/44
U-69	VIIC	Ulrich Gräf	1935	12/15	2/17/43
U-71	VIIC	Walter Flachsenberg	1928	10/08	
		Hardo Rodler von Roithberg	1937A	2/18	5/1/43 R
U-73	VIIB	Helmut Rosenbaum	1932	5/13	
		Horst Deckert	1937A	10/18	12/16/43
U-77	VIIC	Otto Hartmann	1936	4/17	3/29/43
U-81	VIIC	Fritz Guggenberger	1934	3/15	
		Johann-Otto Krieg	1937X	3/19	1/9/44
U-83	VIIB	Hans-Werner Kraus	1934	7/15	
		Ulrich Wörishoffer	1936	3/17	3/4/43
U-84	VIIB	Horst Uphoff	1935	10/16	8/7/43 ?
U-86	VIIB	Walter Schug	1934	10/10	11/28/43 ?
U-87	VIIB	Joachim Berger	1934	6/13	3/4/43
U-88	VIIC	Heino Bohmann	1934	3/14	9/12/42
U-89	VIIC	Dietrich Lohmann	1930	10/09	5/12/43
U-91	VIIC	Heinz Walkerling	1935	5/15	
		Heinz Hungershausen	1936	12/16	2/26/44
U-92	VIIC	Adolf Oelrich	1935	3/16	
		Wilhelm Brauel	1937	9/14	10/4/44 R
U-96	VIIC	Hans-Jürgen Hellriegel	1936	6/17	2/5/43 R
U-97	VIIC	Friedrich Bürgel	1936	10/16	
		Hans-Georg Trox	1936	1/16	6/16/43
U-98	VIIC	Wilhelm Schulze	NA	7/09	
		Kurt Eichmann	1937IV	10/17	11/15/42
U-103	IXB	Gustav-Adolf Janssen	1936	4/15	3/13/44 R
U-105	IXB	Heinrich Schuch	1925	8/06	
		Jürgen Nissen	1936	5/16	6/2/43

R = Retired

? = Cause of loss still in doubt ("missing")

BOAT	TYPE	SKIPPER	CREW	D.O.B.	LOST/ RETIRED
U-106	IXB	Hermann Rasch	1934	8/14	
		Wolf-Dietrich Damerow	1937X	5/19	8/2/43
U-107	IXB	Harald Gelhaus	1935	7/15	
		Volker Simmermacher	1937A	2/19	
		Karl Heinz Fritz	1941I	2/21	8/18/44
U-108	IXB	Klaus Scholtz	1927	3/08	
		Ralf-Reimar Wolfram	1930	3/12	
		Matthias Brünig	1938X	2/20	4/11/44 R
U-109	IXB	Heinrich Bleichrodt	1931	10/09	
		Hans Joachim Schramm	1936	6/16	5/4/43
U-116	XB	Werner von Schmmidt	1926	4/06	
		Wilhelm Grimme	1925	5/07	10/6/42 ?
U-123	IXB	Horst von Schroeter	1937B	6/19	6/17/44
U-124	IXB	Johann Mohr	1934	6/16	4/2/43
U-125	IXC	Ulrich Folkers	1934	3/15	5/6/43
U-126	IXC	Ernst Bauer	1933	2/14	
		Siegfried Kietz	1937A	1/17	7/3/43
U-128	IXC	Ulrich Heyse	1933	9/06	
		Hermann Steinert	1936	12/16	5/17/43
U-129	IXC	Hans-Ludwig Witt	1929	12/09	
		Richard von Harpe	1937X	8/17	8/18/44 R
U-130	IXC	Ernst Kals	1924	8/05	
		Siegfried Keller	1937IV	10/17	3/12/43
U-132	VIIC	Ernst Vogelsang	1931	8/11	11/4/42 ?
U-134	VIIC	Rudolf Schendel	1932	1/14	
		Hans-Günther Brosin	1936	11/16	8/24/43
U-135	VIIC	Friedrich-Hermann Praetorius	1935	2/04	
		Heinz Schütt	1936	11/15	
		Otto Luther	1937B	9/18	7/15/43
U-154	IXC	Walther Kölle	1926	9/07	
		Heinrich Schuch	1925	8/06	
		Oskar Heinz Kusch	1937A	4/18	
		Gerth Gemeiner	1937X	10/18	7/3/44
U-155	IXC	Adolf-Cornelius Piening	1930	9/10	
		Johannes Rudolph	1937B	4/16	
		Ludwig-Ferdinand von Friedeburg	1941V	5/24	
		Erwin Witte	1936	2/11	
		Friedrich Altmeier	1938	7/20	End
U-156	IXC	Werner Hartenstein	1928	2/08	3/8/43
U-159	IXC	Helmut Witte	1934	4/15	
		Heinz Beckmann	1939X	6/13	7/28/43
U-160	IXC	Georg Lassen	1935	5/15	
		Gerd von Pommer-Esche	1937A	1/18	7/14/43
U-161	IXC	Albrecht Achilles	1934	1/14	9/27/43
U-162	IXC	Jürgen Wattenberg	1921	12/00	9/3/42
U-163	IXC	Kurt-Eduard Engelmann	1923	4/03	3/13/43
U-164	IXC	Otto Fechner	1924	11/05	1/6/43
U-165	IXC	Eberhard Hoffmann	1925	5/07	9/27/42 ?
U-171	IXC	Günther Pfeffer	1934	10/14	10/9/42
U-172	IXC	Carl Emmermann	1934	3/15	
		Hermann Hoffmann	1939X	4/21	12/13/43
U-173	IXC	Heinz-Ehler Beucke	1922	1/04	
		Hans-Adolph Schweichel	1936	5/15	11/16/42
U-174	IXC	Ulrich Thilo	1922	1/03	
		Wolfgang Grandefeld	1936	2/17	4/27/43

BOAT	TYPE	SKIPPER	CREW	D.O.B.	LOST/ RETIRED
U-175	IXC	Heinrich Bruns	1931	4/12	4/17/43
U-176	IXC	Reiner Dierksen	1933	3/08	5/15/43
U-179	IXD2	Ernst Sobe	1924	9/04	10/8/42
U-201	VIIC	Günther Rosenberg	1936	1/17	2/17/43
U-202	VIIC	Hans-Heinz Linder	1933	2/13	
		Günter Poser	1936	9/16	6/2/43
U-203	VIIC	Rolf Mützelburg	1932	6/13	
		Hermann Kottmann	1936	12/15	4/25/43
U-205	VIIC	Franz-Georg Reschke	1929	5/08	
		Friedrich Bürgel	1936	10/16	2/17/43
U-209	VIIC	Heinrich Brodda	1921	5/03	5/7/43 ?
U-211	VIIC	Karl Hause	1935	7/16	11/19/43
U-214	VIID	Günther Reeder	1935	11/15	
		Rupprecht Stock	1937A	2/16	
		Gerhard Conrad	1939XII	8/20	7/26/44
U-216	VIID	Karl-Otto Schultz	1934	11/1	10/20/42
U-217	VIID	Kurt Reichenbach-Klinke	1935	2/17	6/5/43
U-218	VIID	Richard Becker	1934	2/11	
		Rupprecht Stock	1937A	2/16	End
U-251	VIIC	Heinrich Timm	1933	4/10	
		Franz Säck	1928	12/09	
		Joachim Sauerbier	1939IX	9/19	4/19/45
U-254	VIIC	Hans Gilardone	1932	7/12	12/8/42
U-255	VIIC	Reinhart Reche	1934	12/14	
		Erich Harms	1939	1/10	
		Helmut Heinrich	NA	10/13	End
U-256	VIIC	Odo Loewe	1934	9/14	
		Wilhelm Brauel	1937	9/14	
		Heinrich Lehmann-Willenbrock	1931	12/11	End
U-259	VIIC	Klaus Köpke	1935	1/15	11/15/42
U-331	VIIC	Hans-Dietrich von Tiesenhausen	1934	2/13	11/17/42
U-332	VIIC	Johannes Liebe	1933	7/13	
		Eberhard Hüttemann	1937X	6/19	4/29/43
U-333	VIIC	Peter Erich Cremer	1932	3/11	
		Lorenz Kasch	1933	8/14	
		Werner Schwaff	1936	3/15	
		Peter Erich Cremer	1932	3/11	
		Hans Fiedler	1936	10/14	7/31/44
U-334	VIIC	Hilmar Siemon	1934	3/15	
		Heinz Ehrich	1937B	9/19	6/14/43
U-355	VIIC	Günter La Baume	1929	4/11	4/1/44
U-371	VIIC	Waldemar Mehl	1933	9/14	
		Horst-Arno Fenski	1937X	11/18	5/4/44
U-373	VIIC	Paul-Karl Loeser	1935	4/15	
		Detlev von Lehsten	1937	8/17	6/8/44
U-375	VIIC	Jürgen Könenkamp	1932	8/13	7/30/43
U-376	VIIC	Friedrich-Karl Marks	1934	6/14	4/6/43 ?
U-377	VIIC	Otto Köhler	1931	11/09	
		Gerhard Kluth	1937B	8/18	1/15/44 ?
U-378	VIIC	Alfred Hoschatt	1927	2/09	
		Erich Mäder	1936	10/18	10/20/43
U-380	VIIC	Josef Röther	1927	10/0	
		Albrecht Brandi	1935	6/14	3/11/44
U-402	VIIC	Siegfried von Forstner	1930	9/10	10/13/43

BOAT	TYPE	SKIPPER	CREW	D.O.B.	LOST/ RETIRED
U-403	VIIC	Heinz-Ehlert Clausen	1932	7/09	
		Karl-Franz Heine	1934	10/15	8/18/43
U-404	VIIC	Otto von Bülow	1930	10/11	
		Adolf Schönberg	1937B	8/18	7/28/43
U-405	VIIC	Rolf-Heinrich Hopmann	1926	3/06	11/1/43
U-406	VIIC	Horst Dieterichs	1934	3/12	2/18/44
U-407	VIIC	Ulrich-Ernst Brüller	1936	9/17	
		Hubertus Korndörfer	1939X	11/19	
		Hans Kolbus	1938	10/19	9/19/44
U-408	VIIC	Reinhard von Hymmen	1933	11/42	11/5/42
U-409	VIIC	Hans-Ferdinand Massmann	1936	6/17	7/12/43
U-410	VIIC	Kurt Sturm	1925	1/06	
		Horst-Arno Fenski	1937	11/18	3/11/44
U-411	VIIC	Gerhard Litterscheid	1935	6/14	
		Johann Spindlegger	1935	7/15	11/13/42
U-431	VIIC	Wilhelm Dommes	1931	4/07	
		Dietrich Schöneboom	1937	12/17	10/21/43
U-432	VIIC	Heinz-Otto Schultze	1934	9/15	
		Hermann Eckhardt	1936	6/16	3/11/43
U-435	VIIC	Siegfried Strelow	1931	4/11	7/9/43
U-436	VIIC	Günther Seibicke	1932	8/11	5/26/43
U-437	VIIC	Werner-Karl Schulz	1928	10/10	
		Hermann Lamby	1936	12/15	10/5/44
U-438	VIIC	Rudolf Franzius	1932	6/11	
		Heinrich Heinsohn	1933	2/10	5/6/43
U-453	VIIC	Egon-Reiner von Schlippenbach	1934	4/14	
		Dierk Lührs	1938	11/19	5/21/44
U-454	VIIC	Burkhard Hackländer	1933	12/14	8/1/43
U-455	VIIC	Hans-Heinrich Giessler	1931	1/11	
		Hans Martin Scheibe	1936	4/18	4/2/44 ?
U-456	VIIC	Max-Martin Teichert	1934	1/15	5/12/43 ?
U-457	VIIC	Karl Brandenburg	1924	7/06	9/16/42
U-458	VIIC	Kurt Diggens	1934	10/13	8/22/43
U-459	XIV	Georg von Wilamowitz-Möllendorf	1914	11/1893	7/24/43
U-460	XIV	Ebe Schnoor	1915XII	6/1895	10/4/43
U-461	XIV	Wolf-Harro Stiebler	1932	8/07	7/30/43
U-463	XIV	Leo Wolfbauer	1913	7/1895	5/16/43
Note: In Volume I, U-501 to U-517 inclusive were misidentified as IXC40s.					
U-504	IXC	Fritz Poske	1923	10/04	
		Wilhelm Luis	1935	12/15	7/30/43
U-505	IXC	Axel-Olaf Loewe	1928	1/09	
		Peter Zschech	1936	10/18	
		Harald Lange	NA	12/03	6/4/44 Captured
U-506	IXC	Erich Würdemann	1933	1/14	7/12/43
U-507	IXC	Harro Schacht	1926	12/07	1/13/43
U-508	IXC	Georg Staats	1935	3/16	11/12/43
U-509	IXC	Karl-Heinz Wolff	1928	10/09	
		Werner Witte	1935	1/15	7/15/43
U-510	IXC	Karl Neitzel	1923	1/01	
		Alfred Eick	1937	3/16	End
U-511	IXC	Friedrich Steinhoff	1935	7/09	
		Fritz Schneewind	1936	4/17	9/16/43 Japan
U-512	IXC	Wolfgang Schultze	1930	10/1	10/2/42
U-513	IXC	Rolf Rüggeberg	1926	3/07	
		Friedrich Guggenberger	1934	3/15	7/19/43

BOAT	TYPE	SKIPPER	CREW	D.O.B.	LOST/ RETIRED
U-514	IXC	Hans-Jürgen Auffermann	1934	10/14	7/8/43
U-515	IXC	Werner Henke	1934	5/08	4/9/44
U-516	IXC	Gerhard Wiebe	1925	1/07	
		Hans-Rutger Tillessen	1934	4/13	
		Friedrich Petran	1938	12/19	End
U-517	IXC	Paul Hartwig	1935	9/15	11/21/42
U-552	VIIC	Erich Topp	1934	7/14	
		Klaus Popp	1935	5/17	
		Günther Lube	1939IX	10/20	End
U-553	VIIC	Karl Thurmann	1928	9/09	1/20/43 ?
U-558	VIIC	Günther Krech	1933	9/14	7/20/43
U-559	VIIC	Hans Heidtmann	1934	8/14	10/30/42
U-561	VIIC	Heinz Schomburg	1935	9/14	
		Fritz Henning	1937A	4/17	7/12/43
U-562	VIIC	Horst Hamm	1935	3/16	2/19/43
U-563	VIIC	Götz von Hartmann	1934	10/13	
		Gustav Borchardt	1937B	12/16	5/31/43
U-564	VIIC	Reinhard Suhren	1935	4/16	
		Hans Fiedler	1936	10/14	6/14/43
U-565	VIIC	Wilhelm Franken	1935	9/14	
		Fritz Henning	1937A	4/17	9/30/44
U-566	VIIC	Gerhard Remus	1936	4/17	
		Hans Hornkohl	1936	4/17	10/24/43
U-569	VIIC	Hans-Peter Hinsch	1934	7/14	
		Hans Johannsen	1935	9/10	5/22/43
U-571	VIIC	Helmut Möhlmann	1933	6/13	
		Gustav Lüssow	1937A	12/17	1/28/44
U-572	VIIC	Heinz Hirsacker	1934	8/14	
		Heinz Kummetat	1937A	11/18	8/3/43
U-575	VIIC	Günther Heydemann	1933	1/14	
		Wolfgang Boehmer	1939XII	8/20	3/13/44
U-582	VIIC	Werner Schulte	1937A	11/12	10/5/42
U-584	VIIC	Joachim Deecke	1933	6/12	
		Kurt Nölke	1935	9/14	
		Joachim Deecke	1933	6/12	10/31/43
U-586	VIIC	Dietrich von der Esch	1934	1/15	
		Hans Götze	1939XI	1/16	7/5/44
U-589	VIIC	Hans-Joachim Horrer	1933	2/08	9/14/42
U-590	VIIC	Heinrich Müller-Edzards	1933/32	3/10	
		Werner Krüer	NA	11/14	7/9/43
U-591	VIIC	Hans-Jürgen Zetzsche	1934	10/15	
		Reimer Ziesmer	1937A	11/17	7/30/43
U-592	VIIC	Karl Borm	1933	8/11	
		Hans Jaschke	1939IX	7/20	1/31/44
U-593	VIIC	Gerd Kelbling	1934	6/15	12/13/43
U-594	VIIC	Friedrich Mumm	1936	1/15	6/4/43
U-595	VIIC	Jürgen Quaet-Faslem	1934	5/13	11/14/42
U-596	VIIC	Günter Jahn	1931	9/10	
		Viktor-Wilhelm Nonn	1937A	4/17	
		Hans Kolbus	1938	10/19	9/25/44
U-597	VIIC	Eberhard Bopst	1933	12/13	10/12/42
U-598	VIIC	Gottfried Holtorf	1935	5/12	7/23/43
U-599	VIIC	Wolfgang Breithaupt	1932	9/13	10/24/42
U-600	VIIC	Bernhard Zurmühlen	1934	3/09	11/25/43
U-601	VIIC	Peter-Ottmar Grau	1934	5/14	
		Otto Hansen	1937IV	4/18	2/25/44
U-604	VIIC	Horst Höltring	1933	6/13	8/11/43

BOAT	TYPE	SKIPPER	CREW	D.O.B.	LOST/ RETIRED
U-605	VIIC	Herbert-Viktor Schütze	1935	2/17	11/14/42
U-607	VIIC	Ernst Mengersen	1933	6/12	
		Wolf Jeschonnek	1938	7/19	7/13/43
U-608	VIIC	Rolf Struckmeier	NA	NA	
		Wolfgang Reisener	1938	10/18	8/10/44
U-609	VIIC	Klaus Rudloff	1935	1/16	2/7/43
U-617	VIIC	Albrecht Brandi	1935	6/14	9/12/43
U-653	VIIC	Gerhard Feiler	1934	9/09	
		Hans-Albrecht Kandler	1937A	10/17	3/15/44
U-657	VIIC	Heinrich Göllnitz	1935	8/09	5/17/43
U-658	VIIC	Hans Senkel	1933	1/10	10/30/42
U-659	VIIC	Hans Stock	1935	8/15	5/4/43
U-660	VIIC	Götz Baur	1935	8/17	11/12/42
U-703	VIIC	Heinz Bielfeld	1934	8/16	
		Joachim Brünner	1937B	4/19	9/16/44 ?
U-704	VIIC	Horst Kessler	1934	8/14	
		Gerhard Nolte	1939X	1/22	End
U-705	VIIC	Karl-Horst Horn	1935	12/16	9/3/42
U-752	VIIC	Karl-Ernst Schroeter	1934	12/12	5/23/43
U-753	VIIC	Alfred Manhardt von Mannstein	1925	3/08	5/13/43
U-755	VIIC	Walter Göing	1934	8/14	5/28/43
U-756	VIIC	Klaus Harney	1934	3/17	9/1/42
September 1942:					
U-118	XB	Werner Czygan	1925	11/04	6/12/43
U-177	IXD2	Robert Gysae	1931	1/11	
		Heinz Buchholz	1929	8/09	2/6/44
U-178	IXD2	Hans Ibbeken	1918	9/1899	
		Wilhelm Dommes	1929	4/07	
		Wilhelm Spahr	1921	4/04	8/20/44 R
U-181	IXD2	Wolfgang Lüth	1933	10/13	
		Kurt Freiwald	1925	10/06	End
U-183	IXC40	Heinrich Schäfer	1925	1/07	
		Fritz Schneewind	1936	4/10	4/23/45
U-212	VIIC	Helmut Vogler	1935	9/16	7/21/44
U-221	VIIC	Hans Trojer	1936	1/16	9/27/43
U-253	VIIC	Adolf Friedrichs	1935	3/14	9/25/42 ?
U-257	VIIC	Heinz Rahe	1935	3/16	2/24/44
U-258	VIIC	Wilhelm von Mässenhausen	1935	1/15	
		Leopold Koch	1937B	9/18	
		Wilhelm von Mässenhausen	1935	1/15	5/20/43
U-260	VIIC	Hubertus Purkhold	1935	6/16	
		Klaus Becker	1939IX	4/20	3/12/45
U-261	VIIC	Hans Lange	1935	5/15	9/15/42
U-262	VIIC	Heinz Franke	1936	11/15	
		Helmut Wieduwilt	1938	11/19	
		Karl-Heinz Laudahn	1939X	9/15	End
U-353	VIIC	Wolfgang Römer	1936	10/16	10/16/42
U-356	VIIC	Georg Wallas	1925	2/5	
		Günther Ruppelt	1937B	9/19	12/27/42
U-382	VIIC	Herbert Juli	1935	6/16	
		Leopold Koch	1937B	9/18	
		Rudolf Zorn	1937B		
		Hans-Dietrich Wilke	1932	6/12	

BOAT	TYPE	SKIPPER	CREW	D.O.B.	LOST/ RETIRED
		Günter Schimmel	1939XII	8/20	End
U-440	VIIC	Hans Geissler	1938	10/16	
		Werner Schwaff	1936	3/15	5/31/43
U-441	VIIC	Klaus Hartmann	1933	12/12	
		Götz von Hartmann	1934	10/13	
		Klaus Hartmann	1933	12/12	6/8/44
U-442	VIIC	Hans-Joachim Hesse	1925	1/06	2/12/43
U-518	IXC	Friedrich-Wilhelm Wissmann	1935	12/15	
		Hans-Werner Offermann	1939IX	7/21	4/22/45
U-602	VIIC	Philipp Schüler	1935	1/11	4/19/43 ?
U-606	VIIC	Hans Klatt	1935	6/16	
		Dietrich von der Esch	1934	1/15	
		Hans-Heinrich Döhler	1937	12/17	2/22/43
U-610	VIIC	Walter von Freyberg-Eisenberg-Allmendingen	1935	11/15	10/8/43
U-615	VIIC	Ralph Kapitzky	1935	6/16	8/7/43
U-618	VIIC	Kurt Baberg	1936	2/17	
		Erich Faust	1939XII	4/21	8/15/44
U-619	VIIC	Kurt Makowski	1936	9/15	10/5/42
U-620	VIIC	Heinz Stein	1937	8/13	2/13/43
U-621	VIIC	Horst Schünemann	1934	1/14	
		Max Kruschka	1937B	5/19	
		Hermann Stuckmann	1939	1/21	8/18/44
U-622	VIIC	Horst-Thilo Queck	1935	1/19	7/24/43
U-625	VIIC	Hans Benker	1936	2/17	
		Siegfried Straub	1939IX	6/18	3/10/44
U-661	VIIC	Erich von Lilienfeld	1935	11/15	10/15/42
U-662	VIIC	Wolfgang Hermann	1928	12/08	
		Heinz-Eberhard Müller	1936	3/16	7/21/43
U-706	VIIC	Alexander von Zitzewitz	1934	3/16	8/2/43
U-757	VIIC	Friedrich Deetz	1935	9/16	1/8/44
OCTOBER 1942:					
U-117	XB	Hans-Werner Neumann	1925	9/06	8/7/43
U-185	IXC40	August Maus	1934	2/15	8/24/43
U-224	VIIC	Hans Karl Kosbadt	1937	12/17	1/13/43
U-263	VIIC	Kurt Nölke	1935	9/14	1/20/44 ?
U-301	VIIC	Willy-Roderich Körner	1935	12/14	1/21/43
U-354	VIIC	Karl-Heinz Herbschleb	1935	10/10	
		Hans-Jürgen Sthamer	1937B	7/19	8/24/44
U-381	VIIC	Wilhelm-Heinrich von Pückler und Limpurg	1934	3/13	5/9/43 ?
U-383	VIIC	Horst Kremser	1936	9/17	8/1/43 ?
U-412	VIIC	Walter Jahrmärker	1935	9/17	10/22/42
U-413	VIIC	Gustav Poel	1936	8/17	
		Dieter Sachee	1939IX	8/17	8/20/44
U-443	VIIC	Konstantin von Puttkamer	1936	7/17	2/23/43
U-465	VIIC	Heinz Wolf	1934	8/14	5/2/43
U-519	IXC	Günter Eppen	1933	8/12	1/30/43 ?
U-520	IXC	Volkmar Schwartzkopff	1934	4/14	10/30/42
U-521	IXC	Klaus Bargsten	1935	10/11	6/2/43
U-522	IXC	Herbert Schneider	1934	6/15	2/23/43
U-611	VIIC	Nikolaus von Jacobs	1933	1/13	12/8/42
U-613	VIIC	Helmut Köppe	1933	4/09	7/23/43
U-624	VIIC	Ulrich von Soden-Fraunhofen	1936	8/13	2/7/43

BOAT	TYPE	SKIPPER	CREW	D.O.B.	LOST/ RETIRED
U-627	VIIC	Robert Kindelbacher	1935	5/15	10/27/42
U-663	VIIC	Heinrich Schmid	1934	5/15	5/8/43 ?
U-664	VIIC	Adolf Graef	1936	4/16	8/9/43
NOVEMBER 1942:					
U-184	IXC40	Günther Dangechat	1935	7/15	11/20/42 ?
U-264	VIIC	Hartwig Looks	1936	6/17	2/19/44
U-336	VIIC	Hans Hunger	1935	3/15	10/5/43
U-439	VIIC	Wolfgang Sporn	1934	9/12	
		Helmut von Tippelskirch	1937A	12/17	5/4/43
U-445	VIIC	Heinz-Konrad Fenn	1937A	7/18	
		Rupprecht Fischler von Treuberg	1939	2/20	8/24/44
U-462	XIV	Bruno Vowe	1923	7/04	7/30/43
U-524	IXC	Walter von Steinaecker	1935	3/17	3/22/43
U-603	VIIC	Hans-Joachim Bertelemann	1936	4/16	
		Rudolf Baltz	1935	7/20	
		Hans-Joachim Bertelsmann	1936	4/16	3/1/44
U-623	VIIC	Hermann Schröder	1937I	4/12	2/21/43
U-628	VIIC	Heinz Hasenschar	1936	9/16	7/3/43
U-758	VIIC	Helmut Manseck	1934	12/14	
		Hans-Arendt Feindt	1939XII	10/21	3/16/45
DECEMBER 1942:					
U-167	IXC40	Kurt Neubert	1936	3/10	
		Kurt Sturm	1925	1/06	4/6/43
U-182	IXD2	Nikolaus Clausen	1929	6/11	5/16/43
U-186	IXC40	Siegfried Hesemann	1935	7/12	5/12/43
U-225	VIIC	Wolfgang Leimkühler	1937A	8/18	2/15/43
U-226	VIIC	Rolf Borchers	1933	11/13	
		Albrecht Gänge	1937B	6/19	11/6/43
U-266	VIIC	Ralf von Jessen	1935	2/17	5/15/43
U-302	VIIC	Herbert Sickel	1935	6/14	4/6/44
U-303	VIIC	Karl-Franz Heine	1934	10/15	5/21/43
U-337	VIIC	Kurt Ruwiedel	1936	9/17	1/3/43 ?
U-357	VIIC	Adolf Kellner	1935	4/10	12/26/42
U-384	VIIC	Hans-Achim von Rosenberg-Gruszczynski	1937A	6/17	3/19/43
U-444	VIIC	Albert Langfeld	1937A	1/18	3/11/43
U-525	IXC40	Hans-Joachim Drewitz	1933	11/07	8/11/43
U-626	VIIC	Hans-Botho Bade	1939X	11/09	12/15/42
U-629	VIIC	Hans-Helmuth Bugs	1937A	3/17	6/7/44
U-631	VIIC	Jürgen Krüger	1937A	7/18	10/17/43
U-632	VIIC	Hans Karpf	1935	5/16	4/6/43
JANUARY 1943:					
U-187	IXC40	Ralph Münnich	1935	2/16	2/4/43
U-223	VIIC	Karl-Jürgen Wächter	1936	5/16	
		Peter Gerlach	1939XI	5/22	3/30/44
U-265	VIIC	Leonhard Auffhammer	1936	6/17	2/3/43
U-267	VIIC	Otto Tinschert	1935	3/19	
		Bernhard Knieper	1941I	3/11	End
U-268	VIIC	Ernst Heydemann	1936	6/16	2/19/43
U-358	VIIC	Rolf Manke	1935	12/15	3/1/44
U-414	VIIC	Walther Huth	1937IV	4/18	5/25/43

BOAT	TYPE	SKIPPER	CREW	D.O.B.	LOST/ RETIRED
U-448	VIIC	Helmut Dauter	1937B	8/19	4/14/44
U-466	VIIC	Gerhard Thäter	1936	11/16	8/19/44
U-468	VIIC	Klemens Schamong	1937A	4/17	8/11/43
U-529	IXC40	Georg-Werner Fraatz	1935	3/17	2/12/43 ?
U-614	VIIC	Wolfgang Sträter	1935	5/16	7/29/43
U-707	VIIC	Günter Gretschel	1936	10/14	11/9/43
February 1943:					
U-119	XB	Alois Zech	1925	9/07	
		Horst-Tessen von Kameke	1935	2/16	6/24/43
U-180	IXD1	Werner Musenberg	1925	9/04	
		Rolf Riesen	1938	12/19	8/23/44 ?
U-190	IXC40	Max Wintermeyer	1934	2/14	
		Hans-Edwin Reith	1939A	1/20	End
U-228	VIIC	Erwin Christophersen	1936	4/15	
		Herbert Engel	1939VII	6/12	10/4/44
U-229	VIIC	Robert Schetelig	1937A	10/18	9/22/43
U-230	VIIC	Paul Siegmann	1935	5/13	
		Heinz-Eugen Eberbach	1939X	7/21	8/21/44
U-305	VIIC	Rudolf Bahr	1935	4/16	1/17/44
U-306	VIIC	Claus von Trotha	1936	3/14	10/31/43
U-338	VIIC	Manfred Kinzel	1935	3/15	9/20/43 ?
U-359	VIIC	Heinz Förster	1940	6/09	7/26/43
U-447	VIIC	Friedrich-Wilhelm Bothe	1936	7/17	5/7/43
U-523	IXC	Werner Pietzsch	1935	4/17	8/25/43
U-526	IXC40	Hans Möglich	1935	1/16	4/14/43
U-527	IXC40	Herbert Uhlig	1935	2/16	7/23/43
U-530	IXC40	Kurt Lange	1922	8/03	
		Otto Wermuth	1939IX	7/20	End (Argentina)
U-616	VIIC	Siegfried Koitschka	1937A	8/17	5/17/44
U-633	VIIC	Bernhard Müller	1937A	10/16	3/10/43
U-634	VIIC	Eberhard Dahlhaus	1938	7/20	8/30/43
U-638	VIIC	Hinrich-Oskar Bernbeck	1934	7/14	
		Oskar Staudinger	1936	5/17	5/5/43
U-641	VIIC	Horst Rendtel	1936	11/16	1/19/44
U-642	VIIC	Herbert Brünning	1935	9/15	7/5/44
U-665	VIIC	Hans-Jürgen Haupt	1935	2/11	3/22/43
U-666	VIIC	Herbert Engel	1939VII	6/12	
		Ernst-August Wilberg	1938I	9/13	2/10/44 ?
U-709	VIIC	Karl-Otto Weber	1936	10/14	
		Rudolf Ites	1936	2/18	3/1/44
U-759	VIIC	Rudolf Friedrich	1935	6/14	7/15/43
March 1943:					
U-168	IXC40	Helmuth Pich	1934	6/14	10/6/44
U-169	IXC40	Hermann Bauer	1936	8/17	3/27/43
U-188	IXC40	Siegfried Lüdden	1936	5/16	8/20/44 R
U-191	IXC40	Helmut Fiehn	1935	2/16	4/23/43
U-195	IXD1	Heinz Buchholz	1929	8/09	
		Friedrich Steinfeldt	1940IV	12/14	End
U-196	IXD2	Eitel-Friedrich Kentrat	1928	9/06	
		Heinz-Werner Striegler	1937B	6/18	11/30/44 ?
U-198	IXD2	Werner Hartmann	1921	12/02	
		Burkhard Heusinger von Waldegg	1938X	5/20	8/12/44
U-269	VIIC	Karl-Heinrich Harlfinger	1936	8/15	
		Otto Hansen	1937A	4/18	

BOAT	TYPE	SKIPPER	CREW	D.O.B.	LOST/ RETIRED
		Georg Uhl	1939IV	1/15	6/25/44
U-270	VIIC	Paul-Friedrich Otto	1937A	4/17	
		Heinrich Schreiber	1937B	4/17	8/13/44
U-339	VIIC	Georg-Wilhelm Basse	1936	8/17	
		Werner Remus	1939X	9/19	End
U-415	VIIC	Kurt Neide	1936	7/16	
		Herbert Werner	1939XII	5/20	7/14/44
U-467	VIIC	Heinz Kummer	1936	5/15	5/25/43
U-469	VIIC	Emil Claussen	1937IV	10/17	3/25/43
U-487	XIV	Helmut Metz	1935	9/06	7/13/43
U-532	IXC40	Otto-Heinrich Junker	1924	7/05	End
U-630	VIIC	Werner Winkler	1936	5/17	5/6/43
U-635	VIIC	Heinz Eckelmann	1937A	7/16	4/5/43
U-639	VIIC	Walter Wichmann	1937B	4/19	8/28/43
U-644	VIIC	Kurt Jensen	1937IV	2/18	4/7/43
U-711	VIIC	Hans-Günther Lange	1937	9/16	5/4/45
APRIL 1943:					
U-189	IXC40	Helmut Kurrer	1935	2/16	4/23/43
U-192	IXC40	Werner Happe	1936	9/15	5/6/43
U-197	IXD2	Robert Bartels	1934	4/11	8/20/43
U-227	VIIC	Jürgen Kuntze	1936	9/17	4/30/43
U-231	VIIC	Wolfgang Wenzel	1934	3/10	1/13/44
U-304	VIIC	Heinz Koch	1939	7/14	5/28/43
U-340	VIIC	Hans-Joachim Klaus	1937A	5/18	11/2/43
U-386	VIIC	Hans-Albrecht Kandler	1937A	10/17	
		Fritz Albrecht	1937B	5/20	2/19/44
U-418	VIIC	Gerhard Lange	1937B	5/20	6/1/43
U-528	IXC40	Georg von Rabenau	1936	7/16	5/11/43
U-531	IXC40	Herbert Neckel	1935	8/16	5/6/43
U-533	IXC40	Helmut Hennig	1936	4/14	10/16/43
U-636	VIIC	Hans Hildebrandt	1936	12/11	
		Eberhard Schendel	1939XII	6/20	4/21/45
U-645	VIIC	Otto Ferro	1940	1/11	12/24/43
U-646	VIIC	Heinrich Wulff	1940	2/08	5/17/43
U-648	VIIC	Peter-Arthur Stahl	1938	8/13	11/22/43 ?
U-650	VIIC	Ernst von Witzendorff	1937A	6/16	
		Rudolf Zorn	1937B	7/17	12/9/44 ?
U-710	VIIC	Dietrich von Carlowitz	1936	7/16	4/24/43
U-731	VIIC	Werner Techand	1937B	1/19	
		Alexander von Keller	1938	3/19	5/15/44
U-732	VIIC	Claus-Peter Carlsen	1937B	10/19	10/31/43
U-760	VIIC	Otto-Ulrich Blum	1936	2/17	9/8/43
U-952	VIIC	Oskar Curio	1937A	2/18	7/5/44
U-954	VIIC	Odo Loewe	1934	9/14	5/19/43
MAY 1943:					
U-170	IXC40	Günther Pfeffer	1934	10/14	
		Hans Gerold Hauber	1933	7/13	End
U-193	IXC40	Hans Pauckstadt	1926	9/06	
		Ulrich Abel	1939	3/12	4/23/44 ?
U-199	IXD2	Hans-Werner Kraus	1934	7/15	7/31/43
U-232	VIIC	Ernst Ziehm	1933	7/14	7/8/43
U-271	VIIC	Curt Barleben	1935	3/09	1/28/44
U-273	VIIC	Hermann Rossmann	1937B	7/18	5/19/43
U-308	VIIC	Karl Mühlenpfort	1940	6/09	6/4/43
U-341	VIIC	Dietrich Epp	1937A	8/17	9/19/43

BOAT	TYPE	SKIPPER	CREW	D.O.B.	LOST/ RETIRED
U-450	VIIC	Kurt Böhme	1937X	1/17	3/10/44
U-488	XIV	Erwin Bartke	1940	4/09	
		Bruno Studt	1939X	4/18	4/26/44
U-535	IXC40	Helmut Ellmenreich	1935	7/13	7/5/43
U-640	VIIC	Karl-Heinz Nagel	1937A	1/17	5/14/43
U-667	VIIC	Heinrich Schroeteler	1936	12/15	
		Karl-Heinz Lange	1937A	2/18	8/25/44 ?
U-669	VIIC	Kurt Köhl	1939XI	12/12	8/29/43 ?
U-951	VIIC	Kurt Pressel	1937B	4/11	7/7/43
U-953	VIIC	Karl-Heinz Marbach	1937IV	7/19	
		Herbert Werner	1939XII	5/20	
		Erich Steinbrink	1938	3/19	End
June 1943:					
U-194	IXC40	Hermann Hesse	1935	3/09	6/24/43
U-200	IXD2	Heinrich Schonder	1935	7/10	6/24/43
U-307	VIIC	Friedrich-Georg Herrle	1939	8/10	
		Erich Krüger	1939X	4/18	4/29/45
U-387	VIIC	Rudolf Büchler	1936	10/15	12/9/44
U-388	VIIC	Peter Sues	1938	9/19	6/20/43
U-417	VIIC	Wolfgang Schreiner	1937A	4/17	6/11/43
U-420	VIIC	Hans-Jürgen Reese	1937A	4/18	10/20/43 ?
U-449	VIIC	Hermann Otto	1934	5/14	6/24/43
U-536	IXC40	Rolf Schauenburg	1934	5/13	11/20/43
July 1943:					
U-277	VIIC	Robert Lübsen	1937A	9/16	5/1/44
U-489	XIV	Adalbert Schmandt	1940I	12/09	8/4/43
U-647	VIIC	Willi Hertin	1935	9/14	7/28/43 ?
U-713	VIIC	Henri Gosejakob	1936	12/15	2/24/44
U-737	VIIC	Paul Brasack	1937	5/16	
		Friedrich-August Gréus	1939A	4/21	12/19/44
U-847	IXD2	Herbert Kuppisch	1933	12/09	8/27/43
August 1943:					
U-220	XB	Bruno Barber	1922	3/04	10/28/43
U-238	VIIC	Horst Hepp	1936	10/17	2/9/44
U-274	VIIC	Günther Jordan	1937	2/19	10/23/43
U-275	VIIC	Helmut Bork	1939	5/10	
		Helmut Wehrkamp	1939XII	3/21	3/10/45
U-309	VIIC	Hans-Gert Mahrholz	1938	10/18	
		Herbert Loeder	1938X	4/19	2/16/45
U-360	VIIC	Klaus Becker	1936	3/18	4/2/44
U-389	VIIC	Siegfried Heilmann	1936	6/17	10/4/43
U-419	VIIC	Dietrich Giersberg	1937A	11/17	10/8/43
U-422	VIIC	Wolfgang Poeschel	1938	3/20	10/4/43
U-643	VIIC	Hans-Harald Speidel	1936	5/17	10/8/43
U-841	IXC40	Werner Bender	1936	10/16	10/17/43
U-956	VIIC	Hans-Dieter Mohs	1937B	9/19	End
U-960	VIIC	Günther Heinrich	1938	1/20	5/19/44
U-963	VIIC	Karl Boddenberg	1933	5/14	
		Rolf-Werner Wentz	1939X	1/20	End
U-1061	VIIF	Otto Hinrichs	NA	11/13	
		Walter Jäger	1943	5/1897	End
September 1943:					
U-279	VIIC	Otto Finke	1936	9/15	10/4/43
U-281	VIIC	Heinz von Davidson	1937A	12/18	End

BOAT	TYPE	SKIPPER	CREW	D.O.B.	LOST/ RETIRED
U-282	VIIC	Rudolf Müller	1937B	6/17	10/29/43
U-426	VIIC	Christian Reich	1936	11/15	1/8/44
U-470	VIIC	Günther Grave	1937A	7/17	10/16/43
U-537	IXC40	Peter Schrewe	1934	12/13	11/10/44
U-539	IXC40	Hans-Jürgen Lauterbach-Emden	1937A	5/19	End
U-540	IXC40	Lorenz Kasch	1933	8/14	10/17/43
U-714	VIIC	Hans-Joachim Schwebcke	1937A	3/18	3/14/45
U-761	VIIC	Horst Geider	1937A	9/18	2/24/44
U-762	VIIC	Wolfgang Hille	1936	3/18	
		Walter Pietschmann	1937B	7/19	2/8/44
U-842	IXC40	Wolfgang Heller	1930	6/10	11/6/43
U-844	IXC40	Günther Möller	1937A	6/18	10/16/43
U-848	IXD2	Wilhelm Rollmann	1936	8/07	11/5/43
U-962	VIIC	Ernst Liesberg	1937B	6/18	4/8/44
U-964	VIIC	Emmo Hummerjohann	1937IV	4/16	10/16/43
U-966	VIIC	Eckehard Wolf	1937B	3/18	11/10/43
U-969	VIIC	Max Dobbert	NA	4/10	8/6/44
OCTOBER 1943:					
U-219	XB	Walter Burghagen	1911	9/1891	End
U-280	VIIC	Walter Hungershausen	1936	3/19	11/16/43
U-343	VIIC	Wolfgang Rahn	1938	10/21	3/10/44
U-391	VIIC	Gert Dültgen	1937	9/18	12/13/43
U-424	VIIC	Günter Lüders	1938	7/20	2/11/44
U-538	IXC40	Johann-Eghert Gossler	1935	11/14	11/21/43
U-542	IXC40	Christian-Brandt Coester	1937	11/19	11/26/43
U-764	VIIC	Hans-Kurt von Bremen	1938	8/18	End
U-843	IXC40	Oskar Herwartz	1935	1/15	4/9/45
U-849	IXD2	Heinz-Otto Schultze	1934	9/15	11/25/43
U-967	VIIC	Herbert Loeder	1938	4/19	
		Albrecht Brandi	1935	6/14	
		Heinz-Eugen Eberbach	1939X	7/21	8/19/44
NOVEMBER 1943:					
U-284	VIIC	Günther Scholz	1938	2/19	12/21/43
U-311	VIIC	Joachim Zander	1936	4/17	4/22/44
U-364	VIIC	Paul-Heinrich Sass	1939	10/19	1/29/44 ?
U-421	VIIC	Hans Kolbus	1938	10/19	4/29/44
U-425	VIIC	Heinz Bentzien	1937	1/17	2/17/45
U-471	VIIC	Friedrich Kloevekorn	1937A	2/18	8/6/44
U-541	IXC40	Kurt Petersen	1936	9/16	End
U-543	IXC40	Hans-Jürgen Hellriegel	1936	6/17	7/2/44
U-544	IXC40	Willy Mattke	1928	1/09	1/16/44
U-672	VIIC	Ulf Lawaetz	1937B	11/16	7/18/44
U-734	VIIC	Hans-Jörg Blauert	1939VIII	3/18	2/9/44
U-739	VIIC	Ernst Mangold	1935	11/17	
		Fritz Kosnick	1936	3/11	End
U-741	VIIC	Gerhard Palmgren	1938X	11/19	8/15/44
U-801	IXC40	Hans-Joachim Brans	1935	8/15	3/17/44
U-850	IXD2	Klaus Ewerth	1925	3/07	12/20/43
U-972	VIIC	Klaus-Dietrich König	1937B	11/15	12/15/43 ?
U-976	VIIC	Raimund Tiesler	1937	3/19	3/25/44
U-981	VIIC	Walter Sitek	1939VIII	1/13	
		Günter Keller	1939XII	8/21	8/12/44

BOAT	TYPE	SKIPPER	CREW	D.O.B.	LOST/ RETIRED
DECEMBER 1943:					
U-390	VIIC	Heinz Geissler	1938	8/17	7/5/44
U-392	VIIC	Henning Schümann	1937B	4/19	3/16/44
U-545	IXC40	Gert Mannesmann	NA	10/10	2/11/44
U-547	IXC40	Kurt Sturm	1925	1/06	
		Heinrich Niemeyer	1939	6/10	12/31/44
U-716	VIIC	Hans Dunkelberg	1937B	8/18	
		Jürgen Thimme	1937A	9/17	End
U-744	VIIC	Heinz Blischke	1938	9/19	3/6/44
U-763	VIIC	Ernst Cordes	1934	6/13	
		Karl-Heinz Schröter	1939IX	3/21	End
U-846	IXC40	Berthold Hashagen	1937	8/09	5/4/44
U-957	VIIC	Gerd Schaar	1937B	3/19	10/19/44
U-965	VIIC	Klaus Ohling	1937A	2/18	
		Günter Unverzagt	1939XII	5/21	3/30/45
U-984	VIIC	Heinz Sieder	1938	6/20	8/20/44
U-1060	VIIF	Herbert Brammer	1937	4/14	10/27/44
JANUARY 1944:					
U-240	VIIC	Günther Link	1937B	3/18	5/14/44 ?
U-276	VIIC	Rolf Borchers	1933	11/13	
		Heinz Zwarg	1937IV	11/17	9/29/44
U-278	VIIC	Joachim Franze	1937A	1/18	End
U-283	VIIC	Günter Ney	1939XII	3/22	2/11/44
U-312	VIIC	Kurt-Heinz Nicolay	1937A	10/17	
		Friedrich-Georg Herrle	1939XII	8/10	
		Jürgen von Gaza	1939X	9/20	End
U-313	VIIC	Friedhelm Schweiger	1937A	3/17	End
U-314	VIIC	Georg-Wilhelm Basse	1936	8/17	1/30/44
U-472	VIIC	Wolfgang-Friedrich von Forstner	1937A	10/16	3/4/44
U-546	IXC40	Paul Just	1936	12/15	4/24/45
U-549	IXC40	Detlev Krankenhagen	1936	7/17	5/29/44
U-802	IXC40	Helmut Schmoeckel	1936	12/17	End
U-845	IXC40	Werner Weber	1925	11/07	3/10/44
U-852	IXD2	Heinz Eck	1934	3/16	5/3/44
U-973	VIIC	Klaus Paepenmöller	1937A	2/18	3/6/44
U-985	VIIC	Horst Kessler	1934	8/14	
		Heinz Wolff	1937A	3/18	11/15/44
U-989	VIIC	Hardo Rodler von Roithberg	1937A	2/18	2/14/45
U-990	VIIC	Hubert Nordheimer	1936	2/17	5/25/44
U-1062	VIIF	Karl Albrecht	1923	4/04	9/30/44
FEBRUARY 1944:					
U-288	VIIC	Willy Meyer	1936	10/12	4/3/44
U-315	VIIC	Herbert Zoller	1938	5/19	End
U-361	VIIC	Hans Seidel	1937A	5/18	7/17/44
U-362	VIIC	Ludwig Franz	1937A	1/18	9/5/44
U-365	VIIC	Heimar Wedemeyer	1934	9/06	
		Diether Todenhagen	1937B	7/20	12/13/44
U-366	VIIC	Bruno Langenberg	1938	11/20	3/5/44
U-550	IXC40	Klaus Hänert	1936	2/18	4/16/44
U-674	VIIC	Harald Muhs	1938	10/19	5/2/44
U-851	IXD2	Hannes Weingaertner	1928	7/08	3/27/44 ?
U-856	IXC40	Friedrich Wittenberg	1937B	10/18	4/7/44
U-959	VIIC	Friedrich Weitz	1938	4/20	5/2/44

BOAT	TYPE	SKIPPER	CREW	D.O.B.	LOST/ RETIRED
U-970	VIIC	Hans-Heinrich Ketels	1937A	3/18	6/8/44
U-986	VIIC	Karl-Ernst Kaiser	1938	4/20	4/17/44
U-1059	VIIF	Günther Leupold	1938	2/91	3/19/44
MARCH 1944:					
U-347	VIIC	Johann de Buhr	1934/40	3/12	7/17/44
U-473	VIIC	Heinz Sternberg	1936	2/17	5/6/44
U-548	IXC40	Eberhard Zimmermann	1937	10/16	
		Erich Krempl	1939IX	5/21	4/19/45
U-673	VIIC	Heinz-Gerd Sauer	1939XII	4/15	
		Ernst-August Gerke	1939XII	5/21	10/24/44
U-740	VIIC	Günther Stark	1936	2/17	6/6/44 ?
U-766	VIIC	Hans-Dietrich Wilke	1939	6/12	End
U-821	VIIC	Ulrich Knackfuss	1938X	6/20	6/10/44
U-961	VIIC	Klaus Fischer	1938	10/19	3/29/44
U-968	VIIC	Otto Westphalen	1938	3/20	End
U-974	VIIC	Heinz Wolff	1937B	3/18	4/19/44
U-992	VIIC	Hans Falke	1939A	6/20	End
U-993	VIIC	Kurt Hilbig	1938	5/19	
		Karl-Heinz Steinmetz	1939XII	2/21	10/4/44
U-1224	IXC40	Georg Preuss	1933	12/16	5/13/44
APRIL 1944:					
U-241	VIIC	Arno Werr	1939IX	12/20	5/18/44
U-292	VIIC41	Werner Schmidt	1939IX	7/20	5/27/44
U-293	VIIC41	Leonhard Klingepor	1937B	6/17	End
U-342	VIIC	Albert Hossenfelder	1935	3/08	4/17/44
U-344	VIIC	Ulrich Pietsch	1936	12/15	8/22/44
U-348	VIIC	Hans-Norbert Schunck	1938	3/20	3/30/45
U-385	VIIC	Hans-Guido Valentiner	1937A	1/19	8/11/44
U-394	VIIC	Wolfgang Borger	1936	4/13	9/2/44
U-668	VIIC	Wolfgang von Eickstedt	1935	12/15	
		Fritz Henning	1937IV	4/17	End
U-736	VIIC	Reinhard Reff	1937	9/13	8/6/44
U-742	VIIC	Heinz Schwassmann	1935	2/16	7/18/44
U-765	VIIC	Werner Wendt	1938	2/16	5/6/44
U-853	IXC40	Helmut Sommer	1935	8/14	
		Günter Kuhnke	1931	9/12	
		Helmut von Frömsdorf	1939IX	3/21	5/6/45
U-859	IXD2	Johann Jebsen	1935	4/16	9/23/44
U-860	IXD2	Paul Büchel	1925	8/07	6/15/44
U-861	IXD2	Jürgen Oesten	1933	10/13	End
U-955	VIIC	Hans-Heinrich Baden	1938	4/15	6/7/44
U-997	VIIC41	Hans Lehmann	1938	9/15	End
U-1222	IXC40	Heinz Bielfeld	1934	8/16	7/11/44
MAY 1944:					
U-233	XB	Hans Steen	1937A	9/07	7/5/44
U-242	VIIC	Karl-Wilhelm Paucke	1938	10/15	
		Heinrich Riedel	1939XII	12/21	4/5/45
U-289	VIIC	Alexander Hellwig	1935	3/16	5/31/44
U-290	VIIC	Helmuth Herglotz	19318	3/18	
		Heintz Baum	1940	11/12	5/5/45
U-476	VIIC	Otto Niethmann	1938	8/19	5/25/44
U-477	VIIC	Karl-Joachim Jenssen	1938	7/20	6/3/44
U-490	XIV	Wilhelm Gerlach	1939XI	5/05	6/12/44
U-534	IXC40	Herbert Nollau	1936	3/16	5/5/45
U-671	VIIC	Wolfgang Hegewald	1937A	7/17	8/4/44

BOAT	TYPE	SKIPPER	CREW	D.O.B.	LOST/ RETIRED
U-675	VIIC	Karl-Heinz Sammler	1937B	1/19	5/24/44
U-719	VIIC	Klaus-Dietrich Steffens	1937A	6/18	6/26/44
U-745	VIIC	Wilhelm von Trotha	1936	8/16	1/30/45 ?
U-767	VIIC	Walter Dankleff	1935II	11/06	6/18/44
U-857	IXC40	Rudolf Premauer	1937B	5/19	4/?/45 ?
U-921	VIIC	Alfred Werner	1938	12/18	9/24/44 ?
U-958	VITC	Gerhard Groth	1937A	8/17	
		Friedrich Stege	1939X	11/20	End
U-975	VIIC	Paul Frerks	NA	6/08	
		Hubert Jeschke	1939IX	4/21	
		Walter-Ernst Koch	1938X	9/19	
		Wilhelm Brauel	1937X	9/14	End
U-987	VIIC	Hilmer Karl Schreyer	1933	8/14	6/15/44
U-988	VIIC	Erich Dobberstein	1938	12/19	6/30/44
U-1191	VIIC	Peter Grau	1939X	3/20	6/12/44 ?
U-1192	VIIC	Herbert Zeissler	1938	9/20	
		Erich Jewinski		3/20	
		Karl-Heinz Meenen		3/21	End
June 1944:					
U-243	VIIC	Hans Märtens	1937A	1/18	7/8/44
U-247	VIIC	Gerhard Matschulat	1938XI	5/20	9/1/44
U-294	VIIC41	Heinz Schütt	1936	11/15	End
U-317	VIIC41	Peter Rahlf	1939IX	3/09	6/26/44
U-318	VIIC41	Josef Will	1939X	4/06	End
U-319	VIIC41	Johannes Clemens	1935	5/11	7/15/44
U-363	VIIC	Werner Nees	1928	2/10	End
U-370	VIIC	Karl Nielsen	1935	9/11	End
U-396	VIIC	Ernst-Günther Unterhorst	1937B	4/19	
		Hillmar Siemon	1934	3/15	4/11/45 ?
U-397	VIIC	Fritz Kallipke	1937XI	11/09	
		Gerhard Groth	1937IV	8/17	End
U-423	VIIC	Klaus Hackländer	1937B	7/16	6/17/44
U-427	VIIC	Karl-Gabriel von Gudenus	1938	10/20	End
U-478	VIIC	Rudolf Rademacher	1937B	2/19	6/30/44
U-480	VIIC	Hans-Joachim Förster	1938	2/20	2/24/45
U-481	VIIC	Ewald Pick	1934XII	5/12	
		Klaus Andersen	1937B	10/18	End
U-677	VIIC	Paul Weber	1937XI	3/13	
		Gerhard Ady	1940X	9/23	4/9/45
U-678	VIIC	Guido Hyronimus	1937X	11/18	7/6/44
U-679	VIIC	Friedrich Breckwoldt	1939XI	6/12	
		Eduard Aust	1939	8/20	1/9/45
U-715	VIIC	Helmut Röttger	1937A	12/18	6/13/44
U-743	VIIC	Helmuth Kandzior	1938	9/19	8/21/44 ?
U-771	VIIC	Helmut Block	1938	4/15	11/11/44
U-804	IXC40	Herbert Meyer	1937III	11/10	4/9/45
U-858	IXC40	Thilo Bode	1936	2/18	End
U-862	IXD2	Heinrich Timm	1933	4/10	End
U-971	VIIC	Walter Zeplien	1937B	9/18	6/24/44
U-980	VIIC	Hermann Dahms	1939	3/16	6/11/44
U-982	VIIC	Ernst-Werner Schwirley	1939XII	6/19	
		Curt Hartmann	1939X	10/20	4/9/45
U-994	VIIC	Wolf Ackermann	1939A	3/21	
		Volker Melzer	1939X	1/18	End
U-995	VIIC41	Walter Köhntopp	1937I	4/11	
		Hans-Georg Hess	1940	5/23	End

BOAT	TYPE	SKIPPER	CREW	D.O.B.	LOST/ RETIRED
U-998	VIIC41	Hans Fiedler	1936	10/14	6/27/44
U-999	VIIC41	Hermann Hansen	1939XI	5/18	
		Wilhelm Peters	1937X	6/16	
		Wolfgang Heibges	1940IV	7/22	End
U-1001	VIIC41	Ernst-Ulrich Blaudow	1935	11/14	4/8/45
U-1007	VIIC41	Hans Hornkohl	1936	4/17	
		Helmut Wicke	1939X	11/20	
		Ernst von Witzendorff	1937IV	6/16	5/2/45
U-1165	VIIC41	Hans Homann	1938	3/18	End
U-1225	IXC40	Ernst Sauerberg	1934	1/14	6/24/44
July 1944:					
U-244	VIIC	Ruprecht Fischer	1937A	11/16	
		Hans-Peter Mackeprang	1935XI	12/11	End
U-250	VIIC	Werner-Karl Schmidt	1935	4/15	7/30/44
U-300	VIIC41	Fritz Hein	1938	12/19	2/22/45
U-310	VIIC	Wolfgang Ley	1938	6/20	End
U-637	VIIC	Günther Zedelius	1935	5/15	
		Fritz Fabricius	1937X	5/19	
		Wolfgang Riekeberg	1937A	10/18	End
U-855	IXC40	Prosper Ohlsen	1936	1/18	9/11/44 ?
U-863	IXD2	Dietrich von der Esch	1934	1/15	9/29/44
U-865	IXC40	Dietrich Stellmacher	1939IV	3/15	9/8/44 ?
U-866	IXC40	Walter Pommerehne	1931	4/08	
		Peter Rogowsky	1938X	6/19	3/18/45
U-1164	VIIC41	Hans Wengel	1937XI	5/14	7/24/44
U-1193	VIIC	Joachim Guse	1939A	6/21	End
U-1221	IXC40	Karl Kölzer	1931	3/12	
		Paul Ackermann	1939XII	9/20	4/3/45
U-1229	IXC40	Armin Zinke	1930	7/08	8/20/44
August 1944:					
U-245	VIIC	Friedrich Schumann-Hindenberg	1932	3/13	End
U-248	VIIC	Bernhard Emde	1937	12/17	
		Johann-Friedrich Loos	1939XII	4/21	1/16/45
U-285	VIIC	Konrad Bornhaupt	1937B	6/20	4/15/45
U-286	VIIC	Willi Dietrich	1928	12/09	4/29/45
U-295	VIIC41	Günter Wieboldt	1937B	2/19	End
U-296	VIIC41	Karl-Heinz Rasch	1934I	4/14	3/12/45 ?
U-299	VIIC41	Helmuth Heinrich	NA	10/13	
		Bernhard Emde	1937	12/17	End
U-398	VIIC	Johann Reckhoff	1928XI	1/11	
		Wilhelm Cranz	1939X	4/15	4/17/45 ?
U-475	VIIC	Otto Stoeffler	1939X	3/10	5/3/45
U-479	VIIC	Friedrich-Wilhelm Sons	1940I	8/10	11/15/44 ?
U-482	VIIC	Hartmut von Matuschka	1934	12/14	12/1/44 ?
U-483	VIIC	Hans-Joachim von Morstein	1928	8/09	End
U-484	VIIC	Wolff-Axel Schaefer	1930	3/11	9/9/44
U-680	VIIC	Max Ulber	1935VII	10/16	End
U-717	VIIC	Siegfried von Rothkirch und Panthen	1938	10/19	End
U-722	VIIC	Hans-Heinrich Reimers	1939/40	10/16	3/27/45
U-735	VIIC	Hans-Joachim Börner	1937X	7/18	12/28/44
U-772	VIIC	Ewald Rademacher	1937A	12/17	12/30/44
U-773	VIIC	Hugo Baldus	1939X	4/21	End
U-868	IXC40	Eduard Turre	1939IX	1/20	End

BOAT	TYPE	SKIPPER	CREW	D.O.B.	LOST/ RETIRED
U-871	IXD2	Erwin Ganzer	1935	12/12	9/26/44
U-925	VIIC	Helmuth Knoke	1941III	8/06	8/24/44 ?
U-978	VIIC	Günther Pulst	1937X	3/18	End
U-979	VIIC	Johannes Meermeier	1937A	11/16	End
U-1004	VIIC41	Hartmuth Schimmelpfennig	1937B	10/19	
		Rudolf Hinz	1939IX	2/20	End
U-1163	VIIC41	Ernst-Ludwig Balduhn	1938	10/19	End
U-1223	IXC40	Harald Bosüner	1934	10/13	
		Albert Kneip	1939IX	7/21	End
U-1227	IXC40	Friedrich Altmeier	1938	7/20	4/9/45
U-1228	IXC40	Friedrich-Wilhelm Marienfeld	1939	3/20	End
U-1230	IXC40	Hans Hilbig	1936	7/17	End
SEPTEMBER 1944:					
U-676	VIIC	Werner Sass	1937B	1/16	2/12/45 ?
U-867	IXC40	Arved von Mühlendahl	1923	11/04	9/19/44
U-991	VIIC	Diethelm Balke	1937B	9/19	End
U-1003	VIIC41	Werner Strübing	1942I	5/07	3/23/45
U-1006	VIIC41	Horst Voigt	1938	10/19	10/16/44
U-1199	VIIC	Rolf Nollmann	1936	12/14	1/21/45
U-1200	VIIC	Hinrich Mangels	1938	8/19	11/11/44
U-1202	VIIC	Rolf Thomsen	1936	5/15	End
U-1226	IXC40	August-Wilhelm Claussen	1937X	3/19	10/23/44 ?
OCTOBER 1944:					
U-246	VIIC	Ernst Raabe	1926	2/07	4/?/45 ?
U-806	IXC40	Klaus Hornbostel	1934	6/16	End
U-870	IXC40	Ernst Hechler	1929	11/07	3/30/45
U-1017	VIIC41	Werner Riecken	1934	6/12	4/29/45
U-1231	IXC40	Hermann Lessing	1921	10/00	
		Helmut Wicke	1939X	11/20	End
U-1232	IXC40	Kurt Dobratz	1922	4/04	
		Götz Roth	1938X	12/19	End
NOVEMBER 1944:					
U-297	VIIC41	Wolfgang Aldegarmann	1939	4/16	11/26/44 ?
U-322	VIIC41	Gerhard Wysk	1938	5/20	11/25/44
U-400	VIIC	Horst Creutz	1935	5/15	12/17/44
U-485	VIIC	Friedrich Lutz	1930	8/11	End
U-486	VIIC	Gerhard Meyer	1935	4/15	4/12/45
U-681	VIIC	Werner Gebauer	1939XII	9/22	3/11/45
U-775	VIIC	Erich Taschenmacher	1938	11/19	End
U-869	IXC40	Helmut Neuerburg	1936	8/17	2/17/45 ?
U-877	IXC40	Eberhard Findeisen	1936	5/16	12/27/44
U-1009	VIIC41	Claus Hilgendorf	1939X	2/12	End
U-1053	VIIC	Helmut Lange	1937A	8/16	2/15/45
U-1209	VIIC	Ewald Hülsenbeck	1938	12/19	12/18/44
U-1233	IXC40	Joachim Kuhn	1931	4/10	
		Heinrich Niemeyer	1939X	6/10	End
U-1276	VIIC41	Karl-Heinz Wendt	1938	2/20	2/20/45
DECEMBER 1944:					
U-325	VIIC41	Erwin Dohrn	1938	3/20	4/7/45 ?
U-825	VIIC	Gerhard Stoelker	1939XI	5/10	End
U-864	IXD2	Ralf-Reimar Wolfram	1930	3/12	2/9/45
U-905	VIIC	Bernhard Schwarting	1936	1/13	3/27/45

BOAT	TYPE	SKIPPER	CREW	D.O.B.	LOST/ RETIRED
U-907	VIIC	Servais Cabolet	NA	4/08	End
U-1018	VIIC41	Walter Burmeister	1937B	2/19	2/27/45
U-1019	VIIC41	Hans Rinck	1941VII	6/12	End
U-1020	VIIC41	Otto-Emil Eberlein	1938I	11/13	12/31/44 ?
U-1021	VIIC41	William Holpert	1934	6/14	3/14/45 ?
U-1055	VIIC	Rudolf Meyer	1938	2/20	4/23/45 ?
U-1172	VIIC41	Jürgen Kuhlmann	1938	3/20	1/27/45
U-1203	VIIC	Sigurd Seeger	1939IX	7/20	End
U-1235	IXC40	Franz Barsch	1930	11/11	4/15/45
U-1278	VIIC41	Erich Müller-Bethke	1937B	7/17	2/17/45
JANUARY 1945:					
U-249	VIIC	Uwe Koch	1936	11/11	End
U-327	VIIC41	Hans Lemcke	1937A	12/18	1/30/45 ?
U-683	VIIC	Günter Keller	1939XII	2/17	2/20/45 ?
U-826	VIIC	Olaf Lübcke	1937B	8/19	End
U-1014	VIIC41	Wolfgang Glaser	1937B	2/19	2/4/45
U-1051	VIIC	Heinrich von Holleben	1938	3/19	1/26/45
U-1058	VIIC	Hermann Bruder	1939XII	3/21	End
U-1195	VIIC	Ernst Cordes	1934	6/13	4/6/45
U-1208	VIIC	Georg Hagene	1927	7/08	2/27/45
U-1302	VIIC41	Wolfgang Herwartz	1937	1/15	3/7/45
U-2324	XXIII	Konstantin von Rappard	1936	6/17	End
FEBRUARY 1945:					
U-399	VIIC	Heinz Buhse	1939X	11/17	3/26/45
U-774	VIIC	Werner Sausmikat	1937B	10/17	4/8/45
U-873	IXD2	Friedrich Steinhoff	1935	7/09	End
U-878	IXC40	Johannes Rodig	1936	3/17	4/10/45
U-879	IXC40	Erwin Manchen	1936	6/18	4/30/45
U-927	VIIC	Jürgen Ebert	1937A	11/16	2/24/45
U-1002	VIIC41	Hans-Werner Boos	1937	2/13	End
U-1005	VIIC41	Hermann Lauth	1939XII	11/20	End
U-1008	VIIC41	Hans Gessner	1938	5/19	5/6/45
U-1022	VIIC41	Hans-Joachim Ernst	1937B	8/18	End
U-1024	VIIC41	Hans-Joachim Gutteck	1935	4/14	4/13/45
U-1064	VIIC41	Hermann Schneidewind	1936	3/07	End
U-1104	VIIC	Rüdiger Perleberg	1933	3/13	End
U-1105	VIIC	Hans-Joachim Schwarz	1938	9/19	End
U-1106	VIIC	Erwin Bartke	1940	4/09	3/29/45
U-1107	VIIC41	Fritz Parduhn	1937B	11/18	4/30/45
U-1109	VIIC41	Friedrich van Riesen	1938	7/11	End
U-1169	VIIC41	Heinz Goldbeck	1936	2/14	3/29/45
U-1206	VIIC	Karl-Adolf Schlitt	1937A	4/18	4/14/45
U-1273	VIIC41	Helmut Knollmann	1937A	8/18	2/17/45
U-1277	VIIC41	Ehrenreich-Peter Stever	1937B	10/18	End
U-1279	VIIC41	Hans Falke	1939A	1/20	2/3/45
U-2322	XXIII	Fridtjof Heckel	1939XII	10/20	End
MARCH 1945:					
U-321	VIIC41	Fritz Berends	1933	9/06	4/2/45
U-324	VIIC41	Ernst Edelhoff	1936	10/17	End
U-326	VIIC41	Peter Matthes	1937B	1/18	4/25/45
U-776	VIIC	Erich Lothar Martin	1937A	6/16	End
U-778	VIIC	Ralf Jürs	1937A	5/19	End
U-805	IXC40	Richard Bernadelli	1932	11/08	End
U-827	VIIC41	Wilhelm Hunck	1937XI	12/14	
		Kurt Baberg	1936	2/17	End

BOAT	TYPE	SKIPPER	CREW	D.O.B.	LOST/ RETIRED
U-874	IXD2	Theodor Petersen	1934I	1/14	End
U-875	IXD2	Georg Preuss	1936	12/16	End
U-880	IXC40	Gerhard Schötzau	1936	4/17	4/16/45
U-881	IXC40	Heinz Frischke	1936	11/12	5/6/45
U-889	IXC40	Friedrich Braeucker	1937A	7/19	End
U-901	VIIC	Hans Schrenk	1937A	9/17	End
U-1023	VIIC	Wolfgang Strenger	1937X	2/19	
		Heinrich Schroeteler	1936	12/15	End
U-1063	VIIC41	Karl-Heinz Stephan	1936	9/15	4/15/45
U-1101	VIIC	Rudolf Dübler	1939XII	10/21	End
U-1171	VIIC41	Hermann Koopmann	1940I	2/10	End
U-1272	VIIC41	Hans Schatteburg	1939XII	5/22	End
U-1305	VIIC41	Helmut Christiansen	1938	9/18	End
U-2321	XXIII	Hans-Heinrich Barschkis	1939XII	4/20	End
April 1945:					
U-234	XB	Johann-Heinrich Fehler	1935	9/10	End
U-1010	VIIC41	Günter Strauch	1934	12/08	End
U-1057	VIIC	Günter Lüth	1937III	3/17	End
U-1065	VIIC41	Johannes Panitz	1937VIII	8/13	4/9/45
U-1274	VIIC41	Hans-Hermann Fitting	1939	5/20	4/16/45
U-2326	XXIII	Karl Jobst	1936	4/13	End
U-2329	XXIII	Heinrich Schlott	1940X	7/22	End
U-2511	XXI	Adalbert Schnee	1934	12/13	End
May 1945:					
U-320	VIIC41	Heinz Emmrich	1941	1/13	5/8/45
U-328	VIIC41	Hans-Ulrich Scholle	1938I	9/09	End
U-977	VIIC	Heinz Schäffer	1939XII	4/21	End (Argentina)

SUMMARY 9/1/42 TO 5/1/45[2]	
Total U-boats deployed:	806
Total U-boats lost:	662
U-boats deployed from 9/1/42:	531
U-boats lost from 9/1/42:	568

1. Official records, vetted and corrected by author and Franks (1995), and Niestlé (1998). For loss and "missing" dates, we are all indebted to the work of Robert M. Coppock, Foreign Documents Section, Naval Historical Branch, British Ministry of Defence. List does not include oceangoing boats in combat in the Baltic Sea.

2. For comparable figures 8/1/39 to 9/1/42, see Appendix 1, Volume I, p. 708.

APPENDIX 2

U-BOAT PATROLS TO THE NORTH ATLANTIC

SEPTEMBER 1942–APRIL 1945

BOAT	TYPE	SKIPPER	SAILED	RETURNED	SHIPS SUNK	TONS
SEPTEMBER 1942:						
U-221	VIIC	Hans Trojer*	9/1	10/22	5	29,681
U-258	VIIC	Wilhelm von Mässenhausen*	9/1	10/27		None
U-618	VIIC	Kurt Baberg*	9/1	10/27	2	10,563
U-440	VIIC	Hans Geissler*	9/1	9/21		None/Abort
U-356	VIIC	Georg Wallas*	9/3	11/4		None
U-615	VIIC	Rolf Kapitsky*	9/5	10/30	2	16,877
U-661	VIIC	Erich von Lilienfeld*	9/5	Lost 10/15	1	3,672
U-461	XIV	Wolf Stiebler	9/7	10/18		None/Supply
U-607	VIIC	Ernst Mengersen	9/8	10/23	1	4,826/Abort
U-261	VIIC	Hans Lange*	9/8	Lost 9/15		None
U-595	VIIC	Jürgen Quaet-Faslem	9/9	10/6		None/Abort
U-260	VIIC	Hubertus Purkhold*	9/10	11/15		None
U-619	VIIC	Kurt Makowski*	9/10	Lost 10/5	2	8,723
U-620	VIIC	Heinz Stein*	9/12	11/12		None/Abort
U-610	VIIC	Walter von Freyberg-Eisenberg-Allmendingen*	9/12	10/31	2	7,913
U-253	VIIC	Adolf Friedrichs*	9/12	Lost 9/25 ?		None
U-582	VIIC	Werner Schulte	9/14	Lost 10/5		None
U-597	VIIC	Eberhard Bopst	9/16	Lost 10/12		None
U-437	VIIC	Werner-Karl Schulz	9/17	11/15		None
U-441	VIIC	Klaus Hartmann*	9/17	11/7		None
U-442	VIIC	Hans-Joachim Hesse*	9/17	11/16	1	1,744
U-118	XB	Werner Czygan*	9/19	10/16		None/Supply
U-382	VIIC	Herbert Juli*	9/19	10/31		None/Abort
U-575	VIIC	Günther Heydemann	9/19	11/8	1	11,330
U-753	VIIC	Alfred Manhardt von Mannstein	9/20	12/9		None
U-254	VIIC	Odo Loewe	9/21	10/22	2	17,749/Abort

* = First patrol of boat or skipper (C.O.)
\+ = Damaged ships or shared credit
M = Mining mission
PR = Provisional refueler
S = Snort boat
W = Weather-reporting mission

BOAT	TYPE	SKIPPER	SAILED	RETURNED	SHIPS SUNK	TONS
U-257	VIIC	Heinz Rahe*	9/21	10/18		None/Abort
U-116	XB	Wilhelm Grimme* (C.O.)	9/22	Lost 10/6 ?		None/Supply
U-353	VIIC	Wolfgang Römer*	9/22	Lost 10/16		None
U-706	VIIC	Alexander Zitzewitz*	9/22	11/7	1	4,265
U-262	VIIC	Heinz Franke	9/24	9/28		None/Abort
U-454	VIIC	Burkhard Hackländer	9/26	12/7		None
U-602	VIIC	Philipp Schüler*	9/26	11/6		None
U-757	VIIC	Friedrich Deetz*	9/26	10/24		None
U-662	VIIC	Wolfgang Hermann*	9/27	11/18		None
U-463	XIV	Leo Wolfbauer	9/28	11/11		None/Supply
U-84	VIIC	Horst Uphoff	9/29	12/7*	½[1]	3,750
U-621	VIIC	Horst Schünemann*	9/29	11/5	1	6,113
Totals:	37 patrols (4 supply)				21½	127,206
OCTOBER 1942:						
U-301	VIIC	Willy Roderich Körner*	10/1	11/6		None
U-381	VIIC	Wilhelm-Heinrich von Pückler und Limpurg*	10/1	11/21		None
U-443	VIIC	Konstantin von Puttkamer*	10/1	11/4	2	17,843
U-458	VIIC	Kurt Diggins	10/1	Into Mediterranean 10/11		
U-563	VIIC	Götz von Hartmann* (C.O.)	10/1	1/6		None
U-611	VIIC	Nikolaus von Jacobs*	10/1	10/6		None
U-625	VIIC	Hans Benker*	10/1	10/6		None
U-262	VIIC	Heinz Franke*	10/3	10/6		None[2]
U-520	IXC	Volkmar Schwartzkopff*	10/3	Lost 10/30		None
U-521	IXC	Klaus Bargsten*	10/3	12/8	1⅓	8,655[3]
U-571	VIIC	Helmut Möhlmann	10/3	11/14		None
U-593	VIIC	Gerd Kelbling	10/3	Into Mediterranean 10/11		
U-660	VIIC	Götz Baur	10/3	Into Mediterranean 10/11		
U-89	VIIC	Dietrich Lohmann	10/4	11/19	2	9,958/Abort
U-402	VIIC	Siegfried von Forstner	10/4	11/20	4½	23,578
U-605	VIIC	Herbert-Viktor Schütze	10/4	Into Mediterranean 10/10		
U-71	VIIC	Hardo Rodler von Roithberg	10/5	11/17		None
U-704	VIIC	Horst Kessler	10/5	11/23	1	4,212/Abort
U-132	VIIC	Ernst Vogelsang	10/6	Lost 11/3	2	11,886
U-436	VIIC	Günther Seibicke	10/6	11/12	2	15,105+
U-438	VIIC	Rudolf Franzius	10/6	11/19	⅓	1,800
U-609	VIIC	Klaus Rudloff	10/6	10/22		None/Abort
U-658	VIIC	Hans Senkel	10/6	Lost 10/30		None
U-522	IXC	Herbert Schneider*	10/8	12/2	4⅓	21,877
U-624	VIIC	Ulrich von Soden-Frauenhofen*	10/10	12/4	4	34,743+
U-117	XB	Hans-Werner Neumann*	10/12	11/22		None/Supply
U-627	VIIC	Robert Kindelbacher*	10/15	Lost 10/27		None
U-224	VIIC	Hans-Karl Kosbadt*	10/17	12/9	2	9,614
U-383	VIIC	Horst Kremser*	10/17	12/9		None+
U-412	VIIC	Walter Jahrmärker*	10/17	Lost 10/22		None
U-519	IXC	Günter Eppen*	10/17	12/29		None
U-606	VIIC	Hans Döhler	10/17	12/5	1	8,225
U-440	VIIC	Hans Geissler	10/19	11/13		None/Abort
U-664	VIIC	Adolf Graef*	10/20	11/10		None/Abort
U-98	VIIC	Kurt Eichmann* (C.O.)	10/22	Lost 11/15		None

BOAT	TYPE	SKIPPER	SAILED	RETURNED	SHIPS SUNK	TONS
U-413	VIIC	Gustav Poel*	10/22	11/25	1	20,1071/Abort[4]
U-613,	VIIC	Helmut Köppe*	10/22	11/27	1	4,252/Abort
U-92	VIIC	Adolf Oelrich	10/24	12/28	1	7,662
U-108	IXB	Ralf-Reimar Wolfram*(C.O.)	10/25	11/26		None/Abort
U-218	VIID	Richard Becker	10/26	11/21		None/Abort
U-185	IXC40	August Maus*	10/27	1/1/43	1	5,476
U-263	VIIC	Kurt Nölke*	10/27	11/29	2	12,376/Abort
U-564	VIIC	Hans Fiedler* (C.O.)	10/27	12/30		None
U-653	VIIC	Gerhard Feiler	10/27	12/29		None
U-566	VIIC	Gerhard Remus	10/28	12/1	1	4,252/Abort
U-130	IXC	Ernst Kals	10/29	12/30	3	34,407
U-465	VIIC	Heinz Wolf*	10/29	12/21		None/Abort
U-86	VIIB	Walter Schug	10/30	1/7/43		None
U-595	VIIC	Jürgen Quaet-Faslem	10/31	Into Mediterranean 11/9		
Totals:	46 patrols (1 supply, 5 to Mediterranean)				$36^{1}/_{2}$	256,028

NOVEMBER 1942 (Torch):

BOAT	TYPE	SKIPPER	SAILED	RETURNED	SHIPS SUNK	TONS
U-91	VIIC	Heinz Walkerling	11/1	12/26		None
U-173	IXC	Hans-Adolph Schweichel* (C.O.)	11/1	Lost 11/16	1	9,359+[5]
U-755	VIIC	Walter Göing	11/1	Into Mediterranean 11/9		
U-407	VIIC	Ernst-Ulrich Brüller	11/2	Into Mediterranean 11/8		
U-617	VIIC	Albrecht Brandi	11/2	Into Mediterranean 11/8		
U-264	VIIC	Hartwig Looks*	11/3	12/4	1	6,696
U-445	VIIC	Heinz-Konrad Fenn*	11/3	1/3/43		None
U-596	VIIC	Günter Jahn	11/4	Into Mediterranean 11/9		
U-259	VIIC	Klaus Köpke	11/5	Into Mediterranean 11/10		
U-380	VIIC	Josef Röther	11/5	Into Mediterranean 11/11		
U-623	VIIC	Hermann Schröder*	11/5	12/26		None
U-663	VIIC	Heinrich Schmid	11/5	12/31	1	5,170/Abort
U-155	IXC	Adolf-Cornelius Piening	11/7	12/30	3	33,520+[6]
U-411	VIIC	Johann Spindlegger* (C.O.)	11/7	Lost 11/13		None
U-515	IXC	Werner Henke	11/7	1/6/43	2	29,573+[7]
U-184	IXC40	Günther Dangschat*	11/9	Lost 11/21 ?	1	3,192+
U-524	IXC	Walter von Steinäcker*	11/9	1/3/43	1	8,194+
U-118	XB	Werner Czygan	11/11	12/13		None/Supply
U-262	VIIC	Heinz Franke	11/11	12/9	2	8,103[8]
U-611	VIIC	Nikolaus von Jacobs	11/11	Lost 12/8		None
U-439	VIIC	Wolfgang Sporn*	11/12	12/24		None
U-758	VIIC	Helmut Manseck*	11/14	12/24		None
U-211	VIIC	Karl Hause	11/16	12/29	1	1,350[9]
U-460	XIV	Ebe Schnoor	11/16	12/19		None/Supply
U-461	XIV	Wolf Stiebler	11/17	1/3/43		None/Supply
U-135	VIIC	Heinz Schütt* (C.O.)	11/21	12/25		None
U-254	VIIC	Hans Gilardone	11/21	Lost 12/8[10]		None
U-600	VIIC	Bernhard Zurmühlen	11/22	12/27	1	6,762
U-373	VIIC	Paul-Karl Loeser	11/22	1/3/43		None
U-610	VIIC	Walter von Freyberg-Eisenberg-Allmendingen	11/22	12/26	1	6,125+
U-221	VIIC	Hans Trojer	11/23	12/23		None/Abort[11]
U-455	VIIC	Hans-Martin Scheibe* (C.O.)	11/24	1/29/43		None
U-553	VIIC	Karl Thurmann	11/24	12/18		None/Abort

BOAT	TYPE	SKIPPER	SAILED	RETURNED	SHIPS SUNK	TONS
U-569	VIIC	Hans-Peter Hinsch	11/25	12/28		None
U-603	VIIC	Hans-Joachim Bertelsmann*	11/25	1/9/43		None/Abort[12]
U-615	VIIC	Ralph Kapitzky	11/25	1/9/43		None
U-618	VIIC	Kurt Baberg	11/25	1/18/43		None[13]
U-604	VIIC	Horst Höltring	11/26	12/31	1	7,057
U-336	VIIC	Hans Hunger*	11/28	1/8/43	1	4,919
U-628	VIIC	Heinz Hasenschar*	11/28	1/8/43	1	5,029
U-443	VIIC	Konstantin von Puttkamer	11/29	Into Mediterranean 12/5		
U-432	VIIC	Heinz-Otto Schultze	11/30	1/5/43	1	310
U-435	VIIC	Siegfried Strelow	11/30	1/10/43	$2\frac{1}{3}$	11,691[14]
U-609	VIIC	Klaus Rudloff	11/30	12/23		None
Totals:	44 patrols (3 supply, 7 to Mediterranean)				$21\frac{1}{3}$	147, 050

December 1942:

BOAT	TYPE	SKIPPER	SAILED	RETURNED	SHIPS SUNK	TONS
U-591	VIIC	Hans-Jürgen Zetsche	12/1	1/12/43	2	7,937+
U-602	VIIC	Philipp Schüler	12/1	Into Mediterranean 12/8		
U-258	VIIC	Wilhelm von Mässenhausen	12/2	12/6	Abort Mediterranean attempt	
U-301	VIIC	Willy-Roderich Körner	12/3	Into Mediterranean 12/9		
U-410	VIIC	Kurt Sturm	12/3	1/3/43	None/Rescue/Abort	
U-225	VIIC	Wolfgang Leimkühler*	12/5	1/8/43	$1\frac{1}{3}$	9,275
U-123	IXB	Horst von Schroeter* (C.O.)	12/5	2/6/43	$1\frac{1}{3}$	5,741+
U-356	VIIC	Günther Ruppelt* (C.O.)	12/5	Lost 12/27	3	13,649+
U-621	VIIC	Max Kruschka* (C.O.)	12/5	1/5/43	2	10,691
U-664	VIIC	Adolph Graef	12/5	1/13/43	1	5,859
U-203	VIIC	Hermann Kottmann	12/6	1/7/43		None
U-463	XIV	Leo Wolfbauer	12/6	1/27/43		None/Supply
U-257	VIIC	Heinz Rahe	12/7	12/14	Abort Mediterranean attempt	
U-409	VIIC	Hans-Ferdinand Massmann	12/7	1/6/43		None
U-626	VIIC	Hans-Botho Bade*	12/8	Lost 12/15		None
U-706	VIIC	Alexander von Zitzewitz	12/8	2/13/43		None
U-125	IXC	Ulrich Folkers	12/9	2/19/43		None
U-514	IXC	Hans-Jürgen Auffermann	12/9	2/12/43	1	7,177+
U-563	VIIC	Götz von Hartmann	12/9	1/14/43	1	4,906
U-384	VIIC	Hans-Achim von Rosenberg-Gruszczynski*	12/12	2/3/43	1	6,155
U-440	VIIC	Hans Geissler	12/12	1/26/43		None/Abort
U-659	VIIC	Hans Stock	12/12	1/5/43		None
U-441	VIIC	Klaus Hartmann	12/13	1/22/43	1	5,822+
U-260	VIIC	Hubertus Purkhold	12/14	2/3/43	1	4,893
U-406	VIIC	Horst Dieterichs	12/14	1/12/43		None+
U-357	VIIC	Adolf Kellner*	12/15	Lost 12/26		None
U-525	IXC40	Hans-Joachim Drewitz*	12/15	3/3/43	1	3,454
U-436	VIIC	Günther Seibicke	12/17	2/19/43	2	14,703
U-444	VIIC	Albert Langfeld*	12/17	2/3/43		None
U-575	VIIC	Günther Heydemann	12/17	2/18/43	1	4,963+
U-381	VIIC	Wilhelm-Heinrich von Pückler und Limpurg	12/19	2/19/43		None/Abort
U-620	VIIC	Heinz Stein	12/19	Lost 2/13	1	6,983
U-631	VIIC	Jürgen Krüger*	12/19	2/4/43	1	3,987
U-662	VIIC	Wolfgang Hermann	12/19	2/7/43	1	5,083
U-333	VIIC	Werner Schwaff* (C.O.)	12/20	2/5/43		None

BOAT	TYPE	SKIPPER	SAILED	RETURNED	SHIPS SUNK	TONS
U-442	VIIC	Hans-Joachim Hesse	12/20	Lost 2/12	2	16,983+
U-404	VIIC	Otto von Bülow	12/21	2/6/43		None/Abort
U-167	IXC40	Helmut Neubert*	12/21	1/16/43		None/Abort
U-257	VIIC	Heinz Rahe (resail)	12/22	2/12/43		None
U-266	VIIC	Ralf von Jessen*	12/22	2/17/43	1	4,077
U-571	VIIC	Helmut Möhlmann	12/22	2/19		None
U-71	VIIC	Hardo Rodler von Roithburg	12/23	2/12/43		None
U-572	VIIC	Heinz Kummetat* (C.O.)	12/23	2/11/43		None
U-337	VIIC	Kurt Ruwiedel*	12/24	Lost 1/3?/43		None
U-632	VIIC	Hans Karpf*	12/24	2/14/43	2	14,963
U-117	XB	Hans-Werner Neumann	12/25	2/17/43		None/Supply
U-96	VIIC	Hans-Jürgen Hellriegel	12/26	2/5		None/Retired
U-598	VIIC	Gottfried Holtorf	12/26	2/8/43		None
U-413	VIIC	Gustav Poel	12/27	2/17/43	2	8,932
U-584	VIIC	Kurt Nölke	12/30	2/21/43		None/Abort
U-594	VIIC	Friedrich Mumm	12/30	2/18/43		None+
U-226	VIIC	Rolf Borchers*	12/31	3/10/43		None
U-303	VIIC	Karl-Franz Heine*	12/31	3/8/43	1	4,959
U-186	IXC40	Siegfried Hesemann*	12/31	3/5/43	3	18,782
U-511	IXC	Fritz Schneewind* (C.O.)	12/31	3/8/43	1	5,004
U-522	IXC	Herbert Schneider	12/31	Lost 2/23	3	25,749+
Totals:	56 patrols (2 supply, 2 to Mediterranean, 2 Mediterranean aborts)				$37^{2}/_{3}$	220,727
January 1943:						
U-69	VIIC	Ulrich Gräf	1/2	Lost 2/17		None
U-268	VIIC	Ernst Heydemann*	1/2	Lost 2/19	1	14,547+
U-607	VIIC	Ernst Mengersen	1/2	3/9	1	11,355
U-201	VIIC	Günther Rosenberg	1/3	Lost 2/17		None
U-224	VIIC	Hans-Karl Kosbadt	1/3	Into Mediterranean 1/17		
U-606	VIIC	Hans-Heinrich Döhler	1/4	Lost 2/22	2	12,302+
U-66	IXC	Friedrich Markworth	1/6	3/24	2	4,425 [15]
U-383	VIIC	Horst Kremser	1/6	3/10		None
U-218	VIID	Richard Becker	1/7	3/10		None/Abort
U-521	IXC	Klaus Bargsten	1/7	3/26	2	7,950
U-414	VIIC	Walter Huth*	1/7	2/19		None/Abort
U-624	VIIC	Ulrich von Soden-Fraunhofen	1/7	Lost 2/7	1	5,112
U-704	VIIC	Horst Kessler	1/7	2/12		None
U-43	IX	Hans-Joachim Schwantke	1/9	3/31	1	5,154
U-87	VIIB	Joachim Berger	1/9	Lost 3/4		None
U-403	VIIC	Heinz-Ehlert Clausen	1/9	3/2	2	13,099
U-438	VIIC	Rudolf Franzius	1/9	2/16		None/Abort
U-558	VIIC	Günther Krech	1/9	3/29	1	9,811 [16]
U-613	VIIC	Helmut Köppe	1/9	2/18		None
U-614	VIIC	Wolfgang Sträter*	1/9	2/26	$1^{1}/_{2}$	10,366/Abort
U-752	VIIC	Karl-Ernst Schroeter	1/9	2/15		None/Abort
U-258	VIIC	Leopold Koch* (C.O.)	1/10	3/4		None
U-264	VIIC	Hartwig Looks	1/10	3/5		None/Rescue/Abort
U-187	IXC40	Ralph Münnich*	1/12	Lost 2/4		None
U-202	VIIC	Günter Poser	1/12	3/26	1	7,989+
U-223	VIIC	Karl-Jürgen Wächter*	1/12	3/6	1	5,649
U-267	VIIC	Otto Tinschert*	1/12	2/18		None/Abort

BOAT	TYPE	SKIPPER	SAILED	RETURNED	SHIPS SUNK	TONS
U-358	VIIC	Rolf Manke*	1/12	3/8	2	9,677
U-466	VIIC	Gerhard Thäter*	1/12	2/11		None
U-707	VIIC	Günter Gretschel*	1/12	3/8	1	7,176
U-456	VIIC	Max-Martin Teichert	1/13	2/26	3	17,333
U-402	VIIC	Siegfried von Forstner	1/14	2/23	6	32,446+
U-262	VIIC	Heinz Franke	1/16	2/15	1	2,864/Abort
U-465	VIIC	Heinz Wolf	1/16	2/18		None/Abort
U-553	VIIC	Karl Thurmann	1/16	Lost 1/20 ?		None
U-609	VIIC	Klaus Rudloff	1/16	Lost 2/7		None
U-454	VIIC	Burkhard Hackländer	1/18	3/8		None
U-504	IXC	Wilhelm Luis* (C.O.)	1/19	3/24		None
U-108	IXB	Ralf-Reimer Wolfram	1/20	2/24		None/Abort
U-608	VIIC	Rolf Struckmeier	1/20	3/29	½	4,636[17]
U-265	VIIC	Leonhard Auffhammer*	1/21	Lost 2/3		None
U-462	XIV	Bruno Vowe	1/22	1/26		None/Supply/Abort
U-89	VIIC	Dietrich Lohmann	1/24	3/28		None
U-135	VIIC	Heinz Schütt	1/24	3/10		None/Abort
U-118	XB	Werner Czygan	1/25	2/26	4	15,124+M[18]
U-332	VIIC	Eberhard Hüttemann	1/28	3/24	½	2,982[19]
U-468	VIIC	Klemens Schamong*	1/28	3/27	1	6,537[20]
U-653	VIIC	Gerhard Feiler[21]	1/28	3/31	1	7,176+
U-753	VIIC	Alfred Manhardt von Mannstein	1/28	3/10		None/Abort
U-439	VIIC	Wolfgang Sporn	1/29	2/2	½	4,675[22]/Abort
U-107	IXB	Harald Gelhaus	1/30	3/25	5	25,177
U-376	VIIC	Friedrich-Karl Marks	1/30	3/13		None/Abort
U-377	VIIC	Otto Köhler	1/30	3/18		None
U-448	VIIC	Helmut Dauter*	1/30	3/25		None
U-519	IXC	Günter Eppen	1/30	Lost 1/30 ?		None
U-529	IXC40	Georg-Werner Fraatz*	1/30	Lost 2/12 ?		None
U-590	VIIC	Heinrich Müller-Edzards	1/31	2/11		None/Abort
U-460	XIV	Ebe Schnoor	1/31	3/5		None/Supply
Totals:	58 patrols (2 supply, 1 to Mediterranean)				41½	284,897

February 1943:

BOAT	TYPE	SKIPPER	SAILED	RETURNED	SHIPS SUNK	TONS
U-621	VIIC	Max Kruschka	2/1	3/23	1	3,355
U-628	VIIC	Heinz Hasenschar	2/1	3/9	1½	9,460[23]
U-225	VIIC	Wolfgang Leinkühler	2/2	Lost 2/15		None
U-623	VIIC	Hermann Schröder	2/2	Lost 2/21		None
U-759	VIIC	Rudolf Friedrich*	2/2	3/14		None
U-437	VIIC	Hermann Lamby* (C.O.)	2/3	3/5		None/Abort
U-230	VIIC	Paul Siegmann*	2/4	3/31	1	2,868
U-359	VIIC	Heinz Förster*	2/4	3/18		None
U-638	VIIC	Hinrich-Oskar Bernbeck*	2/4	3/31		None+
U-92	VIIC	Adolf Oelrich	2/6	3/5	1½	14,664/Abort
U-119	XB	Alois Zech*	2/6	4/11		None/M[24]
U-228	VIIC	Erwin Christophersen*	2/6	3/29		None
U-566	VIIC	Hans Hornkohl* (C.O.)	2/6	3/25		None
U-616	VIIC	Siegfried Koitschka*	2/6	3/26		None
U-84	VIIB	Horst Uphoff	2/7	3/28		None
U-103	IXB	Gustav-Adolf Janssen	2/7	3/26		None
U-405	VIIC	Rolf-Heinrich Hopmann	2/7	3/23	3	11,984+
U-445	VIIC	Heinz-Konrad Fenn	2/7	3/27		None
U-603	VIIC	Hans-Joachim Bertelsmann	2/7	3/26	2½	14,605[25]/Abort
U-382	VIIC	Herbert Juli	2/8	3/8		None+/Abort

BOAT	TYPE	SKIPPER	SAILED	RETURNED	SHIPS SUNK	TONS
U-569	VIIC	Hans Johannsen* (C.O.)	2/8	3/13		None/Abort
U-604	VIIC	Horst Höltring	2/8	3/9	1	1,683/Abort
U-659	VIIC	Hans Stock	2/8	3/20		None
U-410	VIIC	Horst-Arno Fenski* (C.O.)	2/9	3/27	1	7,133+
U-523	IXC	Werner Pietzsch*	2/9	4/16	1	5,848
U-527	IXC40	Herbert Uhlig*	2/9	4/12	2	5,385+
U-91	VIIC	Heinz Walkerling[26]	2/11	3/29	5	35,577
U-526	IXC40	Hans Möglich*	2/11	Lost 4/14		None[27]
U-600	VIIC	Bernhard Zurmühler	2/11	3/26	1	12,156+/Abort
U-461	XIV	Wolf Stiebler	2/13	3/22		None/Supply
U-211	VIIC	Karl Hause	2/13	2/25		None/Abort
U-709	VIIC	Karl-Otto Weber*	2/13	3/18		None/Abort
U-409	VIIC	Hans-Ferdinand Massmann	2/14	4/12	2	9,826
U-432	VIIC	Hermann Eckhardt* (C.O.)	2/14	Lost 3/11	1	1,340[28]
U-664	VIIC	Adolf Graef	2/14	3/28	2	13,466/Abort
U-758	VIIC	Helmut Manseck	2/14	3/30	1	6,813+/Abort
U-106	IXB	Hermann Rasch	2/17	4/4		None
U-591	VIIC	Hans-Jürgen Zetzsche	2/17	4/7	2	11,995
U-435	VIIC	Siegfried Strelow	2/18	3/25		None+/Abort
U-615	VIIC	Ralph Kapitzky	2/18	4/20	1	7,177
U-634	VIIC	Eberhard Dahlhaus*	2/18	3/23	1	7,176
U-462	XIV	Bruno Vowe	2/19	3/11		None/Supply
U-190	IXC40	Max Wintermeyer*	2/20	3/30	1	7,015[29]/Abort
U-229	VIIC	Robert Schetelig*	2/20	4/17	1	4,946+
U-447	VIIC	Friedrich-Wilhelm Bothe*	2/20	3/24		None
U-513	IXC	Rolf Rüggeberg	2/20	4/14		None
U-530	IXC40	Kurt Lange*	2/20	4/22	2	12,063
U-633	VIIC	Bernhard Müller*	2/20	Lost 3/10		None
U-641	VIIC	Horst Rendtel*	2/20	4/11		None
U-642	VIIC	Herbert Brünning*	2/20	4/8	1	2,125
U-665	VIIC	Hans-Jürgen Haupt*	2/20	Lost 3/22	1	7,134
U-172	IXC	Carl Emmermann	2/21	4/17	5	29,162
U-618	VIIC	Kurt Baberg	2/21	5/7		None
U-406	VIIC	Horst Dieterichs	2/22	3/30		None+
U-439	VIIC	Helmut von Tippelskirch* (C.O.)	2/22	3/29		None
U-508	IXC	Georg Staats	2/22	3/15		None/Abort
U-590	VIIC	Heinrich Müller-Edzards	2/22	4/12		None/Abort
U-757	VIIC	Friedrich Deetz	2/22	3/18	2	12,198/Abort
U-338	VIIC	Manfred Kinzel*[30]	2/23	3/24	4	21,927+[31]/Abort
U-86	VIIB	Walter Schug	2/24	4/16		None
U-373	VIIC	Paul-Karl Loeser	2/25	4/13		None
U-666	VIIC	Herbert Engel*	2/25	4/10		None+/Abort
U-306	VIIC	Claus von Trotha*	2/26	5/9	2	17,394
U-167	IXC40	Kurt Sturm* (C.O.)	2/27	Lost 4/6	1	4,621+
U-221	VIIC	Hans Trojer	2/27	3/28	5	30,476
U-305	VIIC	Rudolf Bahr*	2/27	4/12	2	13,045
U-440	VIIC	Hans Geissler	2/27	4/11		None
U-441	VIIC	Klaus Hartmann	2/27	4/11		None
U-130	IXC	Siegfried Keller* (C.O.)	2/28	Lost 3/12	4	16,359
Totals:	69 patrols (2 supply, 1 mine mission)				61	346,312

BOAT	TYPE	SKIPPER	SAILED	RETURNED	SHIPS SUNK	TONS
MARCH 1943:						
U-444	VIIC	Albert Langfeld	3/1	Lost 3/11		None
U-333	VIIC	Werner Schwaff	3/2	4/13	1	5,234[32]
U-336	VIIC	Hans Hunger	3/2	4/11		None
U-67	IXC	Günther Müller-Stöckheim	3/3	4/13		None/Abort
U-109	IXB	Hans Joachim Schramm* (C.O.)	3/3	4/1		None/Abort
U-524	IXC	Walter von Steinäcker	3/3	Lost 3/22	1	8,062
U-159	IXC	Helmut Witte	3/4	4/25	1	5,449
U-188	IXC40	Siegfried Lüdden*	3/4	5/3	1	1,190[33]
U-463	XIV	Leo Wolfbauer	3/4	4/17		None/Supply
U-134	VIIC	Hans-Günther Brosin* (C.O.)	3/6	5/2		None/Abort
U-598	VIIC	Gottfried Holtorf	3/6	5/13		None
U-384	VIIC	Hans-Achim von Rosenberg-Gruszczynski	3/6	Lost 3/19	1	7,252
U-631	VIIC	Jürgen Krüger	3/6	5/10	1	5,158
U-415	VIIC	Kurt Neide*	3/7	5/5	2	10,403
U-610	VIIC	Walter von Freyberg-Eisenberg-Allmendingen	3/8	5/12	1	7,176
U-168	IXC40	Helmut Pich*	3/9	5/18		None
U-592	VIIC	Carl Borm	3/9	4/18		None
U-163	IXC	Kurt-Edward Engelmann	3/10	Lost 3/13		None
U-572	VIIC	Heinz Kummetat	3/10	4/13		None/Abort
U-663	VIIC	Heinrich Schmid	3/10	4/4	1	5,754
U-191	IXC40	Helmut Fiehn*	3/11	Lost 4/23	1	3,025
U-564	VIIC	Hans Fiedler	3/11	4/15		None/Abort
U-260	VIIC	Hubertus Purkhold	3/12	5/22		None
U-257	VIIC	Heinz Rahe	3/14	5/7		None
U-704	VIIC	Horst Kessler	3/14	4/10[34]		None/Retired
U-632	VIIC	Hans Karpf	3/15	Lost 4/6	1	7,065
U-706	VIIC	Alexander von Zitzewitz	3/15	5/11	2	14,385
U-469	VIIC	Emil Claussen*	3/16	Lost 3/25		None
U-635	VIIC	Heinz Eckelmann*	3/16	Lost 4/5	1	5,529
U-169	IXC40	Hermann Bauer*	3/18	Lost 3/27		None
U-630	VIIC	Werner Winkler*	3/18	Lost 5/6	1	9,365
U-455	VIIC	Hans-Martin Scheibe	3/20	4/23	1	3,777 /M[35]
U-404	VIIC	Otto von Bülow	3/21	5/3	3	17,736
U-563	VIIC	Götz von Hartmann	3/21	4/18		None/Abort
U-267	VIIC	Otto Tinschert	3/23	5/21		None
U-270	VIIC	Paul-Friedrich Otto*	3/23	5/15		None/Abort
U-584	VIIC	Joachim Deecke	3/23	5/24	1	5,565
U-594	VIIC	Friedrich Mumm	3/23	4/14		None/Abort
U-662	VIIC	Heinz-Eberhard Müller* (C.O.)	3/23	5/19	2	13,011+
U-532	IXC40	Otto-Heinrich Junker*	3/25	5/15		None/Abort
U-571	VIIC	Helmut Möhlmann	3/25	5/1	1	3,835
U-613	VIIC	Helmut Köppe	3/25	5/6		None
U-71	VIIC	Hardo Rodler von Roithberg	3/27	5/1[36]		None/Abort/Retired
U-124	IXB	Johann Mohr	3/27	Lost 4/2	2	9,547
U-487	XIV	Helmut Metz*	3/27	5/11		None/Supply
U-413	VIIC	Gustav Poel	3/30	6/13		None

BOAT	TYPE	SKIPPER	SAILED	RETURNED	SHIPS SUNK	TONS
U-381	VIIC	Wilhelm-Heinrich Pückler und Limpurg	3/31	Lost 5/9 ?		None
U-438	VIIC	Heinrich Heinsohn* (C.O.)	3/31	Lost 5/6		None[37]
U-117	XB	Hans-Werner Neumann	3/31	5/14		None + M[38]
Totals:	49 patrols (2 supply, 2 mine missions)				26	148,518
April 1943:						
U-108	IXB	Ralf-Reimer Wolfram	4/1	5/15[39]		None/Retired
U-258	VIIC	Wilhelm von Mässenhausen	4/1	Lost 5/20	1	6,198
U-303	VIIC	Karl-Franz Heine	4/1	Into Mediterranean 4/9		
U-414	VIIC	Walter Huth	4/1	Into Mediterranean 4/9		
U-462	XIV	Bruno Vowe	4/1	4/24		None/Supply
U-189	IXC40	Helmut Kurrer*	4/3	Lost 4/23		None
U-203	VIIC	Hermann Kottmann	4/3	Lost 4/25		None
U-648	VIIC	Peter-Arthur Stahl*	4/3	5/19		None[40]
U-552	VIIC	Klaus Popp	4/4	6/13[41]		None
U-209	VIIC	Heinrich Brodda*	4/6	Lost 5/7 ?		None
U-465	VIIC	Heinz Wolf	4/7	4/14		None/Abort
U-264	VIIC	Hartwig Looks	4/8	6/1	3	15,228
U-382	VIIC	Leopold Koch	4/8	4/24		None/Abort
U-628	VIIC	Heinz Hasenschar	4/8	5/19	1½	8,779
U-732	VIIC	Klaus-Peter Carlsen*	4/8	5/15		None/Abort
U-954	VIIC	Odo Loewe*	4/8	Lost 5/19		None
U-175	IXC	Heinrich Bruns	4/10	Lost 4/17		None
U-226	VIIC	Rolf Borchers	4/10	5/17	½	3,567
U-650	VIIC	Ernst von Witzendorff*	4/10	6/28		None
U-358	VIIC	Rolf Manke	4/11	5/16	1	2,864 +
U-92	VIIC	Adolf Oelrich	4/12	6/26		None
U-378	VIIC	Erich Mäder	4/12	6/4		None
U-614	VIIC	Wolfgang Sträter	4/12	5/24		None
U-707	VIIC	Günter Gretschel	4/12	5/31	1	4,635
U-125	IXC	Ulrich Folkers	4/13	Lost 5/6		None
U-192	IXC40	Werner Happe*	4/13	Lost 5/6		None
U-231	VIIC	Wolfgang Wenzel*	4/13	5/30		None/Abort
U-531	IXC40	Herbert Neckel*	4/13	Lost 5/6		None
U-266	VIIC	Ralf von Jessen	4/14	Lost 5/15	3	12,012
U-223	VIIC	Karl-Jürgen Wächter	4/15	5/24		None/Abort
U-377	VIIC	Otto Köhler	4/15	6/7		None/Abort
U-386	VIIC	Hans-Albrecht Kandler*	4/15	5/11	1	1,997/Abort
U-514	IXC	Hans-Jürgen Auffermann	4/15	5/22		None
U-525	IXC40	Hans-Joachim Drewitz	4/15	5/26		None
U-528	IXC40	Georg von Rabenau*	4/15	Lost 5/11		None
U-533	IXC40	Helmut Hennig*	4/15	5/24		None/Abort
U-634	VIIC	Eberhard Dahlhaus	4/15	5/23		None
U-709	VIIC	Karl-Otto Weber	4/15	5/23		None
U-710	VIIC	Dietrich von Carlowitz*	4/15	Lost 4/24		None
U-186	IXC40	Siegfried Hesemann	4/17	Lost 5/12		None
U-383	VIIC	Horst Kremser	4/17	5/25		None
U-448	VIIC	Helmut Dauter	4/17	5/26		None/Abort
U-454	VIIC	Burkhard Hackländer	4/17	5/23		None
U-466	VIIC	Gerhard Thäter	4/17	5/26		None
U-217	VIID	Kurt Reichenbach-Klinke	4/19	Lost 6/5		None/M[42]

BOAT	TYPE	SKIPPER	SAILED	RETURNED	SHIPS SUNK	TONS
U-359	VIIC	Heinz Förster	4/19	5/20		None/Abort
U-403	VIIC	Heinz-Ehlert Clausen	4/19	5/31	½	3,569
U-468	VIIC	Klemens Schamong	4/19	5/29		None/Abort
U-569	VIIC	Hans Johannsen	4/19	Lost 5/22		None
U-616	VIIC	Siegfried Koitschka	4/19	Into Mediterranean 5/7		
U-218	VIID	Richard Becker	4/20	6/2		None/M[43]/Abort
U-402	VIIC	Siegfried von Forstner	4/20	5/26	2	7,627/Abort
U-461	XIV	Wolf Stiebler	4/20	5/30		None/Supply
U-638	VIIC	Oskar Staudinger	4/20	Lost 5/5	1	5,507
U-504	IXC	Wilhelm Luis	4/21	5/28		None
U-459	XIV	Georg von Wilamowitz-Möllendorf	4/21	6/3		None/Supply
U-566	VIIC	Hans Hornkohl	4/22	4/26		None/Abort
U-575	VIIC	Günther Heydemann	4/22	6/11		None
U-604	VIIC	Horst Höltring	4/22	4/26		None/Abort
U-621	VIIC	Max Kruschka	4/22	6/3		None
U-752	VIIC	Karl-Ernst Schroeter	4/22	Lost 5/23		None
U-952	VIIC	Oskar Curio*	4/22	5/31		None/Abort
U-103	IXB	Gustav-Adolf Janssen	4/24	5/26		None
U-107	IXB	Harald Gelhaus	4/24	5/26	1	12,411
U-227	VIIC	Jürgen Kuntze*	4/24	Lost 4/30		None
U-418	VIIC	Gerhard Lange*	4/24	Lost 6/1		None
U-456	VIIC	Max-Martin Teichert	4/24	Lost 5/12 ?	½	3,569
U-607	VIIC	Wolf Jeschonnek*	4/24	6/2	1	5,589
U-645	VIIC	Otto Ferro*	4/24	6/22		None
U-89	VIIC	Dietrich Lohmann	4/25	Lost 5/12	1	3,803
U-230	VIIC	Paul Siegmann	4/25	5/24		None[44]
U-406	VIIC	Horst Dieterichs	4/25	5/11		None[45]/Abort
U-436	VIIC	Günther Seibicke	4/25	Lost 5/26		None
U-600	VIIC	Bernhard Zurmühlen	4/25	5/11		None/Abort
U-659	VIIC	Hans Stock	4/25	Lost 5/4		None[46]
U-410	VIIC	Horst-Arno Fenski	4/26	Into Mediterranean 5/6		
U-332	VIIC	Eberhard Hüttemann	4/26	Lost 4/29		None
U-437	VIIC	Hermann Lamby	4/26	4/30		None/Abort
U-304	VIIC	Heinz Koch*	4/27	Lost 5/28		None
U-439	VIIC	Helmut von Tippelskirch	4/27	Lost 5/4		None
U-445	VIIC	Heinz-Konrad Fenn	4/27	4/30		None/Rescue/Abort
U-447	VIIC	Friedrich-Wilhelm Bothe	4/27	Lost 5/7 in Mediterranean attempt		
U-109	IXB	Hans Joachim Schramm	4/28	Lost 5/4		None
U-91	VIIC	Heinz Hungershausen*	4/29	6/7		None/Abort
U-202	VIIC	Günter Poser	4/29	Lost 6/11		None
U-340	VIIC	Hans-Joachim Klaus*	4/29	5/31		None
U-465	VIIC	Heinz Wolf (resail)	4/29	Lost 5/2		None
U-664	VIIC	Adolf Graef	4/29	6/9		None
U-731	VIIC	Werner Techand*	4/29	6/12		None
U-760	VIIC	Otto-Ulrich Blum*	4/29	5/31		None

Totals: 90 patrols (3 supply, 2 mine missions, 4 to Mediterranean) 19 97,355

May 1943:

U-640	VIIC	Karl-Heinz Nagel*	5/1	Lost 5/14		None
U-405	VIIC	Rolf-Heinrich Hopmann	5/2	5/21		None/Abort
U-636	VIIC	Hans Hildebrandt*	5/2	6/8		None/Norway[47]
U-221	VIIC	Hans Trojer	5/3	7/21	1	9,432
U-214	VIID	Günther Reeder	5/4	5/10		None[48]/Abort
U-228	VIIC	Erwin Christophersen	5/4	7/19		None
U-642	VIIC	Herbert Brünning	5/4	7/6		None

BOAT	TYPE	SKIPPER	SAILED	RETURNED	SHIPS SUNK	TONS
U-657	VIIC	Heinrich Göllnitz	5/4	Lost 5/17		None
U-603	VIIC	Rudolf Baltz* (C.O.)	5/5	7/16	1	4,819
U-663	VIIC	Heinrich Schmid	575	Lost 5/8 ?		None
U-753	VIIC	Alfred Manhardt von Mannstein	5/5	Lost 5/13		None
U-666	VIIC	Herbert Engel	5/6	7/9		None
U-232	VIIC	Ernst Ziehm*	5/8	Lost 7/8		None
U-273	VIIC	Hermann Rossmann*	5/8	Lost 5/19		None
U-336	VIIC	Hans Hunger	5/8	7/17		None
U-463	XIV	Leo Wolfbauer	5/8	Lost 5/16		None/Supply
U-558	VIIC	Günther Krech	5/8	Lost 7/20		None[49]
U-641	VIIC	Horst Rendtel	5/9	7/16		None
U-193	IXC40	Hans Pauckstadt*	5/11	7/23		None
U-229	VIIC	Robert Schetelig	5/11	6/7		None/Abort
U-305	VIIC	Rudolf Bahr	5/12	6/1		None/Abort
U-591	VIIC	Hans-Jürgen Zetzsche	5/12	5/16		None/Abort
U-646	VIIC	Heinrich Wulff	5/12	Lost 5/17		None
U-211	VIIC	Karl Hause	5/13	7/16		None
U-951	VIIC	Kurt Pressel*	5/13	Lost 7/7		None
U-953	VIIC	Karl-Heinz Marbach*	5/13	7/22		None
U-608	VIIC	Rolf Struckmeier	5/15	7/18		None
U-488	XIV	Erwin Bartke*	5/18	7/9		None/Supply
U-214	VIID	Rupprecht Stock* (C.O.) (resail)	5/19	6/26		None +/M[50]
U-435	VIIC	Siegfried Strelow	5/20	Lost 7/9		None
U-467	VIIC	Heinz Kummer	5/20	Lost 5/25		None
U-667	VIIC	Heinrich Schroeteler*	5/20	7/26		None
U-441	VIIC	Götz von Hartmann* (C.O.)	5/22	5/26		None/Abort/Flak[51]
U-594	VIIC	Friedrich Mumm	5/23	Lost 6/4 in Mediterranean attempt		
U-118	XB	Werner Czygan	5/25	Lost 6/12		None/PR
U-341	VIIC	Dietrich Epp*	5/25	7/10		None
U-450	VIIC	Kurt Böhme*	5/25	6/22		None/Abort/PR
U-535	IXC40	Helmut Ellmenreich*	5/25	Lost 7/5		None/PR[52]
U-409	VIIC	Hans-Ferdinand Massmann	5/26	Into Mediterranean 6/5		
U-440	VIIC	Werner Schwaff	5/26	Lost 5/31		None
U-758	VIIC	Helmut Manseck	5/26	6/25		None/Abort
U-170	IXC40	Günther Pfeffer*	5/27	7/9		None/PR[52]
U-669	VIIC	Kurt Köhl*	5/27	7/14		None/Rescue/Abort
U-271	VIIC	Curt Barleben*	5/29	7/16		None/Rescue/Abort
U-308	VIIC	Karl Mühlenpfort*	5/29	Lost 6/4		None
U-530	IXC40	Kurt Lange	5/29	7/2		None/PR[52]
U-563	VIIC	Gustav Borchardt* (C.O.)	5/29	Lost 5/31		None
U-592	VIIC	Carl Borm	5/29	7/14		None/Rescue/Abort
U-455	VIIC	Hans-Martin Scheibe	5/30	7/31		None
Totals:	48 patrols (2 supply, 1 mine mission, 2 to Mediterranean)				2	14,251

June 1943:

BOAT	TYPE	SKIPPER	SAILED	RETURNED	SHIPS SUNK	TONS
U-449	VIIC	Hermann Otto*	6/1	Lost 6/24		None
U-536	IXC40	Rolf Schauenburg*	6/1	7/9		None/PR
U-417	VIIC	Wolfgang Schreiner*	6/3	Lost 6/11		None
U-334	VIIC	Heinz Ehrich* (C.O.)	6/5	Lost 6/14		None
U-135	VIIC	Otto Luther* (C.O.)	6/7	Lost 7/15		None
U-388	VIIC	Peter Sues*	6/8	Lost 6/20		None
U-564	VIIC	Hans Fiedler	6/9	Lost 6/14		None

BOAT	TYPE	SKIPPER	SAILED	RETURNED	SHIPS SUNK	TONS
U-68	IXC	Albert Lauzemis	6/12	6/16		None/Abort
U-194	IXC40	Hermann Hesse*	6/12	Lost 6/24		None
U-420	VIIC	Hans-Jürgen Reese*	6/12	7/16		None/Abort
U-338	VIIC	Manfred Kinzel	6/15	6/21		None/Abort
U-487	XIV	Helmut Metz	6/15	Lost 7/13		None/Supply[53]
U-462	XIV	Bruno Vowe	6/19	6/23		None/Supply/Abort
U-270	VIIC	Paul-Friedrich Otto	6/26	7/2		None/Abort
U-160	IXC	Gerd von Pommer-Esche* (C.O.)	6/28	Lost 7/14		None/PR
U-462	XIV	Bruno Vowe (resail)	6/28	7/6		None/Supply/Abort
U-386	VIIC	Fritz Albrecht* (C.O.)	6/29	7/8		None/Abort
U-505	IXC	Peter Zschech	6/30	7/1		None/Abort
Totals:	17 patrols (2 supply)				None	None
JULY 1943:						
U-267	VIIC	Otto Tinschert	7/4	7/13		None/Abort
U-373	VIIC	Paul-Karl Loeser	7/7	8/16		None/M[54]/Abort
U-441	VIIC	Götz von Hartmann	7/8	7/13		None/Flak/Abort
U-459	XIV	Georg von Wilamowitz-Möllendorf	7/22	Lost 7/24		None/Supply
U-489	XIV	Adalbert Schmandt*	7/22	Lost 8/4		None/Supply[55]
U-647	VIIC	Willi Hertin*	7/22	Lost 7/28 ?		None
U-404	VIIC	Adolf Schönberg* (C.O.)	7/24	Lost 7/28		None
U-614	VIIC	Wolfgang Sträter	7/25	Lost 7/29 in Mediterranean attempt		
U-129	IXC	Richard von Harpe* (C.O.)	7/27	9/5		None/PR
U-461	XIV	Wolf-Harro Stiebler	7/27	Lost 7/30		None/Supply
U-462	XIV	Bruno Vowe	7/27	Lost 7/30		None/Supply
U-504	IXC	Wilhelm Luis	7/27	Lost 7/30		None/PR
U-525	IXC40	Hans-Joachim Drewitz	7/27	Lost 8/11		None/PR
U-106	IXB	Wolf-Dietrich Damerow* (C.O.)	7/28	Lost 8/2		None/PR
U-383	VIIC	Horst Kremser	7/29	Lost 8/1 ?		None
U-454	VIIC	Burkhard Hackländer	7/29	Lost 8/1 in Mediterranean attempt		
U-706	VIIC	Alexander von Zitzewitz	7/29	Lost 8/2 in Mediterranean attempt		
Totals:	17 patrols (4 supply, 4 provisional supply, 3 Mediterranean attempts, 1 flak)				None	None
AUGUST 1943:						
U-68	IXC	Albert Lauzemis	8/l	8/3		None/Recalled
U-437	VIIC	Hermann Lamby	8/1	8/3		None/Recalled
U-448	VIIC	Helmut Dauter	8/1	8/3		None/Recalled
U-505	IXC	Peter Zschech	8/1	8/3		None/Recalled
U-621	VIIC	Max Kruschka	8/22	9/28		None/Flak/Biscay
Totals:	5 patrols					
AUGUST/SEPTEMBER (Group *Leuthen*):						
U-305	VIIC	Rudolf Bahr	8/23	10/16	1	1,190[56]/Abort
U-645	VIIC	Otto Ferro	8/23	10/22	1½	9,175[57]
U-260	VIIC	Hubertus Purkhold	8/25	10/17		None/Abort
U-338	VIIC	Manfred Kinzel	8/25	Lost 9/20 ?		
U-731	VIIC	Werner Techand	8/29	11/1		None/Abort
U-386	VIIC	Fritz Albrecht	8/29	10/8		None/Abort
U-460	XIV	Ebe Schnoor	8/30	Lost 10/4		None/Supply

BOAT	TYPE	SKIPPER	SAILED	RETURNED	SHIPS SUNK	TONS
U-229	VIIC	Robert Schetelig	8/31	Lost 9/22		None
U-341	VIIC	Dietrich Epp	8/31	Lost 9/19		None
U-666	VIIC	Herbert Engel	8/31	9/4		None/Abort
U-758	VIIC	Helmut Manseck	9/1	10/10		None
U-584	VIIC	Joachim Deecke	9/2	Lost 10/31		None
U-402	VIIC	Siegfried von Forstner	9/4	Lost 10/13		None[58]
U-238	VIIC	Horst Hepp*	9/5	10/8	4½	26,636[59]
U-641	VIIC	Horst Rendtel	9/5	10/?		None
U-378	VIIC	Erich Mäder	9/6	Lost 10/20	1	1,920[60]
U-666	VIIC	Herbert Engel (resail)	9/6	10/16	1	1,370[61]/Abort
U-952	VIIC	Oskar Curio	9/6	10/17	2	7,123+[62]
U-270	VIIC	Paul-Friedrich Otto	9/7	10/6	1	1,370[63]/Abort
U-422	VIIC	Wolfgang Poeschel*	9/8	Lost 10/4		None
U-275	VIIC	Helmut Bork*	9/9	10/10		None
U-603	VIIC	Rudolf Baltz	9/9	11/3		None
U-377	VIIC	Gerhard Kluth* (C.O.)	9/9	10/10		None/Abort
Totals:	23 patrols (1 supply)				12	48,784

September 1943:

BOAT	TYPE	SKIPPER	SAILED	RETURNED	SHIPS SUNK	TONS
U-274	VIIC	Günther Jordan	9/1	9/13		None/Abort
U-279	VIIC	Otto Finke*	9/4	Lost 10/5		None[64]
U-963	VIIC	Karl Boddenberg*	9/4	9/17		None/Abort
U-488	XIV	Erwin Bartke	9/7	12/12		Supply
U-413	VIIC	Gustav Poel	9/8	9/18		None/Abort
U-610	VIIC	Walter von Freyberg-Eisenberg-Allmendingen	9/12	Lost 10/8		None
U-419	VIIC	Dietrich Giersberg*	9/13	Lost 10/8		None
U-223	VIIC	Karl-Jürgen Wächter	9/14	Into Mediterranean 9/23		
U-336	VIIC	Hans Hunger	9/14	Lost 10/5		None
U-448	VIIC	Helmut Dauter	9/14	11/3		None/Abort
U-539	IXC40	Hans-Jürgen Lauterbach-Emden*	9/14	10/20		None[65]/Abort
U-643	VIIC	Hans-Harald Speidel*	9/14	Lost 10/8		None
U-389	VIIC	Siegfried Heilmann*	9/18	Lost 10/4		None
U-631	VIIC	Jürgen Krüger	9/18	Lost 10/17		None
U-667	VIIC	Heinrich Schroeteler	9/18	10/11		Abort Mediterranean attempt
U-221	VIIC	Hans Trojer	9/20	Lost 9/27		None
U-455	VIIC	Hans-Martin Scheibe	9/20	11/11		Abort Mediterranean attempt[66]
U-91	VIIC	Heinz Hungershausen	9/21	11/22		None
U-264	VIIC	Hartwig Looks	9/22	10/15		Abort Mediterranean attempt
U-92	VIIC	Horst-Thilo Queck* (C.O.)	9/25	10/7		None/Abort
U-309	VIIC	Hans-Gert Mahrholz*	9/25	11/7		None
U-437	VIIC	Hermann Lamby	9/26	11/19		None
U-231	VIIC	Wolfgang Wenzel	9/27	11/22		None
U-470	VIIC	Günter Paul Grave*	9/28	Lost 10/16		None
U-762	VIIC	Wolfgang Hille*	9/28	11/15		None
Total:	25 patrols (1 supply, 1 to Mediterranean, 3 Mediterranean attempts)				None	None

October 1943:

BOAT	TYPE	SKIPPER	SAILED	RETURNED	SHIPS SUNK	TONS
U-271	VIIC	Kurt Barleben	10/2	11/3		None/Flak/Abort
U-413	VIIC	Gustav Poel	10/2	11/21		None
U-424	VIIC	Günter Lüders*	10/2	12/15		None
U-608	VIIC	Rolf Struckmeier	10/2	11/28		None

BOAT	TYPE	SKIPPER	SAILED	RETURNED	SHIPS SUNK	TONS
U-267	VIIC	Ernst von Witzendorff* (C.O.)	10/3	11/26		None
U-552	VIIC	Klaus Popp	10/3	11/30		None
U-256	VIIC	Wilhelm Brauel* (C.O.)	10/4	11/17		None/Flak/Abort
U-540	IXC40	Lorenz Kasch*	10/4	Lost 10/17		None
U-841	IXC40	Werner Bender*	10/4	Lost 10/17		None
U-953	VIIC	Karl-Heinz Marbach	10/4	11/17		None/Flak/Abort
U-226	VIIC	Albrecht Gänge* (C.O.)	10/5	Lost 11/6		None
U-426	VIIC	Christian Reich*	10/5	11/29	1	6,625
U-592	VIIC	Hans Jaschke* (C.O.)	10/5	11/25		None
U-842	IXC40	Wolfgang Heller*	10/5	Lost 11/6		None
U-963	VIIC	Karl Boddenberg	10/5	12/3		None
U-964	VIIC	Emmo Hummerjohann*	10/5	Lost 10/16		None
U-966	VIIC	Eckehard Wolf*	10/5	Lost 11/10		None[67]
U-969	VIIC	Max Dobbert*	10/5	12/6		None
U-281	VIIC	Heinrich von Davidson*	10/6	11/26		None
U-373	VIIC	Detlev von Lehsten* (C.O.)	10/6	11/26		None
U-575	VIIC	Wolfgang Boehmer* (C.O.)	10/6	11/28		None
U-709	VIIC	Karl-Otto Weber	10/6	11/28		None
U-844	IXC40	Günther Möller*	10/6	Lost 10/16		None
U-843	IXC40	Oskar Herwartz*	10/7	12/15		None
U-420	VIIC	Hans-Jürgen Reese	10/9	Lost 10/20 ?		None
U-648	VIIC	Peter-Arthur Stahl	10/9	Lost 11/22 ?		None[68]
U-405	VIIC	Rolf-Heinrich Hopmann	10/10	Lost 11/1		None[69]
U-212	VIIC	Helmut Vogler	10/11	12/2		None
U-967	VIIC	Herbert Loeder*	10/11	12/1		None
U-280	VIIC	Walter Hungershausen*	10/12	Lost 11/16		None
U-274	VIIC	Günther Jordan	10/13	Lost 10/23		None
U-714	VIIC	Hans-Joachim Schwebcke*	10/13	12/2		None
U-211	VIIC	Karl Hause	10/14	Lost 11/19		None/Flak
U-306	VIIC	Klaus von Trotha	10/14	Lost 10/31		None
U-343	VIIC	Wolfgang Rahn*	10/14	11/26		None
U-586	VIIC	Hans Götze* (C.O.)	10/16	12/3		None
U-642	VIIC	Herbert Brünning	10/16	Into Mediterranean 11/3		
U-707	VIIC	Günter Gretschel	10/16	Lost 11/9		None
U-732	VIIC	Claus-Peter Carlsen	10/16	Lost 10/31 in Mediterranean attempt		
U-340	VIIC	Hans-Joachim Klaus	10/17	Lost 11/2 in Mediterranean attempt		
U-450	VIIC	Kurt Böhme	10/17	Into Mediterranean 11/1		
U-566	VIIC	Hans Hornkohl	10/18	Lost 10/24 in Mediterranean attempt		
U-441	VIIC	Klaus Hartmann	10/19	11/7		None/Flak/Abort
U-262	VIIC	Heinz Franke	10/20	12/7		None
U-282	VIIC	Rudolf Müller*	10/20	Lost 10/29		None
U-333	VIIC	Peter Cremer	10/20	12/1		None/Abort
U-466	VIIC	Gerhard Thäter	10/20	11/19		None/Abort
U-219	XB	Walter Burghagen*	10/22	1/1/44		None/PR
U-228	VIIC	Erwin Christophersen	10/25	12/20		None
U-358	VIIC	Rolf Manke	10/25	12/15		None
U-764	VIIC	Hans-Kurt von Bremen*	10/27	12/11		None/Abort
U-391	VIIC	Gert Dültgen*	10/?	Lost 12/13		None
U-542	IXC40	Christian-Brandt Coester*	10/?	Lost 11/26		None
U-538	IXC40	Johann-Egbert Gossler*	10/?	Lost 11/21		None
Totals:	54 patrols (5 flak, 2 to Mediterranean, 3 Mediterranean attempts, 1 provisional supply)				1	6,625

BOAT	TYPE	SKIPPER	SAILED	RETURNED	SHIPS SUNK	TONS
November 1943:						
U-962	VIIC	Ernst Liesberg*	11/3	12/28		None
U-269	VIIC	Karl-Heinrich Harlfinger	11/4	12/15		None/Abort
U-541	IXC40	Kurt Petersen*	11/4	1/9/44		None
U-421	VIIC	Hans Kolbus*	11/6	1/8/44		None
U-734	VIIC	Hans-Jörg Blauert*	11/6	12/25		None
U-801	IXC40	Hans-Joachim Brans*	11/6	1/8/44		None
U-600	VIIC	Bernhard Zurmühlen	11/7	Lost 11/25		None
U-508	IXC	Georg Staats	11/9	Lost 11/12		None [70]
U-544	IXC40	Willi Mattke*	11/9	Lost 1/16/44		None
U-86	VIIB	Walter Schug	11/11	Lost 11/29 ?		None
U-238	VIIC	Horst Hepp	11/11	12/12		None/Abort
U-618	VIIC	Kurt Baberg	11/11	1/4/44		None [71]
U-672	VIIC	Ulf Lawaetz*	11/13	1/15/44		None
U-625	VIIC	Hans Benker	11/15	1/6/44		None [72]
U-107	IXB	Volker Simmermacher	11/16	1/8/44		None
U-761	VIIC	Horst Geider*	11/17	12/26		None/Abort
U-667	VIIC	Heinrich Schroeteler	11/18	1/6/44		None
U-92	VIIC	Horst-Thilo Queck	11/21	1/18/44		None
U-415	VIIC	Kurt Neide	11/21	1/6/44	1	1,340 [73]
U-653	VIIC	Hans-Albrecht Kandler* (C.O.)	11/21	1/13/44		None
U-230	VIIC	Paul Siegmann	11/22	Into Mediterranean 12/5		
U-629	VIIC	Hans-Helmut Bugs	11/22	1/5/44		None[74]/Abort
U-284	VIIC	Günther Scholz*	11/23	Lost 12/21		None [75]
U-364	VIIC	Paul-Heinrich Sass*	11/23	Lost 1/29/44 ?		None [76]
U-311	VIIC	Joachim Zander*	11/25	1/26/44		None
U-741	VIIC	Gerhard Palmgren*	11/25	1/27/44		None
U-976	VIIC	Raimund Tiesler*	11/25	1/29/44		None
U-471	VIIC	Friedrich Kloevekorn*	11/27	1/29/44		None
U-981	VIIC	Walter Sitek*	11/27	1/30/44		None
U-972	VIIC	Klaus-Dietrich König*	11/30	Lost 12/15		None
Totals:	30 patrols (1 to Mediterranean)					
December 1943:						
U-390	VIIC	Heinz Geisslero	12/2	2/13/44		None
U-645	VIIC	Otto Ferro	12/2	Lost 12/24		None
U-744	VIIC	Heinz Blischke*	12/2	1/15/44	$^1/_2$	3,680
U-846	IXC40	Berthold Hashagen*	12/4	3/3/44		None
U-960	VIIC	Günther Heinrich	12/4	2/3/44	1	7,176
U-302	VIIC	Herbert Sickel	12/6	1/30/44		None
U-392	VIIC	Henning Schümann*	12/6	1/20/44		None
U-270	VIIC	Paul-Friedrich Otto	12/8	1/17/44		None [77]
U-275	VIIC	Helmut Bork	12/8	1/11/44		None [78]
U-305	VIIC	Rudolf Bahr	12/8	Lost 1/17/44	1	1,370 [79]
U-545	IXC40	Gert Mannesmann*	12/9	Lost 2/11/44	$^1/_2$	3,680 [80]
U-382	VIIC	Rudolf Zorn* (C.O.)	12/11	1/26/44	1	1,090 [81]
U-641	VIIC	Horst Rendtel	12/11	Lost 1/19/44		None
U-763	VIIC	Ernst Cordes*	12/14	2/7/44		None [82]
U-377	VIIC	Gerhard Kluth	12/15	Lost 1/15/44 ?		None
U-758	VIIC	Helmut Manseck	12/16	1/20/44		None
U-952	VIIC	Oskar Curio	12/16	Into Mediterranean 1/3/44		
U-260	VIIC	Hubertus Purkhold	12/18	2/27/44		None
U-1062	VIIF	Karl Albrecht	12/18	12/23		None/Supply [83]
U-309	VIIC	Hans-Gert Mahrholz	12/19	2/14/44		None
U-731	VIIC	Alexander von Keller* (C.O.)	12/19	2/18/44		None

BOAT	TYPE	SKIPPER	SAILED	RETURNED	SHIPS SUNK	TONS
U-666	VIIC	Ernst-August Wilberg* (C.O.)	12/25	Lost 2/10/44 ?		None
U-231	VIIC	Wolfgang Wenzel	12/26	Lost 1/13/44		None
U-343	VIIC	Wolfgang Rahn	12/26	Into Mediterranean 1/5/44		
U-953	VIIC	Karl-Heinz Marbach	12/26	2/20/44		None/Flak
U-547	IXC40	Kurt Sturm*	12/28	2/23/44*		None
U-762	VIIC	Walter Pietschmann* (C.O.)	12/28	Lost 2/8/44		None
U-386	VIIC	Fritz Albrecht	12/29	Lost 2/19/44		None
U-445	VIIC	Heinz-Konrad Fenn	12/29	1/10/44		None/Abort
U-757	VIIC	Friedrich Deetz	12/29	Lost 1/8/44		None
U-984	VIIC	Heinz Sieder*	12/30	2/24/44		None
Totals:	30 patrols (2 to Mediterranean)				4	16,996
JANUARY 1944:						
U-373	VIIC	Detlev von Lehsten	1/1	1/4		None[84]/Abort
U-650	VIIC	Ernst von Witzendorff	1/1	3/2		None
U-257	VIIC	Heinz Rahe	1/2	Lost 2/24		None
U-426	VIIC	Christian Reich	1/3	Lost 1/8		None
U-281	VIIC	Heinrich von Davidson	1/5	3/5		None
U-406	VIIC	Horst Dieterichs	1/5	Lost 2/18		None
U-455	VIIC	Hans-Martin Scheibe	1/6	Into Mediterranean 1/22		
U-621	VIIC	Max Kruschka	1/6	1/23		None/Abort
U-764	VIIC	Hans-Kurt von Bremen	1/7	3/14		None
U-571	VIIC	Gustav Lüssow	1/8	Lost 1/28		None[85]
U-592	VIIC	Hans Jaschke	1/10	Lost 1/31		None
U-989	VIIC	Hardo Rodler von Roithberg*	1/11	3/4		None
U-549	IXC40	Detlev Krankenhagen*	1/11	3/26		None
U-271	VIIC	Kurt Barleben	1/12	Lost 1/28		None
U-212	VIIC	Helmut Vogler	1/13	3/12		None
U-283	VIIC	Günter Ney*[86]	1/13	Lost 2/11		None
U-263	VIIC	Kurt Nölke	1/19	Lost 1/20 ?		None[87]
U-608	VIIC	Wolfgang Reisener* (C.O.)	1/19	4/3		None
U-985	VIIC	Horst Kessler*	1/19	3/12	1	1,735
U-441	VIIC	Klaus Hartmann	1/20	3/14		None/Abort
U-714	VIIC	Hans-Joachim Schwebcke	1/20	2/26		None[88]/Abort
U-967	VIIC	Herbert Loeder	1/20	Into Mediterranean 2/12		
U-734	VIIC	Hans-Jörg Blauert	1/21	Lost 2/9		None
U-546	IXC40	Paul Just*	1/23	4/23		None[89]
U-969	VIIC	Max Dobbert	1/24	Into Mediterranean 2/3		
U-91	VIIC	Heinz Hungershausen	1/25	Lost 2/25		None
U-256	VIIC	Wilhelm Brauel	1/25	3/22	1	1,300[90]
U-709	VIIC	Rudolf Ites* (C.O.)	1/25	Lost 3/1		None
U-963	VIIC	Karl Boddenberg	1/26	3/27		None
U-238	VIIC	Horst Hepp	1/27	Lost 2/9		None
U-424	VIIC	Günter Lüders	1/29	Lost 2/11		None
Totals:	31 patrols (3 to Mediterranean)				2	2,035
FEBRUARY 1944:						
U-445	VIIC	Rupprecht Fischler von Treuberg* (C.O.)	2/1	2/27		None/Abort
U-586	VIIC	Hans Götz	2/1	Into Mediterranean 2/13		
U-437	VIIC	Hermann Lamby	2/2	4/1		None
U-413	VIIC	Gustav Poel	2/3	3/27	1	1,100[91]

BOAT	TYPE	SKIPPER	SAILED	RETURNED	SHIPS SUNK	TONS
U-264	VIIC	Hartwig Looks	2/5	Lost 2/19		None/S
U-603	VIIC	Hans-Joachim Bertelsmann	2/5	Lost 3/1		None
U-986	VIIC	Karl-Ernst Kaiser*	2/8	Lost 4/17		None [92]
U-761	VIIC	Horst Geider	2/12	Lost 2/24 in Mediterranean attempt		
U-262	VIIC	Helmut Wieduwilt* (C.O.)	2/14	4/29		None
U-333	VIIC	Peter Cremer	2/14	4/20		None
U-358	VIIC	Rolf Manke	2/14	Lost 3/1	1	1,600 [93]
U-448	VIIC	Helmut Dauter	2/14	Lost 4/14		None
U-962	VIIC	Ernst Liesberg	2/14	Lost 4/8		None
U-552	VIIC	Klaus Popp	2/16	4/22		None/Retired [94]
U-214	VIID	Rupprecht Stock	2/19	4/29		None/M [95]
U-421	VIIC	Hans Kolbus	2/19	Into Mediterranean 3/20		
U-621	VIIC	Max Kruschka	2/21	4/19		None
U-488	XIV	Bruno Studt	2/22	Lost 4/26		None/Supply
U-618	VIIC	Kurt Baberg	2/23	4/8	Abort Mediterranean attempt	
U-672	VIIC	Ulf Lawaetz	2/24	5/12		None
U-744	VIIC	Heinz Blischke	2/24	Lost 3/6	1	1,625+ [96]
U-255	VIIC	Erich Harms* (C.O.)	2/26	4/11	1	1,200 [97]
U-267	VIIC	Otto Tinschert	2/26	5/20		None/S
U-392	VIIC	Henning Schümann	2/29	Lost 3/16 in Mediterranean attempt		
U-575	VIIC	Wolfgang Boehmer	2/29	Lost 3/13	1	1,015/S
U-625	VIIC	Siegfried Straub*	2/29	Lost 3/10		None
U-741	VIIC	Gerhard Palmgren	2/29	5/3		None
Totals:	27 patrols (1 supply, 1 mine mission, 2 to Mediterranean, 3 Mediterranean attempts)				5	6,540

MARCH 1944:

BOAT	TYPE	SKIPPER	SAILED	RETURNED	SHIPS SUNK	TONS
U-415	VIIC	Kurt Neide	3/2	3/31		None/Abort
U-653	VIIC	Hans-Albrecht Kandler	3/2	Lost 3/15		None
U-466	VIIC	Gerhard Thäter	3/4	Into Mediterranean 3/22		
U-92	VIIC	Horst-Thilo Queck	3/5	5/10		None
U-667	VIIC	Heinrich Schroeteler	3/8	5/19		None/S
U-311	VIIC	Joachim Zander	3/9	Lost 4/22	1	10,342
U-629	VIIC	Hans-Helmut Bugs	3/9	3/15		None/Abort
U-302	VIIC	Herbert Sickel	3/11	Lost 4/6	2	9,777
U-970	VIIC	Hans-Heinrich Ketels*	3/16	4/22		None/Recalled
U-471	VIIC	Friedrich Kloevekorn	3/16	Into Mediterranean 3/31		
U-228	VIIC	Erwin Christophersen	3/19	3/26		None/Abort
U-763	VIIC	Ernst Cordes	3/19	3/27		None/Recalled
U-821	VIIC	Ulrich Knackfuss*	3/19	4/12		None/Recalled
U-960	VIIC	Günther Heinrich	3/19	3/27		None/Recalled
U-976	VIIC	Raimund Tiesler	3/20	Lost 3/25		None [98]
U-766	VIIC	Hans-Dietrich Wilke*	3/23	4/16		None/Recalled
U-961	VIIC	Klaus Fischer*	3/25	Lost 3/29		None
U-993	VIIC	Kurt Hilbig*	3/25	4/22		None/Recalled
U-473	VIIC	Heinz Sternberg*	3/27	4/18	1	1,400 [99]
U-740	VIIC	Günther Stark*	3/27	4/21		None/Recalled
Totals:	20 patrols (2 to Mediterranean, 7 recalled)				4	21,519

APRIL 1944:

BOAT	TYPE	SKIPPER	SAILED	RETURNED	SHIPS SUNK	TONS
U-736	VIIC	Reinhard Reff*	4/1	5/26		None/W
U-342	VIIC	Albert Hossenfelder	4/3	Lost 4/17		None
U-765	VIIC	Werner Wendt*	4/3	Lost 5/6		None
U-385	VIIC	Hans-Guido Valentiner*	4/5	6/4		None/W
U-955	VIIC	Hans-Heinrich Baden*	4/15	Lost 6/7		None [100]/W

BOAT	TYPE	SKIPPER	SAILED	RETURNED	SHIPS SUNK	TONS
U-731	VIIC	Alexander von Keller* (C.O.)	4/18	Lost 5/15 in Mediterranean attempt		
U-193	IXC40	Ulrich Abel* (C.O.)	4/23	Lost 4/23 ?		None
U-473	VIIC	Heinz Sternberg	4/24	Lost 5/6		None
U-960	VIIC	Günther Heinrich	4/27	Into Mediterranean 5/9		
U-846	IXC40	Berthold Hashagen	4/29	Lost 5/4		None [101]
U-853	IXC40	Helmut Sommer*	4/29	7/3		None/Abort/W

Totals: 11 patrols (1 to Mediterranean, 1 Mediterranean attempt)

May 1944:

U-534	IXC40	Herbert Nollau	5/8	8/13		None
U-857	IXC40	Rudolf Premauer*	5/9	8/13		None

Totals: 2 patrols

GROUP DRAGONER (CHANNEL TEST OF SNORT BOATS)

U-764	VIIC	Hans-Kurt von Bremen	5/18	5/27		None/S
U-441	VIIC	Klaus Hartmann	5/20	5/27		None/S
U-984	VIIC	Heinz Sieder	5/22	5/27		None/S
U-953	VIIC	Karl-Heinz Marbach	5/22	5/27		None/S
U-269	VIIC	Georg Uhl* (C.O.)	5/23	5/27		None/S

Totals: 5 patrols

June 1944:

U-804	IXC40	Herbert Meyer*	6/12	6/17		None[102]/S/Abort
U-858	IXC40	Thilo Bode*	6/12	9/27		None/S
U-743	VII	Helmut Kandzior*	6/15	6/21		None[103]/S/Abort
U-1225	IXC40	Ernst Sauerberg*	6/17	Lost 6/24		None/S
U-804	IXC40	Herbert Meyer (resail)	6/19	10/7	1	1,300[104]/S
U-396	VIIC	Ernst-Günther Unterhorst*	6/20	7/3		None/S/Abort
U-865	IXC40	Dietrich Stellmacher*	6/20	7/5		None/S/Abort

Totals: 7 patrols 1 1,300

OVERLORD

U-boats Based in the Arctic Available to Reinforce France (32 Nonsnorts):

GROUP GRIMM (10)

U-307	VIIC	Friedrich-Georg Herrle*
U-313	VIIC	Friedhelm Schweiger*
U-315	VIIC	Herbert Zoller*
U-347	VIIC	Johann de Buhr*
U-362	VIIC	Ludwig Franz*
U-387	VIIC	Rudolf Büchler*
U-668	VIIC	Wolfgang von Eickstedt*
U-742	VIIC	Heinz Schwassmann*
U-997	VIIC41	Hans Lehmann*
U-71L	VIIC	Hans-Günther Lange*

GROUP TRUTZ (7)

U-344	VIIC	Ulrich Pietsch*
U-363	VIIC	Werner Nees*
U-394	VIIC	Wolfgang Borger*

BOAT	TYPE	SKIPPER	SAILED	RETURNED	SHIPS SUNK	TONS
U-425	VIIC	Heinz Bentzien*				
U-737	VIIC	Paul Breasack*				
U-957	VIIC	Gerd Schaar* (scrapped)[105]				
U-987	VIIC	Hilmar-Karl Schreyer*				

RESERVE (15)

U-965	VIIC	Klaus Ohling*
U-312	VIIC	Kurt-Heinz Nicolay*
U-361	VIIC	Hans Seidel*
U-636	VIIC	Rudolf Schendel
U-703	VIIC	Joachim Brünner
U-278	VIIC	Joachim Franzen
U-354	VIIC	Karl-Heinz Herbschleb
U-716	VIIC	Hans Dunkelberg*
U-992	VIIC	Hans Falke*
U-956	VIIC	Hans-Dieter Mohs
U-739	VIIC	Ernst Mangold
U-921	VIIC	Alfred Werner*
U-968	VIIC	Otto Westphalen*
U-995	VIIC41	Walter Köhntopp*
U-365	VIIC	Heimar Wedemeyer*

U-BOATS ORDERED TO SAIL FROM GERMANY OR NORWAY TO REINFORCE FRANCE (27):

SNORT BOATS (17)

U-719	VIIC	Klaus-Dietrich Steffens	5/22	Lost 6/26		None
U-767	VIIC	Walter Dankleff*	5/22	Lost 6/18	1	1,370[106]
U-1191	VIIC	Peter Grau*	5/22	Lost 6/12 ?		None
U-988	VIIC	Erich Dobberstein*	5/23	Lost 6/30	3?	10,368?[107]
U-477	VIIC	Karl-Joachim Jenssen*	5/28	Lost 6/3		None
U-671	VIIC	Wolfgang Hegewald*	5/28	France 7/5		None
U-247	VIIC	Gerhard Matschulat*	5/31	France 7/27	1	207[108]
U-673	VIIC	Heinz Sauer*	6/4	France 7/23		None[109]
U-243	VIIC	Hans Märtens	6/8	Norway 6/11		None/Abort
U-678	VIIC	Guido Hyronimus*	6/8	Lost 7/6		None
U-715	VIIC	Helmut Röttger	6/8	Lost 6/13		None
U-971	VIIC	Walter Zeplein*	6/8	Lost 6/24		None
U-423	VIIC	Klaus Hackländer*	6/9	Lost 6/17		None
U-480	VIIC	Hans-Joachim Förster	6/10	France 7/6		None
U-998	VIIC41	Hans Fiedler*	6/12	Norway 6/17		None/Abort[110]
U-243	VIIC	Hans Märtens (resail)	6/15	Lost 7/8		None
U-478	VIIC	Rudolf Rademacher*	6/20	Lost 6/30		None
Totals:					5?	11,945?

NONSNORTS (10)

U-240	VIIC	Günter Link*	5/13	Lost 5/14 ?		None
U-241	VIIC	Arno Werr	5/13	Lost 5/18		None
U-675	VIIC	Karl-Heinz Sammler	5/18	Lost 5/24		None
U-476	VIIC	Otto Niethmann*	5/20	Lost 5/25		None
U-990	VIIC	Hubert Nordheimer	5/22	Lost 5/25		None
U-292	VIIC41	Werner Schmidt	5/24	Lost 5/27		None
U-294	VIIC41	Heinz Schütt*	5/31	6/21		None/Recalled
U-290	VIIC	Helmuth Herglotz*	6/1	6/16		None/Recalled
U-980	VIIC	Hermann Dahms*	6/3	Lost 6/11		None
U-958	VIIC	Gerhard Groth	6/3	6/23		None/Recalled

BOAT	TYPE	SKIPPER	SAILED	RETURNED	SHIPS SUNK	TONS
U-boat Patrols from French Bases in Defense of Occupied France:						
GROUP LANDWIRT: FROM BREST (25)						
Snort boats (16)[111]						
U-269	VIIC	Georg Uhl	6/6[112]	Lost 6/25		None
U-275	VIIC	Helmut Bork	6/6[113]	6/24		None
U-441	VIIC	Klaus Hartmann	6/6	Lost 6/8[114]		None[115]
U-621	VIIC	Hermann Stuckmann*	6/6	6/9		None/Abort
U-764	VIIC	Hans-Kurt von Bremen	6/6	6/23	1	1,085[116]/Abort
U-953	VIIC	Karl-Heinz Marbach	6/6	6/18		None/Abort
U-984	VIIC	Heinz Sieder	6/6	6/9		None/Abort
U-214	VIID	Rupprecht Stock	6/11	6/14		None/Abort
U-621	VIIC	Hermann Stuckmann (resail)	6/12	6/21	1	1,490[117]
U-984	VIIC	Heinz Sieder (resail)	6/12[118]	7/4	3	21,550+[119]
U-218	VIID	Richard Becker	6/13	7/9		None+[120]/M
U-214	VIID	Rupprecht Stock (resail)	6/16	7/1		None[121]/M
U-821	VIIC	Gerhard Palmgren	6/20	6/28		None/Ammo
U-953	VIIC	Karl-Heinz Marbach (resail)	6/24	7/21	1	1,927+
U-212	VIIC	Helmut Vogler (resail)	6/28	7/4		None/Abort
U-309	VIIC	Hans-Gert Mahrholz (resail)	6/29	776		None+
Nonsnorts (9)						
U-256	VIIC	Wilhelm Brauel	6/6	6/7		None/Abort
U-413	VIIC	Dieter Sachse*	6/6	6/9		None/Abort
U-415	VIIC	Herbert Werner*	6/6	6/7		None[122]/Abort
U-629	VIIC	Hans-Helmut Bugs	6/6	Lost 6/7		None
U-740	VIIC	Günther Stark	6/6	Lost 6/6 ?		None
U-741	VIIC	Ulrich Knackfuss	6/6	Lost 6/10		None
U-963	VIIC	Karl Boddenberg	6/6	6/7		None/Abort
U-989	VIIC	Hardo Rodler von Roithberg	6/6	6/7		None/Abort
U-373	VIIC	Detlev von Lehsten	6/7	Lost 6/8		None
FROM ST. NAZAIRE, LORIENT, AND LA PALLICE (28)						
Snort boats (9)						
U-212	VIIC	Helmut Vogler	6/6[123]	6/8		None/Abort
U-763	VIIC	Ernst Cordes (resail)	6/11	6/16[126]		None/Abort
U-212	VIIC	Helmut Vogler (resail)	6/12	6/16		None/Abort
U-763	VIIC	Ernst Cordes (resail)	6/18	6/19		None/Abort
U-763	VIIC	Ernst Cordes (resail)	6/20	7/14[127]	1	1,499
U-309	VIIC	Hans-Gert Mahrholz	6/21	6/25[124]		None/Ammo
U-390	VIIC	Heinz Geissler	6/21	6/24[125]		None/Ammo
U-212	VIIC	Helmut Vogler (resail)	6/22	6/24		None/Ammo
U-212	VIIC	Helmut Vogler (resail)	6/28	7/4[128]		None
Nonsnorts (19)						
U-981	VIIC	Günther Keller*	6/6	6/17		None/Recalled
U-270	VIIC	Paul-Friedrich Otto	6/6	6/17		None[129]/Recalled
U-260	VIIC	Klaus Becker*	6/6	6/16		None/Recalled
U-382	VIIC	Rudolf Zorn	6/6	6/13		None/Recalled
U-714	VIIC	Hans-Joachim Schwebcke*	6/6	6/15		None/Recalled
U-650	VIIC	Ernst von Witzendorff	6/6	6/15		None/Recalled

BOAT	TYPE	SKIPPER	SAILED	RETURNED	SHIPS SUNK	TONS
U-437	VIIC	Hermann Lamby	6/6	6/15		None/Recalled
U-766	VIIC	Hans-Dietrich Wilke	6/6	6/15		None/Recalled
U-255	VIIC	Erich Harms	6/6	6/15		None[130]/Recalled
U-445	VIIC	Rupprecht Fischler von Treuberg	6/6	6/15		None/Recalled
U-262	VIIC	Helmut Wieduwilt	6/6	6/15		None/Recalled
U-985	VIIC	Heinz Wolff*	6/6	6/15		None/Recalled
U-758	VIIC	Hans-Arendt Feindt*	6/6	6/15		None/Recalled
U-281	VIIC	Heinrich von Davidson	6/6	6/15		None/Recalled
U-228	VIIC	Erwin Christophersen	6/6	6/15		None/Recalled
U-608	VIIC	Wolfgang Reisener	6/6	6/14		None/Recalled
U-993	VIIC	Kurt Hilbig	6/6	6/14		None/Recalled
U-333	VIIC	Peter Cremer	6/6	6/12		None[131]/Abort
U-970	VIIC	Hans-Heinrich Ketels	6/6	Lost 6/8		None

U-Boats Sailing to Repel an Allied Invasion of Norway or Denmark:

GROUP MITTE (26)

						Fate
U-242	VIIC	Karl-Wilhelm Paucke*	6/8	6/26		East Baltic
U-348	VIIC	Hans-Norbert Schunck*	6/8	6/26		East Baltic
U-397	VIIC	Fritz Kallipke	6/8	7/2		Retired/School
U-677	VIIC	Paul Weber	6/8	7/6		Retired/School
U-975	VIIC	Hubert Jeschke*	6/8	7/2		Norway
U-999	VIIC41	Hermann Hansen*	6/8	7/6		Retired/School
U-1001	VIIC41	Ernst-Ulrich Blaudow*	6/8	7/25		East Baltic
U-276	VIIC	Rolf Borchers*	6/10	7/6	Abort	Retired/R&D
U-745	VIIC	Wilhelm von Trotha*	6/10	7/27		East Baltic
U-982	VIIC	Ernst-Werner Schwirley*	6/10	7/6		Retired/School
U-1007	VIIC41	Hans Hornkohl*	6/10	7/6		Baltic
U-1165	VIIC41	Hans Homann*	6/10	8/9		East Baltic
U-290	VIIC	Helmut Herglotz*	6/11	8/9	Abort	East Baltic
U-294	VIIC41	Heinz Schütt*	6/11	6/20		Norway
U-958	VIIC	Gerhard Groth*	6/11	7/27		East Baltic
U-1000	VIIC41	Willi Müller*	6/11	8/9		East Baltic
U-1192	VIIC	Herbert Zeissler*	6/20	7/2		Retired/School
U-317	VIIC41	Peter Rahlf*	6/20	Lost 6/26		
U-771	VIIC	Helmut Block*	6/21	7/15		Arctic
U-994	VIIC	Volker Melzer*	6/22	7/19	Abort	Norway/S
U-293	VIIC41	Leonhard Klingspor*	6/26	7/?		Arctic
U-319	VIIC41	Johannes Clemens*	7/5	Lost 7/15[132]		
U-299	VIIC41	Helmuth Heinrich*	7/5	7/19	Abort	Norway
U-286	VIIC	Willi Dietrich*	7/5	7/19	Abort	Norway
U-295	VIIC41	Günter Wieboldt*	7/13	7/19		Arctic
U-1163	VIIC41	Ernst-Ludwig Balduhn*	7/13	7/19		Arctic

GROUP MITTE RESERVE (7)

U-370	VIIC	Karl Nielsen*	6/9	7/19	Baltic
U-479	VIIC	Friedrich-Wilhelm Sons*	6/9	7/19	Baltic
U-679	VIIC	Friedrich Breckweldt*	6/10	7/19	Baltic
U-310	VIIC	Wolfgang Ley*	6/12	7/19	Arctic
U-318	VIIC41	Josef Will	6/12	7/19	Arctic

BOAT	TYPE	SKIPPER	SAILED	RETURNED	SHIPS SUNK	TONS
U-427	VIIC	Karl-Gabriel von Gudenus*	6/27	7/19		Arctic
U-637	VIIC	Günther Zedelius*	6/xx	7/19		Baltic

U-Boat Patrols from French Bases in July 1944:

U-212	VIIC	Helmut Vogler (resail)	7/5	Lost 7/21		None/S
U-741	VIIC	Gerhard Palmgren	7/5	7/15		None/S/Abort
U-92	VIIC	Wilhelm Brauel	7/6	7/10		None/Port defense
U-672	VIIC	Ulf Lawaetz	7/6	Lost 7/18		None/S
U-989	VIIC	Hardo Rodler von Roithberg	7/6	7/10		None/Port defense
U-415	VIIC	Herbert Werner	7/11	7/12		None/Port defense
U-963	VIIC	Karl Boddenberg	7/11	7/12		None/Port defense/S
U-309	VIIC	Hans-Gert Mahrholz	7/13	8/2		None+/S
U-415	VIIC	Herbert Werner	7/13	Lost 7/14		None/Port defense[133]
U-621	VIIC	Hermann Stuckmann	7/15	8/11	1	2,938 +[134]/S
U-275	VIIC	Helmut Wehrkamp*	7/16	8/1		None/S/Abort
U-993	VIIC	Kurt Hilbig	7/17	7/19		None/Port defense/S
U-963	VIIC	Werner Müller* (C.O.)	7/19	8/21		None/S
U-214	VIID	Gerhard Conrad* (C.O.)	7/22	Lost 7/26		None[135]/S
U-260	VIIC	Klaus Becker	7/22	7/23		None/Port defense
U-608	VIIC	Wolfgang Reisener	7/22	7/23		None/Port defense
U-667	VIIC	Karl-Heinz Lange* (C.O.)	7/22	Lost 8/25 ?	4	10,000[136]/S
U-333	VIIC	Hans Fiedler* (C.O.)	7/23	Lost 7/31		None
U-671	VIIC	Wolfgang Hegewald	7/26	Lost 8/4		None/S
U-984	VIIC	Heinz Sieder	7/26	Lost 8/20		None/S
Totals:	20				5	12,938

Interbase Transfers in France in July:

U-618	VIIC	Erich Faust	7/26	7/30	Naz-Brest
U-766	VIIC	Hans-Dietrich Wilke	7/26	7/29	Naz-Brest

Interbase Transfers in France in August:

U-260	VIIC	Klaus Becker	8/7	8/13	Lorient–La Pallice
U-309	VIIC	Hans-Gert Mahrholz	8/7	8/12	Brest–La Pallice/S
U-608	VIIC	Wolfgang Reisener	8/7	Lost 8/10	Lorient–La Pallice
U-981	VIIC	Günther Keller	8/7	Lost 8/12	Lorient–La Pallice
U-766	VIIC	Hans-Dietrich Wilke	8/8	8/24	Brest–La Pallice[137]
U-281	VIIC	Heinrich von Davidson	8/9	8/14	St. Nazaire–La Pallice
U-437	VIIC	Hermann Lamby	8/9	8/13	St. Nazaire–La Pallice
U-763	VIIC	Ernst Cordes	8/9	8/14	Brest–La Pallice
U-270	VIIC	Heinrich Schrelber*	8/10	Lost 8/13	Lorient–La Pallice
U-953	VIIC	Herbert Werner*	8/10	8/18	Brest-Bordeaux
U-618	VIIC	Erich Faust	8/11	Lost 8/15	Brest–La Pallice
U-445	VIIC	Rupprecht Fischler von Treuberg	8/12	8/17	La Pallice–Lorient
U-650	VIIC	Rudolf Zorn*	8/12	8/17	La Pallice–Lorient
U-621	VIIC	Hermann Stuckmann	8/13	Lost 8/18	Brest–La Pallice
U-963	VIIC	Werner Müller	8/13	8/21	Brest–La Pallice
U-107	IXB	Karl-Heinz Fritz*	8/16	Lost 8/18	Lorient–La Pallice

BOAT	TYPE	SKIPPER	SAILED	RETURNED	SHIPS SUNK	TONS
SNORT BOATS EVACUATING FROM FRANCE TO NORWAY, AUGUST–SEPTEMBER 1944:						
U-413	VIIC	Dietrich Sachs	8/2	Lost 8/20	1	2,360
U-480	VIIC	Hans-Joachim Förster	8/3	10/4	4	14,621 [138]
U-736	VIIC	Reinhard Reff	8/5	Lost 8/6		None
U-764	VIIC	Hans-Kurt von Bremen	8/6	9/19	1	638
U-741	VIIC	Gerhard Palmgren	8/8	Lost 8/15		None
U-989	VIIC	Hardo Rodler von Roithberg	8/9	9/25	1	1,791+
U-385	VIIC	Hans-Guido Valentiner	8/9	Lost 8/11		None
U-218	VIID	Rupprecht Stock* (C.O.)	8/10	9/23		None [139]
U-548	IXC40	Günther Pfeffer* (C.O.)	8/11	9/28		None
U-228	VIIC	Herbert Engel* (C.O.)	8/12	9/20		None***
U-275	VIIC	Helmut Wehrkamp	8/13	9/18		None***
U-92	VIIC	Wilhelm Brauel* (C.O.)	8/16	9/29		None***
U-993	VIIC	Karl-Heinz Steinmetz* (C.O.)	8/17	9/18		None***
U-190	IXC40	Hans-Edwin Reith* (C.O.)	8/22	10/1		None
U-650	VIIC	Rudolf Zorn*	8/22	9/22		None
U-445	VIIC	Rupprecht Fischler von Treuberg	8/22	Lost 8/24		
U-262	VIIC	Helmut Wieduwilt	8/23	11/1		None
U-758	VIIC	Hans-Arendt Feindt	8/23	10/10		None
U-763	VIIC	Kurt Braun*	8/23	9/25		None
U-547	IXC40	Heinrich Niemeyer	8/24	9/27		None
U-437	VIIC	Hermann Lamby	8/24	9/22		None***
U-534	IXC40	Herbert Nollau	8/25	10/24		None
U-857	IXC	Rudolf Premauer	8/25	10/7		None
U-247	VIIC	Gerhard Matschulat	8/26	Lost 9/1		None
U-714	VIIC	Hans-Joachim Schwebcke	8/27	10/24		None
U-853	IXC40	Günter Kuhnke	8/27	10/11		None
U-309	VIIC	Hans-Gert Mahrholz	8/29	10/9		None
U-963	VIIC	Karl Boddenberg	8/29	10/7		None
U-985	VIIC	Heinz Wolff	8/30	10/23		None***
U-953	VIIC	Herbert Werner	8/31	10/11		None
U-256	VIIC	Heinrich Lehmann-Willenbrock	9/3	10/17		None***
U-260	VIIC	Klaus Becker	9/3	10/17		None
U-281	VIIC	Heinrich von Davidson	9/4	10/28		None
U-155	IXC	Ludwig von Friedeburg*	9/9	10/17		None
U-382	VIIC	Hans-Dietrich Wilke*	9/10	10/19		None
U-673	VIIC	Ernst-August Gerke*	9/14	10/19		None***
U-267	VIIC	Bernhard Knieper*	9/23	10/29		None
Totals:	37				7	19,410

SNORT-BOAT PATROLS FROM NORWAY, JULY–DECEMBER 1944:

JULY 1944:

U-855	IXC40	Prosper Ohlsen	7/3	Lost 9/11 ?	None/PR
U-300	VIIC41	Fritz Hein*	7/18	8/17	None/Abort

Totals: 2 patrols (1 supply)

*** = Lost, destroyed, or decommissioned upon arrival in Norwegian waters from France (8)

BOAT	TYPE	SKIPPER	SAILED	RETURNED	SHIPS SUNK	TONS
AUGUST 1944:						
U-396	VIIC	Ernst-Günther Unterhorst	8/6	8/16		None/Abort
U-772	VIIC	Ewald Rademacher*	8/13	10/6		None/W
U-245	VIIC	Friedrich Schumann-Hindenberg*	8/14	10/24		None/W
U-482	VIIC	Hartmut von Matuschka*	8/14	9/26	5	32,671[140]
U-484	VIIC	Wolff-Axel Schaefer*	8/14	Lost 9/9		None
U-680	VIIC	Max Ulber*	8/14	9/8		None/Abort
U-296	VIIC41	Karl-Heinz Rasch*	8/16	9/29		None
U-248	VIIC	Bernhard Emde*	8/17	10/14		None
U-743	VIIC	Helmut Kandzior	8/21	Lost 8/21 ?		None
U-1004	VIIC41	Hartmuth Schimmelpfennig*	8/22	10/23		None
U-244	VIIC	Ruprecht Fischer	8/23	10/10		None
U-285	VIIC	Konrad Bornhaupt*	8/24	9/18		None/Abort
U-925	VIIC	Helmuth Knoke*	8/24	Lost 8/24 ?		None
U-398	VIIC	Johann Reckhoff*	8/26	10/14		None
U-979	VIIC	Johannes Meermeier*	8/29	10/10		None+[141]
Totals:	15 patrols (2 weather)				5	32,671
SEPTEMBER 1944:						
U-1228	IXC40	Friedrich-Wilhelm Marienfeld*	9/5	9/20		None/Rescue
U-1227	IXC40	Friedrich Altmeier*	9/12	12/26	1	1,370[142]
U-1199	VIIC	Rolf Nollmann*	9/14	11/5		None
Totals:	3 patrols			1	1,370	
OCTOBER 1944:						
U-300	VIIC41	Fritz Hein	10/4	12/2	3	7,819
U-483	VIIC	Hans-Joachim von Morstein*	10/5	11/21	1.	1,300[143]/Abort
U-246	VIIC	Ernst Raabe*	10/7	11/11		None/Abort
U-1200	VIIC	Hinrich Mangels*	10/7	10/15		None/Abort
U-978	VIIC	Günther Pulst*	10/9	12/16	1	7,176+
U-1006	VIIC41	Horst Voigt*	10/9	Lost 10/16		None
U-1003	VIIC41	Werner Strübing*	10/11	12/16		None
U-773	VIIC	Hugo Baldus*	10/15	11/18		None/Supply
U-722	VIIC	Hans-Heinrich Reimers*	10/16	11/20		None/Supply
U-1200	VIIC	Hinrich Mangels	10/17	Lost 11/11		None/W
U-991	VIIC	Diethelm Balke*	10/18	12/25		None
U-396	VIIC	Ernst-Günther Unterhorst	10/21	12/19		None
U-680	VIIC	Max Ulber	10/26	11/08		None/Abort
U-1202	VIIC	Rolf Thomsen	10/30	1/1/45	1	7,176+
Totals: 15 patrols (2 supply)					7	28,971
NOVEMBER 1944:						
U-296	VIIC41	Karl-Heinz Rasch	11/4	12/25		None
U-1053	VIIC	Helmut Lange*	11/7	1/22/45		None/W
U-979	VIIC	Johannes Meermeier	11/9	1/16/45		None
U-870	IXC40	Ernst Hechler*	11/12	2/20/45	3	6,462[144]
U-680	VIIC	Max Ulber	11/13	1/18/45		None
U-322	VIIC41	Gerhard Wysk*	11/15	Lost 11/25		None

BOAT	TYPE	SKIPPER	SAILED	RETURNED	SHIPS SUNK	TONS
U-400	VIIC	Horst Creutz*	11/15	Lost 12/17		None
U-482	VIIC	Hartnut von Matuschka	11/18	Lost 12/1 ?	1	8,300 [145]
U-775	VIIC	Erich Taschenmacher*	11/18	12/22	1	1,300 [146]/Abort
U-772	VIIC	Ewald Rademacher	11/19	Lost 12/30	4	21,053+[147]
U-1020	VIIC41	Otto-Emil Eberlein*	11/24	Lost 12/31 ?		None+[148]
U-1209	VIIC	Ewald Hülsenbeck*	11/24	Lost 12/18		None
U-297	VIIC41	Wolfgang Aldegarmann*	11/26	Lost 11/26 ?		None
U-877	IXC40	Eberhard Findeisen*	11/26	Lost 12/27		None
U-486	VIIC	Gerhard Meyer*	11/28	1/5/45	4	20,036 [149]
U-1009	VIIC41	Claus Hilgendorf*	11/28	12/3		None/Abort
U-485	VIIC	Friedrich Lutz*	11/29	2/2/45		None
Totals:	17 patrols				13	57,151
December 1944:						
U-275	VIIC	Helmut Wehrkamp	12/2	12/12		None/Abort
U-248	VIIC	Johann-Friedrich Loos* (C.O.)	12/3	Lost 1/16/45		None/W
U-722	VIIC	Hans-Heinrich Reimers	12/7	12/29		None/Supply
U-773	VIIC	Hugo Baldus	12/7	1/10/45		None/Supply
U-650	VIIC	Rudolf Zorn	12/9	Lost 12/9 ?		None
U-325	VIIC41	Erwin Dohrn*	12/11	2/14/45		None
U-905	VIIC	Bernhard Schwarting*	12/11	2/1/45		None/Abort
U-1009	VIIC41	Dietrich Zehle*	12/11	2/8/45		None/W
U-1055	VIIC	Rudolf Meyer*	12/11	2/8/45	4	19,413+
U-278	VIIC	Joachim Franze	12/12	12/20		None/Abort
U-244	VIIC	Ruprecht Fischer	12/12	12/23		None/Abort
U-312	VIIC	Friedrich-Georg Herrle*	12/13	1/3/45		None/Abort
U-1172	VIIC41	Jürgen Kuhlmann*	12/13	Lost 1/27/45 ?	2	2,751+[150]
U-739	VIIC	Ernst Mangold	12/16	12/21		None/Abort
U-285	VIIC	Konrad Bornhaupt	12/20	1/31/45		None/Abort
U-313	VIIC	Friedhelm Schweiger*	12/23	2/15/45		None
U-278	VIIC	Joachim Franze	12/24	2/11/45		None+
U-315	VIIC	Herbert Zoller*	12/25	1/6/45		None/Abort
U-764	VIIC	Hans-Kurt von Bremen	12/26	2/10/45		None
U-825	VIIC	Gerhard Stoelker*	12/29	2/18/45	1	8,300+
U-1017	VIIC41	Werner Riecken*	12/29	2/28/45	3	17,733
U-1051	VIIC	Heinrich von Holleben*	12/29	Lost 1/26/45		None
Totals:	22 patrols				10	48,197

Snort-Boat Patrols from Norway, January–May 1945:

BOAT	TYPE	SKIPPER	SAILED	RETURNED	SHIPS SUNK	TONS
January 1945:						
U-245	VIIC	Friedrich Schumann-Hindenberg	1/?	2/19	1	7,240+[151]
U-1199	VIIC	Rolf Nollmann	1/1	Lost 1/21	1	7,176
U-907	VIIC	Servais Cabolet*	1/4	3/16		None/W
U-480	VIIC	Hans-Joachim Förster	1/6	Lost 2/24	1	1,644
U-244	VIIC	Ruprecht Fischer	1/9	3/13		None
U-275	VIIC	Helmut Wehrkamp	1/13	2/10		None[152]/Abort
U-1208	VIIC	Georg Hagene*	1/14	Lost 2/27	1	925 [153]
U-963	VIIC	Rolf-Werner Wentz* (C.O.)	1/16	3/4		None

BOAT	TYPE	SKIPPER	SAILED	RETURNED	SHIPS SUNK	TONS
U-1058	VIIC	Hermann Bruder*	1/16	3/18		None
U-1203	VIIC	Sigurd Seeger	1/17	3/31	1	580 [154]
U-1014	VIIC41	Wolfgang Glaser*	1/18	Lost 2/4		None
U-300	VIIC41	Fritz Hein	1/21	Lost 2/22	1	9,551+
U-1018	VIIC41	Walter Burmeister*	1/21	Lost 2/27	2	16,699
U-868	IXC40	Eduard Turre	1/22	2/18		None/Supply [155]
U-1276	VIIC41	Karl-Heinz Wendt*	1/27	Lost 2/20		None
U-1004	VIIC	Rudolf Hinz*	1/28	3/21	2	2,293 [156]
U-1104	VIIC41	Rüdiger Perleberg*	1/28	3/22		None
U-2324	XXIII	Hans-Heinrich Hass*	1/29	2/24		None
U-327	VIIC41	Hans Lemcke*	1/30	Lost 1/30 ?		None
U-1279	VIIC41	Hans Falke*	1/30	Lost 2/3		None
U-927	VIIC	Jürgen Ebert*	1/31	Lost 2/24		None
Totals:	21 patrols (1 supply)				10	30,726

FEBRUARY 1945:

BOAT	TYPE	SKIPPER	SAILED	RETURNED	SHIPS SUNK	TONS
U-683	VIIC	Günter Keller*	2/6	Lost 2/20 ?		None
U-1302	VIIC41	Wolfgang Herwartz*	2/6	Lost 3/7	4	10,312+
U-2322	XXIII	Fridtjof Heckel*	2/6	3/3	1	1,317+
U-483	VIIC	Hans Joachim von Morstein	2/7	3/?		None/Abort
U-309	VIIC	Herbert Loeder*	2/8	Lost 2/16		None
U-399	VIIC	Heinz Buhse*	2/8	Lost 3/26	2	7,546
U-775	VIIC	Erich Taschenmacher	2/8	3/19		None
U-989	VIIC	Hardo Rodler von Roithburg	2/8	Lost 2/14		None
U-1064	VIIC41	Hermann Schneidewind*	2/8	4/10	1	1,564/W
U-1019	VIIC41	Hans Rinck*	2/10	4/10		None
U-1278	VIIC41	Erich Müller-Bethke*	2/11	Lost 2/17		None
U-878	IXC40	Johannes Rodig*	2/12	3/20	1	672/Supply [157]
U-1022	VIIC41	Hans-Joachim Ernst*	2/12	4/2	2	1,720
U-315	VIIC	Herbert Zoller	2/15	4/25		None+
U-965	VIIC	Günter Unverzagt*	2/15	2/26		None/Abort
U-681	VIIC	Werner Gebauer*	2/16	Lost 3/11		None
U-773	VIIC	Hugo Baldus	2/19	4/15		None
U-1003	VIIC41	Werner Strübing	2/19	Lost 3/23		None
U-1021	VIIC41	William Holpert*	2/20	Lost 3/14		None
U-1169	VIIC41	Heinz Goldbeck*	2/20	Lost 3/29		None
U-260	VIIC	Klaus Becker	2/21	Lost 3/12		None [158]
U-722	VIIC	Hans-Heinrich Reimers	2/21	Lost 3/27	1	2,190
U-953	VIIC	Herbert Werner	2/21	4/3		None
U-1002	VIIC41	Richard Boos*	2/21	4/10		None
U-1005	VIIC41	Hermann Lauth*	2/21	3/21		None/Abort
U-246	VIIC	Ernst Raabe	2/22	Lost 4/1 ?	1	1,370 [159]
U-1195	VIIC	Ernst Cordes	2/24	Lost 4/6	2	18,596
U-275	VIIC	Helmut Wehrkamp	2/25	Lost 3/10	1	4,934 [160]
U-978	VIIC	Günther Pulst	2/25	4/18		None
U-296	VIIC41	Karl-Heinz Rasch	2/28	Lost 3/12 ?		None [161]
U-1273	VIIC41	Helmut Knollmann	2/28	Lost 2/17		None [162]
Totals:	31 patrols (1 supply)				16	50,221

MARCH 1945:

BOAT	TYPE	SKIPPER	SAILED	RETURNED	SHIPS SUNK	TONS
U-1024	VIIC41	Hans-Joachim Gutteck*	3/3	Lost 4/13		None+ [163]
U-242	VIIC	Heinrich Riedel*	3/4	Lost 4/5		None

BOAT	TYPE	SKIPPER	SAILED	RETURNED	SHIPS SUNK	TONS
U-714	VIIC	Hans-Joachim Schwebcke	3/4	Lost 3/14	2	1,651[164]
U-1202	VIIC	Rolf Thomsen	3/4	4/27		None+
U-778	VIIC	Ralf Jürs*	3/6	4/7		None/Abort
U-965	VIIC	Günter Unverzagt	3/6	Lost 3/30		None
U-1023	VIIC41	Heinrich Schroeteler	3/7	5/10	1	335[165]/U.K.
U-826	VIIC	Olaf Lübcke*	3/11	5/11		None/U.K.
U-1001	VIIC41	Ernst-Ulrich Blaudow	3/12	Lost 4/8		None
U-1063	VIIC41	Karl-Heinz Stephan*	3/12	Lost 4/15		None
U-2321	XXIII	Hans-Heinrich Barschkis*	3/12	4/13	1	1,406
U-396	VIIC	Hillmar Siemon*	3/13	Lost 4/11 ?		None/W
U-905	VIIC	Bernhard Schwarting	3/13	Lost 3/27		None
U-774	VIIC	Werner Sausmikat*	3/15	Lost 4/8		None
U-321	VIIC41	Fritz Berends*	3/17	Lost 4/2		None
U-868	IXC40	Eduard Turre	3/19	4/8		None/Supply[166]
U-249	VIIC	Uwe Kock*	3/22	3/25		None/Abort
U-325	VIIC41	Erwin Dohrn	3/22	Lost 4/7 ?		None+
U-218	VIID	Rupprecht Stock	3/23	5/30	1	200/M[167]
U-1106	VIIC	Erwin Bartke*	3/23	Lost 3/29		None
U-1109	VIIC41	Friedrich van Riesen*	3/23	4/6		None/Abort
U-485	VIIC	Friedrich Lutz	3/24	4/24		None[168]
U-776	VIIC	Lothar Martin*	3/24	U.K.		None
U-324	VIIC41	Ernst Edell Hoff*	3/24	3/30		None/Abort
U-285	VIIC	Konrad Bornhaupt	3/26	Lost 4/15		None
U-326	VIIC41	Peter Matthes*	3/29	Lost 4/25		None
U-979	VIIC	Johannes Meermeier	3/29	5/?	1	348+
U-1107	VIIC41	Fritz Parduhn*	3/30	Lost 4/30	2	15,209
U-293	VIIC41	Leonhard Klingpor	3/31	5/?	1	878
U-636	VIIC	Eberhard Schendel* (C.O.)	3/31	Lost 4/21		None
U-956	VIIC	Heinz-Dieter Mohs	3/31			None/U.K.
Totals:	31 patrols (1 supply)				9	20,027
April 1945:						
U-739	VIIC	Fritz Kosnick* (C.O.)	4/1	5/4		None
U-1009	VIIC41	Claus Hilgendorf	4/1	5/10		None/W/U.K.
U-825	VIIC	Gerhard Stoelker	4/3	U.K.		None
U-2324	XXIII	Konstantin von Rappard*	4/3	4/25	1	1,150
U-249	VIIC	Uwe Koch	4/4	U.K.		None
U-1065	VIIC41	Johannes Panitz*	4/4	Lost 4/9		None/M[169]
U-901	VIIC	Hans Schrenk*	4/5	5/15		None
U-1055	VIIC	Rudolf Meyer	4/5	Lost 4/23 ?		None/M[170]
U-1274	VIIC41	Hans-Hermann Fitting*	4/5	Lost 4/16	1	8,966
U-1305	VIIC41	Hans Christiansen*	4/5	5/10		None/U.K.
U-2322	XXIII	Fridtjof Heckel	4/5	5/5		None
U-878	IXC40	Johannes Rodig	4/6	Lost 4/10		None/Supply[171]
U-516	IXC	Friedrich Petran* (C.O.)	4/6	U.K.		None/Supply[172]
U-486	VIIC	Gerhard Meyer	4/7	Lost 4/12		None[173]
U-1206	VIIC	Karl-Adolf Schlitt*	4/7	Lost 4/14		None[174]
U-245	VIIC	Friedrich Schumann-Hindenberg	4/9	5/10	2	9,847[175]
U-541	IXC40	Kurt Petersen	4/11	5/14	Gib.	None
U-2329	XXIII	Heinz Schlott*	4/12	4/26		None+

BOAT	TYPE	SKIPPER	SAILED	RETURNED	SHIPS SUNK	TONS
U-1105	VIIC41	Hans-Joachim Schwarz*	4/13	5/10	1	1,300[176]/U.K.
U-1017	VIIC	Werner Riecken	4/14	Lost 4/29		None
U-244	VIIC	Hans-Peter Mackeprang* (C.O.)	4/15	U.K.		None
U-1010	VIIC41	Günter Strauch*	4/15	5/14		None/U.K.
U-1277	VIIC41	Ehrenreich Stever*	4/15	Lost 6/3		None[177]
U-251	VIIC	Joachim Sauerbier* (C.O.)	4/17	Lost 4/19		None
U-398	VIIC	Wilhelm Cranz* (C.O.)	4/17	Lost 4/17 ?		
U-1109	VIIC41	Friedrich van Riesen	4/18	U.K.		None
U-2326	XXIII	Karl Jobst*	4/19	4/28		None/Abort
U-637	VIIC	Wolfgang Riekeberg*	4/23	4/28		None[178]/Abort
U-963	VIIC	Rolf-Werner Wentz	4/23	5/?		None/M[179]
U-975	VIIC	Wilhelm Brauel*	4/23	4/28		None/M[180]/Recall
U-328	VIIC41	Hans-Ulrich Scholle*	4/25	U.K.		None
U-485	VIIC	Friedrich Lutz	4/26	Gib.		None
U-1057	VIIC	Günter Lüth*	4/26	5/9		None
U-1165	VIIC41	Hans Homann	4/26	5/?		None
U-1058	VIIC	Hermann Bruder	4/28	U.K.		None
U-2511	XXI	Adalbert Schnee*	4/30	5/6		None
Totals:	36 patrols (2 supply)				5	21,263

May 1945:

BOAT	TYPE	SKIPPER	SAILED	RETURNED	SHIPS SUNK	TONS
U-255	VIIC	Helmut Heinrich*	5/1	U.K.		None/M[181]
U-764	VIIC	Hans-Kurt von Bremen	5/1	U.K.		None
U-2336	XXIII	Emil Klusmeier*	5/1	5/14	2	4,669[182]
U-977	VIIC	Heinz Schäffer	5/2	8/17		None/Argentina
U-2326	XXIII	Karl Jobst	5/3	U.K.		None
U-320	VIIC41	Heinz Emmrich*	5/5	Lost 5/8		None
Totals:	6 patrols				2	4,669

U-boats Lost at War's End En Route from Germany to Norway:

U-236	VIIC	Herbert Mumm*	Lost 5/5
U-393	VIIC	Friedrich-Georg Herrle*	Lost 5/4
U-534	IXC40	Herbert Nollau	Lost 5/5[183]
U-579	VIIC	Hans-Dietrich Schwarzenberg*	Lost 5/5
U-733	VIIC	Ulrich Hammer*	Lost 5/5
U-746	VIIC	Ernst Lottner*	Lost 5/5
U-1007	VIIC41	Karl-Heinz Raabe*	Lost 5/2
U-1008	VIIC41	Hans Gessner*	Lost 5/6
U-1210	VIIC	Paul Gabert*	Lost 5/3
U-2338	XXIII	Hans-Friedrich Kaiser*	Lost 5/4
U-2359	XXIII	Gustav Bischoff*	Lost 5/2
U-2365	XXIII	Uwe Christiansen*	Lost 5/5
U-2503	XXI	Karl-Jürgen Wächter*	Lost 5/3
U-2521	XXI	Joachim Methner*	Lost 5/4
U-2524	XXI	Ernst von Witzendorff*	Lost 5/3
U-3032	XXI	Horst Slevogt*	Lost 5/3
U-3523	XXI	Willi Müller*	Lost 5/5

1. Shared credit with U-402 for 7,460-ton English freighter Empire Sunrise.
2. Sailed from Bergen to North Atlantic, but on 10/6 temporarily diverted with U-611 and U-625 to Narvik. The U-625 remained in the Arctic force, but U-262 and U-611 rejoined the Atlantic force on 11/11.
3. Shared one-third credit with U-438 and U-522 for British freighter Hartington.
4. The British troopship Warwick Castle, in convoy MKF 1, returning to England, November 14, 1942.
5. Inflicted severe damage on the modern American destroyer Hambleton, at anchor in Fédala, Morocco.
6. Includes the British "jeep" carrier Avenger.
7. Sank the 665-foot, 18,000-ton British troopship Ceramic, from which only one of 656 persons survived; sank the British destroyer-tender Hecla, and severely damaged the British destroyer Marne.
8. Including Norwegian corvette Montbretia.
9. British destroyer Firedrake.
10. Accidentally rammed and sunk by U-221.
11. Rammed and sank U-254 on 12/8/42 and damaged herself.
12. Bertelsmann fell ill.
13. Shot down a Sunderland of Canadian Squadron 422.
14. Shared one-third credit with U-123 and U-225 for 7,068-ton British Empire Shackleton.
15. Landed agent in area of Mauritania–Río de Oro, Spanish Sahara.
16. Administered coup de grace to ship damaged by U-202.
17. Shared one-half credit with U-614 for sinking the 9,272-ton British freighter Daghild, which had been damaged by U-402.
18. Laid minefield on 2/1/43 at the western mouth of the Strait of Gibraltar. Victims included the British corvette Weybourn.
19. Shared credit with U-603 for sinking 5,964-ton Norwegian freighter Stigstad.
20. Administered coup de grace to ship earlier damaged by U-638.
21. Detected and reported fast convoy Halifax 229.
22. Shared credit with U-92 for sinking 9,350-ton tanker N. T. Nielson Alonso.
23. Shared credit with U-600 for sinking 4,391-ton Norwegian freighter Ingria.
24. Laid mines off Reykjavik, all of which failed. Thereafter served as provisional U-tanker for ten VIIs.
25. Shared credit with U-332 for 5,964-ton Norwegian freighter Stigstad.
26. Detected and reported fast convoy Halifax 229.
27. May have sunk 3,921-ton British freighter Guido.
28. British destroyer Harvester.
29. Control directed U-190, outbound from Kiel on her maiden patrol, to give all possible fuel to Wolfbauer in the XIV tanker U-463 and put into France. This enabled Wolfbauer to refuel many more VIIs.
30. Detected and reported Slow Convoy 122.
31. Shot down Halifax on 3/22, captured one aircrew.
32. Shot down a Wellington.
33. British four-stack destroyer Beverley.
34. To Training Command.
35. Laid minefield at Casablanca on 4/10/43. Sank the French freighter Rouennais.
36. Rammed by U-631 on 4/17. Retired to Training Command.
37. Shot down aircraft on April 5.
38. Laid minefield at Casablanca on 4/11/43. Damaged two freighters. Thereafter refueled around ten IXs in the Azores area.
39. To Training Command.
40. Shot down aircraft in Biscay on 5/17/43.
41. While homebound, badly damaged by a B-24 in the Bay of Biscay.
42. Laid mines in St. George's Channel.

43. Laid unsuccessful minefield in North Channel on 5/4.
44. Shot down a Swordfish from Biter.
45. Collided with U-600 on 5/5 and both boats returned to France.
46. Collided with U-439 on 5/3, and both boats sank.
47. After one patrol in the Atlantic, transferred to the Arctic.
48. Was to mine Dakar but was hit by a Whitley in Biscay and aborted with damage and wounded skipper.
49. Probably shot down an American B-24 of Squadron 19 on 7/20.
50. Resailed under a new skipper and laid a minefield off Dakar on 6/6/43.
51. First "flak" boat. Shot down a Sunderland on 5/24 but aborted with battle damage.
52. Diverted to be provisional tankers, U-170, U-530, U-535, and U-536 gave all possible fuel to U-tanker U-488 or to other inbound and outbound attack boats.
53. Shot down a Wildcat fighter from Core.
54. U-373 was to mine Port Lyautey but was damaged by an aircraft and aborted.
55. Shot down the Sunderland that sank the U-boat.
56. The 1,190-ton Canadian destroyer St. Croix, sunk with one of the first T-5 Wren (Gnat) homing torpedoes used in combat.
57. Shared credit with U-238 for 7,176-ton Frederick Douglass.
58. Shot down airplane in Biscay.
59. Refueled and sailed from Norway with U-275 and U-422. Shared credit with U-645 for Frederick Douglass.
60. Polish destroyer Orkan.
61. British frigate Itchen.
62. Including the 925-ton British corvette Polyanthus.
63. British frigate Lagan.
64. Landed agent on Iceland on 9/25.
65. Shot down British Lancaster bomber.
66. Later collided with U-631 and aborted.
67. After severe damage by aircraft, grounded on the coast of Spain and scuttled.
68. Shot down a B-24 of Squadron 53.
69. Rammed and sunk by the American destroyer Borie, which also sank from collision damage.
70. Probably shot down the U.S. Navy B-24 that sank it.
71. Rescued twenty-one survivors of the German destroyer Z-27 and shot down a Sunderland.
72. Benker killed in air attack 1/2/44.
73. British destroyer Hurricane.
74. Rescued crew of scuttled U-284 and returned to France.
75. Incurred heavy sea damage and scuttled.
76. Shot down the Wellington that sank her, piloted by Leighton D. Richards.
77. Shot down attacking B-17.
78. Skipper Bork came down with appendicitis.
79. British frigate Tweed.
80. Scuttled after receiving severe damage from Allied aircraft; one crewman was killed, the rest rescued by U-714.
81. American destroyer Leary.
82. Shot down a British B-24 and a British Halifax in the Bay of Biscay.
83. She and a surface-ship escort shot down two Beaufighters.
84. Severely damaged in Biscay by two aircraft.
85. Sunk by a B-24 of U.S. Navy Squadron VB 103.
86. Age twenty-one, the youngest skipper yet in the Atlantic force.
87. Shot down a Leigh Light–equipped Wellington.
88. Rescued fifty-six-man crew of the scuttled U-545 on 2/11 and returned to France.
89. Shot down a British Mosquito.
90. British sloop Woodpecker.
91. British destroyer Warwick.

92. As an R&D experiment, U-986 was fitted with antiaircraft-rocket arrays around the conning tower.
93. British frigate Gould.
94. To Training Command.
95. Laid unproductive minefield off Casablanca on 3/31/44.
96. Including British LST 362.
97. American destroyer escort Leopold. Thereafter boat was ordered to the Mediterranean, but Allied forces turned her back.
98. Hit by six Allied aircraft, which killed four and severely wounded three men. German forces rescued the other crew.
99. Designated a "picket" boat, she was fitted with several radar detectors and search radars. She hit the American destroyer escort Donnell with a T-5. It was towed to harbor but was a complete loss.
100. Shot down a B-24 of British Squadron 120.
101. Shot down a Halifax of British Squadron 58 before being sunk by a Canadian Wellington of Squadron 407.
102. Hit by aircraft.
103. Sailed from Kiel to Norway. Hit in North Sea by aircraft, put into Bergen for extended repairs. Resailed in August.
104. American destroyer escort Fiske.
105. Rammed by a German vessel and decommissioned in Narvik.
106. British frigate Mourne.
107. Some sources credited U-988 with sinking three ships for 10,368 tons in late June, including the 925-ton British corvette Pink, and two British freighters. Alex Niestlé writes that it is likely U-988 was sunk on 6/30, a revision which supports that case.
108. The trawler Noreen Mary.
109. While testing a new bridge configuration, the boat made a weather patrol to the Atlantic that terminated in France by mistake.
110. The boat was decommissioned because of severe battle damage.
111. Seven snort boats sailed from Brest on D day, June 6. Authors often put this number at eight, but the eighth snort boat, U-212, sailed from La Pallice that day.
112. Put into Guernsey.
113. Put into Guernsey.
114. Shot down a B-24.
115. Shot down a B-24.
116. Damaged British frigate Blackwood, which sank under tow.
117. American LST 280.
118. Put into Guernsey.
119. Wrecked American Liberty ships Henry G. Blasdel, John A. Treutlen, and James A. Farrell. Damaged British frigate Goodson and American Liberty ship Edward M. House.
120. Planted minefield off Lands End on 7/1. A mine damaged the 7,200-ton British freighter Empire Halberd.
121. Planted minefield off Plymouth. No success.
122. Werner claimed he shot down an aircraft, perhaps a B-24.
123. From La Pallice and again on 6/12 and 6/22, then put into Brest.
124. Put into Brest.
125. Put into Brest.
126. Put into Brest.
127. Put into Brest.
128. Put into Brest.
129. Shot down a B-17 and a B-24.
130. Battle and mechanical damage forced her retirement in St. Nazaire on 8/19.
131. Shot down a British Sunderland.
132. Clemens apparently shot down the attacking B-24.

133. Hit a mine off Brest and was scrapped.
134. Sank British troopship (LSI) Prince Leopold, possibly damaged other ships.
135. Was to lay a minefield off Lands End, but lost beforehand.
136. Including the 925-ton Canadian corvette Regina, the 1,653-ton American LST 921, and the 246-ton American LCI 99.
137. Because of heavy battle damage the boat was retired in La Pallice.
138. Including the 925-ton Canadian corvette Alberni and the 850-ton British minesweeper Loyalty.
139. Laid minefield off Plymouth.
140. Including British corvette Hurst Castle.
141. Damaged American Navy supply ship Yukon.
142. Canadian frigate Chebogue, towed in but a total loss.
143. British frigate Whitaker, towed in but a total loss.
144. Includes 1,600-ton American LST 359 and the 335-ton Free French patrol craft L'Enjoue. In addition, Hechler severely damaged the American destroyer escort Fogg.
145. British "jeep" carrier Thane, severely damaged and not repaired during the war.
146. British frigate Bullen.
147. Includes the 7,177-ton British troopship (LSI) Empire Javelin.
148. Damaged 1,700-ton British destroyer Zephyr.
149. Includes the 11,509-ton British troopship Leopoldville and British frigates Capel and Affleck, the latter towed in but a total wreck.
150. Damaged British frigate Manners.
151. Sailed from Heligoland to the mouth of the Thames River and returned to Heligoland.
152. Put into St. Nazaire with a broken snorkel.
153. British corvette Vervain.
154. British ASW trawler Ellesmere.
155. Took ammo and other supplies to St. Nazaire.
156. Includes the 980-ton Canadian corvette Trentonian.
157. Sank Canadian minesweeper Guyeborough and took ammo and other supplies to St. Nazaire.
158. Hit a mine off Fastnet, southern Ireland, and scuttled. The crew got ashore in Ireland.
159. Canadian frigate Teme.
160. After snorkel repairs, sailed from St. Nazaire to resume patrol.
161. At the time, her loss was incorrectly credited to a B-24 of British Squadron 120 piloted by L. J. White. Franks (1995) writes that White probably attacked U-1003 for damage.
162. Hit a mine in Horten and sank before embarking on patrol.
163. Abandoned and captured but sank under tow.
164. Including 425-ton Norwegian minesweeper Nordhav II.
165. Norwegian minesweeper NYMS 382.
166. Returned from St. Nazaire to Norway.
167. Laid minefield in Firth of Clyde, sank British trawler Ethel Crawford.
168. Refueled in La Pallice for a patrol off Gibraltar.
169. Was to lay minefield at Dundee but sunk beforehand.
170. Was to lay minefield at Cherbourg but sunk beforehand.
171. Lost on return from St. Nazaire to Norway.
172. Embarked ammo and other supplies for St. Nazaire, but did not complete the mission.
173. Sunk by British submarine Tapir.
174. Ran aground off Peterhead, Scotland, and abandoned.
175. Made a second patrol from Heligoland, returned to Bergen.
176. British frigate Redmill, a total wreck.
177. Scuttled off the Portuguese coast; crew survived.
178. Three days after sailing, two British PT boats attacked, killing the skipper, Riekeberg. The engineer, Klaus Weber, returned the boat to Stavanger.
179. Was to lay minefield at Portland Bill but mission canceled. Later grounded on Portuguese coast and scuttled; crew survived.

180. Was to lay minefield at Hartlepool but mission canceled.
181. Recommissioned in St. Nazaire. Laid minefield at Les Sables l'Olonne.
182. Off the Firth of Forth, sank the last two freighters of the war: the 1,800-ton Norwegian Sneland and the 2,900-ton British Avondale Park.
183. Raised in 1993, barged to Liverpool for display.

APPENDIX 3

ALLIED CARGO-CONVOY SAILINGS ON THE NORTH ATLANTIC RUN

In the "Critical Period": September 1942–May 1943[1]

EASTBOUND			WESTBOUND		
CONVOY	ESCORT	LOSSES	CONVOY	ESCORT	LOSSES
September 1942: (19)					
HX 205	B-6	____	ONS 126[2]	B-3	____
HX 206	B-1	____	ON 127	C-4	8[3]
HX 207	B-3	____	ONS 128	B-2	____
HX 208[4]	B-2	____	ON 129	C-2	1
SC 98	C-3	____	ONS 130	B-4	____
SC 99	C-1	____	ON 131	C-3	2
SC 100	A-3	5	ONS 132	B-6	____
SC 101	C-4	1	ON 133	C-1	____
SC 102	C-2	____	ONS 134	B-1	____
RB 1	RN	4[5]			
October 1942: (16)					
HX 209	B-4	1	ON 135	A-3	____
HX 210	C-3	____	ONS 136	B-3	4
HX 211	C-1	____	ON 137	C-4	2
HX 212	A-3	6	ONS 138	B-2	____
SC 103	B-7	____	ON 139	C-2	2
SC 104	B-6	8	ONS 140	B-4	____
SC 105	B-1	____	ON 141	C-3	____
SC 106	B-3	____			
SC 107	C-4	15[6]			

November 1942: (15)

Note: In November 1942, Axis submarines in all waters sank 126 Allied ships for 802,160 gross tons, the best month of the war for the U-boats (see Appendix 20). Some historians and authors use the November 1942 figures to assert or imply that in so doing, German U-boats very nearly cut the vital North Atlantic convoy "lifeline" between the Americas and the British Isles. In fact, Jürgen Rohwer *(Successes)* states that German U-boats operating against the North Atlantic convoy "lifeline" in November sank twenty-nine cargo ships for 166,662 gross tons: fifteen loaded eastbound ships from Slow Convoy 107 for 82,817 tons, six empty westbound ships from Outbound North (Slow) 144 for 26,321 tons, and one ship each from Slow Convoy 109, Outbound North 143, and Outbound North 145 for an aggregate 19,524 tons, plus five cargo vessels sailing outside convoys for 38,000 tons. The other ninety-seven ships for 635,492 tons, Rohwer states, were sunk in other waters—for example, thirty in the Indian Ocean. For other examples, see Plates 3 and 4.

HX 213	B-2	____	ONS 142	B-7	____
HX 214	B-4	____	ON 143	C-1	1
HX 215	B-1	____	ONS 144	B-6	6[7]
HX 216	B-7	____	ON 145	A-3	1

EASTBOUND			WESTBOUND		
CONVOY	ESCORT	LOSSES	CONVOY	ESCORT	LOSSES
SC 108	C-2	—	ONS 146	B-3	1[8]
SC 109	C-3	1[9]	ON 147	C-4	—
SC 110	C-1	—	ONS 148	B-2	—
			ON 149	C-2	1[10]

December 1942: (16)

HX 217	B-6	2	ONS 150	B-4	—
HX 218	B-3	—	ON 151	B-1	—
HX 219	B-2	—	ONS 152	C-3	2
HX 220	B-4	—	ON 153	B-7	4[11]
SC 111	A-3	—	ONS 154	C-1[12]	14[13]
SC 112	C-4	—	ON 155	B-6	—
SC 113	C-2	—	ONS 156	A-3	1
SC 114	B-1	—	ON 157	B-3	—

January 1943: (13)

HX 221	C-3	—	ONS 158	C-4	—
HX 222	C-1[14]	1[15]	ON 159	B-2	—
HX 223	A-3	2	ONS 160	C-2	—
HX 224	C-4[16]	3[17]	ON 161	B-4	—
SC 115	B-7	—	ON 162	B-1	—
SC 116	B-6	—	ONS 163	C-3	—
SC 117	B-3	2			

February 1943: (12)

HX 225	C-2[18]	—	ON 164	B-7	—
HX 226	C-3	—	ONS 165	B-6	2
HX 227	B-6	2[19]	ON 166	A-3	14[20]
SC 118	B-2	10[21]	ONS 167	B-3	2
SC 119	B-1	—	ON 168	B-5	1[22]
SC 120	B-7	—	ONS 169	B-4	2

March 1943: (16)

Note: In March 1943, Axis submarines in all waters sank 110 Allied ships for 633,731 tons, the third-best month of the war in tonnage sunk by U-boats (see Appendix 18, Volume I, and Appendix 20, this volume). Rohwer states that of the 110 ships lost, forty loaded eastbound ships were sunk on the North Atlantic "lifeline" from convoys Halifax 227, 228, 229, 230, and Slow Convoys 121 and 122, three empty westbound ships from Outbound North 168 and Outbound North (Slow) 169, and four other ships sailing outside convoys. Total in the North Atlantic area in March: forty-seven ships, the worst Allied setback of the war on that "lifeline." The other sixty-three ships, Rohwer states, were sunk in other waters—for example, twenty-three in the Mediterranean Sea and the Indian Ocean.

HX 228	B-3 (Bogue)	5[23]	ON 170	B-2	—
HX 229	B-4	13	ONS 171	B-1	—
HX 229A	EG-40[24]	—	ON 172	C-3	—
HX 230	B-1	1	ON 173	B-7	—
SC 121	A-3	12[25]	ON 174	B-3	—
SC 122	B-5	9	ON 175	A-3	—
SC 123	B-2 (Bogue)	—	ONS 1[26]	B-6	—
SC 124	C-3	—	ONS 2	C-1	—

April 1943: (18)

HX 231	B-7	6	ON 176	B-4	2[27]
HX 232[28]	B-3	4	ON 177	C-4	—
HX 233	A-3	1	ON 178	B-1	3
HX 234	B-4	2	ON 179	C-2	—
HX 235	C-4 (Bogue)[29]	—	ON 180	C-3	—

EASTBOUND			WESTBOUND		
CONVOY	ESCORT	LOSSES	CONVOY	ESCORT	LOSSES
SC 125[30]	B-6	____	ON 181	B-3	____
SC 126	B-5	____	ONS 3	EG-40	____
SC 127	C-1	____	ONS 4	B-2 (Biter)[31]	____
SC 128	EG-40	____	ONS 5	B-7	13
MAY 1943: (15)					
HX 236	B-1	____	ON 182	C-5[32]	____
HX 237[33]	C-2 (Biter)	3	ON 183	B-4	____
HX 238	C-3	____	ON 184	C-1 (Bogue)	____
HX 239	B-3 (Archer)	____	ONS 6	B-6	____
HX 240	C-5	____	ONS 7	B-5	1
SC 129	B-2 (Biter)	2	ONS 8	C-4	____
SC 130	B-7 (Archer)[34]	____	ONS 9[35]	B-2 (Biter)	____
SC 131	B-6	____			

Totals: 140 convoys of about 7,000 ships, assuming an average 50 ships per convoy. 211 ships lost to U-boats (3 percent), of which 121 (less than 2 percent) were eastbound.

---

1. Based on data in Jürgen Rohwer's *Critical Convoy Battles of March, 1943* and *Axis Submarine Successes,* and British Monthly Anti-Submarine Reports and other sources. Losses include stragglers and rompers.
2. ON 125 was the first westbound convoy to terminate in New York.
3. Including Canadian destroyer Ottawa I.
4. HX 208 and SC 102 were the first eastbound convoys to sail from New York. The first departed on 9/17, the second on 9/19. The official Canadian historian wrote that convoys HX 1 to HX 207 from Halifax had sailed with 8,501 ships and SC 1 to SC 94 had sailed with 3,652 ships. SC 95 (8/4/42) to SC 101 (318 ships) sailed from Halifax, not Sydney. All told: 12,471 vessels.
5. Including British destroyer Veteran.
6. All ships of SC 107 were sunk in November.
7. Including Norwegian corvette Montbretia.
8. Sunk in December.
9. Badly damaged on 11/18, this ship, the 9,100-ton American tanker *Brilliant,* sank under tow on 1/25/43.
10. Sunk in December. Two other ships of this convoy were sunk in December after leaving it to sail alone.
11. Including British destroyer Firedrake.
12. On 1/1/43, the escort was reinforced halfway across the Atlantic by a new (1942) U.S. Navy fleet destroyer, *Pringle.* She was one of six U.S. destroyers (DD 476 to DD 481) fitted with a catapult and derrick to launch and recover an OS2U Kingfisher floatplane. The scheme was a failure; all six destroyers were restored to standard fighting configuration.
13. Plus two 10-ton LCVs.
14. Upon arrival in the British Isles, group withdrawn for training.
15. Plus three 143-ton LCT landing craft.
16. Upon arrival in the British Isles, group withdrawn for training.
17. All ships sunk in February.
18. Upon arrival in the British Isles, group withdrawn for training.
19. One of these, the Liberty ship Meriwether Lewis, was sunk in March.
20. Plus two tankers damaged and towed to St. John's.
21. Plus one 143-ton LCT landing craft.
22. Sunk in March.

23. Including British destroyer Harvester. The American "jeep" carrier Bogue hunter-killer group inaugurated operations with convoy Halifax 228, but after a few days she returned to Argentia on 3/14. She resailed 3/20 with SC 123 but returned again to Argentia on 3/30 and then to Boston for repairs.
24. A KM MK escort group that sailed directly from the British Isles on 3/3/43, to St. John's specifically to escort special convoy Halifax 229A.
25. Plus one 143-ton LCT landing craft.
26. After convoy Outbound North (Slow) 171, slow westbound convoys were designated by a new numerical sequence and terminated in Halifax, beginning with Outbound North (Slow) 1.
27. Including ex-American British four-stack destroyer Beverley.
28. Sailed from New York on 4/1 at night in dense fog and became intermingled with convoy UGS 7, resulting in collisions and aborts that reduced ships sailing in HX 232 from fifty to thirty-four.
29. For the first time, on 4/23, Bogue, with five destroyers, sailed with a convoy all the way across the Atlantic to Belfast, where she was fitted with Huff Duff. She returned to the Americas in company with ON 184 in May.
30. Commencing with SC 125 on 3/31, Slow Convoys sailed from Halifax.
31. The British Support Group 5, consisting of the "jeep" carrier Biter and four destroyers, sailed from Iceland on 4/21 and inaugurated westbound operations with Outbound North (Slow) 4. Thus Biter and Bogue were at sea in the Greenland "Air Gap" at the same time.
32. A new Canadian MOEF group: new destroyers Ottawa II and Kootenay and five corvettes, in effect replacing A-3.
33. The British Support Group 5, consisting of "jeep" carrier Biter and three destroyers, inaugurated eastbound operations with HX 237 and SC 129.
34. The British Support Group 4, consisting of the "jeep" carrier Archer, three destroyers, and one sloop, inaugurated eastbound operations with HX 239.
35. The first merchant aircraft carrier (MAC ship), Empire MacAlpine, 8,200 tons, sailed with ONS 9, carrying four Swordfish aircraft. Loaded with grain, she returned to the U.K. with SC 135, which sailed from Halifax on 6/27.

APPENDIX 4

U-BOAT PATROLS TO THE SOUTH ATLANTIC AND INDIAN OCEAN

SEPTEMBER 1942–APRIL 1945

BOAT	TYPE	SKIPPER	SAILED	RETURNED	SHIPS SUNK	TONS
SEPTEMBER 1942:						
U-333	VIIC	Peter Cremer	9/1	10/6		None/Abort
U-460	XIV	Ebe Schnoor	9/2	10/14		None/Supply
U-178	IXD2	Hans Ibbeken*	9/8	1/9/43	6	47,097+
U-552	VIIC	Klaus Popp* (C.O.)	9/10	12/15	1	520
U-181	IXD2	Wolfgang Lüth*	9/12	1/18	12	58,381
U-128	IXC	Ulrich Heyse	9/14	1/7	3	15,551
U-177	IXD2	Robert Gyeae*	9/17	1/22	8	49,371
U-126	IXC	Ernst Bauer	9/19	1/7	3	14,536
U-161	IXC	Albrecht Achilles	9/19	1/9	3	16,284+
Totals:	9 patrols (1 supply)				36	201,740
OCTOBER 1942:[1]						
U-572	VIIC	Heinz Hirsacker[2]	10/12	11/22		None/Abort
U-409	VIIC	Hans-Ferdinand Massmann	10/13	11/5	2	13,924/Abort
U-659	VIIC	Hans Stock	10/13	11/5	1	7,519+/Abort
U-510	IXC	Karl Neitzel	10/14	12/12		None+/Abort
U-604	VIIC	Horst Höltring	10/14	11/5	3	23,245/Abort
U-134	VIIC	Rudolph Schendel	10/15	1/19	1	4,827
U-509	IXC	Werner Witte* (C.O.)	10/15	11/26	4	24,154+/Abort
U-203	VIIC	Hermann Kottmann* (C.O.)	10/15	11/6	2	12,414
U-462	XIV	Bruno Vowe	10/18	12/7		None/Supply
U-103	IXB	Gustav-Adolph Janssen* (C.O.)	10/21	12/29	2	11,431+
U-752	VIIC	Karl-Ernst Schroeter	10/22	12/3		None/Abort
Totals:	11 patrols (1 supply)				15	97,514
NOVEMBER 1942:						
U-D3	Dutch	Hermann Rigele	11/3	1/7/43	1	5,041
U-515	IXC	Werner Henke	11/9	1/14	3	20,913+
Totals:	2 patrols				4	25,954

* = First patrol of boat or skipper
\+ = Damaged ships or shared credit
S = Snort boat
PR = Provisional refueler
GS = Group Seehund[3]
M = Mining mission

BOAT	TYPE	SKIPPER	SAILED	RETURNED	SHIPS SUNK	TONS
DECEMBER 1942:						
U-175	IXC	Heinrich Bruns	12/1	2/24	1	7,177
U-182	IXD2	Nicolai Clausen*	12/9	Lost 5/16/43	5	30,071/GS[3]
U-506	IXC	Erich Würdemann	12/14	5/8/43	2	9,980/GS
U-459	XIV	Georg von Wilamowitz-Möllendorf	12/20	3/8/43	None/Supply	
U-509	IXC	Werner Witte	12/23	5/11/43	2	12,066/GS
U-516	IXC	Gerhard Wiebe	12/23	5/3/43	4	25,596/GS
Totals:	6 patrols (1 supply)				14	84,890
JANUARY 1943:						
U-160	IXC	Georg Lassen	1/6	5/10	7	45,205+/GS
FEBRUARY 1943:						
U-180	IXD1	Werner Musenberg*	2/9	7/2	2	13,298[4]
U-515	IXC	Werner Henke	2/21	6/24	10	58,456
Totals:	2 patrols				12	71,754
MARCH 1943:						
U-198	IXD2	Werner Hartmann*	3/9	9/25	7	36,778
U-123	IXB	Horst von Schroeter	3/13	6/8	5	24,883
U-196	IXD2	Eitel-Friedrich Kentrat*	3/13	10/23	2	12,285
U-105	IXB	Jürgen Nissen	3/16	Lost 6/2	1	4,669
U-126	IXC	Siegfried Kietz*	3/20	Lost 7/3	1	7,177[5]
U-195	IXD1	Heinz Buchholz*	3/20	7/23	2	14,391+
U-181	IXD2	Wolfgang Lüth	3/23	10/14	10	45,331
U-178	IXD2	Wilhelm Dommes	3/28	8/29[6]	6	32,683
Totals:	8 patrols				34	178,197
APRIL 1943:						
U-177	IXD2	Robert Gysae	4/1	10/1	6	38,017
U-197	IXD2	Robert Bartels*	4/3	Lost 8/20	3	21,267+
U-460	XIV	Ebe Schnoor	4/24	6/25	None/Supply	
Totals:	3 patrols (1 supply)				9	59,284
MAY 1943:						
U-511	IXC	Fritz Schneewind* (C.O.)	5/10	7/17[7]	1	7,194
MAY–JUNE 1943:						
Italian cargo submarines sailing to the Far East:						
Barbarigo		Umberto De Julio	5/?	5/?	Lost/Unknown causes	
Cappellini		Waler Auconi	5/11	8/43[8]	Arrived Singapore	
Giuliani		Mario Tei	5/?	8/43	Arrived Singapore	
Tazzoli		Giuseppe Gaito	5/?	5/?	Lost/Unknown causes	
Torelli		Enrico Groppallo	5/?	8/43	Arrived Singapore	
JUNE 1943:						
U-333	VIIC	Peter Cremer	6/2	8/31		None
U-508	IXC	Georg Staats	6/7	9/14	3	21,112
U-571	VIIC	Gustav Lüssow*	6/8	9/1		None
U-618	VIIC	Kurt Baberg	6/8	9/1	1	5,225
U-306	VIIC	Klaus von Trotha	6/10	8/11		None+
U-358	VIIC	Rolf Manke	6/10	9/1		None
U-257	VIIC	Heinz Rahe	6/12	9/14		None

BOAT	TYPE	SKIPPER	SAILED	RETURNED	SHIPS SUNK	TONS
U-600	VIIC	Bernhard Zurmühlen	6/12	9/9		None
U-382	VIIC	Leopold Koch	6/19	9/7		None
Totals:	9 patrols				4	26,337
JUNE–JULY 1943 (GROUP *MONSUN*):						
U-200	IXD2	Heinrich Schonder*	6/12	Lost 6/24		None[9]
U-188	IXC40	Siegfried Lüdden	6/30	10/31	1	7,176+
U-168	IXC40	Helmut Pich	7/3	11/11	1	2,183+
U-183	IXC40	Heinrich Schäfer	7/3	10/31		None
U-509	IXC	Werner Witte	7/3	Lost 7/15		None
U-514	IXC	Hans-Jürgen Auffermann	7/3	Lost 7/8		None
U-532	IXC40	Otto-Heinrich Junker	7/3	10/31	4	24,484+
U-506	IXC	Erich Würdemann	7/6	Lost 7/12		None
U-533	IXC40	Helmut Hennig	7/6	Lost 10/16		None
U-847	IXD2	Herbert Kuppisch	7/6	7/20		None/Abort
U-516	IXC	Hans-Rutger Tillessen*	7/8	8/23		None/PR[10]
U-847	IXD2	Herbert Kuppisch (resail)	7/29	Lost 8/27		None/PR[11]
Totals:	11 patrols (2 supply)				6	33,843
JULY 1943:						
U-709	VIIC	Karl-Otto Weber	7/5	7/20		None/Abort
U-340	VIIC	Hans-Joachim Klaus	7/6	9/2		None
U-468	VIIC	Klemens Schamong	7/7	Lost 8/11		None
U-757	VIIC	Friedrich Deetz	7/7	9/4	1	4,116
U-86	VIIB	Walter Schug	7/8	9/11		None
U-445	VIIC	Heinz-Konrad Fenn	7/10	9/15		None
U-43	IX	Hans-Joachim Schwantke	7/13	Lost 7/30		None/M[12]
U-403	VIIC	Karl-Franz Heine*	7/13	Lost 8/18		None
Totals:	8 patrols				1	4,116
AUGUST 1943:						
U-515	IXC	Werner Henke	8/29	9/12		None/Abort
SEPTEMBER 1943:						
U-68	IXC	Albert Lauzemis	9/8	12/23	4	17,661
U-848	IXD2	Wilhelm Rollmann*	9/18	Lost 11/5	1	4,573
U-103	IXB	Gustav-Adolf Janssen	9/23	1/1/44	None/M[13]/Retired	
Totals:	3 patrols				5	22,234
OCTOBER 1943:						
U-849	IXD2	Heinz-Otto Schultze*	10/2	Lost 11/25		None
U-764	VIIC	Hans-Kurt von Bremen*	10/27	12/11		None[14]/Abort
NOVEMBER 1943:						
U-510	IXC	Alfred Eick	11/3	4/5/44	6	31,220+
U-515	IXC	Werner Henke	11/9	1/14	4	22,263[15]
U-850	IXD2	Klaus Ewerth	11/18	Lost 12/20		None
U-172	IXC	Hermann Hoffmann*	11/22	Lost 12/13		None
U-178	IXD2	Wilhelm Spahr*	11/27	5/24/44	1	7,244
Totals:	5 patrols				11	60,727
DECEMBER 1943:						
U-505	IXC	Harald Lange*	12/25	1/2/44		None[16]/Abort

BOAT	TYPE	SKIPPER	SAILED	RETURNED	SHIPS SUNK	TONS
JANUARY 1944:						
U-177	IXD2	Heinz Buchholz*	1/2	Lost 2/6		None
U-1062	VIIF	Karl Albrecht*	1/3	4/19		None/Supply
U-532	IXC40	Otto-Heinrich Junker	1/4	4/19	2	9,457+/Abort
U-123	IXB	Horst von Schroeter	1/9	4/24		None/Retired
U-188	IXC40	Siegfried Lüdden	1/9	6/19	7	42,549+
U-66	IXC	Gerhard Seehausen*	1/16	Lost 5/6	4	19,754
U-852	IXD2	Heinz-Wilhelm Eck*	1/18	Lost 5/3	2	9,972[17]
U-IT22	Ital.	Karl Wunderlich*	1/21	Lost 3/11		None/Cargo
Totals:	8 patrols (1 supply)				15	81,732
FEBRUARY 1944:						
U-168	IXC40	Helmut Pich	2/7	3/24	2	5,825+[18]
U-IT24	Ital.	Heinrich Pahls* (resail)	2/8	4/4		None/Cargo/Abort
U-183	IXC40	Fritz Schneewind*	2/10	3/21	2	12,412/Abort
U-1059	VIIF	Günter Leupold*	2/12	Lost 3/19		None/Supply
U-IT23	Ital.	Hans-Werner Striegler	2/13	Lost 2/15		None/Cargo
U-843	IXC40	Oskar Herwartz	2/19	6/11	1	8,261
U-488	XIV	Bruno Studt* (C.O.)	2/22	Lost 4/26		None/Supply
U-801	IXC40	Hans-Joachim Brans	2/26	Lost 3/17		None
U-851	IXD2	Hannes Weingaertner*	2/26	Lost 3/27?		None/Supply
U-IT25	Ital.	Hans-Werner Striegler	2/27	4/3		None/Cargo/Abort
U-537	IXC40	Peter Schrewe	2/29	3/6		None/Abort
Totals:	11 patrols (3 supply)				5	26,498
MARCH 1944:						
U-155	IXC	Johannes Rudolph*	3/11	6/23		None
U-181	IXD2	Kurt Freiwald*	3/16	8/8	4	24,869
U-190	IXC40	Max Wintermeyer	3/16	6/20		None[19]
U-196	IXD2	Eitel-Friedrich Kentrat*	3/16	8/10	1	5,454
U-505	IXC	Harald Lange	3/16	Captured 6/4		None
U-537	IXC40	Peter Schrewe (resail)	3/25	8/2		None
U-543	IXC40	Hans-Jürgen Hellriegel	3/28	Lost 7/2		None[20]/S
U-515	IXC	Werner Henke	3/30	Lost 4/9		None
U-1224	IXC40	Georg Preuss*	3/30	Lost 5/13		None[21]
Totals:	9 patrols			5	30,323	
APRIL 1944:						
U-859	IXD2	Johann Jebsen*	4/4	Lost 9/23	3	20,853+
U-860	IXD2	Paul Büchel*	4/11	Lost 6/15		None
U-198	IXD2	Burkhard Heusinger von Waldegg*	4/20	Lost 8/12	4	22,912
U-861	IXD2	Jürgen Oesten*	4/20	9/22	4	22,048+
U-547	IXC40	Heinrich Niemeyer* (C.O.)	4/30	8/11	3	9,121+/S
Totals:	5 patrols				14	74,934
MAY 1944:						
U-490	XIV	Wilhelm Gerlach*	5/6	Lost 6/12		None/Supply/S
U-183	IXC40	Fritz Schneewind	5/17	7/7	1	5,259[22]
Totals:	2 patrols (1 supply)				1	5,259

BOAT	TYPE	SKIPPER	SAILED	RETURNED	SHIPS SUNK	TONS
June 1944:						
U-862	IXD2	Heinrich Timm*	6/3	9/9	5	28,018 [23]
U-1062	VIIF	Karl Albrecht	6/19	7/2	None/Supply/Abort	
U-546	IXC40	Paul Just	6/25	11/6		None
Totals:	3 patrols (1 supply)				5	28,018
July 1944:						
U-1062	VIIF	Karl Albrecht	7/15	Lost 9/30		None/Supply
U-863	IXD2	Dietrich von der Esch*	7/26	Lost 9/29		None
Totals:	2 patrols (1 supply)					
August 1944:						
U-170	IXC40	Hans-Gerold Hauber* (C.O.)	8/4	11/30		None
U-180	IXD1	Rolf Riesen* (C.O.)	8/20	Lost 8/23?		None/Cargo
U-195	IXD1	Friedrich Steinfeldt* (C.O.)	8/20	12/28		None/Cargo [24]
U-219	XB	Walter Burghagen	8/23	12/11		None/Cargo [25]
U-871	IXD2	Erwin Ganzer*	8/31	Lost 9/26		None
Totals:	5 patrols					
September 1944:						
None						
October 1944:						
U-168	IXC40	Helmut Pich	10/3	Lost 10/6		None
U-181	IXD2	Kurt Freiwald	10/19	1/5/45	1	10,198/Abort [26]
Totals:	2 patrols				1	10,198
November 1944:						
U-537	IXC40	Peter Schrewe	11/9	Lost 11/10		None
U-862	IXD2	Heinrich Timm	11/18	2/15/45	2	14,356
U-510	IXC	Alfred Eick	11/26	12/3		None/Abort
U-196	IXD2	Hans-Werner Striegler	11/30	Lost 11/30?		None
Totals:	4 patrols				2	14,356
December 1944:						
U-843	IXC40	Oskar Herwartz	12/10	Lost 4/9/45		None
January 1945:						
U-510	IXC	Alfred Eick	1/10	4/24	1	7,136
U-532	IXC40	Otto-Heinrich Junker	1/13	U.K.	2	12,954
U-861	IXD2	Jürgen Oesten	1/14	4/18		None
U-195	IXD1	Friedrich Steinfeldt	1/26	3/4		None/PR
Totals:	4 patrols				3	20,090
February 1945:						
U-864	IXD2	Ralf-Reimar Wolfram*	2/6	Lost 2/9		None
March 1945:						
None						
April 1945:						
U-234	XB	Johann-Heinrich Fehler*	4/17	U.S. 5/16		None/Supply
U-183	IXC40	Fritz Schneewind	4/21	Lost 4/23		None
Totals:	2 patrols (1 supply)					

1. All in Group Streitaxt, which encountered and attacked convoy Sierra Leone 125. Of these, only U-134 proceeded to Freetown as planned.
2. Hirsacker relieved, tried for cowardice, found guilty, executed 4/24/43.
3. Group Seehund (GS), which sailed to the South Atlantic, Cape Town, and the Indian Ocean.
4. Transferred the political activist Subhas Chandra Bose, his aide, and cargo to the Japanese submarine I-29, and received cargo in return. Later shot down a Hampden bomber.
5. Hit the American Liberty ship Flora MacDonald, which beached, a total loss.
6. Arrived at the island of Penang, Malaya, to establish a German U-boat base.
7. Arrived in Penang. Designated "Marco Polo I," U-511 was a gift from Hitler to Japan. She arrived in Japan on 9/16/43 and was redesignated RO-500.
8. The Cappellini, Giuliani, and Torelli were seized by the Japanese on 9/8/43, when Italy capitulated. Returned to Germany on about December 1943, redesignated U-IT23, U-IT24, U-IT25. In February 1944, these three ex-Italian boats set off from Penang to France with cargoes. None made it. The surviving two, U-IT24 (ex-Cappellini) and U-IT25 (ex-Torelli), were reseized by the Japanese on 5/8/45, when Germany capitulated and were redesignated I-503 and I-504, respectively.
9. Embarked "coastal troops" *(Küstentruppe)* of the Brandenburg Division, lost with the entire crew in the sinking.
10. Refueled Monsun boats and returned to France.
11. Diverted from Monsun to be a refueler.
12. Was to mine Lagos, but was sunk before the mission was carried out. Possibly shot down an aircraft in Biscay.
13. Laid eight TMC mines at Takoradi on 10/31. After returning, the boat retired to the Baltic.
14. Returned three British POWs to France.
15. Includes British sloop Chanticleer, towed to port but not repaired.
16. Rescued thirty-four German survivors of torpedo boat T-25 and returned to France.
17. Includes Greek freighter Peleus, whose survivors Eck was accused of shooting in the water.
18. En route from Penang to France, rescued 135 survivors of the German tanker Brake and returned to Jakarta, Java.
19. Wintermeyer went on to other duty because of his inability to handle personnel.
20. Diverted from the Americas to be a provisional refueler; thereafter patrolled to Freetown.
21. Another gift from Hitler to Japan ("Marco Polo II"), redesignated RO-501. She sailed from Kiel with a German skipper and a Japanese crew, all killed in the sinking.
22. Patrolled from Penang to the Indian Ocean and returned to Penang.
23. Seized by the Japanese, redesignated I-502.
24. Seized by the Japanese, redesignated I-506.
25. Seized by the Japanese, redesignated I-505.
26. Seized by the Japanese, redesignated I-501.

APPENDIX 5

U-BOAT PATROLS TO THE AMERICAS

SEPTEMBER 1942–APRIL 1945

BOAT	TYPE	SKIPPER	SAILED	RETURNED	SHIPS SUNK	TONS
SEPTEMBER 1942:						
U-203	VIIC	Rolf Mützelburg	8/29	9/18	None [1]/Abort	
U-332	VIIC	Johannes Liebe	9/5	12/6	2	11,004
U-201	VIIC	Günther Rosenberg* (C.O.)	9/6	10/26	3	15,696
U-202	VIIC	Günter Poser* (C.O.)	9/6	10/25	1	1,815+
U-67	IXC	Günther Müller-Stöckheim	9/16	12/21	4	20,467+
U-183	IXC40	Heinrich Schäfer*	9/19	12/23	1	6,089
U-43	IX	Hans-Joachim Schwantke	9/23	12/9	1	9,132
U-160	IXC	George Lassen	9/23	12/9	8	44,865+
U-518	IXC	Friedrich-Wilhelm Wissmann*	9/26	12/15	4	29,748+[2]
U-129	IXC	Hans Witt	9/28	1/6/43	5	32,613
Totals:	11 patrols				30	173,569
OCTOBER 1942:						
U-505	IXC	Peter Zschech* (C.O.)	10/4	12/12	1	7,173/Abort
U-174	IXC	Ulrich Thilo	10/8	1/9/43	5	30,813
U-154	IXC	Heinrich Schuch* (C.O.)	10/12	1/7/43	3	17,936
U-163	IXC	Kurt-Edward Engelmann	10/17	1/6/43	4	17,011+[3]
U-508	IXC	George Staats	10/17	1/6/43	9	50,265
U-608	VIIC	Rolf Struckmeier	10/20	12/9	1	5,621/M[4]
U-511	IXC	Friedrich Steinhoff	10/24	11/28	None [5]/Abort	
Totals:	7 patrols				23	128,819
NOVEMBER 1942:						
U-66	IXC	Friedrich Markworth	11/9	11/11	None/Abort	
U-176	IXC	Reiner Dierksen	11/9	2/18/43	3	12,432
U-517	IXC	Paul Hartwig	11/17	Lost 11/21	None	
U-513	IXC	Rolf Rüggeberg	11/21	12/18	None/Abort	

* = First patrol of boat or skipper (C.O.)
+ = Damaged ships or shared credit
M = Mining mission
S = Snort boat
PR = Provisional refueler
W = Weather-reporting mission

BOAT	TYPE	SKIPPER	SAILED	RETURNED	SHIPS SANK	TONS
U-105	IXB	Jürgen Nissen* (C.O.)	11/23	2/14/43	4	19,844
U-217	VIID	Kurt Reichenbach-Klinke	11/24	2/23/43	2	10,576+
U-124	IXB	Johann Mohr	11/25	2/13/43	5	28,259+
U-109	IXB	Heinrich Bleichrodt	11/28	1/23/43		None/Abort
U-507	IXC	Harro Schacht	11/28	Lost 1/13/43	3	14,230
U-164	IXC	Otto Fechner	11/29	Lost 1/6/43	1	2,608
U-214	VIID	Günther Reeder	11/30	2/24/43	1	4,426
Totals:	11 patrols				19	92,375

December 1942:
None (U-boats en route to the Americas were diverted to convoy attacks in the Middle Atlantic.)

January 1943:

BOAT	TYPE	SKIPPER	SAILED	RETURNED	SHIPS SANK	TONS
U-518	IXC	Friedrich-Wilhelm Wissmann	1/11	4/27	4	22,598
U-156	IXC	Werner Hartenstein	1/16	Lost 3/8		None
U-510	IXC	Karl Neitzel	1/16	4/16	3	18,240+
U-183	IXC40	Heinrich Schäfer	1/30	5/13	1	2,493
Totals:	4 patrols				8	43,331

February 1943:

BOAT	TYPE	SKIPPER	SAILED	RETURNED	SHIPS SANK	TONS
U-68	IXC	Albert Lauzemis* (C.O.)	2/3	5/8	2	10,186
U-155	IXC	Adolf-Cornelius Piening	2/8	4/30	2	7,973
U-185	IXC40	August Maus	2/8	5/3	3	20,504
Totals:	3 patrols				7	38,663

March 1943:

BOAT	TYPE	SKIPPER	SAILED	RETURNED	SHIPS SANK	TONS
U-129	IXC	Hans Witt	3/11	5/29	3	26,590
U-161	IXC	Albrecht Achilles	3/13	6/7	1	255[6]
U-174	IXC	Wolfgang Grandefeld* (C.O.)	3/18	Lost 4/27		None
U-154	IXC	Oskar-Heinz Kusch* (C.O.)	3/20	7/6	1	8,166+
Totals:	4 patrols				5	35,011

April 1943:

BOAT	TYPE	SKIPPER	SAILED	RETURNED	SHIPS SANK	TONS
U-128	IXC	Hermann Steinert* (C.O.)	4/6	Lost 5/17		None
U-176	IXC	Reiner Dierksen	4/6	Lost 5/15	2	4,232
U-262	VIIC	Heinz Franke	4/6	5/25		None
U-376	VIIC	Friedrich-Karl Marks	4/6	Lost 4/6		None[7]
U-119	XB	Horst-Tessen van Kameke* (C.O.)	4/25	Lost 6/24	1	2,937+/M[8]
U-66	IXC	Friedrich Markworth	4/29	9/1	2	20,368+
Totals:	6 patrols				5	27,537

May 1943:

BOAT	TYPE	SKIPPER	SAILED	RETURNED	SHIPS SANK	TONS
U-190	IXC40	Max Wintermeyer	5/1	8/19		None
U-521	IXC	Klaus Bargsten	5/5	Lost 6/2		None
U-67	IXC	Günther Müller-Stöckheim	5/10	Lost 7/16		None
U-527	IXC40	Herbert Uhlig	5/10	Lost 7/23		None
U-199	IXD2	Hans-Werner Kraus*	5/13	Lost 7/31	1	4,161
U-513	IXC	Friedrich Guggenberger*[9]	5/18	Lost 7/19	4	17,151+

BOAT	TYPE	SKIPPER	SAILED	RETURNED	SHIPS SANK	TONS
U-523	IXC	Werner Pietzsch	5/22	5/26		None/Abort
U-172	IXC	Carl Emmermann	5/29	9/7	4	22,946
Totals:		8 patrols			9	44,258
June 1943:						
U-572	VIIC	Heinz Kummetat	6/2	Lost 8/3	3	4,510 [10]
U-510	IXC	Alfred Eick*	6/3	8/29	3	18,865
U-759	VIIC	Rudolf Friedrich	6/7	Lost 7/15	3	12,764
U-590	VIIC	Werner Krüer*	6/8	Lost 7/9	1	5,228
U-185	IXC40	August Maus	6/9	Lost 8/24	5	36,781+ [11]
U-84	VIIB	Horst Uphoff	6/10	Lost 8/7?		None
U-134	VIIC	Hans-Günther Brosin	6/10	Lost 8/24		None [12]
U-653	VIIC	Gerhard Feiler	6/10	9/11		None
U-732	VIIC	Klaus-Peter Carlsen	6/10	8/31		None
U-155	IXC	Adolf-Cornelius Piening	6/12	6/16		None/Abort
U-159	IXC	Heinz Beckmann* (C.O.)	6/12	Lost 7/28		None
U-415	VIIC	Kurt Neide	6/12	9/8		None
U-615	VIIC	Ralph Kapitzky	6/12	Lost 8/6	1	3,177 [13]
U-634	VIIC	Eberhard Dahlhaus	6/12	Lost 8/30		None
U-518	IXC	Friedrich-Wilhelm Wissmann	6/24	7/3		None/Abort
U-604	VIIC	Horst Höltring	6/24	Lost 8/11		None
U-406	VIIC	Horst Dieterichs	6/26	9/15		None
U-591	VIIC	Reimar Ziesmer*	6/26	Lost 7/30		None
U-598	VIIC	Gottfried Holtorf	6/26	Lost 7/23		None
U-662	VIIC	Heinz-Eberhard Müller	6/26	Lost 7/21		None
U-359	VIIC	Heinz Förster	6/29	Lost 7/26		None
U-466	VIIC	Gerhard Thäter	6/29	8/16		None/Abort
U-155	IXC	Adolf-Cornelius Piening (resail)	6/30	8/11		None/PR [14]
Totals:		22 patrols			16	81,325
July 1943:						
U-628	VIIC	Heinz Hasenschar	7/1	Lost 7/3		None
U-648	VIIC	Peter-Arthur Stahl	7/1	8/10		None/PR [15]
U-505	IXC	Peter Zschech	7/3	7/13		None/Abort
U-230	VIIC	Paul Siegmann	7/5	9/8		None/M [16]
U-566	VIIC	Hans Hornkohl	7/5	9/1	1	1,500/M [17]
U-607	VIIC	Wolf Jeschonnek	7/10	Lost 7/13		None/M
U-613	VIIC	Helmut Köppe	7/10	Lost 7/23		None/M
U-664	VIIC	Adolf Graef	7/21	Lost 8/9		None
U-117	XB	Hans-Werner Neumann	7/22	Lost 8/7		None/PR
U-262	VIIC	Heinz Franke	7/24	9/2		None/PR [18]
U-760	VIIC	Otto-Ulrich Blum	7/24	9/8		None/PR [19]
U-107	IXB	Volker von Simmermacher*	7/28	10/3		None+/M
U-218	VIID	Richard Becker	7/29	8/6		None/M/Abort
Totals:		13 patrols			1	1,500
August 1943:						
U-161	IXC	Albrecht Achilles	8/8	Lost 9/27	2	10,760 [20]
U-123	IXB	Horst von Schroeter	8/16	11/7		None
U-523	IXC	Werner Pietzsch	8/16	Lost 8/25		None
U-518	IXC	Friedrich-Wilhelm Wissmann	8/18	12/1		None
U-214	VIID	Rupprecht Stock	8/22	11/30		None/M [21]

BOAT	TYPE	SKIPPER	SAILED	SHIPS RETURNED	SANK	TONS
U-170	IXC40	Günther Pfeffer	8/29	12/23	1	4,663
U-536	IXC40	Rolf Schauenburg	8/29	Lost 11/20		None
U-669	VIIC	Kurt Köhl	8/29	Lost 8/29?		None[22]
Totals:	5 patrols				3	15,133
September 1943:						
U-220	XB	Bruno Barber*	9/8	Lost 10/28	2	7,199/M[23]
U-505	IXC	Peter Zschech	9/18	9/30		None/Abort
U-218	VIID	Richard Becker	9/19	12/8		None/M[24]
U-155	IXC	Adolf Piening	9/21	1/1/44	1	5,393
U-537	IXC40	Peter Schrewe*	9/30	12/8		None[25]
Totals:	5 patrols				3	12,592
October 1943:						
U-154	IXC	Oskar-Heinz Kusch	10/2	12/20		None[26]
U-516	IXC	Hans-Rutger Tillessen	10/4	2/26/44	6	24,745
U-505	IXC	Peter Zschech	10/9	11/7		None[27]/Abort
U-129	IXC	Richard von Harpe	10/12	1/31/44	1	5,441
U-193	IXC40	Hans Pauckstadt	10/12	2/25/44	1	10,172
U-530	IXC40	Kurt Lange	10/16	2/22/44		None+
U-190	IXC40	Max Wintermeyer	10/17	1/15/44		None
Totals:	7 patrols				8	40,358
November 1943:						
U-543	IXC40	Hans-Jürgen Hellriegel*	11/9	1/24/44		None
December 1943:						
None						
January 1944:						
U-539	IXC40	Hans-Jürgen Lauterbach-Emden	1/3	3/21		None/PR[28] S
U-845	IXC40	Werner Weber*	1/8	Lost 3/10		None+/S
U-518	IXC	Hans-Werner Offermann*	1/23	5/7	1	3,401
U-802	IXC40	Helmut Schmoeckel*	1/29	5/2	1	1,621
U-154	IXC	Gerth Gemeiner* (C.O.)	1/31	4/28		None
Totals:	5 patrols (1 supply)				2	5,022
February 1944:						
U-550	IXC40	Klaus Hänert*	2/6	Lost 4/16	1	11,017
U-170	IXC40	Günther Pfeffer	2/9	5/27		None
U-218	VIID	Richard Becker	2/12	5/7		None[29]
U-856	IXC40	Friedrich Wittenberg*	2/24	Lost 4/7		None
U-541	IXC40	Kurt Petersen	2/29	6/22		None
Totals:	5 patrols			1	11,017	
March 1944:						
U-548	IXC40	Eberhard Zimmermann*	3/21	6/24	1	1,445[30]
U-129	IXC	Richard von Harpe	3/22	7/18	2	11,964/Retired
U-68	IXC	Albert Lauzemis	3/27	Lost 4/10		None
U-543	IXC40	Hans-Jürgen Hellriegel	3/28	Diverted to Freetown/S		
Totals:	4 patrols				3	13,409

BOAT	TYPE	SKIPPER	SAILED	SHIPS RETURNED	SANK	TONS
APRIL 1944:						
U-1222	IXC40	Heinz Bielfeld*	4/13	Lost 7/11		None/S
MAY 1944:						
U-539	IXC40	Hans-Jürgen Lauterbach-Emden	5/1	9/17	1	1,517+/S
U-516	IXC	Hans-Rutger Tillessen	5/7	10/1	1	9,887
U-107	IXB	Volker von Simmermacher	5/10	7/22		None+/S
U-549	IXC40	Detlev Krankenhagen	5/14	Lost 5/29	1	8,600+[31]/S
U-530	IXC40	Kurt Lange	5/22	10/1		None[32]/S
U-233	XB	Hans Steen*	5/27	Lost 7/5		None/PR/M[33]
Totals:	6 patrols				3	20,004
JUNE 1944 (ALL SNORT BOATS HEREAFTER):						
U-154	IXC	Gerth Gemeiner	6/20	Lost 7/3		None
U-802	IXC40	Helmut Schmoeckel	6/22	7/8		None/Abort
JULY 1944:						
U-518	IXC40	Hans-Werner Offermann	7/15	10/22	1	7,176[34]
U-802	IXC40	Helmut Schmoeckel	7/16	11/12		None
U-1229	IXC40	Armin Zinke*	7/26	Lost 8/20		None[35]
U-865	IXC40	Dietrich Stellmacher*	7/27	7/28		None/Abort
Totals:	4 patrols				1	7,176
AUGUST 1944:						
U-865	IXC40	Dietrich Stellmacher (resail)	8/1	8/3		None/Abort
U-541	IXC40	Kurt Petersen	8/6	11/6	1	2,140
U-865	IXC40	Dietrich Stellmacher (resail)	8/10	8/13		None/Abort
U-1221	IXC40	Paul Ackermann*	8/20	11/26		None
U-1223	IXC40	Albert Kneip*	8/28	12/14	1	1,370[36]
Totals:	3 patrols				2	3,510
SEPTEMBER 1944:						
U-865	IXC40	Dietrich Stellmacher (resail)	9/8	Lost 9/18?		None
U-867	IXC40	Arved von Mühlendahl*	9/12	Lost 9/19		None
U-1226	IXC40	August-Wilhelm Claussen*	9/30	Lost 10/23?		None
Totals:	3 patrols				None	
OCTOBER 1944:						
U-1230	IXC40	Hans Hilbig*	10/8	1/28/45	1	5,458[37]
U-1228	IXC40	Friedrich-Wilhelm Marienfeld	10/12	12/28	1	950[38]
U-1231	IXC40	Hermann Lessing*	10/15	1/30/45		None
U-806	IXC40	Klaus Hornbostel*	10/30	2/21/45	1	672+[39]
Totals:	4 patrols				3	7,080
NOVEMBER 1944:						
U-1232	IXC40	Kurt Dobratz*	11/12	2/14/45	5	26,900
DECEMBER 1944:						
U-869	IXC40	Helmut Nuuerburg*	12/8	Lost 2/17/45?		
U-1233	IXC40	Hans-Joachim Kuhn*	12/12	12/16		None/Abort

				SHIPS		
BOAT	TYPE	SKIPPER	SAILED	RETURNED	SANK	TONS
U-1233	IXC40	Hans-Joachim Kuhn	12/20	12/21		None/Abort
U-1233	IXC40	Hans-Joachim Kuhn	12/24	3/28		None
Totals:	4 patrols					

Last Patrols to Canada and the U.S.A., January–May 1945:

January 1945:
None

February 1945:

U-866	IXC40	Peter Rogowsky* (C.O.)	2/6	Lost 3/18		None
U-857	IXC40	Rudolf Premauer	2/8	Lost 4/?		None+
U-879	IXC40	Erwin Manchen* (C.O.)	2/11	Lost 4/30	1	6,959
U-190	IXC40	Hans-Edwin Reith	2/22	Canada	1	590[40]
U-853	IXC	Helmut von Frömsdorf* (C.O.)	2/23	Lost 5/6	2	5,783[41]
Totals:	5 patrols				4	13,332

March 1945:

U-858	IXC40	Thilo Bode	3/2	3/10		None/Abort
U-530	IXC40	Otto Wermuth* (C.O.)	3/4	7/11		None/Argentina
U-805	IXC40	Richard Bernardelli*	3/4	3/10		None/Abort
U-548	IXC40	Erich Krempl* (C.O.)	3/7	Lost 4/30	1	8,300+
U-858	IXC40	Thilo Bode (resail)	3/14	U.S.A.		None
U-880	IXC40	Gerhard Schötzau*	3/14	Lost 4/16		None
U-805	IXC40	Richard Bernardelli (resail)	3/17	U.S.A		None
U-1235	IXC40	Franz Barsch	3/20	Lost 4/19		None
U-546	IXC40	Paul Just	3/22	Lost 4/24	1	1,200[42]
U-518	IXC	Hans-Werner Offermann	3/24	Lost 4/22		None
U-881	IXC40	Heinz Frischke	3/26	3/28		None/Abort
Totals:	9 patrols				2	9,500

April 1945:

U-873	IXD2	Friedrich Steinhoff*	4/1	U.S.A.		None
U-889	IXC40	Friedrich Braeucker*	4/6	Canada		None
U-881	IXC40	Dr. Heinz Frischke (resail)	4/7	Lost 5/6		None
U-1228	IXC40	Friedrich-Wilhelm Marienfeld	4/14	U.S.A.		None
U-1231	IXC40	Helmut Wicke* (C.O.)	4/27	U.K.		None
Totals:	5 patrols					None

May 1945:

U-802	IXC40	Helmut Schmoeckel	5/3	U.K.		None
Totals:	1 patrol				6	22,832

1. Mützelburg was killed in a swimming accident at sea.
2. Landed agent in New Brunswick, Canada, 11/9/42.
3. Includes destruction of the American gunboat Erie, prototype of Treasury-class U.S. Coast Guard cutters.

4. Planted a fallow minefield near Ambrose Lightship in the approaches to New York on 11/10/42. Sank the one ship by torpedo.
5. Recalled to attack Torch forces, but Steinhoff fell ill and aborted.
6. While outbound, met inbound blockade-runners Regensburg and Pietro Orseolo and gave them Metox gear.
7. Was assigned to carry out a special mission to pick up POWs who were to escape from a prison camp in Canada. After U-376 was correctly assumed to be sunk outbound in Biscay, the mission into the Gulf of St. Lawrence was carried out by the "backup," U-262. Mission unsuccessful.
8. Outbound, served as a provisional tanker for boats on the North Atlantic run; thereafter laid mines off Halifax on 6/1/42, which sank one ship and damaged another.
9. Guggenberger, who gained fame on U-81 in the Mediterranean for sinking the British carrier Ark Royal, was initially reassigned to commission a new U-boat, but was diverted to France to command U-513.
10. Probably shot down a U.S. Navy Mariner on 8/3.
11. Shot down a Whitley in Biscay on 6/14 and a U.S. Navy B-24 on 8/11.
12. Shot down ASW blimp K-74 near Key West, Florida.
13. Shot down a U.S. Navy Mariner patrol plane.
14. En route to Brazil, diverted to refuel three Monsun boats and returned to France.
15. Refueled U-527 and returned to France.
16. U-230 and U-566 laid minefields at Norfolk on 7/27 and 7/30, respectively, and U-107 laid a field at Charleston on 8/28. No field produced a sinking, but U-566 sank with torpedoes the yacht Alva, built in Kiel and commissioned as the gunboat Plymouth. U-607 was to lay a field at Kingstown, Jamaica, but was sunk outbound in Biscay. U-613 was to lay a field at Jacksonville, Florida, but was lost en route. U-117 was to lay a field at New York but was diverted to be a refueler and was lost. U-218 was to lay a field in Trinidad but aborted in Biscay.
17. Shot down a Ventura.
18. Possibly shot down an aircraft from Card.
19. Damaged and interned for the rest of the war in Vigo, Spain.
20. Outbound, met the inbound Japanese submarine "Flieder," or I-8.
21. Laid mainefield off Panama on 10/10.
22. Was assigned to carry out special mission Kiebitz (Lapwing) to pick up German POWs, including Otto Kreschmer, who were to escape from a camp in Canada. After the boat was sunk in the Bay of Biscay, the mission was assigned to the backup, U-536.
23. Laid minefield off St. John's, Newfoundland, on 10/9.
24. Laid minefield at Trinidad on 10/27.
25. Special mission to establish automatic weather station at Martin Bay on the coast of Labrador, 10/23.
26. After this patrol, on 1/26/44, the Kriegsmarine court-martialed Kusch for sedition. Found guilty, he was shot on 5/12/44.
27. Zschech committed suicide on 10/24. First watch officer Paul Meyer assumed command and brought the boat home.
28. First boat to sail on a combat patrol with a snorkel.
29. Laid minefield off Trinidad on 10/27.
30. The Canadian frigate Valleyfield.
31. Sank the American "jeep" carrier Block Island and damaged the American destroyer escort Barr.
32. Met inbound Japanese submarine code-named "Föhre," formerly code-named "Tanne."
33. Was to lay minefield off Halifax, but sunk beforehand.
34. The 7,200-ton American Liberty ship George Ade, which Offermann damaged on 9/12, towed to an anchorage by Escape. A hurricane sank George Ade in the anchorage.
35. Was to land an agent, Oskar Mantel, in the Gulf of Maine, but was sunk beforehand. Mantel was among the forty survivors who were rescued by American forces.
36. Canadian frigate Magog, towed to port a total wreck.

37. Also landed two agents, William C. Colepaugh and Eric Gimpel, in Frenchman Bay, Maine, on 11/29/44.
38. Canadian corvette Shawinigan.
39. Canadian minesweeper Clayoquot.
40. Canadian minesweeper Esquimalt.
41. Includes 430-ton American subchaser Eagle 56.
42. American destroyer escort Frederick C. Davis.

APPENDIX 6

U-BOATS ASSIGNED TO THE ARCTIC AREA

SEPTEMBER 1942–APRIL 1945

BOAT		SKIPPER	ARRIVED	DEPARTED/LOST	
IN SERVICE 9/1/42: (23)					
U-88	VIIC	Heino Bohmann	4/42	9/12/42	Lost
U-209	VIIC	Heinrich Brodda	2/42	2/43	
U-251	VIIC	Heinrich Timm	4/42	7/43	
U-255	VIIC	Reinhardt Reche	6/42	11/43	
U-334	VIIC	Hilmar Siemon	3/42	5/43	
U-355	VIIC	Günter La Baume	6/42	4/1/44	Lost
U-376	VIIC	Friedrich-Karl Marks	3/42	2/43	
U-377	VIIC	Otto Köhler	2/42	2/43	
U-378	VIIC	Alfred Hoschatt	3/42		
		Erich Mäder	10/42	4/43	
U-403	VIIC	Heinz-Ehlert Clausen	3/42	12/42	
U-405	VIIC	Rolf-Heinrich Hopmann	3/42	12/42	
U-408	VIIC	Reinhard von Hymmen	5/42	11/5/42	Lost
U-435	VIIC	Siegfried Strelow	2/42	11/42	
U-436	VIIC	Günther Seibicke	2/42	10/42	
U-456	VIIC	Max-Martin Teichert	6/42	12/42	
U-457	VIIC	Karl Brandenburg	6/42	9/16/42	Lost
U-586	VIIC	Dietrich von der Esch	3/42	9/43	
U-589	VIIC	Hans-Joachim Horrer	2/42	9/14/42	Lost
U-591	VIIC	Hans-Jürgen Zetzsche	3/42	12/42	
U-592	VIIC	Karl Borm	2/42	2/43	
U-601	VIIC	Peter-Ottmar Grau	7/42		
		Otto Hansen	11/43	2/25/44	Lost
U-657	VIIC	Heinrich Göllnitz	4/42	4/43	
U-703	VIIC	Heinz Bielfeld	6/42		
		Joachim Brünner	5/43	9/16/44?	Lost
BOATS ARRIVING AFTER 9/1/42:					
U-212	VIIC	Helmut Vogler	9/42	10/43	
U-606	VIIC	Hans Klatt	9/42		
		Dietrich von der Esch	9/42		
		Hans Döhler	10/42	10/42	
U-622	VIIC	Horst-Thilo Queck	9/42	7/24/43	Lost
U-625	VIIC	Hans Benker	9/42	10/43	
U-354	VIIC	Karl-Heinz Herbschleb	10/42		
		Hans-Jürgen Sthamer	2/44	8/24/44	Lost

* = First patrol of boat or skipper (C.O.)

BOAT		SKIPPER	ARRIVED	DEPARTED/LOST	
U-629	VIIC	Hans-Helmut Bugs	12/42	10/43	
U-302	VIIC	Herbert Sickel	12/42	10/43	
U-269	VIIC	Karl-Heinrich Harlfinger*	3/43	10/43	
U-339	VIIC	Georg-Wilhelm Basse	3/43	4/43[1]	Retired
U-467	VIIC	Heinz Kummer*	3/43	4/43	
U-639	VIIC	Walter Wichmann*	3/43	8/28/43	Lost
U-644	VIIC	Kurt Jensen*	3/43	4/7/43	Lost[2]
U-711	VIIC	Hans-Günther Lange*	3/43	5/4/45	Lost
U-974	VIIC	Heinz Wolff	3/43	4/19/44	Lost[7]
U-646	VIIC	Heinrich Wulff*	4/43	4/43	
U-636	VIIC	Hans Hildebrandt*	4/43		
		Eberhard Schendel	2/44	2/45	
U-307	VIIC	Friedrich-Georg Herrle*	6/43		
		Erich Krüger	12/44	4/29/45	Lost
U-387	VIIC	Rudolf Büchler*	6/43	12/9/44	Lost
U-277	VIIC	Robert Lübsen*	7/43	5/1/44	Lost
U-713	VIIC	Henri Gosejakob*	7/43	2/24/44	Lost
U-737	VIIC	Paul Brasack*	7/43		
		Friedrich August Gréus*	11/44	12/19/44	Lost
U-360	VIIC	Klaus Becker*	8/43	4/2/44	Lost
U-956	VIIC	Heinz-Dieter Mohs	8/43	End	
U-960	VIIC	Günther Heinrich*	8/43	12/44	
U-716	VIIC	Hans Dunkelberg*	12/43		
		Jürgen Thimme*	1/45	End	
U-957	VIIC	Gerd Schaar*	12/43	10/21/44	Retired[3]
U-965	VIIC	Klaus Ohling*	12/43	10/44	
U-278	VIIC	Joachim Franze*	1/44	End	
U-314	VIIC	Georg-Wilhelm Basse*	1/44	1/30/44	Lost
U-425	VIIC	Heinz Bentzien*	1/44	2/17/45	Lost
U-312	VIIC	Kurt-Heinz Nicolay*	1/44	11/44	
		Friedrich-Georg Herrle	12/44		
		Jürgen von Gaza	2/45	End	
U-313	VIIC	Friedhelm Schweiger*	1/44	End	
U-366	VIIC	Bruno Langenberg*	1/44	3/5/44	Lost
U-472	VIIC	Wolfgang-Friedrich von Forstner*	1/44	3/4/44	Lost
U-674	VIIC	Harald Muhs*	1/44	5/2/44	Lost
U-739	VIIC	Ernst Mangold*	1/44	2/45	
		Fritz Kosnick*	3/45	End	
U-973	VIIC	Klaus Paepenmöller*	1/44	3/6/44	Lost[4]
U-990	VIIC	Hubert Nordheimer*	1/44	5/25/44	Lost
U-288	VIIC	Willi Meyer*	2/44	4/3/44	Lost
U-315	VIIC	Herbert Zoller*	2/44	12/44	
U-361	VIIC	Hans Seidel*	2/44	7/17/44	Lost
U-959	VIIC	Friedrich Weitz*	2/44	5/2/44	Lost
U-362	VIIC	Ludwig Franz*	3/44	9/5/44	Lost[5]
U-673	VIIC	Heinz Sauer	3/44	6/4/44[6]	
U-968	VIIC	Otto Westphalen*	3/44	End	
U-289	VIIC	Alexander Hellwig*	5/44	5/31/44	Lost
U-347	VIIC	Johann de Buhr*	5/44	7/17/44	Lost
U-668	VIIC	Wolfgang von Eickstedt*	5/44		
		Fritz Henning*	4/45	End	
U-742	VIIC	Heinz Schwassmann*	5/44	7/18/44	Lost
U-293	VIIC41	Leonhard Klingspor	6/44	12/44	
U-344	VIIC	Ulrich Pietsch*	6/44	8/22/44	Lost
U-363	VIIC	Werner Nees*	6/44	End	
U-365	VIIC	Heimar Wedemeyer*	6/44		
		Diether Todenhagen*	11/44	12/13/44	Lost

BOAT		SKIPPER	ARRIVED	DEPARTED/LOST	
U-394	VIIC	Wolfgang Borger*	6/44	9/2/44	Lost
U-921	VIIC	Alfred Werner*	6/44	9/24/44?	Lost
U-987	VIIC	Hilmer Karl Schreyer*	6/44	6/15/44	Lost
U-992	VIIC	Hans Falke*	6/44	End	
U-995	VIIC41	Walter Köhntopp*	6/44		
		Hans-Georg Hess*	9/44	End	
U-997	VIIC41	Hans Lehmann*	6/44	End	
U-310	VIIC	Wolfgang Ley	7/44	End	
U-771	VIIC	Helmut Block	7/44	11/11/44	Lost
U-1163	VIIC41	Ernst-Ludwig Balduhn	7/44	End	
U-295	VIIC41	Günter Wieboldt	8/44	End	
U-286	VIIC	Willi Dietrich*	8/44	4/29/45	Lost
U-1165	VIIC	Hans Homann	8/44	End	
U-299	VIIC41	Helmuth Heinrich*	8/44		
		Bernhard Emde*	12/44	End	
U-318	VIIC41	Josef Will	8/44	End	
U-427	VIIC	Karl-Gabriel von Gudenus	11/44	End	
U-294	VIIC	Heinz Schütt	3/45	End	
U-481	VIIC	Klaus Andersen	4/45	End	

1. After surviving an air attack, returned to Baltic and Training Command.
2. The new VII U-644, commanded by twenty-four-year-old Kurt Jensen, joined the Arctic force in mid-March. Doubtless guided by Enigma decrypts, on 4/7 the British submarine Tuna, commanded by Desmond Martin, found and sank U-644 on her first patrol, near the island of Jan Mayen. Probably with Enigma help, a week later Martin found another Arctic VII, U-302, commanded by Herbert Sickel, but Martin missed with eight torpedoes.
3. Boat rammed by a German ship and decommissioned. Later repaired and recommissioned.
4. In experimental status with a Type VI conning tower.
5. In experimental status with a Type V conning tower.
6. In experimental status with a Type VI conning tower. Sailed to France on this date, arriving 7/23.
7. Sunk off Bergen on 4/19 by the Norwegian submarine Ula.

APPENDIX 7

U-BOATS TRANSFERRED TO THE MEDITERRANEAN SEA

SEPTEMBER 1942–APRIL 1944

BOAT	TYPE	SKIPPER	ARRIVED	LOST
IN SERVICE 9/1/42: (15)				
U-371	VIIC	Waldemar Mehl	5/24/42 [1]	
		Horst-Arno Fenski	3/24/44 [2]	5/4/44
U-97	VIIC	Friedrich Bürgel	5/16/42	
		Hans-Georg Trox	2/4/43	6/16/43
U-559	VIIC	Hans-Otto Heidtmann	9/26/42	10/30/42
U-331	VIIC	Hans-Dietrich von Tiesenhausen	9/30/41	11/17/42
U-205	VIIC	Franz-Georg Reschke	11/11/41	
		Friedrich Bürgel	10/19/42	2/17/43
U-81	VIIC	Friedrich Guggenberger	11/12/41	
		Johann-Otto Krieg	12/23/42	1/9/44
U-565	VIIC	Wilhelm Franken	3/18/42 [3]	
		Fritz Henning	10/7/43	9/30/44
U-431	VIIC	Wilhelm Dommes	11/24/41 [4]	
		Dietrich Schöneboom	1/6/43	10/21/43
U-562	VIIC	Horst Hamm	11/27/41 [5]	2/19/43
U-375	VIIC	Jürgen Könenkamp	12/9/41 [6]	7/30/43
U-453	VIIC	Egon-Reiner von Schlippenbach	12/9/41 [7]	
		Dierk Lührs	12/2/43	5/21/44
U-77	VIIC	Otto Hartmann	8/30/42 [8]	3/29/43
U-83	VIIB	Hans-Werner Kraus	12/18/41	
		Ulrich Wörishoffer	9/21/42	3/4/43
U-73	VIIB	Helmut Rosenbaum	1/14/42	
		Horst Deckert	9/10/42	12/16/43
U-561	VIIC	Robert Bartels	1/15/42	
		Heinz Schomburg	9/5/42	
		Fritz Henning	7/1/43	7/12/43
BOATS ARRIVING AFTER SEPTEMBER 1942:				
U-605	VIIC	Herbert-Viktor Schütze	10/10/42	11/14/42
U-458	VIIC	Kurt Diggins	10/11/42	8/22/43
U-593	VIIC	Gerd Kelbling	10/11/42 [9]	12/13/43
U-660	VIIC	Götz Baur	10/11/42	11/12/42
U-407	VIIC	Ernst-Ulrich Brüller	11/9/42 [10]	
		Hubertus Korndörfer	1/14/44	
		Hans Kolbus	9/??/44	9/19/44
U-617	VIIC	Albrecht Brandi	11/8/42 [11]	9/12/43
U-595	VIIC	Jürgen Quaet-Faslem	11/9/42	11/14/42
U-596	VIIC	Günter Jahn	11/9/42	
		Victor-Wilhelm Nonn	6/26/43	
		Hans Kolbus	4/30/44	9/25/44

BOAT	TYPE	SKIPPER	ARRIVED	LOST
U-755	VIIC	Walter Göing	11/9/42	5/28/43
U-259	VIIC	Klaus Köpke	11/11/42	11/15/42
U-380	VIIC	Josef Röther	11/11/42[12]	
		Albrecht Brandi	11/11/43	3/11/44
U-443	VIIC	Konstantin von Puttkamer	12/5/42[13]	2/23/43
U-602	VIIC	Philipp Schüler	12/8/42[14]	4/23/43
U-301	VIIC	Willy-Roderich Körner	12/9/42	1/21/43
U-224	VIIC	Hans Karl Kosbadt	1/9/43	1/13/43
U-303	VIIC	Karl-Franz Heine	4/9/43	5/21/43
U-414	VIIC	Walther Huth	4/9/43	5/25/43
U-410	VIIC	Horst-Arno Fenski	5/6/43[15]	3/11/44
U-616	VIIC	Siegfried Koitschka	5/6/43[16]	5/14/44
U-409	VIIC	Hans-Ferdinand Massmann	6/5/43	7/12/43
BOATS ARRIVING AFTER SEPTEMBER 1943:				
U-223	VIIC	Karl-Jürgen Wächter	9/??/43[17]	
		Peter Gerlach	12/17/44	3/30/44
U-450	VIIC	Kurt Böhme	11/1/43	3/10/44
U-642	VIIC	Herbert Brünning	11/3/43	7/5/44
U-230	VIIC	Paul Siegmann	12/5/43[18]	
		Heinz-Eugen Eberbach	8/??/44	8/21/44
U-952	VIIC	Oskar Curio	1/3/44	7/5/44
U-343	VIIC	Wolfgang Rahn	1/5/44	3/10/44
U-455	VIIC	Hans-Martin Scheibe	1/22/44	4/2/44?
U-969	VIIC	Max Dobbert	2/3/44	8/6/44
U-586	VIIC	Hans Götz	2/13/44	7/5/44
U-967	VIIC	Herbert Loeder	2/13/44	
		Albrecht Brandi	3/19/44[19]	
		Heinz-Eugen Eberbach	7/??/44	8/19/44
U-421	VIIC	Hans Kolbus	3/20/44	4/29/44
U-466	VIIC	Gerhard Thäter	3/22/44	8/19/44
U-471	VIIC	Friedrich Kloevekorn	3/31/44	8/6/44
U-960	VIIC	Günther Heinrich	4/30/44	5/19/44

SUMMARY

Total U-Boats into the Mediterranean:	62
U-Boats lost:	62[20]
U-boats lost from 9/1/42:	49
Total manpower lost (captured):	1,893 (930)[21]

---

1. Sank 700-ton British minesweeper Hythe on 10/11/43 and the 1,600-ton American destroyer Bristol on 10/13/43.
2. Damaged French destroyer escort Sénégalais on 5/4/44.
3. Sank the 1,500-ton British destroyer Partridge on 12/18/42 and on 12/22/42 damaged the 16,300-ton British troopship Cameronia.
4. Sank the 2,000-ton British destroyer Martin on 11/10/42, and the 1,600-ton Dutch destroyer Isaac Sweers on 11/13/42.
5. Sank the 23,700-ton British troopship Strathallan on 12/21/42, with five thousand soldiers on board. Ship sank slowly with "small" loss of life.
6. Damaged the 2,650-ton British minelayer-cruiser Manxman.
7. Planted minefields at Brindisi and Bari, on the east coast of Italy, on 11/11/43. Mines damaged the 1,700-ton British destroyer Quail beyond repair and sank the 800-ton British minesweeper Hebe.

8. Damaged the 1,200-ton British sloop Stork on 11/12/42.
9. Sank 1,600-ton American LST 387 and 1,600-ton British LST 333 on 6/22/43, the 800-ton American minesweeper Skill on 8/25/43, and the 1,000-ton British Hunt-class destroyers Tynedale and Holcombe on 12/12/43.
10. Sank the 20,000-ton British troopship Viceroy of India on 11/12/42, damaged the 8,800-ton British cruiser Newfoundland on 7/23/43, and damaged the 9,100-ton British cruiser Birmingham on 11/28/43.
11. Sank the 2,650-ton British minelayer-cruiser Welshman on 2/1/43 and 1,050-ton British Hunt-class destroyer Puckeridge on 9/6/43.
12. Sank the 11,000-ton Dutch troopship Nieuw Zeeland on 11/12/42.
13. Sank the 1,000-ton British Hunt-class destroyer Blean on 12/11/42.
14. Damaged the 1,500-ton British destroyer Porcupine on 12/18/42.
15. Sank 5,300-ton British light cruiser Penelope and American LST 348 off Anzio on 2/20/44.
16. Sank 1,600-ton American destroyer Buck on 10/9/43.
17. Hit the 1,300-ton British frigate Cuckmere with a T-5 on 12/11/43. Ship scrapped. Hit 1,900-ton British destroyer Laforey on 3/30/44. Ship scrapped.
18. Sank the 1,600-ton British LST 418 off Anzio on 2/16/44, 1,600-ton British LST 305 on 2/20/44, and 335-ton American PC on 5/9/44.
19. Sank the 1,300-ton American destroyer escort Fechteler on 5/15/44.
20. Eleven U-boats were destroyed in ports by USAAF heavy bomber air raids.
21. The manpower loss figures in Volume I are not correct. It should be 452, of whom 220 were captured.

APPENDIX 8

HUFF DUFF

Many authorities have asserted that in World War II, land and shipboard high-frequency direction finding (HF/DF or Huff Duff) should rank right up with radar and codebreaking as an anti–U-boat weapon.

Until recently, little was known about Huff Duff and its evolution. Historian Kathleen Broome Williams admirably filled that gap in 1996 with the publication of her book *Secret Weapon: U.S. High-Frequency Direction Finding in the Battle of the Atlantic.* The following is condensed from her book.

In the 1930s, scientists and engineers in a number of countries secretly developed electronic devices for the specific purpose of taking a bearing on the transmissions of radio traffic in the high-frequency ranges. The military establishments were especially interested in a device capable of nearly instantaneous detection of the new, extremely brief transmissions of German U-boats that were manifest in their prewar exercises and operations.

In several nations, soon to become allies against the Axis, engineers produced Huff Duff devices, albeit slowly.

In Great Britain, the R&D on land and shipboard Huff Duff proceeded under the direction of Robert Watson-Watt, the so-called father of radar. The first British version for shipboard use, FH 1, was installed on the destroyer Hesperus on March 12, 1940, and later that year on a few other convoy escorts and rescue ships. Owing to topside stability problems and electronic interferences, in the early stages of development it was not possible to fit both radar and Huff Duff on the same ship. Inasmuch as British warship captains preferred radar over the less reliable Huff Duff, the latter had a lower R&D priority, and development lagged.

Slowly, British engineers produced improved Huff Duff models FH 2 and FH 3. In October 1941, the FH 3 was first installed on the ex-American Coast Guard cutter Mendota, serving in the Royal Navy as the sloop Culver, along with Type 271 centimetric-wavelength radar. Culver sailed as an escort to West Africa. On the return voyage, as an escort in convoy Sierra Leone 98, Culver was sunk on January 31, 1942, by U-105, a calamity that did nothing to build confidence in Huff Duff.[1]

By that time, according to Williams, about twenty-five convoy escorts and rescue vessels were fitted with British FH 3 Huff Duff sets. In March 1942, yet another improved model, FH 4, was fitted on the ex-American destroyer Twiggs, serving in the Royal Navy as Leamington. This set performed better, and the Admiralty ordered a total of thirty FH 4s for delivery by the end of the year. By August 1942, seventy Royal Navy vessels were fitted with Huff Duff, mostly FH 3s. It was not until mid-1943 that shipboard Huff Duff sets were commonplace in the Royal Navy, and they were still very much hush-hush.[2]

In France, prewar R&D on Huff Duff was carried out at the Laboratoire Téléphonique in Paris, a subsidiary of International Telephone and Telegraph (ITT). Maurice E. Deloraine was the director of the lab; Henri Busignies was the leading expert on Huff Duff. This work paralleled that of the British, with whom the French shared electronic secrets until the Germans overran France in May 1940.

By that time, Busignies had built four Huff Duff models that were approximately the equivalent of the British FH 3s. They were automatic and "instantaneous," fitted with a cathode-ray tube on which a lingering "blip" was displayed, like a radar set. The antenna, based on the universally used Adcock, incorporated a "sense" feature, developed by the Pole W. Struszynski, that distinguished between the actual signal bearing and its reciprocal echo, a breakthrough of transcendent importance. The invading Germans insisted that ITT keep the Paris lab going, but Deloraine, Busignies, and nine other top engineers destroyed the Huff Duff sets and fled with their families to Lisbon with Huff Duff drawings and some key components. These French boarded an American tramp steamer, Siboney, and reached Hoboken, New Jersey, on December 31, 1940.

The president of ITT, Sosthenes Behn, directed these French engineers to join ITT's New York lab, then arranged a meeting between Deloraine and Busignies and representatives of the U.S. Army and Navy. The Americans were distrustful of Behn and ITT because of its business ties to the Germans and refused to give ITT or the French an unlimited security clearance. However, Maxwell K. Goldstein, the U.S. Navy's Huff Duff expert at the Naval Research Laboratory, already embarked on creating a chain of Atlantic shore–based Huff Duff stations, immediately recognized the advantages of the Busignies design, and the Navy (but not the Army) gave ITT and the Frenchmen a "limited" security clearance and a contract to build four Busignies Huff Duff sets for shipboard use.

The U.S. Navy, experimenting with its own shipboard Huff Duff models as well as the British FH 3s, was slow to embrace the Busignies Huff Duff. Like the British, American warship captains preferred radar over Huff Duff. That preference, plus the distrust of ITT's loyalty and the withholding of full security clearances for the French engineers, delayed the development of Huff Duff in the United States for months. Tests on the four Busignies sets did not take place until October 1941. Moreover, the reviews were not raves.

Finally, in May 1942, the U.S. Navy embraced Huff Duff. Maxwell Goldstein carried out comparative tests on the new destroyer Corry, fitted with both the British FH 3 and the Busignies model, designated DAQ to distinguish it from the DAJ sets in its shore-based system. Williams wrote that Goldstein chose the DAQ over the British FH 3 and that on June 26, 1942, Admiral King ordered half of all new U.S. destroyers and destroyer escorts to be fitted with DAQs or any improved models. Altogether, Williams wrote, ITT produced about four thousand Huff Duff sets for the U.S. military in World War II. The U.S. Navy presented ITT president Sosthenes Behn and the ITT company high awards. The Americans also awarded Deloraine and Busignies Certificates of Commendation "for outstanding service" in the Allied cause but never granted them unrestricted security clearances.

The popular rush to credit radar, and later codebreaking, for the defeat of the U-boat left the equally effective but less glamorous and more difficult to understand Huff Duff in the shadows.

---

1. See Volume I, pp. 475–77 and p. 497.
2. As usual, the Canadians were last to receive Huff Duff in quantity. In 1942, the destroyer Restigouche was the first Canadian warship to be fitted with a Huff Duff set. It was said to have been "scrounged" by her captain from a British shipyard.

APPENDIX 9

PRINCIPAL NORTH ATLANTIC CARGO CONVOYS INBOUND TO THE BRITISH ISLES

September 1, 1942–December 31, 1944

Number of Ships Arriving and Losses to Enemy Action[1]

MONTH	HALIFAX, N.S.	SYDNEY, N.S.	FREETOWN, S.L.	CU/UT[2]	TOTALS
1942					
September[3]	182	187 (6)	77	—	446 (6)
October	157 (7)	189 (8)	84 (12)	—	430 (27)
November	152	148 (15)	42	—	342 (15)
December	168 (2)	159	—	—	327 (2)
Totals:	659 (9)	683 (29)	203 (12)		1,545 (50)
1943					
January	103 (6)[4]	151 (2)	—	—	254 (8)
February	186 (2)	121 (10)[5]	—	—	307 (12)
March	198 (19)	164 (21)[6]	—	—	362 (40)
April	247 (13)	150[7]	85 (4)	9	482 (17)
May	215 (3)	178 (2)	54 (1)	—	447 (6)
June	322	93	127	15	542
July	307	194	93	23	594
August	276	147	86	—	509
September	317	199	123	31	670
October	226	77 (2)[8]	69	25	397 (2)
November	298	63	114 (2)	20	495 (2)
December	263	124	128	56	571
Totals:	2,958 (43)	1,661 (37)	879 (7)	179 (0)[9]	5,667 (87)
1944					
January	218	52	101	65	436
February	252	29	161	45	487
March	258	94	110	94 (2)[10]	556 (2)
April	292	40 (3)	146	80	558 (3)
May	411[11]	48	126	171	756
June	418	—[12]	103	93	614
July	407	—	108	143	658
August	496	—	110	117 (1)[13]	723 (1)
September	439 (2)	—	103	134	676 (2)
October	372	72	91	125	660
November	246	110	105	137[14]	598
December	276	156	130	126	688
Totals:	4,085 (2)	601 (3)	1,394 (0)	1,330 (3)[15]	7,410 (8)
Grand Totals:	7,702 (54)	2,945 (69)	2,476 (19)	1,462 (3)	14,632 (145)[16]

1. Sources: The numbers of ships arriving in convoys are derived from British Monthly Anti-Submarine Reports, January 1942 to December 1944. The ship loss figures in those reports closely match those of Rohwer's *Axis Submarine Successes.* The Rohwer figures are used here. Note well that these figures do not include independent sailings and losses. For earlier years, see Vol. I, Plate 10 and Plate 13, pp. 424 and 698, respectively.
2. Tanker convoys (CU) sailed from the Caribbean and New York to the U.K. in 1943 and via New York in 1944. From August 1943, troop convoys (UT) for Overlord sailed from New York, sometimes merged with CU convoys. Note that tanker convoys from the Caribbean to the Mediterranean battle zone (TM, OT) are not included in this table.
3. From 9/18/42, onward, HX convoys sailed from New York. SC convoys also sailed from New York from September 1942 to April 1943.
4. Plus three 143-ton LCTs.
5. Plus one 143-ton LCT.
6. Plus two 143-ton LCTs.
7. From June 17, 1943, to the end of the war, SC convoys sailed from Halifax.
8. Includes Polish destroyer Orkan in convoy SC 143.
9. Beginning 3/23/43, CU 1, 2, 3, and 4 sailed at 14.5 knots from the Caribbean; CU 5 from New York; CU 6 from the Caribbean; CU 7, 8, and 9 from New York. Beginning on 8/21/43, UT 1 to 6 sailed at 15 knots from New York. The total, 179 vessels, includes 159 tankers and 20 troopships in UT 1 to UT 6.
10. American destroyer escort Leopold in CU 16 and American tanker Seakay in CU 17.
11. From May to September 1944, HX convoys from New York were subdivided into fast, medium, and slow.
12. Ships of SC convoys sailed in HX convoys June–September 1944.
13. American tanker Jacksonville in CU 36.
14. Eight other tankers of CU convoys sailed directly to France in November.
15. Fast tanker convoys CU 10 to CU 51 sailed about every twelve days from New York, as did the fast troop convoys UT 7 onward. Beginning on 5/3/44, CU 23, 24, 24B, 28, 33, 34 and 35 merged with UT troop convoys 12 to 18, and were temporarily redesignated TCU convoys. After July 1944, the troopship convoys resumed separate status, sailing from New York again as UT.
16. Ship losses amounted to 1 percent of total.

APPENDIX 10

ALLIED AIRCRAFT DEPLOYED IN ASW ROLES IN THE NORTH ATLANTIC AREA[1]

(BY TYPES AND SQUADRONS, SEPTEMBER–OCTOBER 1942)

In the early fall of 1942 there were about seven hundred Allied aircraft assigned to frontline antisubmarine warfare (ASW) units based around the perimeter of the North Atlantic where Allied convoys sailed. This figure does not include U.S. Army Air Forces (USAAF) and U.S. Navy (USN) units in southern Florida assigned to the Gulf Sea Frontier nor those units assigned to the Caribbean and Panama Sea Frontiers. Nor does it include about 150 USN single-engine floatplanes (OS2U, etc.) or the thirty-nine blimps assigned to the Eastern Sea Frontier (ESF). If all of these aircraft were to be included, the total would easily exceed one thousand.

The nearly seven hundred aircraft of the frontline units listed here include about 275 capable of long-range and/or very-long-range missions:

138	Catalinas/Cansos
48	Sunderlands
42	B-24 Liberators
36	B-17 Flying Fortresses
12	Halifaxes

U.S. East Coast/Bermuda[2]

VP 31	USN	12 PBY-5A Catalinas[3]	
VP 74	USN	12 PBM-1 Mariners[4]	
VP 82	USN	12 PBO-1 Hudsons[5]	
VP 92	USN	12 PBY-5A Catalinas[6]	
VP 93	USN	12 PBY-5A Catalinas[7]	
VP 94	USN	12 PBY-5A Catalinas[8]	
PZ 11	USN	8 Blimps	
PZ 12	USN	8 Blimps	
PZ 14	USN	8 Blimps	
PZ 21	USN	15 Blimps[9]	
28	USAAF[10]	B-25s	Westover, Massachusetts
7	USAAF	B-18s	Long Island, New York
11	USAAF	B-25s	Dover, Delaware
12	USAAF	B-17s	Langley, Virginia
2	USAAF	B-18s	Langley, Virginia
15	USAAF	B-34s[11]	Langley, Virginia
10	USAAF	A-29s	Cherry Point, North Carolina
14	USAAF	DB-7Bs	Jacksonville, Florida
12	USAAF	B-34s	Jacksonville, Florida

Newfoundland/Nova Scotia

5	RCAF	12 Cansos[12]
10	RCAF	12 Digbys[13]
11	RCAF	12 Hudsons

113	RCAF	12 Hudsons
116	RCAF	12 Catalinas
117	RCAF	12 Cansos
119	RCAF	12 Hudsons
145	RCAF	12 Hudsons
162	RCAF	12 Cansos
VP 84	USN	12 PBY-5A Catalinas [14]
20	USAAF	12 B-17s at Gander

Iceland

330	RAF	6 Catalinas and 6 Northrop float planes (Norwegian-manned)
269	RAF	20 Hudsons
120	RAF	6 B-24 Liberators
VP 73	USN	12 Catalinas [15]

Hebrides

58	RAF	20 Whitleys (reequipping with Halifaxes)
206	RAF	12 B-17s
228	RAF	12 Sunderlands

Northern Ireland

120	RAF	3 B-24s
201	RAF	12 Sunderlands
220	RAF	12 B-17s

Faeroes

210	RAF	12 Catalinas

Northwest Scotland

48	RAF	20 Hudsons
179	RAF	6 Wellingtons
612	RAF	8 Whitleys

Southern England

10	RAAF	12 Sunderlands
51	RAF	20 Whitleys
77	RAF	20 Whitleys
172	RAF	10 Wellingtons
304	RAF	16 Wellingtons (Polish-manned)
311	RAF	16 Wellingtons (Czech-manned)
461	RAAF	12 Sunderlands
500	RAF	20 Hudsons
502	RAF	12 Halifaxes
10 [16]	OTU	8 Whitleys

Gibraltar

179	RAF	12 Wellingtons
202	RAF	12 Catalinas
233	RAF	12 Hudsons
48	RAF	12 Hudsons

EQUIPPING IN SOUTHERN ENGLAND:

224	RAF	12 B-24s

PREPARING TO LEAVE THE U.S. FOR MOROCCO (TORCH) BUT DIVERTED TO ENGLAND:

ASW 1	USAAF	9 B-24s
ASW 2	USAAF	12 B-24s

1. Sources: War Diary, USN, ESF, September–December 1942; War Diary, USN Fleet Air Wing 7; War Diary, USN Fleet Air Wing 15; USN Administrative Histories No. 44 and No. 142; British Monthly Anti-Submarine Reports, September and October 1942; Craven and Cate, vols. 1 and 2; Douglas, vol. 2 (1986); Morison, vol. 1.
2. American ASW air units assigned to operational control of the Eastern Sea Frontier (ESF) completed training and/or reequipping with new aircraft and were held in place or transferred. Generally speaking, in September 1942, the ESF controlled about three hundred combat-ready ASW aircraft (186 Navy, 112 USAAF) and twenty-four blimps. The naval aircraft included twenty-four PBY-5A Catalinas or PBM-1 Mariners; the Army aircraft included about twenty-four B-17s and B-18s.
3. Activated 10/15/42; based in Rhode Island and North Carolina.
4. Reequipping with PBM-3C Mariners, a new but much-delayed and unsatisfactory aircraft. In spring 1943, the squadron was transferred to Brazil.
5. These Hudsons had been diverted from an allotment for the RAF. Squadron reequipped with Catalinas, then PV-1 Venturas. Returned to Argentia with Catalinas when reequipped with PV-3s, redesignated VB 125 on 11/16/42.
6. Transferred to Morocco on 11/13/42 for Torch.
7. Reequipped with PV-1 Venturas and redesignated VB 126.
8. Based in North Carolina, South Carolina, and Florida.
9. Activated 11/1/42 in Florida.
10. The designation of Army Air Forces ASW groups and squadrons changed too frequently in the fall of 1942 to identify here. Generally speaking, the ESF exercised operational control of about one dozen squadrons of USAAF Bombardment Groups 2 and 13. The locations, numbers, and types of ASW aircraft units shown remained fairly constant.
11. The B-34 was the USAAF version of the USN PV-1 Ventura, an upgraded Hudson. However, it was not a satisfactory aircraft. The USAAF also based at Langley the ASW R&D Sea-Search Attack Development Unit (SADU), comprising the 1st Attack Group, 2nd Attack Squadron, and 3rd Attack Squadron.
12. Canadian version of the USN Catalina.
13. Canadian version of the USAAF B-18.
14. At Argentia. Transferred to Iceland 10/29/42. Replaced in Newfoundland and Nova Scotia by Catalina Squadrons VP 82 and VP 93.
15. Transferred to Northern Ireland 10/29/42, thence to Morocco on 11/13/42 for Torch. Replaced in Iceland by VP 84.
16. RAF Operational Training Unit, Bomber Command, at St. Eval.

APPENDIX 11

THE LONG- AND VERY-LONG-RANGE ALLIED ASW AIRCRAFT SITUATION IN THE NORTH ATLANTIC

(BY TYPES AND SQUADRONS, MARCH 1943)[1]

Generally, historians and authors of the Battle of the Atlantic substantially understate the numbers of Allied ready or near ready long- and very-long-range ASW aircraft in the North Atlantic area. Assuming an aircraft with a combat radius of at least five hundred nautical miles to be "long range" for ASW purposes, a reliable figure is sixty-one squadrons comprised of 732 aircraft. Although many units were in transfer, working up, or otherwise in flux, the following is a reasonable snapshot of the situation for March 1943 by aircraft type, squadron, and location.

CONSOLIDATED B-24 LIBERATOR (TOTAL: 204 AIRCRAFT)

Frontline Units (5):		
120 (VLR)	RAF	Iceland
86 (VLR)	RAF	Northern Ireland
224	RAF	Southern England
1	USAAF	U.K. to Morocco 3/9/43
2	USAAF	U.K. to Morocco 3/9/43
En Route (3):		
4	USAAF	U.S.A. to Newfoundland to U.K. 6/30/43
19	USAAF	U.S.A. to Newfoundland to U.K. 7/7/43
VB 103	USN	U.S.A. to Newfoundland to U.K. 8/16/43
Equipping or Working Up (9):		
10	RCAF	Newfoundland 4/43–6/43
53	RAF	Southern England 6/43
59 (VLR)	RAF	Northern Ireland 5/1/43
6	USAAF	U.S.A. to Newfoundland to U.K. 9/43
22	USAAF	U.S.A. to Newfoundland to U.K. 9/43
VB 105	USN	U.S.A. to U.K. 9/18/43
VB 110	USN	U.S.A. to U.K. 9/21/43
VB 111	USN	U.S.A. to Morocco 11/1/43
VB 112	USN	U.S.A. to Morocco 11/17/43

BOEING B-17 FLYING FORTRESS (TOTAL: 36 AIRCRAFT)

Frontline Units (3):		
20	USAAF	Newfoundland to USA/East Coast
206	RAF	Scotland
220	RAF	Scotland

HANDLEY PAGE HALIFAX (TOTAL: 24 AIRCRAFT)

Frontline Units (2):

58	RAF	Southern England
502	RAF	Southern England

CONSOLIDATED CATALINA/CANSO AND MARTIN MARINER FLYING BOATS (TOTAL: 168 AIRCRAFT)

Frontline Units (14):

VP 31	USN	U.S.A./East Coast
VP 74	USN	Bermuda (Mariners)
VP 81	USN	U.S.A./East Coast
VP 201	USN	U.S.A./East Coast (Mariners)
5	RCAF	Newfoundland
116	RCAF	Newfoundland
117	RCAF	Newfoundland
162	RCAF	Newfoundland
VP 84	USN	Iceland
330	RAF/Norwegian	Iceland
202	RAF	Gibraltar
VP 73	USN	Port Lyautey, Morocco
VP 92	USN	Port Lyautey, Morocco

Equipping or Working Up:

VP 63	USN	U.S.A. to Newfoundland to U.K. 7/23/43

SHORT SUNDERLAND FLYING BOAT (TOTAL: 96 AIRCRAFT)

Frontline Units (8):

246	RAF	Scotland
422	RCAF	Scotland
201	RAF	Ireland
228	RAF	Ireland
423	RCAF	Ireland
119	RAF	Southern England
10	RAAF	Southern England
461	RAAF	Southern England

LOCKHEED USAAF B-34/USN PV VENTURA (SAME AIRCRAFT) (TOTAL: 96 AIRCRAFT)

Frontline Units (8):

7	USAAF	U.S.A./East Coast
11	USAAF	U.S.A./East Coast
15	USAAF	U.S.A./East Coast
16	USAAF	U.S.A./East Coast
VB 125 (ex-VP 82) USN	Newfoundland to U.S.A. 6/18/43	
VB 126 (ex-VP 93) USN	Newfoundland to U.S.A. 6/18/43	

Working Up:

VB 127	USN	U.S.A. to Morocco 9/6/43[2]
VB 128	USN	U.S.A. to Iceland 9/5/43[3]

VICKERS ARMSTRONG WELLINGTON (TOTAL: 60 AIRCRAFT)

Frontline Units (4):

304	RAF/Polish	Southern England
311	RAF/Czech	Southern England
172	RAF	Southern England
179	RAF	Gibraltar

Working Up:

407	RCAF	Southern England

NORTH AMERICAN AVIATION B-25 MITCHELL (TOTAL: 48 AIRCRAFT)

Frontline Units (4):

3	USAAF	U.S.A./East Coast
5	USAAF	U.S.A./East Coast
13	USAAF	U.S.A./East Coast
14	USAAF	U.S.A./East Coast

Totals at a glance:

B-24 Liberators	17 Squadrons	204
B-17 Flying Fortresses	3 Squadrons	36
Halifaxes	2 Squadrons	24
Catalinas/Cansos and Mariners	14 Squadrons	168
Sunderlands	8 Squadrons	96
Venturas/B-34s	8 Squadrons	96
Wellingtons	5 Squadrons	60
B-25 Mitchells	4 Squadrons	48
Totals:	61 Squadrons	732 aircraft

1. Assumes the standard twelve aircraft per squadron. Does not include Hudsons, Whitleys, B-18s, or long- or very-long-range Allied ASW squadrons in the Gulf of Mexico, Caribbean Sea, and Latin America.
2. Relieved USN Patrol Squadron VP 92 (Catalinas).
3. Relieved USN Patrol Squadron VP 84 (Catalinas).

APPENDIX 12

ATLANTIC FORCE U-BOATS THAT ABORTED PATROLS

JANUARY 1–JUNE 30, 1943[1]

The horrendous loss of U-boats sailing to the North Atlantic in the first half of 1943 (eighty-six)[2] has been documented in this volume (see Appendix 2) and in other publications. Although seldom mentioned, in this same period, eighty-three other U-boats were forced to abort patrols and return to French bases. Seven of these patrolled for fifty days or more, a normal outing for a Type VII, so patrol days lost was not a significant factor. However, the patrol days lost by the other seventy-six aborting boats was another noteworthy setback for the Atlantic U-boat force. Quite a few of these U-boats incurred heavy battle damage and were in repair for extended periods, a further loss of patrol days. Almost every abort shown here was a nerve-racking experience for the crew. In a few instances, crewmen were killed or wounded. The aborting boats were:

BOAT	TYPE	SAILED	RETURNED	DAYS OUT	CAUSE OF ABORT	RESAILED
SAILING IN DECEMBER 1942: (5)						
U-410	VIIC	12/3	1/3	32	Rescue	2/9
U-440	VIIC	12/12	1/26	46	Low fuel	2/27
U-167	IXC40	12/21	1/16	27	Skipper injured	2/27
U-404	VIIC	12/21	2/6	49	Accident	3/21
U-584	VIIC	12/30	2/21	54	Mechanical	3/23
SAILING IN JANUARY 1943: (16)						
U-218	VIID	1/7	3/10	62	Mechanical	4/20
U-414	VIIC	1/7	2/19	44	Bomb, aircraft	4/1
U-438	VIIC	1/9	2/16	39	Bomb, aircraft & destroyer	3/31
U-614	VIIC	1/9	2/26	49	Bomb, aircraft	4/12
U-752	VIIC	1/9	2/15	38	Bomb, aircraft	4/22
U-264	VIIC	1/10	3/5	55	Rescue	4/8
U-267	VIIC	1/12	2/18	38	Bomb, aircraft & destroyer	3/23
U-262	VIIC	1/16	2/15	31	Bomb, aircraft & destroyer	4/6
U-465	VIIC	1/16	2/18	34	Bomb, aircraft	4/7
U-108	IXB	1/20	2/24	36	Bomb, aircraft	4/12
U-462	XIV	1/22	1/26	5	Mechanical	2/19
U-135	VIIC	1/24	3/10	46	Low fuel	6/7
U-753	VIIC	1/28	3/10	42	Depth charge by USCG cutter	5/5
U-439	VIIC	1/29	2/2	5	Mission canceled	2/22
U-376	VIIC	1/30	3/13	43	Battle damage	4/6
U-590	VIIC	1/31	2/11	12	Mechanical	2/22
SAILING IN FEBRUARY 1943: (18)						
U-437	VIIC	2/3	3/5	31	Mechanical	4/26
U-92	VIIC	2/6	3/5	28	Not known	4/12
U-603	VIIC	2/7	3/26	48	Mechanical	5/5

BOAT	TYPE	SAILED	RETURNED	DAYS OUT	CAUSE OF ABORT	RESAILED
U-382	VIIC	2/8	3/8	29	Depth charge by escort	4/8
U-569	VIIC	2/8	3/13	34	Depth charge by escort	4/19
U-604	VIIC	2/8	3/9	30	Bomb, aircraft	4/22
U-600	VIIC	2/11	3/26	44	Mechanical	4/25
U-211	VIIC	2/13	2/25	13	Bomb, aircraft	5/13
U-709	VIIC	2/13	3/18	34	Radio out	4/15
U-664	VIIC	2/14	3/28	43	Mechanical	4/29
U-758	VIIC	2/14	3/30	45	Bomb, aircraft	5/26
U-435	VIIC	2/18	3/25	36	Mechanical	5/20
U-190	IXC40	2/20	3/30	39	Refueler	5/1
U-508	IXC	2/22	3/15	24	Bomb, aircraft	6/17
U-590	VIIC	2/22	4/12	50	Mechanical	6/8
U-757	VIIC	2/22	3/24	31	Backblast of ammo ship	7/7
U-338	VIIC	2/23	3/24	30	Bomb, aircraft	6/15
U-666	VIIC	2/25	4/10	45	Bomb, aircraft	5/6
SAILING IN MARCH 1943: (10)						
U-109	IXB	3/3	4/1	31	Mechanical	4/28
U-67	IXC	3/3	4/13	4	Bomb, aircraft	5/10
U-134	VIIC	3/6	5/2	58	Bomb, aircraft	6/10
U-572	VIIC	3/10	4/13	35	Rammed, destroyer	6/2
U-564	VIIC	3/11	4/15	36	Depth charge by aircraft	6/9
U-563	VIIC	3/21	4/18	29	Bomb, aircraft	5/29
U-270	VIIC	3/23	5/15	43	Depth charge by destroyer	6/26
U-594	VIIC	3/23	4/14	23	Bomb, aircraft	5/23
U-532	IXC40	3/25	5/15	52	Depth charge by destroyer	7/3
U-71	VIIC	3/27	5/1	36	Rammed by U-631, retired	5/31
SAILING IN APRIL 1943: (21)						
U-465	VIIC	4/7	4/14	8	Bomb, aircraft	4/29
U-382	VIIC	4/8	4/24	17	Depth charge by destroyer	6/19
U-732	VIIC	4/8	5/15	38	Depth charge by destroyer	6/10
U-231	VIIC	4/13	5/30	48	Bomb, Bogue aircraft	9/27
U-223	VIIC	4/15	5/24	40	Depth charge by destroyer	9/??
U-377	VIIC	4/15	6/7	54	Depth charge by escorts	9/9
U-386	VIIC	4/15	5/11	27	Aircraft/destroyer	6/29
U-533	IXC40	4/15	5/24	40	Rammed by corvette	7/6
U-448	VIIC	4/17	5/26	40	Mechanical	9/6
U-359	VIIC	4/19	5/20	32	Escort (U-223)	6/29
U-468	VIIC	4/19	5/29	41	Bomb, Bogue aircraft	7/7
U-218	VIID	4/20	6/2	44	Depth charge by destroyer	7/29
U-402	VIIC	4/20	5/26	37	Depth charge by corvette	9/4
U-566	VIIC	4/22	4/26	5	Bomb, aircraft	7/5
U-604	VIIC	4/22	4/26	5	Mechanical	6/24
U-952	VIIC	4/22	5/31	40	Depth charge by frigate	9/6
U-406	VIIC	4/25	5/11	17	Collision (U-600)	6/26
U-600	VIIC	4/25	5/11	17	Collision (U-406)	6/12
U-437	VIIC	4/26	4/30	5	Bomb, aircraft	9/26
U-445	VIIC	4/27	4/30	4	Rescue (U-437)	7/10
U-91	VIIC	4/29	6/7	42	Rescue (U-762)	9/21
SAILING IN MAY 1943: (11)						
U-405	VIIC	5/2	5/21	20	Bomb, aircraft	10/10
U-214	VIID	5/4	5/10	7	Bomb, aircraft	8/22
U-229	VIIC	5/11	6/7	28	Bomb, aircraft	8/31
U-305	VIIC	5/12	6/1	21	Bomb, Bogue aircraft	8/23
U-591	VIIC	5/12	5/16	5	Skipper wounded	6/26

BOAT	TYPE	SAILED	RETURNED	DAYS OUT	CAUSE OF ABORT	RESAILED
U-441	VIIC	5/22	5/26	5	Bomb, aircraft	7/8
U-450	VIIC	5/25	6/22	29	Depth charge by aircraft	10/17
U-758	VIIC	5/26	6/25	31	Bomb, Bogue aircraft	9/1
U-669	VIIC	5/27	7/14	49	Rescue (U-420)	8/29
U-271	VIIC	5/29	7/16	49	Rescue (U-420)	10/2
U-592	VIIC	5/29	7/14	47	Rescue (U-420)	10/2
SAILING IN JUNE 1943: (2)						
U-68	IXC	6/12	6/16	5	Aircraft, skipper wounded	9/8
U-338	VIIC	6/15	6/21	7	Depth charge by aircraft	8/25

Total: 83 aborts

---

1. Sources: U-boat Control War Diary (BdU KTB); Franks, *Search, Find and Kill* (1995); and others.
2. Twenty-seven U-boats sailing to other areas were lost in the same six months, including two accidents in the Baltic (U-5, U-649); see appendices 4, 5, 6, and 7. Four boats were retired for a total loss of 117 U-boats at the battlefronts from 1/1/43 to 6/30/43.

APPENDIX 13

ALLIED HEAVY-BOMBER RAIDS ON U-BOAT FACILITIES[1]

1943–1944

In January 1943, RAF Bomber Command and the newly established American Eighth Air Force commenced an intense, two-year bombing campaign against the U-boat bases in France and the U-boat building yards in Germany. As shown in the figures below, in the first three months of 1943 on about 5,000 sorties Allied bombers dropped about 12,000 tons of bombs. These aircraft leveled French seaports and damaged German cities but had no notable success against the U-boat pens and building yards. In this same three months, RAF Bomber Command in about 550 sorties also planted about 900 mines off the French bases and assisted the RAF Coastal Command offshore antisubmarine patrols in about 600 sorties. The mines probably sank one U-boat, U-526; the Bomber Command antisubmarine patrols produced no kills.

ALLIED AIR RAIDS IN 1943:

	TARGET	AGENCY	NO. AIRCRAFT	BOMBS (TONS)
JANUARY:				
3	St. Nazaire	USAAF	68	153
14–15	Lorient	RAF	101	231
15–16	Lorient	RAF	133	291
23	Brest	USAAF	19	40
23	Lorient	USAAF	35	77
23–24	Lorient	RAF	111	293
26–27	Lorient	RAF	137	203
26–27	Bordeaux	RAF	3	4
27	Wilhelmshaven	USAAF	53	118
27	Emden	USAAF	2	4.9
28–30	Lorient	RAF	81	155
30	Emden	RAF	6	9
30–31	Hamburg	RAF	99	339
FEBRUARY:				
3–4	Hamburg	RAF	142	392
4	Emden	USAAF	39	84.6
4–5	Lorient	RAF	120	213
7–8	Lorient	RAF	302	769
11–12	Wilhelmshaven	RAF	140	431
13–14	Lorient	RAF	437	1,169
16	St. Nazaire	USAAF	65	160
16–17	Lorient	RAF	363	1,003
18–19	Wilhelmshaven	RAF	185	596
19–20	Wilhelmshaven	RAF	311	761
21–22	Bremen	RAF	129	424
24–25	Wilhelmshaven	RAF	105	192

ALLIED AIR RAIDS IN 1943:

	TARGET	AGENCY	NO. AIRCRAFT	BOMBS (TONS)
27	Brest	USAAF	60	138
28	Wilhelmshaven	USAAF	65	142.7
28–Mar 1	St. Nazaire	RAF	413	1,129
MARCH:				
3–4	Hamburg	RAF	344	896
6	Lorient	USAAF	80	145.1
6	Brest	USAAF	15	39
18	Bremen (Vegesack)	USAAF	97	230.3
22	Wilhelmshaven	USAAF	84	230
22–23	St. Nazaire	RAF	284	914
28–29	St. Nazaire	RAF	297	673
APRIL:				
2	St. Nazaire	RAF	50	171.6
2	Lorient	RAF	40	118.1
4	Kiel	RAF	519	1,380.7
16	Lorient	USAAF	59	131.2
16	Brest	USAAF	19	46.4
20	Stettin	RAF	326	847.1
28	Wilhelmshaven	RAF	6	4
MAY:				
1	St. Nazaire	USAAF	29	50.9
14	Kiel	USAAF	126	236
15	Emden	USAAF	59	77.2
15	Heligoland	USAAF	76	166.1
17	Lorient	USAAF	118	258.9
17	Bordeaux	USAAF	34	76.3
19	Kiel	USAAF	101	207.1
19	Flensburg	USAAF	55	119.6
21	Wilhelmshaven	USAAF	78	172.3
21	Emden	USAAF	46	99.1
29	St. Nazaire	USAAF	147	247.3
29	La Pallice	USAAF	34	88.3
29	Rennes	USAAF	57	118.3
JUNE:				
11	Wilhelmshaven	USAAF	168	271
11	Cuxhaven	USAAF	30	67
13	Bremen	USAAF	102	226.6
13	Kiel	USAAF	44	89
28	St. Nazaire	USAAF	152	267.9
JULY:				
4	La Pallice	USAAF	71	122.8
24–25	Hamburg	RAF	740	2,296.5
24	Trondheim	USAAF	41	72.3
25	Hamburg	USAAF	68	139.3
25	Kiel	USAAF	67	149.8
26	Hamburg	USAAF	54	112.8
27–28	Hamburg	RAF	739	2,417.1
29	Kiel	USAAF	90	185.6
29–30	Hamburg	RAF	726	2,382.5

ALLIED AIR RAIDS IN 1943:

	TARGET	AGENCY	NO. AIRCRAFT	BOMBS (TONS)
AUGUST:				
2–3	Hamburg	RAF	425	1,425.9
24	Bordeaux	USAAF	58	126
SEPTEMBER:				
16	Nantes	USAAF	78	207.6
16	La Pallice	USAAF	72	160
23	Nantes	USAAF	107	275.3
27	Emden	USAAF	178	451.4
OCTOBER:				
1–2	Hagen	RAF	240	1,249.6
2	Emden	USAAF	307	851.1
8	Bremen	USAAF	274	608.5
8	Vegesack	USAAF	48	127.2
8–9	Bremen	RAF	107	298.3
9	Gdynia	USAAF	127	275
9	Danzig	USAAF	23	44.9
NOVEMBER:				
3	Wilhelmshaven	USAAF	539	1,293
13	Bremen	USAAF	114	233.9
26	Bremen	USAAF	422	1,075.8
29	Bremen	USAAF	138	366.2
DECEMBER:				
11	Emden	USAAF	523	1,256.1
13	Kiel	USAAF	349	787.3
13	Bremen	USAAF	174	408.1
13	Hamburg	USAAF	116	236.5
16	Bremen	USAAF	528	1,346.4
20	Bremen	USAAF	465	981.8
Total 1943:			15,398	40,121.3

ALLIED AIR RAIDS IN 1944:

JANUARY:				
4	Kiel	USAAF	445	879.4
5	Kiel	USAAF	215	457.2
5–6	Stettin	RAF	348	1,122.8
FEBRUARY:				
3	Wilhelmshaven	USAAF	552	1,151.3
20	Rostock	USAAF	76	155.7
24	Rostock	USAAF	255	539
25–26	Augsburg	RAF	528	1,828.3
MARCH:				
29–20	Kiel	RAF	28	35.5
APRIL:				
6–7	Hamburg	RAF	NA	NA
9	Warnemunde	USAAF	86	178.2
11	Stettin	USAAF	87	180.7
11	Rostock	USAAF	173	361.5
18	Cuxhaven	USAAF	12	20.9

ALLIED AIR RAIDS IN 1944:

	TARGET	AGENCY	NO. AIRCRAFT	BOMBS (TONS)
23–24	Mannheim	RAF	25	34.2
26–27	Hamburg	RAF	NA	NA
28–29	Hamburg	RAF	NA	NA
MAY:				
13	Stettin	USAAF	213	409.2
13	Stralsund	USAAF	56	90
19	Kiel	USAAF	49	97.4
22	Kiel	USAAF	292	562.8
JUNE:				
18	Brunsbüttel	USAAF	54	117.6
18	Hamburg	USAAF	489	1,101.3
18	Bremerhaven	USAAF	94	211.5
18	Wesermünde	USAAF	40	98.2
20	Brunsbüttel	USAAF	12	31
24	Bremen	USAAF	49	101.8
22–23	Hamburg	RAF	101[2]	140.4
24	Wesermünde	USAAF	53	113.8
JULY:				
6	Kiel	USAAF	230	588.1
18	Kiel	USAAF	106	225.8
18	Cuxhaven	USAAF	54	107.9
23–24	Kiel	RAF	612	2,916.3
NA	Bremen	RAF	36	55.1
AUGUST:				
4	Kiel	USAAF	89	225.9
4	Schlutup	USAAF	12	27.9
6	Kiel	USAAF	58	142.8
27	Heligoland	USAAF	11	24.6
27	Heligoland	USAAF	34	87.5
30	Kiel	USAAF	284	620.7
NA	Bordeaux (5)[3]	RAF	168	803.6
NA	La Pallice (8)	RAF	285	1,214.5
NA	Lorient	RAF	28	145.7
NA	Brest (2)	RAF	25	117.9
NA	Bremen	RAF	273	1,130.9
NA	Kiel	RAF	722	2,854.8
NA	Stettin	RAF	822	2,729.8
SEPTEMBER:				
NA	Bremen	RAF	76	95.7
NA	Bremerhaven	RAF	208	863.9
NA	Kiel	RAF	565	1,451.5
OCTOBER:				
6	Hamburg	USAAF	8	21
15	Heligoland	USAAF	23	70
30	Heligoland	USAAF	26	80
30	Cuxhaven	USAAF	34	81
30	Bremen	USAAF	1	3
30	Wesermünde	USAAF	20	48
NA	Bergen	RAF	183	791.9
NA	Bremen	RAF	246	998.8

ALLIED AIR RAIDS IN 1944:

	TARGET	AGENCY	NO. AIRCRAFT	BOMBS (TONS)
NOVEMBER:				
4	Hamburg	USAAF	181	436.25
21	Hamburg	USAAF	345	936
NA	Trondheim	RAF	18	2.8
DECEMBER:				
1	Hagen	RAF	465	1,817.3
19	Gdynia[4]	RAF	227	817
31	Hamburg	USAAF	72	187
Totals 1944:			10,652	31,923.65
Totals 1943–1944:			26,050	72,044.95

1. Source: U.S. Strategic Bombing Survey, NARA, RG 243, Box 47.
2. Includes April RAF raids on Hamburg.
3. Number in parentheses specifies number of separate raids that day.
4. Alternate target: Bad weather obscured the primary target in Germany.

APPENDIX 14

AMERICAN DESTROYER ESCORT (DE) PRODUCTION[1]

January 1–July 1, 1943

Designed specifically for open-ocean convoy escort, the urgently needed American destroyer escort (or DE) building program was postponed or delayed time and time again in 1942 by President Roosevelt, who assigned higher priorities to the merchant-ship and landing-craft building programs. As a result, the first two American-built DEs were not commissioned until January 20, 1943. As shown below, in the first half of 1943, January to June inclusive, fifty-five DEs were commissioned in U.S. shipyards in six different states. Of the first fifty-five ships, twenty-one were sent directly to the Pacific, five were assigned to ASW schools, and seven were transferred to the Royal Navy, leaving only twenty-two of the American DEs in the Atlantic, of which six were converted to fast transports (APDEs). By war's end, American yards had completed 565 DEs in six classes, of which seventy-eight were transferred to the Royal Navy and twelve to other navies. The preferred version was a 306-foot vessel of 1,400 tons with a top speed of twenty-one knots and sufficient fuel capacity to cross the Atlantic nonstop.[2]

NAME	HULL NO.	WHERE BUILT	COMMISSIONED	INITIAL DUTY
Baynton	1	MA	1/20*	Atlantic
Brennan	13	CA	1/20	School
Doherty	14	CA	2/6	Pacific
Austin	15	CA	2/13	Pacific
Bazely	2	MA	2/18*	Atlantic
Andres	45	PA	3/15	School
Berry	3	MA	3/15*	Atlantic
Edgar Chase	16	CA	3/20	School
Blackwood	4	MA	3/27*	Atlantic
Reuben James	153	VA	4/1	Atlantic
E. C. Daly	17	CA	4/3	Pacific
Edsall	129	TX	4/10	School
Evarts	5	MA	4/15	Atlantic
Gilmore	18	CA	4/17	Pacific
Wyffels	6	MA	4/21	Atlantic
Sims	154	VA	4/24	Atlantic (APDE)[3]
Griswold	7	MA	4/28	Pacific
Jacob Jones	130	TX	4/29	Atlantic
Buckley	51	MA	4/30	School
Burden R. Hastings	19	CA	5/1	Pacific
Decker	47	PA	5/3	Atlantic
Steele	8	MA	5/4	Pacific
Carlson	9	MA	5/10	Pacific
Levy	162	NJ	5/13	Pacific
Lehardy	20	CA	5/15	Pacific
Bebas	10	MA	5/15	Pacific

NAME	HULL NO.	WHERE BUILT	COMMISSIONED	INITIAL DUTY
Dobler	48	PA	5/17	Atlantic
Hammann	131	TX	5/17	Atlantic
Bull	52	MA	5/19*	Atlantic
Hopping	155	VA	5/21	Atlantic (APDE)
Crouter	11	MA	5/25	Pacific
McConnell	163	NJ	5/28	Pacific
Harold C. Thomas	21	MA	5/31	Pacific
Charles Lawrence	53	MA	5/31	Atlantic (APDE)
Robert E. Perry	132	TX	5/31	Atlantic
Stewart	238	TX	5/31	Atlantic
Burges	12	MA	6/2*	Atlantic
Pillsbury	133	TX	6/7	Atlantic
Reeves	156	VA	6/9	Atlantic (APDE)
Daniel T. Griffen	54	MA	6/9	Atlantic (APDE)
Donell	49	PA	6/10	Pacific
Seid	256	MA	6/11	Pacific
Wileman	22	CA	6/11	Pacific
Osterhaus	164	NJ	6/12	Pacific
Sturtevant	239	TX	6/16	Atlantic
Smartt	237	MA	6/18	Atlantic
Donaldson	55	MA	6/18*	Atlantic
Engstrom	50	PA	6/21	Pacific
Parks	165	NJ	6/23	Pacific
Pope	134	TX	6/25	Atlantic
Walter S. Brown	258	MA	6/25	Atlantic
Donnell	56	MA	6/26	Atlantic
Flaherty	135	TX	6/26	Atlantic
Charles R. Greet	23	CA	6/26	Pacific
Weber	675	MA	6/30	Atlantic (APDE)

* = Transferred to the Royal Navy on this date

---

1. Source: *Dictionary of American Naval Fighting Ships.*
2. American yards also produced a similar escort vessel based on the British River-class frigate and therefore designated "frigate" (or PF). Of the ninety-eight such vessels completed, seventy-seven were manned by the U.S. Coast Guard and twenty-one (PF 72–PF 92) were transferred to the Royal Navy in late 1943 and 1944. The Royal Navy thus received a total of ninety-nine America-built ocean-convoy escorts: seventy-eight destroyer escorts and twenty-one frigates.
3. (APDE) designates ships converted to fast troop transports.

APPENDIX 15

SPECIAL OIL AND TROOPSHIP CONVOYS FOR TORCH AND THE BRITISH ISLES

1943–1944

To supply Torch operations with oil, gasoline, and other petroleum products, in early 1943 the Allies established a special tanker-convoy system running between the Americas and North Africa. The first two of these convoys, which sailed from Trinidad in January 1943, were British: the 8.5-knot "slow" TM 1 (nine tankers), escorted by a British destroyer and three corvettes, and the twelve-knot "fast" TMF 2 (five tankers), escorted by three British destroyers. U-boats found and devastated TM 1, sinking seven of nine tankers; TMF 2 was not attacked. Thus the casualty rate in these British operations was seven of fourteen tankers, or 50 percent.

In February 1943, the U.S. Navy assumed full responsibility for these convoys, which were redesignated superfast (14.5-knot) OT (Oil for Torch). OT 1 (four tankers) and OT 2 (five tankers) sailed from Aruba on 2/5 and 2/20, respectively, each with an escort group of three American destroyers. Commencing in May 1943, when these tankers and escorts returned to Aruba, they reloaded, sailed in a "shuttle" to New York, unloaded cargoes into an "oil pool," and returned to Aruba to reload for another transatlantic voyage to Africa. Subsequently the oil in the New York pool was transshipped to the British Isles in tankers sailing on the North Atlantic run.

The OT convoys increased in size to an average of about seven tankers and sailed about once a month. In all of 1943, seventy-six fast tankers in eleven OT convoys reached Gibraltar, made the return voyage, and the round-trip shuttle to New York, with no losses inflicted by the enemy. In June 1944, the Allies terminated this system with OT 15, and thereafter these fast tankers sailed in the Middle Atlantic UGF convoys. The four OT convoys that sailed in 1944 consisted of an aggregate of thirty-six ships. Again, there were no losses. Altogether, between February 1943 and June 1944, 112 fast tankers in fifteen U.S. Navy OT convoys sailed to Gibraltar and returned without a loss.

In response to pleas from London for a great increase in oil shipments in order to rebuild shrinking stocks, to sustain the swelling strategic bombing campaign against Germany, and to prepare for Overlord, in March 1943 the Allies established a special convoy system, CU, running between Curaçao and the United Kingdom. Composed initially of twelve fast ("Greyhound") tankers per convoy, escorted by six or seven American destroyers, these special 14.5-knot oil convoys sailed about once a month for Liverpool and returned to Curaçao. Like the OT convoys, these tankers also reloaded for a shuttle run to the "oil pool" in New York and then returned to Curaçao to reload for another transatlantic voyage to Liverpool.

The first convoy of the new CU UC system, designated UC 1, left the British Isles in mid-February 1943. Composed of thirty-two westbound vessels (seventeen tankers in ballast, fifteen freighters), it was commanded by a British commodore and was escorted by a mix of nine British and American destroyers. U-boats attacked UC 1 west of the Canary Islands on February 22–23, sinking three tankers and damaging two. Thereafter the U.S. Navy assumed full responsibility for CU UC convoys. CU 1 (nine tankers) departed Curaçao on March 20 with an escort of American destroyers and reached the British Isles without any losses, as did CU 2, 3, 4, and 6. Commencing with CU 7, the intervening round-trip New York shuttle was discontinued. CU 5, 7, 8, and 9 sailed Curaçao–New York–Liverpool separately from Slow and Halifax convoys on the North Atlantic run. Altogether, nine CU UC convoys, comprised of 163 tankers, sailed from the Caribbean and New York to the British Isles in 1943 with the loss of three tankers. In 1944, forty-three CU convoys, comprised of 2,842 ships, sailed from Curaçao to New

York to Liverpool and the reverse. Two tankers and one destroyer escort (Leopold) were lost in that year.

Beginning on August 21, 1943, the Allies, building up for Overlord, inaugurated a new fast troopship-convoy system running between New York and the British Isles, designated UT. To April 6, 1944, eleven 15-knot UT convoys, comprised of a total of 271 troopships (an average eighteen ships and ten escorts each in 1943 and about twenty-five ships and thirteen escorts each in 1944) transported 592,041 troops across the ocean with no losses.[1]

As D day for Overlord, June 6, 1944, approached, the CU (oil) and UT (troop) convoys from New York were temporarily merged: CU 23 absorbed UT 12 to become TCU 23; CU 24 absorbed UT 13 to become the two-section TCU 24A and TCU 24B; CU 28 absorbed UT 14 to become TCU 28; CU 30 absorbed UT 17 to become TCU 30; CU 33 absorbed UT 19 to become TCU 33; and CU 35 absorbed UT 21 to become TCU 35. After July 1944, the merging of these convoys was terminated and each system reacquired its independence.

From April 1944 to May 1945 (V-E Day) UT and TCU convoys delivered 945,261 troops to Europe.

To recap the numbers of loaded ships and losses in these sailings, *eastbound* only:

	TM/OT	CU	UT	TOTAL
1943	90 (7)[2]	163	107	360 (7)
1944	36	1,402 (2)[3]	164	1,602 (2)
Totals:	126 (7)	1,565 (2)	271	1,962 (9)

1. This eastbound troop haul is in addition to troops transported by the superfast "monster" ocean liners such as Queen Mary and Queen Elizabeth, which sailed alone.
2. All ships in British convoy TM 1.
3. One ship each from American convoys CU and 17 and CU 36.

APPENDIX 16

THE TOP TWENTY U-BOAT SKIPPERS[1]

1939–1945

German U-boat skippers sank about 2,900 Allied ships of about 14.6 million gross tons in World War II. Twenty skippers accounted for about 20 percent of all sinkings and about 23 percent of the tonnage. In detail:

SKIPPER	SHIPS SUNK	TONNAGE	U-BOAT(S)
Otto Kretschmer	$42^1/_2$	238,327	U-23, U-99
Wolfgang Lüth	47	229,000	U-9, U-138, U-43, U-181
Günther Prien	$32^1/_3$	211,393	U-47
Viktor Schütze	36	187,279	U-25, U-103
Erich Topp	34	185,434	U-57, U-552
Herbert Schultze	28	183,432	U-48
Heinrich Lehmann-Willenbrock	25	183,223	U-5, U-96, U-256
Karl-Friedrich Merten	27	170,163	U-68
Heinrich Liebe	$31^1/_2$	171,003	U-38
Heinrich Bleichrodt	28	162,491	U-48, U-109
Georg Lassen	26	156,082	U-160
Joachim Schepke	37	155,882	U-3, U-19, U-100
Carl Emmermann	27	152,904	U-172
Ernst Kals	21	150,991	U-130
Werner Henke	$25^1/_2$	160,081	U-515
Adolf Piening	26	141,521	U-155
Robert Gysae	24	139,413	U-98, U-177
Engelbert Endrass	25	137,990	U-46, U-567
Johann Mohr	29	135,067	U-124
Klaus Scholtz	26	130,667	U-108
Totals:	$597^5/_6$	3,377,349	

1. Sources: Tarrant (1989); Rohwer, *Successes* (1983).

APPENDIX 17

THE TOP TWENTY U-BOATS[1]

1939–1945

BOAT	SKIPPER(S)	SHIPS SUNK	TONNAGE
U-48	Herbert Schultze Hans-Rudolf Rösing Heinrich Bleichrodt	54½	320,429
U-99	Otto Kretschmer	35½	238,327
U-123	Karl-Heinz Moehle Reinhard Hardegen Horst von Schroeter	41½	209,817
U-124	Georg-Wilhelm Schulz Johann Mohr	48	224,053
U-103	Viktor Schütze Werner Winter Gustav-Adolf Janssen	45	238,398
U-107	Günter Hessler Harald Gelhaus	38	212,802
U-68	Karl-Friedrich Merten Albert Lauzemis	33	198,022
U-96	Heinrich Lehmann-Willenbrock Hans-Jürgen Hellriegel	28½	185,027
U-66	Richard Zapp Friedrich Markworth Gerhard Seehausen	33	197,316
U-47	Günther Prien	32⅓	211,393
U-38	Heinrich Liebe Heinrich Schuch	32½	172,696
U-130	Ernst Kals Siegfried Keller	25	167,345
U-160	Georg Lassen	26	156,082
U-515	Werner Henke	25½	160,081
U-172	Carl Emmermann	27	152,904
U-552	Erich Topp Klaus Popp	31½	163,512
U-129	Nikolaus Clausen Hans-Ludwig Witt Richard von Harpe	29	143,792
U-155	Adolf Piening	26	141,521
U-46	Herbert Sohler Engelbert Endrass	25	140,408
U-181	Wolfgang Lüth Kurt Freiwald	27	138,779
Totals:		663+	3,772,704

1. Source: Rohwer, *Successes* (1983).

APPENDIX 18

U-BOATS SCUTTLED OR DISMANTLED AT WAR'S END (222)

NAME	TYPE	WHERE	NAME	TYPE	WHERE
8	IIB	Wilhelmshaven	446	VIIC	Kiel
14	IIB	Wilhelmshaven	474	VIIC	Kiel
17	IIB	Wilhelmshaven	475	VIIC	Kiel
29	VII	Flensburg	552	VIIC	Wilhelmshaven
30	VII	Flensburg	554	VIIC	Wilhelmshaven
37	IX	Wilhelmshaven	560	VIIC	Kiel
38	IX	Weser Estuary	612	VIIC	Warnemunde
46	VIIB	Flensburg	704	VIIC	Vegesack
48	VIIB	Neustadt	708	VIIC	Wilhelmshaven
52	VIIB	Neustadt	717	VIIC	Flensburg
56	IIC	Kiel	721	VIIC	Geltinger
57	IIC	Kiel	747	VIIC	Hamburg
58	IIC	Kiel	748	VIIC	Kiel Canal
59	IIC	Kiel	750	VIIC	Flensburg
60	IIC	Wilhelmshaven	763	VIIC	Königsberg
61	IIC	Wilhelmshaven	792	XVIIA	Kiel Canal
62	IIC	Wilhelmshaven	793	XVIIA	Kiel Canal
71	VIIC	Wilhelmshaven	794	XVIIA	Geltinger
120	IIB	Weser Estuary	795	XVIIA	Kiel
121	IIB	Weser Estuary	822	VIIC	Weser Estuary
137	IID	Wilhelmshaven	827	VIIC41	Flensburg
139	IID	Wilhelmshaven	828	VIIC	Weser Estuary
140	IID	Wilhelmshaven	876	IXD2	Eckernförde
141	IID	Wilhelmshaven	903	VIIC	Geltinger
142	IID	Wilhelmshaven	904	VIIC	Eckernförde
146	IID	Wilhelmshaven	922	VIIC	Kiel
148	IID	Wilhelmshaven	924	VIIC	Kiel
151	IID	Wilhelmshaven	929	VIIC41	Warnemunde
152	IID	Wilhelmshaven	958	VIIC	Kiel
256	VIIC	Bergen	963	VIIC	Portugal
267	VIIC	Geltinger	979	VIIC	Amrum Island
287	VIIC	Elbe Estuary	999	VIIC41	Flensburg
290	VIIC	Flensburg	1016	VIIC41	Geltinger
316	VIIC	Travemunde	1025	VIIC41	Flensburg
323	VIIC41	Nordenham	1056	VIIC	Geltinger
324	VIIC41	Bergen	1101	VIIC	Geltinger
339	VIIC	Wilhelmshaven	1132	VIIC	Flensburg
349	VIIC	Geltinger	1161	VIIC	Flensburg
351	VIIC	Hörup	1162	VIIC	Geltinger
370	VIIC	Geltinger	1168	VIIC41	Flensburg
382	VIIC	Wilhelmshaven	1170	VIIC41	Travemunde
397	VIIC	Geltinger	1192	VIIC	Kiel
428	VIIC	Kiel Canal	1193	VIIC	Geltinger

NAME	TYPE	WHERE	NAME	TYPE	WHERE
1196	VIIC	Travemunde	2539	XXI	Kiel
1201	VIIC	Hamburg	2540	XXI	Flensburg
1204	VIIC	Geltinger	2541	XXI	Geltinger
1205	VIIC	Kiel	2543	XXI	Kiel
1207	VIIC	Geltinger	2544	XXI	Aarhus
1223	IXC40	Wesermünde	2545	XXI	Kiel
1234	IXC40	Hörup	2546	XXI	Kiel
1275	VIIC41	Kiel	2548	XXI	Kiel
1277	VIIC41	Portugal	2551	XXI	Flensburg
1303	VIIC41	Flensburg	2552	XXI	Kiel
1304	VIIC41	Flensburg	3001	XXI	Weser Estuary
1306	VIIC41	Geltinger	3002	XXI	Travemunde
1308	VIIC41	Warnemunde	3004	XXI	Hamburg
1405	XVIIB	Eckernförde	3005	XXI	Weser Estuary
1406	XVIIB	Cuxhaven	3006	XXI	Wilhelmshaven
2327	XXIII	Hamburg	3009	XXI	Weser Estuary
2330	XXIII	Kiel	3010	XXI	Travemunde
2332	XXIII	Hamburg	3011	XXI	Travemunde
2333	XXIII	Geltinger	3013	XXI	Travemunde
2339	XXIII	Geltinger	3014	XXI	Neustadt
2343	XXIII	Geltinger	3015	XXI	Geltinger
2346	XXIII	Geltinger	3016	XXI	Travemunde
2347	XXIII	Geltinger	3018	XXI	Travemunde
2349	XXIII	Geltinger	3019	XXI	Travemunde
2352	XXIII	Hörup	3020	XXI	Travemunde
2355	XXIII	Laboe	3021	XXI	Travemunde
2357	XXIII	Geltinger	3022	XXI	Kiel
2358	XXIII	Geltinger	3023	XXI	Travemunde
2360	XXIII	Geltinger	3024	XXI	Neustadt
2362	XXIII	Geltinger	3025	XXI	Travemunde
2364	XXIII	Geltinger	3026	XXI	Travemunde
2366	XXIII	Geltinger	3027	XXI	Travemunde
2367	XXIII	Baltic	3028	XXI	Kiel
2368	XXIII	Geltinger	3029	XXI	Kiel
2369	XXIII	Geltinger	3030	XXI	Eckernförde
2370	XXIII	Hamburg	3031	XXI	Kiel
2371	XXIII	Hamburg	3033	XXI	Flensburg
2501	XXI	Hamburg	3034	XXI	Flensburg
2504	XXI	Hamburg	3037	XXI	Travemunde
2505	XXI	Hamburg	3038	XXI	Kiel
2507	XXI	Geltinger	3039	XXI	Kiel
2508	XXI	Kiel	3040	XXI	Kiel
2510	XXI	Travemunde	3044	XXI	Geltinger
2512	XXI	Eckernförde	3501	XXI	Weser Estuary
2517	XXI	Geltinger	3502	XXI	Hamburg
2519	XXI	Kiel	3503	XXI	Baltic
2520	XXI	Kiel	3504	XXI	Wilhelmshaven
2522	XXI	Geltinger	3506	XXI	Hamburg
2525	XXI	Geltinger	3507	XXI	Travemunde
2526	XXI	Travemunde	3509	XXI	Weser Estuary
2527	XXI	Travemunde	3510	XXI	Geltinger
2528	XXI	Travemunde	3511	XXI	Travemunde
2531	XXI	Travemunde	3513	XXI	Travemunde
2533	XXI	Travemunde	3516	XXI	Travemunde
2534	XXI	Baltic	3517	XXI	Travemunde
2535	XXI	Travemunde	3518	XXI	Kiel
2536	XXI	Travemunde	3521	XXI	Travemunde
2538	XXI	Aerø Island	3522	XXI	Travemunde

NAME	TYPE	WHERE	NAME	TYPE	WHERE
3524	XXI	Geltinger	4704	XXIII	Hörup
3525	XXI	Kiel	4705	XXIII	Kiel
3526	XXI	Geltinger	4707	XXIII	Geltinger
3527	XXI	Weser Estuary	4709	XXIII	Kiel
3528	XXI	Weser Estuary	4710	XXIII	Geltinger
3529	XXI	Geltinger	4711	XXIII	Kiel
3530	XXI	Kiel	4712	XXIII	Kiel
4701	XXIII	Hörup	UA	Turk	Kiel
4702	XXIII	Geltinger	UB	HMS *Seal*	Kiel
4703	XXIII	Geltinger	UD1	Dutch	Kiel

APPENDIX 19

U-BOATS SURRENDERED AT WAR'S END (174)

NAME	TYPE	WHERE	NAME	TYPE	WHERE
92	VIIC	Norway	516	IXC	U.K.
123	IXB	France	530	IXC40	Argentina
143	IID	Heligoland	532	IXC40	U.K.
145	IID	Heligoland	539	IXC40	Norway
149	IID	Heligoland	541	IXC40	Gibraltar
150	IID	Heligoland	555	VIIC	Hamburg
155	IXC	Wilhelmshaven	637	VIIC	Norway
170	IXC40	Norway	668	VIIC	U.K.
181	IXD2	Far East*	680	VIIC	Wilhelmshaven
190	IXC40	Canada	712	VIIC	Norway
195	IXD1	Far East*	716	VIIC	U.K.
218	VIID	Norway	720	VIIC	Wilhelmshaven
219	XB	Far East*	739	VIIC	Emden
234	XB	U.S.A.	758	VIIC	Kiel
244	VIIC	U.K.	760	VIIC	U.K.
245	VIIC	Norway	764	VIIC	U.K.
249	VIIC	U.K.	766	VIIC	France
255	VIIC	U.K.	773	VIIC	Norway
262	VIIC	Kiel	775	VIIC	Norway
278	VIIC	U.K.	776	VIIC	U.K.
281	VIIC	U.K.	778	VIIC	Norway
291	VIIC	Cuxhaven	779	VIIC	Wilhelmshaven
293	VIIC41	U.K.	802	IXC40	U.K.
294	VIIC41	U.K.	805	IXC40	U.S.A.
295	VIIC41	U.K.	806	IXC40	Aarhus
298	VIIC41	Norway	825	VIIC	U.K.
299	VIIC41	Norway	826	VIIC	U.K.
310	VIIC	Norway	858	IXC40	U.S.A.
312	VIIC	U.K.	861	IXD2	Norway
313	VIIC	U.K.	862	IXD2	Far East*
315	VIIC	Norway	868	IXC40	Norway
318	VIIC41	U.K.	873	IXD2	U.S.A.
324	VIIC41	Norway	874	IXD2	Norway
328	VIIC41	Norway	875	IXD2	Norway
363	VIIC	U.K.	883	IXD42	Wilhelmshaven
368	VIIC	Wilhelmshaven	889	IXC40	Canada
369	VIIC	Norway	901	VIIC	Norway
427	VIIC	U.K.	907	VIIC	Norway
437	VIIC	Norway	926	VIIC	Norway
481	VIIC	U.K.	928	VIIC	Norway
483	VIIC	Norway	930	VIIC	Norway
485	VIIC	Gibraltar	953	VIIC	Norway
510	IXC	France	956	VIIC	U.K.

NAME	TYPE	WHERE	NAME	TYPE	WHERE
968	VIIC	U.K.	1272	VIIC41	Norway
975	VIIC	Norway	1301	VIIC41	Norway
977	VIIC	Argentina	1305	VIIC41	U.K./USSR
978	VIIC	Norway	1307	VIIC41	Norway
985	VIIC	Norway	2321	XXIII	Norway
991	VIIC	Norway	2322	XXIII	Norway
992	VIIC	U.K.	2324	XXIII	Norway
994	VIIC	Norway	2325	XXIII	Norway
995	VIIC41	Norway[1]	2326	XXIII	U.K.
997	VIIC41	U.K.	2328	XXIII	Norway
1002	VIIC41	Norway	2329	XXIII	Norway
1004	VIIC41	Norway	2334	XXIII	Norway
1005	VIIC41	Norway	2335	XXIII	Norway
1009	VIIC41	U.K.	2336	XXIII	Kiel
1010	VIIC41	U.K.	2337	XXIII	Norway
1019	VIIC41	Norway	2341	XXIII	Cuxhaven
1022	VIIC41	Norway	2345	XXIII	Norway
1023	VIIC41	U.K.	2348	XXIII	Norway
1052	VIIC	Norway	2350	XXIII	Norway
1057	VIIC	Norway/USSR[2]	2351	XXIII	Flensburg
1058	VIIC	U.K./USSR	2353	XXIII	Norway/USSR
1061	VIIF	Norway	2354	XXIII	Norway
1064	VIIC41	Norway/USSR	2356	XXIII	Cuxhaven
1102	VIIC	Howacht	2361	XXIII	Norway
1103	VIIC	Cuxhaven	2363	XXIII	Norway
1104	VIIC	Norway	2502	XXI	Norway
1005	VIIC	U.K.	2506	XXI	Norway
1108	VIIC41	Norway	2511	XXI	Norway
1109	VIIC41	U.K.	2513	XXI	Norway
1110	VIIC41	Wilhelmshaven	2518	XXI	Norway
1163	VIIC41	Norway	2529	XXI	Norway/USSR
1165	VIIC41	U.K.	3008	XXI	Kiel
1171	VIIC41	Norway	3017	XXI	Norway
1194	VIIC	Cuxhaven	3035	XXI	Norway/USSR
1197	VIIC	Bremen	3041	XXI	Norway/USSR
1198	VIIC	Cuxhaven	3514	XXI	Norway
1202	VIIC	Norway	3515	XXI	Norway/USSR[3]
1203	VIIC	Norway	4706	XXIII	Norway
1228	IXC40	U.S.A.	UD2	X-Dutch	Kiel
1230	IXC40	Heligoland	UD3	X-Dutch	Kiel
1231	IXC40	U.K./USSR	UD4	X-Dutch	Kiel
1232	IXC40	Weser Estuary	UD5	X-Dutch	Kiel
1233	IXC40	Wilhelmshaven	U-IT24		Far East*
1271	VIIC41	Norway	U-IT25		Far East*

* When Germany surrendered, Japan commandeered these six U-boats in the Far East.

1. After postwar service in the Norwegian Navy, U-995 was returned to Germany to become a museum display ashore at the German Naval Memorial, Laboe.
2. Norway/USSR or U.K./USSR: U-boats in British control designated for transfer to the Soviet Union as war prizes.
3. In addition to the four Type XXI U-boats allocated to the USSR as war prizes, Soviet forces seized at Danzig U-3531 to U-3548 (less U-3532). The first three of these seventeen boats were 85 percent completed; the next eight boats, 65 percent completed; the last six, less than 65 percent completed.

APPENDIX 20

ALLIED AND NEUTRAL SHIPS AND TONNAGE SUNK BY GERMAN AND ITALIAN SUBMARINES IN WORLD WAR II

SEPTEMBER 1, 1942–MAY 8, 1945[1]

	1942		1943		1944		1945	
January[2]			(44)	307,196	(11)	74,816	(14)	67,410
February			(67)	362,081	(14)	66,043	(18)	75,911
March			(110)	633,731	(16)	94,721	(15)	65,901
April			(50)	287,137	(9)	62,149	(12)	65,532
May			(45)	237,182	(4)	24,423	(4)	10,722
June			(17)	76,090	(12)	57,406		
July			(46)	237,777	(14)	61,395		
August			(20)	92,443	(17)	91,454		
September	(96)	461,794	(16)	98,852	(8)	50,790		
October	(89)	583,690	(20)	91,295	(4)	1,659		
November	(126)	802,160	(9)	30,726	(5)	25,193		
December	(64)	337,618	(8)	55,794	(11)	53,268		
Totals:	(375)	2,185,262	(452)	2,510,304	(125)	663,308	(63)	284,476

Grand Total: (1,015) 5,358,874

1. Source: Tarrant (1989). Number of ships lost in parentheses; tonnage is GRT. Note: Losses include ships in convoy or sailing alone and those that fell victim to submarine-laid mines. Comparable Admiralty loss figures to Axis submarines do not include victims of submarine-laid mines.
2. For figures from September 1939 to December 1941 and January to August 1942, see Volume 1, Appendix 18, p. 771.

ACKNOWLEDGMENTS AND SOURCES

This history is based on eleven years of continuous research in archives and published works. For the German side, it relies heavily on the daily war diaries of German naval headquarters in Berlin and U-boat headquarters at various locations, and on the war diaries (or patrol reports) of individual U-boats. For the Allied side, it relies heavily on after-action reports from convoys and from warships and aircraft that tangled with U-boats, on interrogation reports of captured German and Italian submariners, and on codebreaking documents in London and Washington.

The war diaries of the various U-boat commands, amounting to thousands of pages (most translated into English) are immensely detailed. They include sailing and return dates and daily positions (known and assumed) of all U-boats on patrol, names, composition and action of groups ("wolf packs"), sightings, chases and sinkings of Allied ships, battle damage or mechanical breakdowns incurred, information regarding offensive and defensive weapons, and assessments of strategy and tactics by Karl Dönitz and others. Using these diaries and confirmed Allied ship losses to U-boats as compiled by others, a mass of newly released intelligence documents derived from the German naval Enigma decrypts, and data from other sources, including individual U-boat war diaries and interviews with captains and crewmen, it has been possible to re-create almost all significant features of the patrols of virtually all the U-boats.

Although this study is based for the most part on primary documents—war diaries, after-action reports, unit histories, and the like—I have, of course, consulted published sources. These vary quite widely in authenticity, reliability, and literary quality. Those I found of greatest merit include the official and semiofficial Allied war histories; all the writings of the esteemed German scholars Professor Jürgen Rohwer, Eberhard Rössler, Jak Mallmann Showell, and Axel Niestlé as well as the works of Günther Hessler and Karl Dönitz. Also of special notice are the works of the British authors Geoffrey P. Jones and Norman L. R. Franks, who have diligently probed official British archives to record specific U-boat kills by British and other Commonwealth air and naval forces. For equally competent and reliable research of this type, the American authors Philip K. Lundeberg, William T. Y'Blood, and Max Schoenfeld and the Canadian authors W.A.B. Douglas, Michael L. Hadley, and Marc Milner must be mentioned.

Herr Horst Bredow, director of the impressive Stiftung Traditionsarchive Unterseeboote in Cuxhaven, Germany, provided much general help as well as background and specific documents of great value. One is a list (in booklet form) of all German U-boats built in World War II. The data for each boat include type, place of construction, dates of launching and commissioning and assignment to battlefront flotilla (or schools, and so on), skippers and dates they commanded, and final fate of boat and crew. Another document is a compilation of Allied warships and merchant ships that were sunk by each U-boat, broken down by skippers of those individual U-boats. Herr Bredow also helped arrange our interviews with German U-boat veterans.

The most tedious and exacting challenge in this work was the compilation of accurate lists of Allied ships sunk by U-boats and, conversely, U-boats sunk by the Allies. Many such lists published in earlier years, including official government lists, are not accurate. In more recent times, British, German, and other scholars have vetted and published these lists and continue to vet them as new information comes to light. For ships sunk by U-boats, we have, of course, relied on the 1983 edition of Professor Rohwer's indispensable *Axis Submarine Successes 1939–1945.* Regrettably, a new (1998) edition was not available in time for us to consult, but it definitely should be used by others who study this period of history. For U-boats sunk by the Allies, we have relied on the first (1998) edition of *German U-boat Losses During World War II,* by Axel Niestlé, a work of awesome detail and accuracy and therefore also indispensable.

Many other persons assisted us in our research, and for that help we are deeply grateful. We would especially like to thank Marcia Carr; my wife's brother, Charles H. ("Ham") Rutledge; and Frederic Sherman. Marcia, the chief librarian of the Washington Island Library, obtained for us literally hundreds of books and periodicals (some of them quite obscure) through the Wisconsin Interlibrary Loan system. Ham Rutledge, a professional computer wizard, created a program to compile the indices and nursed Joan through countless PC complications and challenges. Purely as a favor, our dear friend Fred, a retired newspaper editor, read and suggested corrections on the manuscripts of both volumes before I turned them over to the publisher. His suggestions, gratefully received, significantly improved the manuscripts.

We are also deeply indebted to the noted Enigma historian Ralph Erskine, who lives in Northern Ireland. He read the pages in Volume II that pertain to Enigma and Allied bombes, correcting errors and freely sharing his vast knowledge of Enigma with us. It needs pointing out that much of this story was not declassified by NSA until the spring of 1996 and that many more thousands of documents remain to be released before historians are satisfied that the full story is available from primary documents.

Finally, we thank the many persons at Random House, Inc., who supported this work and helped see it to completion. These include, notably, our editor, the incomparable Robert D. Loomis; our production editor, Sybil Pincus; and our copy editor, Chuck Thompson.

Others who have helped us over the years in (audiotaped) interviews or by correspondence include Joachim Ahme; Debbie Anderson (née Desch); Phillip Bochichio; Horst Bredow; Gus Britton; Colin Burke; Otto von Bülow; Robert M. Coppock; Joseph J. Eachus; Alfred Eich; Wolfgang von Eickstedt; Carl Emmermann; Kristina Engstrom; Wilhelm Grap; Lucille Gutterman; Reinhard Hardegen; Hans-Georg Hess; Veronica Mackey Hulick; Walter Kaeding; Frank Kaspras; Siegfried Koitschka; Hans-Günther Lange; Georg Lassen; Robert W. Love, Jr.; Bruce I. Meader; Hans Meckel; Allan Rockwell McCann; George P. McGinnis; Timothy P. Mulligan; Jürgen Oesten; Helmut Pich; Georg von Rabenau; Alfred Radermacher; Jürgen Rohwer; Hans-Rudolf Rösing; Heinrich Schroeteler; Friedrich Schumann-Hindeberg; Herbert Sohler; Hans-Harald Speidel; Werner Techand; Louis W. Tordello; Robert H. Weeks; Otto Westphalen.

The massive research collected in the preparation of this work, including thousands of pages of documents and microfilm and microfiche, has been deposited with my papers for *Silent Victory: The U.S. Submarine War Against Japan* and other books and papers relating to my professional and personal activities at the American Heritage Center, University of Wyoming in Laramie. Serious researchers of World War II naval operations and Allied codebreaking should find this collection especially of value.

UNPUBLISHED DOCUMENTS

From the Naval Historical Center (NHC/NARA)

When I began research for *Hitler's U-boat War,* I found a rich source of primary documents at the Naval Historical Center (NHC), located at the Washington, D.C., Navy Yard. In the mid-1990s, almost all of this material was transferred to the National Archives and Records Administration (NARA) in College Park, Maryland, a suburb of Washington. Many of the documents are copied onto microfilm and duplicates are obtainable from NARA.

In our work at the Center, as in other work before, we were ably—and cheerfully—assisted by Bernard Cavalcante and Kathy Lloyd of the staff of the Operational Archives (hereafter NAVOPARCH). We owe them many thanks. We also wish to thank Dr. Timothy Francis in the Ship's History Division and the staff of the Navy Library. Unpublished documents at the Center that were especially useful:

Administrative Histories of the U.S. Navy in World War II. Rare typescripts at the Navy Library, NHC. Some histories are available on microfiche. A printed guide to the histories is also available. We consulted:

#44 Fleet Air Wings.
#138 Commander in Chief, U.S. Atlantic Fleet. 2 vols. 758 pp. Appendices.
#139 Commander Task Force Twenty-Four. Vol. 2. 208 pp. Appendices. See also the document "Task Force 24" listed below.
#141 Destroyers, Atlantic Fleet. 80 pp. Appendices.
#142 Air Force Atlantic Fleet History. 208 pp.

#146 Commander South Atlantic Force. 245 pp.
#160 Commander Caribbean Sea Frontier. 44 pp. Appendices.
#161 History of the Eastern Sea Frontier. 67 pp.
#162 Commander Gulf Sea Frontier. 337 pp. Appendices. Authorship attributed to Jack A. Reynolds.
#164 Aruba-Curaçao Command Headquarters. 57 pp. Appendices.
#165 The Guantánamo Sector. 458 pp. Appendices.
#166 The Trinidad Sector. 195 pp. Appendices. Authorship attributed to Robert F. Millett and Kenneth S. Wales.
#168 Naval Operating Base, Iceland. 107 pp.

Assmann, Kurt. "Headline Diary." 228 pp. In English. GNR Boxes T-64 and T-78. (Microreels T-10, T-11, T-54.)

Assmann, Kurt, and Walter Gladisch. "Aspects of the German Naval War." Essay. 29 pp. In English. GNR Boxes T-64 and T-81.

"Blockade Running Between Japan and Germany." 8/27/45. Essay. 34 pp. GNR Box T-78. (Microreel T-23.)

Boehm, Hermann. "The War at Sea." Essay. 11 pp. In English. GNR Box T-66. (Microreel T-47.)

Clark, William Bell. "Submarines in the Western Hemisphere 1942 and 1943." 3 vols. (Scrapbooks of newspaper clippings re U-boat campaign.) Unique. Navy Library, NHC.

Daily Position Reports of Allied Warships, Merchant-Ship Convoys, and Axis Submarines. (On large Atlantic maps.) Chief of Naval operations: World War II Command File.

Dönitz, Karl. "Capitulation Address." 5 pp. In English. GNR Box T-66.

———. "The Conduct of the War at Sea." 34 pp. Essay. In English. 1/15/46. GNR Box T-66. (Microreel 1985.)

———. Documents about or relating to. From German records and other sources. Includes his official fitness reports (in German), a secret USN interrogation of him on 8/16/45, and a copy of the USSBS interrogation of him on 6/28/45 (see NARA documents). GNR Box T-87 TR-50. (Microreel T-50.)

———. "Talk to the Officers' Corps." [Circa 5/8/45.] In English. GNR Box T-66.

Dossiers of Some German U-boat Officers. (Microreel T-51.)

1. Wilhelm Canaris
2. Karl Dönitz
3. Hans-Georg von Friedeburg
4. Werner Hartmann
5. Fritz-Julius Lemp
6. Heinrich Liebe
7. Karl-Heinz Moehle
8. Günther Prien
9. Erich Raeder
10. Joachim Schepke
11. Viktor Schütze

Freiwald, Kurt. [C.O. *U-181*.] "U-boat Activity in the Indian Ocean." 1/13/50. Essay. 16 pp. In English. GNR Box T-66. (Microreels T-27 and T-47.)

Fuerbringer, Wagner. "The *U-47*'s Scapa Flow Undertaking." 4/3/48. Essay. 6 pp. In English. GNR Box T-66. (Microreel T-47.)

German Arctic Operations. Twenty essays based on data provided by German naval officers who fought in the Arctic. GNR Box T-94. (Microreel T-48, Misc. Series 118-A to 118-U.) See especially:

118-M U-boat War versus USSR shipping, 23 pp.
118-O U-boat mine laying, 6 pp.
118-S U-boat Ops, technical, 13 pp.

German Arctic Operations. The Arctic sea route of the German auxiliary cruiser *Komet,* 8/14/40 to 9/5/40. Admiralty Report 12/4/45. GNR Box T-80.

German Midget Submarines: *Marder, Biber, Molch, Hecht, Seehund.* GNR Box T-95.

German Minesweeping and Estimated Shipping Losses to Allied Mines. Two reports by USN Historical Team, 1950. 43 pp. GNR Box T-93.

German Naval Air 1933–1945. Historical essay, based on German Naval Staff documents. Office of Naval Intelligence, 1/15/47. 37 pp. (Microreel T-48, Misc. Series, Item 4.)

German Naval Policy in Face of the Air Menace from the West (Summary). Report of British Bomber Survey Unit, 9/7/45. 85 pp. GNR Box T-79.

German Submarine Type XXI. Method of production. Admiralty Report of January 1945. (Based on about 5,000 documents captured at the Hermann Göring Werke, Strassburg.) 27 pp. GNR Box T-79.

German Submarine Type XXI. Report from USN Portsmouth Naval Shipyard, March 1946. (Technical evaluation.) Submarines/Undersea Warfare Division. Series 3, File 3, Box 9. (Microreel NRS 517.)

German Technical Aid to Japan: A Survey by the Division of Naval Intelligence. 6/15/45. GNR Box T-95.

"German U-boats from Which Prisoners Were Taken During Hostilities by British and American Forces." 15 pp. N.d. (Postwar.) Lists showing U-boat, type, date, skipper, Allied agency responsible for the destruction, and numbers of officers and enlisted men captured per boat. GNR Box T-76.

Godt, Eberhard. "Critical Review" of an essay, *"Die Unterseebootswaffe im Dritien Weltkrieg"* ["The Submarine Arm in World War II"], by Karl-Heinz Moehle. 11/27/50. 20 pp. In English. GNR Box T-67.

———. "The War At Sea." Essay. 17 pp. November 3, 1945. GNR Box T-64. (Microreel 1985.)

Handbook for U-boat Commanders, 1942 edition. 117 pp. In English. (Microreel T-50, Item TR 41.) See similar item by E. J. Coates, listed in Books section.

Heye, Hellmuth. "The Naval Aspects of the War." Essay. 33 pp. In English. GNR Box T-66. (Microreel NRS 1985.)

———. Operation of German Small Battle Units (KdK). (Midget Submarines.) 5/22/45. 8 pp. GNR Box T-100.

Holtorf, Erich, and Alfred Behr. "Defensive Measures Against Enemy Type XXI and Walter Type XXVI U-boats." 2/14/51. 14 pp. In English. GNR Box T-68.

———. "Fighting Enemy Submarines with Three-Dimensional Torpedoes." 33 pp. In English. GNR Box T-69.

———. "German Torpedo Fire-Control Systems in WW II." 5/22/51. Essay. 17 pp. In English. GNR Box T-69. (Microreel NRS T-47.)

———. "LUT Torpedo Firing Method from Depth." 2/26/51. Essay. 18 pp. In English. GNR Box T-69.

Interrogation of U-boat Survivors, 1942–1944 (American "post mortems"): History, sinking and technical details of some U-boats destroyed by American forces, based on information from POW survivors. Most of these are extensive reports running to scores of pages and in a few cases, many more. Except in the five instances noted, these documents are also on microfilm (NRS 1979-107 and NRS 1980-28). An NRS number in parentheses designates additional information on other microfilm from the American forces that made the kill.

No. 1. U-85 (NRS 1973-98)
No. 2. U-352 (NRS 1973-106)
No. 3. U-701 (NRS 1973-110)
No. 4. U-210
No. 5. U-94
No. 6. U-162
No. 7. U-595
No. 8. U-164
No. 9. U-512
No. 10. U-606
No. 11. U-203 (NRS 1973-105)
No. 12. U-569
No. 13. U-128 (NRS 1973-99)
No. 14. U-521 (NRS 1973-107)
No. 15. U-118
No. 16. U-67
No. 17. U-598
No. 18. U-513

No. 19. U-527
No. 20. U-487 (not micro)
No. 21. U-615 (not micro)
No. 22. U-199
No. 23. U-591 (not micro)
No. 24. U-409 (not micro)
No. 25. U-662 (not micro)
No. 26. U-185 and U-604
No. 27. U-664
No. 28. U-848 and U-841
No. 29. U-172 (NRS 40)
No. 30. U-231
No. 31. U-761
No. 32. U-575
No. 33. U-801
No. 34. U-177 and U-195
No. 35. U-856 (NRS 1983-34)
No. 36. U-515 and U-68 (NRS 1980-64)
No. 37. U-1059
No. 38. U-66 (NRS 281)
No. 39. U-860
No. 40. U-371 and U-410 (NRS 1976-30)
No. 41. U-616 (NRS 1972-101)
No. 42. U-490
No. 43. U-453
No. 44. U-960
No. 45. U-233
No. 46. U-1229

Note: Rough drafts and duplicates of the above and in some cases added documents and photos may also be found in NARA, Record Groups 38, 80, and 165. See below.

In addition, documents relating to the following U-boats, which surrendered after hostilities, may be found in the Command File:

U-234
U-805
U-1228
U-1230

Documents regarding the sinking or surrender of the following U-boats by or to American forces are on microfilm:

NRS 153	U-858	NRS 1973-102	U-175
NRS 202 and 1974-35	U-505	NRS 1973-103	U-176
NRS 321	U-405	NRS 1973-104	U-182
NRS 328	U-550	NRS 1973-108	U-548
NRS 1973-100	U-157	NRS 1979-109	U-857
NRS 1973-109	U-576	NRS 1977-69	U-853
NRS 1973-101	U-166		

Kennedy, Joseph P., Jr. Papers relating to the Navy career and wartime death of. (Microreel NRS 1974-74.)

King, Ernest J. Papers of. Series XI, Box 13. Folder: "Review of Marshall, Arnold and King correspondence re ASW, 1942–1943."

Knowles, Kenneth A., H.Q. USN, and K. E. Donegar, H.Q. British Admiralty. "German U-boat Fleet in World War II: Final Disposition." (Sunk, scuttled, etc.) 9/1/45. 144 pp. GNR Box T-97. (Microreel NRS T-48, Misc. Series Item 155.)

Leuthen, Group. Attack on convoy ON 202 ("*Zaunkönig* convoy"). September 1943. Narrative, translated from German with a Dönitz comment. 13 pp. GNR Misc. Series, Box T-95.

Location of U.S. Naval Forces. Chief of Naval Operations: World War Two Command File. (A daily listing of the location and readiness of all warships and patrol bombers.)

Lockwood, C[harles] A. Jr. (Naval Attaché, London.) "Translation of Operation Order of 5/20/41 captured from German tanker *Gedania.*" 14 pp. GNR Box T-96.

Low, Francis S. "A Personal Narrative of Association with Fleet Admiral Ernest J. King, U.S. Navy." 49 pp. 1961. (Microreel NRS 1975-61.)

Lüth, Wolfgang. "Problems of Leadership in a Submarine." Or, alternatively, "On Being a U-boat Captain." 15 pp. GNR Boxes T-69 and T-84. (Microreel NRS 1973-110.)

Lüdden, Siegfried. Document re Far East U-boat operations he prepared at sea 5/6/44. Captured by French Resistance forces. Forwarded to ONI 11/9/44. 14 pp. In English. GNR Box T-76. (Microreel NRS T-23.)

Mejer, Otto, and H. Reinecke. "Cooperation of U-boats and *Luftwaffe* in Attacks on Convoys." 8 pp. In English. GNR Box T-69. (Microreel NRS T-47.)

Merker, Otto. USN interview with, re German shipbuilding, with emphasis on Types XXI and XXIII U-boats. (Microreel NRS T-25.)

Metcalf, Martin K. See Tenth Fleet.

Moehle, Karl-Heinz. "Report on, with Reference to Orders Alleged to Have Been Given to the 5th U-Boat Flotilla." Box T-77. (Laconia order interpretation.)

Mommsen, Hans-Günther. USN interview with, re labor and materials for German shipbuilding. (Microreel NRS T-25.)

Peters, Rudolph. (FdU U-boats, Arctic 1942.) "Submarine War in the Arctic Ocean." 55 pp. In English. GNR Boxes T-69 and T-92. (Microreel NRS T-30.)

"Q-Ships, Reports and Documents Concerning Operations in World War II." *(Atik, Asterion, Eagle, Big Horn, Irene Forsyte.)* World War Two Command File. See also ESF War Diary, Oct. 1943, ch. 2. Approx. 190 pp. (Microreels NRS 478 and NRS 1975-94.) See also War Diary, ESF, etc.

Raeder, Erich. Memo to Admiral [Kurt] Assmann re Hitler's decision to mount Barbarossa, the invasion of the USSR. 1/10/44. GNR Box T-80.

Rösing, Hans-Rudolf. USN interview with, re U-boat logistics and French Bases. (Microreels NRS T-22 and NRS T-25.)

Ruge, Friedrich, et al. "The Soviet Union as Opponents at Sea." The naval war between Germany and the Soviet Union, 1941–1945, as experienced and analyzed by the Germans. GNR Box T-70. (Microreel NRS T-33.) Also published in book format by USNI: See Ruge.

Schill, Group. Attack on convoy MKS 28/SL 138, October 1943. Narrative, translated from German with a Dönitz comment. 13 pp. GNR Misc. Series, Box T-95.

Schlicke, Heinz. "Electronic Research in the German Navy." Transcripts of ten lectures given to the U.S.N. 7/19/45 to 7/31/45. In English. GNR Box T-73. (Microreel NRS T-40.)

Schrader, Albert E. "War Diary, Naval Attaché, Berlin 9/1/39 to 3/24/41." (Microreel NRS 542.)

Schuessler, Captain. "The [German] Navy's Battle Against the Treaty of Versailles, 1919–1935." Essay. 53 pp. In English; pp. 26–34 re submarines. GNR Boxes T-73 and T-84. (Microreels NRS T-34 and NRS 1985.)

Schuster, Captain, and Otto Schniewind. "The War at Sea." 76 pp. GNR Box T-73. (Microreel NRS 1985.)

Stark, Harold R. Private papers and letters of, from London to SecNav, Cominch et al., re antisubmarine warfare, 1942–1945. About 200 pp. (Microreel NRS 235.)

Talbot, Melvin F. (USN observer at the Nuremberg Trials.) "The Case Against Grand Admiral Doentiz." 7/12/46. Typescript. 51 pps. GNR Box T-105.

Task Force 24, History of. (January–December 1941.) 150 pp. World War Two Command File. (Microreel NRS II-453.) See also USN Administrative Histories.

Tenth Fleet. "Assessment Committee: ASW by 'Incident' Number in World War II." (A chronological index to documents re 9,328 "incidents" or Allied attacks on U-boats.) (Microreel NRS 167.)

———. "Assessment Committee: Reports on Damage to Enemy Submarines, 6/4/42–1/7/46." Rpts nos. 1 to 72. World War Two Command File, Box 260.

———. Convoy and Routing. Extracts of miscellaneous documents from the files: RCAF weekly ASW intelligence summaries, 3/21/43–6/14/44. Letter, Noble to King, enclosing minutes and addenda of the 21st meeting of War Cabinet Anti–U-boat Committee, 6/23/43. Atlantic Convoy Conference, February and March 1943: Minutes, subcommittee reports, etc. Documents and messages re convoy policy and operations 7/25/42–12/3/43. (Microreel NRS 1969-57.)

———. "History of the Anti-Submarine Measures." World War Two Command File. 67 pp. Plus 18-page "Chronology." (Microreel NRS II-457.)

———. "History of Convoy and Routing." World War Two Command File. 145 pp. By Martin K. Metcalf. 1949. (Microreel NRS 1971-36.)

U-Boat Standing Orders. 143 pp. In English. GNR Boxes T-91 and T-92.

United States, German, Italian, and Japanese Submarine Losses in World War II. Edition of 1963. (Microreel NRS 1976-107.) See also listing at Naval History Division in Books section.

United States Navy. *Anti-Submarine Bulletin.* ("Yellow Peril," so-called because the cover is yellow.) A monthly publication, June 1943 to May 1945, and a 44-page "Summary." World War Two Command File, Boxes 259 and 260. "Summary" only on microfilm. (NRS 1973-4.) A once highly classified account of the Battle of the Atlantic, containing technical details about Allied and Axis weaponry, statistical charts of shipping losses, etc. An invaluable source similar to the British Monthly Anti-Submarine Report. (See Public Record Office.)

War Diary, Eastern Sea Frontier. December 1941 to September 1943. World War Two War Diary Collection. (7 Microreels, NRS 1971-48.) Index, 12/41 to 12/44. (Microreel NRS 1988-23.)

War Diary, Fleet Air Wing 7. World War II. (Microreel NRS 1971-102.)

War Diary, Fleet Air Wing 15. World War II. (Microreel NRS 1974-54.)

War Diary and History, U.S.N. Parol Squadron VP 83 (in May 1943, redesignated VB 107), 9/15/41–10/1/45. Prepared by Boyce S. McCoy.

War Diary (*Kriegstagebuch* or KTB) of the Commander in Chief, Submarines (*Des Führers/Befehlshabers der Unterseeboote,* or FdU/BdU). In English. GNR Boxes T-40 to T-44. (5 Microreels, KTB, nos. 1–5.) Also available in German on microfilm at NARA: See Mulligan guide.

The KTB of BdU stops at 1/15/45. However, as Mulligan points out on p. 2 of his guide, reports of U-boat operations from 1/15/45 to 4/21/45 may be found elsewhere (in German) on microreels 3900 and 1755-1759, 1995. Also, there is a missing section, 10/16/43 to 10/31/43, in the BdU/KTB. The original is held by the *Bundes-Abt. Militärchiv* in Freiburg, Germany, item RM 87/32. This missing section can also be partly recovered by consulting the U-boat summaries in the SKL War Dairy (see below) for that period.

War Diary (KTB) FdU U-boats Italy/Mediterranean (*Italien/Mittelmeer*) 12/8/41 to 12/31/43. In English. GNR Boxes T-45 to T-48. Also available in German on microfilm at NARA: See Mulligan guide.

War Diary (KTB) FdU U-boats Italy/Mediterranean (*Italien/Mittelmeer*) 7/15/42 to 12/31/42 (period preceding and following Torch). In English. NARA, RG 457, NSA Historical Collection, NR 3547, Box 110.

War Diary (KTB) FdU U-boats Italy/Mediterranean (*Italien/Mittelmeer*) 1/16/44 to 9/7/44. Rough translation into English. GNR Box T-60. Also available in German on microfilm at NARA: See Mulligan guide.

War Diary (KTB) FdU Norway *(Norwegen)* 1/18/43 to 10/15/44. In English. GNR Boxes T-49 to T-53. Also available in German on microfilm at NARA; See Mulligan guide.

War Diary (KTB) Naval Group Command, West. 6/1/44 to 6/30/44. (Period of the Normandy Invasion.) 124 pp. In English. GNR Box T-82 TR-5. (Microreel NRS T-7.)

War Diary (KTB) of the Operations Division (*der Seekriegsleitung,* or SKL) Part A Naval H.Q., Berlin 1939–1945. Boxes T-1 to T-39 In English, but with significant gaps. (16 Microreels, TM 100A to TM 100P.) Also available in German on microfilm at NARA: See Mulligan guide.

———. Extracts 11/5/42–11/12/42 re U-boat Ops in Mediterranean vs. Torch, 30 pp. In English (filling a gap). GNR Box T-82 TR-1.

———. Extracts of Appendix, "Supplement to the Submarine Situation": 10/1/42 to 12/31/42 re U-boat Ops in South Atlantic versus Torch 11/8/42 to 11/16/42. In English. 5 pp. GNR Box T-92.

War Diaries (KTBs) of U-boats. Extracts in English:

BOAT	DATE	COMMENT	MICROREEL	FILE NO.
U-28	9/14/39	vs. *Vancouver City*	T-23	
U-31	9/24/39	vs. *Hazelside*	T-23	
U-47	10/8/39–10/21/39	In Scapa Flow	T-50	Item TR 18
U-37	5/27/40	vs. *Sheaf Mead*	T-23	
U-100	11/27/40–1/1/41	Lorient-Kiel	T-50	Item TR 19
U-110	3/9/41–3/29/41	Kiel-Lorient	T-50	Item TR 19
U-142	7/25/41–8/31/41	E. Baltic	T-48	MS Item 15
U-652	9/4/41–9/5/41	vs. *USS Greer*	T-48	MS Item 149
U-106	10/29/41–10/31/41	vs. *USS Salinas*	T-48	MS Item 146
U-552	10/31/41–11/1/41	vs. *USS Reuben James*	T-48	MS Item 148
U-701	12/27/41–4/1/42	Drumbeat plus	T-50	Item TR 22

U-132	1/29/42	vs. *USCG Hamilton*	T-48	MS Item 147
U-355	8/25/42–3/6/43	Arctic	T-50	Item TR 20
U-172	10/5/42–10/9/42	Cape Town	T-48	MS Item 90
U-68	10/5/42–10/8/42	Cape Town	T-48	MS Item 88
U-380	11/4/42–11/14/42	vs. Torch	T-48	MS Item 89
U-205	11/7/42–11/11/42	vs. Torch	T-48	MS Item 89
U-458	11/8/42–11/15/42	vs. Torch	T-48	MS Item 89
U-605	11/9/42	vs. Torch	T-48	MS Item 89
U-331	11/9/42	vs. Torch	T-48	MS Item 89
U-561	11/10/42–11/12/42	vs. Torch	T-48	MS Item 89
U-431	11/10/42–11/14/42	vs. Torch	T-48	MS Item 89
U-77	11/10/42–11/11/42	vs. Torch	T-48	MS Item 89
U-73	11/10/42–11/14/42	vs. Torch	T-48	MS Item 89
U-593	11/11/42–11/13/42	vs. Torch	T-48	MS Item 89
U-407	11/11/42	vs. Torch	T-48	MS Item 89
U-595	11/12/42–11/14/42	vs. Torch	T-48	MS Item 89
U-18	6/16/43–7/22/43	Black Sea	T-48	MS Item 155
U-505	12/25/43–6/4/44	2 patrols	NRS 1974-35	
U-763	7/5/44–7/9/44	vs. Overlord	T-48	MS Item 91
U-745	8/1/44–10/20/44	E. Baltic	T-48	MS Item 16
U-312	12/24/44–12/29/44	Scapa Flow try	T-48	MS Item 91
U-2326	5/4/45–5/12/45	Patrol	T-48	MS Item 14

In addition, there are brief extracts or summaries from U-boat war diaries, in English, that are not on microfilm:

BOAT	DATE	COMMENT	GNR BOX
U-26	9/16/39	1st patrol	T-81
U-30	9/16/39	1st patrol	T-81
U-31	9/16/39	1st patrol	T-81
U-34	9/16/39	1st patrol	T-81
U-35	9/16/39	1st patrol	T-81
U-28	11/17/39	vs. *Sliedrecht*	T-82
U-48	9/17/40	vs. *City of Benares*	T-78
U-147	12/11/40–5/15/41	Patrols	T-81
U-44	1/16/40	vs. *Panachandros*	T-82
U-106	1/17/41	vs. *Zealandic*	T-78
U-94	1/20/41	vs. *Florian*	T-81
U-96	4/17/41	vs. *Almeda Star*	T-82
U-123	5/19/41–6/5/42	Patrols	T-81
U-69	7/3/41	vs. *R. L. Holt*	T-81
U-74	11/7/41	vs. *Nottingham*	T-78
U-213	5/14/42	Lands agent	T-78
U-68	6/15/42	vs. *Frimaire*	T-81
U-201	7/6/42	vs. *Avila Star*	T-78
U-172	10/10/42	vs. *Orcades*	T-78
U-178	10/10/42	vs. *Duchess of Atholl*	T-78
U-615	10/23/42	vs. *Empire Star*	T-78
U-604	10/30/42	vs. *President Doumer*	T-78
U-752	11/17/42	vs. liner	T-78
U-172	11/23/42	vs. *Benlomond*	T-78
U-515	12/6/42	vs. *Ceramic*	T-78
U-456	2/23/43	vs. *Kyleclare*	T-81
U-129	4/2/43	vs. *Melbourne Star*	T-78
U-129	5/6/44	vs. *Anadyr*	T-82

Wehr, Oskar, Konteradmiral. Proceedings of the court-martial of him and others for German torpedo failures. 5/27/41. About 250 pp. In German. (Microreel NRS T-26.)

Weichold, Eberhard. "Axis Naval Policy in the Mediterranean, 1939–1943." 130 pp. In English. GNR Box T-76.

———. "German Naval Defense [in 1944] Against the Allied Invasion." 195 pp. In English. GNR Box T-74. (Microreel NRS T-32.)

———. "Survey from Naval Point of View of the Organization of the GAF for Ops over the Sea 1939–1945." In English. GNR Box T-75. (Microreel NRS T-41.)

———. "War at Sea in the Mediterranean." 2/26/47. Essay. 80 pp. In English. GNR Box T-75. (Microreel NRS T-47.)

Whitehead, Thor. "Iceland and the Struggle for the North Atlantic 1940–1941." MA thesis, University of Georgia, 1972. (Microreel NRS 516.)

Worthington, Joseph M. "A Biography of [Commander-in-Chief, Atlantic Fleet] Admiral Royal E. Ingersoll, U.S. Navy." 2 vols. Typescript. 1,009 pp. (2 microreels, NRS 1971-129.) Contains copies of numerous official dispatches re Atlantic Fleet Ops and convoying (etc.) from King to Ingersoll and vice versa and between King and others.

Also at the National Archives and Records Administration (NARA)

Apart from the foregoing, there are literally tens of thousands of primary documents and microfilms of primary documents at the National Archives and Records Administration (NARA) that deal with the U-boat campaigns of World War II. These include, significantly, microfilms of the entire German naval archives, captured at Castle Tambach (near Coburg) by Allied ground forces in April 1945 and removed to England and microfilmed.

The documents relating to the U-boat war at NARA are filed in various categories known as record groups. Because of the vast sizes of these groups, a researcher must be rigidly selective and focus narrowly on those documents that are obviously of exceptional value. In our many visits to NARA, two able officials guided us in our searches and helped arrange the copying of thousands of pages and numerous microreels of documents: John E. Taylor, archivist, and Dr. Timothy P. Mulligan, a specialist in captured German and related records.

Among the captured German records at NARA, those of particular value are the war diaries (*Kriegstagebuchs* or KTBs) of the three major U-boat commands (Atlantic, Mediterranean, Norwegian) and of 889 individual U-boats. The bulk of these records, known as Microfilm Publication T 1022, was reproduced in 1945–47 by the U.S. Navy Office of Naval Intelligence on 147 rolls of microfilm. These microreels (in German) may be purchased singly for a modest fee. Dr. Mulligan has produced an invaluable guide to these microreels (and instructions for ordering same) that can be obtained at NARA (see Mulligan in Books section). As related, the KTBs of the Atlantic U-boat command (as well as that of SKL, Berlin) are available in English on paper and microfilm. The KTBs of the Norwegian and Mediterranean U-boat commands are available in English on paper (but not microfilm).

The KTBs of the U-boats that survived and returned to base are especially valuable. They include a day-by-day account of the patrol, attacks on enemy shipping, Allied counterattacks, unusual events, meetings at sea with other U-boats, and verbatim official radio messages to and from the boat. A detailed "shooting report" for each torpedo expended is usually appended to the patrol report. The last voyages of many U-boats that failed to return have been summarized (and hypothesized) by U-boat Control based on orders and radio messages, sinking reports, interception of Allied ASW reports, and so on.

Note: Some of the following listed record groups at NARA, which we searched, contain copies of declassified Admiralty documents emanating from the Naval Intelligence Division (NID) that London passed to Washington during the war years.

RECORD GROUP 38 (OFFICE OF THE CHIEF OF NAVAL OPERATIONS)

Apart from the material transferred from NHC:

Chart Room Files.

Various boxes. These chronological files contain copies of the entire wartime operational communications of the Commander in Chief (COMINCH) Ernest J. King, both incoming and outgoing. Of particular interest, of course, are the messages pertaining to U-boat operations, convoy composition, convoy routing, convoy escorts, and other aspects of the Battle of the Atlantic. Seldom cited by naval historians, these documents are of unsurpassed value for insights into American, British, and Canadian thinking about the U-boat war, specific policies adopted, steps taken, and warship movements.

We limited our search of these documents to the periods 1/1/42 to about 6/1/42, when Drumbeat, the German U-boat campaign in the Americas, was in progress, and 2/1/43 to 4/1/43, when the Atlantic Convoy Conference convened. Naval historians who have castigated Admiral King for his alleged indifference to German U-boat depredations in American waters will be surprised at the wealth of information in these files that supports a contrary case.

OFFICE OF NAVAL INTELLIGENCE (ONI)

NAVAL ATTACHÉ REPORTS 1944–47: BOXES 1 TO 16 AND 214, 327, 469.

These documents, especially those from USN officers in London (COMNAVEU and COMTWELFTHFLEET), contain a great deal of technical and operational information about U-boats and ASW derived from British sources, including British interrogations of U-boat POWs. Of exceptional interest:

Box 3: British summaries of information on U-boats, 1944–45.

Translation of a German handbook for the tactical use of the German Naval Acoustic Torpedo (GNAT or T-5 Wren), 10/5/44.

Minutes of the "GNAT Panel" meeting of 10/17/44.

Box 4: Radar detection of the Schnorkel.

Box 5: British investigation of the characteristics of the German Naval Acoustic Torpedo (GNAT), 1/16/45.

U-boat Flotillas and Personnel per February 1944. (A total of 365 U-boats assigned by number and skipper names.)

Box 6: Further British investigation of German Naval Acoustic Torpedo (GNAT), 2/17/45.

Box 7: Minutes of the British Aircraft Anti-U-boat Committee, 2/8/45, 3/20/45, and 4/5/45.

Box 15: "Estimate of Russian Exploitation of German Submarine Types" (XXI, XXIII, Walter boats, etc.), 4/19/48.

Box 16: Summary Report of Type XXI and other U-boats.

Box 327: First Interrogation Report of Personnel of the German 29th U-boat Flotilla, Toulon, France, 11/13/44. 12 pp. Information and some operational history of the following:

U-230	U-562
U-343	U-565
U-410	U-586
U-421	U-642
U-455	U-952
U-466	U-967
U-471	U-969

Box 469: Summary of information on German U-boats (less torpedo data). Extraordinarily thorough 37-page document (or "handbook") prepared by E.G.N. Rushbrooke, Director of Naval Intelligence, Admiralty, 11/29/43.

Handbook for the operations of the Type XXI U-boat. 42 pp. In English, 7/10/44.

Report on the capture in Toulon, France, of prefabricated sections and machinery sufficient to assemble two Type XXIII U-boats, 2/2/45.

Subject File, 1942–1945, OP16Z (from Algiers to British N.I.D./1 PW.) British Final Reports. Box 2.

History, sinking, and technical details of thirty-six U-boats destroyed by British forces, based on information obtained from POW survivors—the final British "post mortems." U-boats covered in this series:

U-223	U-413	U-681	U-1003
U-243	U-425	U-715	U-1006
U-269	U-448	U-736	U-1018
U-270	U-450	U-741	U-1024
U-300	U-473	U-765	U-1063
U-385	U-550	U-767	U-1195
U-390	U-608	U-852	U-1199
U-399	U-671	U-877	U-1206
U-407	U-672	U-971	U-1209

Note: Duplicates of some of these documents may be found in RG 80 and RG 165 (see Mulligan guide) and at PRO (see below).

Subject File, 1942–1945, OP16Z (BAD Correspondence 1943–1944). Report re German code "Ireland" in POW mail, 10/12/43. Box 2. 2 pp.

Subject File, 1942–1945 OP16Z (Naval Messages to PW Special, 1945). Box 13.

Memo on the code used in correspondence by German U-boat prisoners of war in World War II. 1. Plus appendix of sample correspondence, 7/27/45.

In addition, boxes 214, 327, and 469 contain information about:

U-300
U-575
U-732

Special Activities Branch, OP16Z. Interrogation Reports (final and rough).

1. History and technical details of forty-six U-boats destroyed by American forces and one *(U-168)* by Dutch forces, based on information from POW survivors. In most cases the final reports duplicate the American "post mortems" listed above (noted

below in parenthesis) but in many cases the roughs contain interesting additional information and photos. (See also Record Groups 59, 80, and 165.) The destroyed U-boats dealt with in this category are:

U-66 (PM 38)	U-203 (PM 11)	U-515 (PM 36)	U-616 (PM 41)
U-67 (PM 16)	U-210 (PM 4)	U-521 (PM 14)	U-662 (PM 23)
U-85 (PM 1)	U-231 (PM 30)	U-527 (PM 19)	U-664 (PM 27)
U-118 (PM 15)	U-233 (PM 45)	U-546	U-761 (PM 31)
U-128 (PM 13)	U-352 (PM 2)	U-569 (PM 12)	U-801 (PM 33)
U-162 (PM 6)	U-371 (PM 40)	U-575 (PM 32)	U-841 (PM 28)
U-164 (PM 8)	U-409 (PM 24)	U-591 (PM 23)	U-848 (PM 28)
U-168	U-453 (PM 43)	U-595 (PM 7)	U-960 (PM 44)
U-172 (PM 29)	U-487 (PM 20)	U-598 (PM 17)	U-1059 (PM 37)
U-177 (PM 34)	U-490 (PM 42)	U-604 (PM 26)	U-1229 (PM 46)
U-185 (PM 26)	U-512 (PM 9)	U-606 (PM 10)	
U-199 (PM 22)	U-513 (PM 18)	U-615 (PM 21)	

2. History and/or technical details of ten U-boats that surrendered to American (US), Canadian (C), or Argentine (A) authorities after cessation of hostilities:

U-190 (C)	U-873 (US)
U-234 (US)	U-889 (C)
U-530 (A)	U-977 (A)
U-805 (US)	U-1228 (US)
U-858 (US)	U-1230 (US)

RECORD GROUP 59 (U.S. DEPARTMENT OF STATE CENTRAL DECIMAL FILES)

Items 862.30/7-1045 through 8-2145 and 862.30/8-445 through 8-2145 contain information about two U-boats that surrendered in 1945 in Argentina. These were:

U-530
U-977

RECORD GROUP 80 (GENERAL RECORDS, SECRETARY OF THE NAVY)

Box 2334. "Official German Naval Reaction to the Subordination of the German Navy to the Supreme Command of the Armed Forces." Historical essay based on interrogations of Grand Admiral Karl Dönitz, VAdm. Otto Schniewind, VAdm. von der Borne, and Otto Mejer. 17 pp. N.d. (Postwar.)

Various boxes in this record group contain some information on U-boats. These boxes have been identified as such: 665, 666, 1679, 1829, 1830. U-boats covered:

U-66	U-183	U-223	U-371	U-523
U-118	U-231	U-300	U-490	U-515

RECORD GROUP 165 (WAR DEPARTMENT GENERAL STAFF)

Records of the G-2 (Intelligence) Division (MIS-Y). Boxes 364, 441 to 571, 599 to 621, 640, 645, 669, 712, 724 to 735, 745, and 746. Records and documents re U-boats, ships, and naval material based on interrogation of or eavesdropping on German POWs. (Some of these reports duplicate or supplement previously described American or British "post mortems.") U-boats and Italian submarines covered:

U-66	U-223	U-464	U-593	U-805	Archimede
U-67	U-231	U-487	U-595	U-841	Calvi
U-68	U-233	U-490	U-598	U-848	Cabolto
U-73	U-234	U-512	U-604	U-852	Millo
U-94	U-331	U-513	U-606	U-856	

U-118	U-335	U-515	U-607	U-858
U-128	U-352	U-517	U-615	U-860
U-162	U-353	U-521	U-616	U-873
U-164	U-357	U-527	U-636	U-877
U-172	U-371	U-530	U-660	U-960
U-177	U-379	U-532	U-662	U-977
U-185	U-407	U-546	U-664	U-1059
U-195	U-409	U-559	U-681	U-1163
U-199	U-451	U-569	U-701	U-1209
U-203	U-453	U-575	U-761	U-1229
U-210	U-461	U-591	U-801	U-2326

In addition, the following boxes contain documents of unusual interest:

724: Bound Volume, tabbed.

Tab A: An Appreciation of the Air Effort Against Submarines [U-boats] prepared by U.S.A.A.F. Eighth Air Force January 1943. 25 pp.
Tab B: U.S.A.A.F. Anti-Submarine Command Monthly Summary, January 1943. 36 pp. Technical and attack data, history of the command and Track Charts of convoys SC 104 and SC 107, etc.

"Schnorchel": report on by USN OP16Z. 2/15/45. 28 pp.

727: POW Interrogations 5G-55NA #643 from *U-118* 8/23/43. 11 pp. Description of Enigma machine (*Schluessel* "M") and operating instructions; description of U-boat's Array Sonar (Type G.H.G. with 48 sensors); description of U-boat radio equipment and antennae.

745: Digests of U-boat [Technical] Information from German POW Sources. Digest 1 (12/4/43) to Digest 59 (6/25/45). About 200 pp.

746: Intelligence Report of 1/21/46 re why it was a mistake to transfer all naval armament production to Speer's ministry in June 1943. Based on interview with Hans Günter Mommsen (chief, Naval Matériels).

RECORD GROUP 218 (U.S. JOINT CHIEFS OF STAFF)

Joint New Weapons Committee Subject File: May 1942–1945. Boxes 1 and 18.

Box 1: Correspondence re ASW between Dr. Vannevar Bush, director of the Office of Scientific Research and Development (or his surrogates) and the JCS. 1/4/43 to 3/5/43.

Box 18: Draft manuscript: "Trends in Submarine Warfare." Typescript. 42 pp. N.d. (circa July 1942). An American summary of ASW weaponry of the past, present, and immediate future and recommendations for lines of R&D to pursue.

Report: "Carriers for ASW Equipment." 14 pp. 7/18/42. A summary of USN ships and aircraft capable of ASW and the weaponry they carry, together with an analysis of U-boat characteristics and operations.

RECORD GROUP 238 (WORLD WAR II CRIMES)

This group contains the official documents of the War Crimes Trials at Nuremburg. We confined our research to two boxes, 25 and 75.

Box 25: "Jackson Files" (main office files of the U.S. chief prosecutor, Robert H. Jackson). Interrogation summaries and analysis: Defendants Dönitz through Ribbentrop. See Dönitz.

Box 75: "Defense Document Books": Bormann, Dönitz, Franks. See Dönitz documents, Folders #1 and #2.

RECORD GROUP 243 (UNITED STATES STRATEGIC BOMBING SURVEY, OR USSBS)

Final Reports 92 to 100, with support documents. Boxes 47, 49, and 50.

Box 47: Final Report 92. "German Submarine Industry." 108 pp.

Exhibit M-1, M-2, and M-3: Allied aircraft attacks on U-boat yards at Hamburg, Bremen, and Kiel.

Box 49: Final Report 92all. Bombing of Submarine Base, Brest, France. 10 pp.

Box 50: Final Report 92a17. Interviews of German submarine builders. See transcripts of four such interviews:

Karl Dönitz on 6/28/45.
Eberhard Godt on 7/15/45.
Otto Merker (chief, naval shipbuilding) on 6/20/45.
H. Günter Mommsen, (naval matériels) on 6/28/45.

Minutes of the [German] Central Planning Committee for 5/4/43 (Dönitz presentation re U-boat war and supply lines) and 12/21/45 (Speer presentation re electric motor production) and brief excerpts from other meetings. Excerpts of speeches by Speer re "electro" U-boats on 8/3/44 and 1/13/45.

RECORD GROUP 457

This collection contains all the documents relating to the Allied penetration of German naval Enigma that have been released to the public by the National Security Agency (NSA) through 1998. The documents include not only translated Enigma decrypts but also technical and historical studies of the U-boat war based on the decrypts, the daily exchanges of U-boat information between the USN, RCN, and RN Submarine Tracking Rooms, daily and weekly summaries of U-boat activities, and the like.

We used two separate and indispensable guides to these documents: a general guide prepared by the Modern Military Branch at NARA (36 pages, n.d.) and a meticulous computerized guide cataloged and indexed by U-boat subject matter, prepared by Irwin G. Newman, a declassification consultant and archivist for the U.S. Naval Cryptologic Veterans Association (64 pages, dated 9/11/92).

Documents of this group that were exceptionally helpful:

DOCUMENT	SHORT TITLE
SRH 003	Influence of U.S. Cryptologic Organizations on the Digital Computer Industry, Samuel S. Snyder. 38 pp.
SRH 008, SRH 009, SRH 024, SRH 025	History of Communications Intelligence in the Battle of the Atlantic. 4 vols. 720 pp. (See also microreel NRS 78.)
SRH 019	Axis submarine blockade running, 1942–44. 33 pp.
SRH 020	Narrative Combat Intelligence Center Joint Intelligence Center Pacific Ocean Area, 8 November 1945. 20 pp.
SRH 037	Reports Received by U.S. War Dept. on the Use of Ultra in European Theater, World War II. October 1945. 33 pp.
SRH 149	Brief History of Communications Intelligence in the U.S. 22 pp.

SRH 152	History Review of OP20G. 13 pp.
SRH 197	Organization, Liaison, and Coordination of USN Communications Intelligence, 1941–45. 39 pp.
SRH 201	Admonitions to U-boats, 1943–45. 208 pp.
SRH 208, SRH 236	ASW Reports, C in C to Admiralty and vice versa, 1942–45. 495 pp. and 2,869 pp.
SRH 232	U.S. Navy C in C Radio Intelligence Appreciation Concerning German U-boat Activity in the Far East, January–April 1945. 9 pp.
SRH 260	OP20G File of Memoranda, Reports, and Messages on German Blockade-Runners (World War II), 1943–44. 238 pp. (Extracts.)
SRH 279	Communications Intelligence Organization, 1942–46. 82 pp.
SRH 305	History of Communications Intelligence in the "undeclared war." 29 pp. (See Safford article.)
SRH 306	Exploits and Commendations of OP20G in World War II. 151 pp.
SRH 355	Naval Security Group History to World War II, by Capt. J. S. Holtwick, Jr. June 1971. 464 pp.
SRH 367, SRH 368	Evaluations of the role of Communications Intelligence in the Battle of the Atlantic. 90 pp. and 111 pp.
SRH 403	Wenger Papers. 78 pp.
SRMN 022	USN log of Allied attacks reported by damaged U-boats, 11/6/42 to 12/30/43. 311 pp.
SRMN 023	USN log of U-boat attacks on Allied shipping, as reported by U-boats, 11/4/42 to 5/10/45. 578 pp.
SRMN 030	U-boat trends, 9/1/42 to 5/1/45. 120 pp.
SRMN 031	U-boat position estimates, 6/10/42 to 11/6/42. 152 pp.
SRMN 032	U-boat tracking room ops, 1/2/43 to 6/6/45. 281 pp.
SRMN 035	Admiralty–C in C Ultra message exchange, 6/25/42 to 10/17/44. 104 pp.
SRMN 036	U-boat situation estimates, 6/15/42 to 5/21/45. 185 pp.
SRMN 037	U-boat Intelligence summaries, 1/1/43 to 5/16/45. 655 pp.
SRMN 038	Functions of the "Secret Room." 10 pp.
SRMN 040	U-boat fleet at end of World War II. 52 pp.
SRMN 041	Liquidation of U-boats, 1942–45. 245 pp.
SRMN 043	U-boats and Overlord. 28 pp.
SRMN 046	The U-boat problem, 6/4/42 to 5/16/45. 103 pp.
SRMN 048	U-boat positions and status, 12/42 to 5/45. 191 pp.
SRMN 049	"Secret Room" assessments of attacks on U-boats, July 1943 to July 1944. 236 pp.
SRMN 051, SRMN 051A	OP20G memos on U-boat activities, 12/42 to 5/45. 540 pp. and 214 pp.
SRMN 053	U-boats east of Cape Town, 7/44 to 5/45. 75 pp.
SRMN 054	Special [Technical] Studies re U-boats. 866 pp.
SRMN 055	Forecasts and statistics re U-boat activities, 1/26/44 to 7/11/44. 47 pp.
SRMN 056	U-boat successes against Allied ships, 1/41 to 4/45. 74 pp.

In addition, some researchers may profit by consulting NARA Entry 9010 of this series: "German Navy/U-boat Messages Translations and Summaries: 1941 to 1945." This massive document series in 67 boxes is 29 feet long and consists of 49,668 Enigma messages to U-boats, translated into English and filed chronologically, 1/2/41–7/9/45.

In 1996 the NSA turned over to NARA about 1.3 million more documents relating to the breaking of World War II Axis codes. These documents, also in Record Group 457, are cataloged in a list of 4,923 very briefly described items. Of particular interest to this book is item NR 1736, "Bombe History." This is an excellent 11-page single-spaced document describing the history of building the American four-rotor bombes for breaking naval Enigma, prepared 4/24/44 by Howard T. Engstrom, Ralph I. Meader, and Joseph N. Wenger, the three men who ran the project. (RG 457, Box 705.)

The catalog of the 4,923 listed items is available at NARA. The catalog (over two hundred pages) can also be downloaded from NARA's home page on the Internet.

At the Library of Congress: Manuscript Division

The papers of Ernest Joseph King. Fifteen linear feet, about 10,000 items.

1. General Correspondence, 1908–57. Containers 1–18. See especially boxes 8, 9, 12, 14.
2. Subject File, 1924–57. Containers 19–26. See especially boxes 21 (General Board) and 22 (Anti-Submarine 1942–1944 and Memoranda for SecNav).
3. Escort-of-Convoy Instructions (Revised 11/17/41). U.S. Atlantic Fleet. 11 pp. (LANTFLT 9A).

Miscellaneous papers (in German) relating to the following U-boats (containers 161–72; microreels 78–86):

U-148	U-480	U-552	U-858	U-977
U-172	U-505	U-585	U-873	U-1058
U-234	U-530	U-805	U-967	U-1064

At the British Public Record Office

Records of the Royal Navy and of British codebreakers in World War II are kept in the British Public Record Office (PRO) in Kew, a suburb of London. There are finding aids available for these records, which are computerized. Numerous records relating to this history have been microfilmed.

We limited our research mostly to those documents that deal with U-boat operations, U-boat sinkings, and information on U-boats gained from interrogation of German U-boat POWs. Most of the Enigma codebreaking documents ("Ultra") relating to U-boats are filed under the broad category ADM 223. Most of the pertinent naval documents are filed under categories ADM 1, ADM 199, and ADM 237. The minutes of the weekly meetings of the Battle of the Atlantic and Anti-U-boat committees plus important addenda are filed in ADM 205 (see also War Cabinet file CAB 86). Official internal Admiralty monographs and histories (BR series) relating to U-boats are filed in ADM 186 and ADM 234. The documents at PRO that we consulted for this book:

PAPERS OF THE FIRST SEA LORD (ADM 205)

205/11 Minutes of the Battle of the Atlantic Committee, 4/18/41 to 7/26/41.

205/21 Special Studies:

Interim progress report re ASW by naval adviser to First Sea Lord (C. V. Usborne), 1/20/42.

Japanese naval purchases from Germany (per NID), 2/26/42.

Visit of G. R. Bromet and George E. Creasy to the U.S. and Canada to assess ASW. Reports of 2/24/42.

Control of shipping in the West Atlantic during U-boat campaign. Part 1: Institution of Convoy System. Part 2: Routing of British-managed shipping. 6/14/42.

Criticism of Allied ASW by Air Officer Commander in Chief, Coastal Command (Philip Joubert) as of September 1942 and partial responses to the criticism by the First Sea Lord's ASW advisers at a meeting, 9/27/42.

205/23 Minutes of the Battle of the Atlantic Committee, 9/2/41 to 6/30/42.

205/27 Correspondence with Prime Minister [Churchill], 1943.

205/30 Minutes of the [War Cabinet] Anti U-boat Committee and Summary of Achievements, 12/3/42 to 12/23/43.

205/35 Correspondence with Prime Minister [Churchill], 1944.

205/36 Minutes of the [War Cabinet] Anti U-boat Committee 1944.

205/44 Minutes of the [War Cabinet] Anti U-boat Committee 1945.

205/59 Prisoners of War (German).

ADMIRALTY CENTER FOR SCIENTIFIC INFORMATION (ADM 213)

213/573 German submarine construction: "History of Walter Submarine Projects," including postwar interviews with the commanders of the Walter Type XVIIB *U-1406* (Werner Klug) and *U-1407* (Horst Heitz).

213/574 Correspondence between Karl Dönitz and Helmut Walter re new U-boat designs and equipment. In English.

German Submarine Construction: "History of the Type XXI."

STATION RECORDS: WESTERN APPROACHES (ADM 217)

Convoy narratives and U-boat sinkings. U-boat kills reported. See below.

NAVAL INTELLIGENCE PAPERS (ADM 223)

223/8 Special Studies:

Percentage of losses imposed on German U-boats, 8/13/43.

Enemy appreciation of Allied ASW aircraft, 8/24/43.

U-boats in the Indian Ocean, 9/5/43.

Rate of expenditure of U-boats, 10/9/43.

223/15 Ultra. Weekly U-boat situation reports, 12/20/41 to 6/28/43. 216 pp.

223/16 Ultra. U-boat appreciations and stories of convoy battles, 12/41 to 11/43. 136 pp. Convoys detailed:

SC 118	HX 229	ON 166	HG 76	SL 138/MKS 28
SC 122	HX 231	ON 167	TM 1	OS 57/KMS 31
SC 143		ON 202	UC 1	MKS 29
		ONS 5		SL 139/MKS 30
		ONS 18		

Special Studies:

Estimated number of U-boats at sea September 1939–February 1943, 2/19/43.

Admiralty appreciation of U-boat situation, 8/1/43.

U-boats in Caribbean and South America, summer 1943, 8/30/43.

Fuel consumption of U-boats, 9/22/43.

U-boat campaign in Cape area and Indian Ocean, summer 1943, 8/10/43.

223/18 Ultra. Weekly U-boat situation reports and miscellaneous Signal Intelligence, 7/5/43 to 12/27/43. 113 pp. (On microreel.)

223/19 Ultra. U-boat appreciations and stories of convoy battles, 9/43 to 3/44. 97 pp. Convoys detailed:

JW 56A	RA 57
JW 56B	ONS 29
JW 57	ON 224

Special Studies:

U-boat operations off South Africa: March–July 1943, 10/24/43.

Resumption of U-boat operations against convoys, 9/20/43.

Claims by U-boats in 1943: Analysis by Naval Section, Bletchley Park (J.H.C. Whitehead). Report of 2/22/44.

Experience of U-boat skippers now on operations. 3/2/44.

U-boat campaign in the Indian Ocean: September–December 1943. Report of 3/18/44.

U-boat war: 1/12/44 to 3/12/44. Report of 3/14/44.

223/21 Ultra. Weekly U-boat situation reports, 10/16/44 to 5/21/45.

223/42 Godt address to U-boat commanders. 6/14/45. 2 pp.

223/88 Special Study: Admiralty use of Special Intelligence in Battle of [the] Atlantic. 7 pp. N.d. (1945?)

Admiralty Use of Special Intelligence in Naval Operations, by G[eoffrey] E. Colpoys, Officer in Charge, Operations Intelligence Center. 379 pp.

223/96 Ultra. Weekly U-boat situation reports, 10/26/42 to 1/25/43.

223/98 Ultra. Weekly U-boat situation reports, 5/31/43 to 9/13/43.

223/152 *U-570,* capture of and technical surveys.

223/170 Ultra. Weekly U-boat situation reports 9/20/43 to 12/13/43.

223/171 Ultra. Weekly U-boat situation reports, 12/20/43 to 3/20/44.

Special Study: The achievements of individual U-boats in 1943. Naval Section (J.H.C. Whitehead), Bletchley Park, 3/21/44.

223/172 Ultra. Weekly U-boat situation reports, 3/20/44 to 10/9/44 and convoy battles in April and August 1944:

JW 58
JW 59

Special Studies:

Note on U-boats in the Mediterranean, 4/18/44.

Experience of U-boat skippers now on operations, 5/8/44.

Movement of U-boats into the English Channel, 5/19/44.

Minutes of meeting re publicity on U-boat kills, 7/10/44.

Experience of U-boat skippers now on operations, 7/12/44.

U-boats sunk or lost, September 1939 to September 1944. Rodger Winn analysis of 10/1/44.

223/220 Booklet, *The Battle of the Atlantic* (September 1939–December 1943), 25 pp.

ATTACKS ON U-BOATS, ASSESSMENTS, INTERROGATION OF POWS, ETC.

Filed in: ADM l: Admiralty and Secretariat Papers.
ADM 199: War History Cases and Papers.
ADM 217: Station Records: See above.

The following U-boats are described in documents as noted in ADM 1 and ADM 199. (Attacks, sinkings, captures, etc.)

U-16	199/128, 199/133, 199/206
U-21	1/17588, 1/16848
U-23	1/16848
U-26	199/131
U-27	199/126
U-31	199/121
U-32	199/121
U-33	199/123
U-34	1/17590
U-35	199/128
U-39	199/126
U-40	199/133
U-46	199/127
U-47	199/127, 199/141, 199/1122
U-63	199/122
U-70	199/1122
U-71	199/1128
U-73	199/1259
U-75	199/1134
U-76	199/1227
U-79	199/1334
U-86	199/505
U-91	1/17561
U-93	199/1255
U-94	199/1245, 199/1247, 199/1254
U-95	199/1134
U-99	199/1127
U-100	199/1127
U-104	199/121
U-110	(Captured) 199/1123, 1/11133
U-131	199/1133
U-162	199/1247
U-175	199/2020, 199/1419
U-187	199/1409, 1/14304
U-194	199/1413
U-202	199/1491, 199/2020
U-203	199/1411
U-205	199/432, 1/14342
U-210	199/267
U-216	199/1253
U-233	199/1491, 199/2023, 1/15794
U-242	199/139
U-243	199/139
U-243	199/520
U-245	199/504
U-249	1/17665
U-252	199/1252
U-270	199/522
U-279	199/1415
U-286	199/139
U-307	199/139, 1/17649
U-333	199/1245, 199/1254, 1/17561
U-334	199/1413
U-340	199/2025
U-341	199/1413
U-353	199/1267
U-378	199/505
U-379	199/1267
U-383	199/1419
U-387	199/503
U-385	199/522
U-400	199/503
U-404	199/1245
U-407	199/500
U-409	217/7
U-413	199/498
U-417	199/1413
U-419	199/1415
U-432	1/16277
U-433	199/1134, 199/1135
U-434	199/1133
U-443	199/432
U-444	1/16277
U-450	1/15796
U-451	199/1133
U-454	199/1420
U-457	199/1251
U-458	1/14532, 1/14581
U-459	199/1491, 199/1419
U-461	199/1419
U-462	199/1491, 199/1419
U-464	199/1247, 199/1251
U-473	1/17556
U-482	1/17668
U-489	199/1413
U-501	199/1129
U-506	199/1491
U-530	199/808
U-540	199/1415
U-546	1/17649
U-551	199/1127
U-556	199/1128
U-558	199/1491
U-559	199/1259, 1/14256
U-568	1/12278
U-570	(Captured) 199/1129, 1/11275, 1/11826
U-581	199/1255
U-607	199/1491
U-608	199/139
U-637	199/139
U-643	199/1415, 199/2023, 1/14780
U-651	199/1128
U-655	199/1246, 199/1250
U-660	199/719
U-662	1/17561
U-678	217/90
U-706	199/1491, 199/1419
U-715	199/519
U-732	199/2025
U-736	217/88
U-741	199/1498
U-744	199/1491, 199/2029, 217/95, 217/108
U-752	199/1412
U-765	1/17556
U-844	199/1415
U-852	199/518, 199/1458
U-870	1/17561
U-971	1/15791
U-977	199/908
U-979	199/139, 199/524
U-1006	199/501
U-1023	1/17340
U-1024	1/17666, 1/17649

U-1056	1/17274	U-1407	1/17561	U-3017	1/18949
U-1209	199/503	U-2008	1/17561	U-3519	1/18765
U-1232	1/17561	U-2326	199/1139, 1/17661	U-3528	1/18765
U-1405	1/17561	U-2336	199/139		
U-1406	1/17561	U-3008	1/17561		

Italian Submarines:

Asteria	199/432	Durbo	199/135
Avorio	199/432	Glauco	199/1132
Baracca	199/1132	Gondar	199/135
Berillo	199/1132	Lafole	199/135
Bianchi	199/1132	Naiade	199/135
Cabolto	199/1259	Ondina	199/1258
Caracciolo	199/1134	Perla (captured)	199/1258
DiBruno	199/131	Veniero	199/1258

Some of the foregoing document series also include special ASW studies. See for example:

199/1245 The air offensive against U-boats (ORS Report 174A). July 1941–December 1941. Dated 7/10/42. Italian U-boats, Intelligence Report 11/21/42.

199/124–915 Attempt to capture U-boats—orders for operation. Dated 6/5/40.

199/1491 Summary of [ASW] operations in the Bay [of Biscay]. 6/14/43 to 9/21/43.

199/2032–2056 U-boat "incidents." Daily log of Allied ships sunk; U-boats sighted, attacked, or sunk; POWs taken, etc. (See similar document at NARA, listed under Tenth Fleet.)

1/17561 Postwar interviews of U-boat POWs conducted by Gilbert Howland Roberts, commander of the RN "Anti–U-boat School":

Eberhard Godt, 5/23/45
Günther Hessler, 5/24/45
Kurt Dobratz, 5/24/45
Ernst Hechler, 5/24/45
Lieutenant Burkner, 5/24/45
Waldemar Mehl, 5/25/45
Heinz Walkering, 5/27/45
Peter Cremer, 5/29/45

1/17617 Summary of [U-boat] information supplied by Eberhard Godt on 5/12/45. 49 pp., plus addenda, which includes a German list of 635 U-boat losses, acknowledged to be incomplete.

199/135 Reports of C in C, Mediterranean Station, re Allied attacks on Axis submarines in the Mediterranean. Dated 11/5/40, 3/13/41, 4/5/41, 8/9/41, and 3/22/42.

199/139 Currents and tides in the Straits [sic] of Gibraltar. Essay by A. L. Maidens. 8 pp. "Measures taken to prevent U-boats from penetrating territorial waters and entering the Mediterranean." Report of C in C, Mediterranean Station. 19 pp.

MONTHLY ANTI-SUBMARINE REPORT SEPTEMBER 1939–DECEMBER 1945 6 VOLS. 2,284 PP. (ON MICROFILM.)

A once highly classified account of the Battle of the Atlantic in a series of monthly booklets. Produced by the Admiralty intelligence division, the issues contain detailed narratives of convoy battles, U-boat kills, descriptions of Allied and Axis weaponry, statistical charts of shipping losses and damage by type and nationality, new ship construction by types, as well as information from interrogations of POWs, and so on. Although the primary focus is on naval actions, the contributions of RAF Coastal Command to ASW operations are not slighted. The issues contain no reference to codebreaking; nonetheless, they remain indispensable to historians of the U-boat war. Of special interest are the narrative accounts of U-boat kills and convoy battles, as noted below.

ADM 199/2057 VOL. 1 (9/39 TO 12/40), 331 PP.

U-BOATS:

U-13	U-39	Durbo
U-26	U-40	Galileo Galilei (captured)
U-27	U-42	Gondar
U-31	U-49	Liuzzi
U-33	U-55	Luigi Galvante
U-35	U-63	

CONVOYS:

HX 55	SC 2	OA 204
HX 66A	SC 6	OB 202
HX 79		
HX 83		

ADM 199/2058 VOL. 2 (1/41 TO 12/41), 446 PP.

U-BOATS:

U-32	U-111	Adua
U-70	U-138	Anfitrite
U-76	U-501	Baracca
U-95	U-566	Ferraris
U-99	U-570	Glauco
U-100	U-651	Naiade
U-110		

CONVOYS:

SC 3	HX 90	SL 73	HG 53	OB 251	OS 10
SC 19	HX 121	SL 81	HG 64	OB 290	
SC 26	HX 133	SL 87	HG 75	OB 318	
SC 42		SL 89	OG 47	OB 336	
SC 57					

ADM 199/2059 VOL. 3 (1/42 TO 12/42), 475 PP.

U-BOATS:

U-85	U-379	Cobolto
U-94	U-433	Emo
U-95	U-434	Ondina
U-131	U-464	Peria (captured)
U-162	U-568	Pietro Calvi
U-210	U-574	
U-335	U-581	
U-353	U-701	
U-372		

CONVOYS:

SC 67	ON 55	SL 98	HG 76	OS 12	HX 217
SC 94	ON 59	SL 109	HG 84	OS 28	PQ 10

SC 104	ON 122	SL 118	MKF 1(Y)
SC 107	ON 138		

ADM 199/2060 Vol. 4 (1/43 to 12/43), 393 pp.

U-BOATS:

U-118	U-432	U-523
U-135	U-439	U-528
U-175	U-444	U-533
U-185	U-454	U-559
U-187	U-458	U-604
U-202	U-468	U-606
U-203	U-487	U-607
U-205	U-506	U-659
U-224	U-512	U-660
U-331	U-513	U-706
U-357	U-517	U-732
U-409	U-521	U-752

CONVOYS:

SC 118	HX 228	ON 144	ONS 18	KMS 10
SC 121	HX 229	ON 202	ONS 20	TM 1
SC 122	HX 263	ON 206		OS 44
SC 130		ON 207		XK 2
SC 143		ON 208		SL 126
				SL 138/MKS 28

ADM 199/2061 Vol. 5 (1/44 to 12/44), 415 pp.

U-BOATS:

U-177	U-407	U-744
U-188	U-536	U-761
U-223	U-539	U-852 (photos)
U-247	U-616	U-960
U-340		

CONVOYS:

SL 139/MKS 30	RA 57	JW 62
SL 140/MKS 31	JW 56A	JW 59
	JW 56B	RA 62
	RA 59	HXS 300

ADM 199/2062 Vol. 6 (1/45 to 12/45), 224 pp.

U-BOATS:

U-300	U-681 (Photos)	U-1024

CONVOYS:

HX 332	TBC 135
HX 346	

This volume also contains a number of essays summarizing certain aspects of the U-boat war. See especially "The Radio War," "Statistical Summary of the War on British, Allied and Neutral Merchant Shipping," "Scientific History of Anti-Submarine Weapon Development," and "Final Assessments." The last booklet in this volume contains a 14-page document based on 1945 interviews with Karl Dönitz, who outlines in detail the "phases" of the U-boat war as he saw them.

British "post mortems" (Special File)

At the Admiralty Office of History: Five oversize, bound volumes:

U-boats

1939:	1940:	1941:	1942:	1943:	1944:
U-27	U-13	U-70	U-92	U-73	U-91
U-35	U-26	U-76	U-201	U-175	U-257
U-39	U-31	U-95	U-331	U-187	U-264
U-40	U-32	U-99	U-335	U-202	U-358
U-42	U-33	U-100	U-353	U-224	U-386
	U-49	U-110	U-357	U-301	U-406
	U-55	U-111	U-374	U-340	U-472
	U-63	U-131	U-379	U-419	U-744
		U-138	U-464	U-426	U-845
		U-433	U-517	U-432	U-973
		U-434	U-660	U-439	
		U-451		U-444	
		U-501		U-454	
		U-556		U-459	
		U-570		U-461	
		U-574		U-468	
		U-651		U-489	
				U-523	
				U-528	
				U-536	
				U-558	
				U-593	
				U-607	
				U-659	
				U-706	
				U-752	

Italian Submarines

Anfitrite	Cabolto	Glauco	Perla
Asteria	Calvi	Gondar	Saint Bon
Avorio	Caracciolo	Millo	Tritone
Baracca	Durbo	Naiade	
Berillo	Ferraris	Ondina	

"Hessler History"

The U-boat War in the Atlantic: 1939–1945, by Günther Hessler, assisted by Alfred Hoschatt and Jürgen Rohwer. 396 pp. plus charts.

Written for the British Admiralty and the U.S. Navy in the immediate postwar years by Dönitz's son-in-law, who made use of the secret War Diary of U-boat Control (FdU/KTB), this is the only known "official" German history of the U-boat war. Translated by unidentified Admiralty linguists, it has been microfilmed. In 1989, HMSO published a revised and corrected version of this indispensable work in one volume (see Books section) with an introduction by Andrew J. Withers, RN.

ADM 186/802 Vol. 1 (BR 305-1): August 1939 to December 1941
ADM 234/67 Vol. 2 (BR 305-2): January 1942 to May 1943
ADM 234/68 Vol. 3 (BR 305-3): June 1943 to May 1945

BOOKS

Abbazia, Patrick. *Mr. Roosevelt's Navy: The Private War of the U.S. Atlantic Fleet, 1939–1942*. Annapolis: Naval Institute Press, 1975.

Addington, Larry H., et al., eds. *Selected Papers from the Citadel Conference on War and Diplomacy 1978*. Charleston, S.C.: Citadel Press, 1979. See paper by Boyd.

Admiralty. *The Battle of the Atlantic. The Official Account of the Fight Against the U-boats, 1939–1945*. Official History. London: His Majesty's Stationery Office (HMSO), 1946.

———. *British Vessels Lost at Sea 1939–45*. (Warships, Merchant Ships.) HMSO, 1947. Rpt. Cambridge: Patrick Stephens, 1976.

———. *The Defeat of the Enemy Attack on Shipping, 1939–45: A Study of Policy and Operations* (by F. W. Barley and D. Waters). Official History. Two vols. (1A and 1B). London: HMSO, 1957.

———. *Submarines*. Vol. 3 of *Operations in Far Eastern Waters*. Official History. London: HMSO, 1955.

Alman, Karl [Karl the German; pseud. for Franz Kurowski]. Many books, published in Germany 1971–1988, about the U-boat war, the U-boat "aces" or "knights," and Dönitz. In a detailed analysis of these books, the Canadian historian Michael L. Hadley (*Count Not the Dead*, 1995) has aptly described them as "hackwork." They include hardbacks and paperbacks in the Landser Military Series and from other publishers about: Albrecht Brandi (1988), Engelbert Endrass (1978), Werner Henke (1971), Hans-Günther Lange (1972), Georg Lassen (1976 and 1982), Heinrich Lehmann-Willenbrock (1978), Wolfgang Lüth (1988), Rolf Mützelburg (1971), Johann Mohr (1975), Günther Prien (1981), Joachim Schepke (1980), Helmut Witte (1977). Much of the same material is rehashed in the following (or vice versa):

———. *An alle Wölff: Angriff!* [*To All Wolves: Attack!*]. Lichtsatz: Podzun-Pallas, 1986.

———. *Angriff, ran, versenken!* [*Attack, At 'Em, Sink!*]. Preface by Karl Dönitz. Rastatt/Baden: Erich Pabel, 1975.

———. *Graue Wölfe in blauer See* [*Gray Wolf in the Blue Sea*]. [Mediterranean]. Rastatt: Manfred Pawlak, 1985.

———. *"Graue Wölfe"—Wilde See: Januar/Februar 1943*. [*Gray Wolf—Wild Sea*]. Rastatt/Baden: Erich Pabel, 1973.

———. *Die letzte Feindfahrt: Mai 1943* [*The Last War Patrol*]. Rastatt/Baden: Erich Pabel, 1973.

———. *Ritter der Sieben Meerr* [*Knights of the Seven Seas*]. (Stories of 18 U-boat aces.) Rastatt: Pabel AG, 1975.

Anderson, Frank J. *Submarines, Submariners, Submarining: A Checklist*. Hamden, Conn.: Shoestring Press, 1963.

Andrew, Christopher, ed. *Codebreaking and Signals Intelligence*. London: Frank Cass and Company Limited, 1986. See papers by Denniston, Morris, and Welchman. [A hardback edition of volume 1, number 1, of the quarterly British periodical *Intelligence and National Security*.]

———. *Her Majesty's Secret Service*. New York: Viking, 1986.

Andrew, Christopher, and David Dilks, eds. *The Missing Dimension: Governments and Intelligence Communities in the Twentieth Century*. Chicago: University of Illinois Press, 1984. See papers by Rohwer and Stengers.

Andrew, Christopher, and J. Noakes, eds. *Intelligence and International Relations, 1900–1945*. Exeter: Exeter University Publications, 1987. See papers by Beesly, Bennett, Chapman, Hinsley, Rohwer, and Thomas.

Arnold, Henry H. *Global Mission*. New York: Harper and Brothers, 1949.

Auphan, Paul and Jacques Mordal [pseud. for Hervé Cras]. *The French Navy in World War II*. Trans. A.C.J. Sabalot. Annapolis: Naval Institute Press, 1959.

Axis Submarine Losses: See Naval History Division.

Bagnasco, Erminio. *Submarines of World War Two*. Annapolis: Naval Institute Press, 1977.

Bailey, Thomas A., and Paul B. Ryan. *Hitler vs. Roosevelt: The Undeclared Naval War*. New York: The Free Press, 1979.

Barnett, Correlli. *Engage the Enemy More Closely*. (Royal Navy in World War II.) New York: W. W. Norton & Co., 1991.

Bauer, Hermann. *Als Führer der U-boote im Weltkriege, 1914–1918* [*As Commander of U-boats in World War I*]. Leipzig: Koehler & Amelang, 1942.
———. *Das Unterseeboot.* Berlin: E. S. Mittler & Sohn, 1931.
Baxter, James Phinney 3rd. *Scientists Against Time.* Boston: Little, Brown and Company, 1950.
Beach, Edward L. *The United States Navy: 200 Years.* New York: Henry Holt & Co., 1986.
Beaver, Paul. *U-boats in the Atlantic: A Selection of German Wartime Photographs from the Bundesarchiv, Koblenz.* (Picture book.) Cambridge, U.K.: Patrick Stephens Limited, 1979.
Beesly, Patrick. *Room 40: British Naval Intelligence, 1914–1918.* San Diego: Harcourt, Brace, Jovanovich, 1982.
———. *Very Special Admiral: The Life of J. H. Godfrey, CB.* London: Hamish Hamilton, 1980.
———. *Very Special Intelligence.* London: Hamish, 1977.
Behrens, C[atherine] B. A. *Merchant Shipping and the Demands of War.* London: HMSO, 1955.
Bekker, Cajus D. [Hans Dieter Berenbrock]. *Defeat At Sea* or *Swastika at Sea* [*Einzelkhampfer auf See*]. New York: Ballantine, 1956.
———. *The German Navy: 1939–45.* (Picture book.) Trans. G. Stalling. New York: Dial, 1974.
———. *Hitler's Naval War* [*Verdammte See*]. Trans. Frank Ziegler. London: Macdonald & Janes, 1974.
———. *X-Men.* Maidstone: George Mann Ltd., 1973.
Bennett, Ralph. *Ultra in the West.* New York: Charles Scribner's Sons, 1979.
Bird, Keith W. *Weimar, the German Naval Officer Corps and the Rise of National Socialism.* Amsterdam: B. R. Grüner, 1977.
Blair, Clay, Jr. *Silent Victory: The U.S. Submarine War Against Japan.* Philadelphia: J. B. Lippincott Company, 1975.
Bloch, Gilbert. *Enigma avant Ultra* [*Enigma Before Ultra*]. Paris: Privately printed, 1988. For excerpts, see Articles section.
Böddeker, Gunther. *Die Boote im Netz* [*Caught in the Net*]. Bergsch Gladbach: Gustav Lubbe, 1981.
Böddeker, Gunther, and Paul K. Schmidt. *Die Gefangenen; Leben und Uberleben* [*Prisoners: Life and Survival*]. Frankfurt: Ullstein, 1980.
Bonatz, Heinz. *Seekrieg im Äther* [*Naval Radio War*]. Herford: E. S. Mittler & Sohn GmbH, 1981.
Botting, Douglas, et al., eds. *The U-boats.* The Seafarers Series. Alexandria, Va.: Time-Life Books, 1979.
Boutilier, James A., ed. *The RCN in Retrospect: 1910–1968.* Vancouver: University of British Columbia Press, 1982. See papers by Beesly, Douglas and Rohwer, Lund, Milner.
Boyd, Carl. *The Extraordinary Envoy: General Hiroshi Oshima and Diplomacy in the Third Reich, 1934–1939.* Washington, D.C.: University Press of America, 1980.
———. *Hitler's Japanese Confidant.* Lawrence: University of Kansas Press, 1993.
Boyd, Carl, and Akihiko Yoshida. *The Japanese Submarine Force and World War II.* Annapolis: Naval Institute Press, 1995.
Bradley, Omar N., and Clay Blair. *A General's Life.* New York: Simon & Schuster, 1983.
Bragadin, Marc' Antonio. *The Italian Navy in World War II.* Trans. Gale Hoffman. Annapolis: Naval Institute Press, 1957.
Breemer, Jan. *Soviet Submarines.* London: Jane's Information Group, 1989.
Brennecke, Hans Jochen. *Der Fall Laconia: Ein Hohes Lied der U-boot Waffe* [*The Laconia Case: A Song of Songs in the U-boat Force*]. Biberach an der Riss: Koehlers, 1959.
———. *Haie im Paradies: Der Deutsche U-boot Krieg im Asiens Gewässern 1943–1945* [*Sharks in Paradise: The German U-boat War in Asian Waters, 1943–1945*]. Preetz/Holstein: Ernst Gerdes, 1961.
———. *The Hunters and the Hunted* [*Jäger-Gejagte: Deutsche U-Boote 1939–1945*]. Trans. R. H. Stevens. New York: W. W. Norton, 1957.
———. *Unser Boot und Wir im Mittelmeer: Die Feindfahrten eines deutschen Unterseebootes in Wort and Bild.* [*Our Boat and Us in the Mediterranean: The War Patrols of Some German U-boats in Words and Pictures*]. (Picture book.) Berlin: Otto von Holten, 1943.
———. *Die Wende im U-boot Krieg* [*The Turnabout in the U-Boat War*]. Herford: Koehlers, 1984.
Breyer, Siegfried and Gerhard Koop. *The German Navy at War.* 2 vols. Vol. 2: *U-boats.* Trans. Edward Force. West Chester, Pa.: Schiffer Publishing Limited, 1989.
Brinkley, David. *Washington Goes to War.* New York: Alfred A. Knopf, Inc., 1988.
Brooks, Geoffrey. See Hirschfeld.

Brown, Anthony Cave. *Bodyguard of Lies.* New York: Harper & Row, 1975.

———. *"C": The Secret Life of Sir Stewart Graham Menzies.* New York: Macmillan Publishing Company, 1987.

Brustat-Naval, Fritz and Teddy Suhren. *Nasses Eichenlaub* [*Soaked Oak Leaves*]. Herford: Koehlers-Mittler, 1983.

Bryant, Arthur. *Triumph in the West.* Garden City: Doubleday & Company, Inc., 1959.

———. *The Turn of the Tide.* Garden City: Doubleday & Company, Inc., 1957.

Bryant, Ben. *Submarine Commander.* London: William Kimber, 1958.

Buchheim, Lothar-Günther. *The Boat* [*Das Boot*]. (Fiction.) Trans. Denver and Helen Lindley. New York: Alfred A. Knopf, Inc., 1975.

———. *Jäger im Weltmeer* [*Hunters on the World's Oceans*]. Preface by Karl Dönitz. Berlin: Suhrkamp, 1943.

———. *U-Boat War* [*U-Boot Krieg*]. Trans. Gudie Lawaetz. Afterword by Michael Salewski. New York: Bantam Books, 1979.

———. *Die U-Boot-Faher: Die Boot, die Bestazungen, und ihr Admiral* [*The Submariners: The Boat, the Crews, and Their Admiral*]. Munich: Bertelsmann, 1985.

Buderi, Robert. *The Invention That Changed the World.* (Radar.) New York: Simon & Schuster, 1996.

Buechner, Howard A., and Wilhelm Bernhart. *Adolf Hitler and the Secrets of the Holy Lance.* (Fiction.) Metairie, La.: Thunderbird Press, Inc., 1988.

Buell, Thomas B. *Master of Seapower: A Biography of Fleet Admiral Ernest J. King.* Boston: Little, Brown and Company, 1980.

Bunker, John. *Heroes in Dungarees.* (Merchant Mariners.) Annapolis: Naval Institute Press, 1995.

———. *Liberty Ships: The Ugly Ducklings of World War II.* Annapolis: Naval Institute Press, 1972.

Burchard, J. E. *Q.E.D.: MIT in World War II.* New York: John Wiley, 1948.

Burke, Colin [B.]. *Information and Secrecy.* Lanham, Md.: The Scarecrow Press, Inc., 1994.

Busch, Harald. *Totentanz der Siebenmeere: Todbringende Gesspensterjagd* [*Death Dance of the Seven Seas: Death-dealing Phantom Hunt*]. Rastatt/Baden: Erich Pabel, 1960.

———. *U-Boats at War: That's the Way It Was* [*So War der U-Boot Krieg*]. Trans. L.P.R. Wilson. New York: Ballantine, 1955.

———. *U-Boot auf Feindfahrt: Bildberichte vom Einsatz im Atlantik* [*U-boat on Patrol*]. Gütersloh: Bertelsmann, 1942.

Busch, Rainer, and Hans-Joachim Röll. *Die deutschen U-boot Kommandanten. Rastatt:* Erich Pabel-Arthur Moewig, January 1992.

Butcher, Harry C. *My Three Years with Eisenhower.* New York: Simon and Schuster, 1946.

Bykofsky, Joseph, and Harold Larson. *The U.S. Army Transportation Corps.* (In World War II.) Part 1, vol. 3: *Operations Overseas.* Washington, D.C.: Office of the Chief of Military History, Dept. of the Army,* 1957. See also Wardlow.

Calvocoressi, Peter. *Top Secret Ultra.* New York: Pantheon Books, 1980.

Cameron, John, ed. *War Crimes Trials.* Vol. 1: *The Peleus Trial.* London: William Hodge Co., Ltd., 1948.

Campbell, Ian, and Donald Macintyre. *The Kola Run: A Record of Arctic Convoys, 1941–1945.* London: Muller, 1958.

Campbell, John. *Naval Weapons of World War II.* Annapolis: Naval Institute Press, 1985.

Cantwell, John D. *The Second World War: A Guide to Documents in the Public Record Office.* London: HMSO, 1993.

Carver, Michael, ed. *The Warlords.* Boston: Little, Brown & Co. 1976. See paper by Kemp.

Chalmers, W. S. *Max Horton and the Western Approaches.* London: Hodder & Stoughton, 1954.

Chandler, Alfred D., Jr., et al., eds. *The Papers of Dwight David Eisenhower: The War Years.* 5 vols. Baltimore: Johns Hopkins Press, 1970.

Chapman, Paul. *Submarine Torbay.* London: Robert Hale, 1986.

Charles, Roland W. *Troopships of World War II.* Washington, D.C.: Army Transportation Assn., 1947.

*Hereafter OCMH.

Cherry, Alex. *Yankee, RN.* London: Jarrolds, 1953.
Churchill, Winston S. *The Second World War.* 6 vols. Boston: Houghton Mifflin Company, 1948–1953.
Clark, Ronald. *The Man Who Broke Purple.* Boston: Little, Brown and Company, 1977.
Clausen, Henry C. and Bruce Lee. *Pearl Harbor: Final Judgement.* New York: Crown Publishers, Inc., 1992.
Cline, Ray S. *Washington Command Post: The Operations Division.* Washington, D.C.: OCMH, 1951.
Coates, E. J., ed. *The U-boat Commander's Handbook.* 1943 ed. Trans. U.S. Navy. Gettysburg, Pa.: Thomas Publications, 1989. (See similar document in NAVOPARCH.)
Cocchia, Aldo. *Submarines Attacking.* Trans. from Italian by Margaret Gwyer. London: William Kimber, 1956.
Cohen, Eliot A., and John Gooch. *Military Misfortunes: The Anatomy of Failure in War.* New York: The Free Press, 1990.
Collier, Richard. *The Road to Pearl Harbor: 1941.* New York: Atheneum, 1981.
Compton-Hall, Richard. *Submarine Warfare—Monsters and Midgets.* New York: Sterling Publishing Company, 1985.
———. *The Underwater War, 1939–1945.* Poole-Dorset: Blanford Press, 1982.
Connell, G. Gordon. *Fighting Destroyer: The Story of HMS Petard.* London: William Kimber, 1976.
Conot, Robert E. *Justice at Nuremberg.* New York: Harper & Row, 1983.
Craven, Wesley Frank, and James Lea Cate, eds. *The Army Air Forces in World War II.* 7 vols. Vol. 1: *Plans and Early Operations.* Vol. 2: *Europe: Torch to Pointblank.* Chicago: The University of Chicago Press, 1948-1958.
Cremer, Peter, with Fritz Brustat-Naval. *U-boat Commander.* Trans. Lawrence Wilson. Annapolis: Naval Institute Press, 1984.
Cunningham, Andrew B. *A Sailor's Odyssey.* London: Hutchison, 1951.
Dalton, Curt. *Keeping the Secret: The Waves and NCR, 1943–1946.* (Bombe operators.) Dayton, Ohio: Privately printed, 1997.
Davidson, Eugene. *The Trial of the Germans.* New York: The Macmillan Company, 1966.
Davis, George T. *A Navy Second to None.* New York: Harcourt, Brace & Co., 1940.
Davis, Vincent. *The Admiral's Lobby.* Chapel Hill: University of North Carolina Press, 1967.
Deighton, Len. *Blood, Tears and Folly.* New York: Harper Collins, 1993.
Dictionary of American Naval Fighting Ships. 8 vols. Washington, D.C.: U.S. Government Printing Office, 1959.
Dönitz, Karl. *Die Fahrtender* Breslau *im Schwazen Meer* [*The Voyages of the* Breslau *in the Black Sea*]. Berlin: Ullstein, 1917.
———. *Mein wechselvolles Leben.* [*My Changing Life*]. Göttingen: Musterschmidt, 1968.
———. *Memoirs: Ten Years and Twenty Days* [*Zehn Jahre und Zwanzig Tage*]. Trans. R. H. Stevens and David Woodward. Afterword by Jürgen Rohwer. Annapolis: Naval Institute Press, 1990.
———. *40 Fragen an Karl Dönitz* [*40 Questions to Karl Dönitz*]. Munich: Bernard & Graefe, 1979.
———. *Die U-bootswaffe* [*The U-boat Arm*]. Berlin: E. S. Mittler & Sohn, 1940.
Dollinger, Hans. *The Decline and Fall of Nazi Germany and Imperial Japan.* New York: Bonanza Books, 1965.
Dorr, Manfred. *Die Ritterkreuzträgen der deutschen Wehrmacht. Teil VI: U-boote.* [*The Knight's Cross Holders in the German Military. Part 6: U-boats*]. Osnabruck: Biblio-Verlag, 1988.
Douglas, W.A.B. *The Creation of a National Air Force.* Vol. 2. Toronto: University of Toronto Press, 1986.
———, ed. *The RCN in Transition: 1910–1985.* Vancouver: University of British Columbia Press, 1988. See papers by Douglas and Rowher, Hadley, and Milner.
Drea, Edward J. *MacArthur's Ultra.* Lawrence: University Press of Kansas, 1992.
Dreyer, Admiral Sir Frederic C. *The Sea Heritage.* London: Museum Press Limited, 1955.
Drummond, John Dorman. *H.M. U-boat.* (*U-570.*) London: W. H. Allen, 1958.
Dupuy, Trevor Nevitt. *The Naval War in the West: The Wolf Packs.* (Juvenile.) New York: Franklin Watts, 1963.
Easton, Alan H. *50 North: An Atlantic Battleground.* (War memoir of a Canadian skipper who commanded two corvettes, a frigate, and a destroyer.) London: Eyre and Spottiswoode, 1963.
Elliott, Peter. *Allied Escort Ships of World War II.* Annapolis: Naval Institute Press, 1977.

Ellis, John. *Brute Force: Allied Strategy and Tactics in the Second World War.* New York: Viking, 1990.
Enders, Gerd. *Auch kleine Igel haben Stacheln: Deutsche U-Boote im Schwarzen Meer* [*Even Small Hedgehogs Have Quills: German U-boats in the Black Sea*]. Herford: Koehlers, 1984.
Essex, James W. *Victory in the St. Lawrence: Canada's Unknown War.* (Versus U-boats.) Erin, Ont.: Boston Mills Press, 1984.
Fahey, James C. *The Ships and Aircraft of the U.S. Fleet.* Annapolis: Naval Institute Press, 1976.
Farago, Ladislas. *The Game of Foxes.* New York: David McKay Company, Inc., 1971.
———. *The Tenth Fleet.* New York: Ivan Obolensky, Inc., 1962.
Fehrenbach, T. R. *F.D.R.'s Undeclared War, 1939 to 1941.* New York: David McKay Company, Inc., 1967.
Fischer, Gerald J. *A Statistical Summary of Shipbuilding Under the U.S. Maritime Commission During World War II.* Historical Reports of War Administration, United States Maritime Commission, No. 2, 1949.
Fisher, David E. *A Race on the Edge of Time: Radar—The Decisive Weapon of World War II.* New York: McGraw-Hill, 1987.
Frank, Wolfgang. *Prien greift an* [*Prien Attacks*]. Hamburg: Deutche Hausbücherei, 1941, 1942.
———. *Der Stier von Scapa Flow: Leben und Taten des U-Boot-Kommandanten Günther Prien* [*The Bull of Scapa Flow: The Life and Facts of Günther Prien*]. Oldenburg: G. Stalling, 1958.
———. *Die Wölfe und der Admiral: Triumph und Tragik der U-Boote* [*The Wolves and the Admiral: Triumph and Tragedy of the U-boats*]. Oldenburg: G. Stalling, 1953. Trans. into English by R.O.B. Long and published as *The Sea Wolves.* New York: Rinehart, 1953.
Franks, Norman L. R. *Conflict over the Bay.* (Of Biscay.) London: William Kimber, 1986.
———. *Search, Find and Kill: Coastal Command's U-boat Successes.* Bourne End, Bucks, England: Aston Publications, 1990. An updated and extensively corrected version was published in 1995 by Grub Street (London).
Freiden, Seymour, and William Richardson, eds. *The Fatal Decisions.* New York: Berkley Publishing Corp., 1958.
Frey, John W., and H. Chandler Ide, eds. *History of the Petroleum Administration for War, 1941–1945.* Washington, D.C.: Government Printing Office, 1946.
Freyer, Paul Herbert. *Der Tod auf allen Meeren* [*Death on All Seas*]. Berlin: Militar-Verlag, 1971.
Friedman, Norman. *U.S. Destroyers: An Illustrated Design History.* Annapolis: Naval Institute Press, 1982.
Friedrich, Otto. *Before the Deluge.* New York: Harper & Row, 1972.
Führen, Franz. *Kapitänleutnant Schepke erzählt* [*Schepke Narrates*]. Foreword by Karl Dönitz. Minden: Wilhelm Kohler, 1943.
Gabler, Ulrich. *U-Bootbau* [*U-boat Construction*]. Bonn: Wehr and Wissen, 1978.
Gallagher, Thomas. *The X-Craft Raid.* (On *Tirpitz.*) New York: Harcourt Brace Jovanovich, 1971.
Gallery, Daniel V. *Clear the Decks!* New York: William Morrow & Co., 1951.
———. *Twenty Million Tons Under the Sea.* Chicago: H. Regnery, 1956.
Gannon, Michael. *Operation Drumbeat.* New York: Harper & Row, 1990.
Gansberg, Judith M. *Stalag: U.S.A.* New York: Thomas Y. Crowell Company, 1977.
Garland, Albert N. and Howard McGaw Smyth, assisted by Martin Blumenson. *Sicily and the Surrender of Italy.* Washington, D.C.: OCHM, 1965.
Garlínski, Józef. *The Enigma War.* New York: Charles Scribner's Sons, 1979.
Gasaway, E[lizabeth] B[lanchard]. *Grey Wolf, Grey Sea.* (*U-124.*) New York: Ballantine Books, 1970.
Gebhard, Louis A. *Evolution of Naval Radio-Electronics and Contributions of the Naval Research Laboratory.* Washington, D.C.: Government Printing Office, 1979.
Gentile, Gary. *Track of the Gray Wolf.* (Drumbeat.) New York: Avon Books, 1989.
Gibson, Richard H., and Maurice Prendergast. *The German Submarine War: 1914–1918.* New York: Richard R. Smith, Inc., 1931.
Giese, Fritz. *Die deutsche Marine: 1920–1945* [*The German Navy: 1920–1945*]. Frankfurt: Verlag für Wehrwesen–Bernard & Graefe, 1956.
Giese, Otto, and James E. Wise, Jr. *Shooting the War.* (With camera, from U-boats.) Annapolis: Naval Institute Press, 1994.

Gilbert, Martin. *Winston S. Churchill.* 8 vols. Vol 6: *Finest Hour, 1939–41.* London: Book Club Assn., 1983. Vol 8: *Road to Victory, 1942–45.* London: Heinemann, 1986.

Gleichauf, Justin F. *Unsung Sailors: The Naval Armed Guard in World War II.* Annapolis: Naval Institute Press, 1990.

Glueck, Sheldon. *The Nuremberg Trial and Aggressive War.* New York: Kraus Reprint Corp., 1966.

Goodhart, Philip. *Fifty Ships That Saved the World.* Garden City: Doubleday, 1965.

Goralski, Robert, and Russell W. Freeburg. *Oil and War: How the Deadly Struggle for Fuel in World War II Meant Victory or Defeat.* New York: William Morrow and Co., 1987.

Gordon, Don E. *Electronic Warfare: Element of Strategy and Multiplier of Combat Power.* New York: Pergamon Press, 1981.

Görlitz, Walter. *History of the German General Staff, 1657–1945.* Trans. Brian Battershaw. New York: Praeger, 1953.

———. *Karl Dönitz: Der Grossadmiral.* Göttingen: Musterschmidt, 1972.

Grant, Robert M. *U-boats Destroyed.* New York: Putnam, 1964.

Gray, Edwyn. *The Devil's Device: Robert Whitehead and the History of the Torpedo.* Annapolis: Naval Institute Press, 1975.

———. *The Killing Time: The U-boat War, 1914–1918.* New York: Charles Scribner's Sons, 1972.

———. *Submarine Warriors.* Novato, Calif.: Presidio Press, 1988.

———. *The Underwater War: Submarines—1914–1918.* New York: Charles Scribner's Sons, 1971.

Greenfield, Kent Roberts, ed. *Command Decisions.* Washington, D.C.: OCMH, 1960. See paper by Leighton.

Gretton, Peter. *Convoy Escort Commander.* London: Cassell & Company, Ltd. 1964.

———. *Crisis Convoy: The Story of HX 231.* Annapolis: Naval Institute Press, 1975.

———. *Winston Churchill and the Royal Navy.* New York: Coward, McCann, 1968.

Griess, Thomas E., ed. *The Second World War: Europe and the Mediterranean.* Wayne, N.J.: Avery Pub. Group Inc., 1989. See paper by Buell.

Griffin, Gwyn. *An Operational Necessity.* (Fictional account of *Peleus.*) New York: G. P. Putnam's Sons, 1967. The German edition was titled *Der letze Zeuge* [*The Last Witness*].

Gröner, Erich. Rev. and expanded by Dieter Jung and Martin Maass. *German Warships, 1815–1945* [*Die deutschen Kriegsschiffe, 1815–1945*]. 3 vols. Vol. 2: *U-boats and Mine Warfare Vessels.* London: Conway Maritime Press Ltd., 1990, and Annapolis: Naval Institute Press, 1991. Originally published by Erich Gröner in 6 volumes by Bernard & Graefe, Koblenz. Updated and republished in 1985 by Bernard & Graefe, attributed thusly: "Drawings by Erich Gröner, Peter Mickel, and Franz Mrva."

Grossnick, Roy A., et al. *United States Naval Aviation: 1910–1995.* Washington, D.C.: Naval Historical Center, Dept. of the Navy, 1997. (Also available from Navy Historical Center in CD-ROM with added material.)

Gunton, Dennis. *The Penang Submarines.* (Operations, 1942–45.) Penang, Malaysia: City Council of George Town, 1970.

Guske, Heinz. *The War Diaries of* U-764: *Fact or Fiction?* Gettysburg, Pa.: Thomas Publications, 1992.

Hackmann, Willem. *Seek and Strike: Sonar, Anti-submarine Warfare and the Royal Navy, 1914–54.* London: HMSO, 1984.

Hadley, Michael L. *Count Not the Dead.* (U-boat mythology.) Annapolis: Naval Institute Press, 1995.

———. *U-boats Against Canada.* McGill: Queen's University Press, 1985.

Hague, Arnold. *Destroyers for Great Britain.* Annapolis: Naval Institute Press, 1988.

Hall, Hessel Duncan. *North American Supply.* History of the Second World War United Kingdom Civil Series. Ed. Sir Keith Hancock. London: HMSO, 1955.

Hall, Hessel Duncan, and C. G. Wrigley. *Studies of Overseas Supply.* History of the Second World War United Kingdom Civil Series. Ed. Sir Keith Hancock. London: HMSO, 1956.

Halpern, Paul G. *A Naval History of World War I.* Annapolis: Naval Institute Press, 1994.

———. *The Naval War in the Mediterranean, 1914–18.* Annapolis: Naval Institute Press, 1987.

Hancock, W. Keith, ed. *Statistical Digest of the War.* Rpt. London: HMSO, 1975.

Hardegen, Reinhard. *"Auf Gefechtestationen": U-Boote im Einsatz gegen England und Amerika* [*Action Stations: U-boats Against England and America*]. Foreword by Karl Dönitz. Leipzig: Boreas, 1943.

Hartmann, Werner. *Feind im Fadenkreuz: U-Boot auf Jagd im Atlantik* [*Enemy in My Sights: U-boat at War in the Atlantic*]. Preface by Karl Dönitz. Berlin: Verlag die Heimbrucherei, 1942.

Hashimoto, Mochitsura. *Sunk: The Story of the Japanese Submarine Fleet, 1941–1945.* Trans. E.H.M. Colgrave. New York: Henry Holt & Co., 1954.

Herlin, Hans. *The Survivor: The True Story of the Sinking of the Doggerbank.* Trans. John Brownjohn. London: Leo Cooper, 1994.,

———. *Verdammter Atlantik. Schicksale deutscher U-Boot Fahrer* [*Damned Atlantic: The Fate of the German U-boat War*]. Munich: Wilhelm Heyne, 1982.

Herwig, Holger H. *Politics of Frustration: The United States in German Naval Planning, 1889–1941.* Boston: Little, Brown and Company, 1976.

Herzog, Bodo. *Die deutschen U-boote, 1906 bis 1945* [*German Submarines, 1906–1945*]. Munich: J. F. Lehmanns, 1959.

———. *60 Jahre deutscher U-Boote, 1906–1966* [*60 Years of German Submarines, 1906–1966*]. Munich: J. F. Lehmanns, 1968.

———. *U-Boote im Einsatz* [*U-boats in Action*]. (Photo book in both German and English.) Dorheim: Polzun, 1970.

Herzog, Bodo, and Günter Schomaekers. *Ritter der Tiefe: Graue Wölfe* [*Knight of the Deep: Gray Wolves*]. Munich: Welsermühl, 1976.

Hess, Hans Georg. *Die Männer von* U-995. [*The Men of* U-995]. Oldenburg: Stalling Maritim, 1979. Rpt. Wumstorf-Idensen: HESS-PRESS, 1987. (Also in English.)

Hessler, Günter, assisted by Alfred Hoschatt and Jürgen Rohwer. *The U-boat War in the Atlantic, 1939–1945.* 3 vols. in one. London: HMSO, 1989. (See also PRO documents and microfilms.)

Hezlet, Arthur R. *Electronics and Sea Power.* New York: Stein and Day, 1975.

———. *The Submarine and Sea Power.* New York: Stein and Day, 1967.

Hickam, Homer H., Jr. *Torpedo Junction* (Drumbeat.) Annapolis: Naval Institute Press, 1989.

Hildebrand, Hans H., and Walter Lohmann. See Lohmann.

Hinsley, F[rancis] H[arry] et al. *British Intelligence in the Second World War.* 5 vols. Vol. 1 (1979), 2 (1981), 3, part 1 (1984), 3, Part 2 (1988). (3,182 pp.) London: HMSO, 1979–88.

Hirschfeld, Wolfgang. *Feindfahrten: Das Logbuch eines U-Boot-Funkers* [*War Patrol: The Diary of U-boat Radio Operators*]. Vienna: Paul Neff, 1982, and Annapolis: Naval Institute Press, 1996. The latter, entitled *Hirschfeld: The Story of a U-boat NCO, 1940–1946,* was translated and expanded by Geoffrey Brooks, who shares authorship ("as told to").

———. *Das Letzte Boot: Atlantik Farewell* [*The Last Boat: Atlantic Good-bye*]. Munich: Universitas, 1989. (As a POW, 1945–46.)

Hitchcock, Walter T., ed. *The Intelligence Revolution: Proceedings of the 13th Military History Symposium, USAF Academy, 1988.* Washington, D.C.: 1991. See papers by Andrew, Hinsley, Rohwer, and Weinberg.

Hodges, Andrew. *Alan Turing: The Enigma.* New York: Touchstone Books, 1983.

Hoehling, Adolph A. *The Fighting Liberty Ship.* (War memoir.) Kent, Ohio: Kent State University Press, 1990.

Högel, Georg. *Embleme Wappen Malings* [*Coats of Arms in Color*]. Herford: Koehlers, 1987.

Holley, I. B., Jr. *Ideas and Weapons.* Hamden, Conn.: Archon Books, 1971.

Hough, Richard. *The Longest Battle: The War at Sea, 1939–45.* New York: Morrow, 1987.

Hough, Richard, and Denis Richards. *The Battle of Britain.* New York: W. W. Norton & Company, 1989.

Howarth, Stephen, ed. *Men of War: Great Naval Leaders of World War II.* New York: St. Martin's Press, 1993. See profiles by Bird, J. David Brown, Herzog, Kemp, Love, Padfield, van der Vat, Wilson, and Winton.

Howard, Stephen, and Derek Law, eds. *The Battle of the Atlantic, 1939–1945.* 50th Anniversary International Naval Conference [at Liverpool]. Annapolis: Naval Institute Press, 1994. See papers by Adams, Allard, Boog, D. K. Brown, Buxton, Goldrick, Hobbs, Kessler, Lundeberg, Lyon, Neitzel, Niestlé, Probert, Pugh, Rahn, Rhys-Jones, Rohwer, Rössler, Santoni, Sutcliffe, Thowsen, Topp, Weir, and Zimmerman.

Howe, George F. *The Mediterranean Theater of Operations, Northwest Africa: Seizing the Initiative in the West.* Washington, D.C.: OCMH, 1957.
———. *United States Cryptographic History.* Ft. Meade, Md.: National Security Agency, 1980.
Howeth, Linwood S. *History of Communications: Electronics in the United States Navy.* Washington, D.C.: GPO, 1963.
Howse, H. Derek. *Radar at Sea: The Royal Navy in World War 2.* London: The Macmillan Press Ltd., 1993.
Hoyt, Edwin P. *The Death of the U-boats.* New York: McGraw-Hill, 1987.
———. *The Sea Wolves.* New York: Avon Books, 1987.
———. *Submarines at War.* New York: Stein & Day, 1983.
———. *U-Boats: A Pictorial History.* New York: McGraw-Hill, 1987.
———. *U-Boats Offshore.* New York: Stein & Day, 1978.
———. *The U-boat Wars.* New York: Arbor House, 1984.
Hughes, Terry, and John Costello. *The Battle of the Atlantic.* New York: Dial Press/James Wade, 1977.
Ickes, Harold L. *Fightn' Oil.* New York: Alfred A. Knopf, 1943.
Ingraham, Reg. *First Fleet: The Story of the U.S. Coast Guard at War.* Indianapolis: Bobbs-Merrill, 1944.
Irving, David. *The Destruction of Convoy PQ-17.* New York: Richardson & Steirman, 1987.
Jackson, Carlton. *Forgotten Tragedy: The Sinking of HMT Rohna.* Annapolis: Naval Institute Press, 1996.
Jackson, Robert H. *The Case Against the Nazi War Criminals.* New York: Alfred A. Knopf, 1946.
Jacobsen, Hans-Adolf, and Jürgen Rohwer, eds. *Decisive Battles of World War II: The German View.* Trans. Edward Fitzgerald. New York: G. P. Putnam's Sons, 1965. See paper by Rohwer.
Jameson, William. *The Most Formidable Thing.* London: Rupert-Hart-Davis, 1965.
Jane's Fighting Ships of World War II, 1946/1947. Rpt. New York: Military Press, 1989.
Johnson, Brian. *The Secret War.* New York: Methuen, 1978.
Johnson, Robert Erwin. *Guardians of the Sea: History of the United States Coast Guard 1915 to the Present.* Annapolis: Naval Institute Press, 1989.
Jones, Geoffrey Patrick. *Autumn of the U-boats.* London: William Kimber, 1984.
———. *Defeat of the Wolf Packs.* London: William Kimber, 1986.
———. *The Month of the Lost U-boats.* London: William Kimber, 1977.
———. *Submarines Versus U-boats.* London: William Kimber, 1986.
Jones, R[eginald] V[ictor]. *The Wizard War.* New York: Coward, McCann & Geohegan, Inc., 1978.
Just, Paul. *Vom Seeflieger zum Uboot-Fahrer* [*From Naval Aviator to U-boat Skipper*]. Stuttgart: Motorbuch Verlag, 1979.
Kahn, David. *The Codebreakers.* New York: Macmillan, 1967.
———. *Hitler's Spies.* New York: Macmillan, 1978.
———. *Seizing the Enigma.* Boston: Houghton Mifflin Company, 1991.
Kaplan, Philip and Jack Currie. *Wolfpack: U-boats at War, 1939–1945.* Annapolis: Naval Institute Press, 1997.
Karig, Walter, with Earl Burton and Stephen L. Freeland. *Battle Report: The Atlantic War.* New York: Farrar and Rinehart, Inc., 1946.
Keatts, Henry C., and George C. Farr. *Dive into History: U-boats.* Houston: Pisces Books/Gulf Publishing Co., 1994.
Keegan, John. *The Price of Admiralty: The Evolution of Naval Warfare.* New York: Viking, 1989.
———. *The Second World War.* New York: Viking, 1989.
Kelshall, Gaylord T. M. *The U-boat War in the Caribbean.* Annapolis: Naval Institute Press, 1994.
Kemp, Peter K. *Decision at Sea: The Convoy Escorts.* New York: Elsevier-Dutton, 1978.
———. *H.M. Submarines.* London: Jenkins, 1952.
Kennedy, Paul. *The Rise and Fall of British Naval Mastery.* Malabar, Fla.: Krieger, 1982.
Kesselring, Albert. *A Soldier's Record.* New York: William Morrow & Company, 1954.
Kimball, Warren F., ed. *Churchill and Roosevelt: The Complete Correspondence.* 3 vols. Princeton, N.J.: Princeton University Press, 1984.

———. *The Most Unsordid Act: Lend Lease, 1939–1941.* Baltimore: Johns Hopkins Press, 1969.

King, Ernest J., and Walter Muir Whitehill. *Fleet Admiral King: A Naval Record.* New York: W. W. Norton & Company, Inc., 1952.

Klenck, Walter [Horst Freiherr von Luttitz]. *Wer das Schwert Nimmt: Erleben im Luft- und Seekrieg, 1940–1945* [*He Who Takes Up the Sword: Experience in Air and Sea Warfare, 1940–1945*]. (Fictionalized war memoir by a *Kriegsmarine* officer describing his experiences in the *Luftwaffe* and those of U-boat skipper Oskar Kusch, crew of 1937A, who was executed for sedition.) München: Universitas, 1987.

Knox, Dudley W. *The Eclipse of American Sea Power.* New York: American Army and Navy Journal, Inc., 1922.

———. *A History of the United States Navy.* New York: G. P. Putnam's Sons, 1935.

Kozaczuk, Wladyslaw. *Enigma.* Trans. Christopher Kasparek. Fredrick, Md.: University Publications of America, 1984.

Krammer, Arnold. *Nazi Prisoners of War in America.* Chelsea, Mich.: Scarborough House, 1991.

Kurowski, Franz: See Karl Alman.

Land, Emory S. *Winning the War with Ships.* New York: Robert M. McBride Co., Inc., 1958.

Lane, Frederic C. *Ships for Victory.* Baltimore: Johns Hopkins Press, 1951.

Langer, William L., and S. Everett Gleason. *The Undeclared War, 1940–1941.* New York: Harper & Brothers Publishers, 1953.

Larrabee, Eric. *Commander in Chief: Franklin Delano Roosevelt, His Lieutenants, and Their War.* New York: Harper & Row, 1987.

Layton, Edwin T., with Roger Pineau and John Costello. *"And I Was There."* New York: William Morrow and Company, Inc., 1985.

Leahy, William D. *I Was There.* New York: McGraw-Hill, 1950.

Leighton, Richard M., and Robert W. Coakley. *Global Logistics and Strategy, 1940–1943.* Washington, D.C.: OCMH, 1955.

Lenton, H. T. *British Escort Ships.* New York: Arco Publishing Company, Inc., 1974.

———. *German Submarines.* 2 vols. (vest-pocket size). Garden City: Doubleday & Co., Inc., 1965.

Leutze, James R. *Bargaining for Supremacy: Anglo-American Naval Collaboration, 1937–1941.* Chapel Hill: University of North Carolina Press, 1977.

Lewin, Ronald. *The American Magic.* New York: Farrar, Straus and Giroux, 1982.

———. *Ultra Goes to War.* London: Hutchinson, 1978.

Liddell Hart, B. H. *History of the Second World War.* New York: Paragon Books, 1979.

Loewenheim, Francis L., Harold D. Langley, and Manfred Jonas, eds. *Roosevelt and Churchill: Their Secret Wartime Correspondence.* New York: Saturday Review Press/E. P. Dutton & Co., 1975

Lohmann, Walter. *Kameraden auf See, zwischen Minen und Torpedoes* [*Shipmates at Sea, Between Mines and Torpedoes*]. Berlin: N.p., 1943.

Lohmann, Walter, and Hans H. Hildebrand. *Die Deutsche Kriegsmarine, 1939–1945.* 3 vols. (See biographies of German naval officers.) Bad Nauheim: Podzun, 1956–1964. Rare. (Copies at NAVOPARCH, GNR Box T-123, Navy Library, and at NARA, Foreign Records Branch.)

Lott, Arnold S. *Most Dangerous Sea.* (Mine warfare.) Annapolis: Naval Institute Press, 1959.

Love, Robert William. Jr., ed. *Changing Interpretations and New Sources in Naval History: Papers from the Third USN Academy History Symposium.* New York: Garland, 1980. See papers by Beesly, Knowles, and Rohwer.

———. *The Chiefs of Naval Operations.* Annapolis: Naval Institute Press, 1980.

———. *History of the U S. Navy.* 2 vols. Harrisburg, Pa.: Stackpole Books, 1992.

Low, Archibald M. *Mine and Countermine.* New York: Sheridan House, 1940.

———. *The Submarine at War.* New York: Random House, 1942.

Lüdde-Neurath, Walter. *Regierung Dönitz* [*The Dönitz Administration*]. Gottingen: Musterschmidt, 1953.

Lund, Paul, and Harry Ludlam. *Night of the U-boats.* (Convoys SC 7 and HX 79.) London: W. Foulshamn & Co. Ltd., 1973.

Lüth, Wolfgang, and Claus Korth. *Boot Greift wieder an: Ritterkreuzträger Erzählen* [*U-boat Strikes Again: Tales of the Knight's Cross*]. Berlin: Erich Klinghammer, 1944.

Lynch, Thomas G. *Canada's Flowers: History of the Corvettes of Canada.* Halifax, N.S.: Nimbus Publishing Ltd., 1981.

Macintyre, Donald. *The Naval War Against Hitler.* London: B. T. Batsford Ltd., 1971.

———. *U-boat Killer.* London: Weidenfeld & Nicolson, 1956.

Madsen, Chris. *The Royal Navy and German Naval Disarmament 1942–1947.* Portland, Oreg.: Frank Cass Publishers, 1998.

Manchester, William. *The Arms of Krupp.* Boston: Little, Brown and Company, 1968.

Manson, Janet M. *Diplomatic Ramifications of Unrestricted Submarine Warfare, 1939–1941.* Westport, Conn.: Greenwood Press, 1990.

March, Edgar J. *British Destroyers: A History of Development, 1892–1953.* London: Seelkey Service, 1961.

Mars, Alastair. *British Submarines at War: 1939–1945.* London: William Kimber, 1971.

Martienssen, Anthony K., ed. *Fueher Conferences on Naval Affairs.* (Extensive notes made by Raeder and Dönitz in conferences with Hitler and entered in the official *Kriegsmarine* record. Captured at Castle Tambach and translated into English by American and British linguists. Edited of verbosity and overly technical details by the Admiralty. Published by HMSO with "background commentary" on the general war situation added by the Admiralty.) Republished in Brassey's *Naval Annual.* New York: The Macmillan Company, 1948.

———. *Hitler and His Admirals.* New York: E. P. Dutton, 1949.

Maser, Werner. *Nuremberg: A Nation on Trial.* Trans. Richard Barry. New York: Charles Scribner's Sons, 1979.

Mason, David. *U-boat: The Secret Menace.* London: Pan, 1972.

Massie, Robert K. *Dreadnought: Britain, Germany, and the Coming of the Great War.* New York: Random House, 1991.

Masterman, J. C. *The Double-Cross System in the War of 1939 to 1945.* New Haven: Yale University Press, 1972.

Matloff, Maurice. *Strategic Planning for Coalition Warfare 1943–1944.* Washington, D.C.: OCMH, 1959.

Matloff, Maurice, and Edwin M. Snell. *Strategic Planning for Coalition Warfare 1941–1942.* Washington, D.C.: OCMH, 1953.

Maurer, Maurer. *Air Force Combat Units of World War II.* Washington, D.C.: U.S. Government Printing Office, 1961.

McCormick, Harold J. *Two Years Behind the Mast.* (War memoir of a Naval Armed Guard officer) Manhattan, Kans: Sunflower University Press, 1991.

McCue, Brian. *U-boats in the Bay of Biscay.* Washington, D.C.: National Defense University Press, 1990.

McLachlan, Donald. *Room 39.* (British Naval Intelligence in World War II.) New York: Atheneum, 1968.

Meigs, Montgomery C. *Slide Rules and Submarines.* Washington, D.C.: National Defense University Press, 1989.

Merten, Karl-Friedrich, and Kurt Baberg. *Nein! So war das nicht* [*No! It Was Not Like That*]. (Refuting Buchheim's *U-boot Krieg.*) West Germany: J. Reiss Verlag, 1985.

Messenger, Charles. *World War II in the Atlantic.* New York: Gallery Books, 1990.

Metzler, Jost. *Sehrohr Südwärts!* [*Periscopes southwards!*]. Berlin: William Limpert, 1943. Trans. into English and published as *The Laughing Cow.* London: William Kimber, 1955.

Middlebrook, Martin. *The Battle of Hamburg: Allied Bomber Forces Against a German City in 1943.* New York: Charles Scribner's Sons, 1981.

———. *Convoy.* (SC 122, HX 229, and HX 229A.) New York: William Morrow, 1976.

Mielke, Otto. *225 Tage Auf Feindfahrt.* [*A War Patrol of 225 Days*]. (By *U-196.*) Munich: Arthur Moewig, 1956.

Millett, Allan R., and Williamson Murray, eds. *Military Effectiveness,* Volume 2. Boston: Allen & Unwin, 1988. See paper by Boyd.

Milner, Marc. *North Atlantic Run.* Annapolis: Naval Institute Press, 1985.
———. *The U-boat Hunters.* (RCN versus German submarines.) Annapolis: Naval Institute Press, 1994.
Monsarrat, Nicholas. *The Cruel Sea.* (Fiction.) London: Cassell & Co., Ltd, 1951.
Montagu, Ewen. *Beyond Top Secret Ultra.* New York: Coward, McCann, Geoghegon, Inc., 1978.
Moore, Arthur R. A. *A Careless Word . . . A Needless Sinking.* (List of U.S. merchant ship losses.) Kings Point, N.Y.: Merchant Marine Museum, 1983.
Moore, John Hammond. *The Faustball Tunnel.* (Escape of U-boat POWs.) New York: Random House, 1978.
Morgan, Ted. *FDR: A Biography.* New York: Simon & Schuster, 1985.
Morison, Samuel Eliot. *History of United States Naval Operations in World War II.* 15 vols. Vol. 1: *The Battle of the Atlantic, September 1939–May 1943.* Vol. 2: *Operations in North African Waters: October 1942–June 1943.* Vol. 9: *Sicily-Salerno-Anzio, January 1943–June 1944.* Vol. 10: *The Atlantic Battle Won, May 1943–May 1945.* Vol. 15: *The Invasion of France and Germany, 1944–1945.* Rpt. Boston: Little, Brown, 1984.
Morse, Philip M. *In at the Beginnings: A Physicist's Life.* Cambridge: MIT Press, 1977.
Morton, Lewis. *Strategy and Command: The First Two Years.* Washington, D.C.: OCMH, 1962.
Mulligan, Timothy P. *Lone Wolf: The Life and Death of U-boat Ace Werner Henke.* Westport, Conn.: Praeger, 1993.
———, comp. *Records Relating to U-boat Warfare, 1939–1945.* (Guides to the Microfilmed Records of the German Navy, 1850–1945.) Washington, D.C.: National Archives and Records Administration, 1985.
Naval History Division. *United States Submarine Losses [in] World War II. With an Appendix of Axis Submarine Losses, Fully Indexed.* Washington, D.C.: GPO, 1963. (Also available at NARA on microfilm NRS 1976–107.)
Neave, Airey. *On Trial at Nuremberg.* Boston: Little, Brown and Company, 1978.
Nicosia, Francis R., and Lawrence D. Stokes, eds. *Germans Against Nazism: Non-Conformity, Opposition and Resistance in the Third Reich.* New York: Berg, 1991. See paper by Walle.
Niestlé, Axel. *German U-boat Losses During World War II.* Annapolis: Naval Institute Press, 1998.
Noli, Jean. *Les loups de l'Admiral [The Admiral's Wolf Pack].* Trans. J. F. Bernard. Garden City: Doubleday, 1974.
Nuremberg: Trial of the Major War Criminals Before the International Military Tribunal. 42 vols. Nuremberg: U.S. Government Printing Office, 1947–49. Vol. 5 (Dönitz) and Vol. 13 (Raeder).
Ott, Wolfgang. *Sharks and Little Fish [Haie und kleine Fische].* (Fiction.) Trans. Ralph Manheim. New York: Ballantine Books, 1966.
Padfield, Peter. *Dönitz: The Last Führer.* London: Victor Gollancz, 1984.
———. *War Beneath the Sea.* New York: John Wiley & Sons, Inc., 1995.
Page, Robert Morris. *The Origin of Radar.* New York: Doubleday, 1962.
Palencia, Mario Moya. *1942: Mexicanos al grito de guerra [1942: Mexicans Cry War].* Mexico: Miguel Ängel Porrüa, 1992.
Parrish, Thomas. *The Ultra Americans.* New York: Stein & Day, 1985.
Payton-Smith, D[ereck] J[oseph]. *Oil: A Study of Wartime Policy and Administration.* London: HMSO, 1971.
Peillard, Léonce. *The Laconia Affair.* Trans. Oliver Coburn. New York: G. P. Putnam's Sons, 1963.
Peter, Karl. *Acht Glas, Ende der Wache: Erinner eines Seeoffiziers der Crew 38 [Eight Bells, End of the Watch: Remembrances of a Naval Officer of Crew 38].* Munich: Preussischer Militar-Verlag, 1988.
Phillips, Cabell. *The 1940s: Decade of Triumph and Trouble.* New York: Macmillan Publishing Co., Inc., 1975.
Pitt, Barrie, et al., eds. *The Battle of the Atlantic.* New York: Time-Life Books, 1977.
Plottke, Herbert. *Ein U-Boot-Drama: Die Letzen Feindfahrten von* U-172 [*U-boat Drama: The Last War Patrol of* U-172]. Rastatt: Erich Pabel, 1987.
Pogue, Forrest C. *George C. Marshall.* 4 vols. Vol. 2: *Ordeal and Hope, 1939–1942.* Vol. 3: *Organizer of Victory, 1943–1945.* New York: Viking, 1963–1987.
———. *The Supreme Command.* Washington, D.C.: OCMH, 1954.
Poolman, Kenneth. *Allied Escort Carriers of World War Two in Action.* London: Blandford Press, 1988.

———. *Escort Carriers of World War II.* (Paper.) London: Arms and Armor Press, 1989.
Pope, Dudley. *73 North: The Defeat of Hitler's Navy.* Annapolis: Naval Institute Press, 1958.
Postan, M. M. *British War Production.* London: HMSO, 1952.
Potter, E[lmer] B[elmont] and C[hester] W. Nimitz, eds. *Sea Power: A Naval History.* Englewood Cliffs, N.J.: Prentice-Hall, 1960.
Powers, Thomas. *Heisenberg's War: The Secret History of the German Bomb.* New York: Knopf, 1993.
Prager, Hans Georg. *Blohm and Voss.* (U-boat builders.) Trans. Frederick A. Bishop. London: Brassey's Publishers, Ltd., 1977.
Preston, Antony. *Submarines.* New York: St. Martin's Press, 1982.
———. *U-boats.* New York: E. P. Dutton, 1978.
Price, Alfred. *Aircraft Versus Submarines.* Annapolis: Naval Institute Press, 1974.
Prien, Günther. *Mein Weg nach Scapa Flow* [*My Road to Scapa Flow*]. Berlin: Im Deutschem Verlag, 1940. Trans. into English by George Vatine and published as *I Sank the Royal Oak.* London: Gray's Inn Press, 1954. American ed.: *U-boat Commander.* New York: Award Books, 1969.
Puttkamer, Karl Jesko von. *Die Unheimliche See* [*The Dreadful Sea*]. 1952.
Quine, W[illard] V[an Orman]. *The Time of My Life.* Cambridge: MIT Press, 1985.
Rachlis, Eugene. *They Came to Kill.* (Saboteurs.) New York: Random House, 1961.
Raeder, Erich. *My Life* [*Mein Leben*]. Trans. Henry W. Drexel. Annapolis: United States Naval Institute Press, 1960.
Range, Clemens. *Die Ritterkreuzträger der Kriegsmarine.* Stuttgart: Motorbuch, 1974.
Rayner, D[enis] A[rthur]. *Escort: The Battle of the Atlantic.* London: William Kimber, 1955.
Riesenberg, Felix. *Sea War: The Story of the U.S. Merchant Marine in World War II.* New York: Rinehart, 1963.
Rink, Hermann. *Kurs Amerika* [*Course America*]. Berlin: Die Wehrmacht, 1943.
Robertson, Terence. *Escort Commander.* (Johnny Walker.) London: Evans Brothers, 1956.
———. *The Golden Horseshoe.* London: Evans Brothers, Ltd., 1955. American edition: *Night Raider of the Atlantic.* New York: E. P. Dutton & Co. Inc., 1956. German edition: *Der Wolf im Atlantik: Die Kriegeerlebnisse Otto Kretschmer* [*Wolf in the Atlantic: The Wartime Experiences of Otto Kretschmer*]. Wels: Welscrmühl, 1969.
Rohwer, Jürgen. *Axis Submarine Successes, 1939–1945* [*Die U-Boot-Erfolge Der Achsenmachte, 1939–1945*]. Introductory material translated by John A. Broadwin. Annapolis: Naval Institute Press, 1983.
———. *The Critical Convoy Battles of March, 1943.* Translated by Derek R. Masters and A. J. Barker. Annapolis: Naval Institute Press, 1977.
———, ed. *Decisive Battles of World War II: The German View.* See Jacobsen.
———. *Die Versenkung der judischen Fluchtlinastransporter . . . im Schwarzen Meer* [*The Sinking of the Jewish Refugee Ship in the Black Sea*]. Frankfurt: Bernard and Graefe, 1965.
Rohwer, Jürgen, and Gerd Hümmelchen. *Chronology of the War At Sea: 1939–45* [*Chronik des Seekrieges: 1939–45*]. Trans. Derek R. Masters. 2 vols. Vol. 1: 1939–1942; Vol. 2: 1943–1945. New York: Arco Publishing Co., 1972–73.
———. *Chronology of the War at Sea, 1939–1945: The Naval History of World War Two.* Annapolis: Naval Institute Press, 1992. (*Chronology* Vols. 1 and 2 updated and combined into a single volume.)
Rohwer, Jürgen, and Eberhard Jäckel, *Die Funkaufklärung und ihre Rolle im Zweiten Weltkrieg* [*The Role of Radio Intelligence in World War II*]. Stuttgart: Motorbuch, 1979.
Roscoe, Theodore. *United States Destroyer Operations in World War II.* Annapolis: Naval Institute Press, 1953.
Rosenman, Samuel I., comp. and ed. *The Public Papers and Addresses of Franklin D. Roosevelt.* 13 vols. Vol. II: *Humanity on the Defensive.* New York: Russell and Russell, 1942.
Roskill, S[tephen] W[entworth]. *A Merchant Fleet in War.* (The story of Alfred Holt & Co., 1939–1945.) London: Collins, 1962.
———. *Naval Policy Between the Wars.* 2 vols. Vol. 1: *The Period of Anglo-American Antagonism, 1919–1929.* London: William Collins Sons & Co., 1968. Vol. 2: *The Period of Reluctant Rearmament, 1930–1939.* Annapolis: Naval Institute Press, 1976.

———. *The Secret Capture.* (Re *U-110,* etc.) London: Collins, 1954.
———. *The War at Sea: 1939–1945.* 3 vols. (1, 2, 3, parts 1 and 2.) London: HMSO, 1954–61.
Rössler, Eberhard. *The U-boat.* Trans. Harold Erenberg. London: Arms & Armour Press, 1981.
Ruge, Friedrich. *Sea Warfare: 1939–1945.* Trans. by M. G. Saunders. London: Cassell & Co. Ltd., 1957.
———. *The Soviets as Naval Opponents, 1941–1945.* Trans. Thomas Koines. Annapolis: Naval Institute Press, 1979.
Runyan, Timothy J., and Jan M. Copes, eds. *To Die Gallantly: The Battle of the Atlantic.* Boulder: Westview Press, 1994. See papers by Allard, Barlow, J. D. Brown, King, Love, Lundeberg, Meany, Milner, Rahn, Rohwer, Sarty, Steury, Syrett, Valle.
Rusbridger, James, and Eric Nave. *Betrayal at Pearl Harbor.* New York: Summit Books, 1991.
Rust, Eric C. *Naval Officers Under Hitler: The Story of Crew 34.* New York: Praeger, 1991.
Salewski, Michael. *Die deutsche Seekriegeleitung, 1939–1945* [*Direction of the German Sea War, 1929–1945*]. 3 vols. Munich: Bernard & Graefe, 1970–75.
Sawyer, Leonard Arthur, and W. H. Mitchell. *The Liberty Ships: The History of the "Emergency" Type Cargo Ships Constructed in the U.S. During World War II.* Newton Abbot: David & Charles (Publishers) Limited, 1970.
Schäffer, Heinz. *U-boat 977.* New York: W. W. Norton & Co., Inc., 1952.
Scheina, Robert L. *U.S. Coast Guard Cutters and Craft of World War II.* Annapolis: Naval Institute Press, 1982.
Schepke, Joachim. *U-Bootfahrer von heute: Erzahlt und Gezeichnet von einen U-Boot-Kommandanten* [*Submariners of Today: Narrated by a U-boat Commander*]. Berlin: Im Deutschen, 1940.
Schoenfeld, Max. *Stalking the U-boat.* (By the USAAF.) Washington, D.C.: Smithsonian Press, 1994.
Schofield, B[rian] B. *The Russian Convoys.* London: B. T. Batsford Ltd., 1964.
Schofield, William G. *Eastward the Convoys.* (War memoir of an Armed Guard officer.) New York: Rand McNally & Co., 1965.
Schull, Joseph. *Far Distant Ships.* (Royal Canadian Navy in World War II.) Ottawa: Queen's Printer, 1952.
Schutze, Hans G. *Operation unter Wasser.* Herford: Koehler, 1985.
Seth, Ronald. *The Fiercest Battle.* (Convoy ONS 5.) New York: W. W. Norton & Company, 1961.
Shirer, William L. *Berlin Diary.* New York: Alfred A. Knopf, 1941.
———. *The Rise and Fall of the Third Reich.* New York: Simon & Schuster, 1960.
Showell, Jak P. Mallmann. *The German Navy in World War II.* London: Arms & Armour Press, 1979.
———. *U-Boat Command and the Battle of the Atlantic.* London: Conway Maritime Press Ltd, 1989.
———. *U-boats Under the Swastika.* London: Allen, 1973.
Simpson, B. Mitchell, III. *Admiral Harold R. Stark: Architect of Victory, 1939–1945.* Columbia, S.C.: University of South Carolina Press, 1989.
Slessor, John C. *The Central Blue.* London: Cassell, 1956.
Smith, Bradley F. *The Ultra-Magic Deals.* San Francisco: Presidio, 1992.
Snyder, Louis L. *Hitler's Elite.* (Nazi notables.) New York: Hippocrene Books, 1989.
Sohler, Herbert. *U-Bootkrieg und Volkerrecht* [*U-boat War and International Law*]. Frankfurt: E. S. Mittler & Sohn, 1956.
Southall, Ivan F. *They Shall Not Pass Unseen.* (History of RAAF Squadron 461.) Sydney: Angus & Robertson, 1956.
Spector, Ronald H. *Eagle Against the Sun.* New York: Free Press/Macmillan, 1985.
Speer, Albert. *Inside the Third Reich.* London: Weidenfeld, 1970.
———. *Spandau: The Secret Diaries.* New York: Macmillan, 1976.
Spindler, Arno, ed. *Der Handelskrieg mit U-Booten* [*Trade War with Submarines*]. 5 vols. Berlin: E. S. Mittler und Sohn, 1932–44 and London: Cassell & Co., Ltd., 1966.
Spooner, A[nthony]. *In Full Flight.* (War memoir of a Coastal Command Squadron Leader.) London: Macdonald, 1965.
Stafford, Edward P. *Subchaser.* Annapolis: Naval Institute Press, 1988.
Stephen, Martin. *The Fighting Admirals: British Admirals of the Second World War.* Annapolis: Naval Institute Press, 1991.

Stern, Robert C. *Type VII U-boats.* Annapolis: Naval Institute Press, 1991.

———. *U-boats in Action.* (Paper.) Warren, Mich.: Squadron/Signal Pub. Inc., 1977.

Sternhell, Charles M., and Alan M. Thorndike. *Anti-Submarine Warfare in World War II.* Rpt. Alexandria, Va.: Center for Naval Analyses, 1977.

Stevenson, William. *A Man Called Intrepid: The Secret War.* New York: Harcourt Brace Jovanovich, 1976.

Stimson, Henry L., and McGeorge Bundy. *On Active Service in Peace and War.* New York: Harper & Bros., 1947.

Syrett, David. *The Defeat of the German U-boats: The Battle of the Atlantic.* Columbia, S.C.: University of South Carolina Press, 1994.

Tarrant, V. E. *The Last Year of the Kriegsmarine: May '44–May '45.* London: Arms and Armor Press, 1994.

———. *The U-boat Offensive: 1914–1945.* Annapolis: Naval Institute Press, 1989.

Tate, Merze. *The United States and Armaments.* Cambridge: Harvard University Press, 1948.

Taylor, Telford. *The Anatomy of the Nuremberg Trials.* New York: Knopf, 1992.

Terraine, John. *Business in Great Waters: The U-boat Wars, 1916–1945.* New York: G. P. Putnam's Sons, 1989.

Terrell, Edward. *Admiralty Brief: The Story of Inventions That Contributed to Victory in the Battle of the Atlantic.* London: George G. Harrap, 1958.

Thomas, Charles S. *The German Navy in the Nazi Era.* Annapolis: Naval Institute Press, 1990.

Thomas, Lowell, *Raiders of the Deep.* (U-boats in WW I.) New York: Garden City Pub. Co., 1928.

Thompson, H. K., Jr., and Henry Strutz, eds. *Doenitz at Nuremberg: A Reappraisal.* New York: Amber Publishing Corp., 1976.

Time-Life Books Series. *The Third Reich. War on the High Seas* (1990) and *Wolf Packs* (1989). Alexandria, Va.: Time-Life Books Inc.

Tirpitz, Alfred P. von. *My Memoirs.* 2 vols. New York: Dodd, Mead, & Co., 1919.

Toland, John. *Adolph Hitler.* New York: Doubleday, 1976.

Topp, Erich. *The Odyssey of a U-boat Commander* [*Fackelnüber dem Atlantik: Lebensbericht eines U-Boot Kommandante*]. Trans. Eric C. Rust. Westport, Conn.: Praeger, 1992.

Tucker, Gilbert Norman. *The Naval Service of Canada: Its Official History.* 2 vols. Vol. 2: *Activities on Shore During the Second World War.* Ottawa: King's Printer, 1952.

Tuleja, Thaddeus V. *Twilight of the Sea Gods.* (German Navy.) New York: W. W. Norton & Co., Inc., 1958.

Turner, L.C.F., H. R. Gordon-Cumming, and J. E. Betzler. *War in the Southern Oceans, 1939–45.* New York: Oxford University Press, 1961.

Tusa, Ann, and John Tusa. *The Nuremberg Trial.* New York: Atheneum, 1984.

Vaeth, J. Gordon. *Blimps and U-boats.* Annapolis: Naval Institute Press, 1992.

van der Vat, Dan. *The Atlantic Campaign.* New York: Edward Burlingame/Harper and Row, 1988.

———. *The Grand Scuttle.* Annapolis: Naval Institute Press, 1986.

Vause, Jordan. *U-boat Ace: The Story of Wolfgang Lüth.* Annapolis: Naval Institute Press, 1990.

———. *Wolf: U-boat Commanders in World War II.* Annapolis: Naval Institute Press, 1997.

Von der Porten, Edward P. *The German Navy in World War II.* New York: Thomas Y. Crowell Company, 1969.

Waddington, Conrad H. *O.R. in World War II: Operational Research Against the U-boat.* London: Elek Science, 1973.

Wardlow, Chester. *The U.S. Army Transportation Corps.* (In World War II.) Part 1, vol. 1: *Responsibilities, Organization and Operations.* Part 1, vol. 2: *Movements, Training and Supply.* Washington, D.C.: OCMH, 1951, 1956. See also Bykofsky and Larson.

Warren, C.E.T., and James Benson. *Will Not We Fear.* (Capture of HMS *Seal.*) New York: William Sloane Associates, 1961.

Waters, John M., Jr. *Bloody Winter.* (War memoir of a Coast Guard officer.) Annapolis: Naval Institute Press, 1987.

Watson, D. M., and H. E. Wright. *Radio Direction Finding.* London: Van Nostrand Reinhold Company, 1971.

Watts, Anthony John. *The U-Boat Hunters.* London: Macdonald and Jane's, 1976.

Weaver, Harry J. *Nightmare at Scapa Flow.* (*U-47* sinks *Royal Oak.*) Oxfordshire: Cressrelles, 1980.

Weinberg, Gerhard L. *A World at Arms.* New York: Cambridge University Press, 1994.

Weir, Gary E. *Building American Submarines, 1919–1940.* Washington, D.C.: Naval Historical Center, 1991.

———. *Forged in War.* (U.S. submarines.) Washington, D.C.: Naval Historical Center, 1993.

Welchman, Gordon. *The Hut Six Story.* New York: McGraw-Hill Company, 1982.

Wemyss, D.E.G. *Walker's Groups in the Western Approaches.* Liverpool: The Liverpool Post and Daily Echo, Ltd., 1948. Rpt. as *Relentless Pursuit.* London: William Kimber, 1955.

Werner, Herbert A. *Iron Coffins* [*Die Eisernensärge*]. (War memoir of a U-boat officer.) New York: Holt, Rinehart and Winston, 1969.

West, Nigel [Rupert Allason]. *GCHO.* London: George Weidenfeld & Nicolson, Ltd., 1986.

———. *The Sigint Secrets: The Signals Intelligence War, 1900 to Today, Including the Persecution of Gordon Welchman.* (Paper.) New York: Quill/William Morrow, 1988.

Westwood, David. *The Type VII U-Boat.* Annapolis: Naval Institute Press, 1984.

Wheeler, Gerald E. *Kinkaid of the Seventh Fleet.* Washington, D.C.: Naval Historical Center, 1995.

Wheeler-Bennett, John W. *Pipe Dream of Peace.* New York: William Morrow Company, 1935.

Whinney, Bob [Reginald]. *The U-boat Peril: An Antisubmarine Commander's War.* London: Blandford Press, 1987.

Whitley, M. J. *Destroyer! German Destroyers in World War II.* Annapolis: Naval Institute Press, 1983.

Wiggins, Melanie. *Torpedoes in the Gulf: Galveston and the U-boats, 1942–1943.* College Station: Texas A&M University Press, 1995.

Williams, Kathleen Broome. *Secret Weapon.* (High frequency direction finding in World War II.) Annapolis: Naval Institute Press, 1996.

Williams, Mark. *Captain Gilbert Roberts, RN, and the Anti-U-Boat School.* London: Cassell, Ltd. 1979.

Williamson, Gordon. *The Iron Cross.* Poole: Blandford Press, 1984.

Williamson, Gordon, and Darko Pavlovic. *U-Boat Crews 1914–45.* (Elite Series, 60.) (Paper.) London: Osprey Publishing Co., 1995.

Willmott, H. P. *The Great Crusade: A New Complete History of the Second World War.* New York: The Free Press, 1989.

Willoughby, Malcolm F. *The U.S. Coast Guard in World War II.* Annapolis: Naval Institute Press, 1957.

Winks, Robin W. *Cloak and Gown.* (Yale alumni in World War II intelligence.) New York: William Morrow and Company, Inc., 1987.

Winterbotham, F. W. *The Ultra Secret.* New York: Dell Books, 1974.

Winton, John. *Convoy: The Defence of Sea Trade: 1890–1990.* London: Michael Joseph, 1983.

———. *Ultra at Sea.* London: Leo Cooper, 1988.

Wise, James E., Jr. *Sole Survivors of the Sea.* (From lost ships.) Baltimore: The Nautical & Aviation Publishing Company of America, 1994.

Wolfe, Robert, ed. *Captured German and Related Records: A National Archives Conference.* Athens, Ohio: Ohio University Press, 1974.

Y'Blood, William T. *Hunter-Killer.* (U.S. "jeep" carriers versus U-boats.) Annapolis: Naval Institute Press, 1983.

Yergin, Daniel. *The Prize.* (History of oil.) New York: Simon & Schuster, 1991.

Young, Edward. *One of Our Submarines.* (War memoir of a British submarine officer.) London: Hart Davis, 1952. American edition published as *Undersea Patrol.* New York: McGraw-Hill, 1952.

Zimmerman, David. *The Great Naval Battle of Ottawa.* (Royal Canadian Navy politics in World War II.) Toronto: University of Toronto Press, 1989.

ARTICLES, ESSAYS, PROFILES, AND SCHOLARLY PAPERS

Cross-references in this list refer the reader to the Books section.

Adams, Thomas A. "The Control of British Merchant Shipping." See Howarth and Law, eds.

Alden, Carroll Storrs. "American Submarine Operations in the War." *United States Naval Institute Proceedings,** June 1920.

Alden, John D. "Dutch Submarines in World War II: The European Theater." *Submarine Review,* April 1994.

———. "Dutch Submarines in World War II: The Far East." *Submarine Review,* April 1993.

Allard, Dean C. "Introduction: An American Assessment." See Runyan and Copes, eds.

———. "A United States Overview." See Howarth and Law, eds.

Althoff, William F. "Airships." *USNIP,* January 1988.

Ancell, Robert M. Jr. "Grand Admiral Doenitz: Reflections at 80." *USNIP,* March 1973.

Andrew, Christopher M. "Gordon Welchman, Sir Peter Marychurch and 'The Birth of Ultra.'" *Intelligence and National Security.* May 1986.

———. "Intelligence Collaboration Between Britain and the United States During the Second World War." See Hitchcock, ed.

Armstrong, W.H.R. "The Sea Devils of the Caribbean." *Journal of the Barbados Museum and Historical Society,* November 1960.

Assmann, Kurt. "The Invasion of Norway." Trans. Roland E. Krause. *USNIP,* April 1952.

———. "Operation Sea Lion." Trans. Roland E. Krause. *USNIP,* January 1950.

———. "Stalin and Hitler." Trans. Roland E. Krause. "Part I: The Pact With Moscow," *USNIP,* June 1949; "Part II; The Road to Stalingrad," *USNIP,* July 1949.

———. "Why U-boat Warfare Failed." *Foreign Affairs,* July 1950.

Atha, Robert I. "Bombe! I Could Hardly Believe It." *Cryptologia,* 1985.

Auphan, Paul. "The French Navy Enters World War II." *USNIP,* June 1956.

Barker, Edward L. "German Naval Aviation." *USNIP,* July 1950.

Barlow, Jeffrey G. "The Views of Stimson and Knox on Atlantic Strategy and Planning." See Runyan and Copes, eds.

Beach, Edward L. "Culpable Negligence." (Re USN torpedo failures.) *American Heritage,* December 1980.

———. "Down by Subs." (Operation Drumbeat.) *USNIP,* April 1991.

Beesly, Patrick. "British Naval Intelligence in Two World Wars." See Andrew and Noakes, eds.

———. "Convoy PQ 17: A Study of Intelligence and Decision-Making." *Intelligence and National Security,* April 1990.

———. "Operational Intelligence in the Battle of the Atlantic: The Role of the Royal Navy's Submarine Tracking Room." See Boutilier, ed.

———. "Special Intelligence and the Battle of the Atlantic: The British View." See Love, ed.

Belke, T. J. "'Roll of Drums.'" *USNIP,* April 1983.

Belote, James H. "The Development of German Naval Policy: 1933–1939." PhD dissertation, University of California, Berkeley, 1954.

Bennett, Ralph. "Army Ultra in the Mediterranean Theatre: Darkness and Light." See Andrew and Noakes, eds.

Bernotti, Romeo. "Italian Naval Policy Under Fascism." *USNIP,* July 1956.

Bird, Keith W. "Erich Raeder." See Howarth, ed.

Bishop, Eleanor C. "The *Campbell*'s Path to Glory." *Naval History,* Spring 1993.

———. "'Hooligan's Navy': Coastal Pickets at War." *Naval History,* Summer 1992.

Bloch, Gilbert. "Enigma Before Ultra." (Excerpts of his book.) Trans. C. A. Deavours. *Cryptologia,* July 1987; October 1987; July 1988.

* Hereafter *USNIP.*

Bloomquist, Dick L. "Air-Independent Submarine Propulsion." *Submarine Review,* July 1993.
Boog, Horst. "*Luftwaffe* Support of the German Navy." See Howarth and Law, eds.
Bowling, Roland A. "Escort of Convoy: Still the Only Way." *USNIP,* December 1969.
Bowman, Richard C. "Organizational Fanaticism: A Case Study of Allied Air Operations Against the U-boat During World War Two." *Air Power Historian,* October 1963.
Boyd, Carl. "American Naval Intelligence of Japanese Submarine Operations Early in the Pacific War." *Journal of Military History,* April 1989.
———. "Japanese Military Effectiveness: The Interwar Period." See Millett and Murray, eds.
———. "The Japanese Submarine Force and the Legacy of Strategic and Operational Doctrine Developed Between the World Wars." See Addington, ed.
———. "The 'Magic' Betrayal of Hitler." Paper presented at The Citadel Symposium on Hitler and the National Socialist Era, April 1980, The Citadel, Charleston, SC.
Bragadin, Marc' Antonio. "Mediterranean Convoys in World War II." *USNIP,* February 1950.
Broad, William J. "Lost Japanese Sub with 2 Tons of Axis Gold Found on Floor of Atlantic." *New York Times,* July 18, 1995.
Brown, David K. "Atlantic Escorts 1939–45." See Howarth and Law, eds.
Brown, J. David. "The Battle of the Atlantic, 1941–1943: Peaks and Troughs." See Runyan and Copes, eds.
———. "John Godfrey." See Howarth, ed.
Brown, Raymond J. "Won by Such as He." (Profile of Johnny Walker, R.N.) *USNIP,* June 1989.
Bruce, Jack D. "Convoy Ahead!" *USNIP,* September 1987.
Buell, Thomas B."The Battle of the Atlantic." See Griess, ed.
Bundy, McGeorge. "Hitler and the Bomb." *New York Times Magazine,* November 13, 1988.
Bunker, John. "One Night of Hell" (*I-8* versus *Jean Nicolet*) *Naval History,* August 1995.
Burdick, Charles. "The Tambach Archive—a Research Note." *Military Affairs,* December 1972.
Burke, Colin. "Commentary: Why Was Safford Pessimistic About Breaking the German Enigma Cipher Machine in 1942." *Cryptologia,* April 1991.
———. "Marvelous Machines, a Bit Too Late." *Intelligence and National Security,* 1998.
Buxton, Ian L. "British Warship Building and Repair." See Howarth and Law, eds.
Cafferky, Shawn. "A Useful Lot, These Canadian Ships: The Royal Canadian Army and Operation Torch, 1942–1943." *Northern Mariner,* October 1993.
Chapman, J.W.M. "Japanese Intelligence 1919–1945: A Suitable Case for Treatment." See Andrew and Noakes, eds.
Chicago Tribune. Special Supplement, Section 2A, December 7, 1966: "New Pearl Harbor Facts! Full Story: How U.S. Got Jap Secrets." See articles by Anonymous (probably Laurence F. Safford), Wayne Thomis, Walter Trohan, Admiral Husband F. Kimmel, C. C. Hiles, Harry Elmer Barnes.
Chiles, James R. "Breaking Codes Was This Couple's Lifetime Career." (Friedmans.) *Smithsonian Magazine,* June 1987.
Christ, Charles J. "The U-boat War in the Caribbean, 1942." *Submarine Review,* October 1985.
Clark, Lloyd. "Escape." (Of U-boat personnel from a U.S. POW camp.) *Arizona Highways,* December 1993.
Clarke, William F. "Government Code and Cypher School: Its Foundation and Development with Special Reference to Its Naval Side." Parts 1, 2, 3. *Cryptologia,* October 1987, January 1988, April 1988.
Cocchia, Aldo. "Italian Submarines and Their Bordeaux Base." *USNIP,* June 1958.
Cole, Paul M. "O.S.S. Documents Predicting U-boat Attack on New York with V-1 Missiles in 1945." Unpublished. Excerpts kindly provided to author.
Colossus [Machine: Three special studies], "The Design of Colossus" by Thomas H. Flowers. Introduction by Howard Campaigne. "The Making of Colossus" by Allen W. M. Coombs. "The Installation and Maintenance of Colossus" by W. W. Chandler. *Annals of the History of Computing,* vol. 5, no. 3, July 1983.
Compton-Hall, Richard. "Holland's *Holland:* An Irish Tale." *USNIP,* February 1991.
Cooper, Harry. "*U-2513* Remembered by Lt. Cdr. M. T. Graham." *Polaris,* February 1994.
Cronenberg, Allen. "U-Boats in the Gulf: The Undersea War in 1942." *Gulf Coast Historical Review,* Spring 1990.

Davis, J. Frank. "Wolf Pack: The German Submarine War in the Atlantic 1939–1943." *Strategy and Tactics,* 1974.
Deac, Wilford P. "America's Undeclared Naval War." *USNIP,* October 1961.
Deavours, C. A., and Louis Kruh. "The Turing Bombe: Was It Enough?" *Cryptologia,* October 1990.
Decker, Hans Joachim. "404 Days! The War Patrol Life of the German *U-505." USNIP,* March 1960.
Denniston, A. G. "The Government Code and Cypher School Between the Wars." See Andrew, ed., *Codebreaking.*
Doenhoff, Richard A. von. "Nuremberg in Perspective." *USNIP,* March 1973.
Douglas, Laurence H. "Submarine Disarmament: 1919–1939." PhD dissertation, Syracuse University, 1969.
Douglas, W.A.B. "Beachhead Labrador." (German automatic weather station.) *Military History Quarterly,* Winter 1995.
Douglas, W.A.B., and Jürgen Rohwer. " 'The Most Thankless Task' Revisited: Convoys, Escorts, and Radio Intelligence in the Western Atlantic, 1941–43." See Boutilier, ed.
———. "Canada and the Wolf Packs, September 1943." See Douglas, ed., *Transition.*
Ehrmann, Howard M. "The German Naval Archives." (Tambach.) See Wolfe, ed.
Erskine, Ralph. "Churchill and the Start of the Ultra-Magic Deals." *Intelligence and Counterintelligence,* vol. 10, no. 1, 1997.
———. "Commentary: Why Was Safford Pesimistic. . . ." *Cryptologia,* April 1991.
———. "From the Archives: U-boat HF WT Signalling." *Cryptologia,* April 1988.
———. "The German Naval Grid in World War II." *Cryptologia,* January 1992.
———. "Naval Enigma: An Astonishing Blunder." *Intelligence and National Security,* vol. 11, no. 3, July 1996.
———. "Naval Enigma: The Breaking of Heimisch and Triton." *Intelligence and National Security,* January 1988.
———. "The Triton Cypher." *Cryptologia,* October 1987.
———. "Ultra and Some U.S. Navy Carrier Operations." *Cryptologia* 19, 1995.
Erskine Ralph, and Frode Weierud. "Naval Enigma: M4 and its Rotors." *Cryptologia,* October 1987.
Ewijk, Pieter L. van. "History of the Dutch Submarine Force." *Submarine Review,* July 1992.
Fioravanzo, Giuseppe. "Italian Strategy in the Mediterranean 1940–43." *USNIP,* September 1958.
Fisher, Robert C. " 'We'll Get Our Own': Canada and the Oil Shipping Crisis of 1942." *Northern Mariner,* April 1993.
Flaherty, Sylvester J. "Convoy Slaughter." (PQ 17.) *Naval History,* March 1988.
Ford, Royal. "Off Coast of Maine, Sub Mystery Surfacing." *Boston Sunday Globe,* January 5, 1997.
Frank, Winn B. "Farewell to the Troopship." *Naval History,* February 1997.
Friedland, Klaus. "Raiding Merchant Shipping: U-boats on the North American Coast, 1942." *American Neptune,* Spring 1991.
Gallery, Daniel V. ". . . Nor Dark of Night." *USNIP,* April 1969.
———. "We Captured a German Sub." *Saturday Evening Post,* September 4, 1945.
Garzke, William H., Jr., and Robert O. Dulin, Jr. "Who Sank the Bismarck?" *USNIP,* June 1991.
German, Japanese and Italian Submarine Losses, World War II. Washington, DC: Chief of Naval Operations, 1946. (Microreel NRS 1976-107.)
Gibson, Charles Dana. "The Far East Odyssey of the *U-IT24." Naval History,* Winter 1990.
Gilbert, Nigel John. "British Submarine Operations in World War II." *USNIP,* March 1963.
Glennon, A. N. "The Weapon That Came Too Late." (The Type XXI Boat.) *USNIP,* March 1961.
Goldrick, James. "Work-Up." See Howarth and Law, eds.
Gordon, Arthur. "The Day the *Astral* Vanished." *USNIP,* October 1965.
Gruner, William P. "The German Type XXVI Convoy Killer Submarine." *Submarine Review,* October 1993.
Güth, Rolf, and Jochen Brennecke. "Hier Irrte Michael Salewski." (Refuting mistakes regarding youthful ages of U-boat skippers.) *Schiff und Zeit,* no. 28, 1988.
Hadley, Michael L. "Inshore ASW in the Second World War: The U-boat Experience." See Douglas, ed., *Transition.*

Hanley, Charles J. "Merchant Marine: The Heroic Fourth Arm of Defense." *American Legion Magazine,* December 1992.

Hazlett, Edward E. "Submarines and the London Treaty." *USNIP,* December 1936.

Heinrichs, Waldo [H., Jr.]. "President Franklin D. Roosevelt's Intervention in the Battle of the Atlantic, 1941." *Diplomatic History,* Fall 1986.

Hersey, John. "*U.S.S. Borie*'s Last Battle." (Versus *U-405.*) *Life,* December 13, 1943.

Herwig, Holger H. "An Introduction to Military Archives in West Germany." *Military Affairs,* December 1972.

———. "Prelude to *'Weltblitzkrieg':* Germany's Naval Policy Towards the United States of America 1939–1941." *Journal of Modern History,* December 1971.

Herzog, Bodo. "Otto Kretschmer." See Howarth, ed.

Herzog, Bodo, and Allison Saville. "Top Submarines in Two World Wars." *USNIP,* September 1961.

Hinsley, F[rancis] H[arry]. "British Intelligence in the Second World War." See Andrew and Noakes, eds.

———. "British Intelligence in the Second World War: An Overview." *Cryptologia,* January 1990.

———. "An Intelligence Revolution." See Hitchcock, ed.

Hobbs, David. "Ship-borne Air Anti-submarine Warfare." See Howarth and Law, eds.

Hubiner, Bert. "We Got That Sonofabitch!" (Japanese *I-52.*) *Naval History,* November-December 1995.

Kahn, David. "An *Enigma* Chronology." *Cryptologia,* July 1993.

———. "Why Weren't We Warned?" (About Pearl Harbor.) *Military History Quarterly,* Autumn 1991.

Kahn, E. J. Jr. "Hand to Hand." (U.S. destroyer escort *Buckley* versus *U-66.*) *New Yorker,* February 8, 1988. Rpt. *Naval History,* Summer 1986.

Kauffman, D. L. "German Naval Strategy in World War II." *USNIP,* January 1954.

Kemp, Peter K. "Dönitz." See Carver, ed.

———. "Sir Dudley Pound." See Howarth, ed.

Kessler, Jean. "U-boat Bases in the Bay of Biscay." See Howarth and Law, eds.

King, Thomas A. "The Merchant Marine Cadet Corps." See Runyan and Copes, eds.

Knowles, Kenneth A. "Ultra and the Battle of the Atlantic: The American View." See Love, ed.

Krause, Roland E. "The German Navy Under Joint Command in World War II." *USNIP,* September 1947.

Krug, Hans-Joachim. "Filming *Das Boot.*" *USNIP,* June 1996.

Kruh, Louis. "British-American Cryptanalytic Cooperation and an Unprecedented Admission by Winston Churchill." *Cryptologia,* April 1989.

———. "Why Was Safford Pessimistic About Breaking the German Enigma Cipher Machine in 1942?" *Cryptologia,* July 1990.

Kurzak, Karl Heinz. "German U-boat Construction." *USNIP,* April 1955.

Langdon, Robert M. "Live Men Do Tell Tales." (Re *Peleus.*) *USNIP,* January 1952.

Lasky, Marvin. "Historical Review of Underwater Technology: 1939–45 with Emphasis on Undersea Warfare." *U.S. Navy Journal of Underwater Acoustics,* vol. 25, 1975, pp. 567–84.

———. "Review of Scientific Effort for Undersea Warfare, 1939–45." *U.S. Navy Journal of Underwater Acoustics,* vol. 25, 1975, pp. 885–918.

Layman, R. D. "U-boat with Wings." *USNIP,* April 1968.

Leighton, Richard M. "U.S. Merchant Shipping and the British Import Crisis." See Greenfield, ed.

Love, Robert W., Jr. "Ernest J. King." See Howarth, ed.

———. "The U.S. Navy and Operation *Roll of Drums,* 1942." See Runyan and Copes, eds.

Lowenthal, Mark M. "Intrepid and the History of World War II." *Military Affairs,* April 1977.

Lujan, Susan M. "Agnes Meyer Driscoll." (American codebreaker.) *Cryptologia,* January 1991.

Lund, W.G.D. "The RCN's Quest for Autonomy in the North Atlantic, 1941–1943." See Boutilier, ed.

Lundeberg, Philip K. "Allied Co-operation." See Howarth and Law, eds.

———. "American Anti-Submarine Operations in the Atlantic, May 1943–May 1945." PhD dissertation, Harvard University, 1953. University Microfilms International #9736996, Ann Arbor, MI. (A copy of the above and a classified version are on file at NAVOPARCH, Naval Historical Center.)

———. "Operation Teardrop Revisited." See Runyan and Copes, eds.

Lyon, David J. "The British Order of Battle." See Howarth and Law, eds.

Macintyre, Donald. "Point of No Return." *USNIP,* February 1964.
———. "Shipborne Radar." *USNIP,* September 1967.
———. "Three Aces—Trumped!" (The death of and capture of Kretschmer, Prien, and Schepke.) *USNIP,* September 1956.
Maher, Robert A., and James E. Wise, Jr. "Stand By for a Ram." (U.S. destroyer *Borie* versus *U-405.*) *Naval History,* Summer 1993 (part 1); October 1993 (part 2).
Markowitz, Arnold. "At Last, Honors for a WW II Hero. . . ." *Miami Herald,* May 17, 1997.
Maurer, Maurer, and Laurence J. Paszek. "Origin of the *Laconia* Order." *Air University Review,* March-April 1964.
McCormick, Harold J. "Convoy Catastrophe." (PQ 17.) *Sea History* 62, Summer 1992.
McLean, Douglas M. "The Battle of Convoy BX 141." *Northern Mariner,* October 1993.
———. "Confronting Technological and Tactical Change: Allied Antisubmarine Warfare in the Last Year of the Battle of the Atlantic." *Naval War College Review,* Winter 1994.
Meany, Joseph F., Jr. "Port in a Storm: The Port of New York in World War II." See Runyan and Copes, eds.
Mellen, Greg, ed. "Rhapsody in Purple: A New History of Pearl Harbor." *Cryptologia,* July 1982 (part 1) and October 1982 (part 2). (A reprint of a manuscript written by Laurence F. Safford, with annotations by Dundas P. Tucker, Charles C. Hiles, and Harry E. Barnes. Original in the papers of Tucker at the American Heritage Center, University of Wyoming.)
Mellin, William F. "To Convoy or Not to Convoy." *USNIP,* March 1980.
Merrill, John. "PMS Blackett" (Profile.) *Submarine Review,* January 1995.
——— "Sonobuoy." *Naval History,* January–February 1994.
Milford, Frederick J. "U.S. Navy Torpedoes," a series of seven articles detailing U.S. submarine torpedo history. *Submarine Review,* April 1996, October 1996, January 1997, April 1997, July 1997, October 1997, January 1998.
———. "More on Fido." (Letter re the Mark XXIV homing torpedo.) *Submarine Review,* April 1996.
Miller, David. "The *Peleus* War Crimes Trial." *Naval History,* February 1997.
———. "World War II Development of Homing Torpedoes, 1940–1946." *Submarine Review,* April 1997.
Milner, Marc. "Inshore ASW: The Canadian Experience in Home Waters." See Douglas, ed., *Transition.*
———. "Royal Canadian Navy Participation in the Battle of the Atlantic Crisis of 1943." See Boutilier, ed.
———. "Squaring Some of the Corners: The Royal Canadian Navy and the Pattern of the Atlantic War." See Runyan and Copes, eds.
Moeser, Vicki. "Unlocking *Enigma*'s Secrets." *Cryptologia,* October 1990.
Morris, Christopher. "Ultra's Poor Relations." (Hand ciphers.) See Andrew, ed., *Codebreaking.*
Mulligan, Timothy [P.]. "The German Navy Evaluates Its Cryptographic Security, October 1941." *Military Affairs,* April 1985.
———. "German U-boat Crews in World War II: Sociology of an Elite." *Journal of Military History,* April 1992.
———. "Tracking *Das Boot:* Records of *U-96* in the National Archives." *Prologue,* Winter 1982.
Neitzel, Sönke. "The Deployment of the U-boats." Trans. Klaus Schmider. See Howarth and Law, eds.
Niestlé, Axel. "German Technical and Electronic Development." See Howarth and Law, eds.
Nimitz, Chester W. "Fleet Admiral Nimitz Replies to Questions in Trial of Gross Admiral Doenitz." *USNIP,* July 1946.
O'Connell, Jerome A. "Radar and the U-boat." *USNIP,* September 1963.
O'Connor, Jerome M. "Secret at Bletchley Park." *Naval History,* December 1997.
Offley, Ed. "Wartime Foes Reunite as Friends." (Re *U-701*) *Norfolk Ledger-Star,* July 7, 8, 9, 1982.
Oliver, Edward F. "Overdue—Presumed Lost." (Tanker S.S. *Astral.*) *USNIP,* March 1961.
Pace, Eric. "Birger Lunde, Norway Seaman." Obituary. *New York Times,* October 1, 1996.
Padfield, Peter. "Karl Dönitz." See Howarth, ed.
Pelick, Thomas J. "Fido—The First U.S. Homing Torpedo." *Submarine Review,* January 1996.
———. "Post WW II Torpedoes: 1945–1950." *Submarine Review,* July 1996.
Picinich, R. G., Jr. "Blimp Blasts Subs." *USNIP,* October 1943.
Poyer, David. "U-boat: The Story of *U-85.*" *Virginia-Pilot and Ledger Star,* April 18, 1982.

Probert, Henry. "Allied Land-Based Anti-Submarine Warfare." See Howarth and Law, eds.
Pugh, Philip. "Military Need and Civil Necessity." See Howarth and Law, eds.
Rahn, Werner. "The Atlantic in the Strategic Perspective of Hitler and Roosevelt, 1940–1941." See Runyan and Copes, eds.
———. "The Campaign: The German Perspective." See Howarth and Law, eds.
———. "Long Range German U-boat Operations in 1942 and Their Logistical Support by U-Tankers." Paper given at USN Academy History Symposium, September 1987.
Reedy, James R., Jr. "Coast Guard Sinking of *U-352*." *World War II Magazine,* May 1996.
Reinecke, H. J. "German Surface Force Strategy in World War II." *USNIP,* February 1957.
Rhys-Jones, Graham. "The German System: A Staff Perspective." See Howarth and Law, eds.
Rohwer, Jürgen. "Allied and Axis Radio-Intelligence in the Battle of the Atlantic: A Comparative Analysis." See Hitchcock, ed.
———. "Codes and Ciphers: Radio Communication and Intelligence." See Runyan and Copes, eds.
———. "Dönitz and the Battle of the Atlantic: A New Perspective." See Dönitz, *Memoirs.*
———. "The Operational Use of 'ULTRA' in the Battle of the Atlantic." See Andrew and Noakes, eds.
———. "Radio Intelligence and Its Role in the Battle of the Atlantic." See Andrew and Dilks, eds.
———. *"Sperrbrecher 104."* (Duty on a Minesweeper.) *Naval History,* February 1994.
———. "The U-boat War Against the Allied Supply Lines." See Jacobsen and Rohwer, eds.
———. "Ultra and the Battle of the Atlantic: The German View." See Love, ed.
———. "'Ultra,' xB-Dienst, und 'Magic.'" *Marine-Rundschar* 76, October 1979.
———. "The Wireless War." See Howarth and Law, eds.
Rohwer, Jürgen, and W.A.B. Douglas. "Canada and the Wolf Packs, September 1943." See Douglas, ed., *Transition.*
———. "'The Most Thankless Task' Revisited." See Boutilier, ed.
Rössler, Eberhard, "U-boat Development and Building." See Howarth and Law, eds.
Rouse, Parke, Jr. "Under the Cloak of Night." *USNIP,* June 1982.
Rousmaniere, John. "The Romance of the Subchasers." *Naval History,* Summer 1992.
Ruge, Friedrich. "Dönitz: The Last *Führer.*" (Comment re Seagren.) *USNIP,* October 1954.
———. "German Naval Strategy Across Two Wars." *USNIP,* February 1955.
Safford, Laurence F. "The Undeclared War: 'History of R.I.' [Radio Intelligence]" 11/15/43 [NARA RG457, SHR 305]. Rpt. *Cryptologia,* special supplement, Summer 1987.
———. See article by Mellen, Greg, ed.
Salewski, Michael. "The Submarine War: A Historical Essay." See Buchheim, *U-boat War.*
Santoni, Alberto. "The Italian Submarine Campaign." See Howarth and Law, eds.
Sarty, Roger. "Ultra, Air Power, and the Second Battle of the St. Lawrence, 1944." See Runyan and Copes, eds.
Saville, Allison W. "The Development of the German U-boat Arm, 1919–1935." PhD dissertation, University of Washington, 1963.
———. "German Submarines in the Far East." *USNIP,* August 1961.
Schäffer, Heinz. "We Escaped in an Outlaw U-boat." *Saturday Evening Post,* November 22, 1952. (Excerpt from his book.)
Schoenfeld, Max. "Winston Churchill as War Manager: The Battle of the Atlantic Committee, 1941." *Military Affairs,* July 1988.
Seagren, Leonard W. "The Last *Führer.*" *USNIP,* May 1954.
Selinger, Franz. "German Midget Submarines." *USNIP,* March 1958.
Smith, Bradley F. "Admiral Godfrey's Mission to America, June/July 1941." *Intelligence and National Security,* September 1986.
Smith, C. Alphonso. "Battle of the Caribbean." *USNIP,* September 1954.
Sokol, A[nthony] E. "German Attacks on the Murmansk Run." *USNIP,* December 1952.
Spilman, C. H. "The German Submarine War." *USNIP,* June 1947.
Stengers, Jean. "Enigma, the French, the Poles and the British, 1931–1940." See Andrew and Dilks, eds.
Steury, Donald P. "The Character of the German Naval Offensive: October 1940–June 1941." See Runyan and Copes, eds.
Stevens, Allan W. "Capital Johnnie Walker. . . ." (Profile.) *World War II Magazine,* May 1996.

Stevenson, Gene C. "Submarine Losses in the Eastern Baltic in World War II." *Warship International,* 1986.

Stratton, Roy O. "German Naval Support Techniques in World War II." *USNIP,* March 1954.

———. "Germany's Secret Naval Supply Service." *USNIP,* October 1953.

Sutcliffe, Paul M. "Operational Research in the Battle of the Atlantic." See Howarth and Law, eds.

Sweetman, Jack. "Destruction of the *Tirpitz*." *USNIP,* November 1994.

———. "The U-boat Peril Overcome." *USNIP,* June 1993.

Syrett, David. "The Battle for Convoy TM 1, January 1943." *American Neptune,* Winter 1990.

———. "The Battle of the Atlantic: 1943, the Year of Decision." *American Neptune,* Winter 1985.

———. "German Meterological Intelligence from the Arctic and North Atlantic, 1940–1945." *Mariner's Mirror,* August 1985.

———. "German U-boat Attacks on Convoy SC 118: 4 February to 14 February 1943." *American Neptune,* Winter 1984.

———. "The Safe and Timely Arrival of Convoy SC 130, 15–25 May 1943." *American Neptune,* Summer 1990.

———. "The Sinking of HMS *Firedrake* and the Battle for Convoy ON 153." *American Neptune,* Spring 1991.

———. "'Situation Extremely Dangerous': Three Atlantic Convoys in February 1943." See Runyan and Copes, eds.

———. "Weather-Reporting U-boats in the Atlantic, 1944–45: The Hunt for *U-248*." *American Neptune,* Winter 1992.

Taylor, Blaine. "Personality: Dönitz." *World War II Magazine,* March 1988.

Thomas, Edward. "The Evolution of the JIC [Joint Intelligence Committee] System up to and During World War II." See Andrew and Noakes, eds.

Thorndike, Joseph J., Jr. "King of the Atlantic." (Profile.) *Life,* November 24, 1941.

Thowsen, Atle. "The Norwegian Merchant Navy in Allied War Transport." See Howarth and Law, eds.

Tollaksen, Duane Morgan. "Last Chapter for *U-853*." *USNIP,* December 1960.

Topp, Erich. "Manning and Training the U-boat Fleet." See Howarth and Law, eds.

Tordella, Louis W. "Commentary: Ultra and the Walkers." *USNIP,* September 1989.

Tucker, Dundas P. See article by Mellen, Greg.

Valle, James E. "United States Merchant Marine Casualties." See Runyan and Copes, eds.

van der Vat, Dan. "Günther Prien." See Howarth, ed.

Walle, Heinrich. "Individual Loyalty and Resistance in the German Military: The Case of Sub-Lieutenant Oskar Kusch." See Nicosia and Stokes, eds.

Webster, W. Russell. "Someone Get That Damned Dog." *Naval History,* November-December 1996.

Weinberg, Gerhard L. "The European Theater: Comment." See Hitchcock, ed.

Weir, Gary E. "A Truly Allied Undertaking: The Progeny of Britain's Empire Liberty [Ship], 1931–43." See Howarth and Law, eds.

Welchman, Gordon. "From Polish Bomba to British Bombe: The Birth of Ultra." See Andrew, ed., *Codebreaking.*

Whipple, A.B.C. "The Education of Willie." (German saboteur.) *Life,* January 22, 1945.

Wiedersheim, William A, III. "Factors in the Growth of the *Reichmarine:* 1919—1939." *USNIP,* March 1948.

———. "Officer Personnel Selection in the German Navy: 1925-1945." *USNIP,* April 1947.

Wilson, Michael. "Sir Max Horton." See Howarth, ed.

Winton, John. "Viscount Cunningham of Hyndhope." See Howarth, ed.

Wise, James E., Jr. "U-boats off Our Coasts." (Photo essay.) *USNIP,* October 1965.

———. "Unsinkable Archie Gibbs." *Naval History,* April 1998.

Zimmerman, David. "Technology and Tactics." See Howarth and Law, eds.

INDEX

This index has three parts: Ships, U-boats, and General. It was compiled by my wife, Joan Blair, and her brother, C. Hamilton Rutledge, who created the software. For technical details consult Hamilton's e-mail address: hamrut@alum.mit.edu

Please note that ships listed in the appendices are not indexed.

SHIPS

B

C

D

E

F

G

H

K

L

M

N

Q

R

T

U-BOATS

GENERAL

C

H

M

N

ABOUT THE AUTHOR

Clay Blair served in combat on a submarine in the Pacific, attended Tulane and Columbia universities, and became the national security correspondent for *Time, Life,* and *The Saturday Evening Post* magazines in Washington, then editor in chief of *The Saturday Evening Post.* He has published hundreds of magazine articles and twenty-four books. These include biographies of Admiral H. G. Rickover; Generals Douglas MacArthur, Omar N. Bradley, and Matthew B. Ridgway; and John F. Kennedy; and, most recently, a definitive account of the conflict in Korea, *The Forgotten War.* He lives with his wife on Washington Island, Wisconsin.

ABOUT THE TYPE

This book was set in Times Roman, designed by Stanley Morison specifically for *The Times* of London. The typeface was introduced in the newspaper in 1932. Times Roman has had its greatest success in the United States as a book and commercial typeface, rather than one used in newspapers.